TRACY ROCKWELL

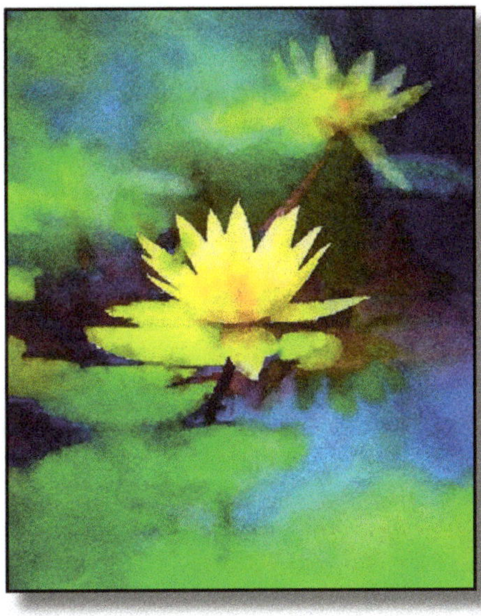

Catalogue raisonné
2000 - 2020

1st Edition

Pegasus Publishing

Tracy Rockwell - Catalogue raisonné
2000 - 2020

Pegasus Publishing
PO Box 980, Edgecliff, NSW, 2027

1st Edition - September, 2021

Orders: pegasuspublishing@iinet.net.au
www.pegasuspublishing.com.au

ISBN:978-1-925909-12-8

Front Cover:
'Life's A Beach [cropped]' (2019), Tamarama Beach, Sydney [ASTB1919].

Back Cover:
'Watsons Bay Twilight' (2016), Watsons Bay, Sydney [ASY(WB)1601].

TRACY ROCKWELL

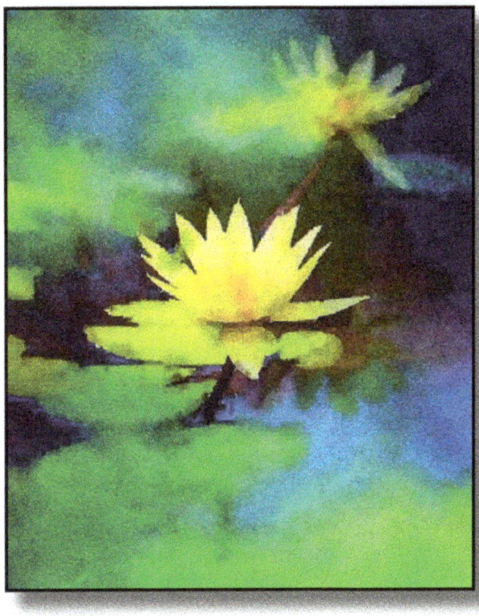

Catalogue raisonné
2000 ~ 2020

1st Edition

Pegasus Publishing

CONTENTS

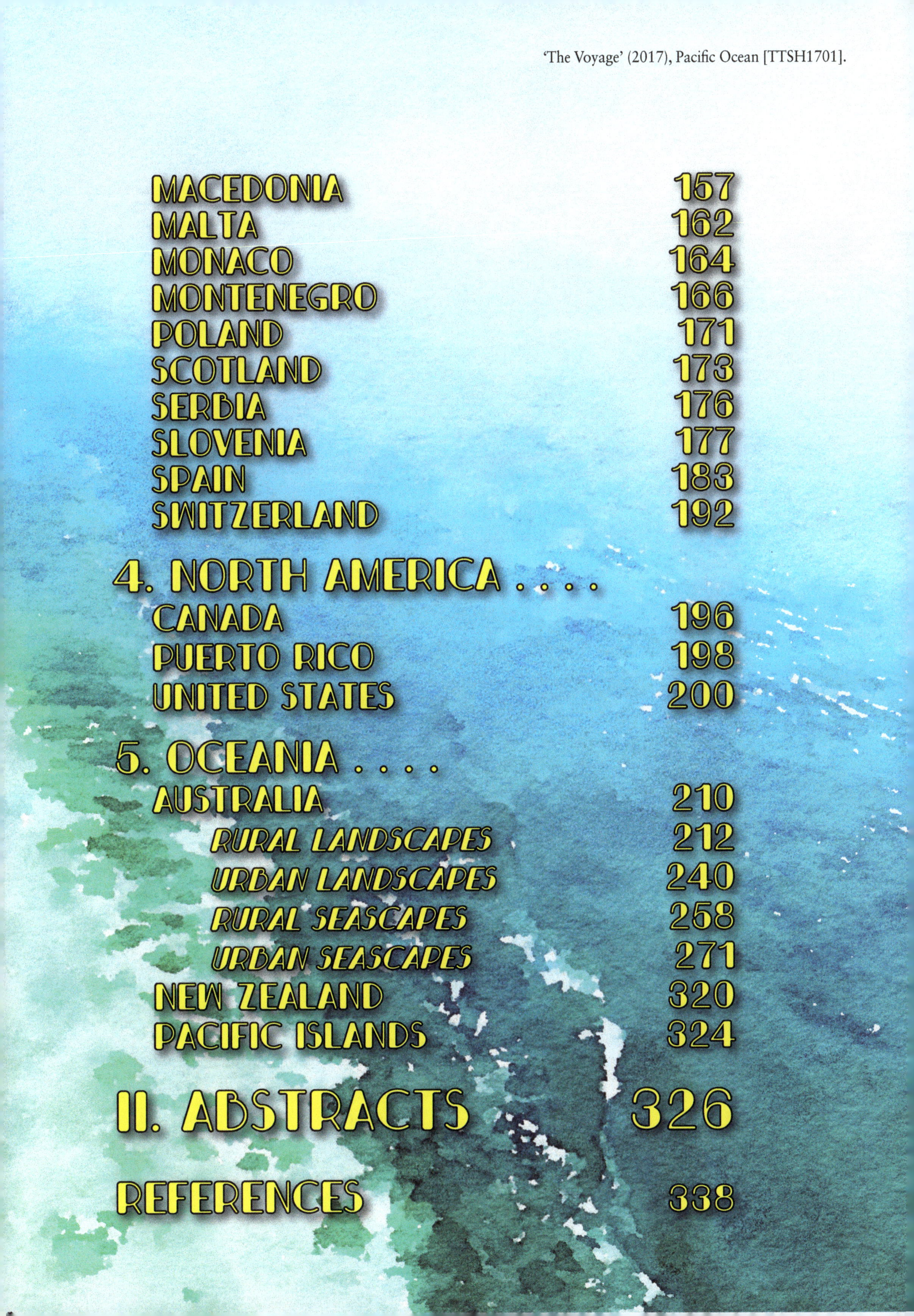

'The Voyage' (2017), Pacific Ocean [TTSH1701].

Preface

This catalogue is a comprehensive, annotated listing of the original artworks categorised to date for the artist Tracy Rockwell in the medium of 'digital art'. The works are described by title, creation date, location and serial number, with each being depicted in such a way that they may be reliably identified by art enthusiasts and third parties.

The Artist

Tracy Rockwell is a Sydney based visual artist and one of Australia's foremost photographers and contemporary impressionists. With a multi-disciplinary background in education, he is inspired by the work of the great impressionists and has resided both in Eugene, Oregon in the USA and for a brief time in Monaco. His work has been featured in numerous exhibitions and galleries across Australia and world-wide. He creates modern impressionist artworks by capturing real-time images that feature the constantly evolving relationship between nature and the human world.

Tracy has travelled widely and tours regularly to gain inspiration, all the time adding to his expanding photographic collection from which he creates unique contemporary impressionistic works of art. Each and every one of these images has its own individual story in terms of when, where, why and how they came about. The interpretation of these works is of course up to each individual, but there is an honesty and appeal to his modern impressionistic pieces that is difficult to achieve through photography alone.

▼'Tracy Rockwell, self-portrait' (2018), Sydney [FPFA1801].

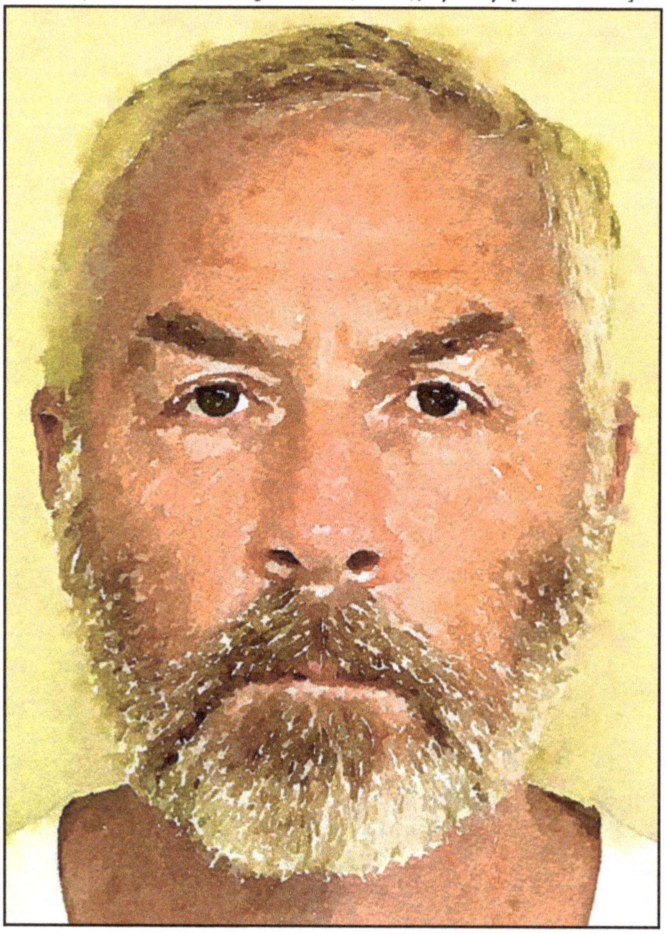

Impressionist Art

The impressionist genre grew out of a 19th-century art movement characterised by relatively small, thin yet visible brush strokes, open composition, emphasis on accurate depiction of light in its changing qualities (often vibrant, and accentuating the effects of the passage of time), with just simple and ordinary subject matter. Impressionism originated with a group of Parisian-based artists whose independent exhibitions brought them to prominence during the 1870's and 1880's.

Radicals in their own time, early impressionists violated the rules of academic and traditional painting. They constructed their pictures from freely brushed colours that took precedence over lines and contours. They also painted realistic scenes of modern life, which often included the outdoors. Previous to the impressionists, landscapes and portraits as well as still lifes were usually painted in a studio.

The impressionists found that they could capture the momentary and transient effects of sunlight by painting outdoors. They portrayed overall visual effects instead of details, and used short 'broken' brush strokes of mixed and pure unmixed colour, not blended smoothly or shaded as was customary at the time, to achieve an effect of intense vibrant colour.

The Method

While some images have been borrowed from copyright free sources (ie. ©), the great majority of these works have been created from Tracy's original photography, the location, lighting and subject of each image being a critical component in the process. His selected images are digitally enhanced to differing degrees in terms of their definition, intensity, saturation, contrast and exposure into their final form. While most of his processed images don't make the cut and are rejected, a small percentage morph into outstanding pieces that are selectively added to a growing portfolio. The end result is an original 'modern impressionistic' digital work of art, which can then be reproduced either on paper or canvas.

Little of Tracy's work consists of an entirely natural land or seascape, with human culture and its affect on the landscape being a prominent feature, mostly present in the form of figures, vehicles, boats or distant structures. Nonetheless, for the most part, these human influences are a welcome rather than an intrusive presence, as many of his works explicitly

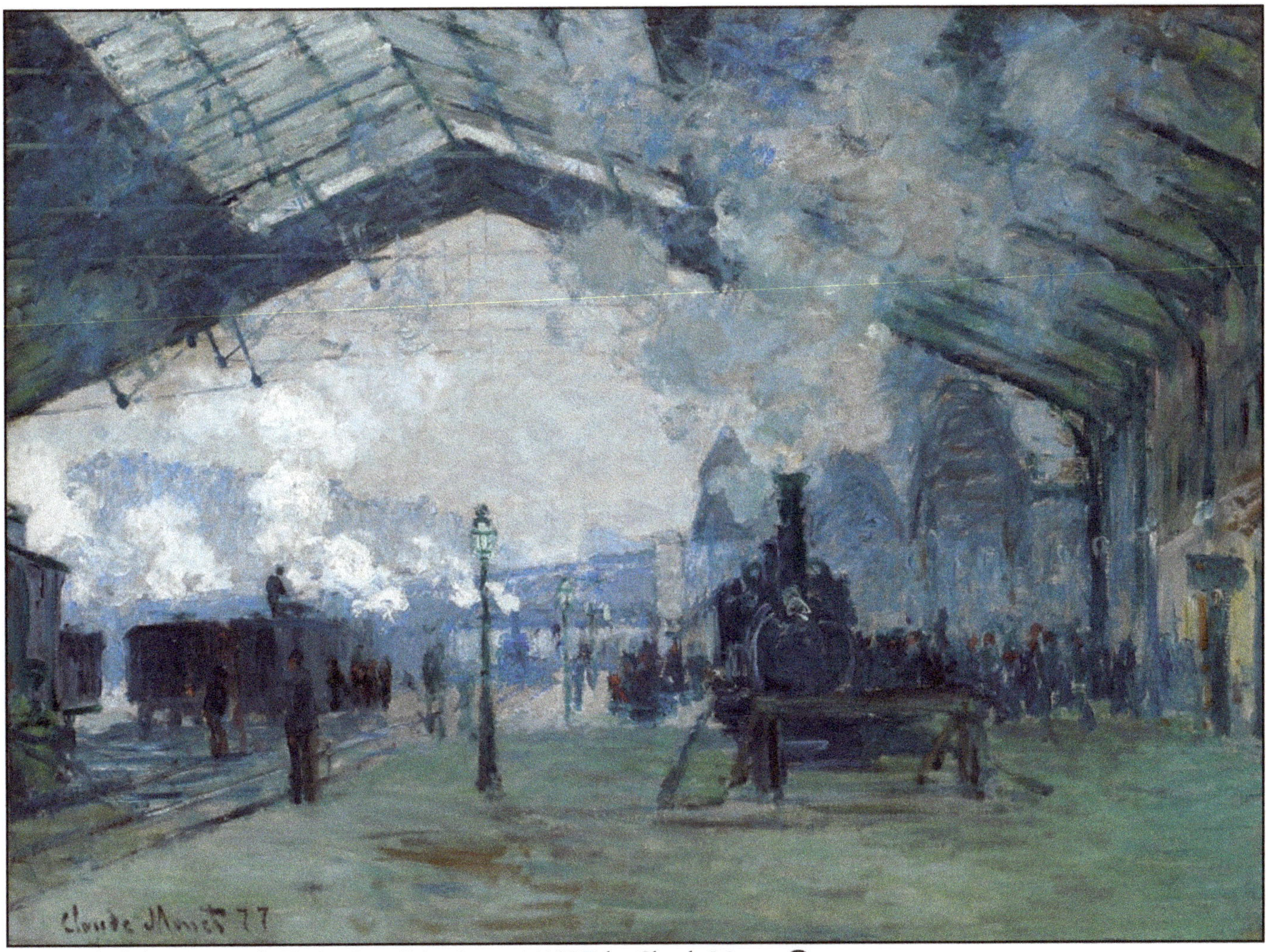

▲'Arrival of the Normandy Train, Gare Saint-Lazare' (1877) by Claude Monet. ©

'The Water Polo Coach' (2015), Lindsay Cotterill, Sydney [FPFA1501].▼

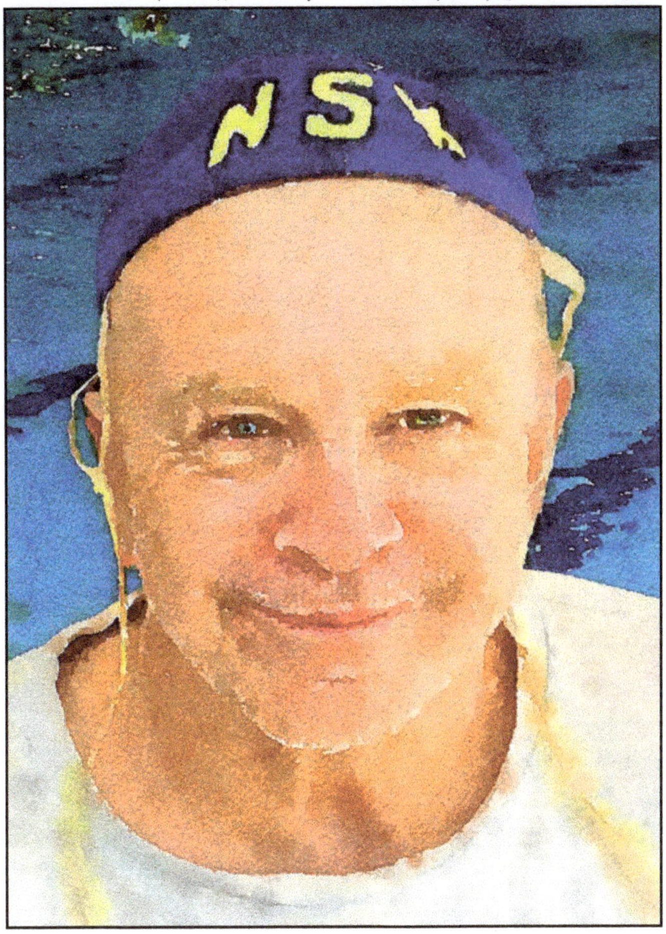

draw their significance, meaning and fascination from a relationship and interaction with people.

While some portraiture has been undertaken, the method employed to create these works is more suited to landscapes, seascapes, abstracts and botanical works rather than the more intricate features required of human characterisation.

> *"My photography and the subsequent processing of images into works of art is both a great passion and provides a wonderful reason for travelling. I've been an amateur photographer since receiving my very first Olympus camera as a young boy. Over the years I've developed an affinity with the essential elements of photography and I take great pleasure from experimentation with light and subject, as well as the composition of my images. In the process I've created quite a collection. Recent developments in digital technology have presented opportunities to transform my images into impressionistic works of art. A great deal of experimentation mixed with inspiration from fellow photographers and artists has led to the creation of the unique images printed in this catalogue."*
>
> *Tracy Rockwell, 2021*

AFRICA

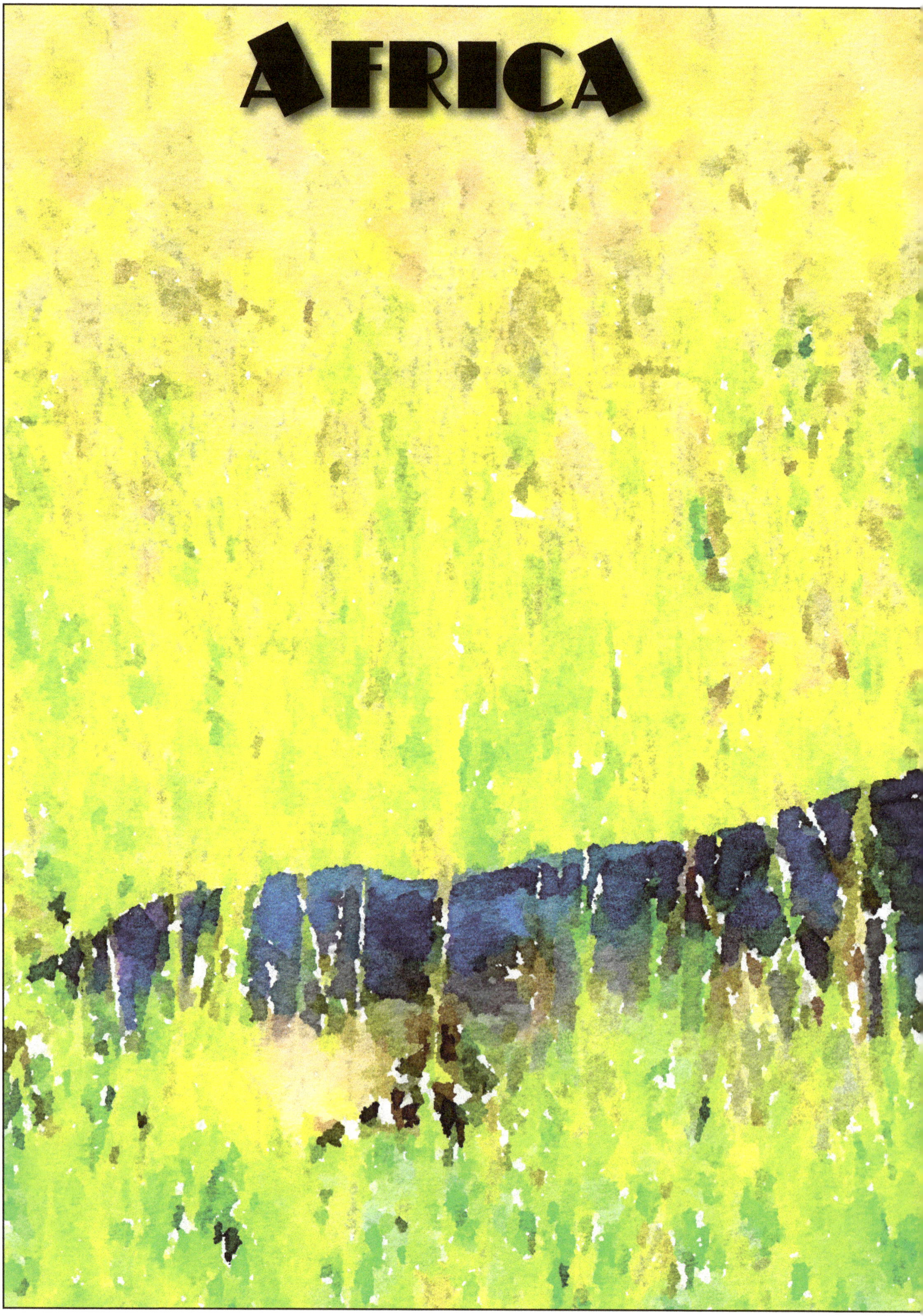

'King Of The Jungle' (2014), Serengeti, Tanzania [FEA1409].

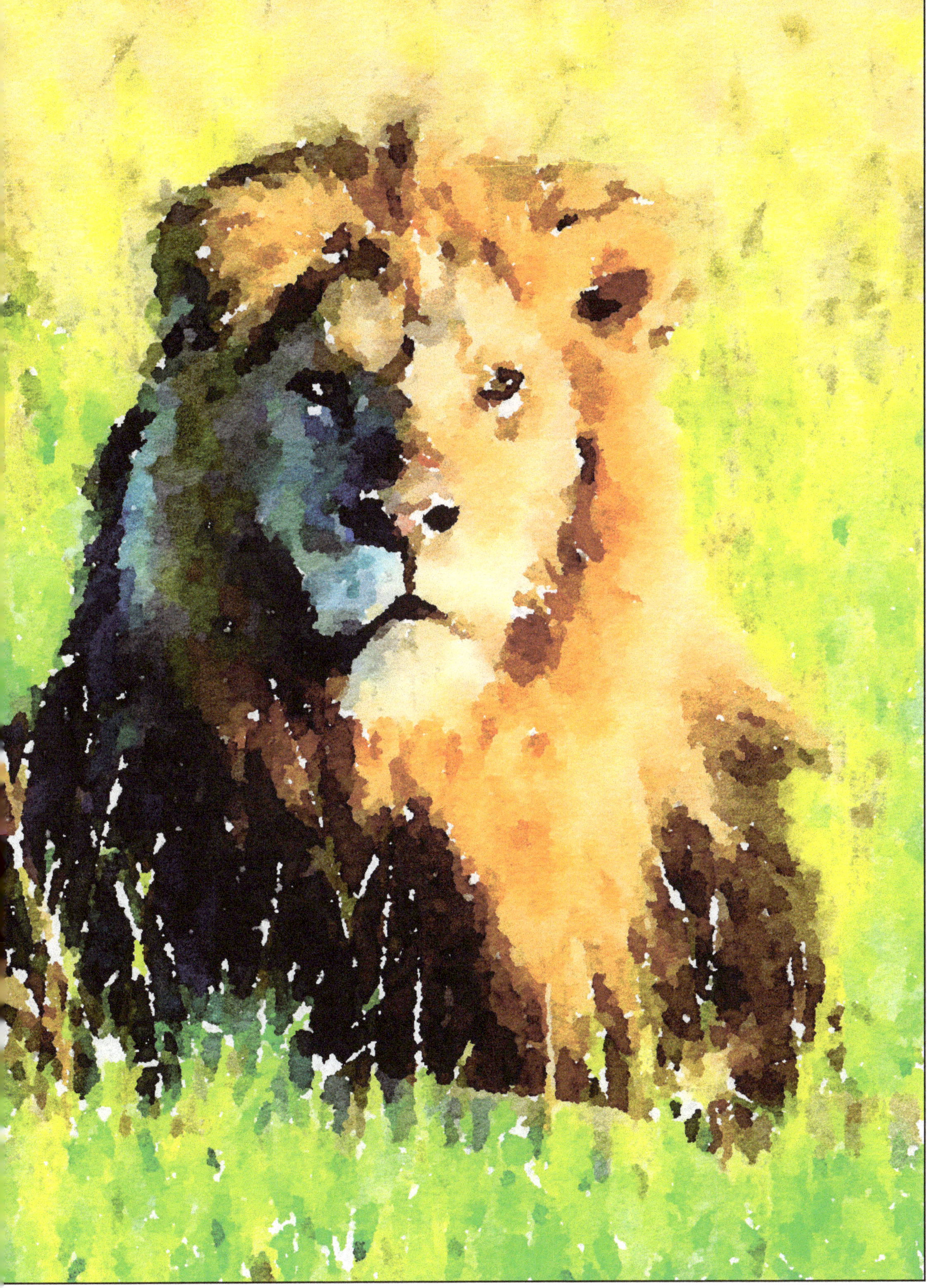

Kenya...

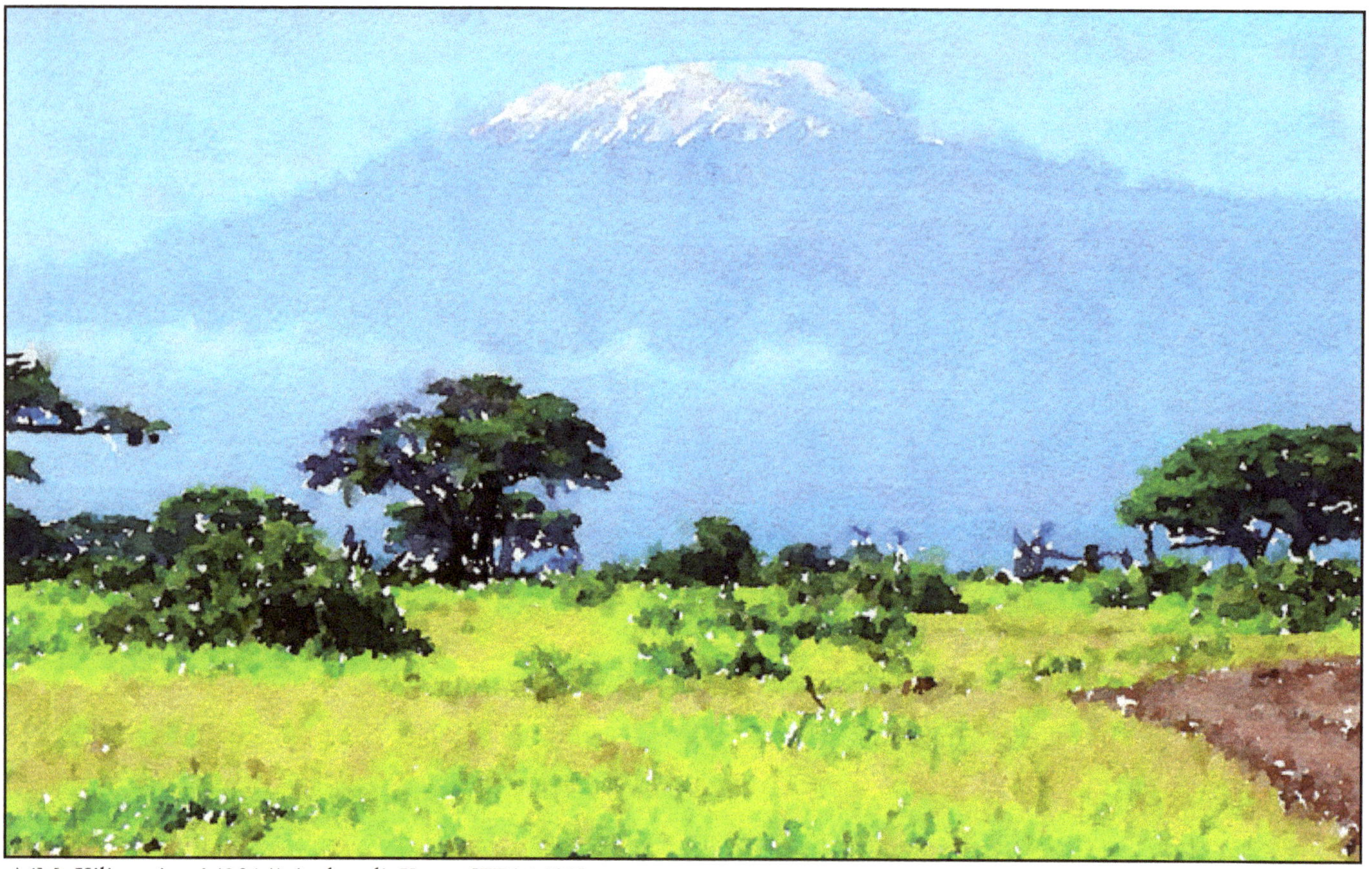

▲'Mt Kilimanjaro' (2014) Amboseli, Kenya [FEA1401].

'Harrowing Hippo' (2014), Kenya. [FEA1402].▼

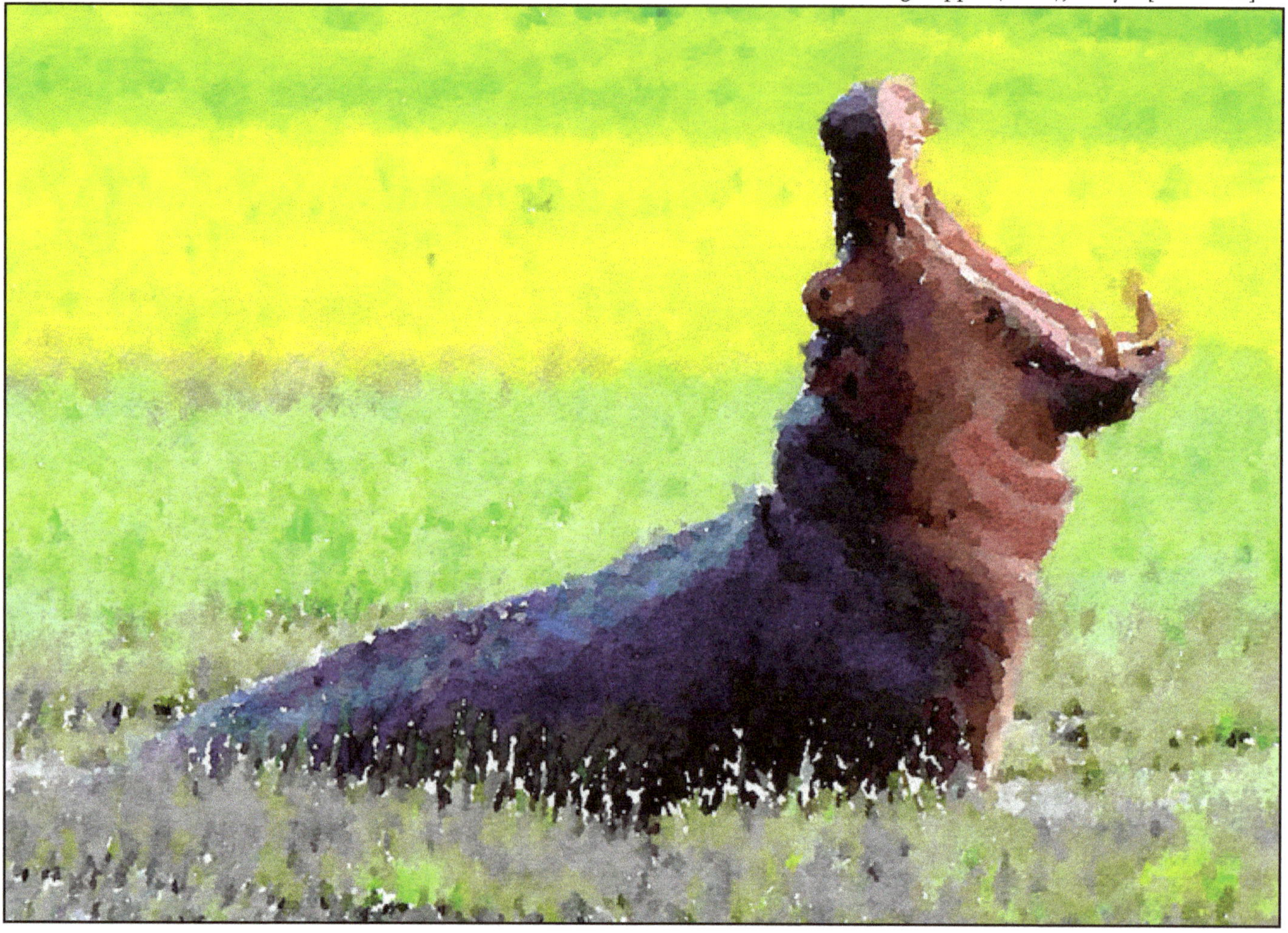

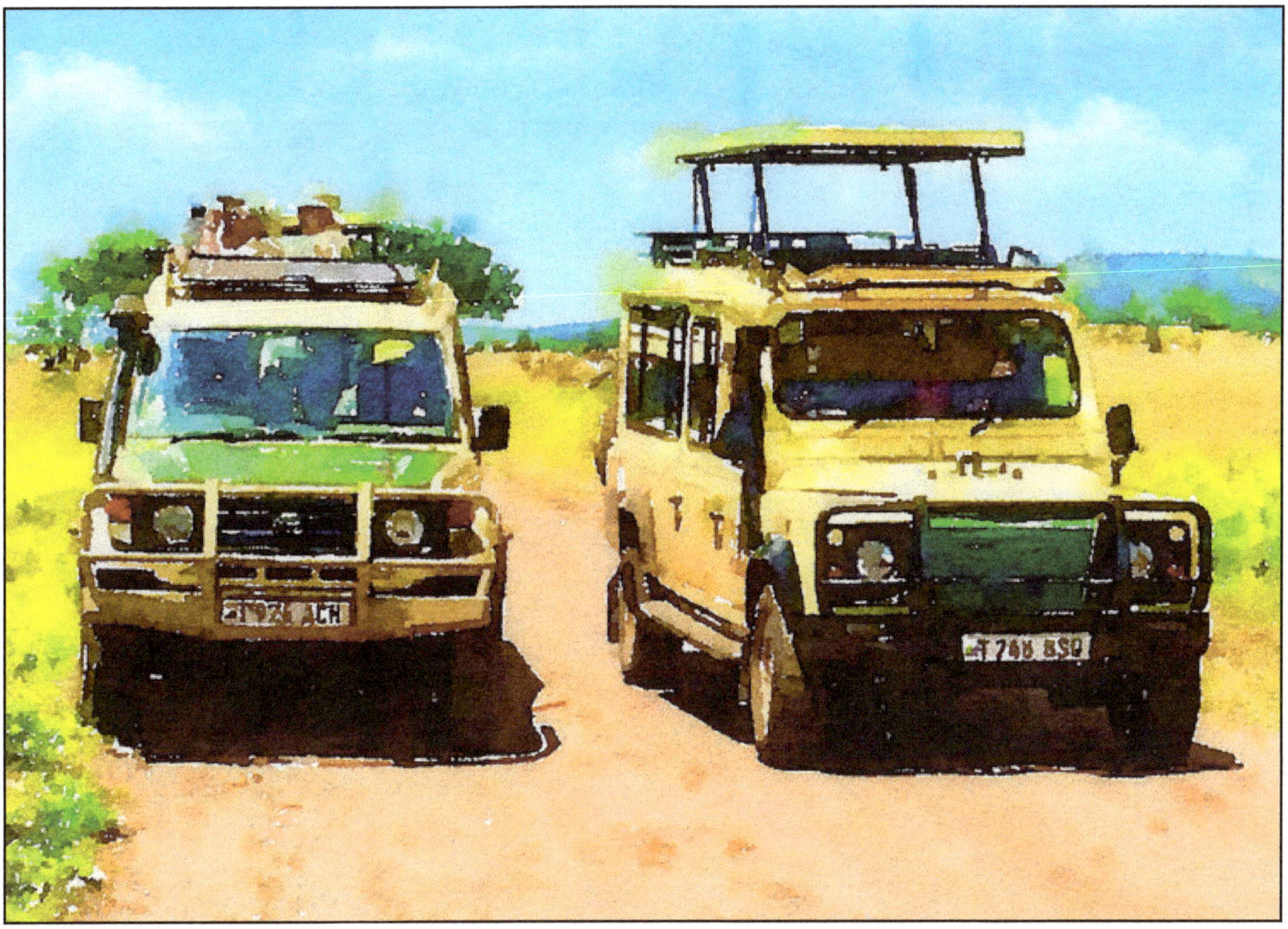

▲'On Safari' (2014), Serengeti, Kenya [FEA1403].

'Cotters Camp' (2014), Serengeti, Kenya [FEA1404].▼

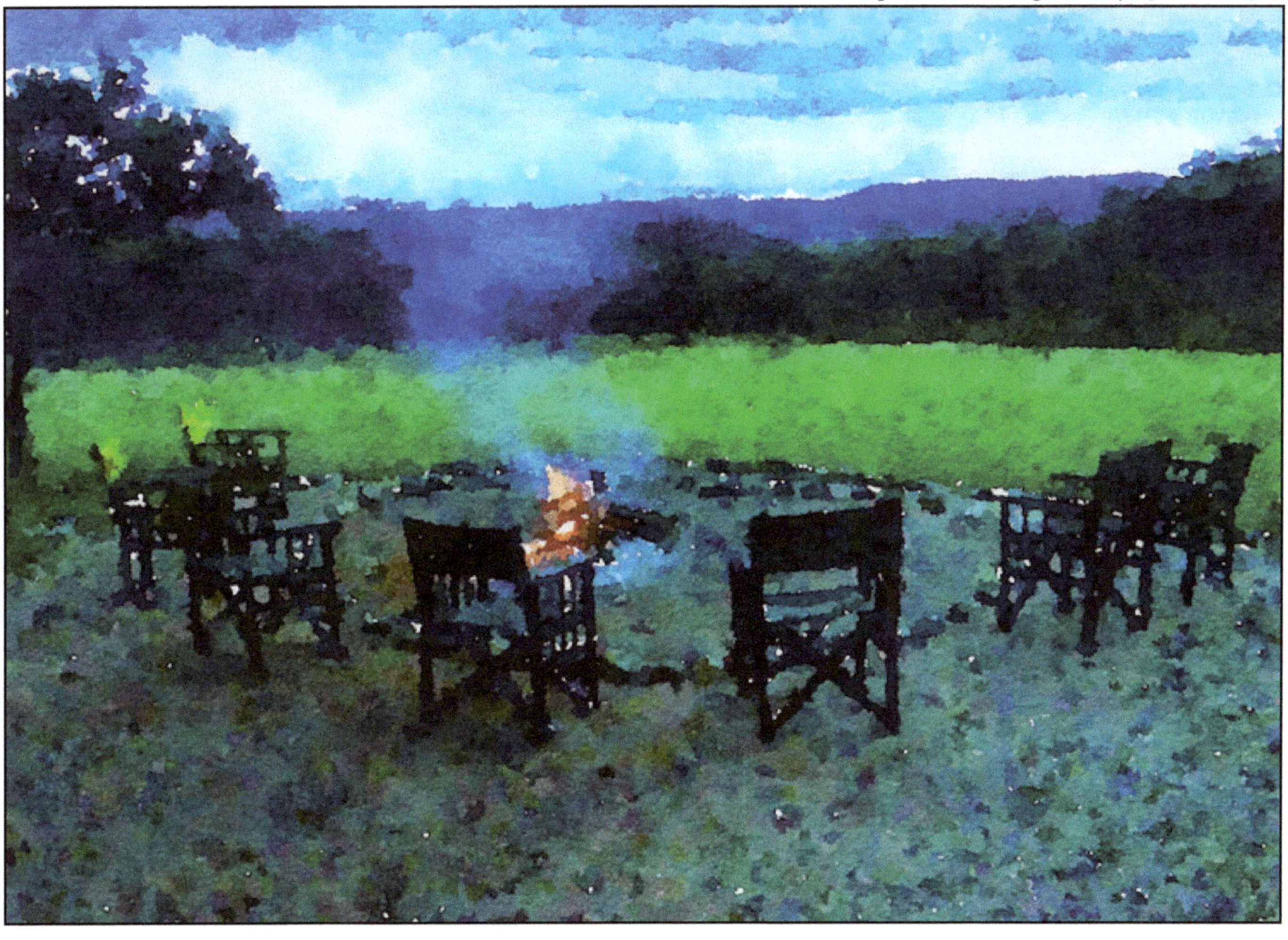

Tanzania...

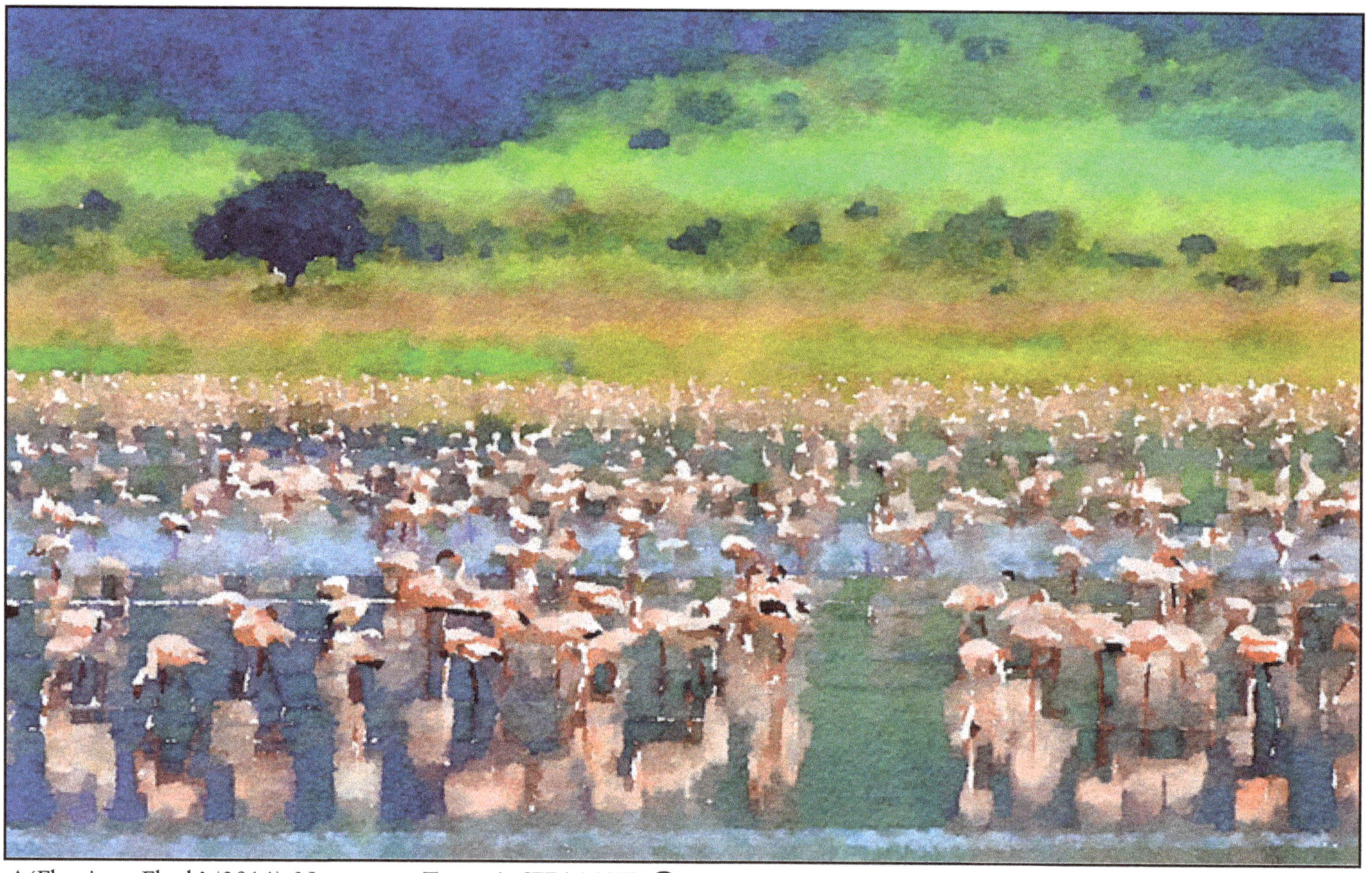

▲'Flamingo Flock' (2014), Ngorogoro, Tanzania [FEA1407]. ©

'Zebra Crossing' (2014), Ngorogoro, Tanzania. [AKR1701].▼

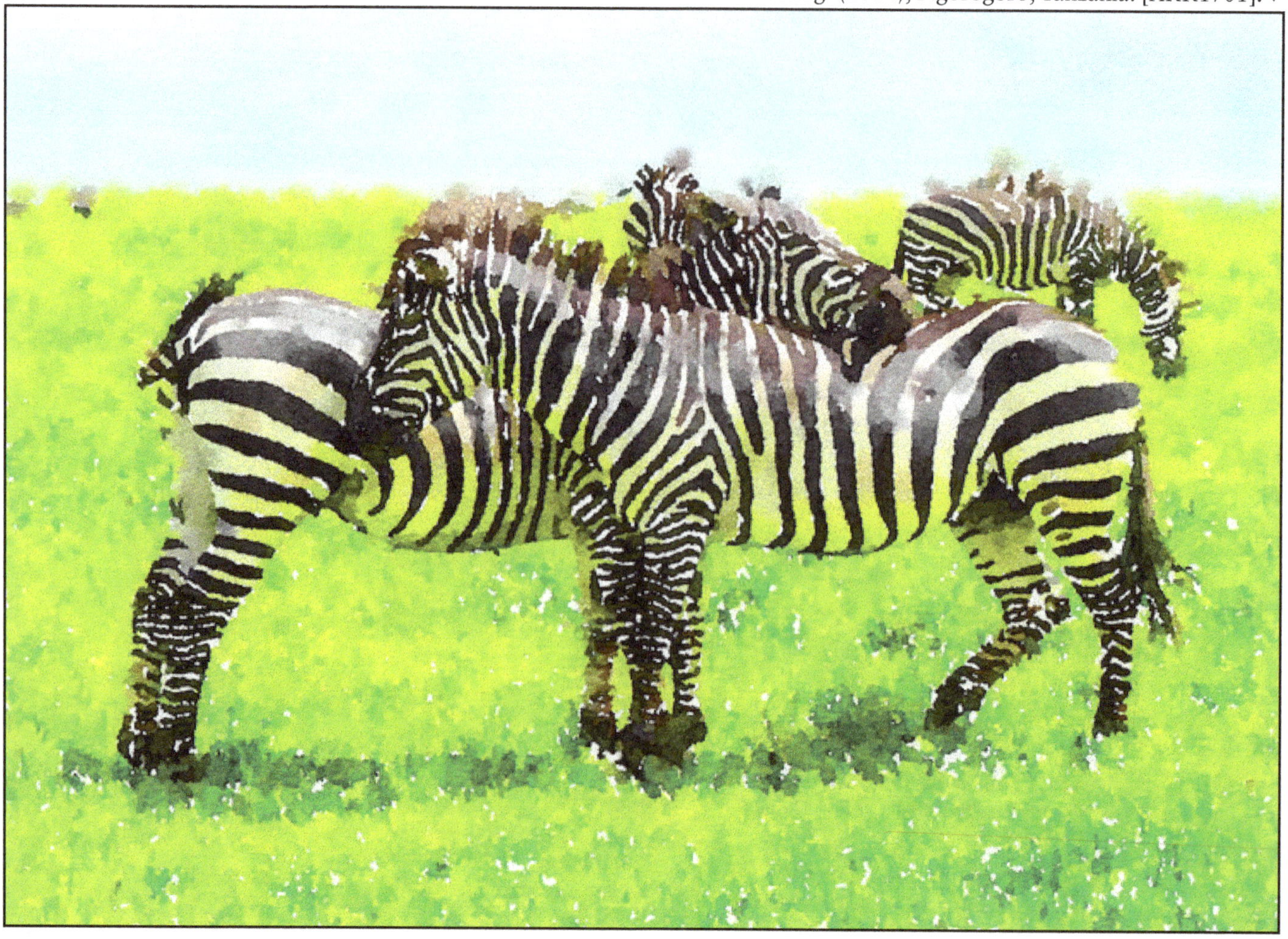

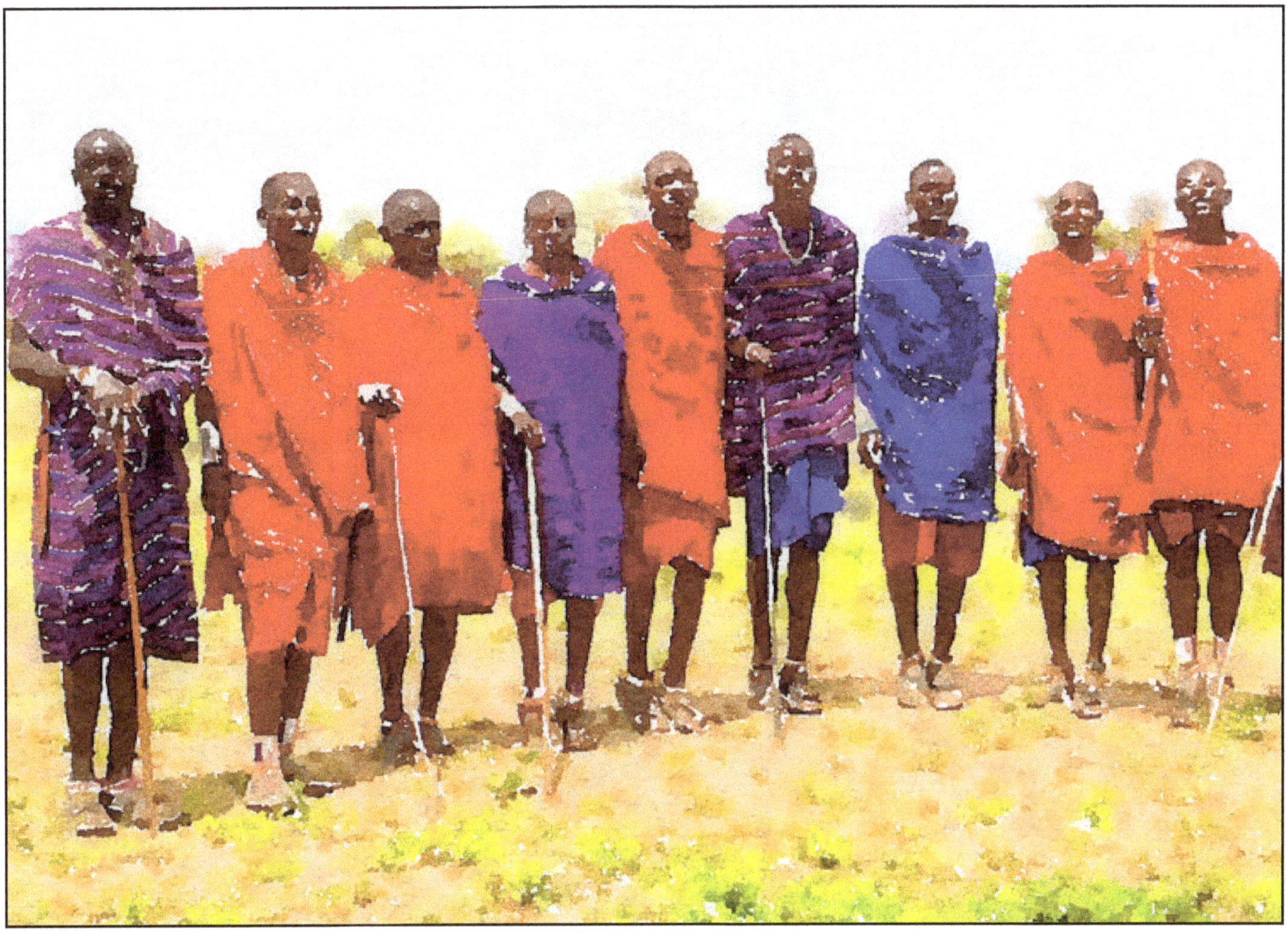

▲'Masai Greeting' (2014), Masai Mara, Tanzania [FEA1406].

'Serengeti Traffic Jam' (2014), Serengeti, Tanzania [FEA1408].▼

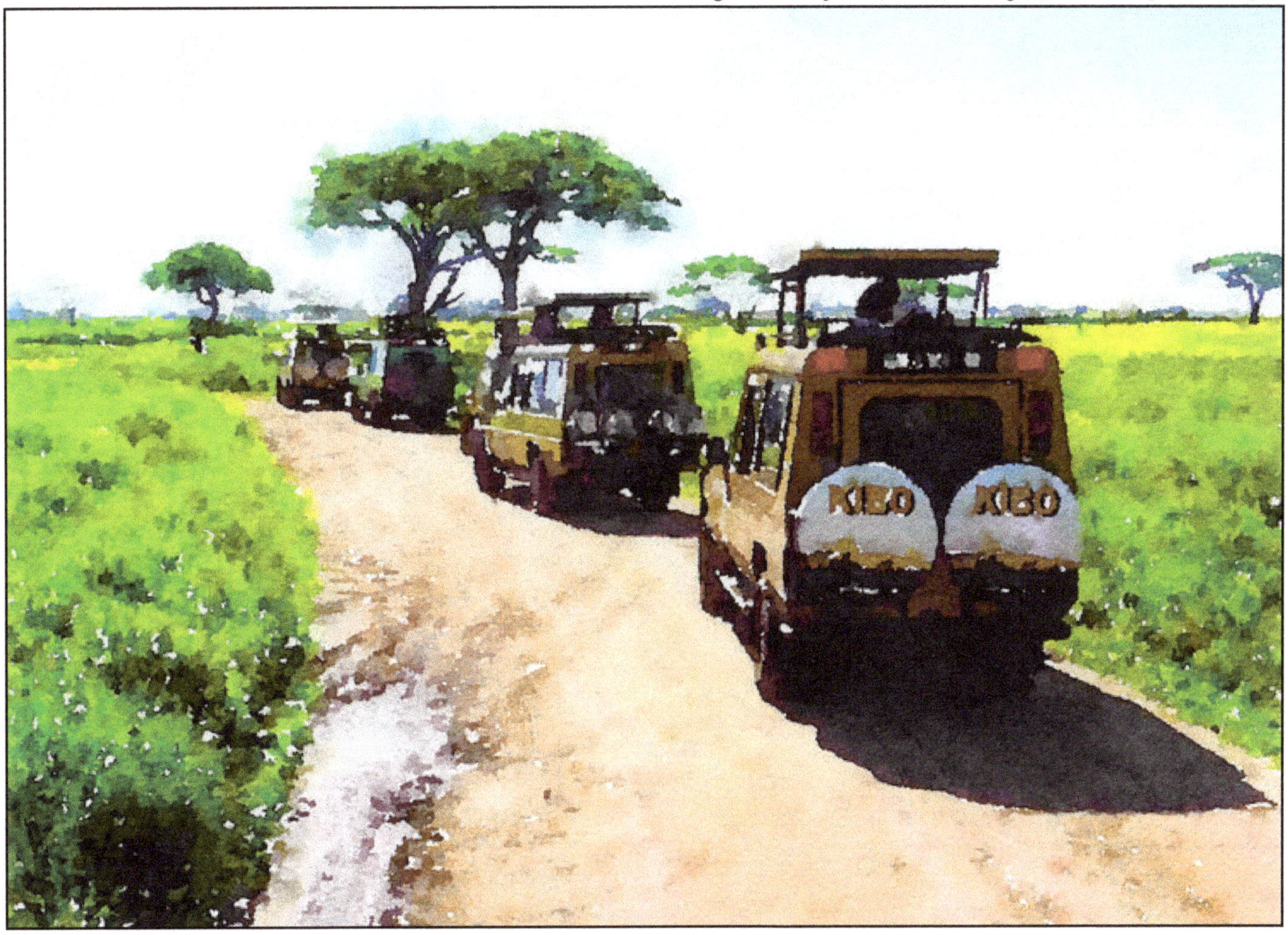

ASIA

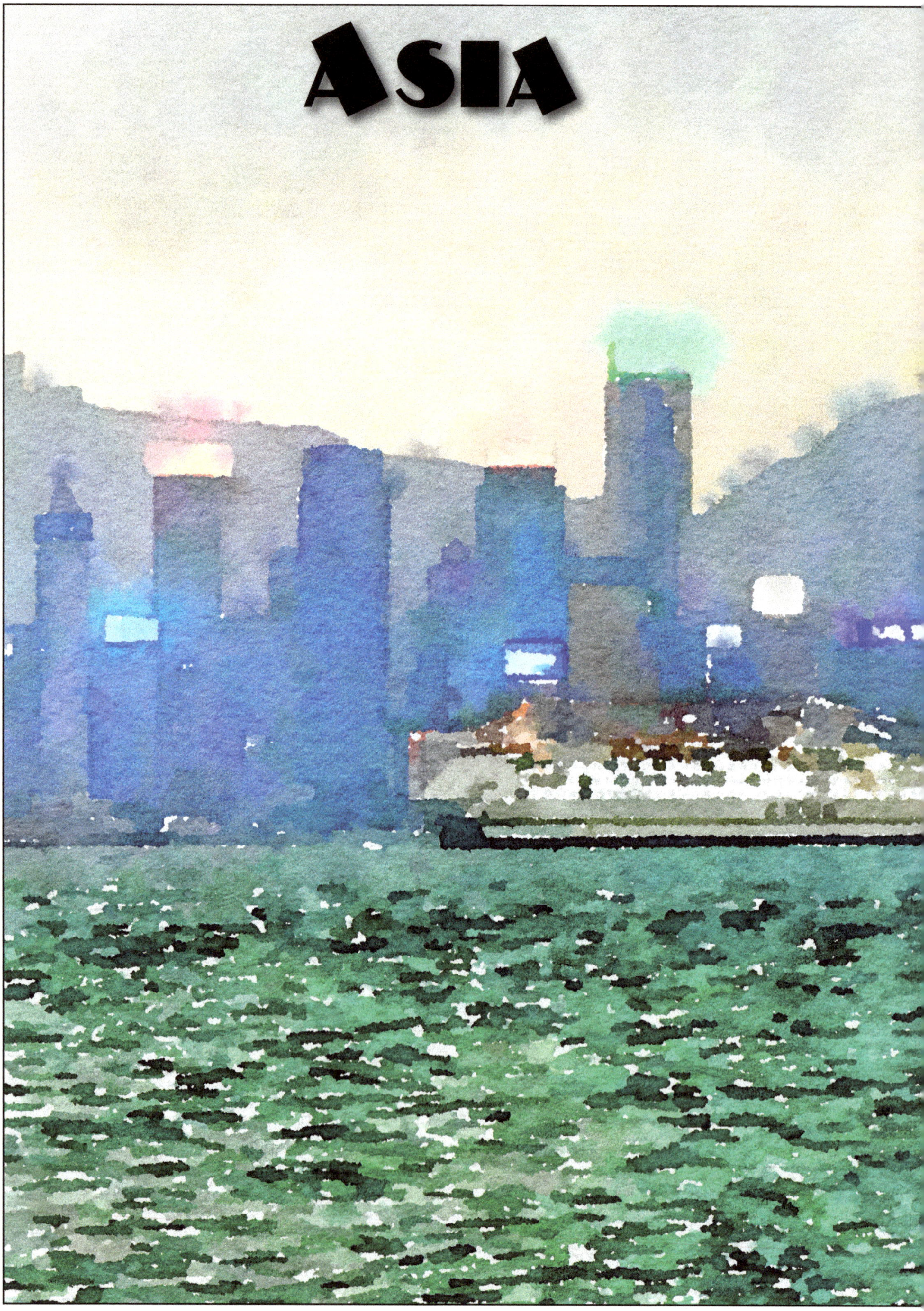

‘Hong Kong Harbour’ (2017), Hong Kong, China [ACN1702].

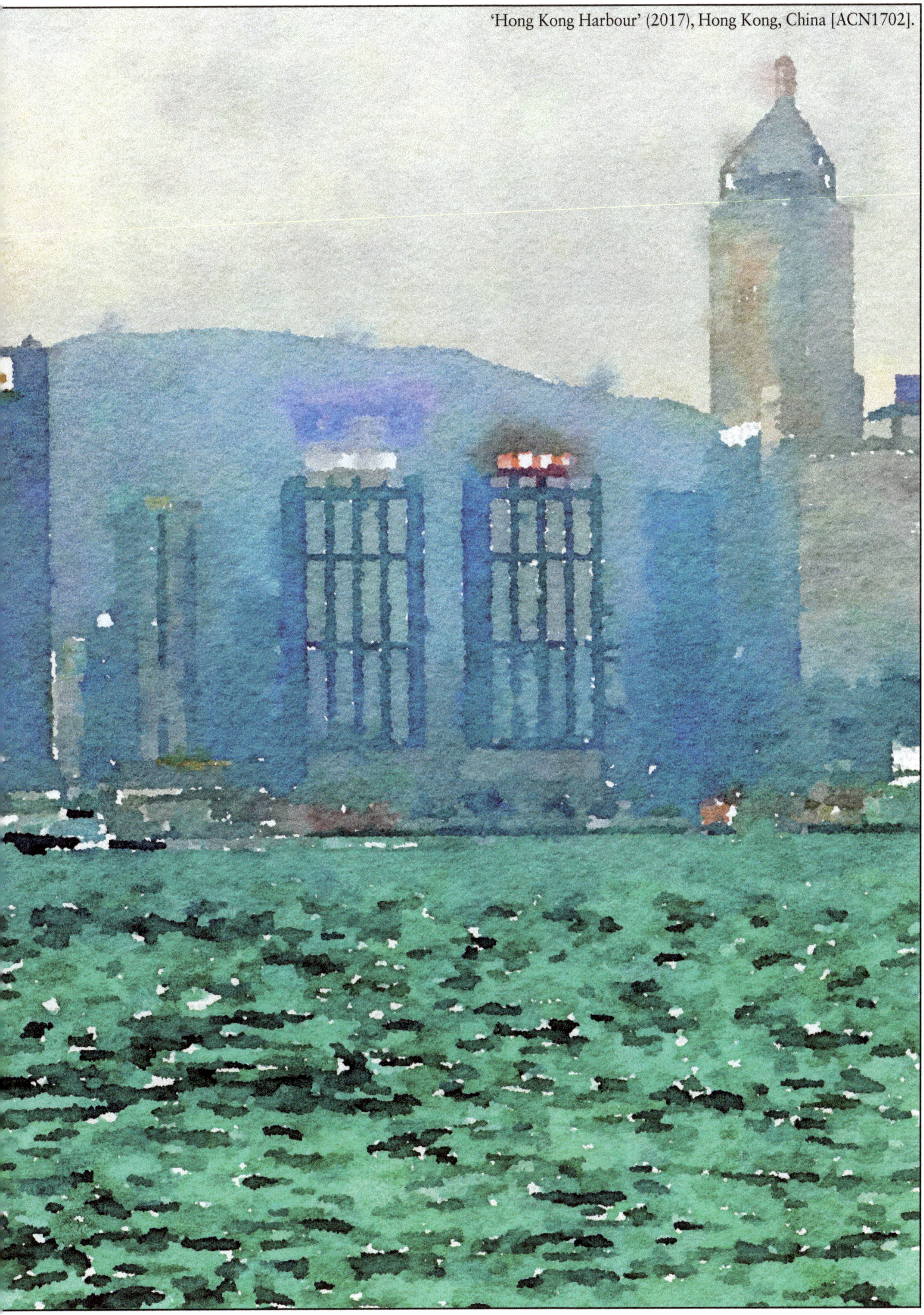

China...

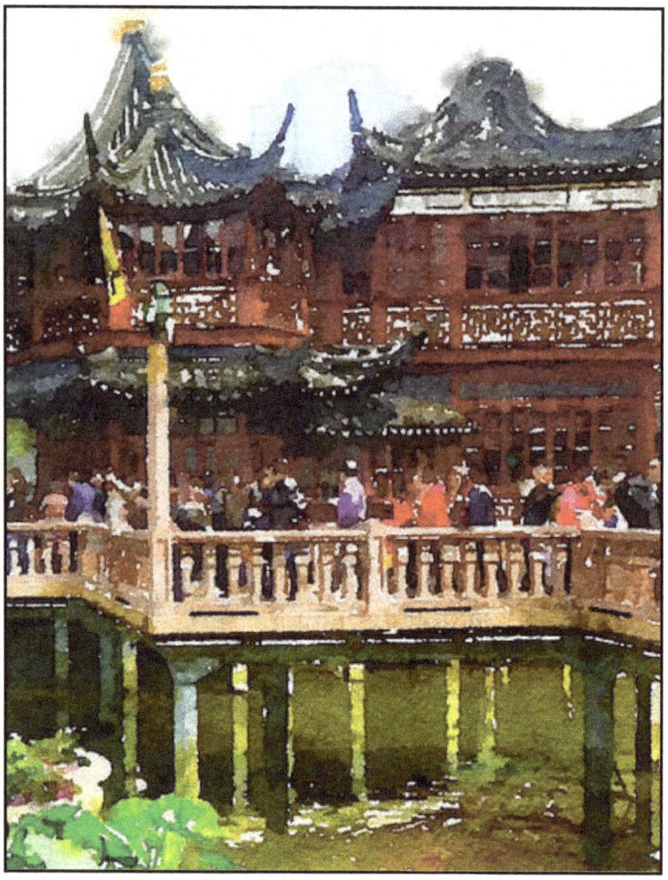

▲'Shanghai Waters' (2017), Shanghai, China [ACN1705].

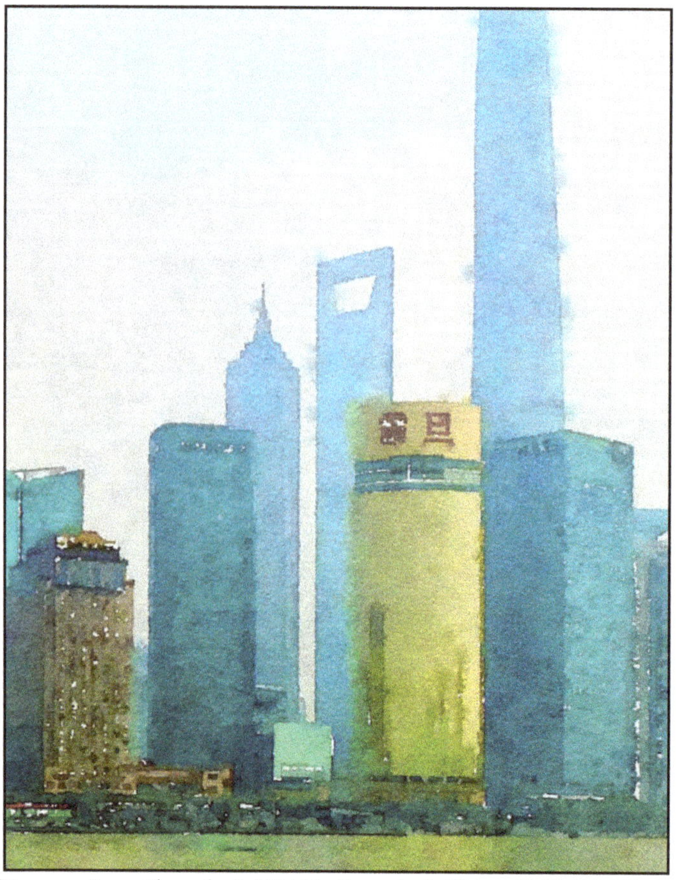

'Towers Over Shanghai' (2017), Shanghai, China [ACN1701].▲

▼'The Lady In Red' (2017), Beijing, China [ACN1704].

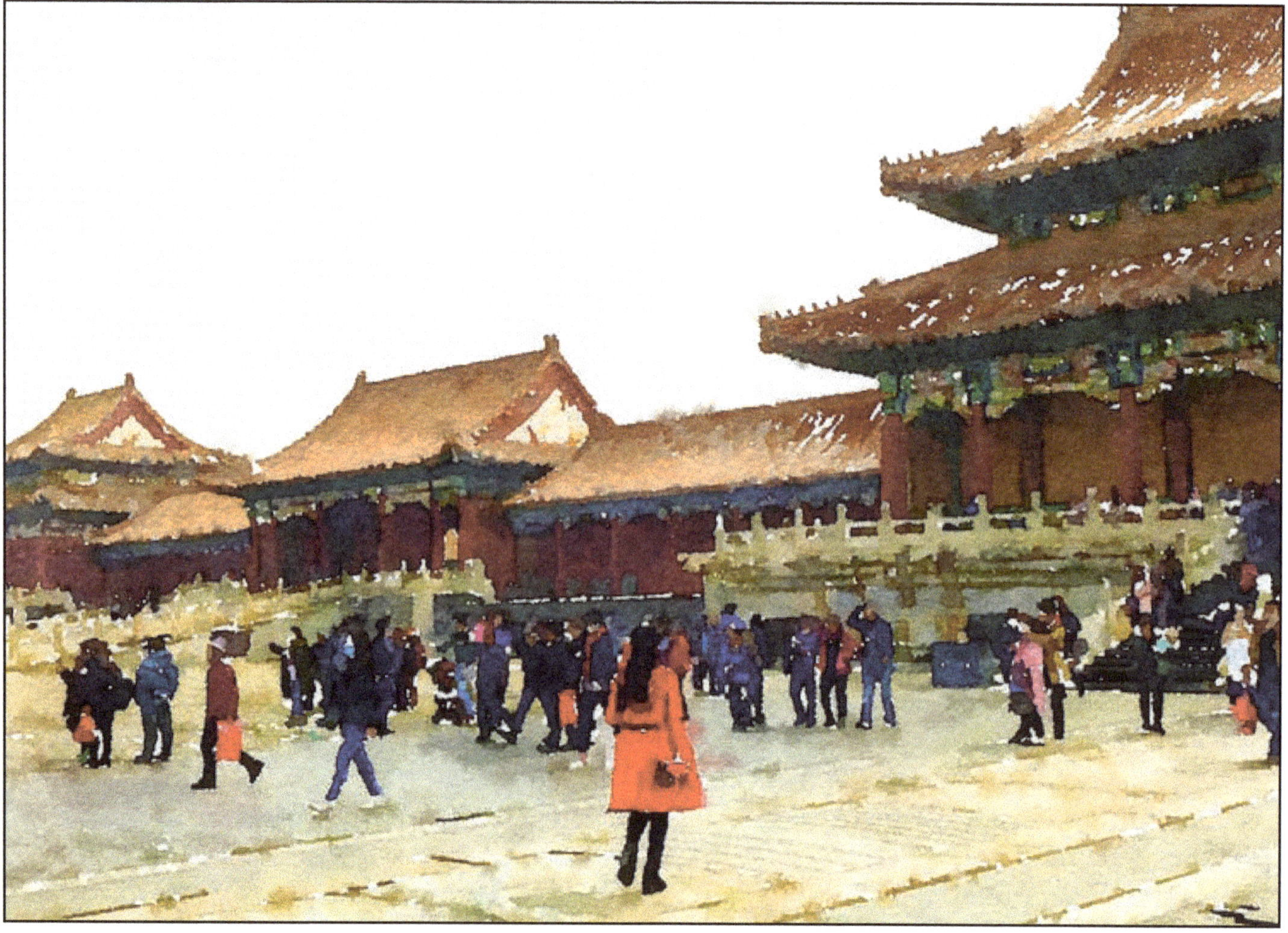

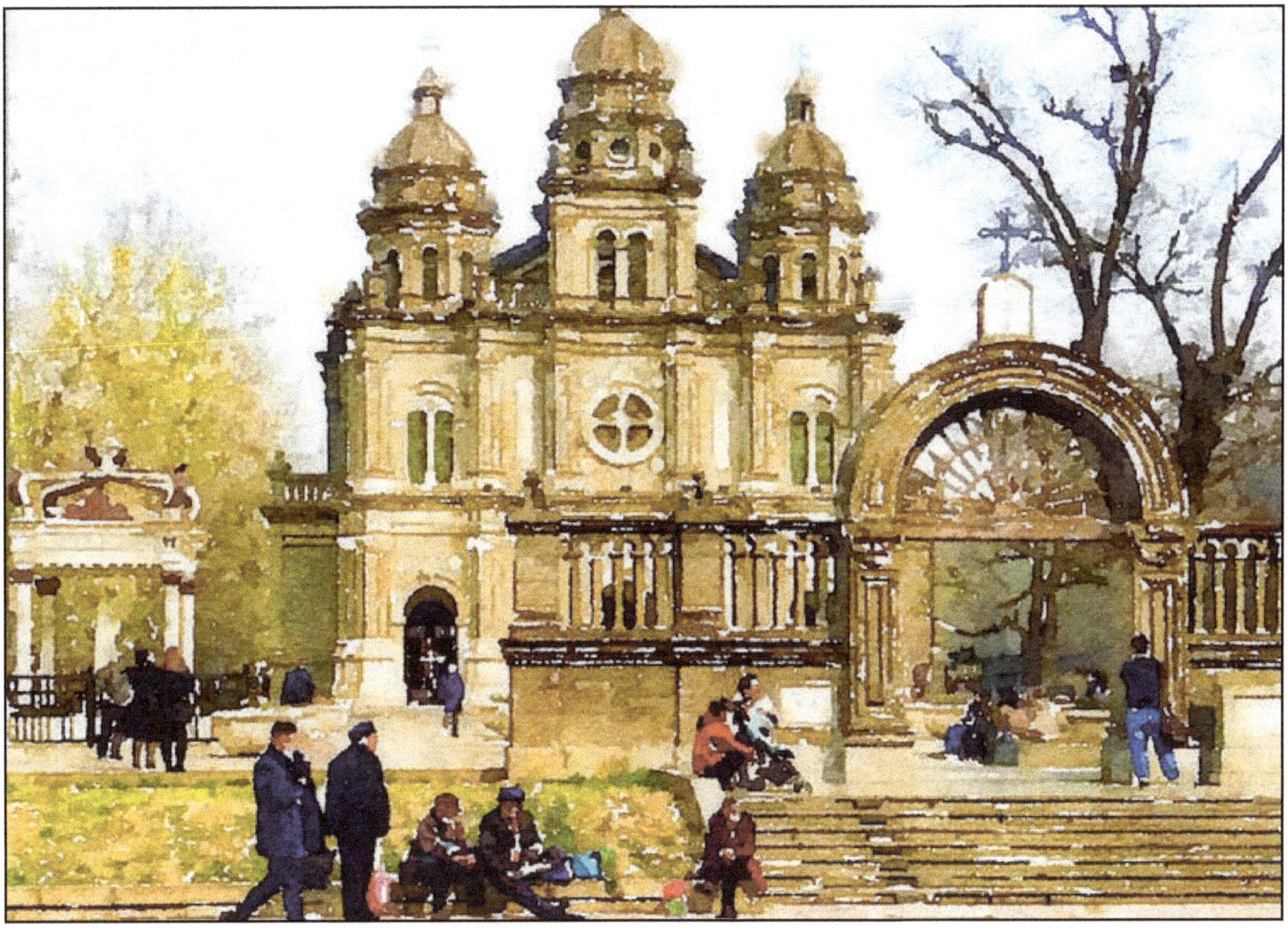

▲'Colonial Legacies' (2017), Beijing, China [ACN1703].

▼ 'Chenxiangge Road' (2017), Shanghai, China [ACN1706].

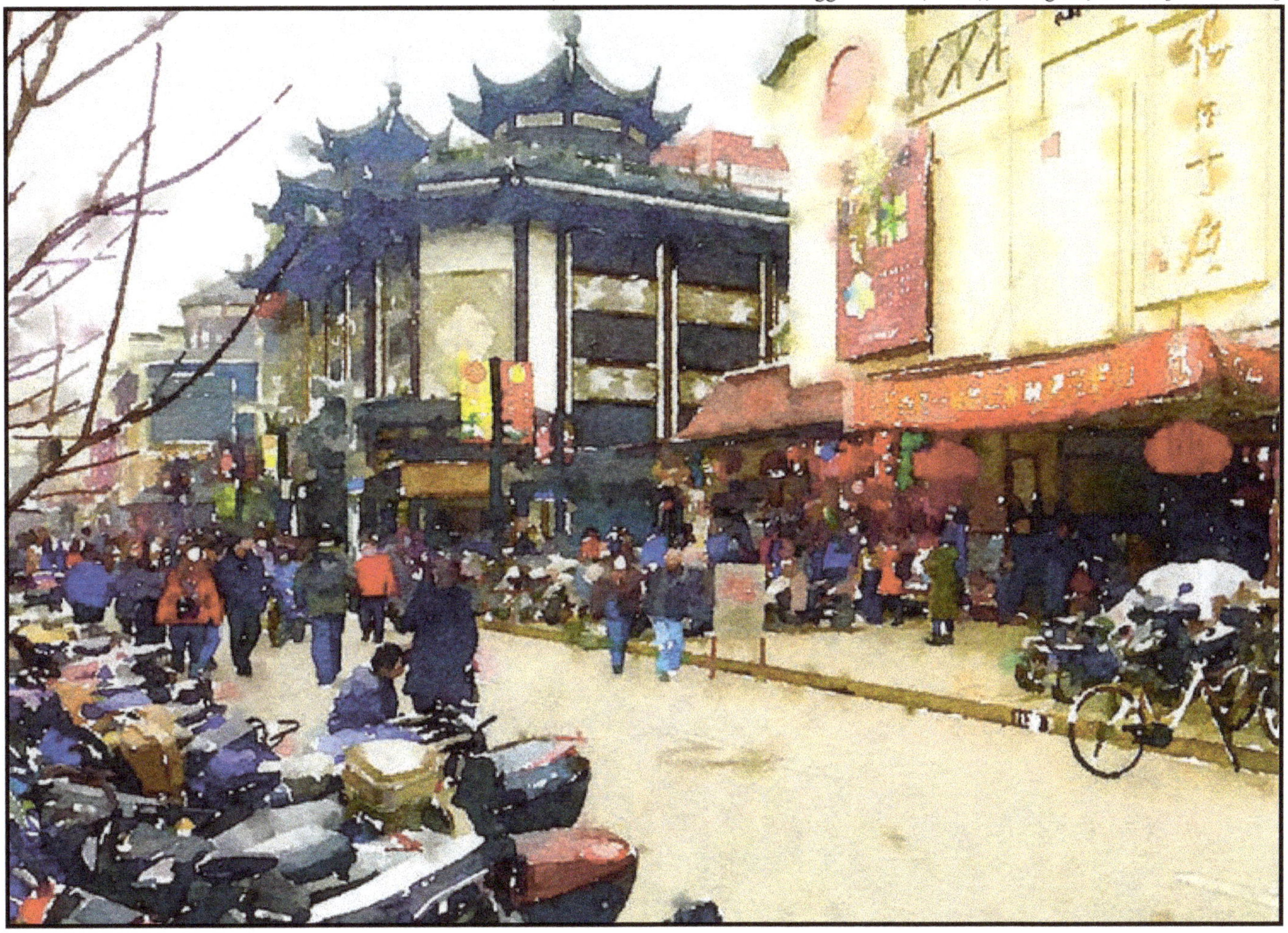

Japan...

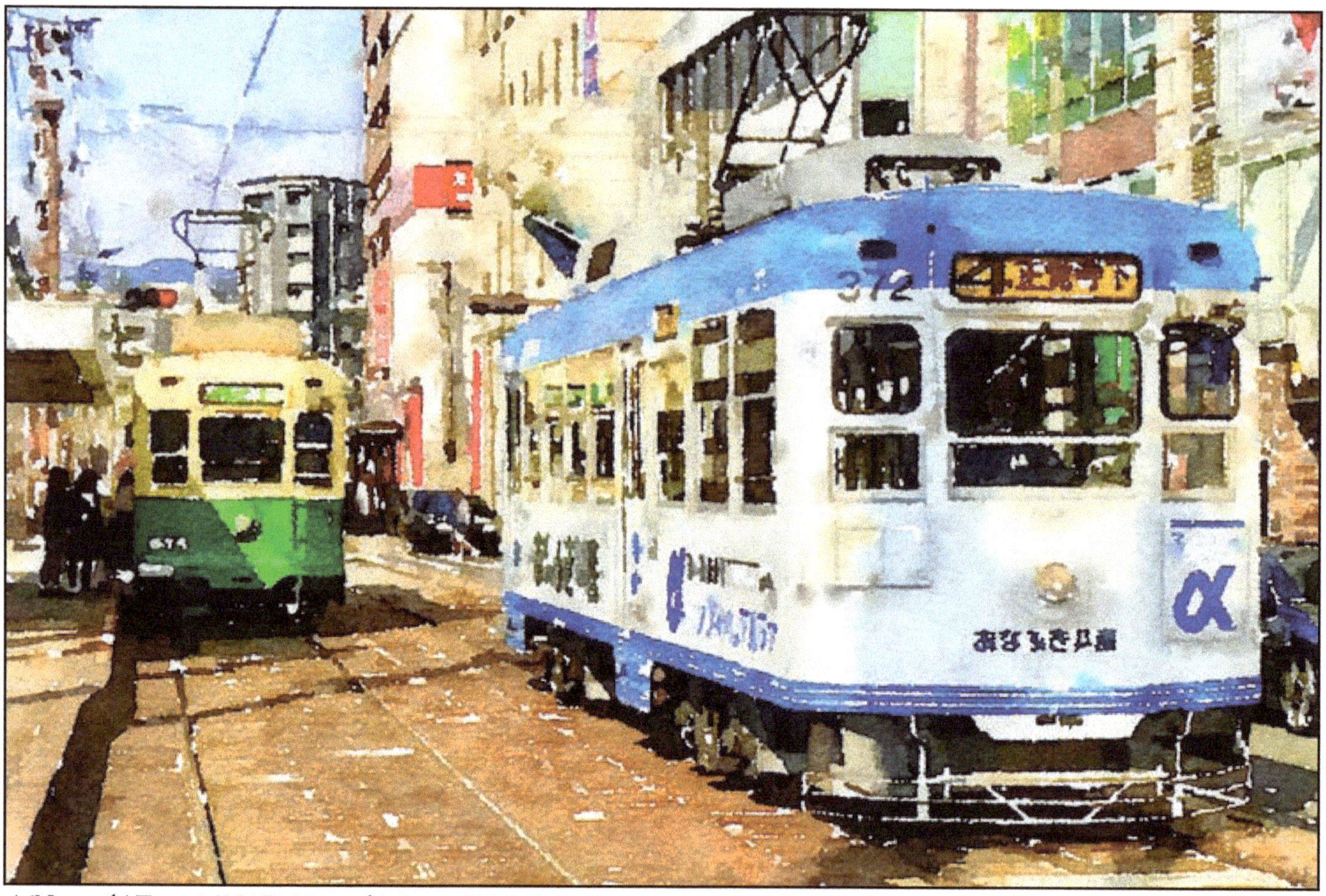

▲'Nagasaki Trams' (2017), Nagasaki, Japan [AJP1701].

'Colorful street signs in Kabukicho, Shinjuku' (2102), Tokyo, Japan [AJP2102]. ⊘▼

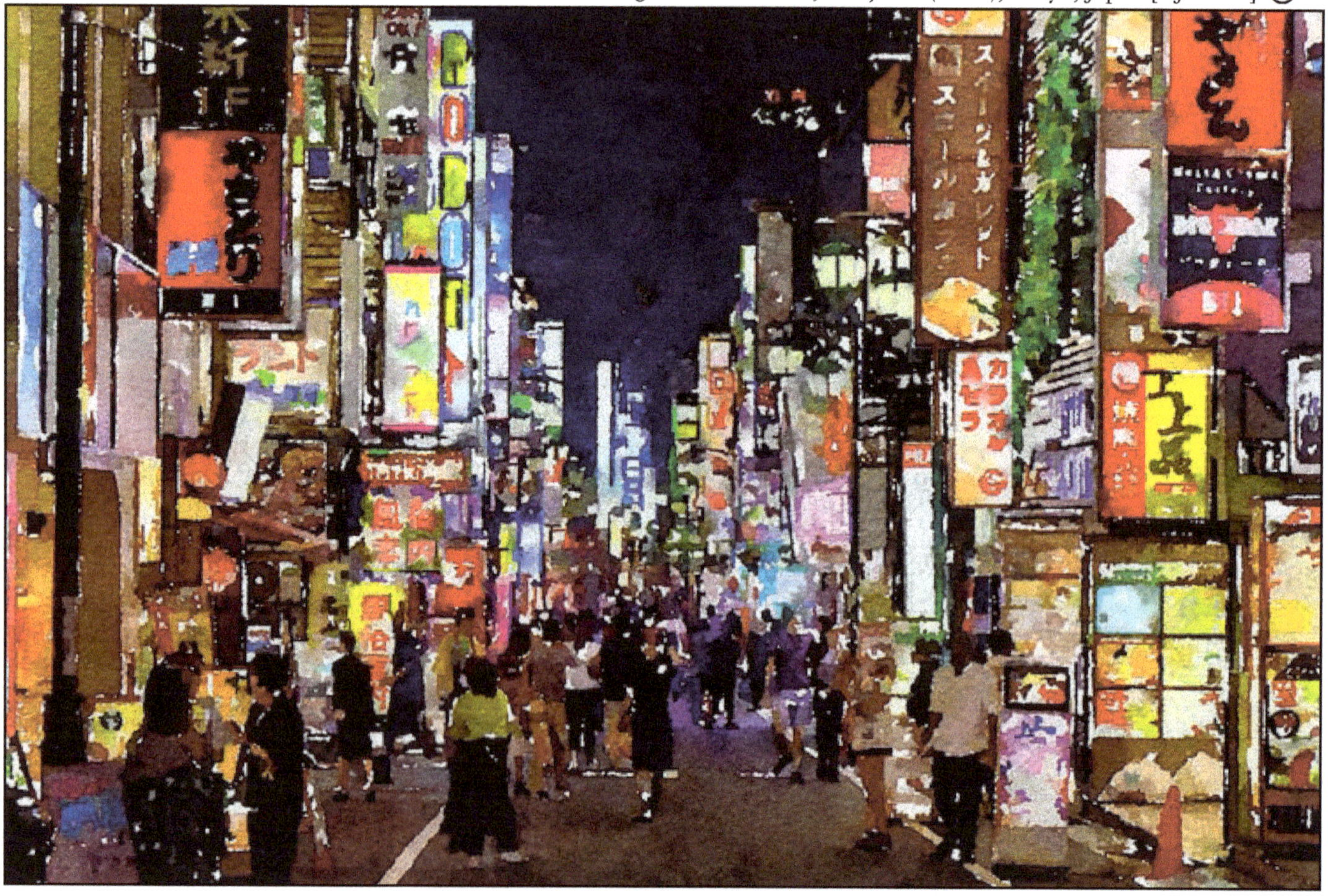

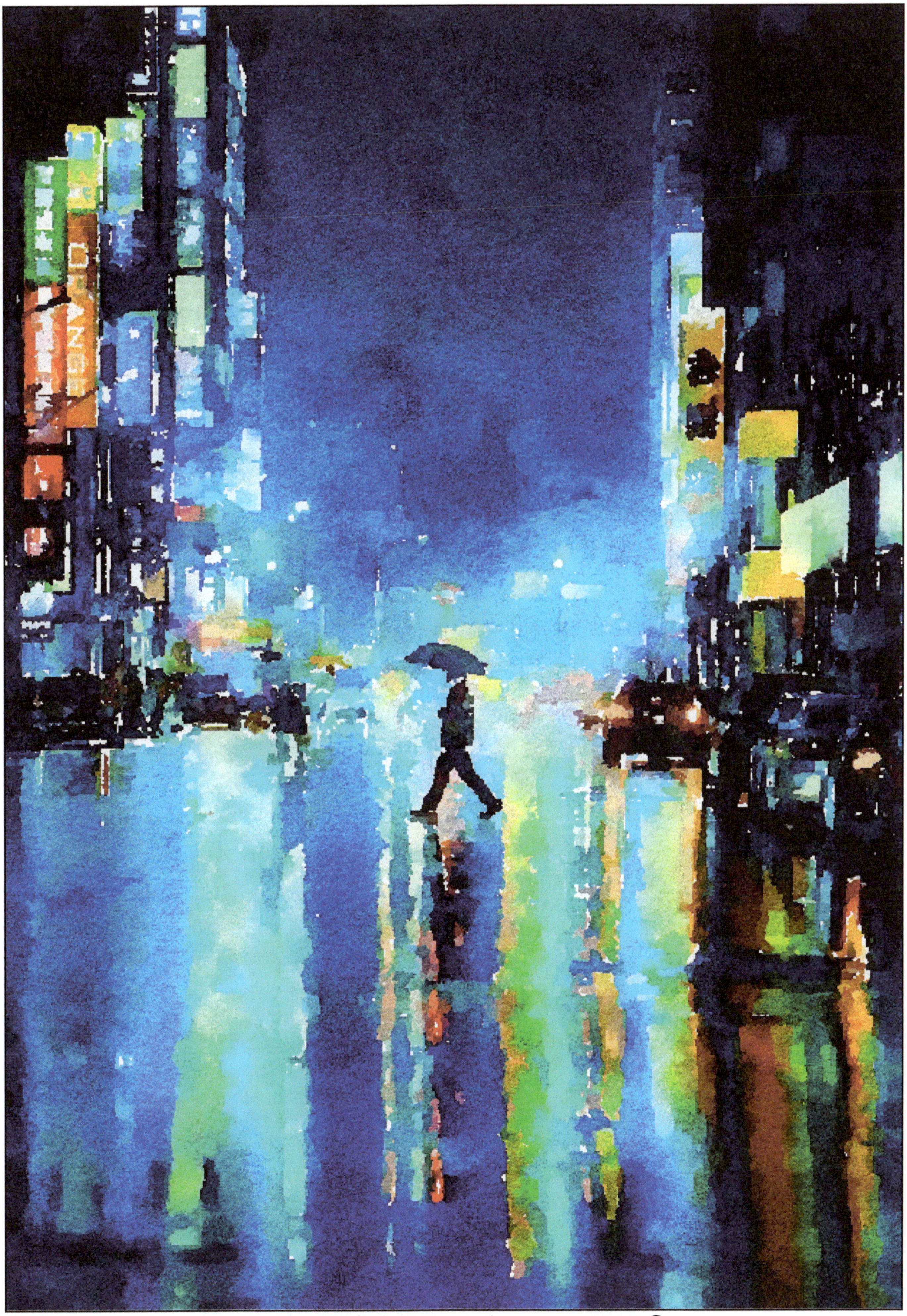

▲'Reflections of Tokyo' (2021), Tokyo, Japan [AJP2101]. ©

Korea...

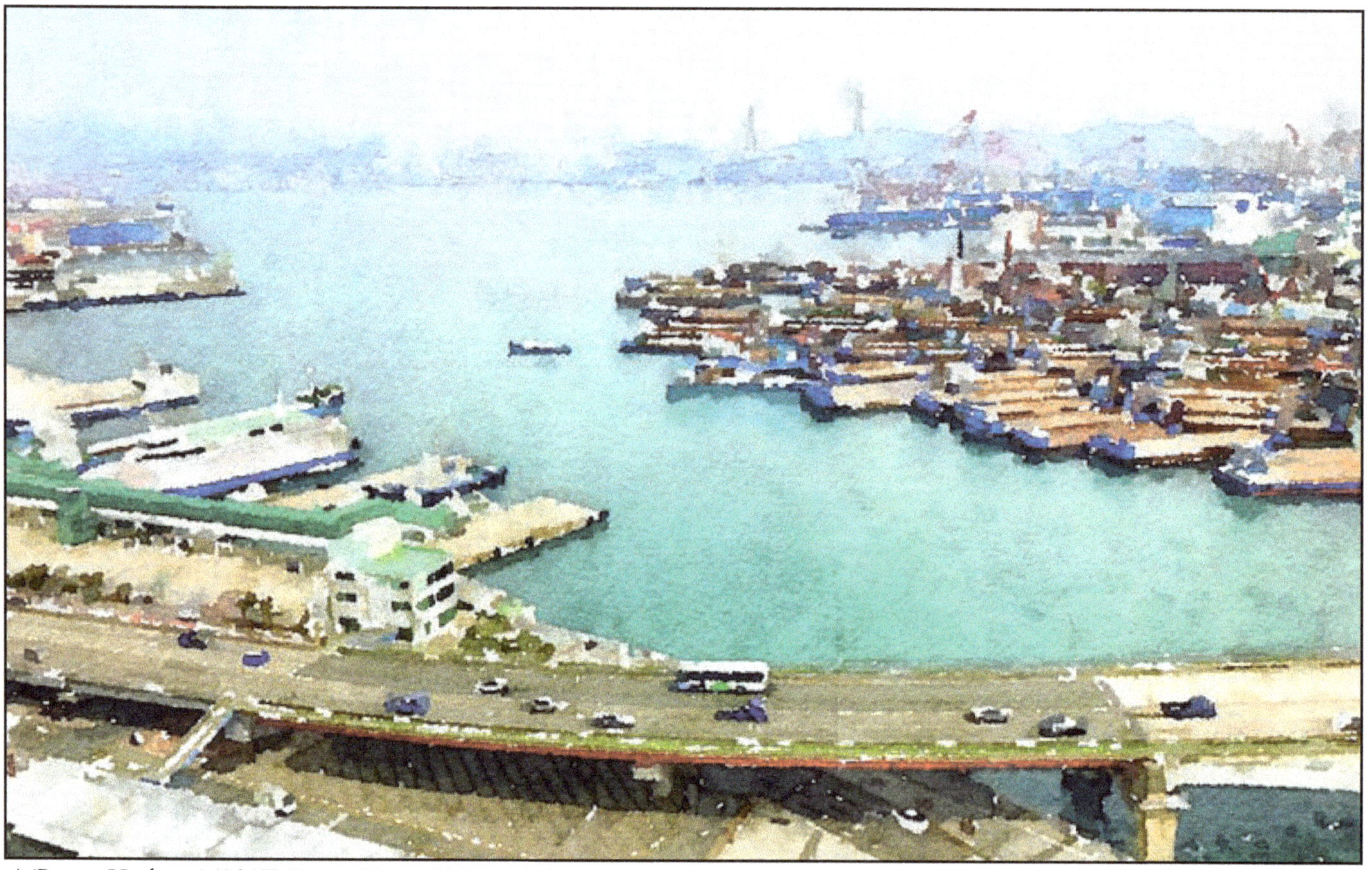

▲'Busan Harbour' (2017) Busan, Korea [AKR1702].

'Dusky Metropolis' (2017), Seoul, Korea. [AKR1701]. ▼

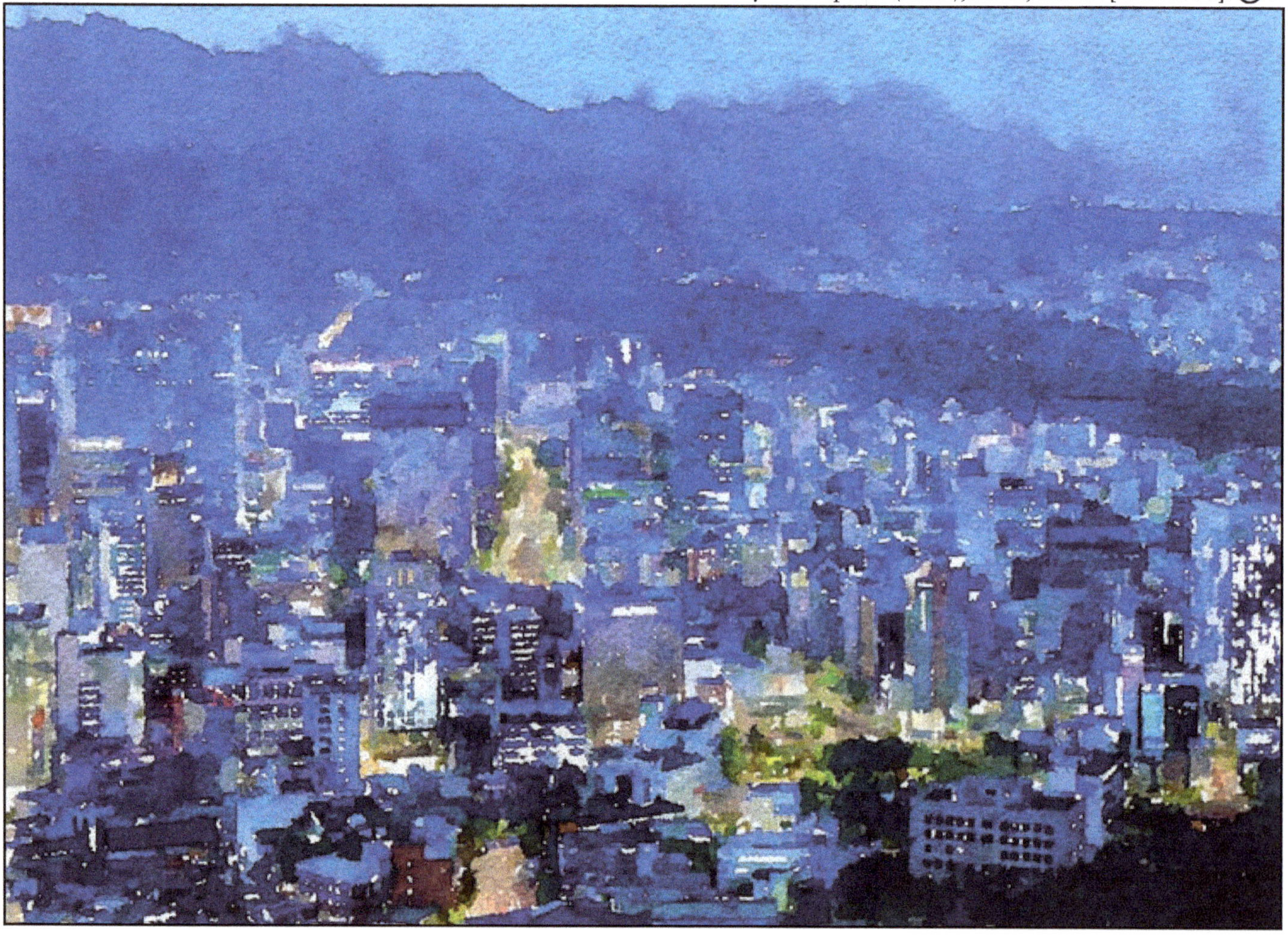

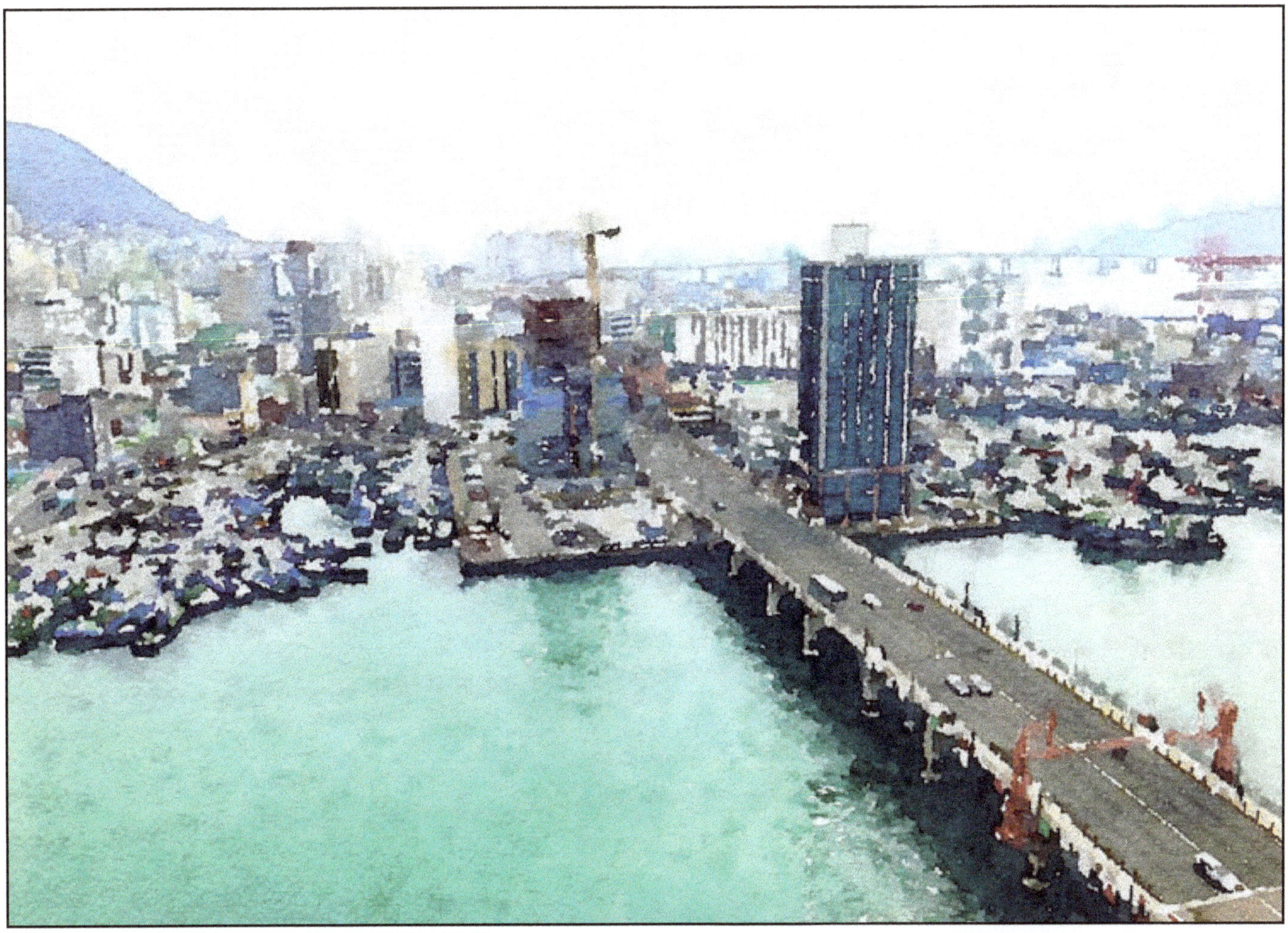

▲'Busan City' (2017), Busan, Korea [AKR1704].

'Busan Harbour Bridge' (2017), Busan, Korea [AKR1703].▼

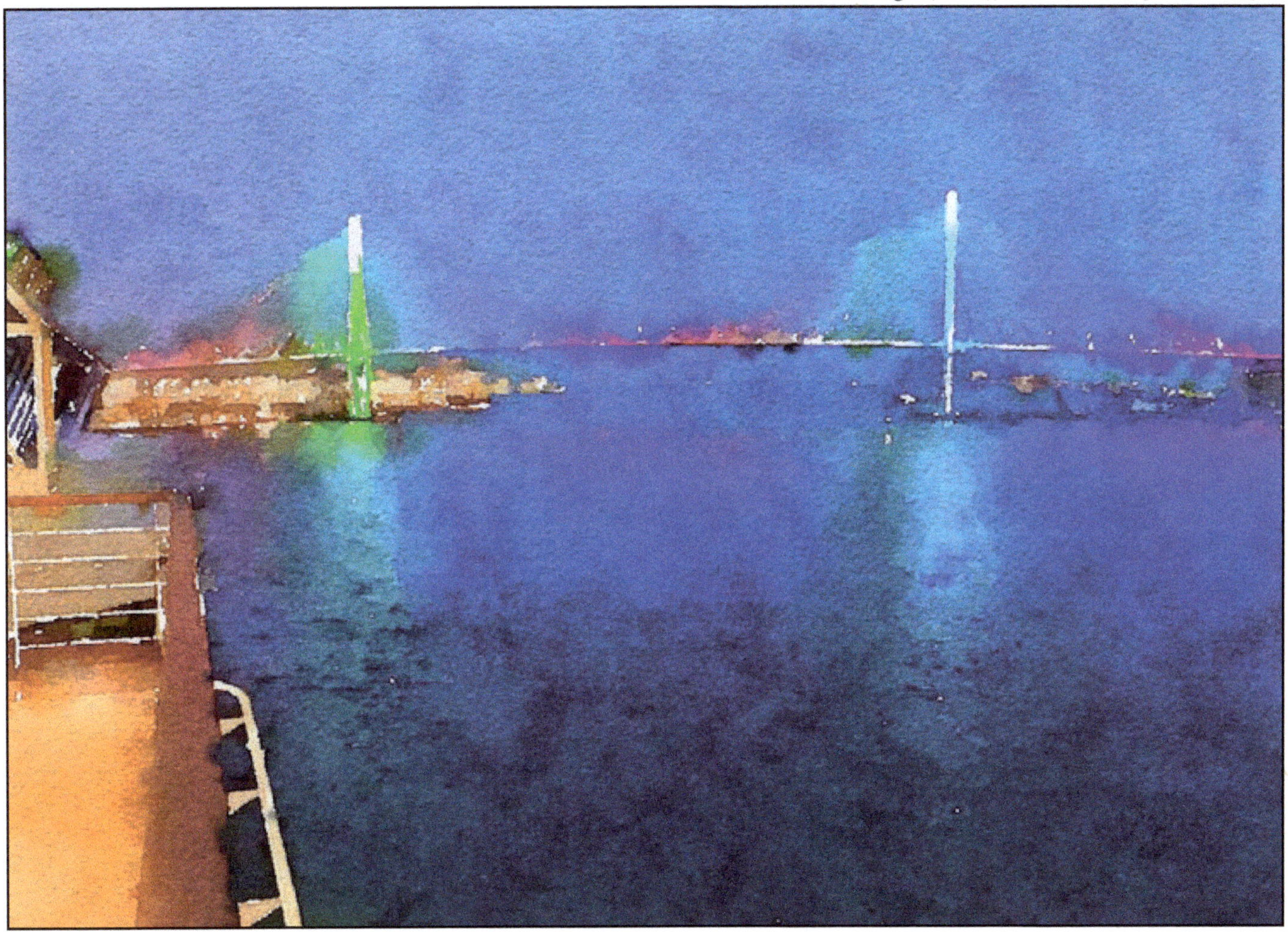

Lebanon...

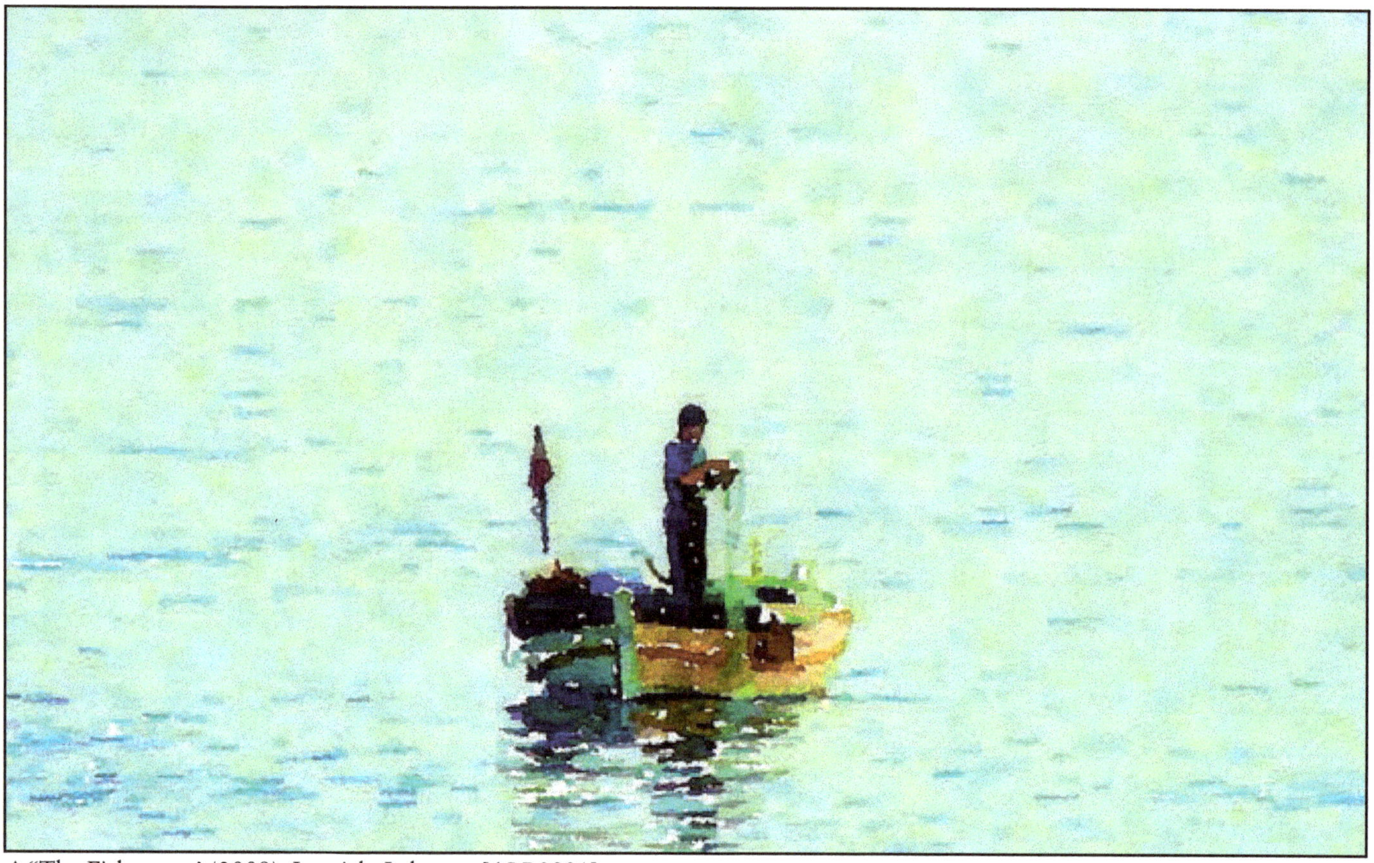

▲"The Fisherman' (2008), Jounieh, Lebanon [ALB0801].

'The Roman Ruins' (2008), Baalbek, Lebanon [ALB0804].▼

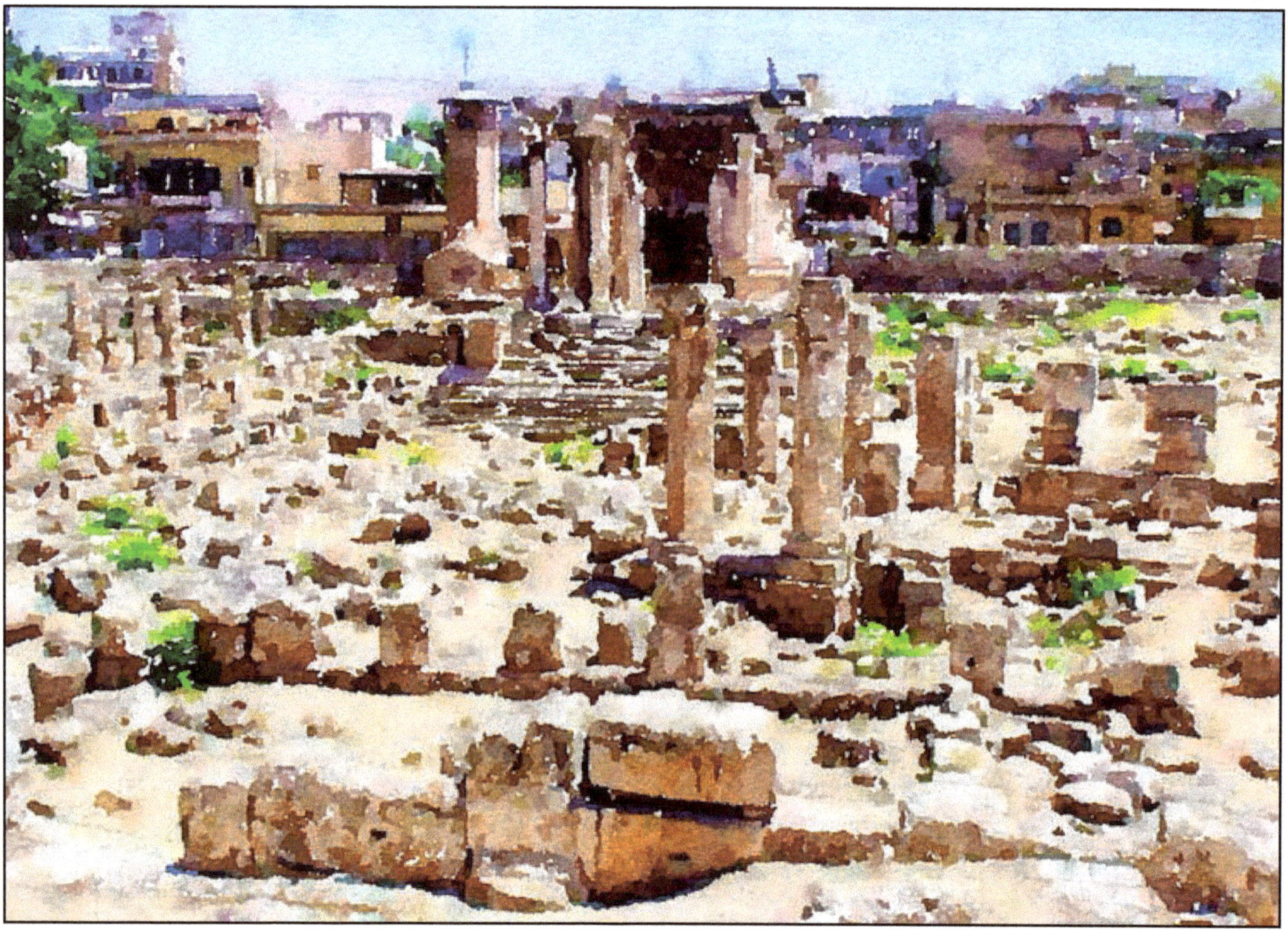

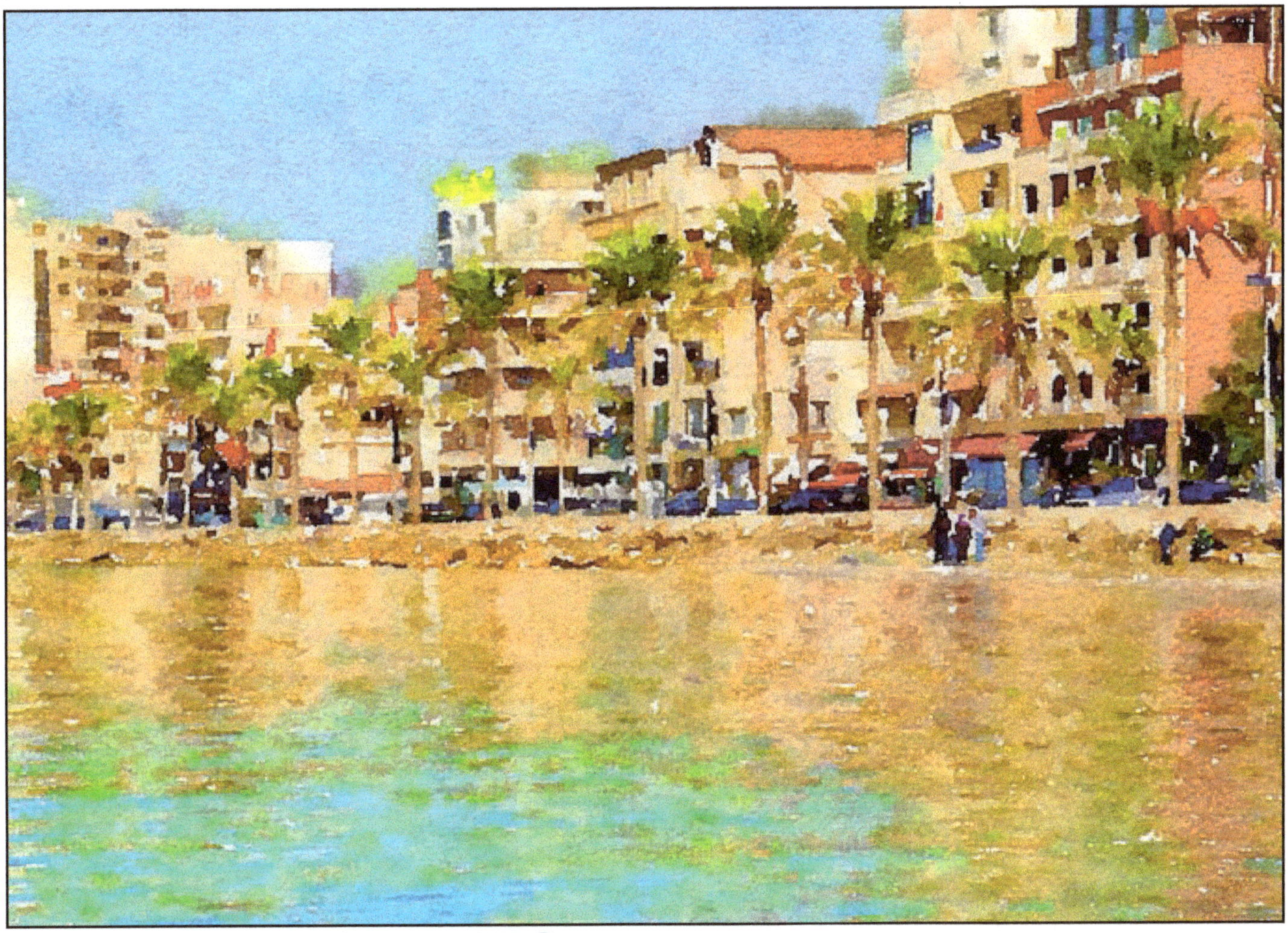

▲'Tyr Waterfront' (2019), Tyr, Lebanon [ALB1902]. ©

'Clearing The Net' (2008), Jounieh, Lebanon [LEB0802].▼

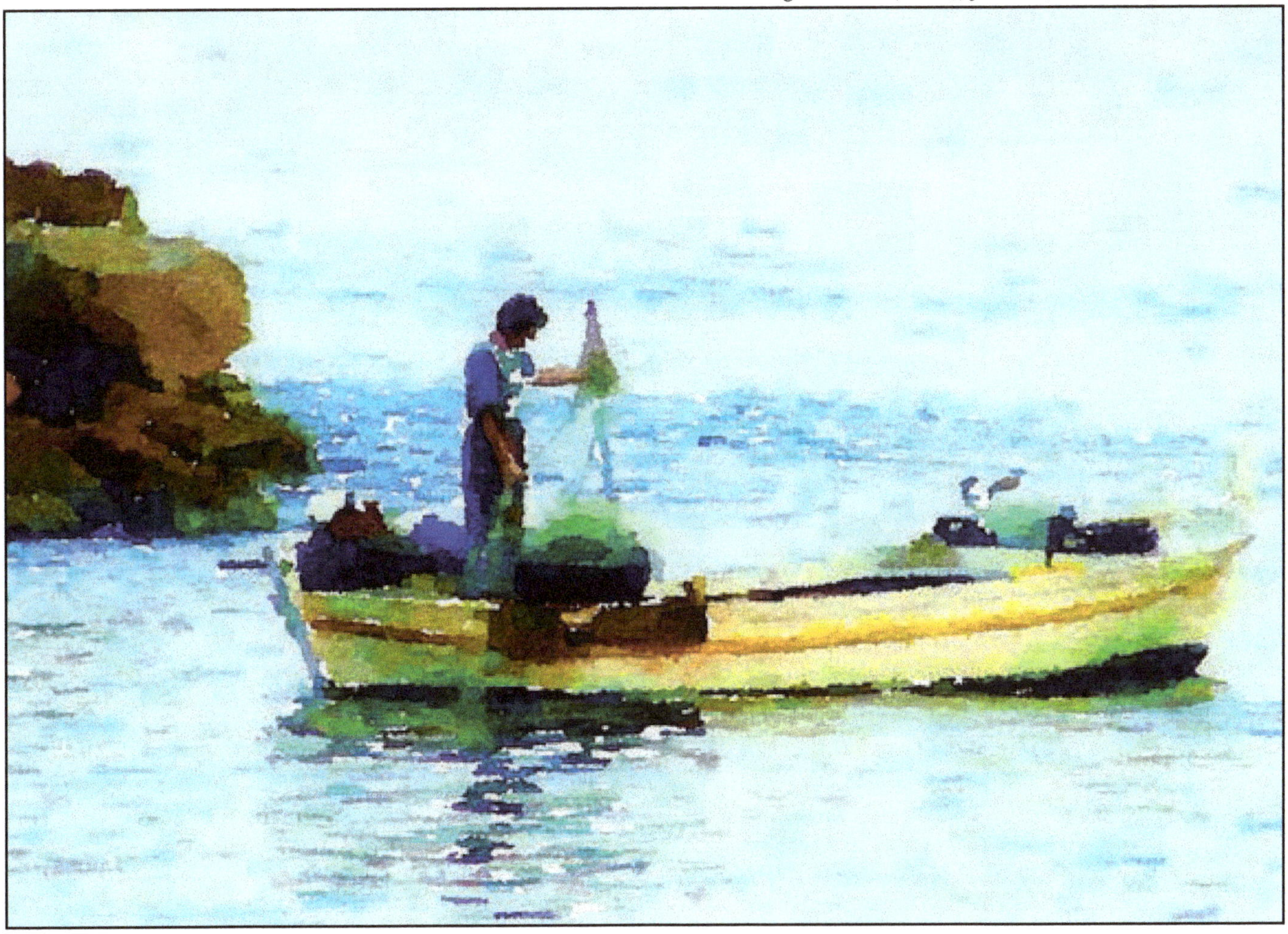

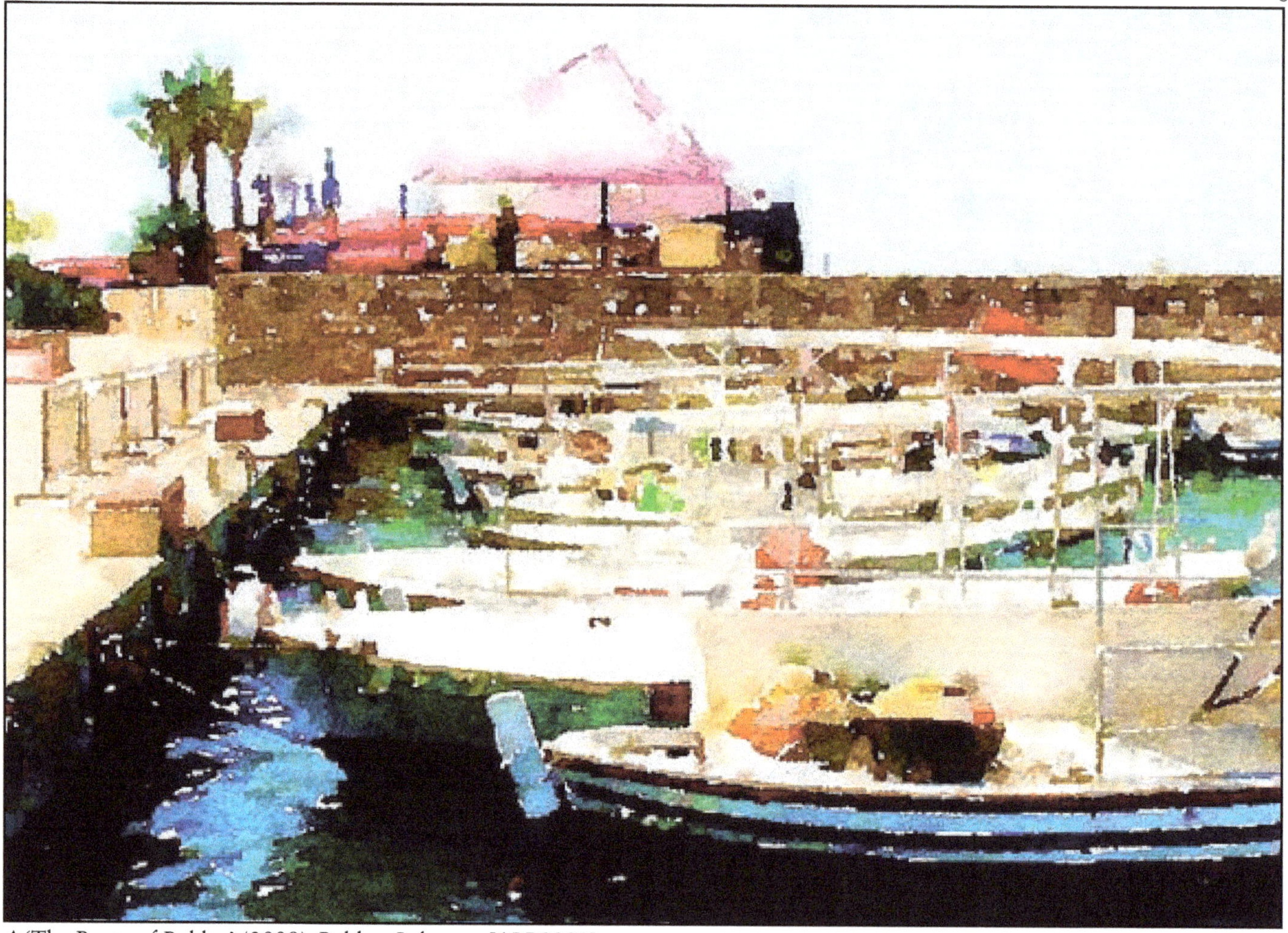

▲'The Boats of Byblos' (2008), Byblos, Lebanon [ALB0803].

'Byblos Harbour' (2019), Byblos, Lebanon [ALB1901]. ▼

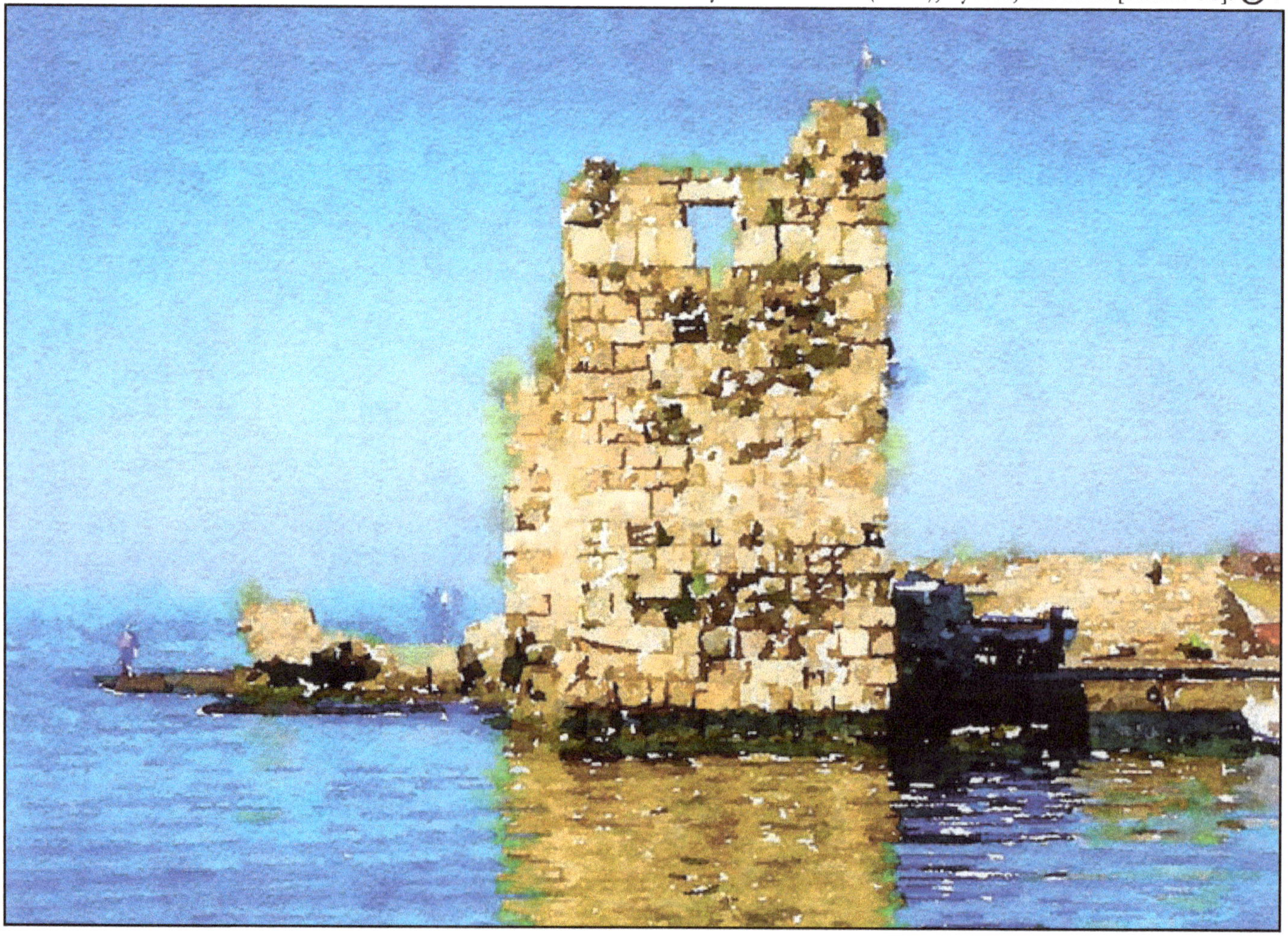

Malaysia...

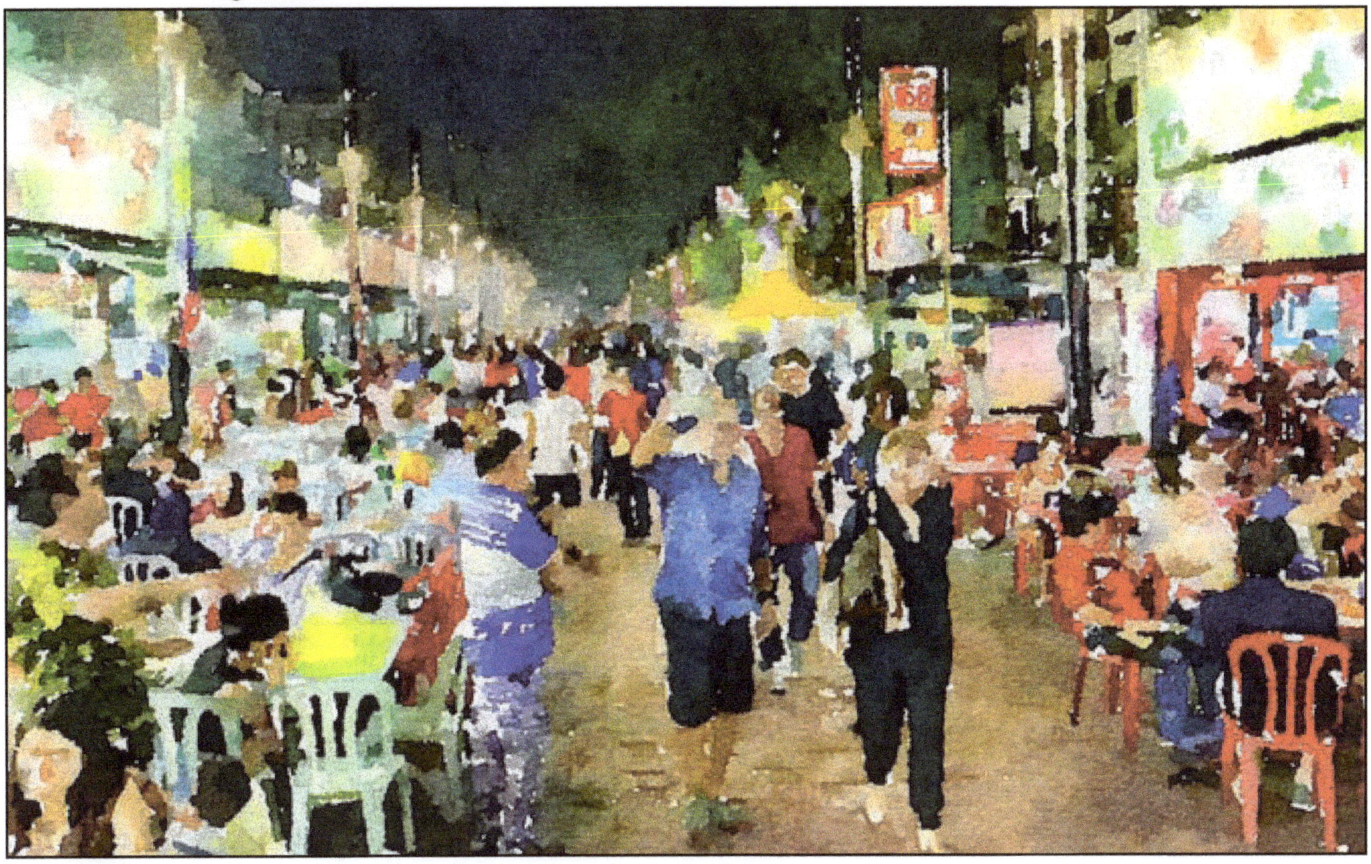

▲'Street Stalls On Jalan Alor' (2017), Kuala Lumpur, Malaysia [AMY1701].

'The Beach At Batu Ferringhi' (2017), Penang, Malaysia [AMY1702].▼

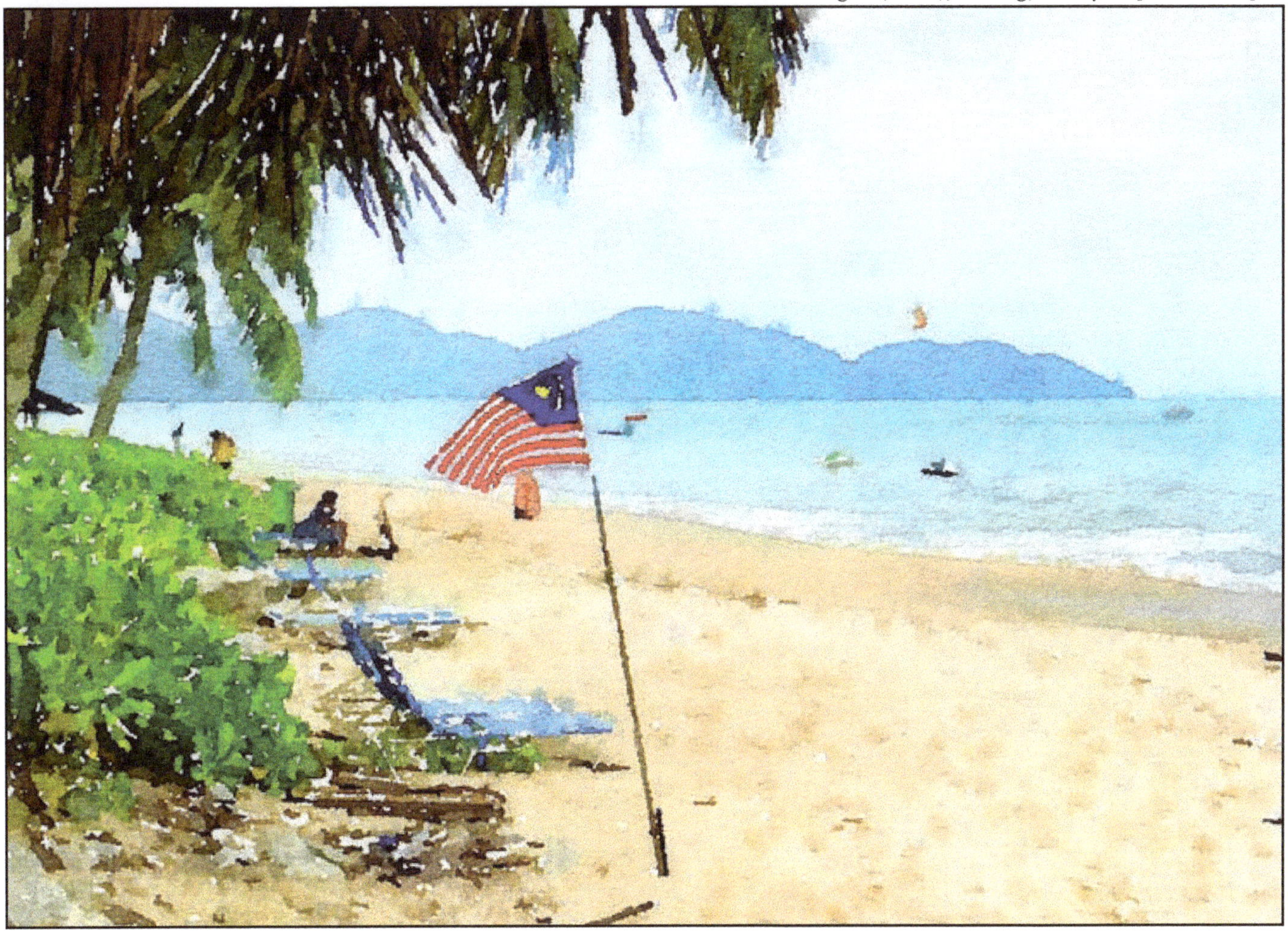

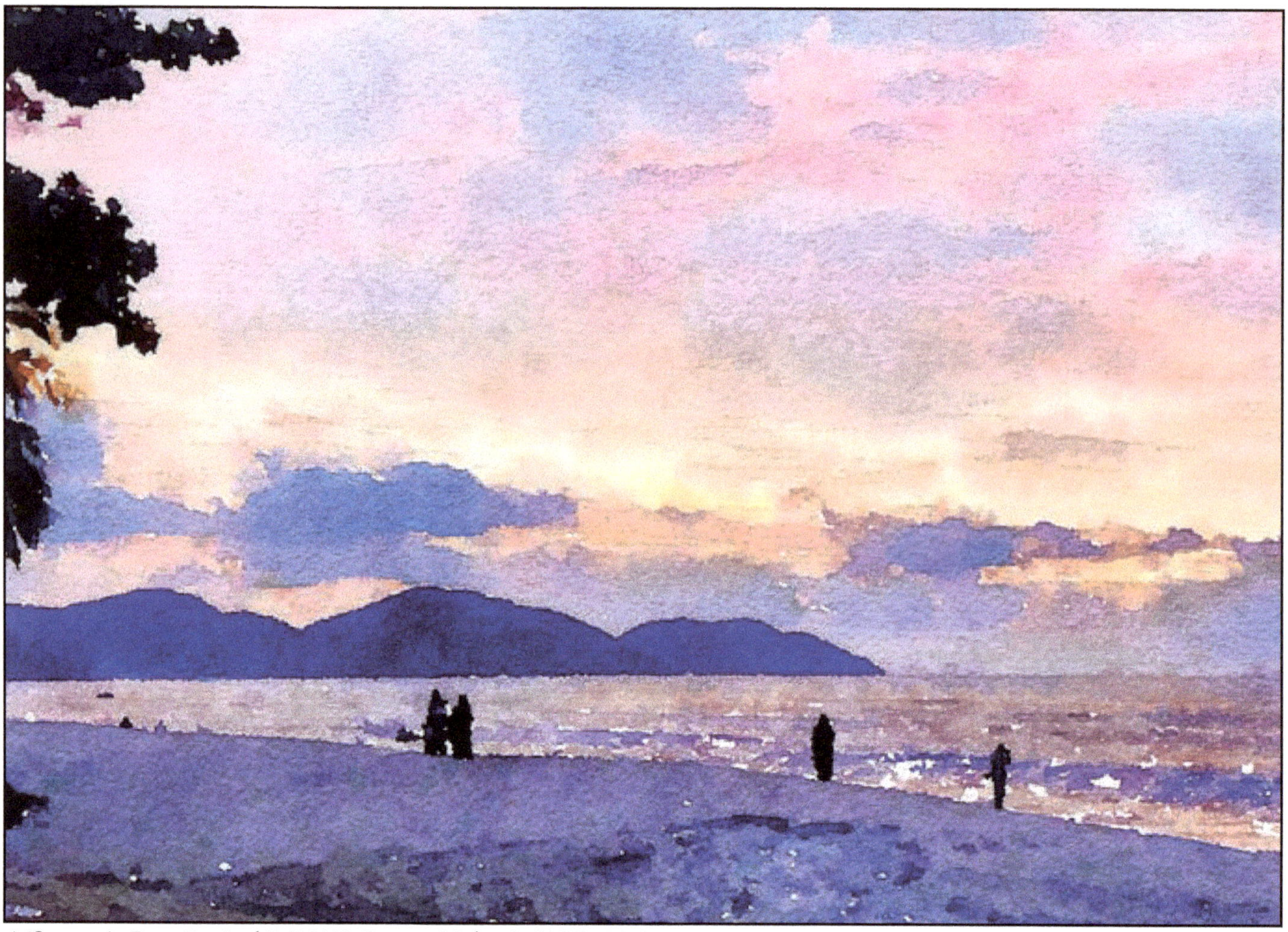

▲'Sunset At Batu Ferringhi' (2017), Penang Malaysia [AKR1703].

'Batu Ferringhi' (2017), Penang, Malaysia [AKR1704].▼

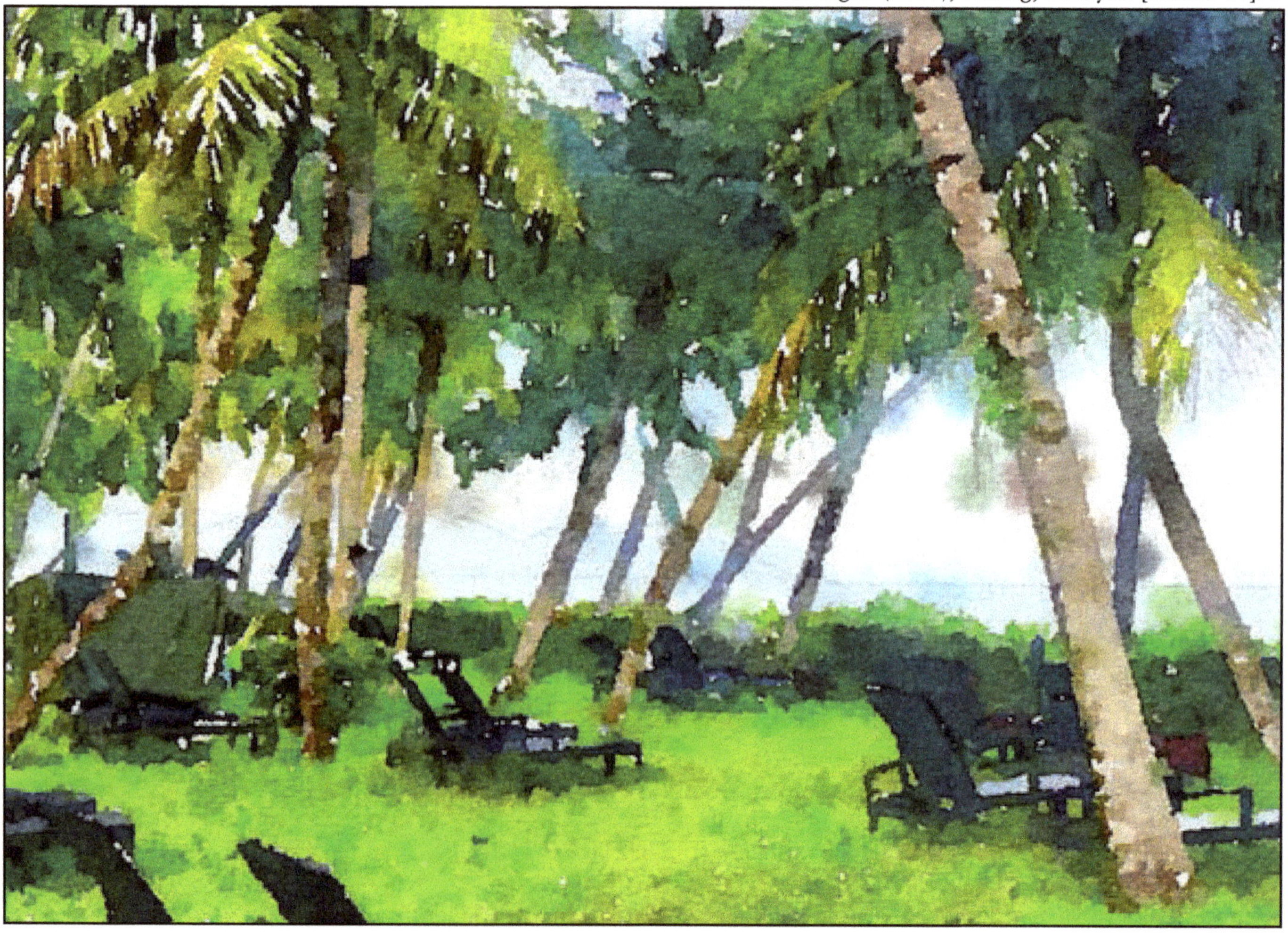

Taiwan...

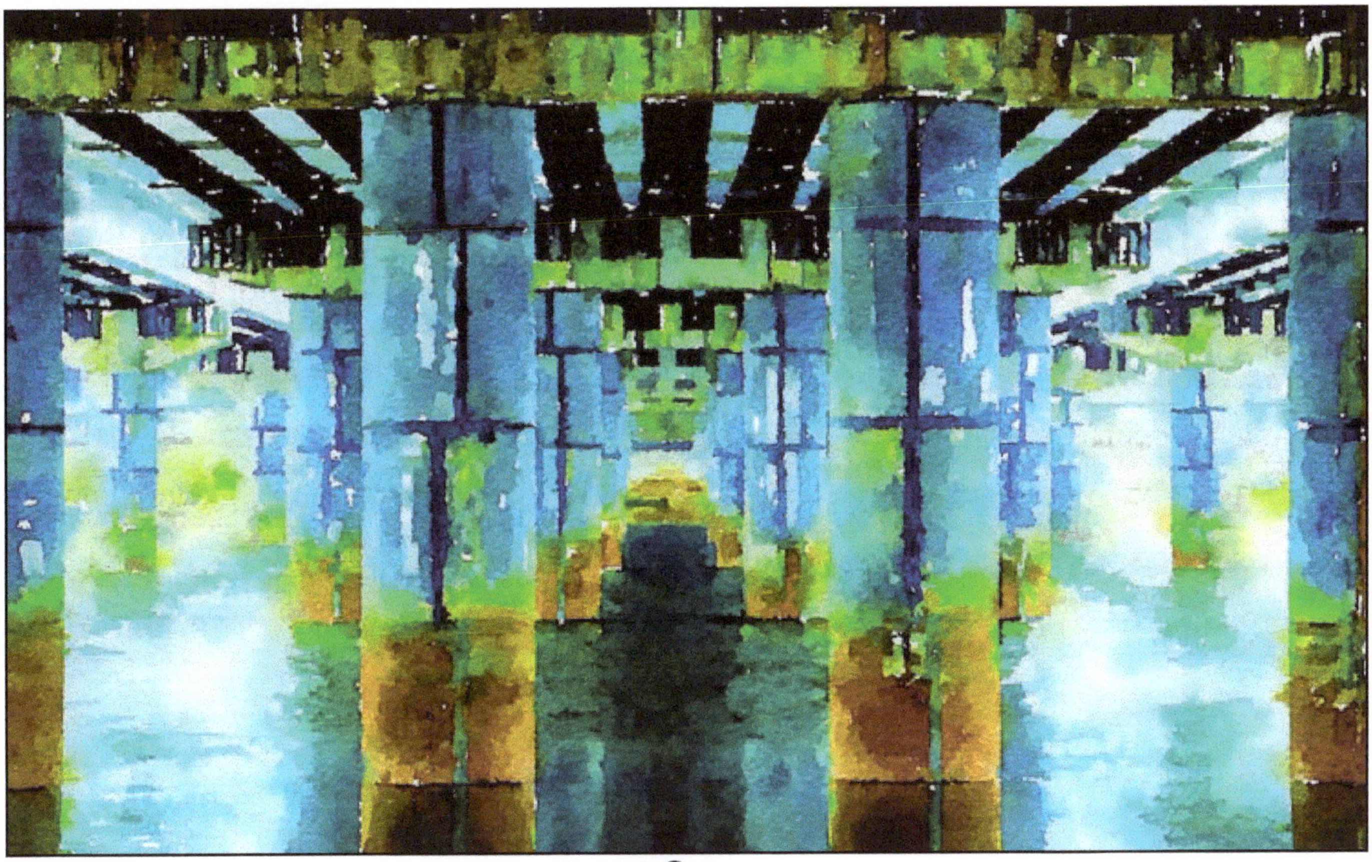

▲'Pilars Of Taipei Bridge' (2021), Taipei, Taiwan [ATA2101].

'Colours of Keelung' (2017), Keelung City, Taiwan [ATA1701].▼

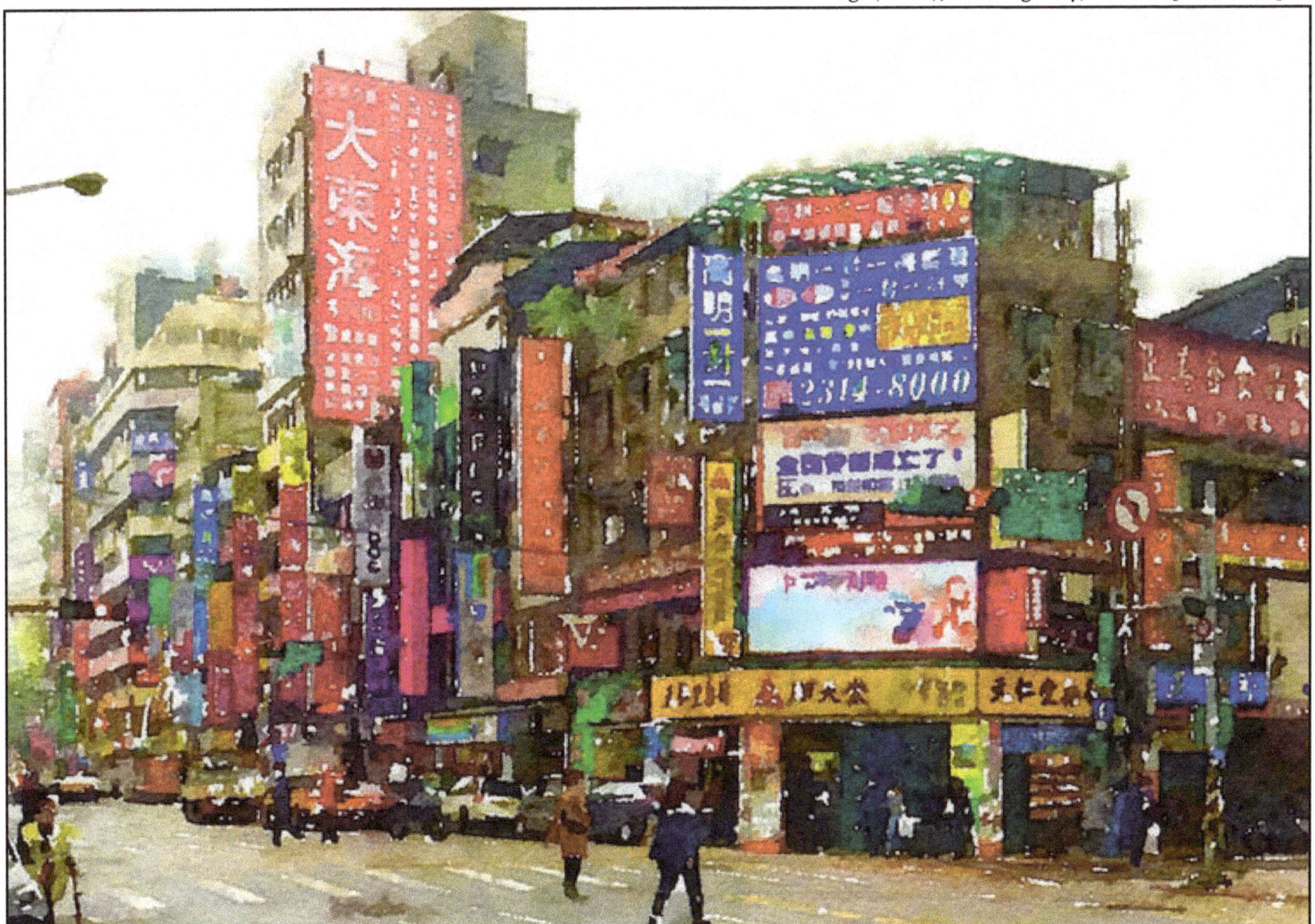

Turkey...

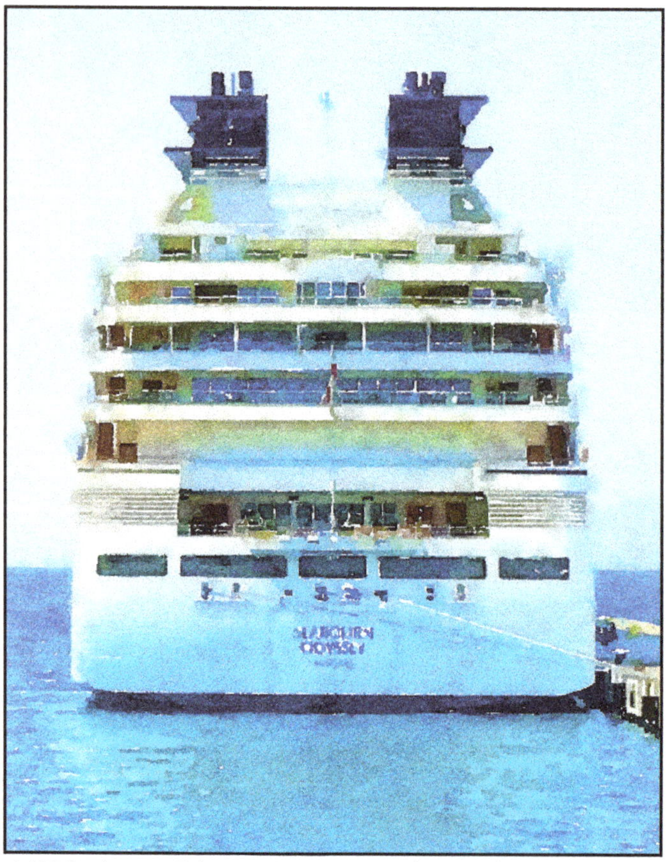

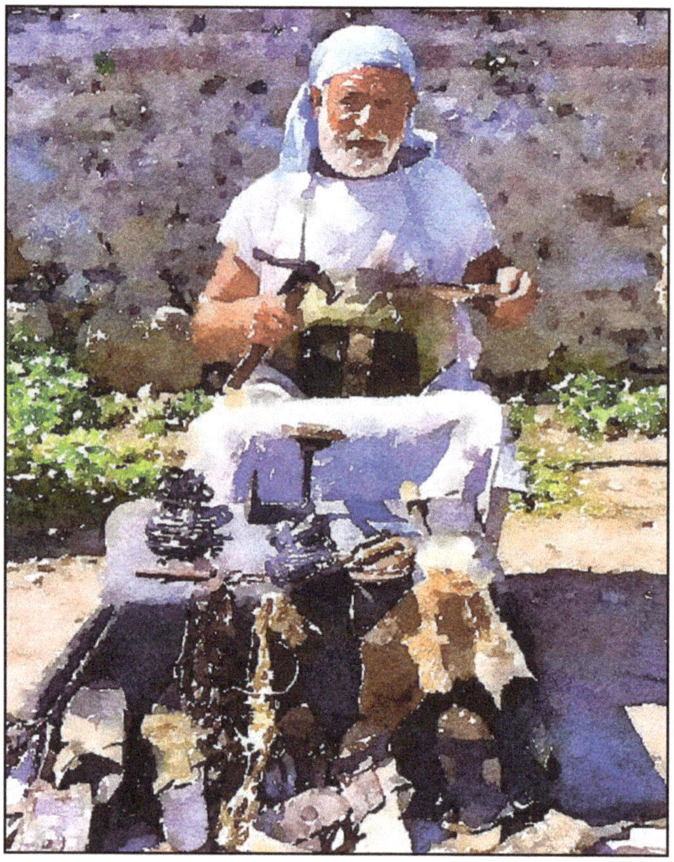

▲'SS Seabourn Odyssey' (2011), Kusadasi, Turkey [TTSH1105].

'The Bootmaker' (2011), Ephesus, Turkey [ATR1104].▲

▼'Sunset Over Bodrum Bay' (2011), Bodrum, Turkey [ATR1101].

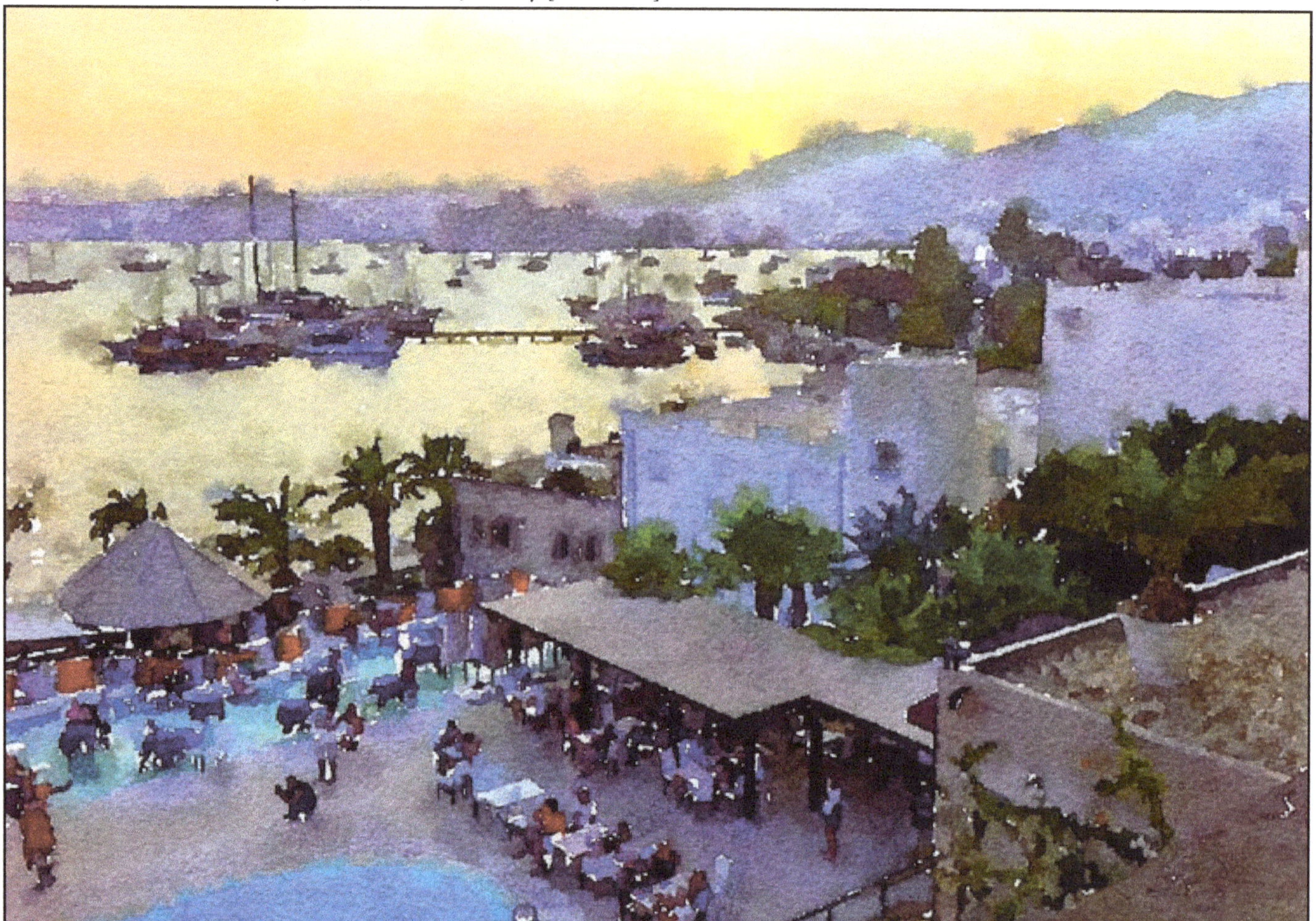

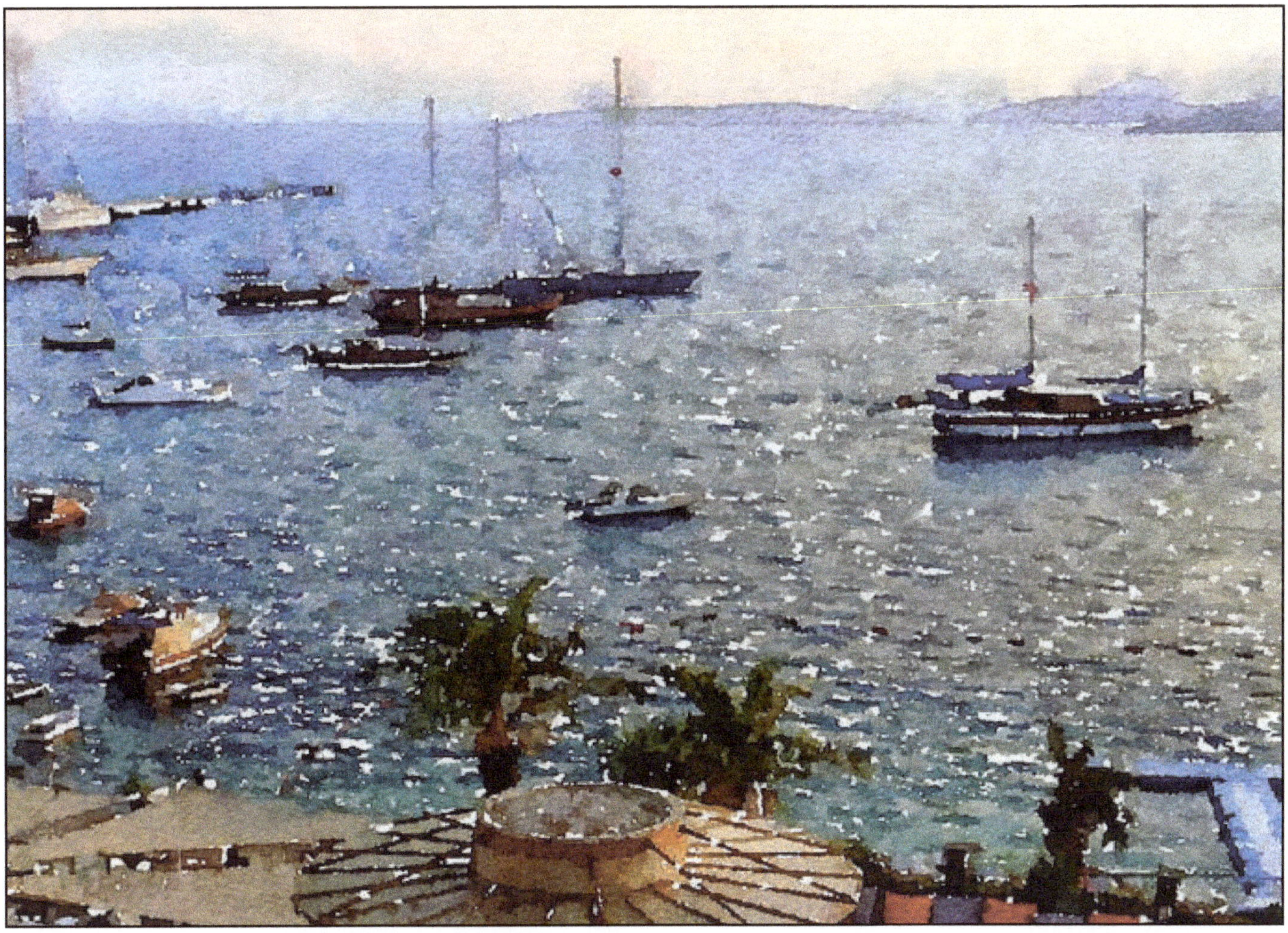

▲'Bodrum Boats' (2011), Bodrum, Turkey [ATR1102].

'Colours Of The Grand Bazaar' (2011), Istanbul, Turkey [ATR1103].▼

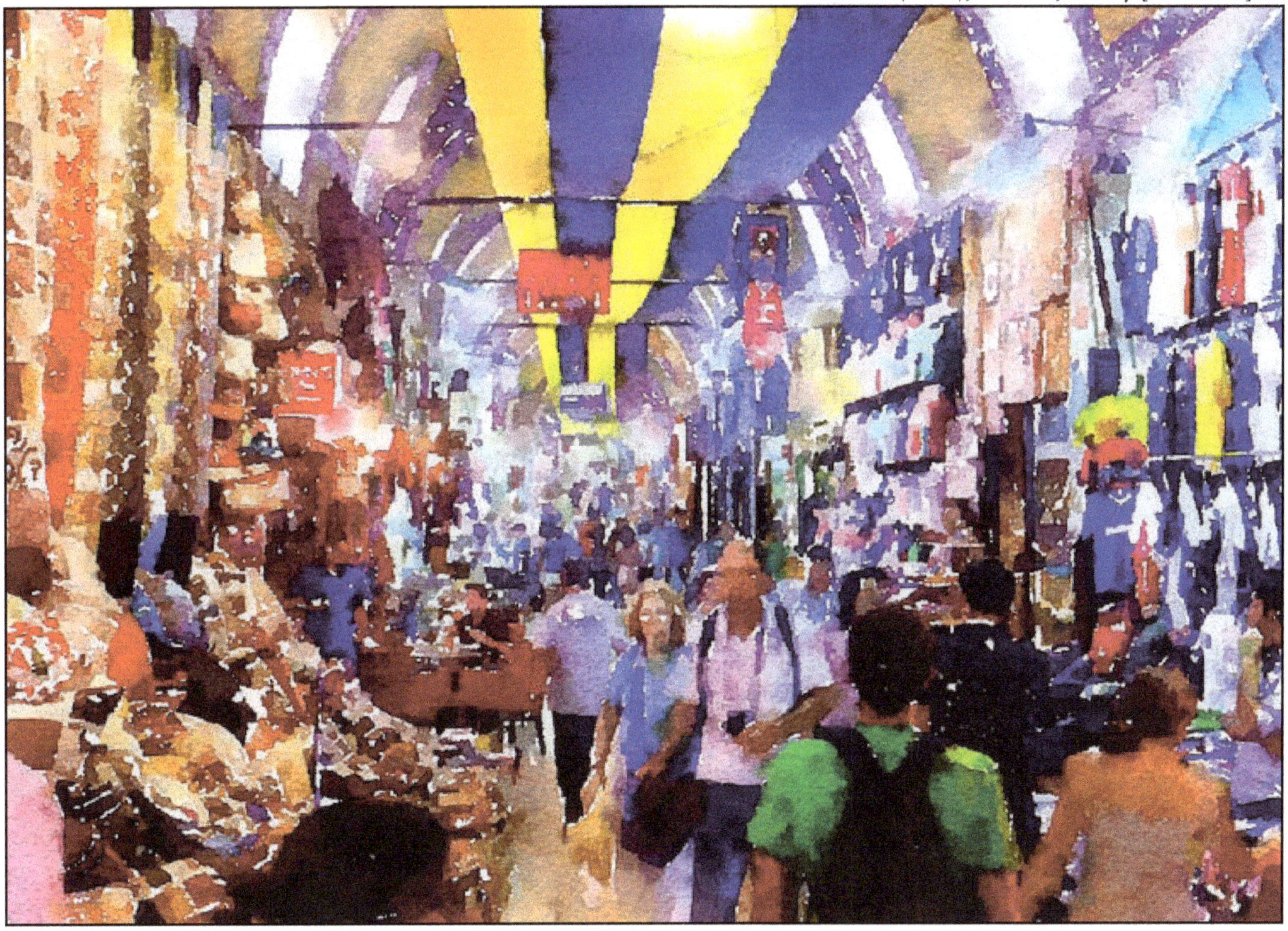

UAE…

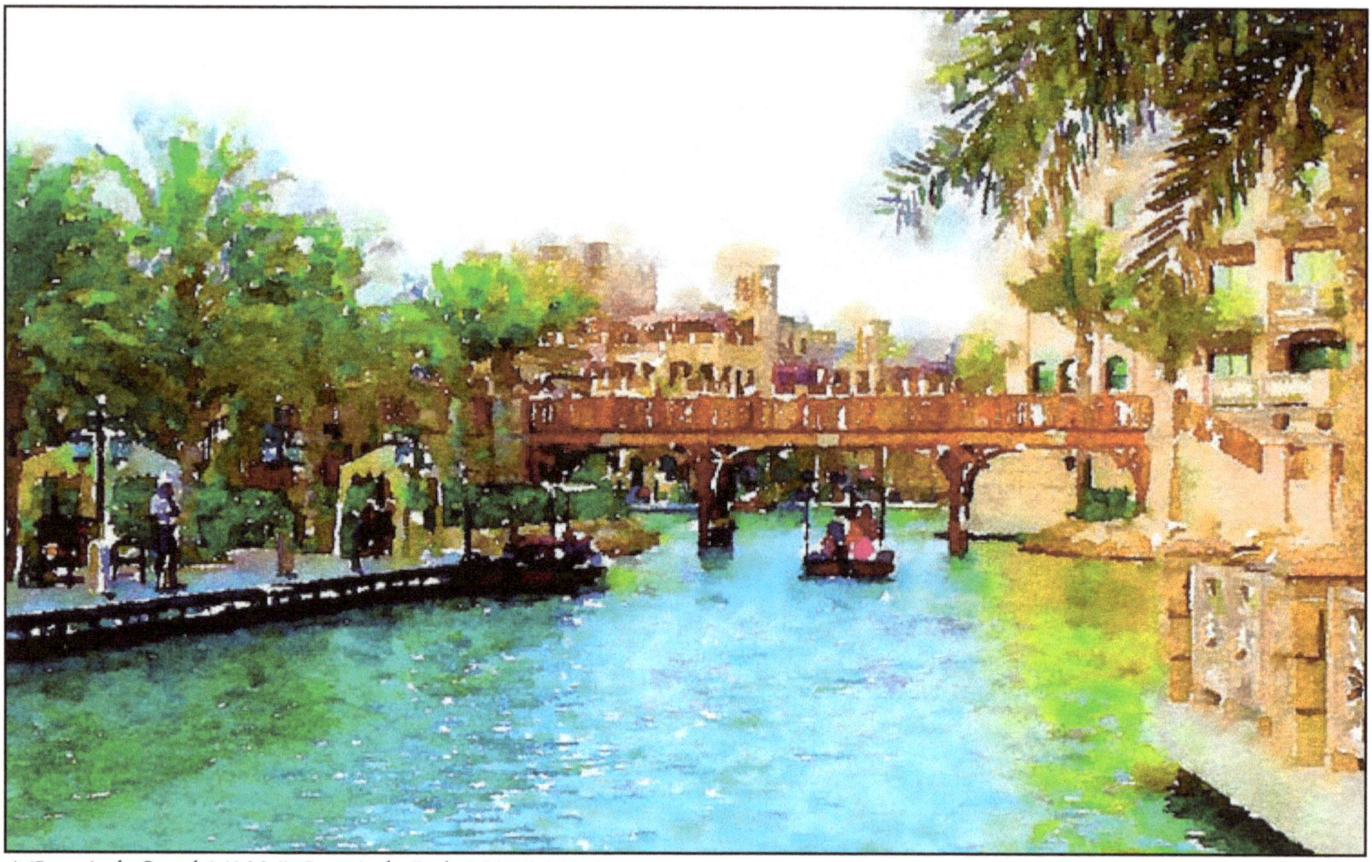

▲'Jumeirah Canals' (2006), Jumeirah, Dubai [AUA0601].

'The Pier At Madinat Jumeirah' (2006), Jumeirah, Dubai [AUA0602].▼

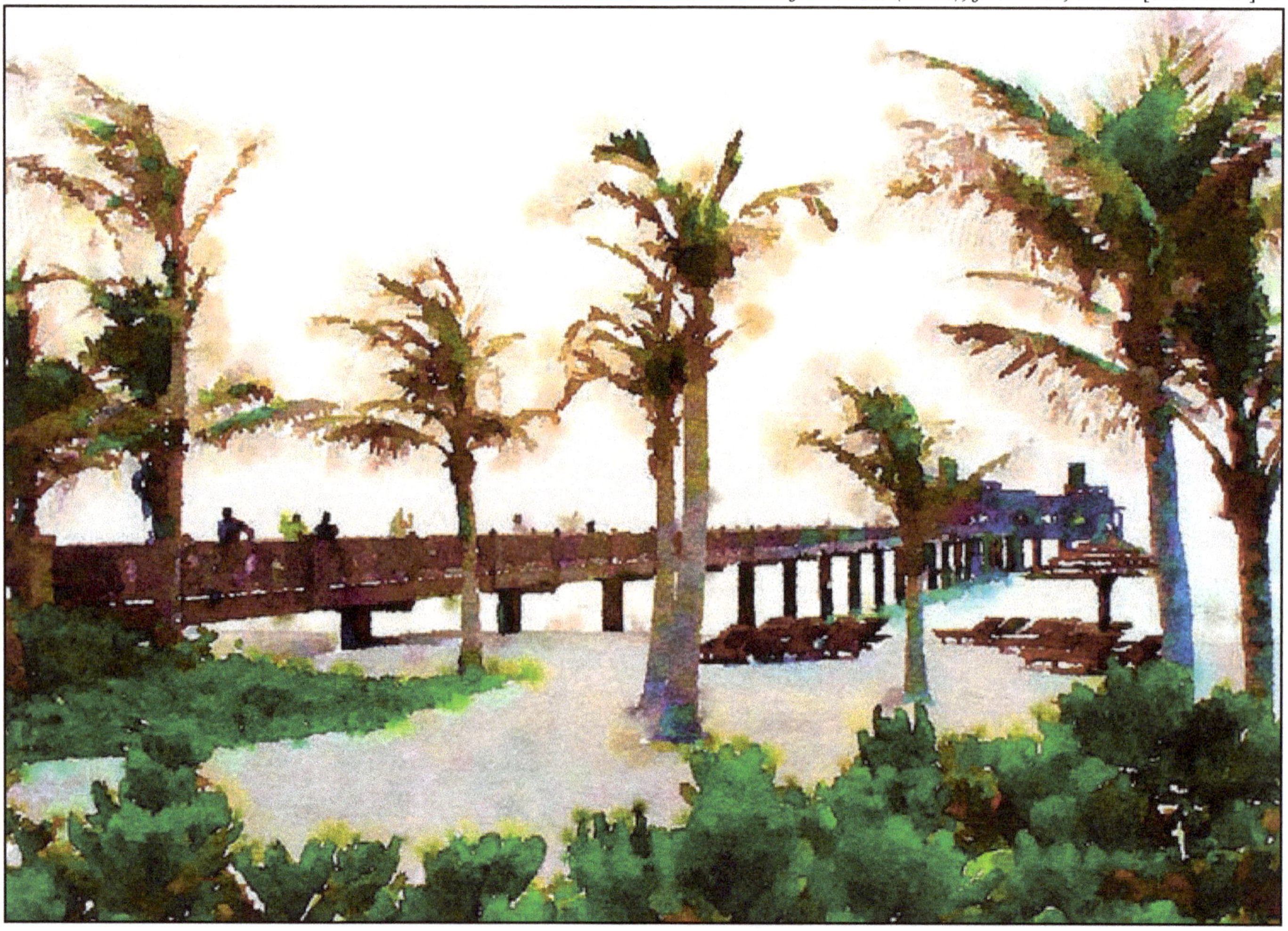

EUROPE

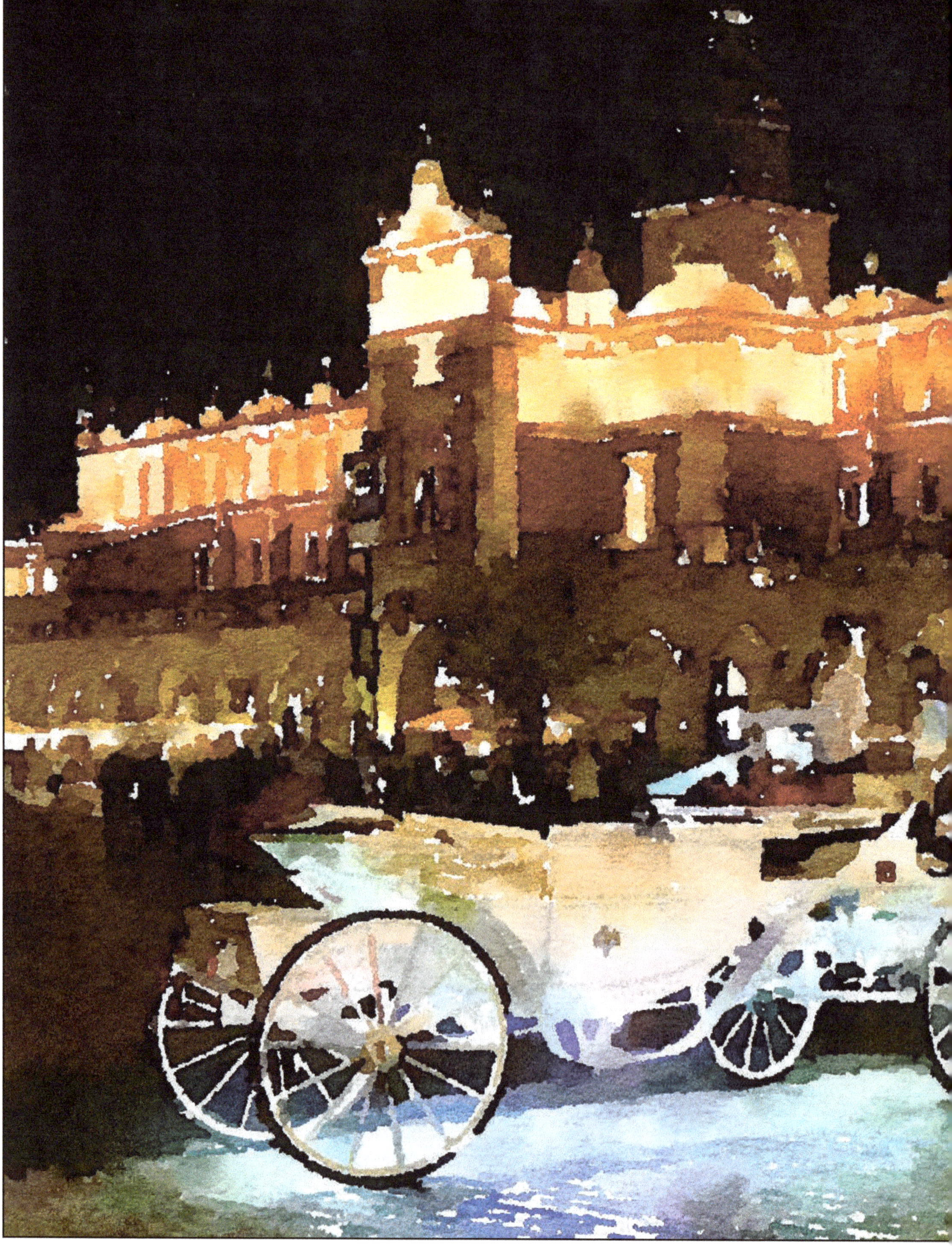

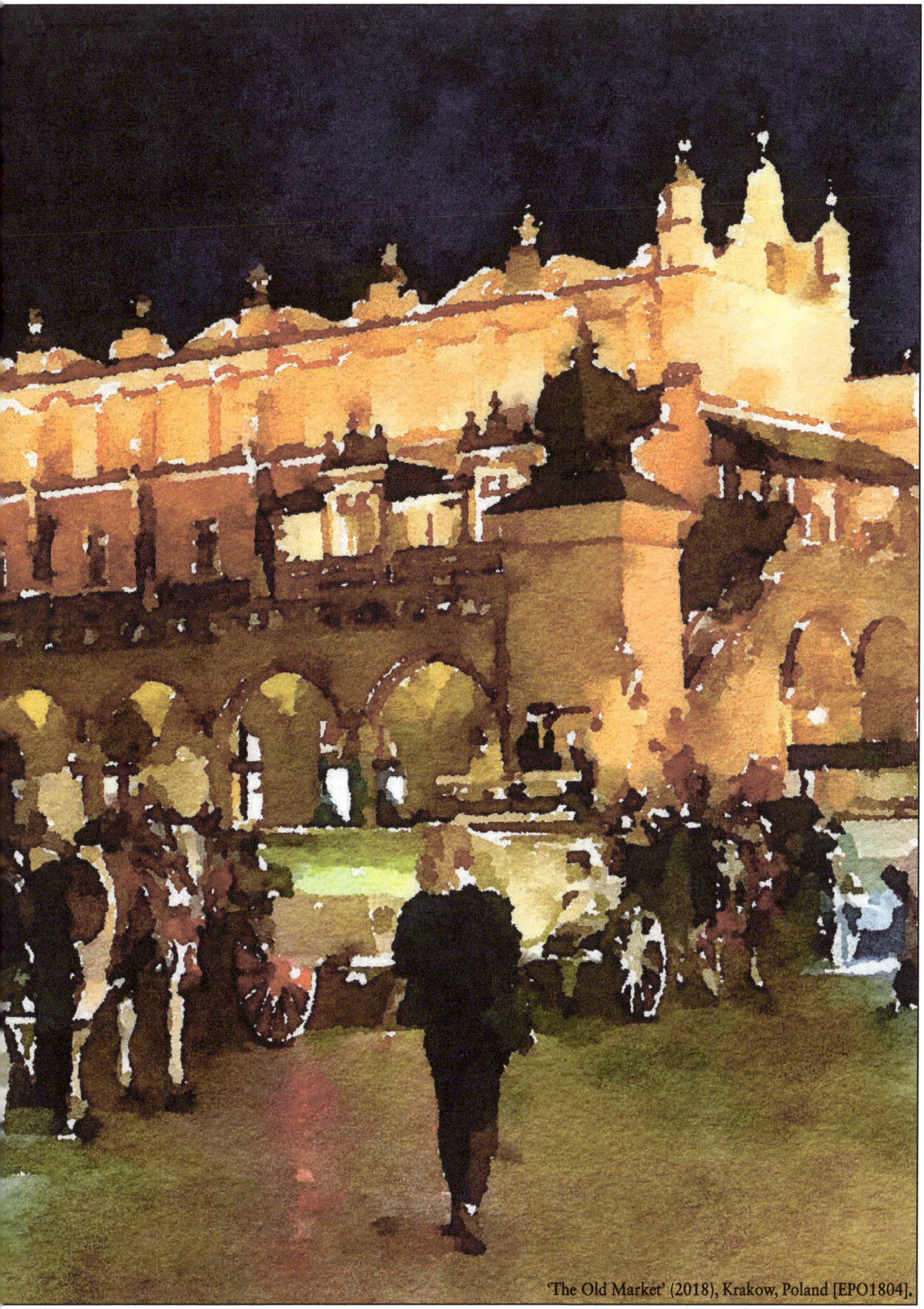

'The Old Market' (2018), Krakow, Poland [EPO1804].

Visiting many of the smaller European countries on my travels through the continent, particularly from around 2010, I generated a great number of images, which in turn have produced some of my most memorable works.

Austria...

Travelling through Austria during the summer of 2018, I encountered Vienna for the very first time and was staggered by both the history and grandeur of the city. Vienna is a photographers dream in featuring ornate and opulent buildings, the streets are filled with old world trams and horse-drawn transport, and it features some of the worlds best restaurants and cafes.

Further afield, the mountains, meadows and lakes of Austria made idyllic backgrounds, resulting in a profusion of photographic opportunities.

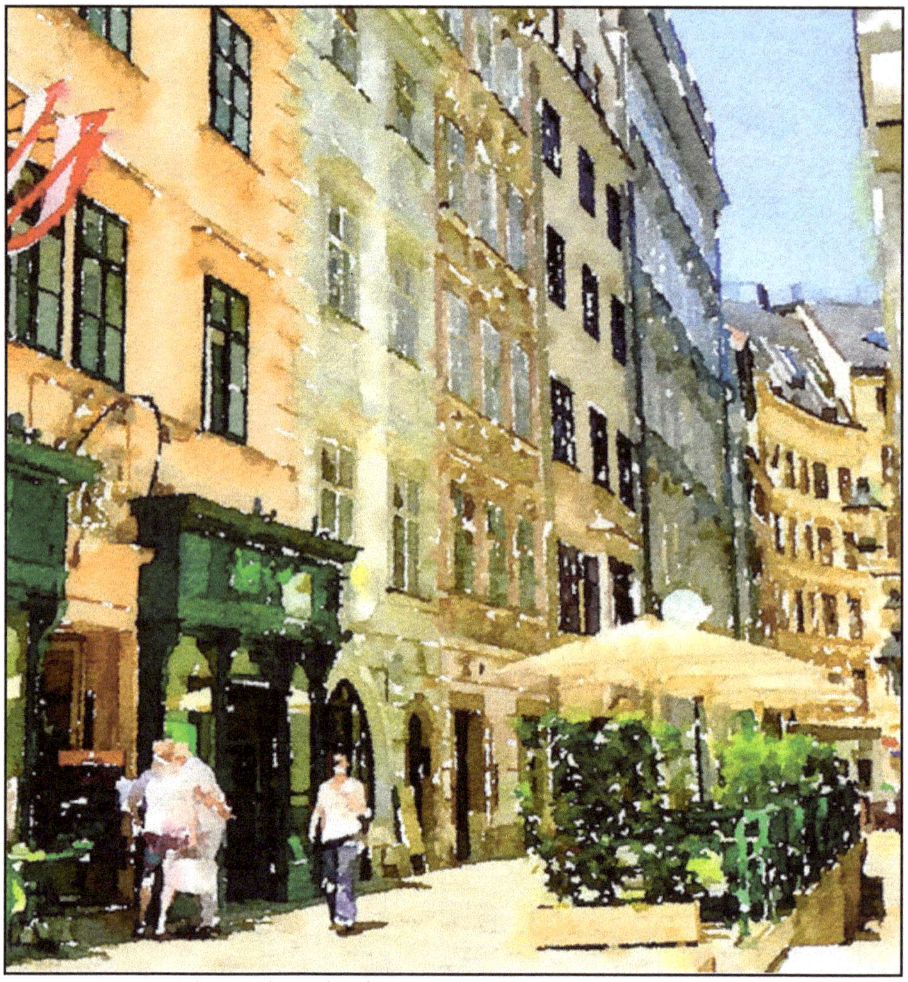

'The Boulevards of Vienna' (2018), Vienna, Austria [EAT(VI)1801].▲

▼'Burgtheater' (2018), Vienna, Austria [EAT(VI)1802].

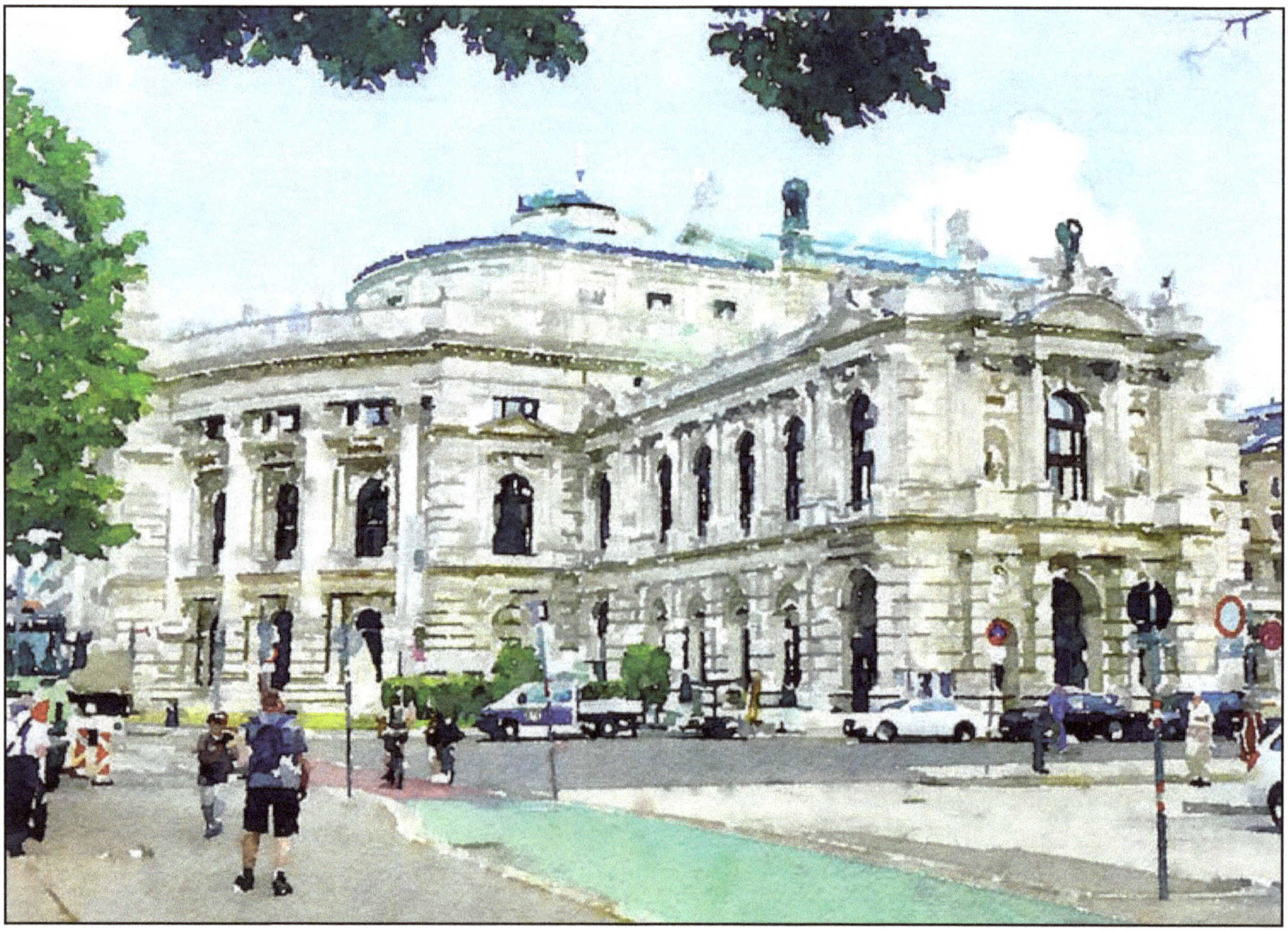

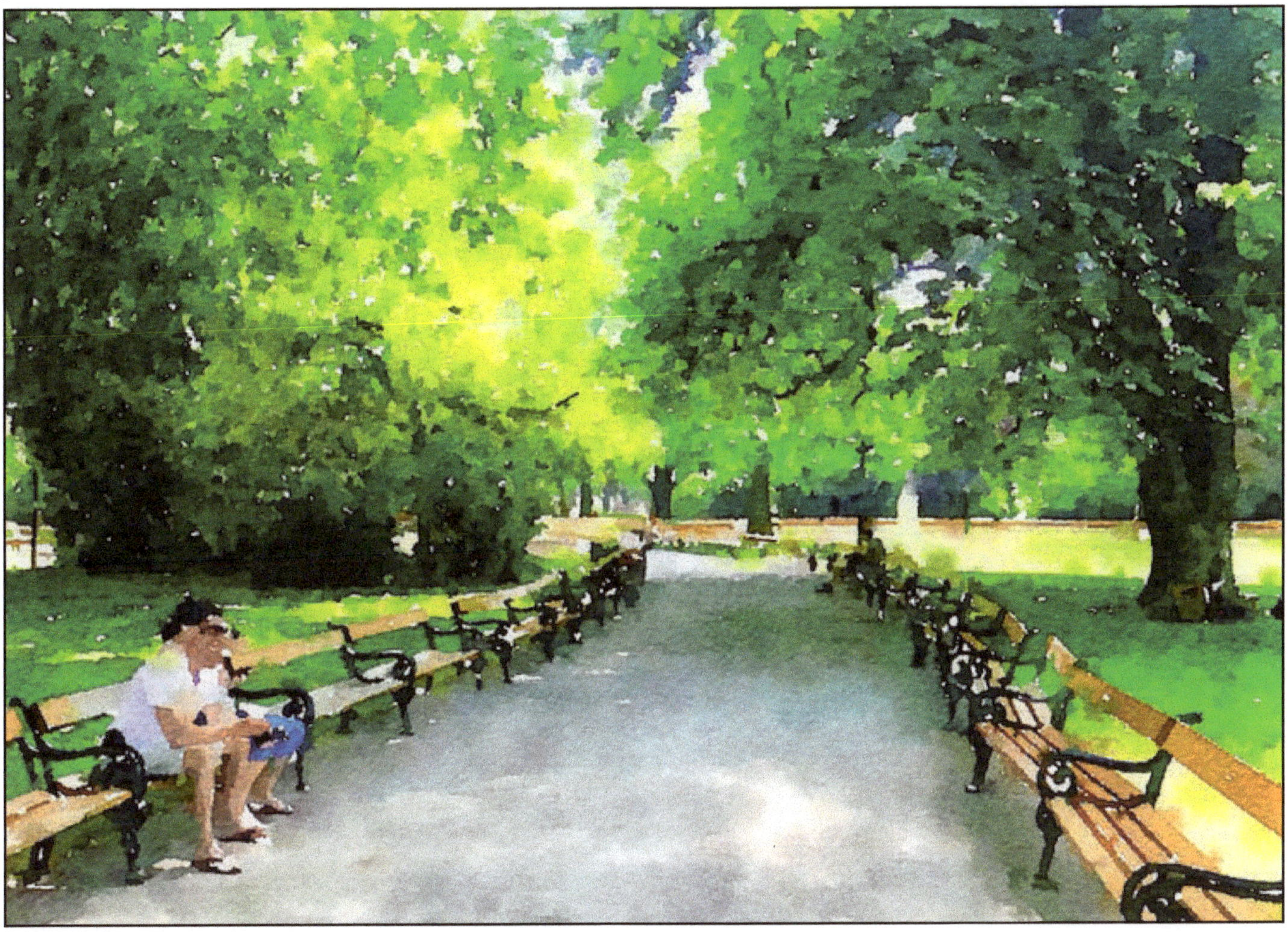

▲'Rathauspark' (2018), Vienna, Austria [EAT(VI)1803].

'The Horse Drawn Carriage' (2018), Vienna, Austria [EAT(VI)1804].▼

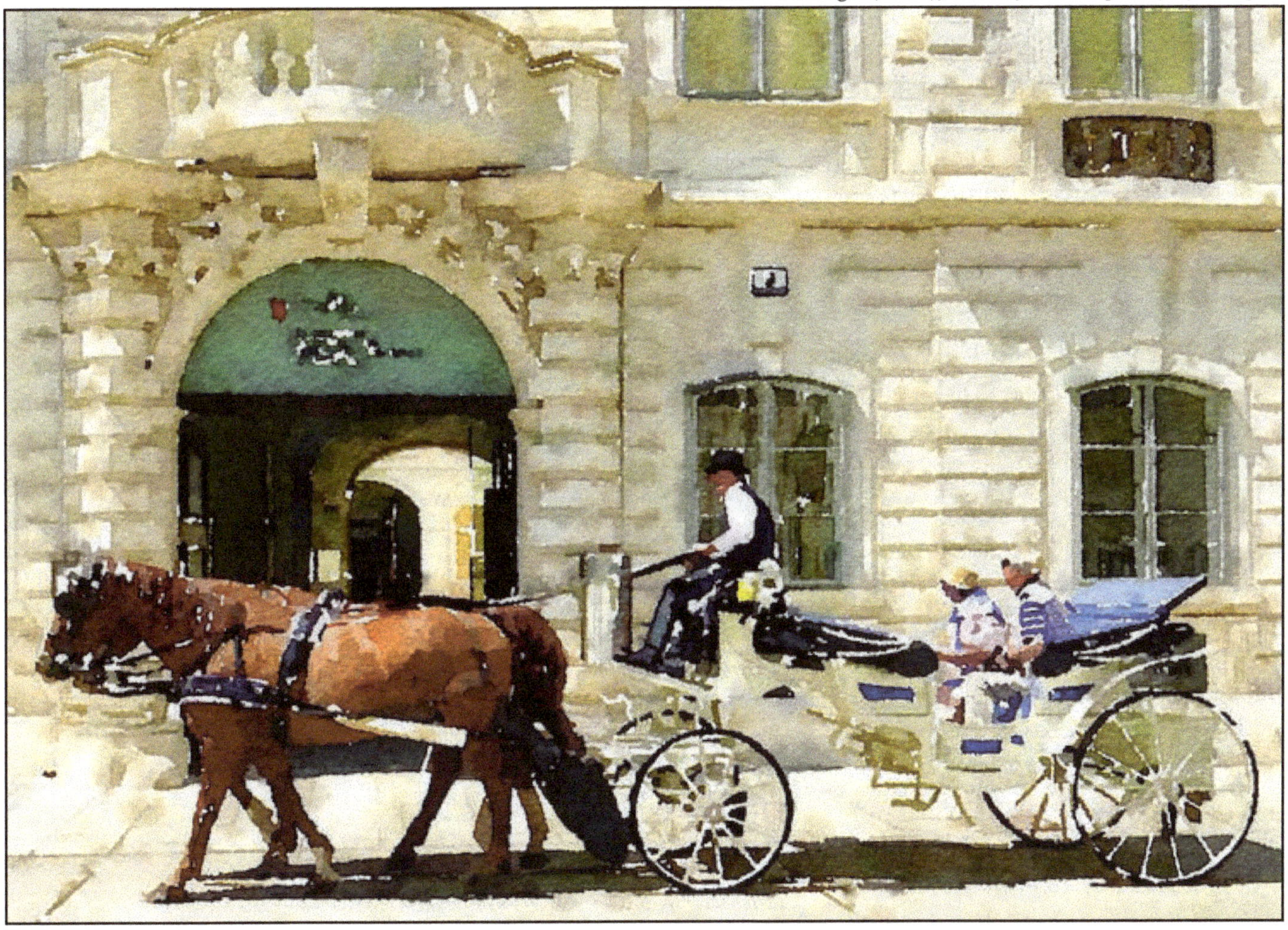

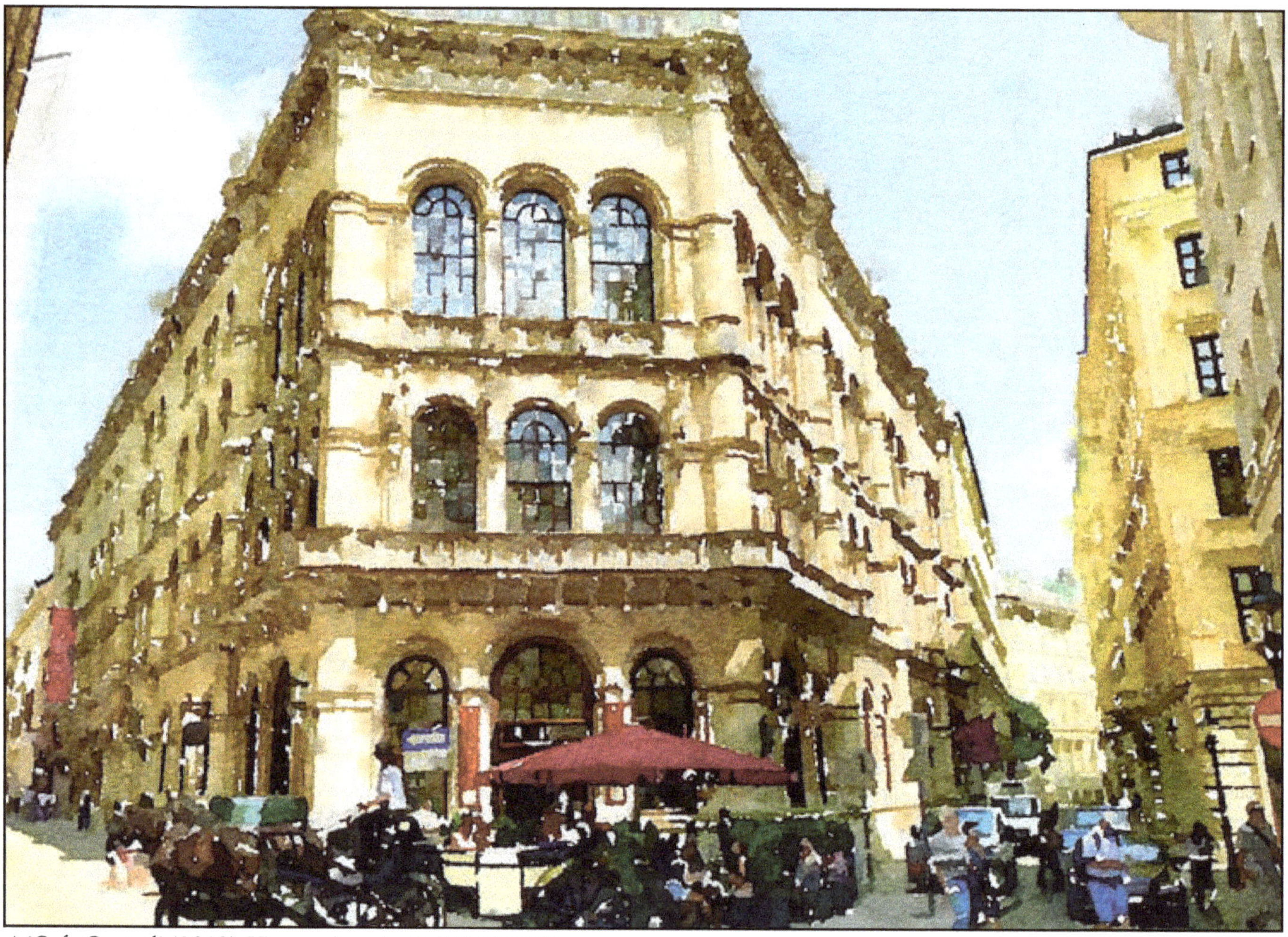

▲'Cafe Central' (2018), Vienna, Austria [EAT(VI)1805].

'Evening At Naschmarkt' (2018), Vienna, Austria [EAT(VI)1806].▼

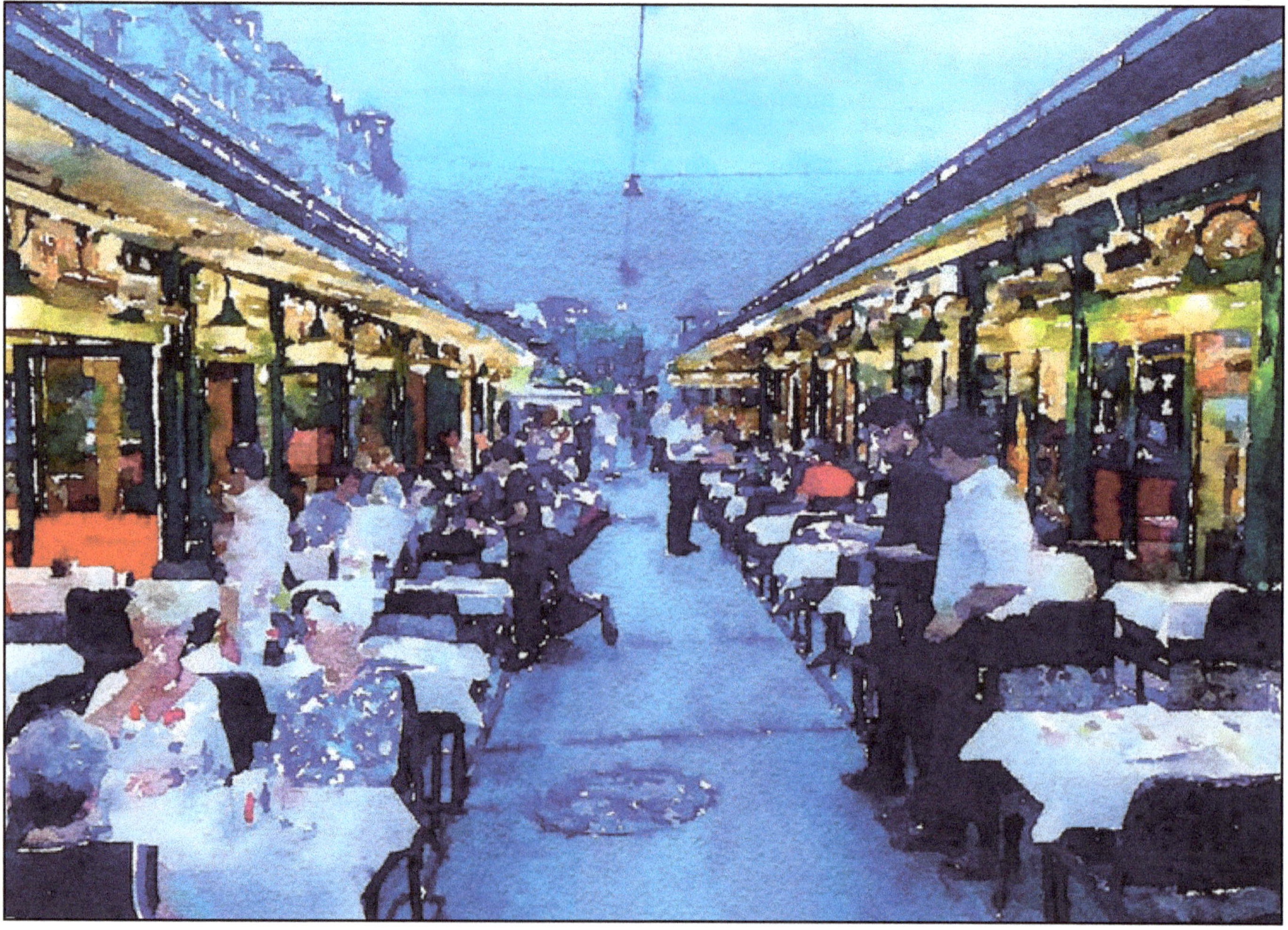

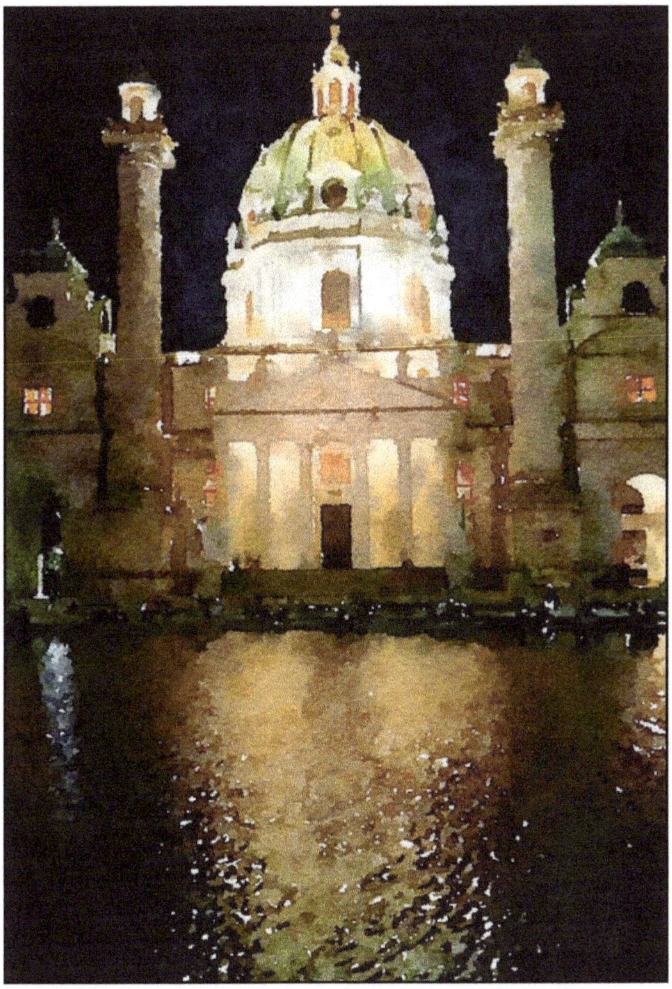

▲'Karlskirche' (2018), Vienna, Austria [EAT(VI)1807].

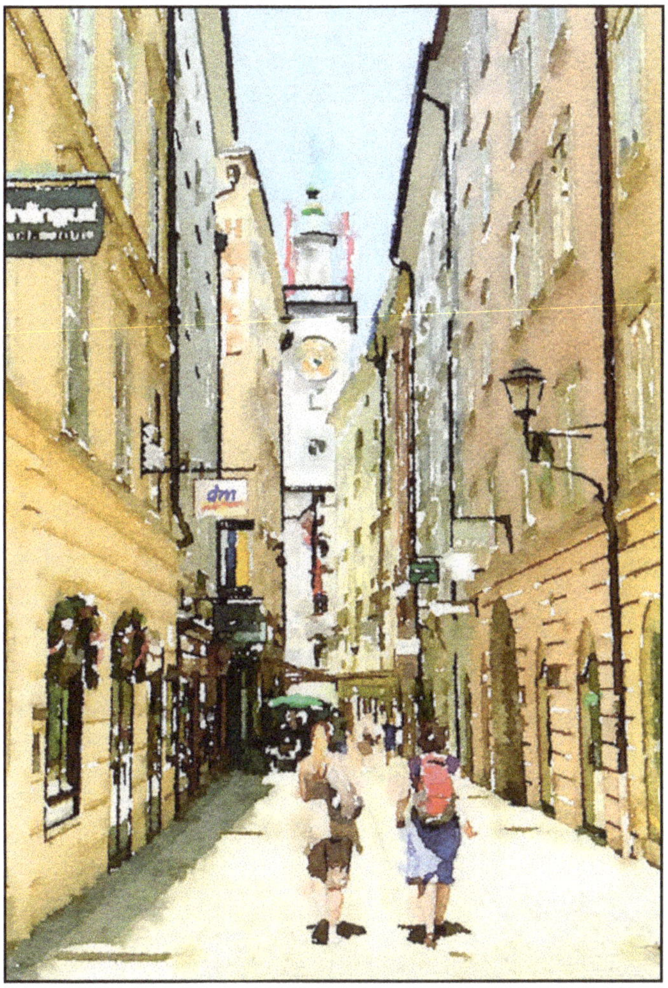

'Sigmund-Hafner Gasse' (2018), Salzburg, Austria [EAT1805].▲

'Das Chalet' St Jakob' (2018), Defereggen, Austria [EAT1801].▼

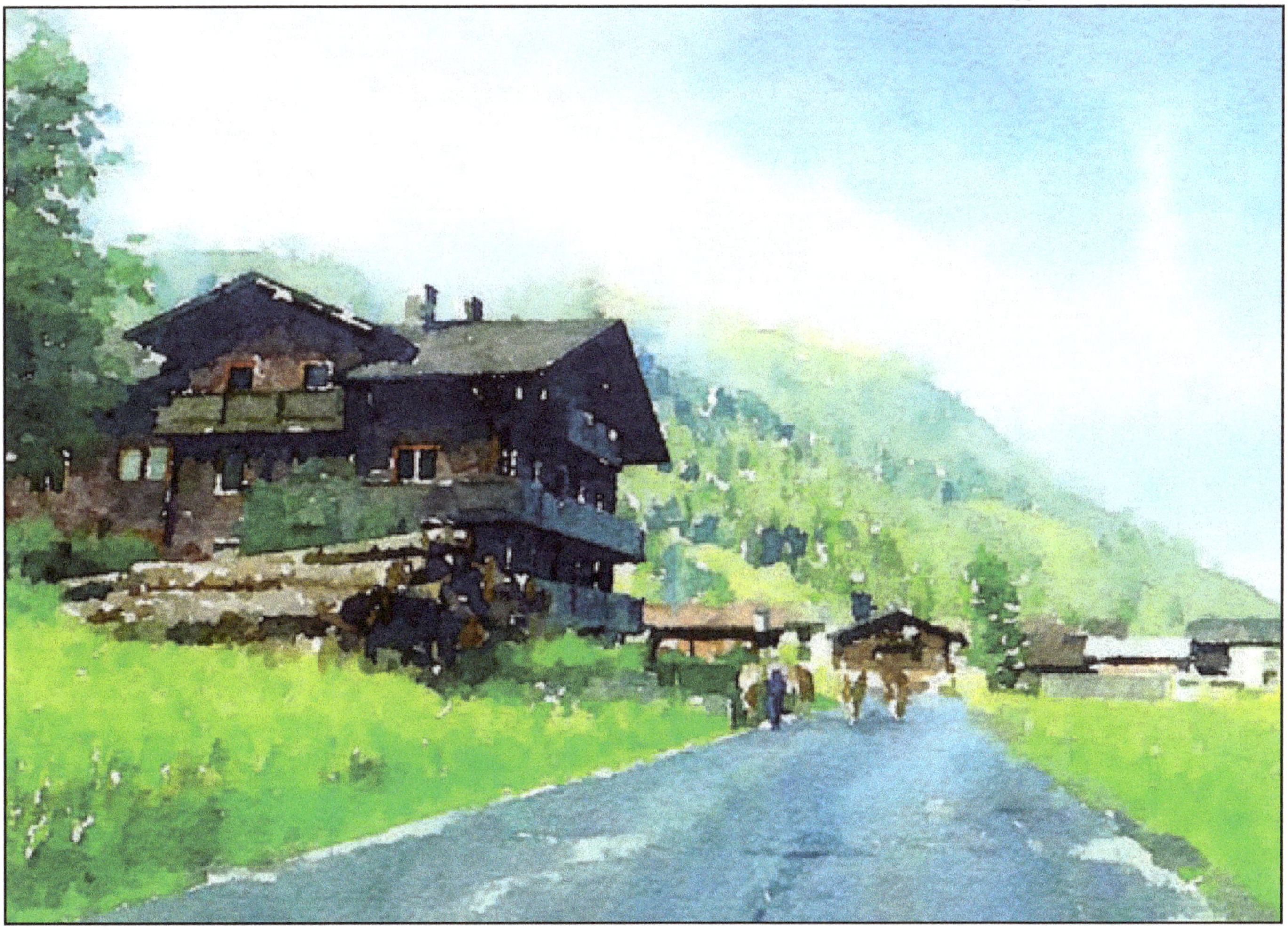

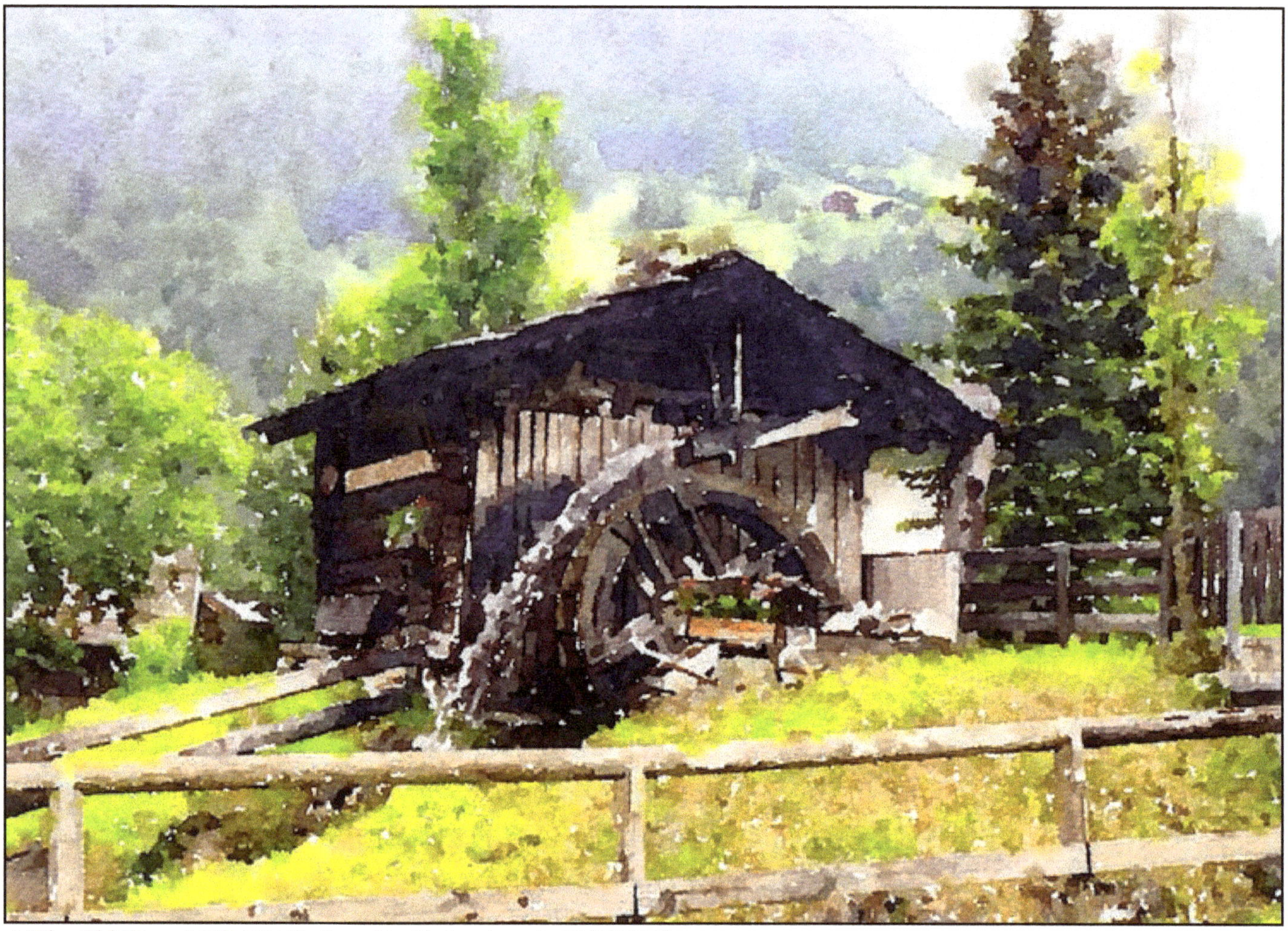

▲'The Old Water Mill' (2018), Grosskirchheim, Austria [EAT1802].

'Village With A View' (2018), Lofer, Austria [EAT1803].▼

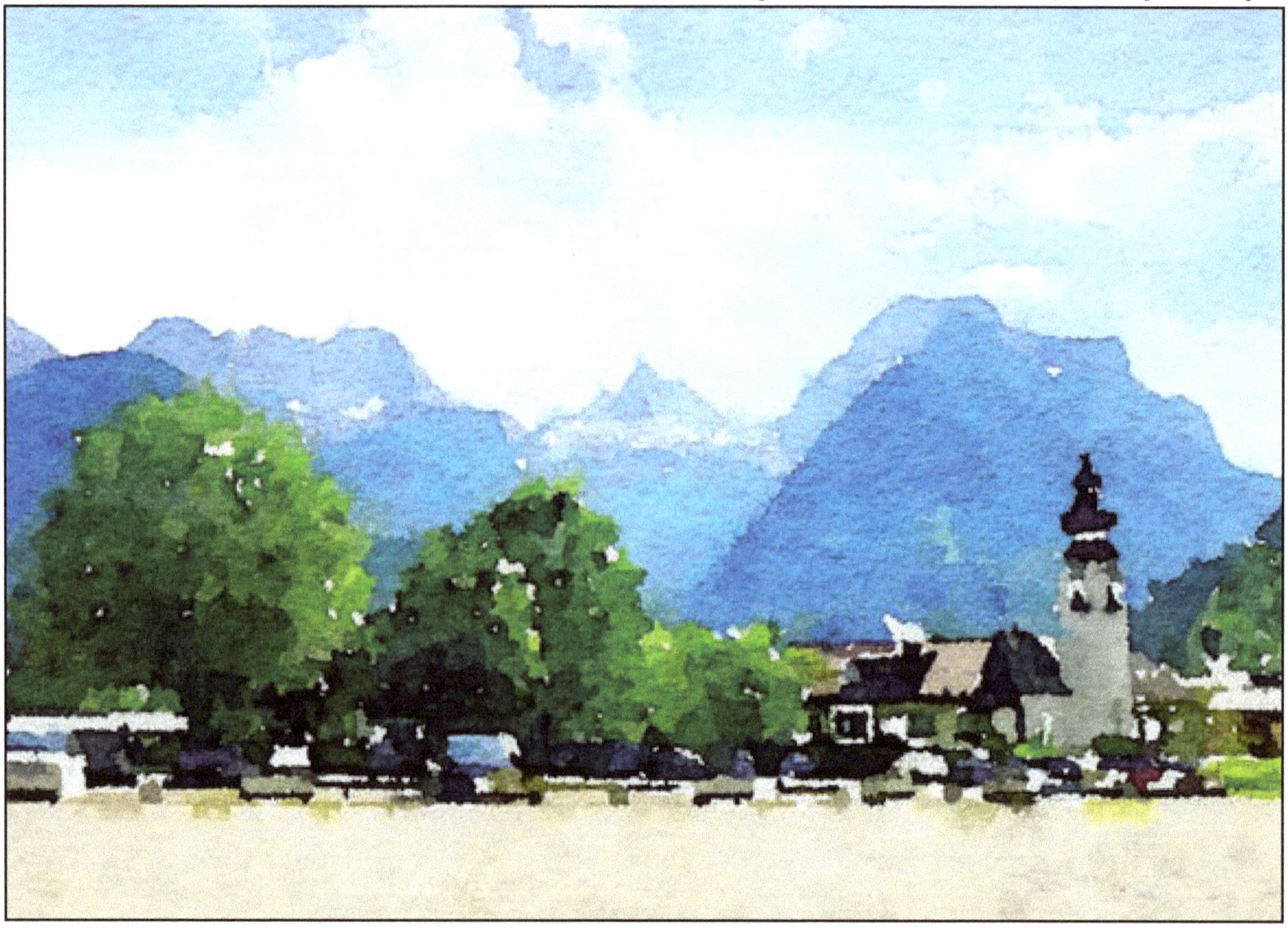

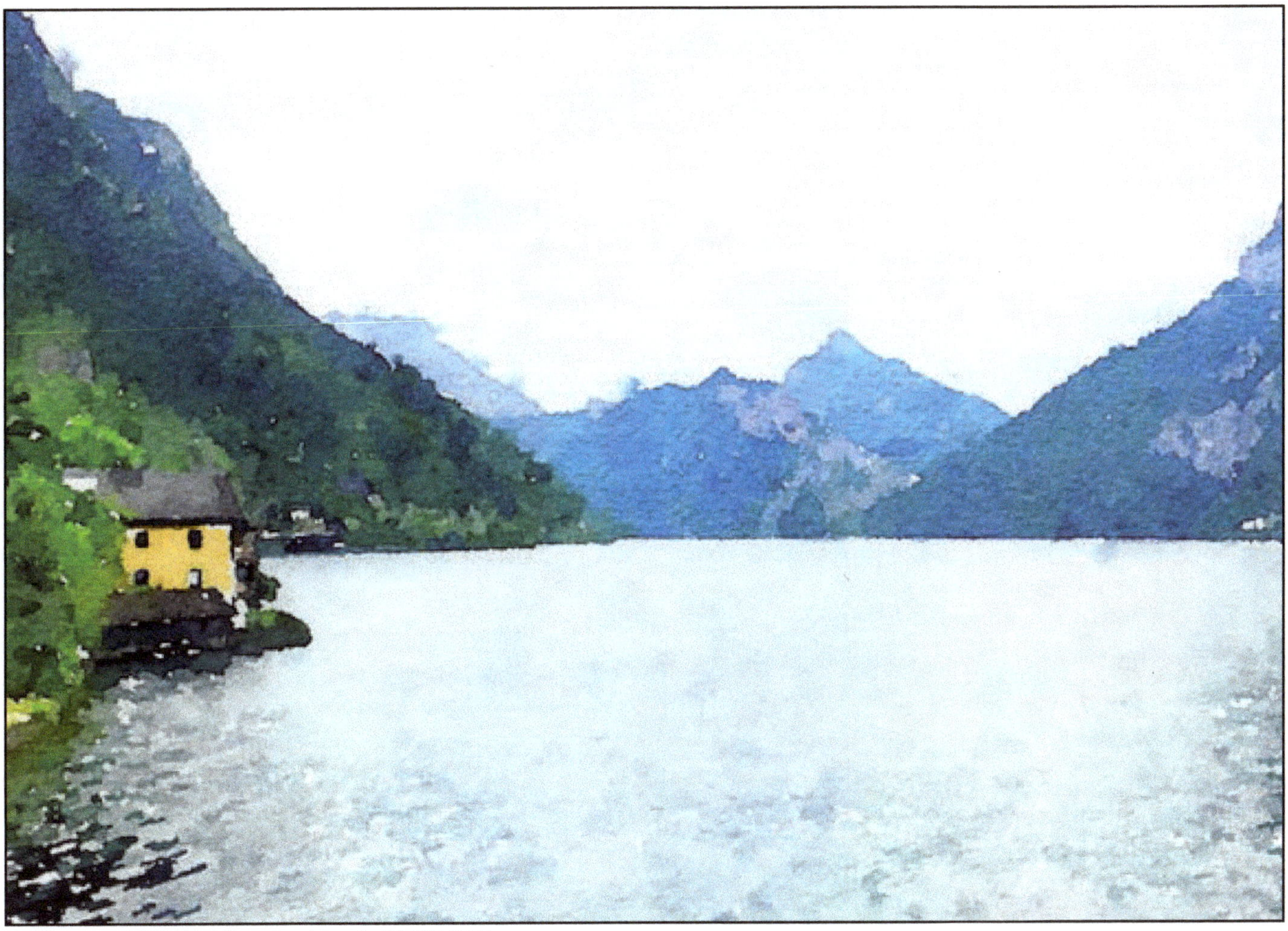

▲'Traunsee' (2018), Ebensee, Austria [EAT1804].

'Melk Abbey' (2018), Melk, Austria [EAT1806].▼

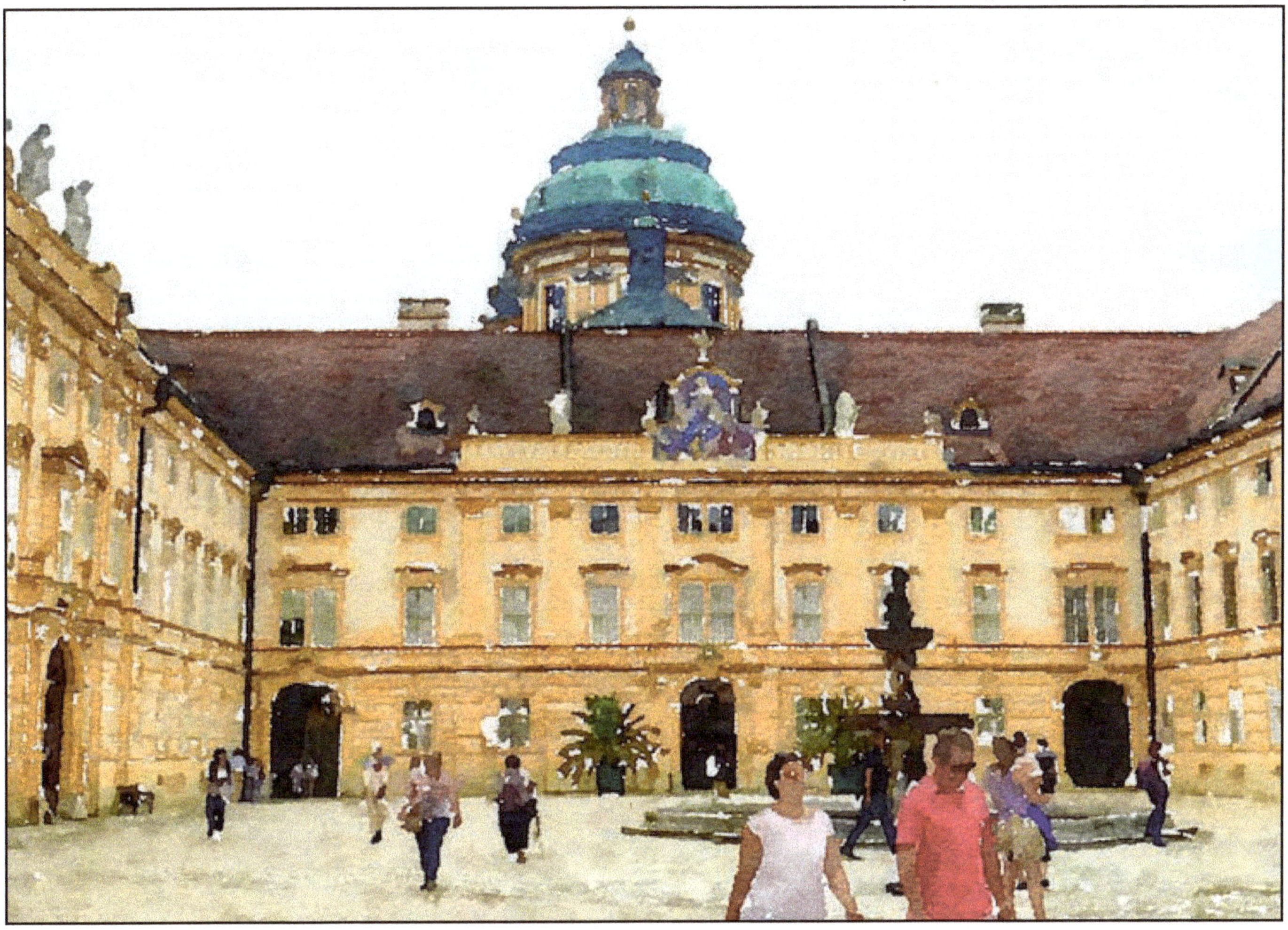

Croatia...

My first visit to Croatia occurred in 2015 when touring the coastal nation aboard a cruise ship. On that occasion, it was the jewel of Dubrovnik that was both so noticeable and captivating. The human activity within its ancient walls as well as its unique harbour on the Adriatic Sea, was a delight to experience. It was on this trip that I was able to venture into Montenegro and Split.

Returning to Croatia in 2018, and making use of a motor vehicle on the second journey, I traversed the entire coastline from south to north, but mostly bypassed the larger cities of Dubrovnik and Split. However, the constant theme throughout was the interplay between the mountains and the sea, which featured some of the most amazing beaches, especially around the more populated areas of Makarska and Omis.

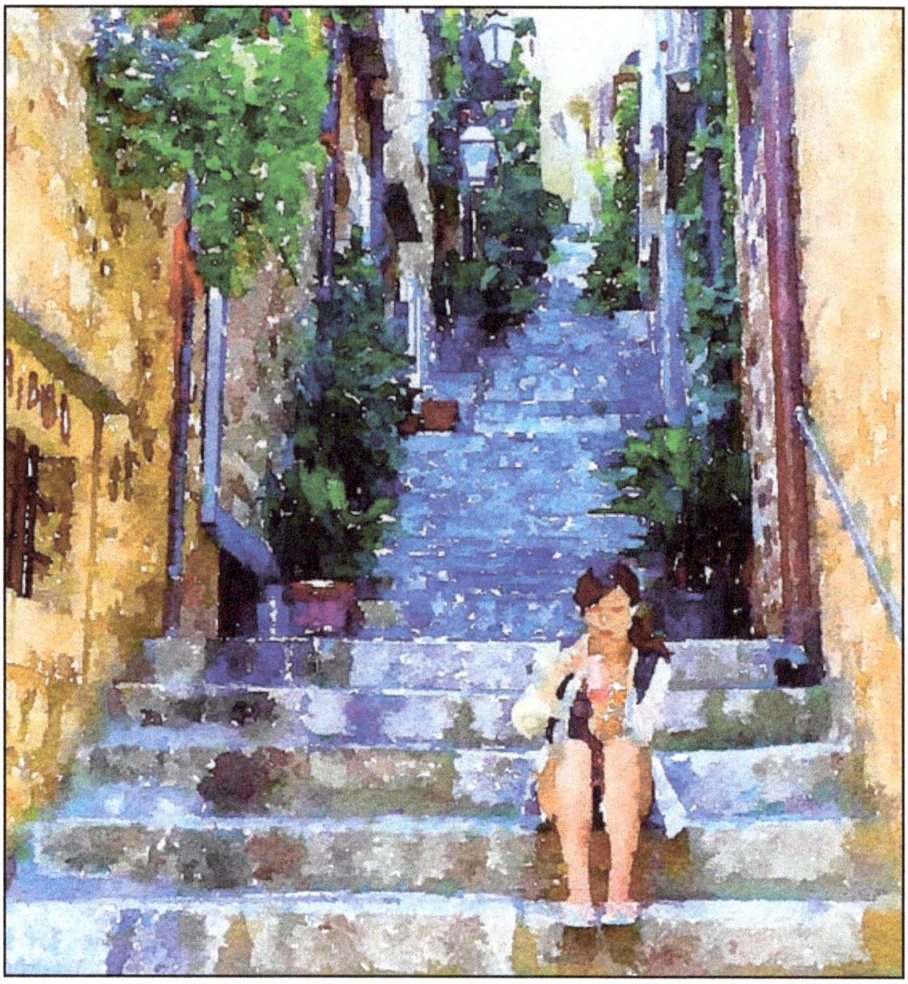

'Lady On The Stairs' (2015), Dubrovnik, Croatia [ECR(DB)1502].▲

▼'View Of The Old City' (2018), Dubrovnik, Croatia [ECR(DB)1801].

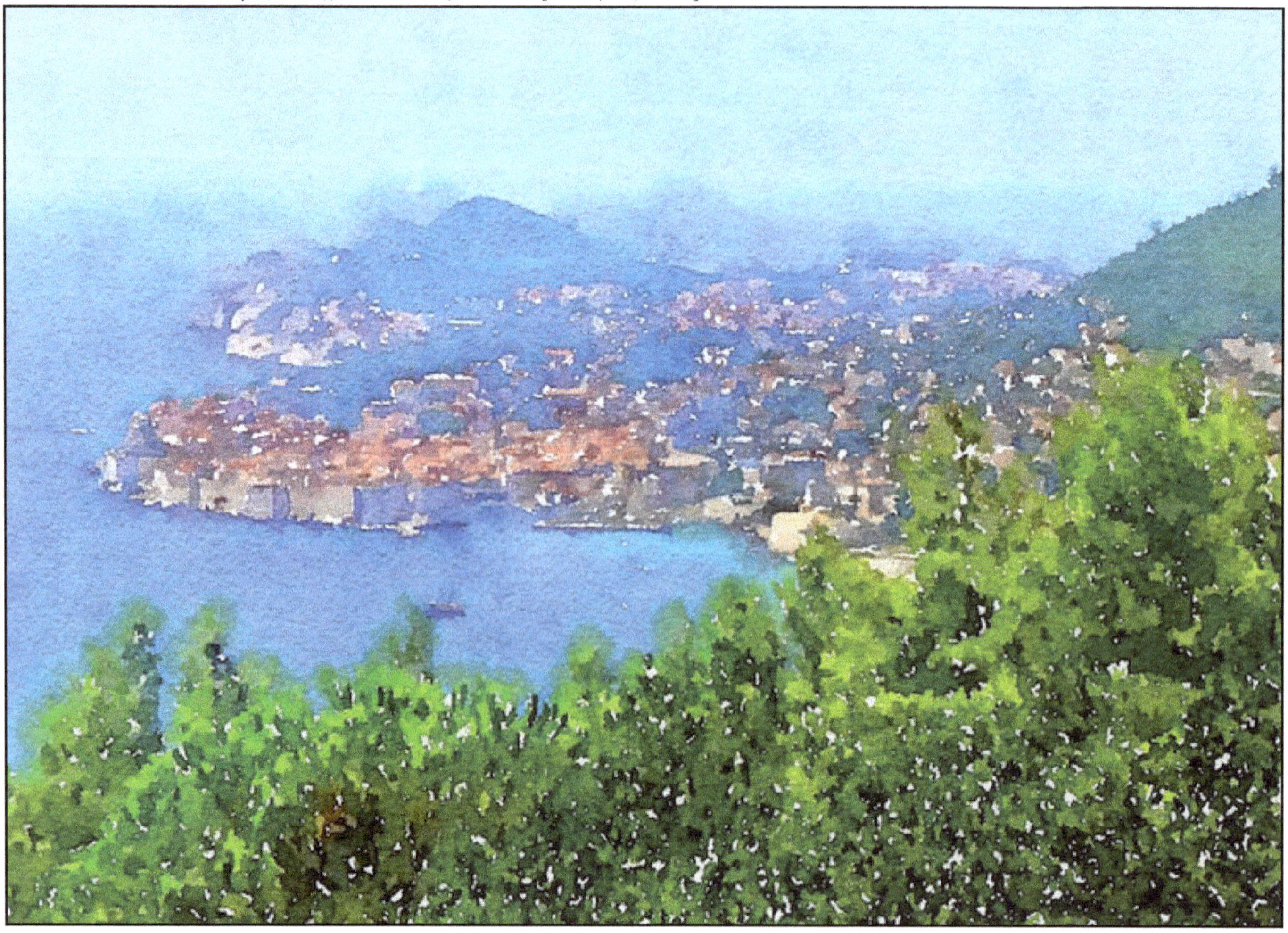

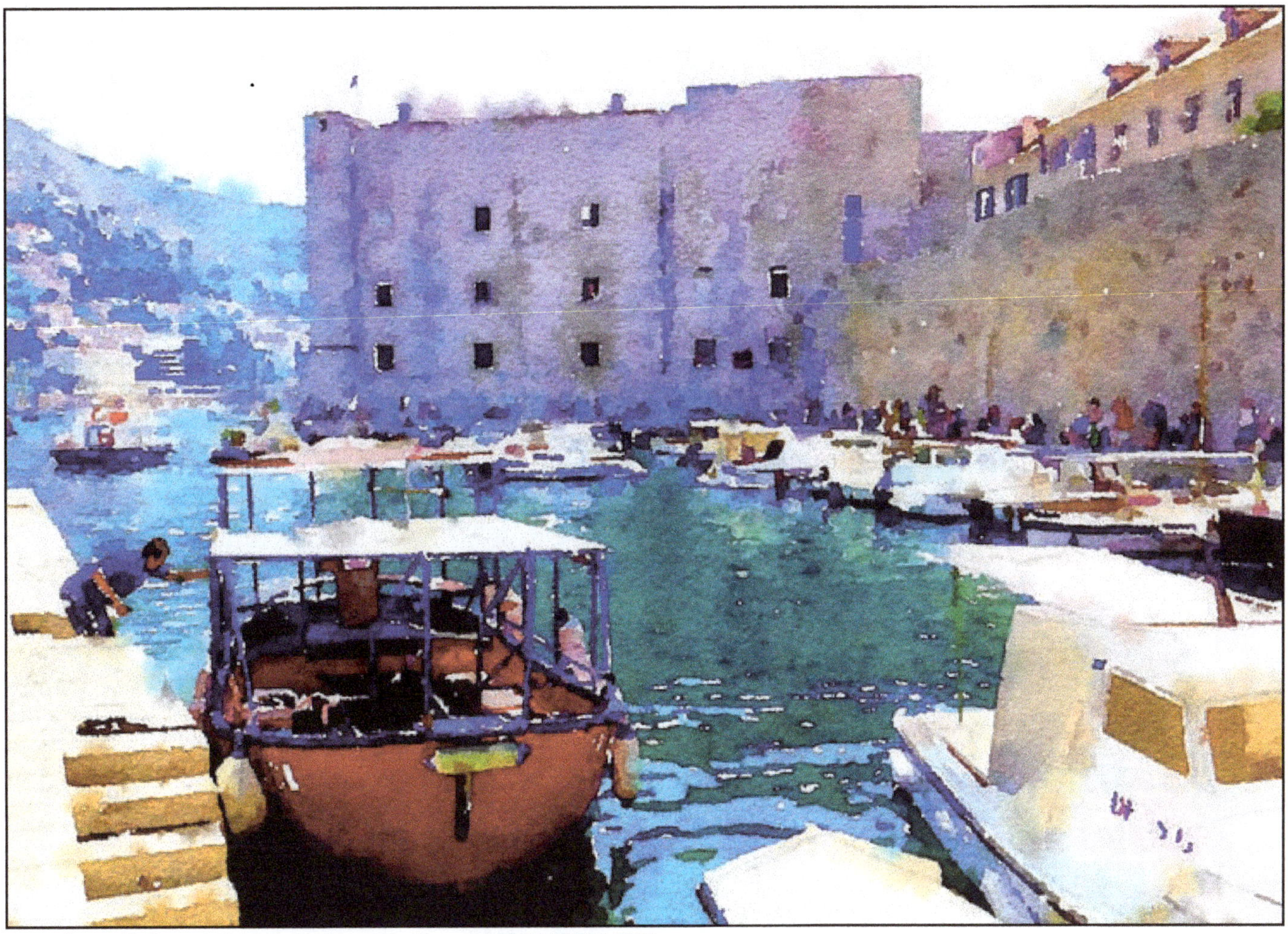

▲'Dubrovnik Boats' (2015), Dubrovnik, Croatia [ECR(DB)1503].

'Dubrovnik Harbour' (2015), Dubrovnik, Croatia [ECR(DB)1504].▼

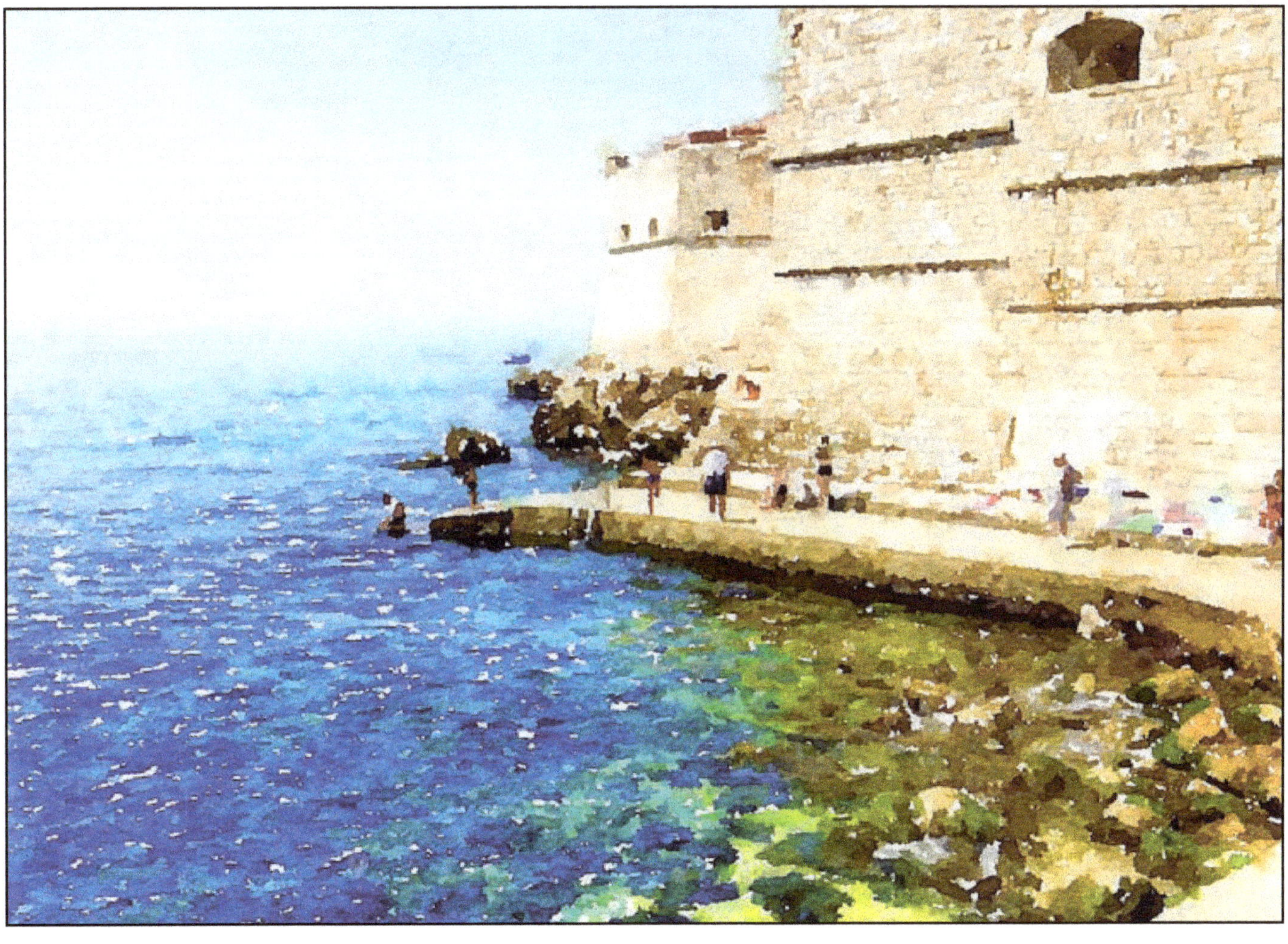

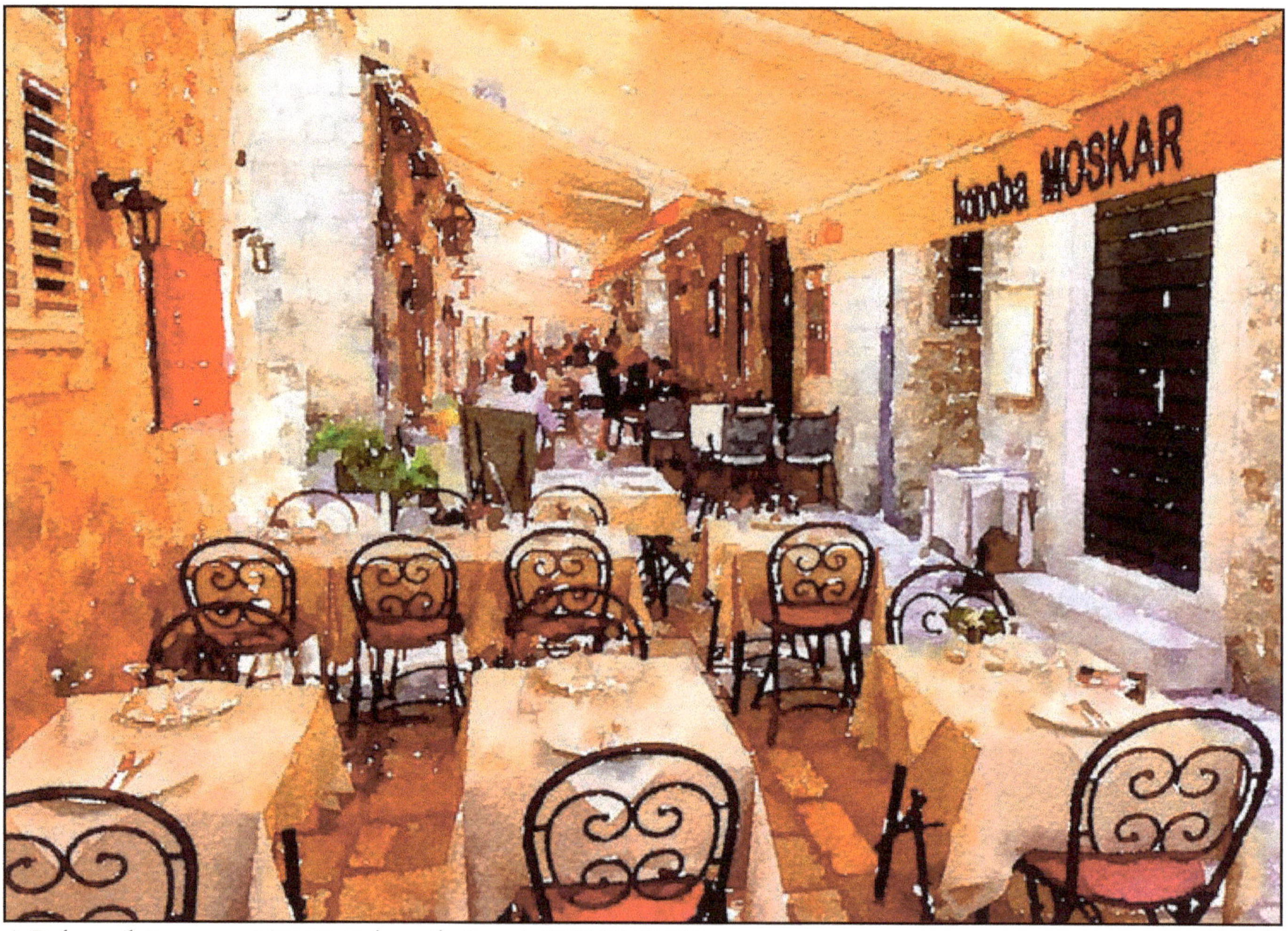

▲'Dubrovnik Restaurant' (2015), Dubrovnik, Croatia [ECR(DB)1501].

'Dubrovnik Nights' (2015), Dubrovnik, Croatia [ECR(DB)1506].▼

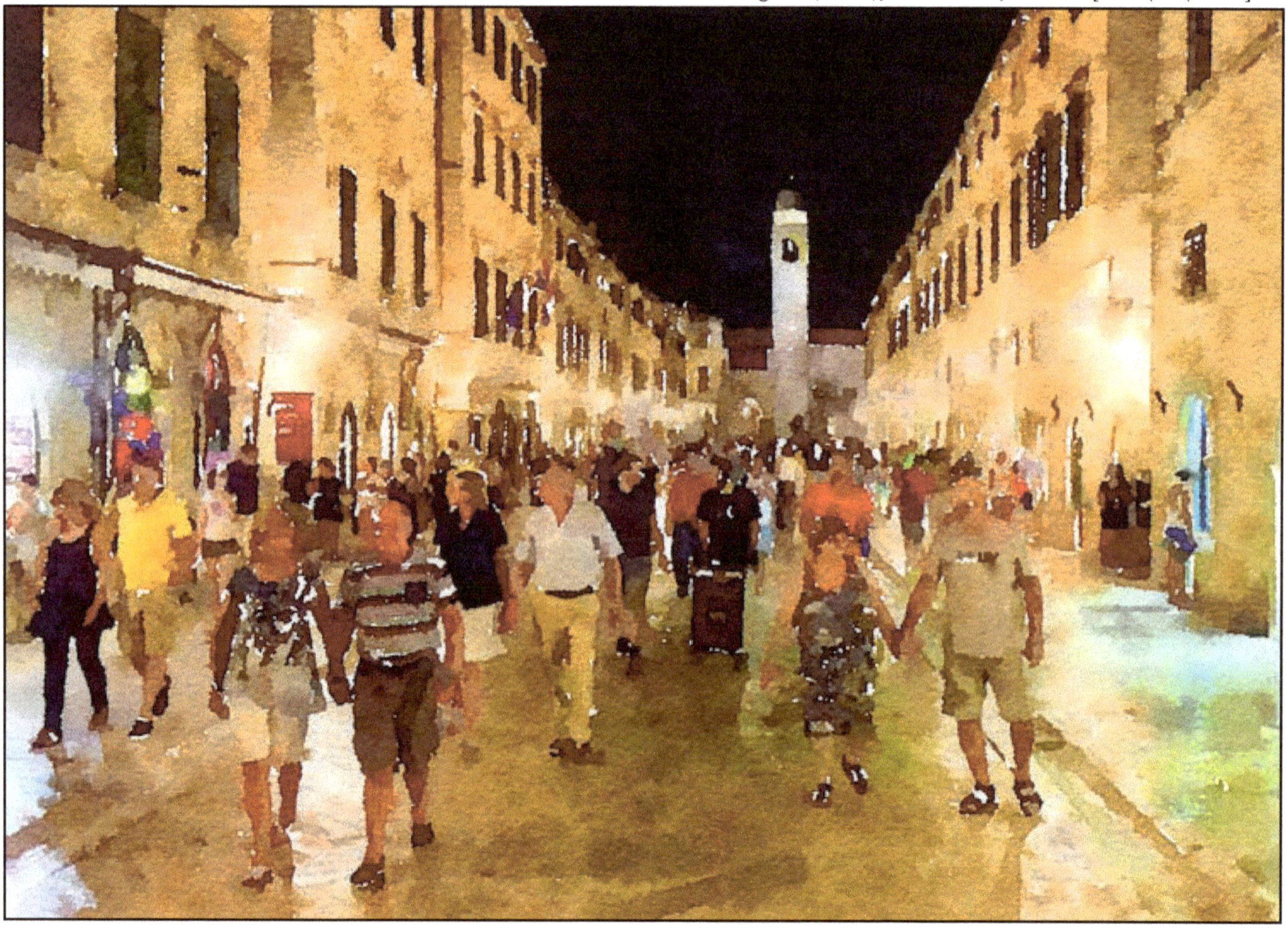

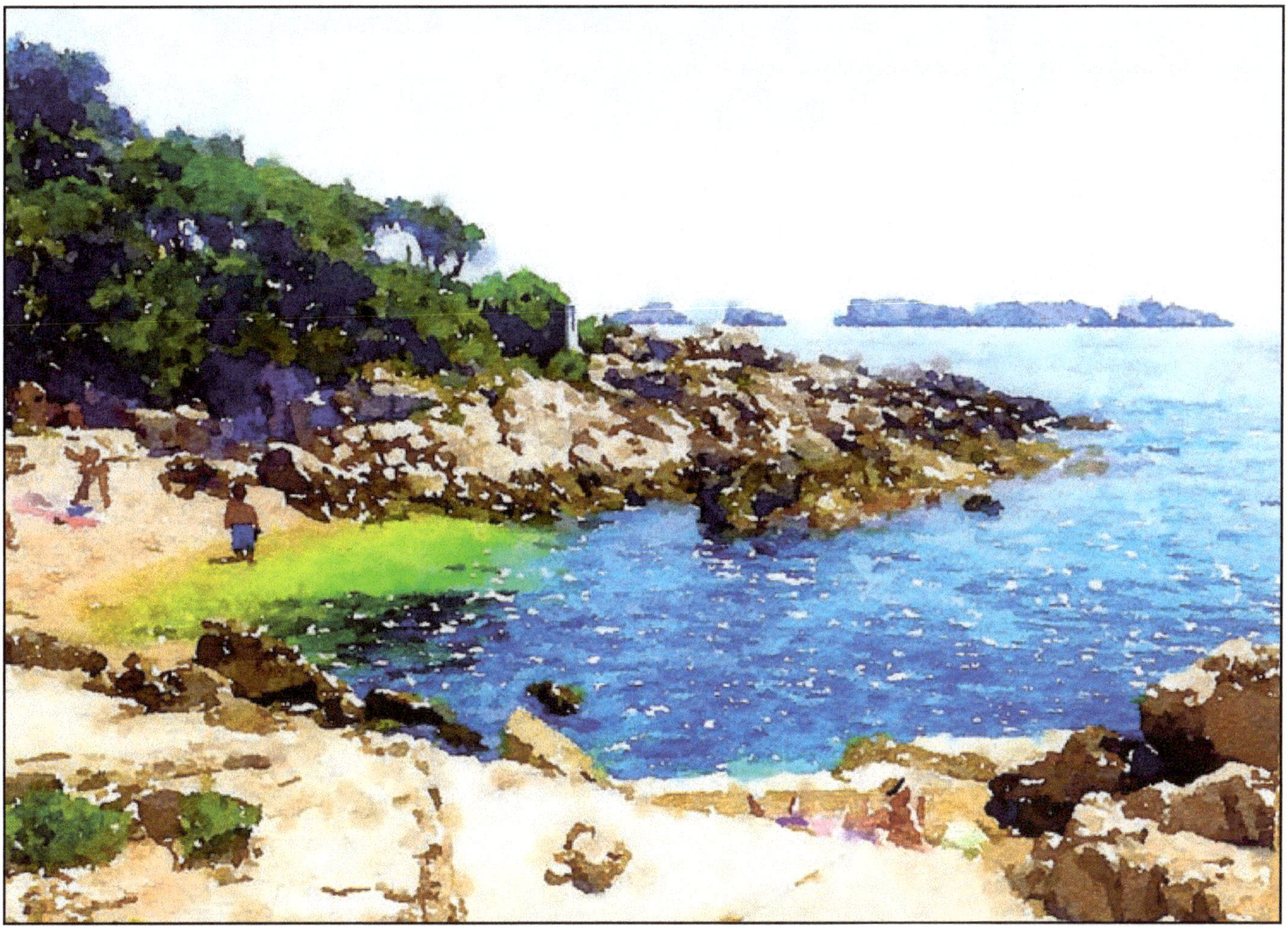

▲'Abyss Beach' (2015), Dubrovnik, Croatia [ECR1505].

'The River Cetina' (2018), Omis, Croatia [ECR1803].▼

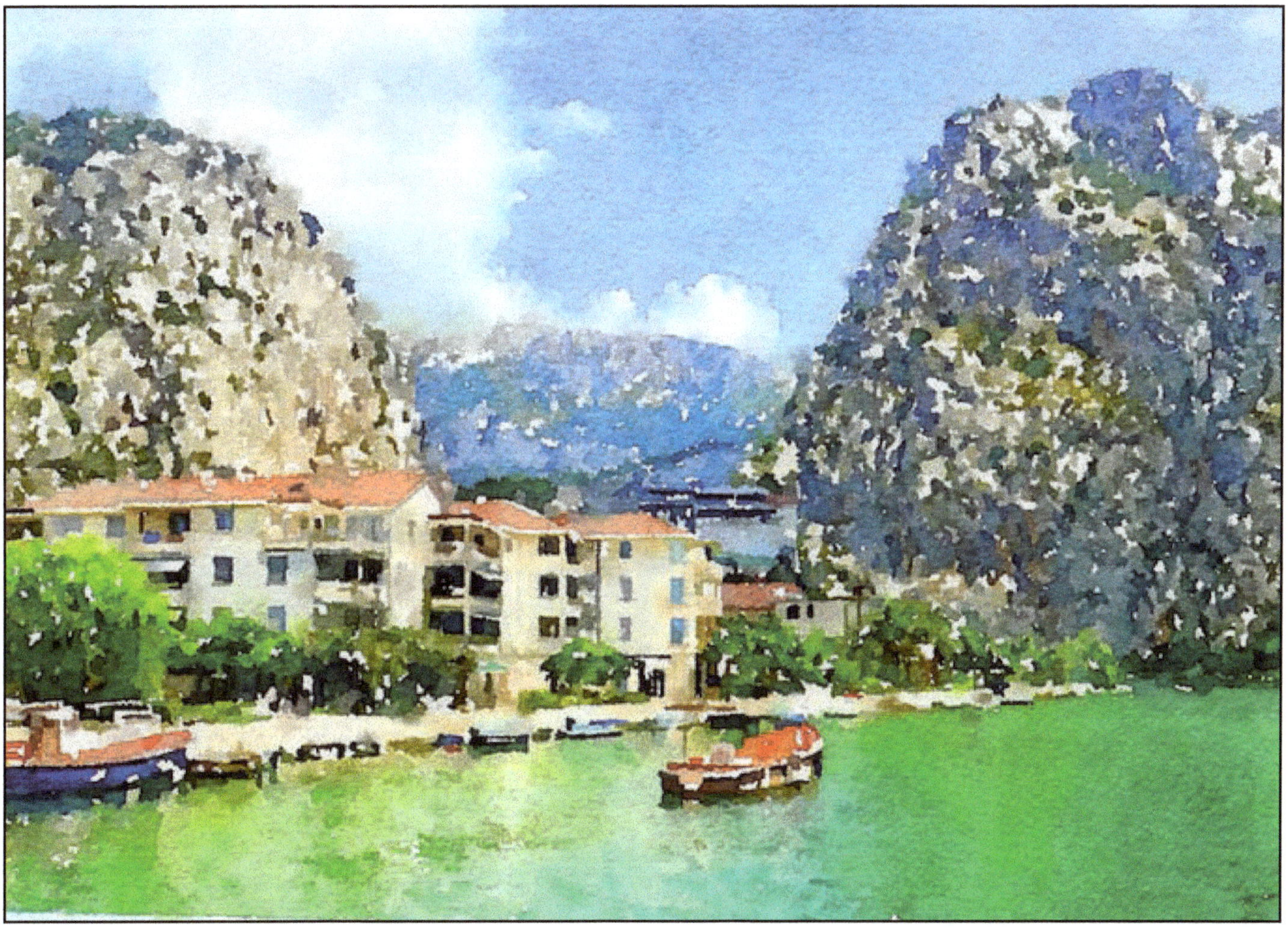

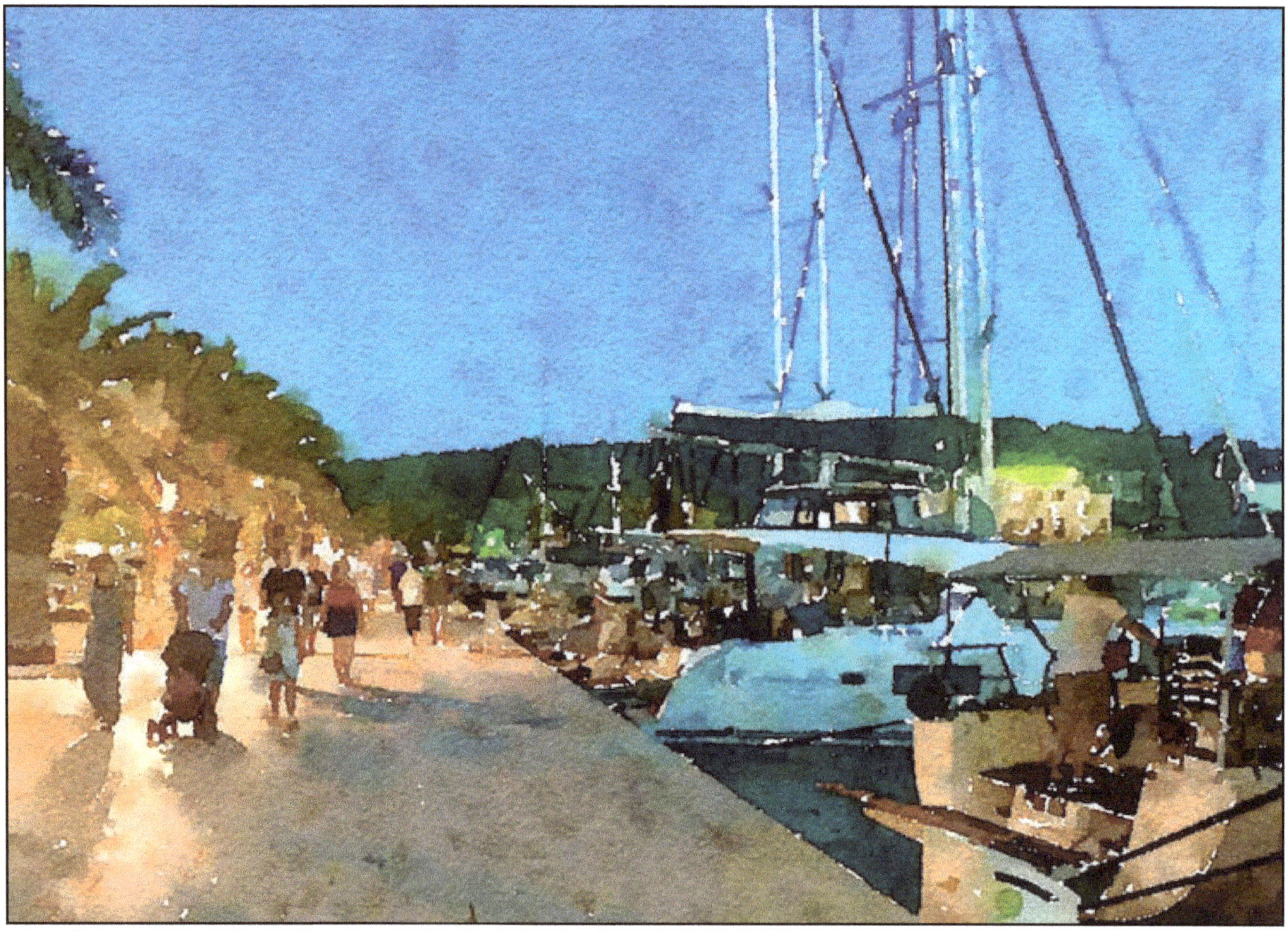

▲'Strolling On Obala Kralja Tomislava' (2018), Makarska, Croatia [ECR1802].

'Makarska Sunset' (2018), Makarska, Croatia [ECR1806].▼

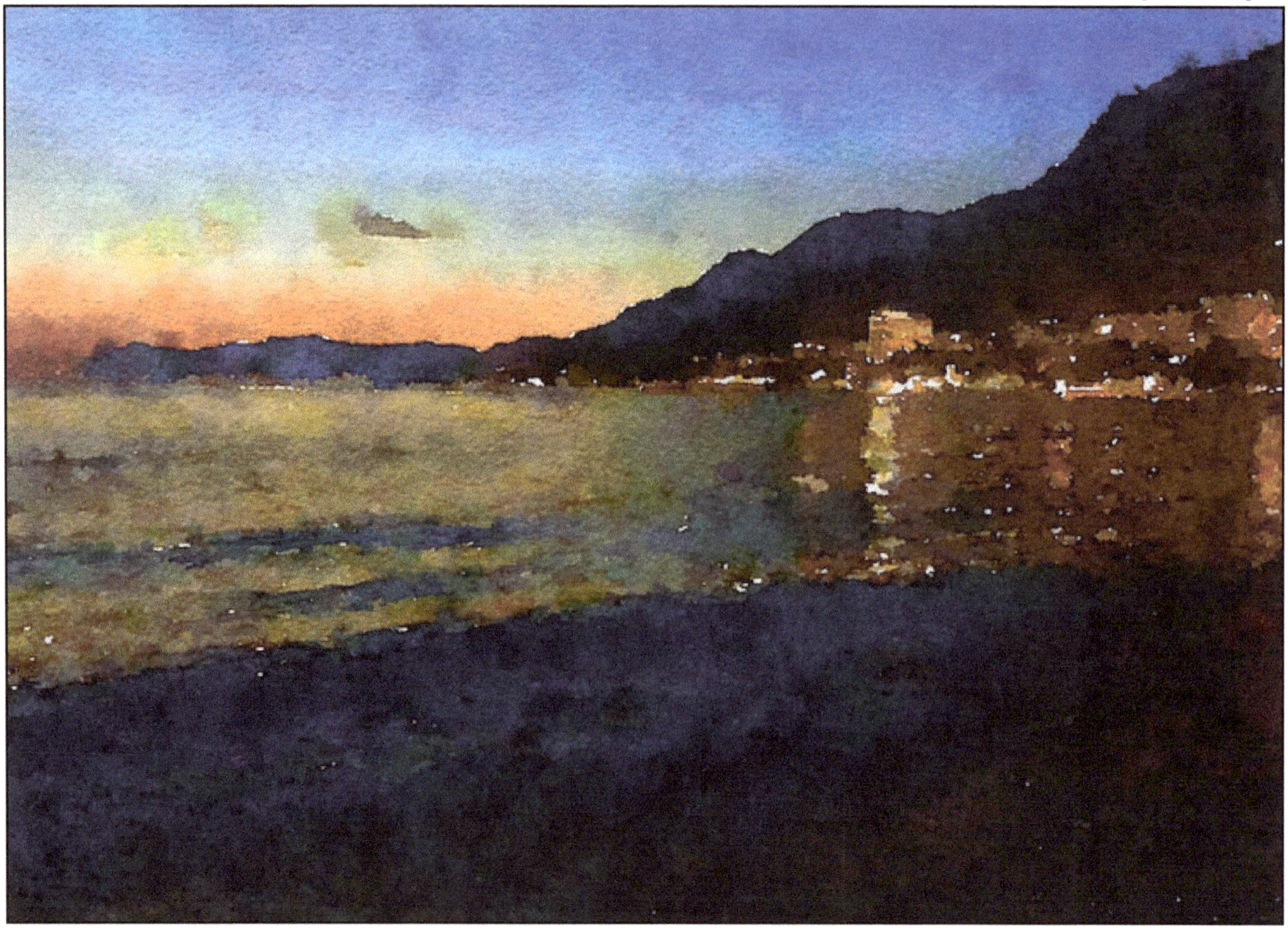

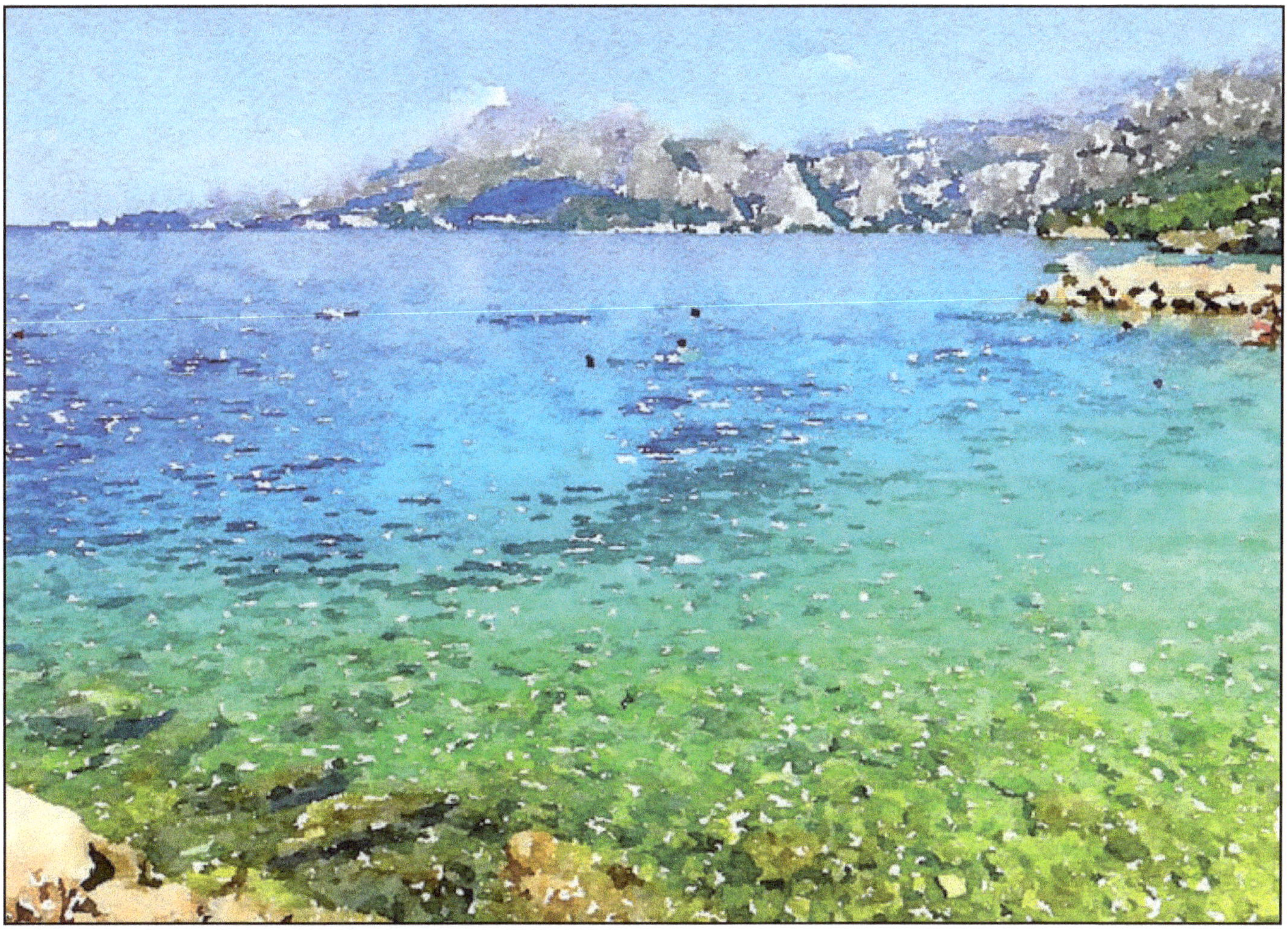

▲'Swimming At Nemira' (2018), Nemira, Croatia [ECR1804].

'The Beach Town' (2018), Klek, Croatia [ECR1807].▼

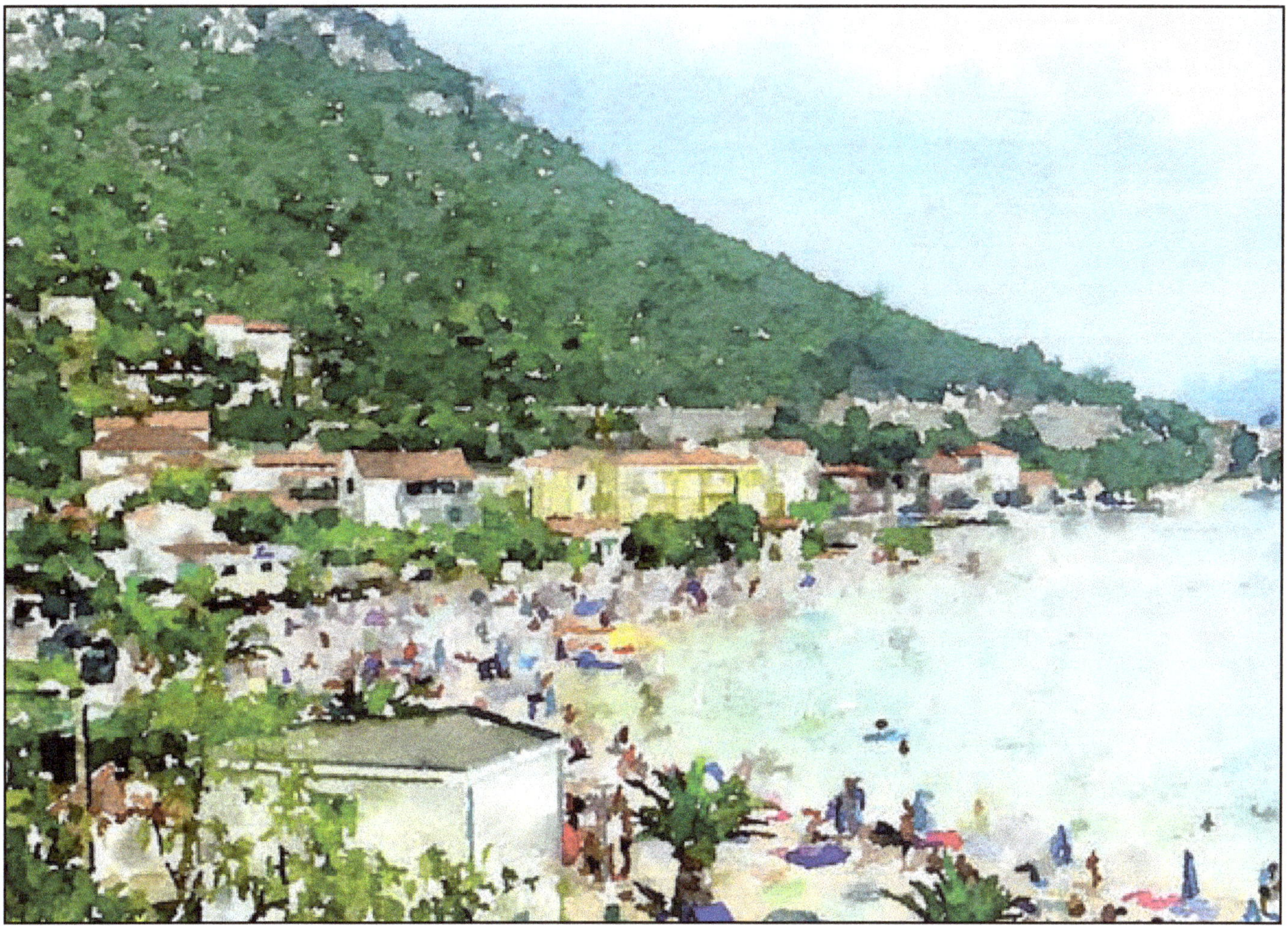

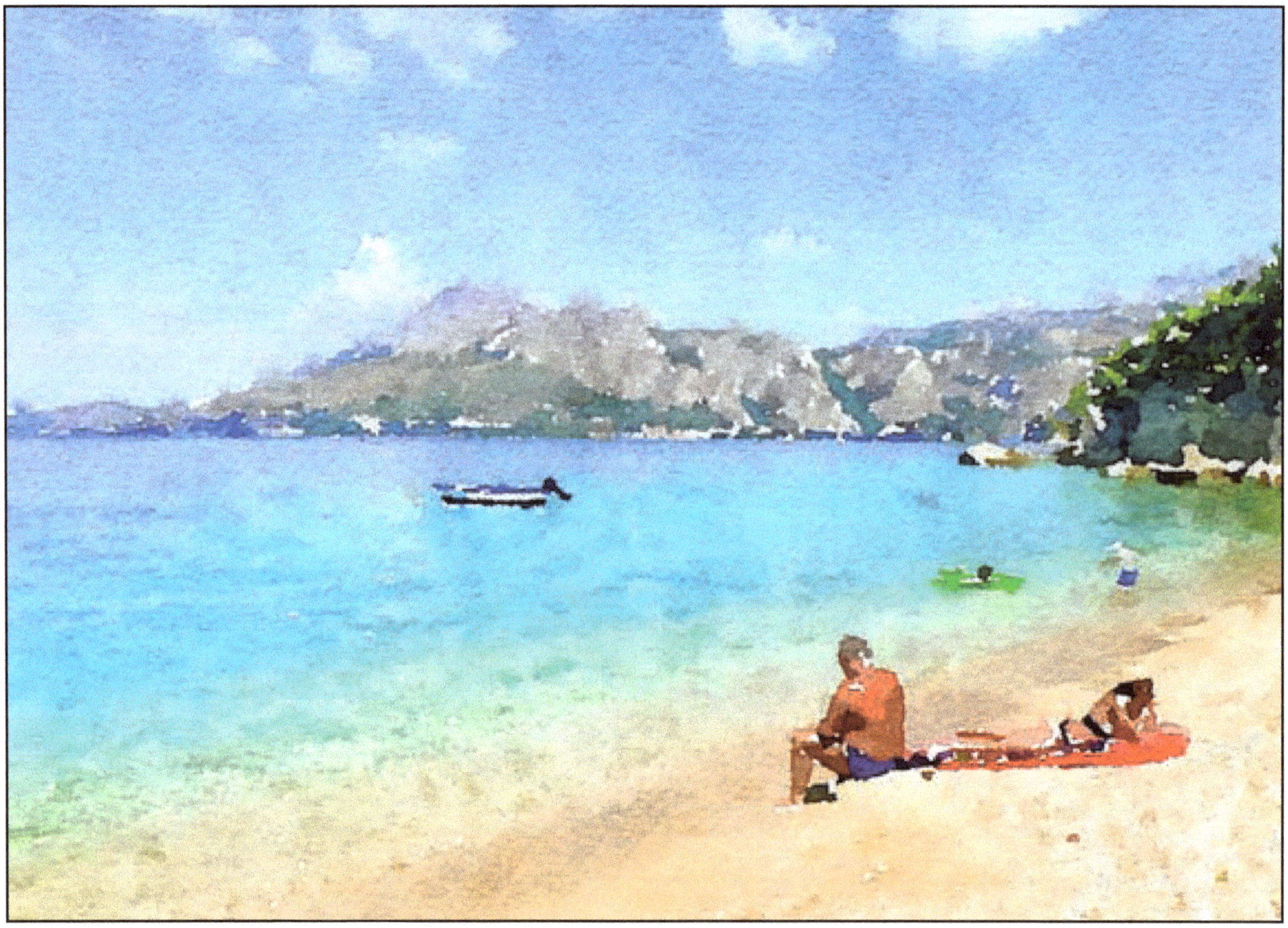

▲'On The Water's Edge' (2018), Nemira, Croatia [ECR1805].

'Old Port Town' (2018), Tribanj, Croatia [ECR1808].▼

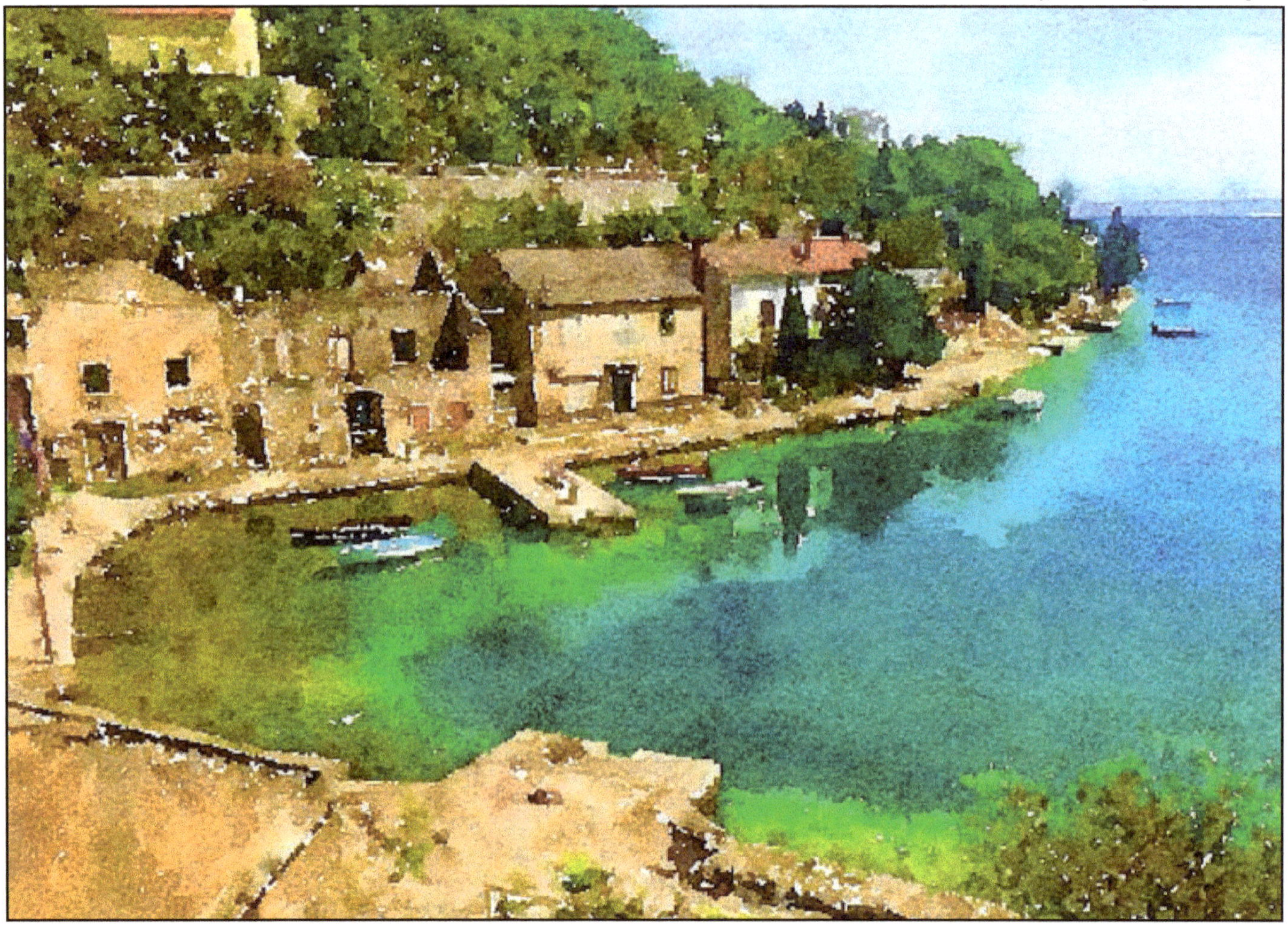

Czech Republic...

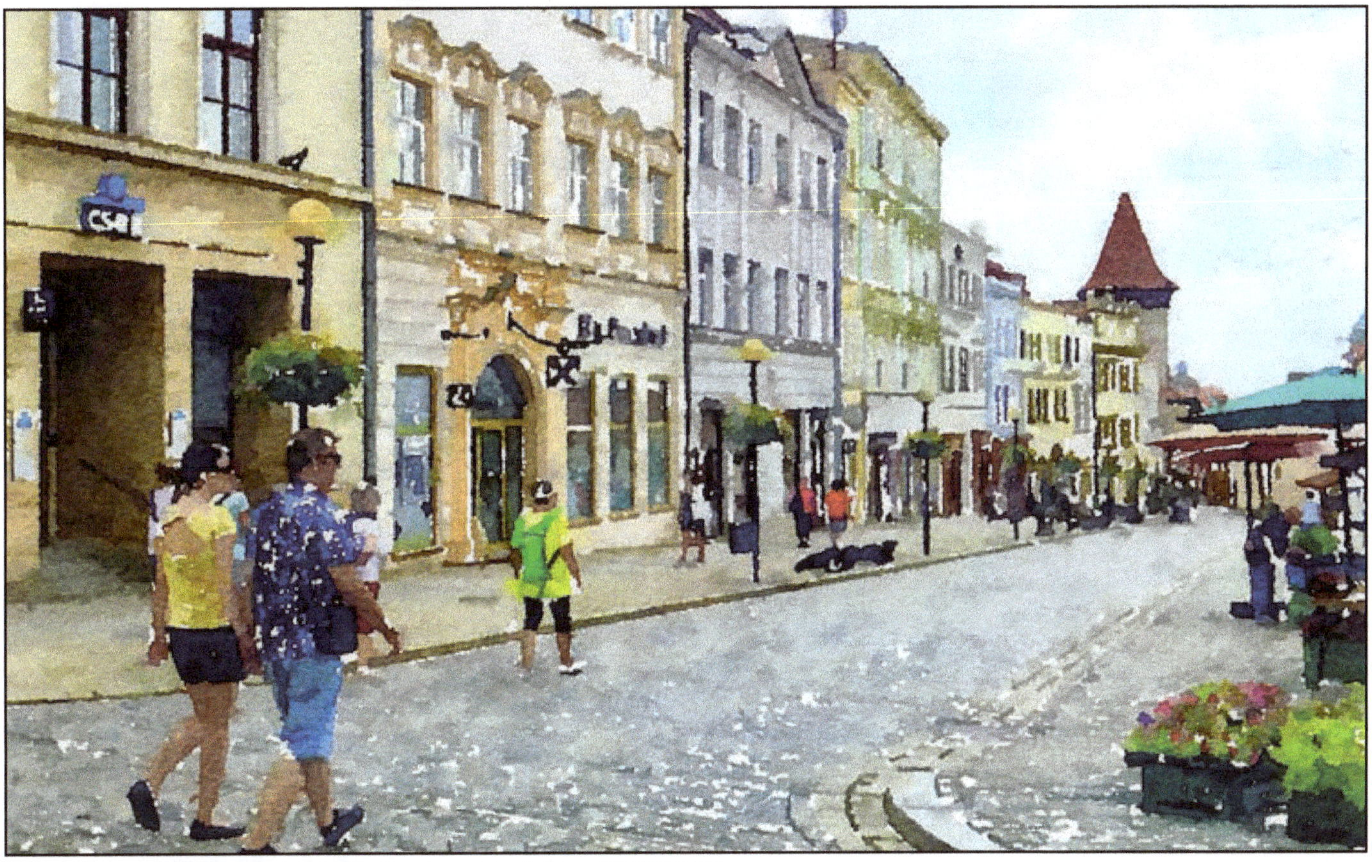

▲'Strolling on Zelenarska' (2018), Znojmo, Czech Rep. [ECZ1801].

'Velka Frantiskanska' (2018), Znojmo, Czech Rep. [ECZ1802].▼

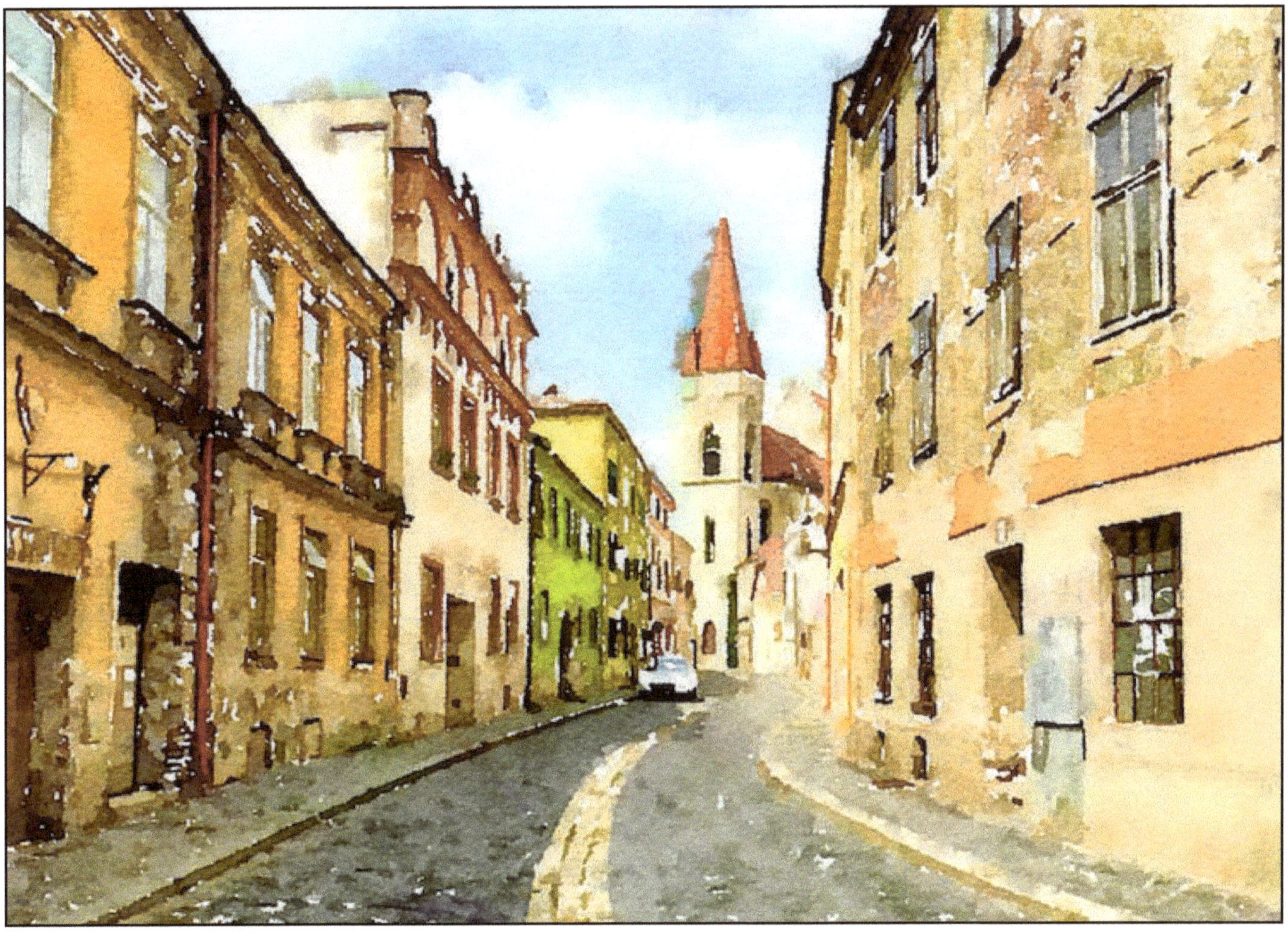

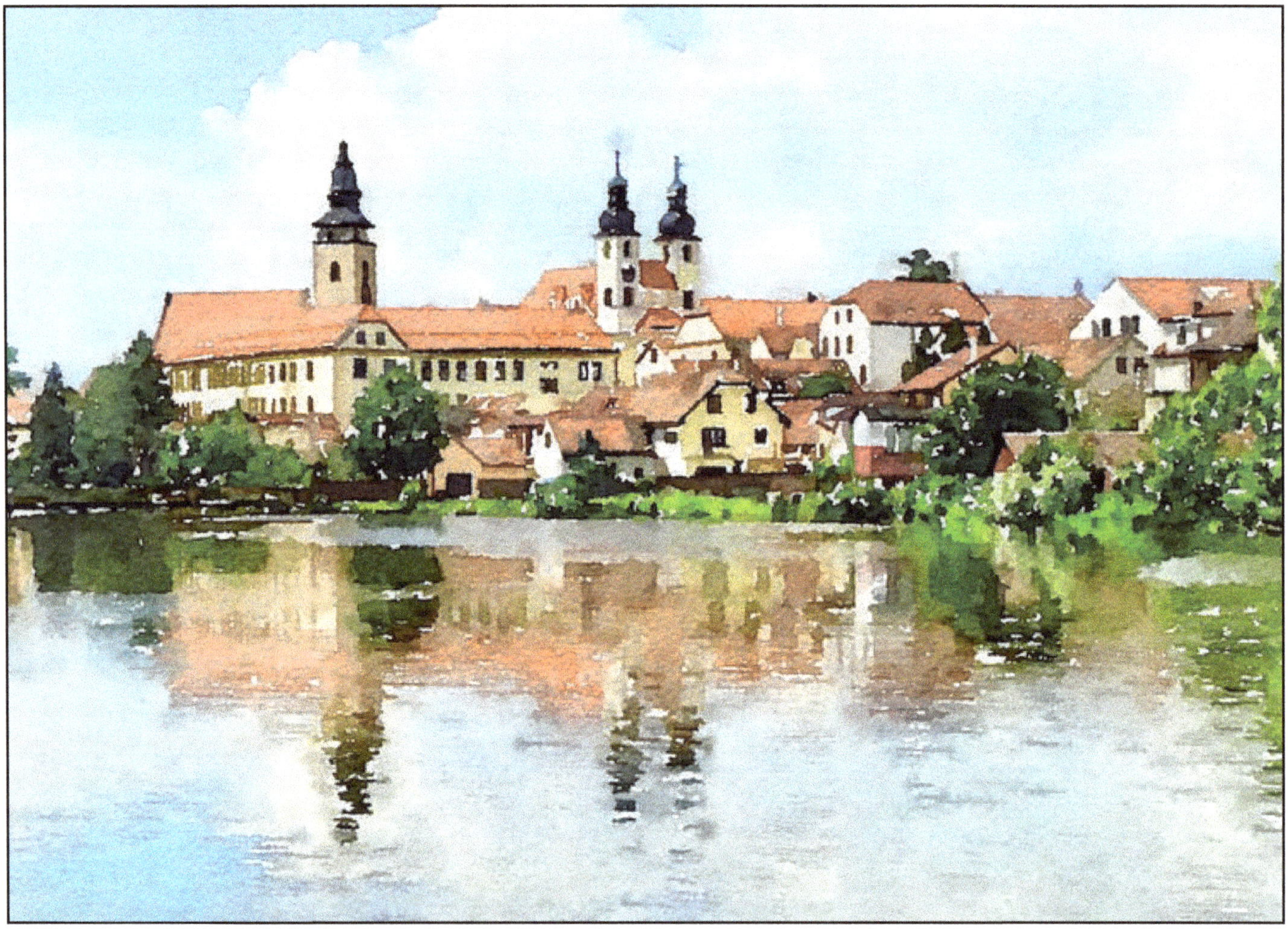

▲'Ulicky Rybnik' (2018), Telc, Czech Rep. [ECZ1803].

'The Facades Of Telc' (2018), Telc, Czech Rep. [ECZ1804].▼

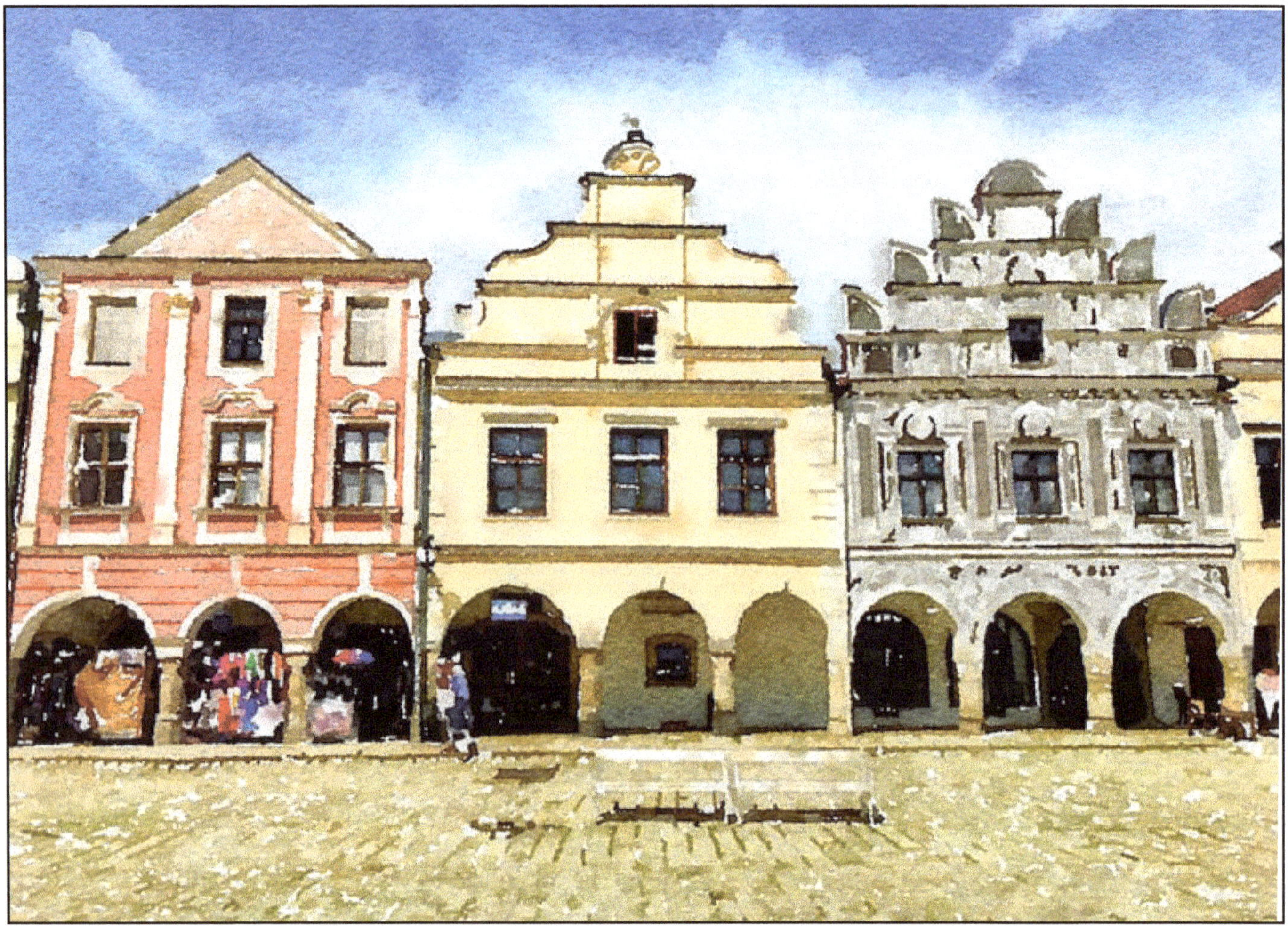

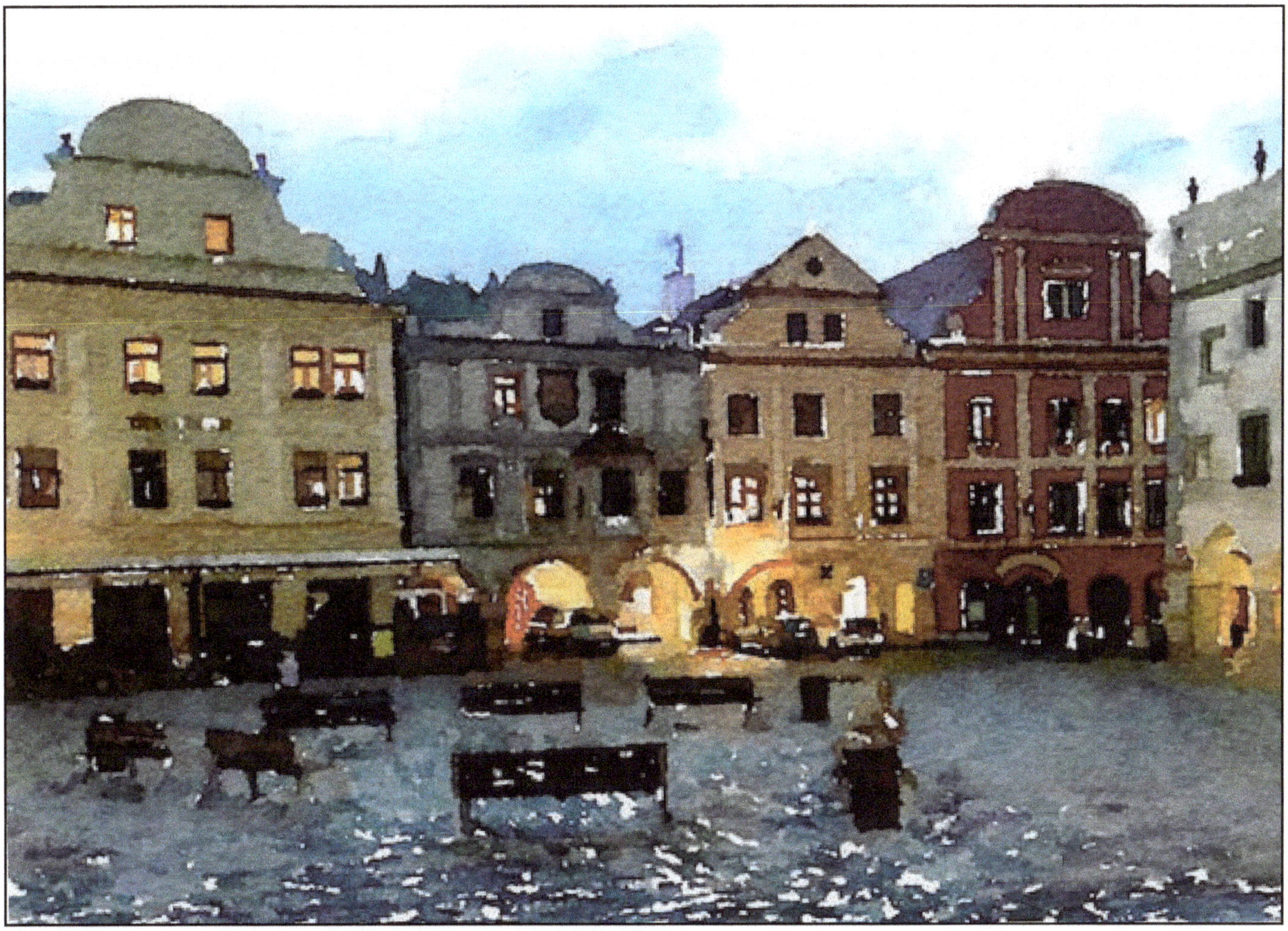

▲'Main Square' (2018), Cesky Krumlov, Czech Rep. [ECZ1805].

'Horni Kaplicka' (2018), Cesky Krumlov, Czech Rep. [ECZ1806].▼

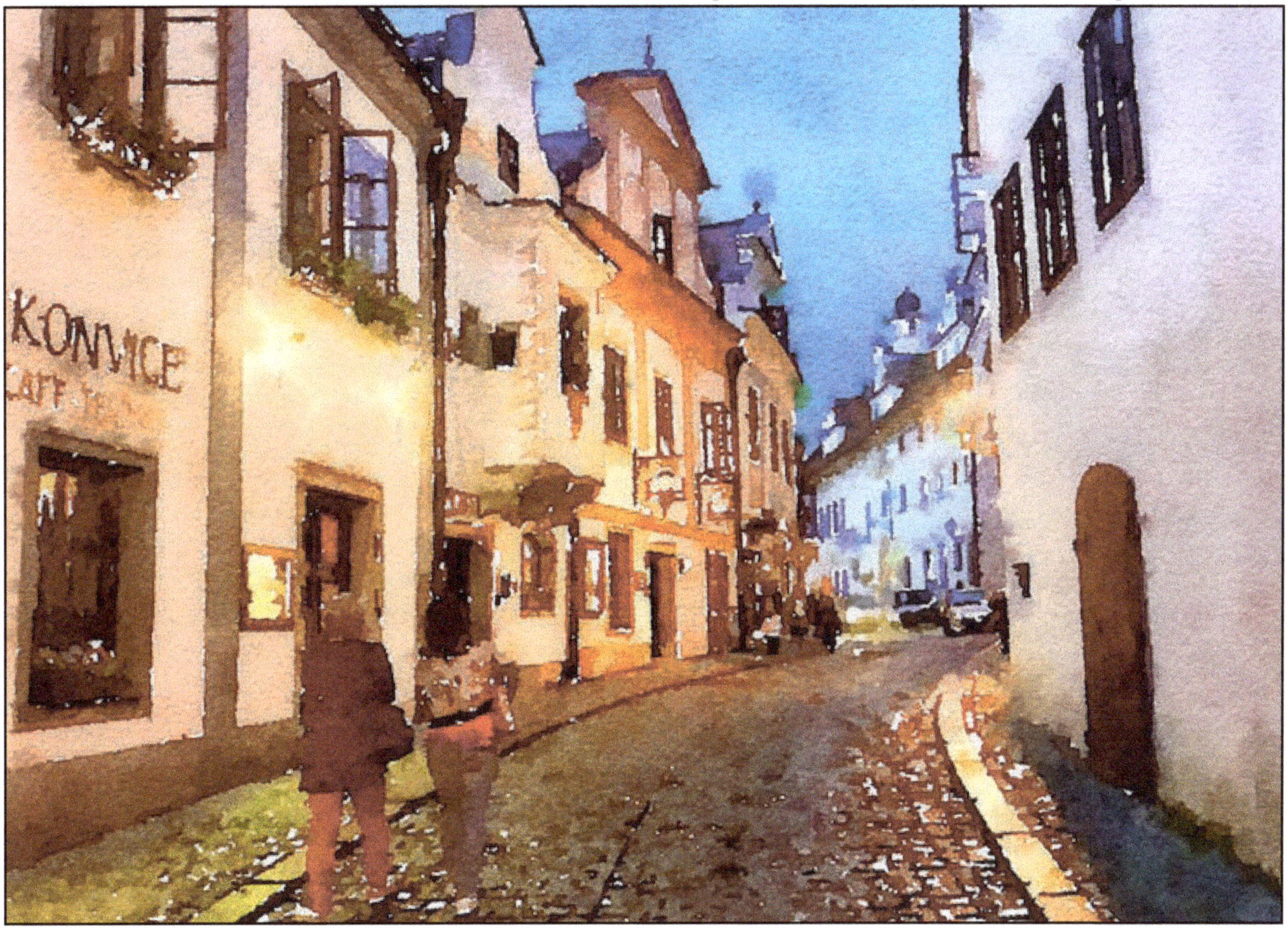

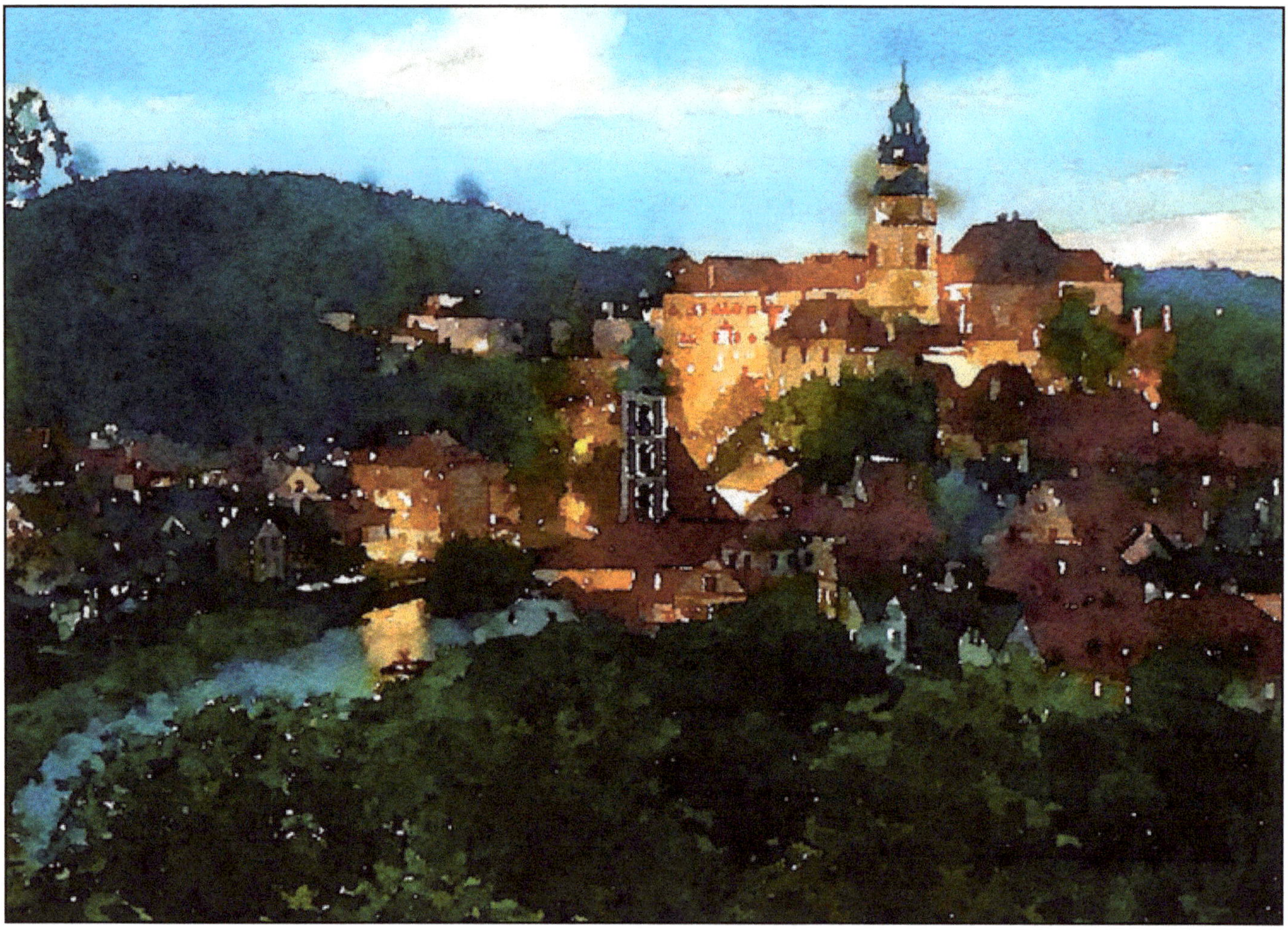

▲'Hradni Castle' (2018), Cesky Krumlov, Czech Rep. [ECZ1807].

'Grand Facades' (2018), Prague, Czech Rep. [ECZ1808].▼

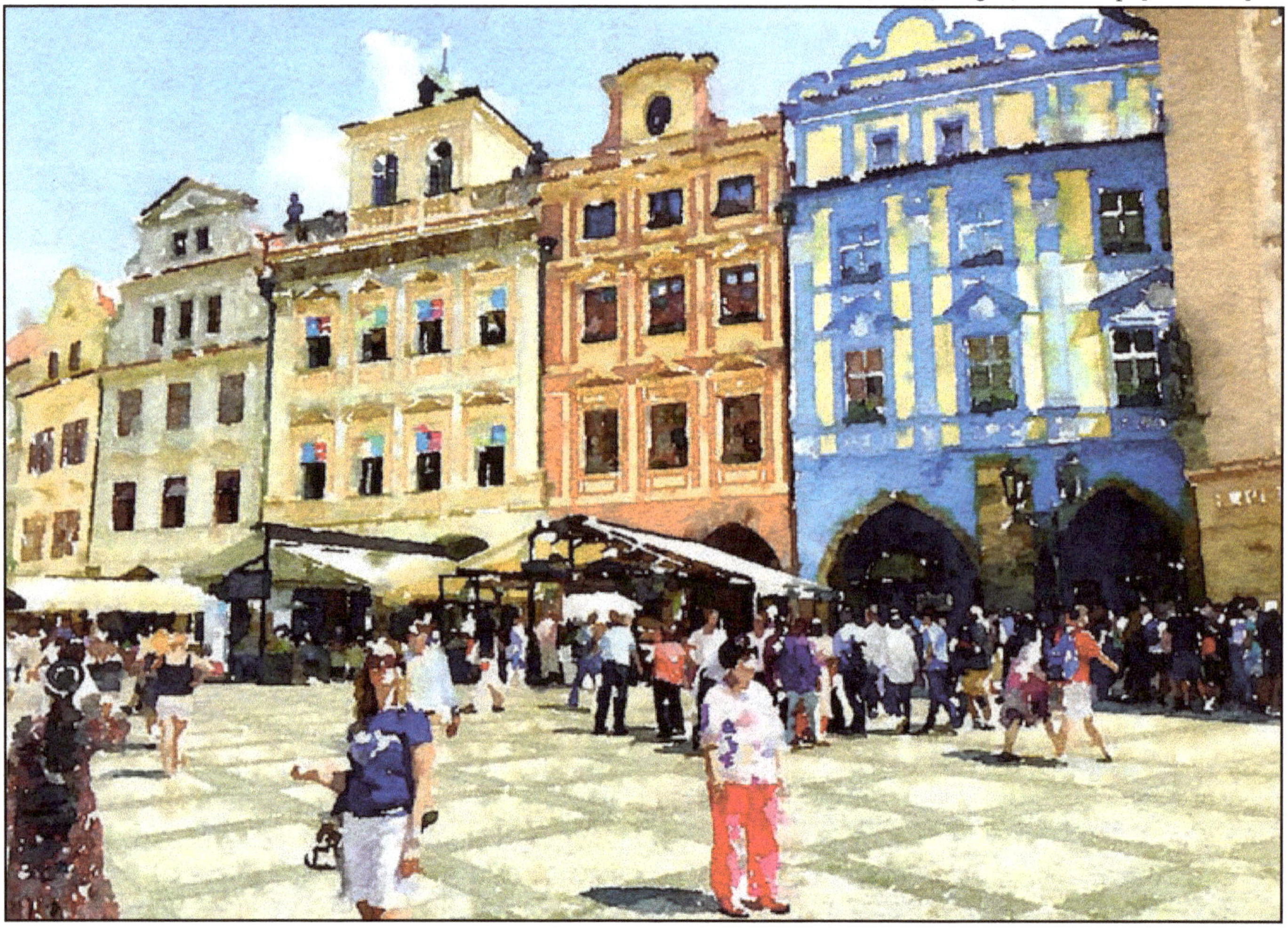

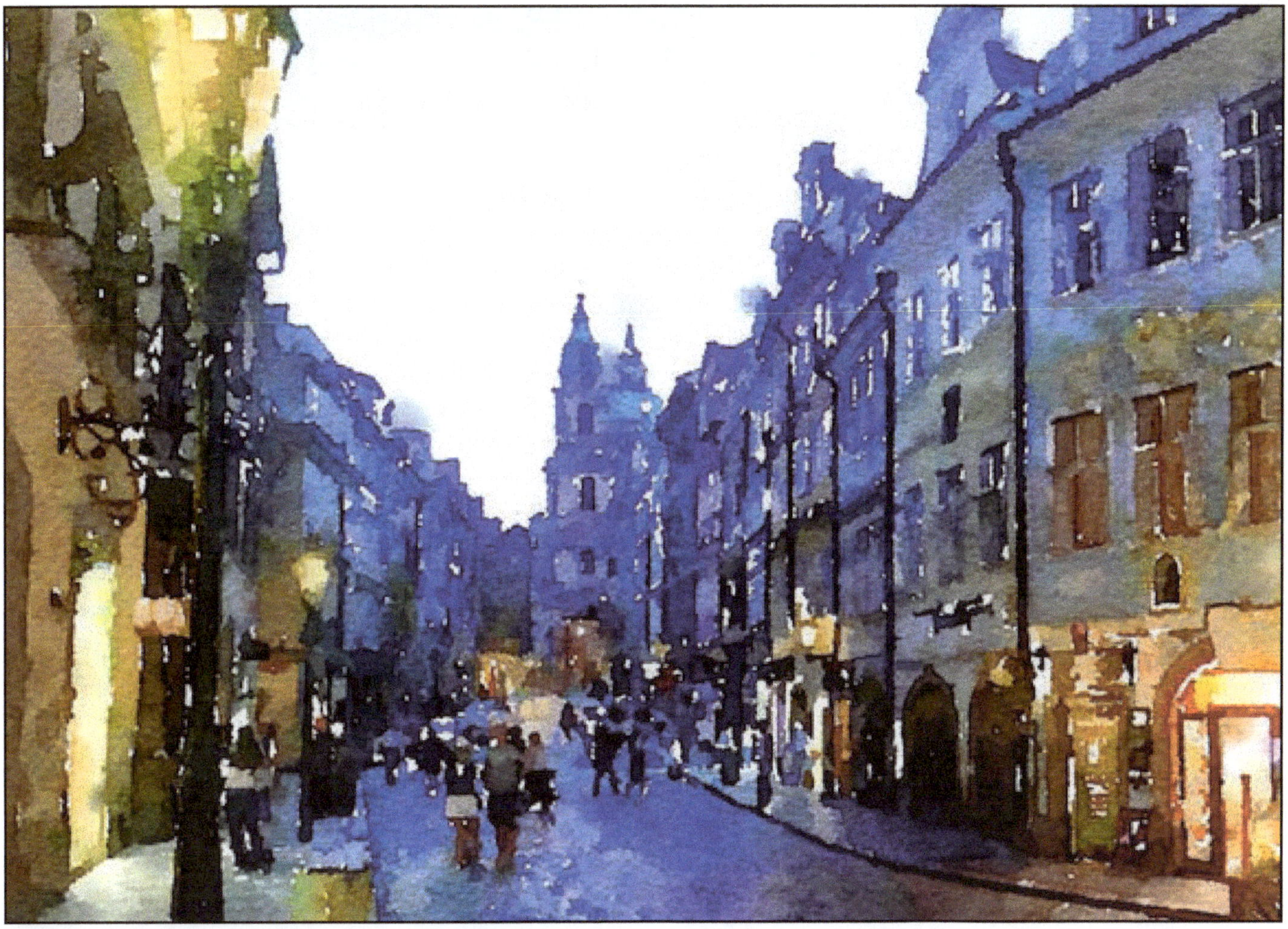

▲'Mostecka' (2018), Prague, Czech Rep. [ECZ1810].

'Vltava Reflections' (2018), Prague, Czech Rep. [ECZ1811].▼

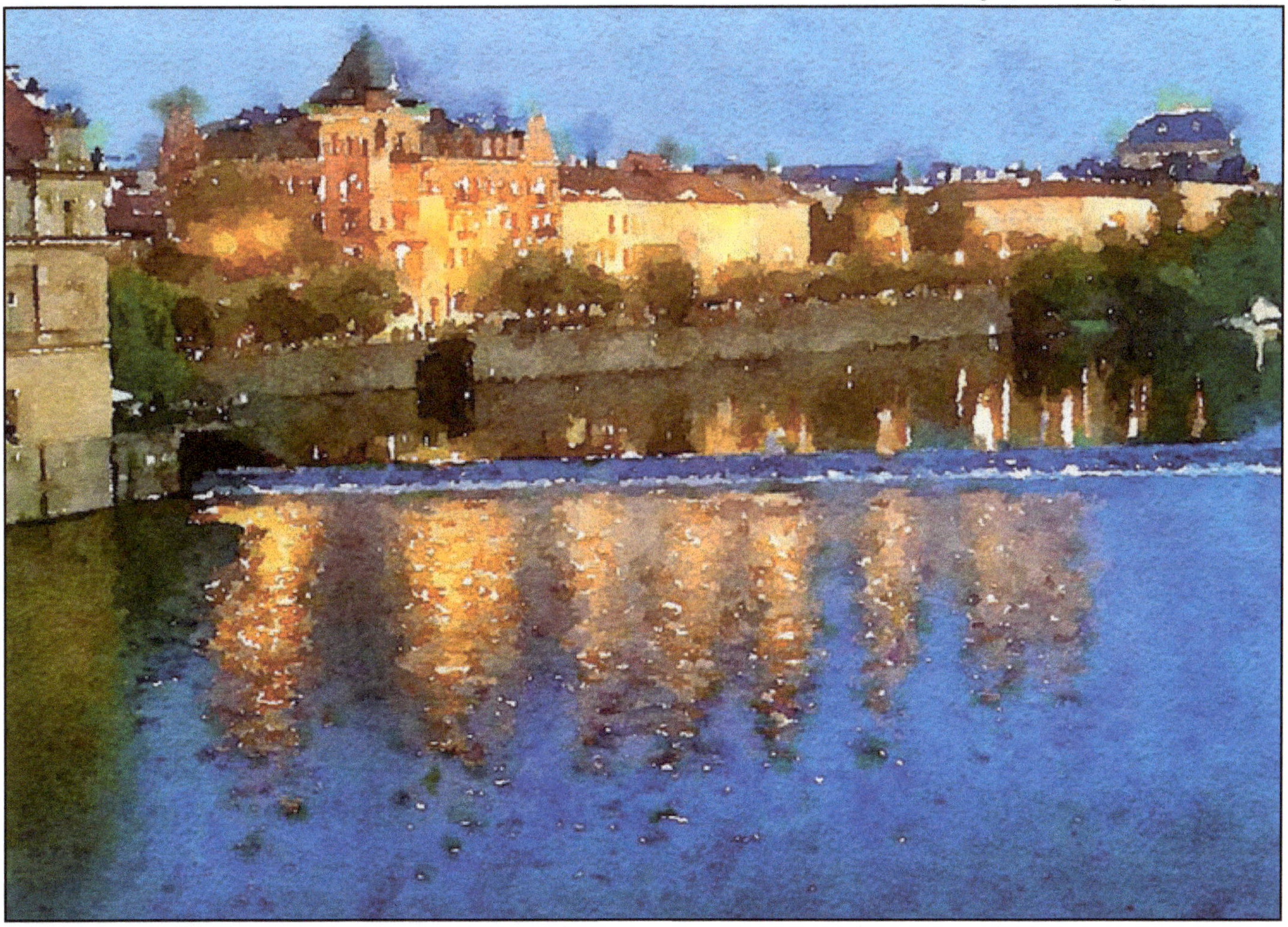

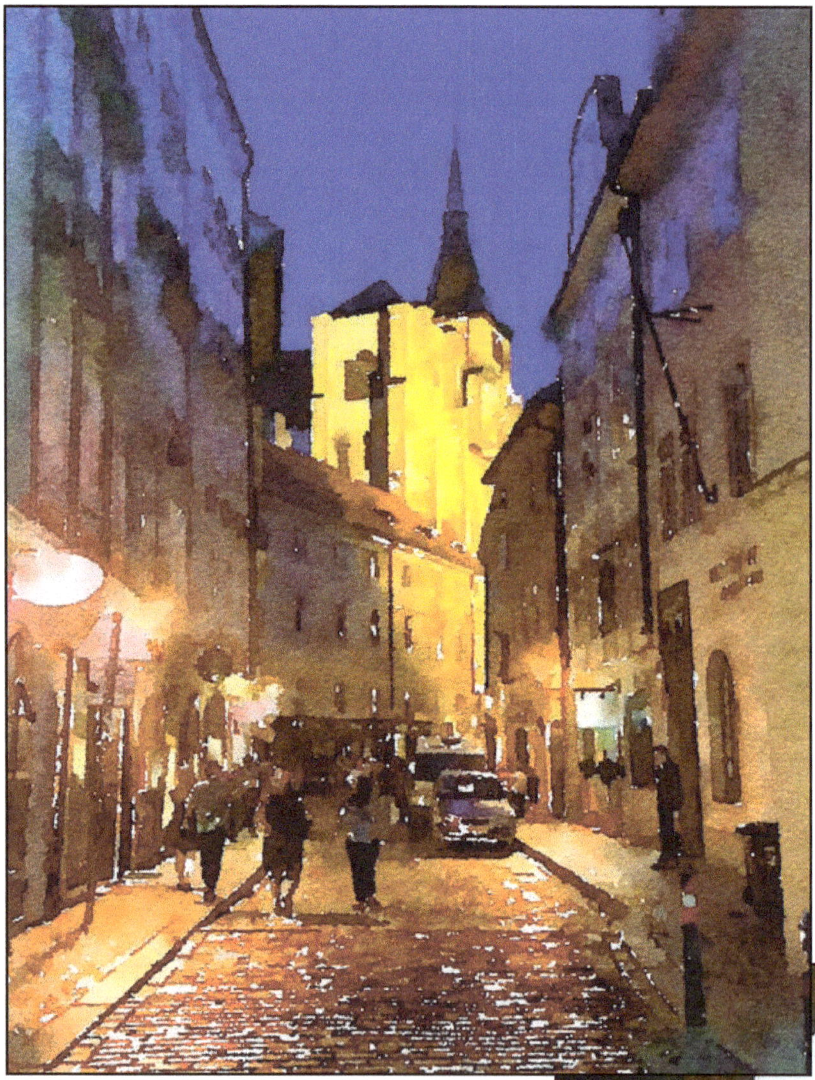

◀'Cobbled Streets' (2018), Prague, Czech Rep. [ECZ1812].

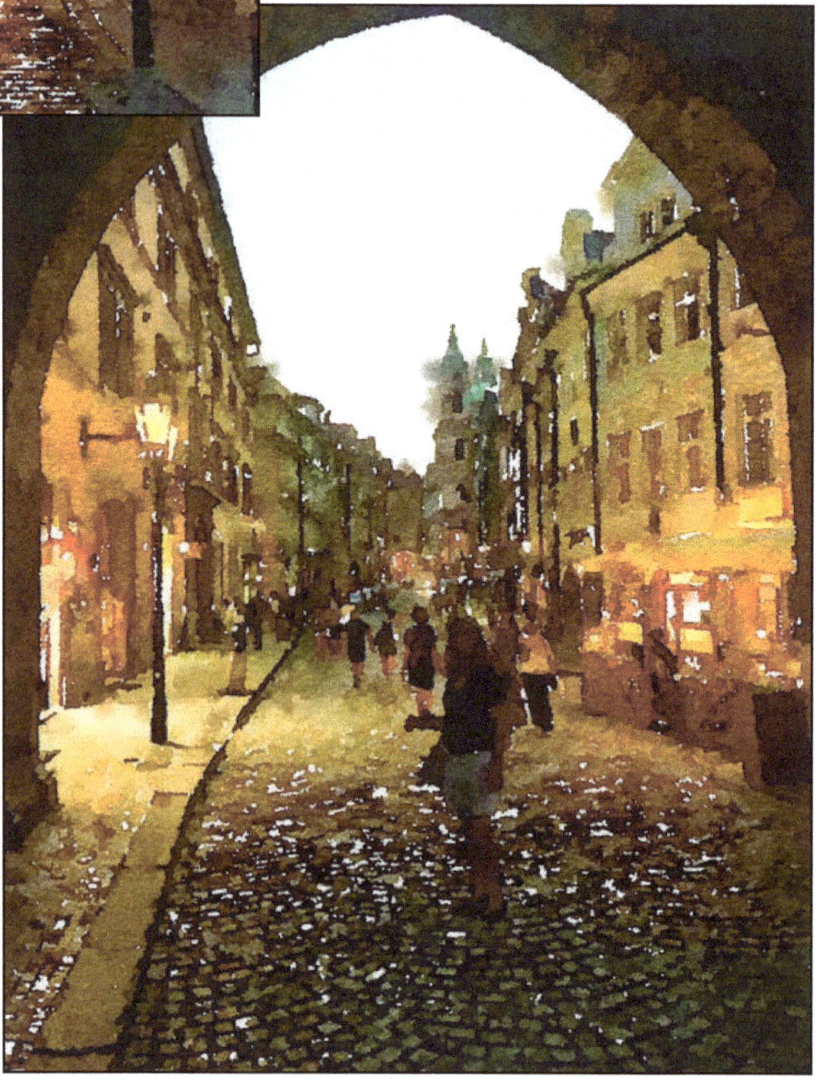

▶'Mostecka From The Bridge Tower' (2018), Prague, Czech Rep. [ECZ1809].

England...

From the time of my first visit to London as a QANTAS steward in 1979, I have been captivated by the 'mother country'. However, few photographs survived from my earlier days and it wasn't until I spent a nine day driving holiday, through the southern counties in 2016, that I was able to capture images that were capable of being converted into works of art.

Heading west from London on that particular tour, I randomly explored the countryside of the southern and western counties, visiting both Berkeley and Arundel castles in the process, and exploring some of the villages of my ancestors in Surrey, Sussex and Hampshire.

It was sheer pleasure to explore and experience the gentle English countryside, the quaint villages and towns of distinct regions, interspersed with glimpses of grand manors and castles appearing at almost every turn. The more I see of England, the more I want to see and nine days was insufficient time to work in such a photographic wonderland, but it provides me with a wonderful excuse to return.

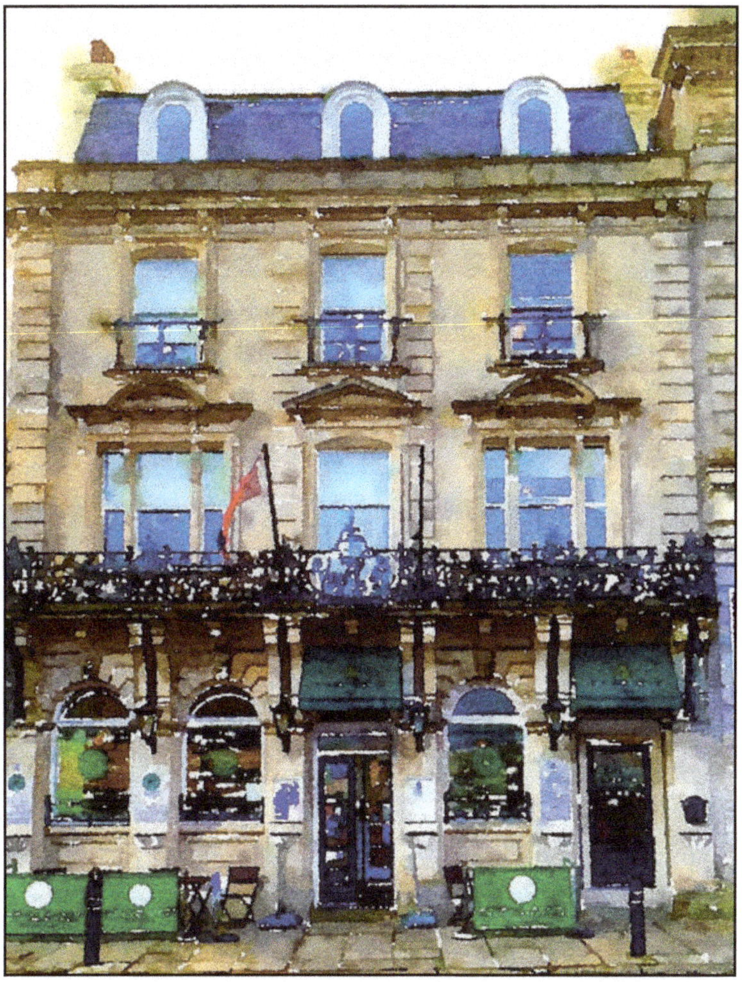

'Portsmouth Hotel' (2016), Portsmouth, Hampshire [EEN1608].▲

▼'Tudor Houses' (2016), Godalming, Surrey [EEN1602].

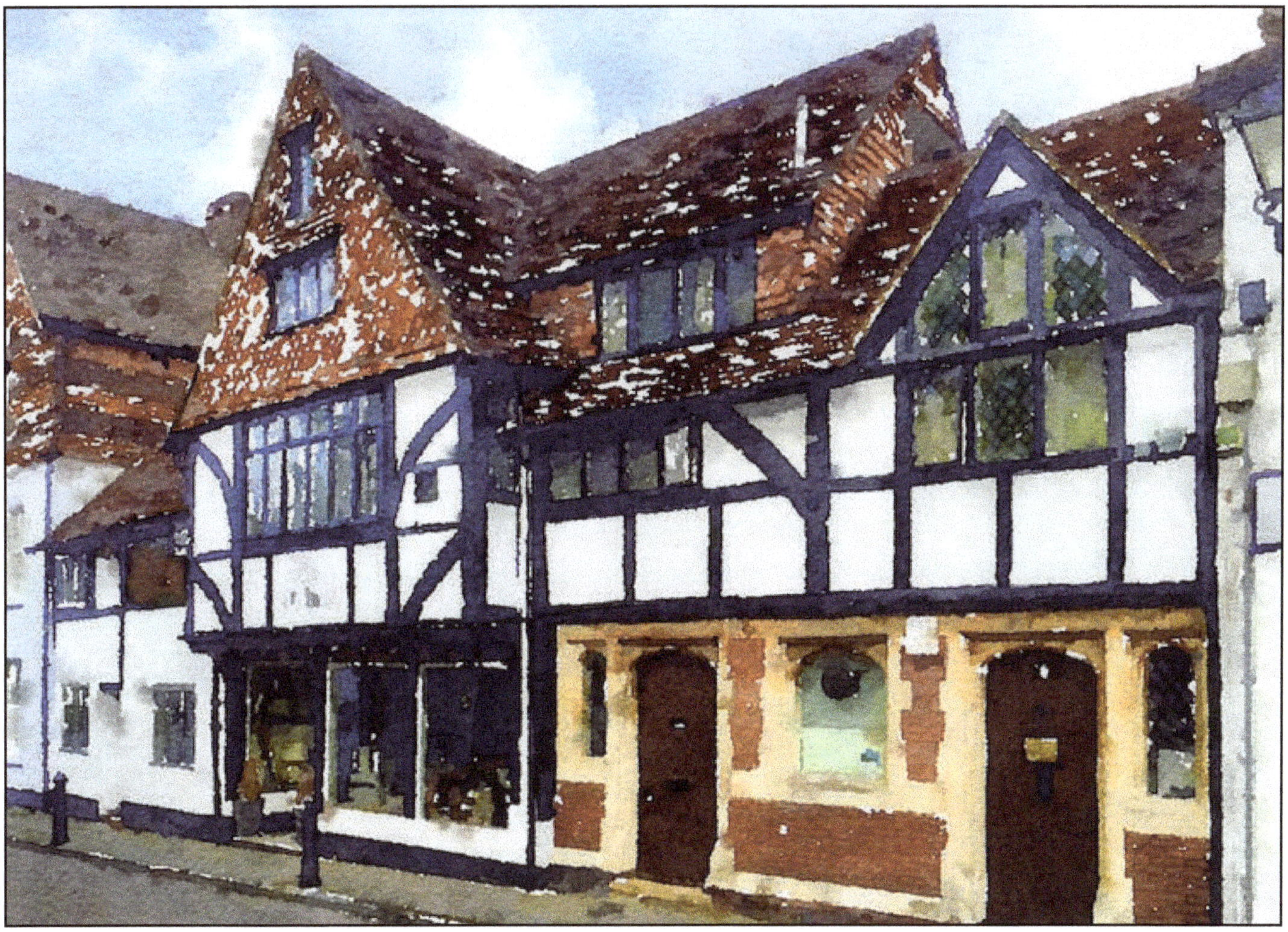

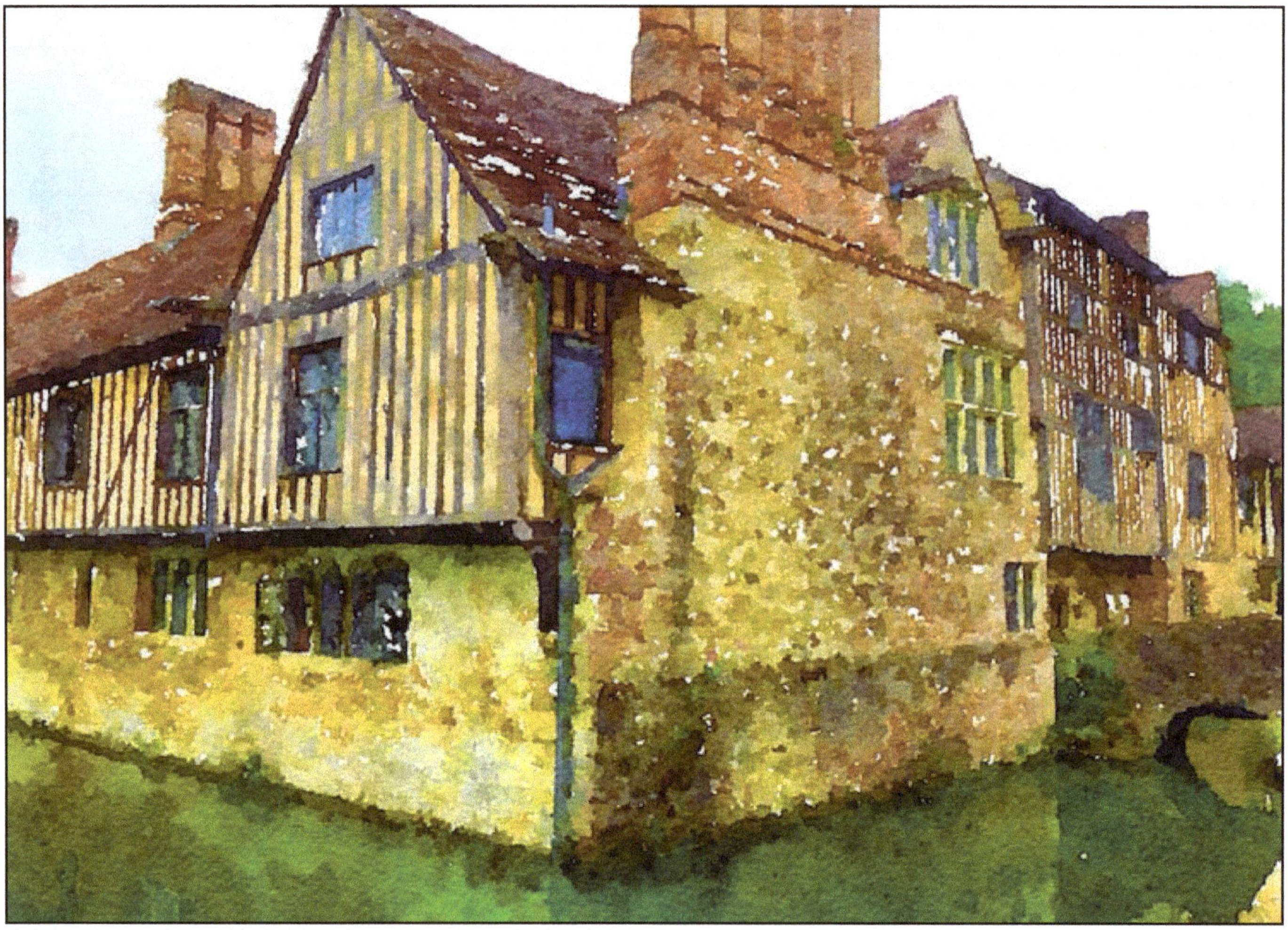

▲'The Manor House' (2016), Ightham Mote, Kent [EEN1603].

'The Old Church' (2016), Brede, Sussex [EEN1604].▼

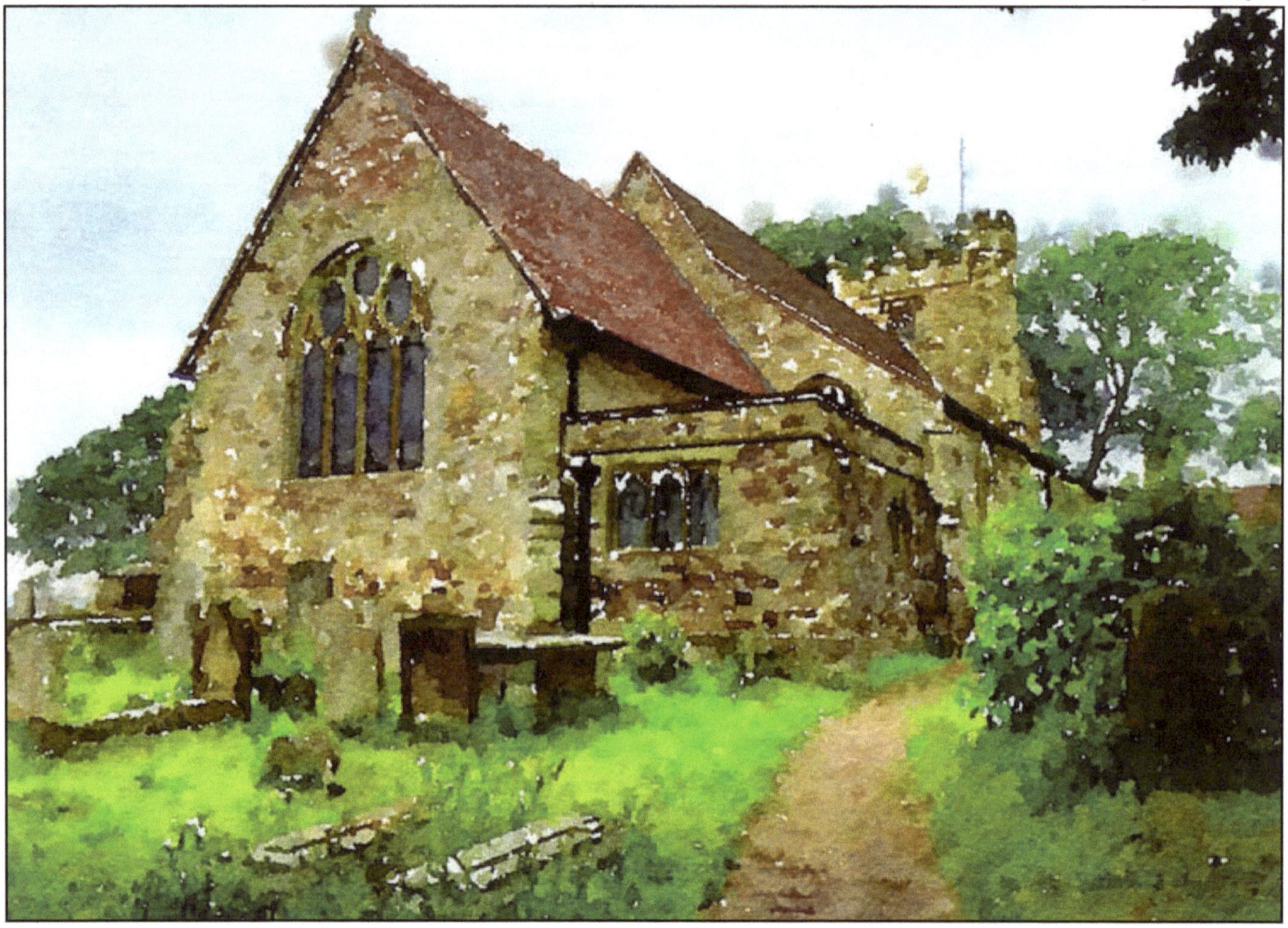

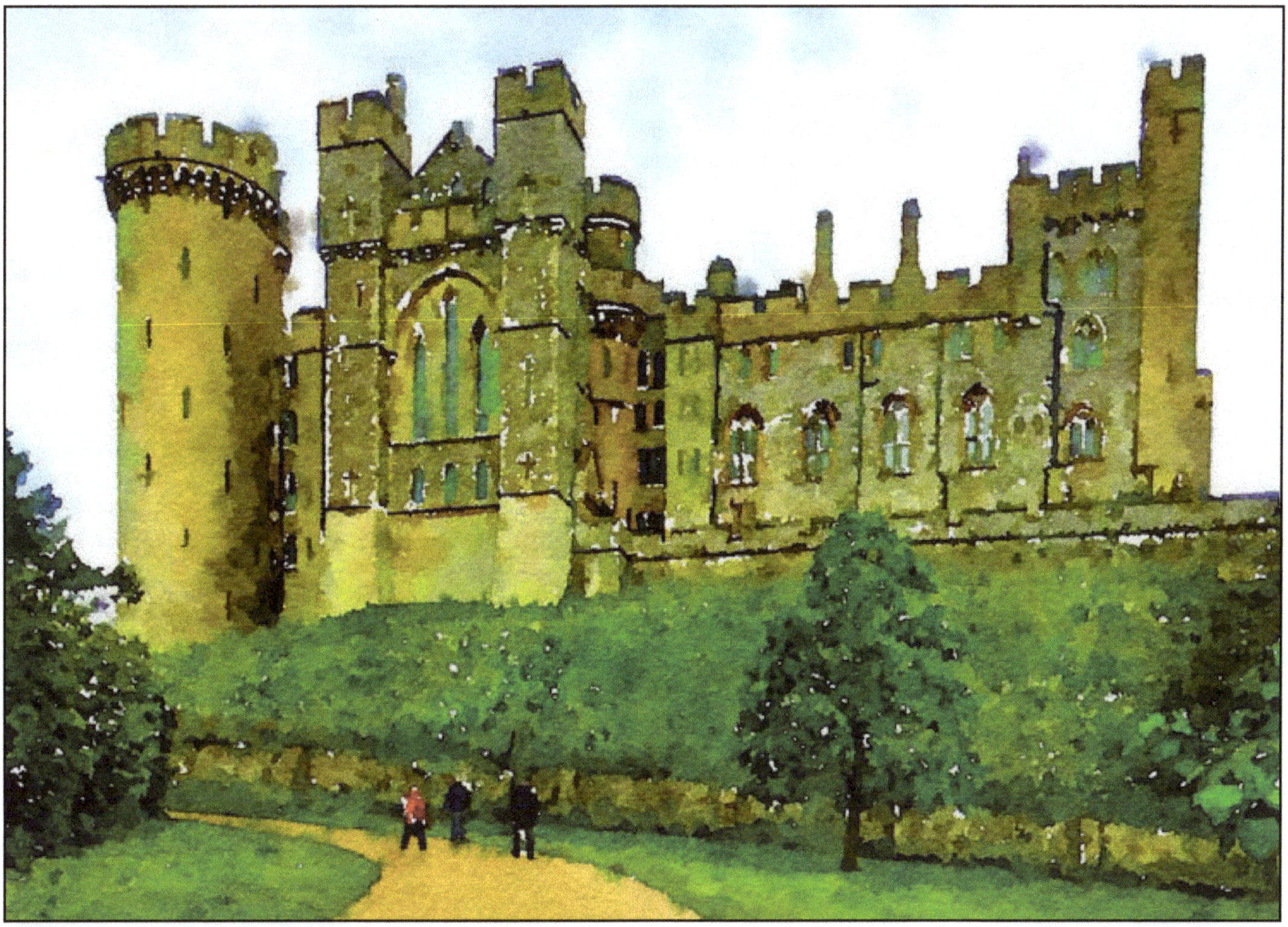

▲'The Castle' (2016), Arundel, West Sussex [EEN1605].

'The Circus' (2016), Bath, Somerset [EEN1609].▼

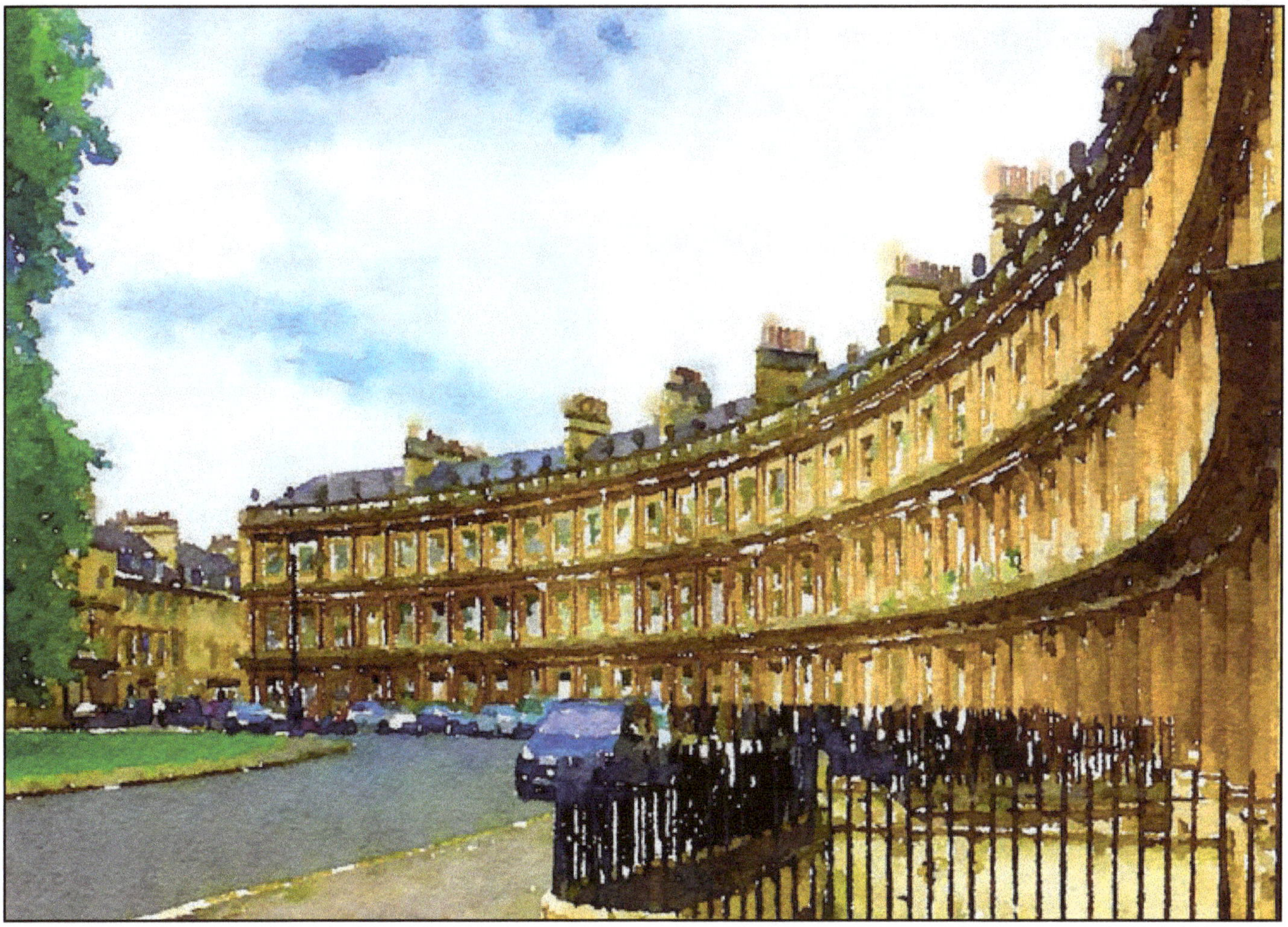

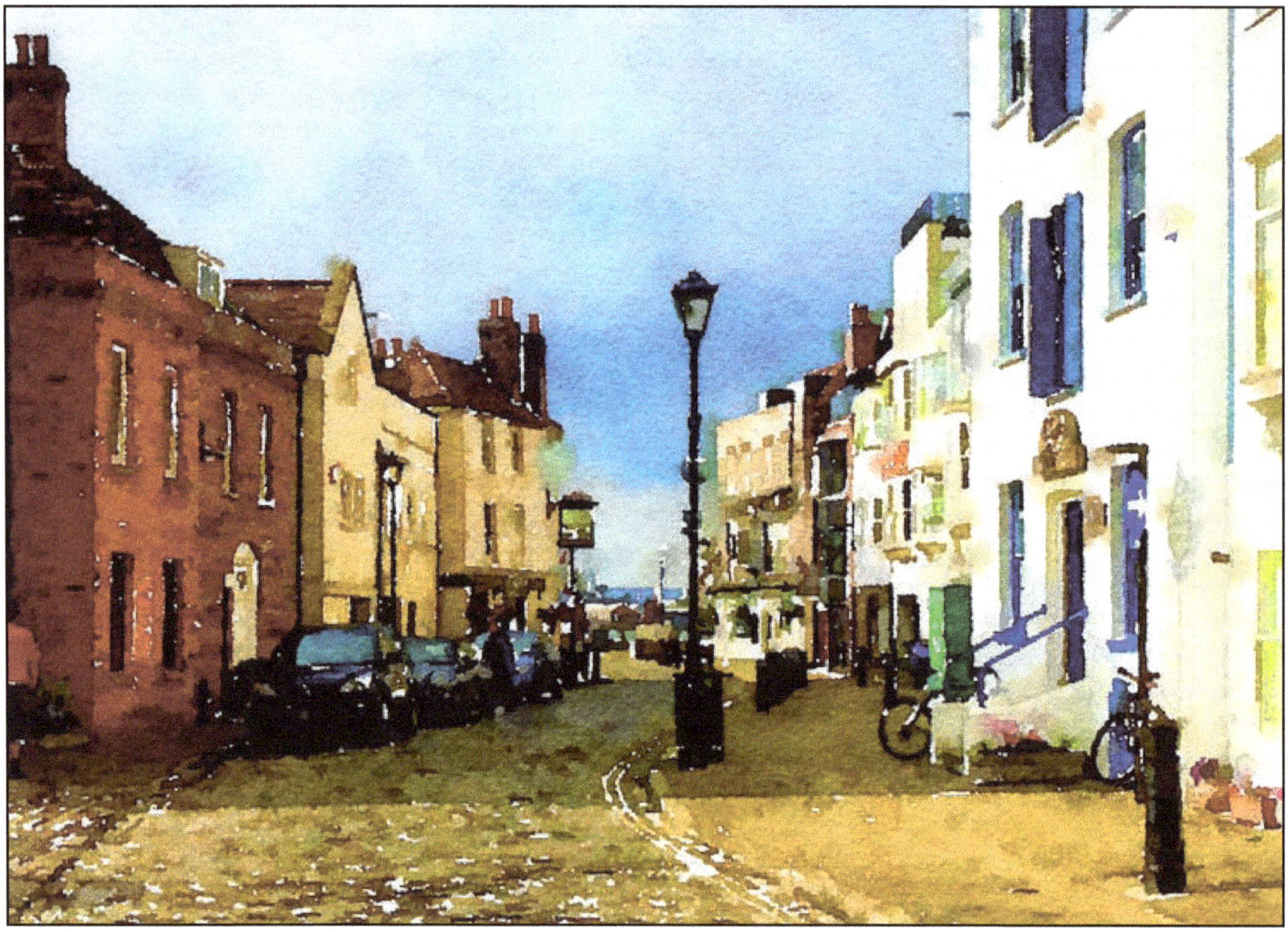

▲'Old Town' (2016), Portsmouth, Hampshire [EEN1607].

'The Steamer' (2016), Dartmouth, Devonshire [EEN1601].▼

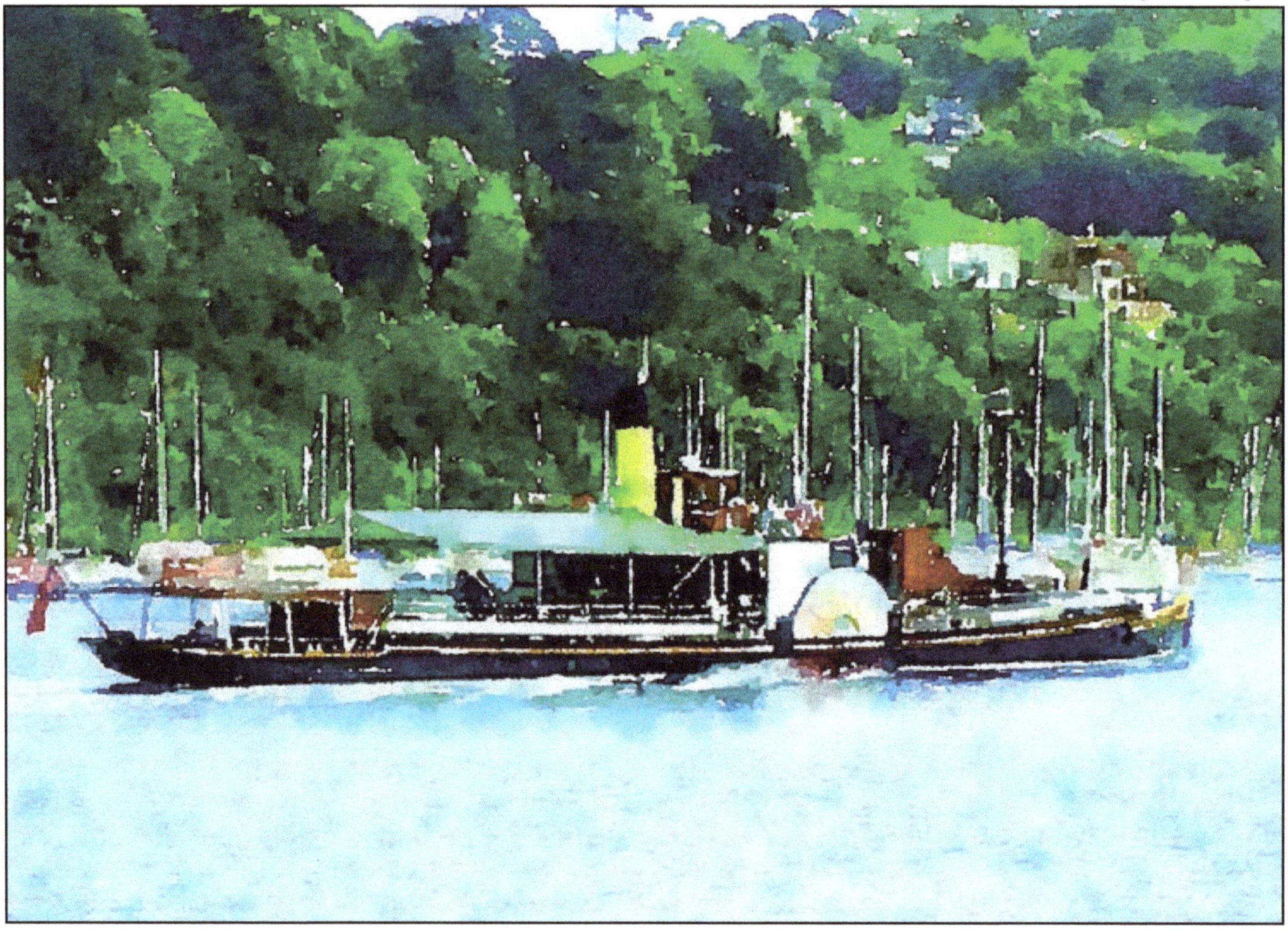

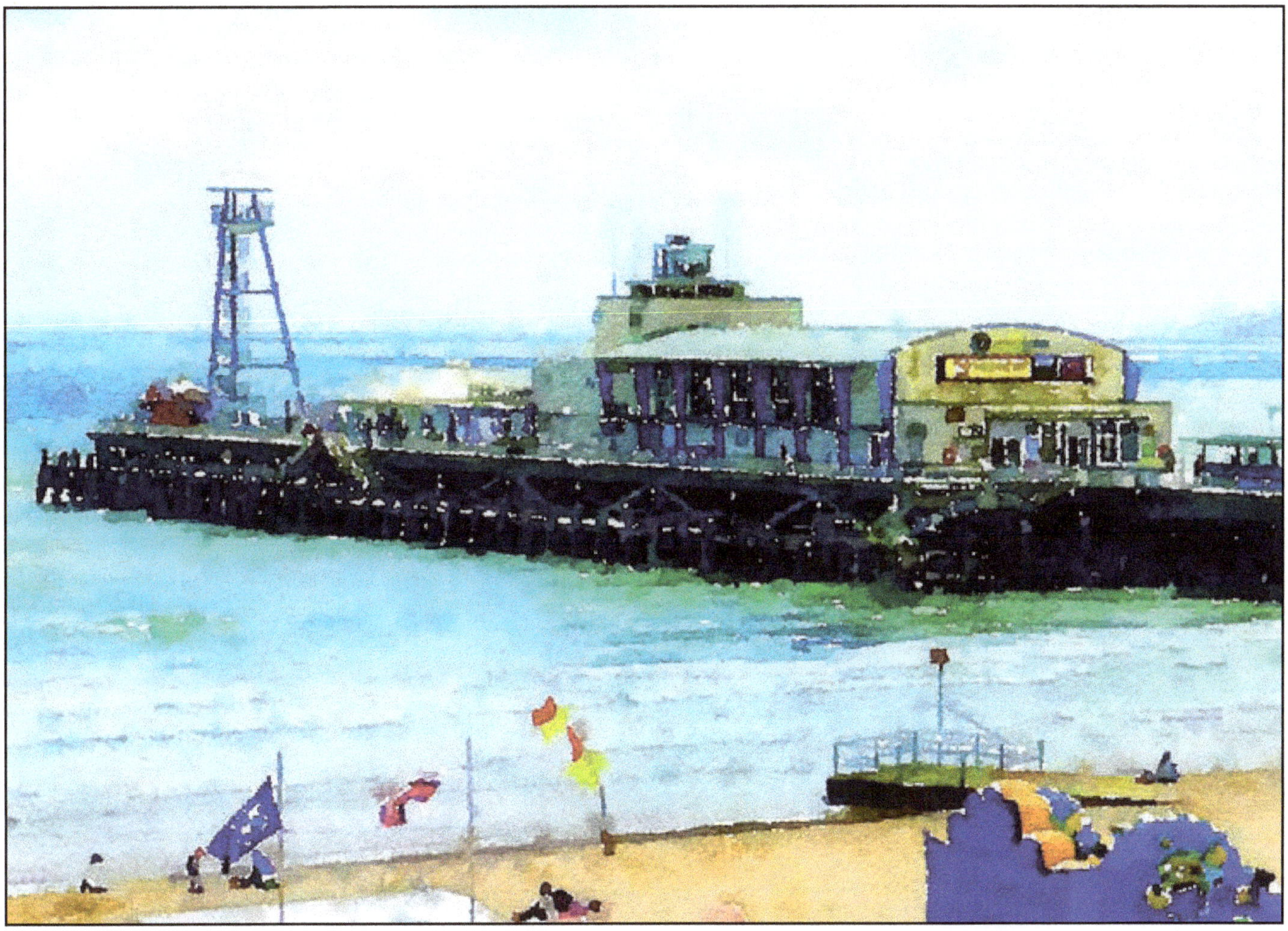

▲'The Pier' (2016), Bournemouth, Dorset [EEN1606].

'The Tower Guards' (2016), London, England [EEN1610].▼

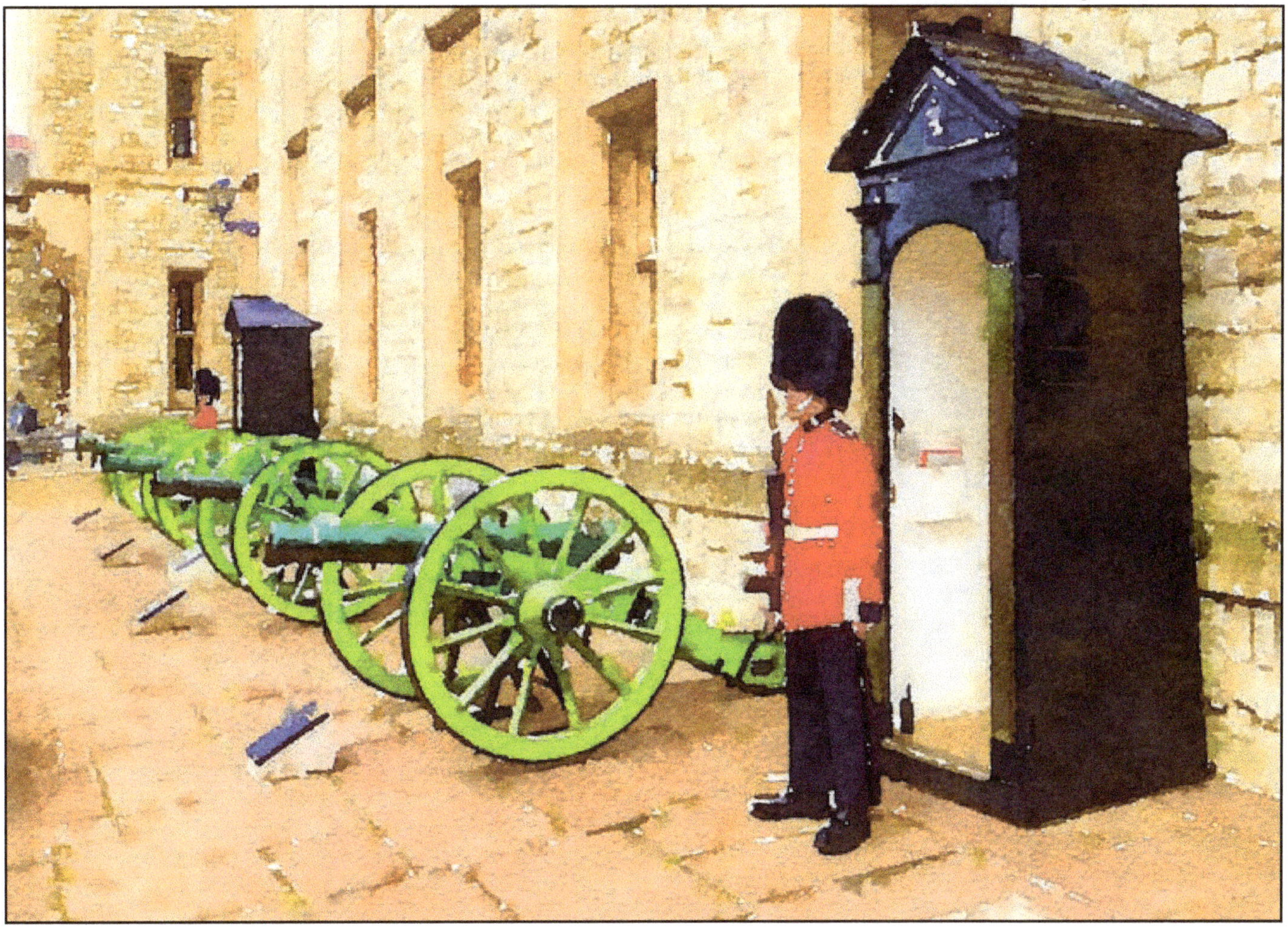

France...

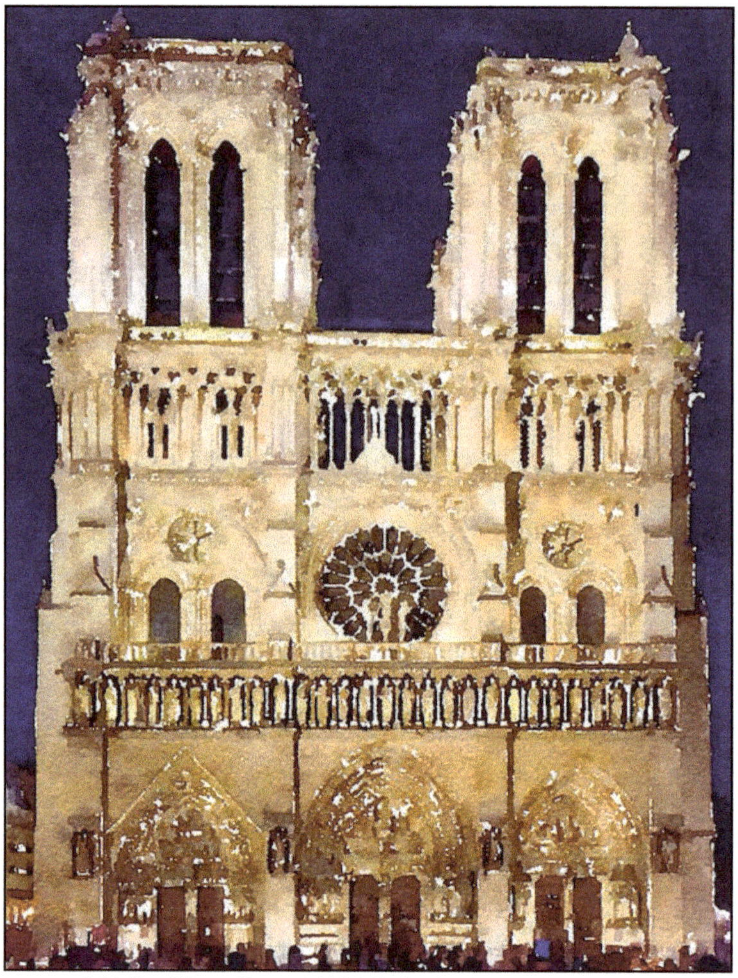

France is undoubtedly a nation of incredible natural features with geographically diverse regions. Despite first visiting Paris in 1980, I didn't have an opportunity to explore France until 2006, when I undertook a six week road tour with my second wife. I arrived again in 2008, this time residing near Monaco at Cap Martin for a number of weeks.

I returned to the the Cote d'Azure in 2010 this time working as a Journey Director for the highly acclaimed travel company 'Bill Peach Journeys', aboard "Seabourne Legend," a luxurious small cruise ship that dropped into many of the smaller French coastal ports. This memorable voyage, billed as the 'Yachtsman's Riviera' called at St Tropez where I spent my 55th birthday at Club 55, and the island of Corsica.

Five years later I re-visited the Cote d'Azure, once again aboard cruise ships in 2015 and 2016, with stop-overs at Toulon, Cassis and Villefranche, this time in company with my partner Rosie. On all these occasions I snapped away and recorded some memorable images of one of the most delightful countries on Earth.

'L'Eglise Notre Dame' (2015), Paris, France [EFR(PA)1503].▲

▼'Saint Severin' (2015), Paris, France [EFR(PA)1501].

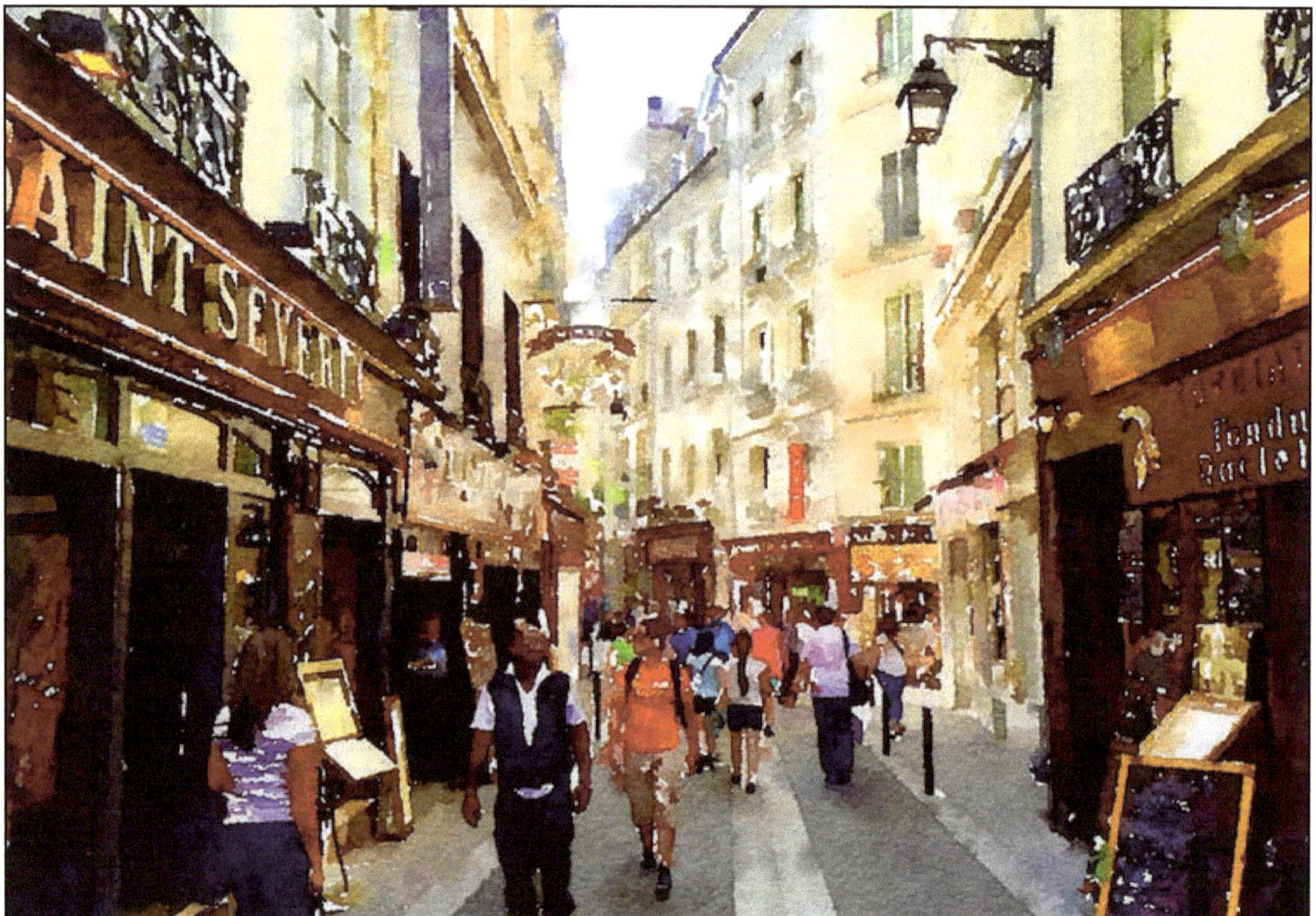

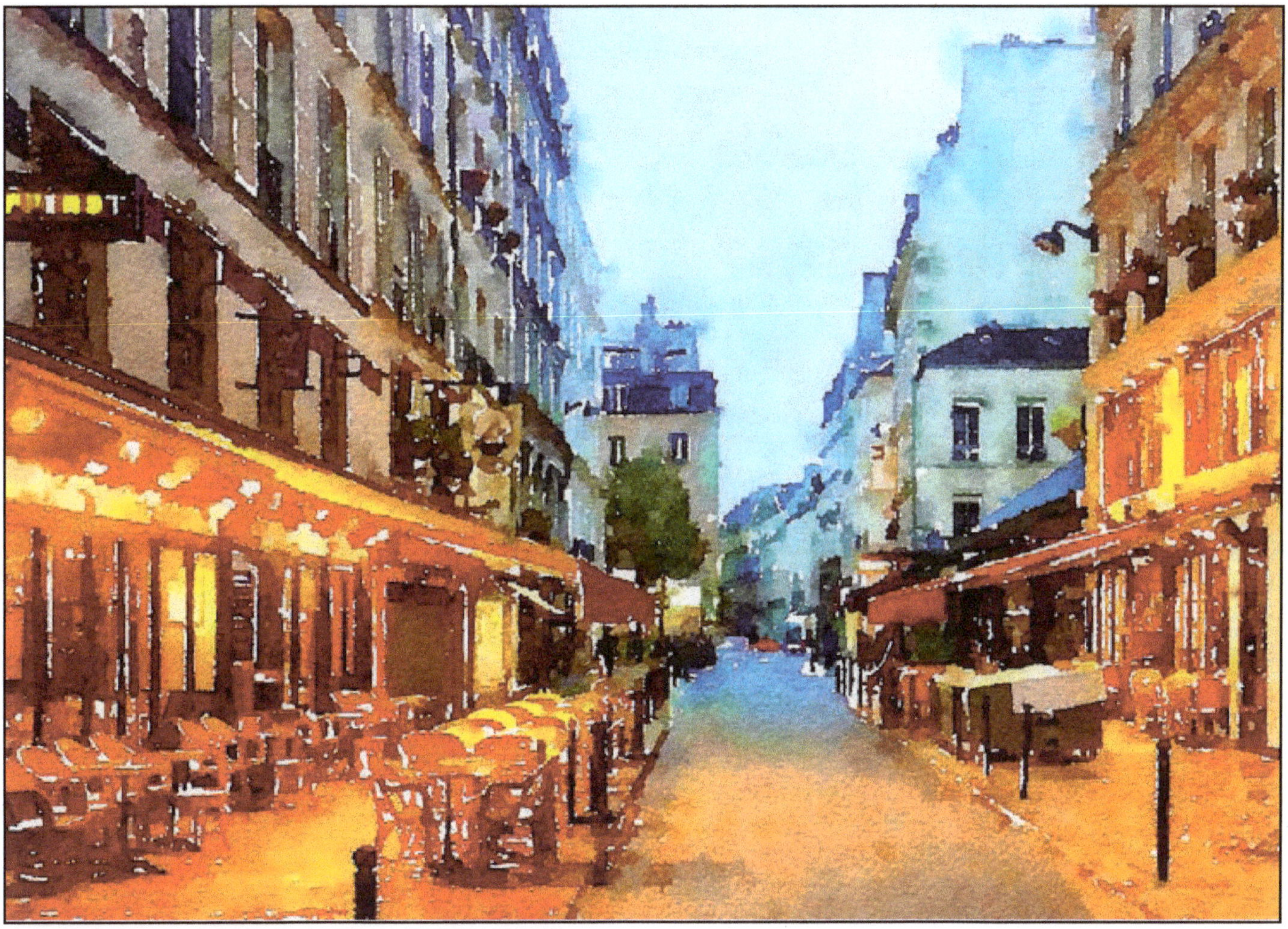

▲'Le Cafe Societe' (2015), Paris, France [EFR(PA)1506].

'La Seine' (2015), Paris, France [EFR(PA)1502].▼

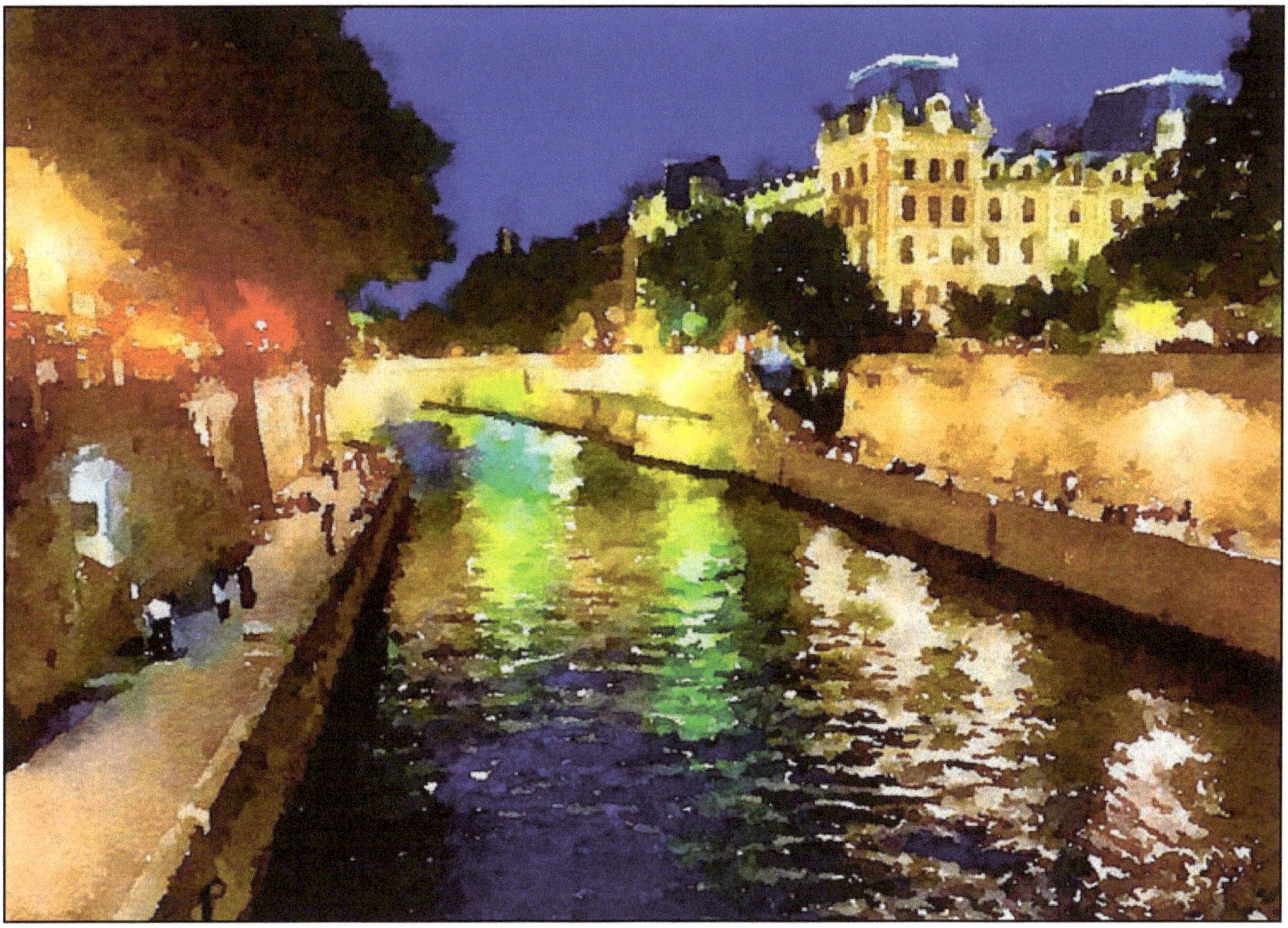

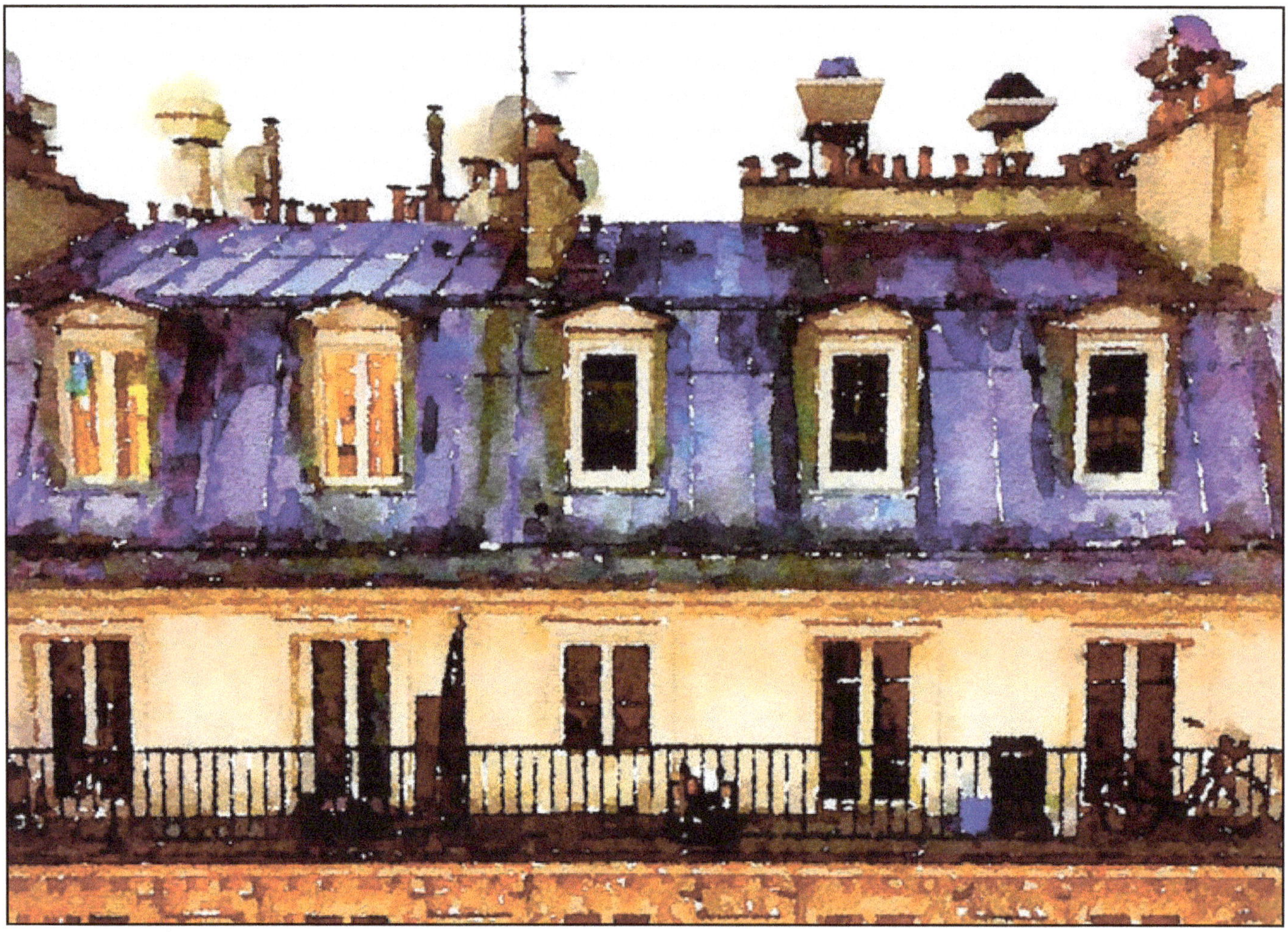

▲'Parisian Rooftops' (2015), Paris, France [EFR(PA)1505].

'The Lights Of Paris' (2015), Paris, France [EFR(PA)1504].▼

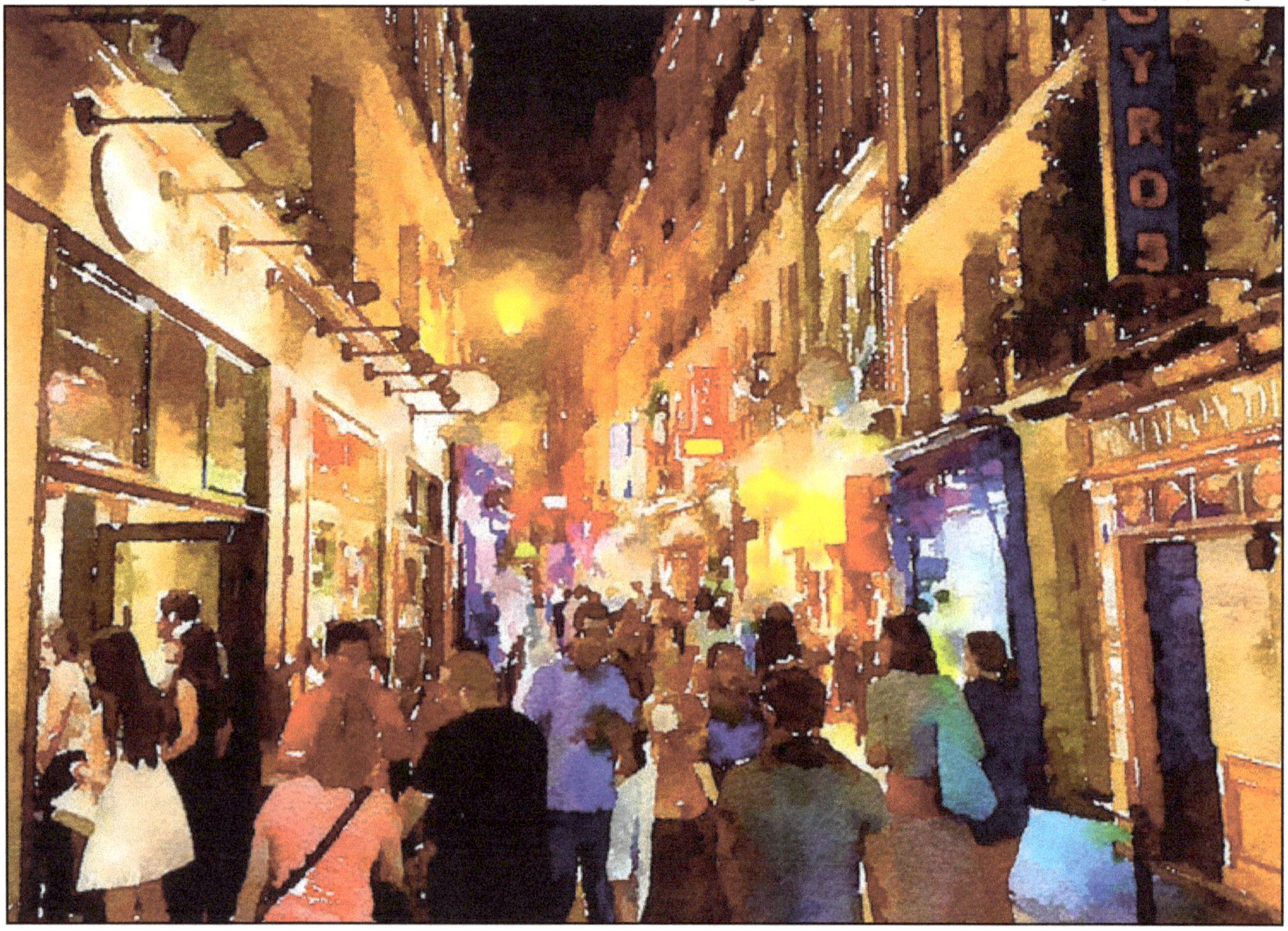

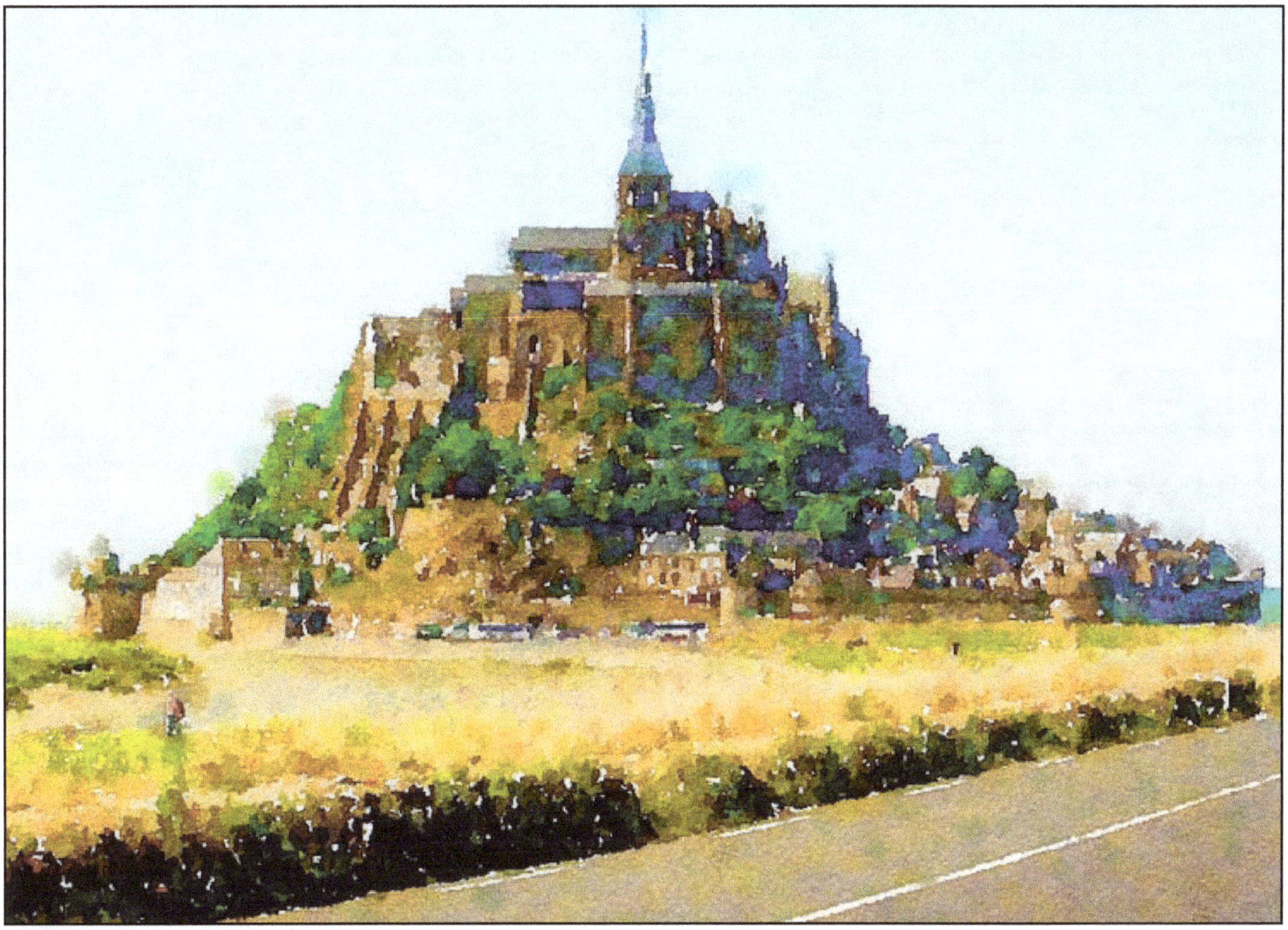

▲'Mont St Michel' (2006), Brittany, France [EFR(BR)0602].

'La Place' (2006), Dinan, France [EFR(BR)0601].▼

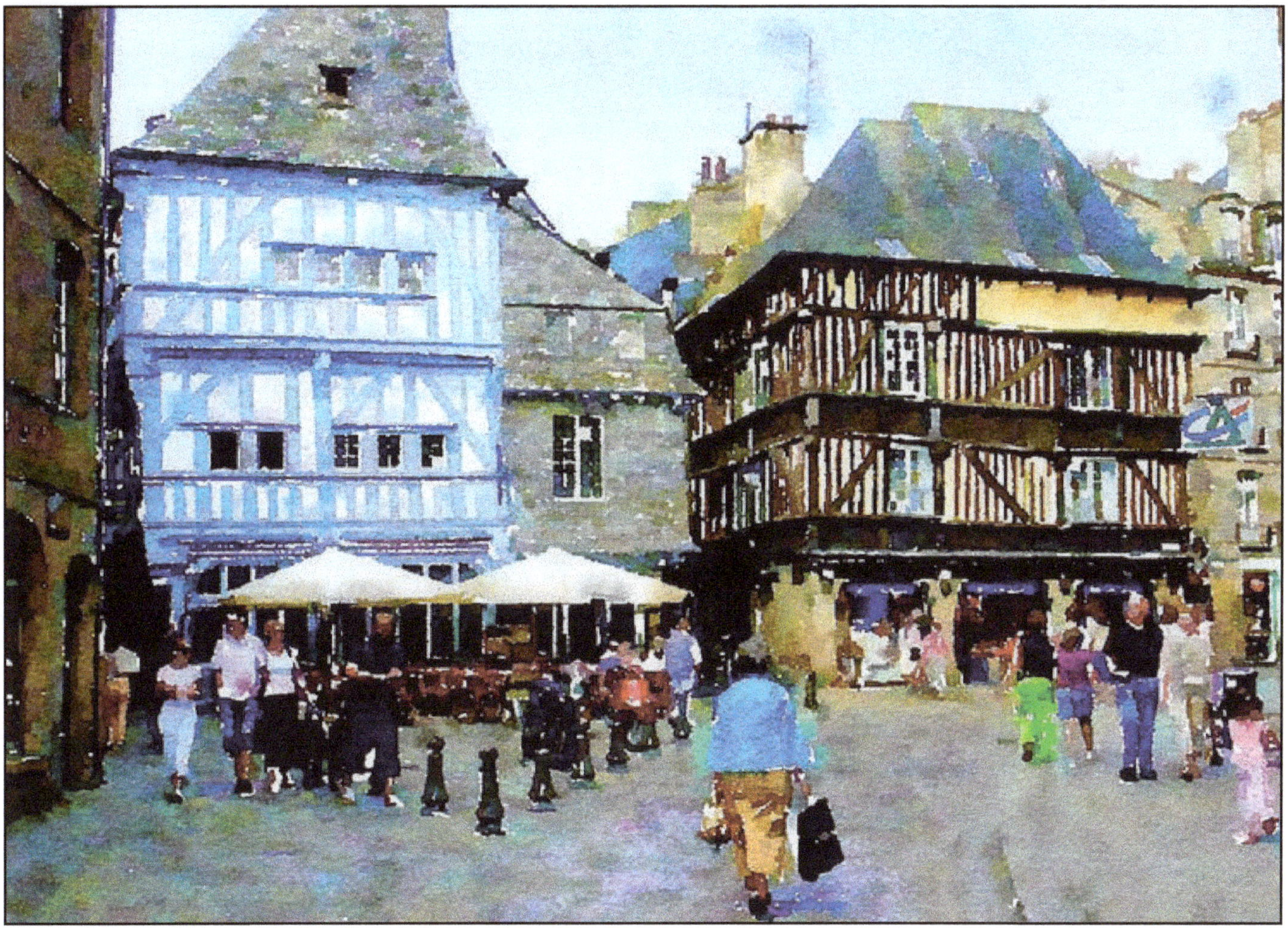

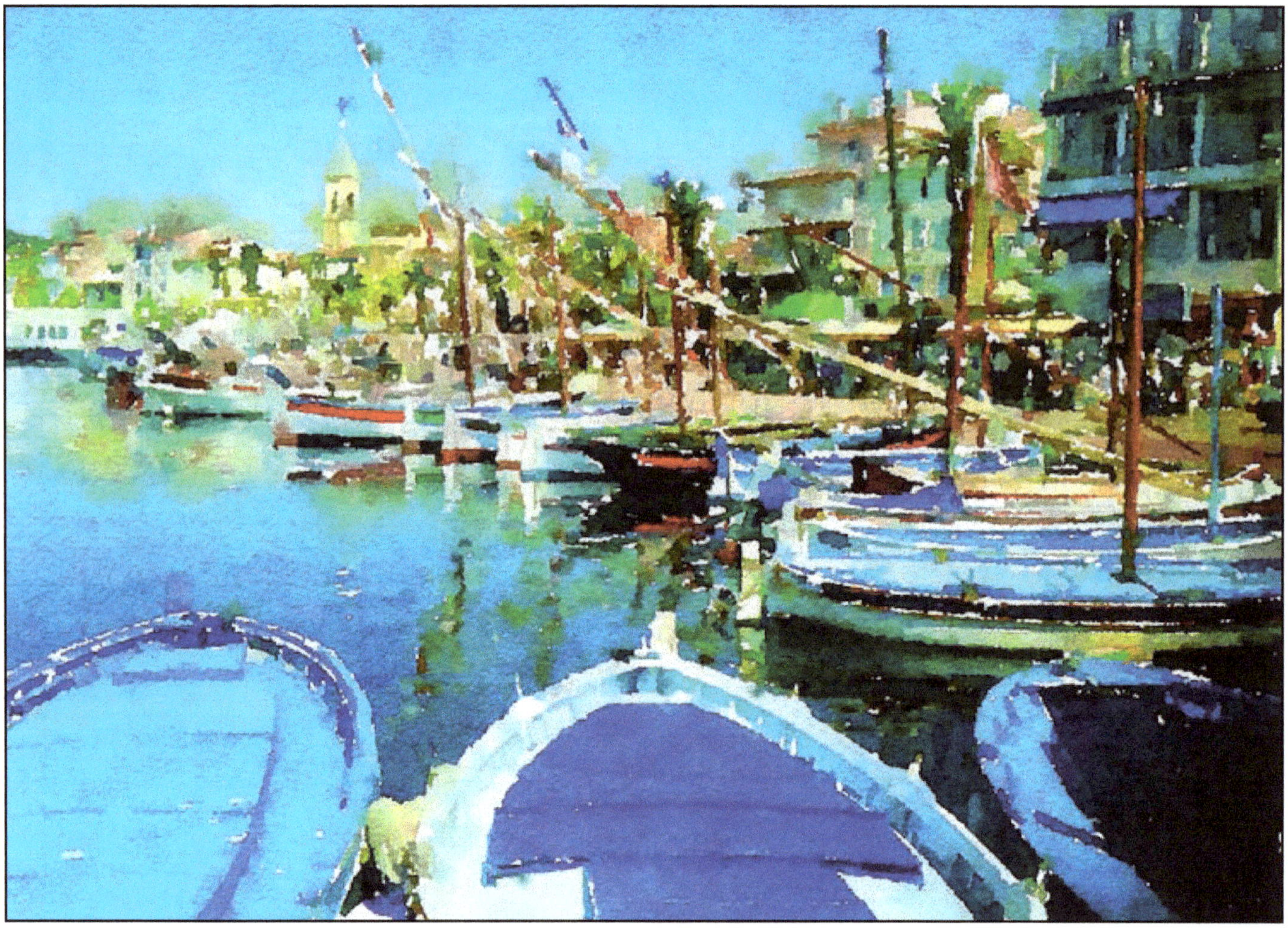

▲'Fisherman Of Cassis' (2010), Cassis, France [EFR(CD)1001].

'The Harbour' (2010), Cassis, France [EFR(CD)1002].▼

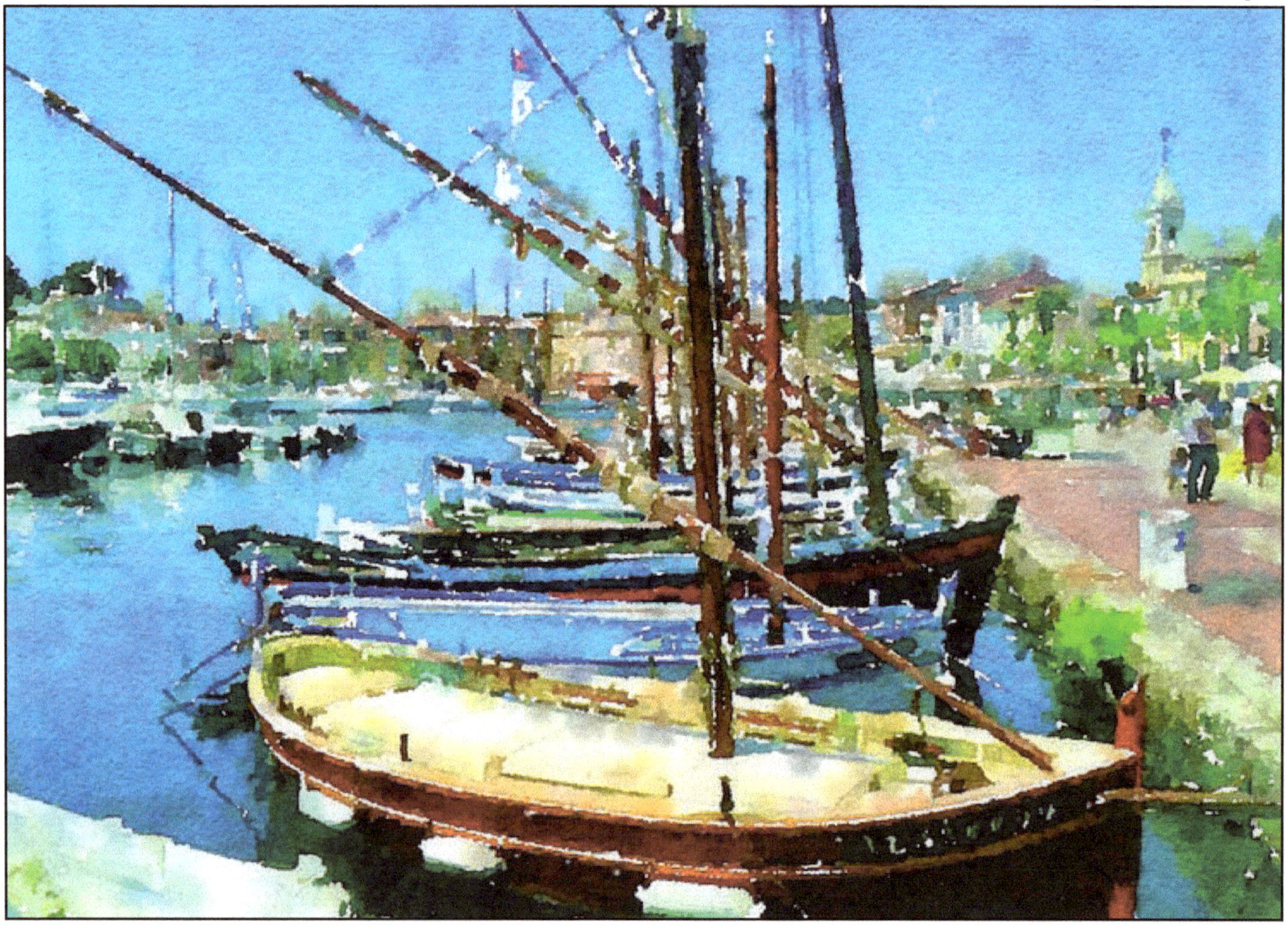

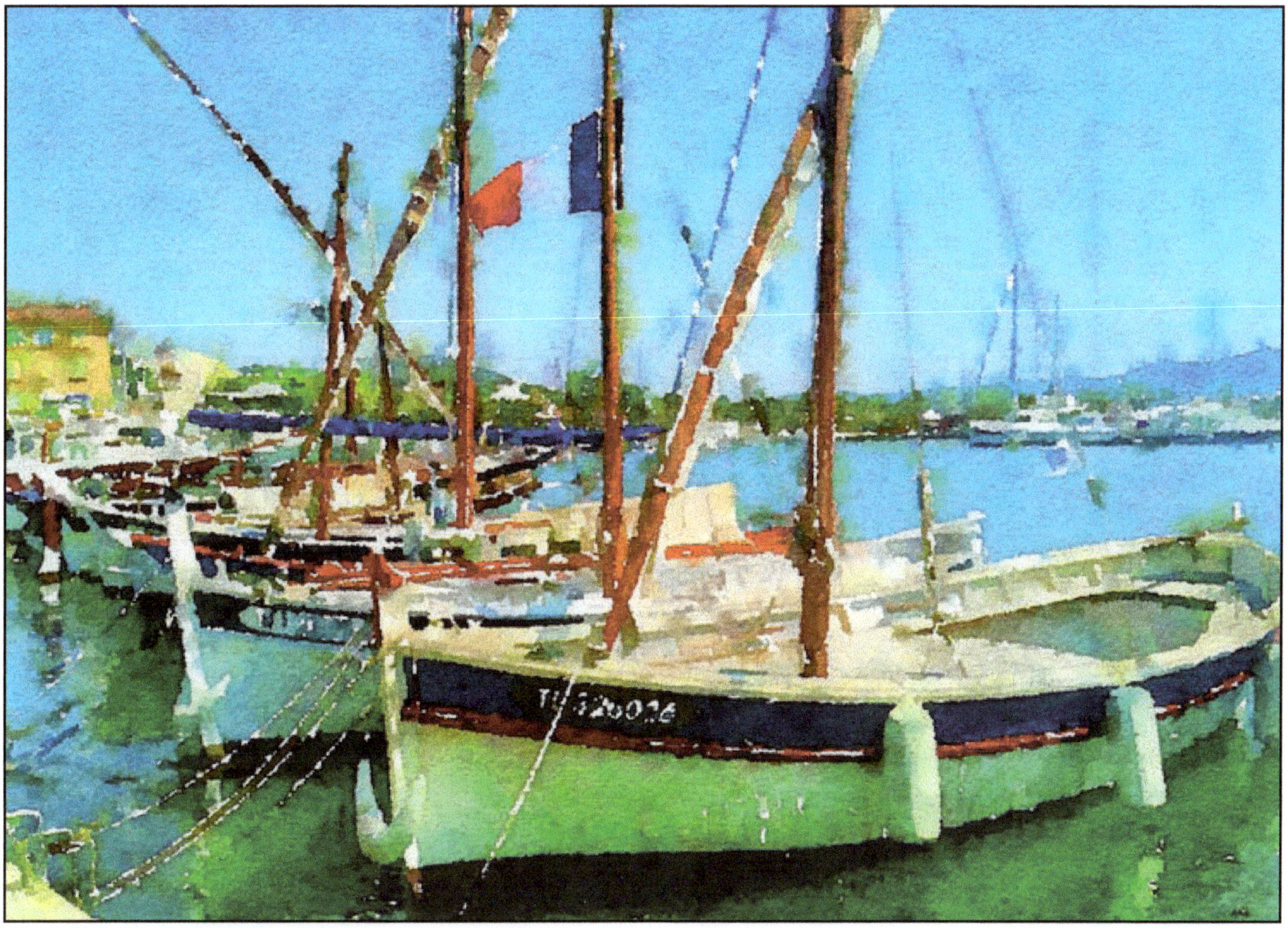

▲'Fishing Fleet' (2010), Cassis, France [EFR(CD)1003].

'The Blue Boats' (2010), Cassis, France [EFR(CD)1004].▼

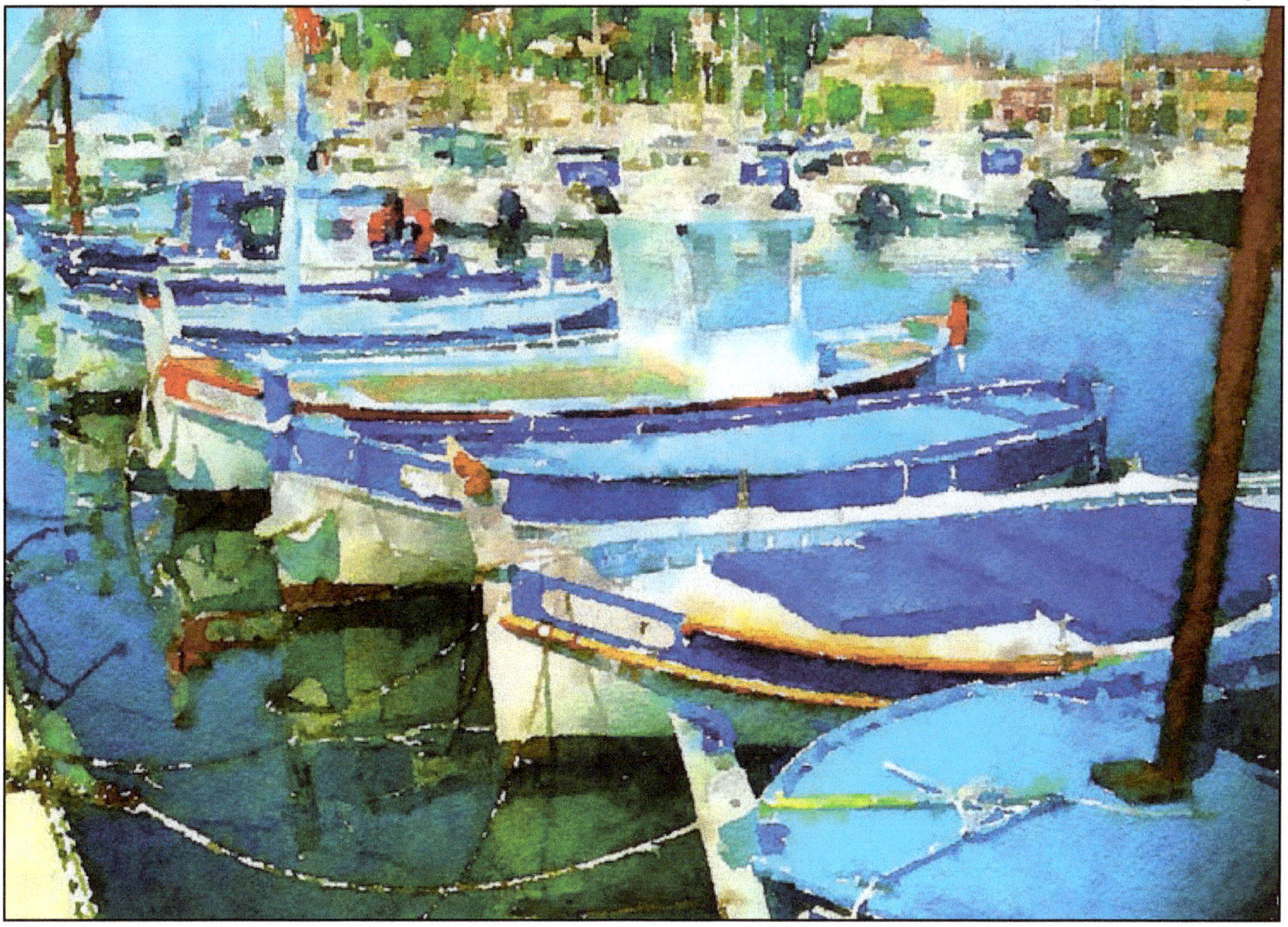

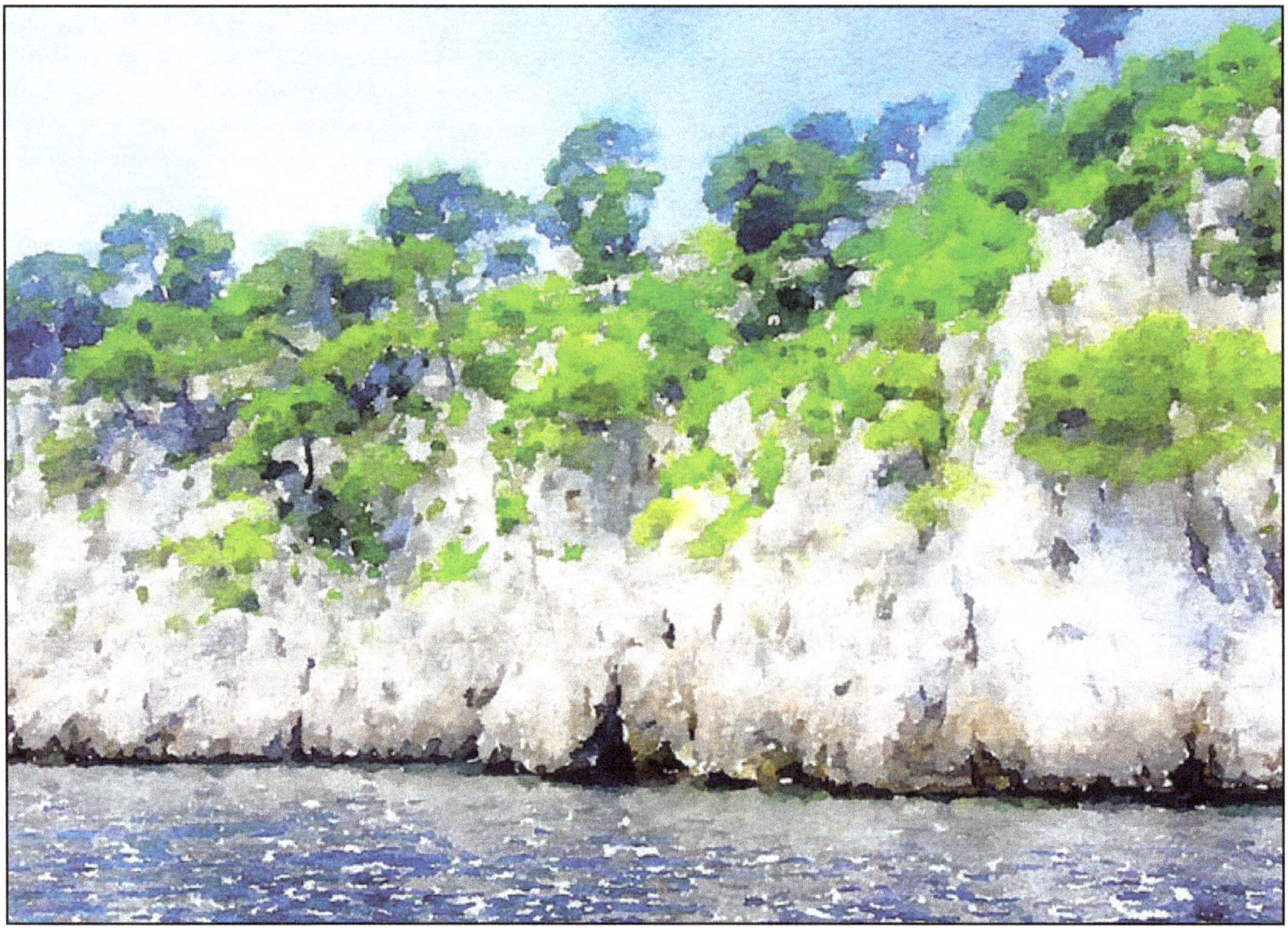

▲'Le Calanque' (2010), Cassis, France [EFR(CD)1005].

'The Inner Harbour' (2010), Cassis, France [EFR(CD)1006].▼

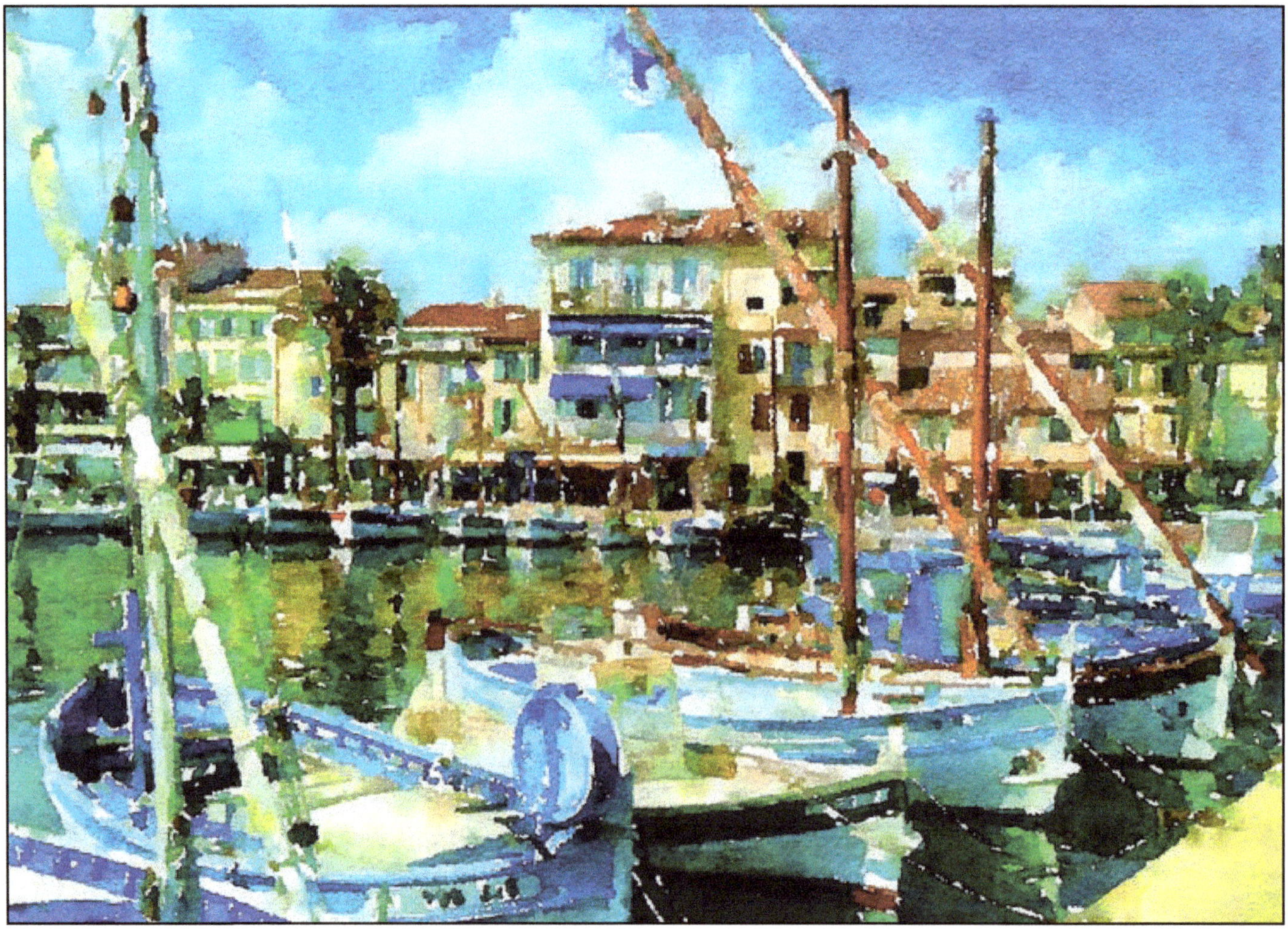

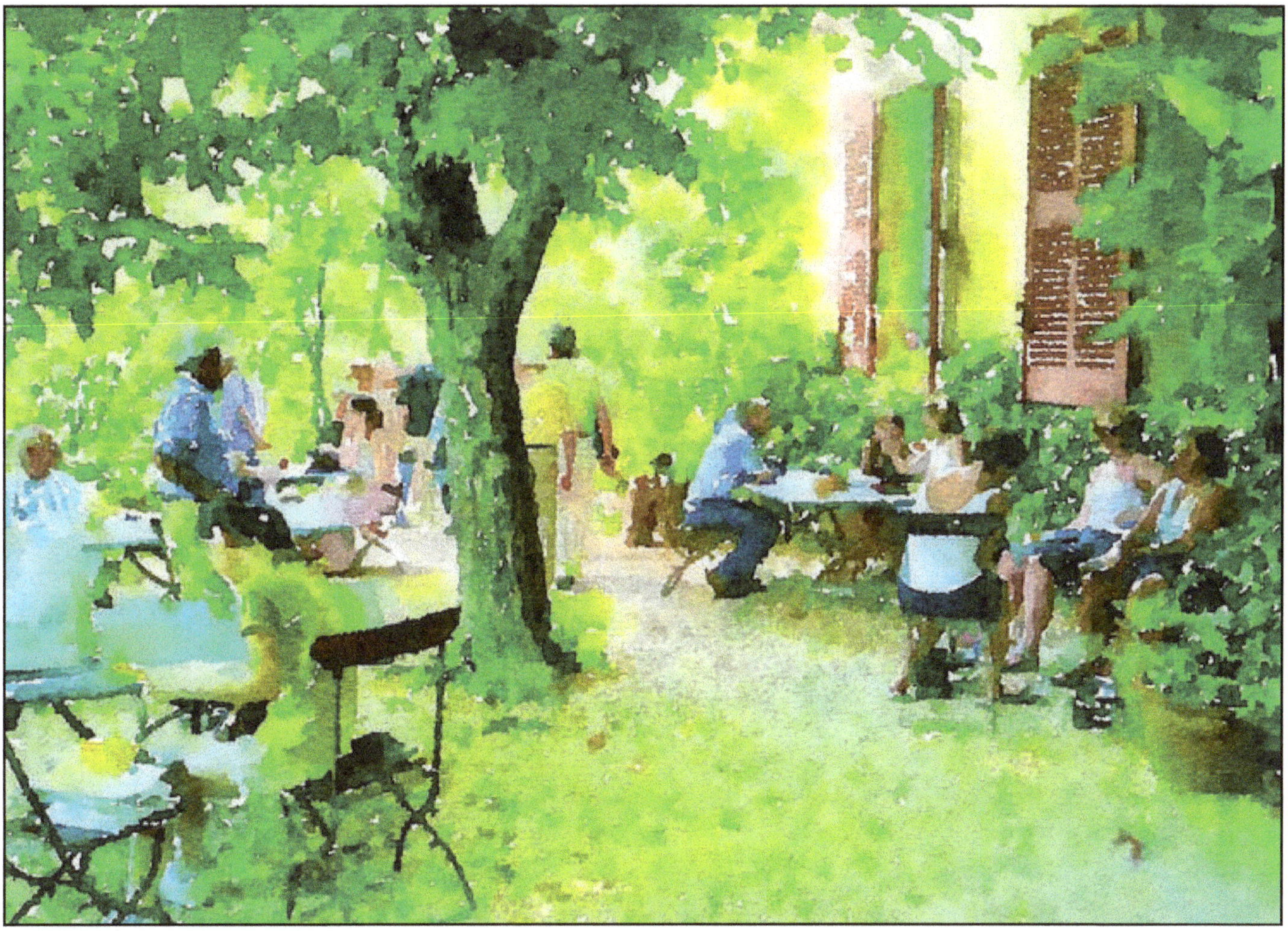

▲'Paul Cezanne Gallery' (2010), Aix En Provence, France [EFR(CD)1007].

'Strolling On Rue Sallier' (2010), Aix En Provence, France [EFR(CD)1008].▼

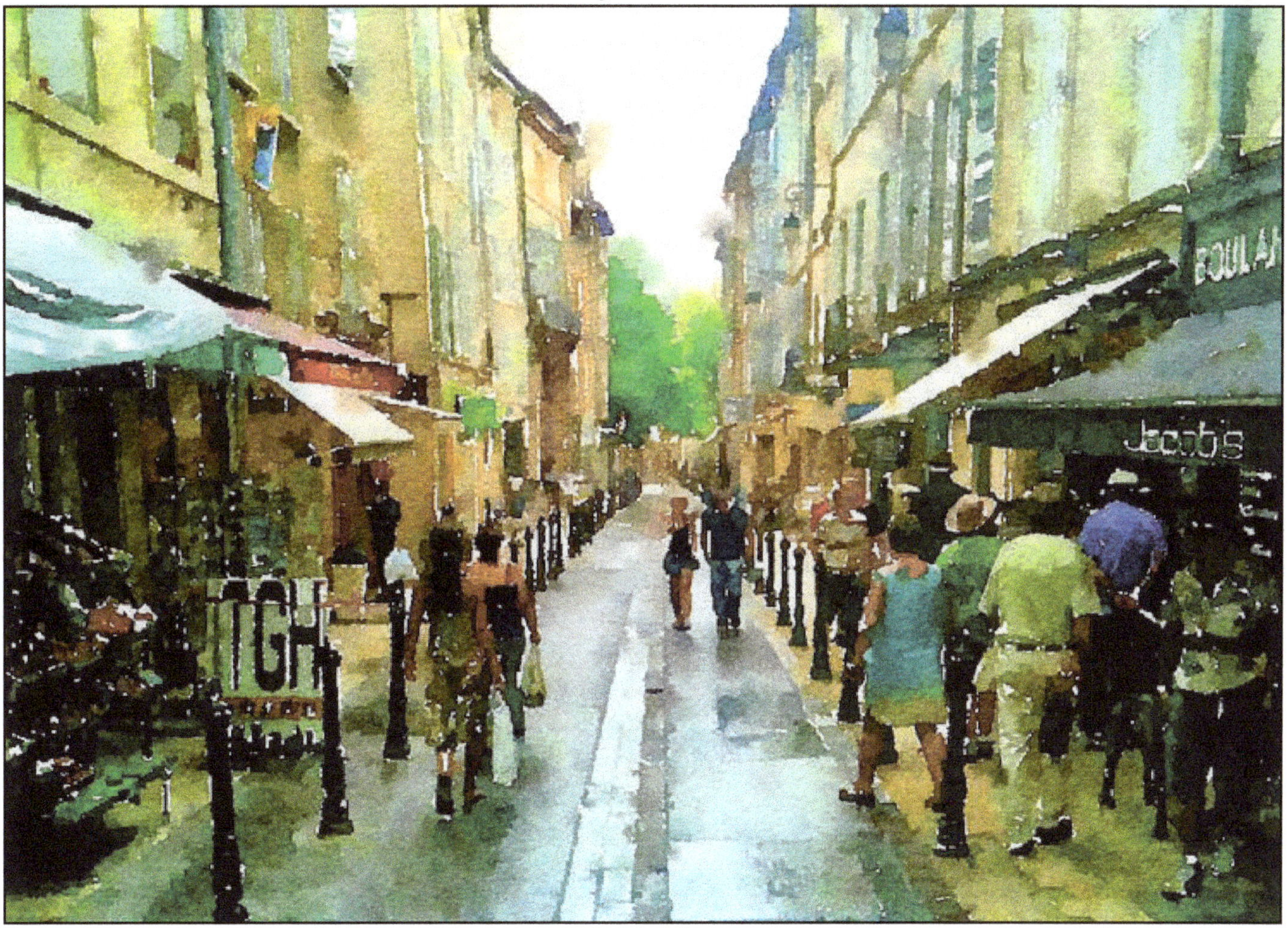

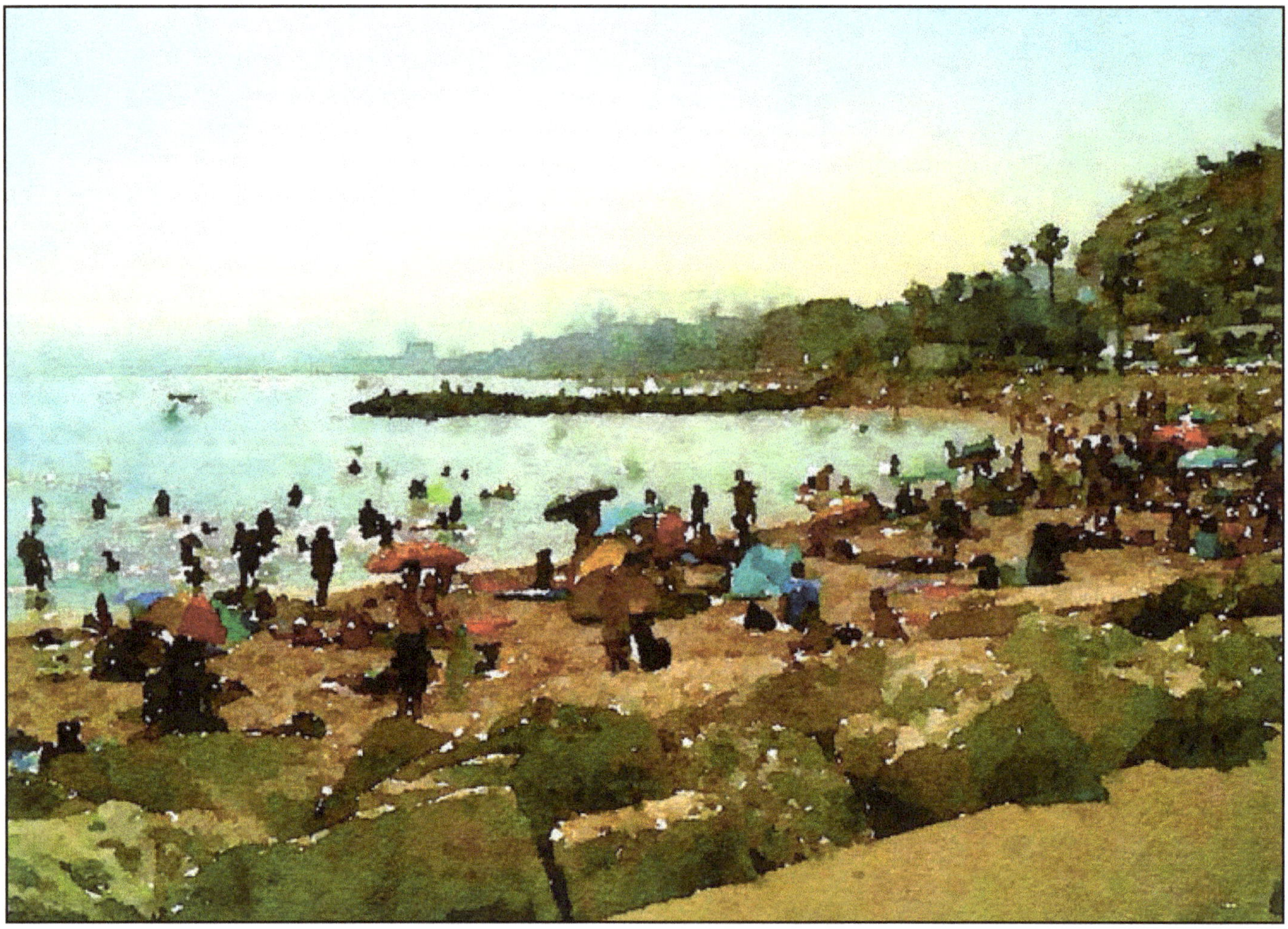

▲'Plage du Midi' (2010), Cannes, France [EFR(CD)1009].

'Riviera Sunbrellas' (20110), Cannes, France [EFR(CD)1010].▼

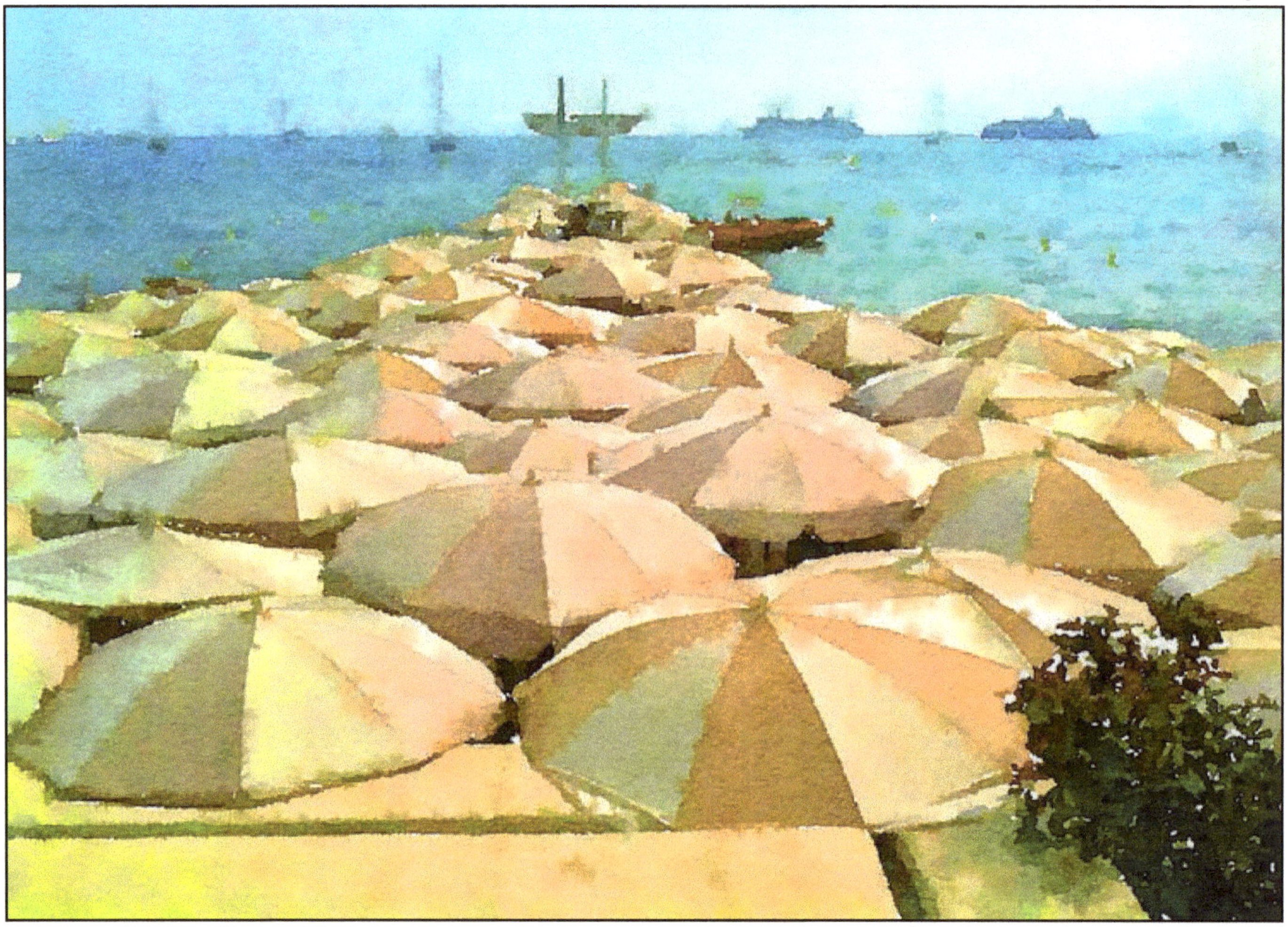

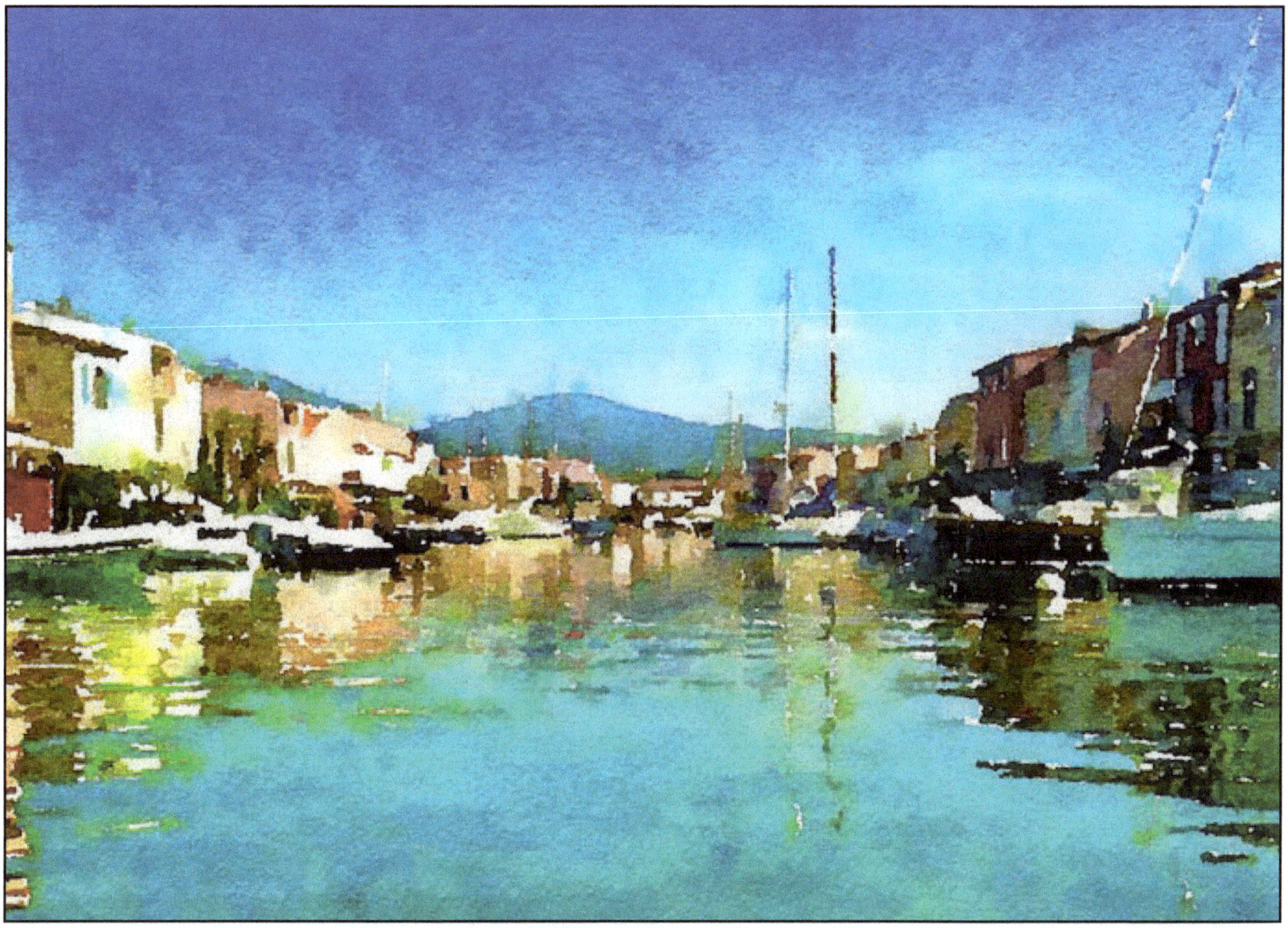

▲'The Grand Canal' (2010), Port Grimaud, France [EFR(CD)1011].

'The Old Villa' (2010), Grimaud, France [EFR(CD)1012].▼

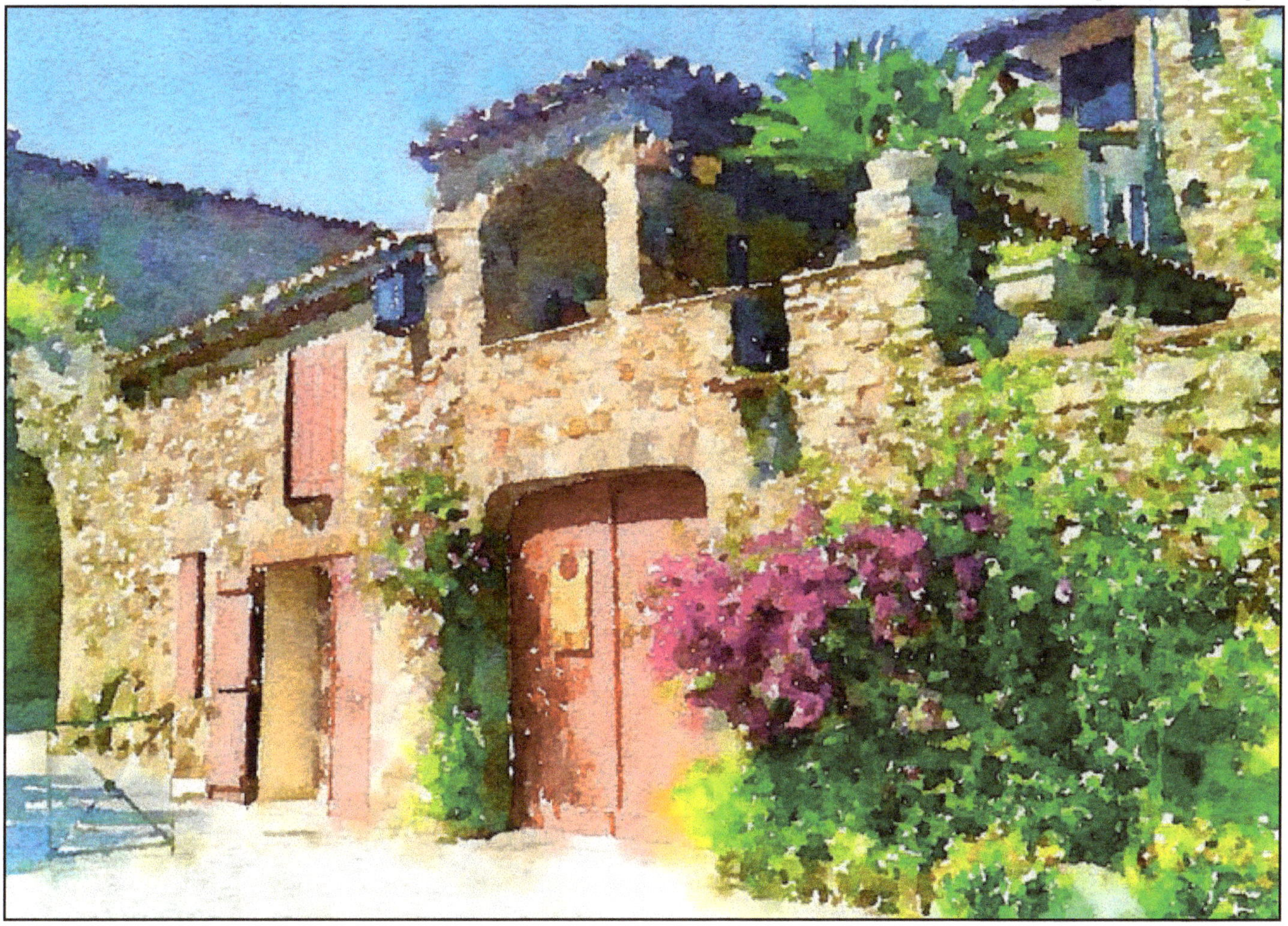

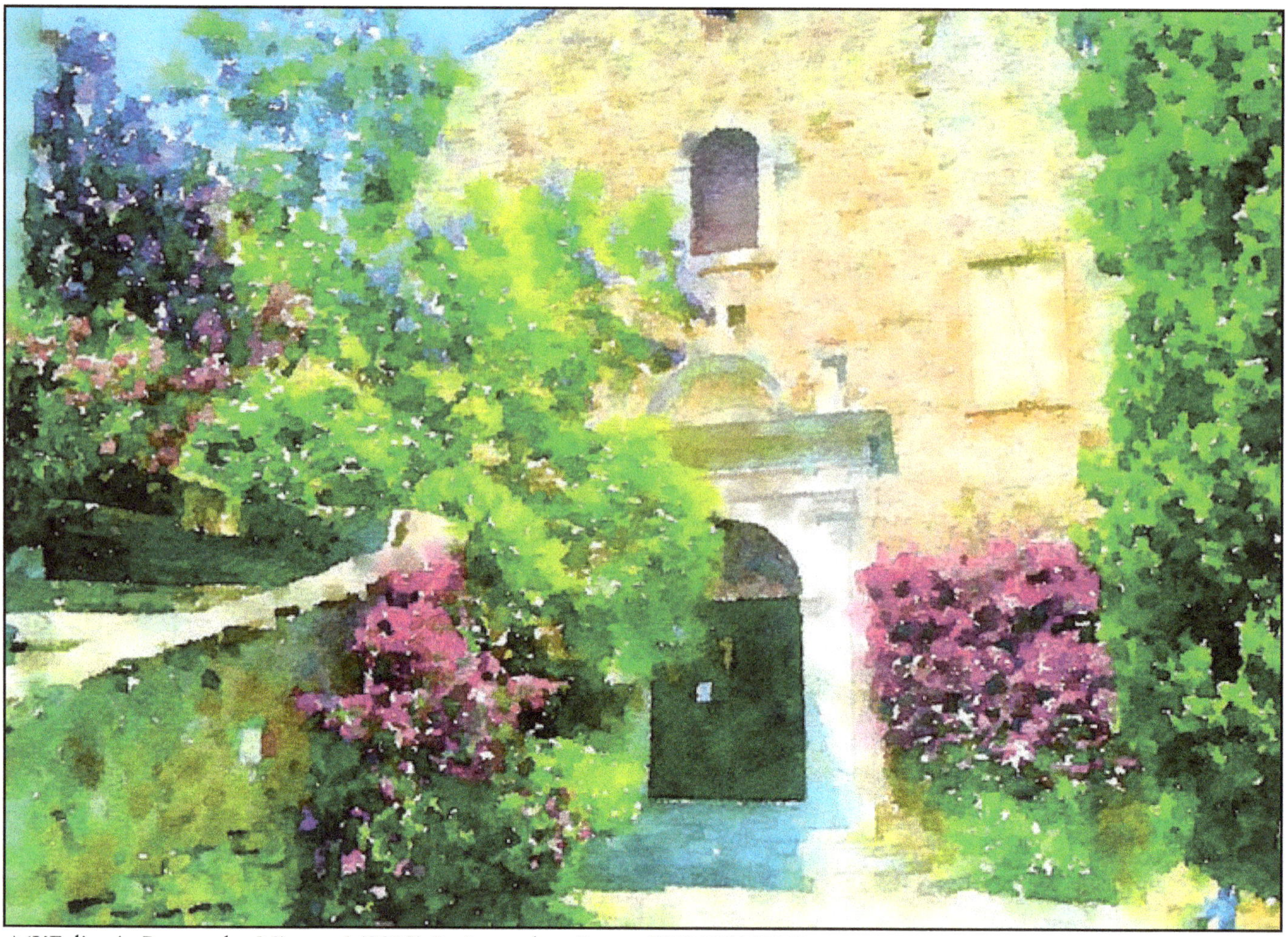

▲'L'Eglise At Bormes-les-Mimosas' (2010), Le Lavandou, France [EFR(CD)1013].

'Rue Saint-Malo' (2006), Bayeaux, France [EFR(NR)0601].▼

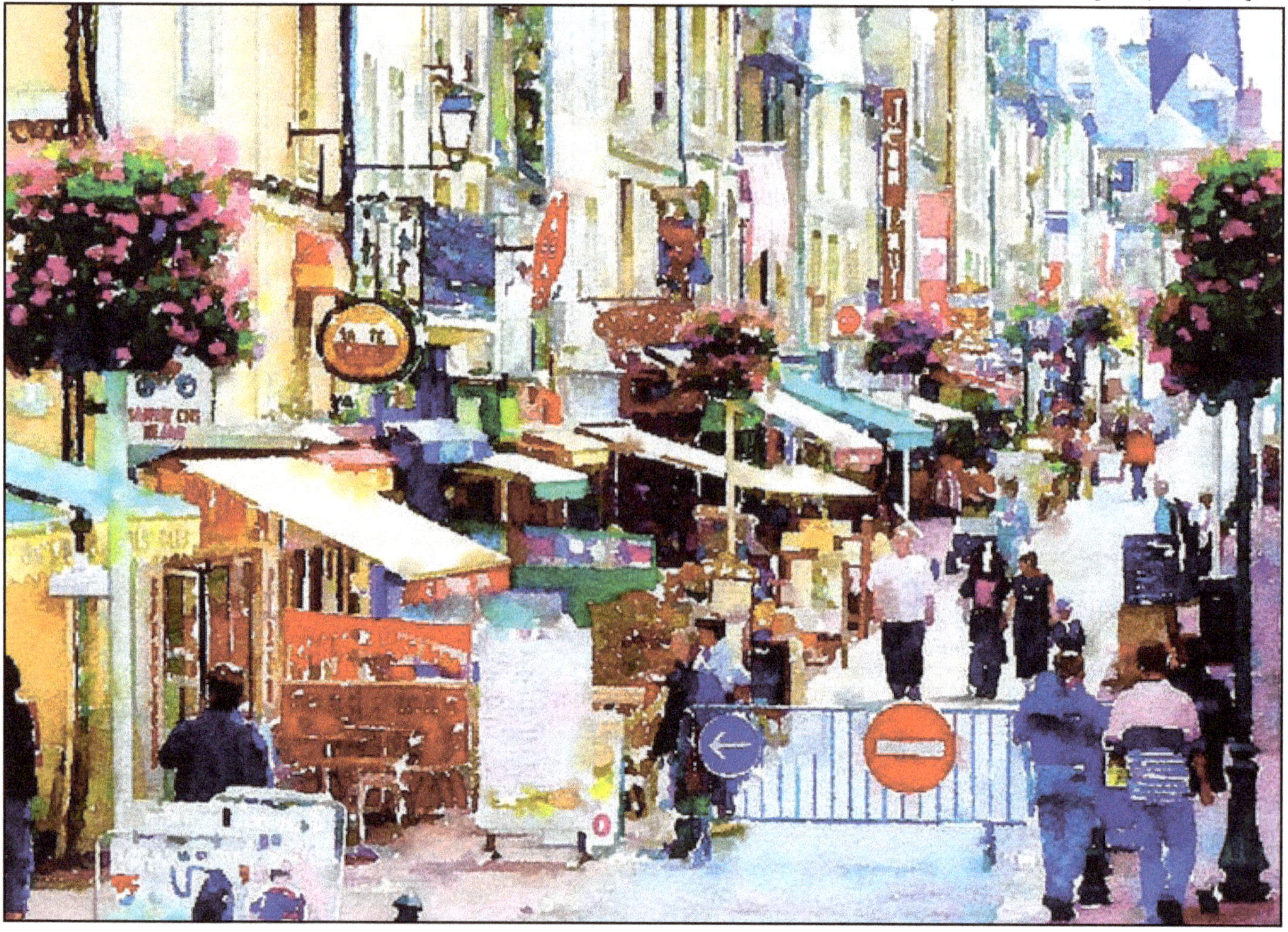

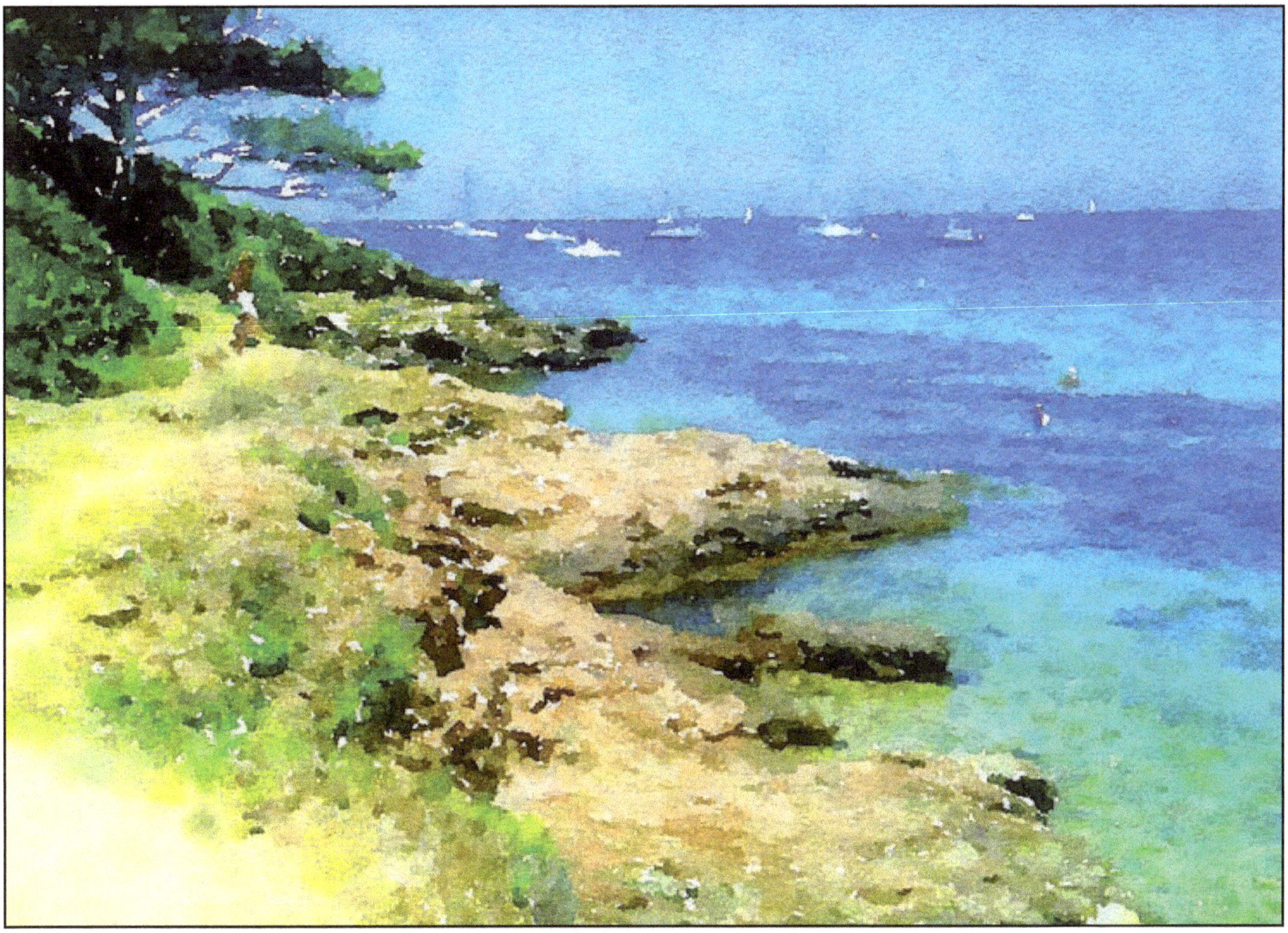

▲'Plage de la Courtade' (2010), Porquerolles, France [EFR(CD)1015].

'Sunbathers At Plage de la Courtade' (2010), Porquerolles, France [EFR(CD)1016].▼

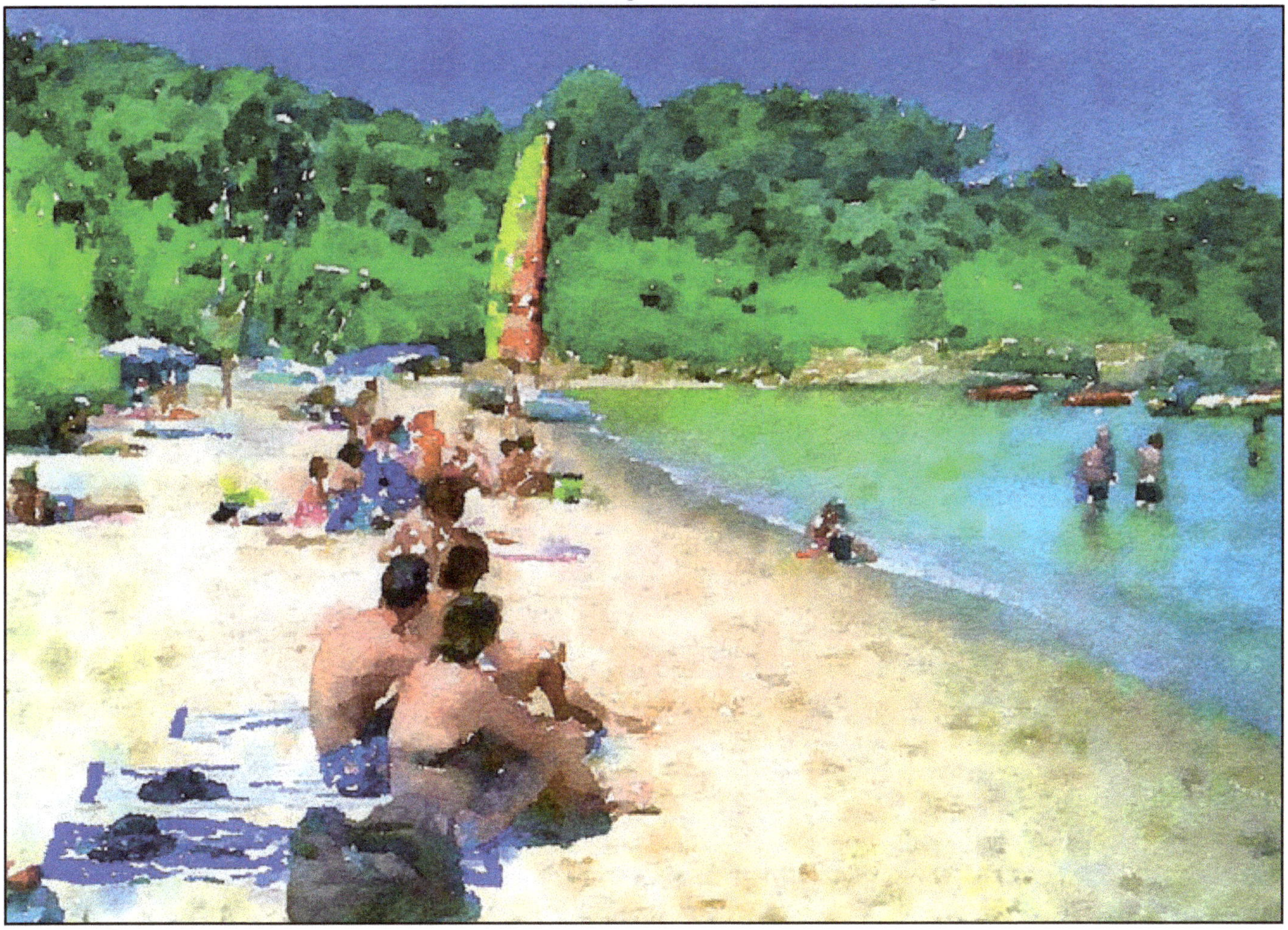

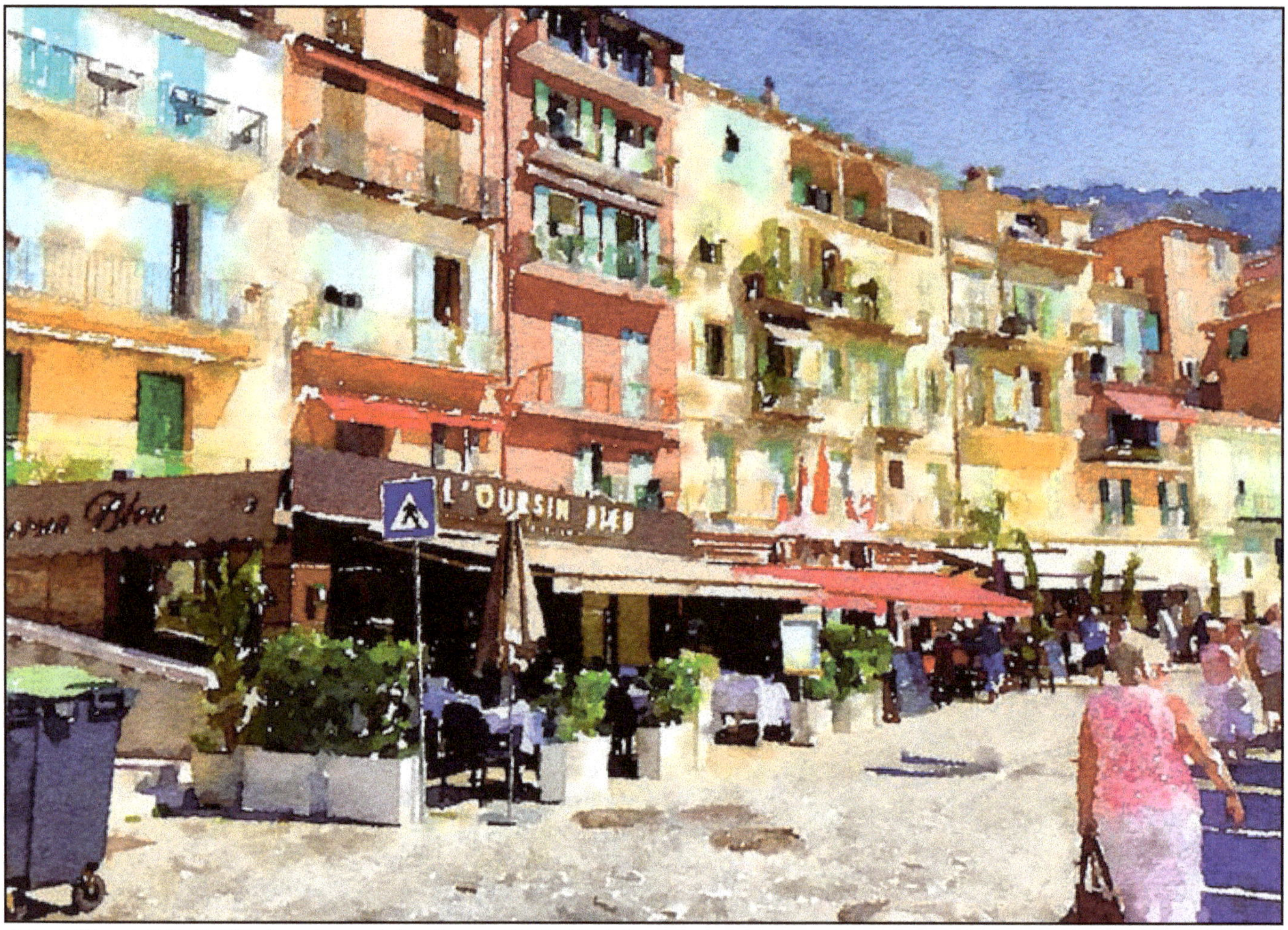

▲'Le Village' (2016), Villefranche sur-Mer, France [EFR(CD)1601].

'La Plage' (2016), Villefranche sur-Mer, France [EFR(CD)1602].▼

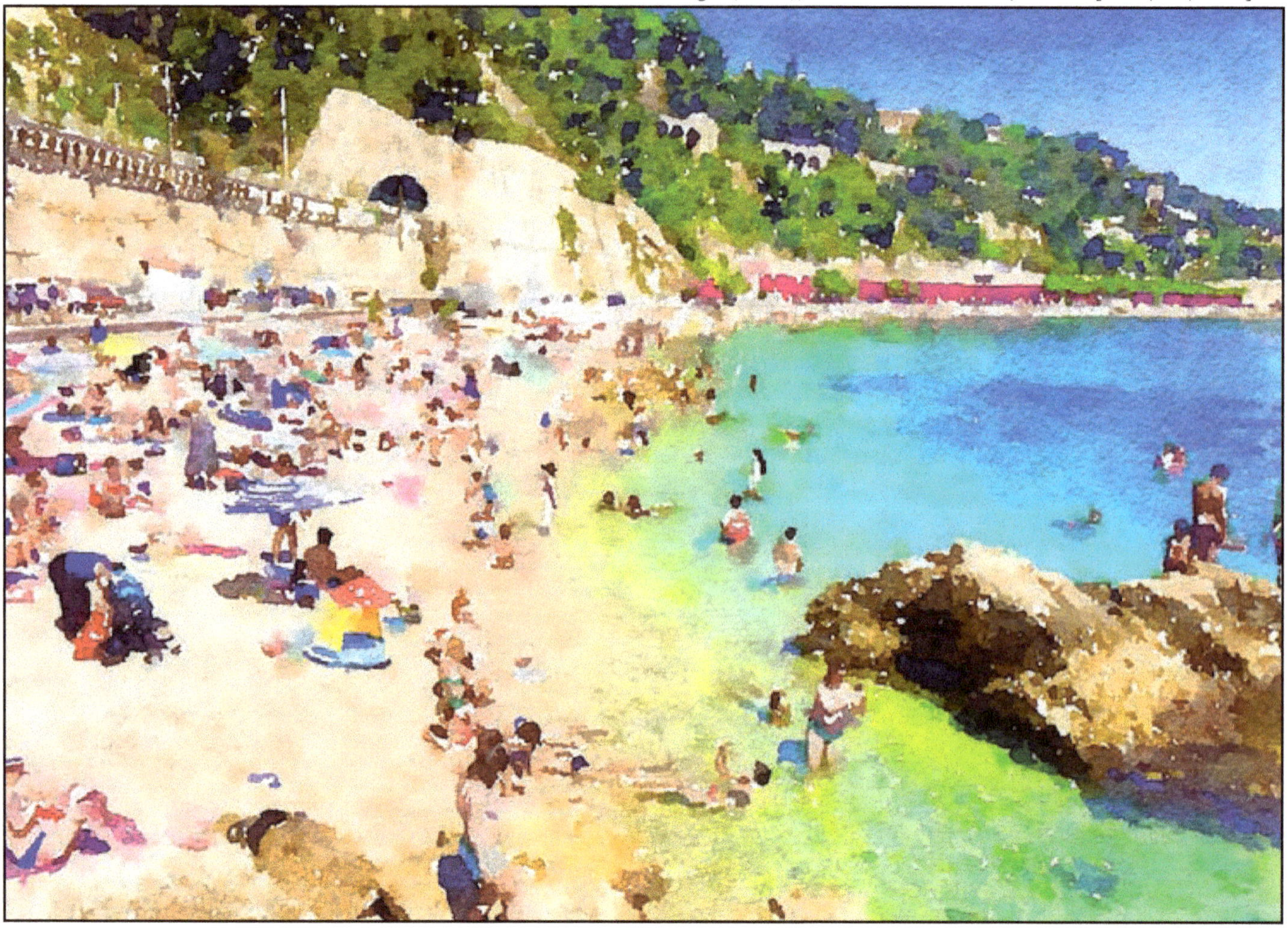

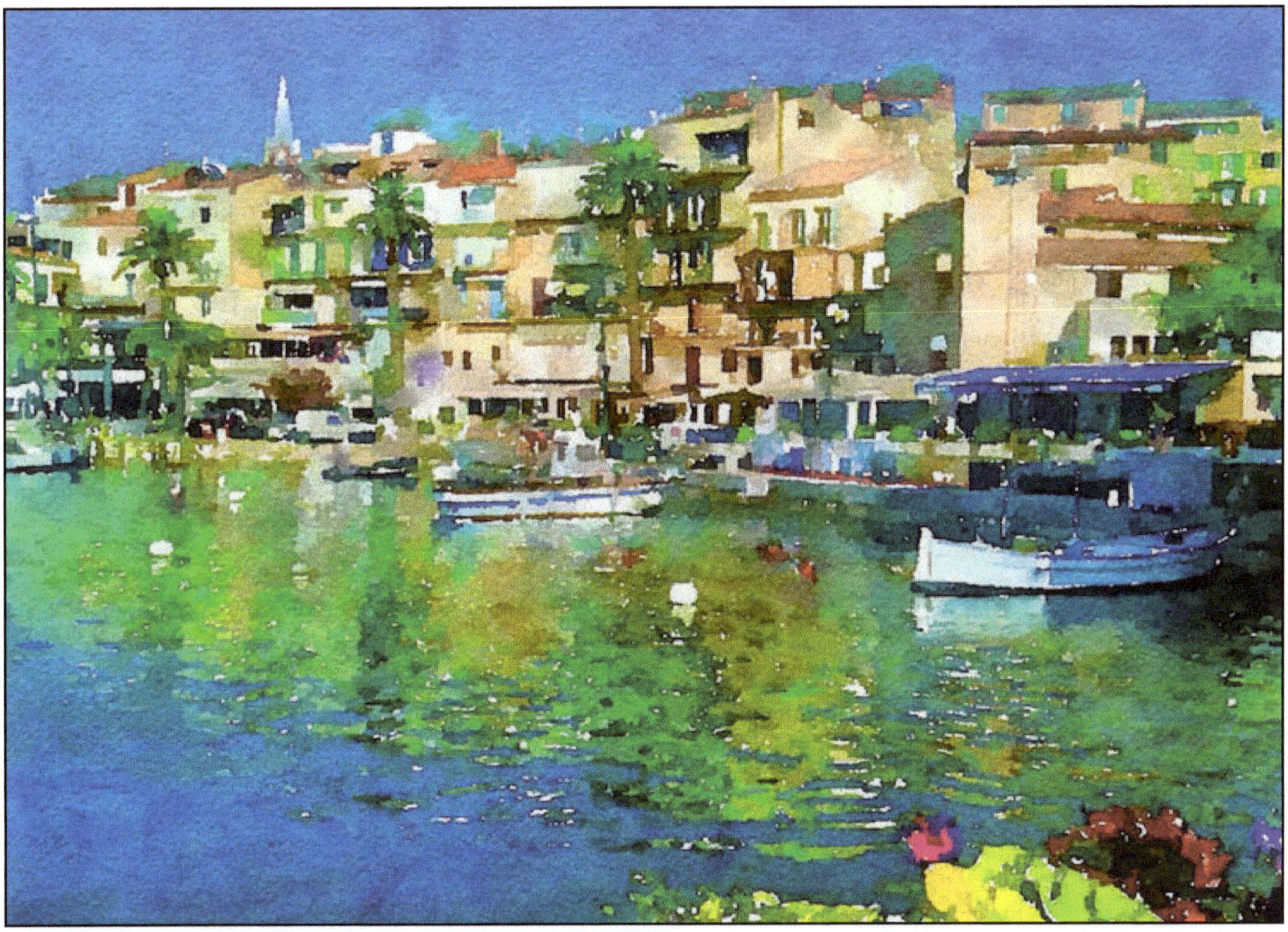

▲'The Harbour at Calvi' (2010), Corsica, France [EFR(CO)1001].

'Le Gare at Ile-Rousse' (2010), Corsica, France [EFR(CO)1002].▼

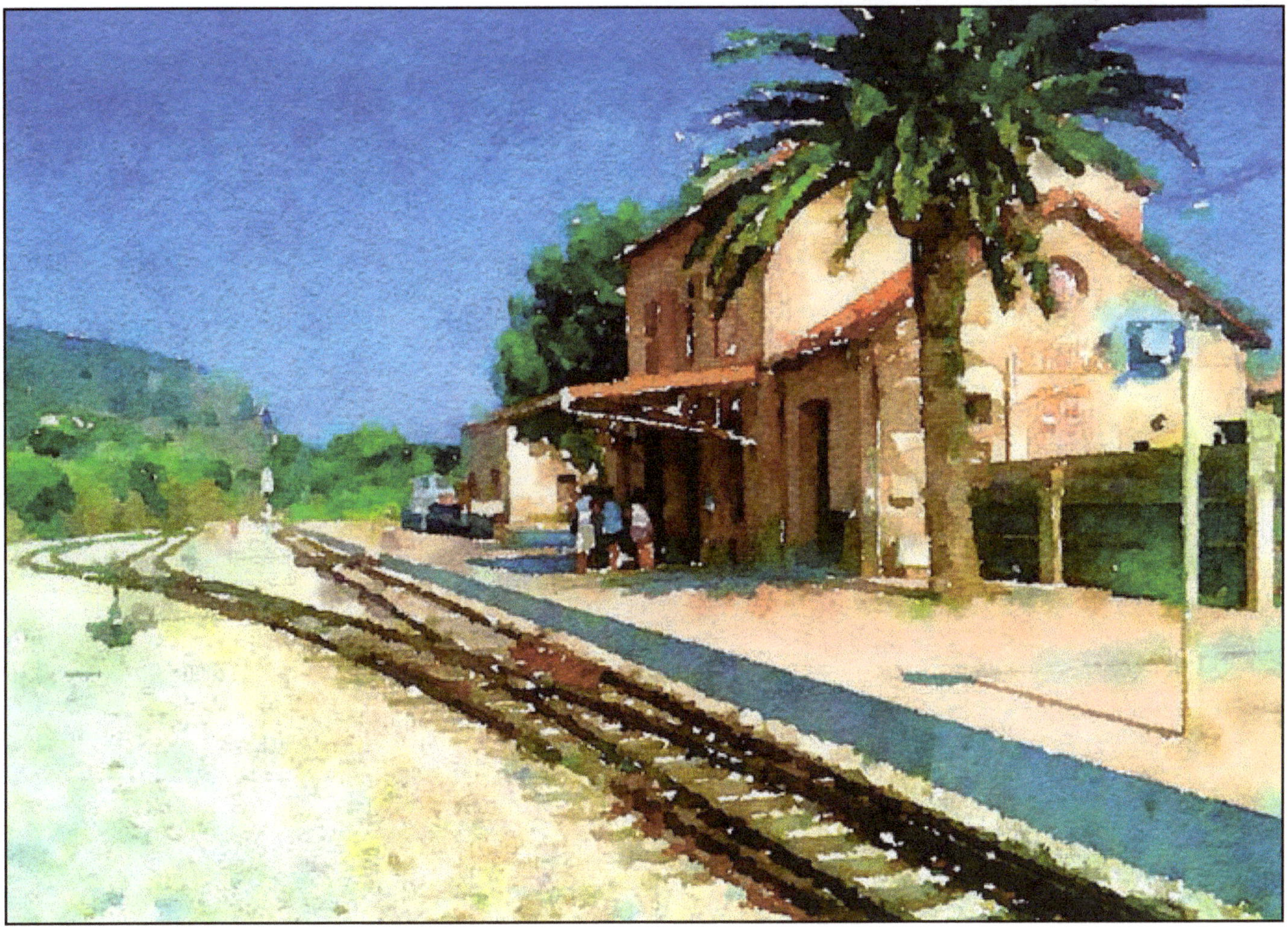

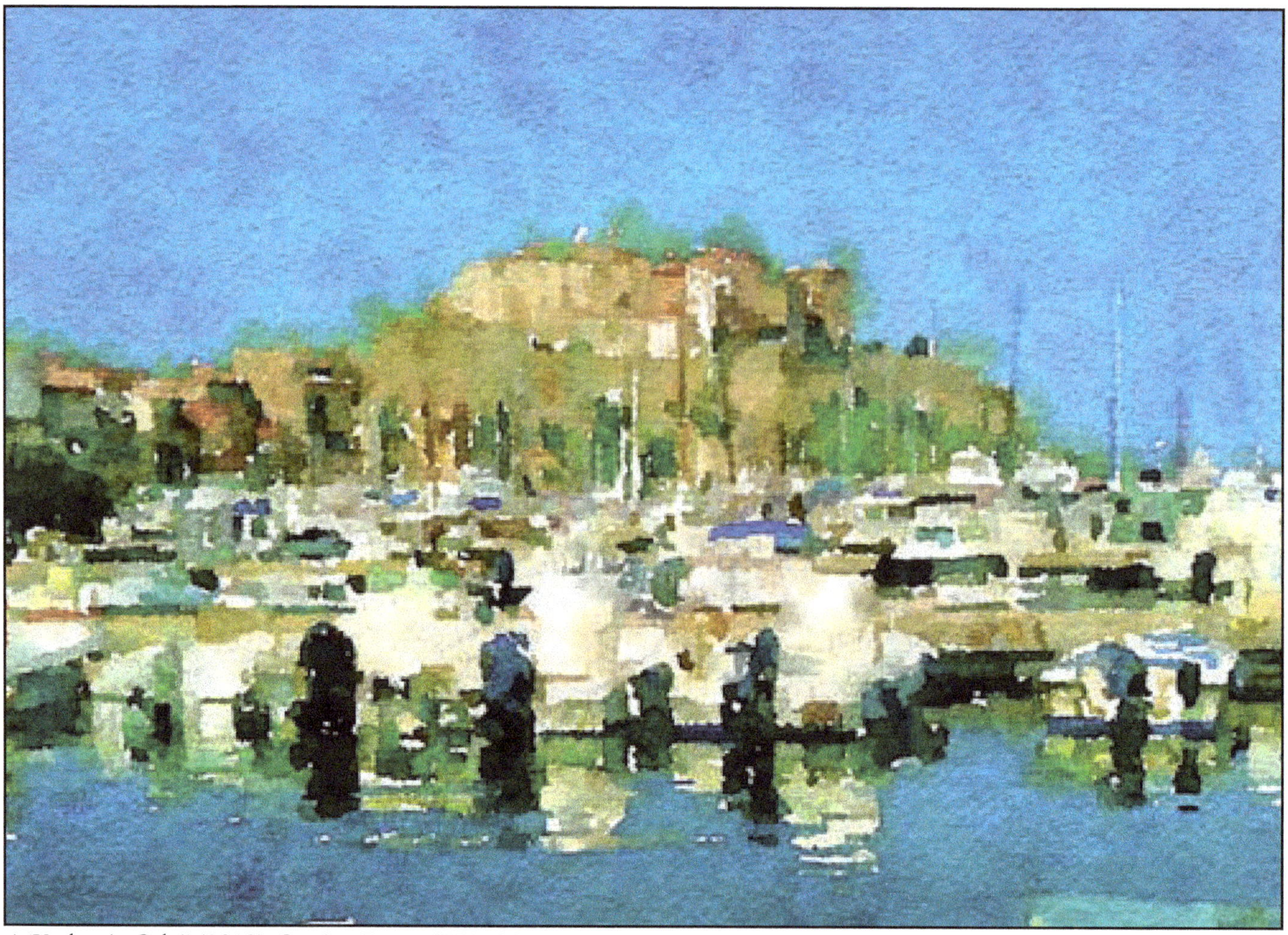

▲'Yachts At Calvi' (2010), Corsica, France [EFR(CO)1003].

'Early Arrival' (2010), Port Vendres, France [EFR(OC)1001].▼

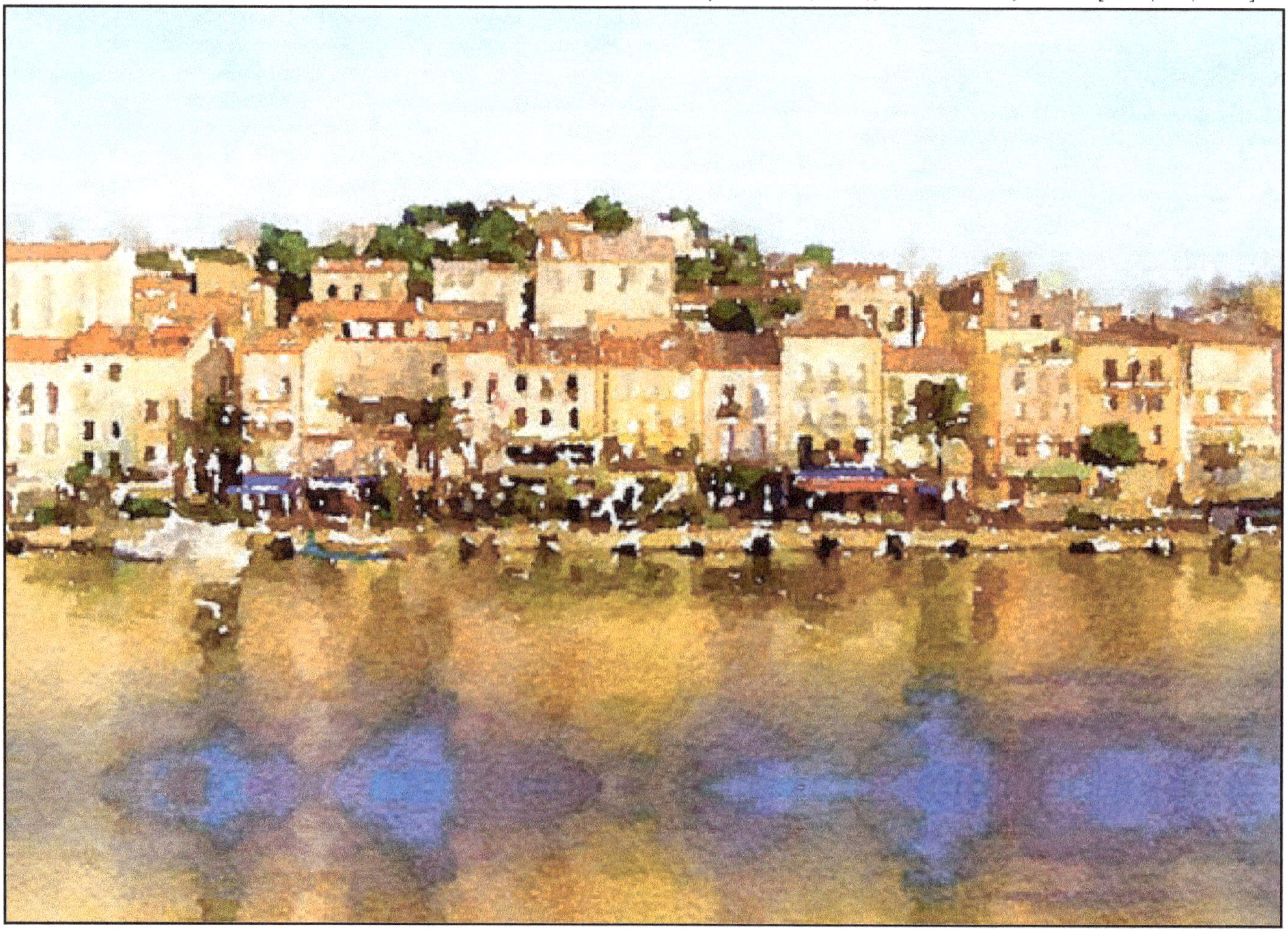

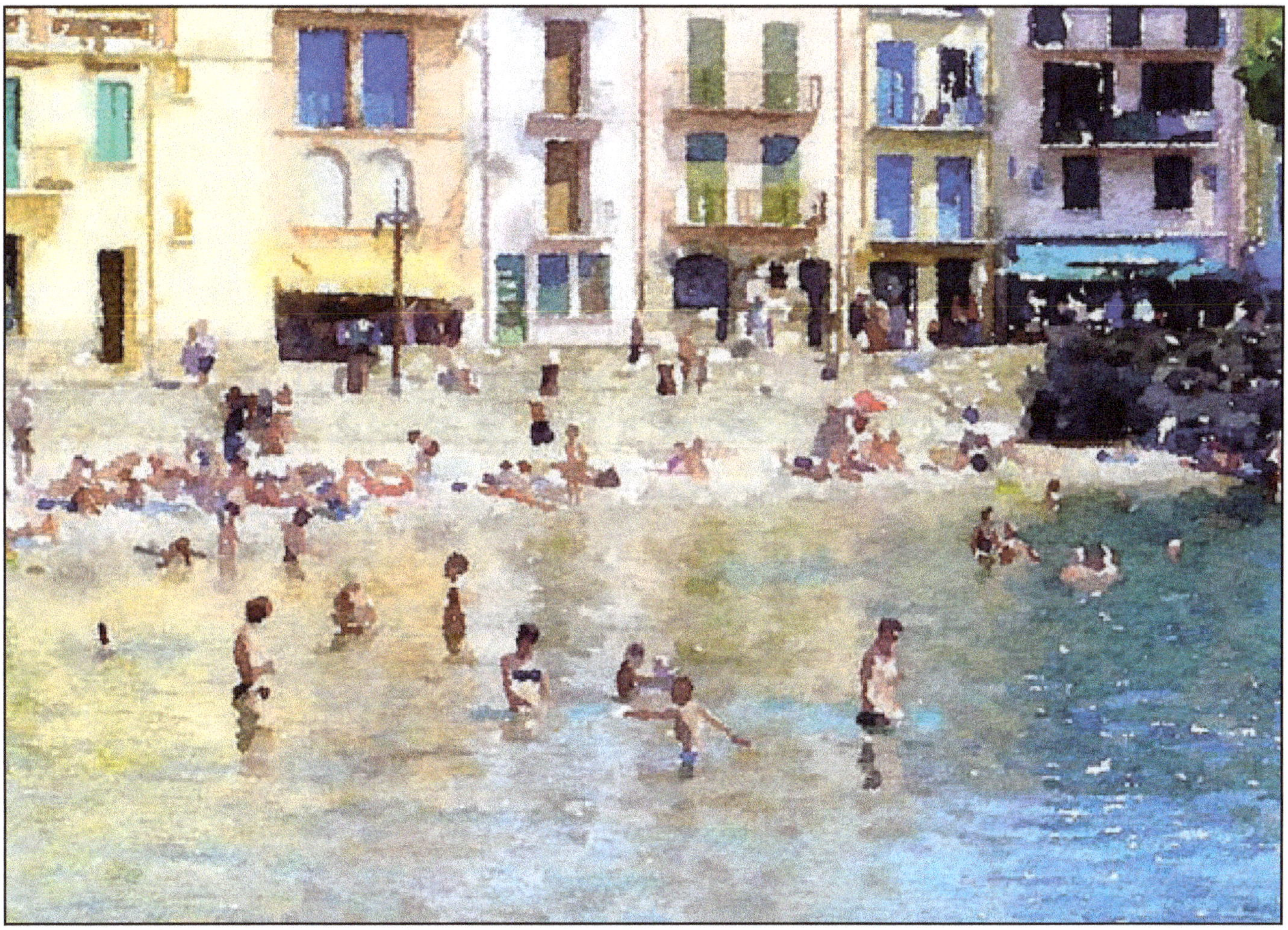

▲'Bathers At Plage Boramar' (2010), Collioure, France [EFR(OC)1002].

'L'Eglise At Plage Boramar' (2010), Collioure, France [EFR(OC)1003].▼

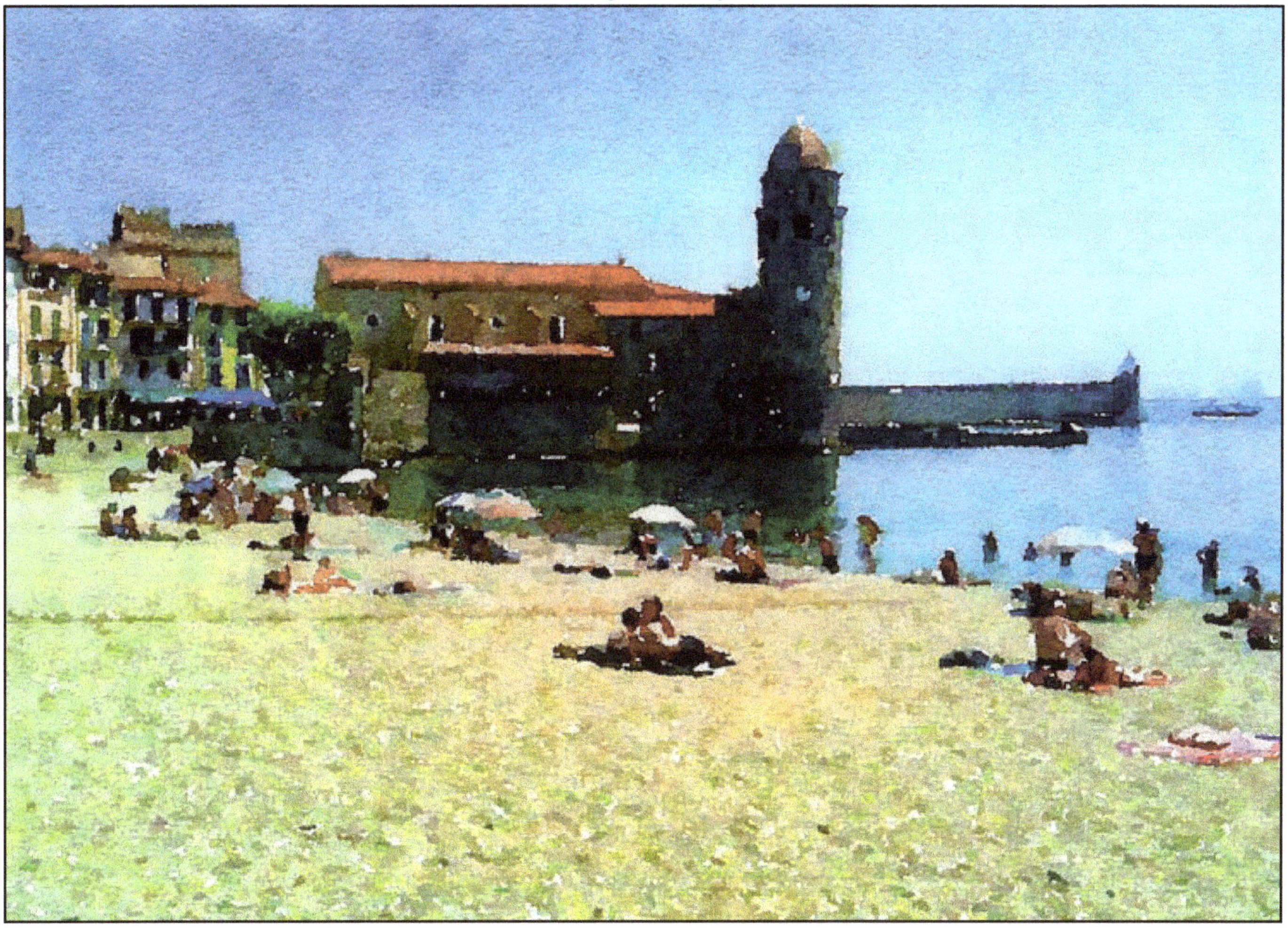

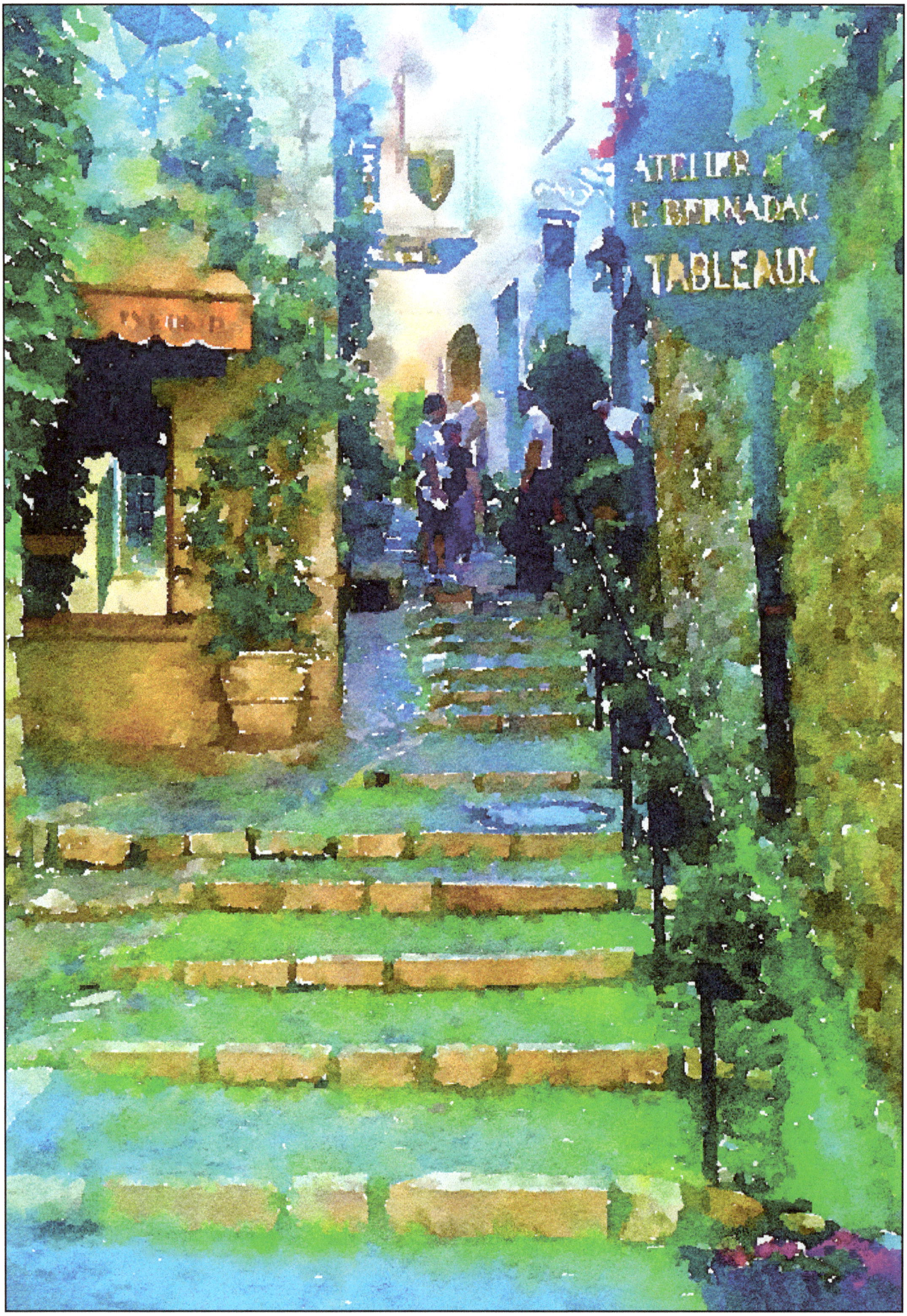

▲'The Old Town' (2010), St Paul de Vence, France [EFR(CD)1014].

Germany...

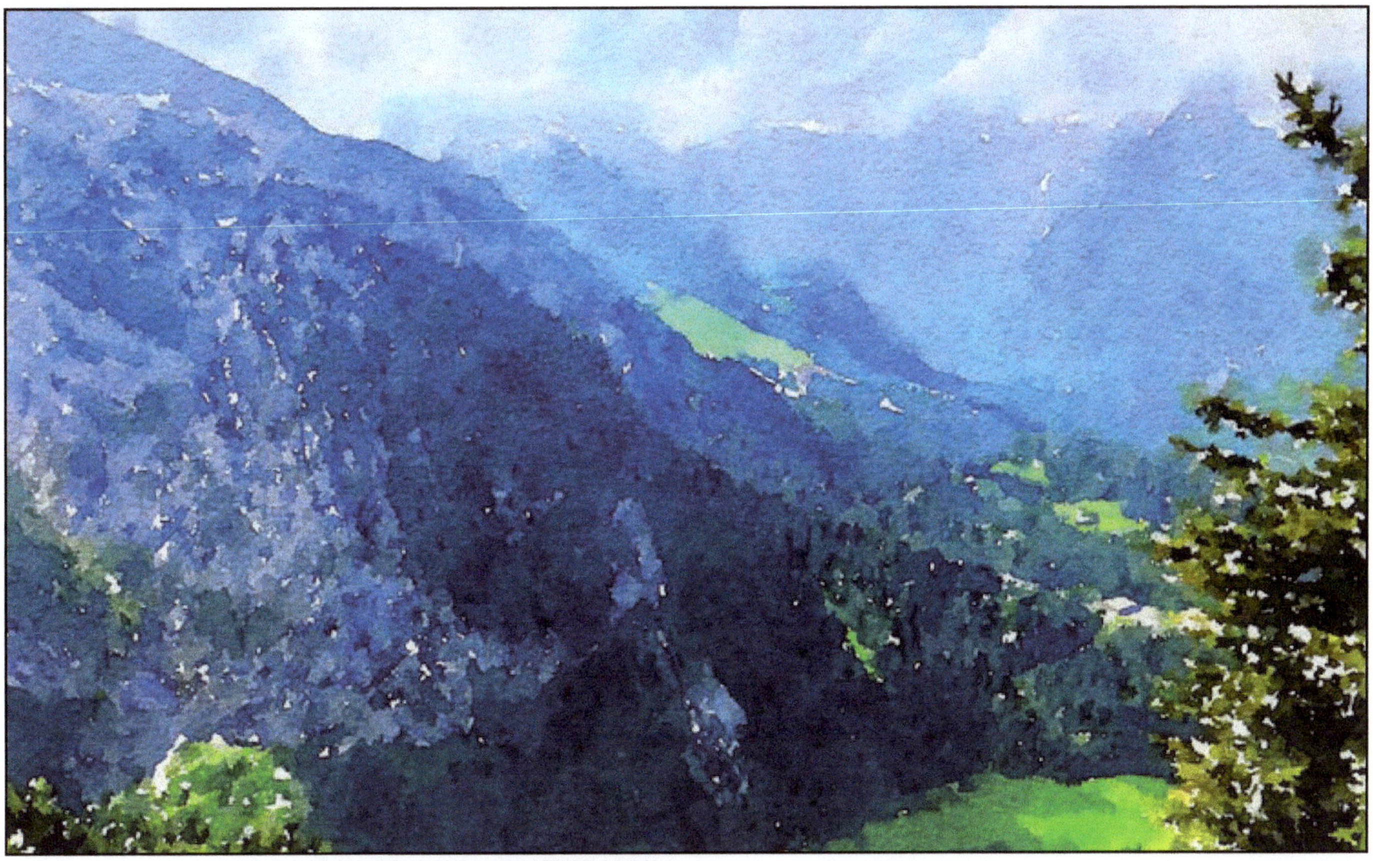

▲'Nationalpark' (2018), Berchtesgaden, Germany [EDE1801].

'The Eagles Nest' (2018), Berchtesgaden, Germany [EDE1802].▼

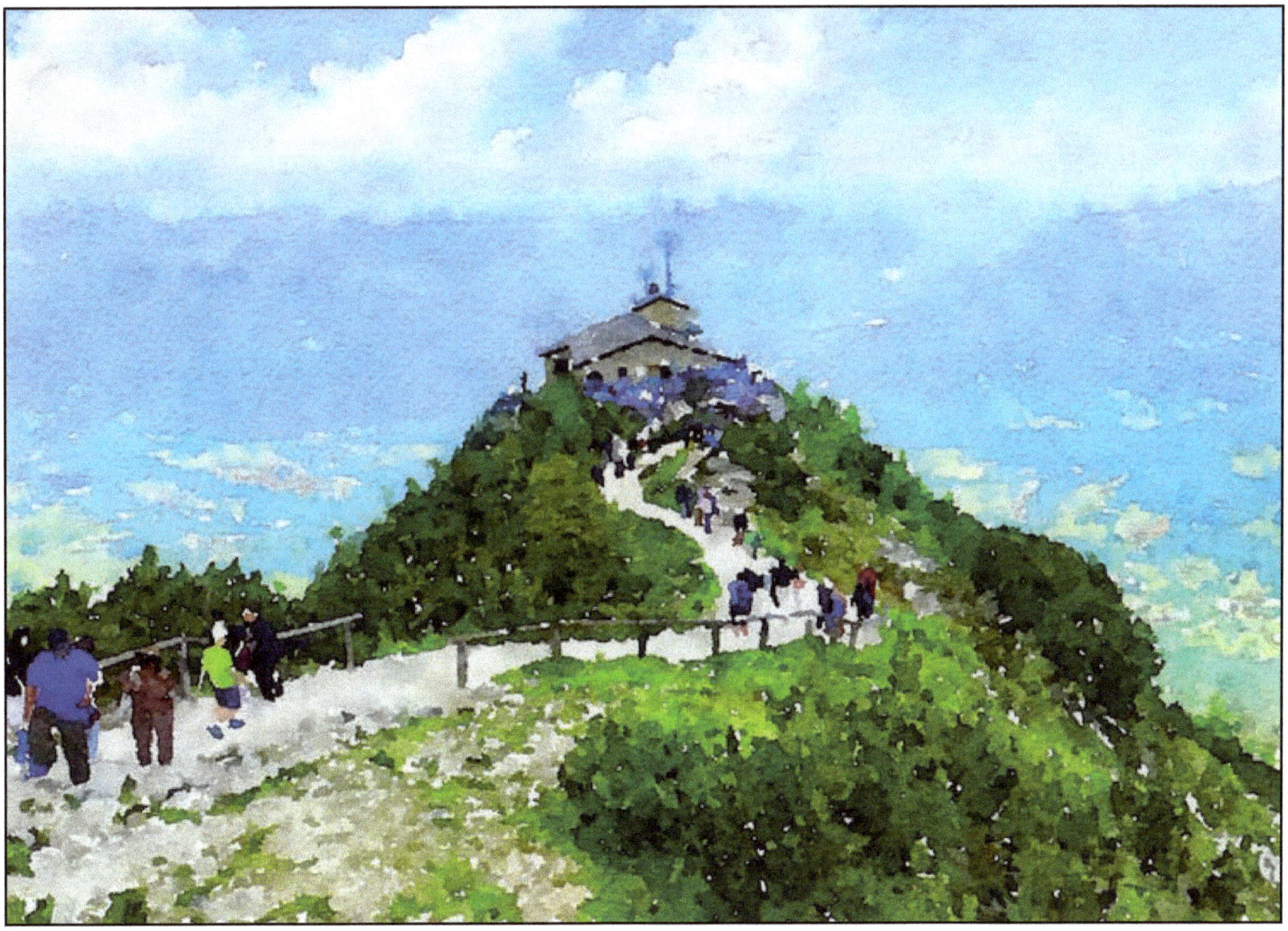

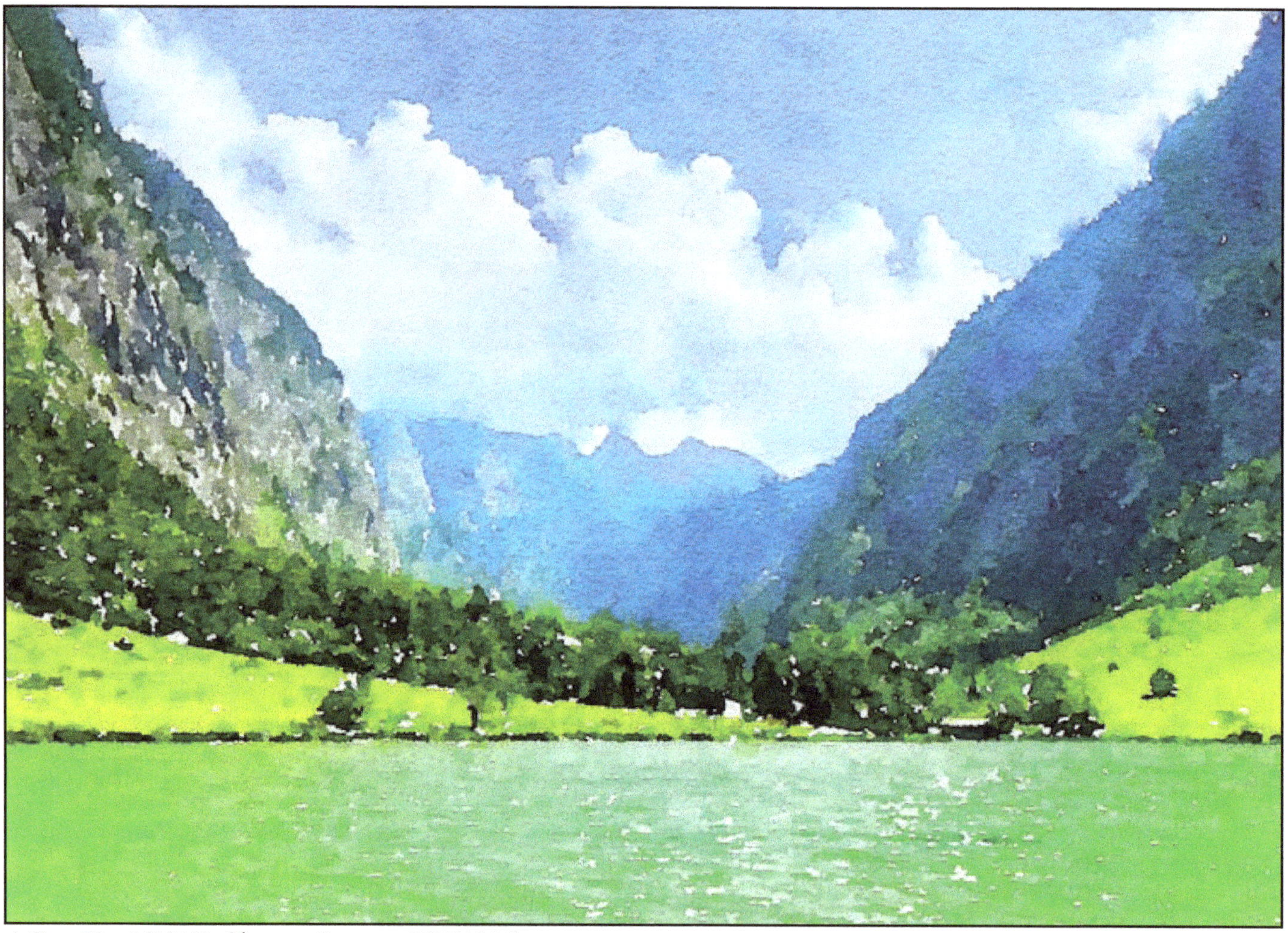

▲'East View' (2018), Obersee, Germany [EDE1805].

'Kirche St Bartholomew' (2018), Konigsee, Germany [EDE1803].▼

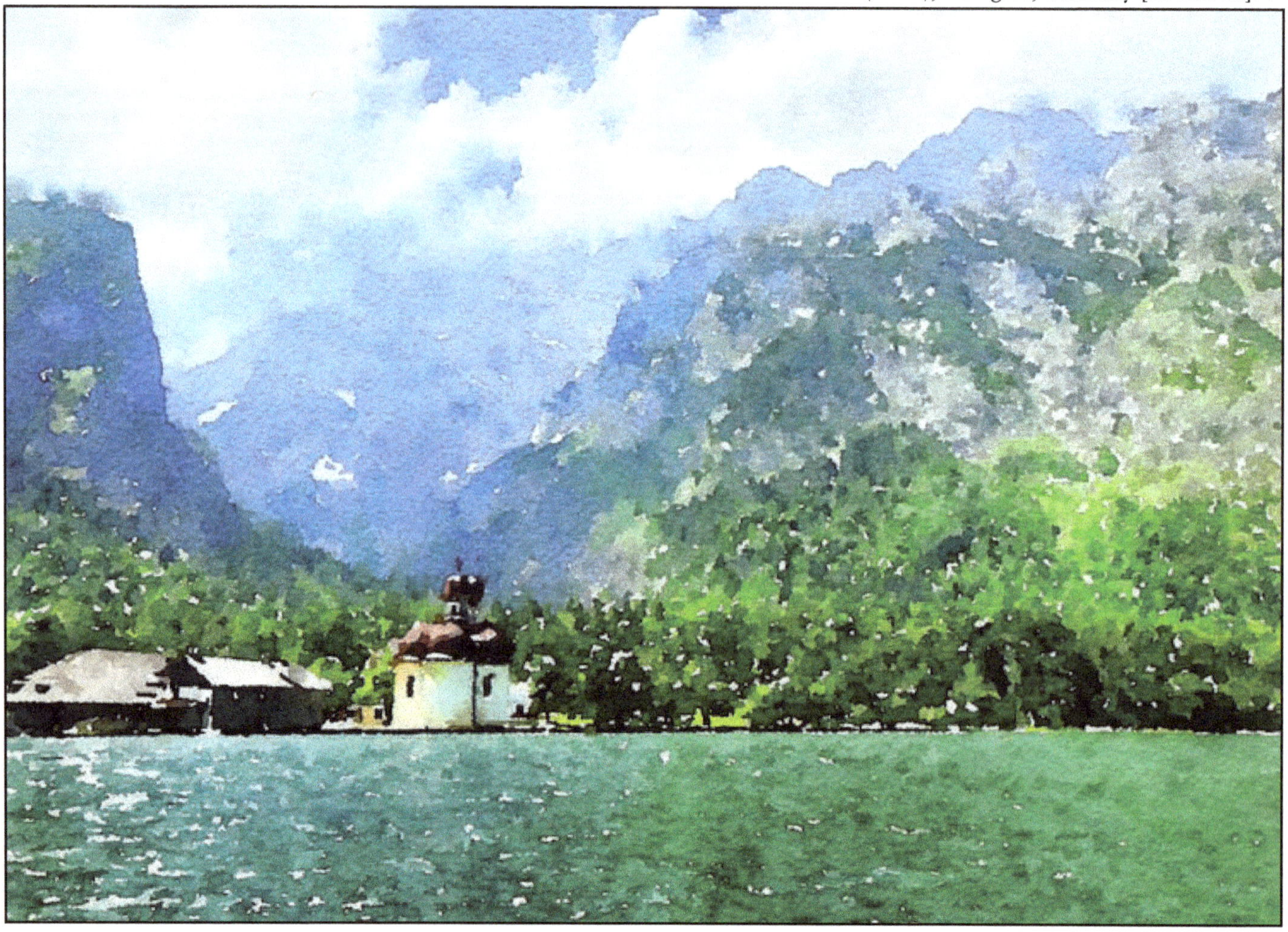

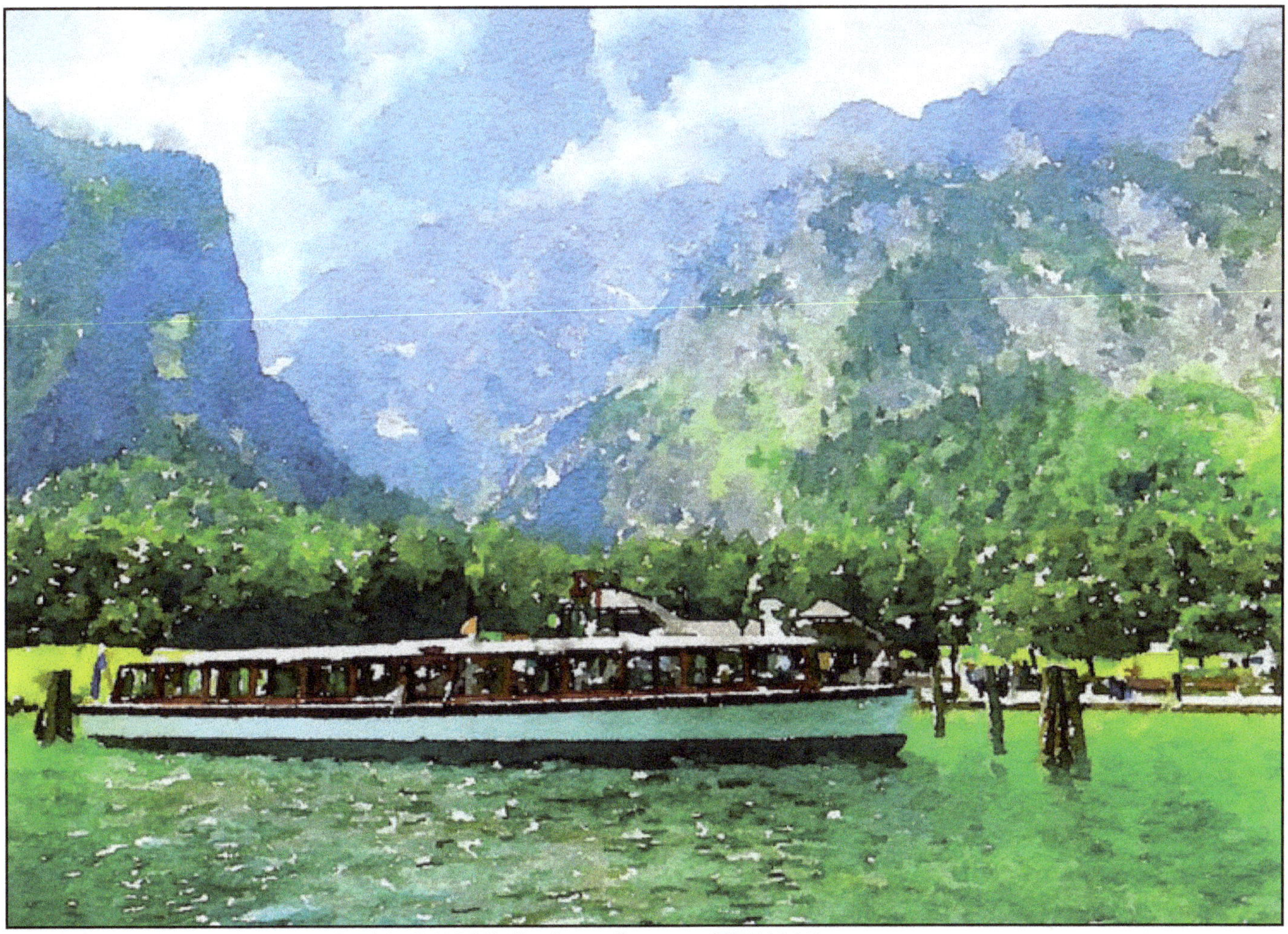

▲'Motor Boat At Mt Watzmann [2713m]' (2018), Konigsee, Germany [EDE1804].

'Chalet At Obersee' (2018), Obersee, Germany [EDE1806].▼

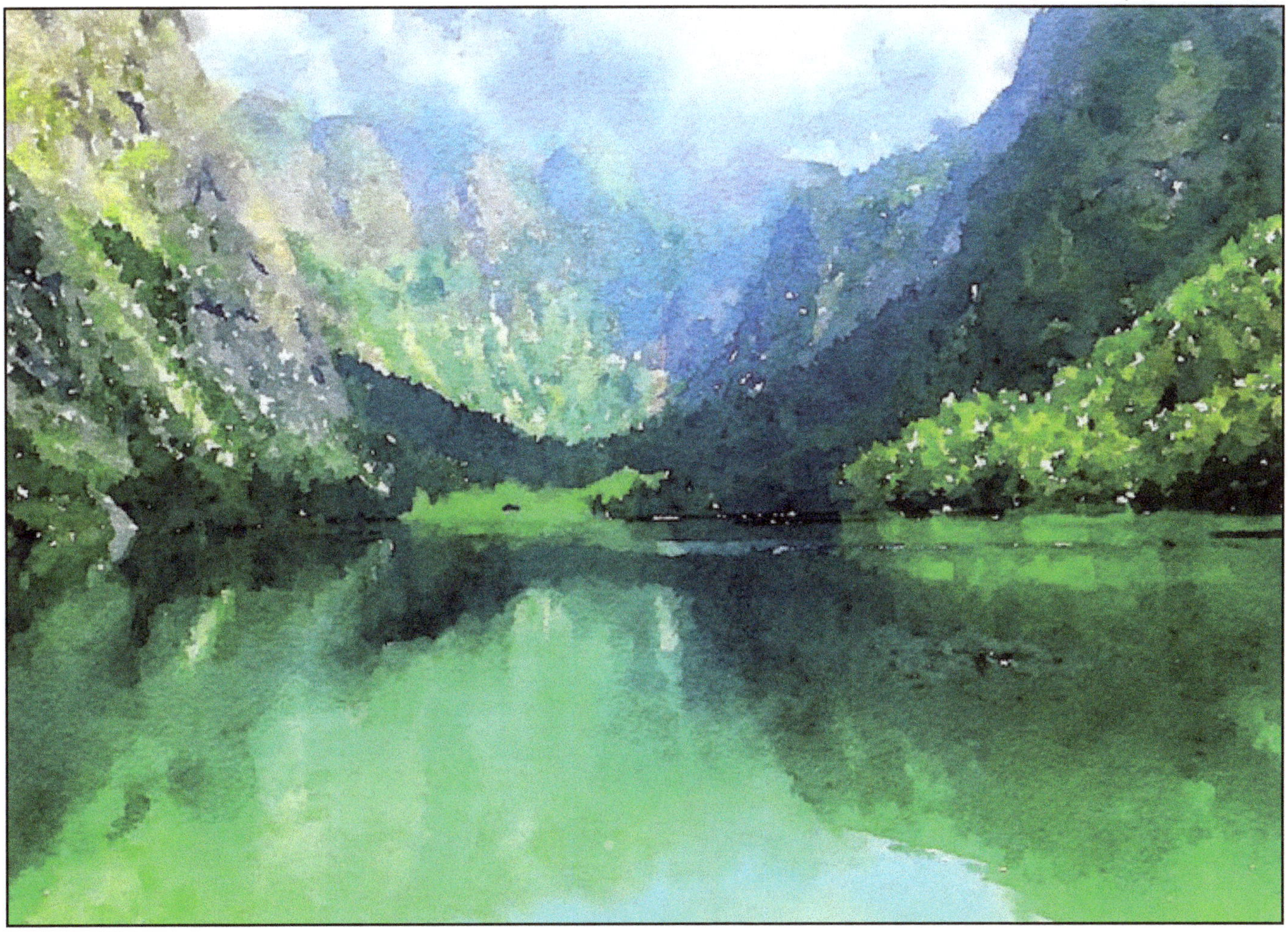

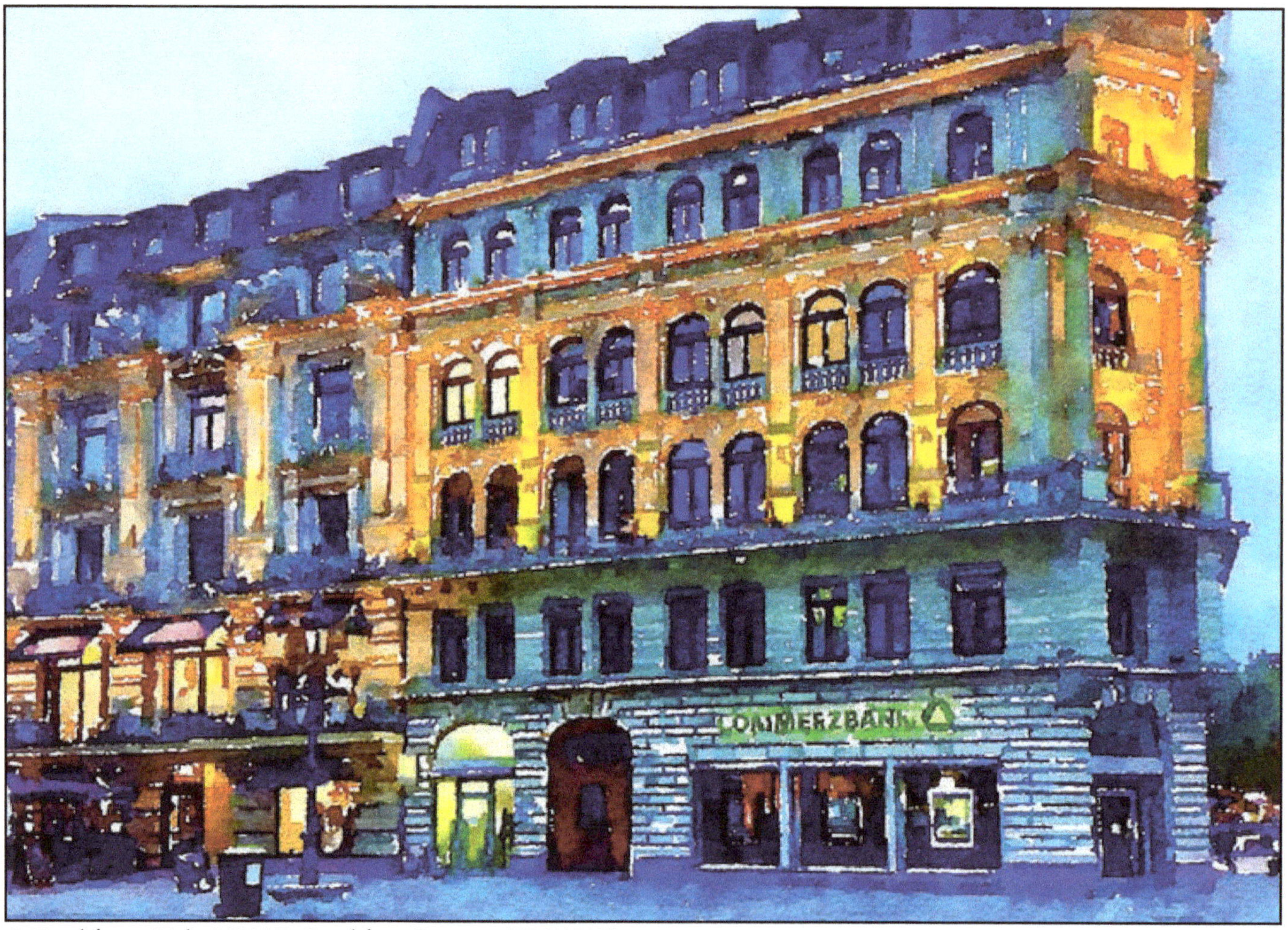

▲'Frankfurter Lights' (2018), Frankfurt, Germany [EDE1807].

'Evening At Augustinerstrasse' (2018), Mainz, Germany [EDE1808].▼

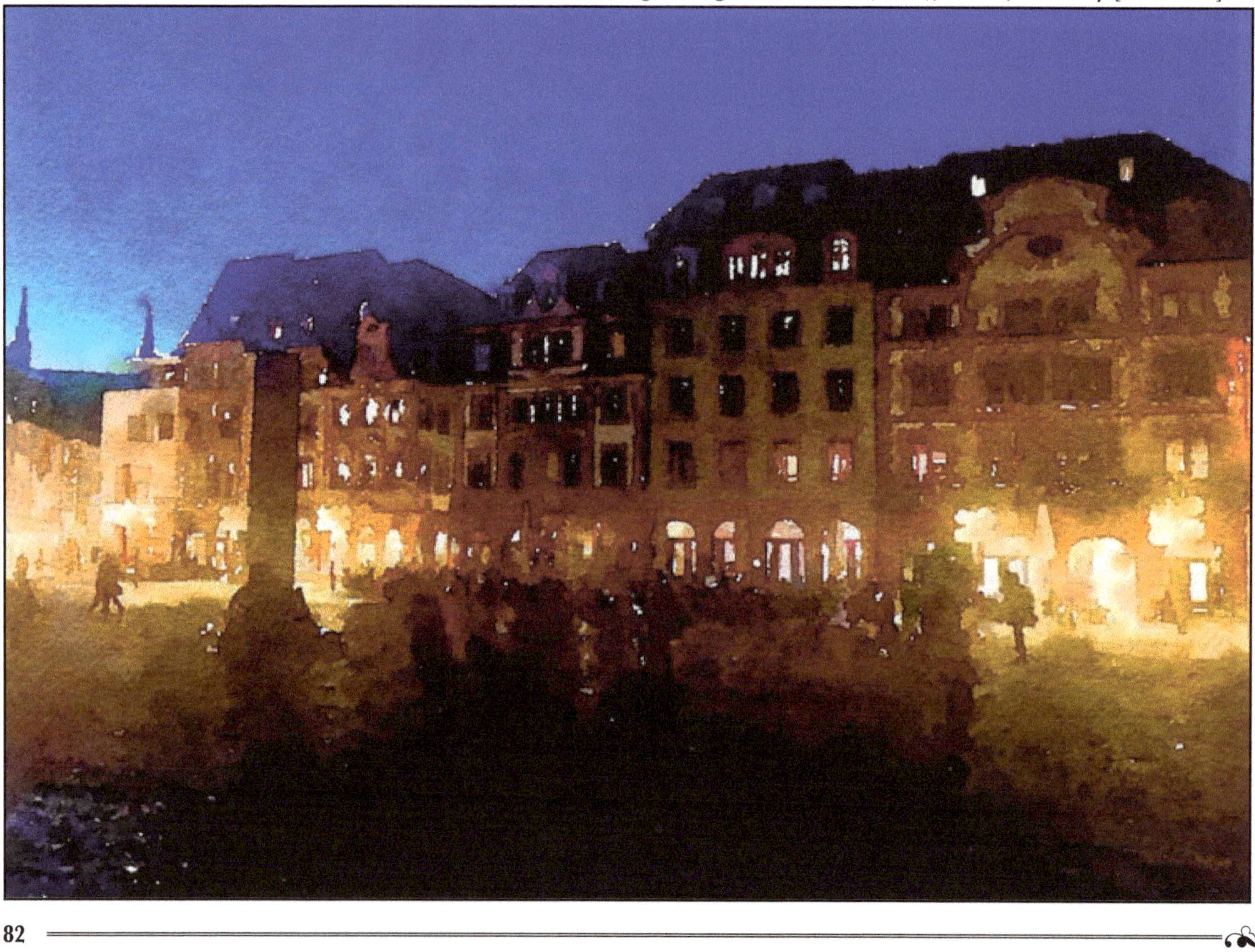

Gibraltar...

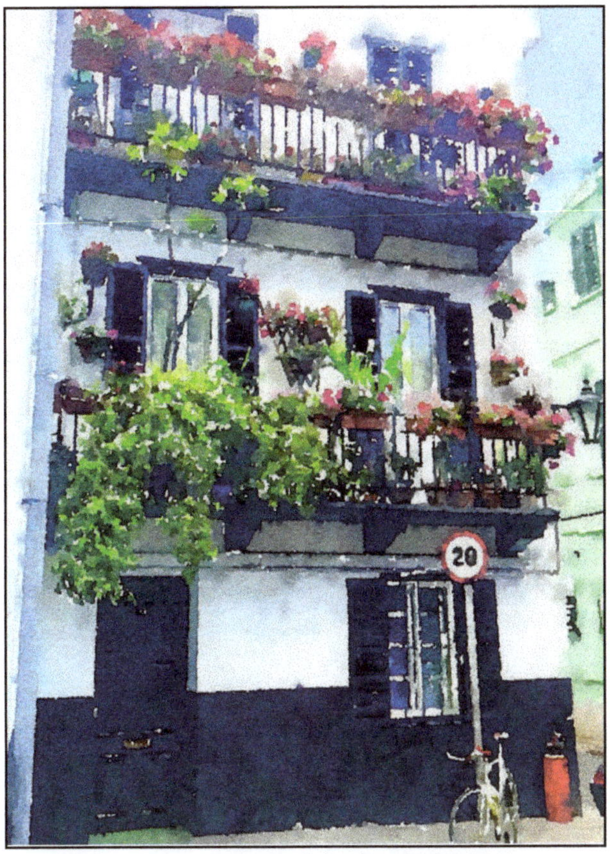

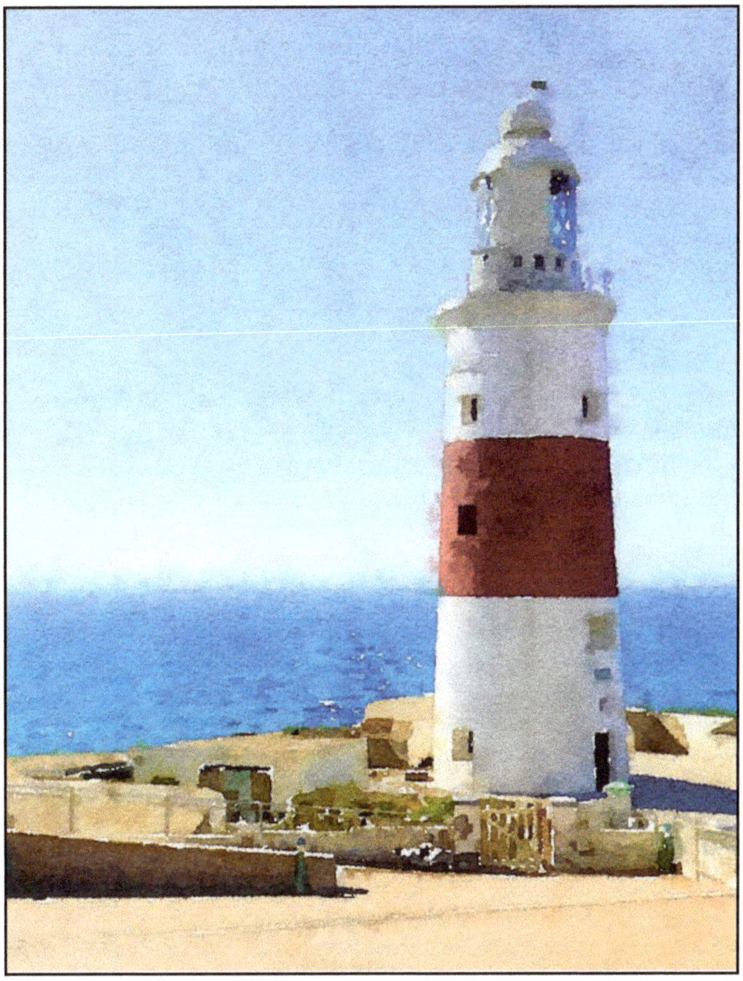

▲'Gibraltar Home' (2018), Gibraltar [EGI1803].

'The Lighthouse' (2018), Gibraltar [EGI1802].▲

▼'The Rock Of Gibraltar' (2018), Gibraltar [EGI1801].

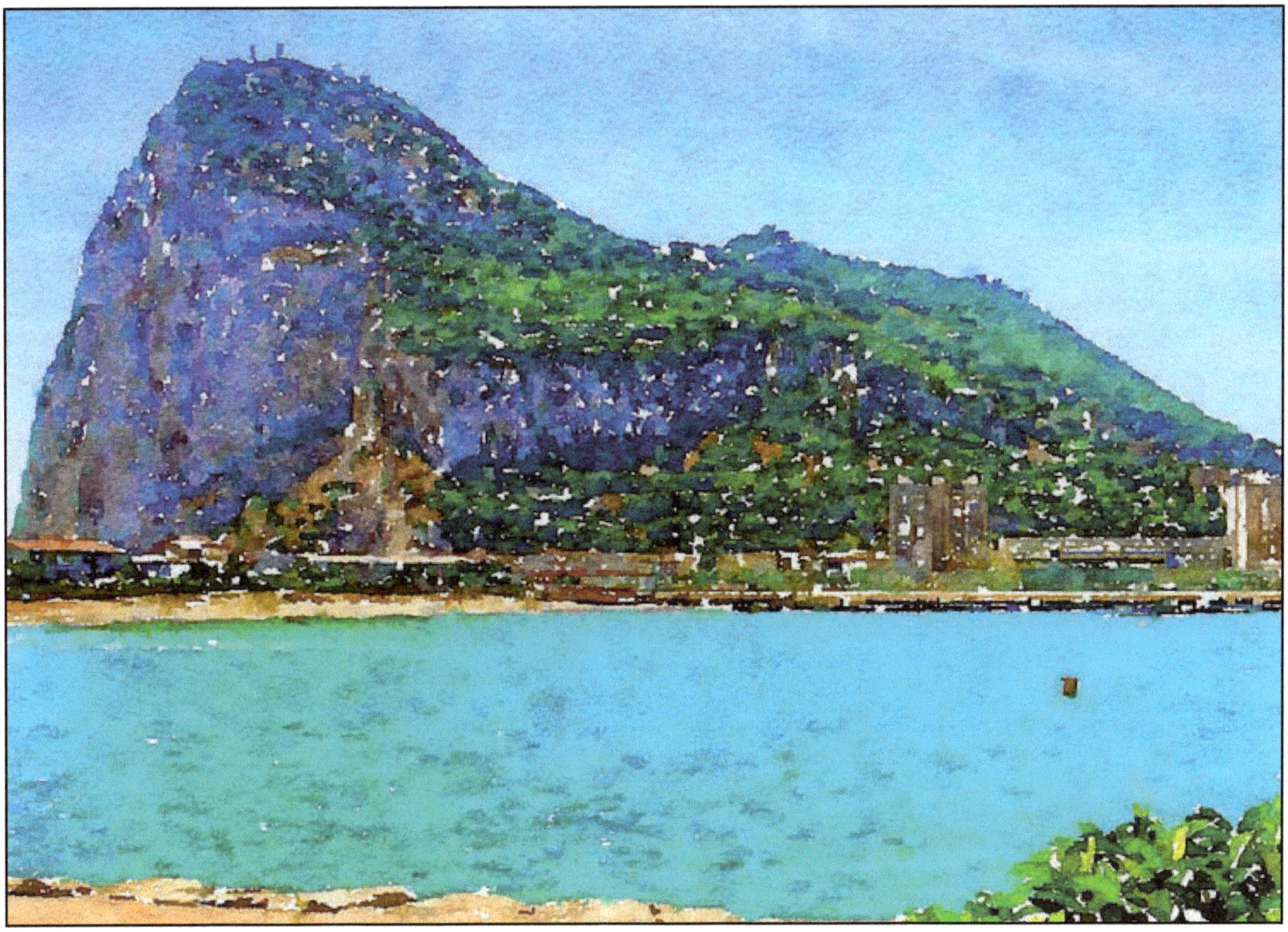

Greece...

Ahhh Greece! The sheer volume of images in this catalogue from this magnificent country testifies to my love of the Hellenes. An aquatic paradise, it is for me the jewel of the Meditteranean, ranking second in my opinion to Australia as my preferred place of residence.

I was first exposed to Greece in 1979, when taken to the island of Spetses on a three-day layover by fellow QANTAS crew, which I took advantage of on later occasions. It was however, another 30 years before I could return aboard the cruise ship "Seabourne Odyssey" in 2011, when my passion for Greece was revived.

Since then I have returned in 2013 aboard a cruise ship, and have spent 2015 and 2016 on the islands of Skiathos and Alonnisos respectively. My most recent and protracted tour of Greece was on a driving holiday in company with Rosie in 2018, where we criss-crossed the various regions. We found some incredible locations like Fiskardo on the island of Kefalonia, but spent most of our time exploring and relaxing on the amazing peninsulas of the Peloponnesus... Greece in spring and summer is what life is all about!

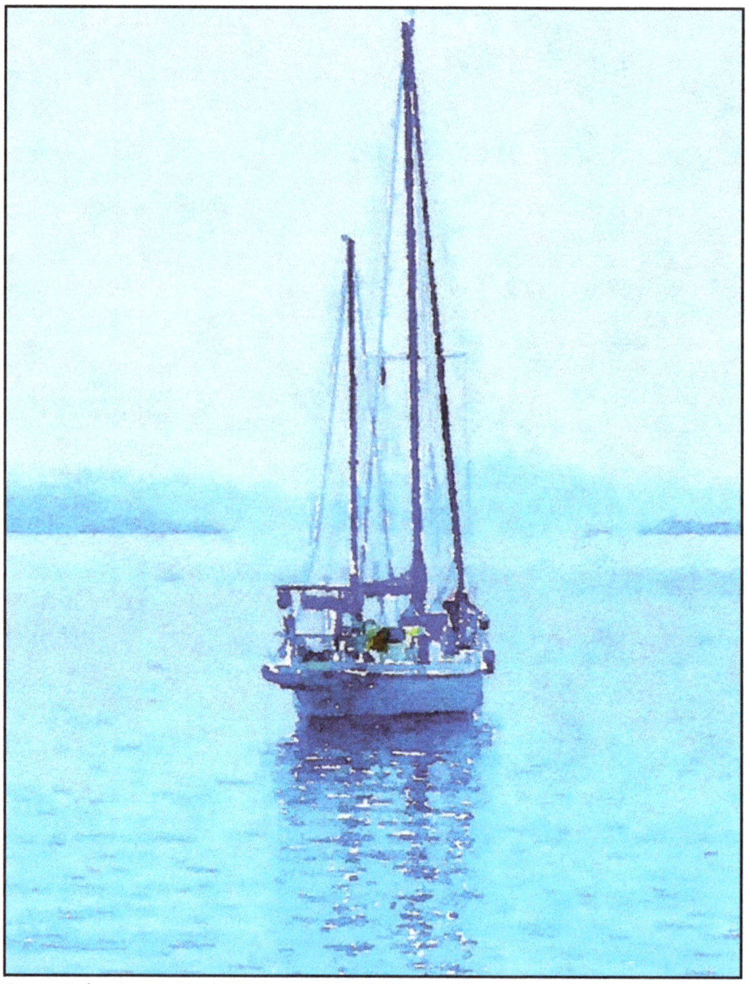

'Overnight Stay' (2018), Pagasetic Gulf, NE Greece [EGR(NE)1805].▲

▼'Lake Ioannina' (2018), Ioannina, NW Greece [EGR(NW)1801].

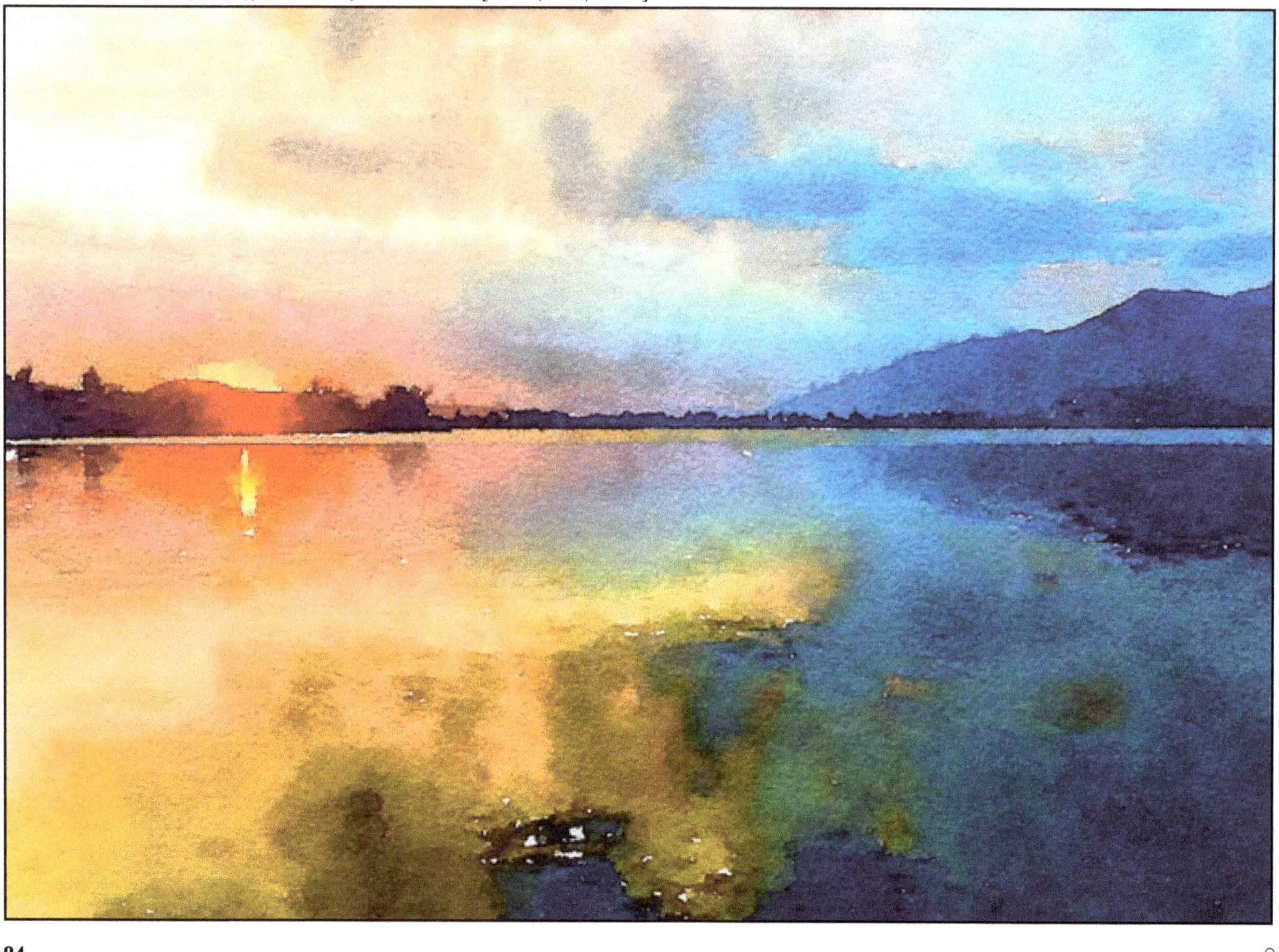

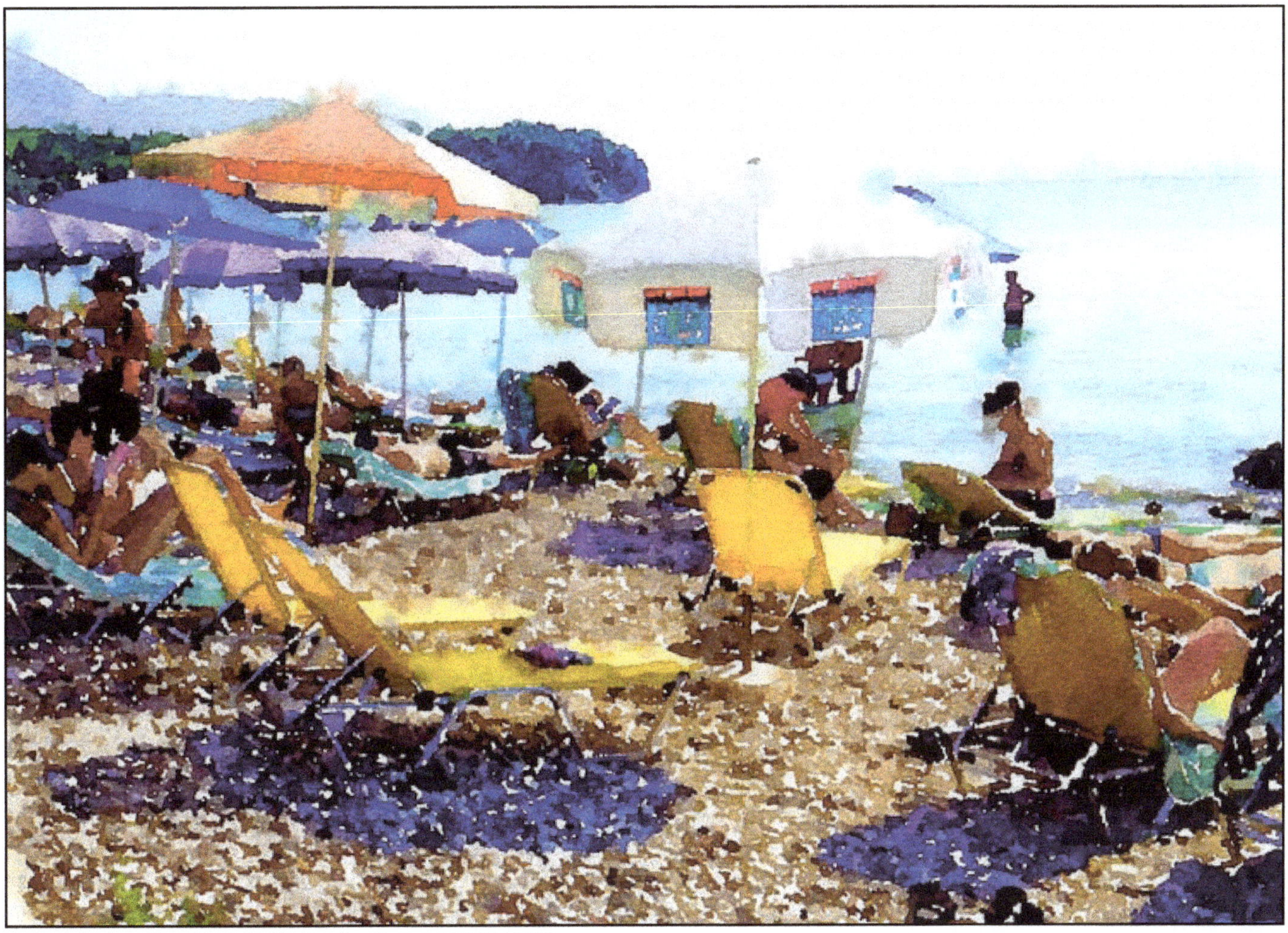

▲'Sotiriotissa Beach' (2013), Corfu, Greece [EGR1301].

'The Lagoon' (2018), Lefkada, NW Greece [EGR(NW)1803].▼

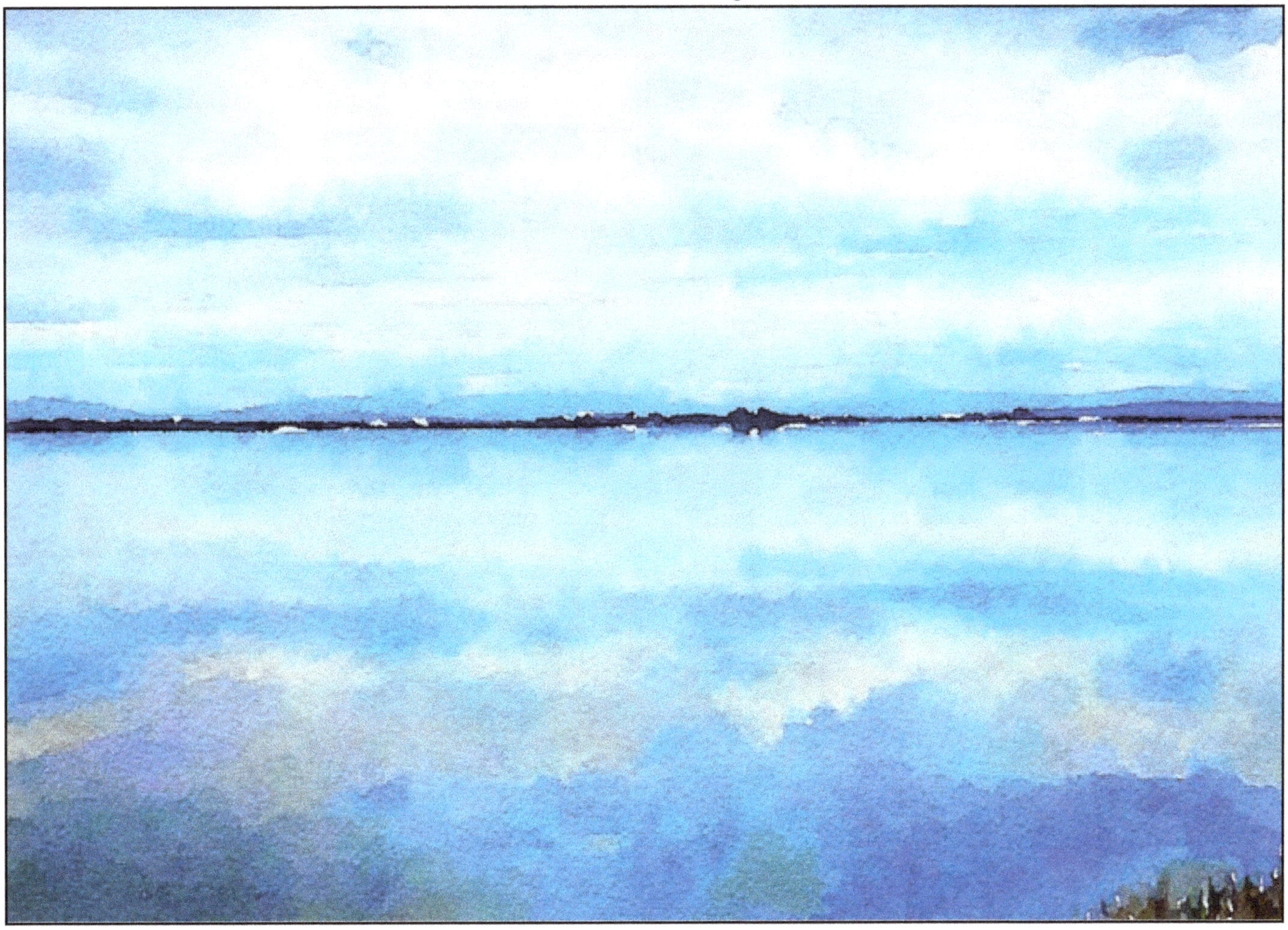

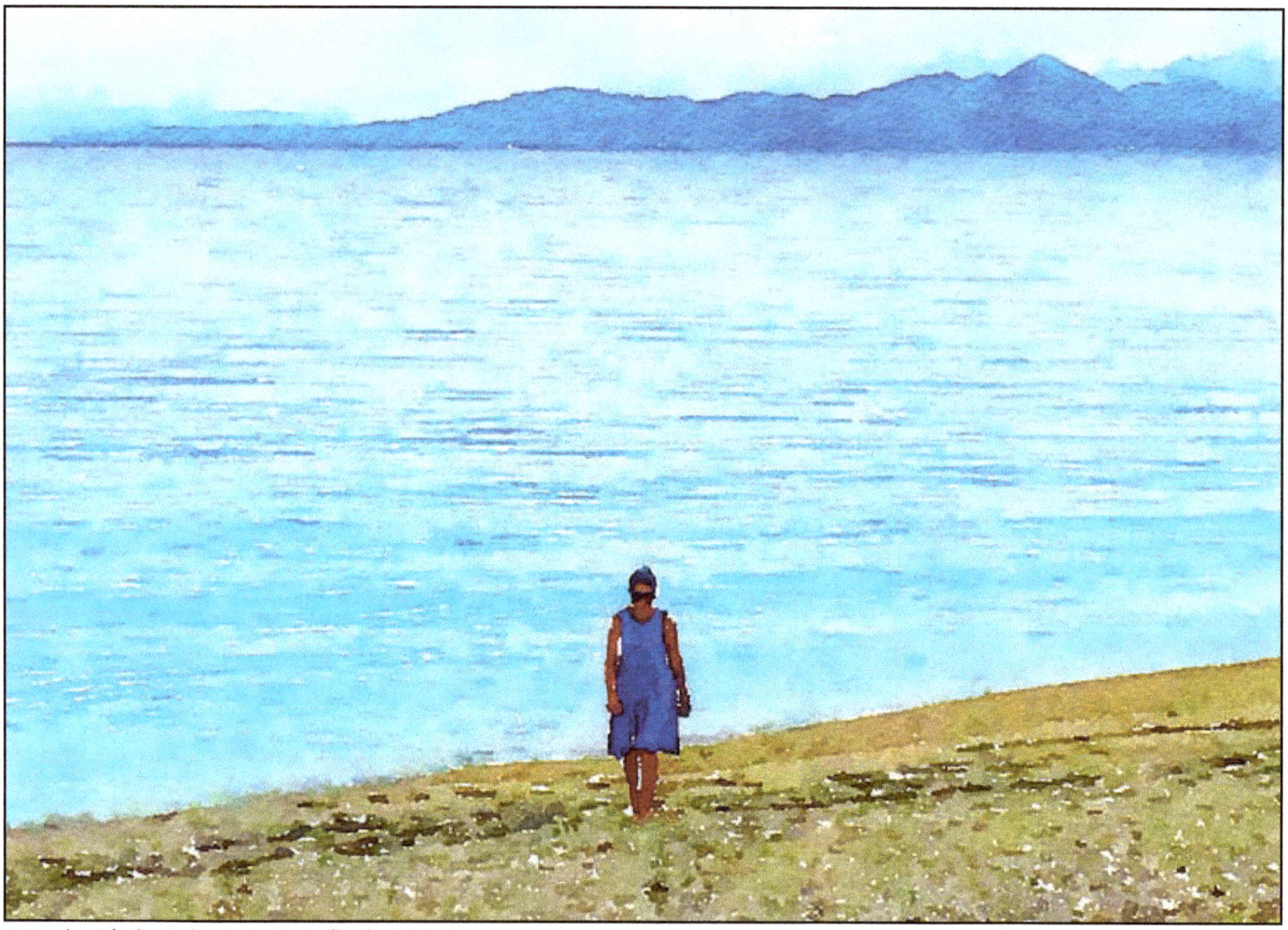

▲'Lady Of The Lake' (2018), Lefkada, NW Greece [EGR(NW)1802].

'Port Nydri' (2018), Lefkada, NW Greece [EGR(NW)1804].▼

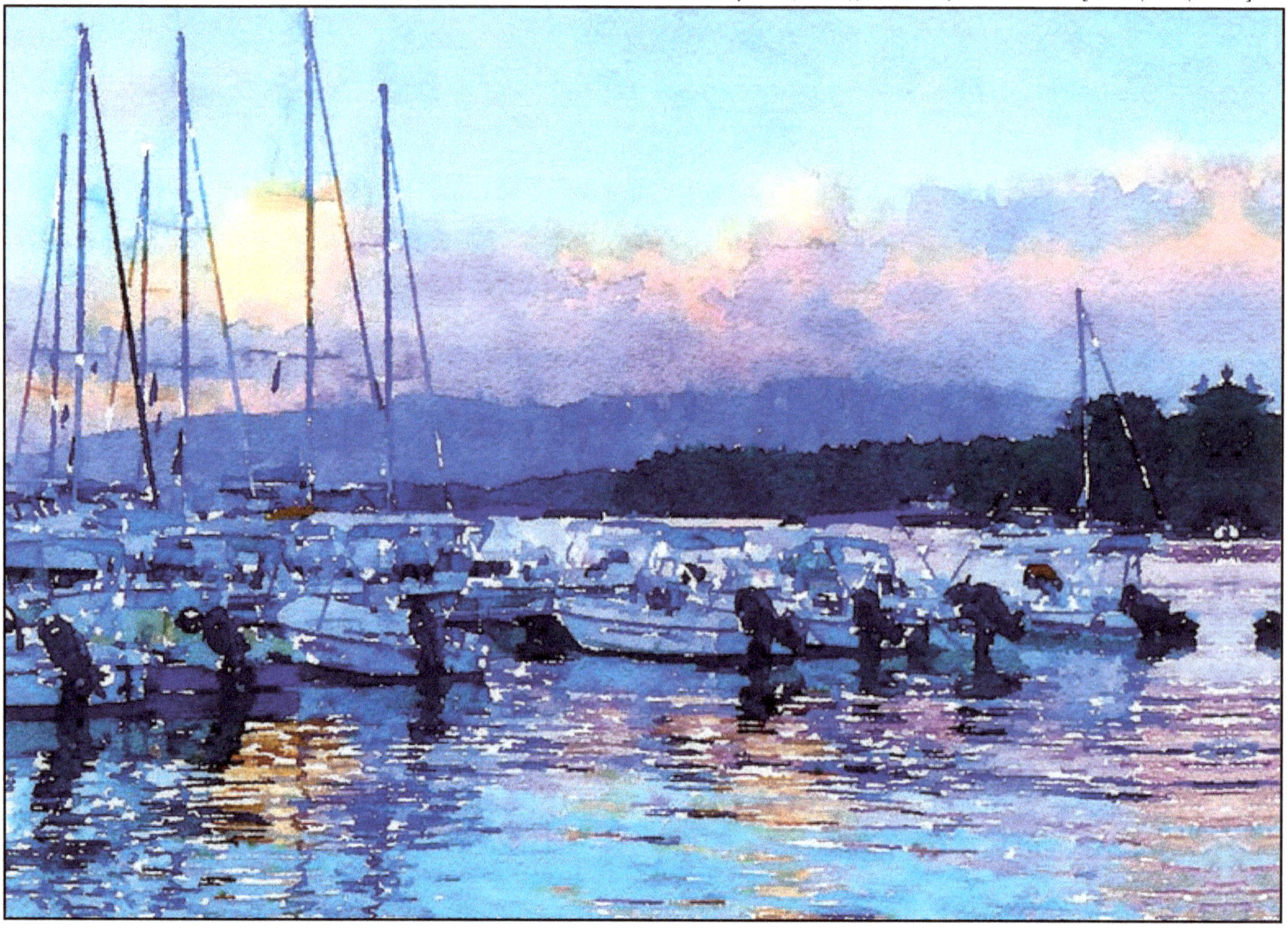

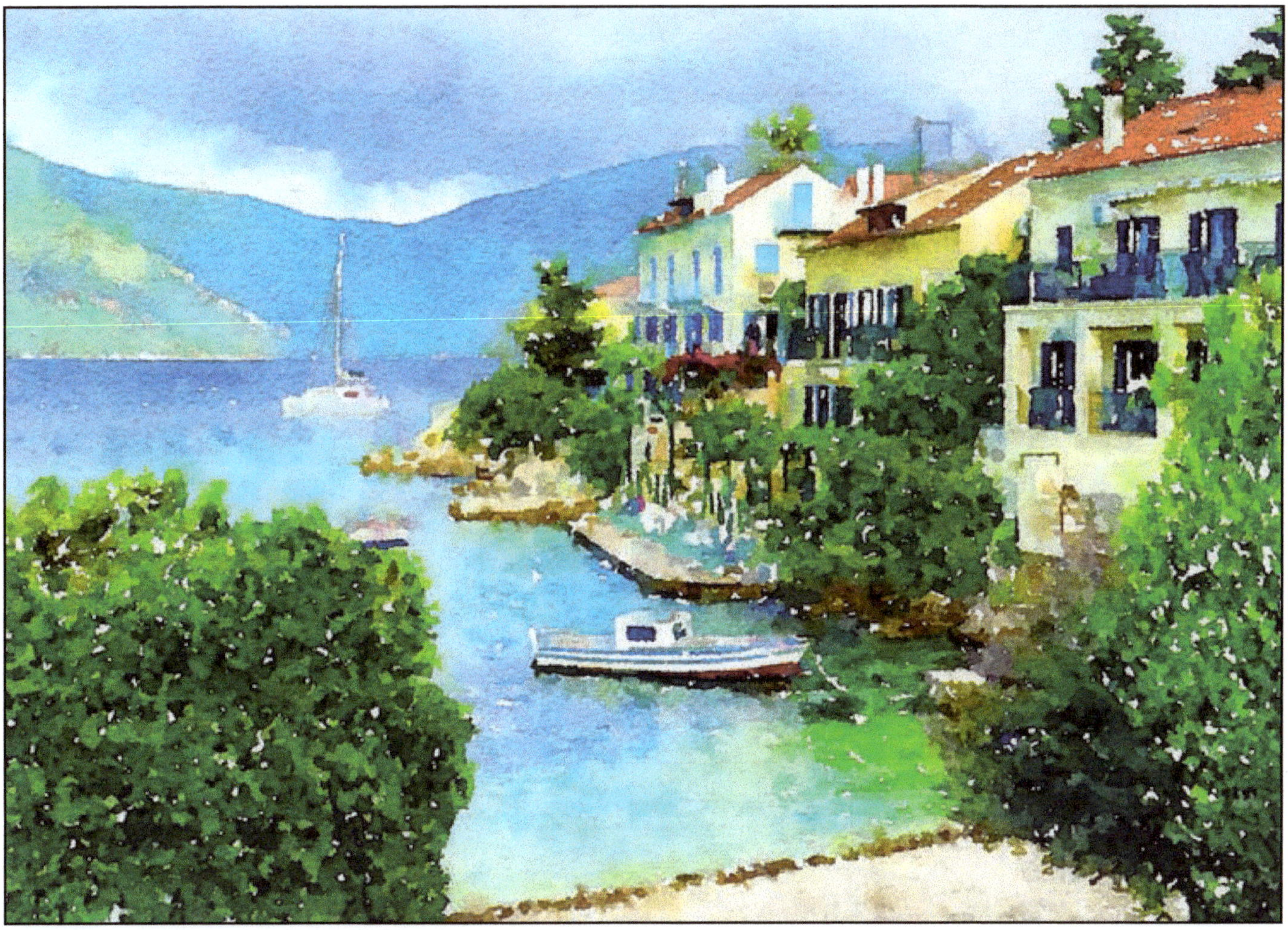

▲'The Villa's Of Fiskardo' (2018), Kefalonia, Greece [EGR(NW)1805].

'Foki Beach, Fiskardo' (2018), Kefalonia, Greece [EGR(NW)1806].▼

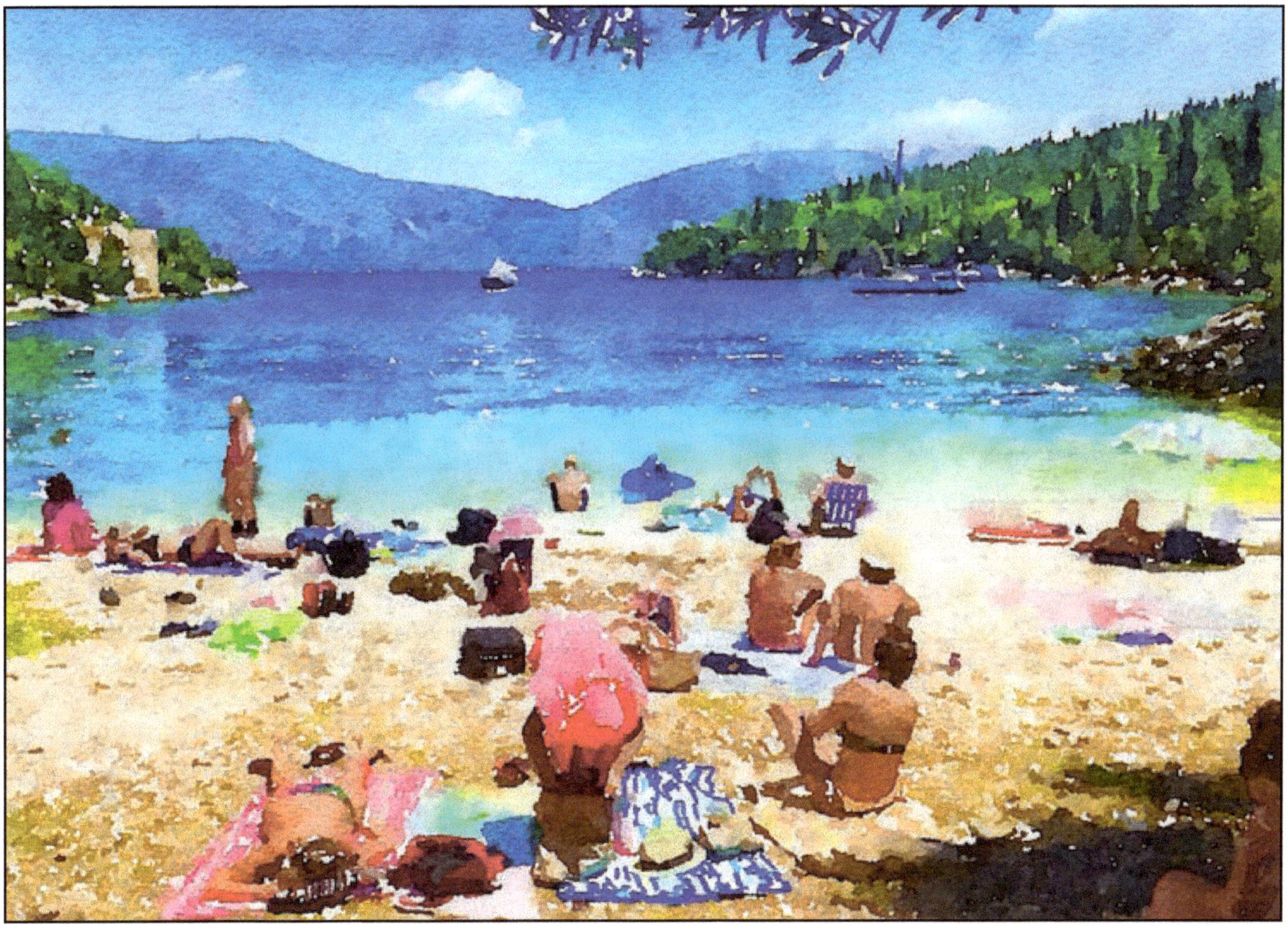

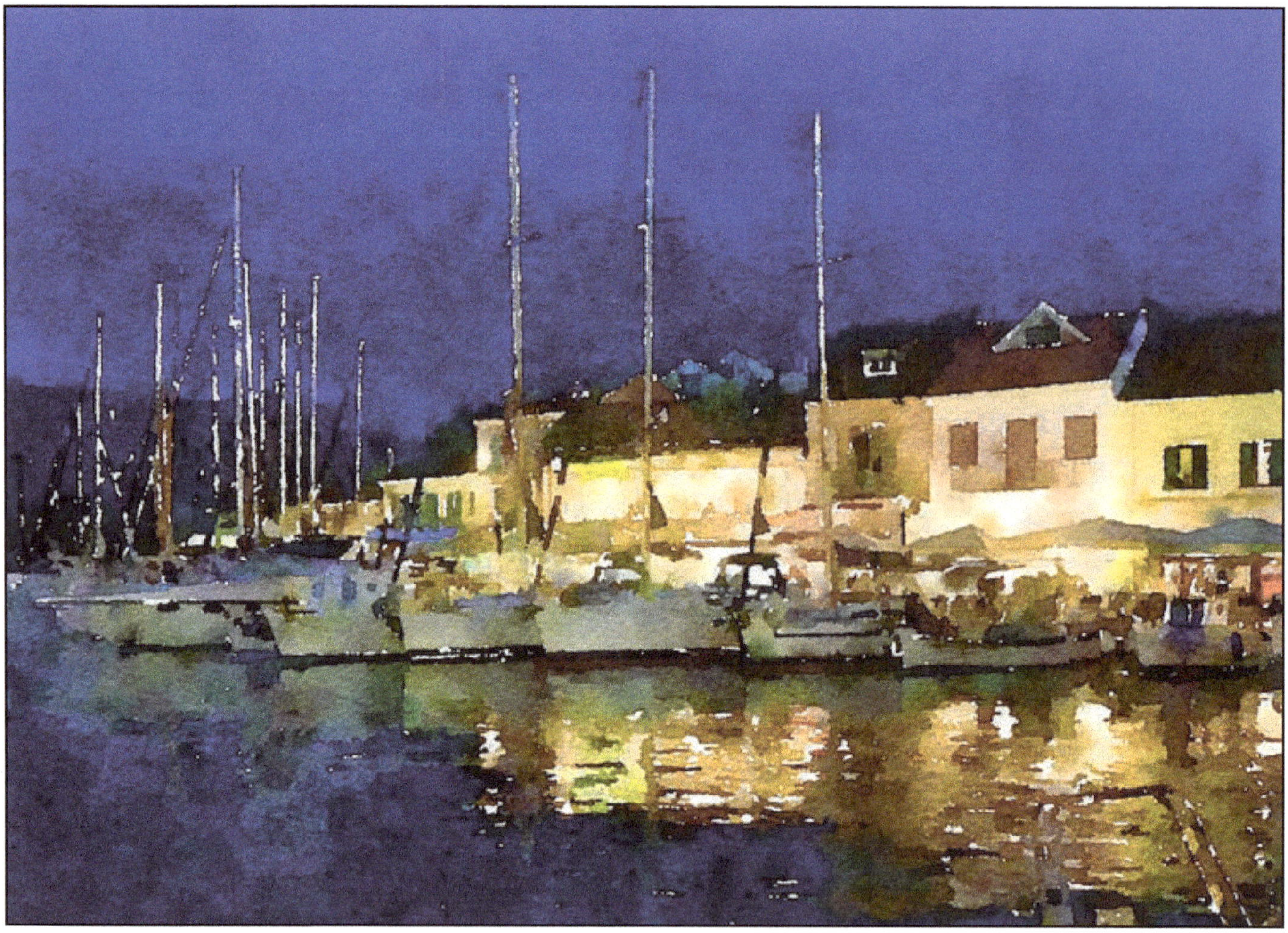

▲'Fiskardo Sailboats' (2018), Kefalonia, Greece [EGR(NW)1807].

'The Lights Of Fiskardo' (2018), Kefalonia, Greece [EGR(NW)1808].▼

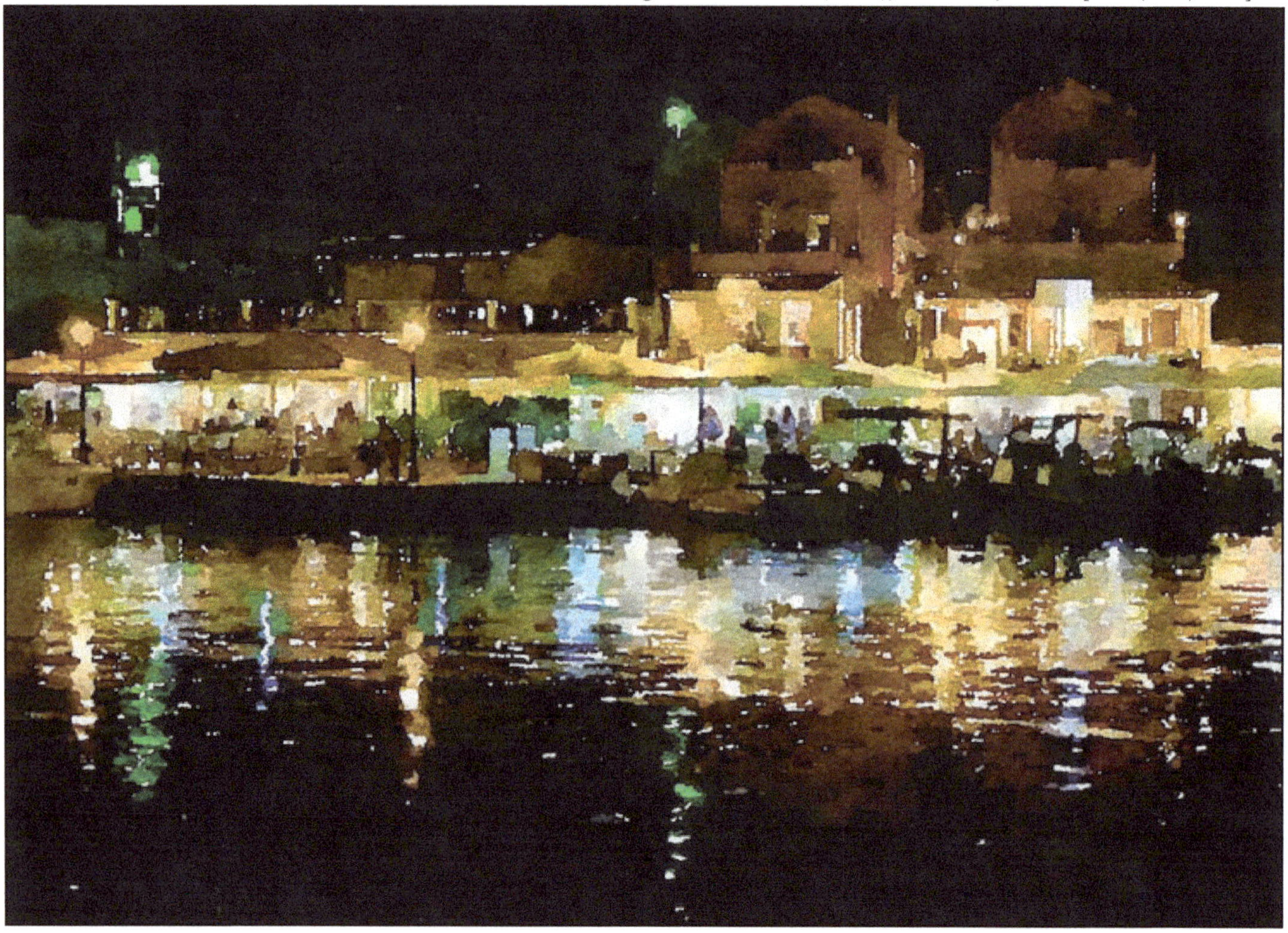

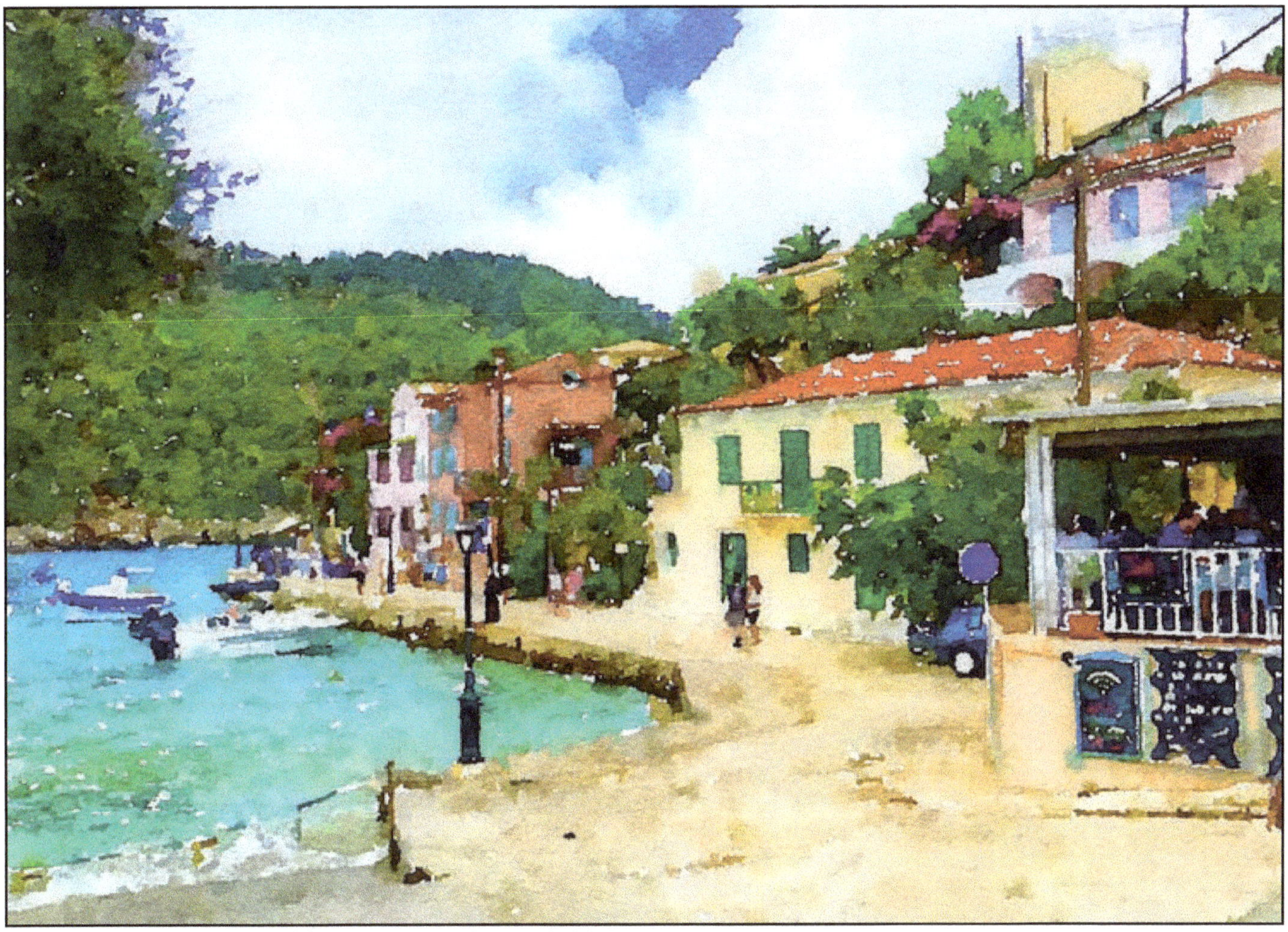

▲'Asos Harbour' (2018), Kefalonia, Greece [EGR(NW)1809].

'Myrtos Beach' (2018), Kefalonia, Greece [EGR(NW)1810].▼

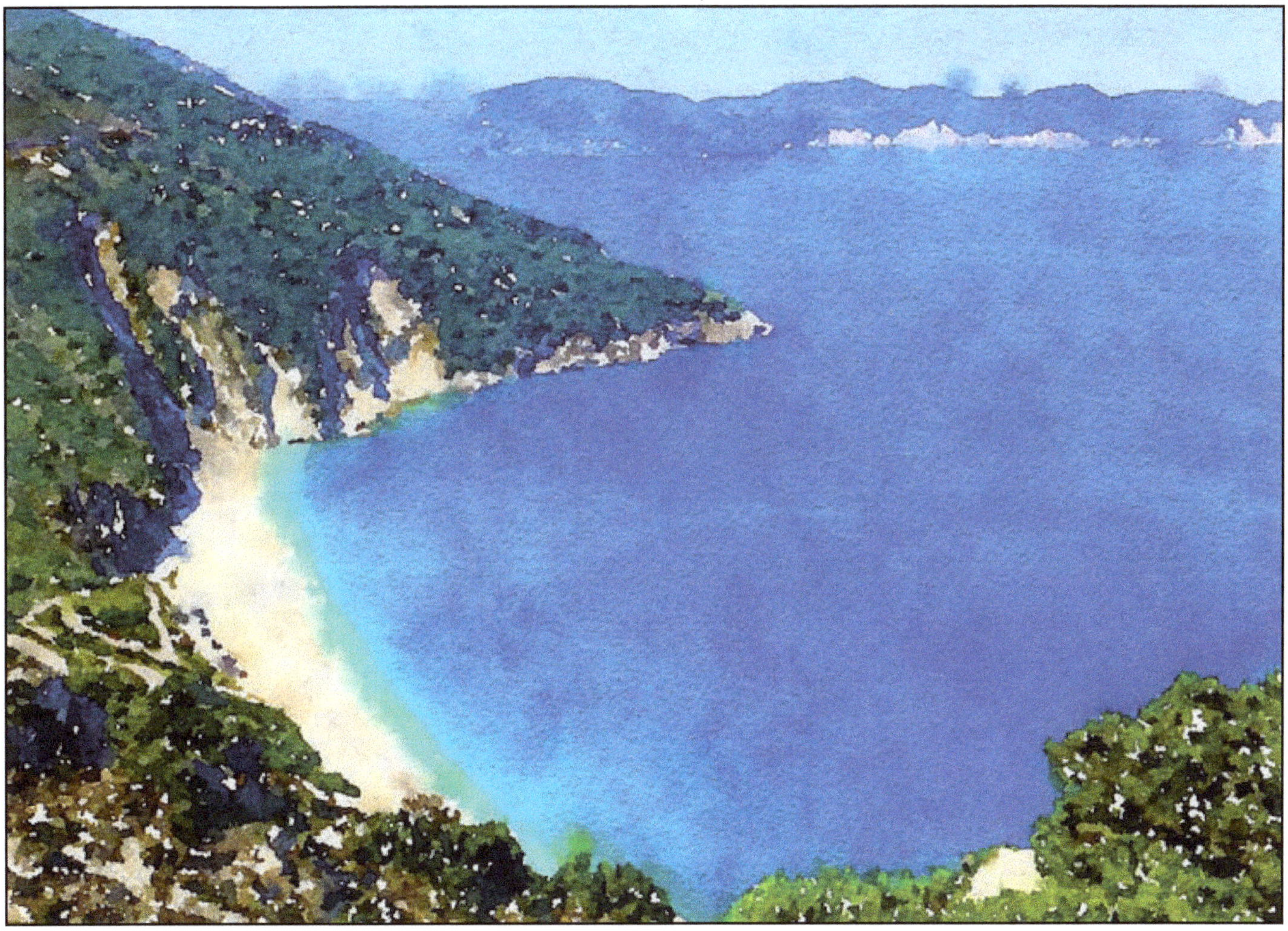

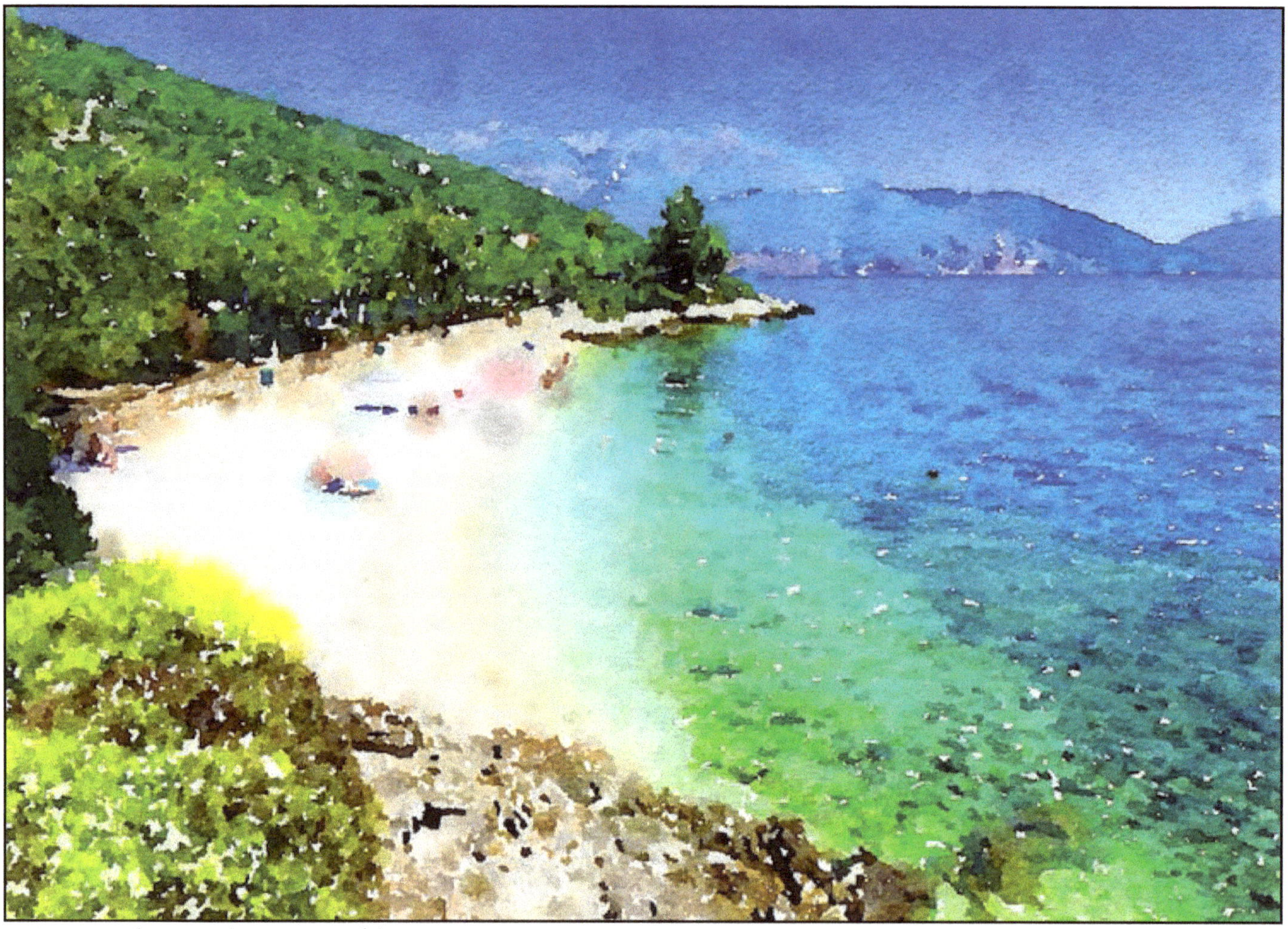

▲'Agia Paraskevi Beach' (2018), Kefalonia, Greece [EGR(NW)1811].

'Moorings At Gargalianoi' (2018), Peloponnese, Greece [EGR(PE)1801].▼

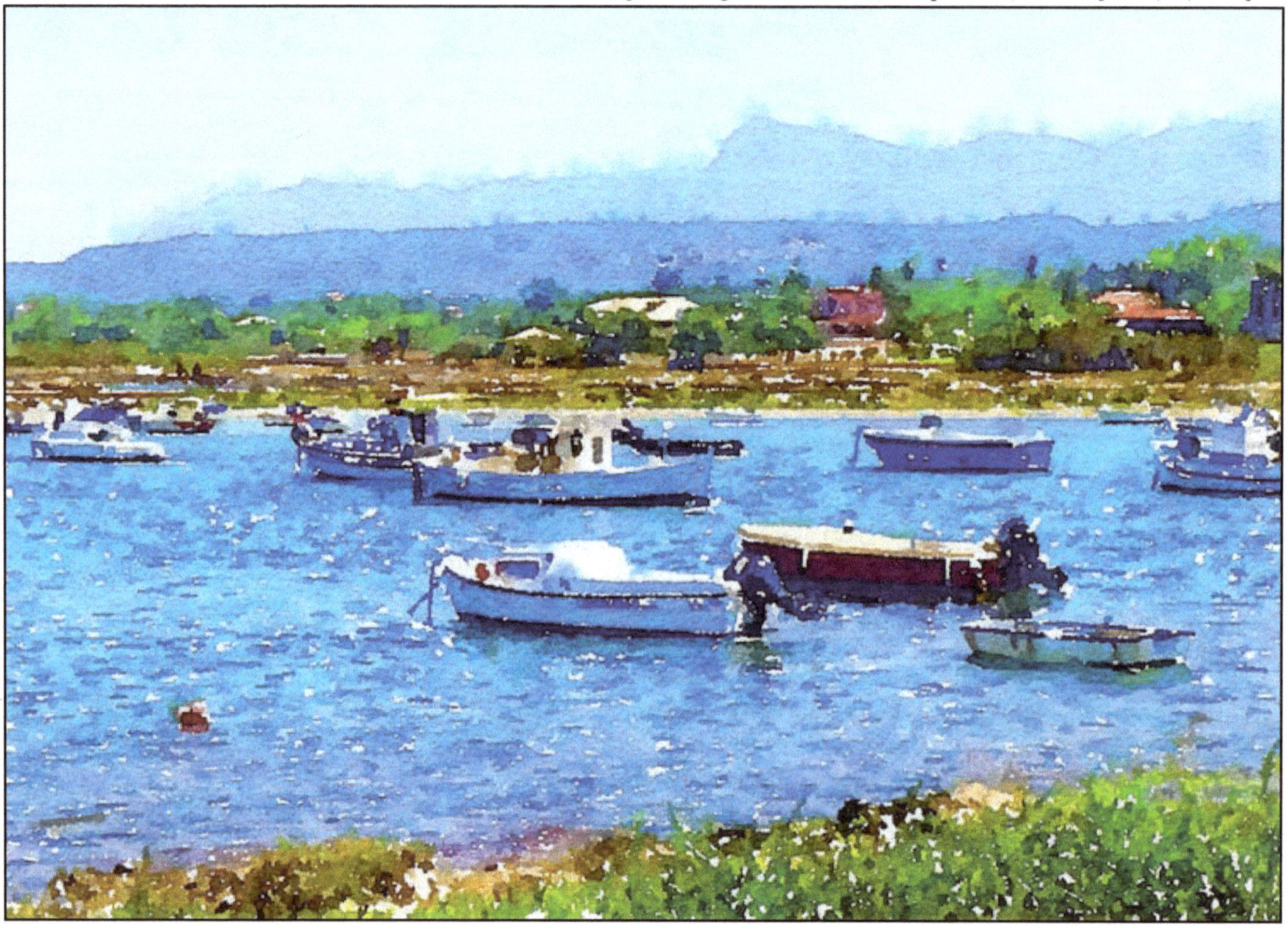

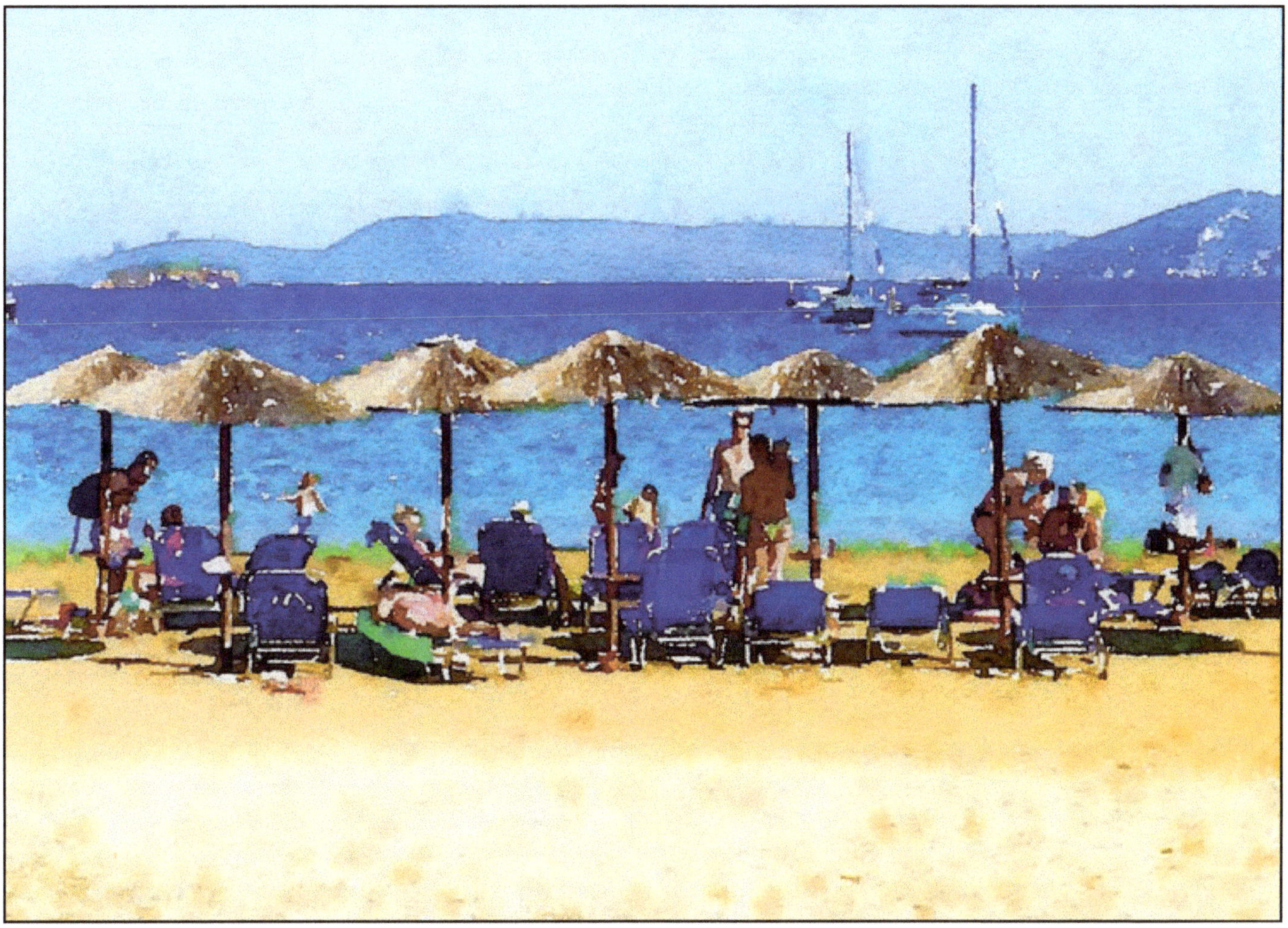

▲'Paralia Methonis' (2018), Peloponnese, Greece [EGR(PE)1802].

'Cretan Beach, Methoni' (2018), Peloponnese, Greece [EGR(PE)1803].▼

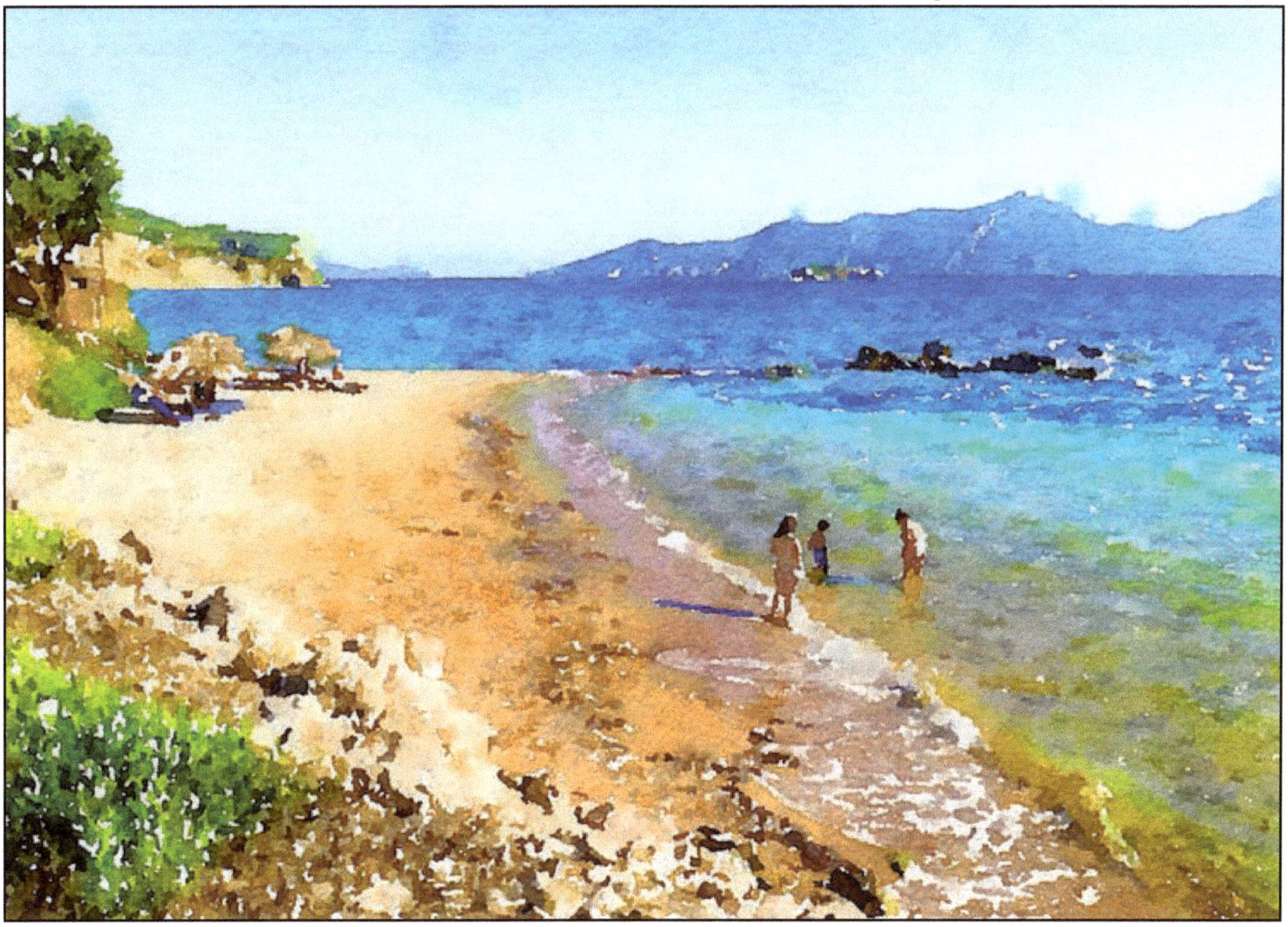

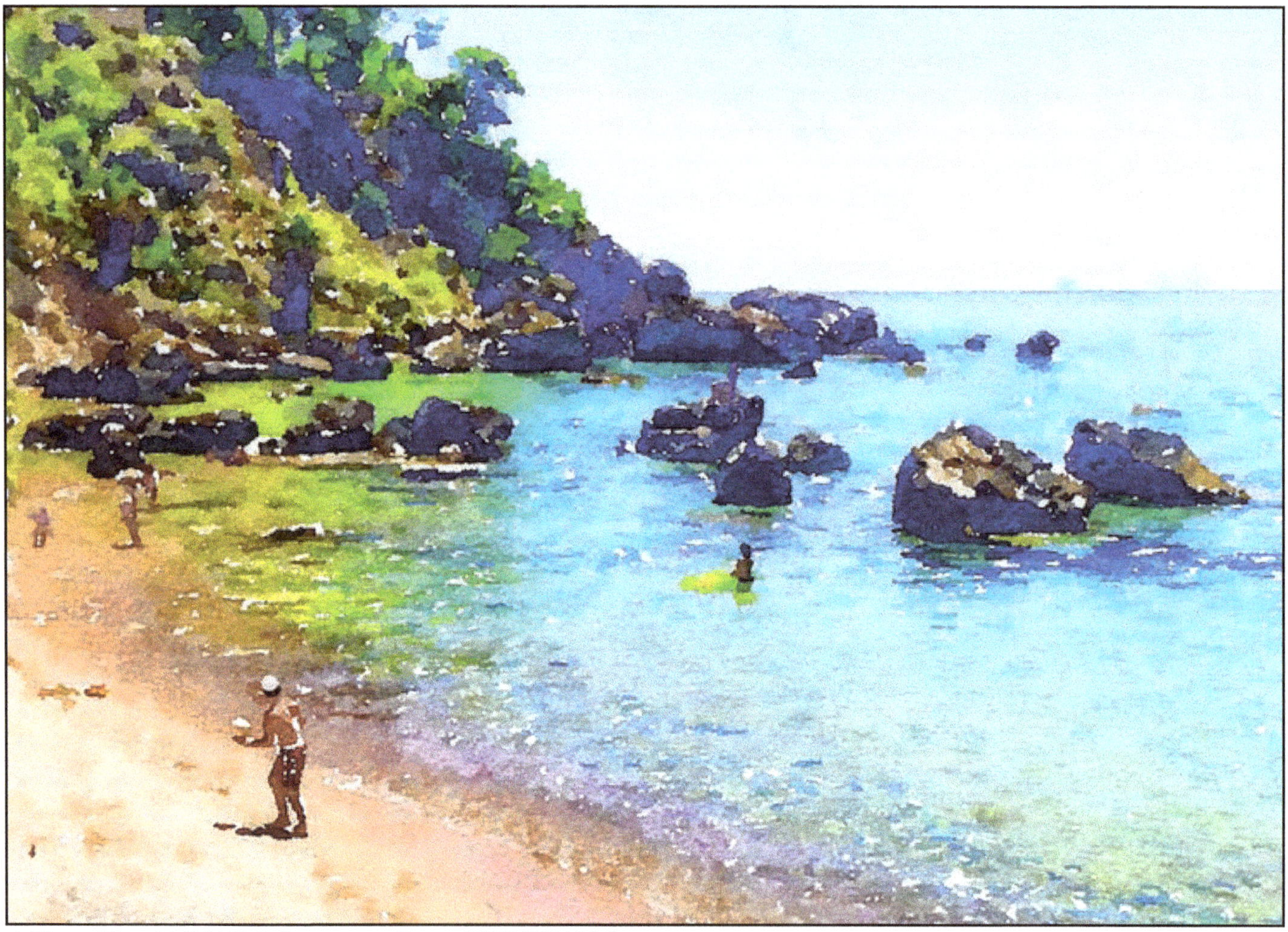

▲'Koroni Beach' (2018), Peloponnese, Greece [EGR(PE)1805].

'Cafe At Koroni ' (2018), Peloponnese, Greece [EGR(PE)1804].▼

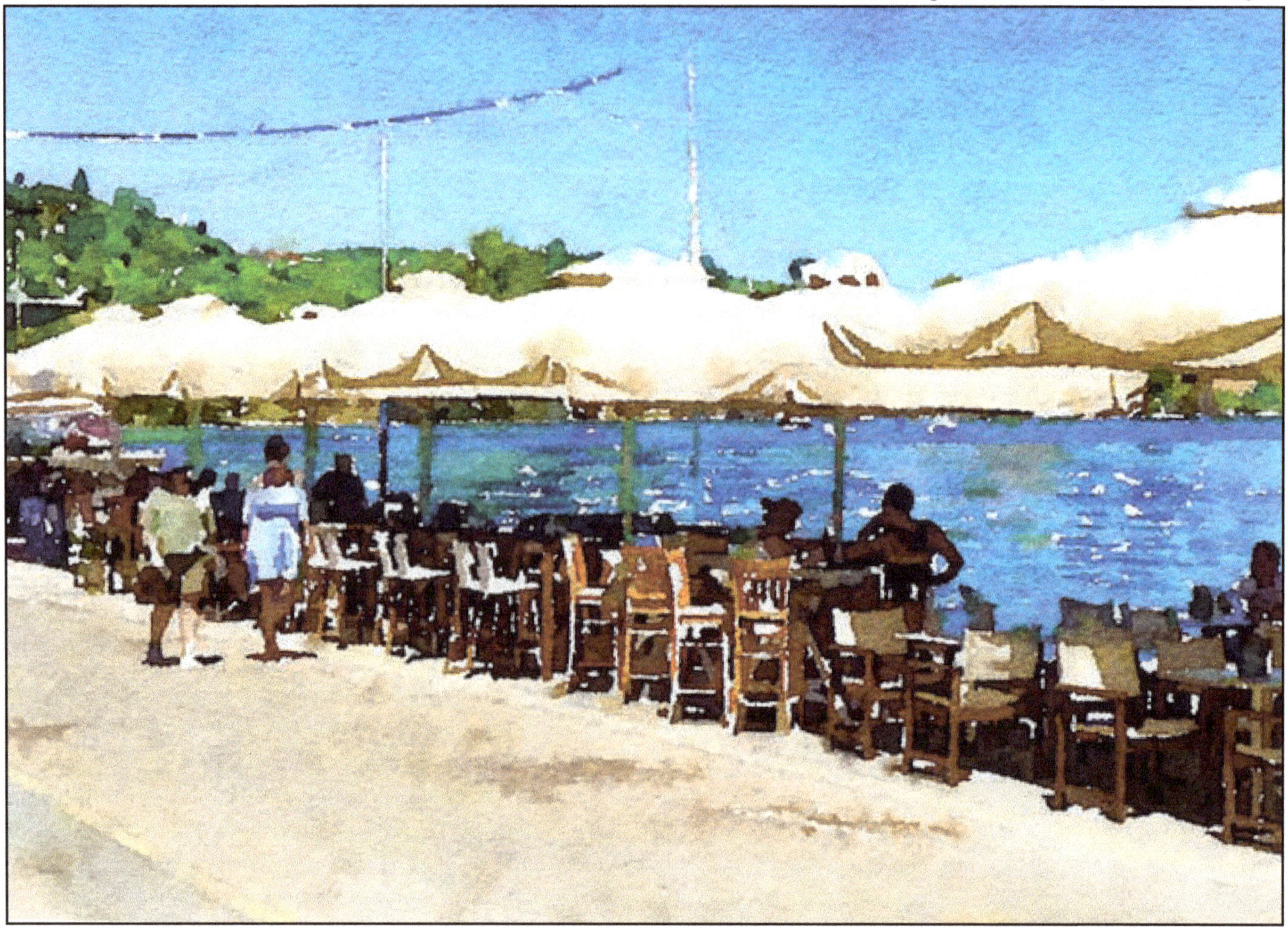

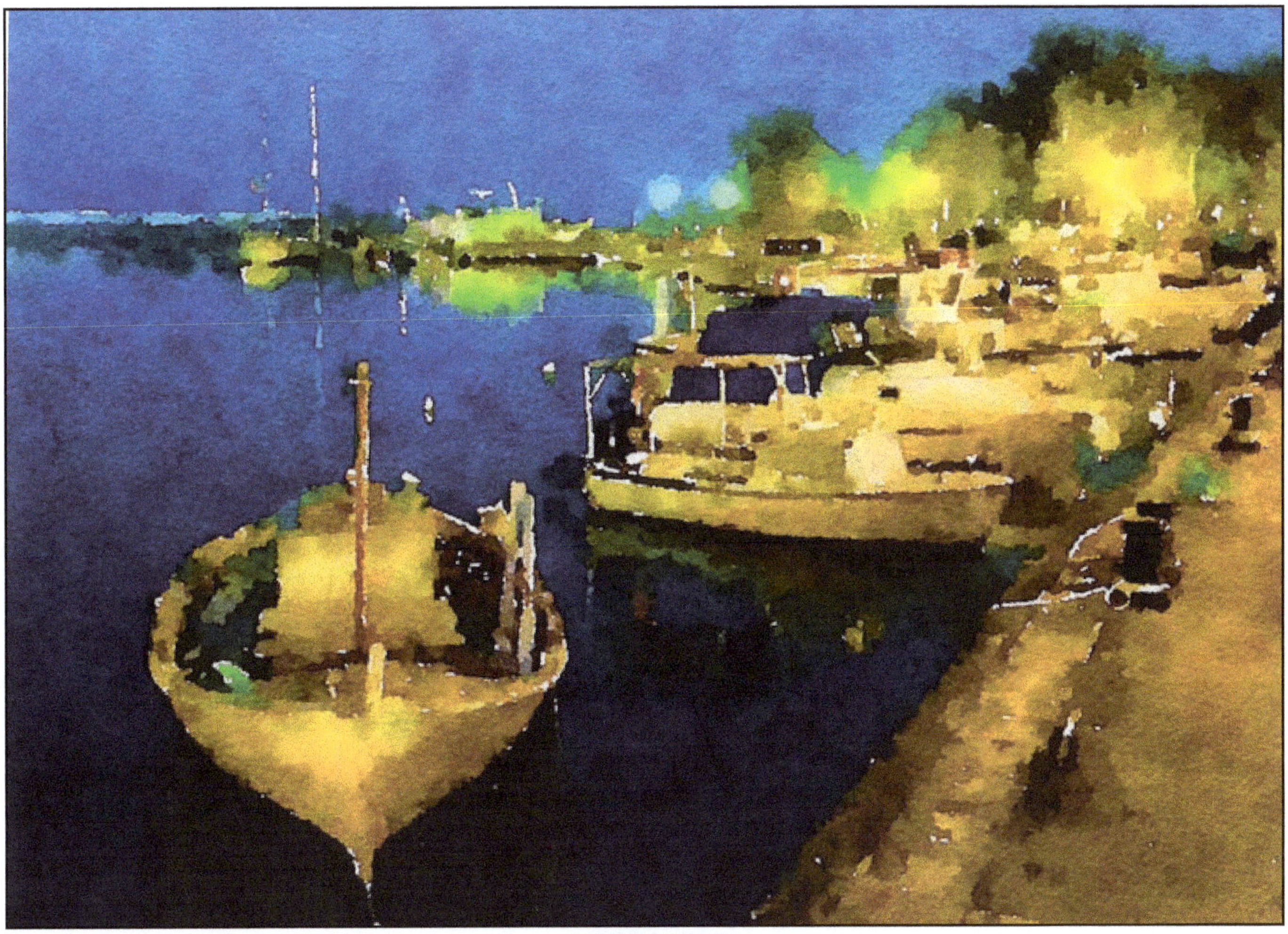

▲ 'Agios Andreas Harbour' (2018), Peloponnese, Greece [EGR(PE)1806].

'Longa Beach' (2018), Peloponnese, Greece [EGR(PE)1807].▼

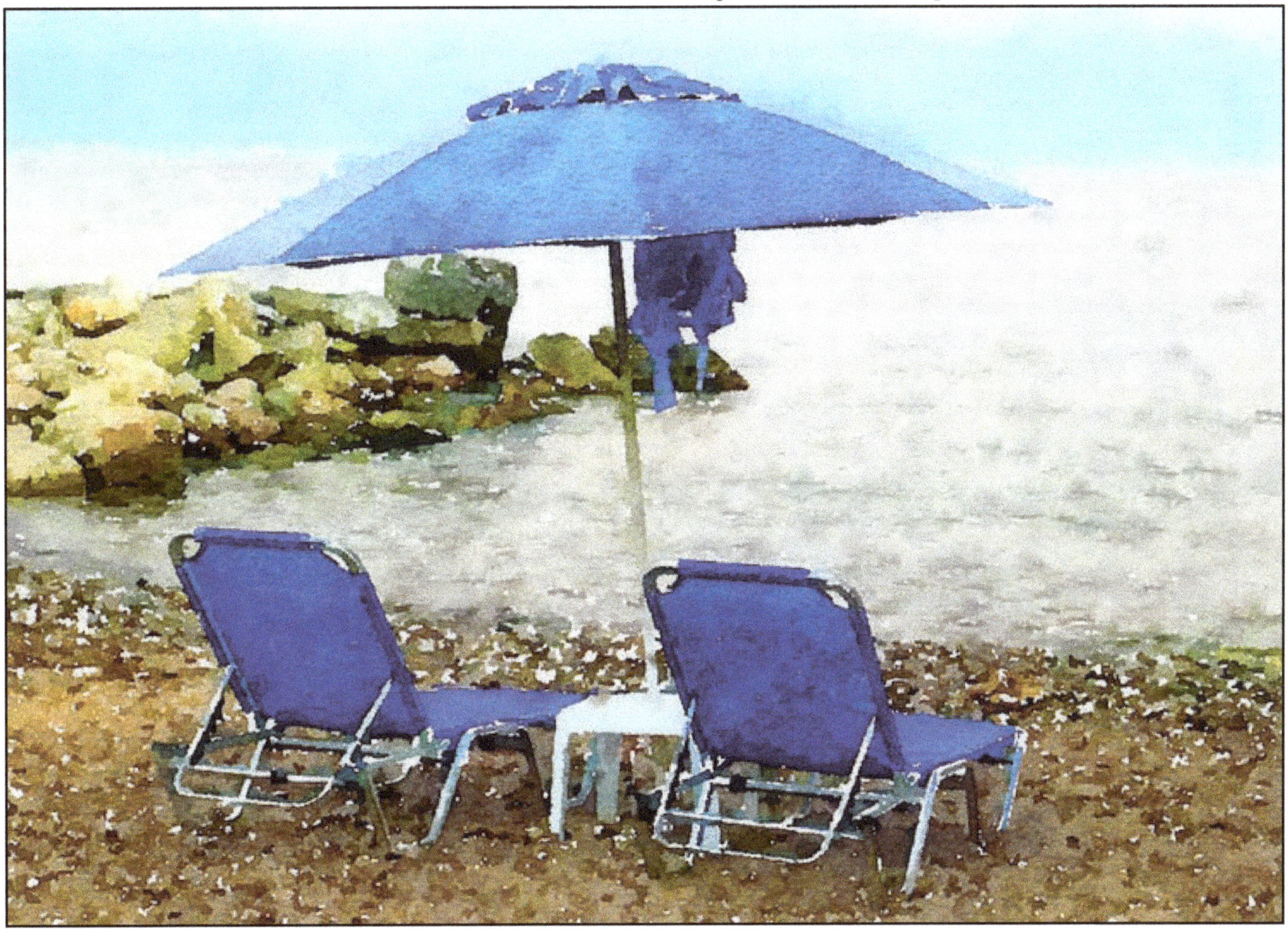

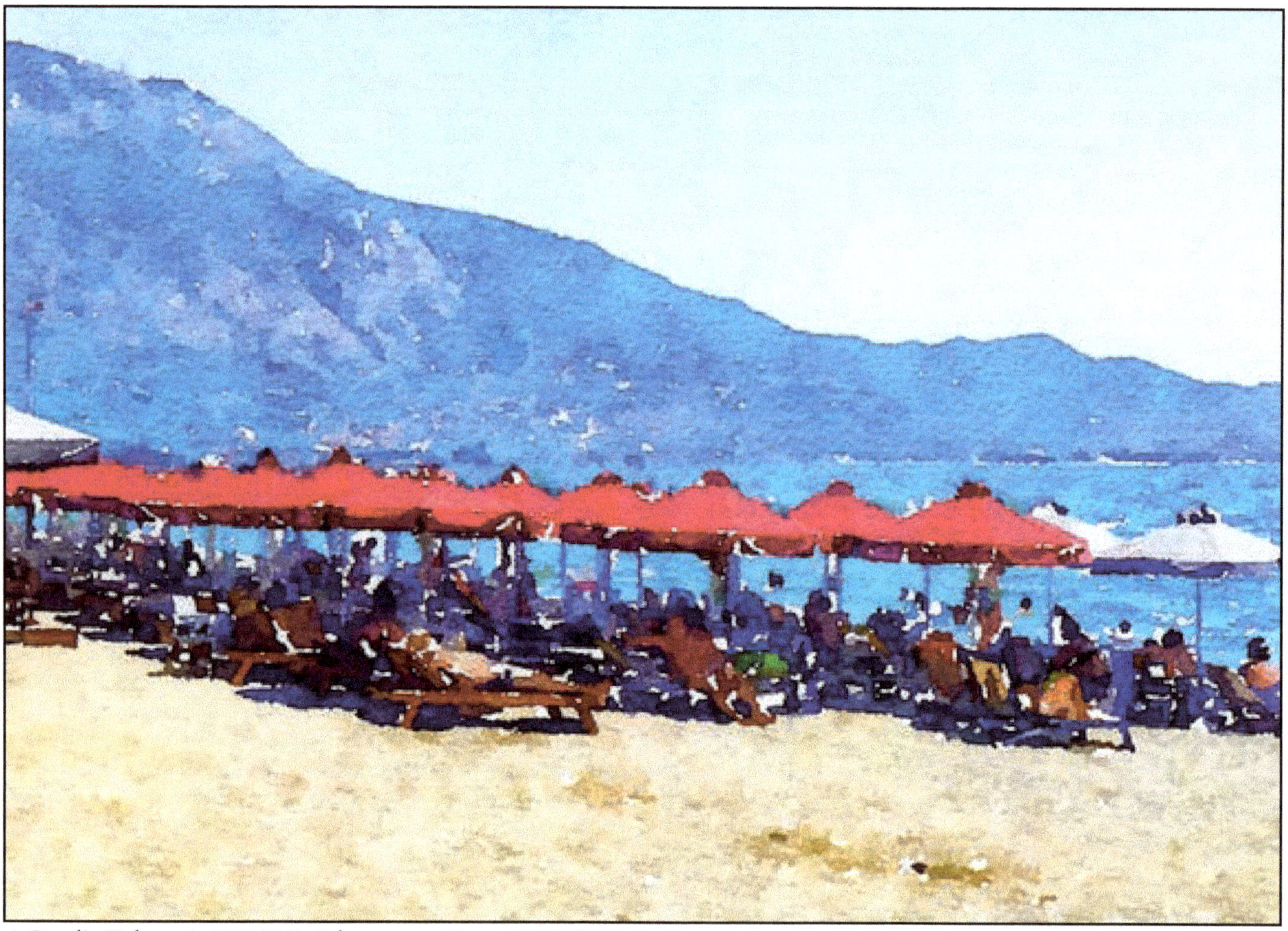

▲'Paralia Kalamatis 1' (2018), Peloponnese, Greece [EGR(PE)1808].

'Paralia Kalamatis 2' (2018), Peloponnese, Greece [EGR(PE)1809].▼

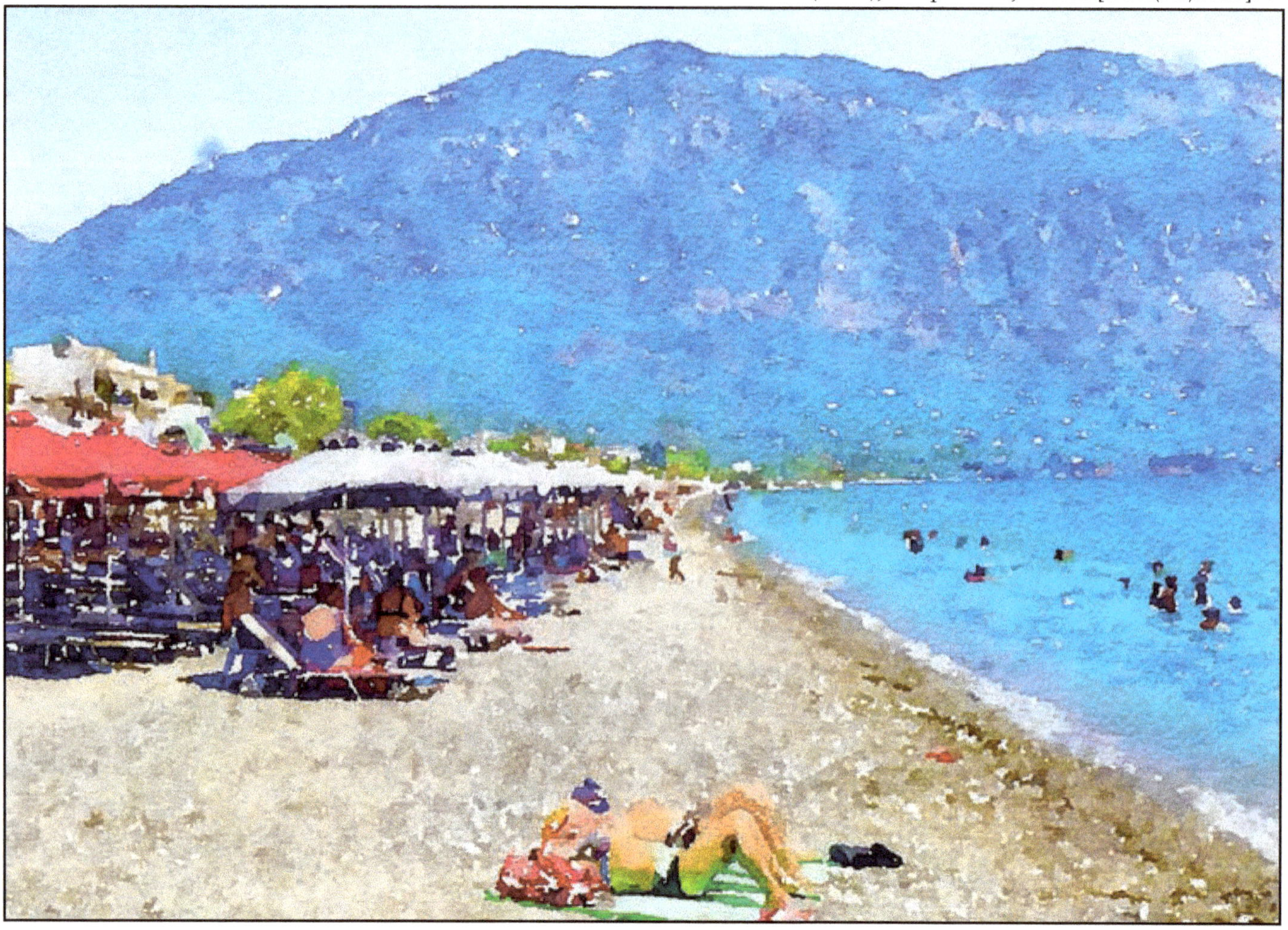

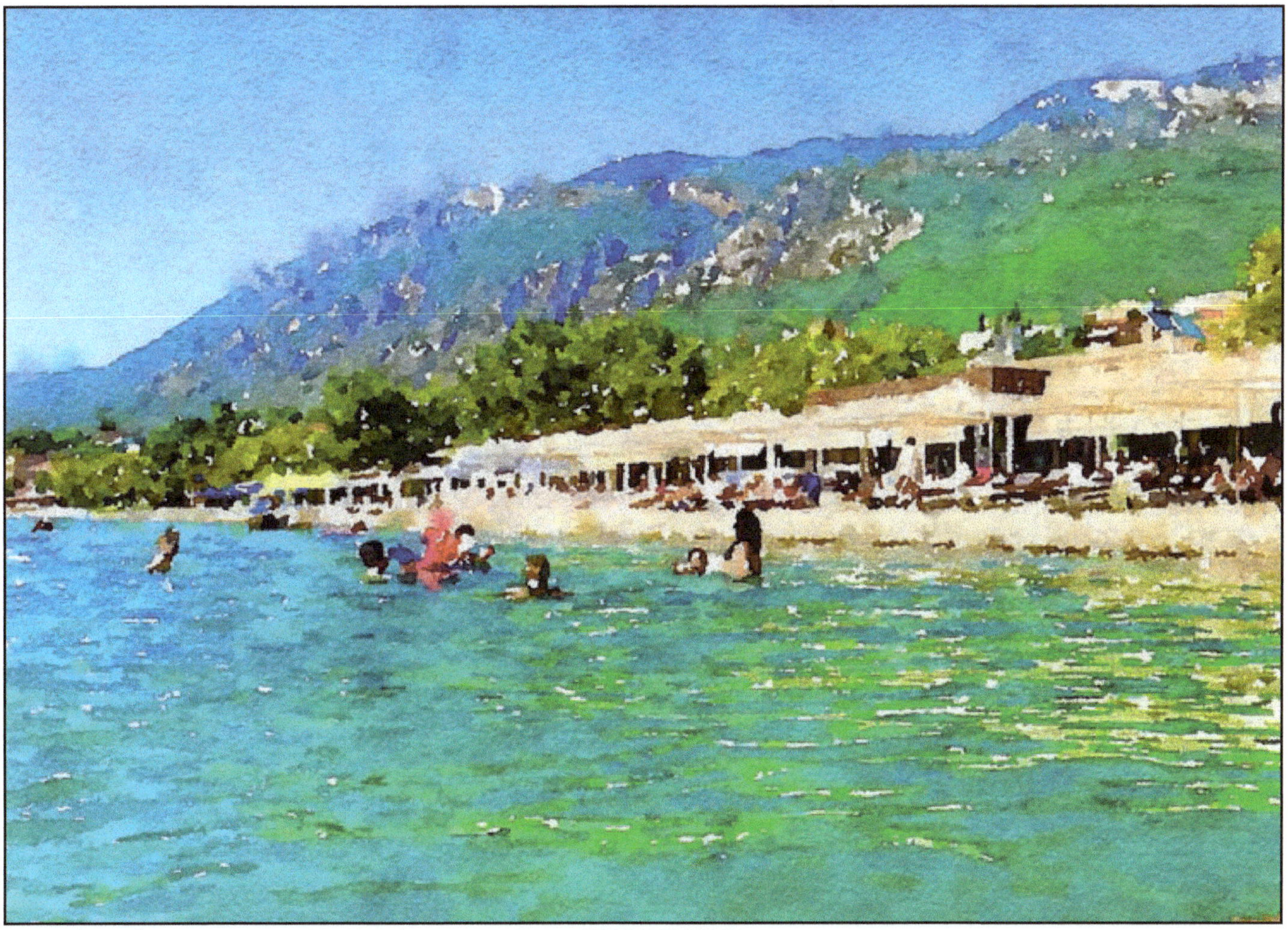

▲'Paralia Mikri Mantinea 1' (2018), Peloponnese, Greece [EGR(PE)1810].

'Paralia Mikri Mantinea 2' (2018), Peloponnese, Greece [EGR(PE)1811].▼

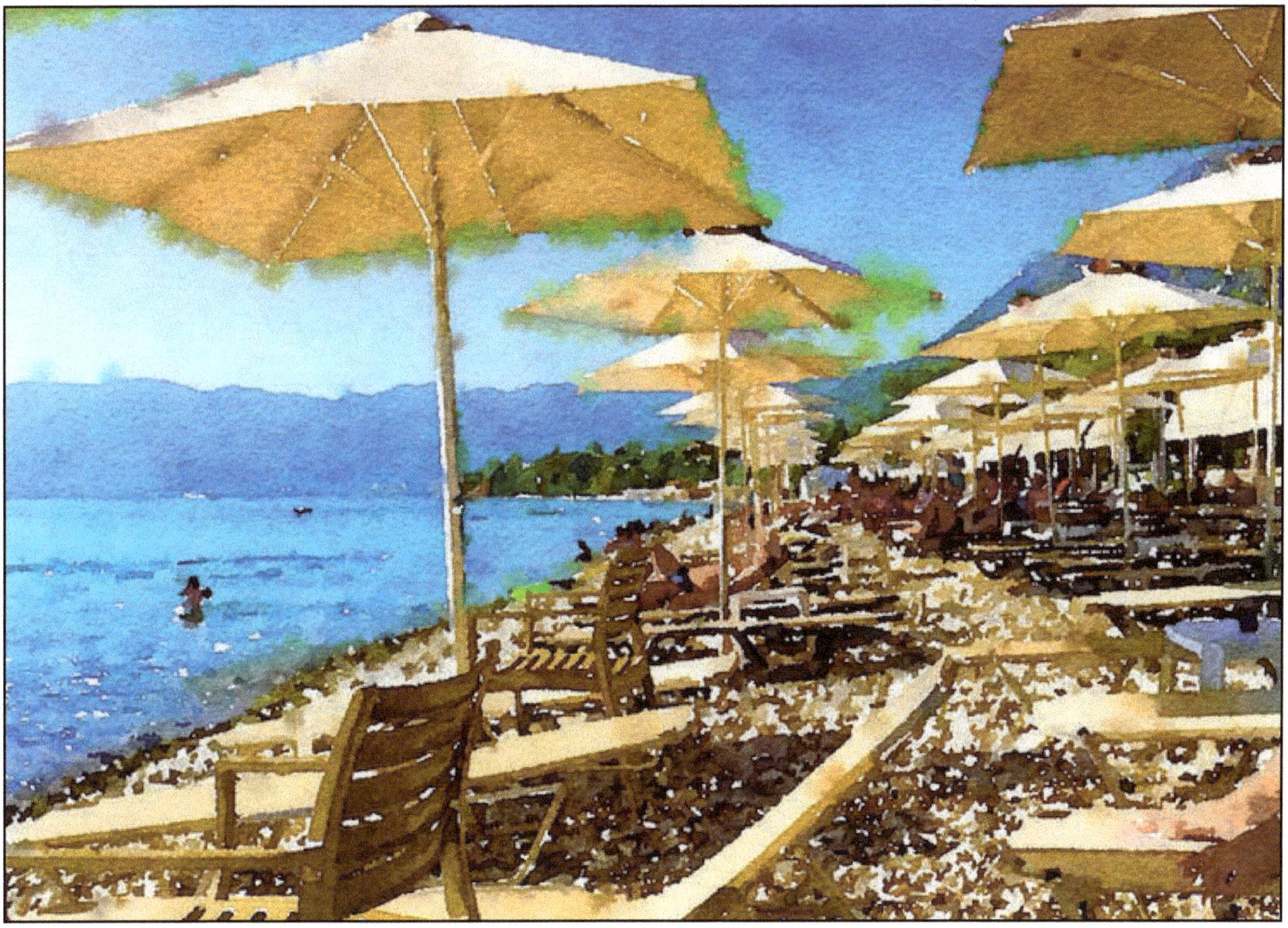

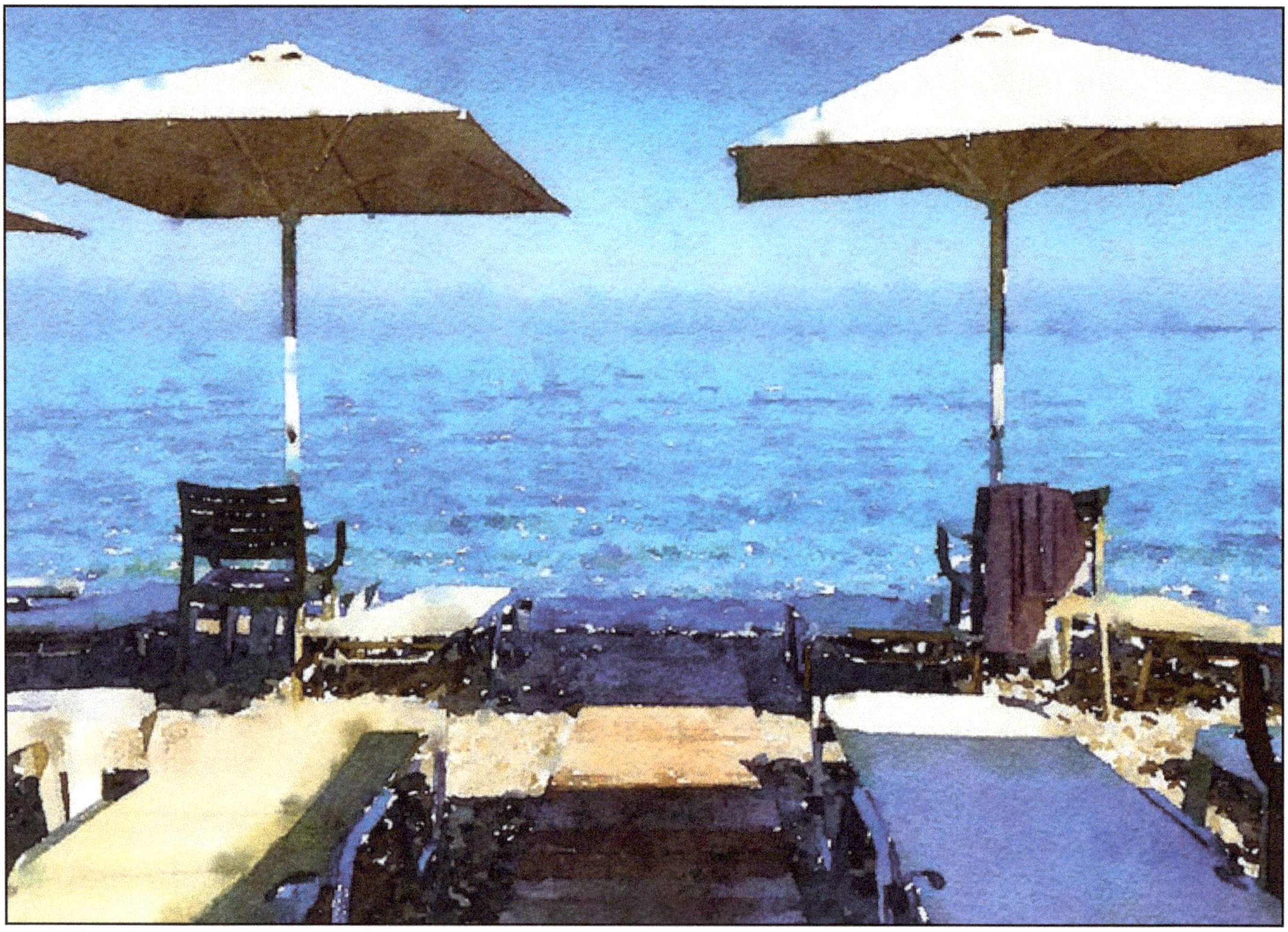

▲'Beach Beds, Mantinea' (2018), Peloponnese, Greece [EGR(PE)1812].

'Paralia Kardamyli' (2018), Peloponnese, Greece [EGR(PE)1813].▼

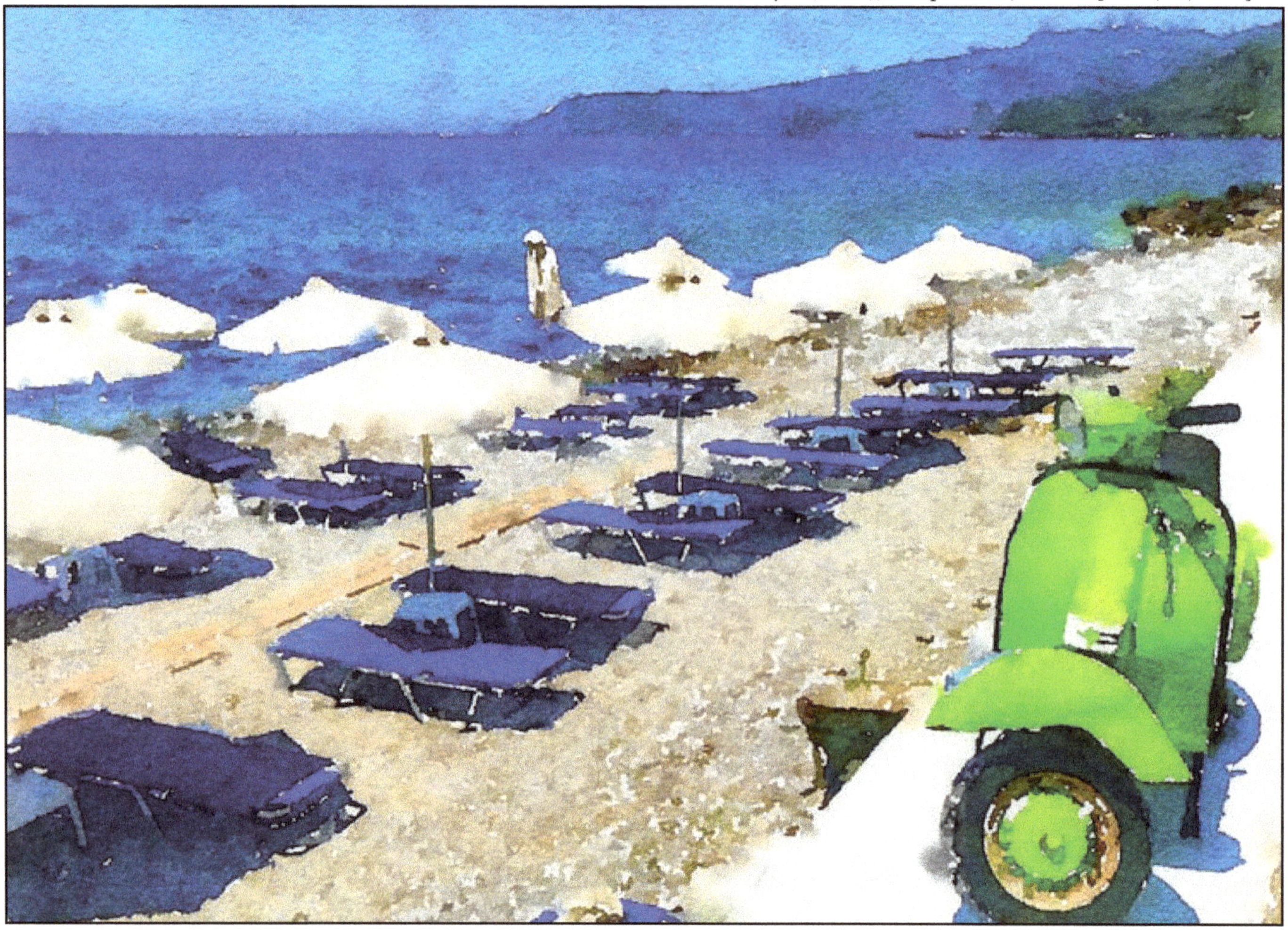

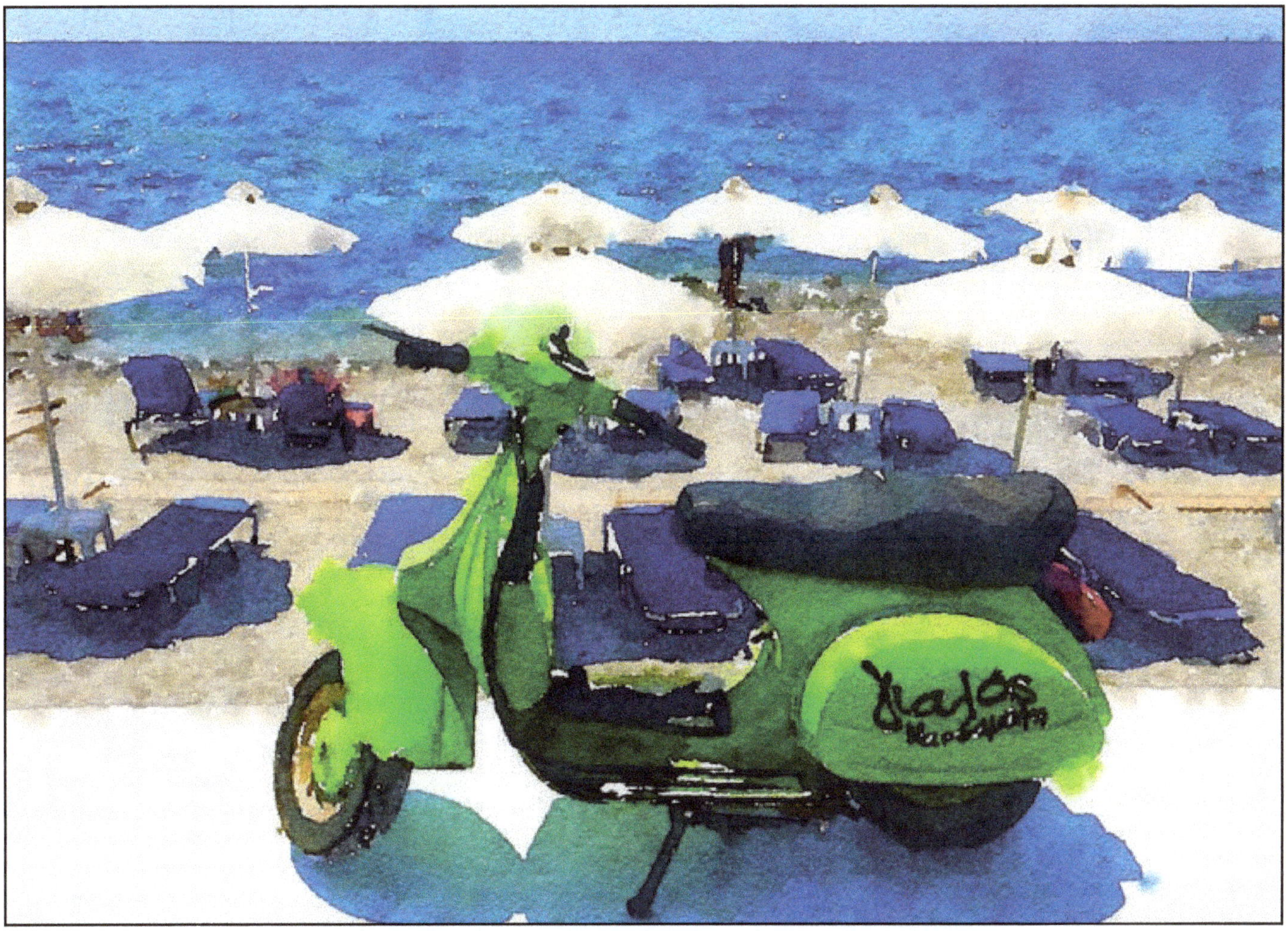

▲'Scooter At Kardamyli' (2018), Peloponnese, Greece [EGR(PE)1814].

'Foneas Beach' (2018), Mani Peninsula, Greece [EGR(PE)1815].▼

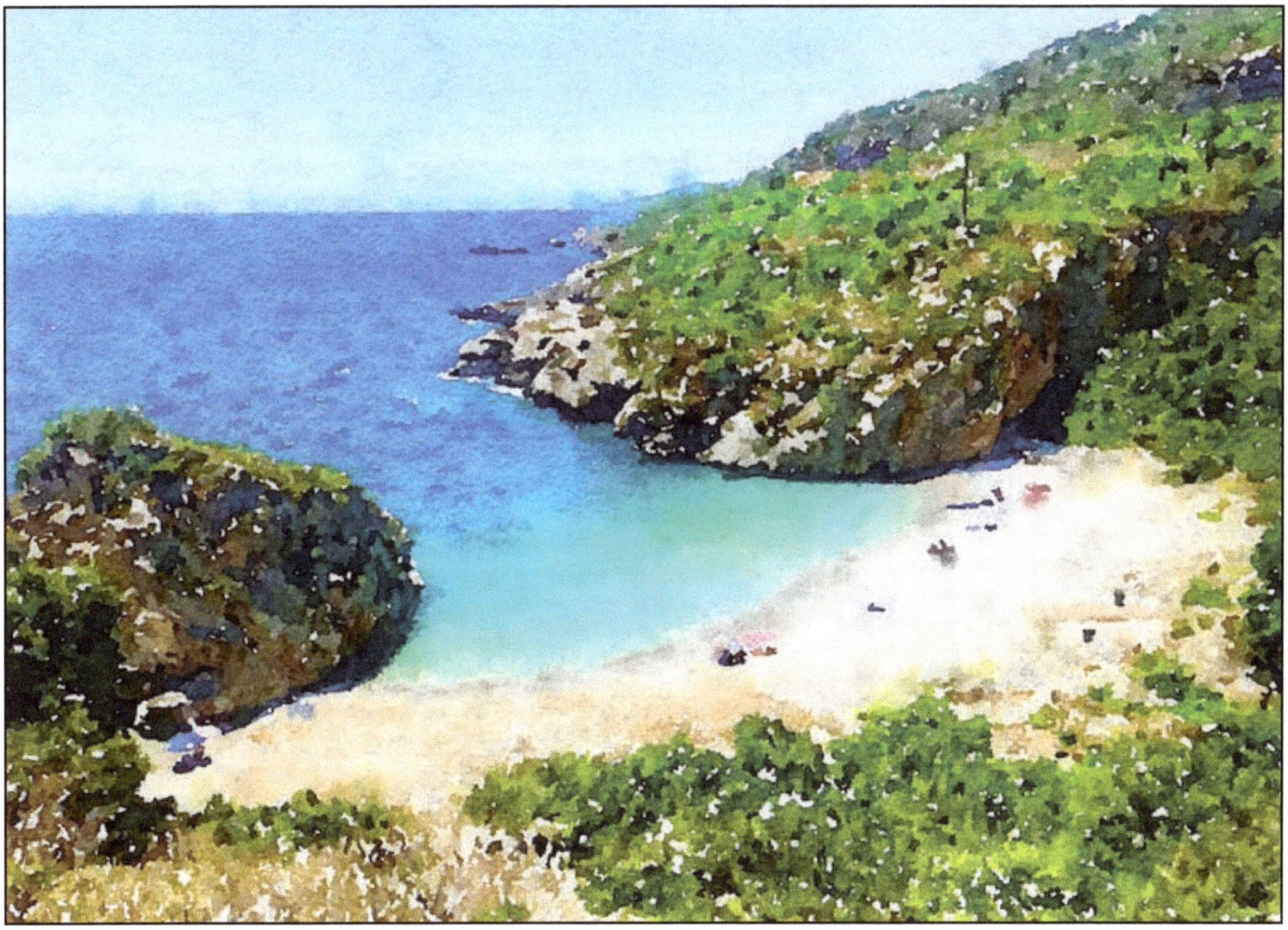

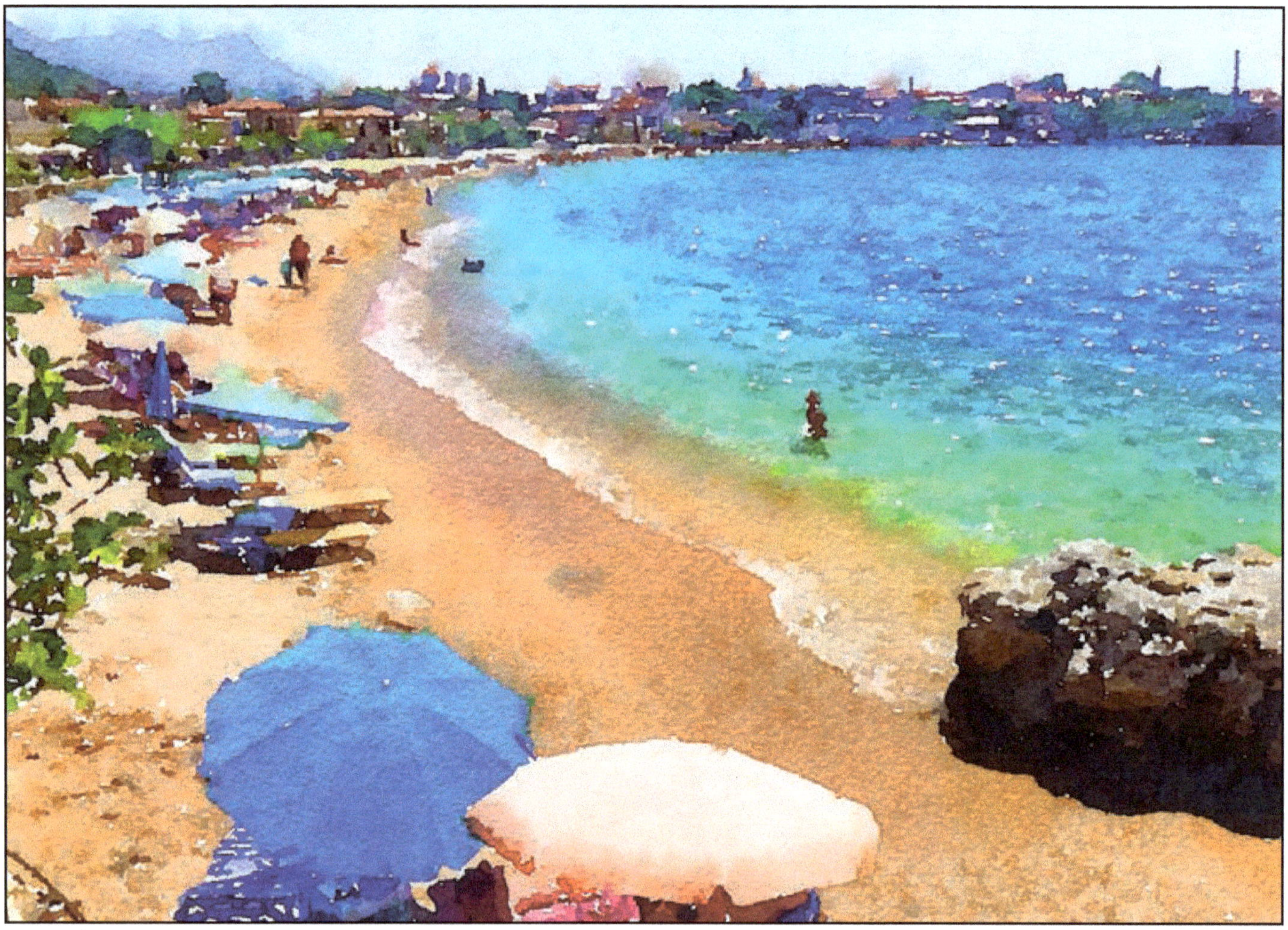

▲'Paralia Stoupa' (2018), Mani Peninsula, Greece [EGR(PE)1816].

'Paralia Itylo' (2018), Mani Peninsula, Greece [EGR(PE)1817].▼

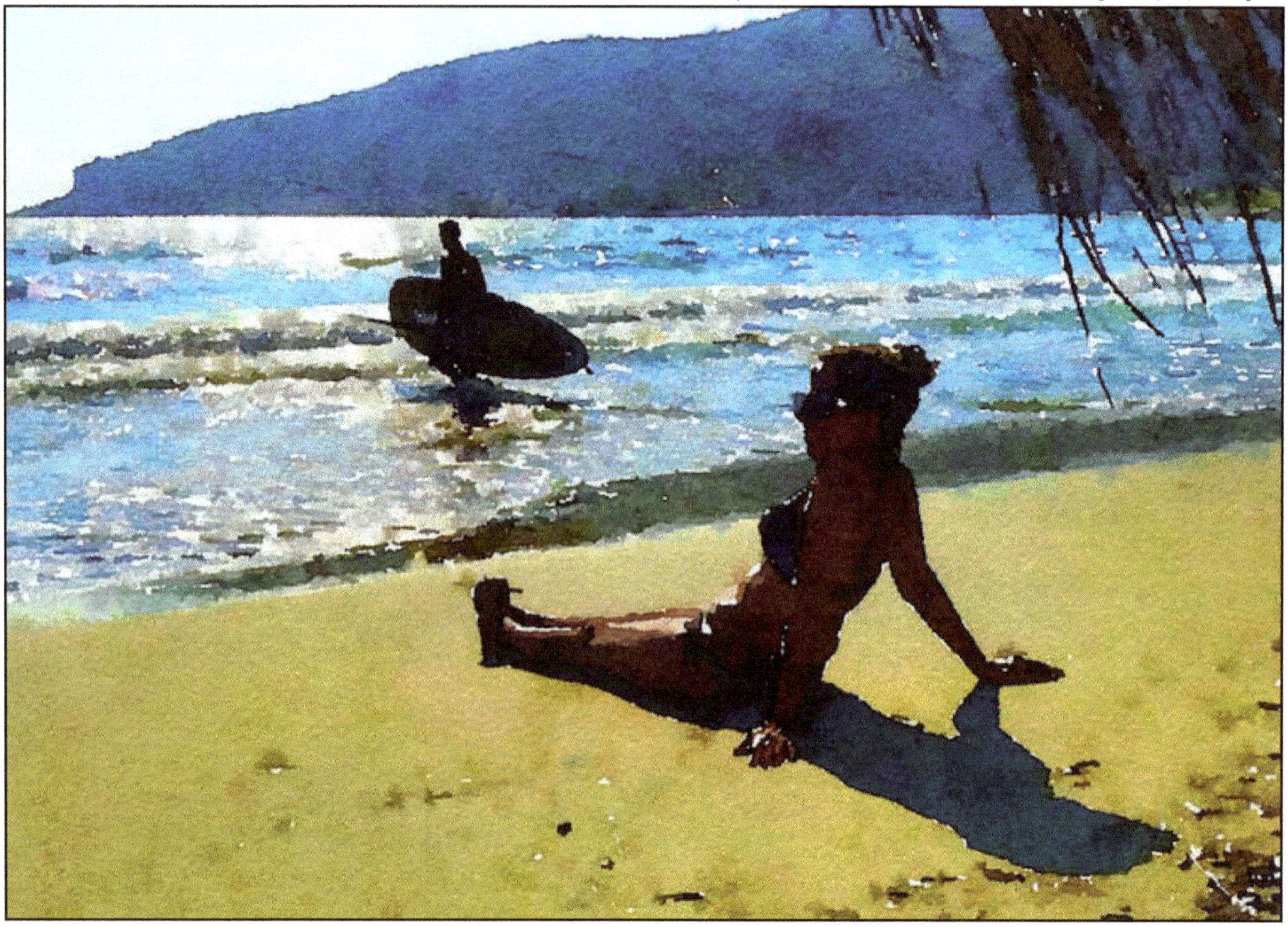

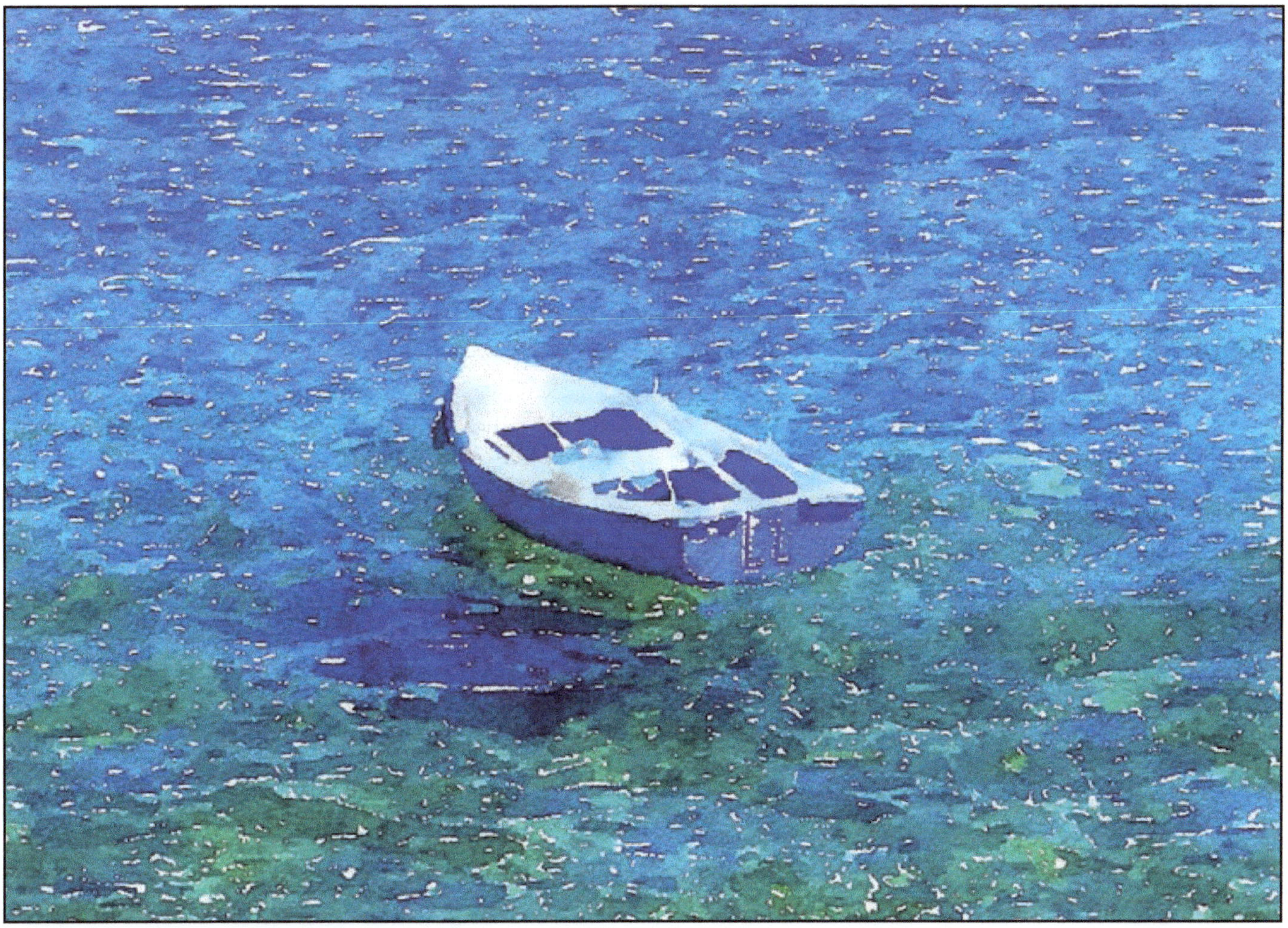

▲'Boats Of Diros' (2018), Mani Peninsula, Greece [EGR(PE)1818].

'Exo Kapoi' (2018), Mani Peninsula, Greece [EGR(PE)1819].▼

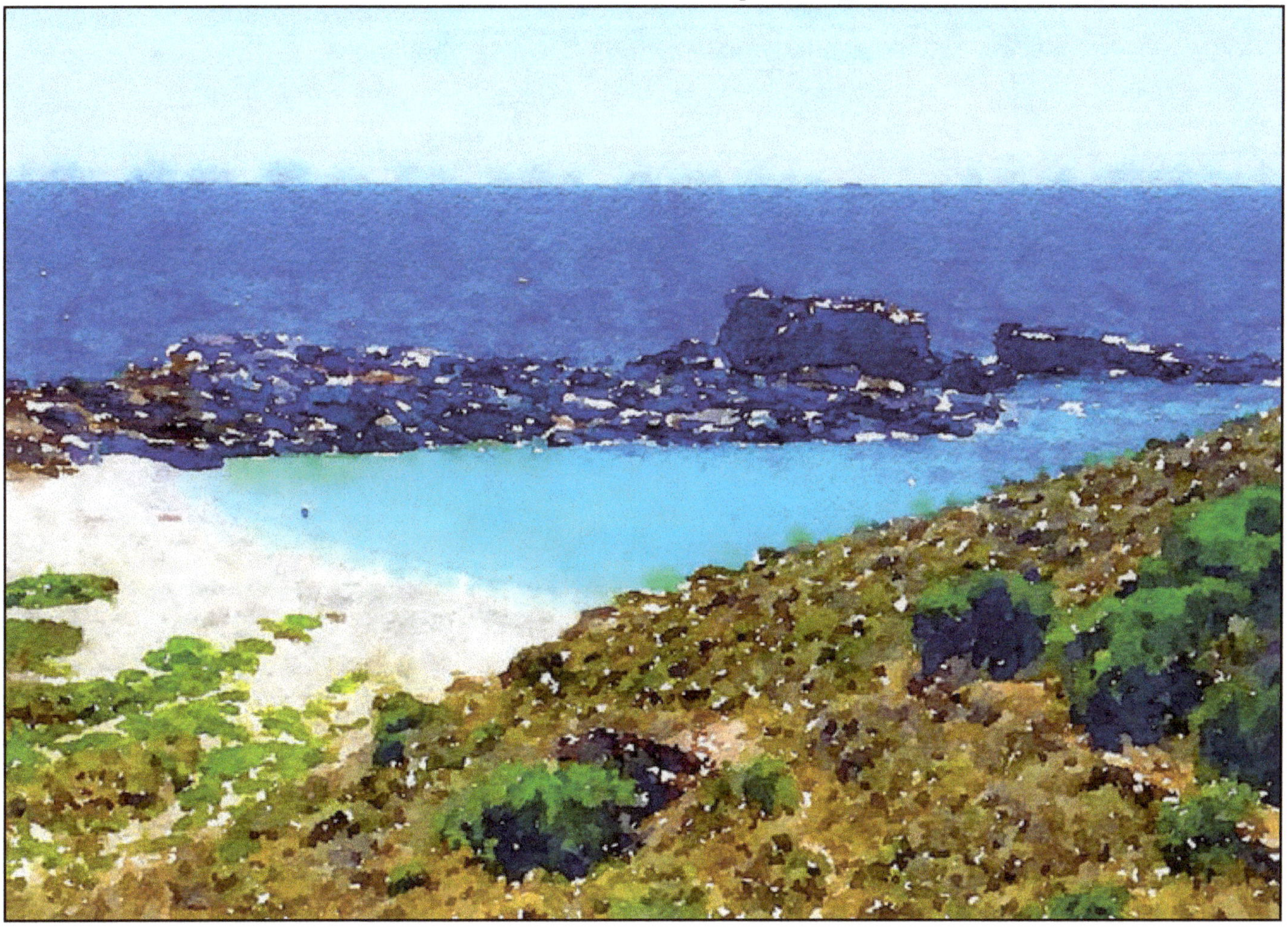

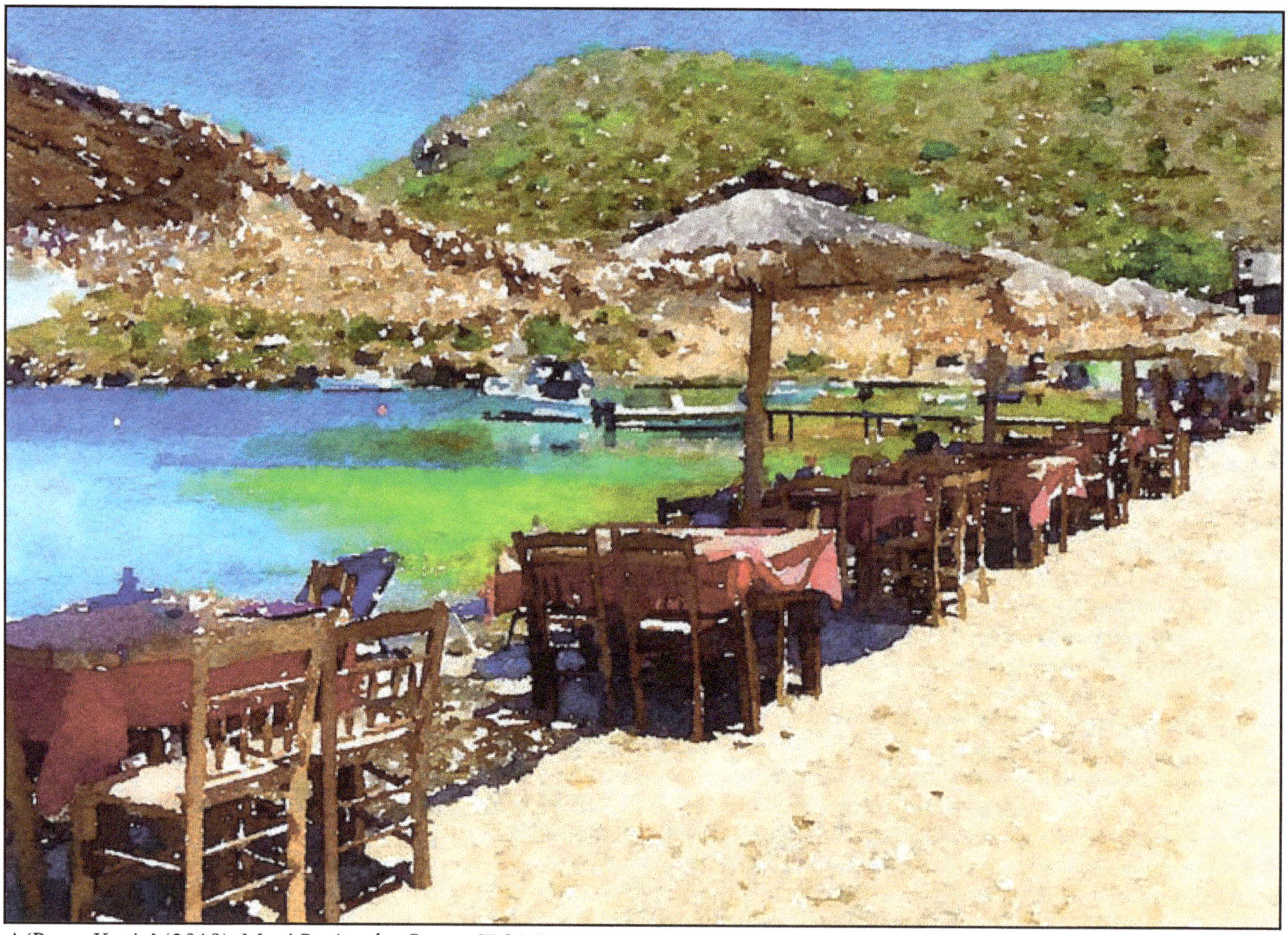

▲'Porto Kagia' (2018), Mani Peninsula, Greece [EGR(PE)1820].

'Road To Monemvasia' (2018), Peloponnese, Greece [EGR(PE)1821].▼

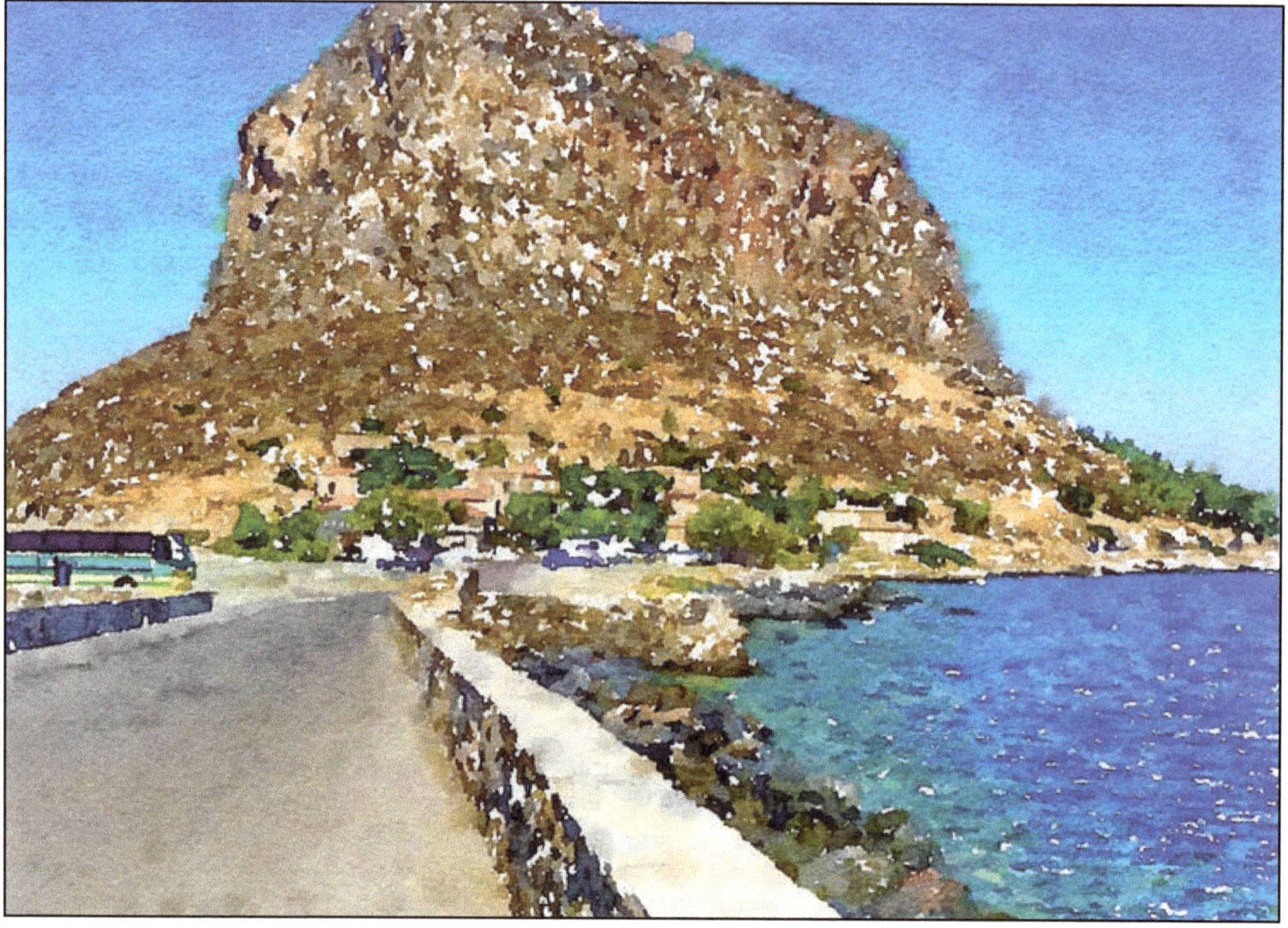

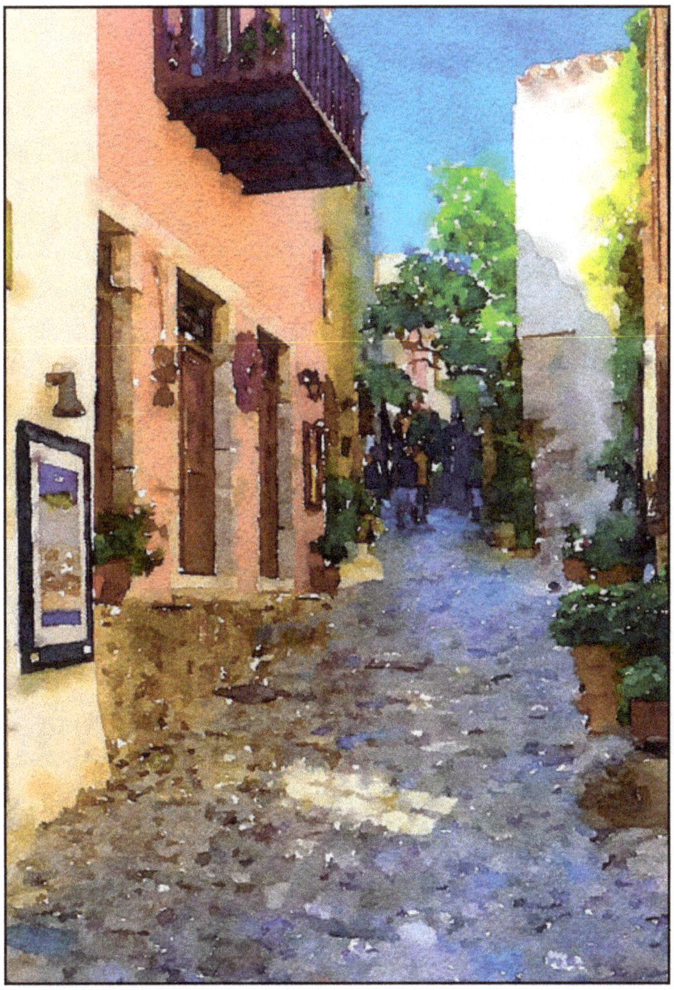

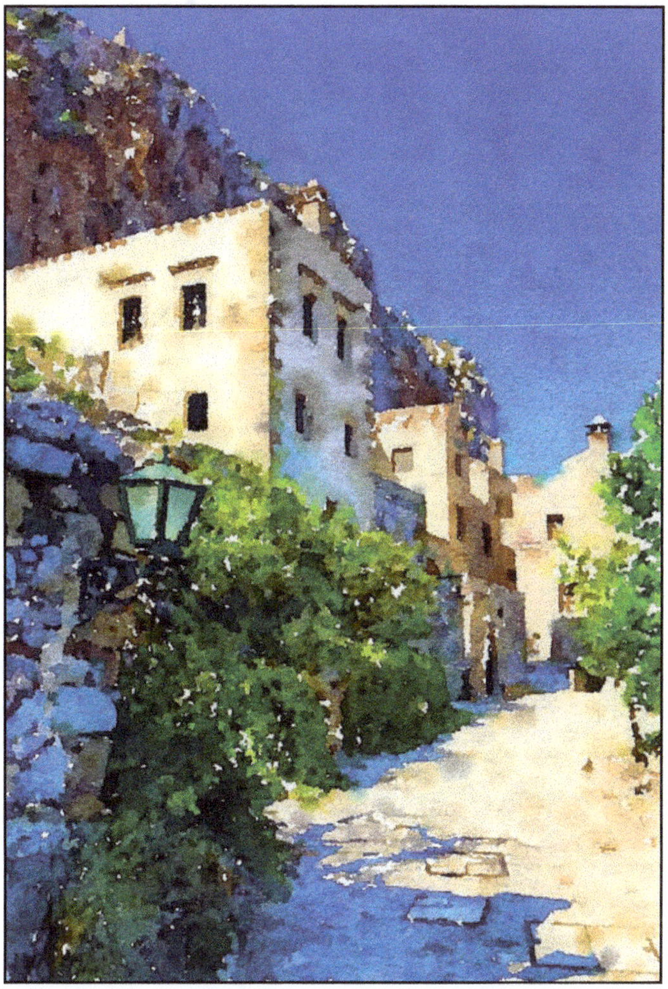

▲'Monemvasia 1' (2018), Peloponnese, Greece [EGR(PE)1822].

'Monemvasia 2' (2018), Peloponnese, Greece [EGR(PE)1822].▲

'Ekklisía Monemvasia'(2018), Peloponnese, Greece [EGR(PE)1823].▼

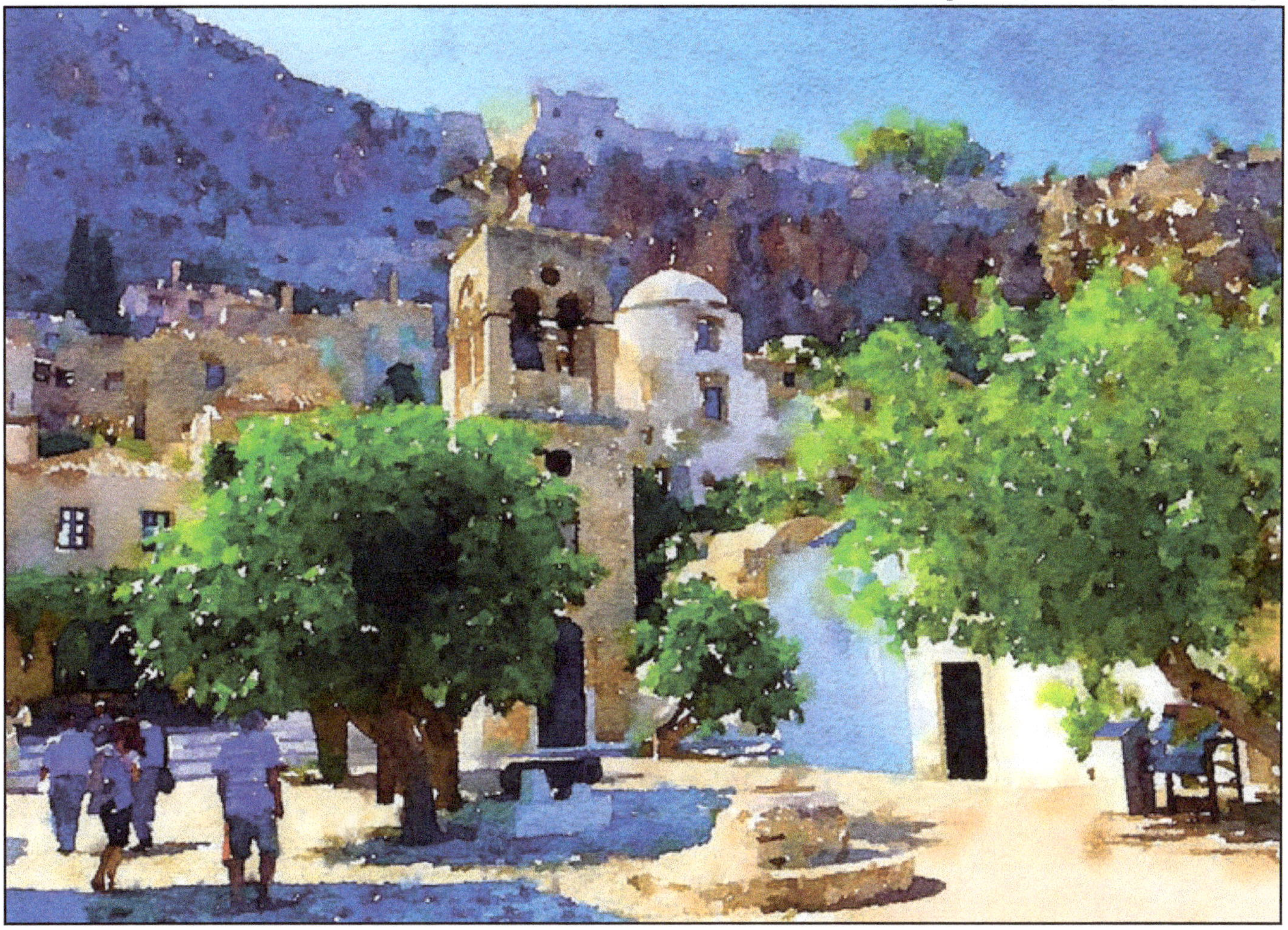

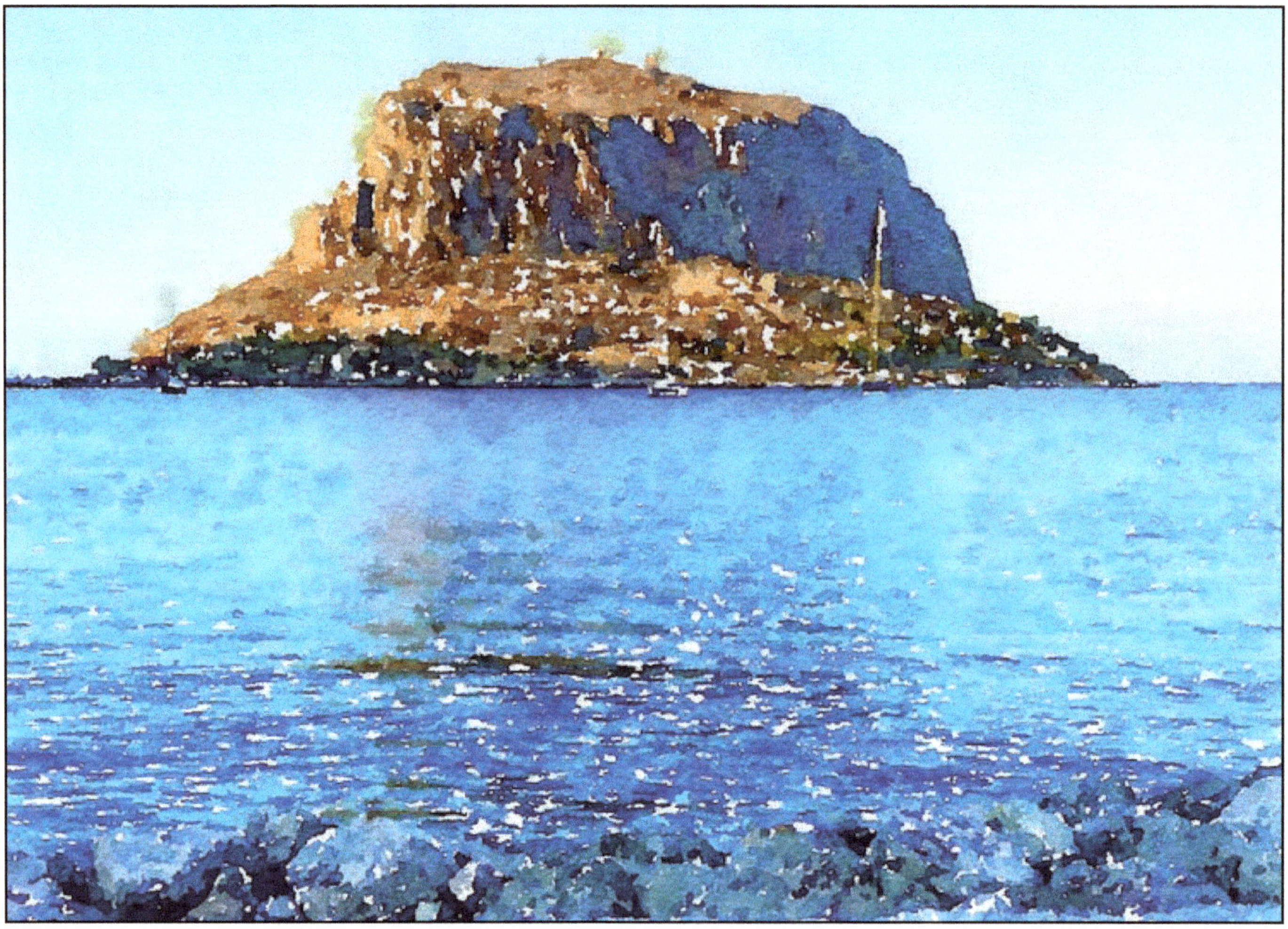

▲'Monemvasia Island' (2018), Peloponnese, Greece [EGR(PE)1825].

'Nafplion Nights' (2018), Peloponnese, Greece [EGR(PE)1826].▼

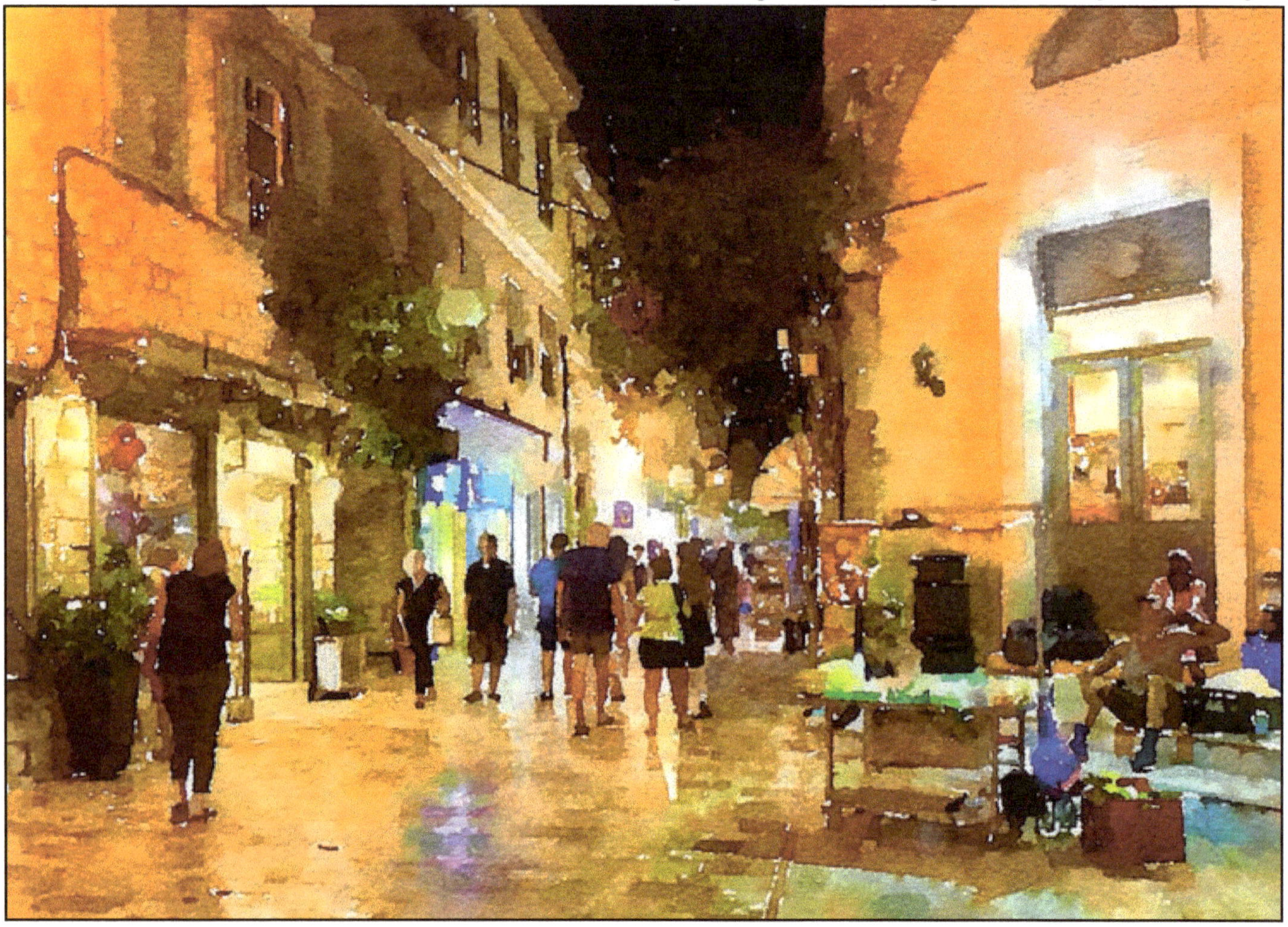

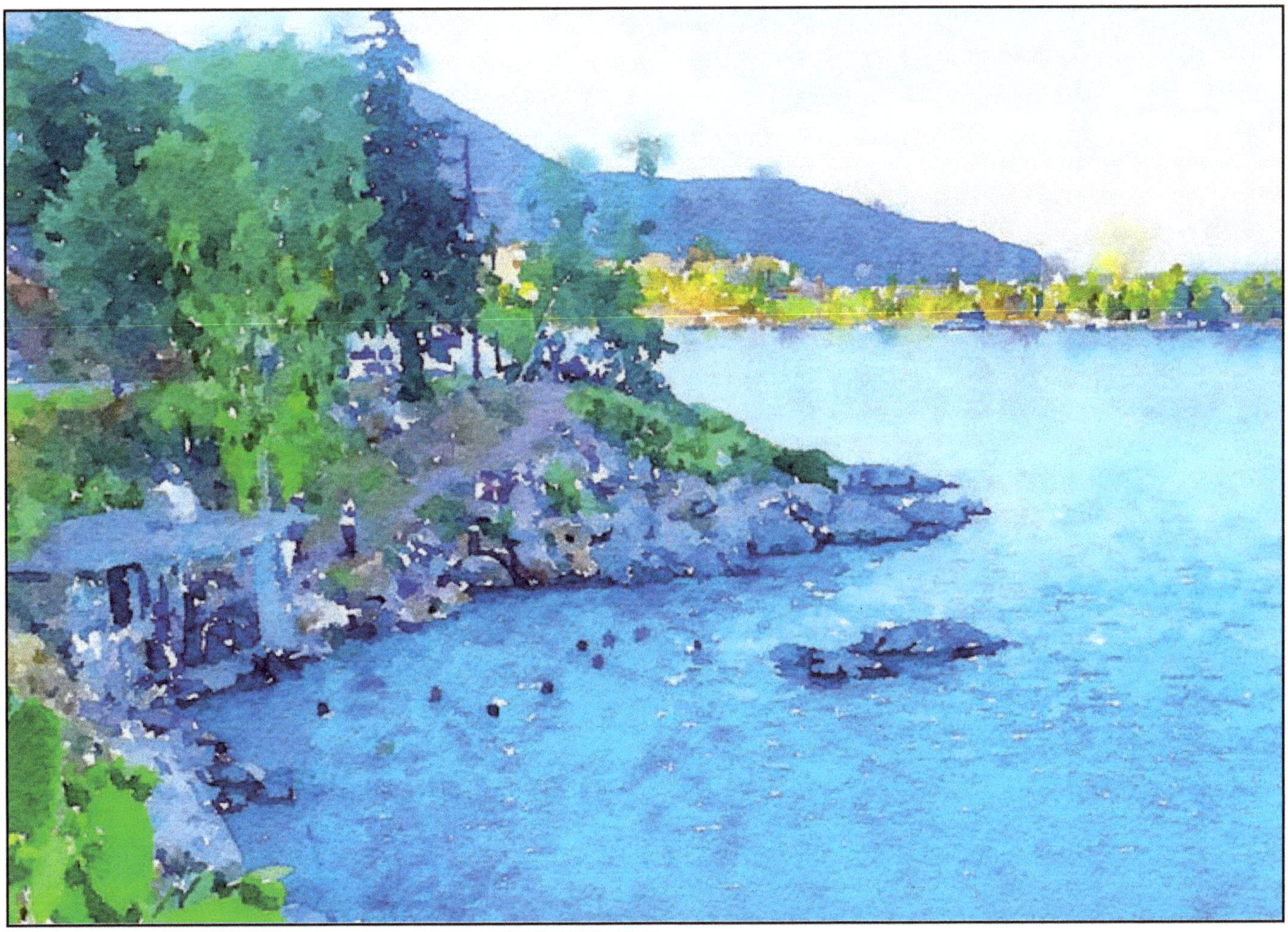

▲'Methana Springs' (2018), Peloponnese, Greece [EGR(PE)1829].

'Golden Waters, Methana' (2018), Peloponnese, Greece [EGR(PE)1828].▼

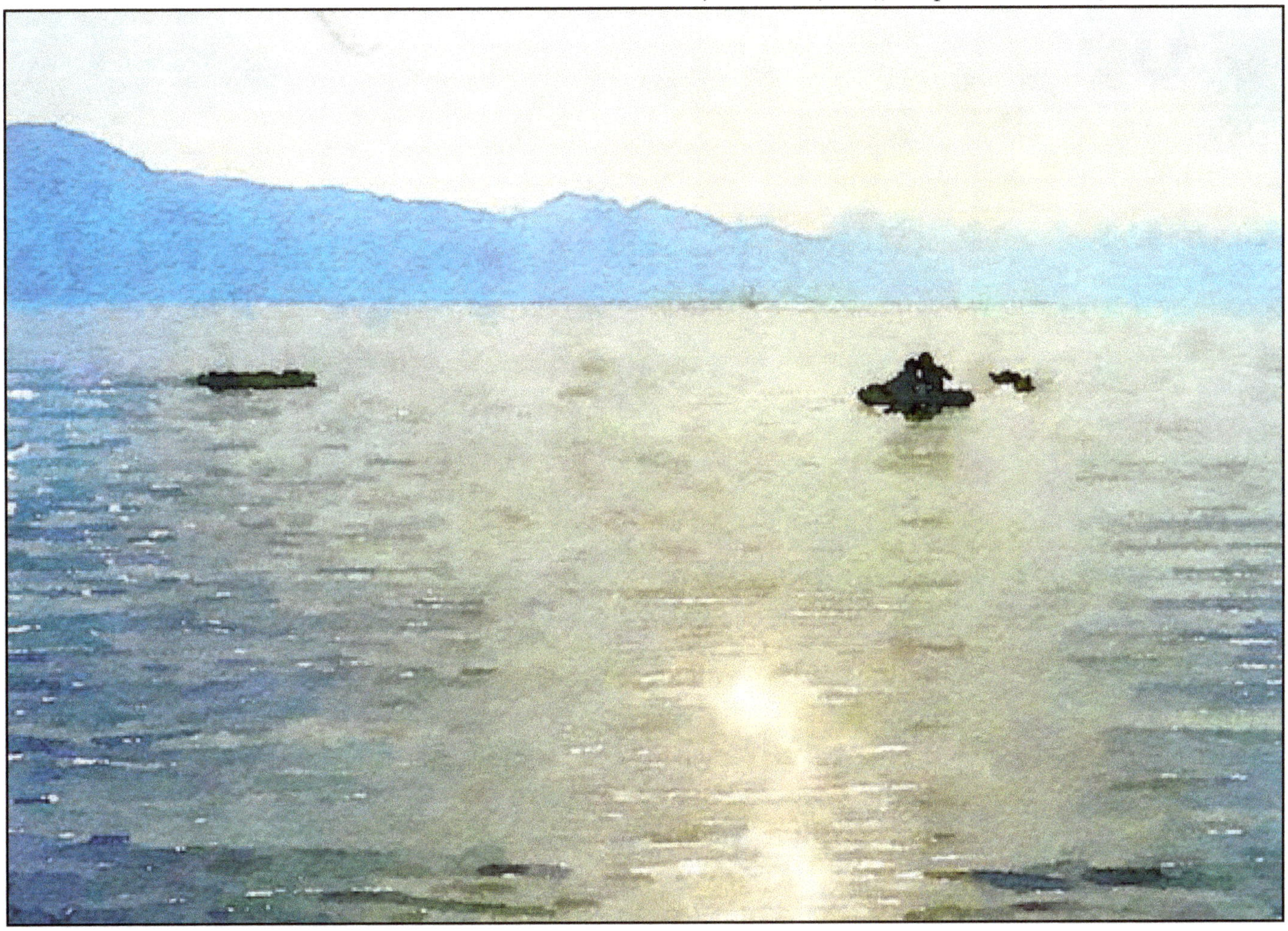

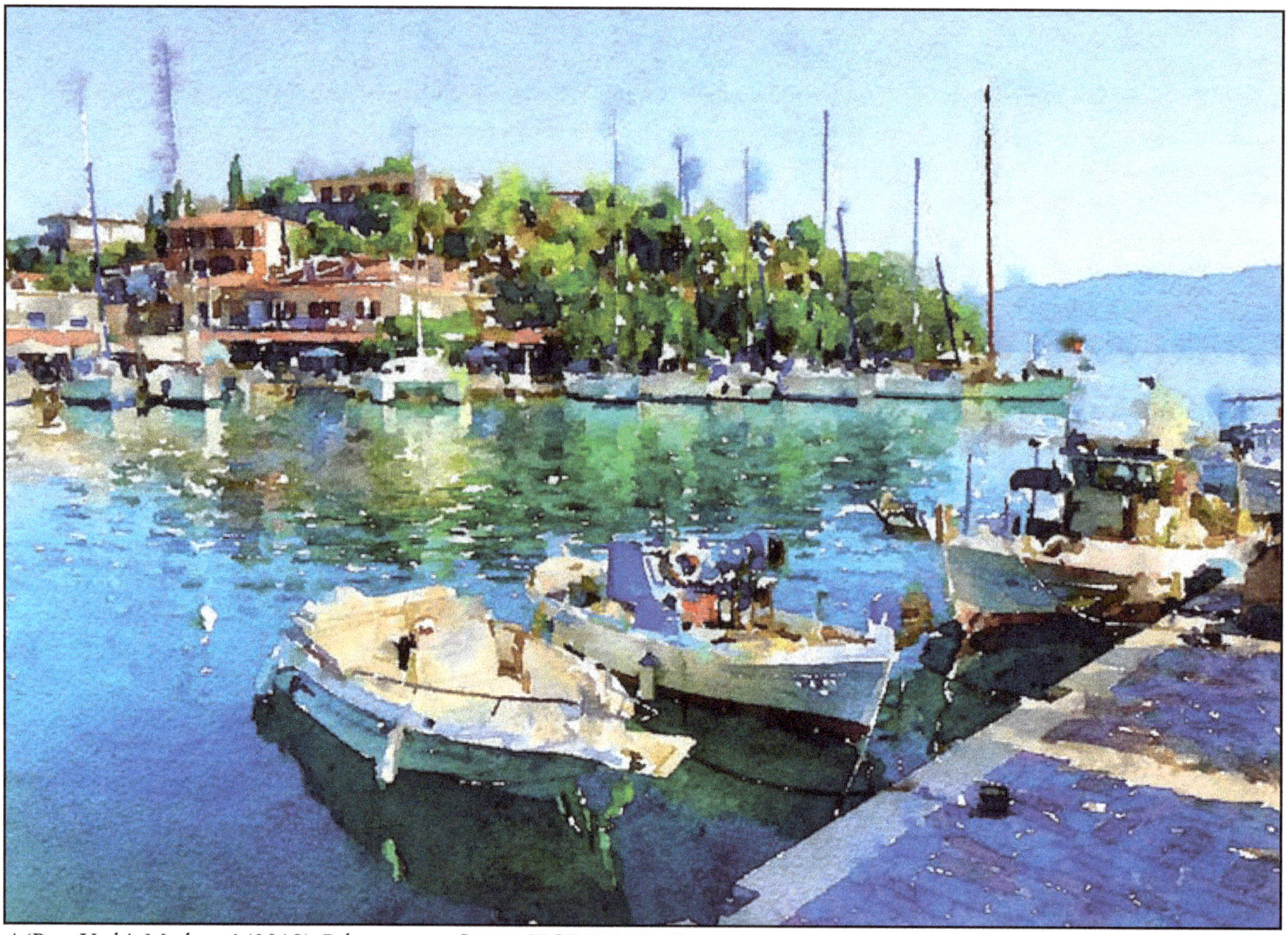

▲'Port Vathi, Methana' (2018), Peloponnese, Greece [EGR(PE)1827].

'Epidaurus' (2018), Peloponnese, Greece [EGR(PE)1830].▼

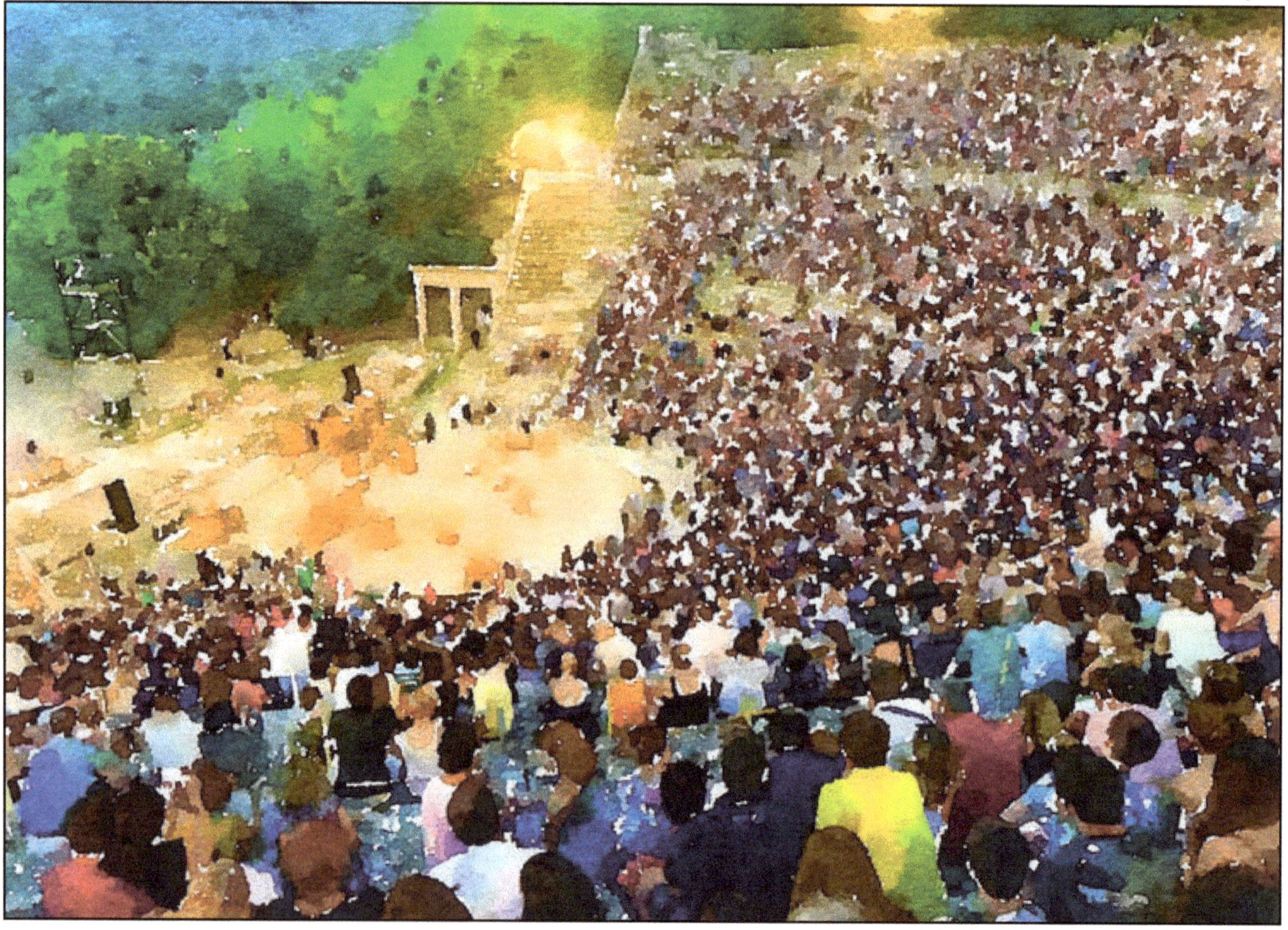

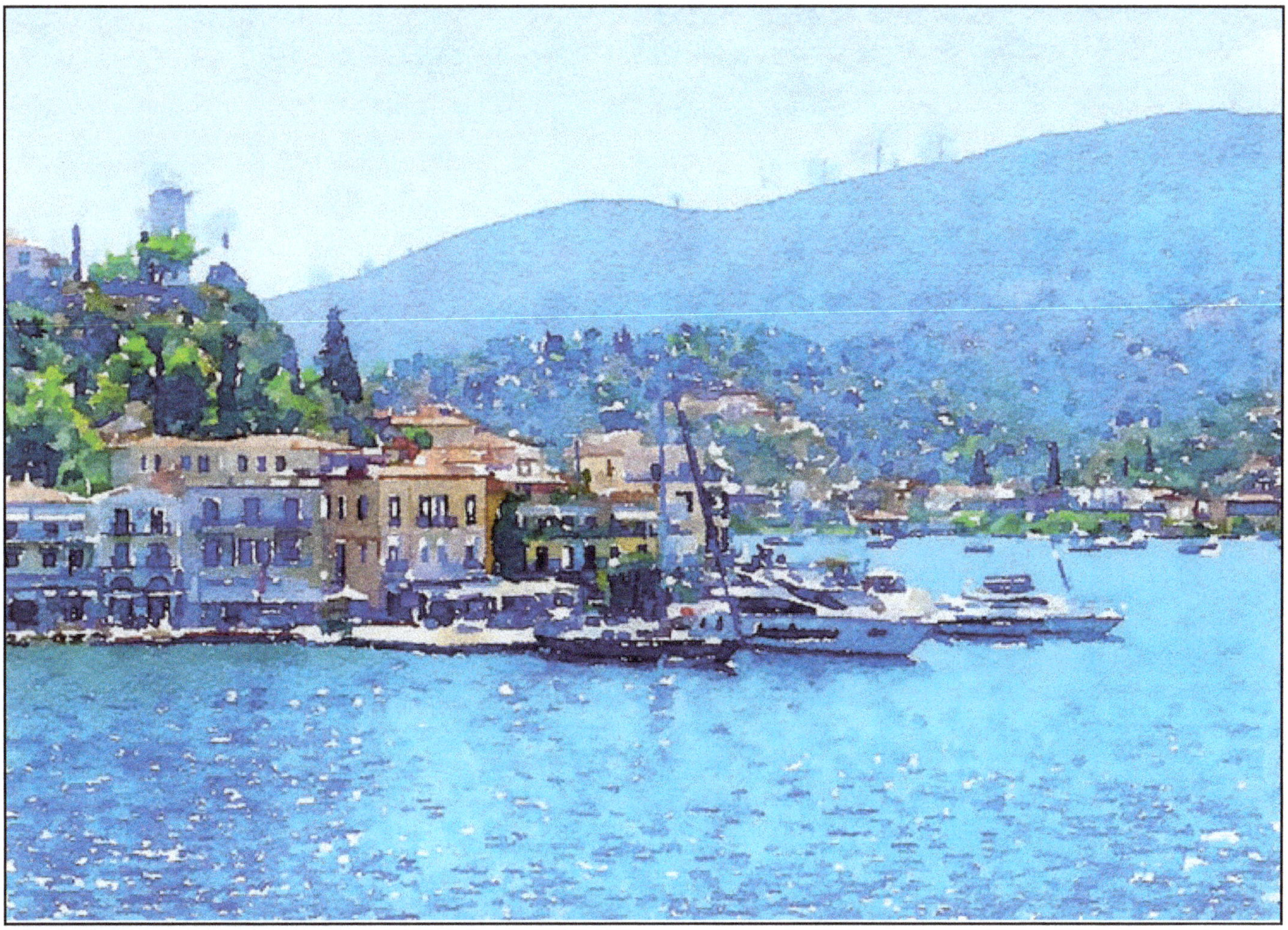

▲'Poros Harbour' (2018), Peloponnese, Greece [EGR(PE)1831].

'The Old Harbour' (2013), Santorini, Greece [EGR1302].▼

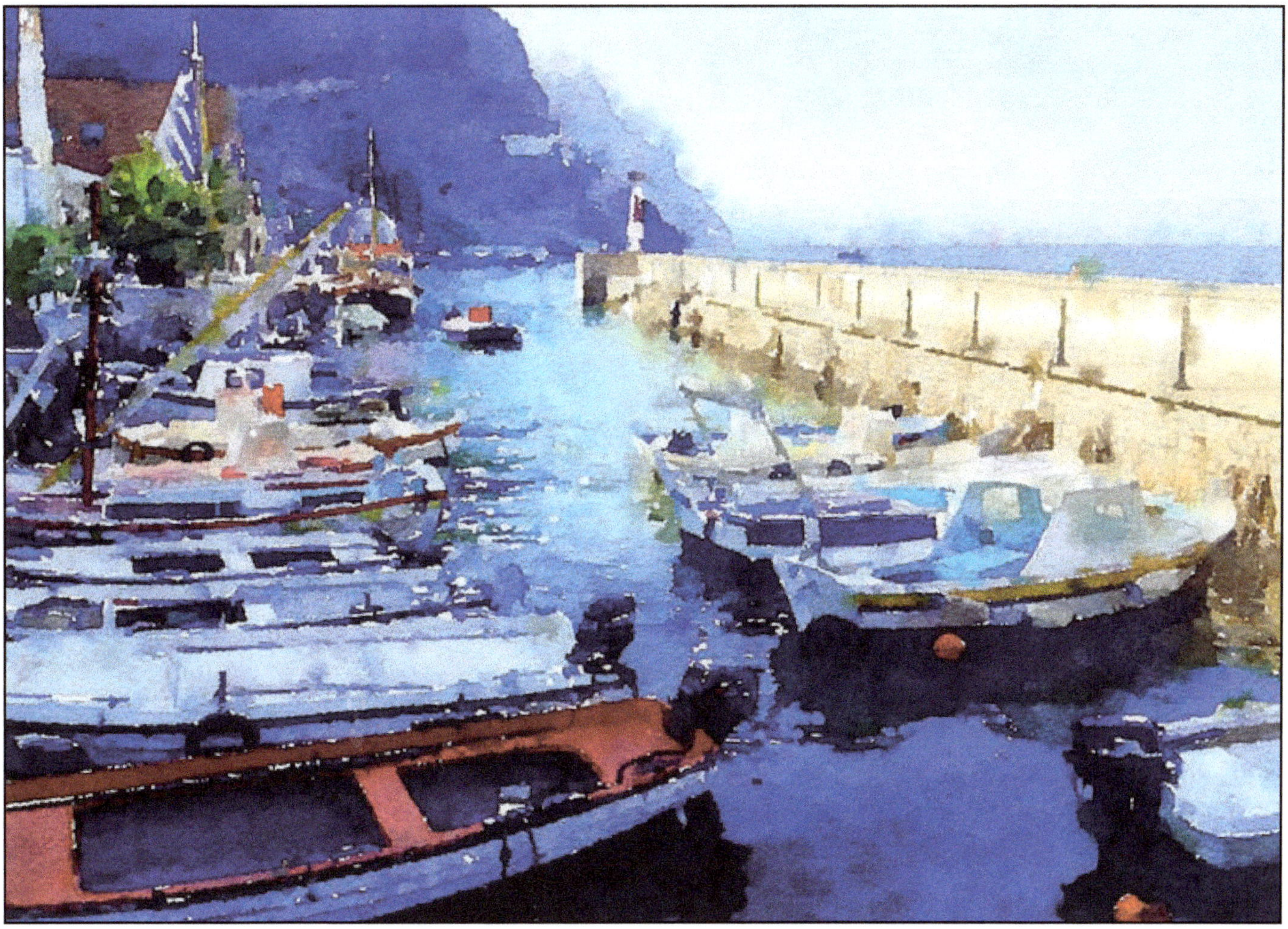

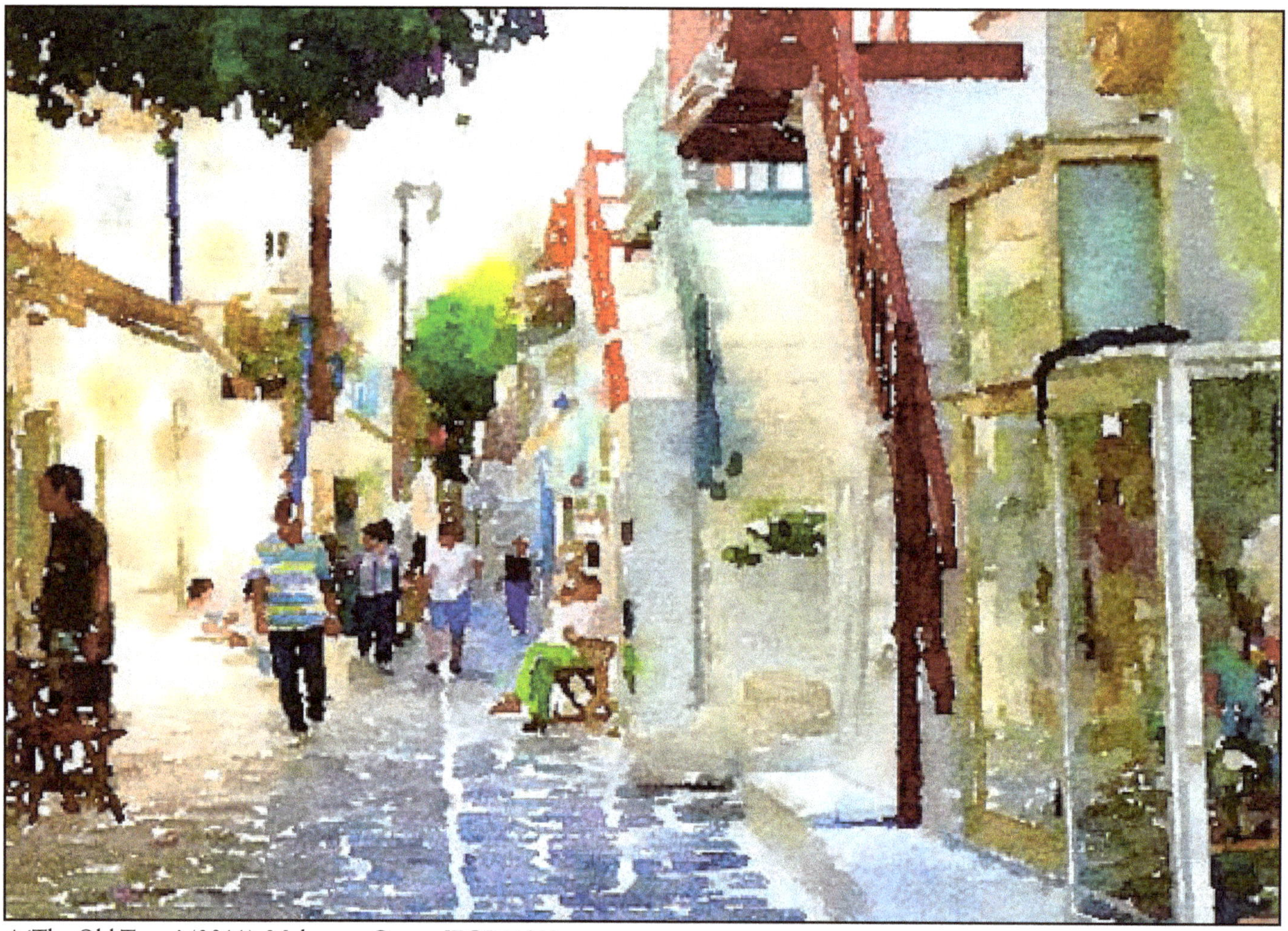

▲'The Old Town' (2011), Mykonos, Greece [EGR1101].

'Hellenes Cuisine' (2011), Mykonos, Greece [EGR1102].▼

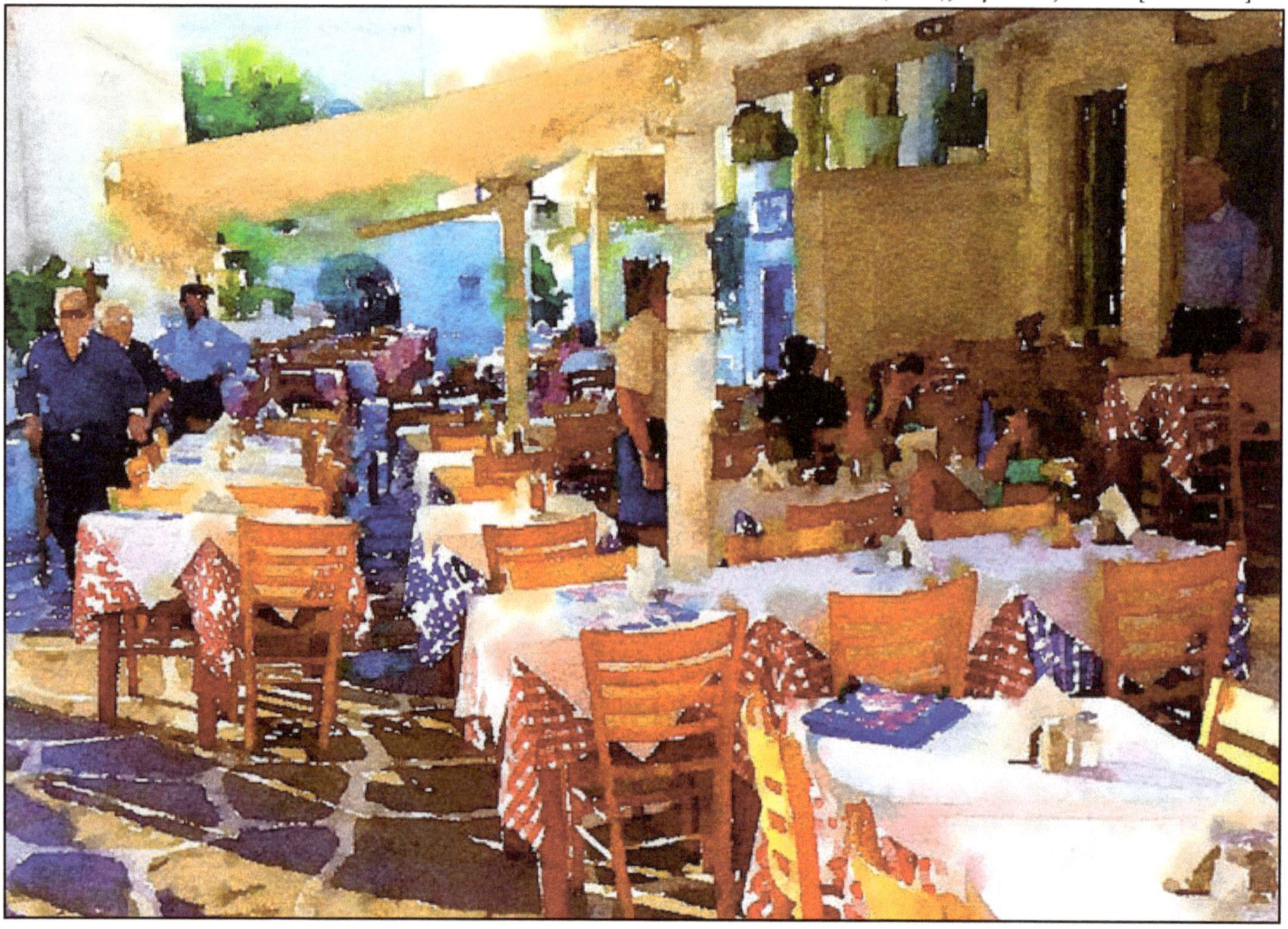

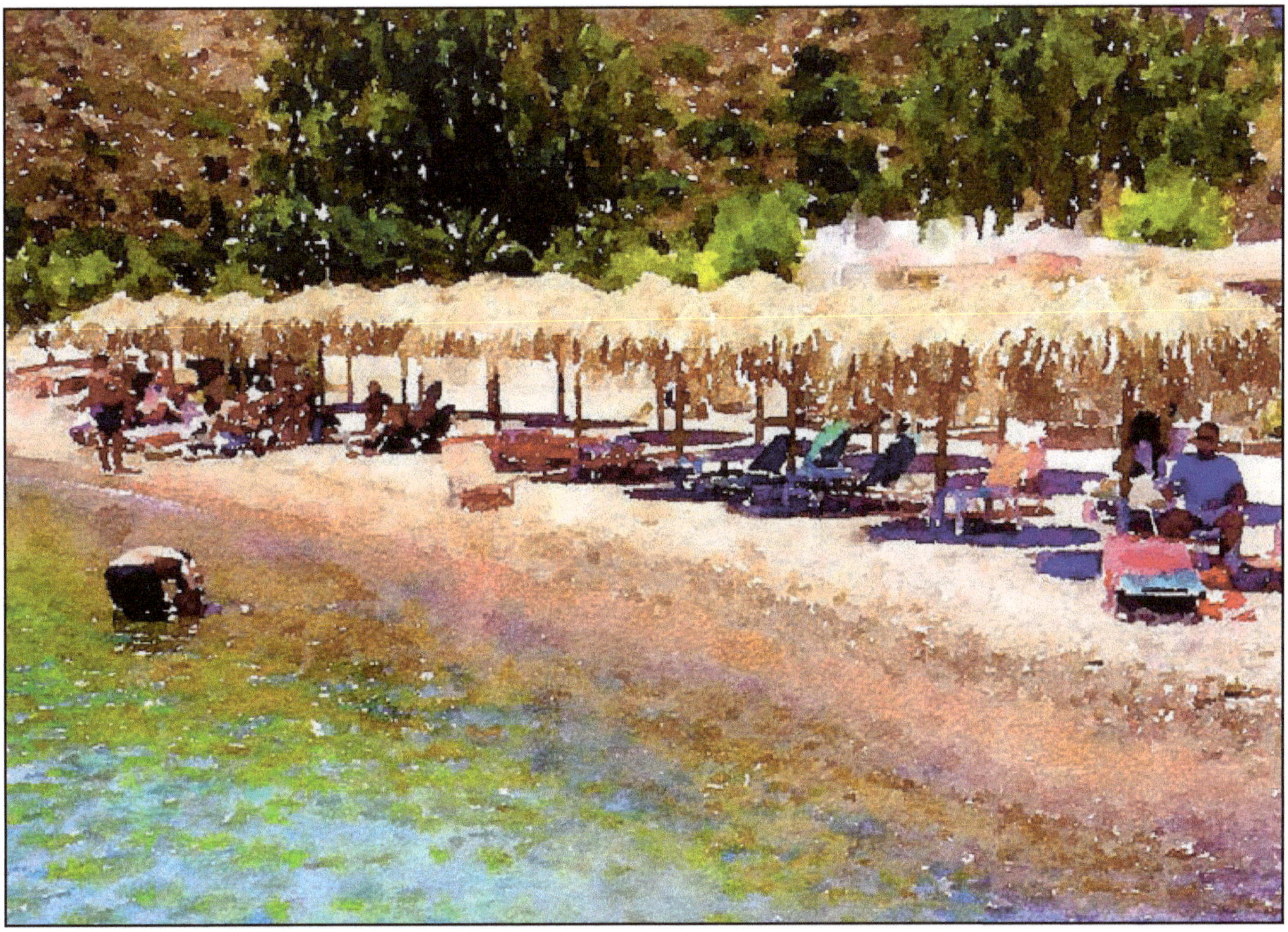

▲'Paralia Kampos' (2011), Patmos, Greece [EGR1103].

'Paralia Vagia' (2011), Patmos, Greece [EGR1104].▼

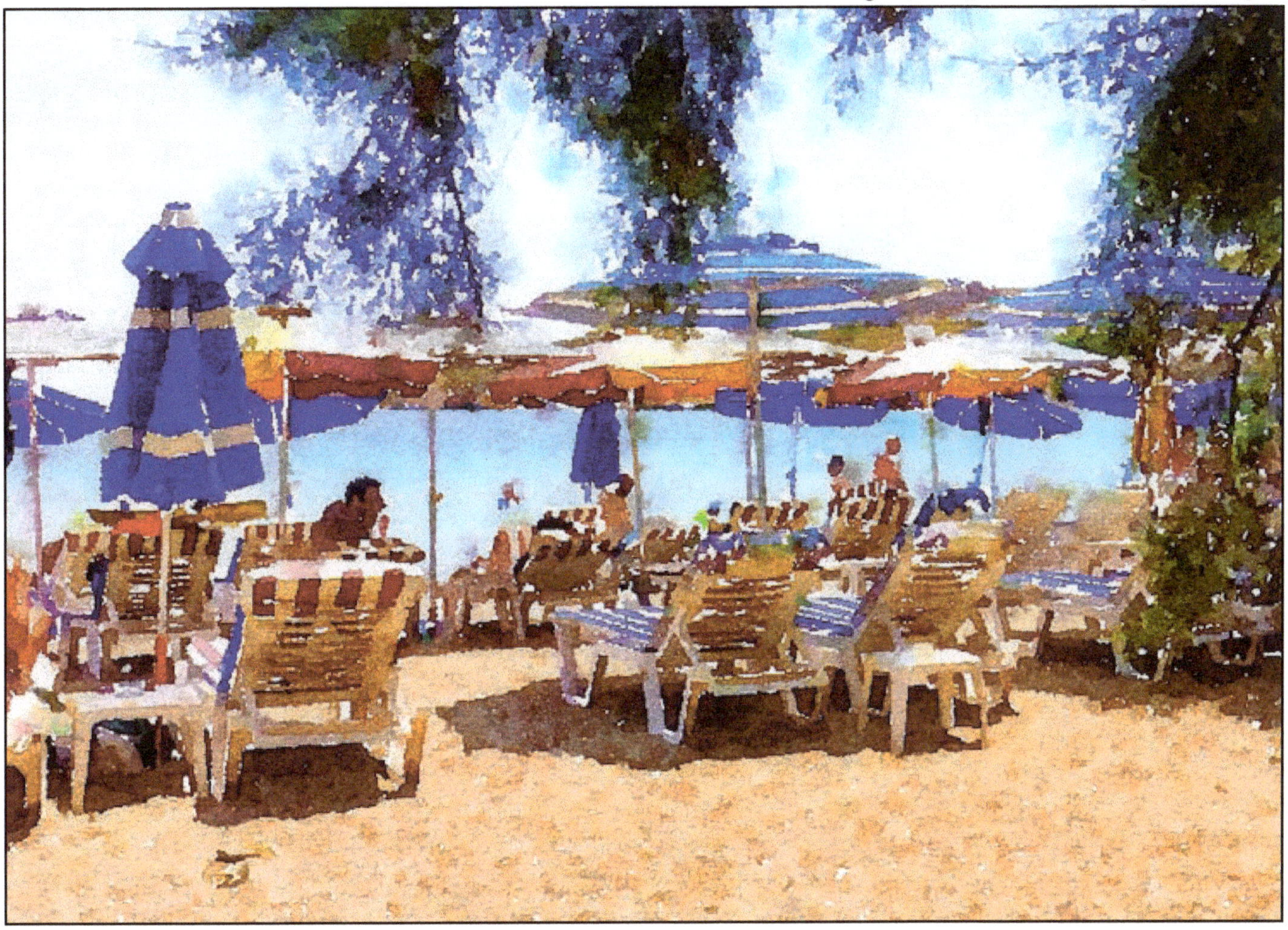

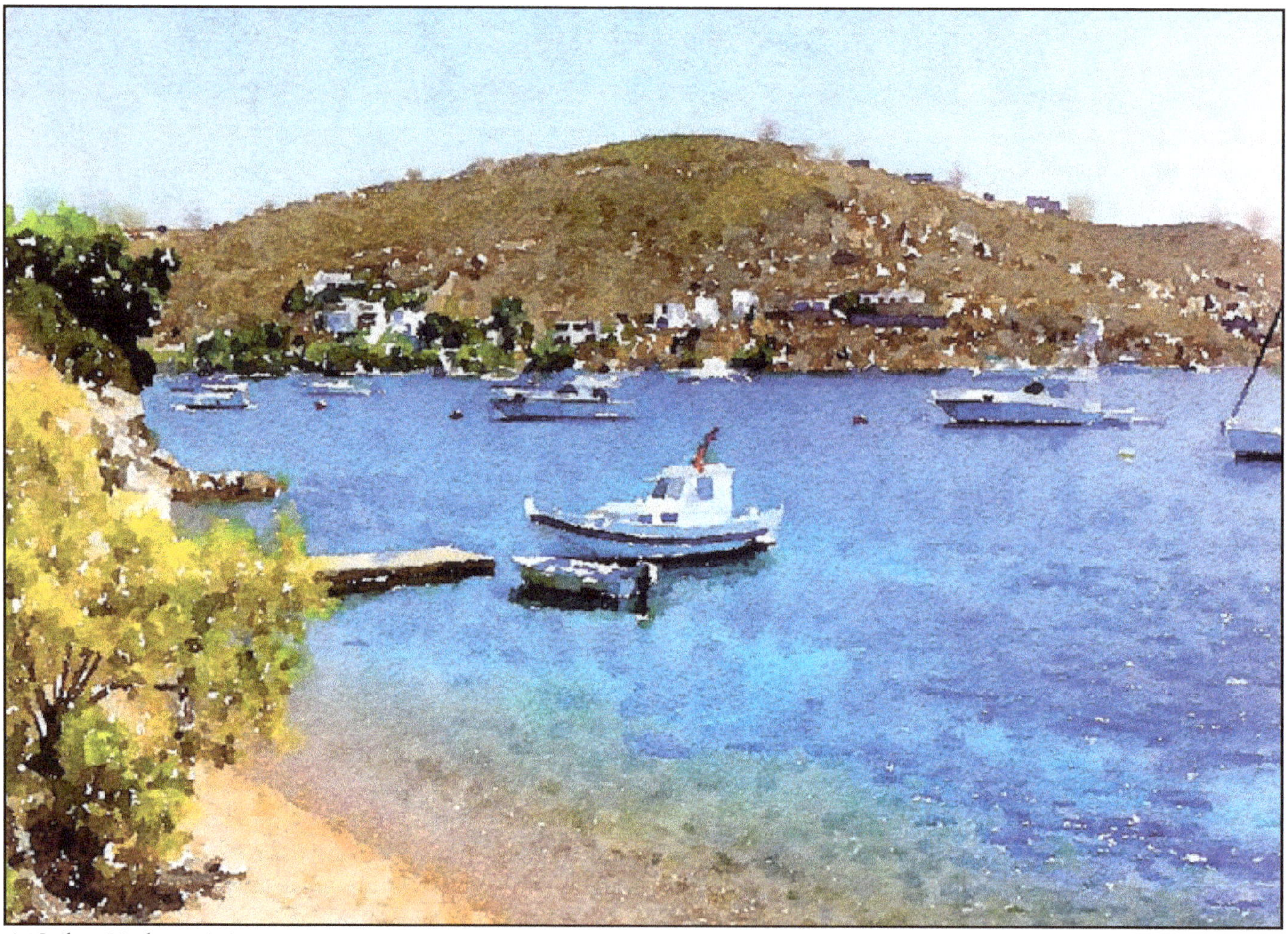

▲'Grikos Harbour' (2011), Patmos, Greece [EGR1105].

'Villa's Of Skiathos' (2015), Skiathos, Greece [EGR1501].▼

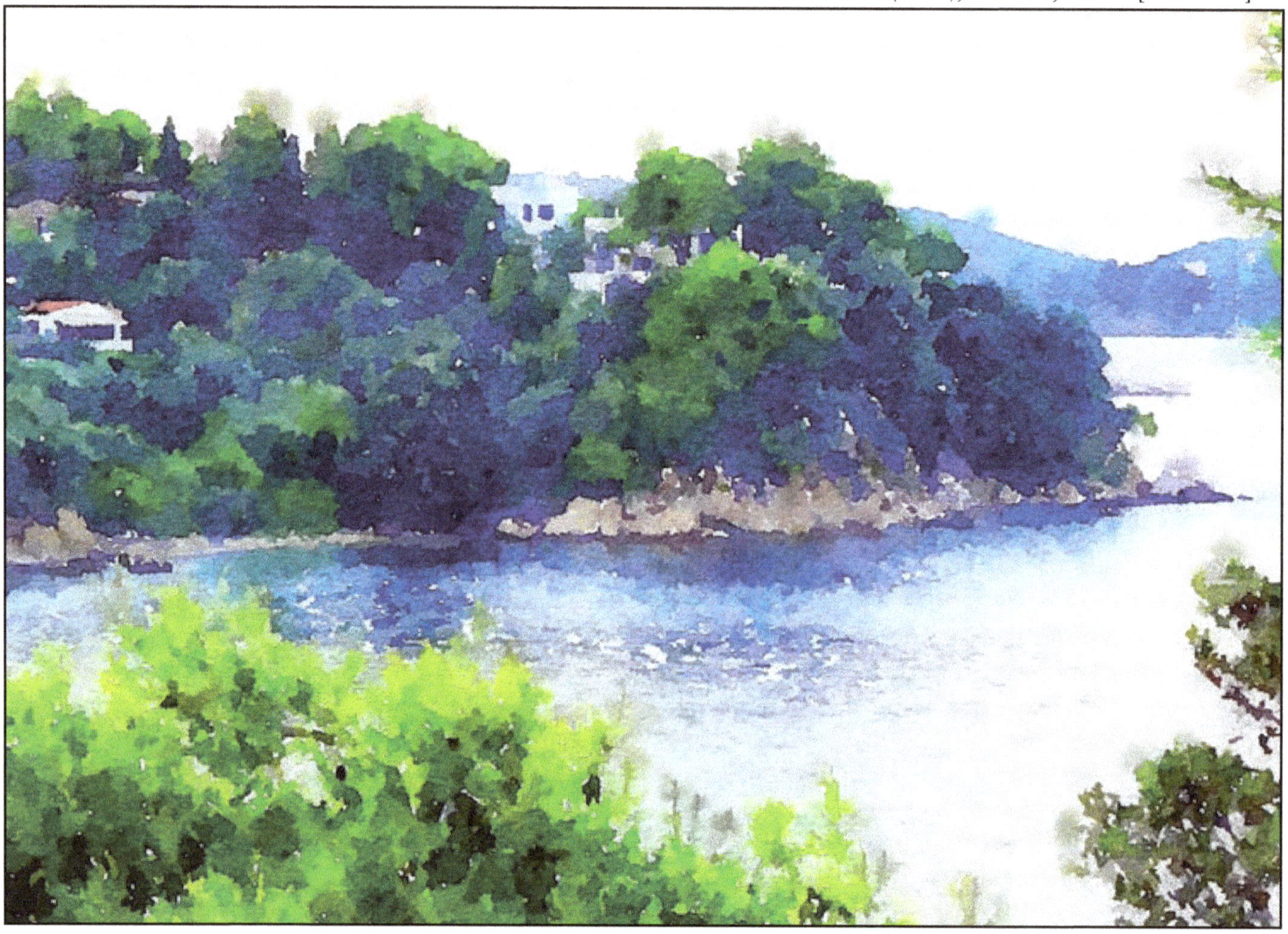

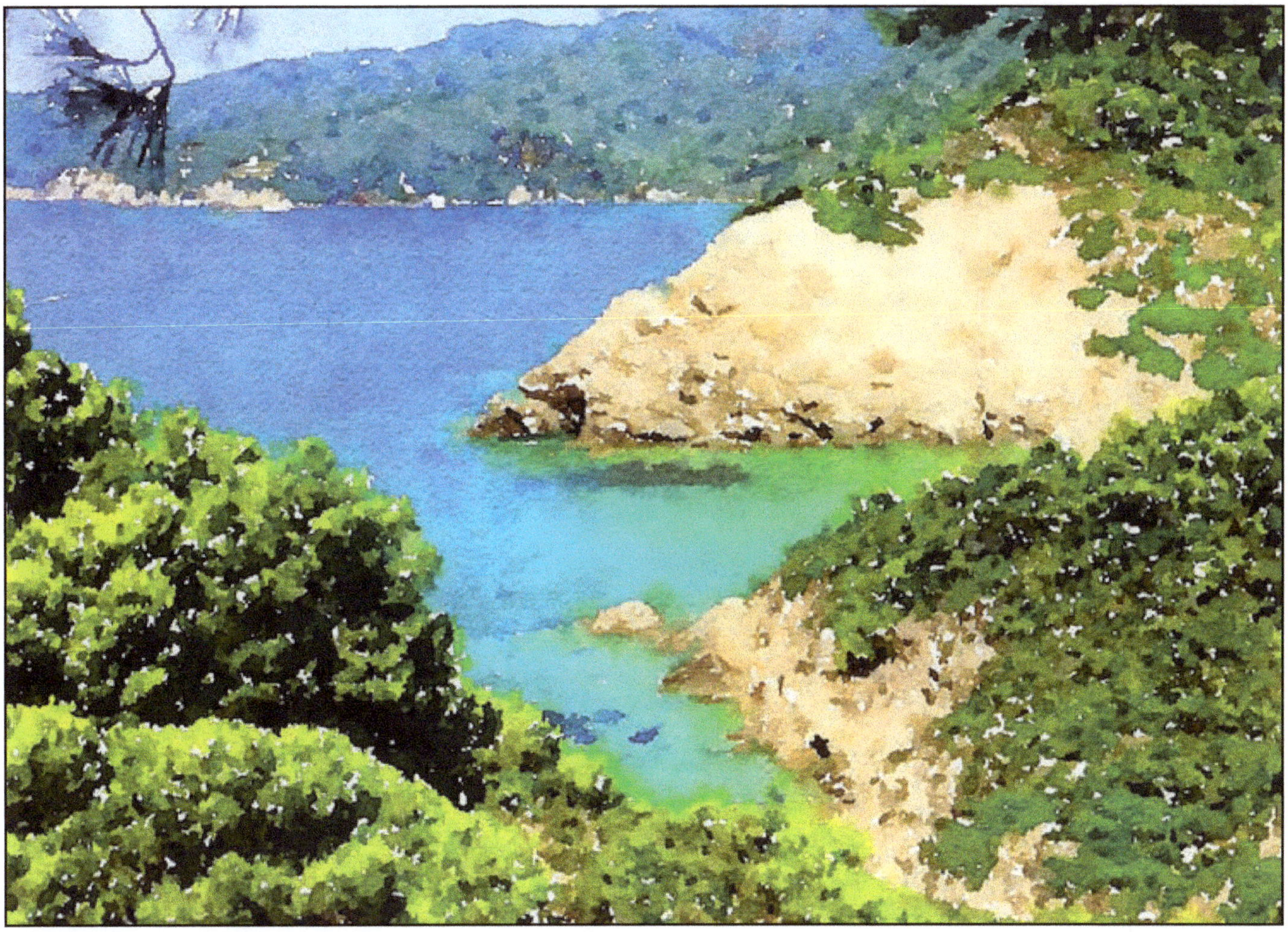

▲'Aselinos Panorama' (2015), Skiathos, Greece [EGR1503].

'The Old Port' (2015), Skiathos, Greece [EGR1509].▼

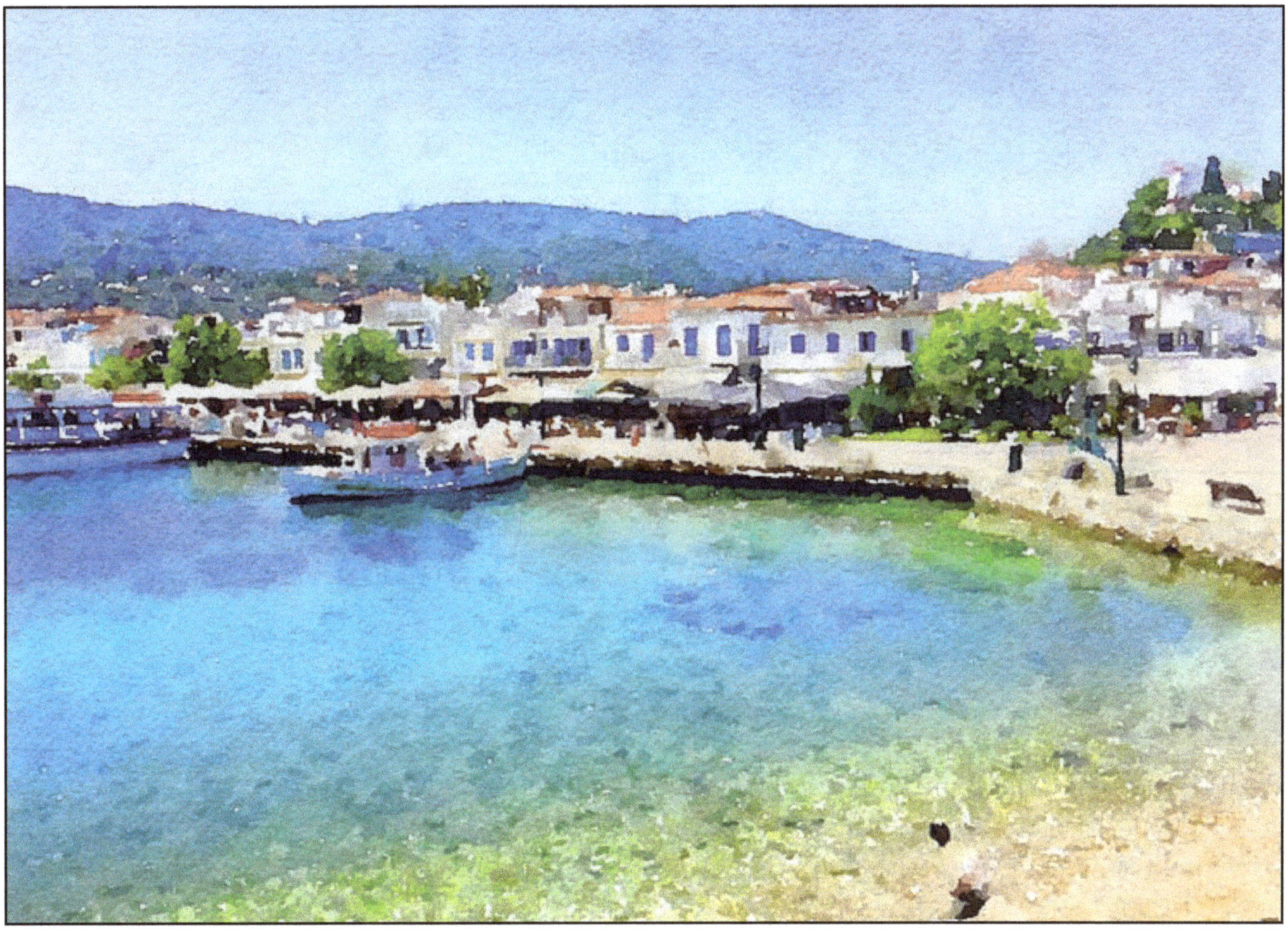

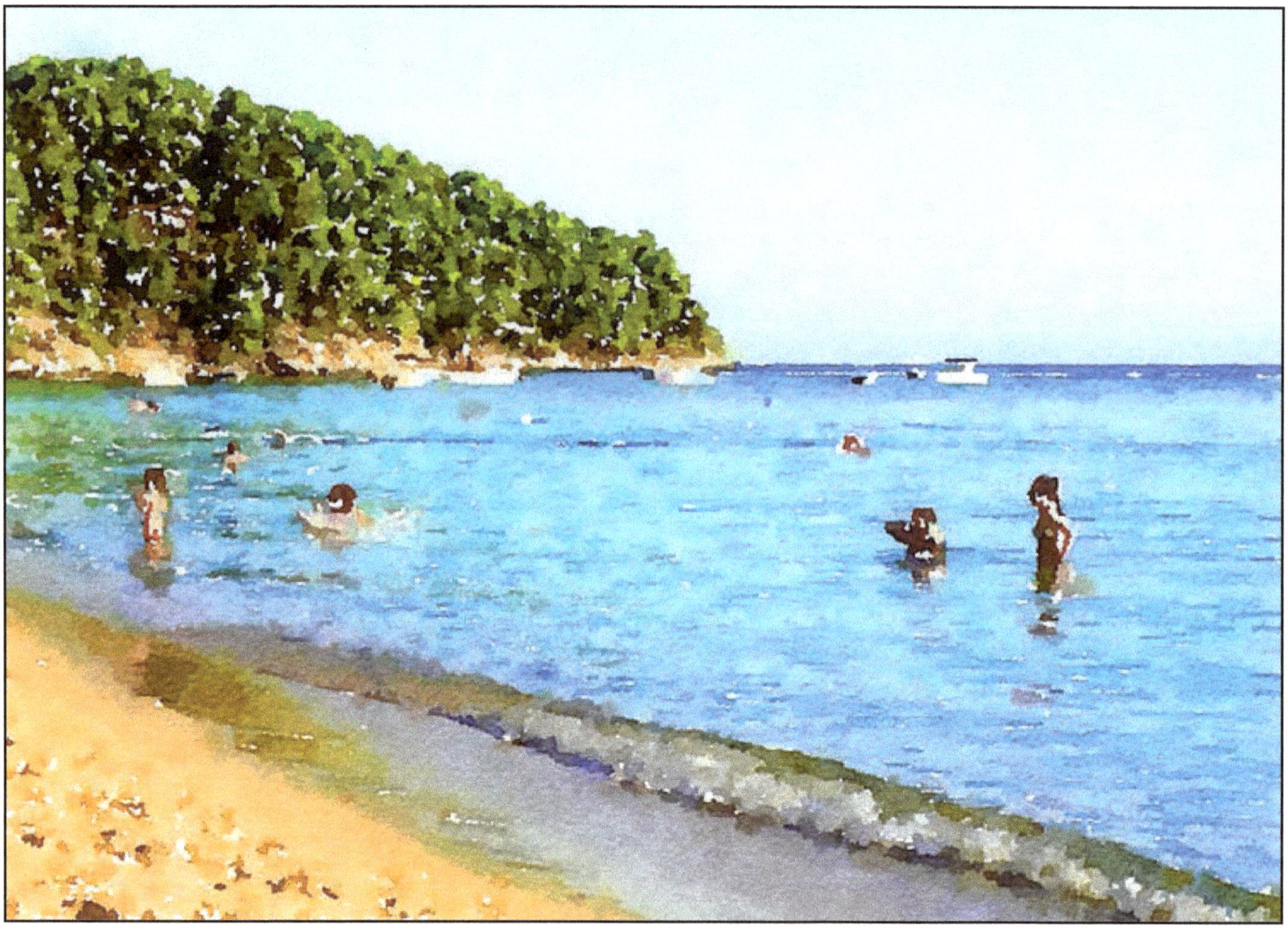

▲'Banana Beach' (2015), Skiathos, Greece [EGR1504].

'Tzaneria Beach' (2015), Skiathos, Greece [EGR1507].▼

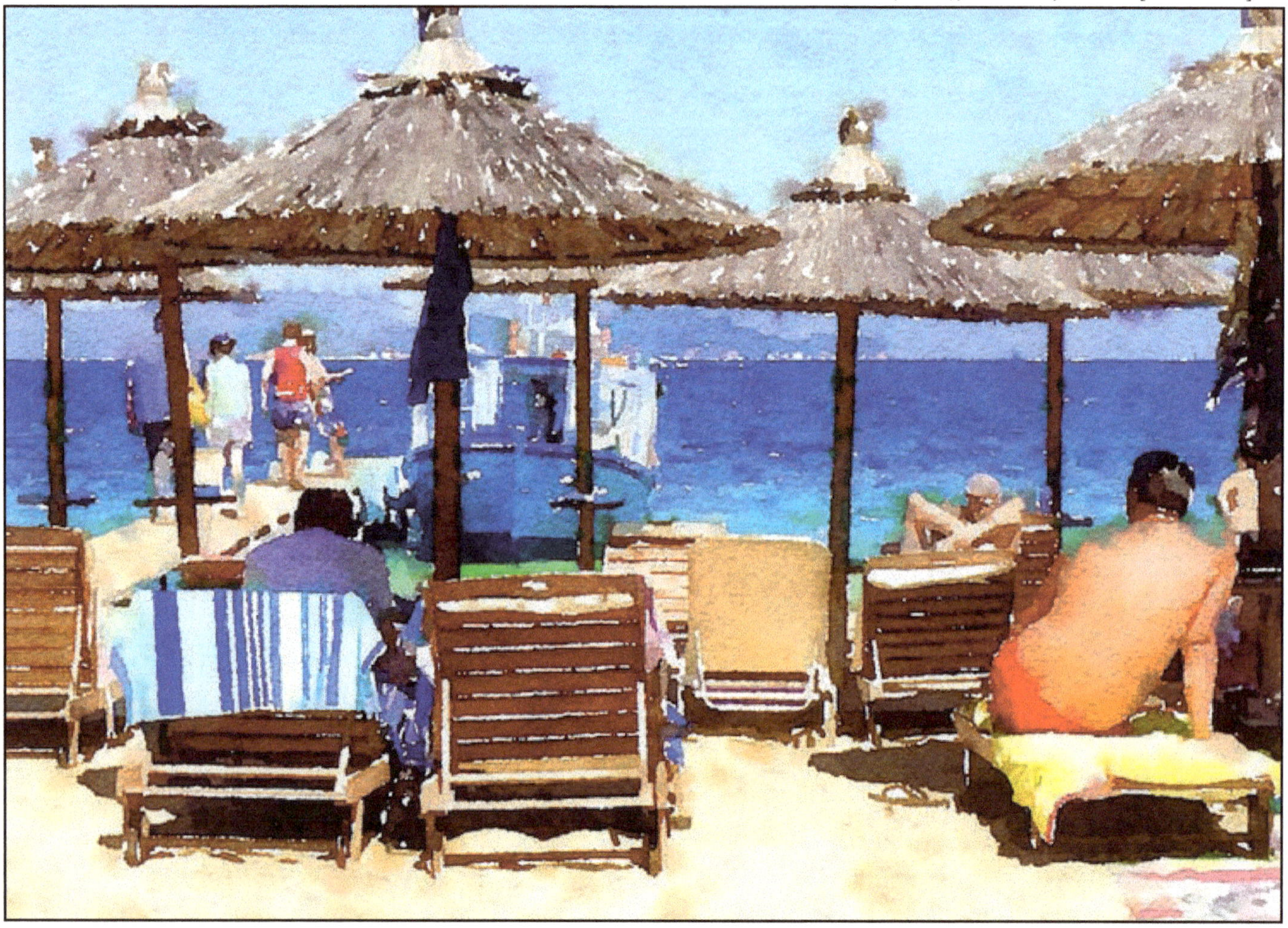

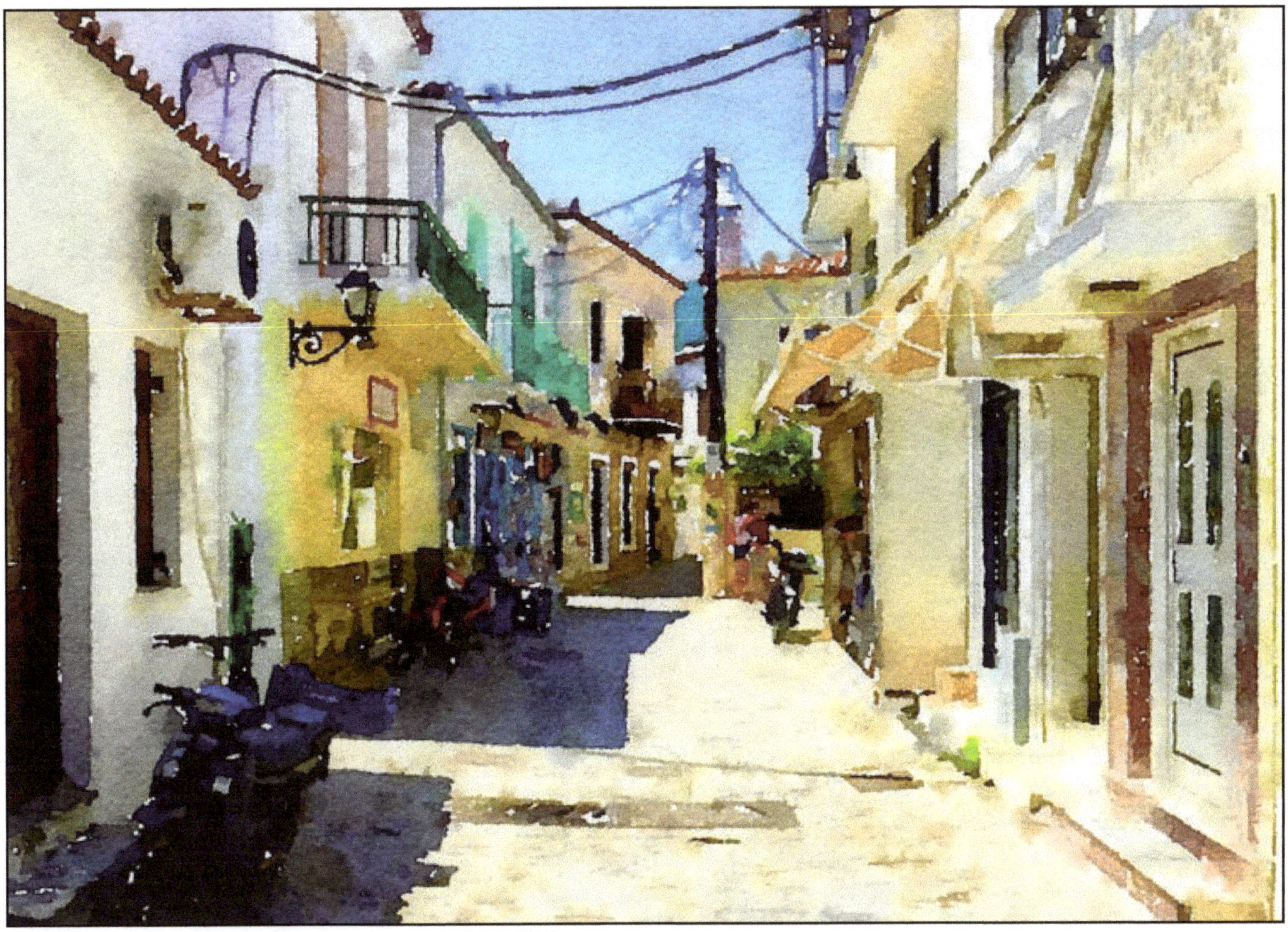

▲'The Old Town' (2015), Skiathos, Greece [EGR1502].

'Sklithri Beach Bistro' (2015), Skiathos, Greece [EGR1505].▼

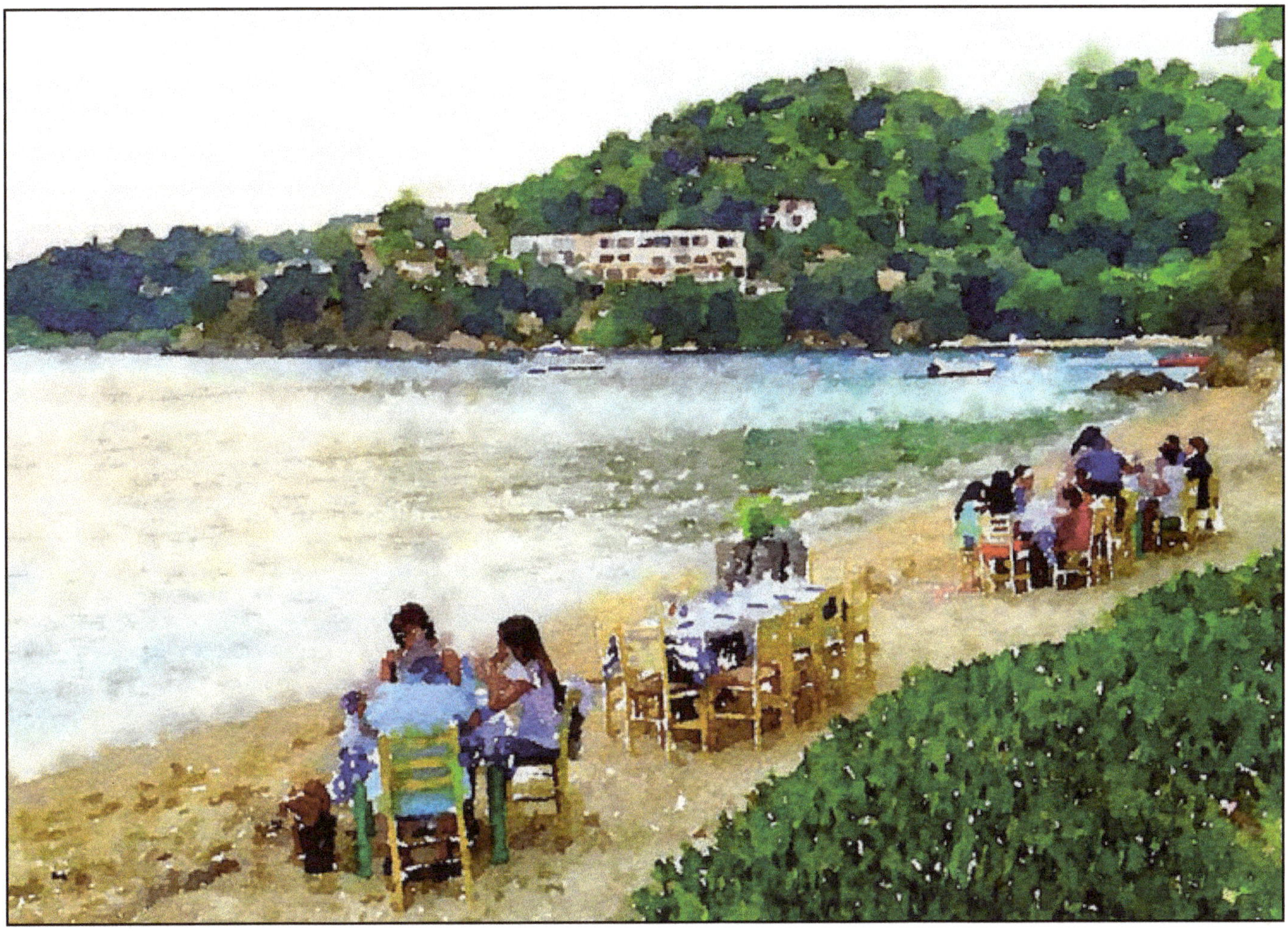

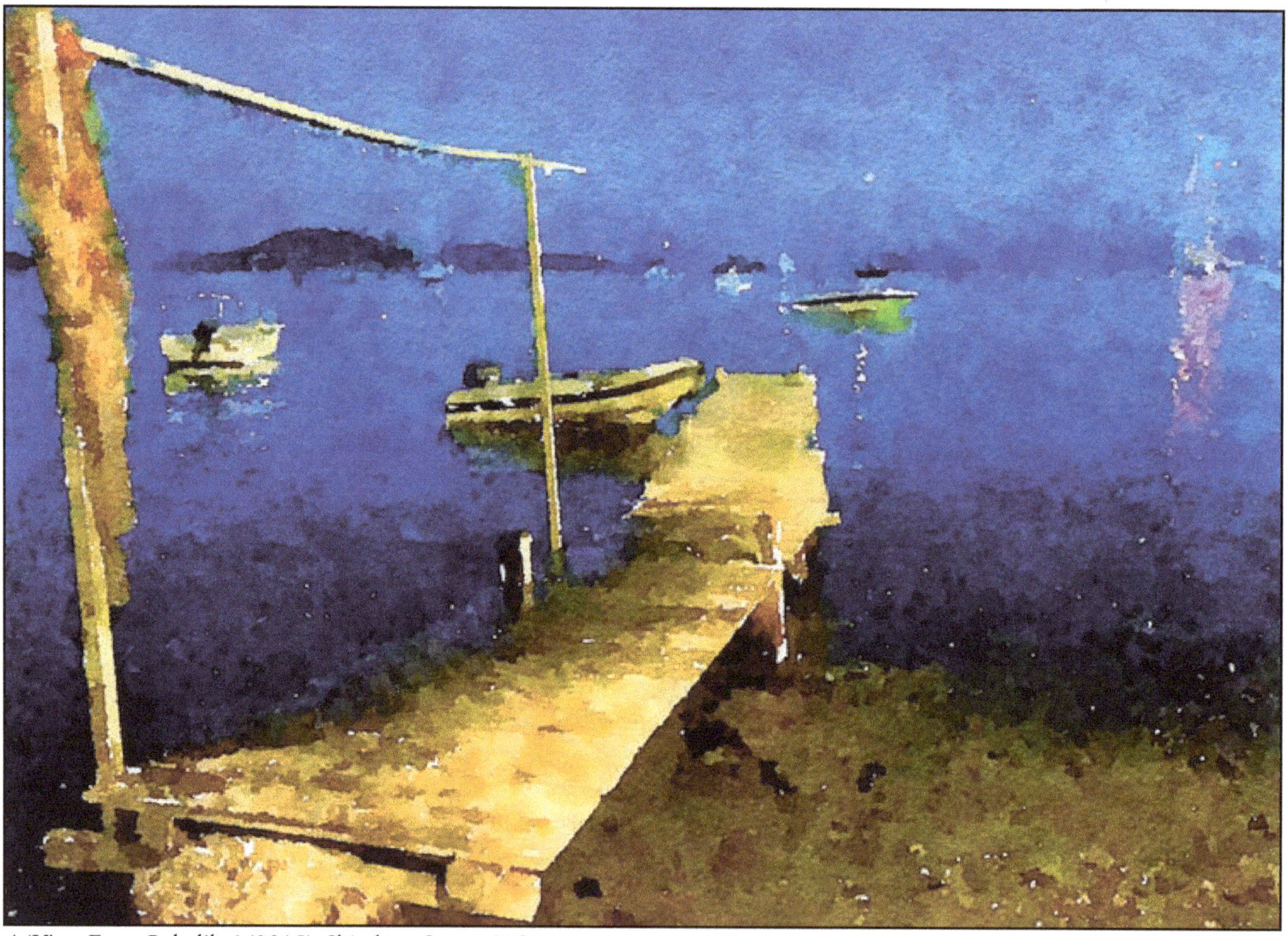

▲'View From Bakaliko' (2015), Skiathos, Greece [EGR1506].

'Skiathos Nights' (2015), Skiathos, Greece [EGR1508].▼

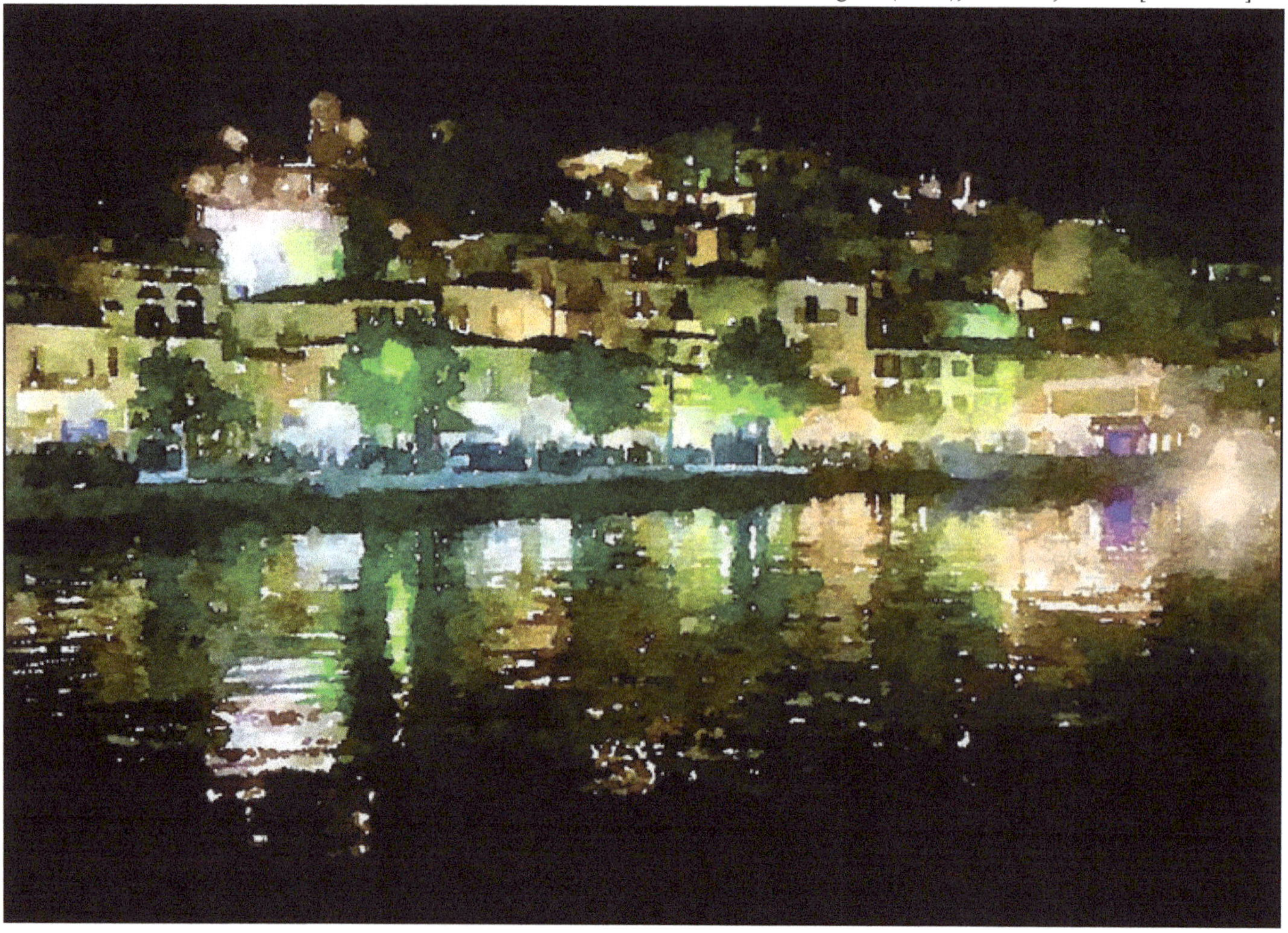

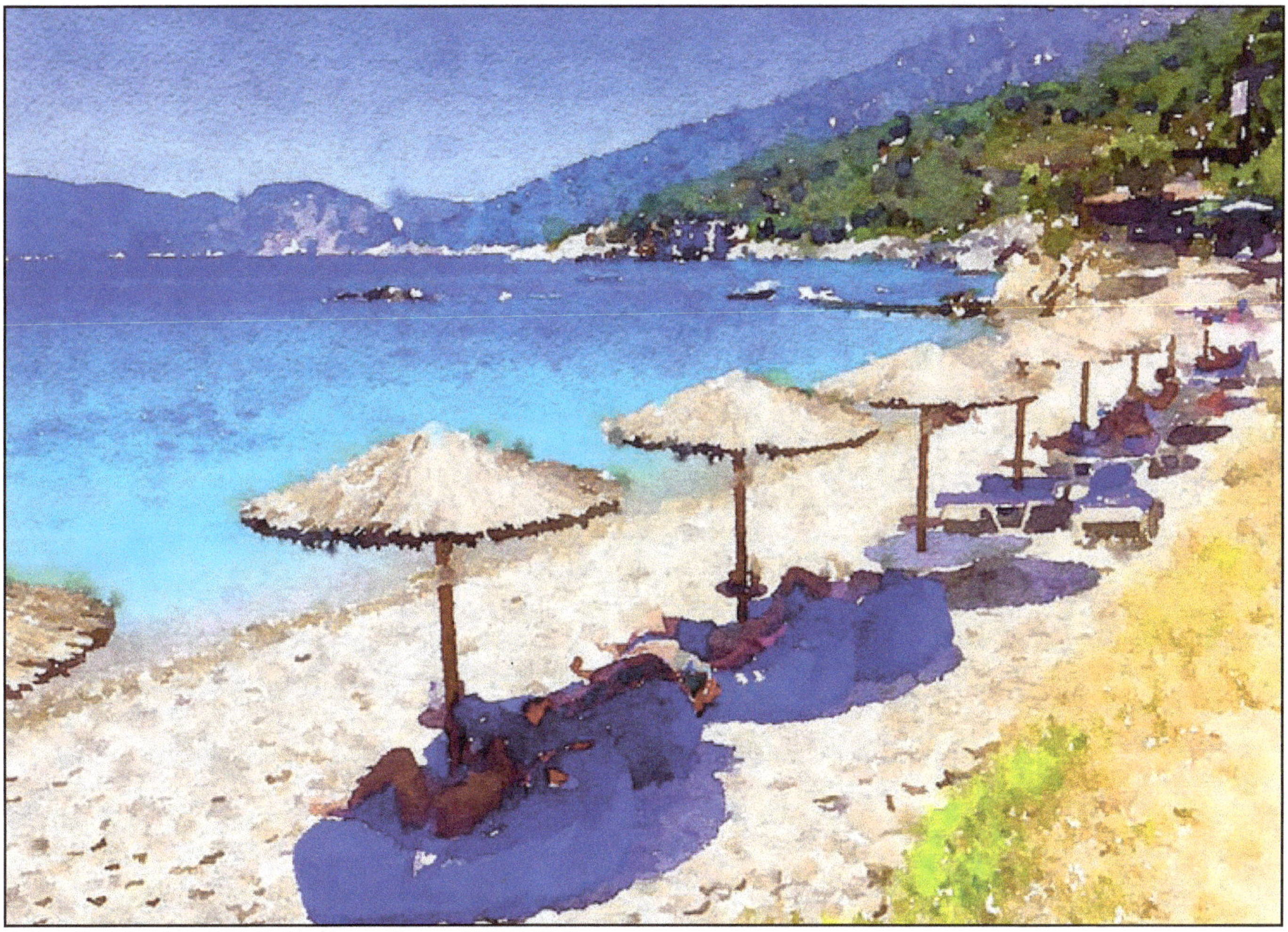

▲'Paralia Megalos' (2016), Alonissos, Greece [EGR1606].

'Aloni Restaurants' (2016), Alonissos, Greece [EGR1607].▼

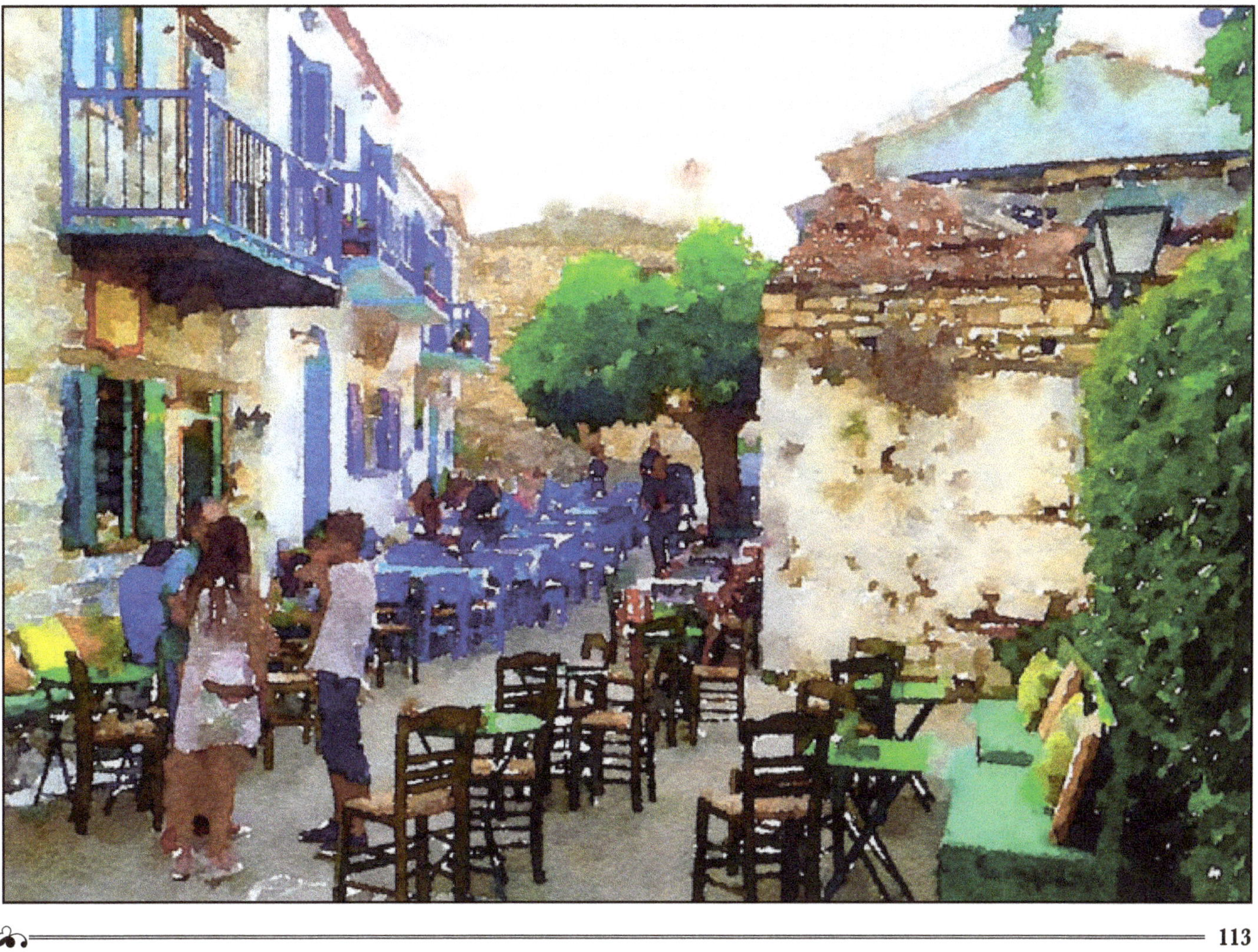

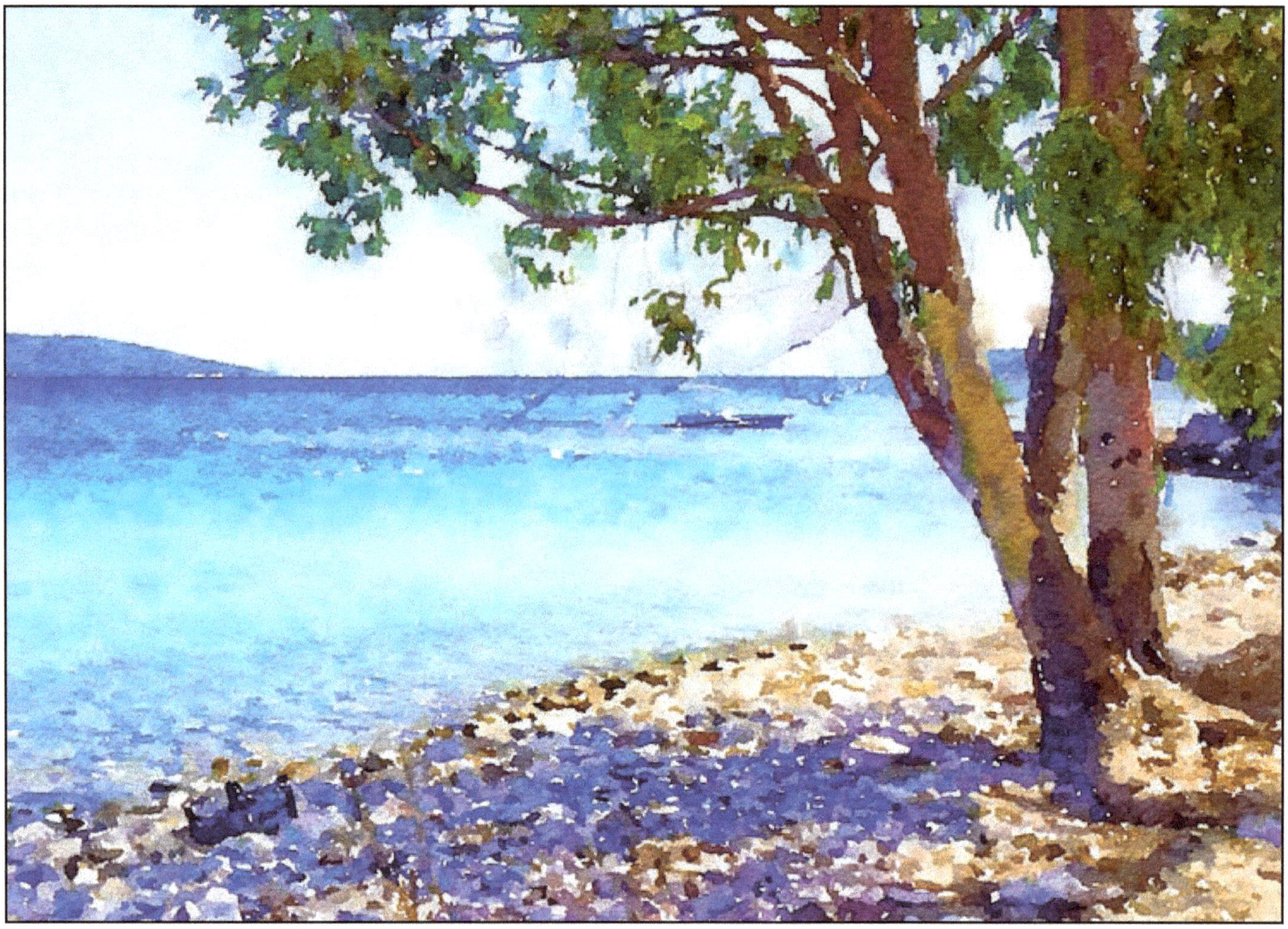

▲'Agios Dimitrios' (2016), Alonissos, Greece [EGR1605].

'Evening In Aloni' (2016), Alonissos, Greece [EGR1602].▼

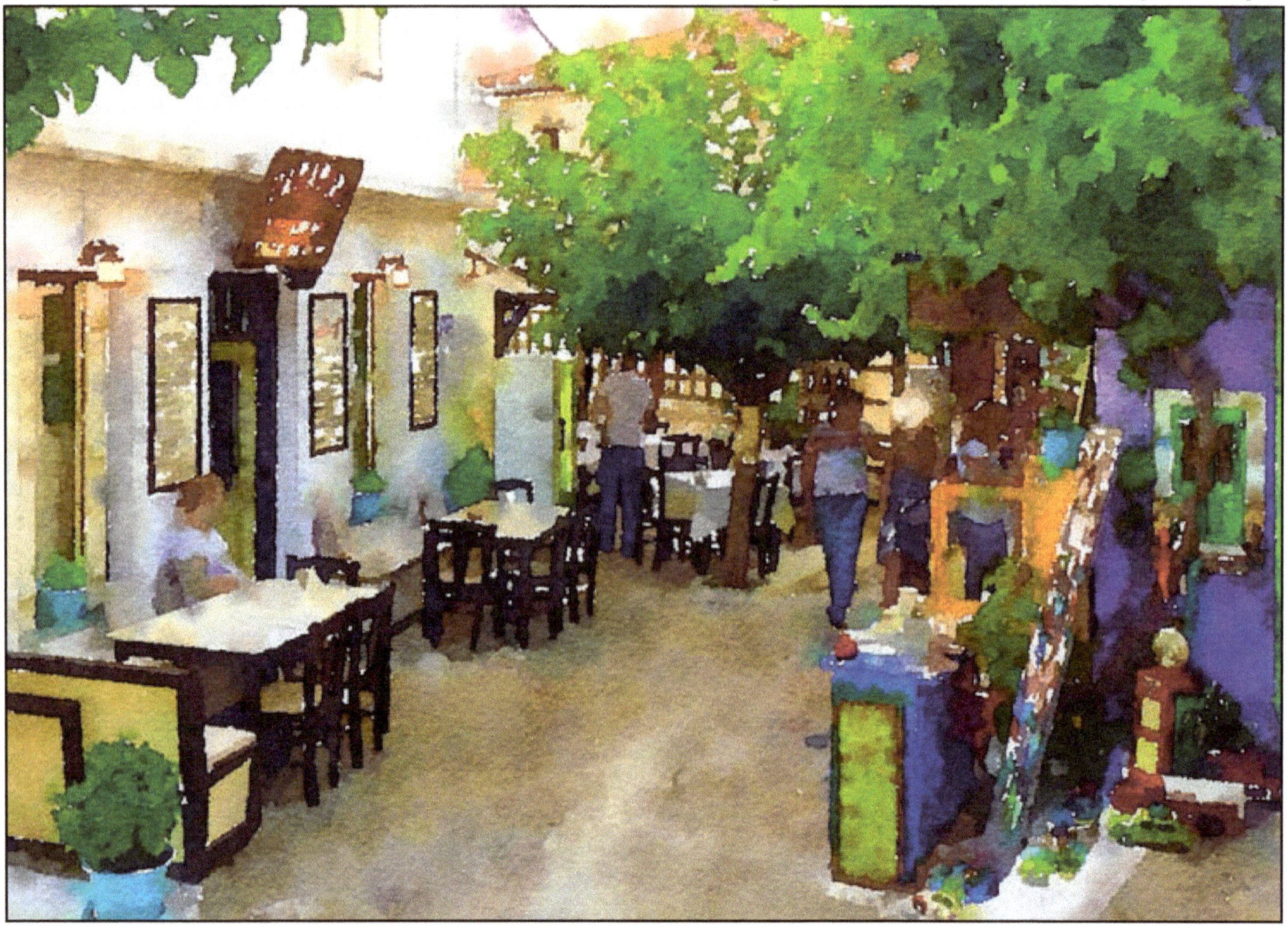

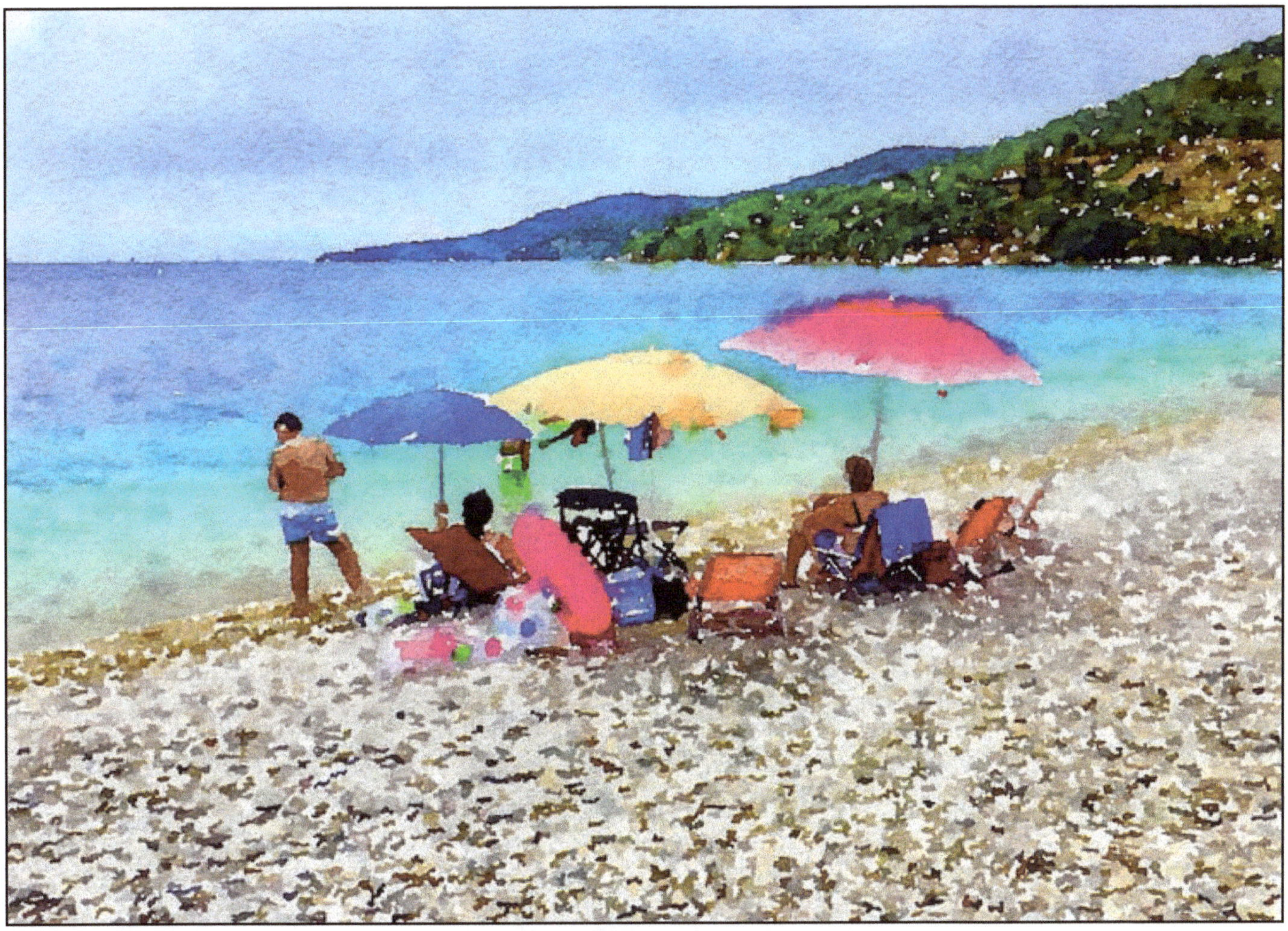

▲'Kokkinokastro Beach' (2016), Alonissos, Greece [EGR1603].

'The Painted Pots Of Alonnisos' (2016), Alonissos, Greece [EGR1601].▼

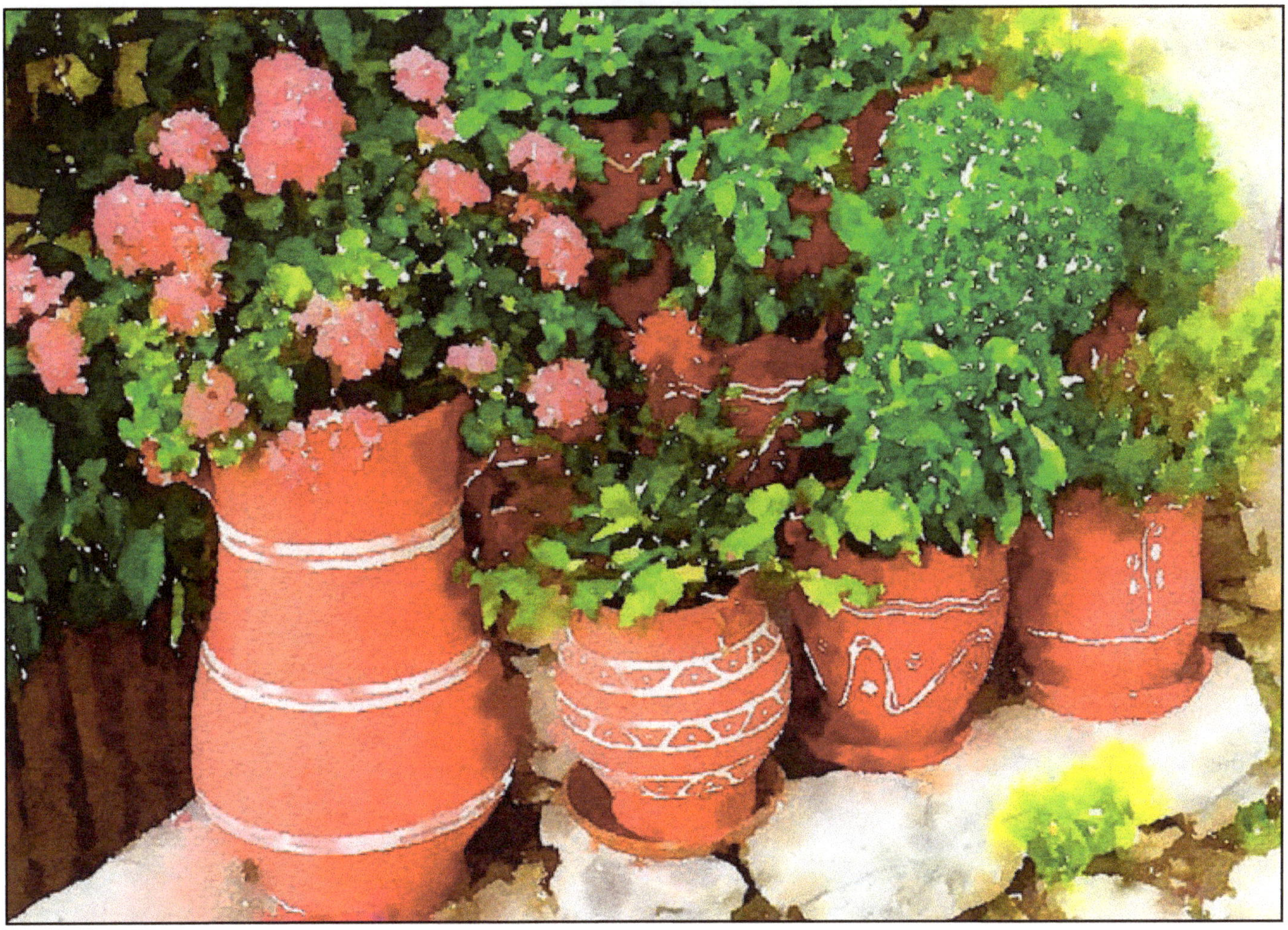

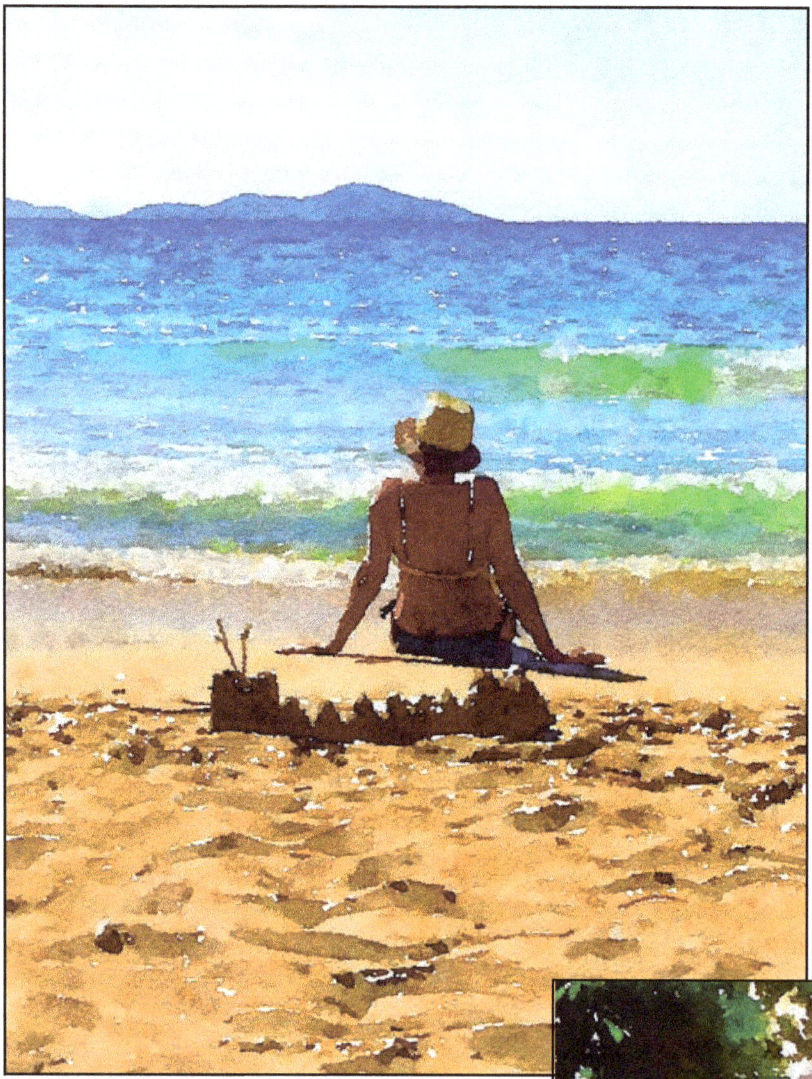

◀'Paralia Chrisi Milia' (2016), Alonissos, Greece [EGR1604].

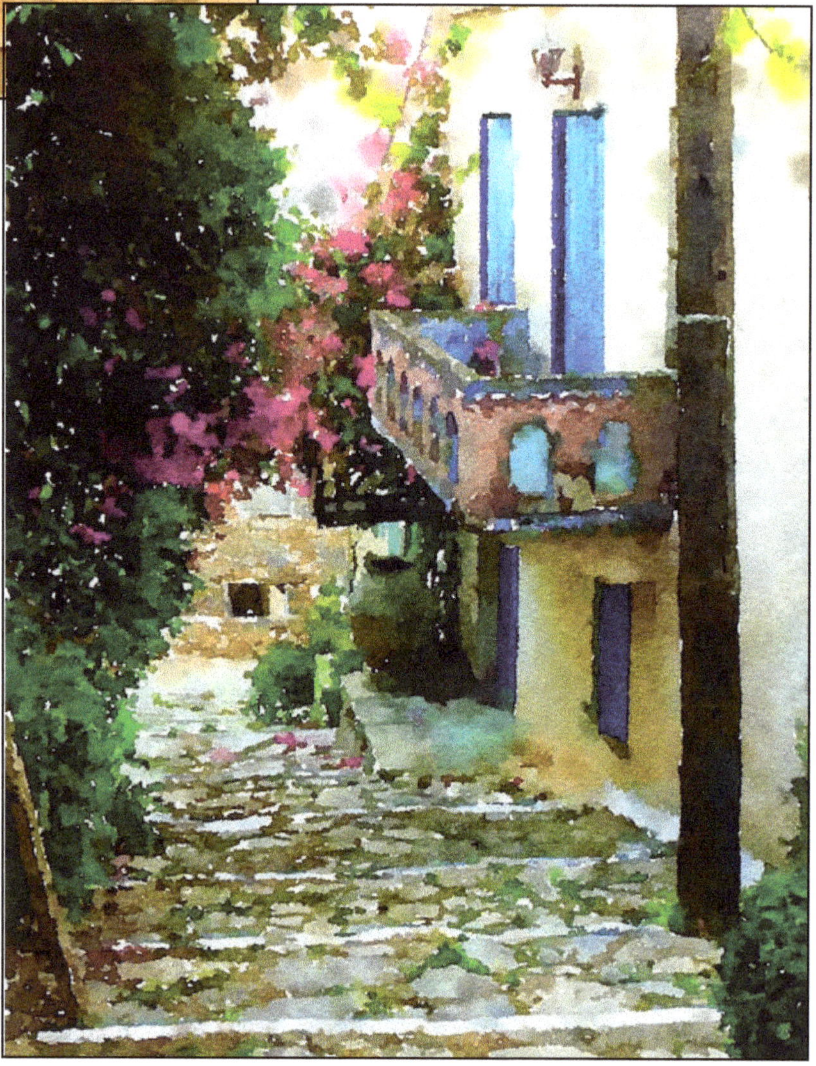

▶'Aloni Old Town' (2016), Alonissos, Greece [EGR1608].

Hungary...

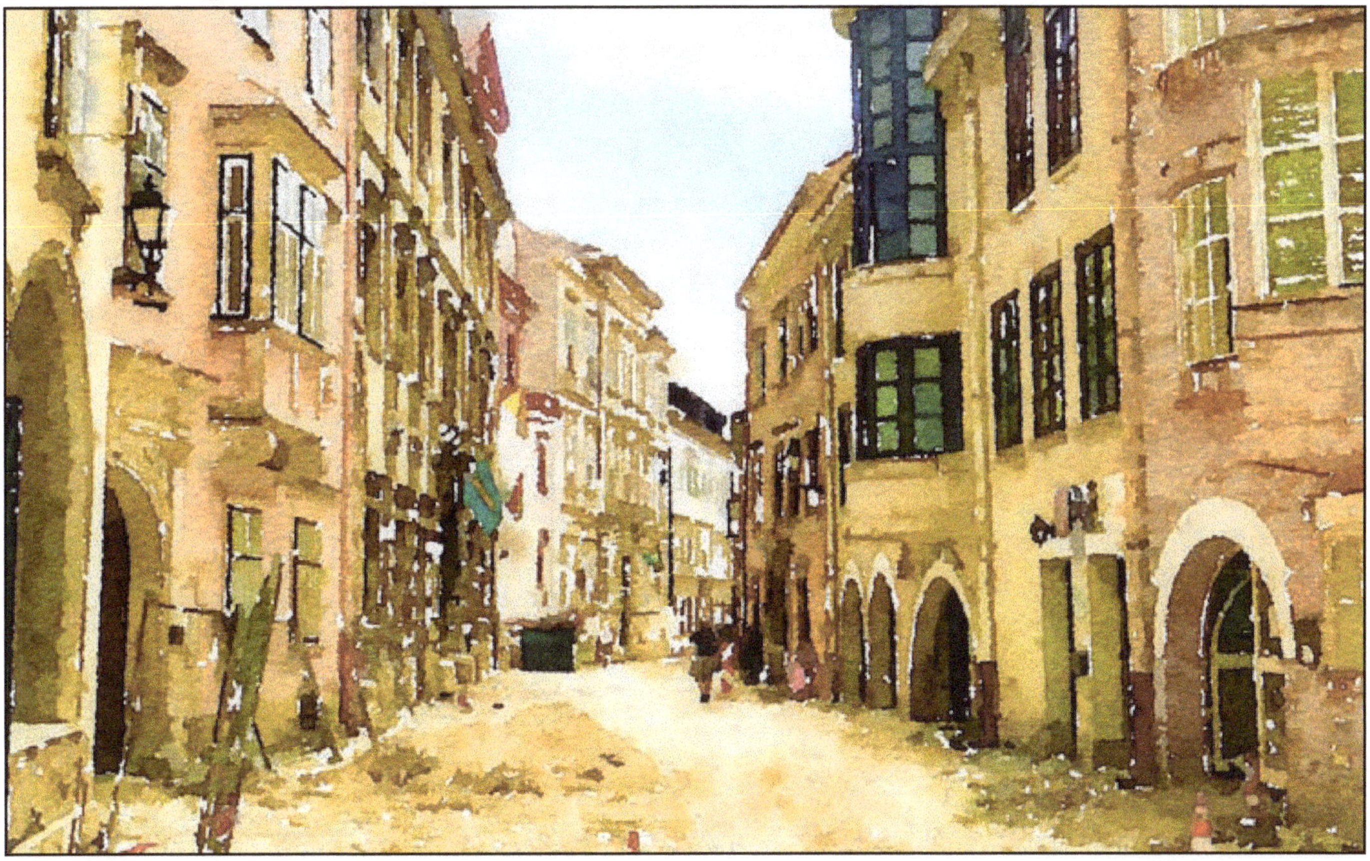

▲'Sveni Gyorgy' (2018), Sopron, Hungary [EHU1801].

'The Village' (2018), Tihany, Hungary [EHU1802].▼

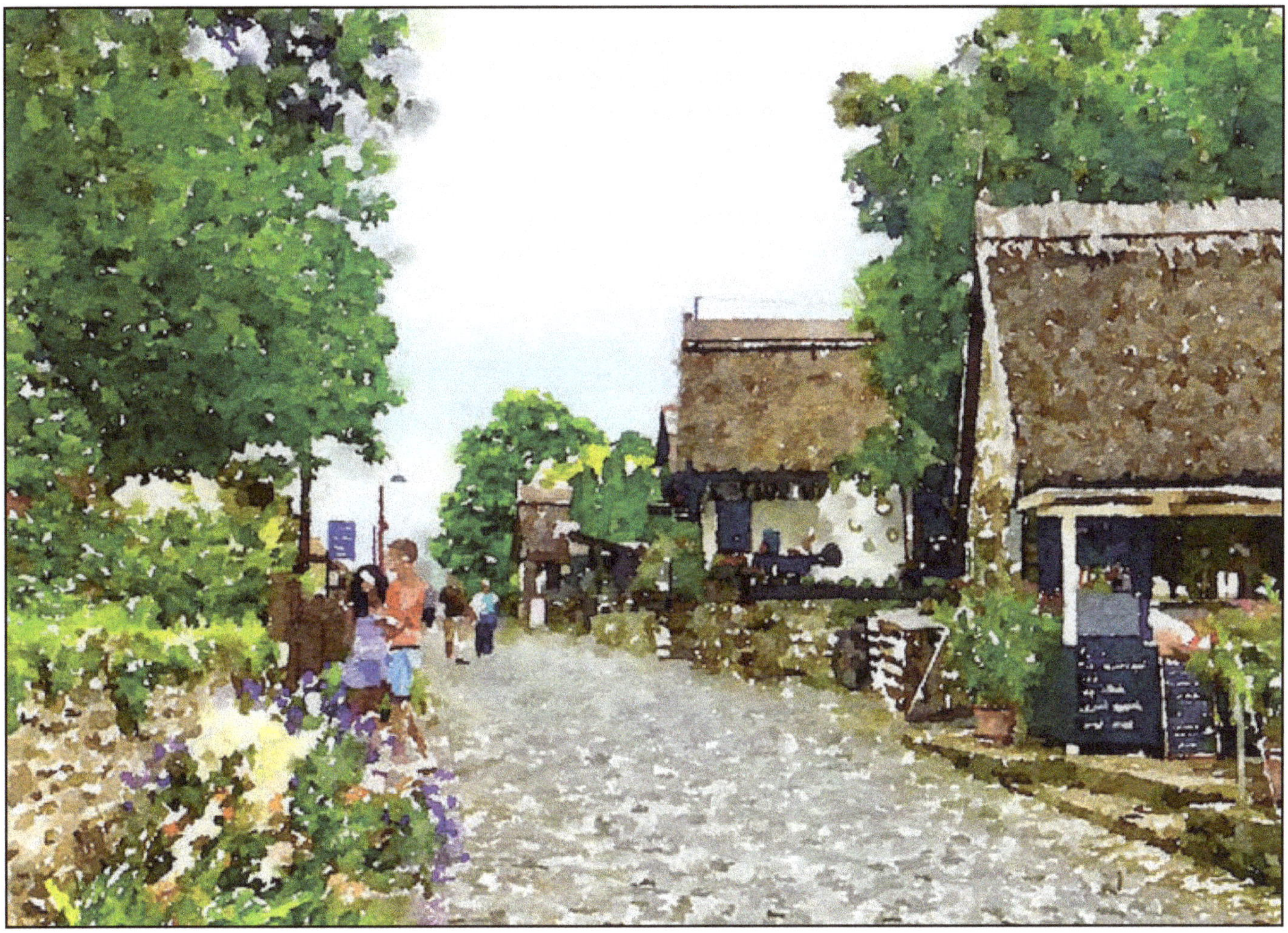

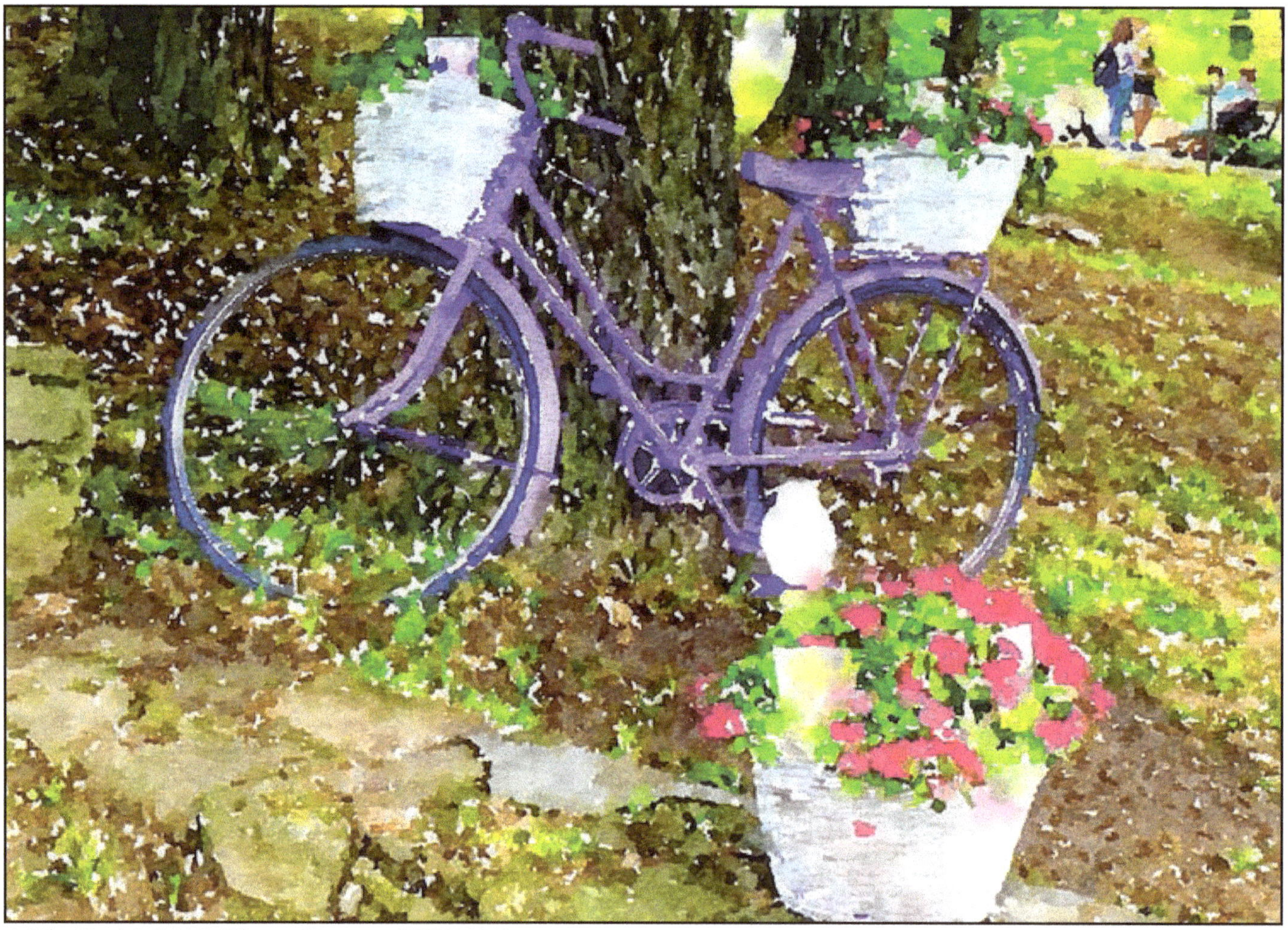

▲'The Picnic' (2018), Tihany, Hungary [EHU1803].

'Zrinyi Utca To St Stephens' (2018), Budapest, Hungary [EHU1809].▼

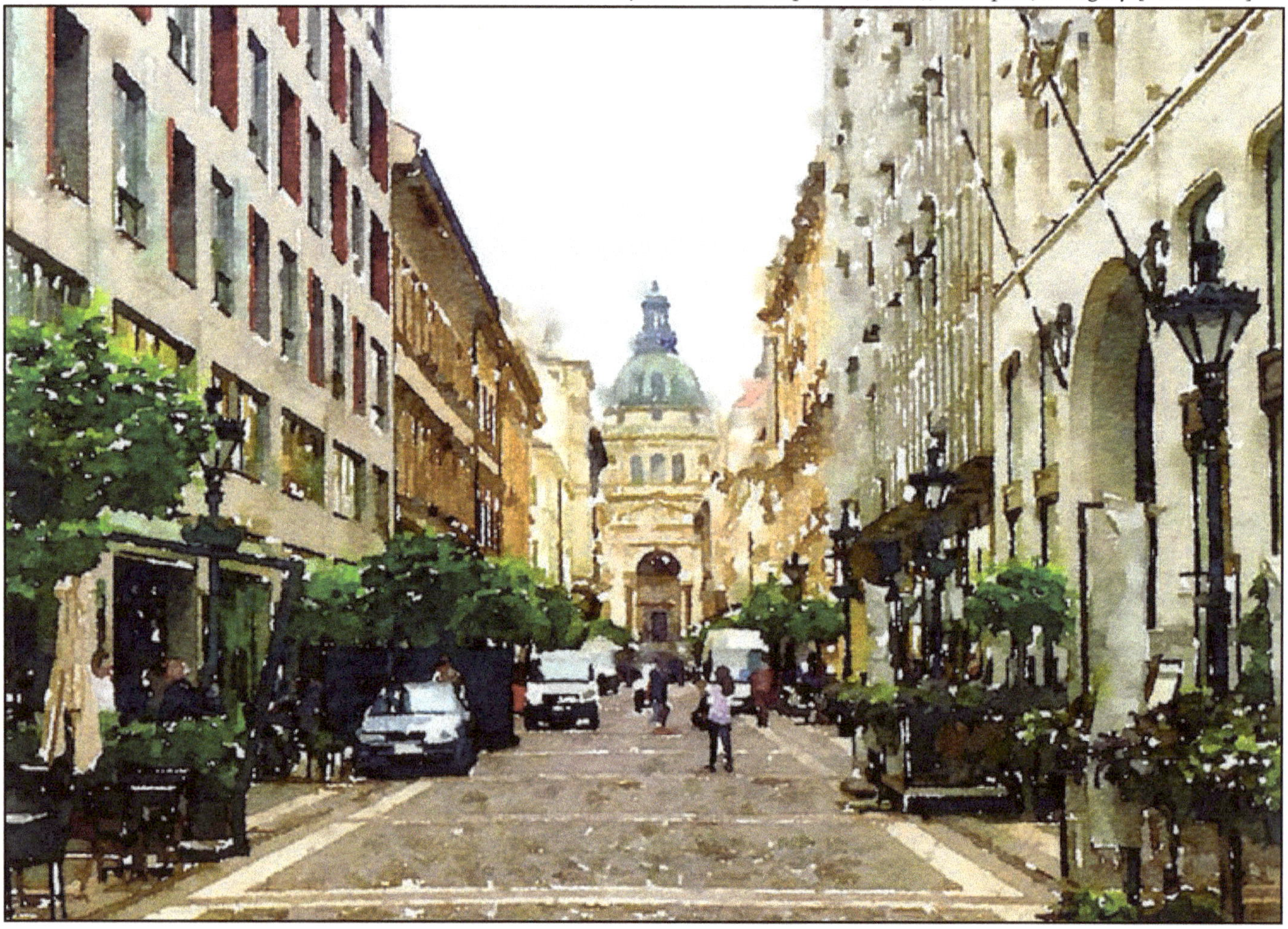

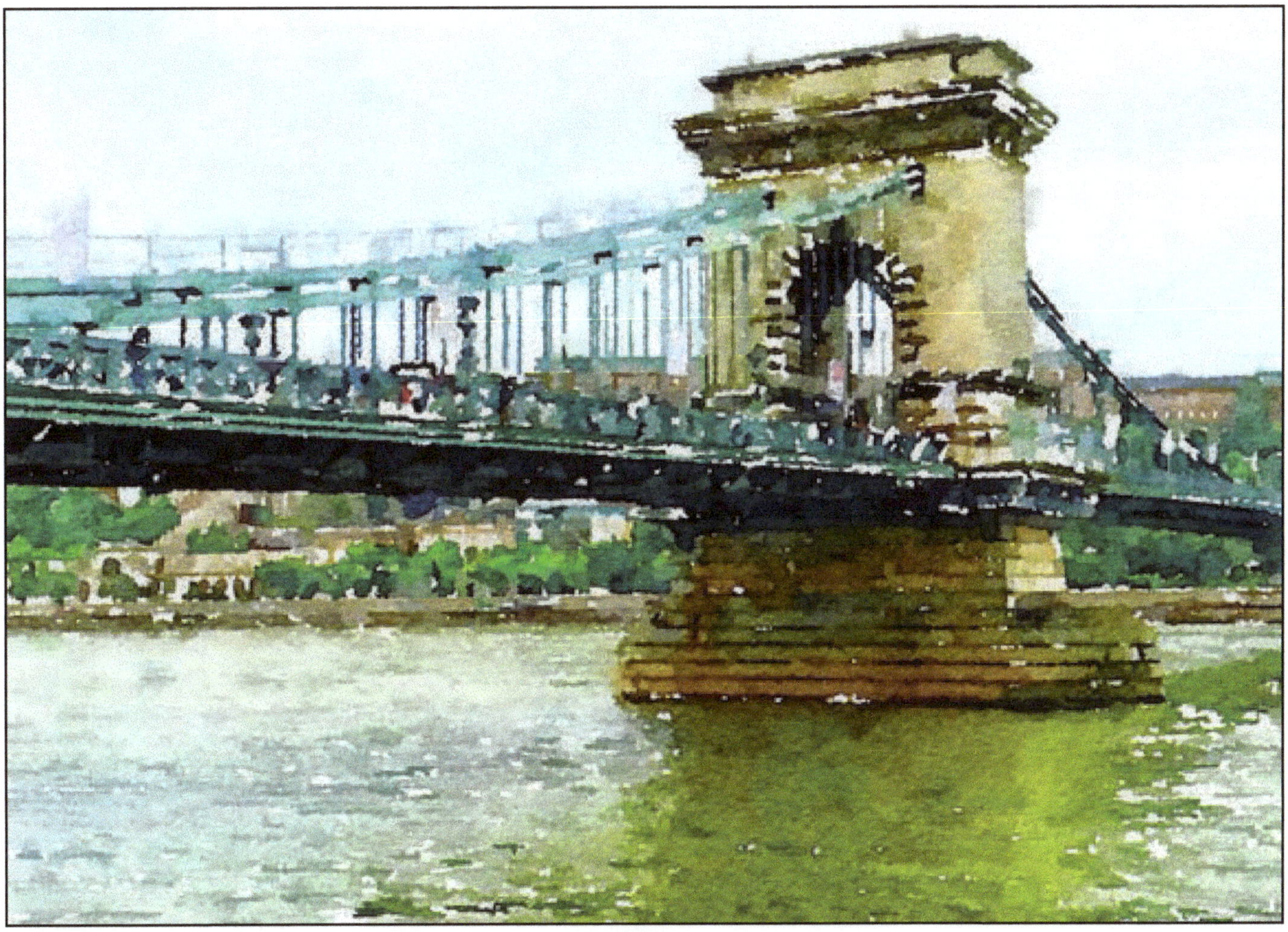

▲'Széchenyi Chain Bridge' (2018), Budapest, Hungary [EHU1811].

'Lights Of Széchenyi Bridge' (2018), Budapest, Hungary [EHU1807].▼

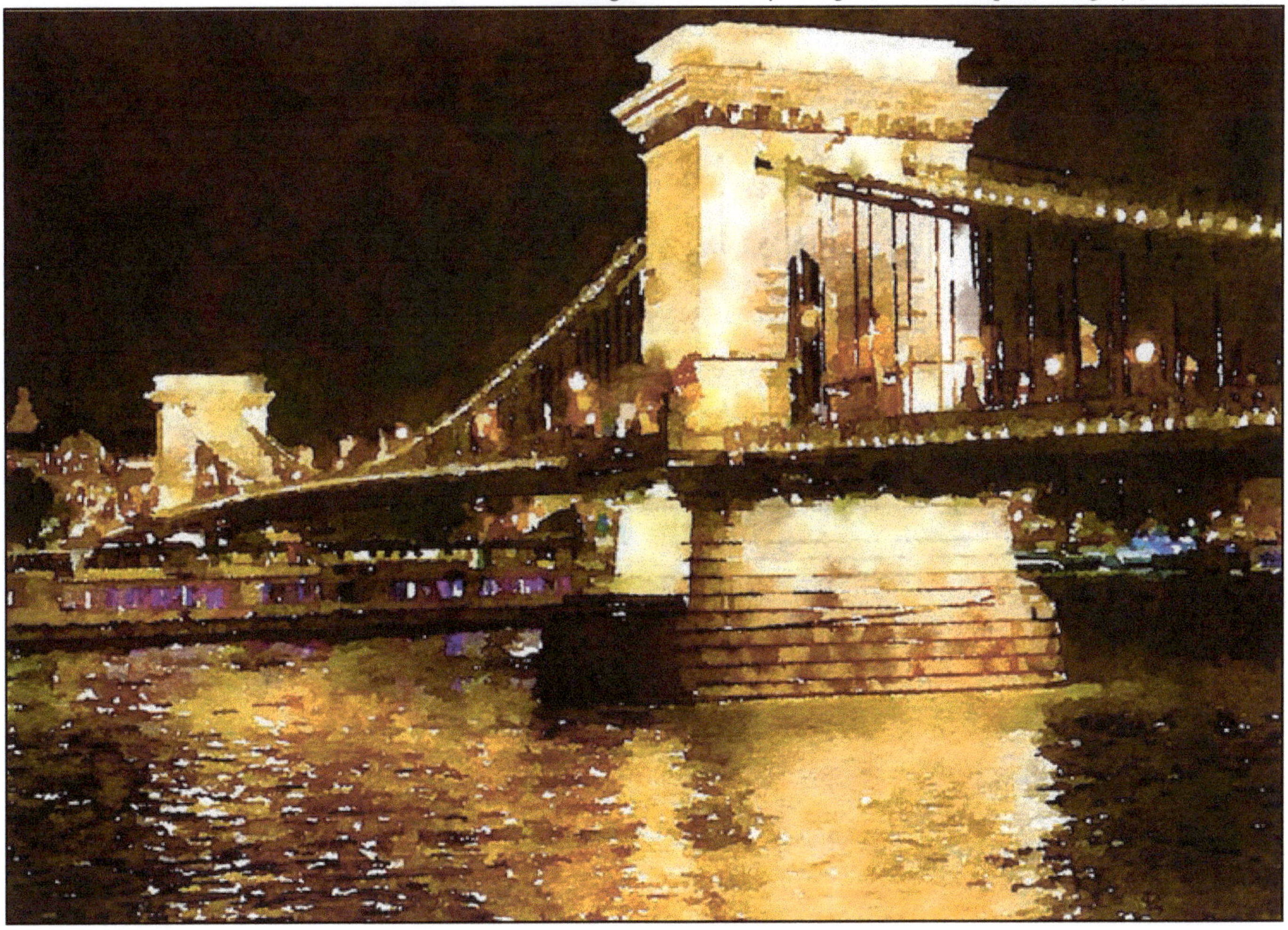

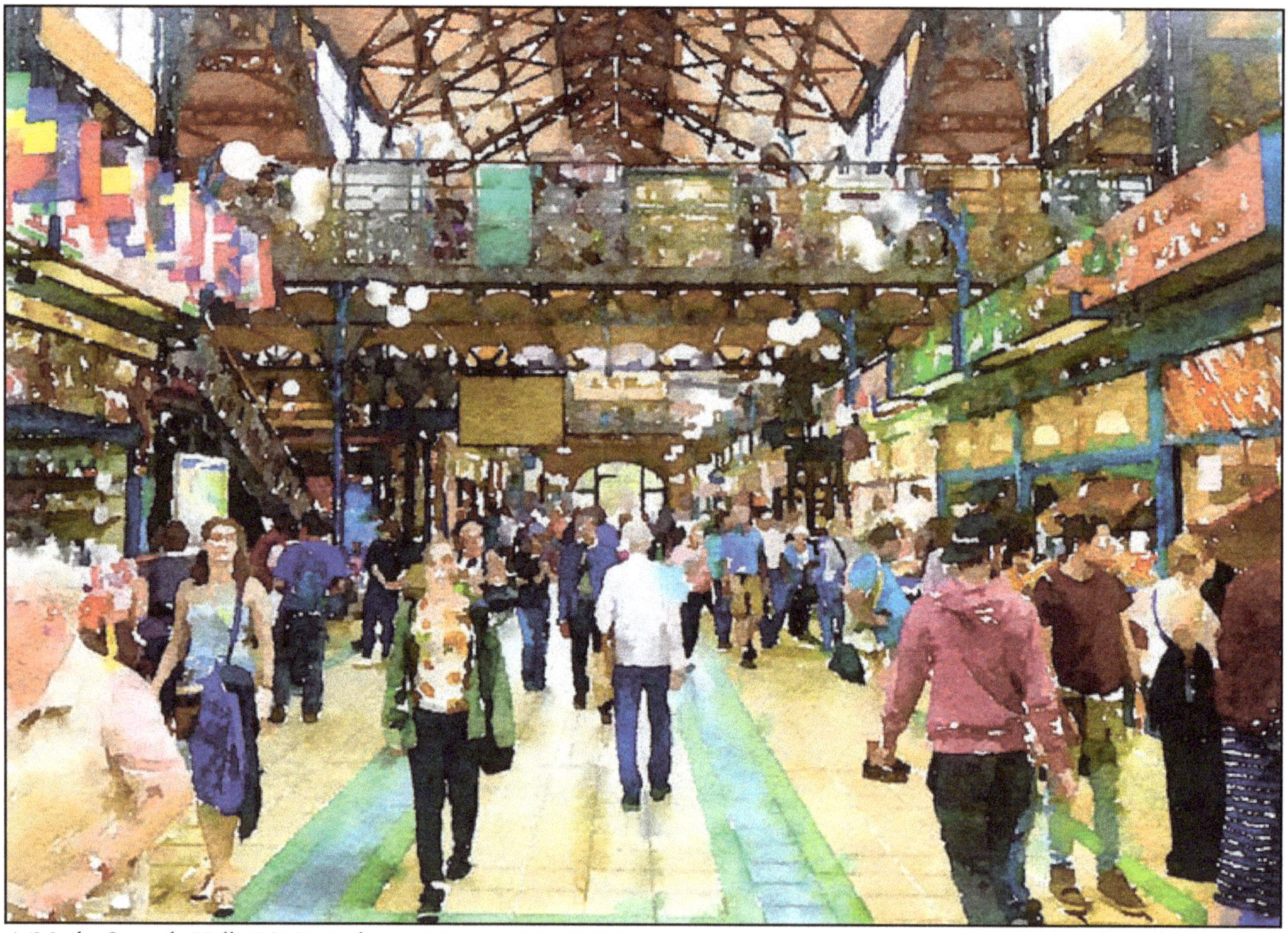

▲'Markt Centrale Hall' (2018), Budapest, Hungary [EHU1813].

'Budapest-Nyugati Station' (2018), Budapest, Hungary [EHU1814].▼

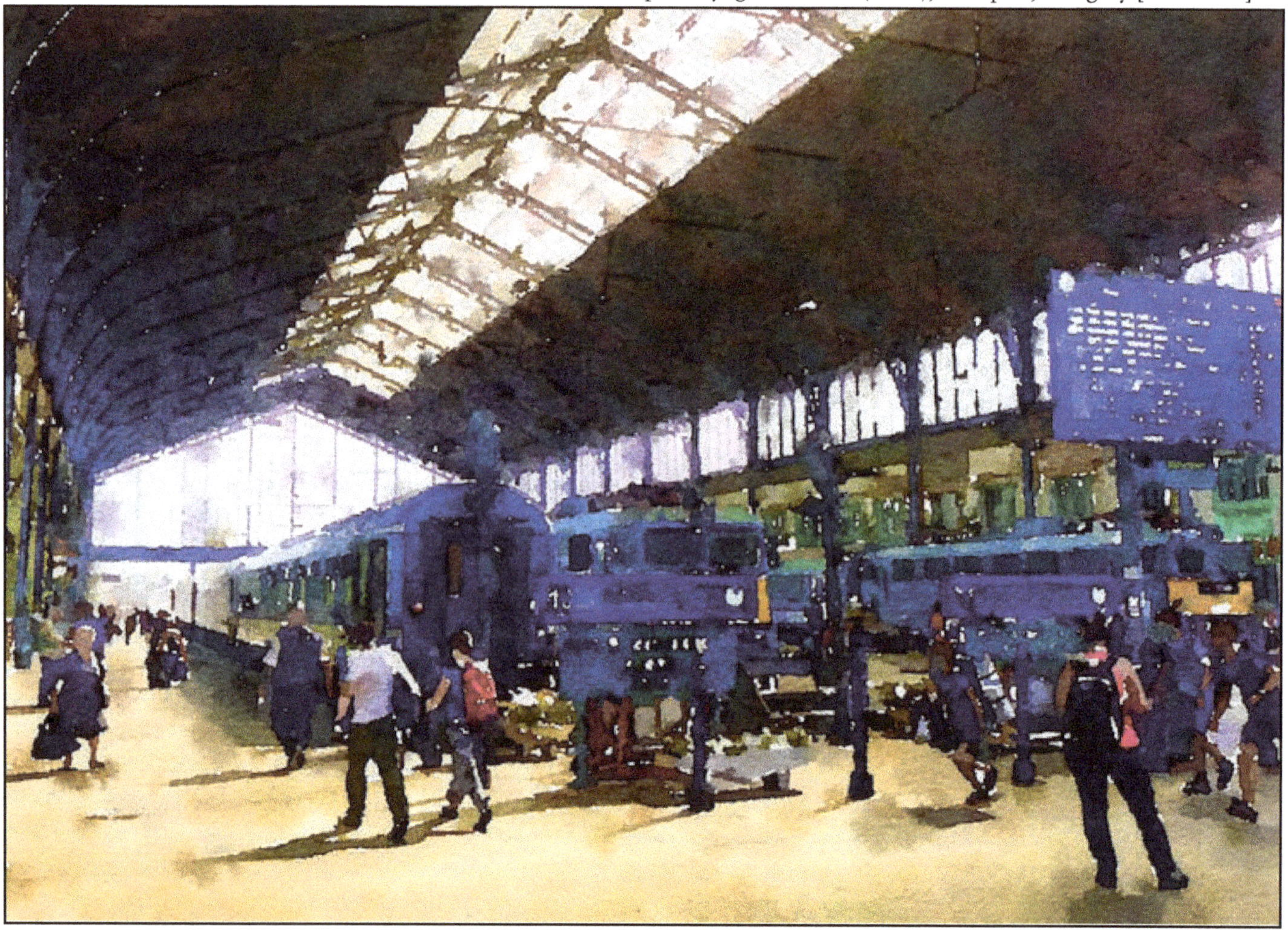

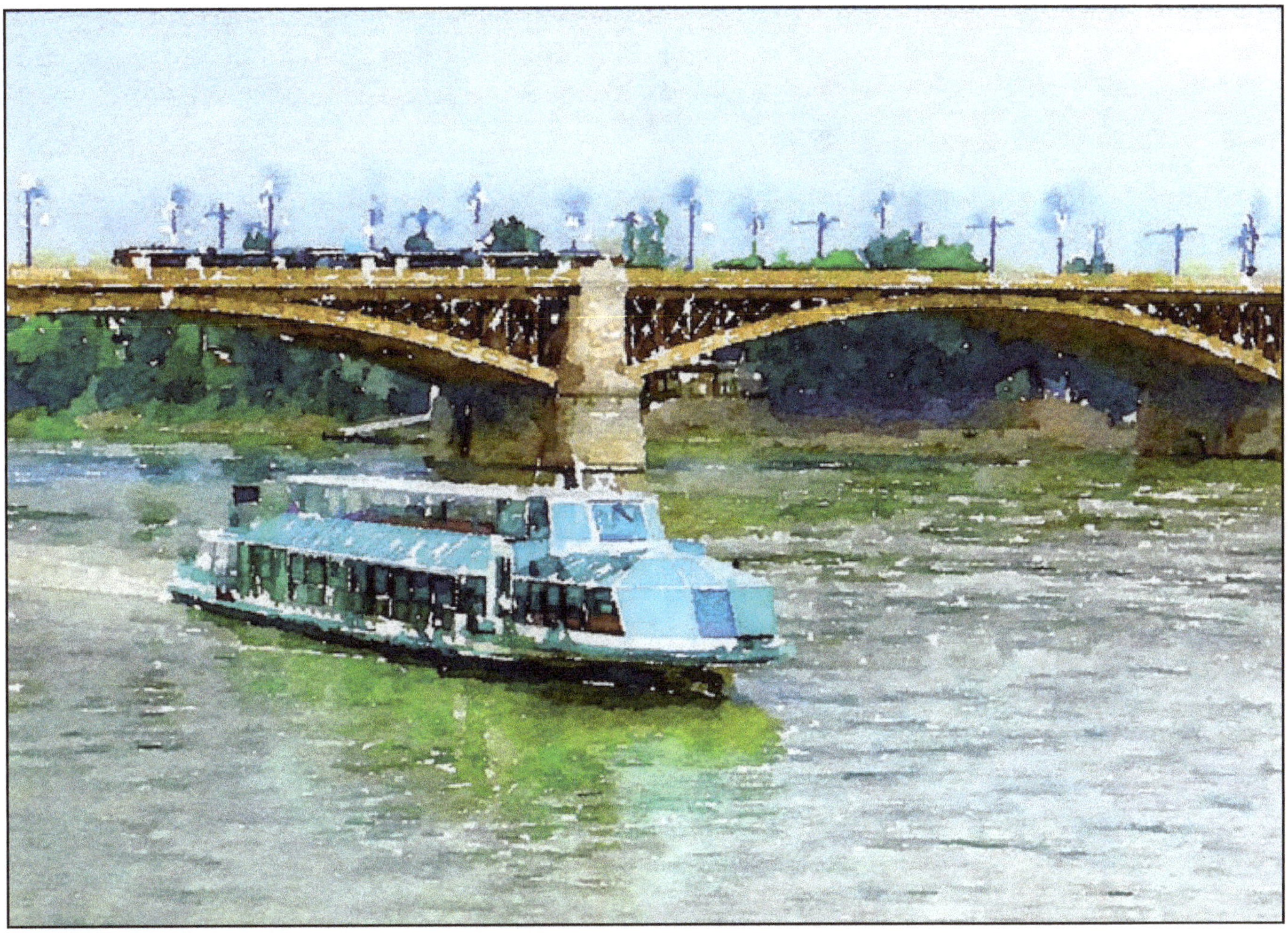

▲'Danube River Traffic' (2018), Budapest, Hungary [EHU1805].

'Houses Of Parliament' (2018), Budapest, Hungary [EHU1804].▼

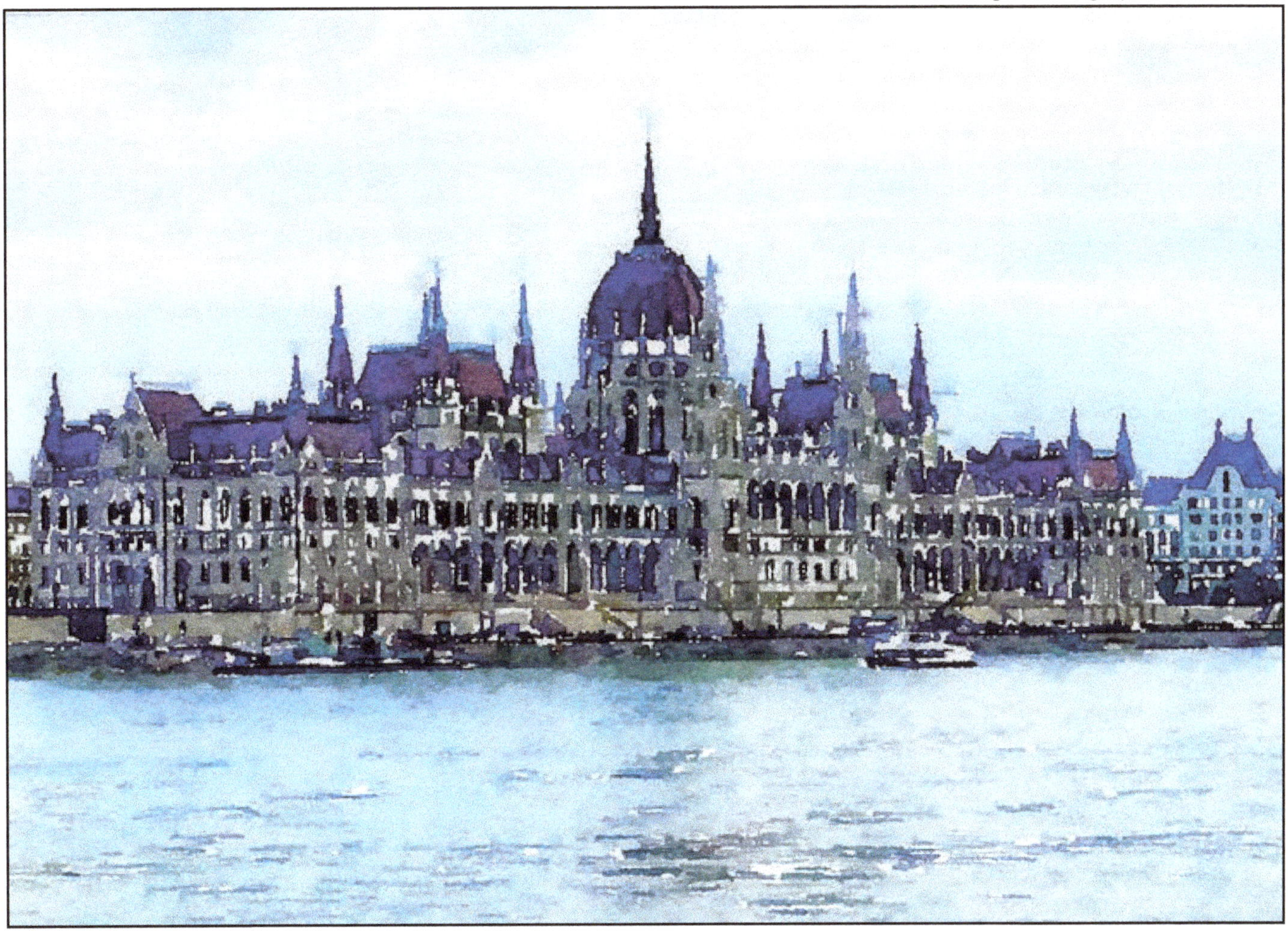

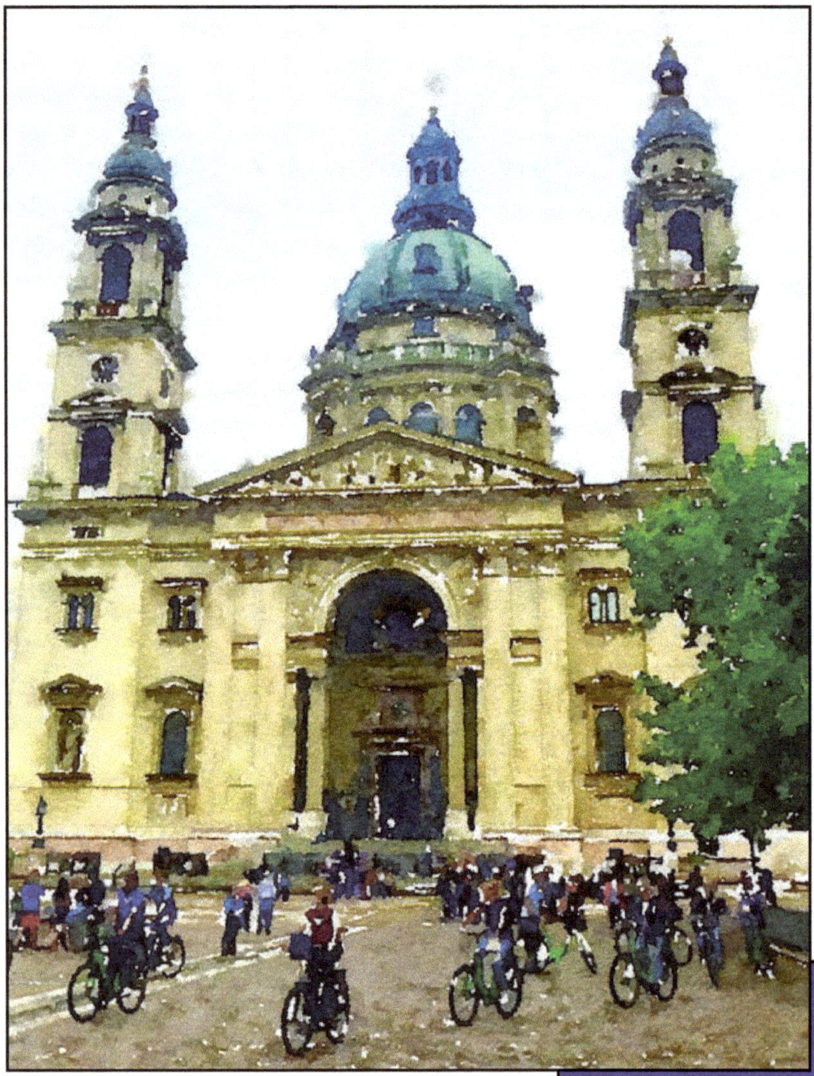

◀'St Stephens Basilica' (2018), Budapest, Hungary [EHU1810].

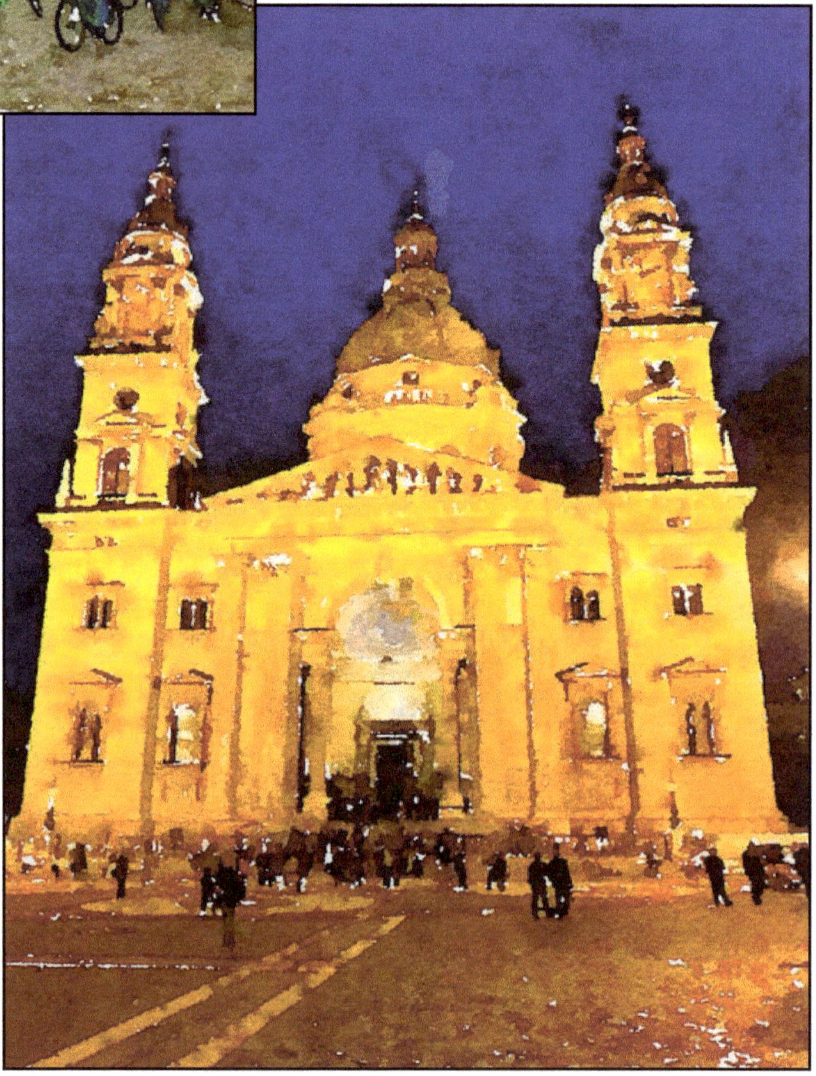

▶'Evening At St Stephens' (2018), Budapest, Hungary [EHU1806].

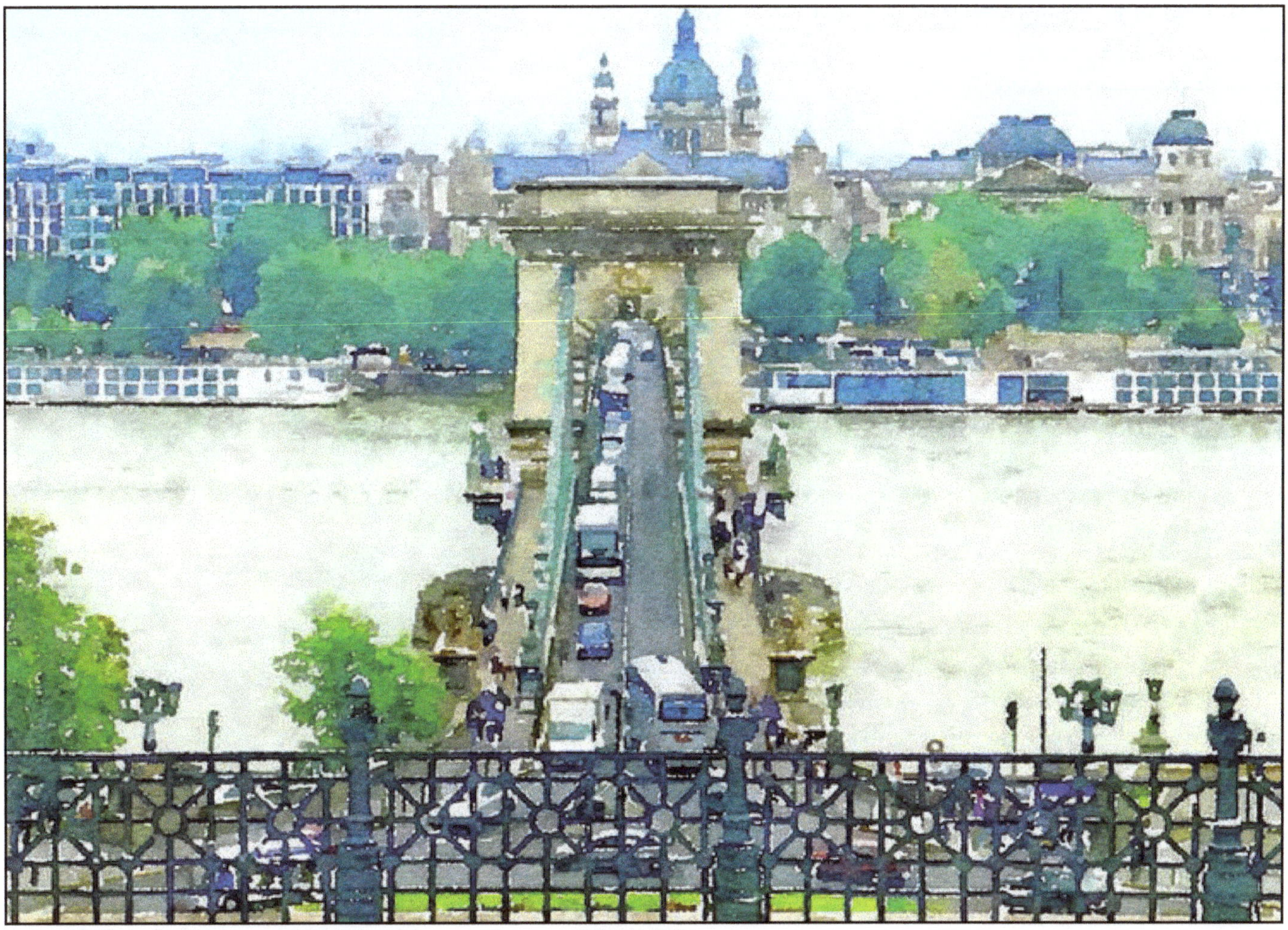

▲'Lánchíd From Alagút-teto' (2018), Budapest, Hungary [EHU1812].

'The Lights Of Parliament' (2018), Budapest, Hungary [EHU1808].▼

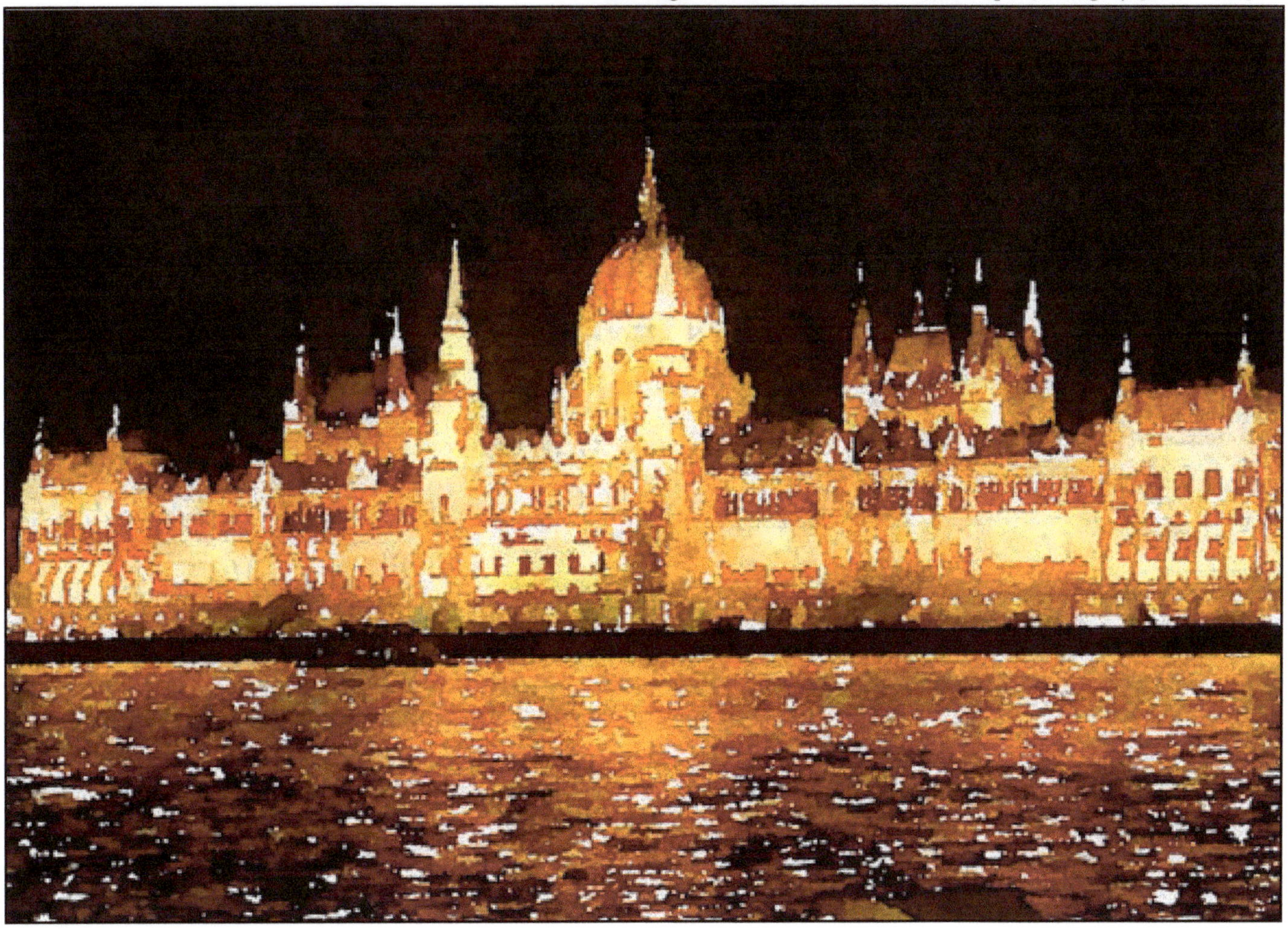

Ireland...

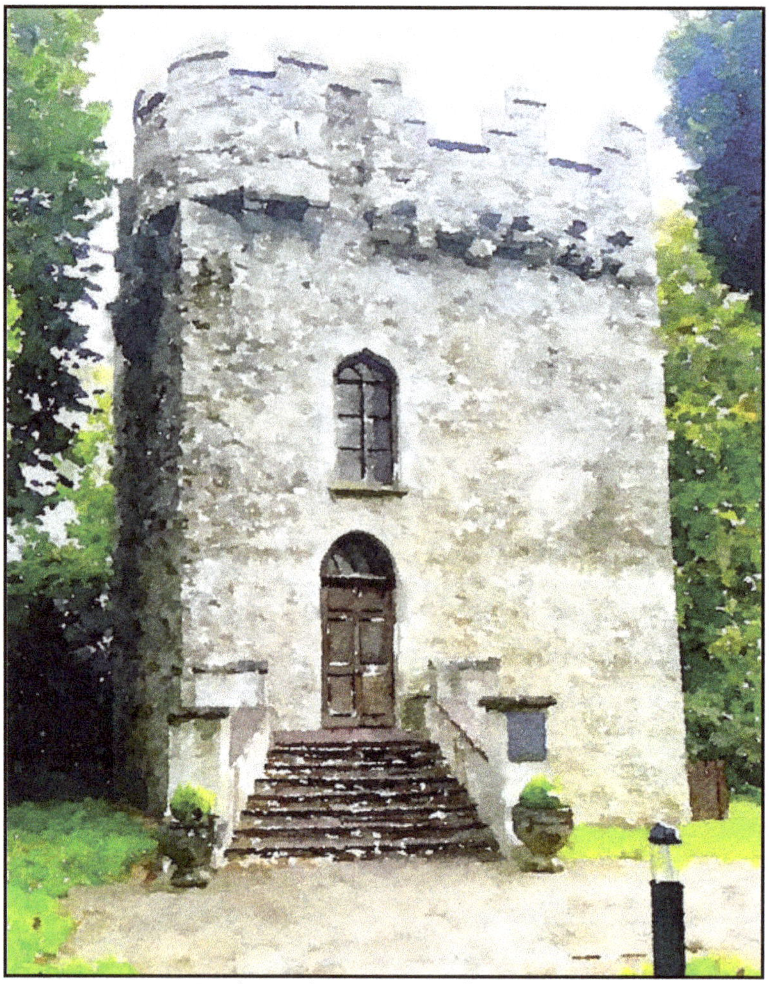

'Castle Dunloe' (2018), Killarney, Ireland [EIE1807].▲

I flew into Belfast in 1993, and travelled by train to Dublin where I then drove to County Cork, but it was a lightning fast trip with no lasting images. By 2016 new research into my Irish ancestry had revealed some fascinating insights and so in late 2018 I managed to organise a three week tour of Scotland and Ireland in conjunction with my old friend and Sydney University colleague, Dr Frank Davidson.

On the Irish leg we departed by road from Dublin and visited Limerick, then Tralee and Killarney before returning to Dublin via Cork City. The primary goal was to visit ancestral land and properties in County Kerry, which included the old family abodes of Dunloe Castle, and the grand houses of Cahernane and Muckross in Killarney.

In the short time I spent on this tour, I was amazed at the natural beauty of Ireland, the history and grandeur of its estates and the friendliness of the people. The end result was a unique collection of images, which have resulted in a few favourite works, but I must return for a longer and more in depth stay, when the time is right.

▼'Shops On Carhan Road' (2018), Cahirsiveen, Ireland [EIE1801].

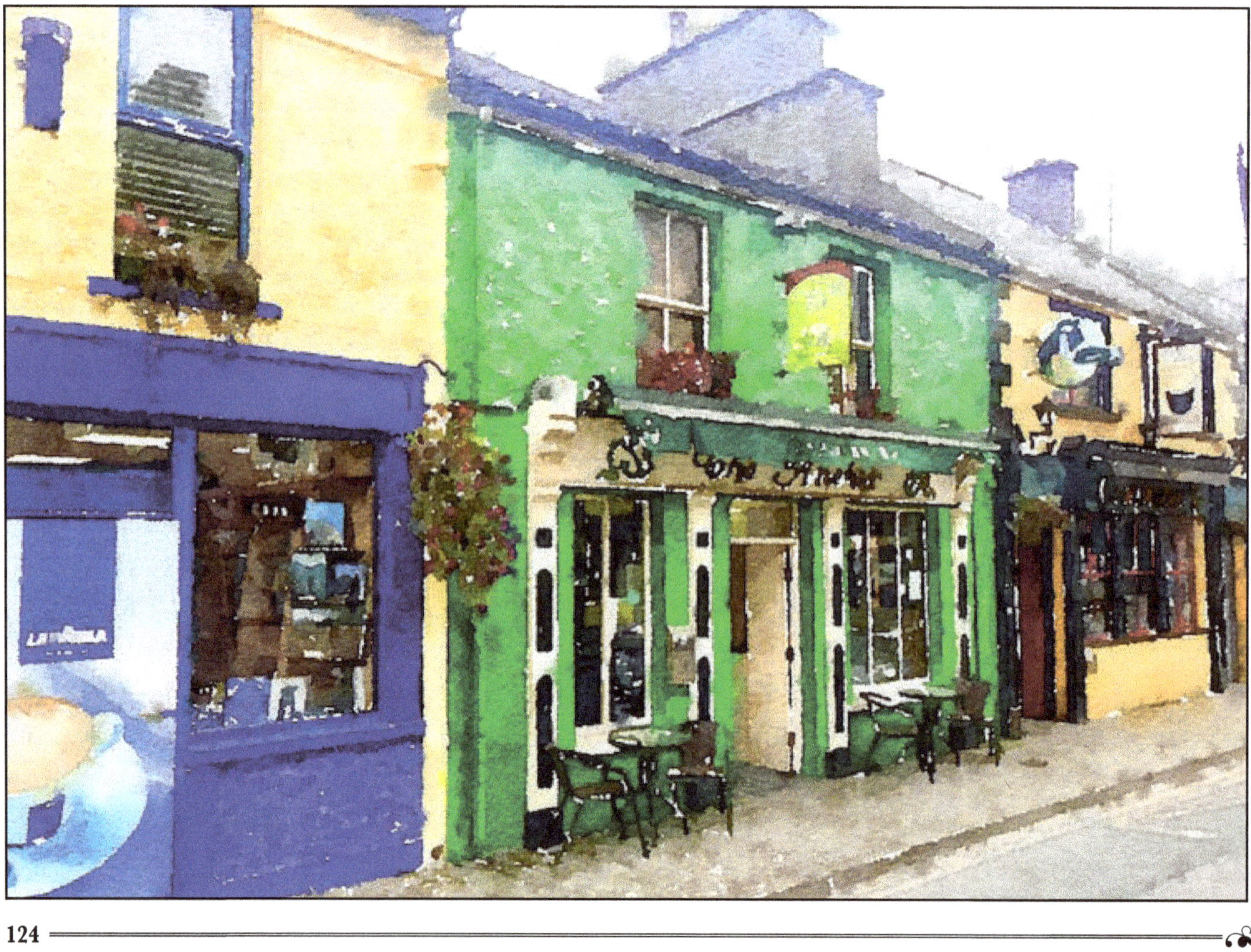

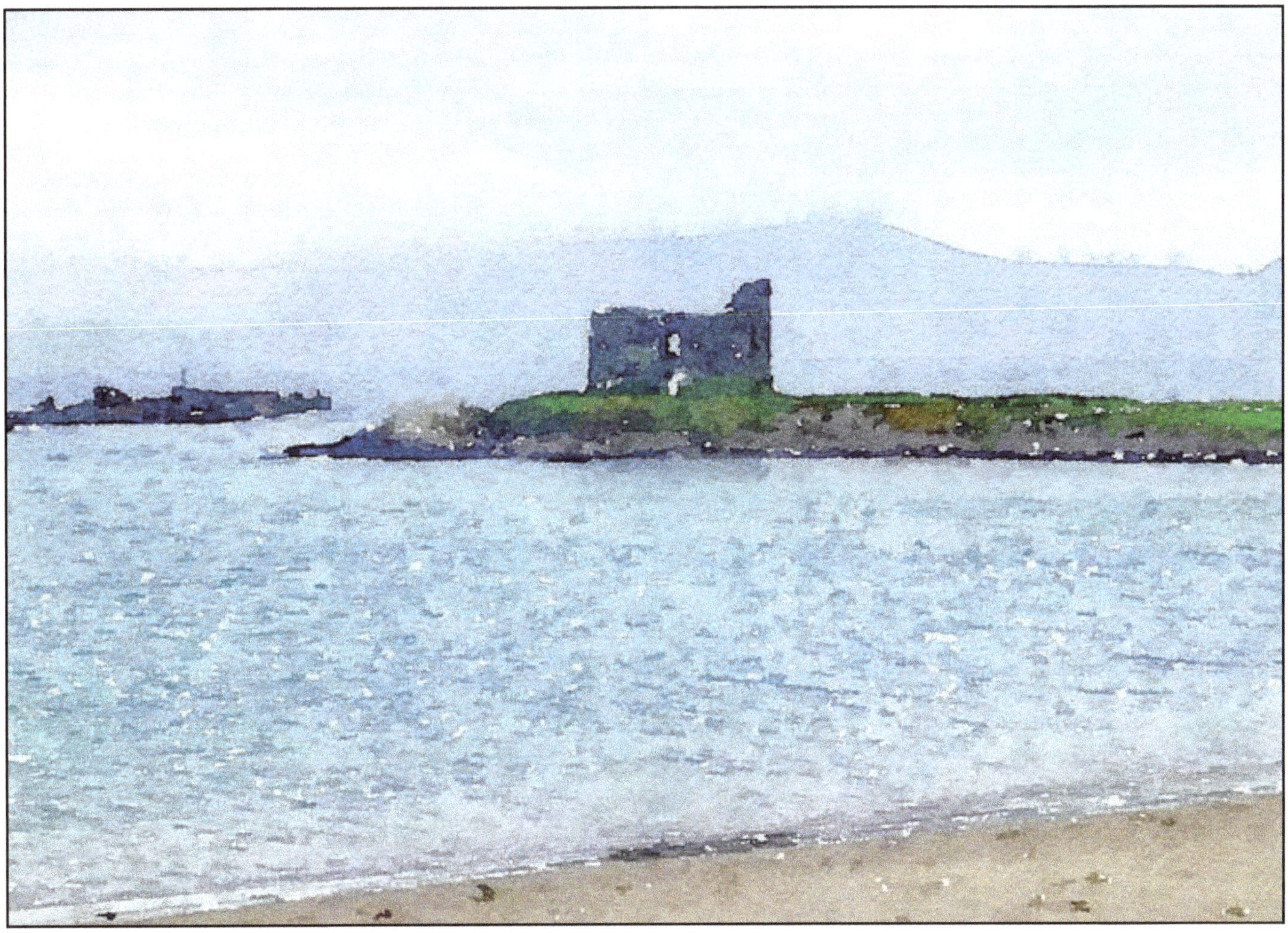

▲'The Castle (1540)' (2018), Ballinskelligs, Ireland [EIE1802].

'View To Ballyoughteragh' (2018), Co. Kerry, Ireland [EIE1803].▼

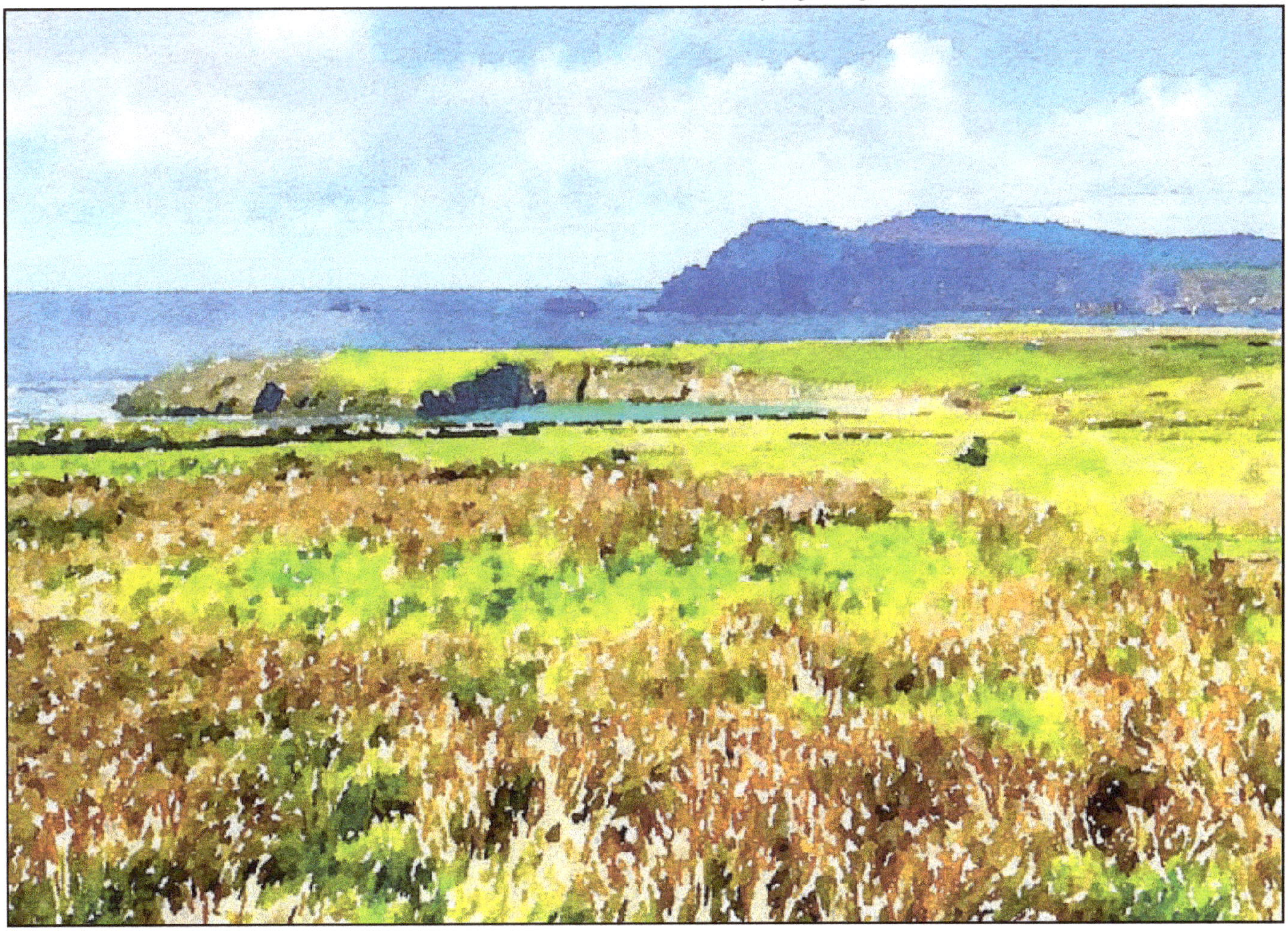

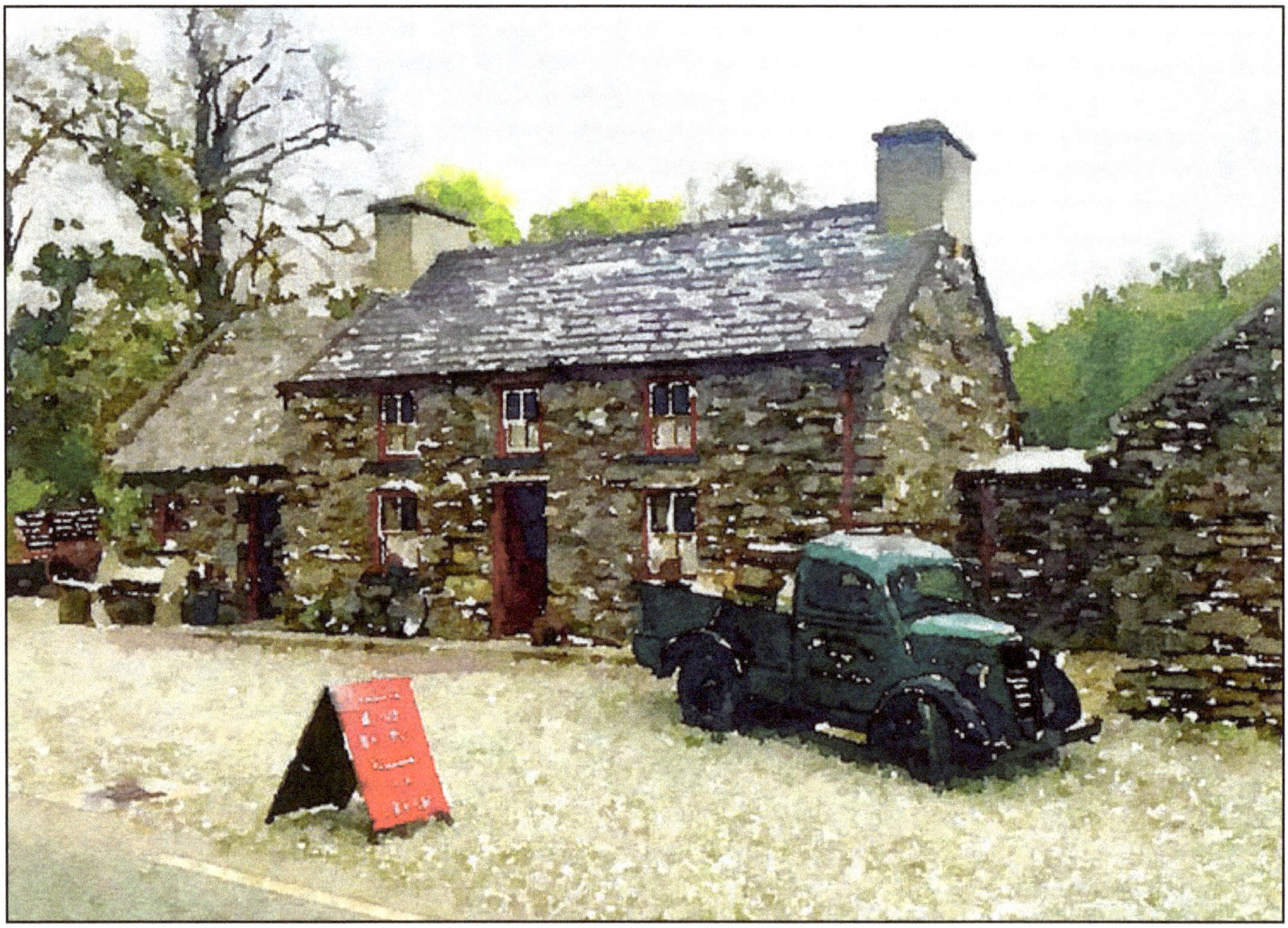

▲'Molly Gallivan's Cottage' (2018), Bonane, Ireland [EIE1804].

'The Three Bayed Cottage' (2018), Co. Kerry, Ireland [EIE1806].▼

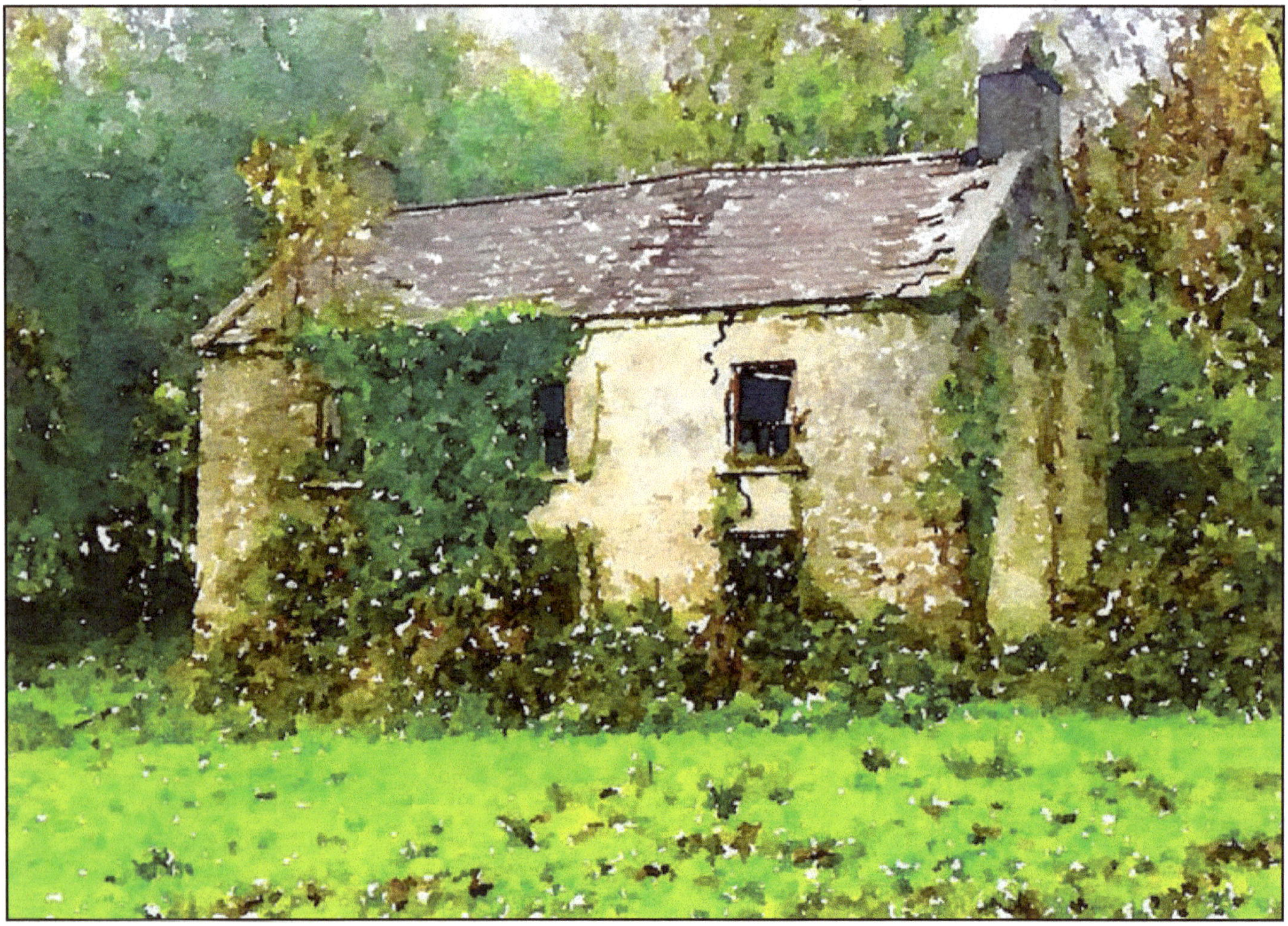

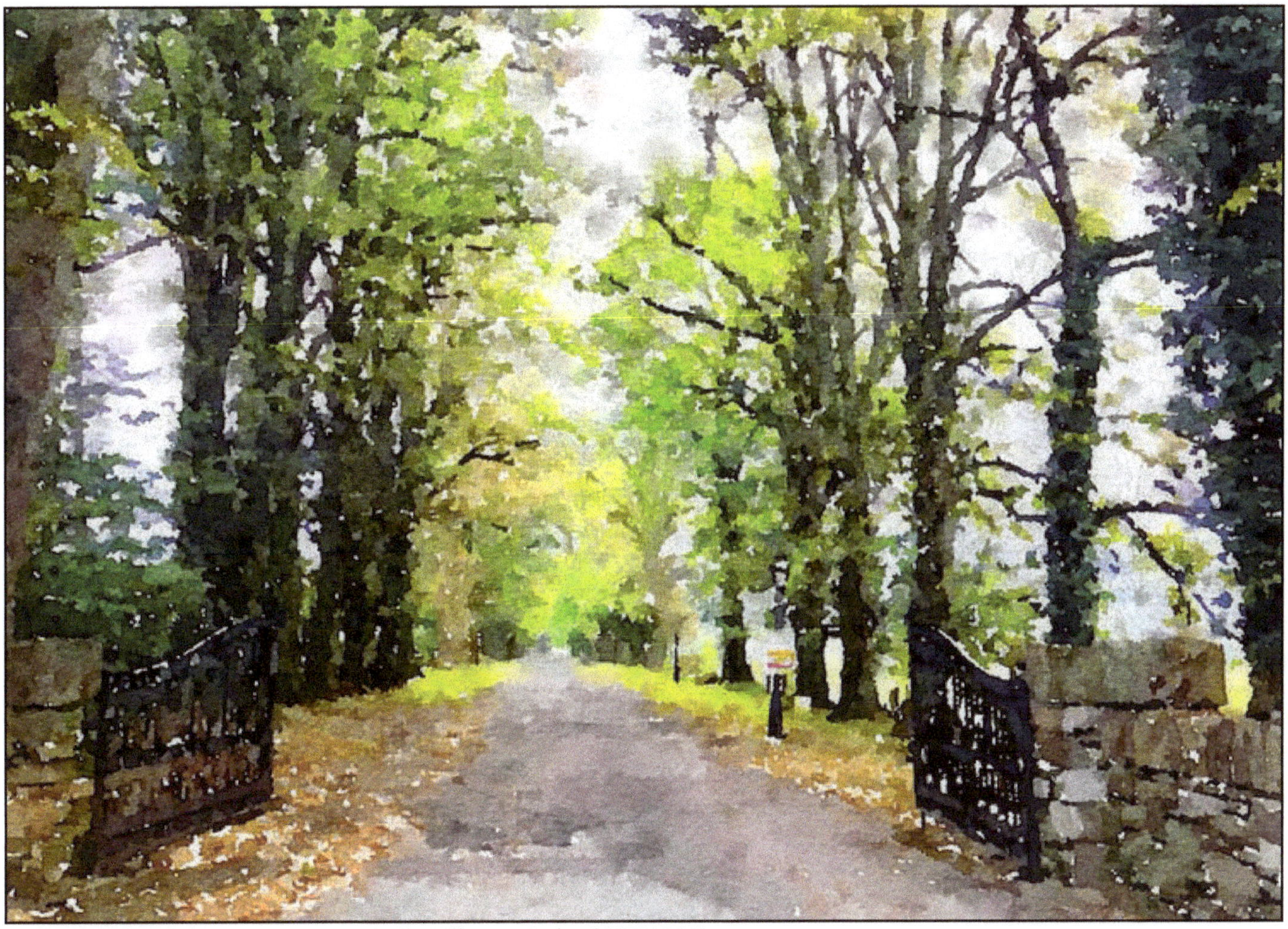

▲'Entrance To Cahernane House' (2018), Killarney, Ireland [EIE1808].

'Cahernane House (1877)' (2018), Killarney, Ireland [EIE1809].▼

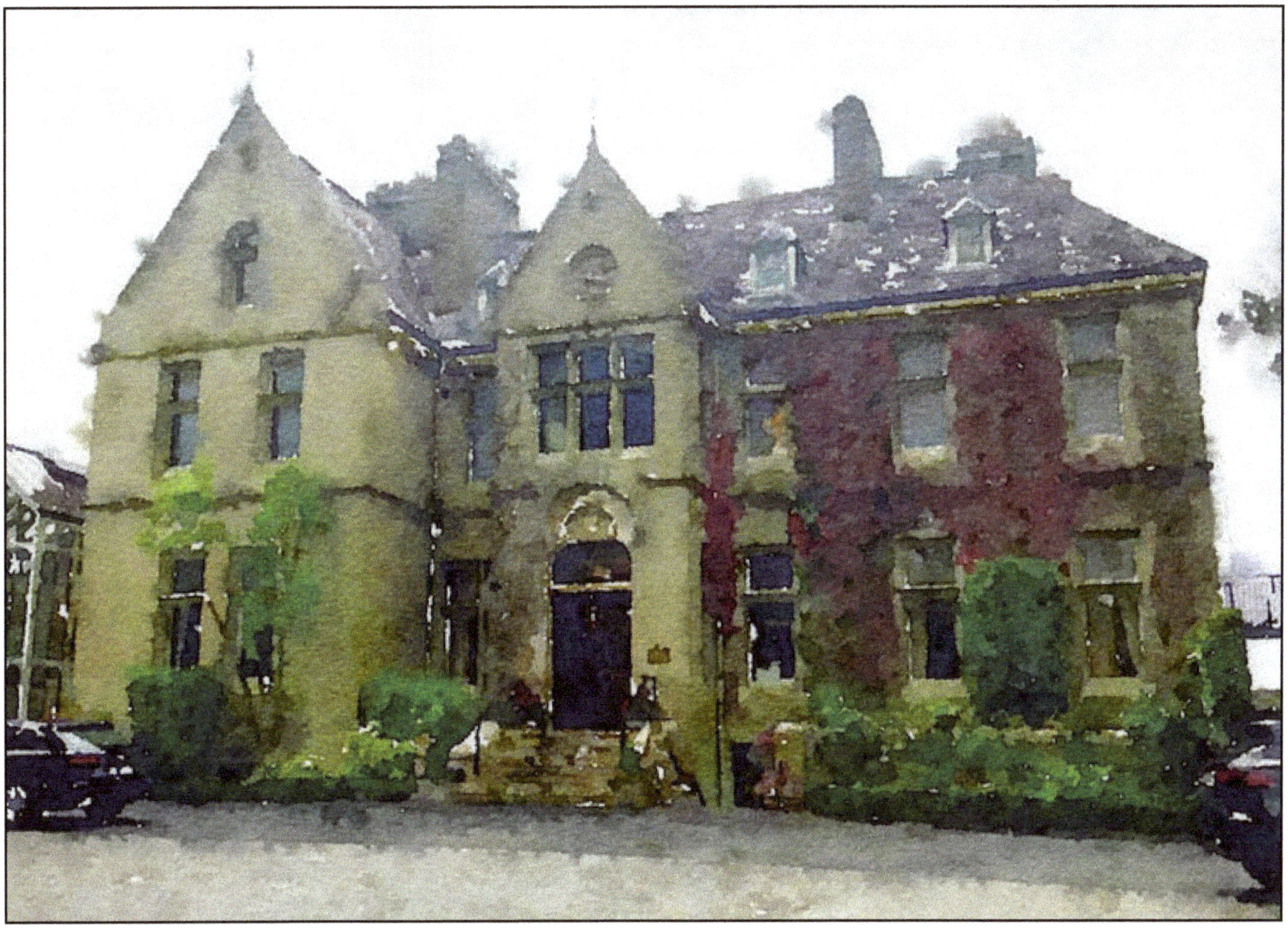

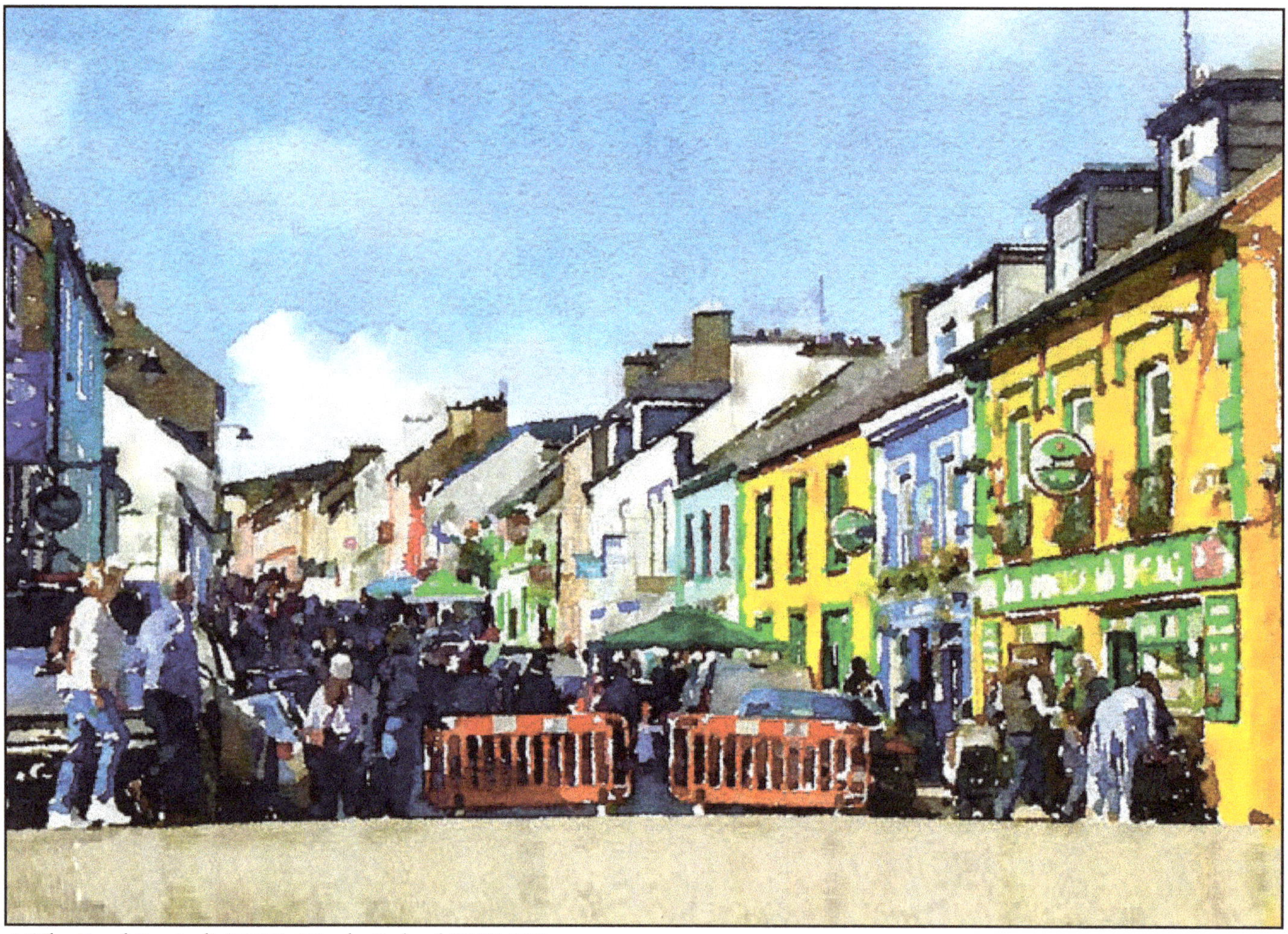

▲'The Food Festival' (2018), Dingle, Ireland [EIE1805].

'Dining Room, Arbutus Hotel' (2018), Killarney, Ireland [EIE1810].▼

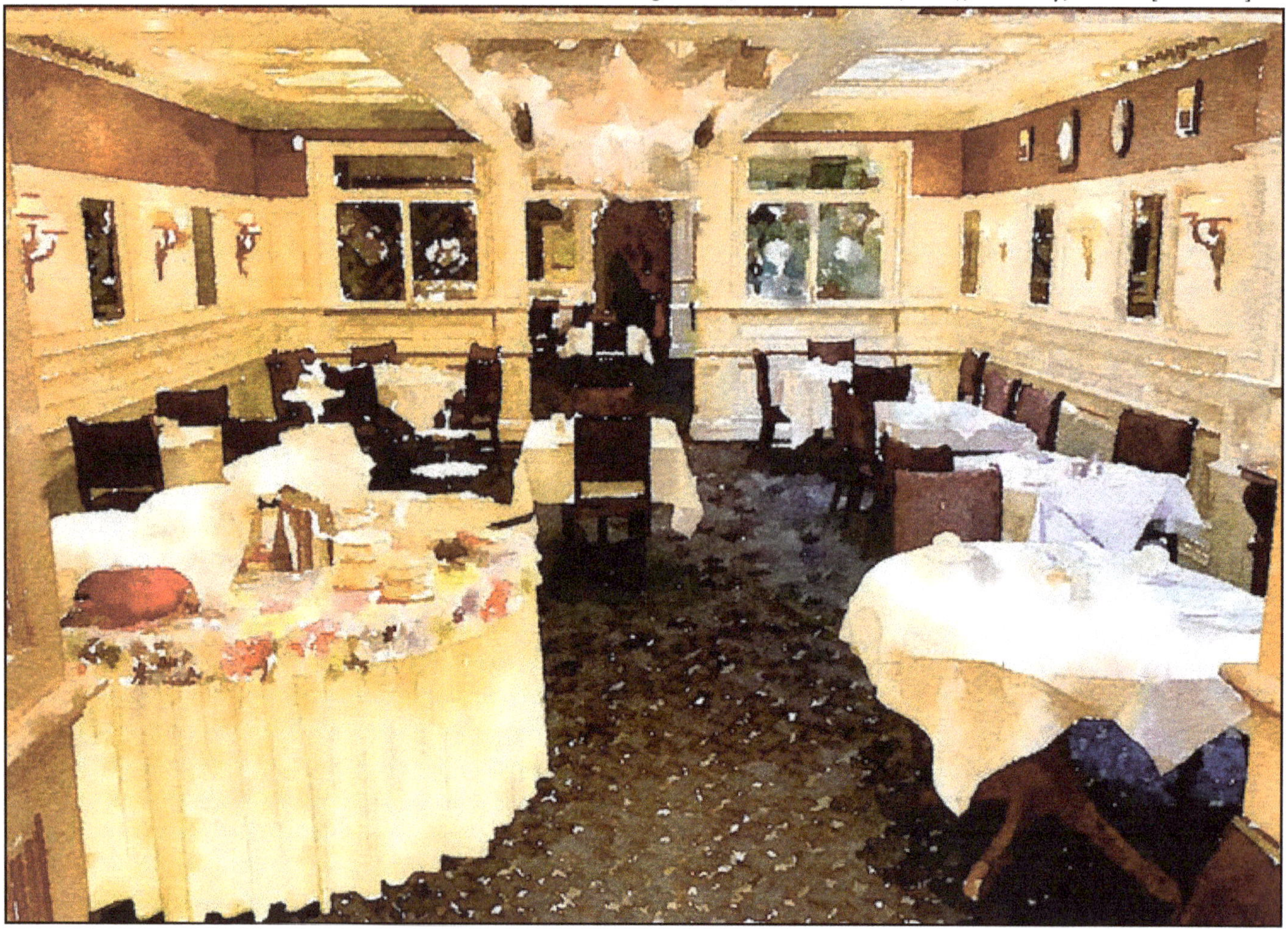

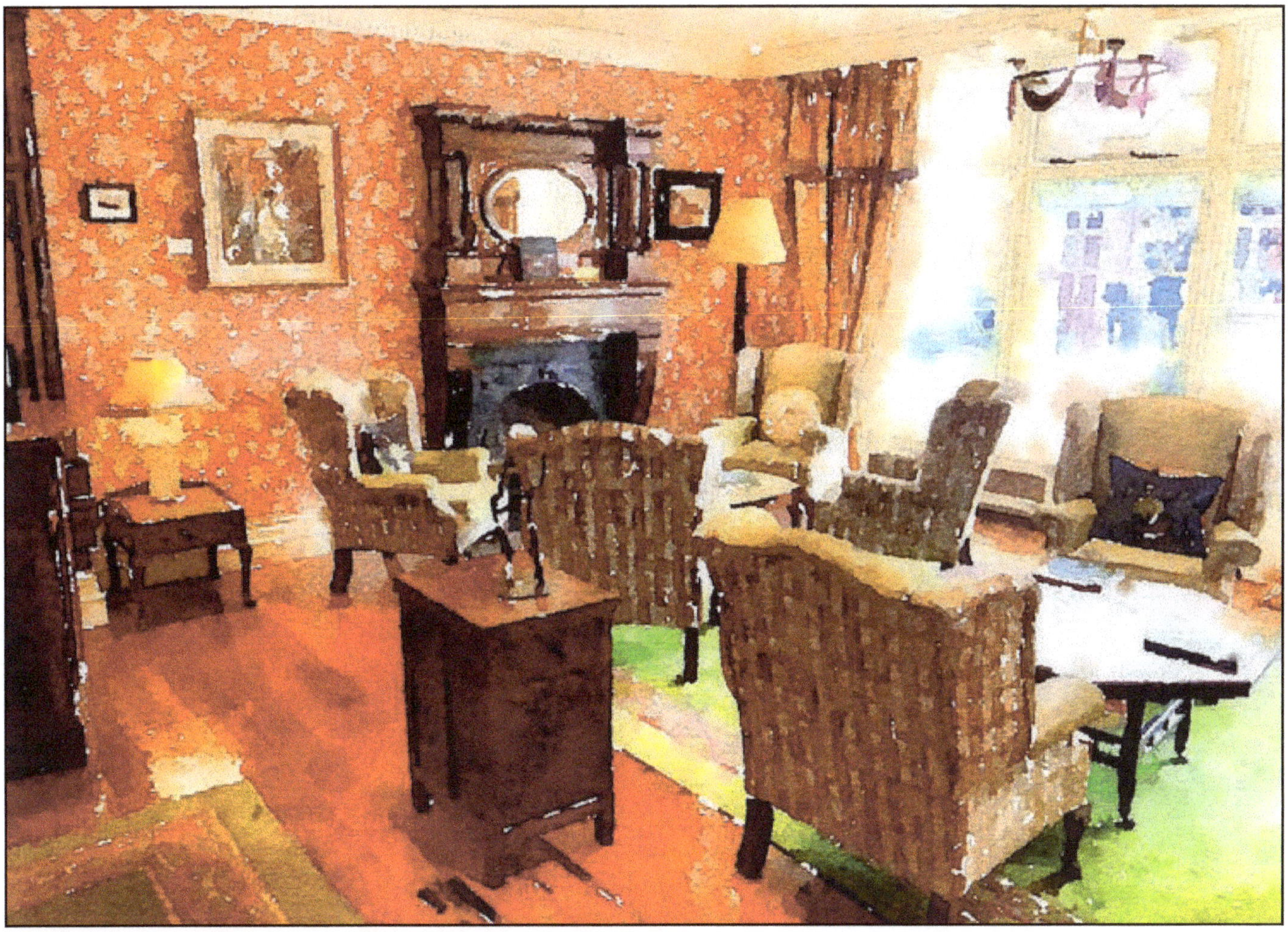

▲'Lounge Room, Arbutus Hotel' (2018), Killarney, Ireland [EIE1811].

'Sitting Room, Arbutus Hotel' (2018), Killarney, Ireland [EIE1812].▼

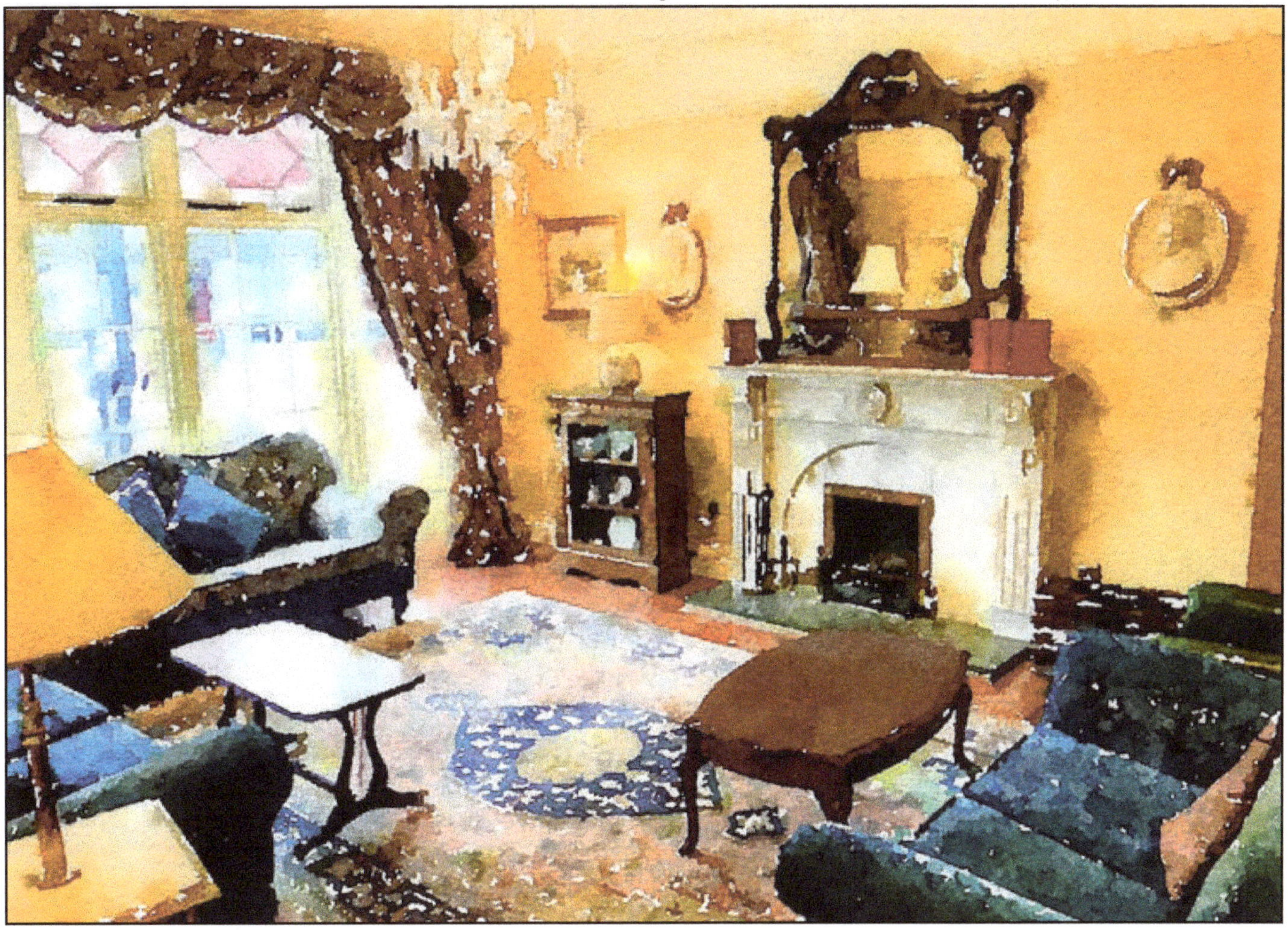

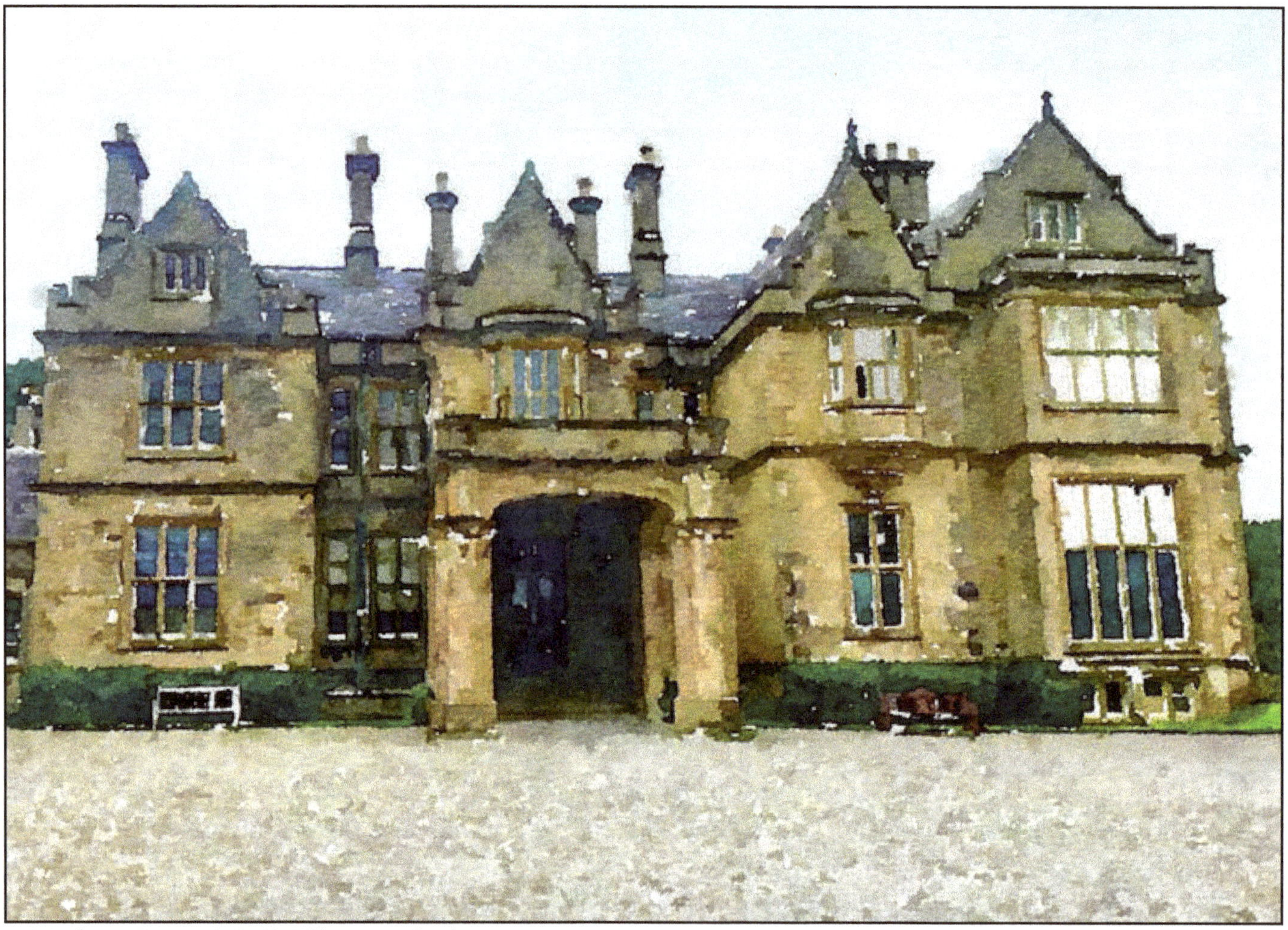

▲'Muckross House' (2018), Killarney, Ireland [EIE1813].

'The Castle (1180)' (2018), Kilkea, Ireland [EIE1815].▼

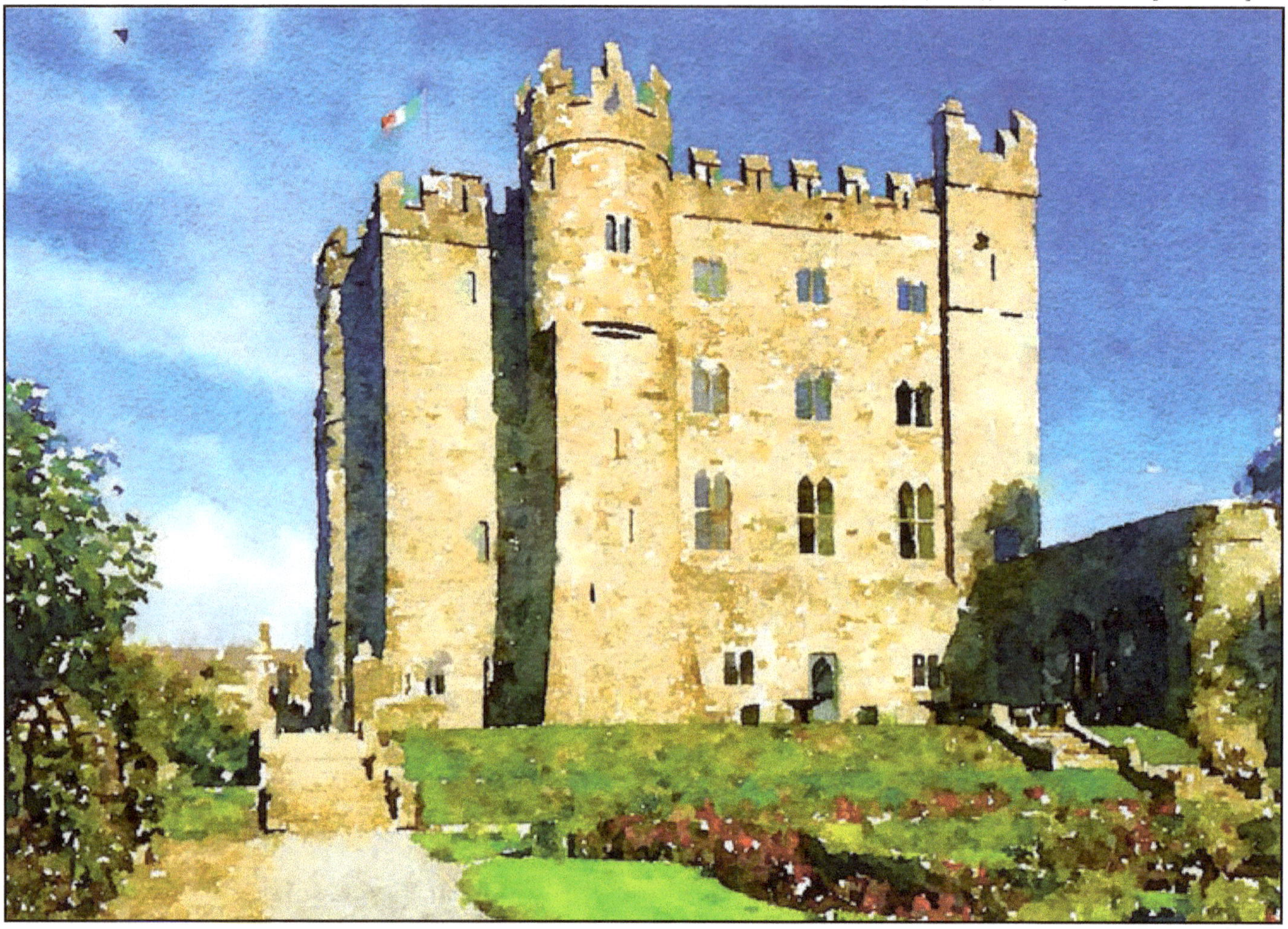

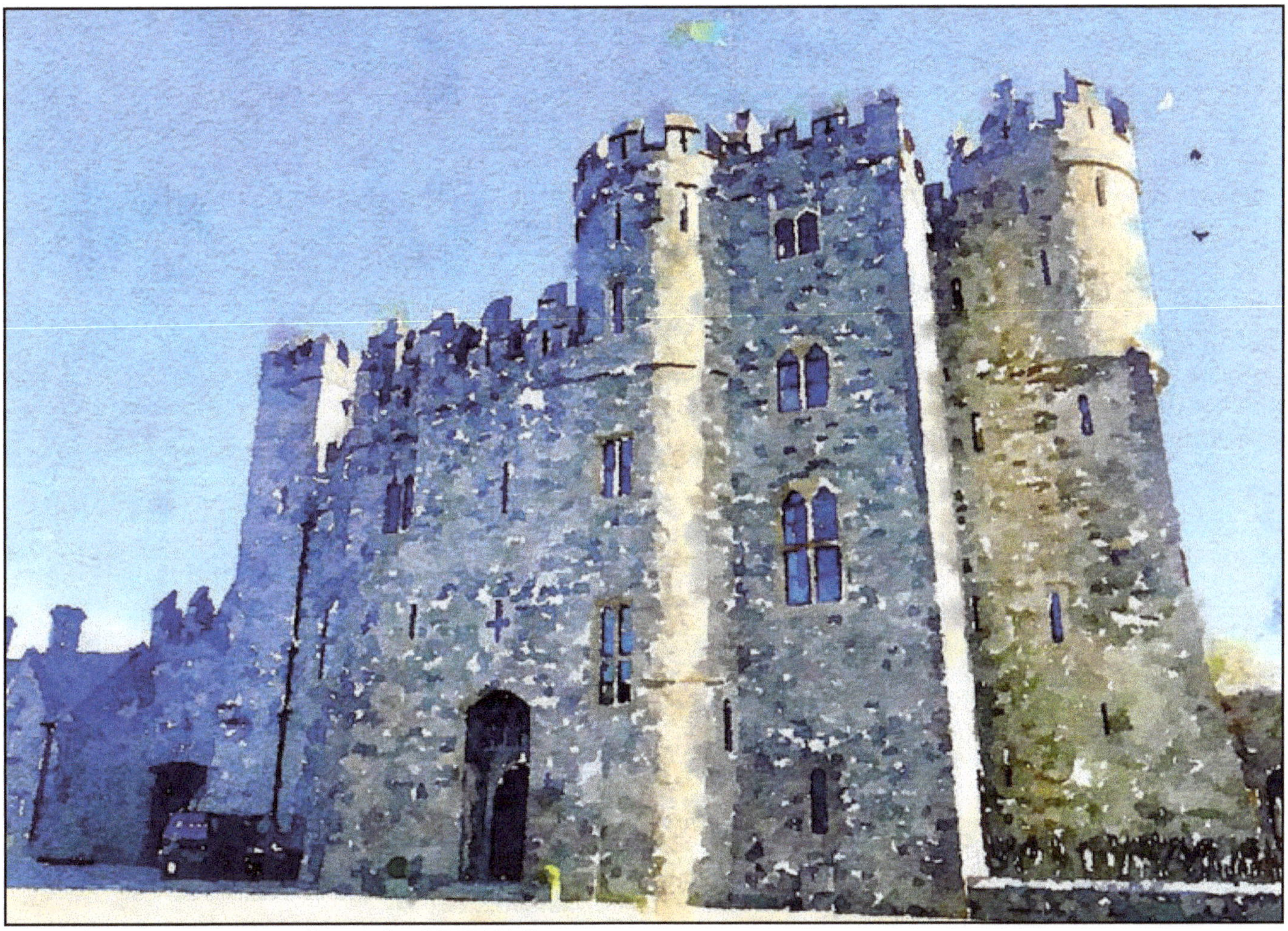

▲ 'Castle Entrance' (2018), Kilkea, Ireland [EIE1814].

'Capital Congestion' (2018), Dublin, Ireland [EIE1816].▼

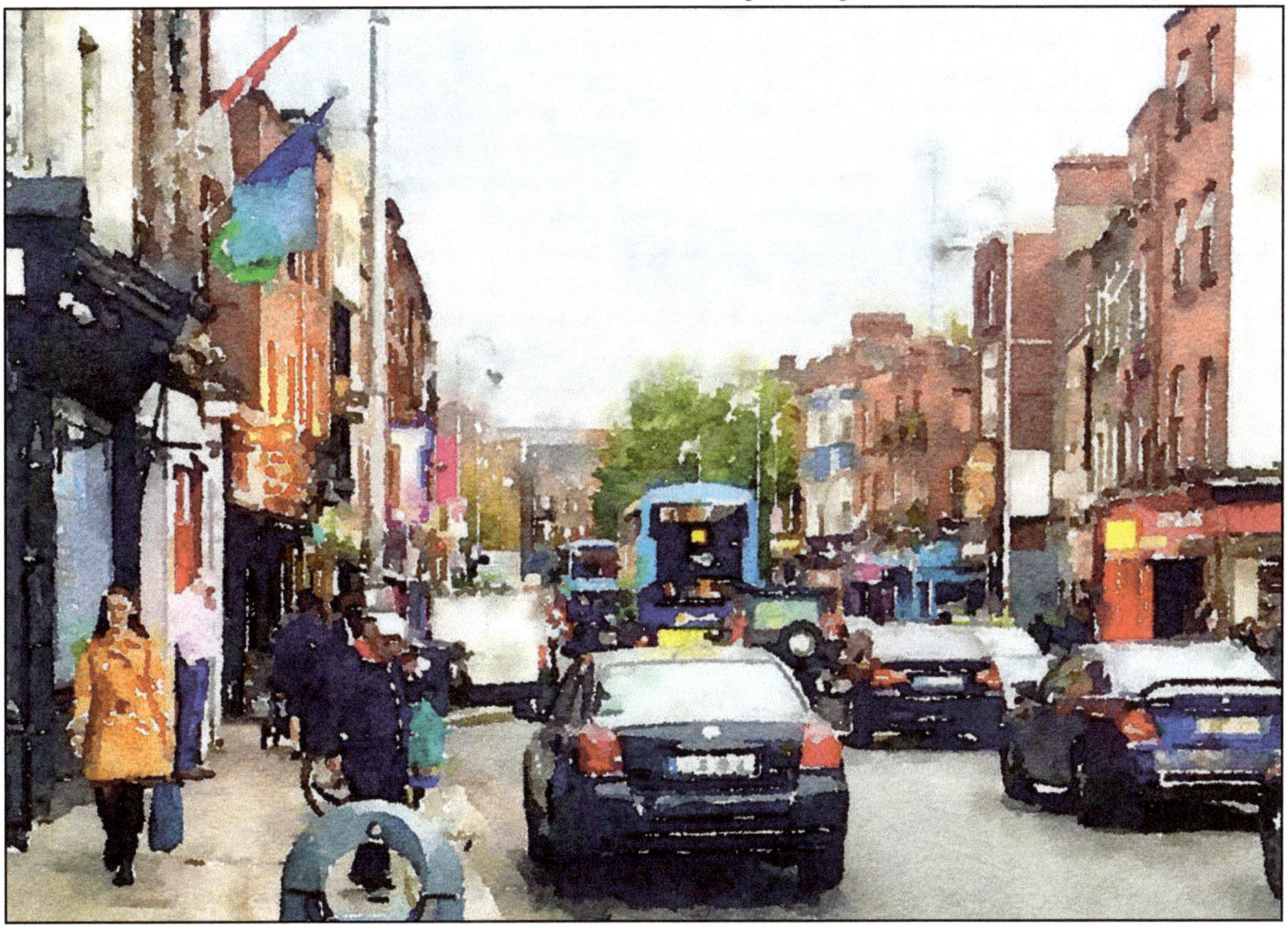

Italy...

I first journeyed to Rome in 1979, spending the briefest eight hour layover as a crew member with QANTAS, but wasn't able to return until 2006, when I undertook a road tour with my second wife. On that occasion I drove along the Ligurian coast and then through Lombardy, but have since returned a number of times.

Visiting Cinque Terre and the island of Elbe in 2010 with 'Bill Peach Journeys', I next journeyed to magnificent Venice in 2013 with my partner Rosie. We reappeared in 2015 visiting Bergamo, Lake Como, the 'Milan Expo' and Sorrento/Positano, before returning once more in 2018 when we spent a full five days exploring the grandeur of Rome.

The Italian countryside, its seascapes, mountains and incredible history are a photographers heaven. I am yet to explore Sardinia and Sicily, which remain on my list of 'must see' regions in one of the most diverse and picturesque lands on the planet.

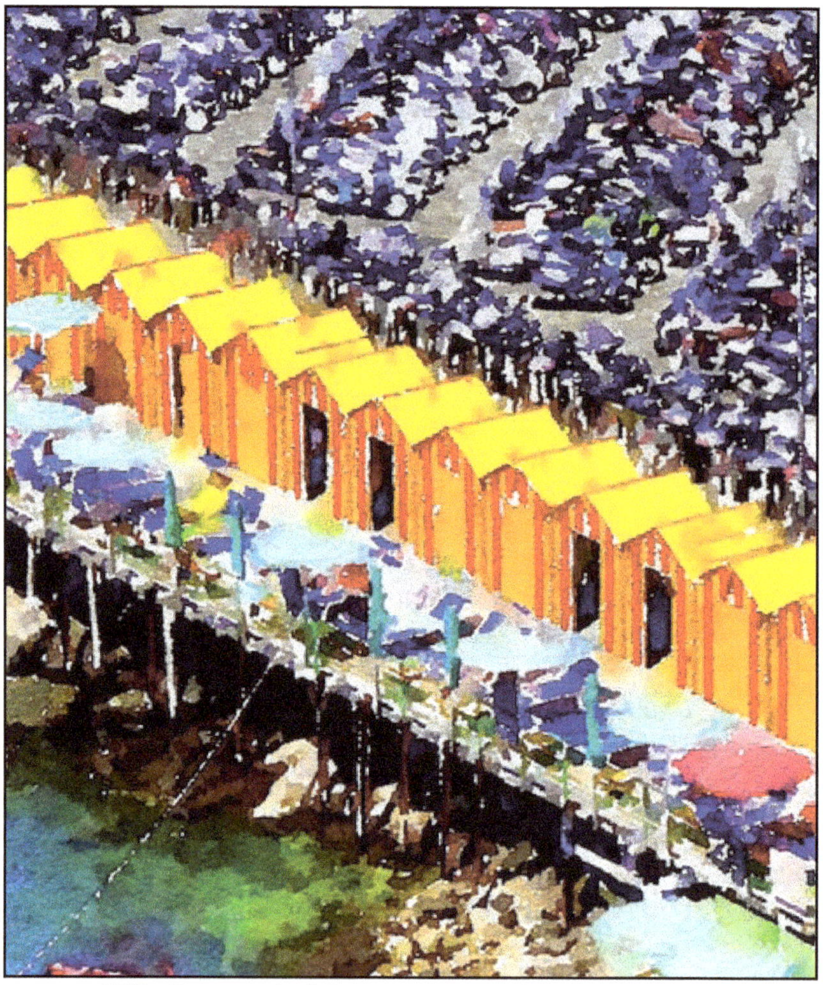

'Villa Communale di Sorrento' (2015), Campania [EIT(CA)1501].▲

▼'Sunbeds In the Sea' (2015), Sorrento, Campania [EIT(CA)1502].

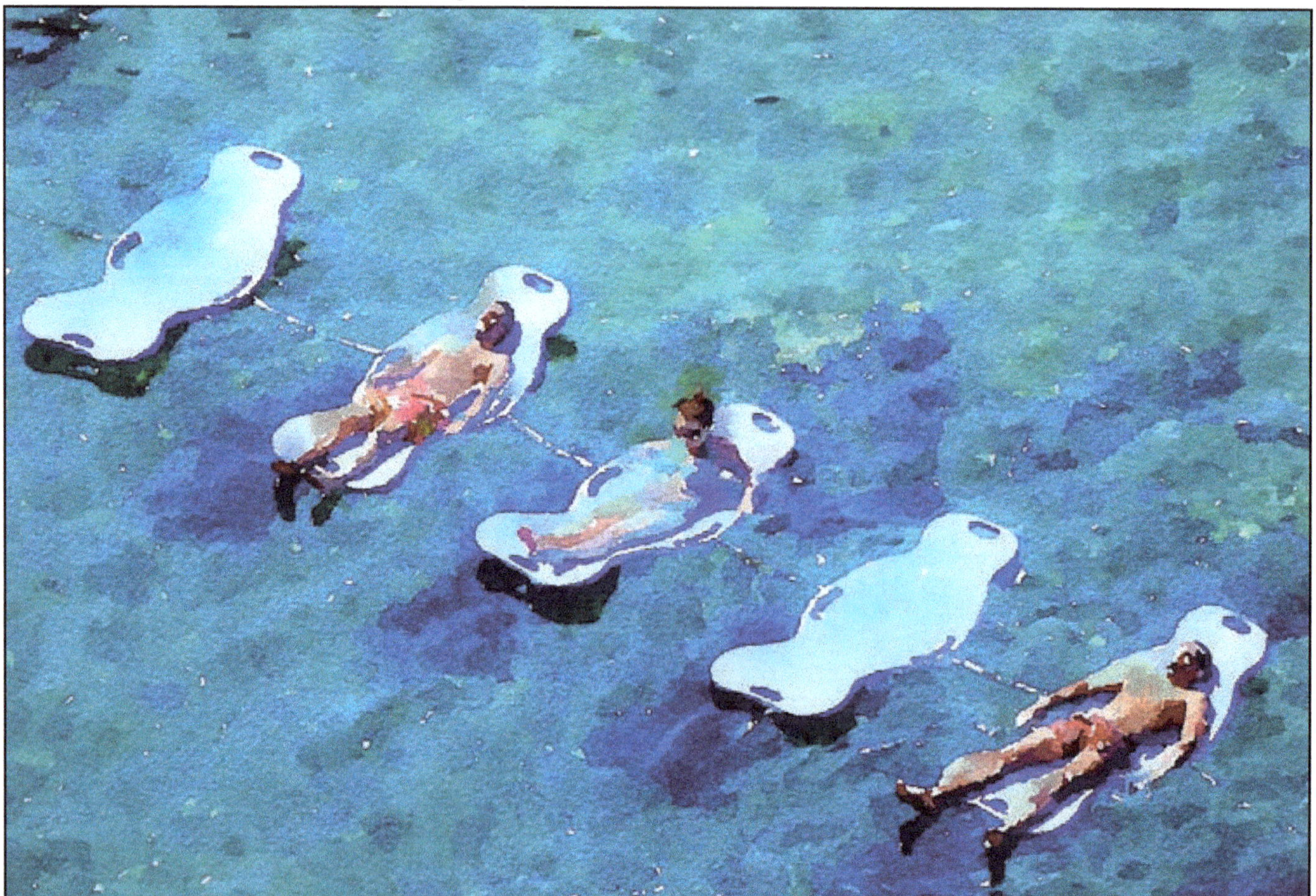

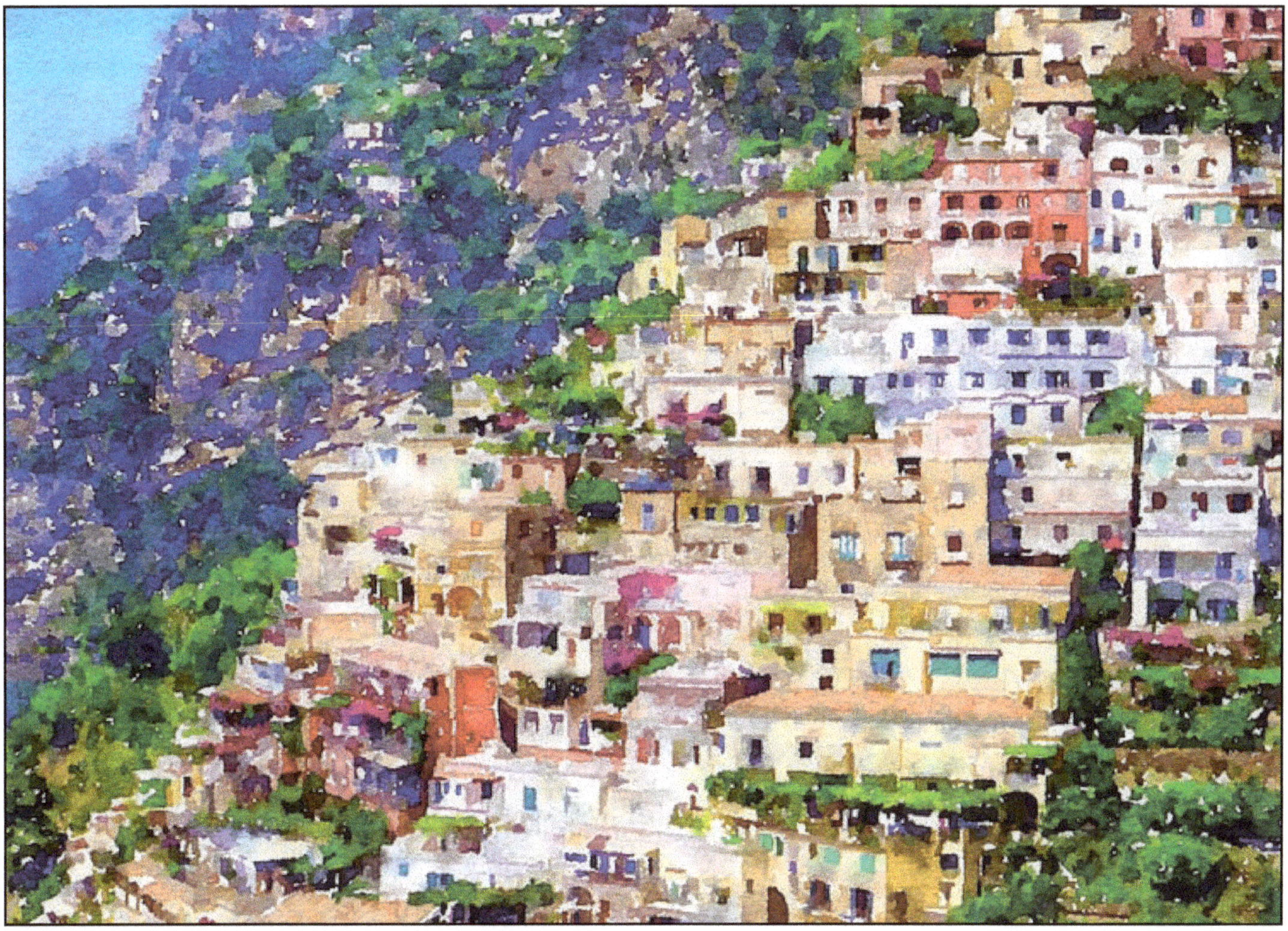

▲'Positano Views' (2015), Sorrento, Campania [EIT(CA)1503].

'Via SaVia Santa Maria delle Grazi' (2015), Sorrento, Campania [EIT(CA)1508].▼

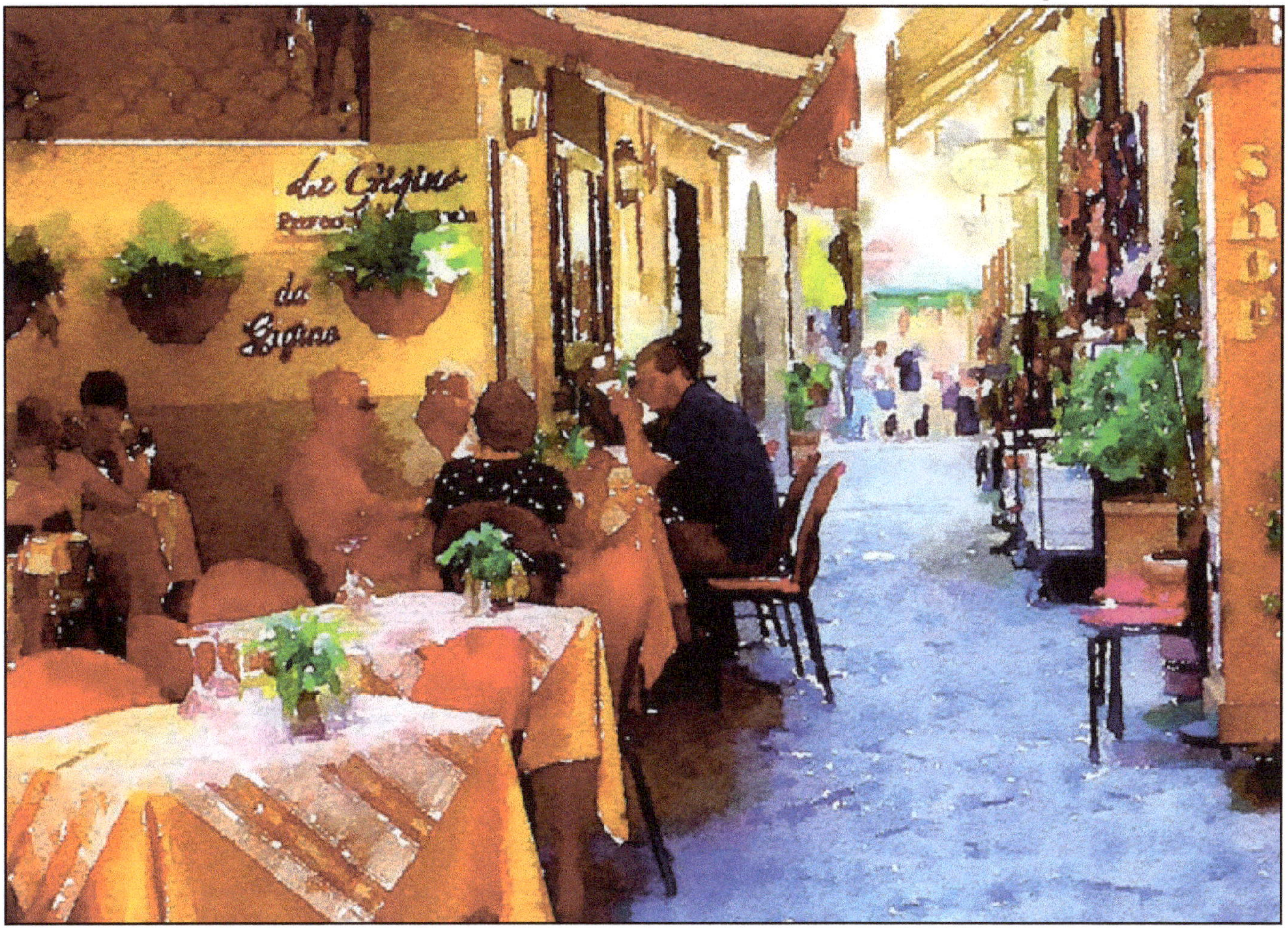

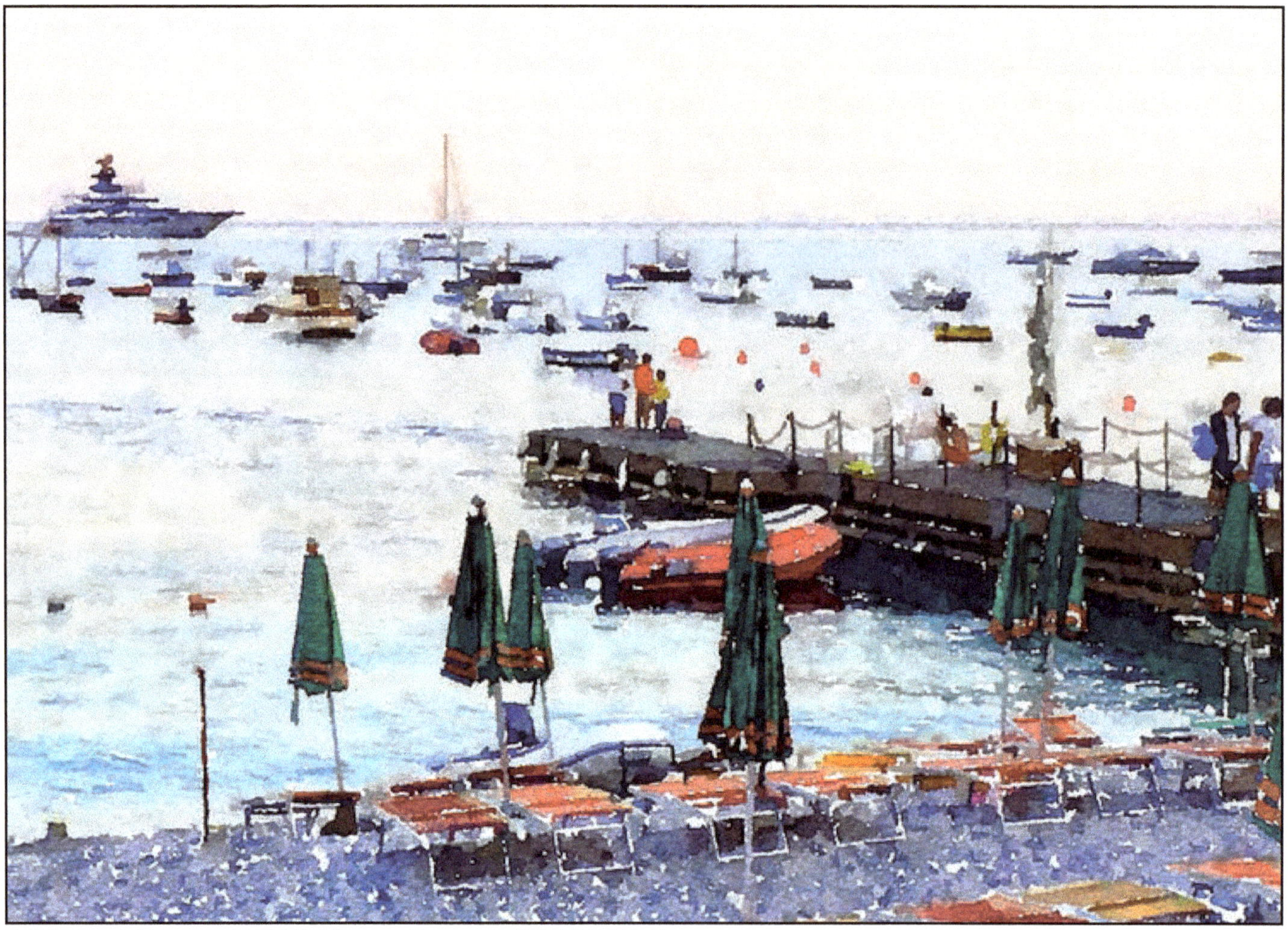

▲'Marina del Cantone' (2015), Nerano, Campania [EIT(CA)1506].

'Marina del Cantone Beach' (2015), Nerano, Campania [EIT(CA)1505].▼

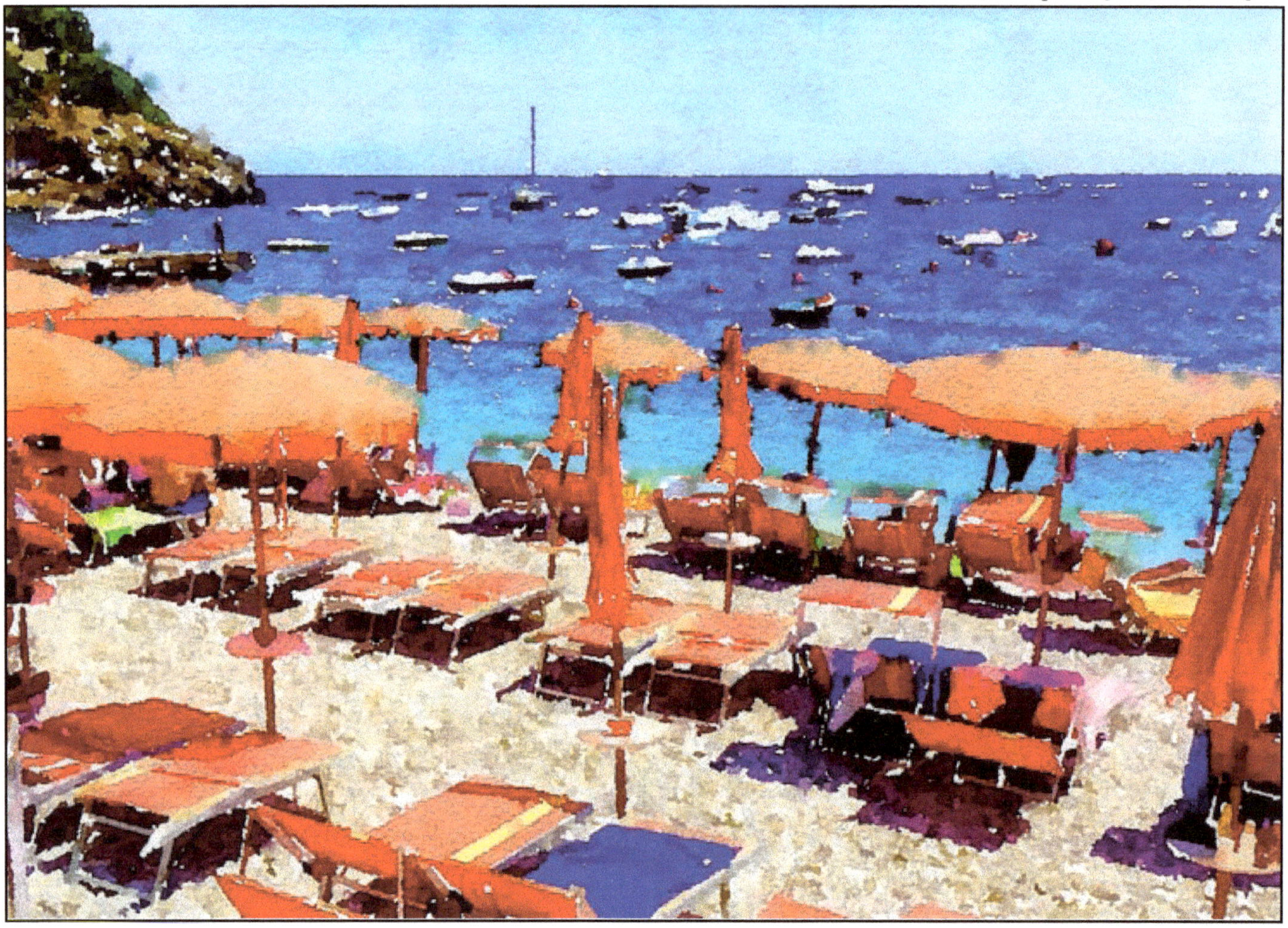

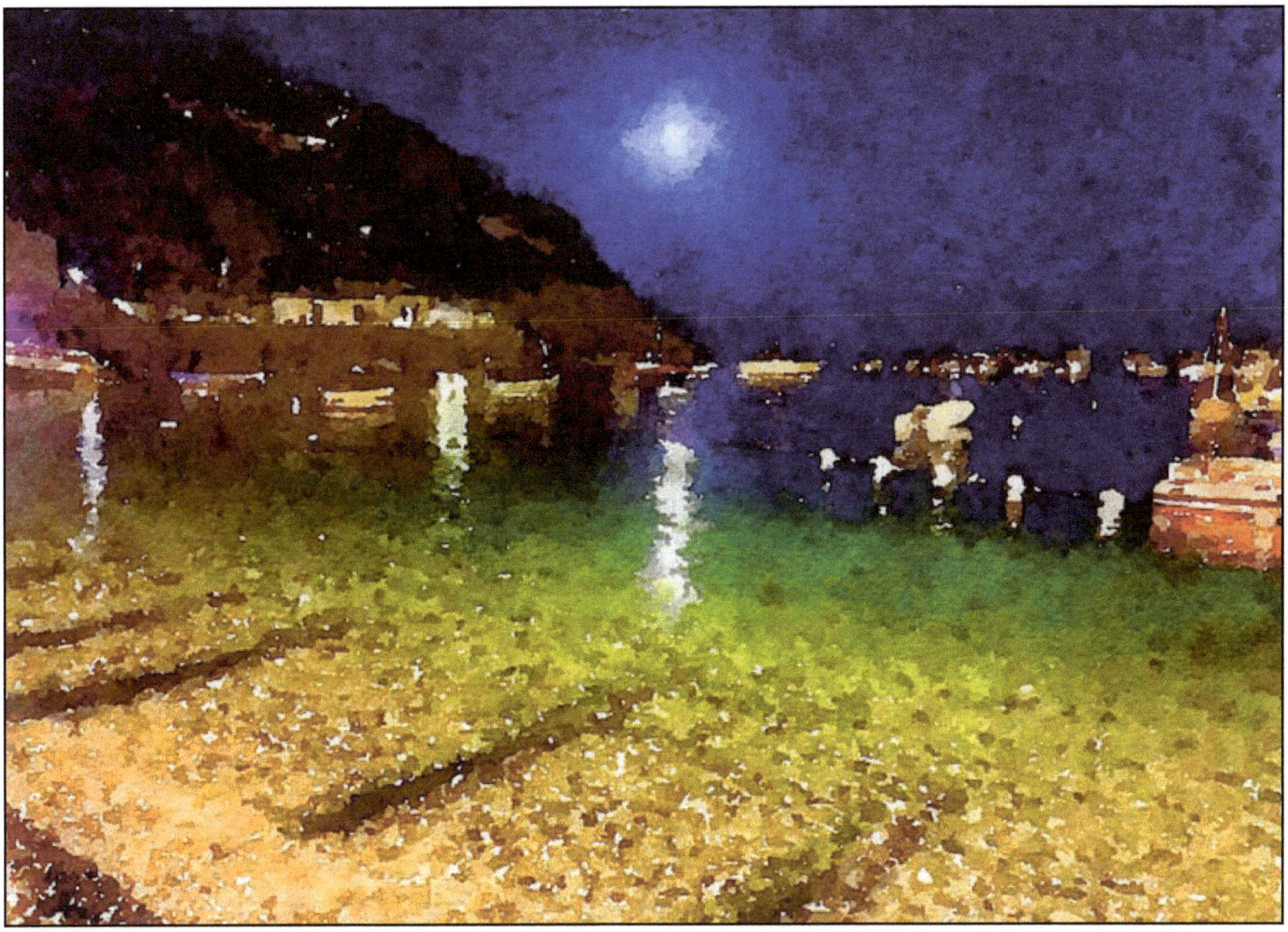

▲'Rising Moon' (2015), Nerano, Campania [EIT(CA)1504].

'Spiaggia di Cala dei Frati' (2010), Portoferraio, Elbe [EIT(EL)1001].▼

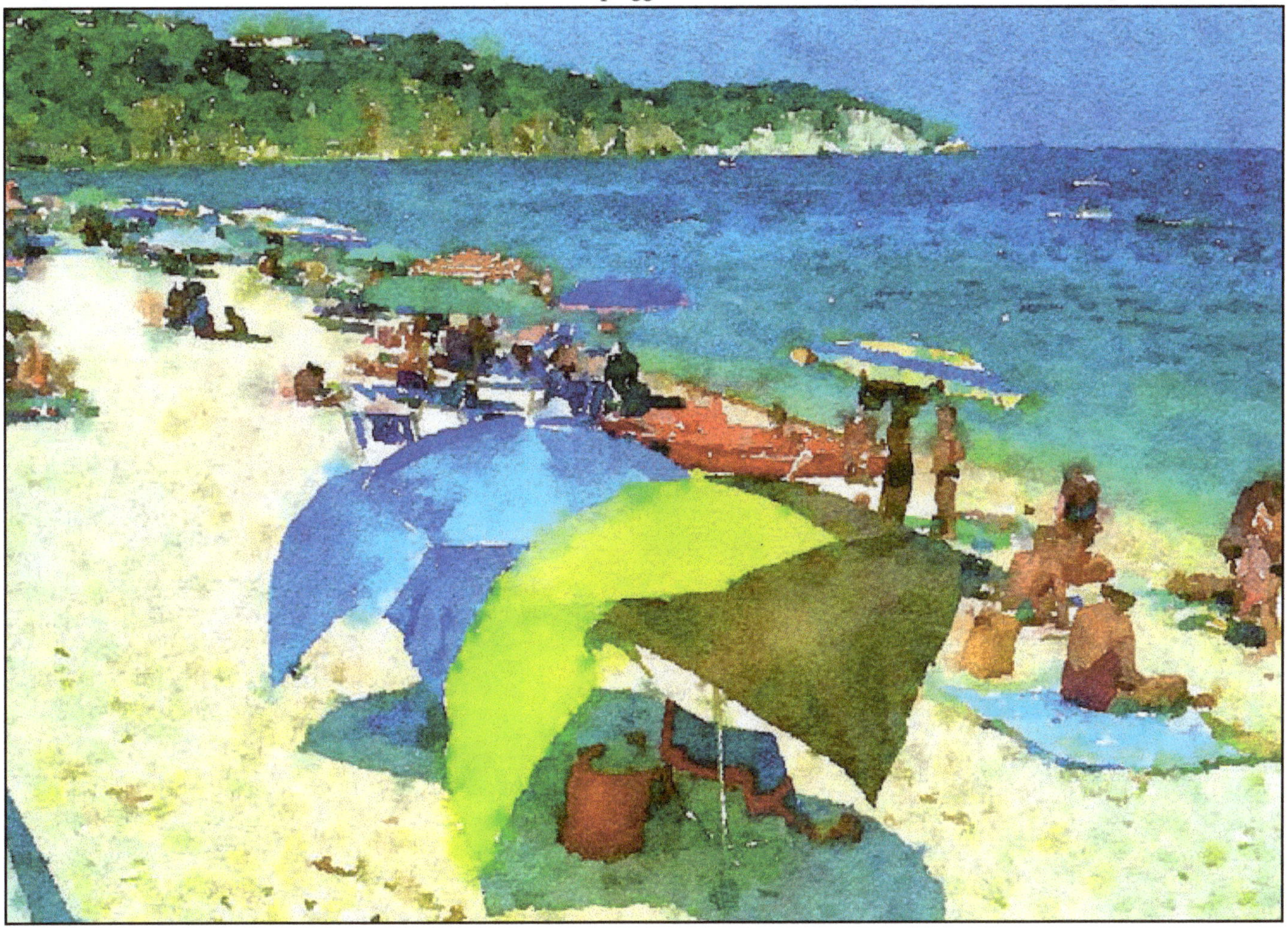

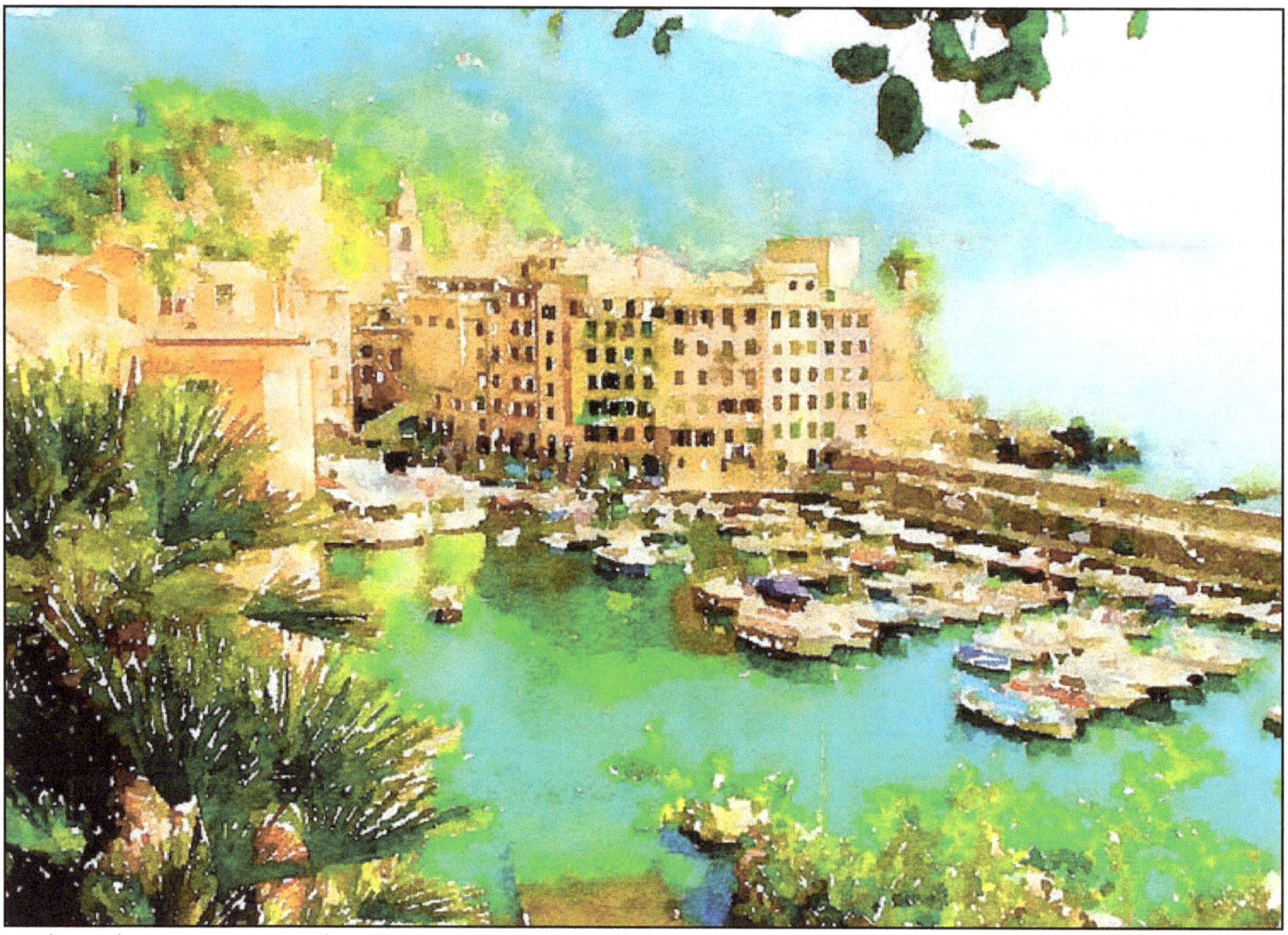

▲'The Harbour' (2006), Camogli, Liguria [EIT(LG)0601].

'The Anchorage' (2006), Portofino, Liguria [EIT(LG)0602].▼

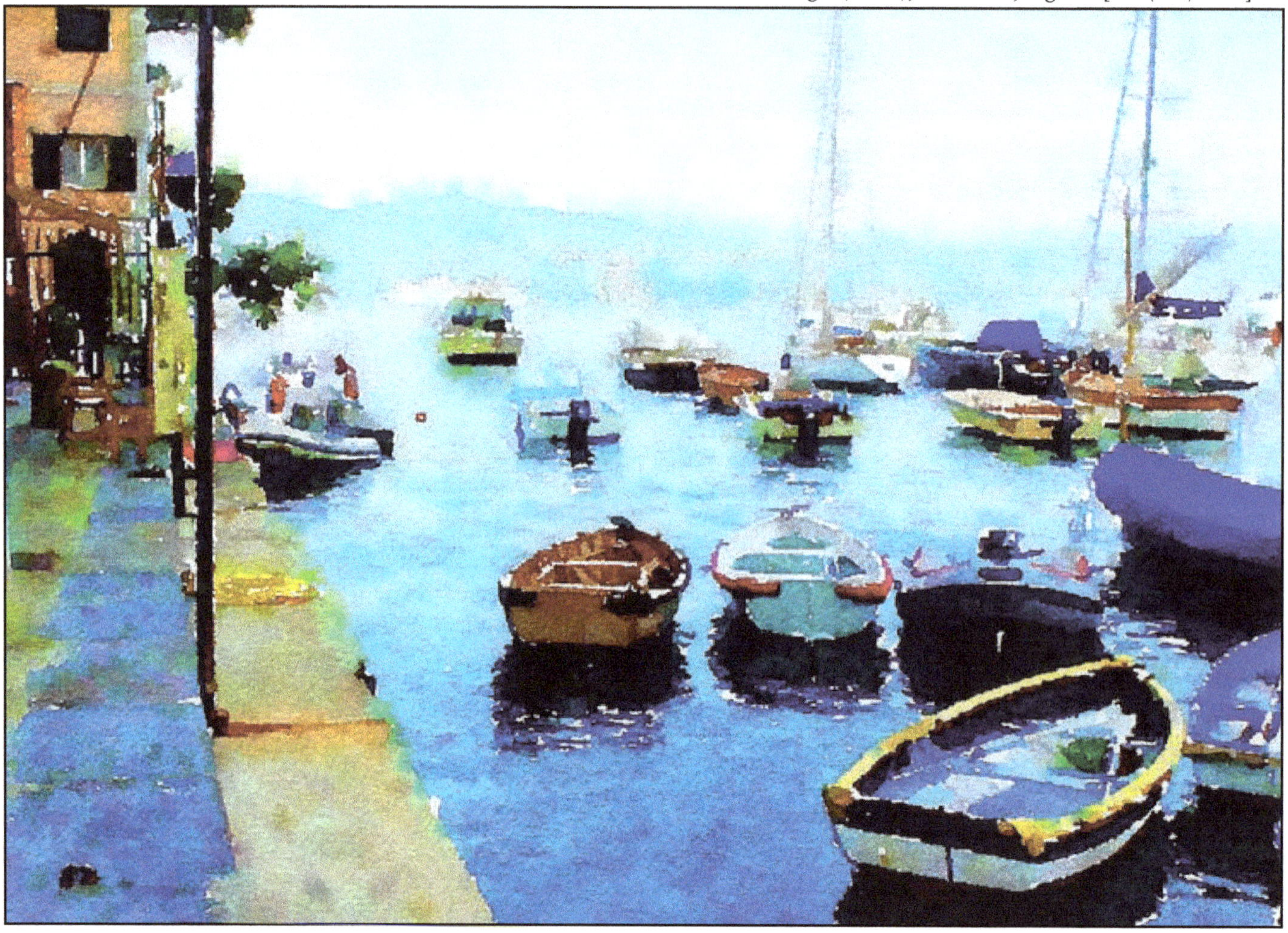

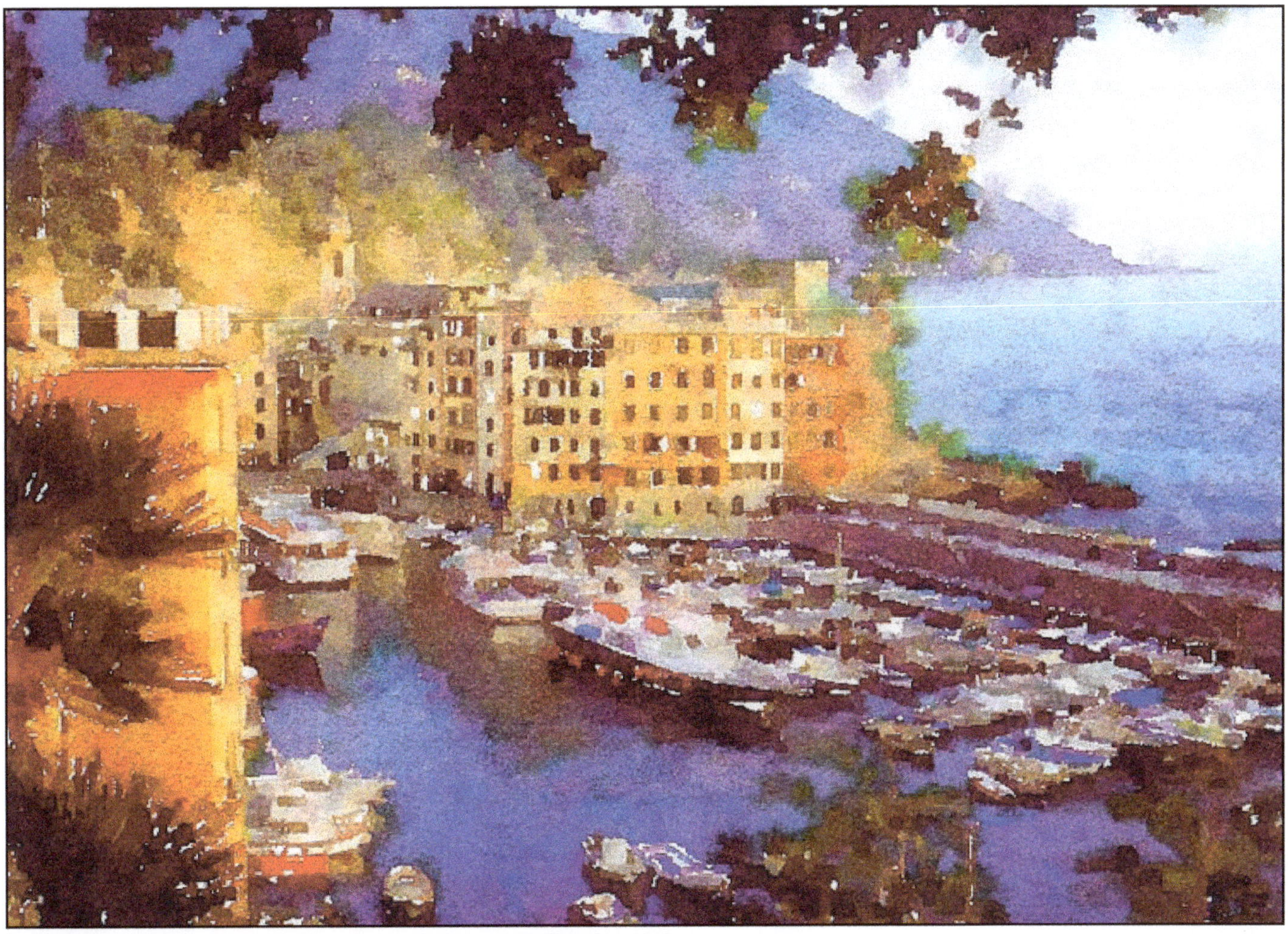

▲'The Boats Of Camogli' (2006), Camogli, Liguria [EIT(LG)0603].

▼'Sorrento Cafe' (2015), Campania [EIT(CA)1507].

'Corsia in Portovenere' (2010), Liguria [EIT(LG)1002].▼

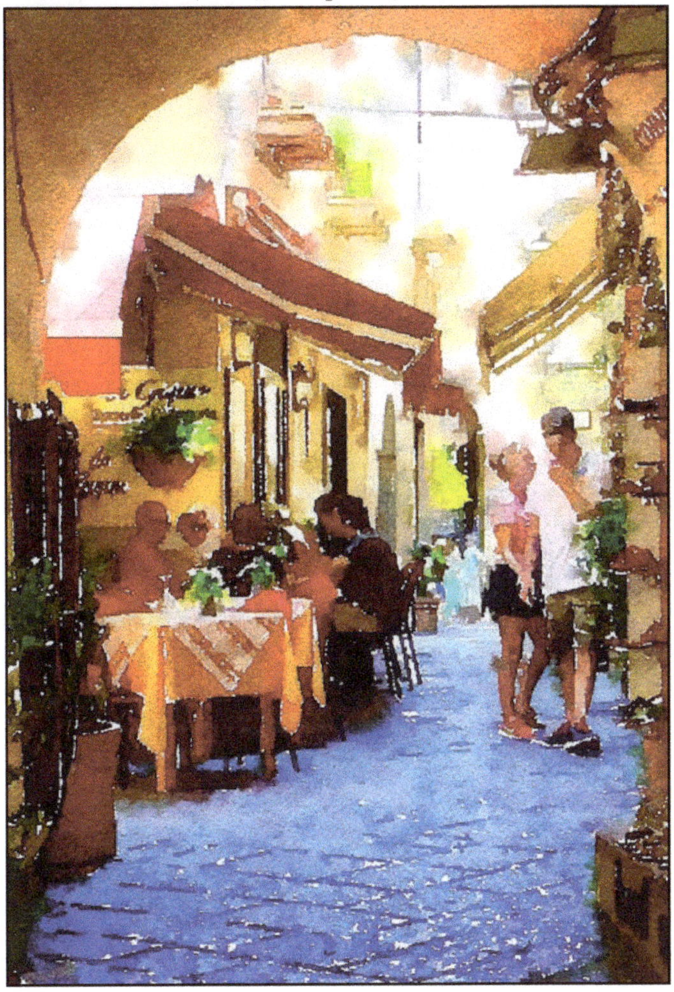

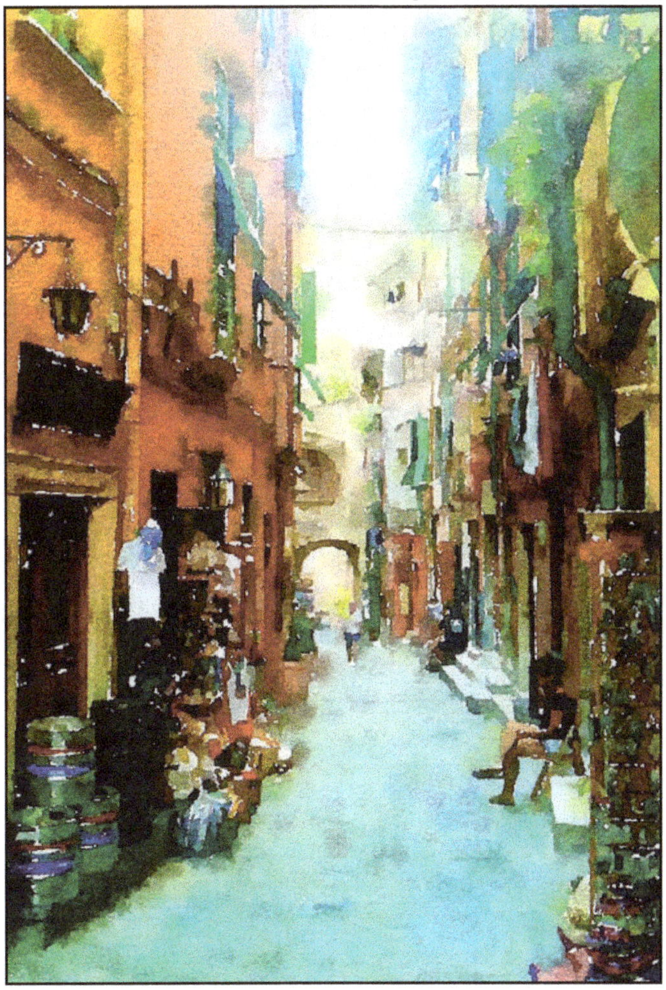

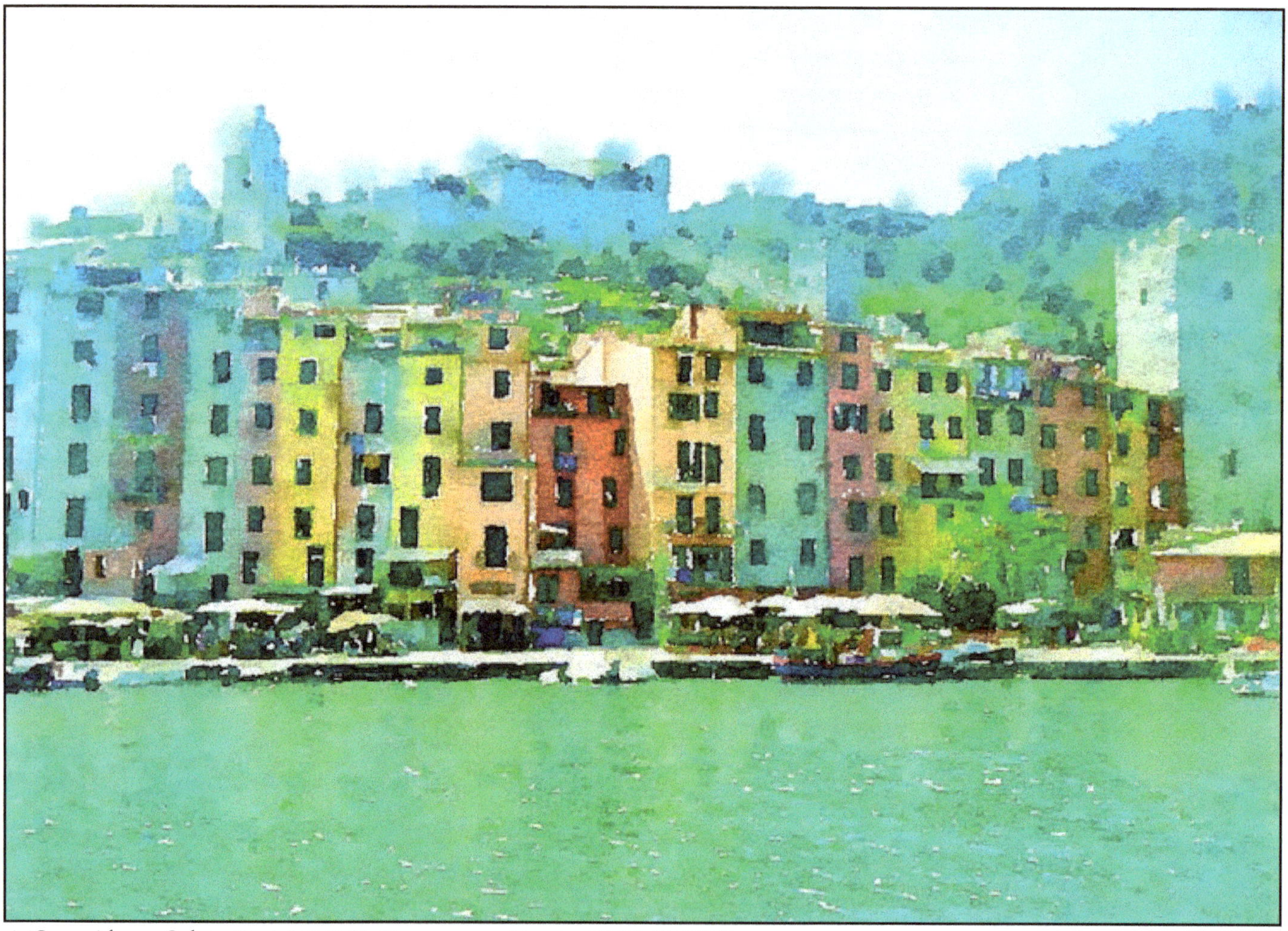

▲'Quayside on Calata Doria' (2010), Portovenere, Liguria [EIT(LG)1001].

'Sunbathing At Portovenere' (2010), Liguria [EIT(LG)1003].▼

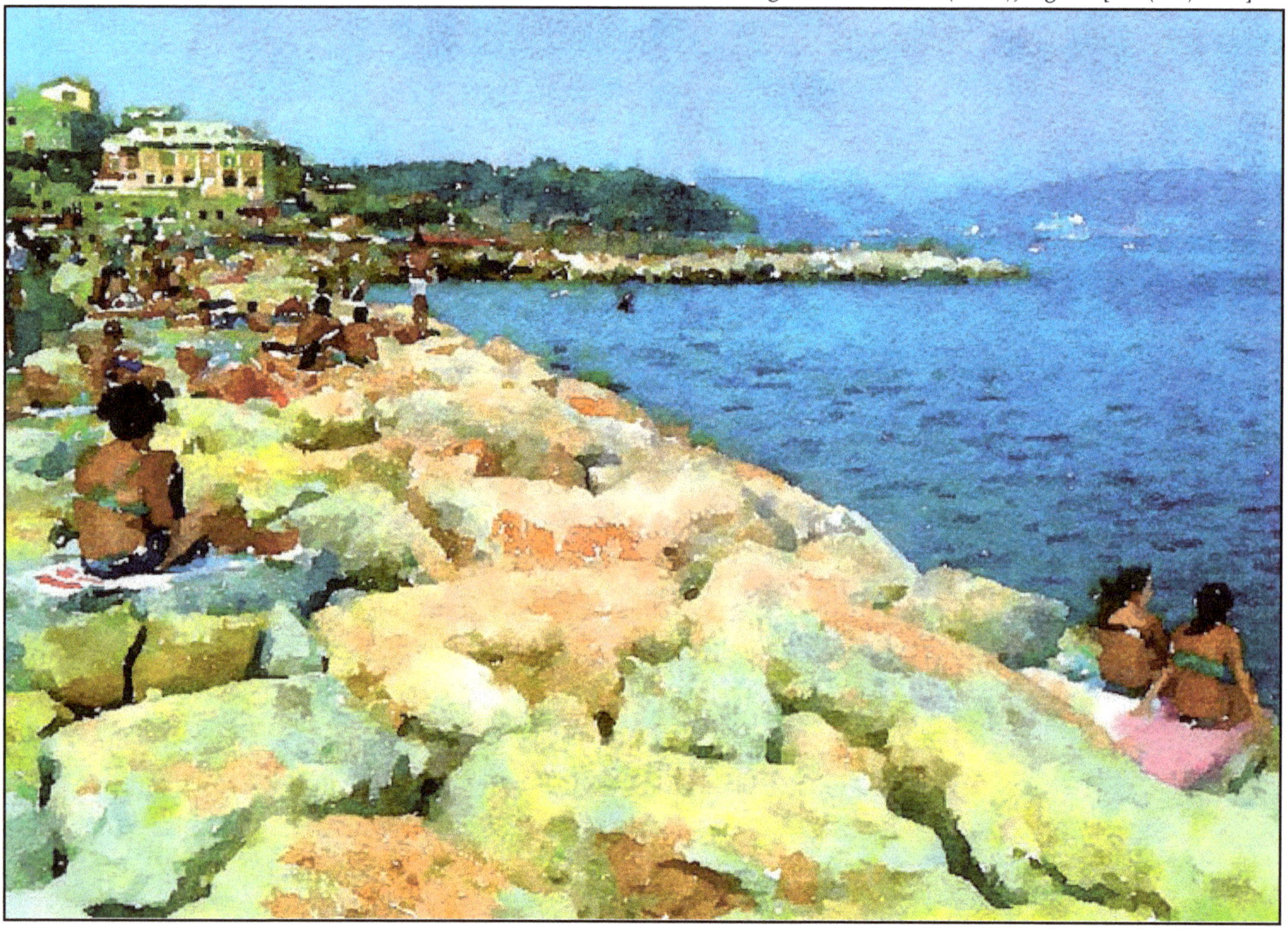

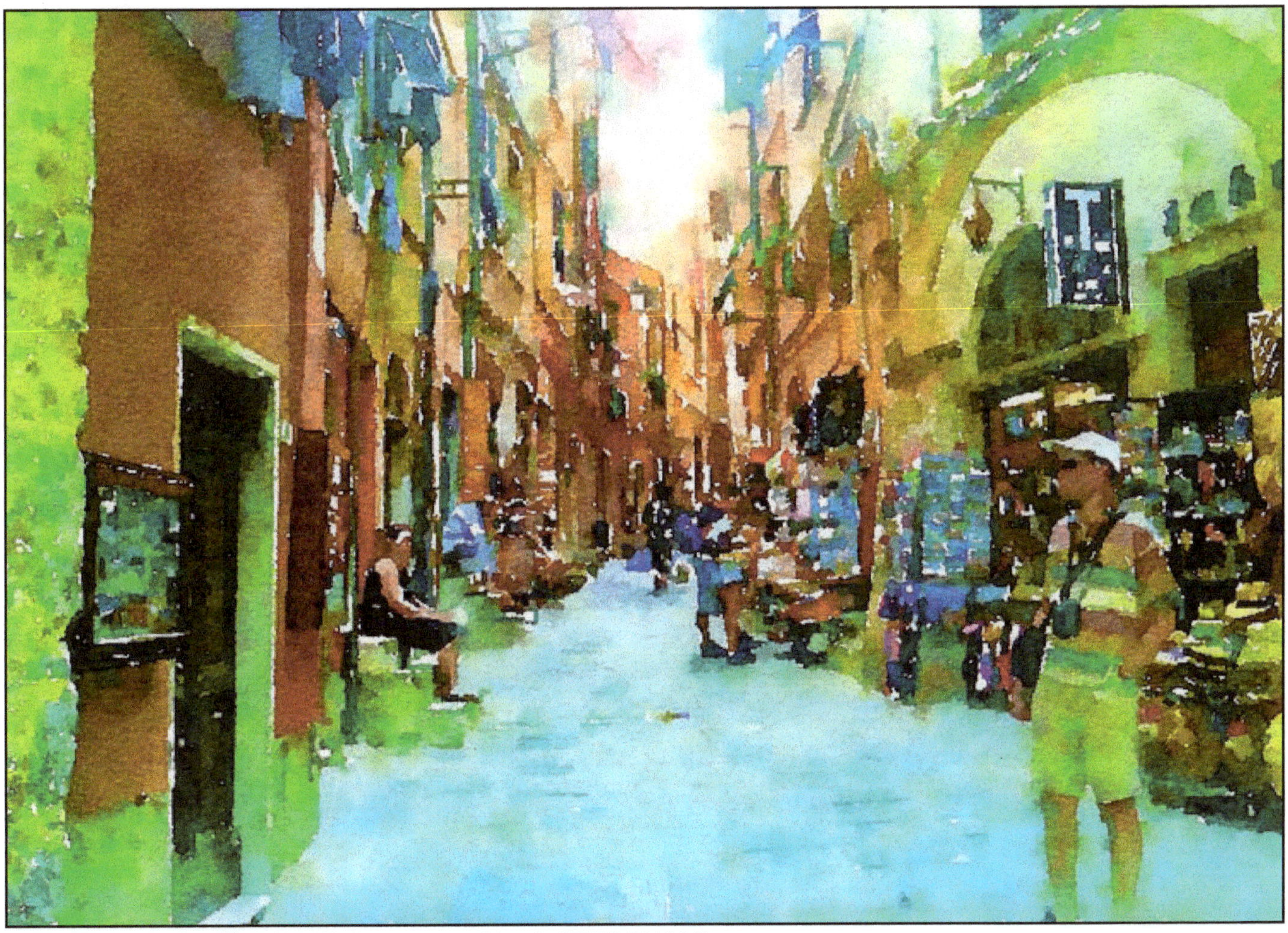

▲'Via Giovanni Capellini' (2010), Portovenere, Liguria [EIT(LG)1004].

'The Marina On Calata Doria' (2010), Portovenere, Liguria [EIT(LG)1005].▼

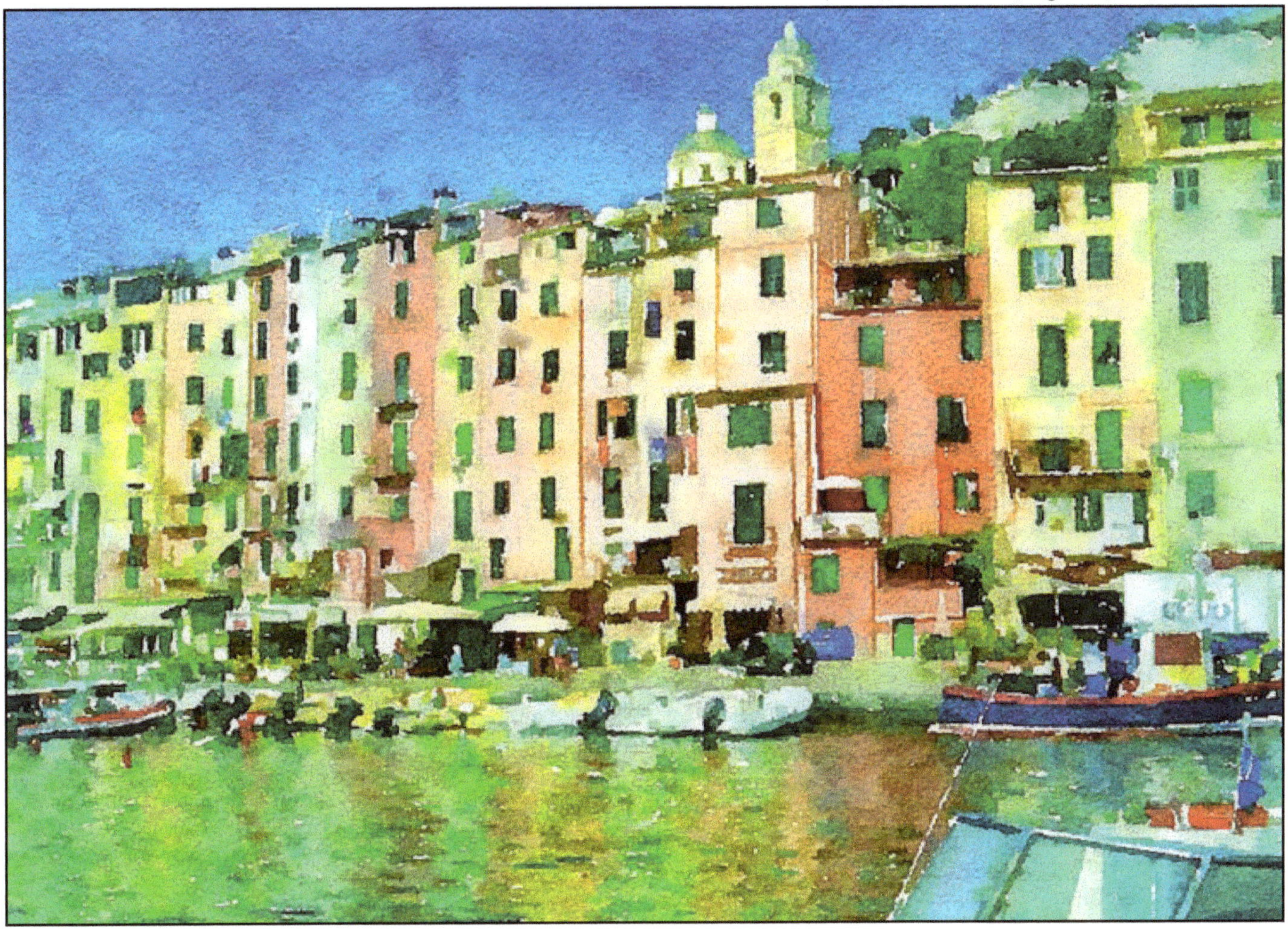

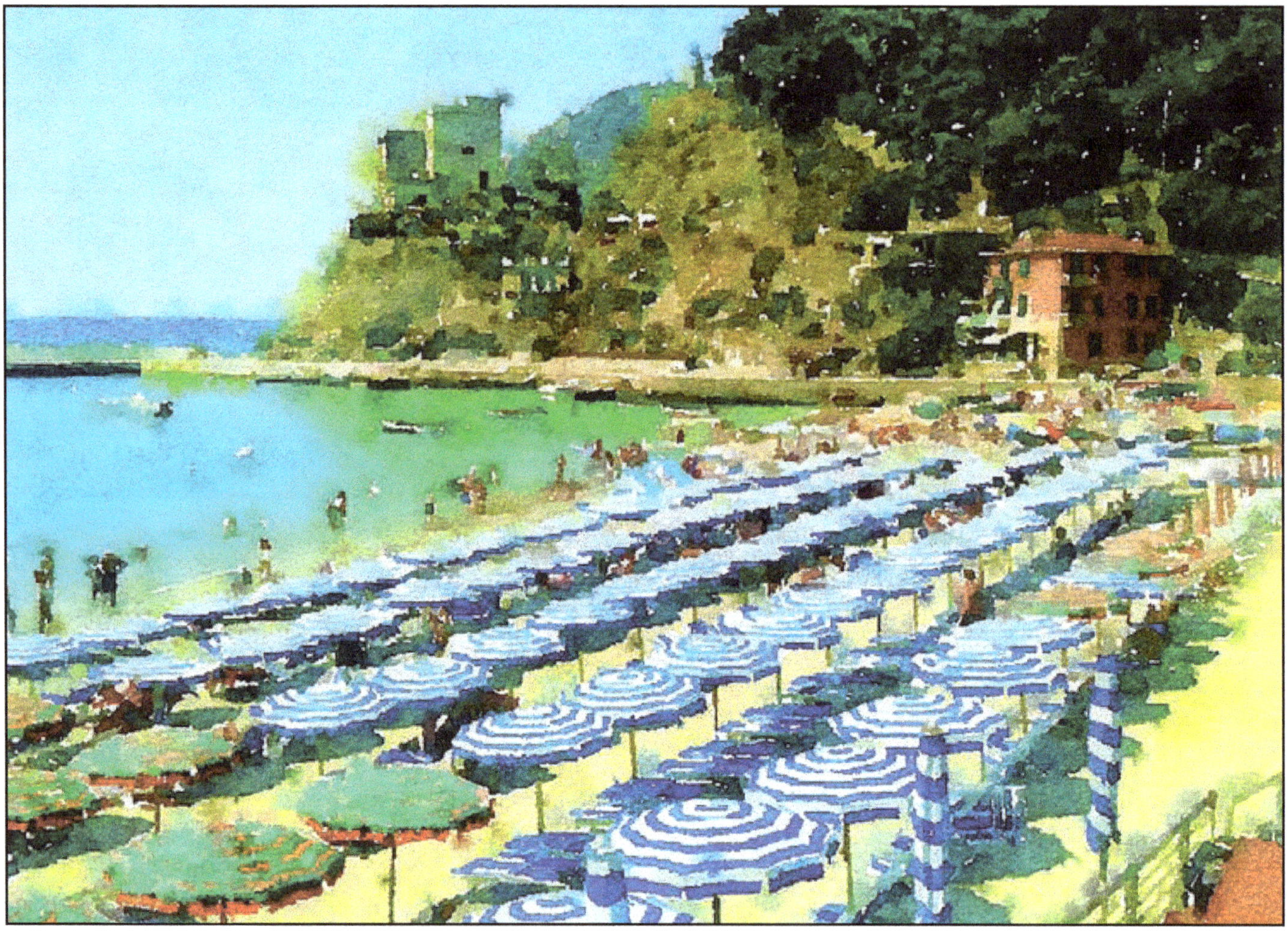

▲'Sunbrella's On The Beach' (2010), Monterosso, Liguria [EIT(LG)1006].

'Sunbathing At Monterosso' (2010), Liguria [EIT(LG)1007].▼

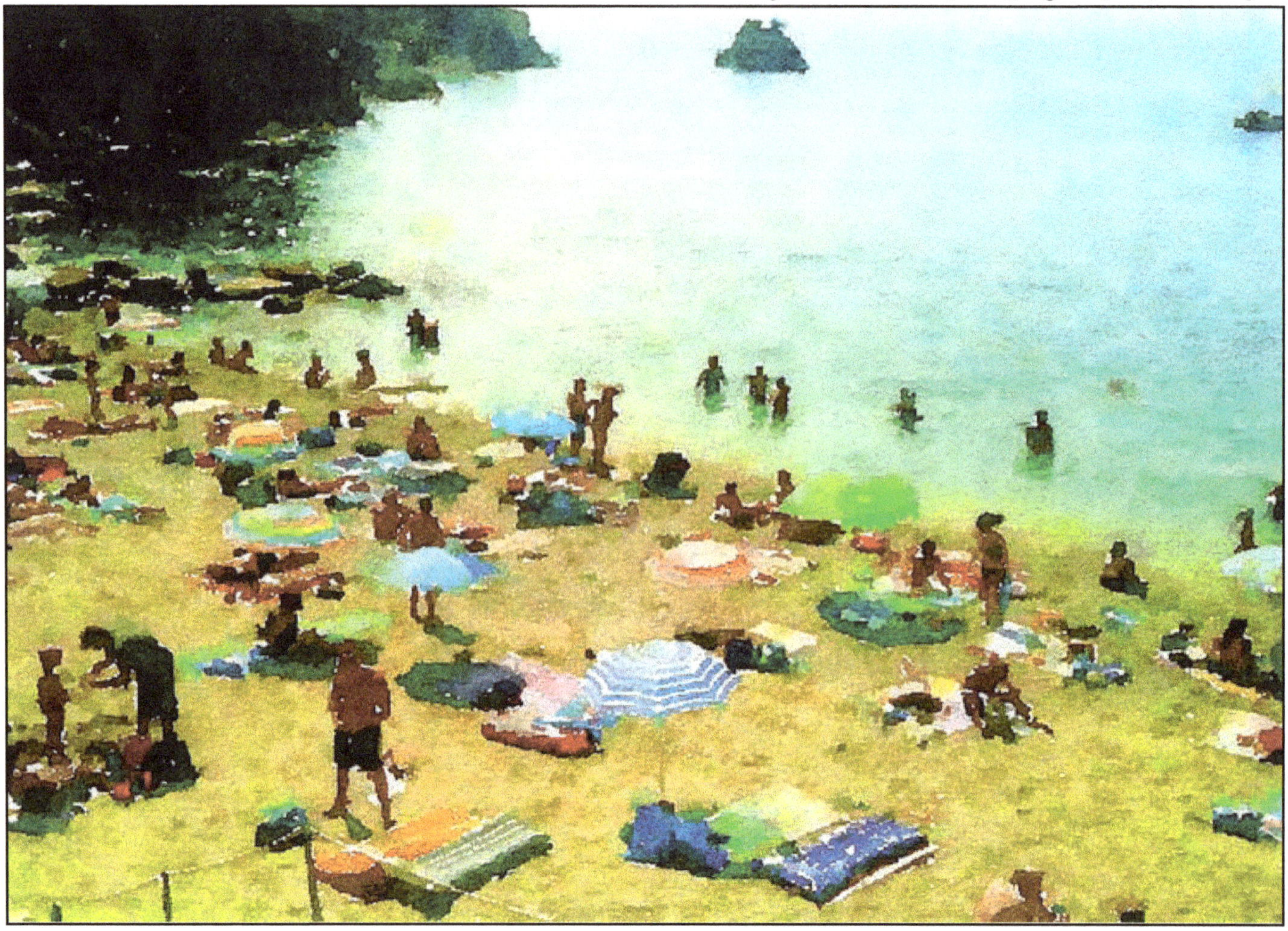

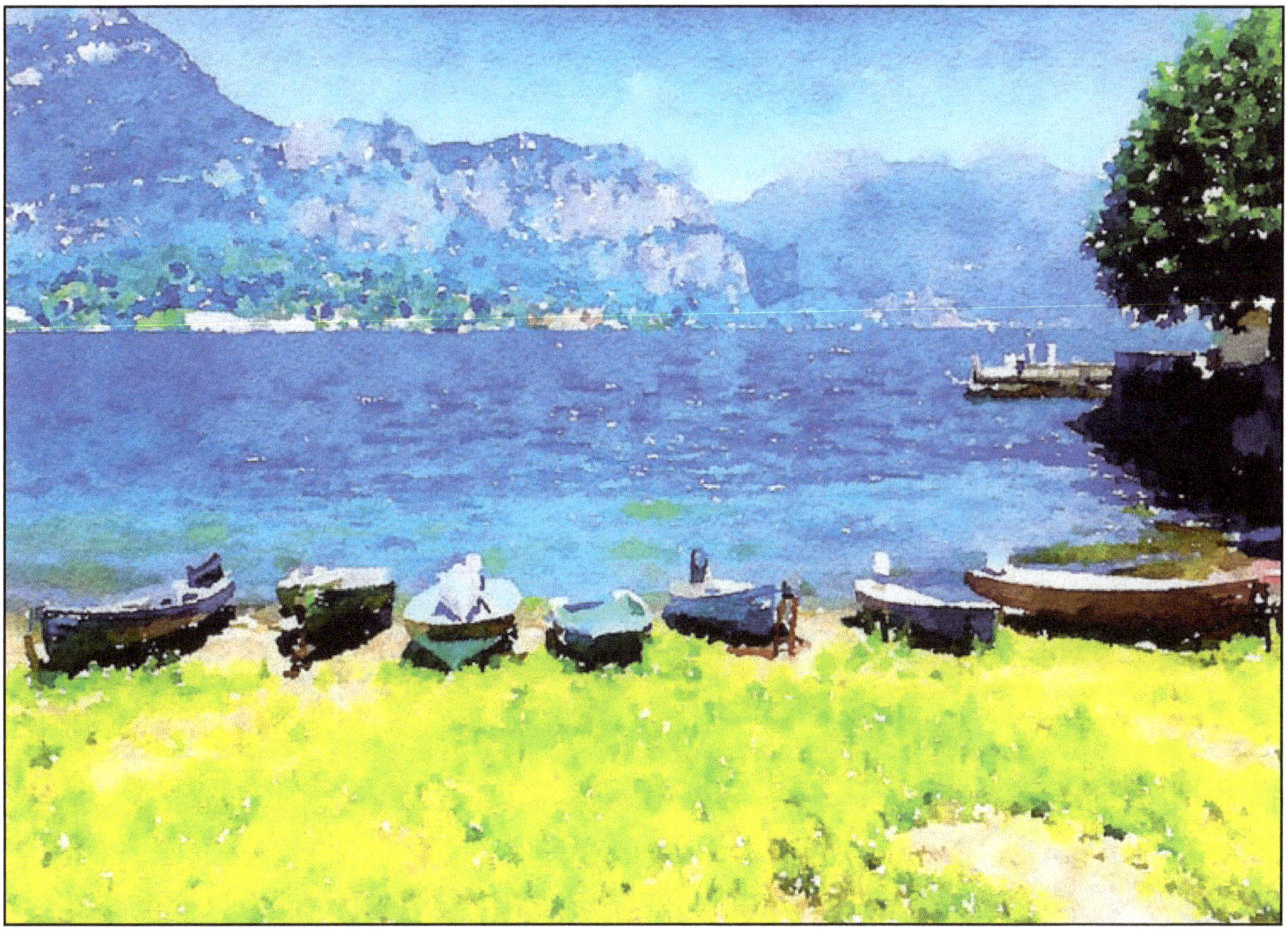

▲'Boats On Lago di Como' (2015), Lombardy [EIT(LO)1506].

'Steinstrand Beach' (2015), Lago di Como, Lombardy [EIT(LO)1507].▼

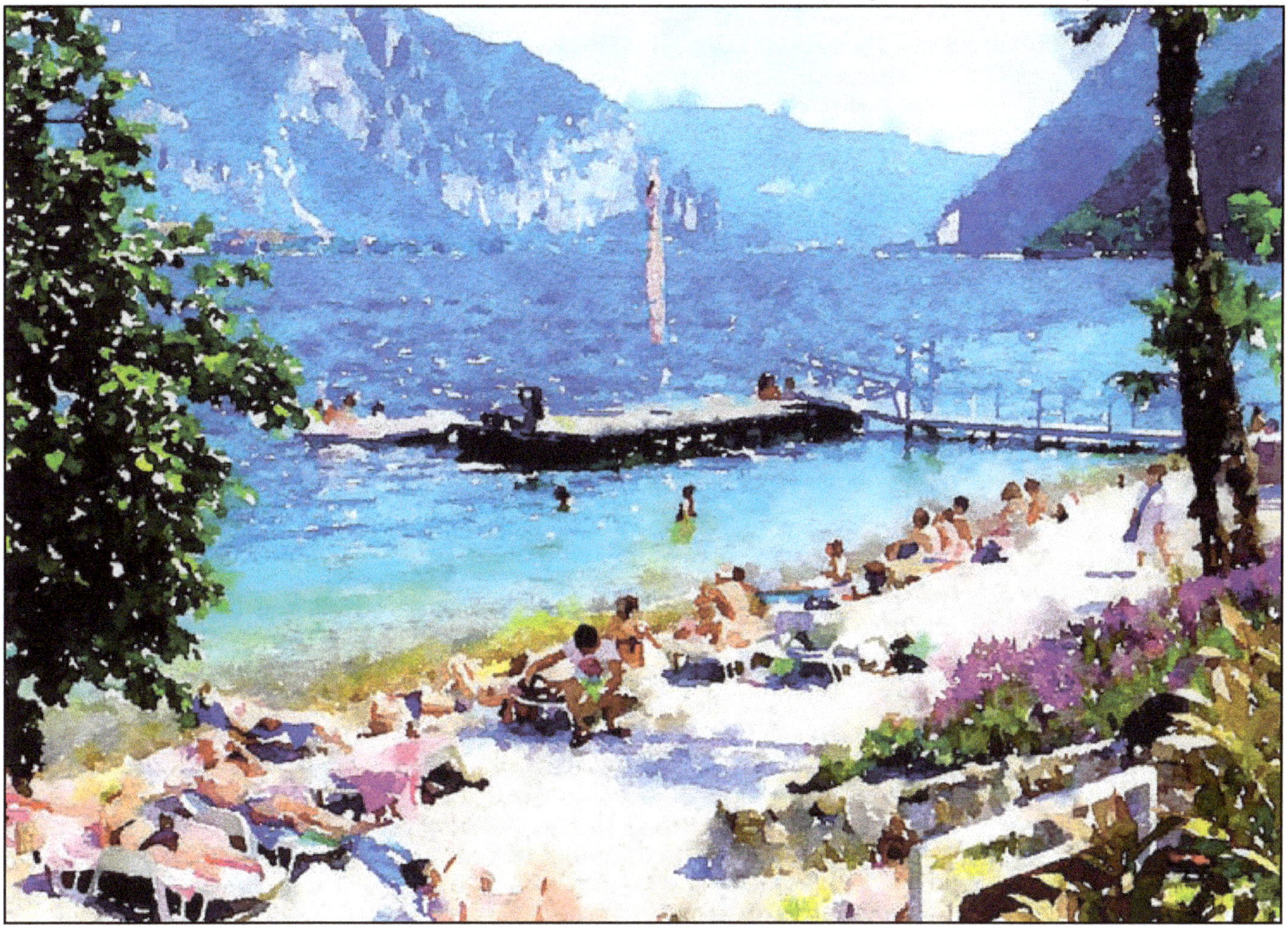

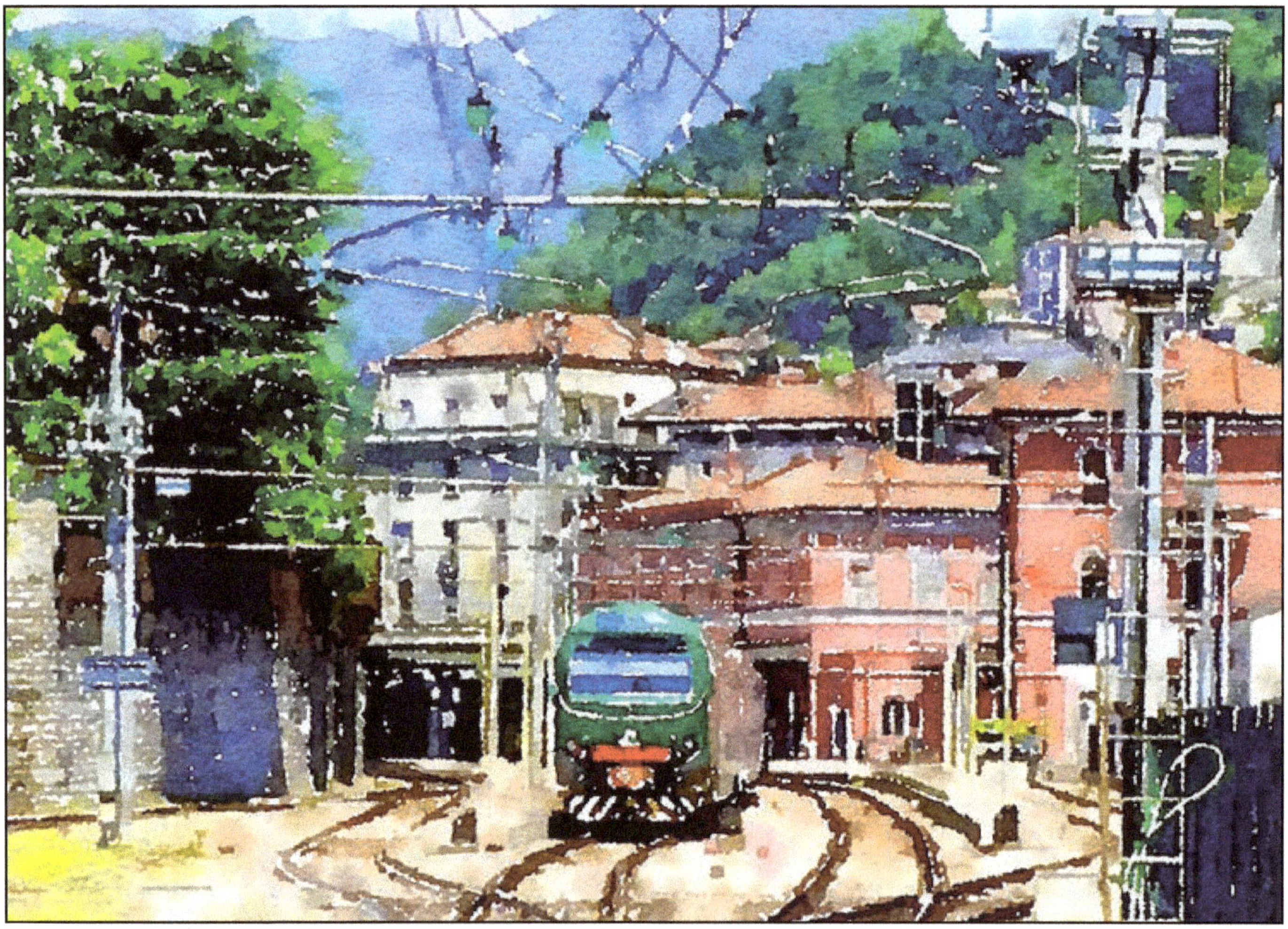

▲'Como Lago Stazione' (2015), Lago di Como, Lombardy [EIT(LO)1509].

▼'The Arches' (2015), Bergamo, Lombardy [EIT(LO)1502].

'Streetwalkers' (2015), Bergamo, Lombardy [EIT(LO)1501].▼

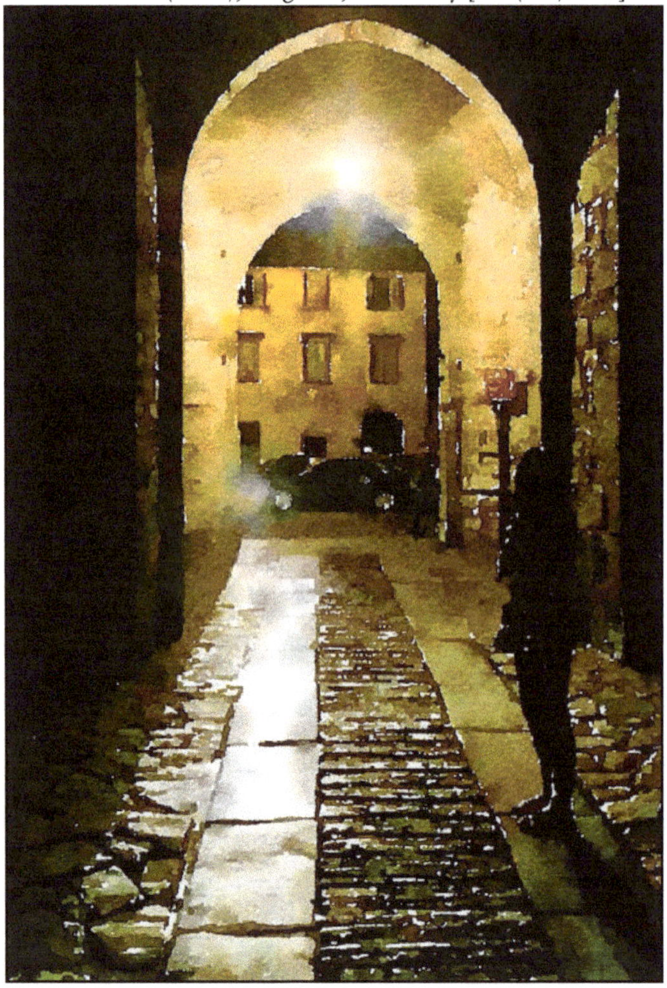

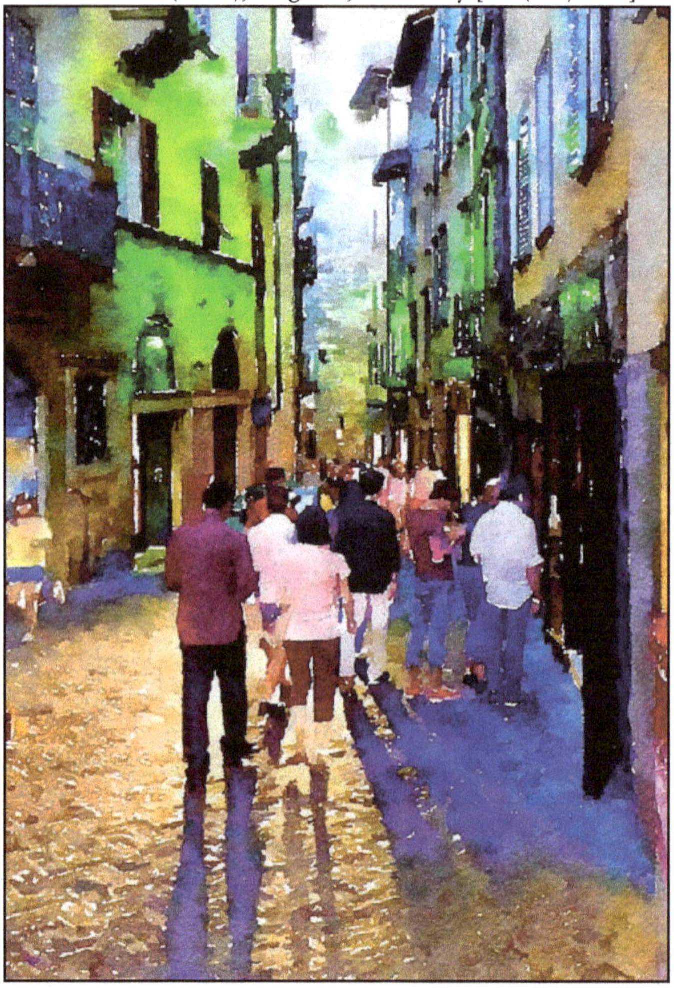

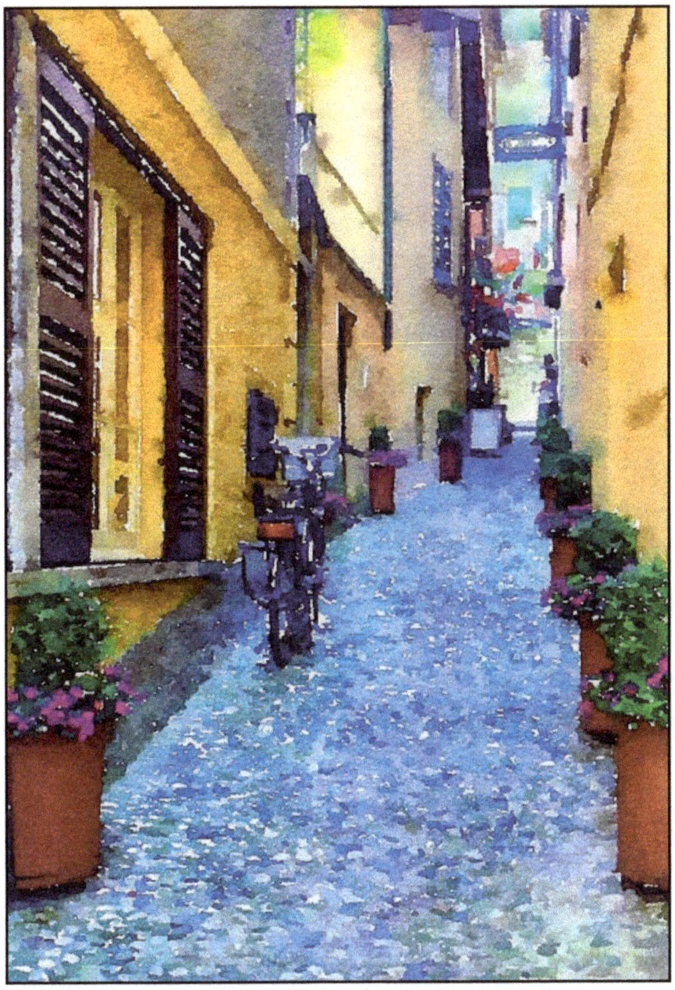

▲'Bellagio Lane' (2015), Lombardy [EIT(LO)1503].

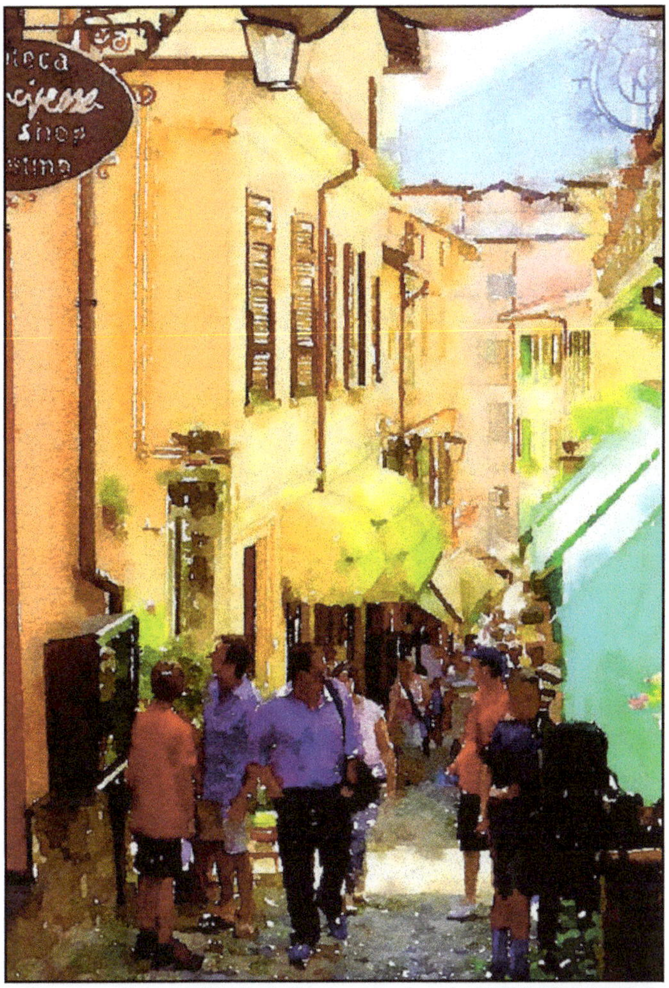

'Streetwalkers' (2015), Bellagio, Lombardy [EIT(LO)1505].▲

'Blossoms Of Bellagio' (2015), Lombardy [EIT(LO)1504].▼

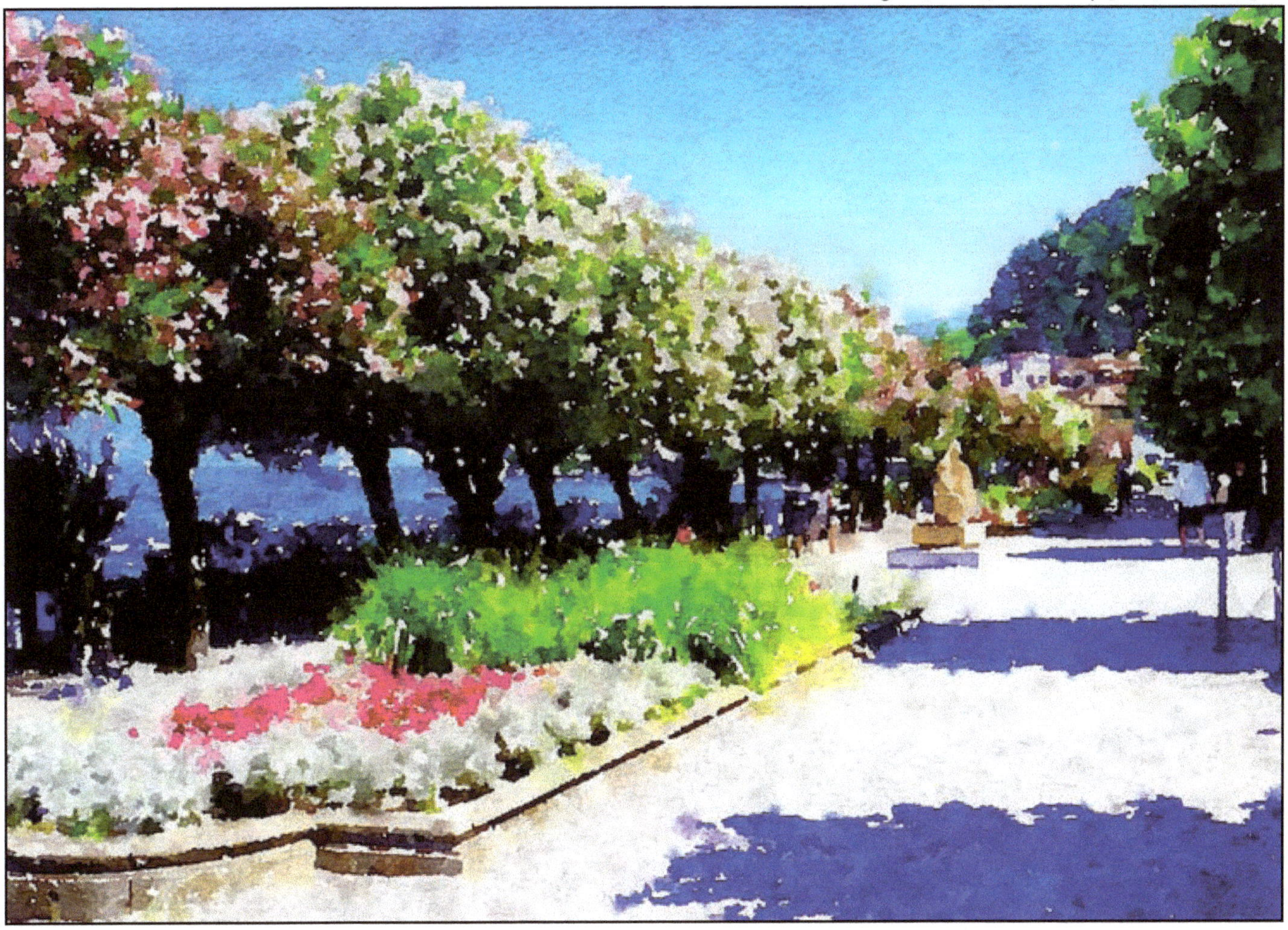

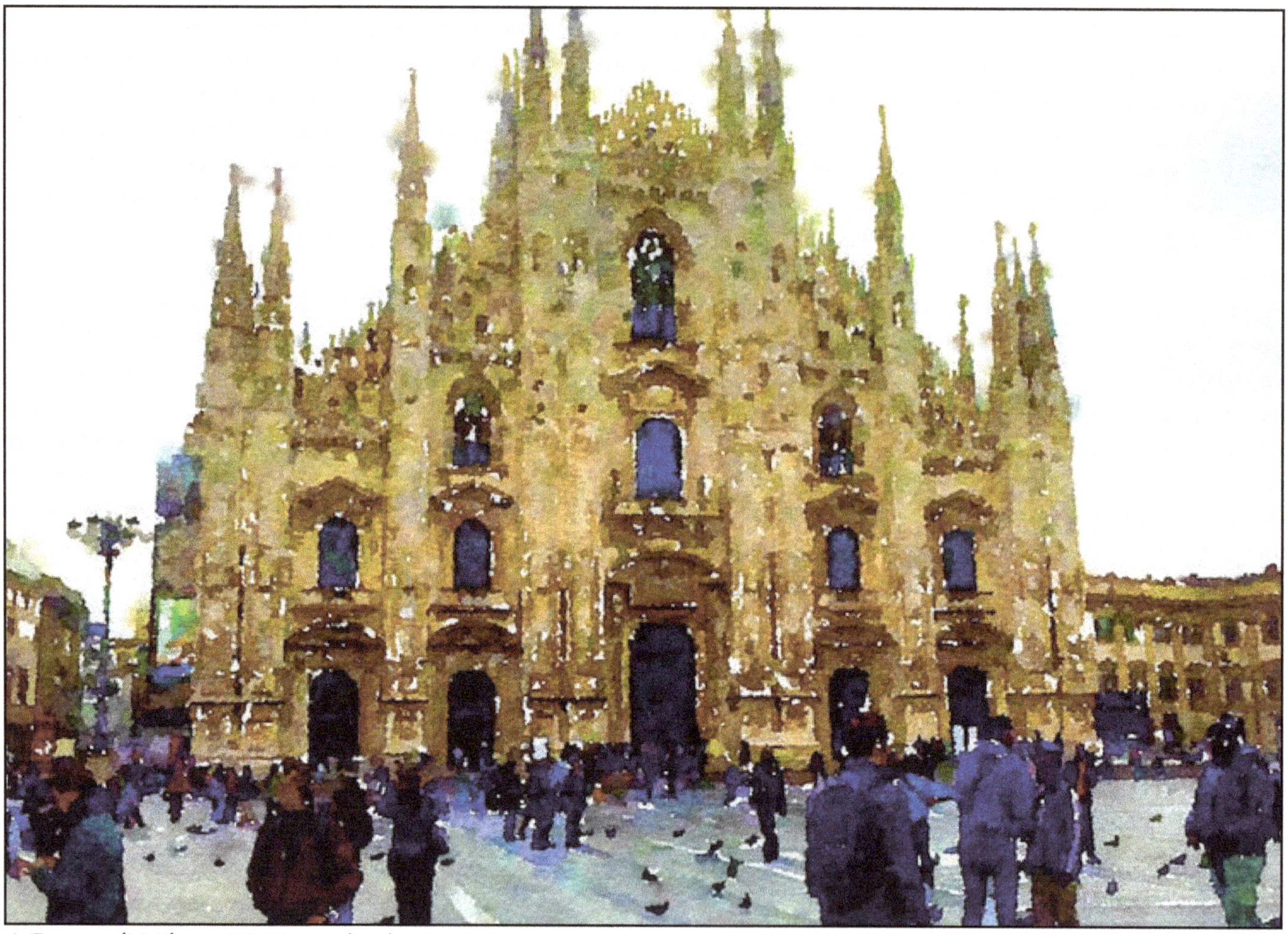

▲'Duomo di Milano' (2015), Lombardy [EIT(LO)1508].

'Milano Stazione' (2015), Lombardy [EIT(LO)1510].▼

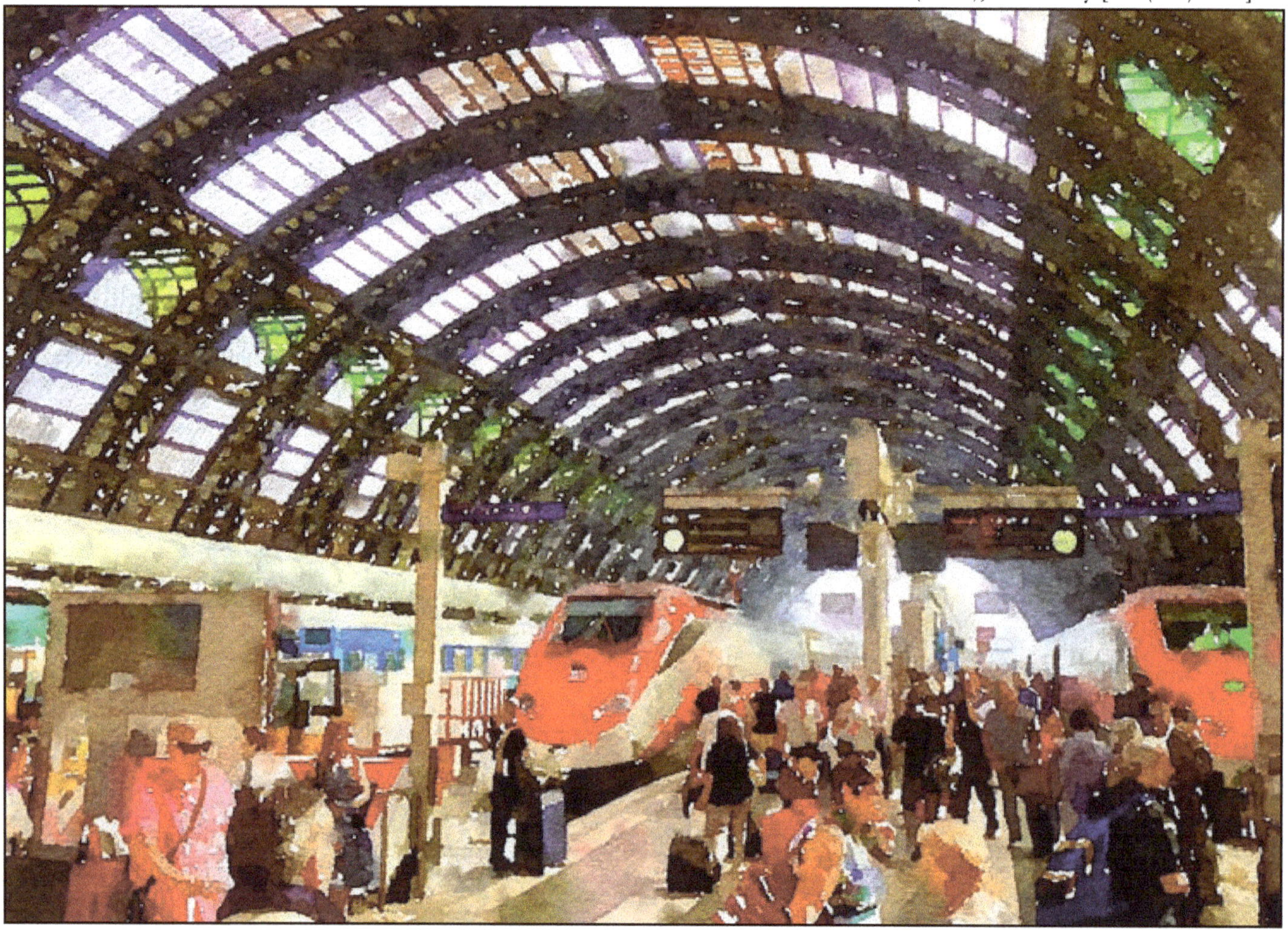

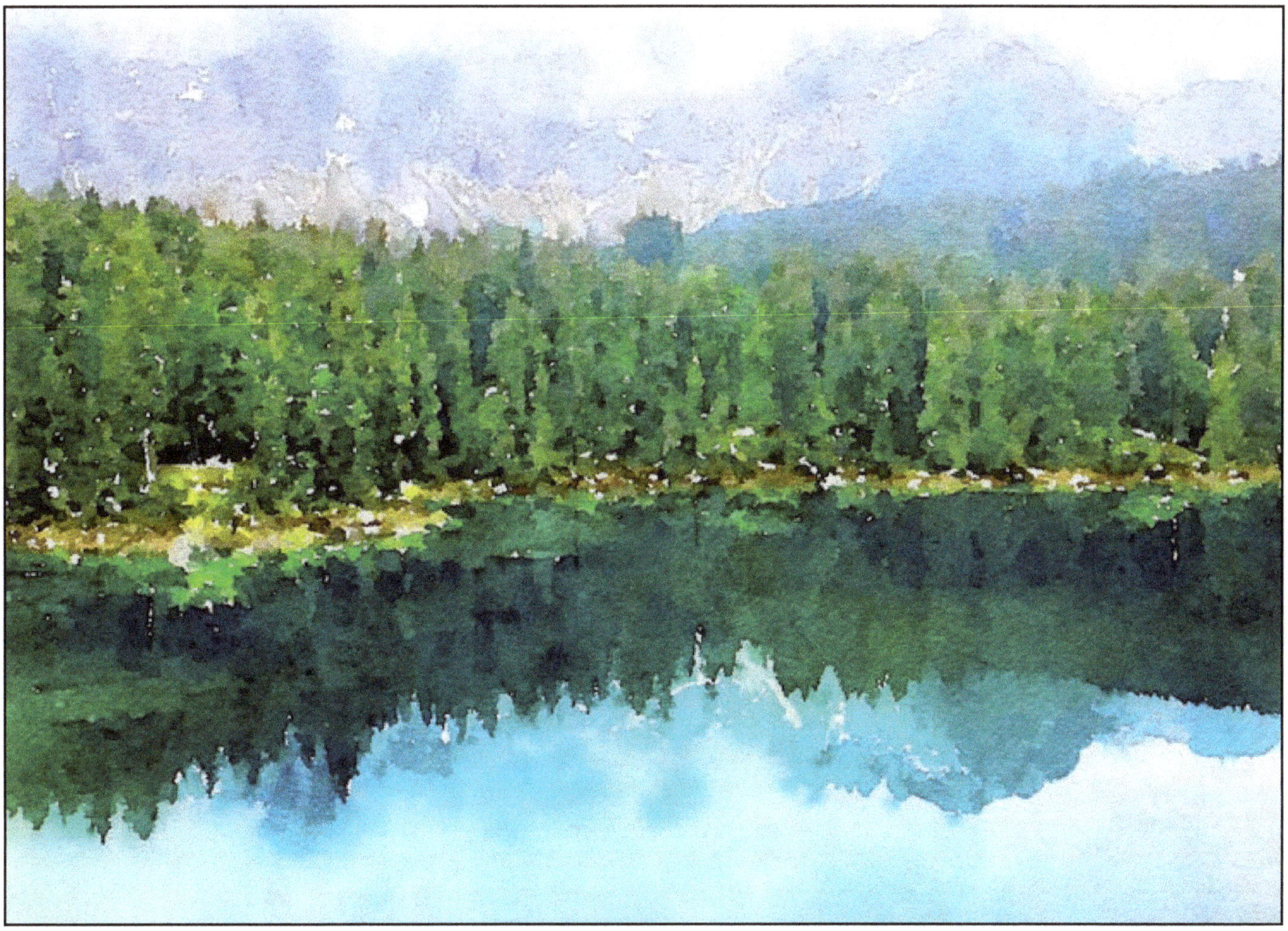

▲'Lago di Carezza' (2018), Karersee, Trentino-Alto [EIT(TA)1801].

'Livinallongo Del Col di Lana' (2018), Trentino-Alto [EIT(TA)1802].▼

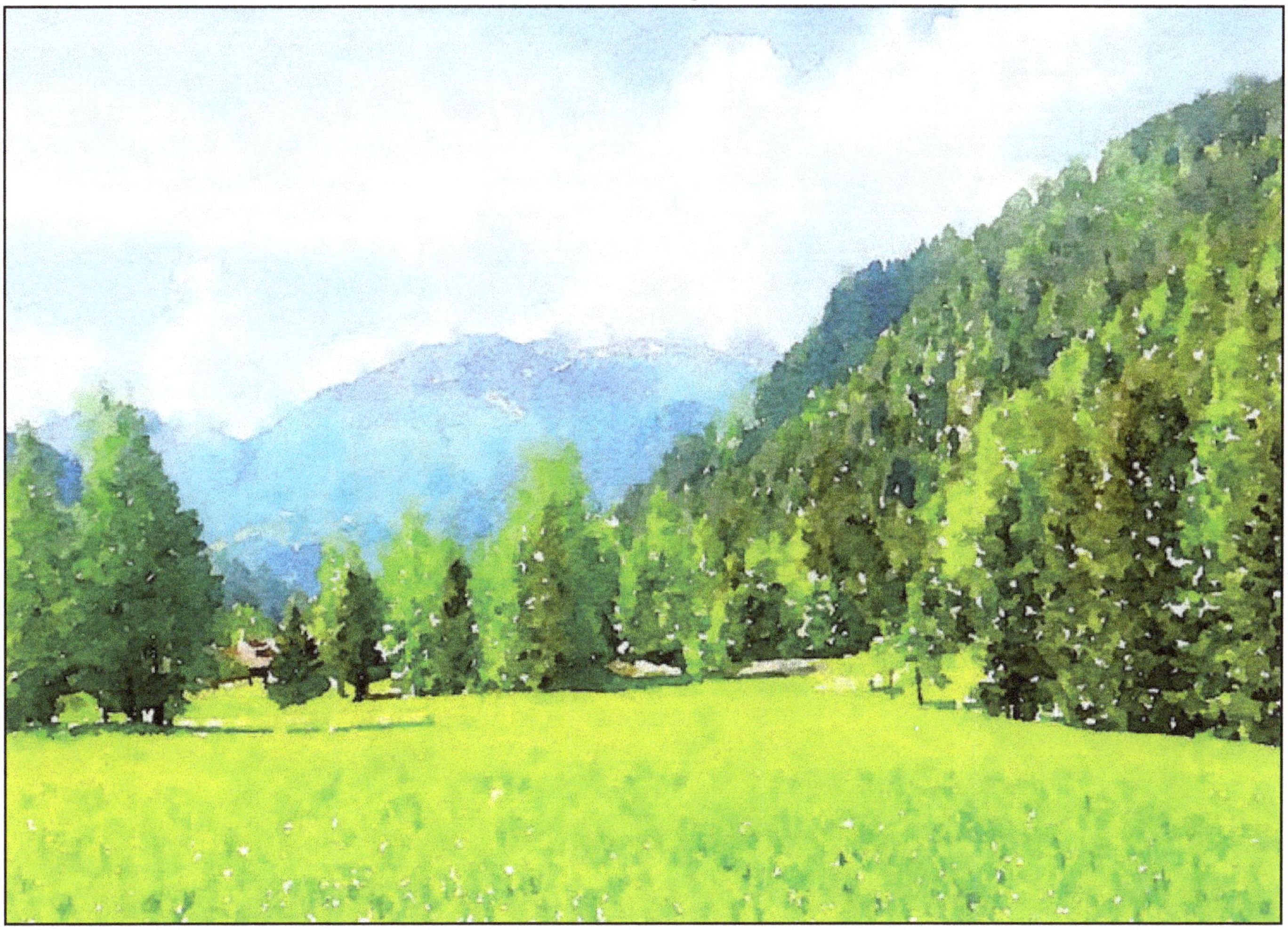

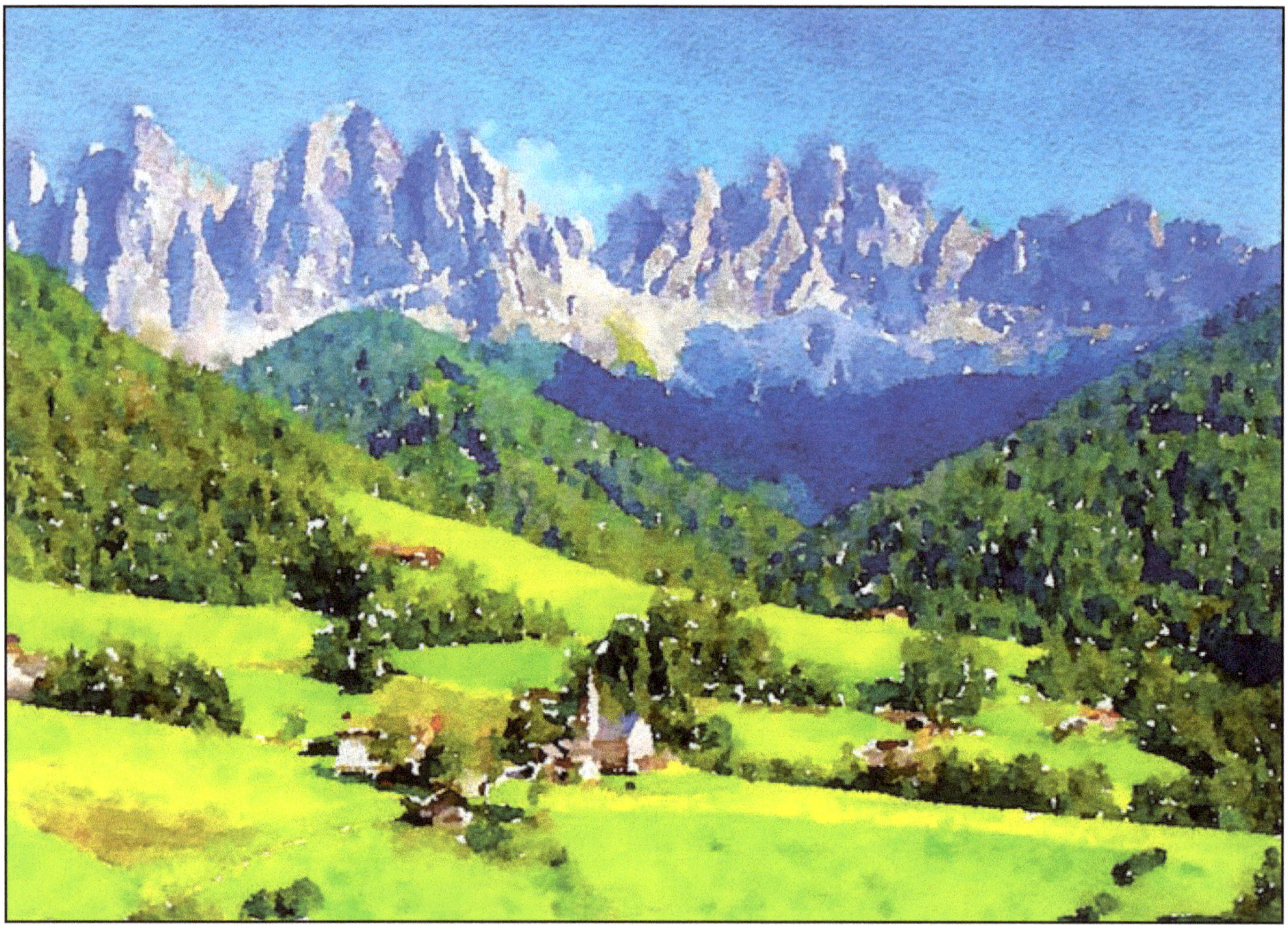

▲'The Dolomites 1' (2018), Trentino-Alto [EIT(TA)1803]. ⊘

'The Dolomites 2' (2018), Trentino-Alto [EIT(TA)1804]. ⊘▼

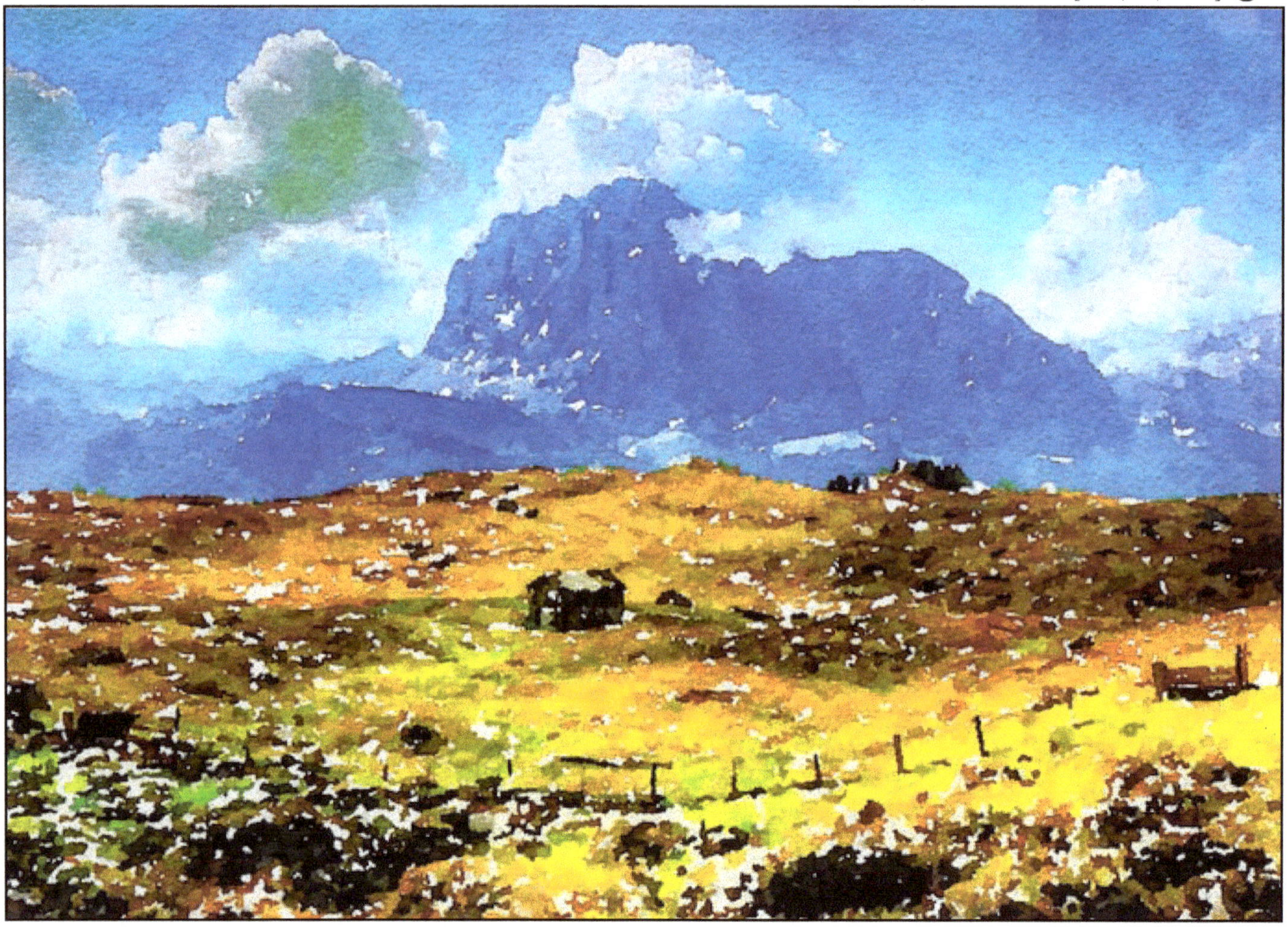

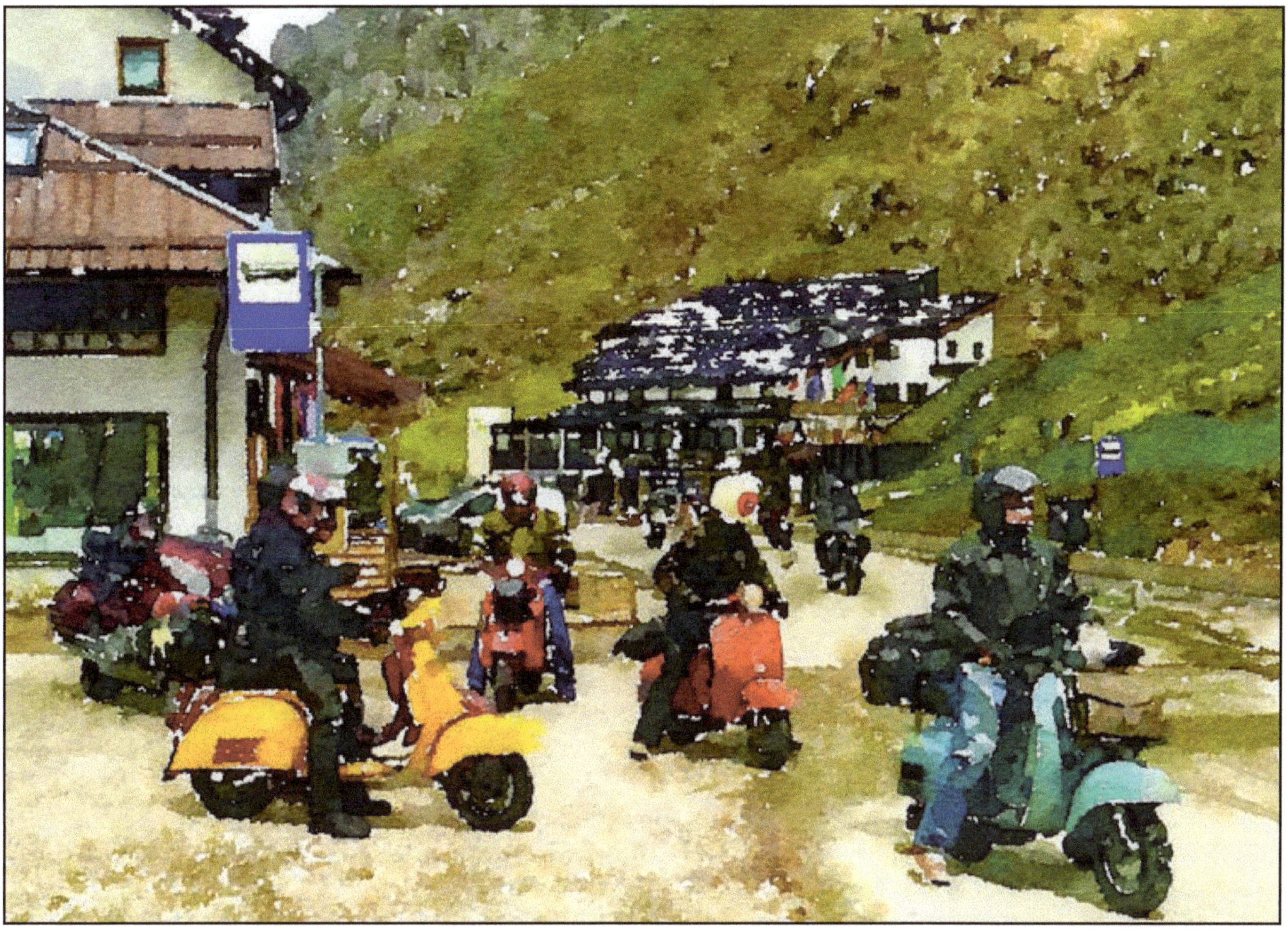

▲'Scooters At Falzarego Pass' (2018), Trentino-Alto [EIT(TA)1808].

'Parco Naturale Tre Cime' (2018), Trentino-Alto [EIT(TA)1805].▼

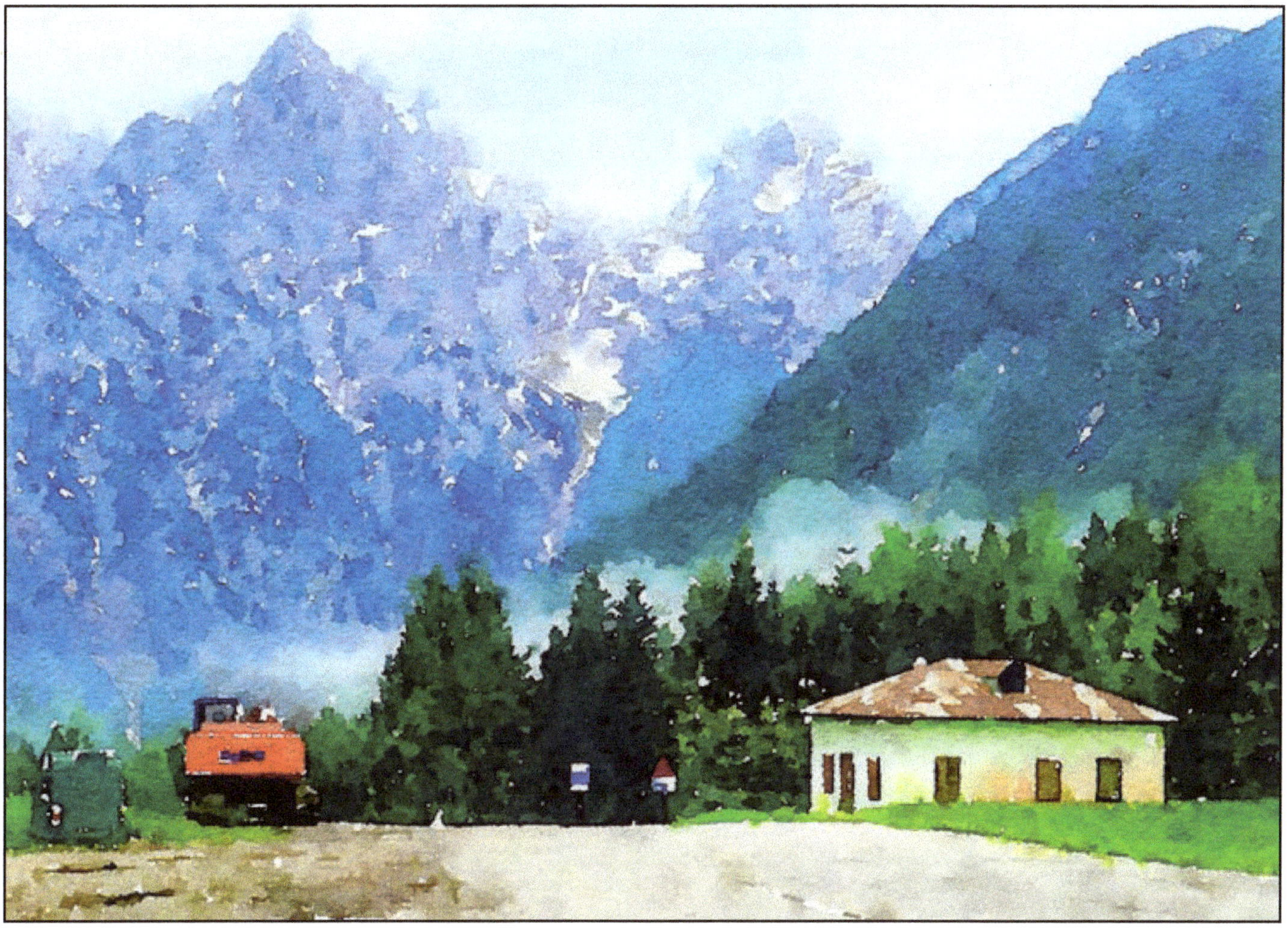

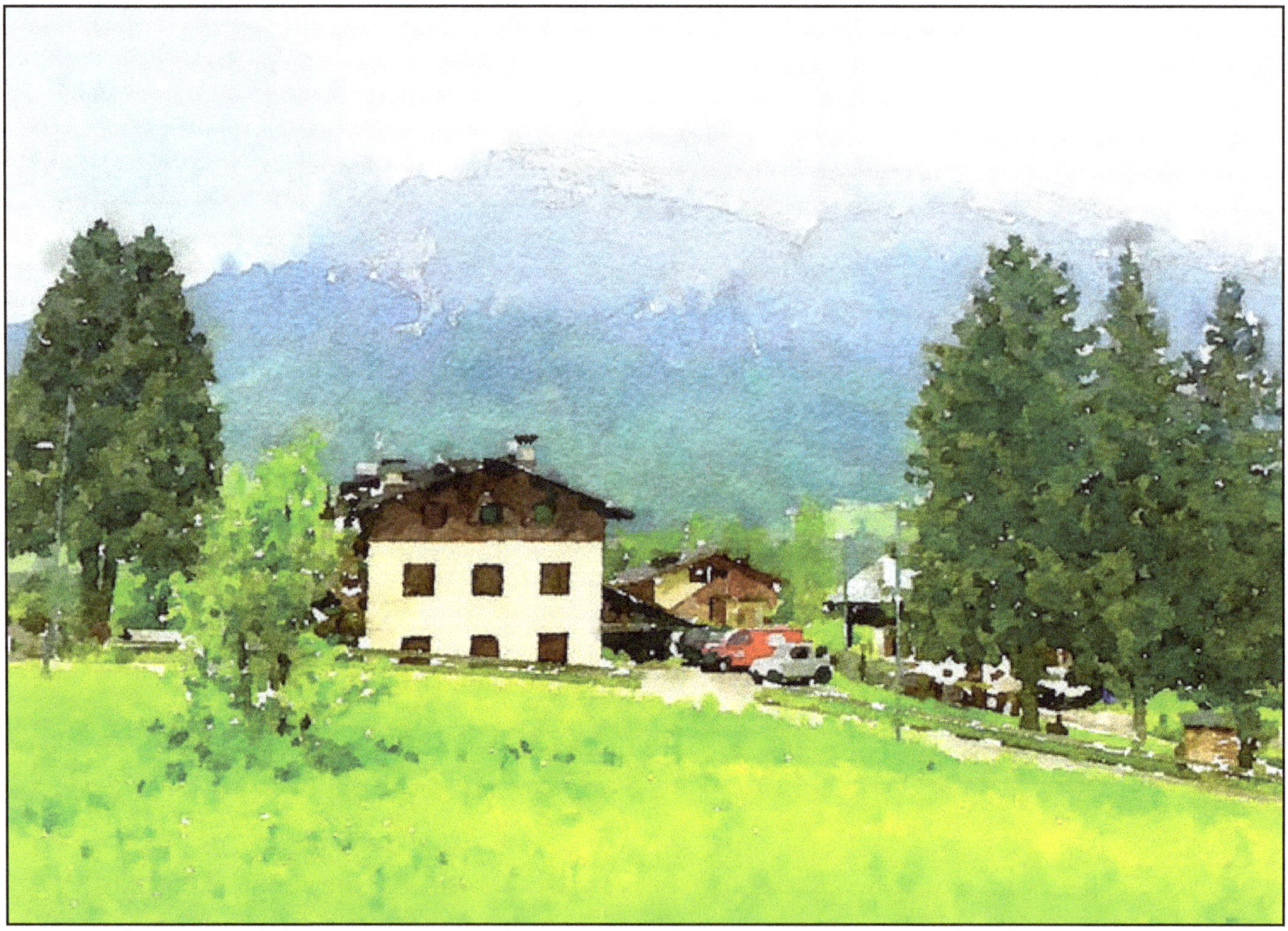

▲'Cortina d'Amprezzo Chalet' (2018), Trentino-Alto [EIT(TA)1806].

'Cortina d'Amprezzo Church' (2018), Trentino-Alto [EIT(TA)1807].▼

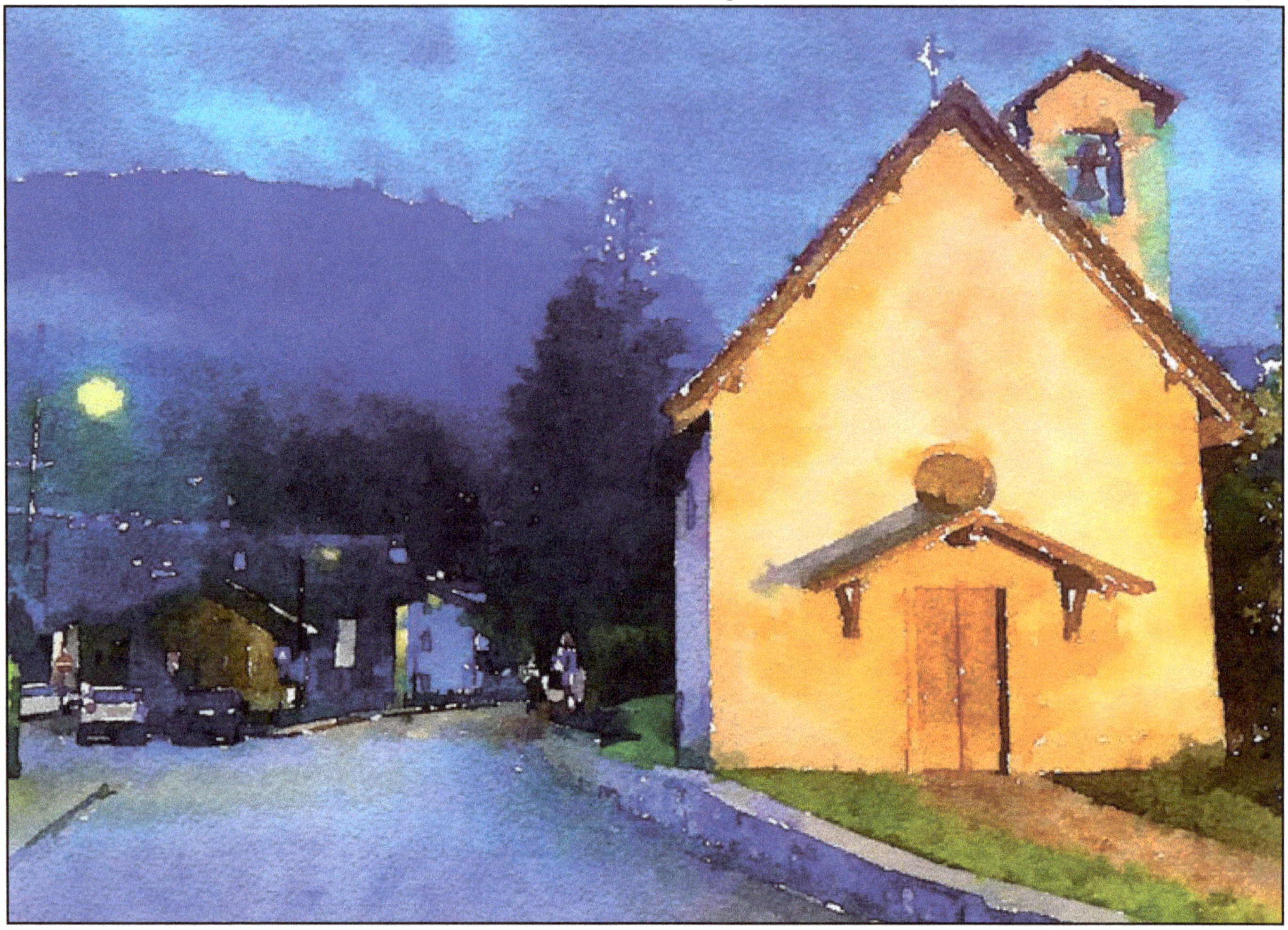

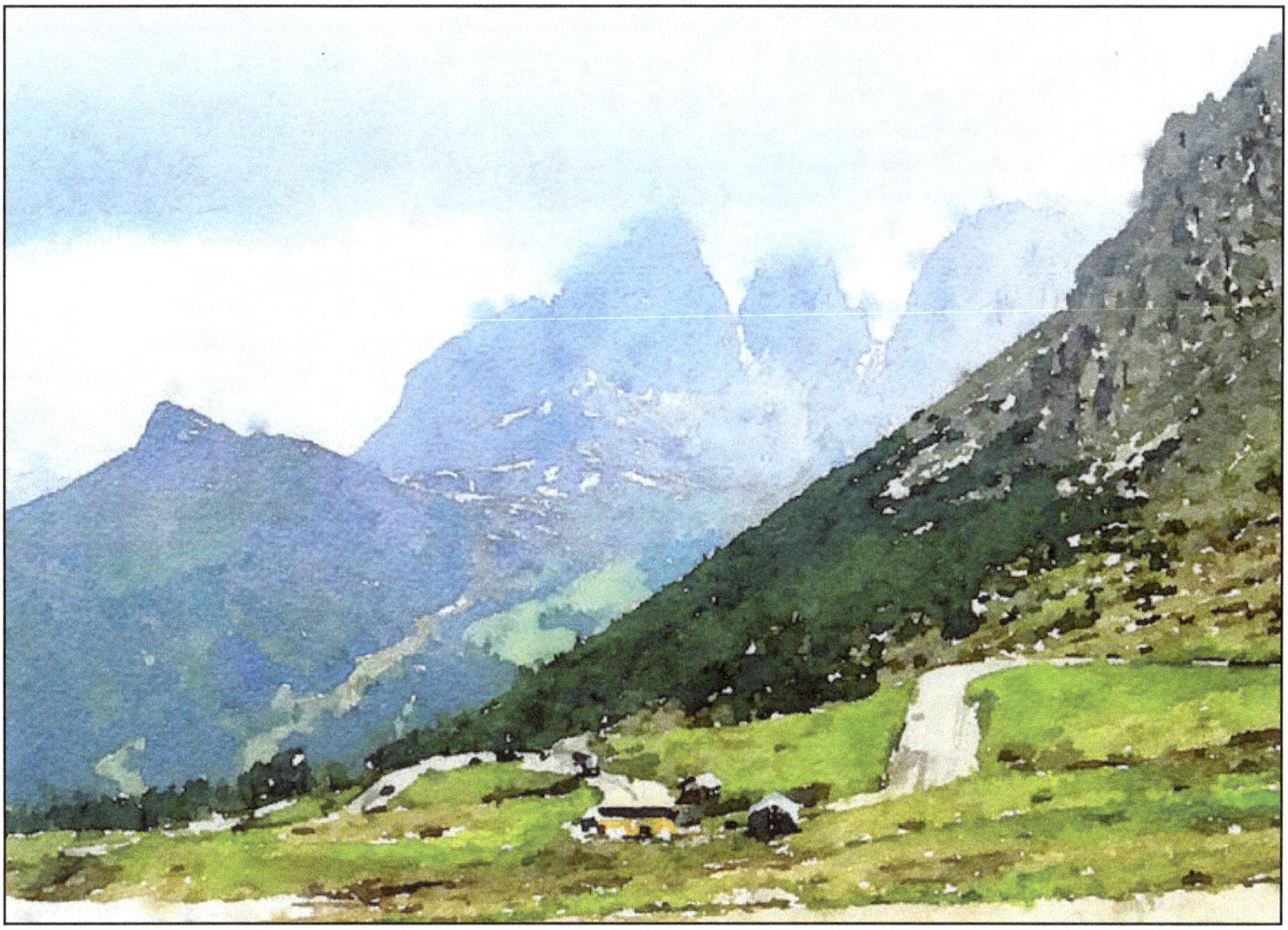

▲'View from Canazei Chalet' (2018), Trentino-Alto [EIT(TA)1809].

'View From Anterselva di Mezzo' (2018), Trentino-Alto [EIT(TA)1810].▼

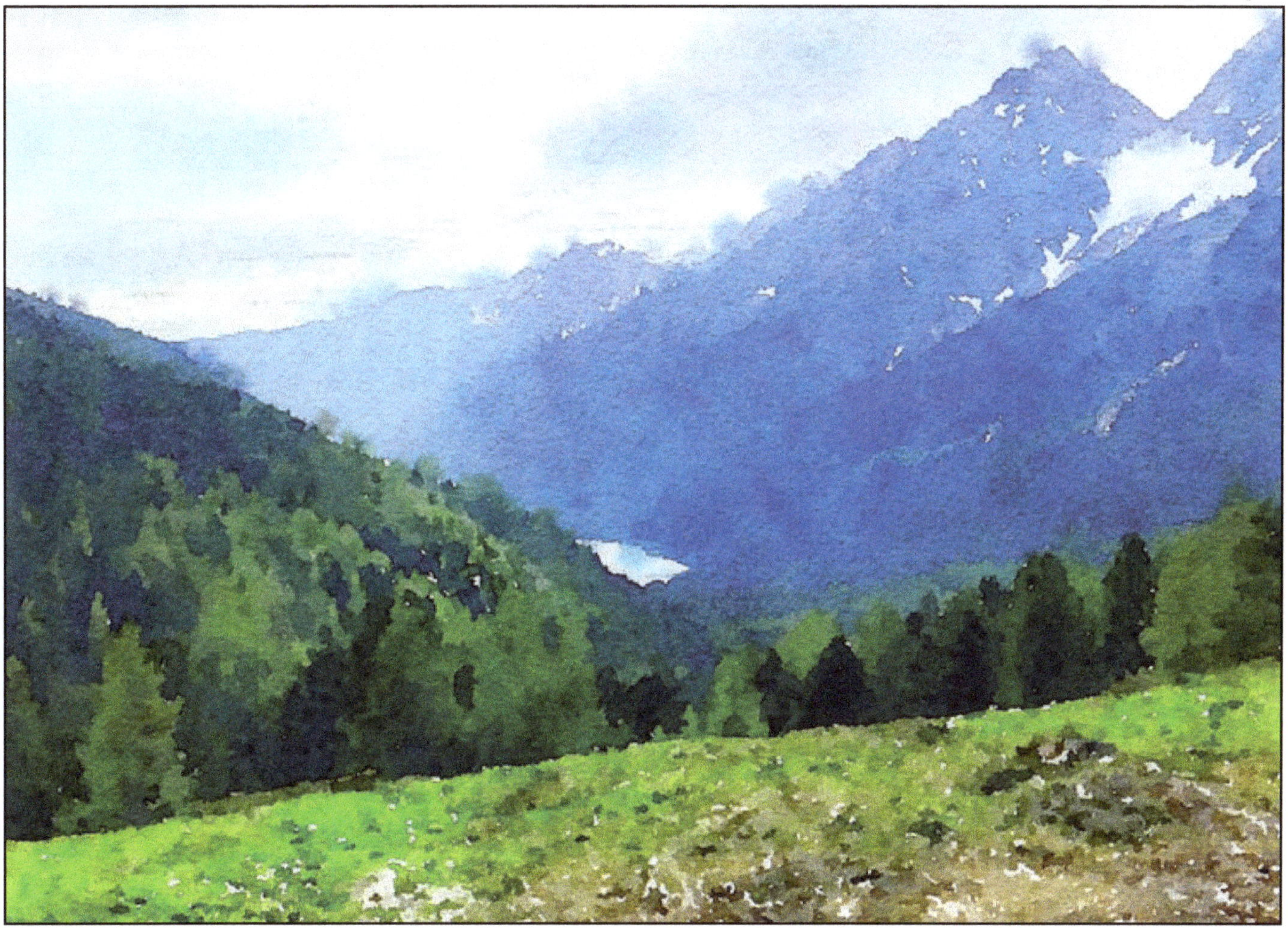

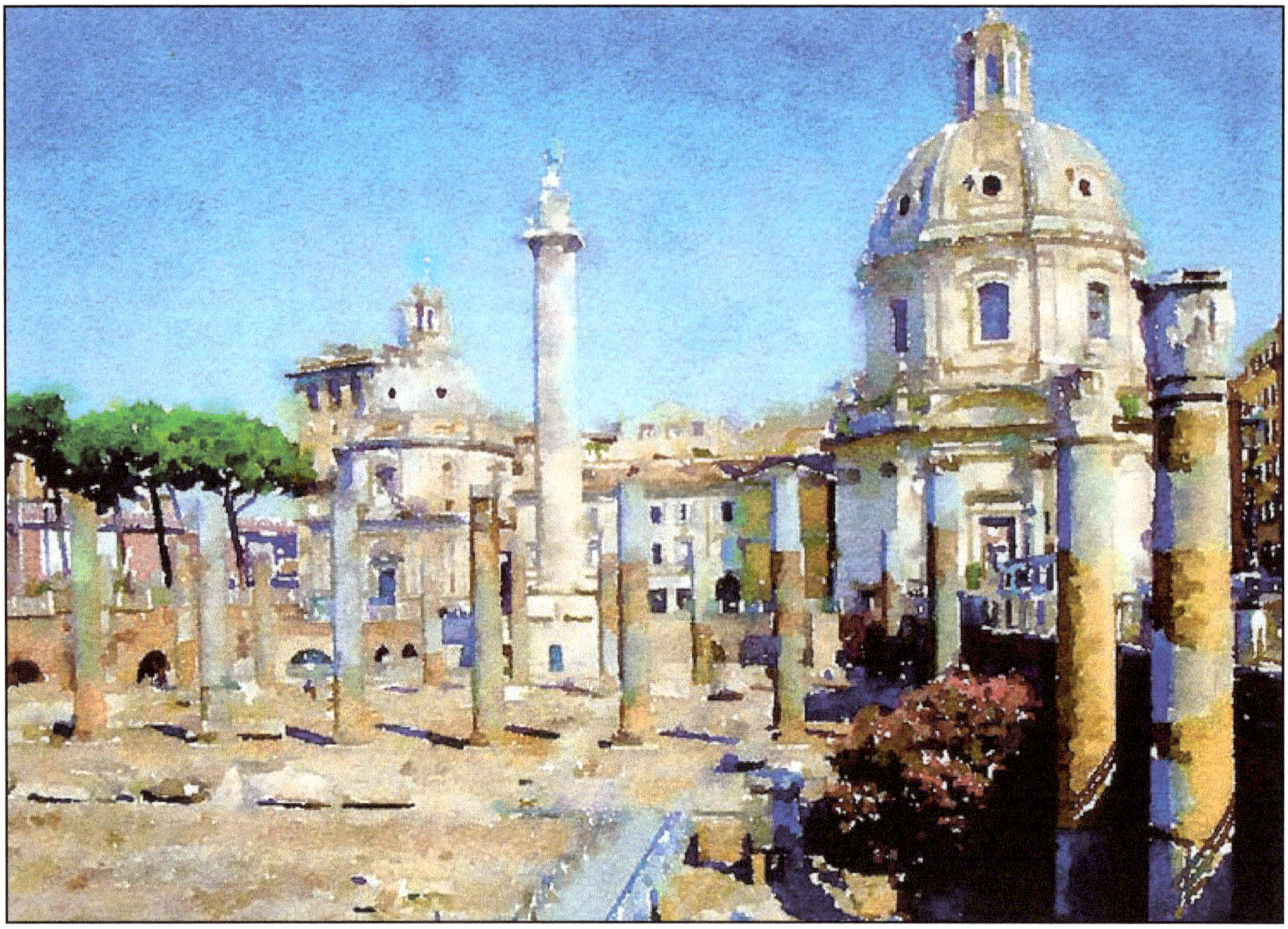

▲'Rome's Ruins' (2010), Rome [EIT(RO)1001].

'The Arch Of Constantine' (2010), Rome [EIT(RO)1002].▼

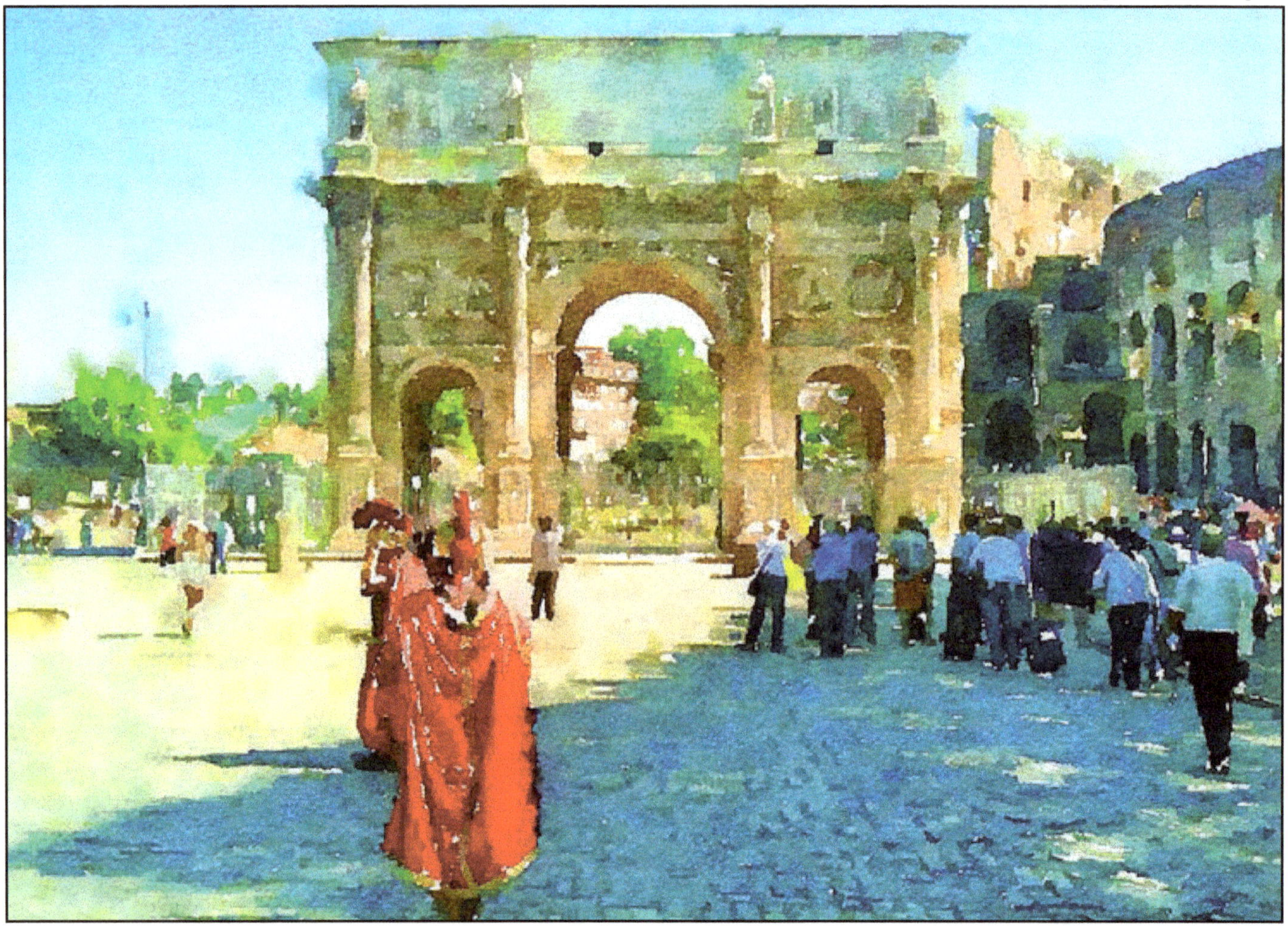

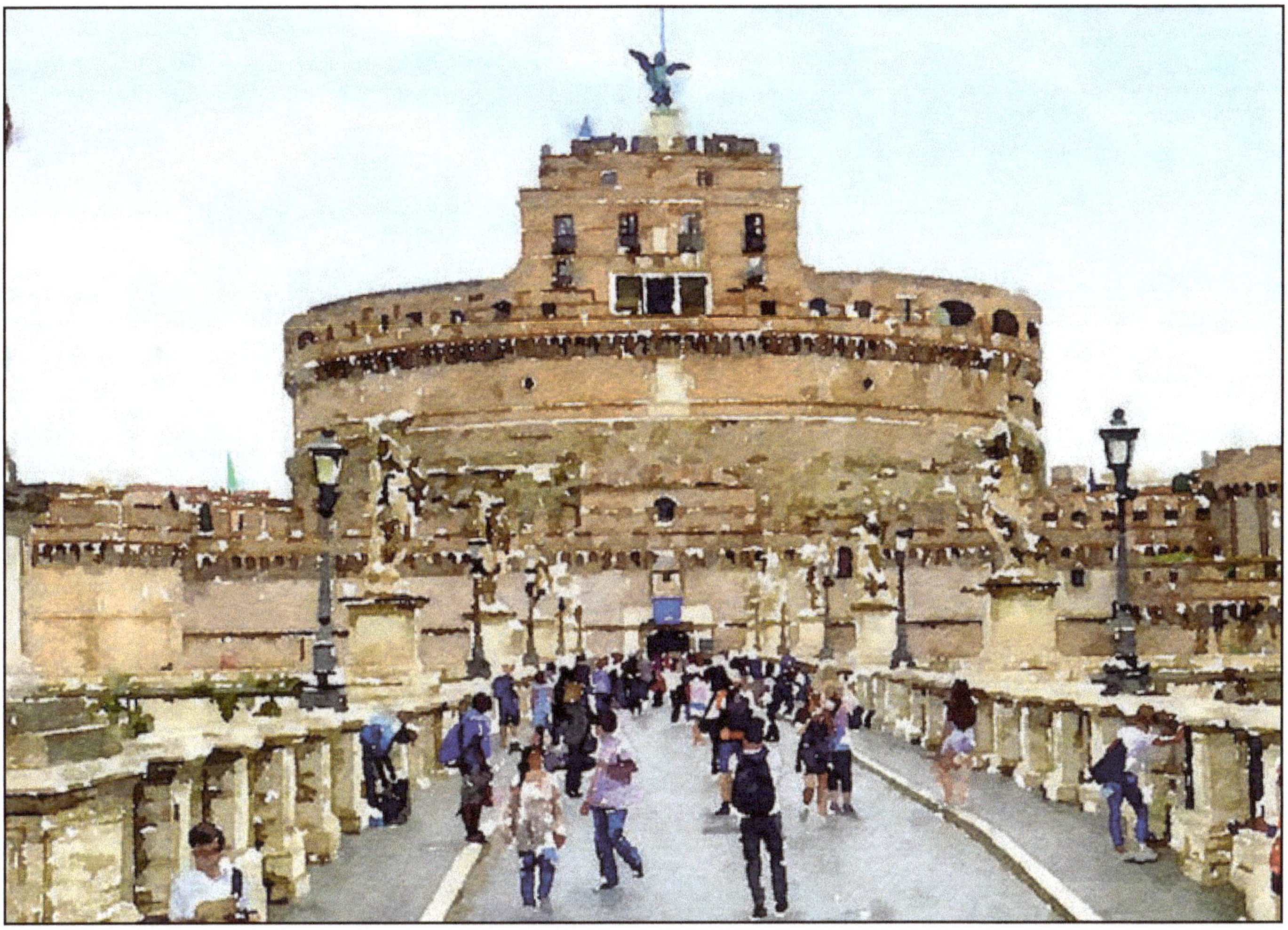

▲'Pont & Castel Sant'Angelo' (2018), Rome [EIT(RO)1802].

'The Colosseum' (2018), Rome [EIT(RO)1803].▼

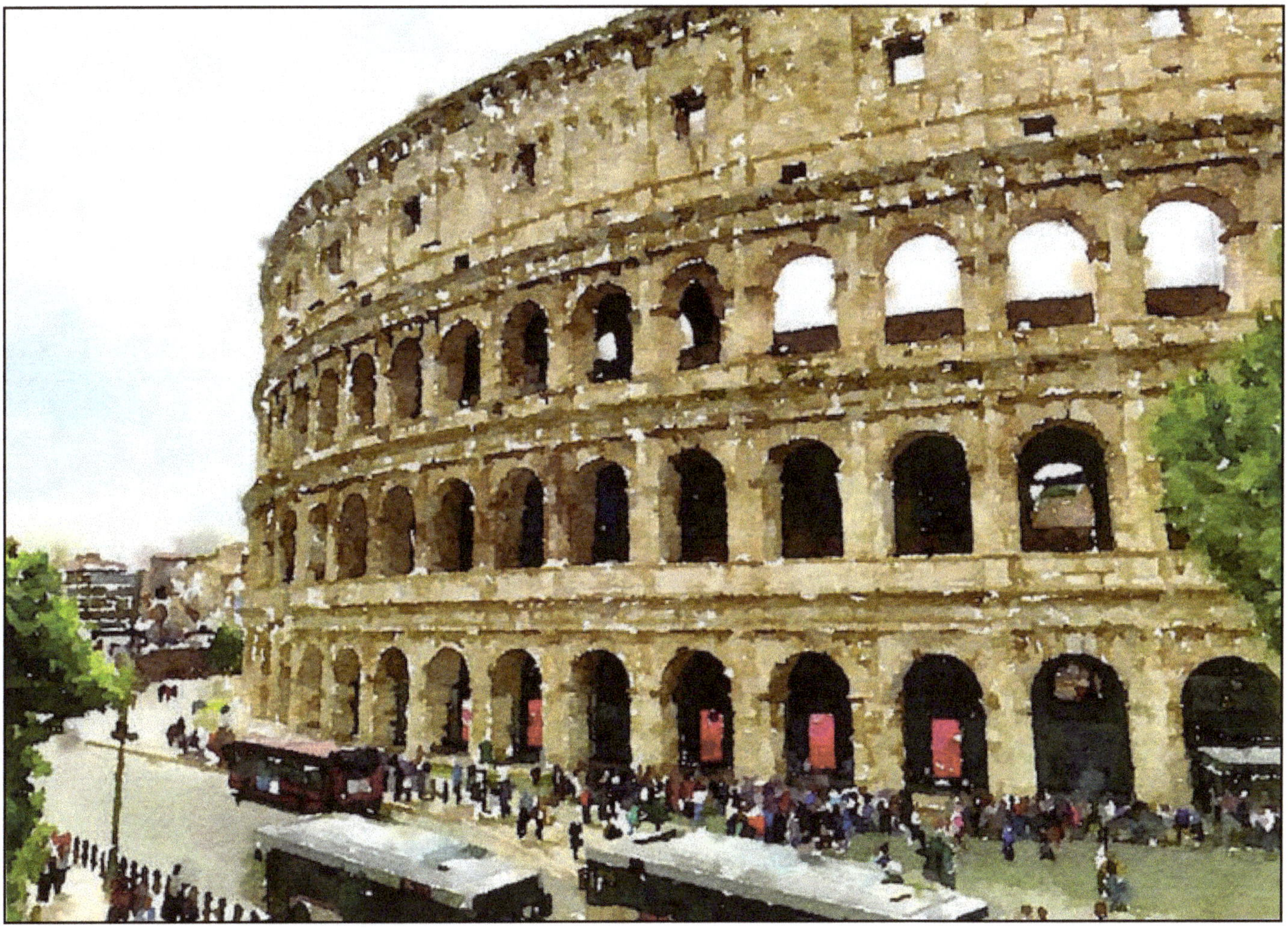

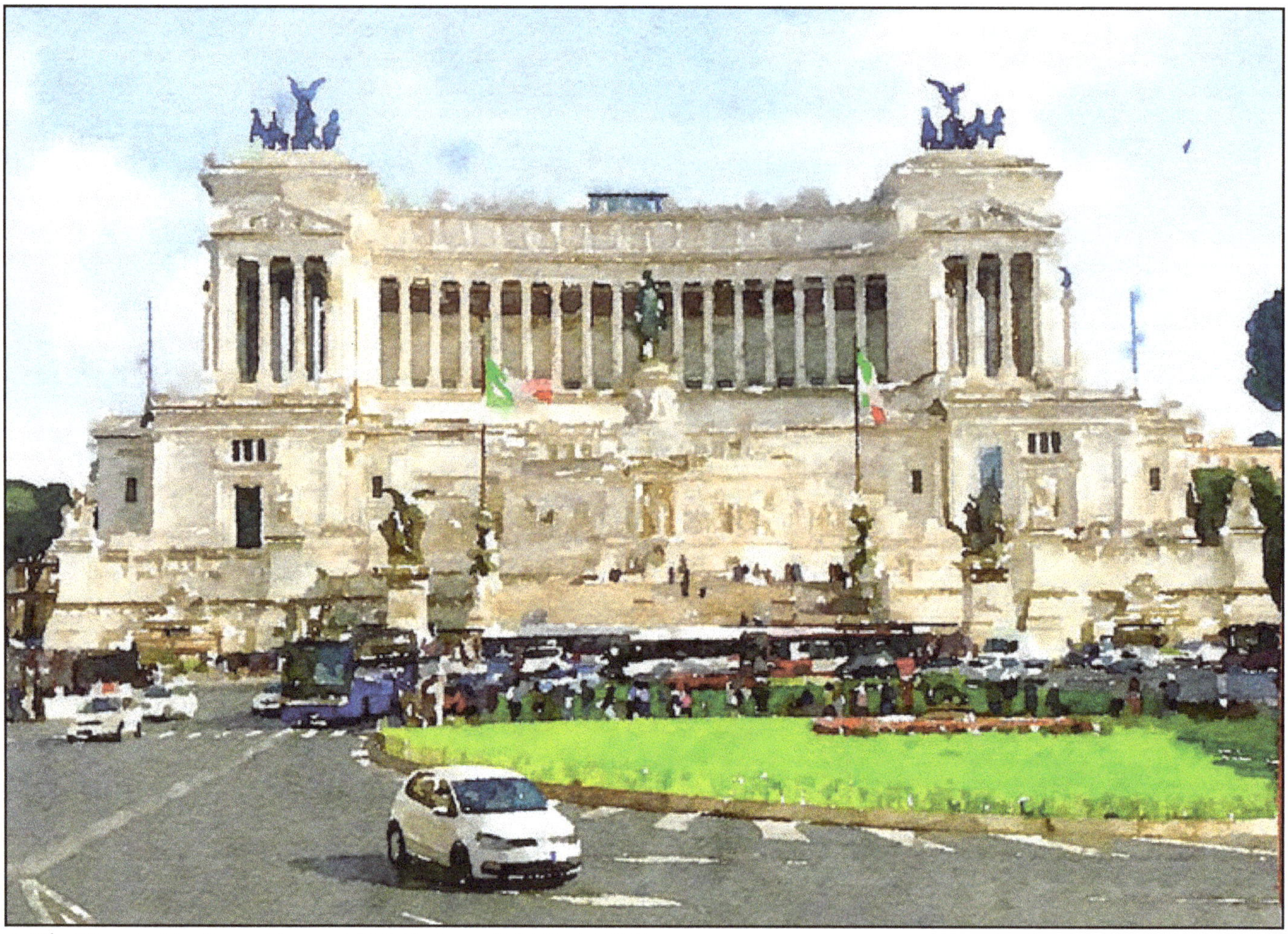

▲'The Vittorio On Piazza Venezia' (2018), Rome [EIT(RO)1804].

▼'Trajan's Column' (2018), Rome [EIT(RO)1801].

'Main Hall of St Peters Basilica' (2018), Vaticano [EIT(RO)1805].▼

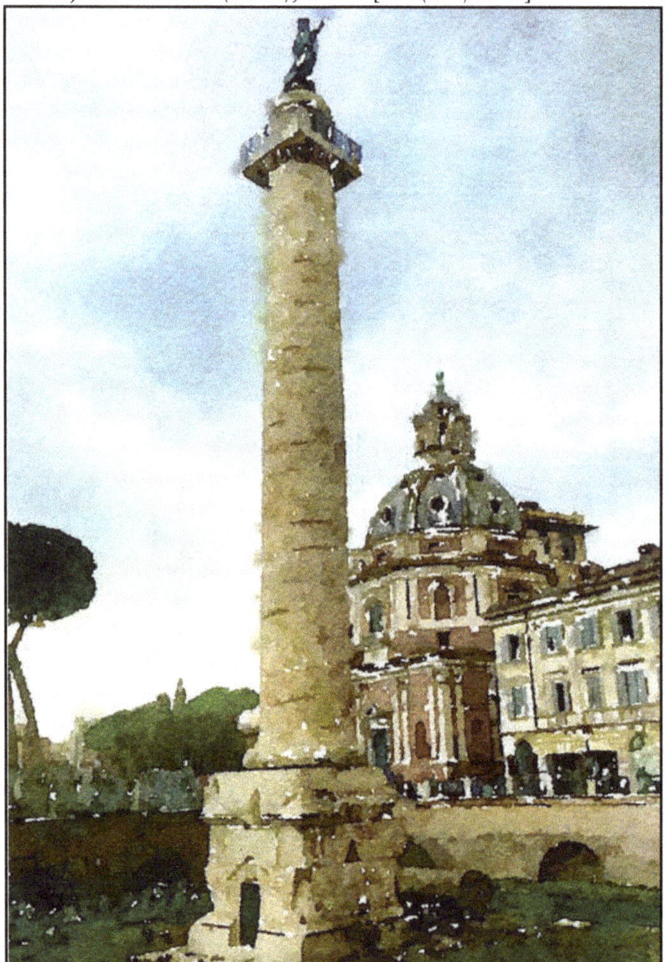

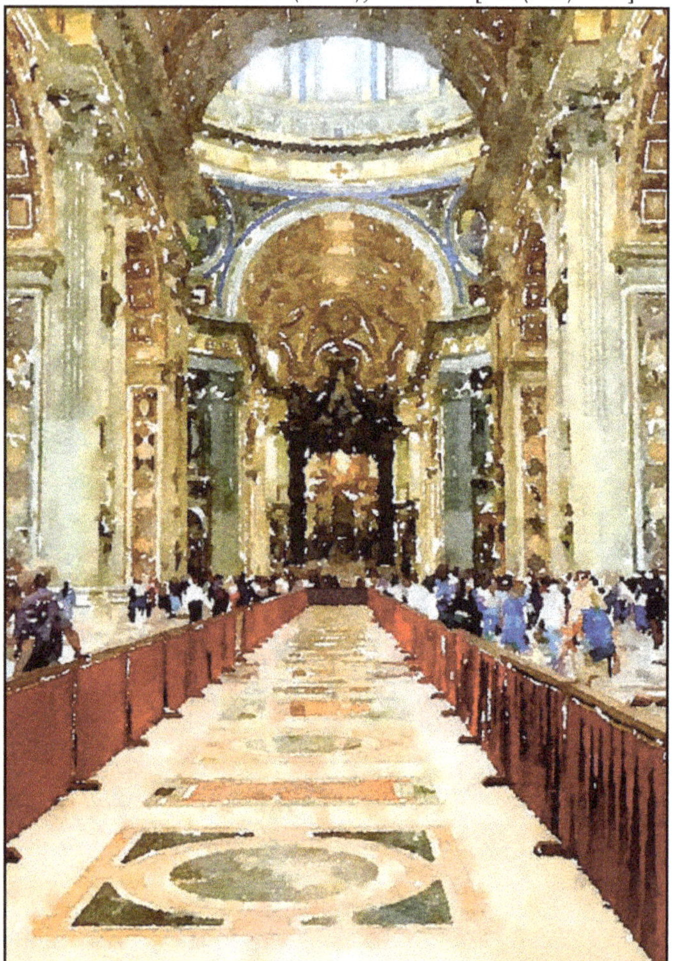

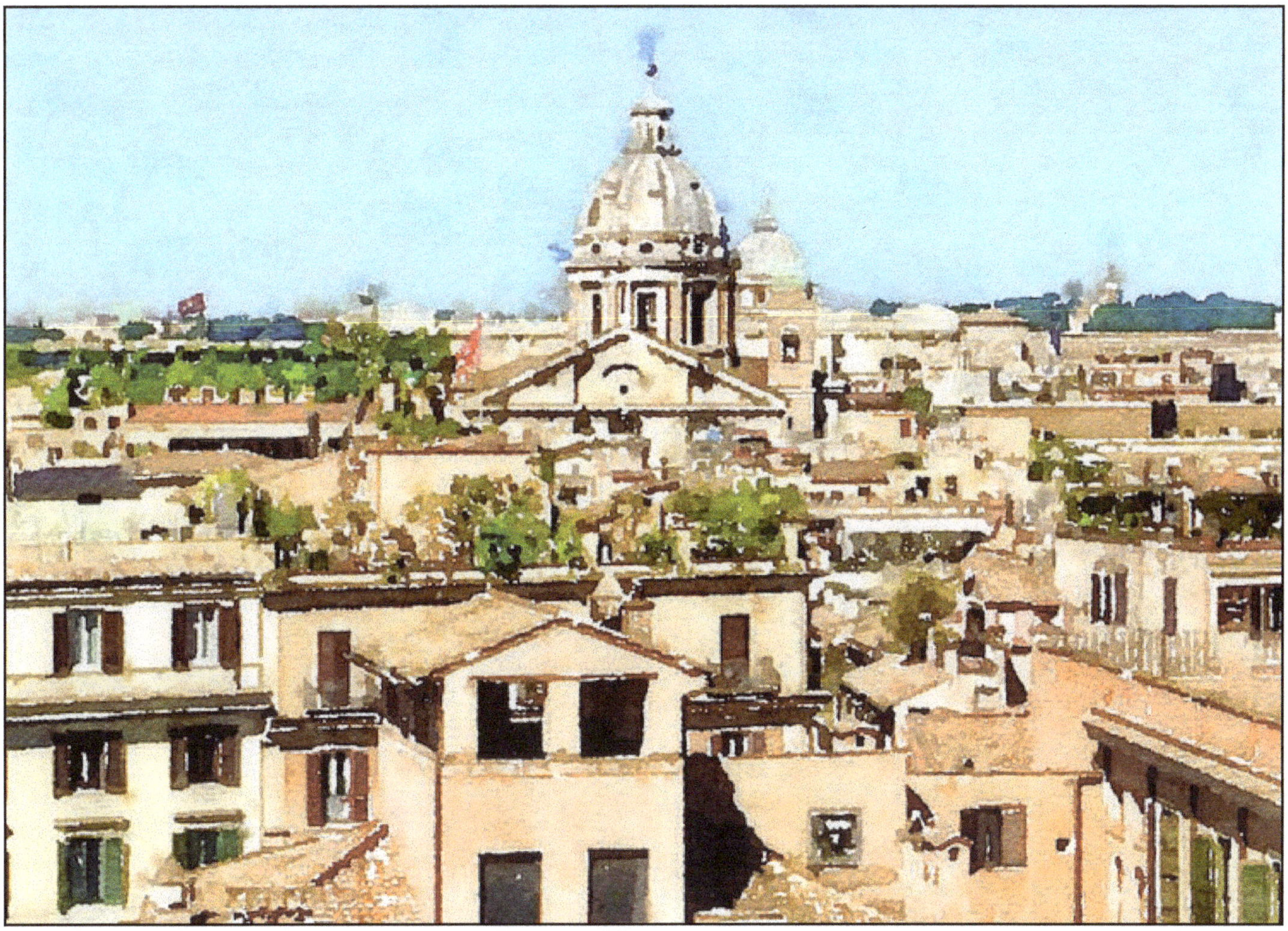

▲'View From Trinita Dei Monti' (2018), Rome [EIT(RO)1809].

'Piazza Venezia' (2018), Rome [EIT(RO)1808].▼

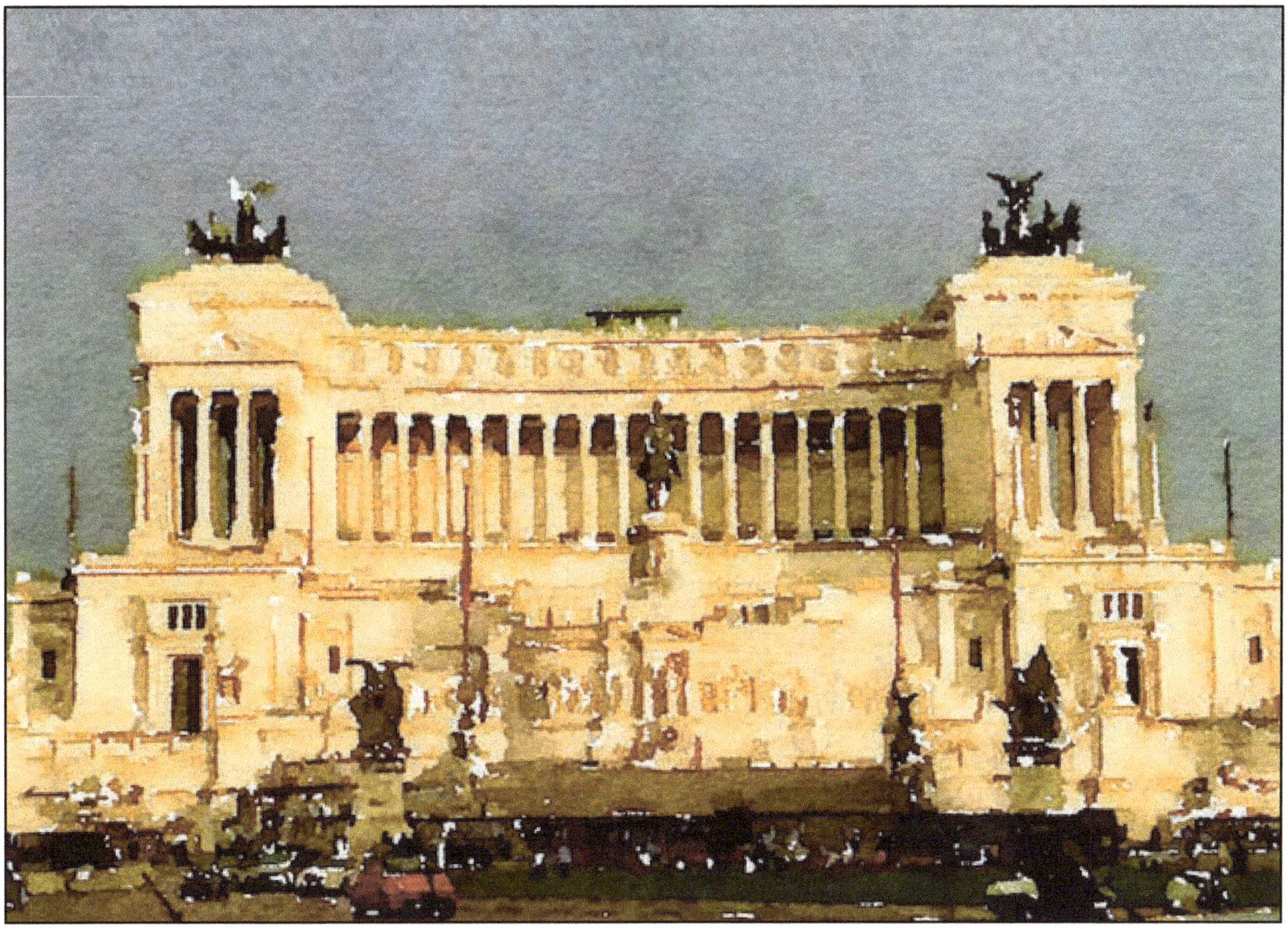

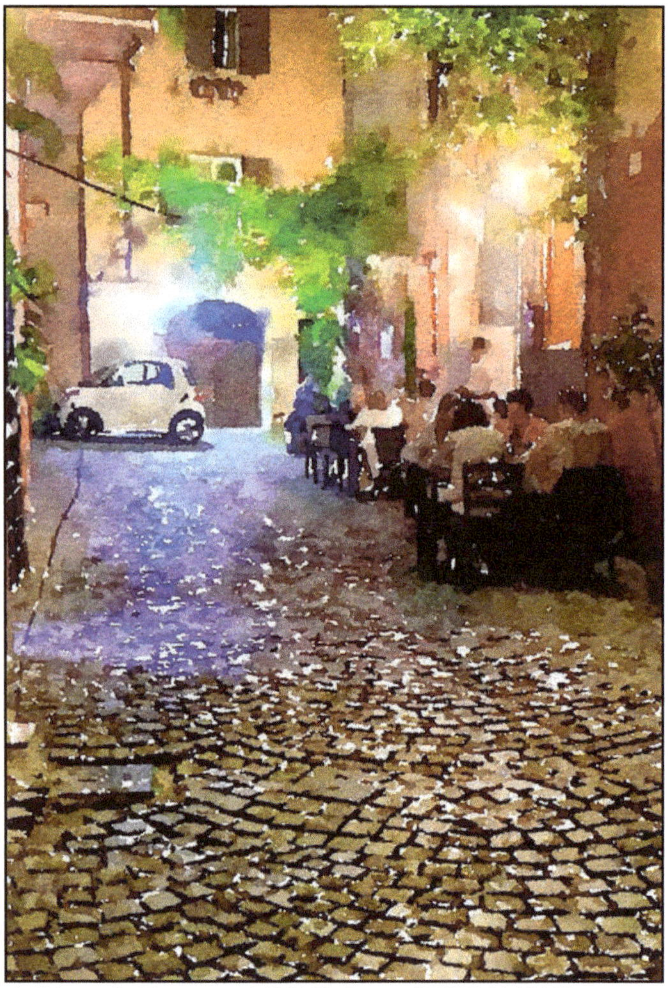

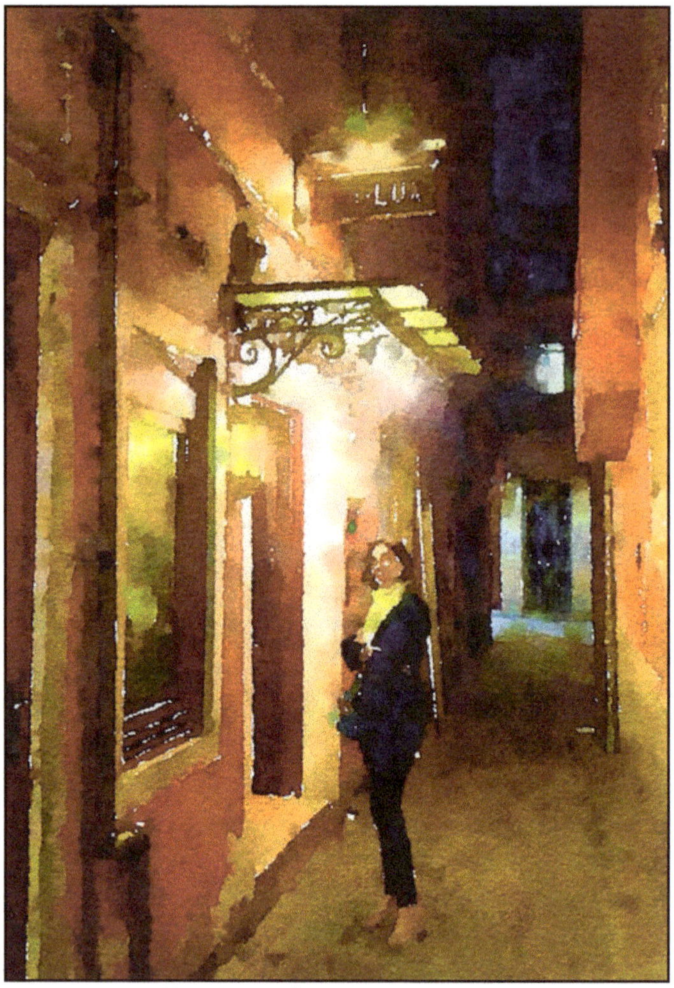

▲'Dinner In Trastevere' (2018), Rome [EIT(RO)1810].

'Venetian Lady' (2013), Venice [EIT(VE)1303].▲

'Ristorante Trastevere' (2018), Rome [EIT(RO)1806].▼

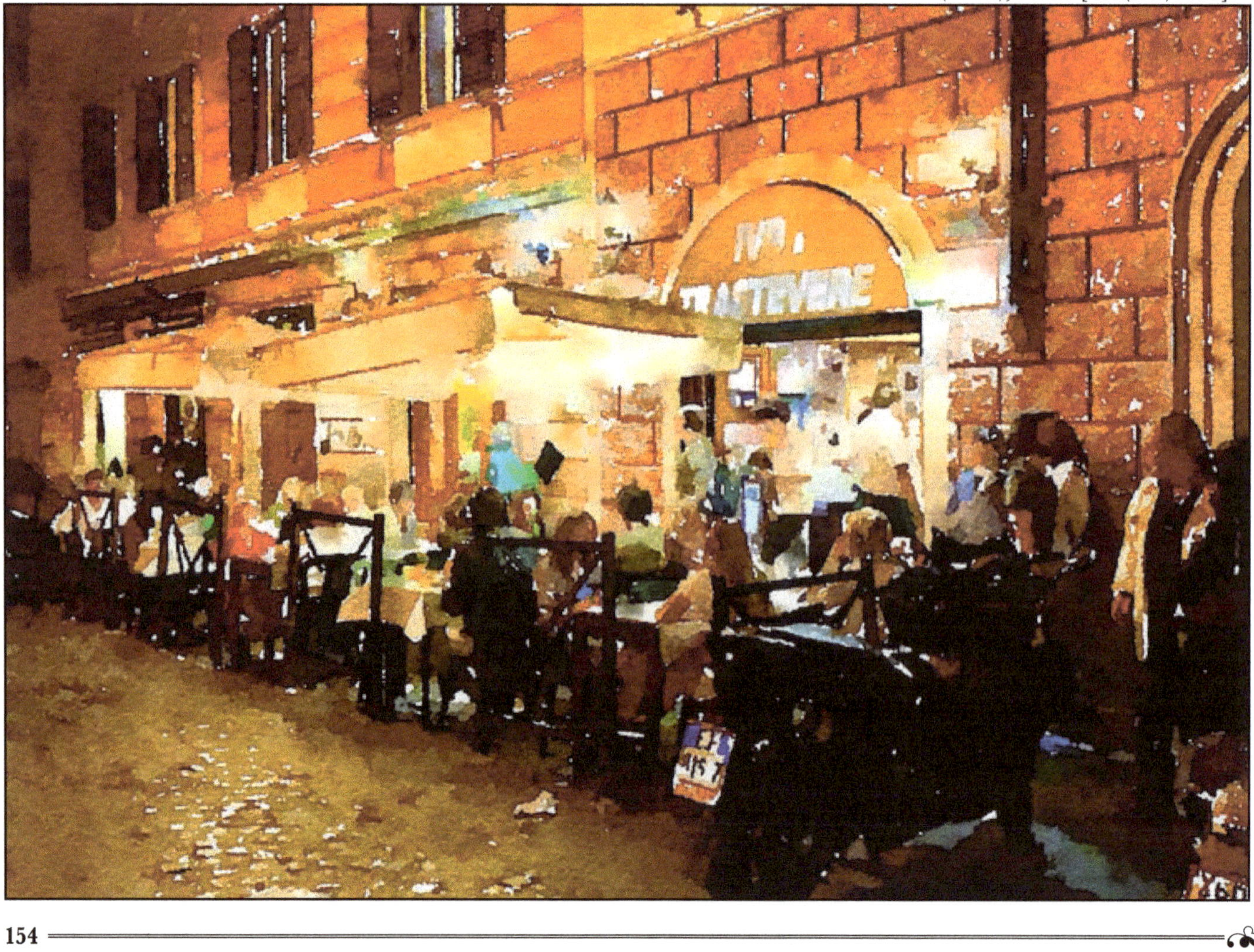

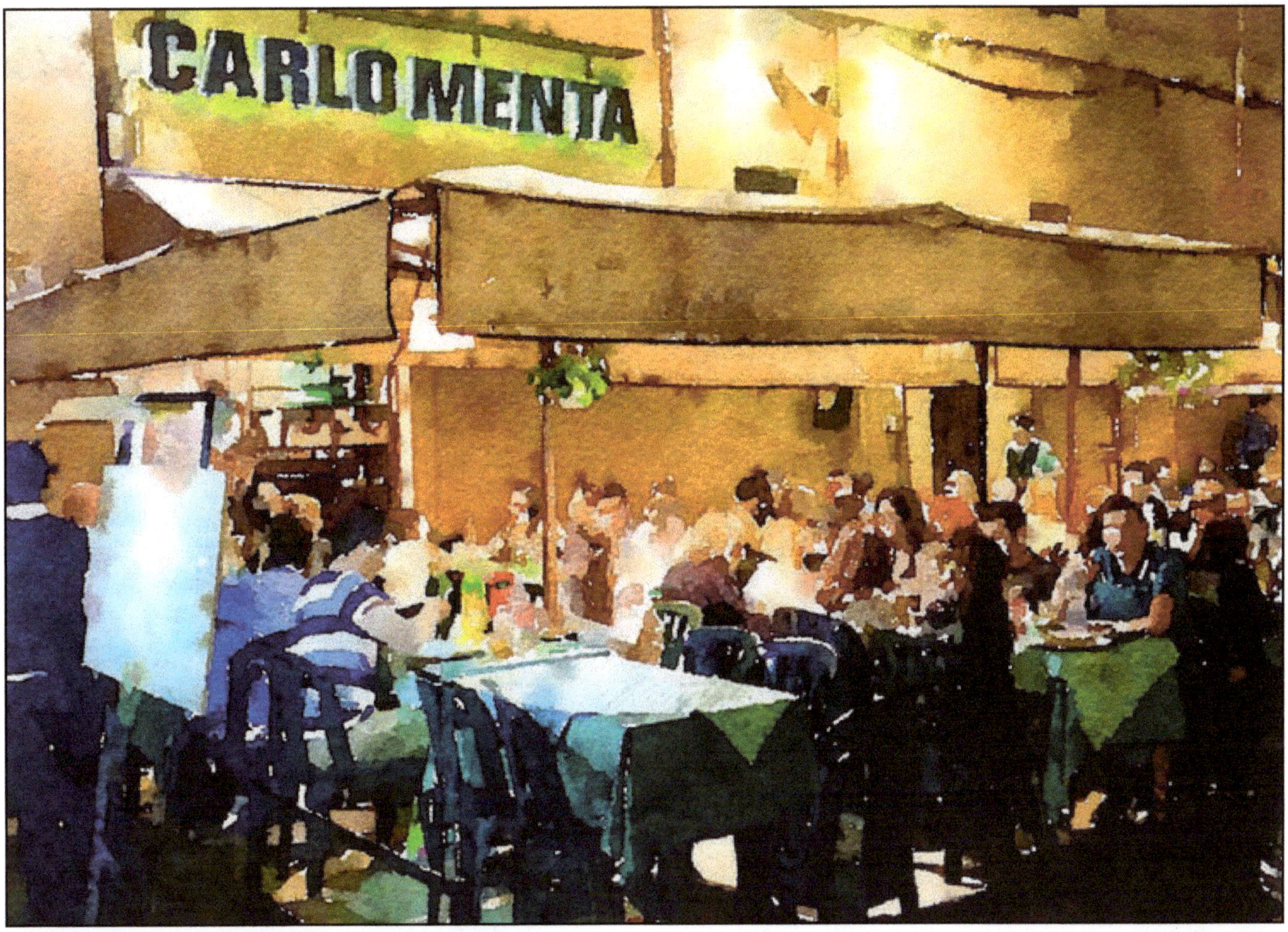

▲'Trastevere Diners' (2018), Rome [EIT(RO)1807].

▼'Venice Canals 1' (2013), Venice [EIT(VE)1301].

'Venice Canals 2' (2013), Venice [EIT(VE)1304].▼

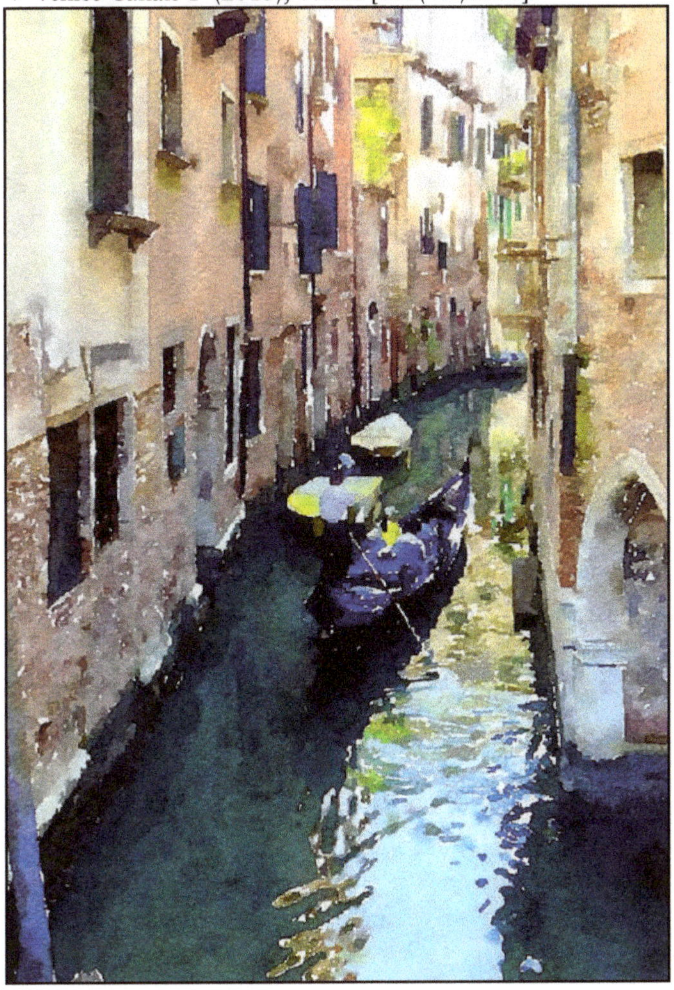

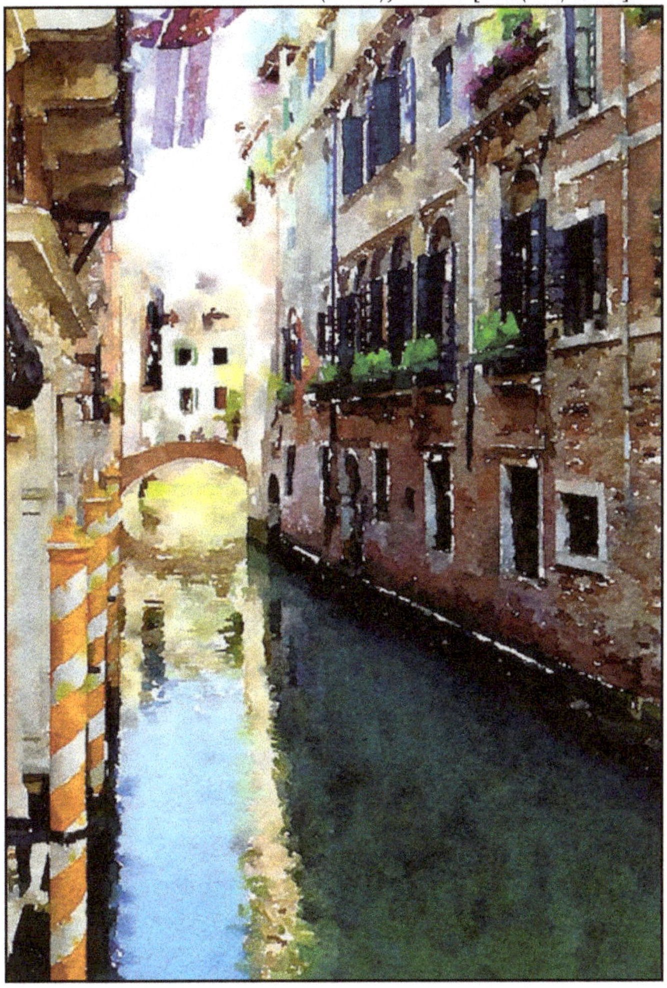

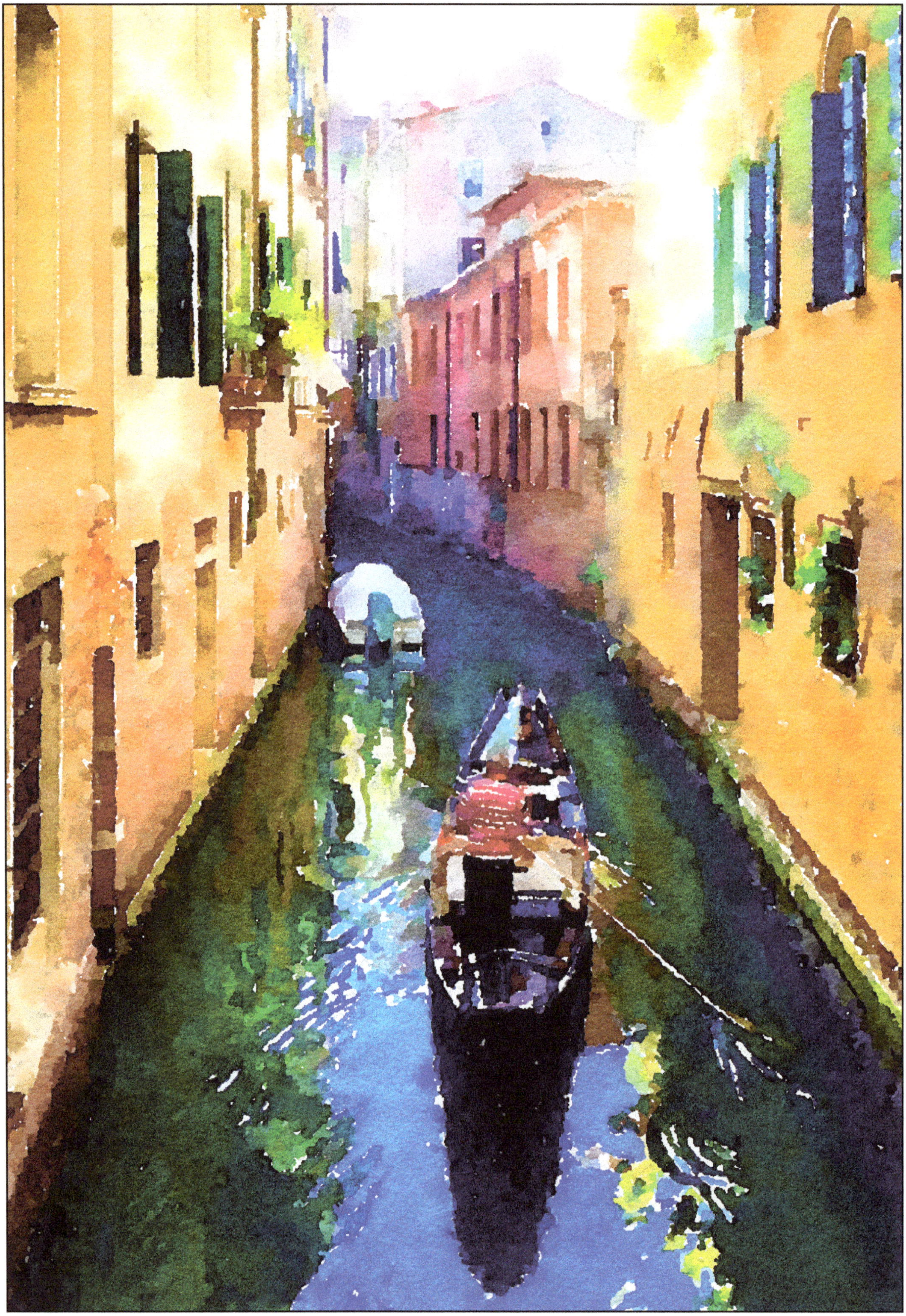

▲'Venetian Canals' (2013), Venice [EIT(VE)1302].

Macedonia...

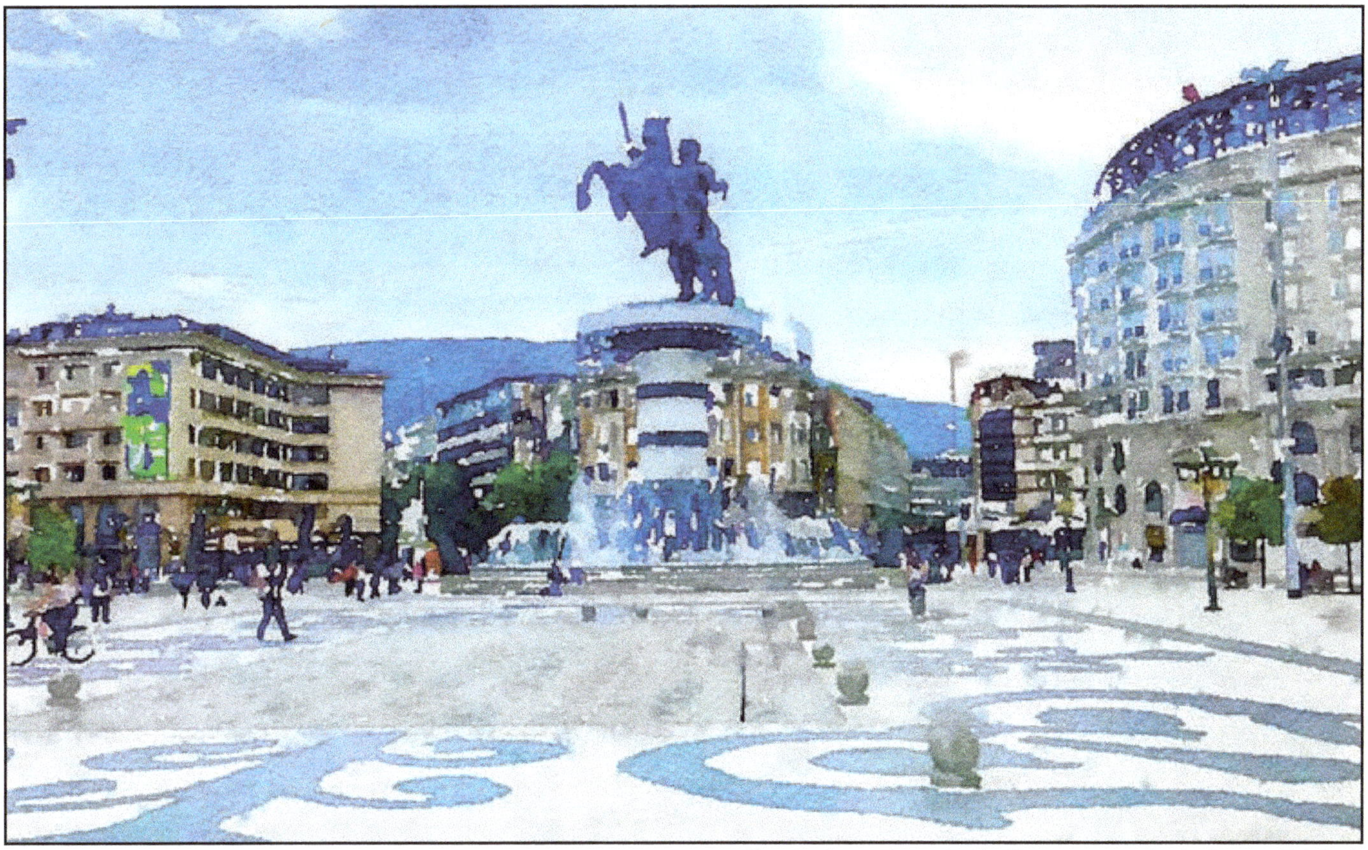

'Skopje Centrale' (2018), Skopje, Macedonia [EMK1805].▲

▼'Archeological Museum' (2018), Skopje, Macedonia [EMK1802].

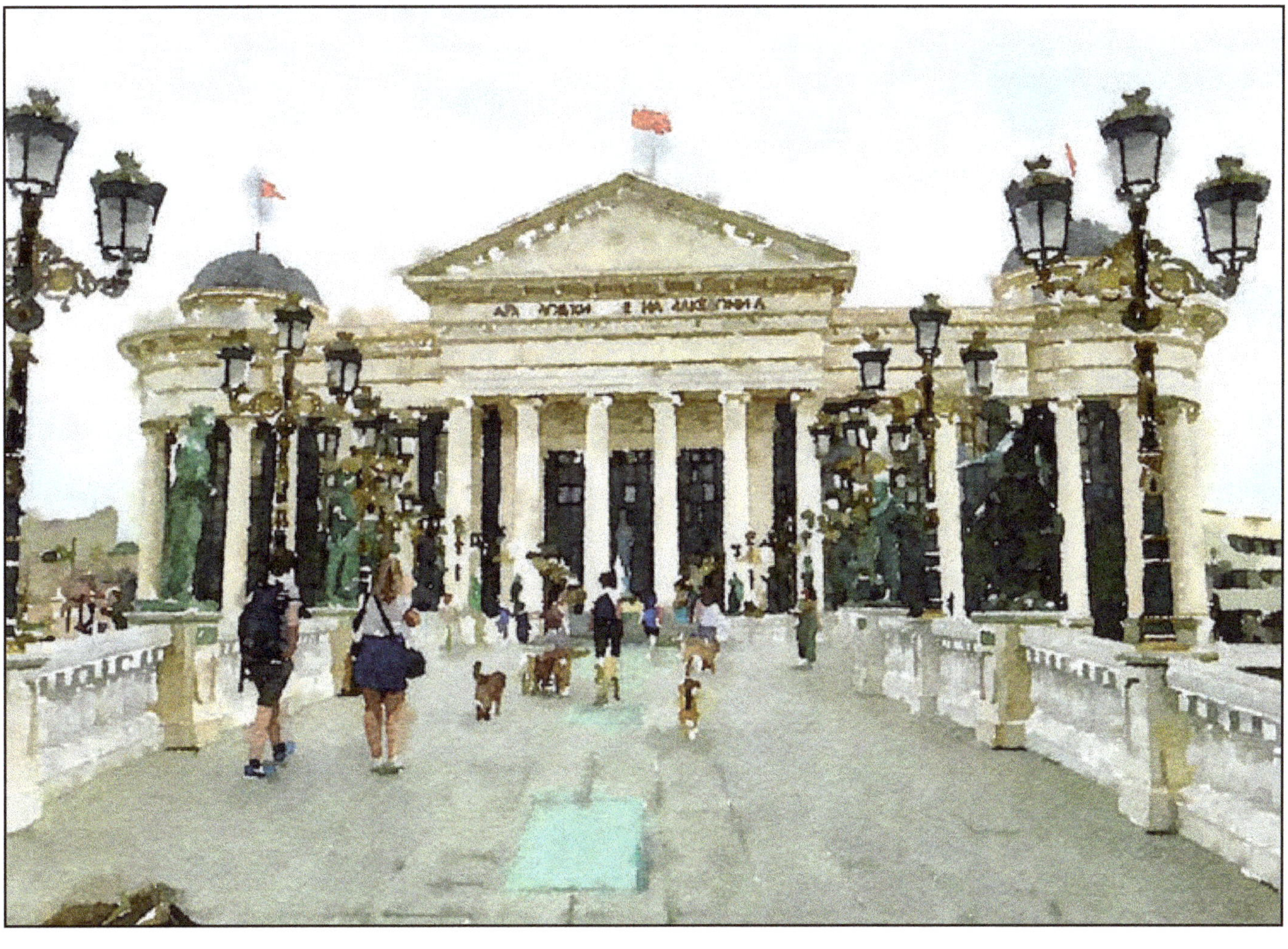

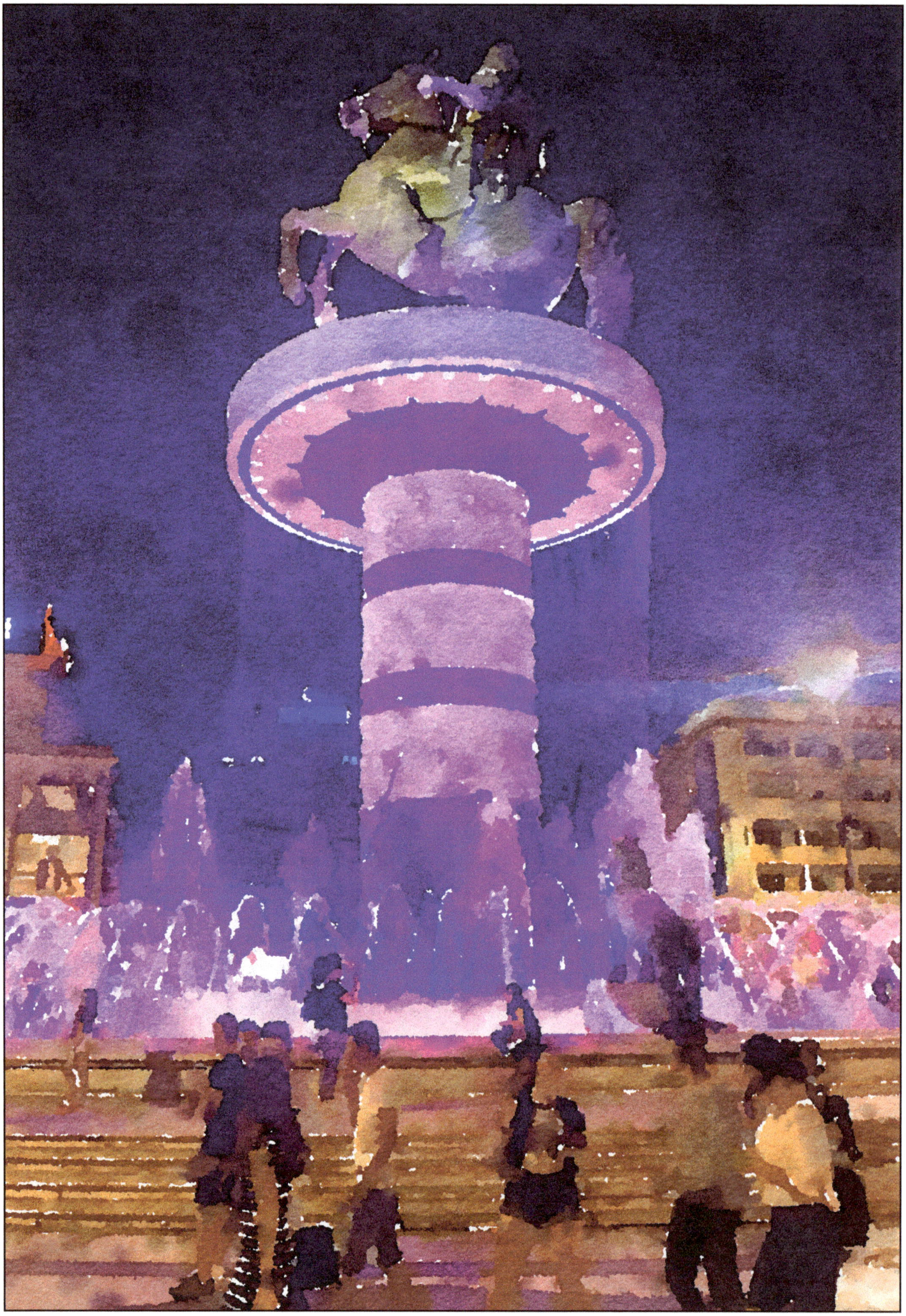

▲'Monument To Alexander' (2018), Skopje, Macedonia [EMK1801].

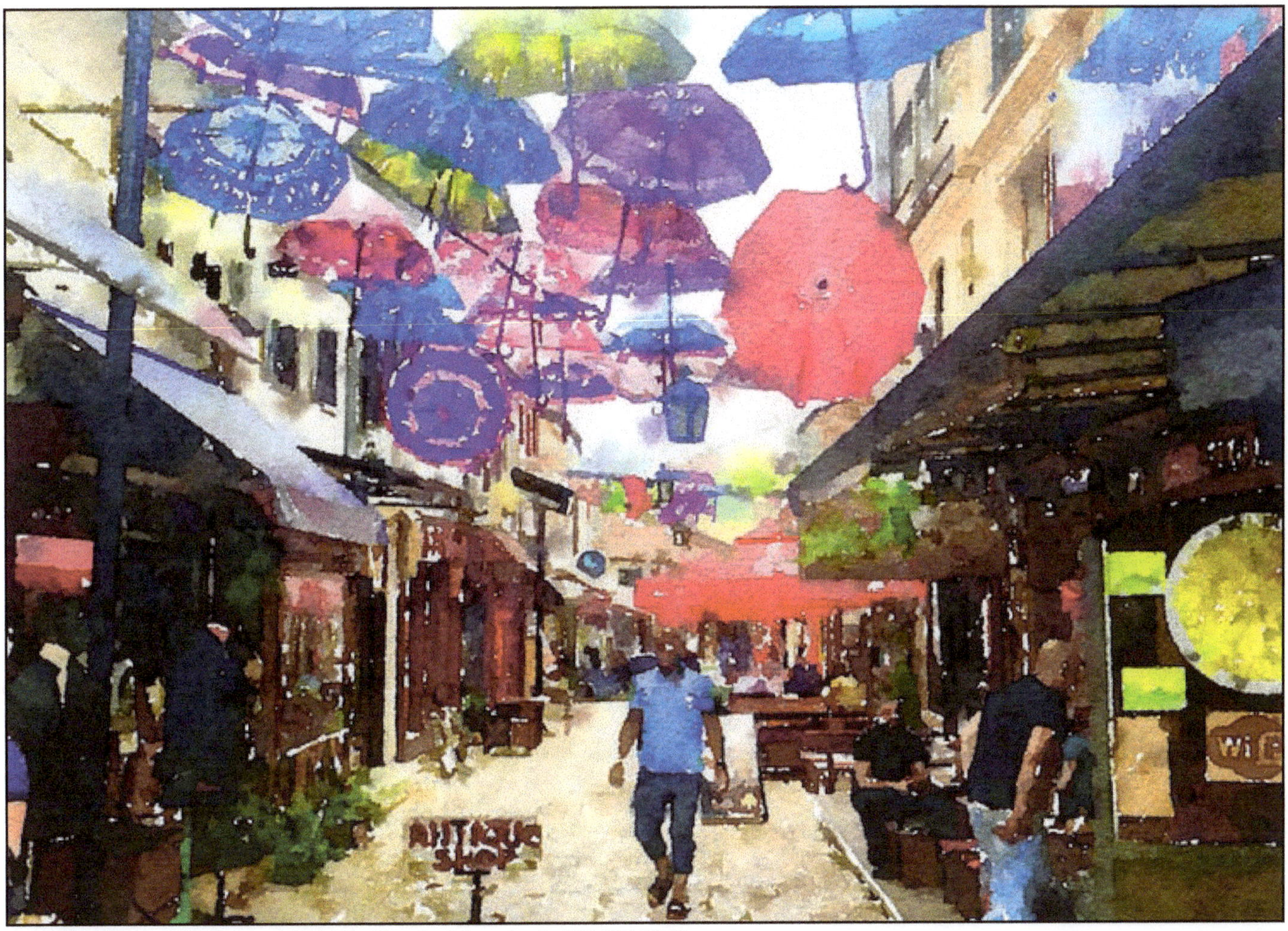

▲'Umbrellas In The Bazaar' (2018), Skopje, Macedonia [EMK1806].

'Macedonia Square' (2018), Skopje, Macedonia [EMK1804].▼

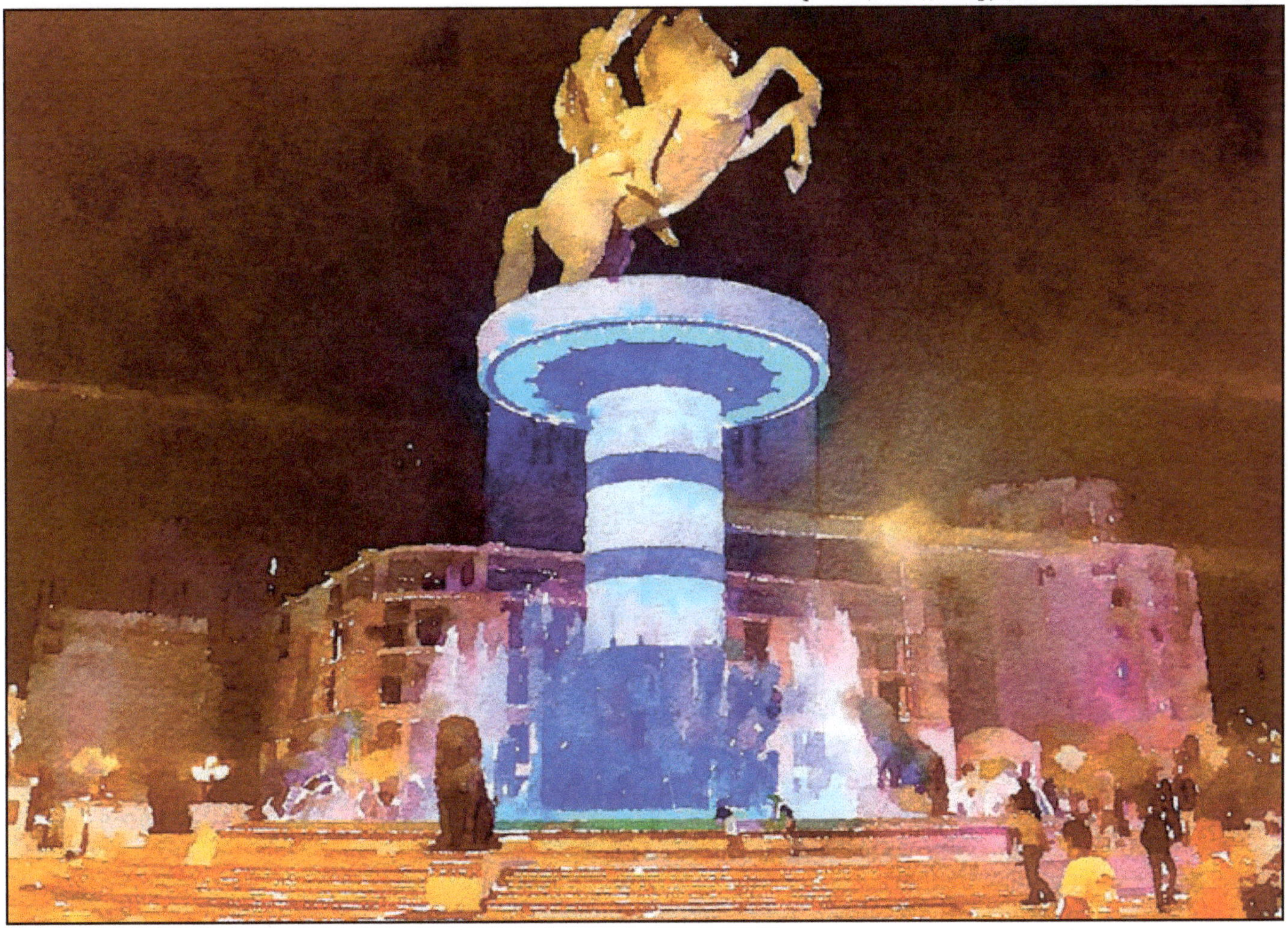

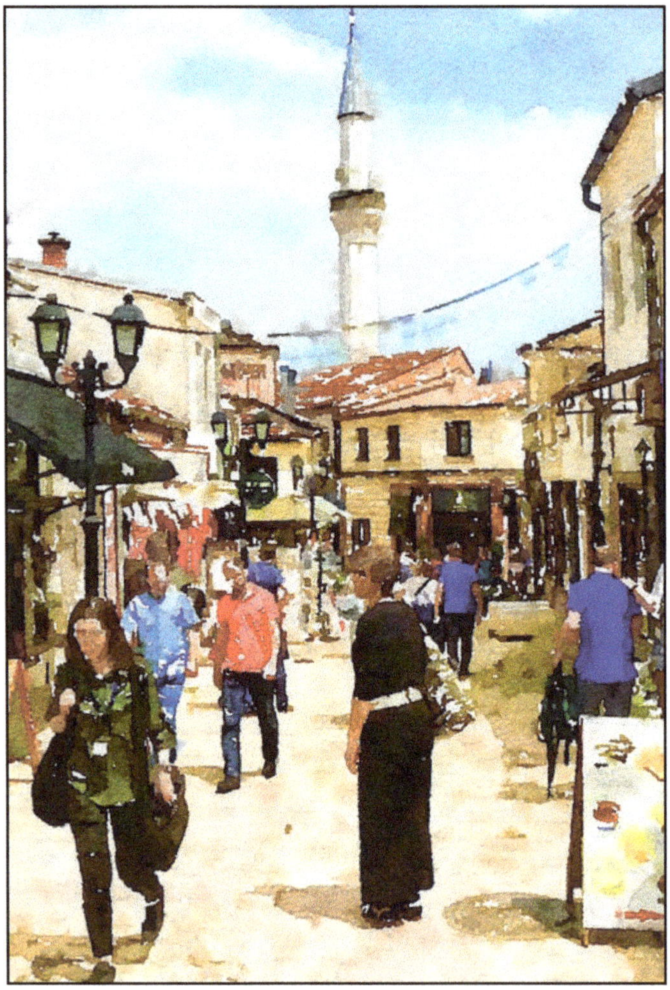

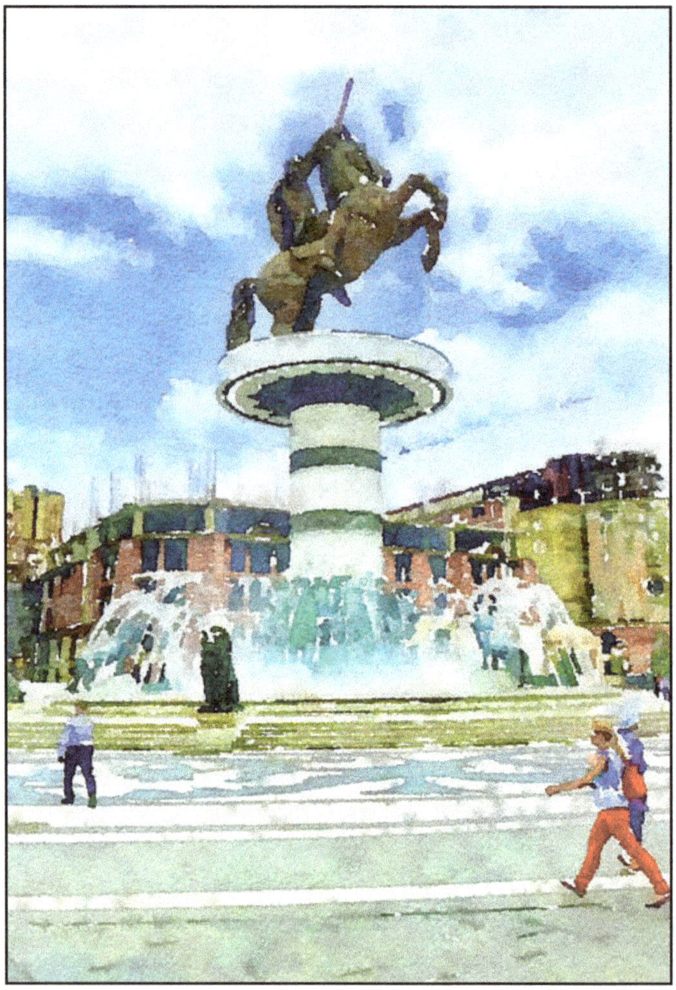

▲'The Bazaar' (2018), Skopje, Macedonia [EMK1807]. 'Alexander The Great' (2018), Skopje, Macedonia [EMK1803].▼

▼'Boats On Lake Ohrid' (2018), Ohrid, Macedonia [EMK1810].

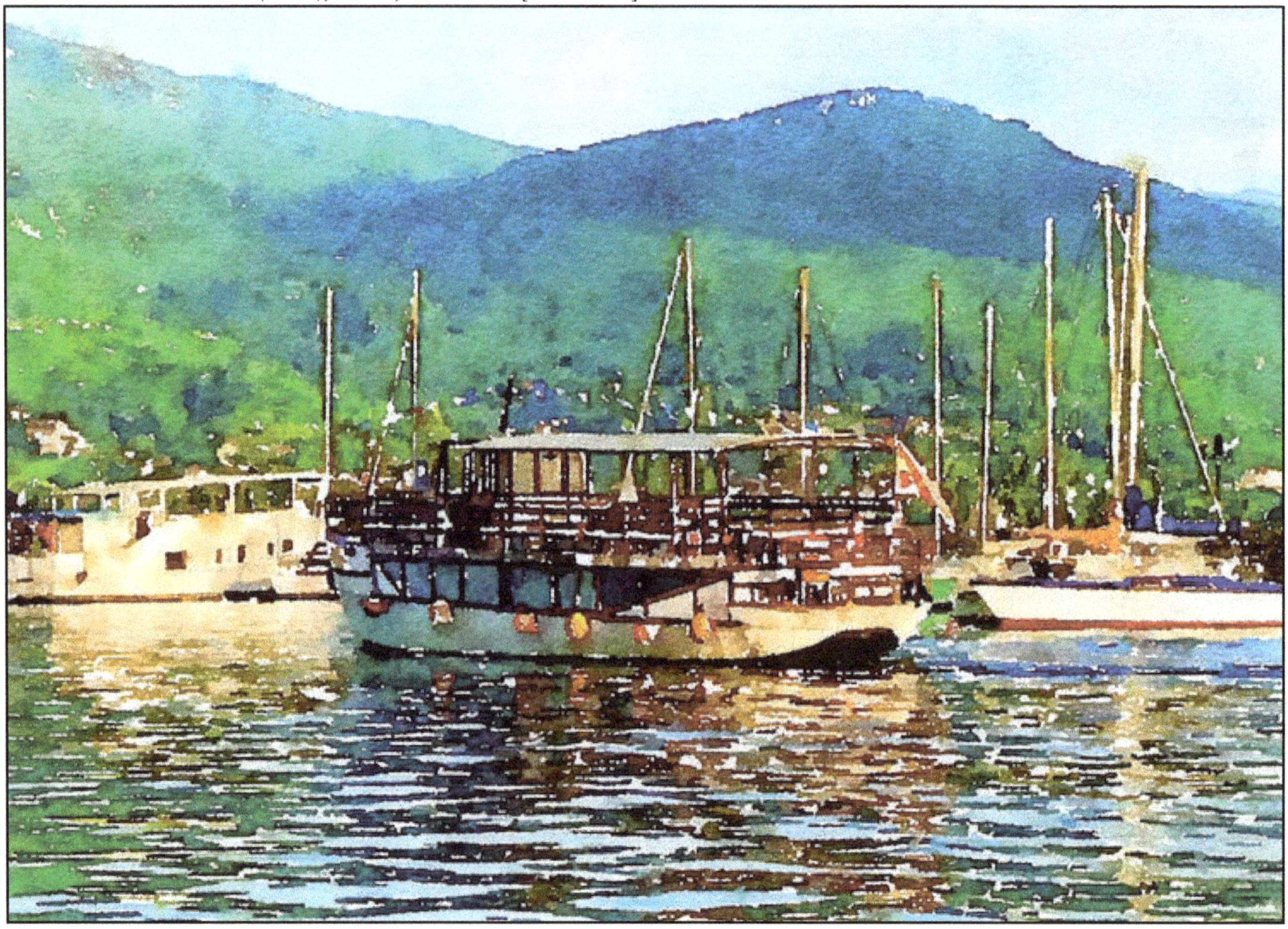

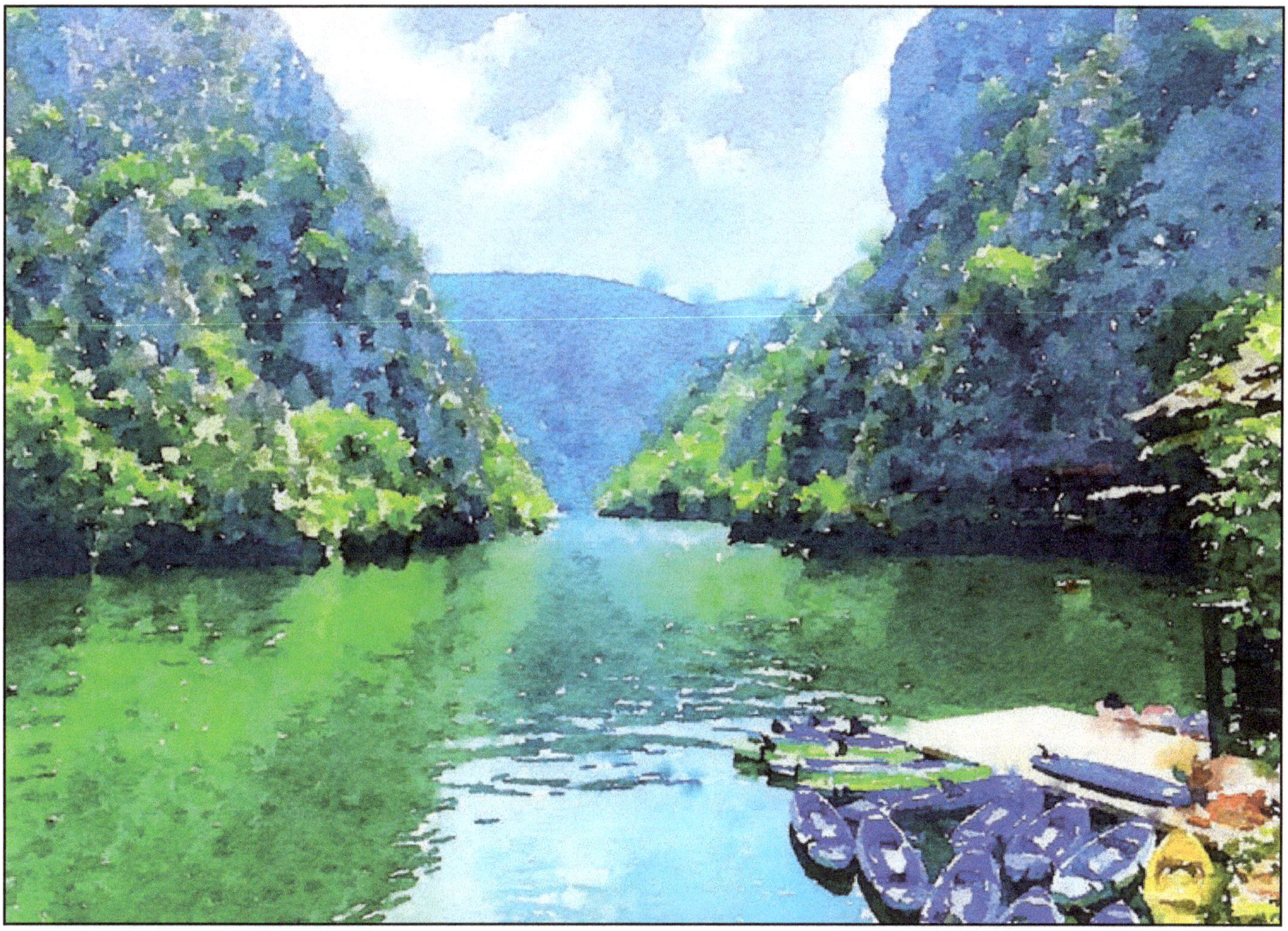

▲'Matka Row Boats' (2018), Matka Canyon, Macedonia [EMK1808].

'Evening On Lake Ohrid' (2018), Ohrid, Macedonia [EMK1809].▼

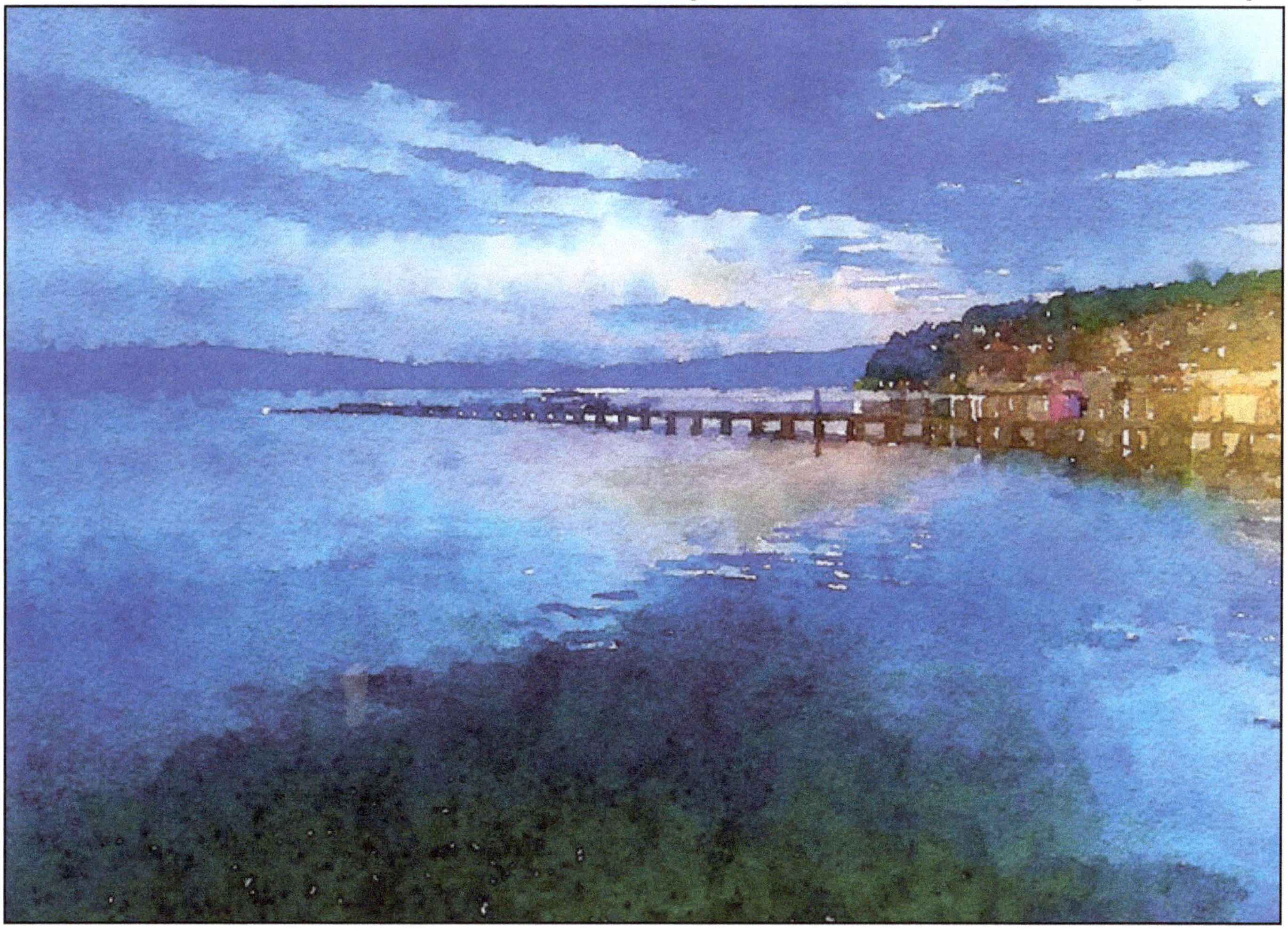

Malta...

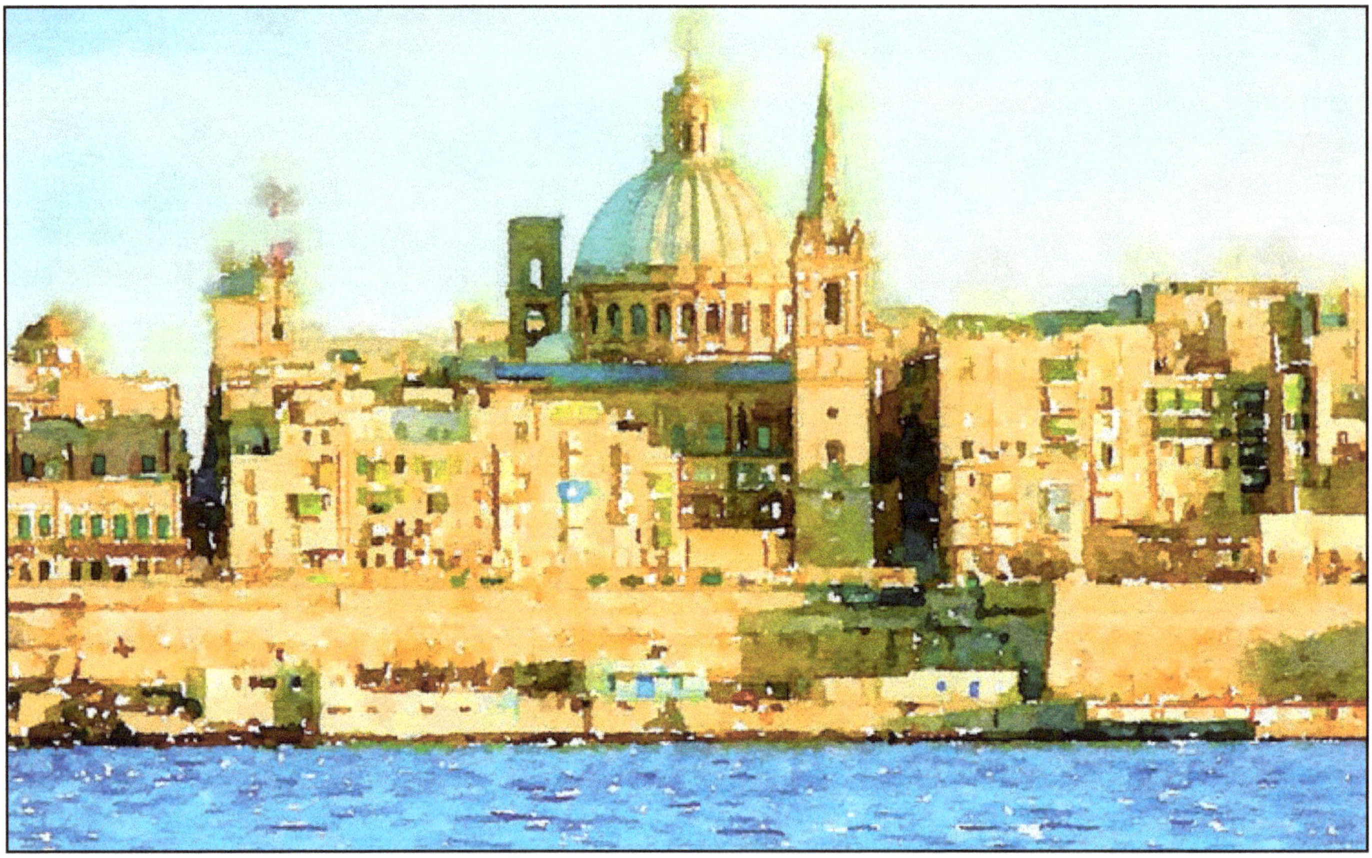

▲'Valletta Skyline' (2016), Malta [EMT1601]. ⓔ

'Sliema Bay' (2016), Malta [EMT1603].▼

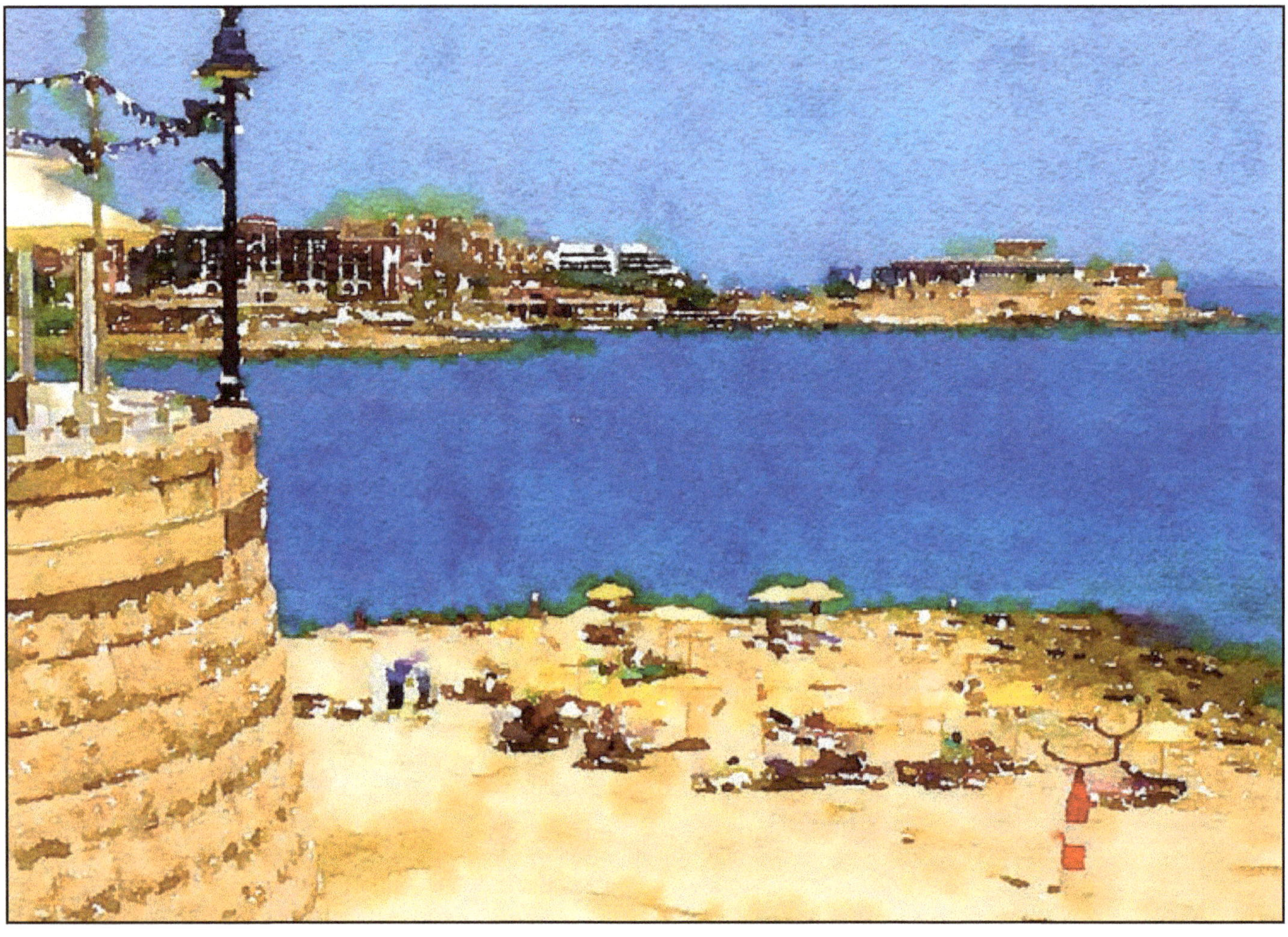

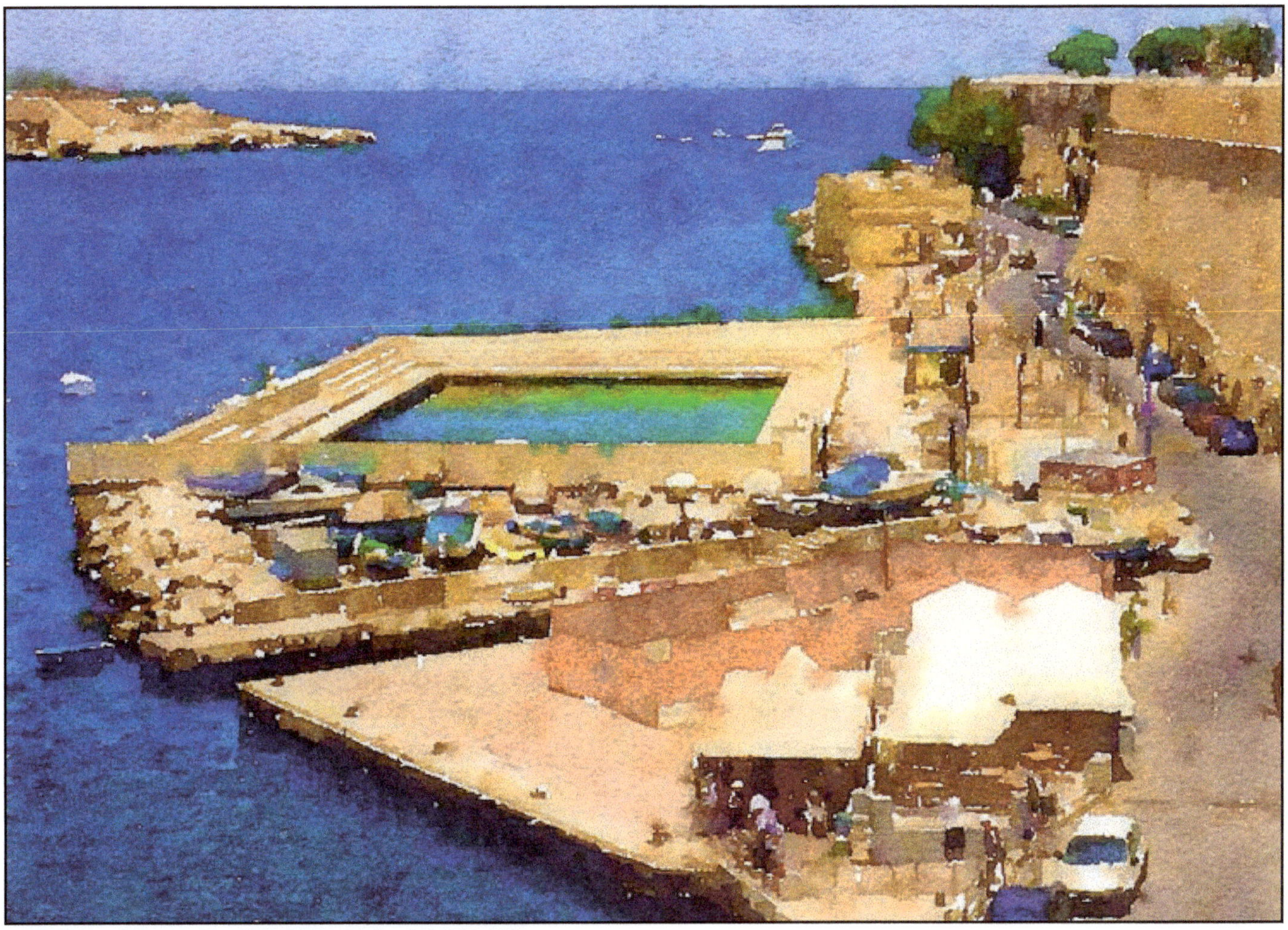

▲'Valletta Olympic Pool' (2016), Malta [EMT1602].

'Sunning On The Rocks' (2016), Malta [EMT1604].▼

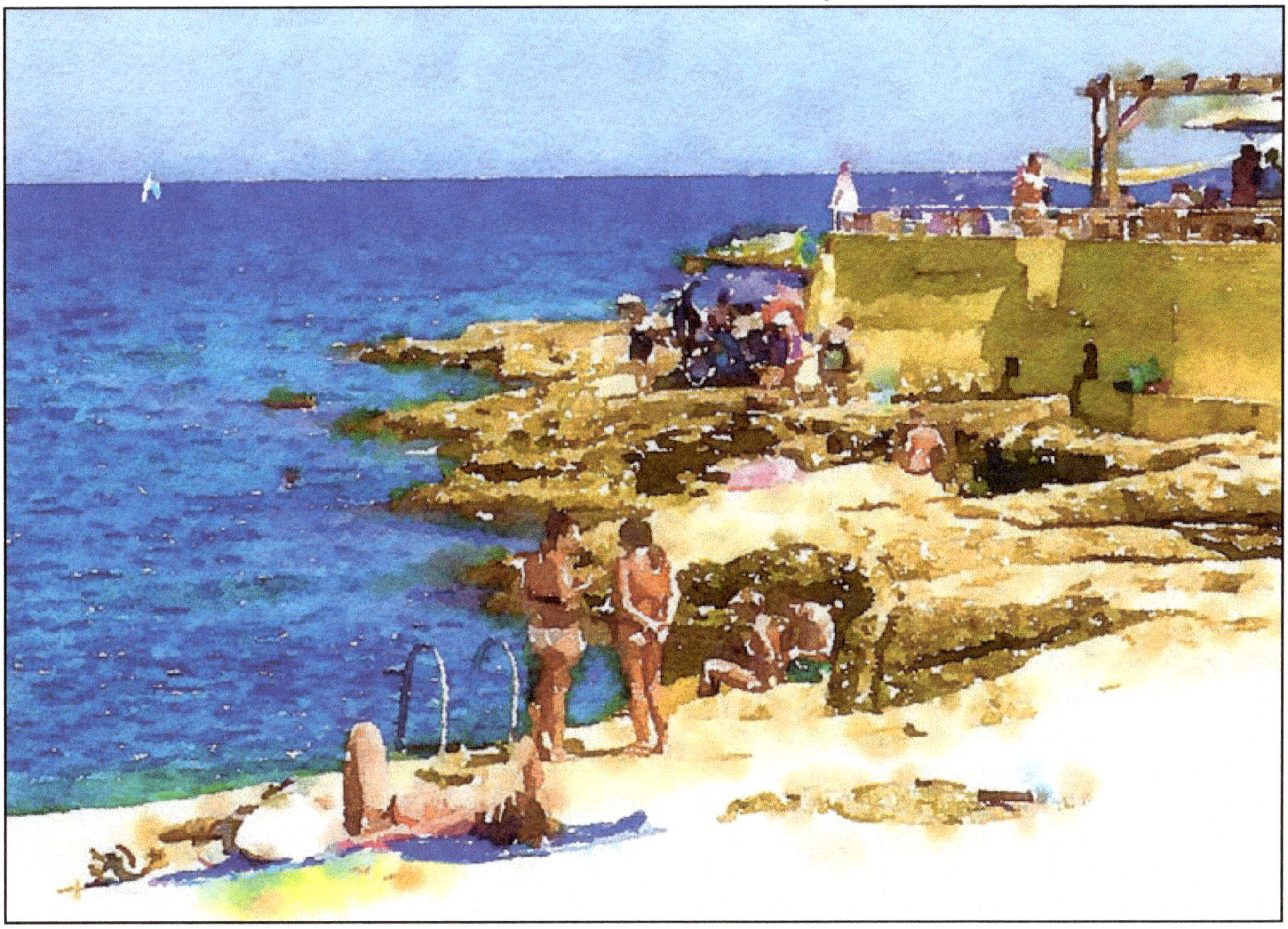

Monaco...

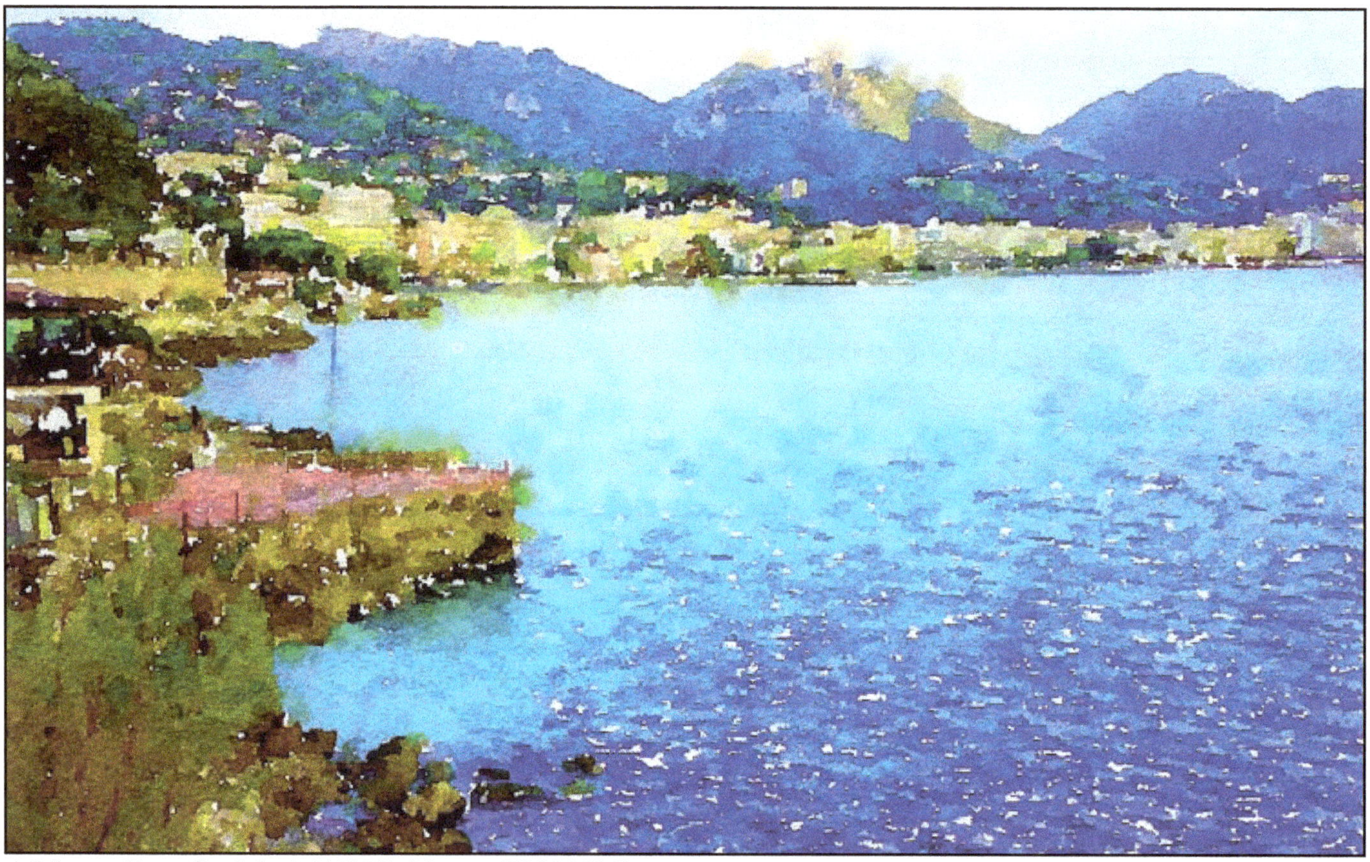

▲'Menton From Cap Martin' (2008), Monaco [EMO0801].

'Port Hercules' (2016), Monaco [EMO1602].▼

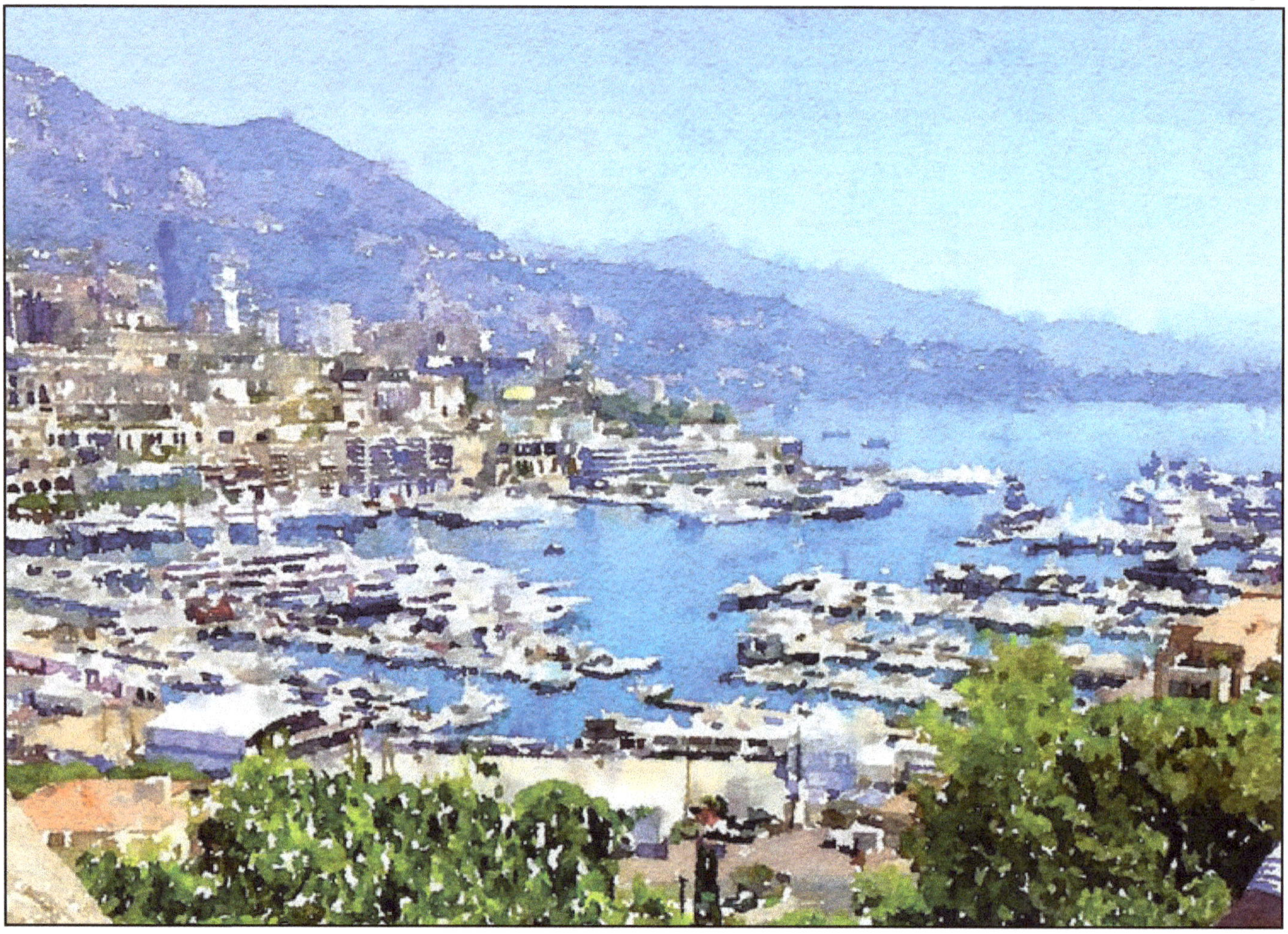

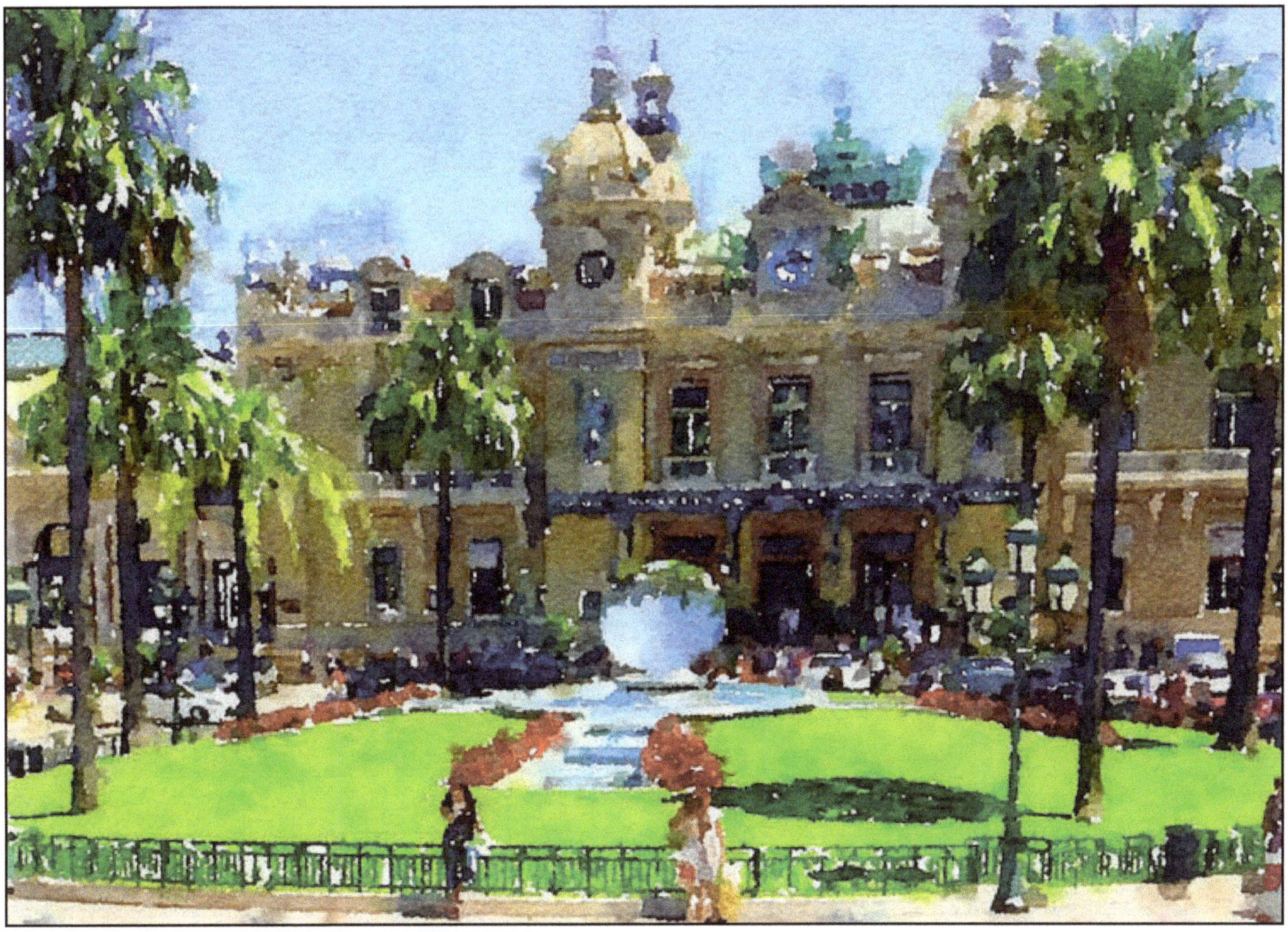

▲'Monte Carlo Casino' (2016), Monaco [EMO1601].

'Lights of Port Hercules' (2010), Monaco [EMO1001].▼

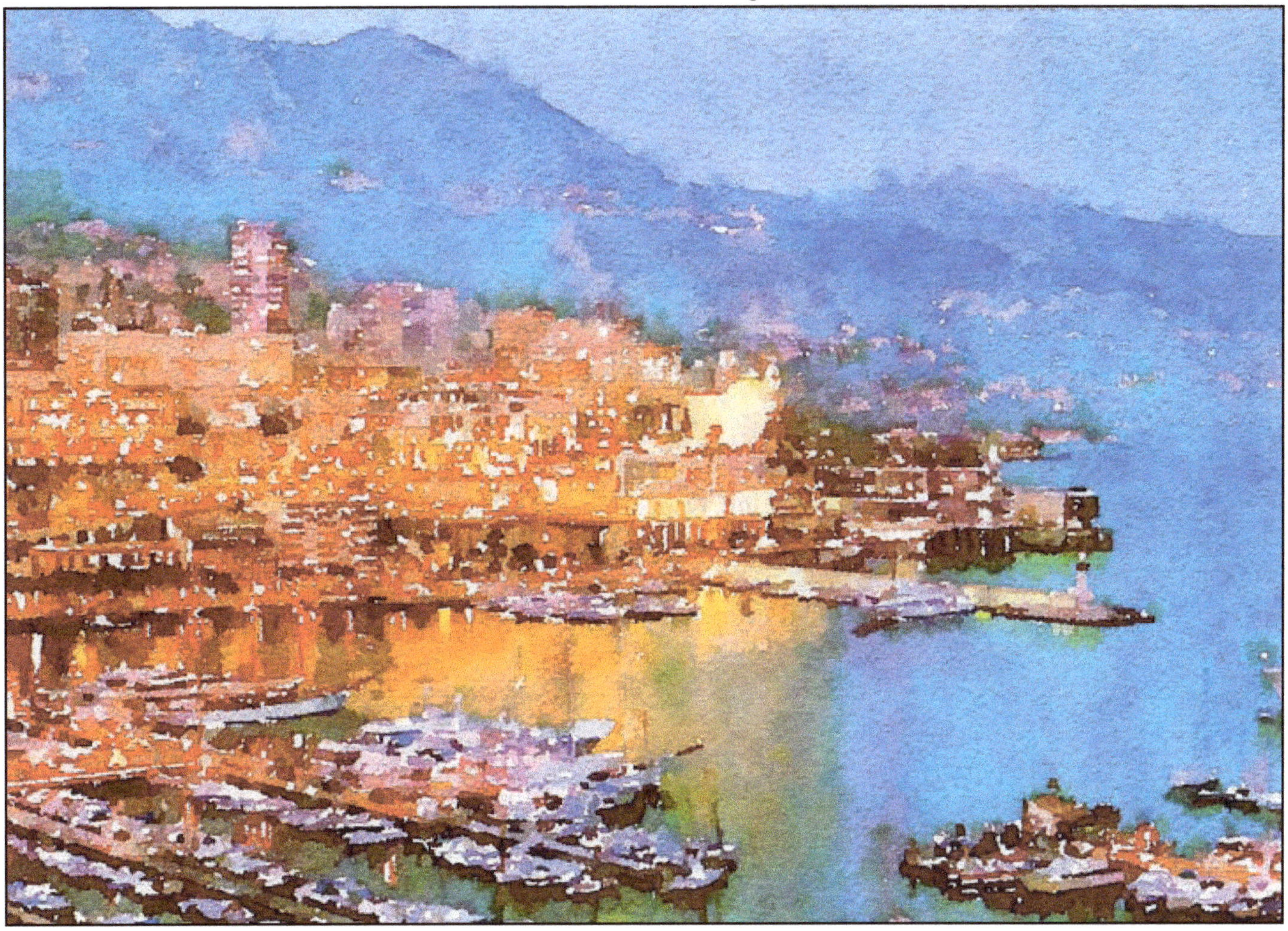

Montenegro...

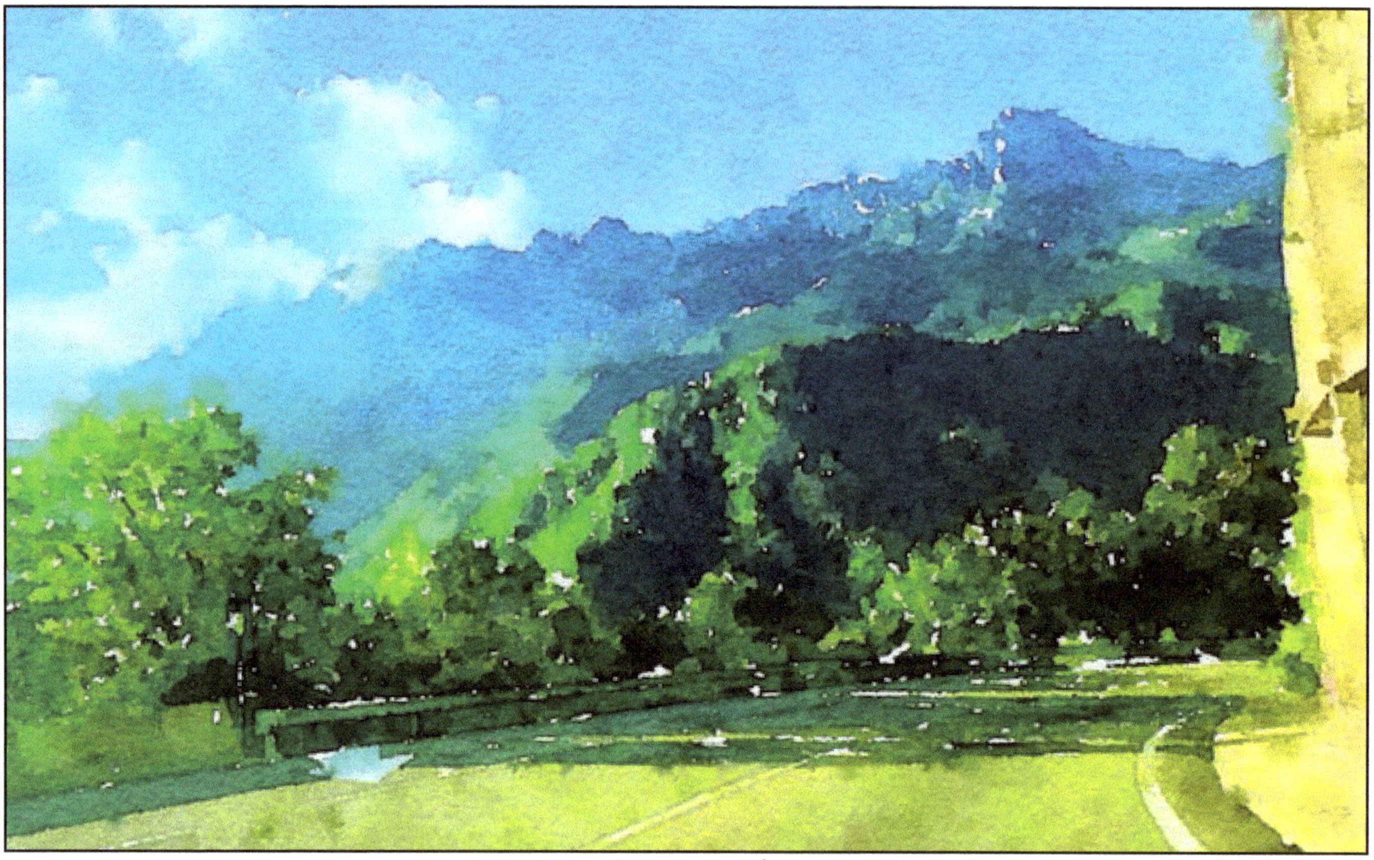

'Mountains Of Montenegro' (2018), Budva, Montenegro [EME1805].▲

▼'Plaža Ricardova Glava' (2018), Budva, Montenegro [EME1806].

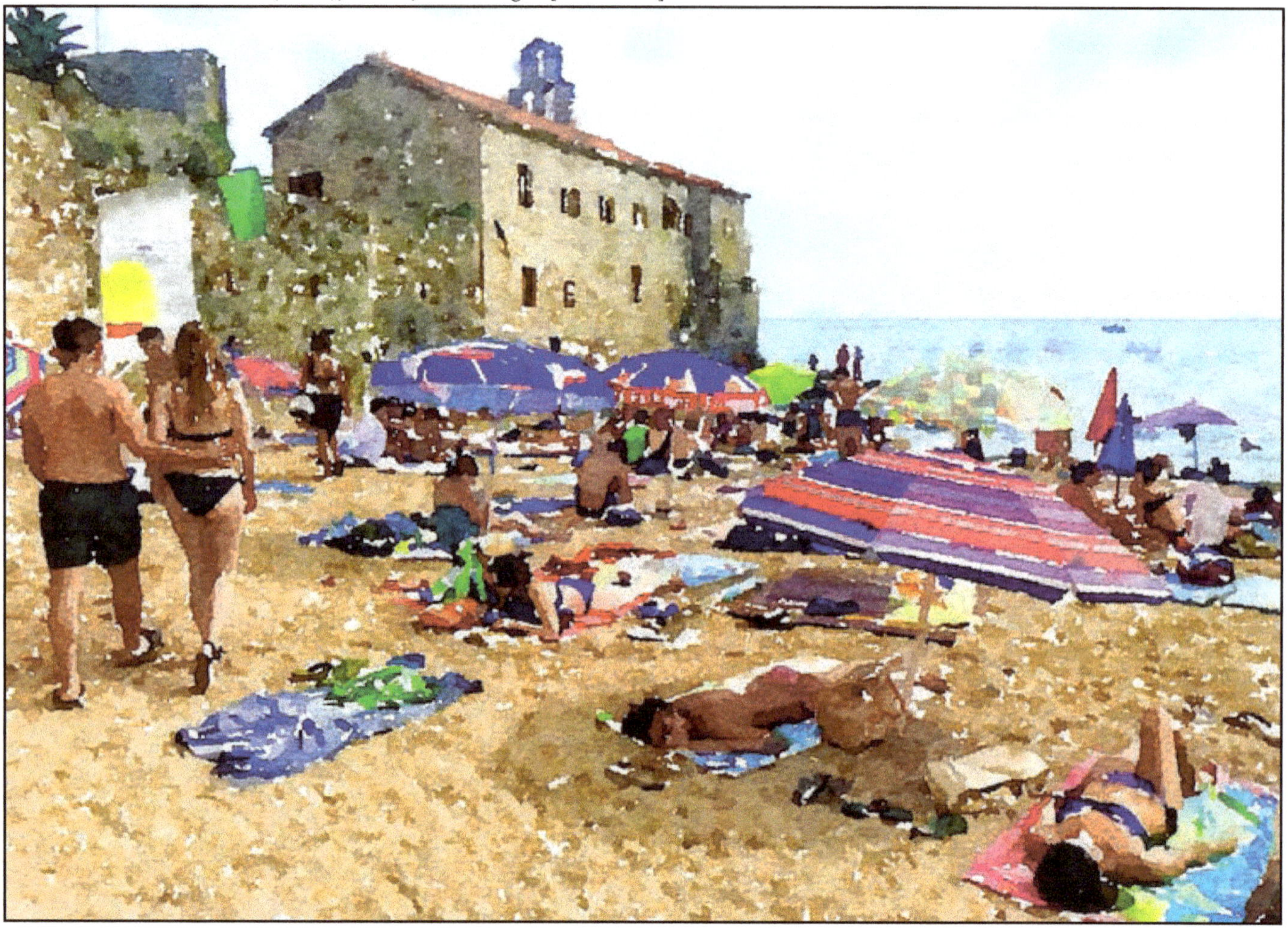

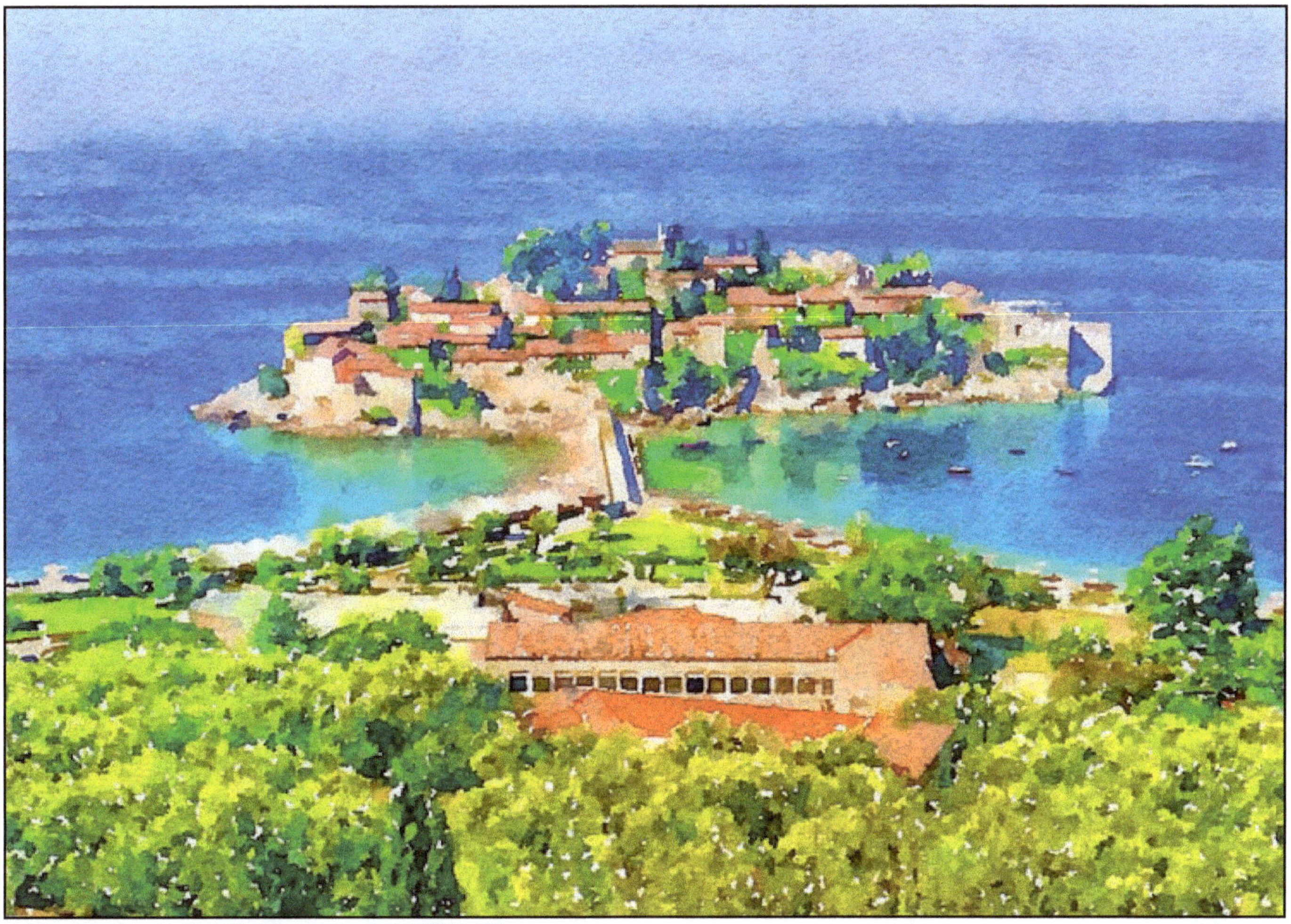

▲'Sveti Stefan 1' (2018), Montenegro [EME1802].

'The Harbour' (2018), Budva, Montenegro [EME1807].▼

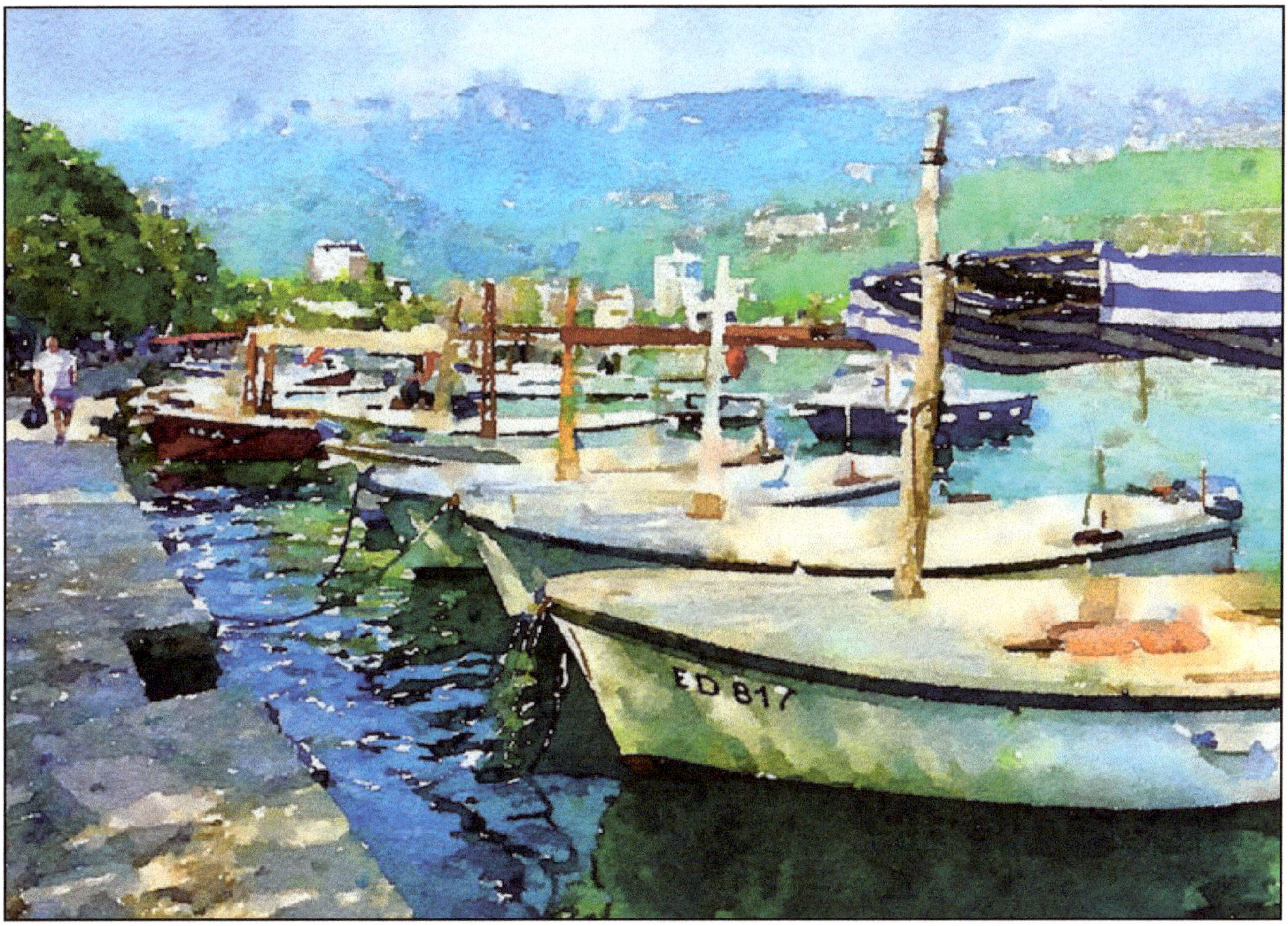

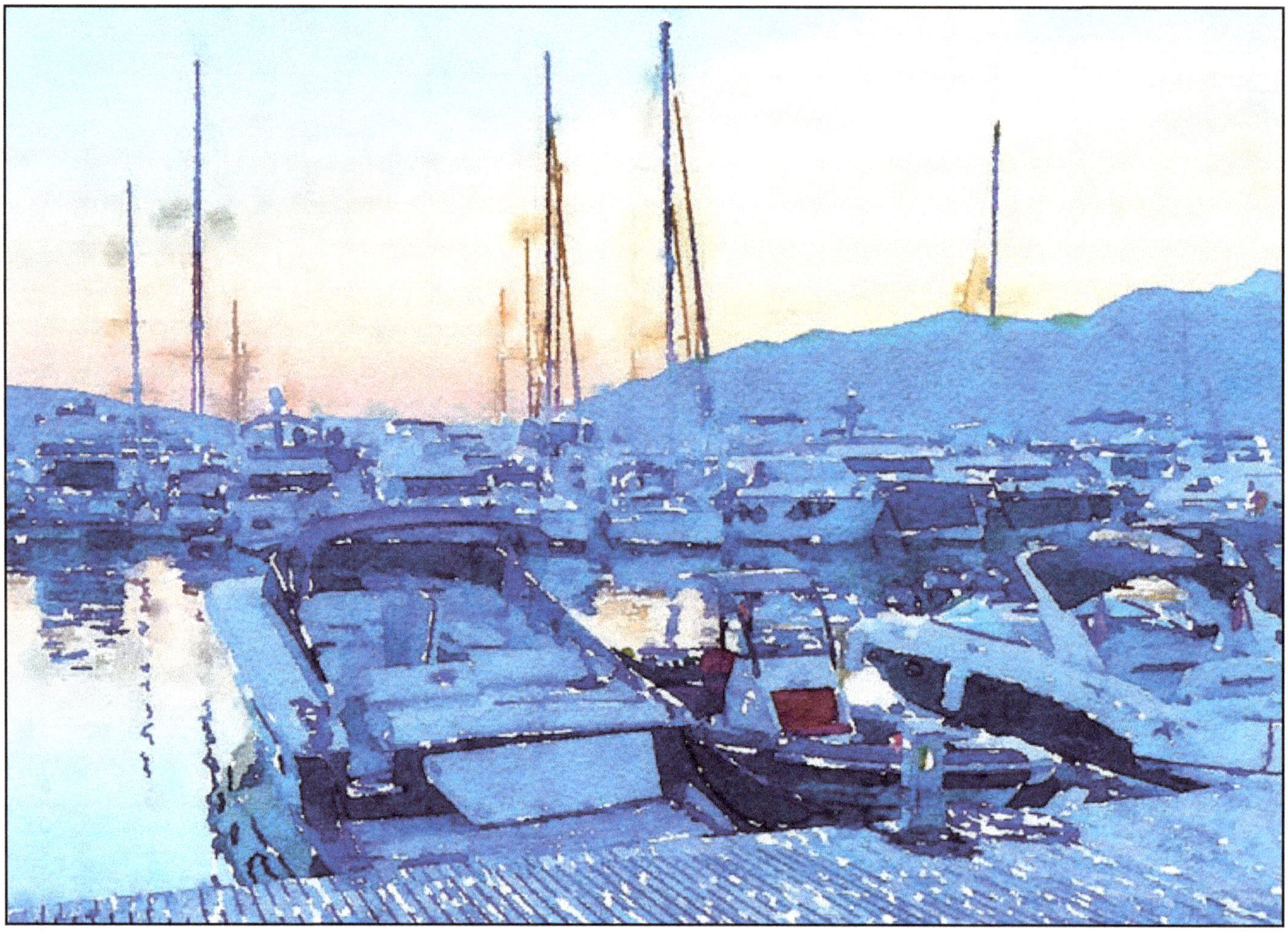

▲'Porto Montenegro' (2018), Montenegro [EME1808].

'Sveti Stefan 3' (2018), Montenegro [EME1804].▼

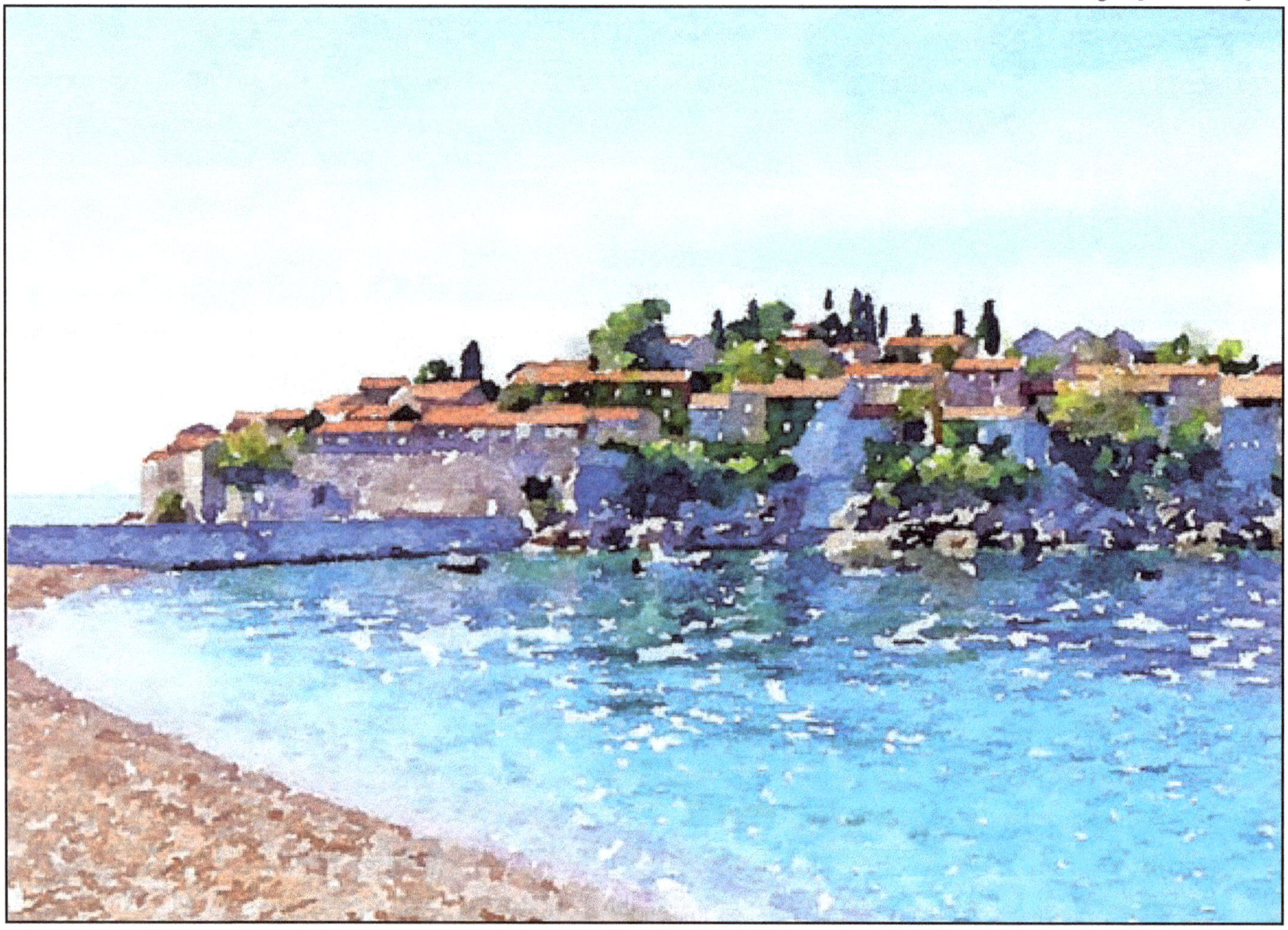

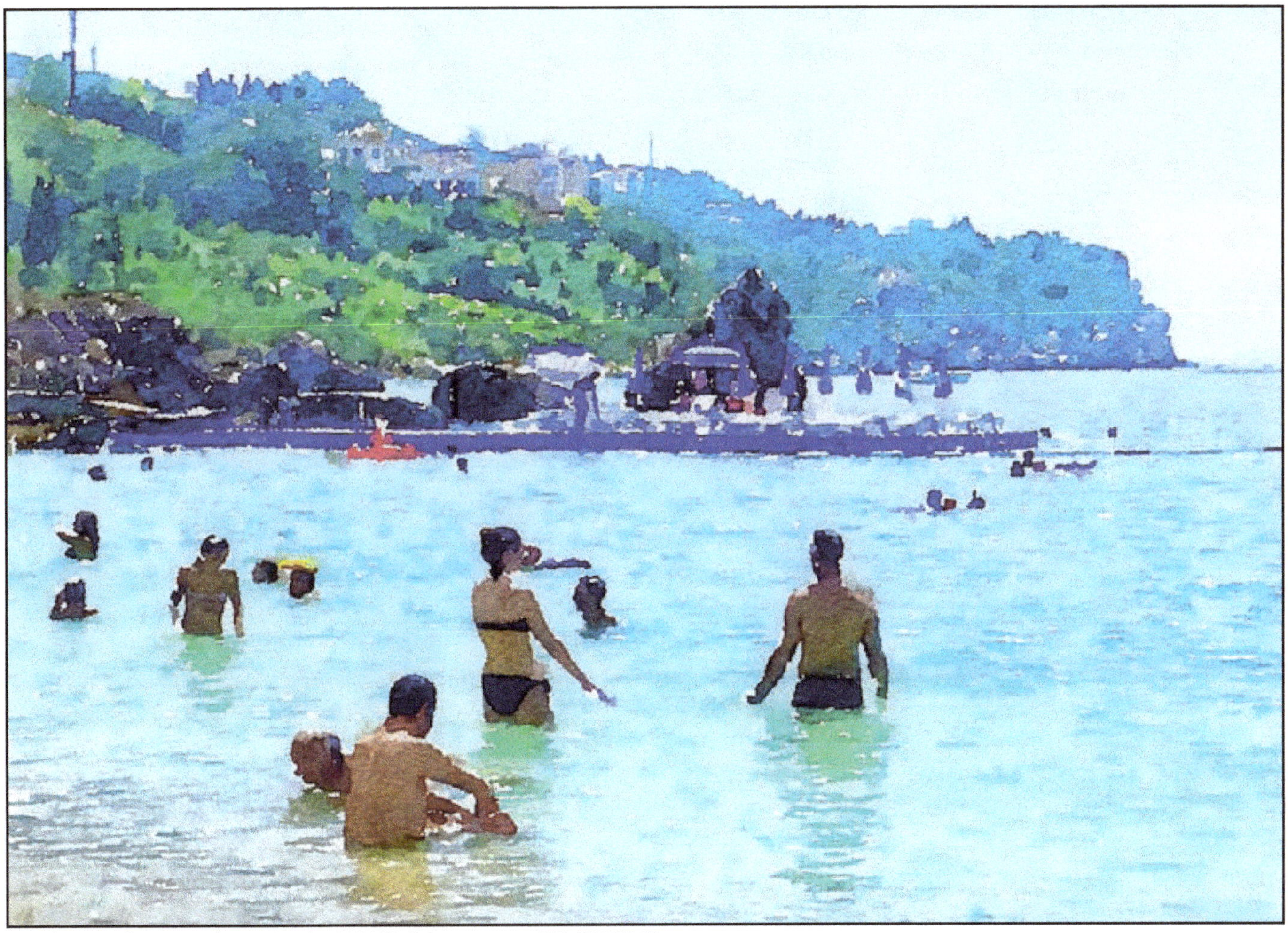

▲'The Beach At Drobni Pijesak' (2018), Montenegro [EME1801].

'Sveti Stefan 2' (2018), Montenegro [EME1803].▼

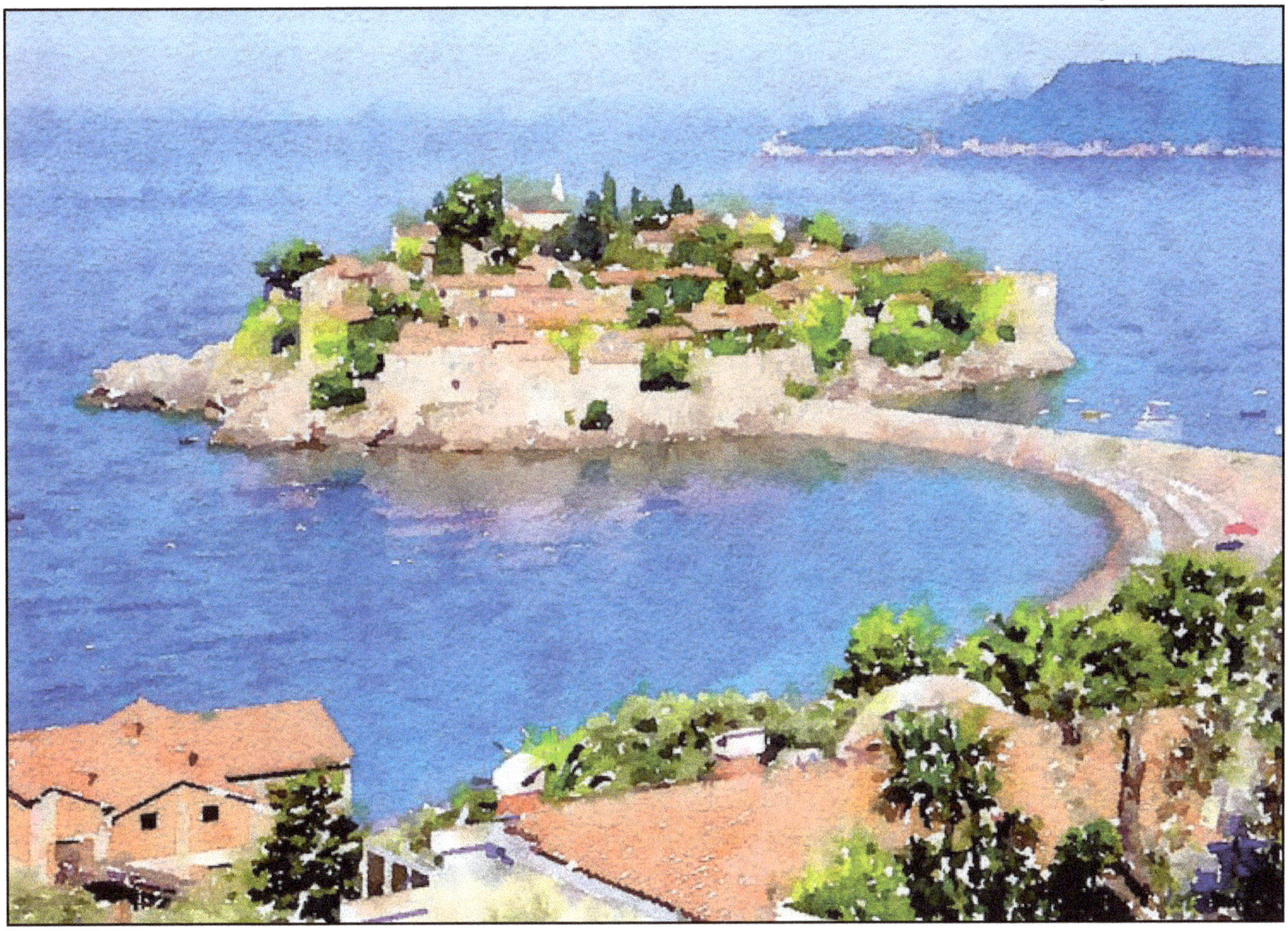

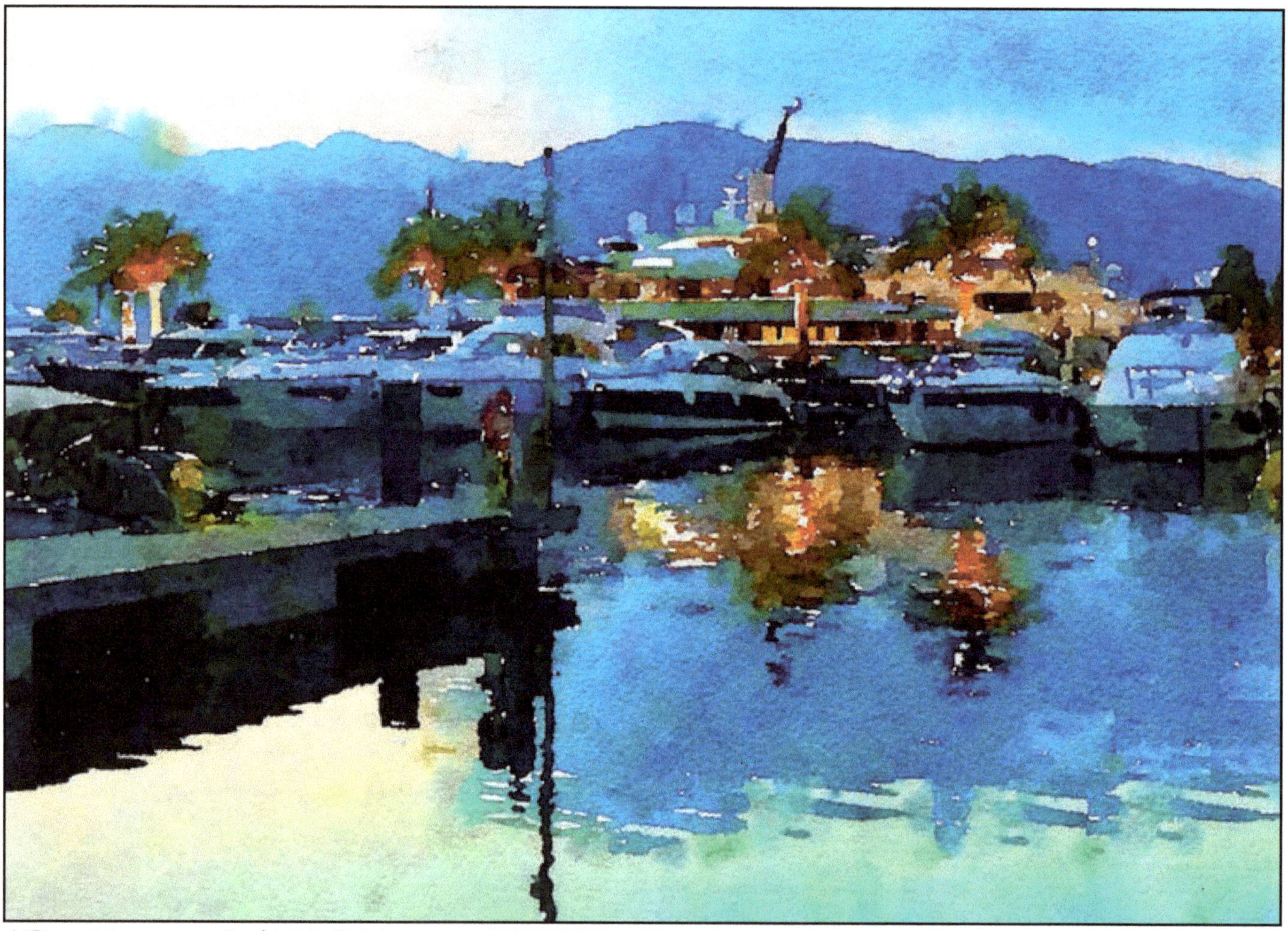

▲'Porto Montenegro Dusk' (2018), Montenegro [EME1809].

'Lepetane-Kamenari Car Ferry' (2018), Montenegro [EME1810].▼

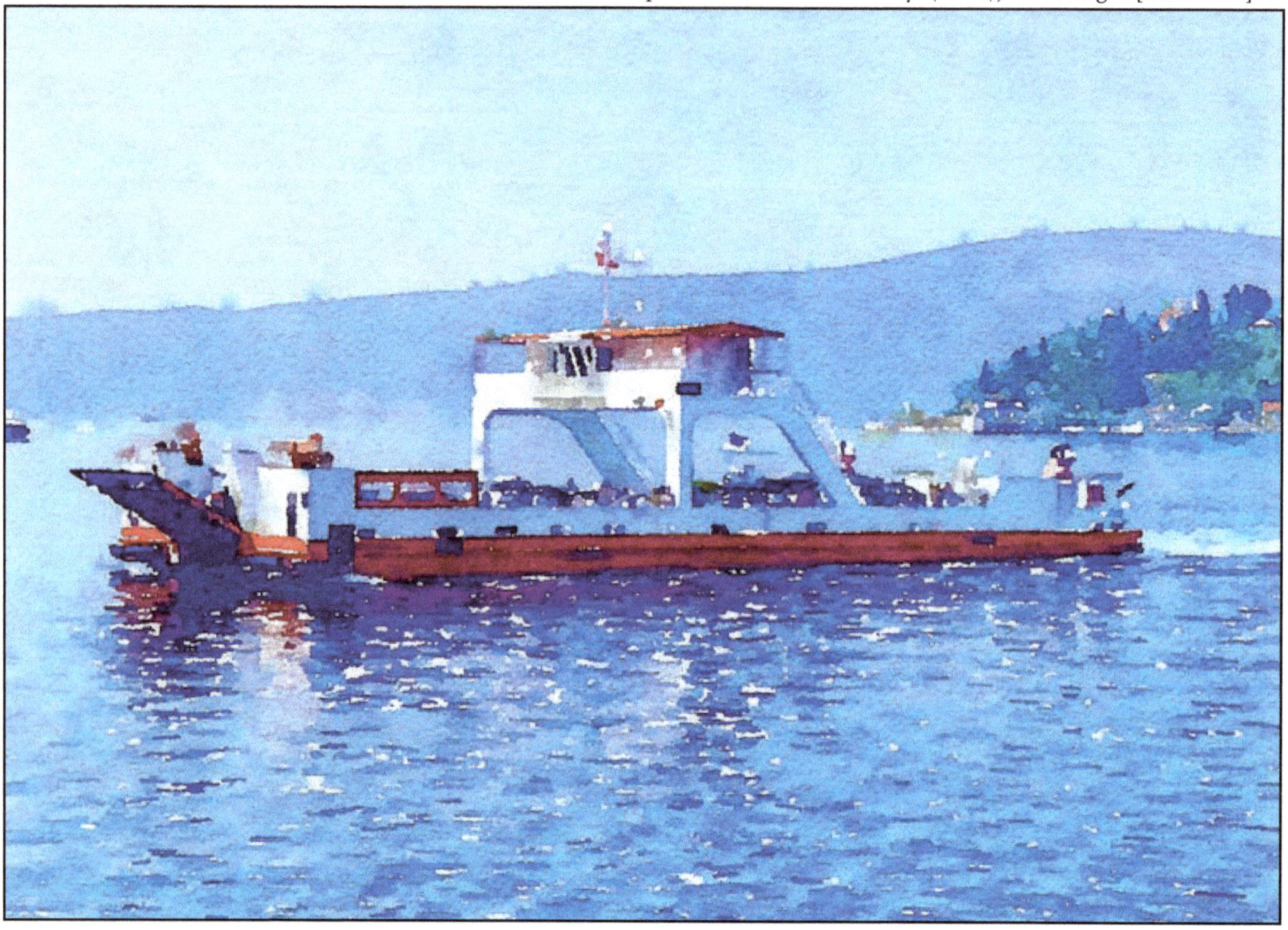

Poland...

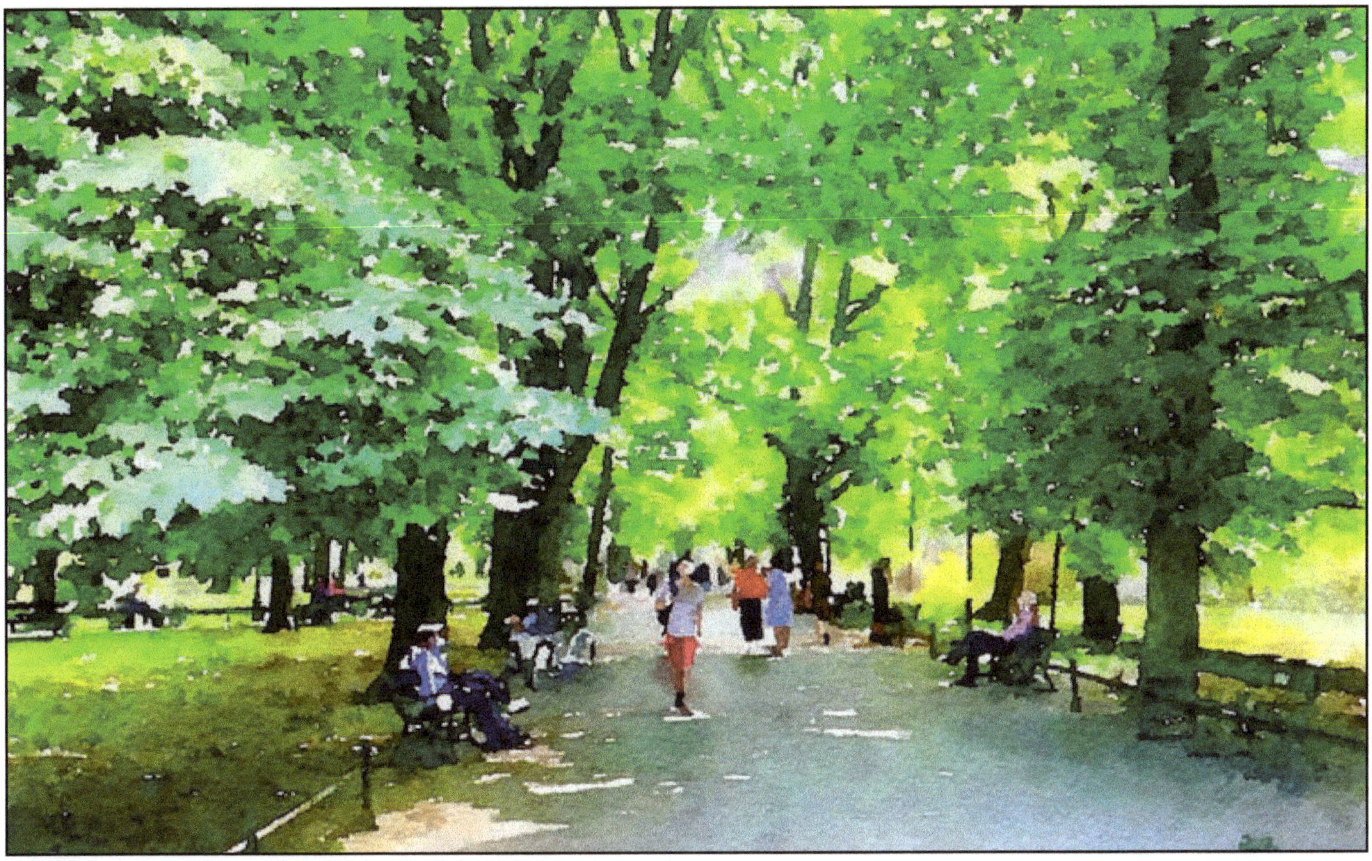

▲'Parkocska' (2018), Krakow, Poland [EPO1803].

'Juliusz Slowacki Theatre' (2018), Krakow, Poland [EPO1801].▼

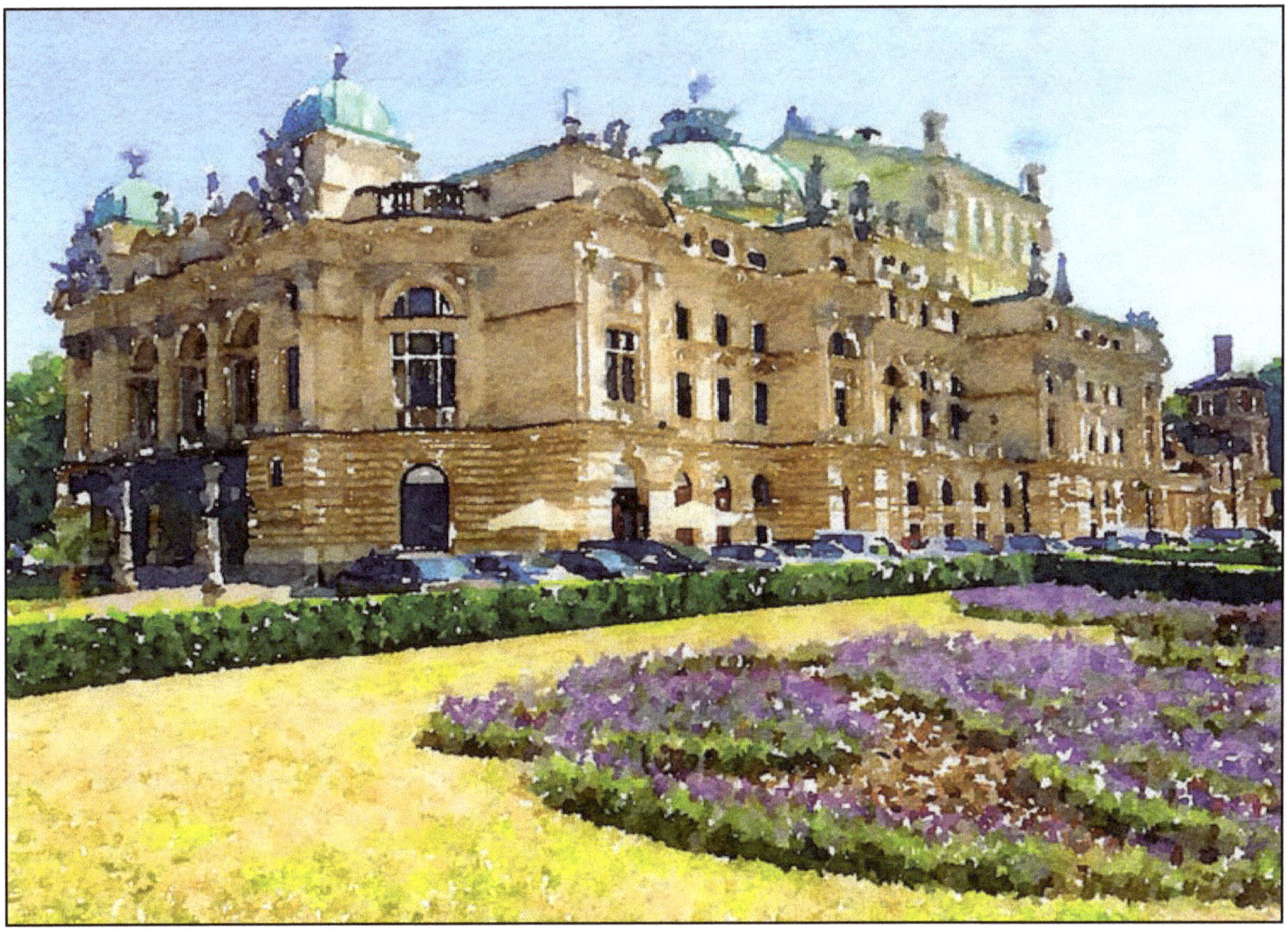

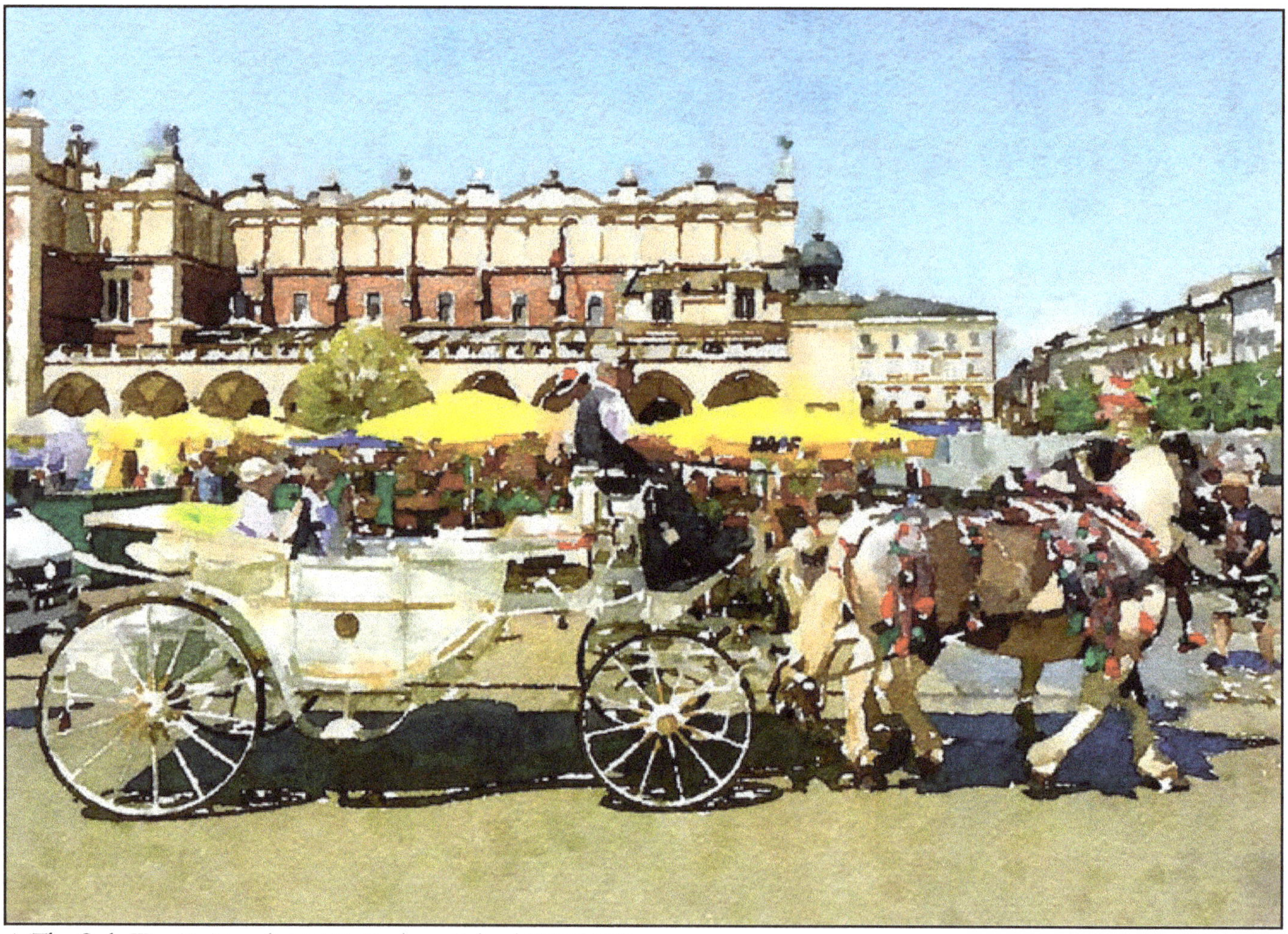

▲'The Only Way To Travel' (2018), Krakow, Poland [EPO1802].

'Ksiaz Castle' (2018), Walbrzych, Poland [EPO1805].▼

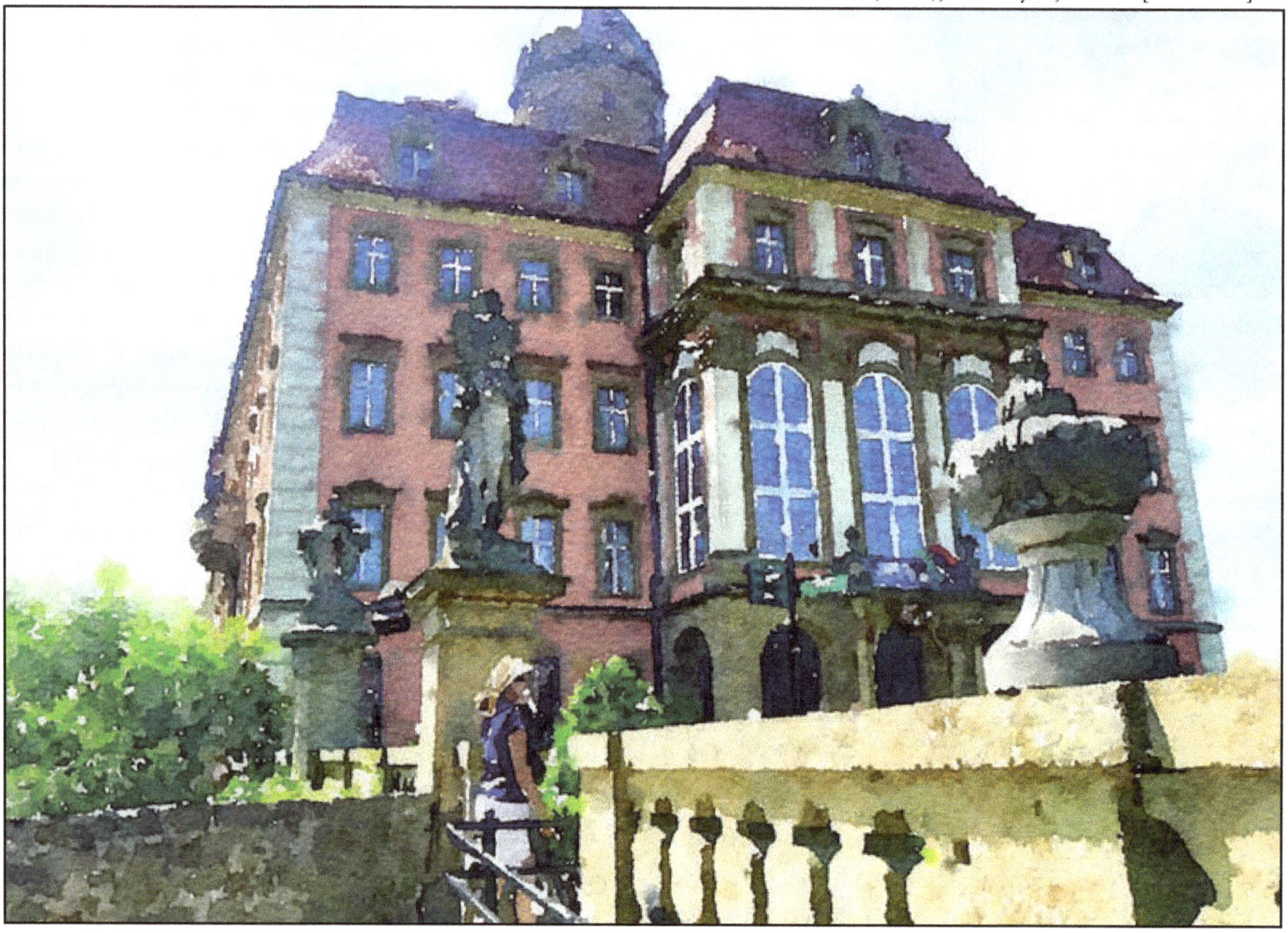

Scotland...

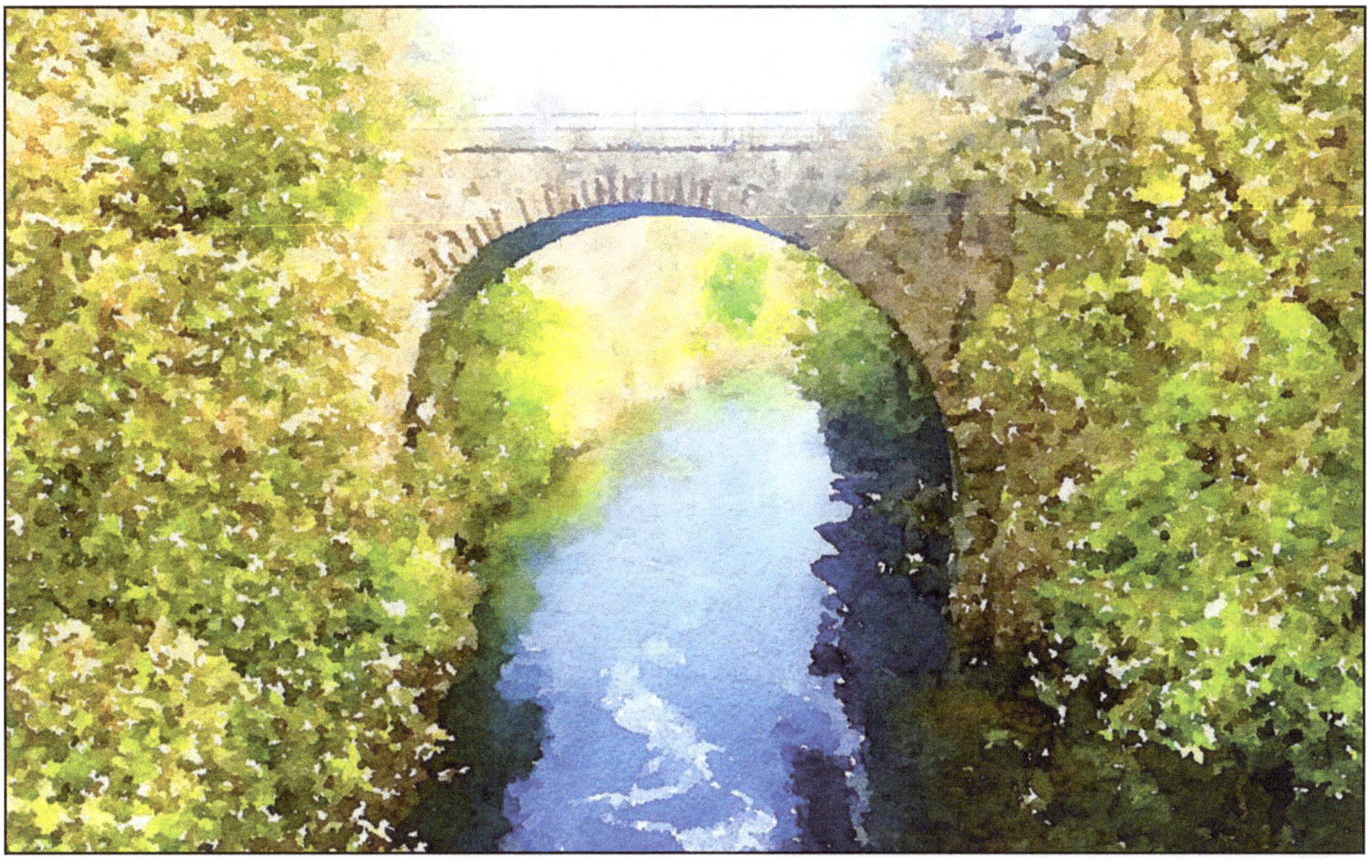

▲'The Rail Bridge' (2018), Brora, Scotland [ESC1805].

'Dunrobin Castle (1401)' (2018), Golspie, Scotland [ESC1801].▼

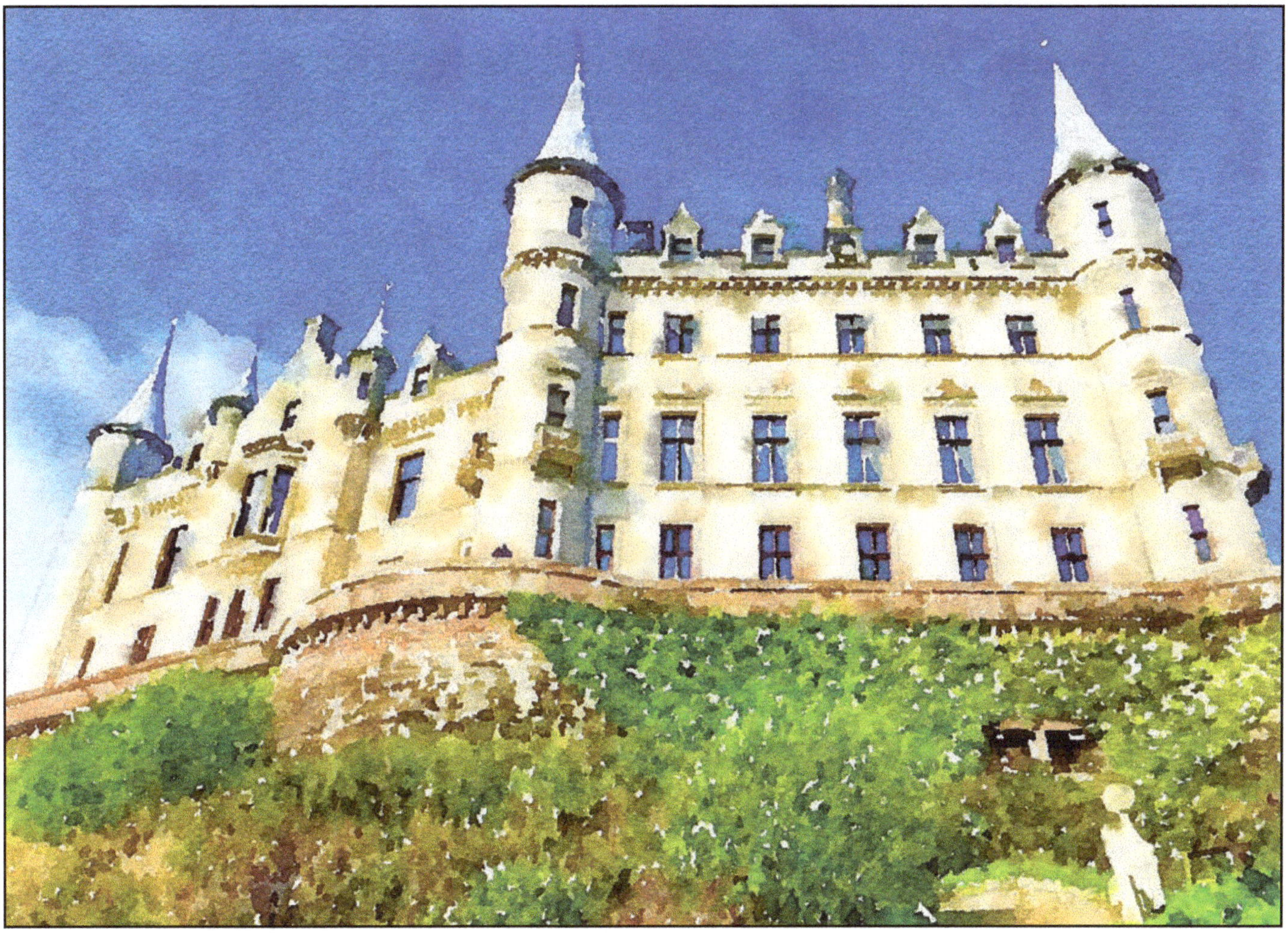

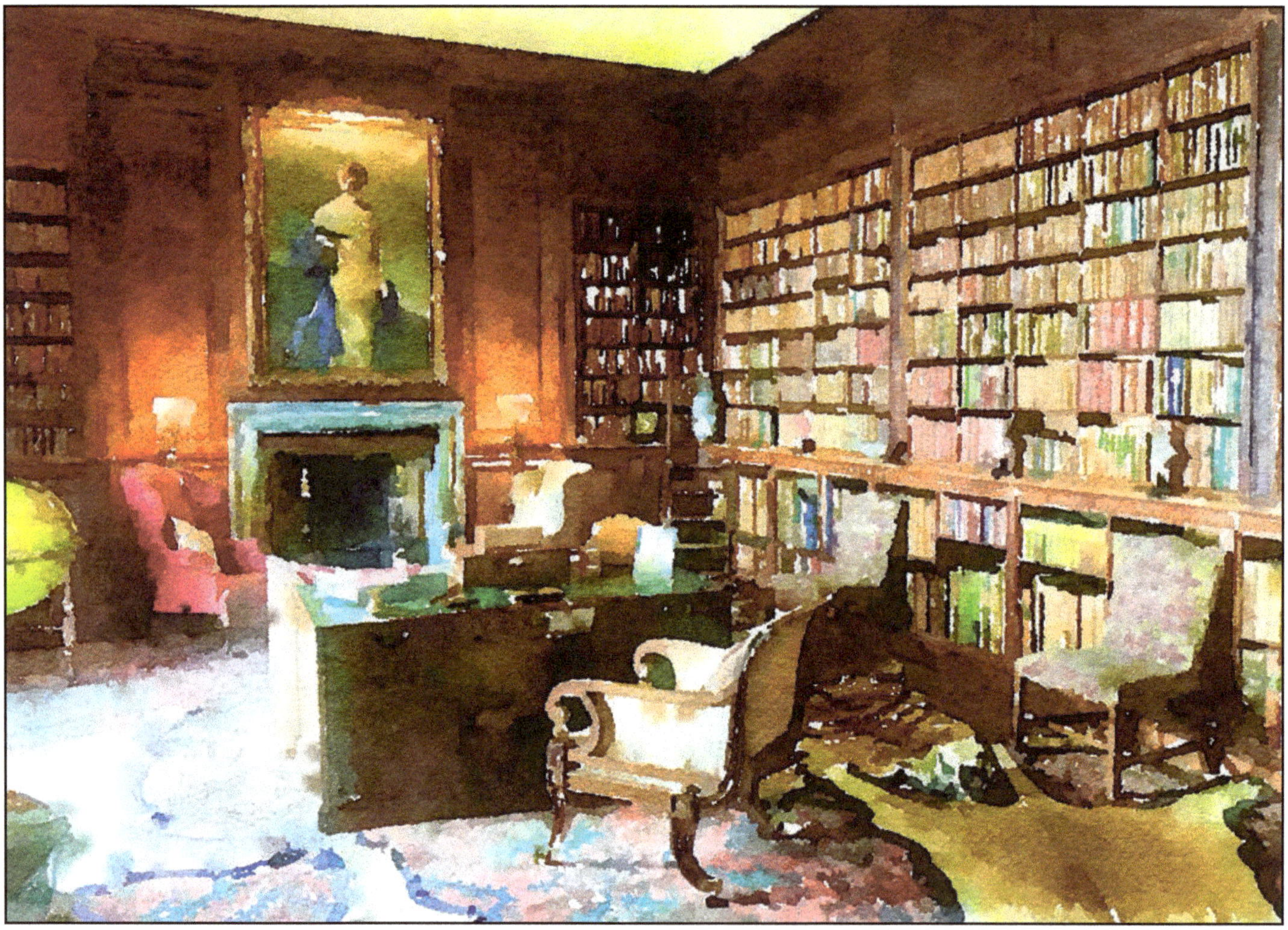

▲'Library, Dunrobin Castle' (2018), Golspie, Scotland [ESC1803].

'Dining Room, Dunrobin Castle' (2018), Golspie, Scotland [ESC1802].▼

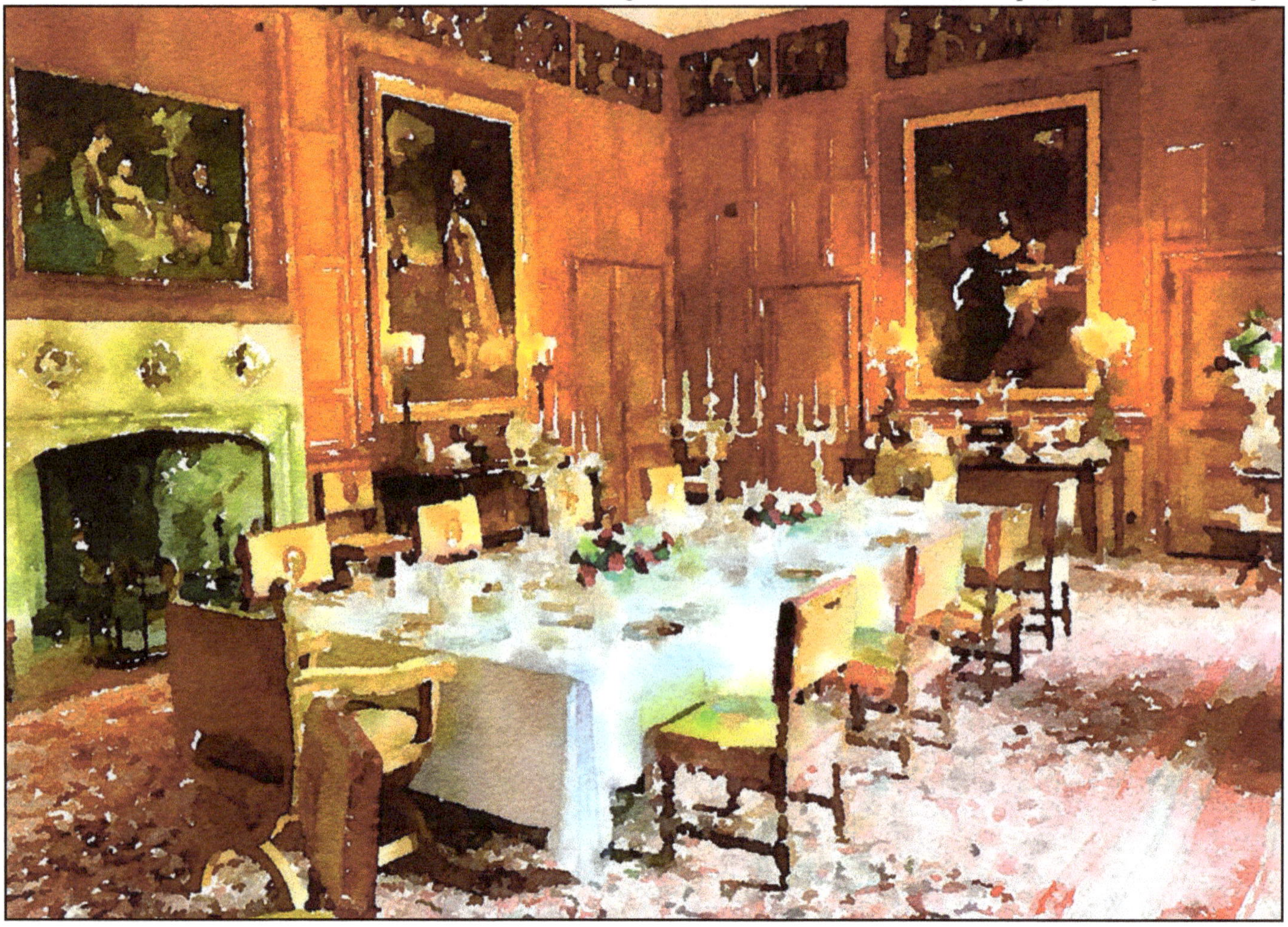

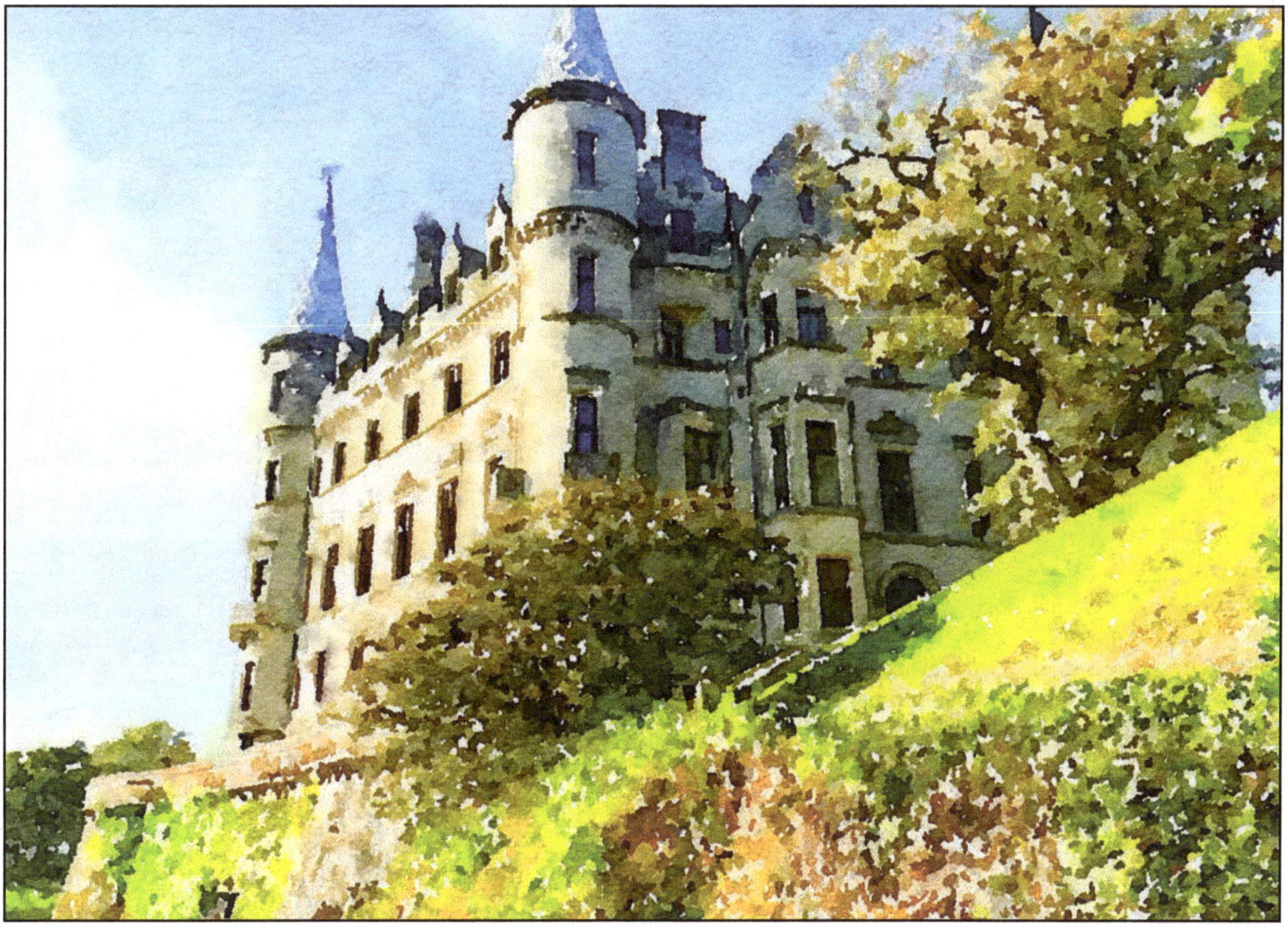

▲'The Towers Of Dunrobin' (2018), Golspie, Scotland [ESC1804].

'The Corner Shop' (2018), Tomintoul, Scotland [ESC1806].▼

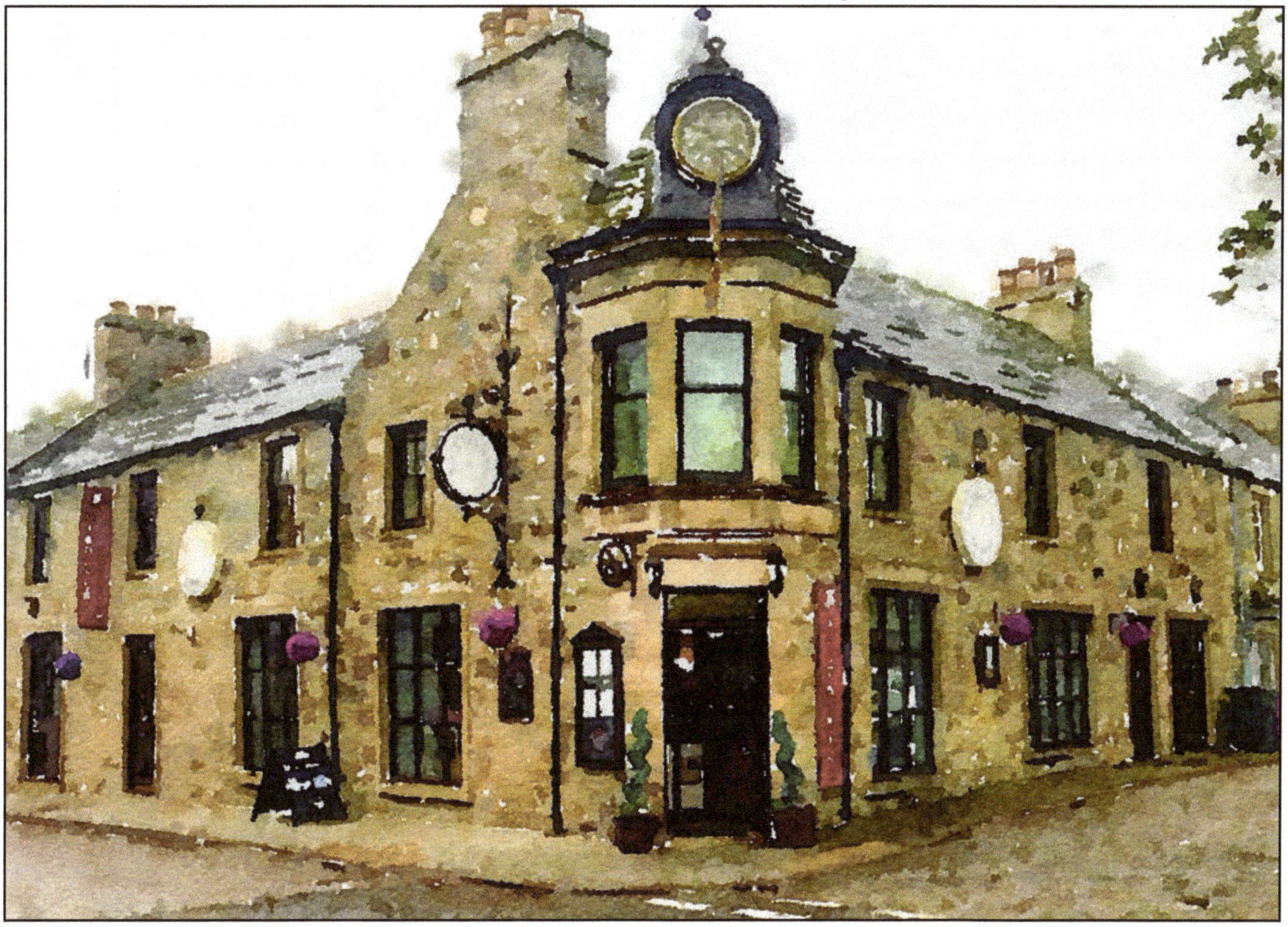

Serbia...

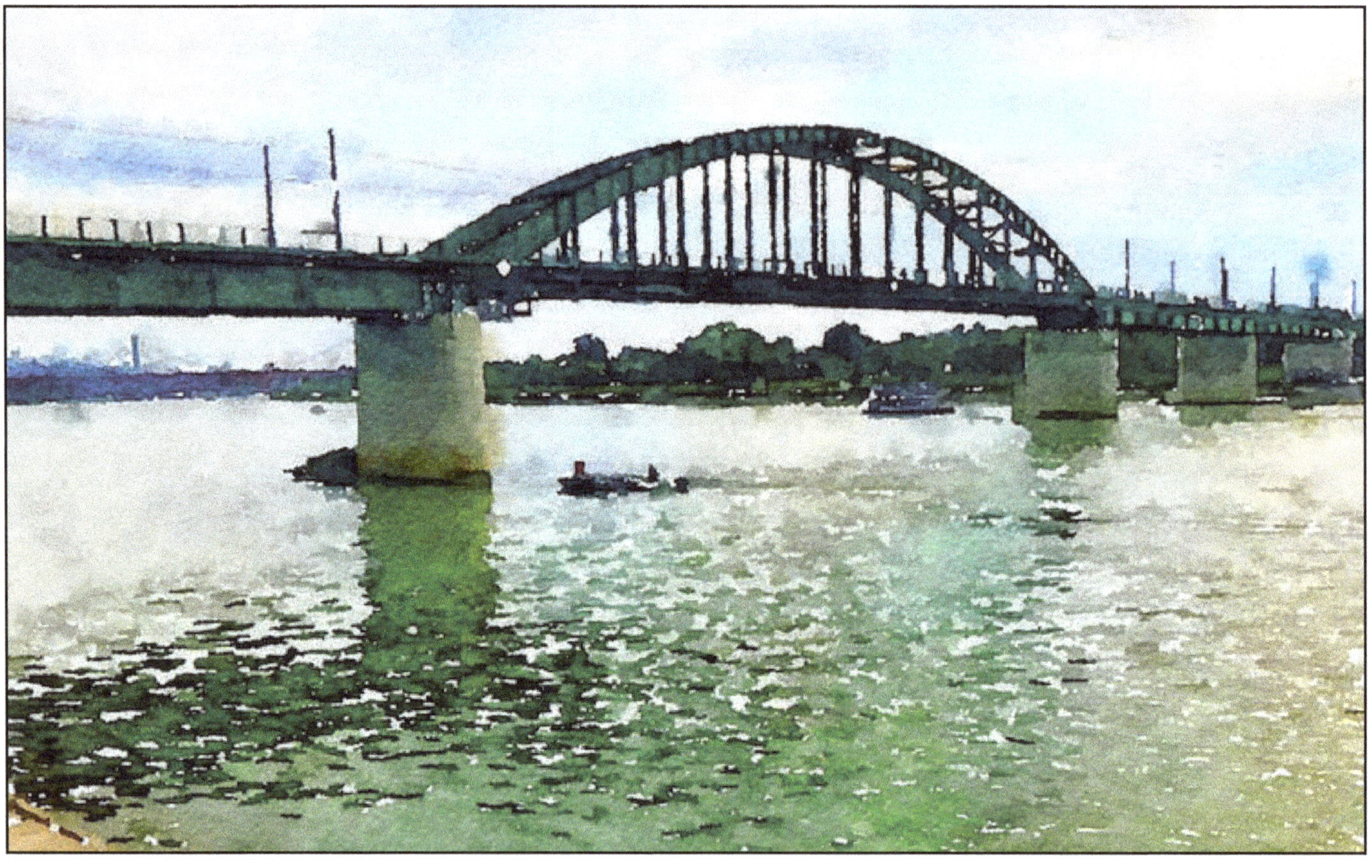

▲'Stari Most' (2018), Belgrade, Serbia [ERS1801].

'Stari Grad' (2018), Belgrade, Serbia [ERS1802].▼

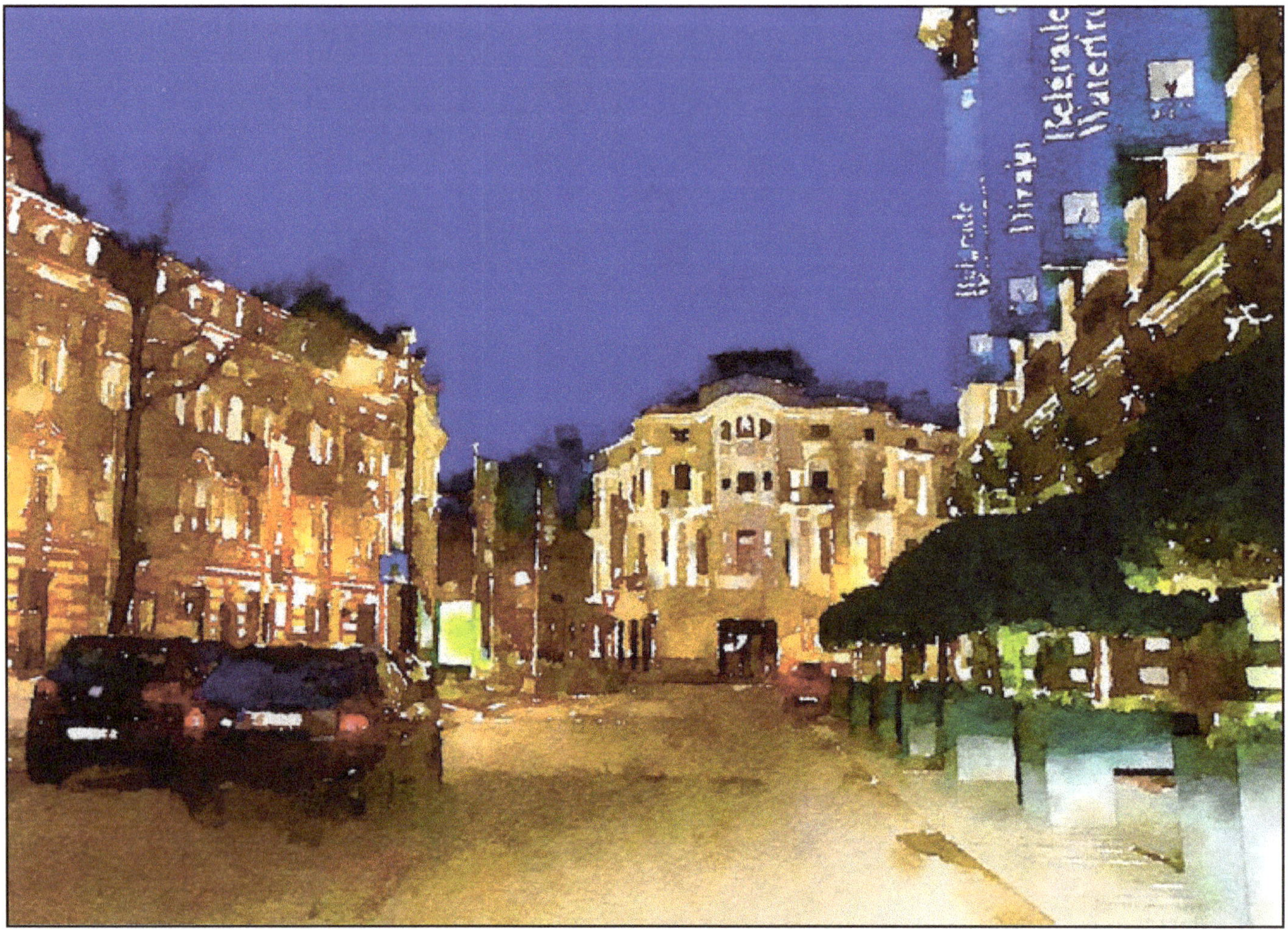

Slovenia...

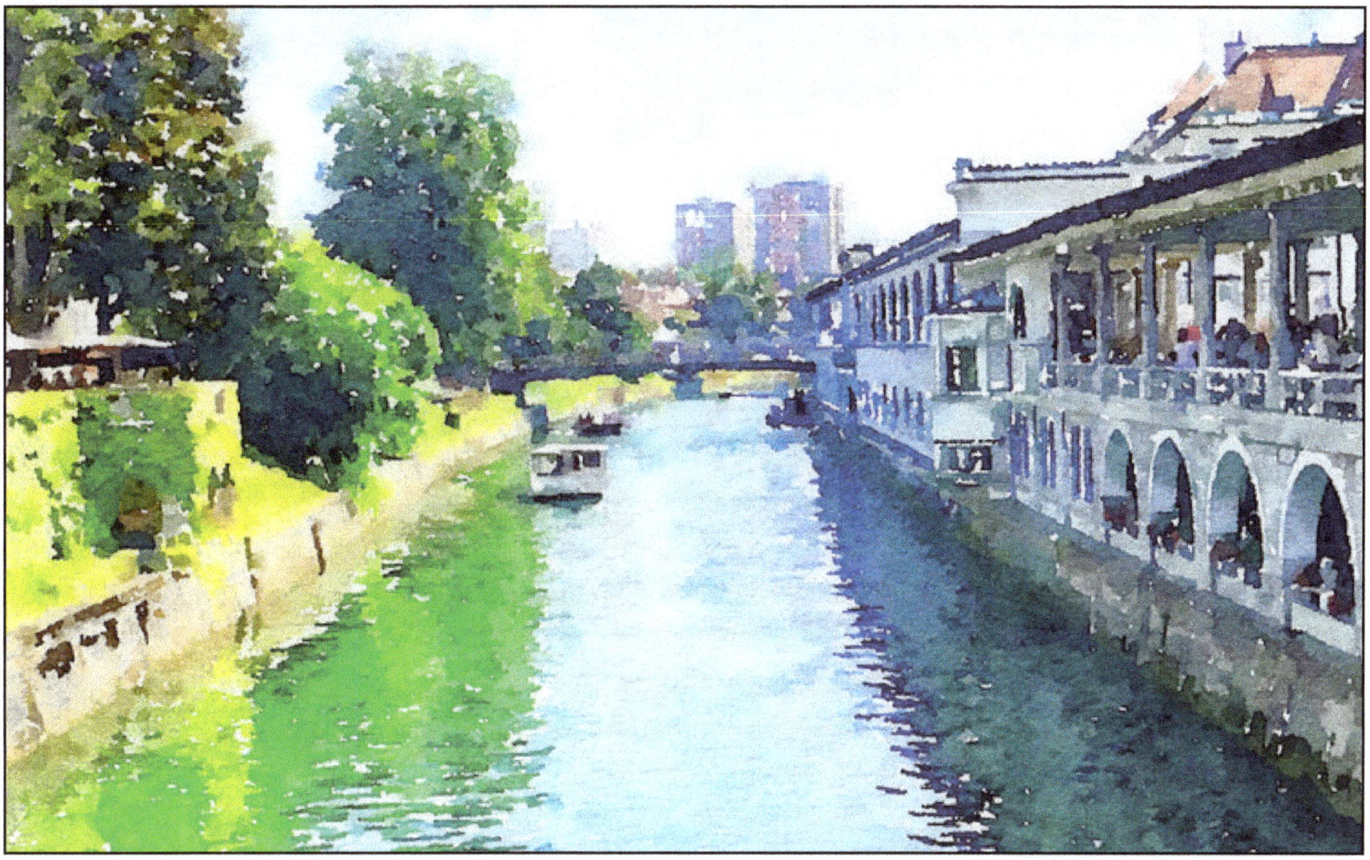

▲'The Ljubljanica River' (2018), Ljubljana, Slovenia [ESL1801].

'Graffiti Street' (2018), Ljubljana, Slovenia [ESL1802].▼

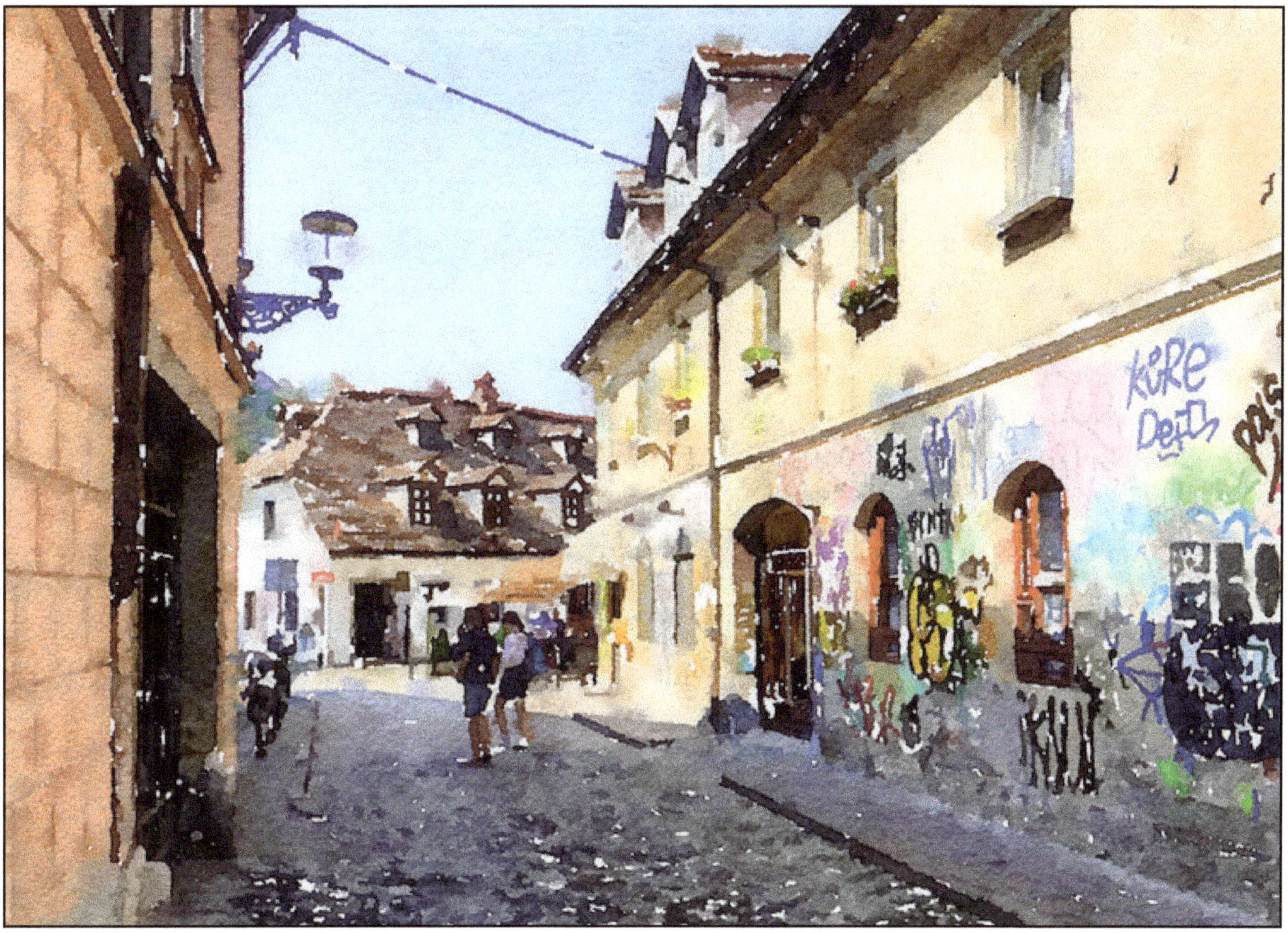

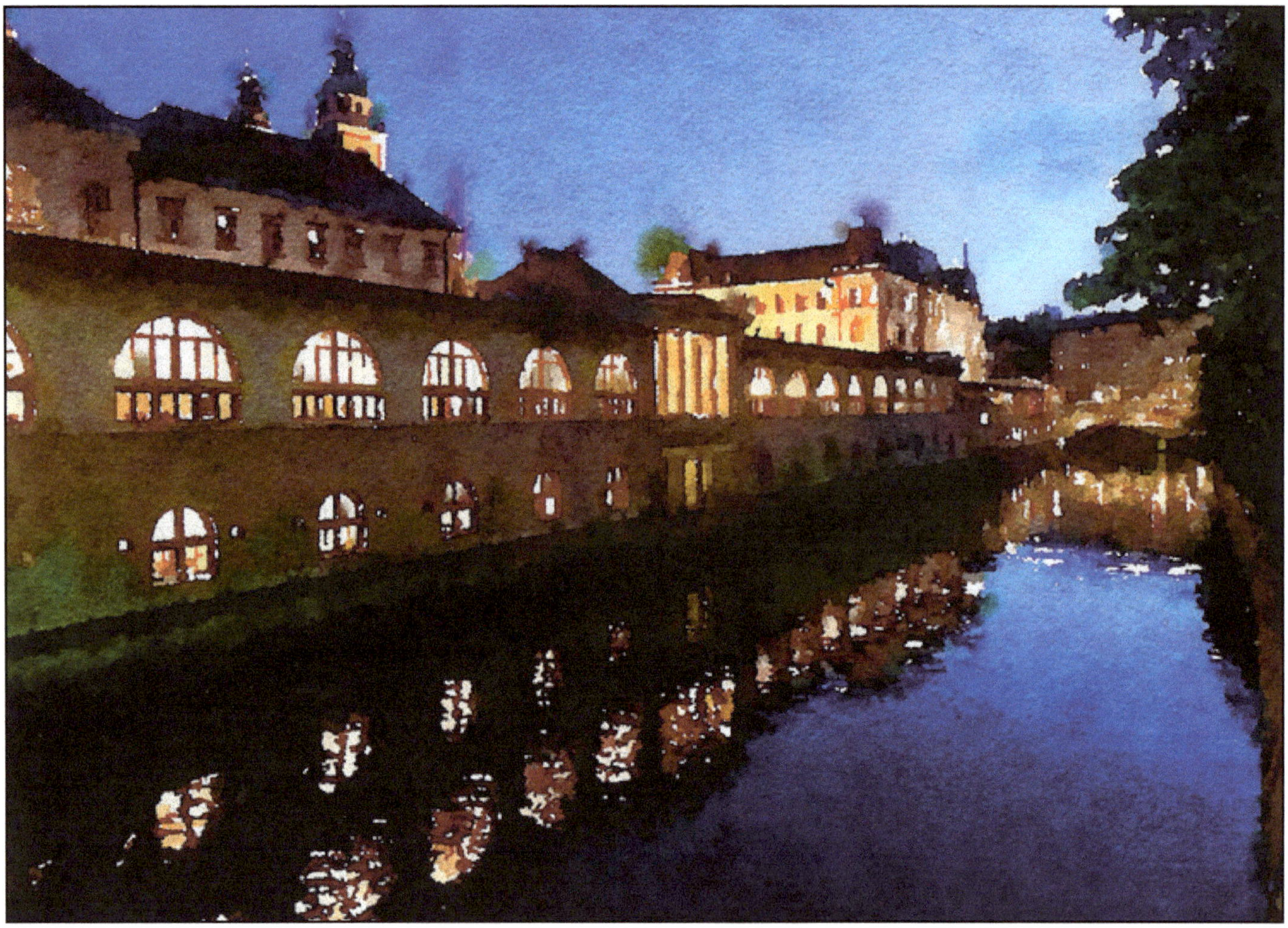

▲'Dusk Over Ljubljana' (2018), Ljubljana, Slovenia [ESL1803].

'The Triple Most' (2018), Ljubljana, Slovenia [ESL1804].▼

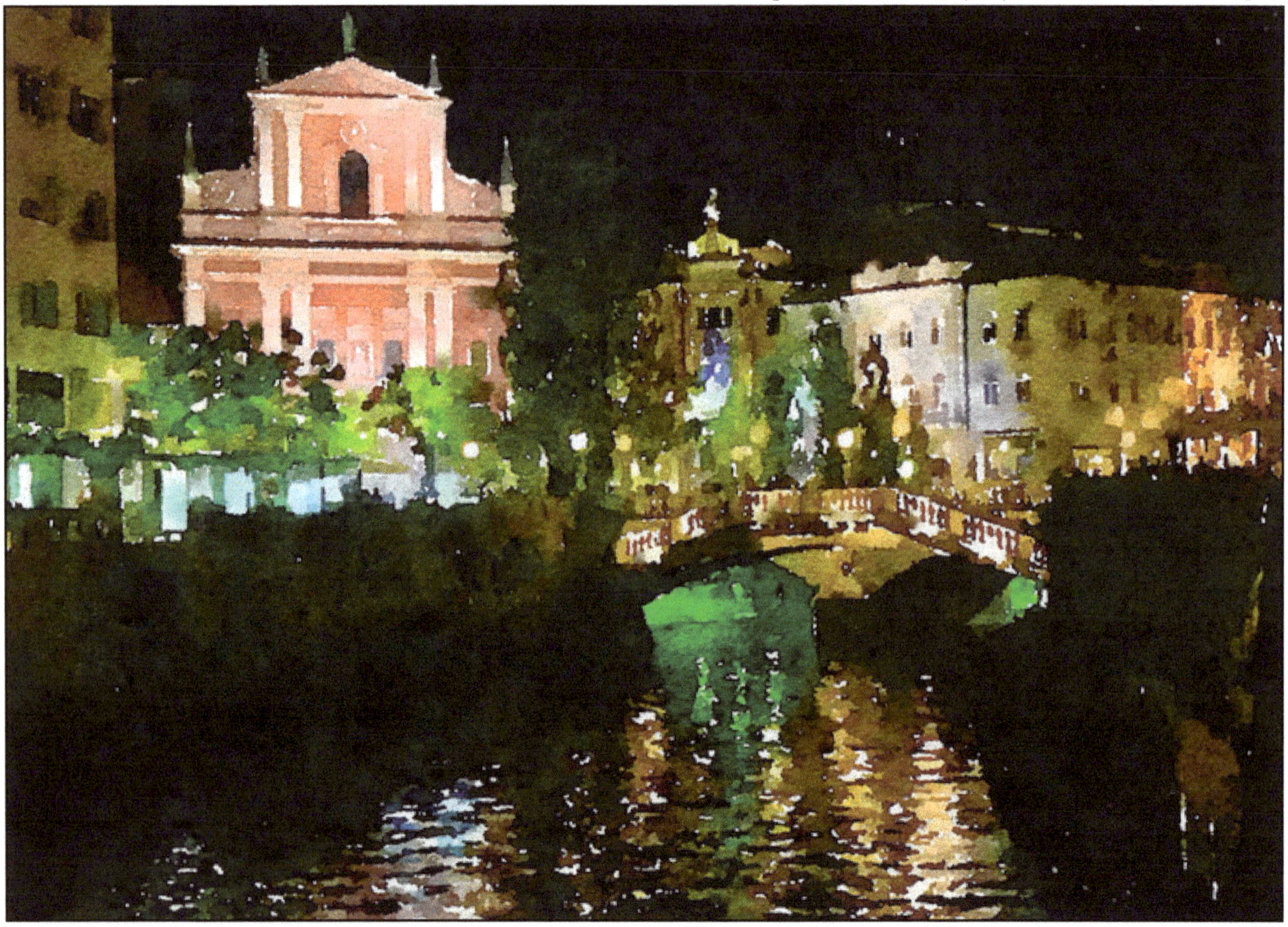

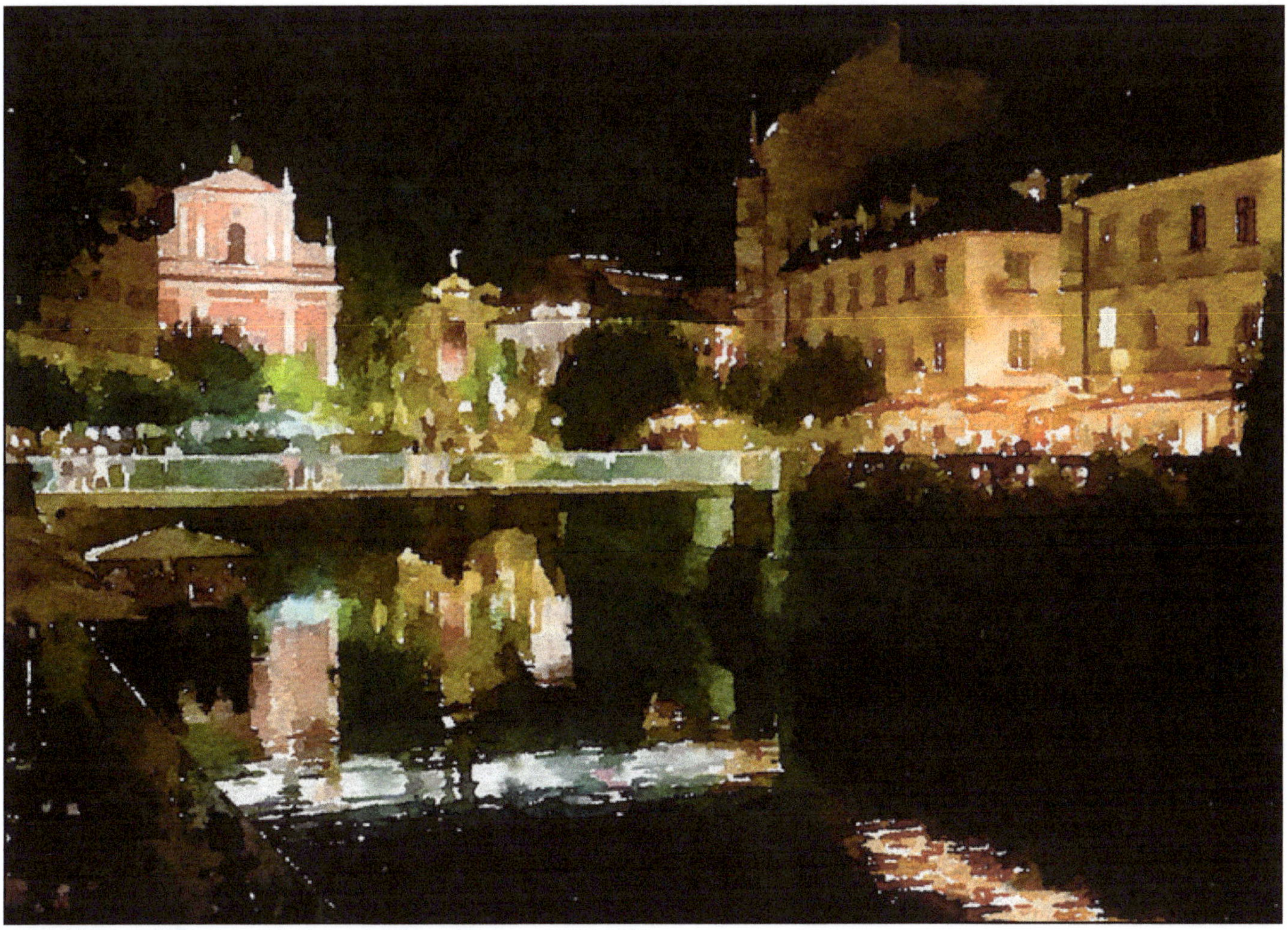

▲'Ljubljanica Reflections' (2018), Ljubljana, Slovenia [ESL1805].

'Eisenkappel' (2018), Vellach, Slovenia [ESL1806].▼

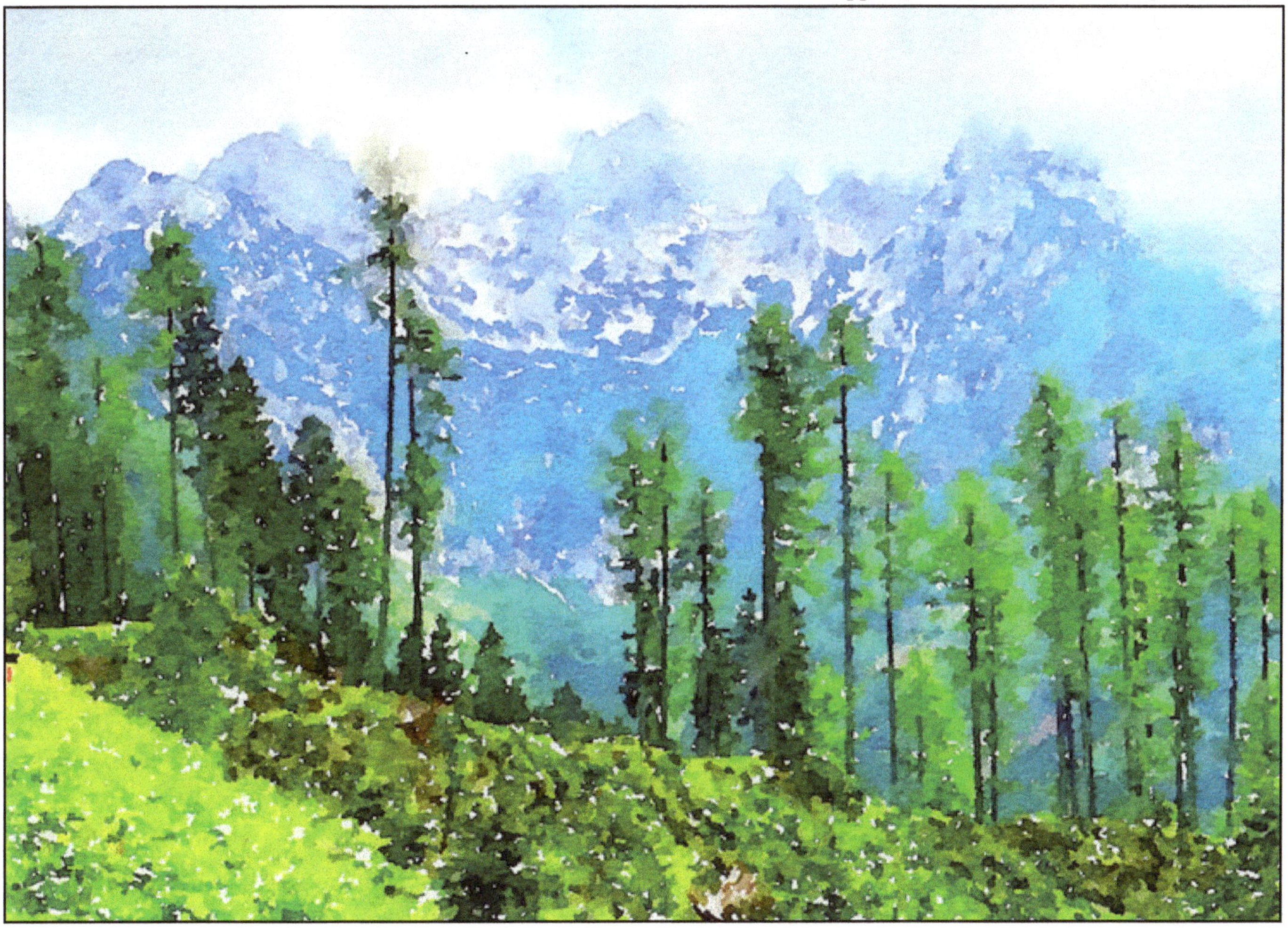

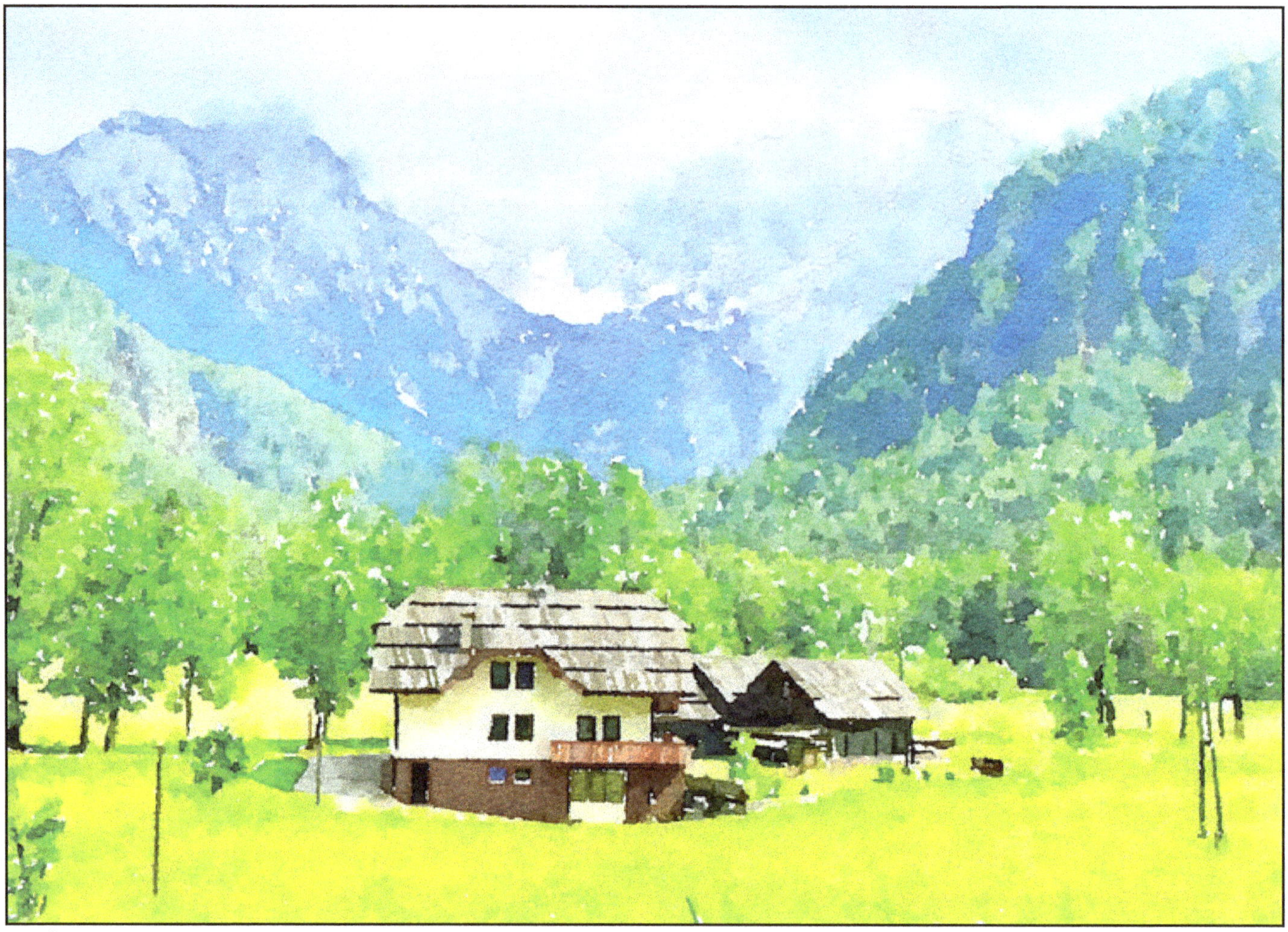

▲'The Farmhouse' (2018), Jezersko, Slovenia [ESL1807].

'Mt Triglav From Gozd Martuljek' (2018), Slovenia [ESL1810].▼

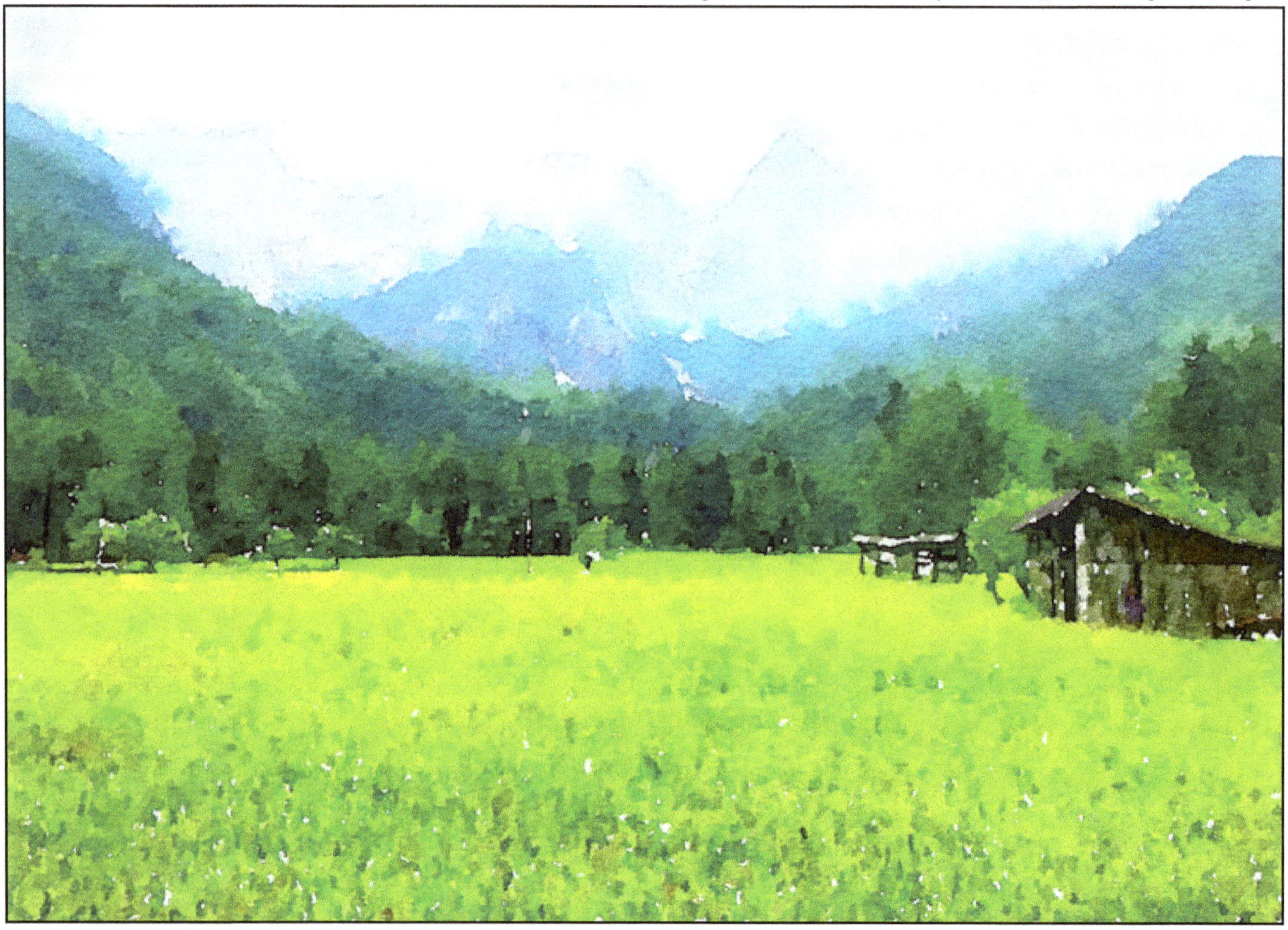

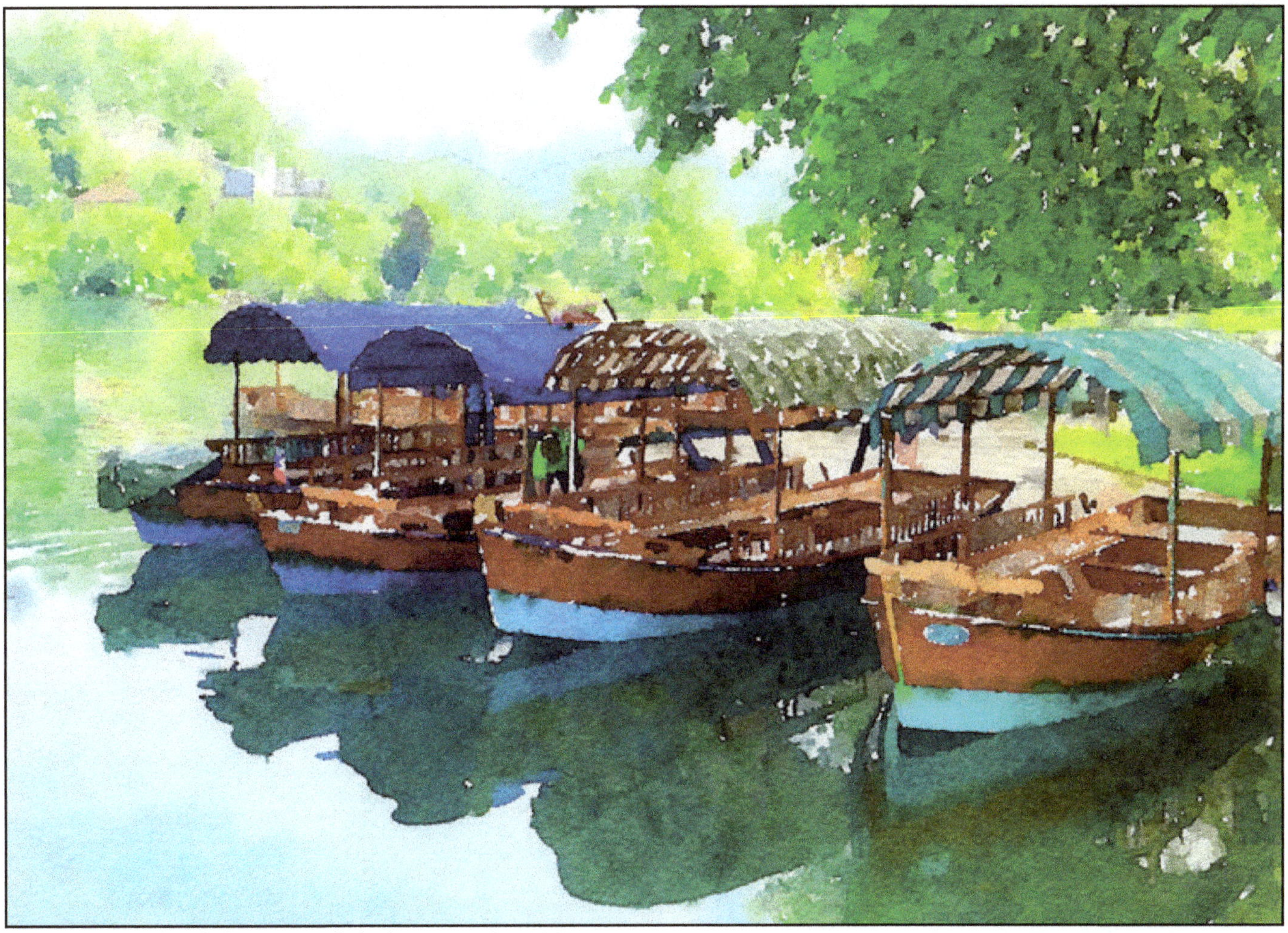

▲'Boats On Lake Bled' (2018), Bled, Slovenia [ESL1808].

'Evening At Lake Bled' (2018), Bled, Slovenia [ESL1809].▼

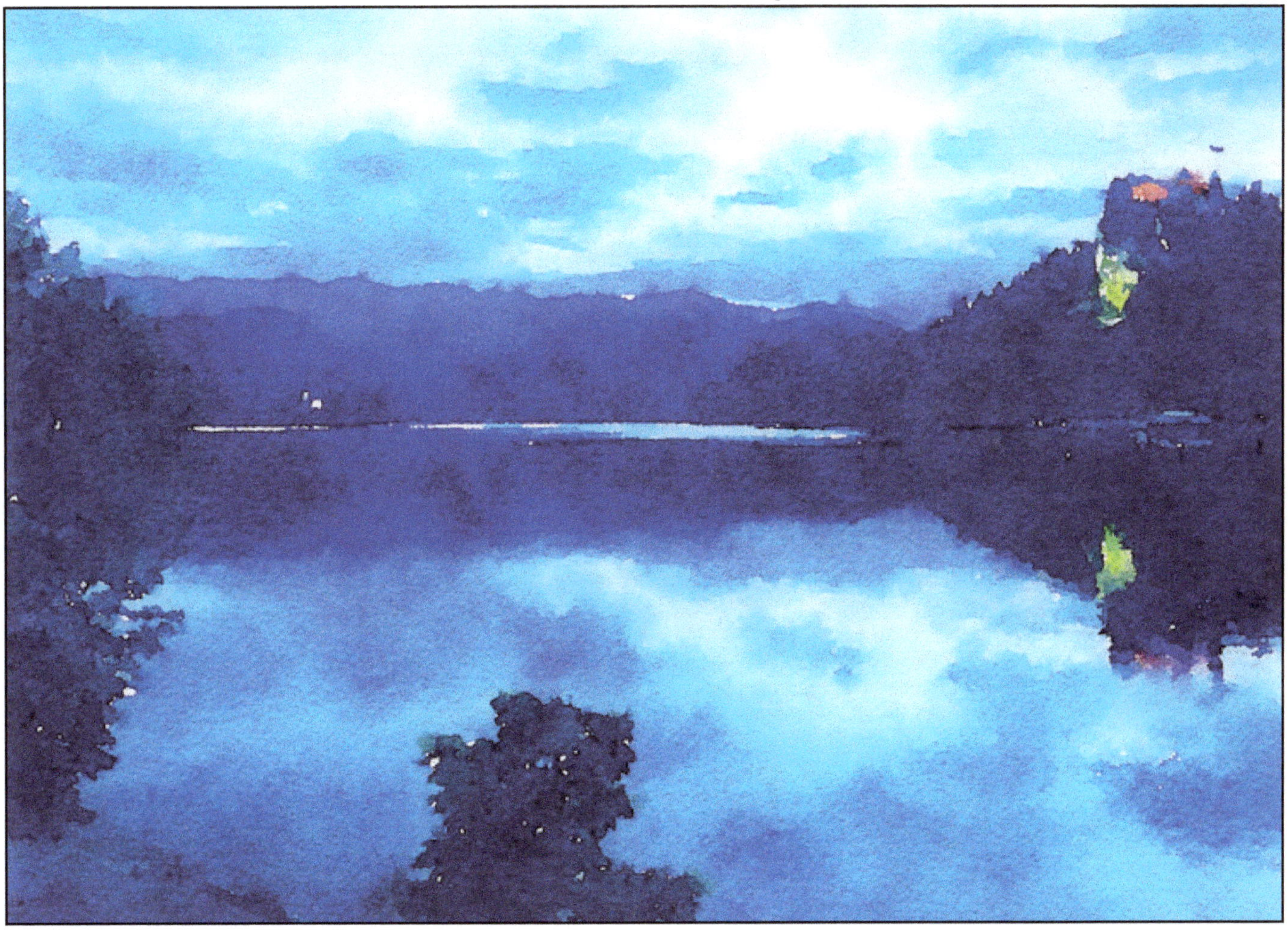

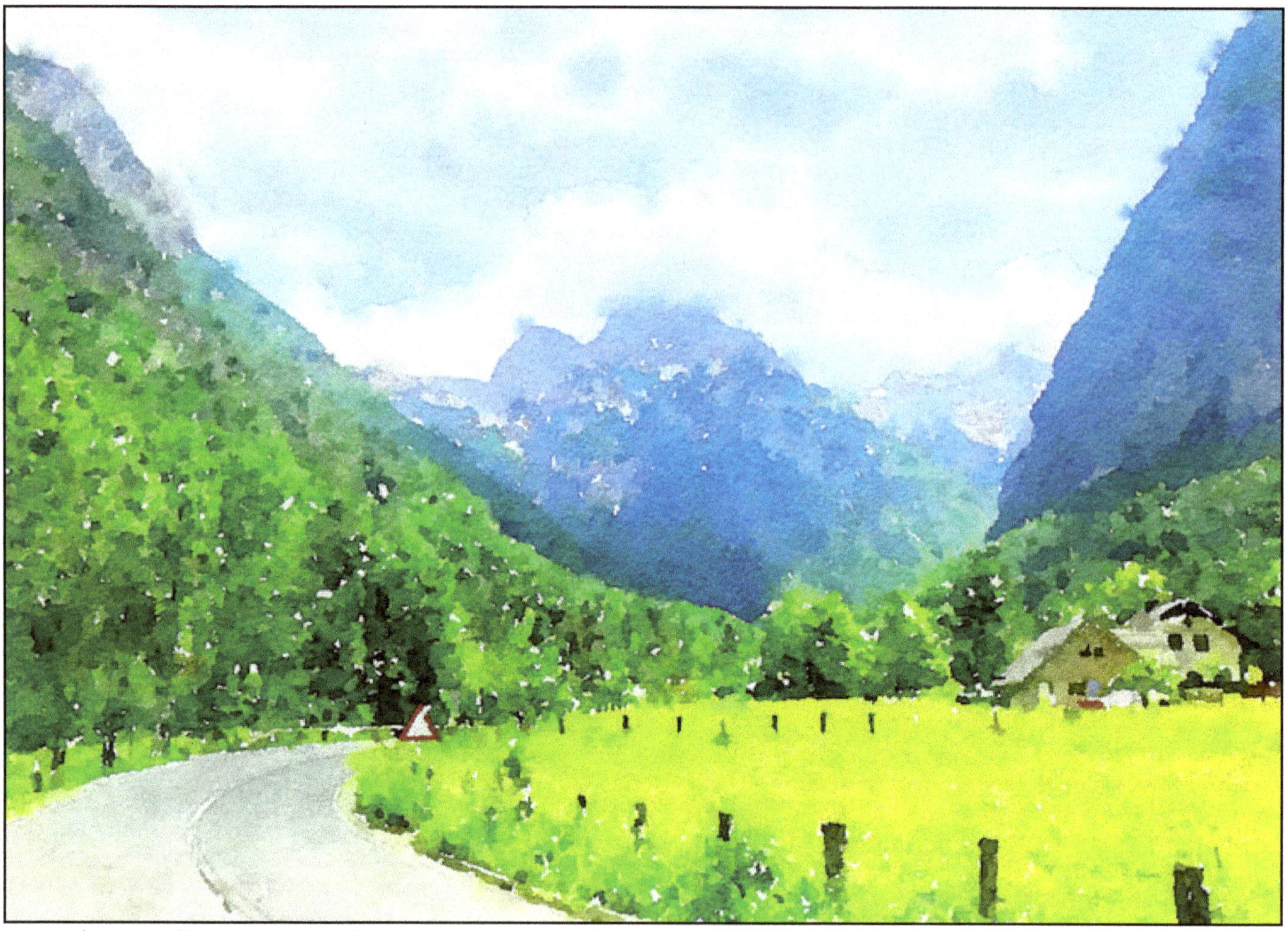

▲'North View Of Mt Triglav' (2018), Trenta, Slovenia [ESL1811].

'The East Railway' (2018), Sava Gorge, Slovenia [ESL1812].▼

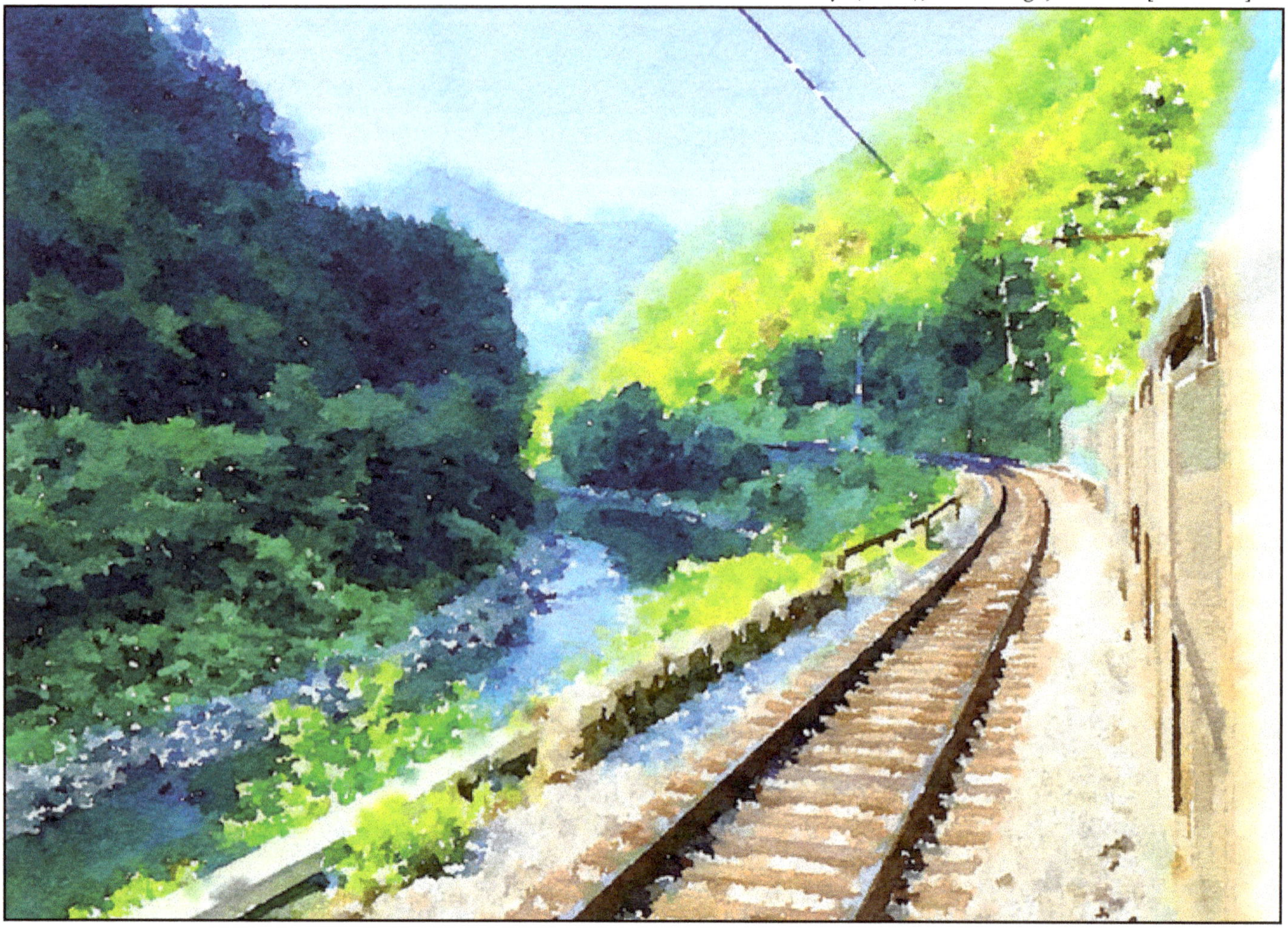

Spain...

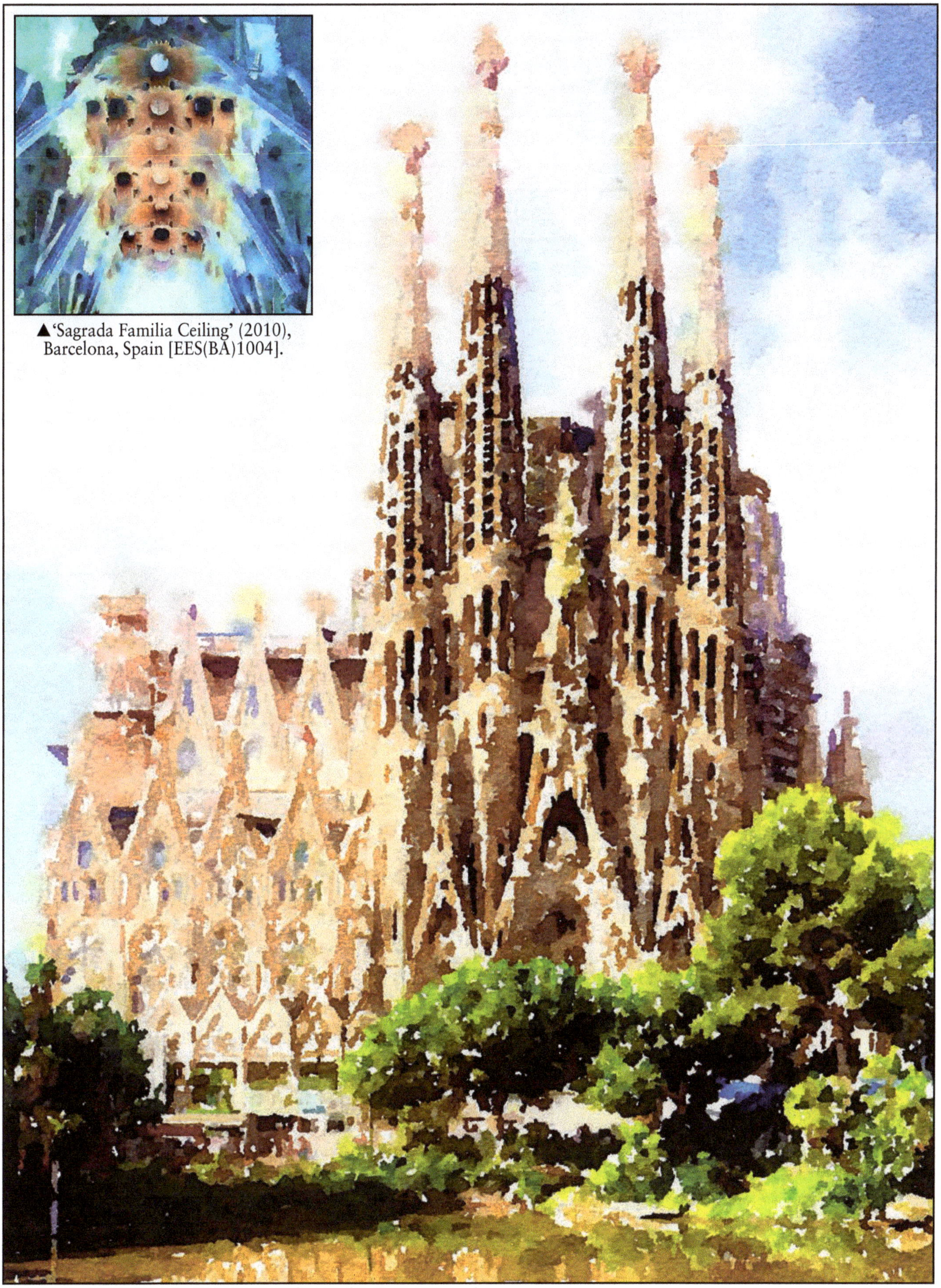

▲'Sagrada Familia Ceiling' (2010), Barcelona, Spain [EES(BA)1004].

▲'Sagrada Familia' (2010), Barcelona, Spain [EES(BA)1006].

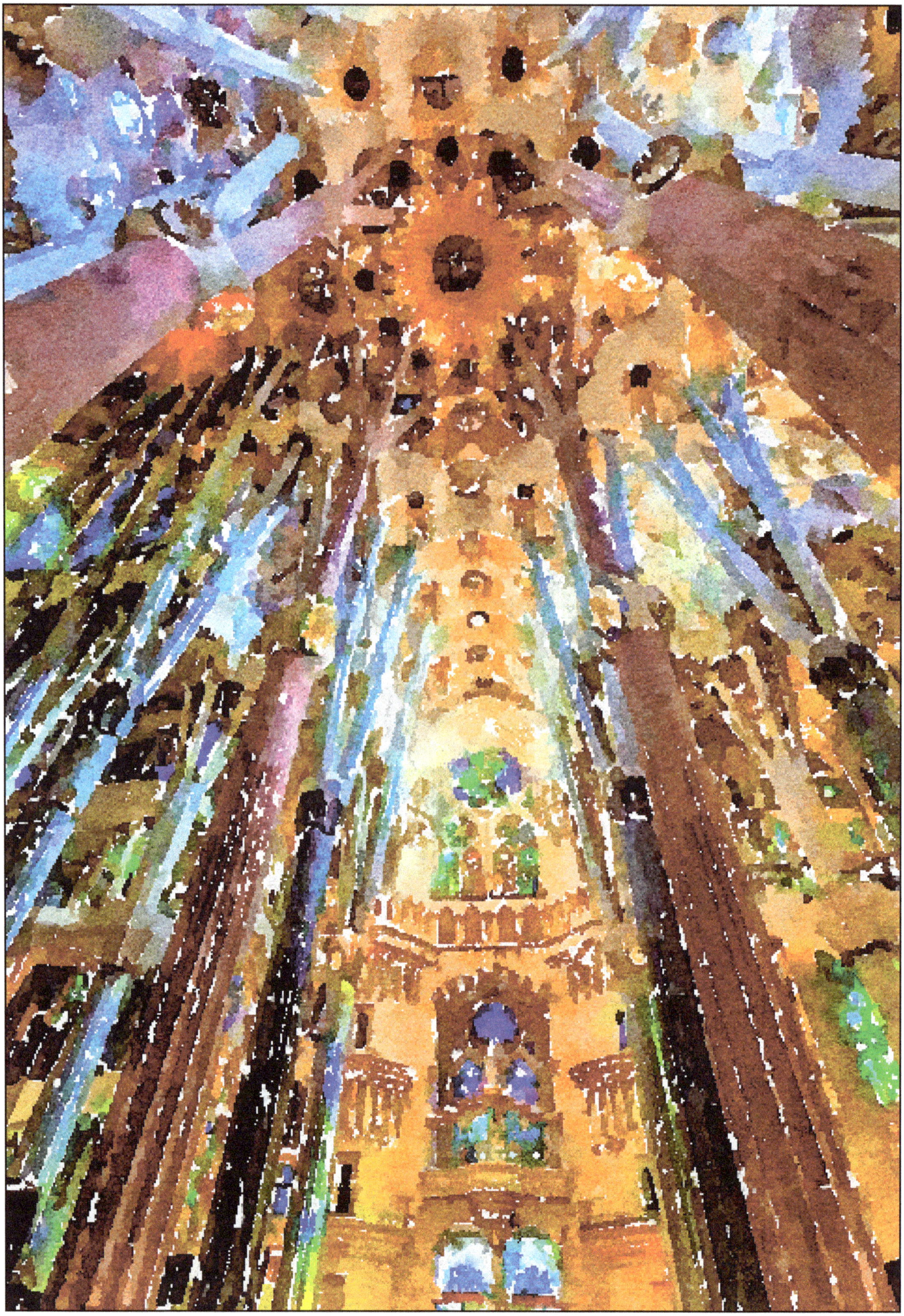

▲'Ceiling Of The Sagrada Familia' (2021), Barcelona, Spain [EES(BA)2102]. ⊘

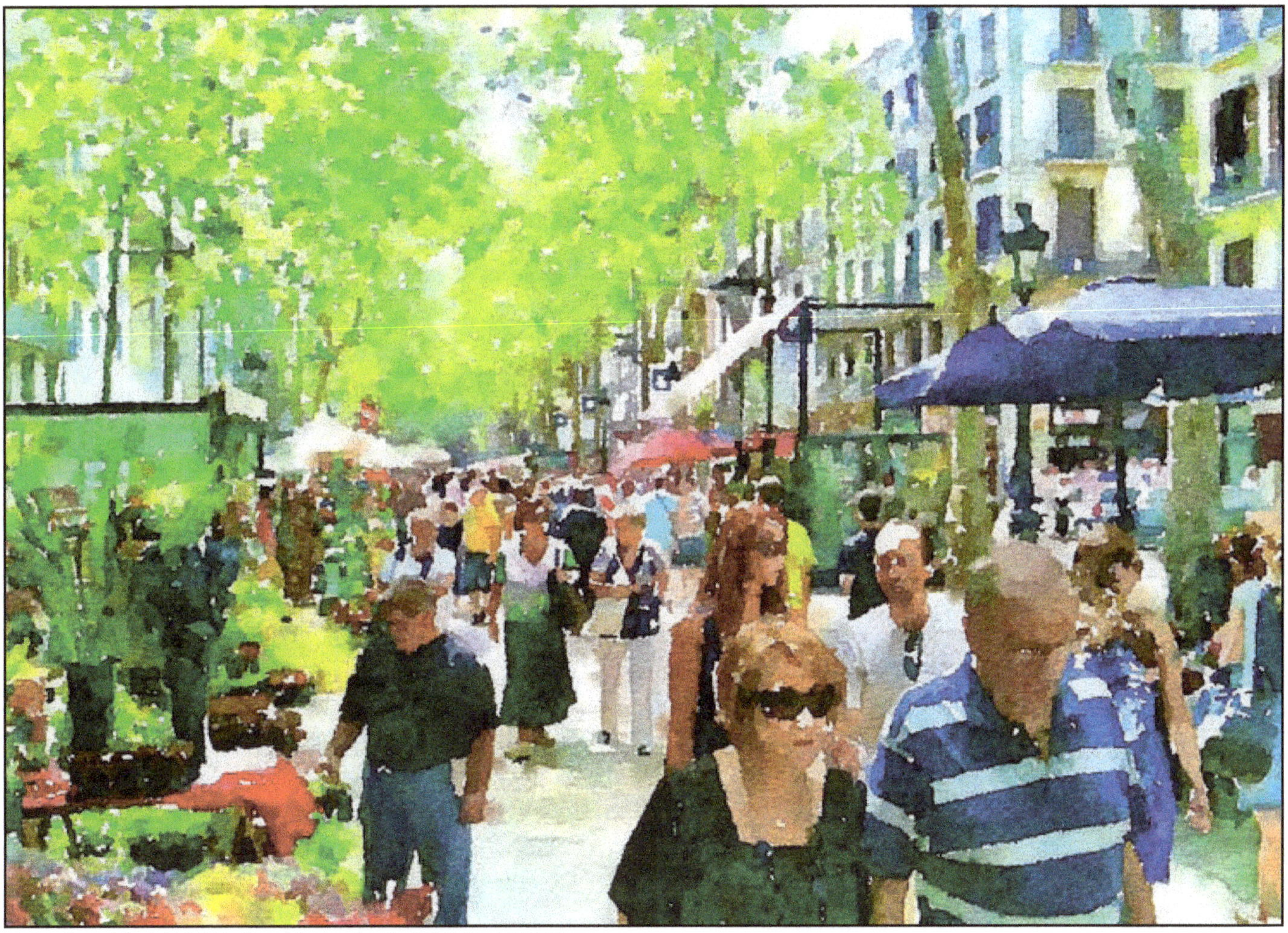

▲'La Ramblas' (2010), Barcelona, Spain [EES(BA)1001].

'Passeig de Gracia' (2010), Barcelona, Spain [EES(BA)1003].▼

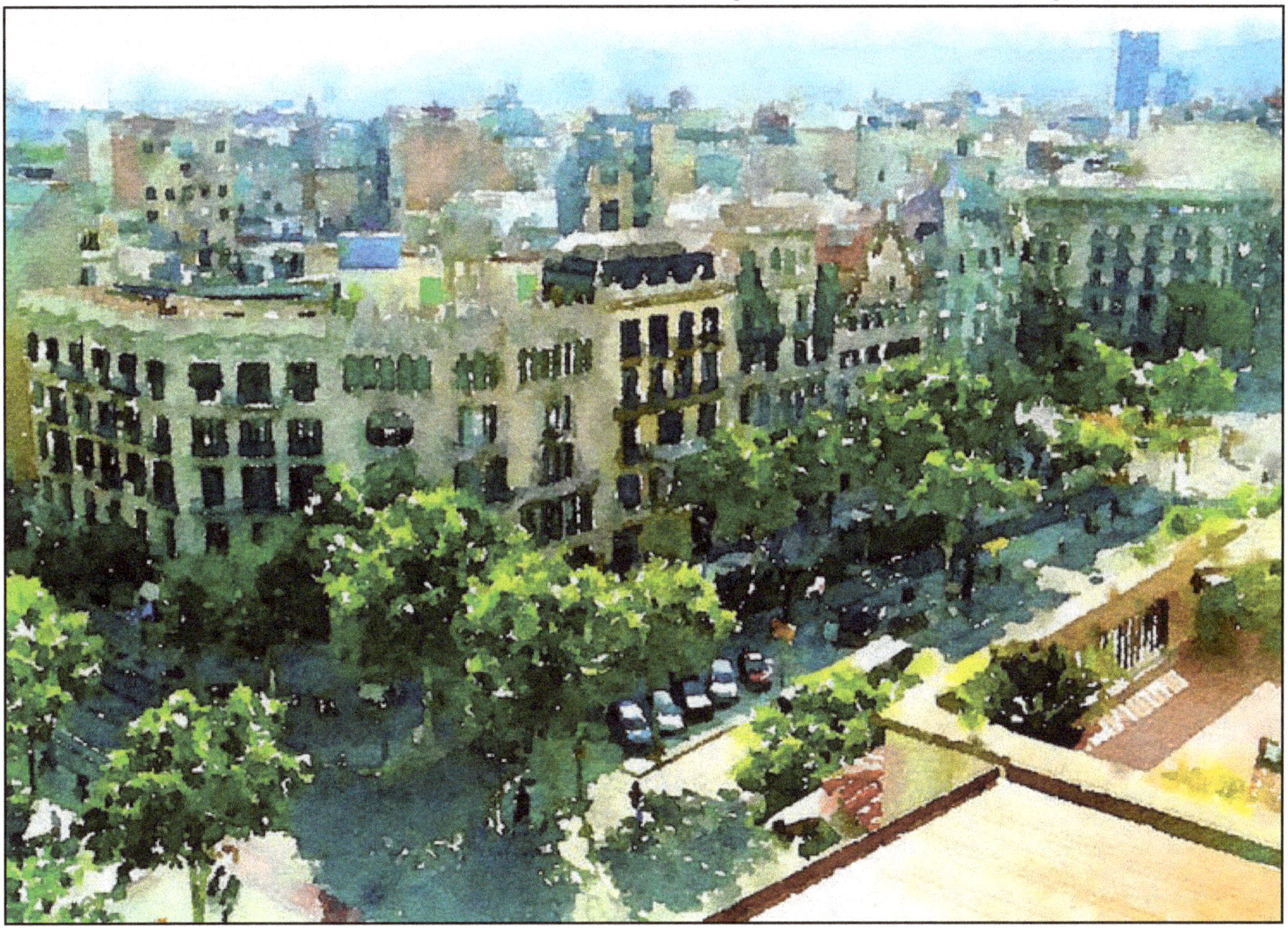

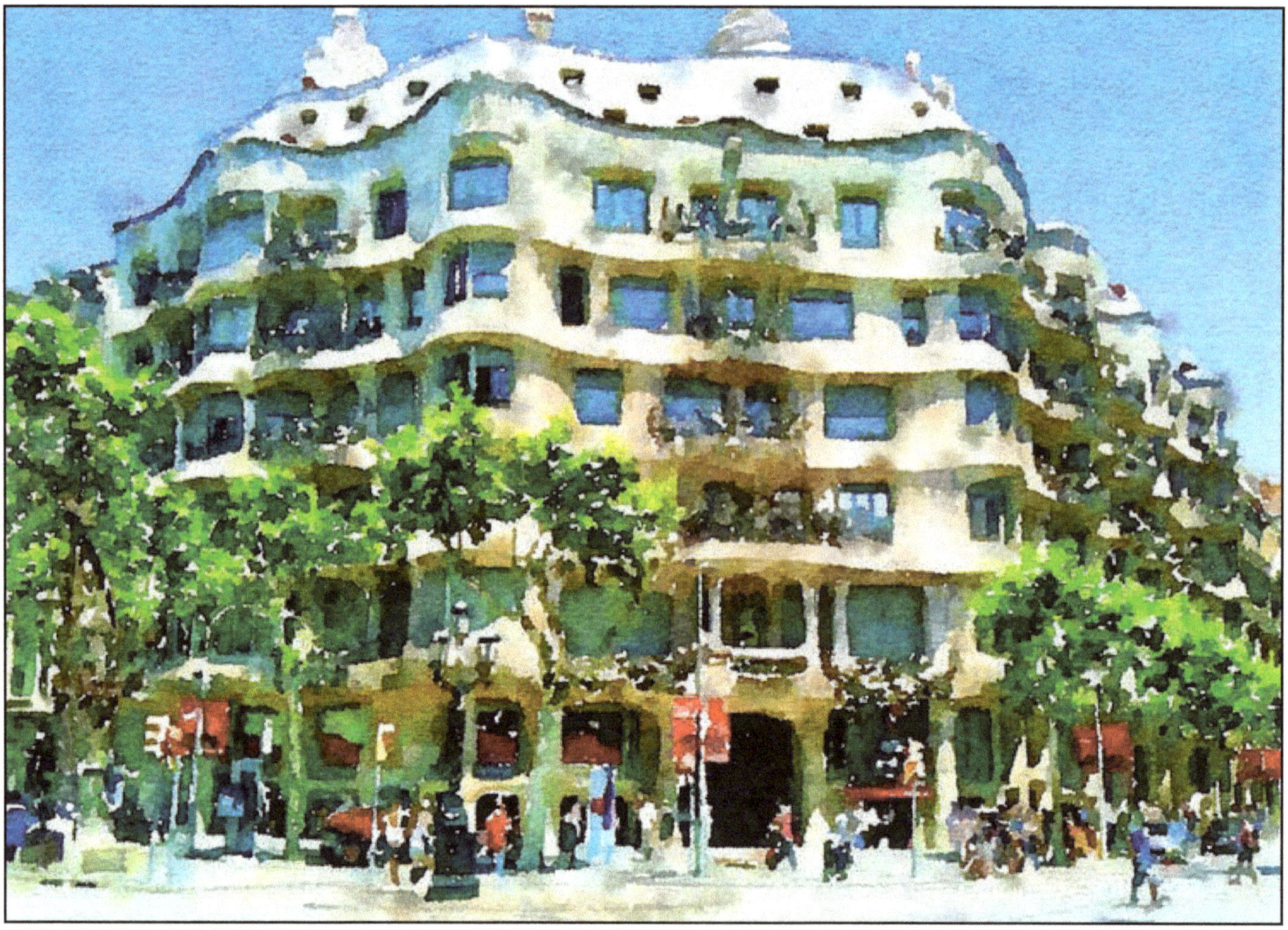

▲'Gaudi's Casa Mila' (2010), Barcelona, Spain [EES(BA)1005].

'Park Guell' (2010), Barcelona, Spain [EES(BA)1002].▼

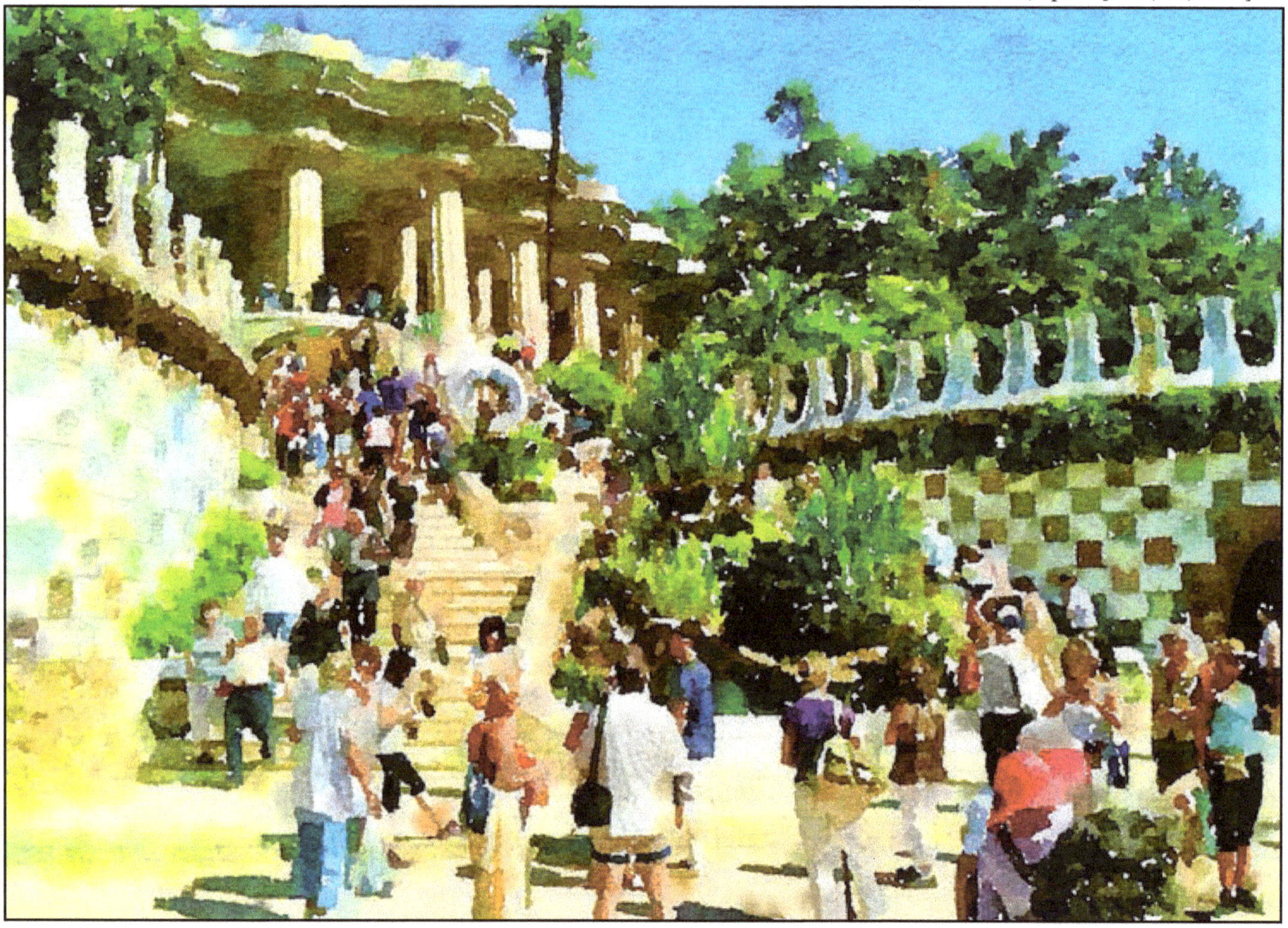

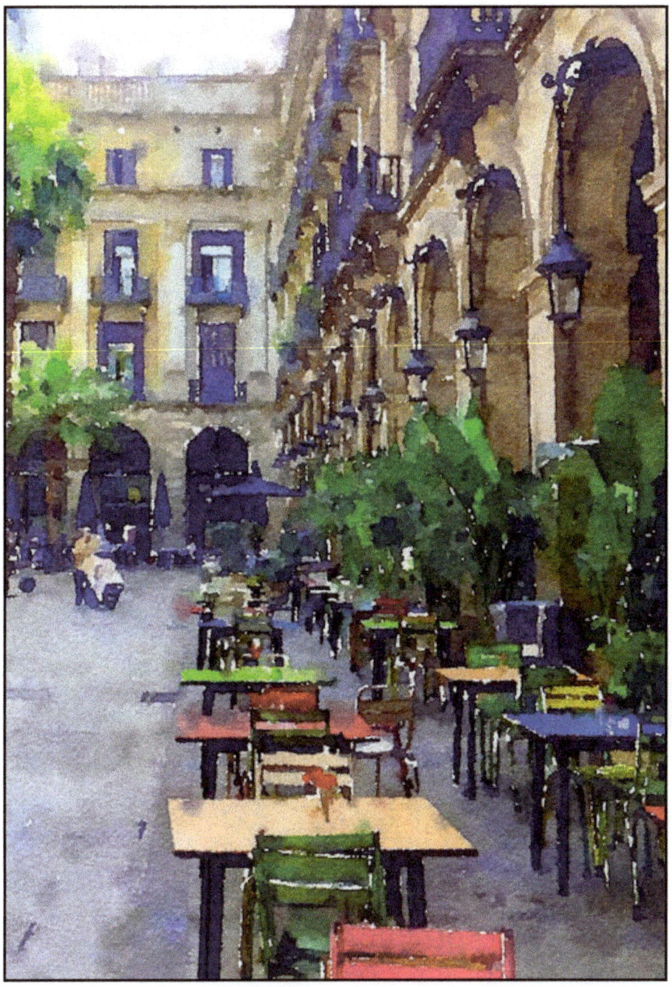

▲'Barcelona Plaza' (2016), Barcelona, Spain [EES(BA)1601].

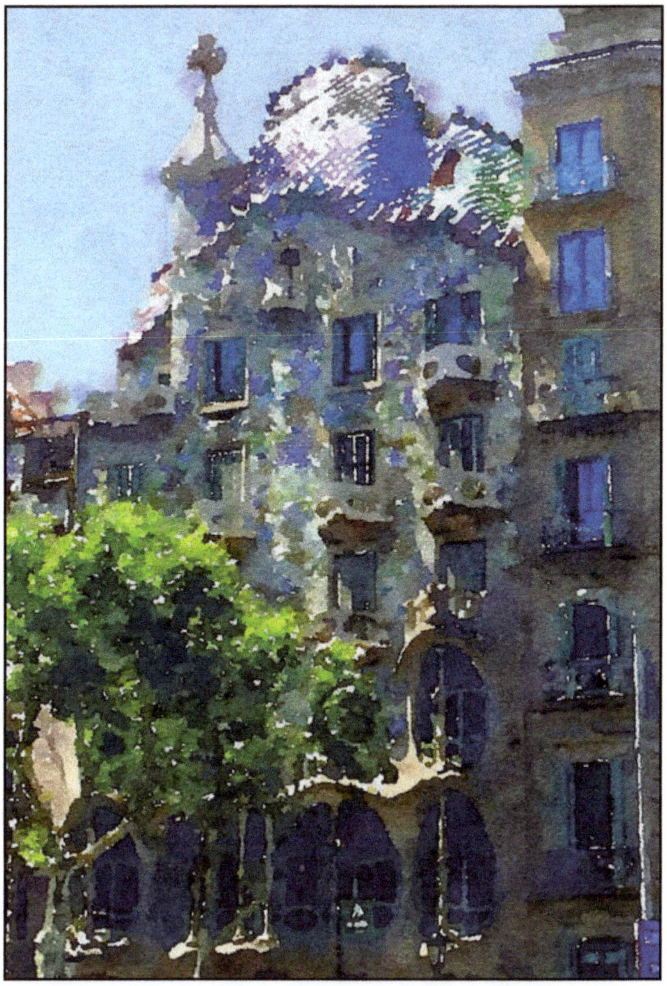

'Apartments Gaudi' (2016), Barcelona, Spain [EES(BA)1602].▲

'The Yacht Harbour' (2018), Alicante, Spain [EES(AL)1802].▼

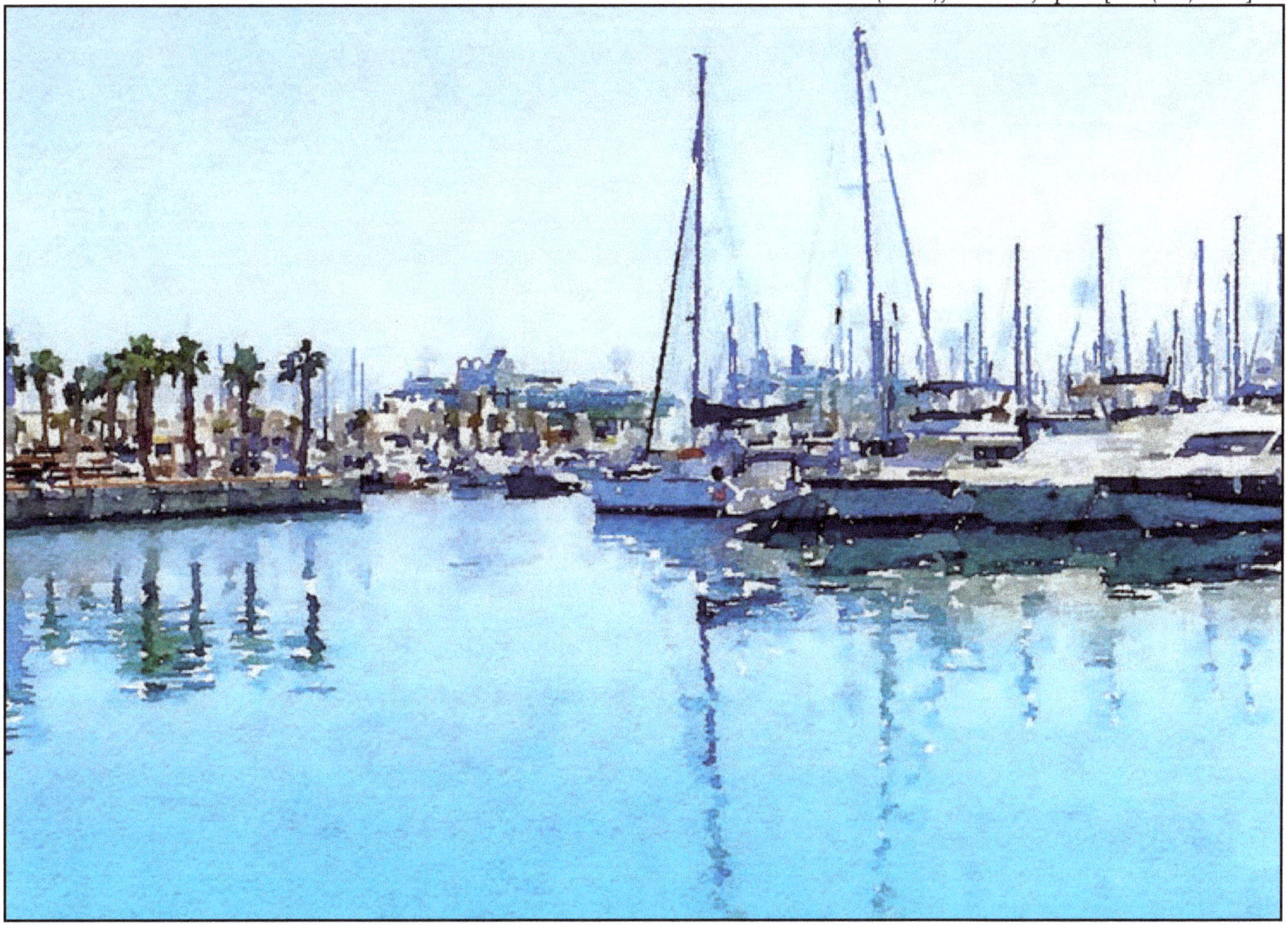

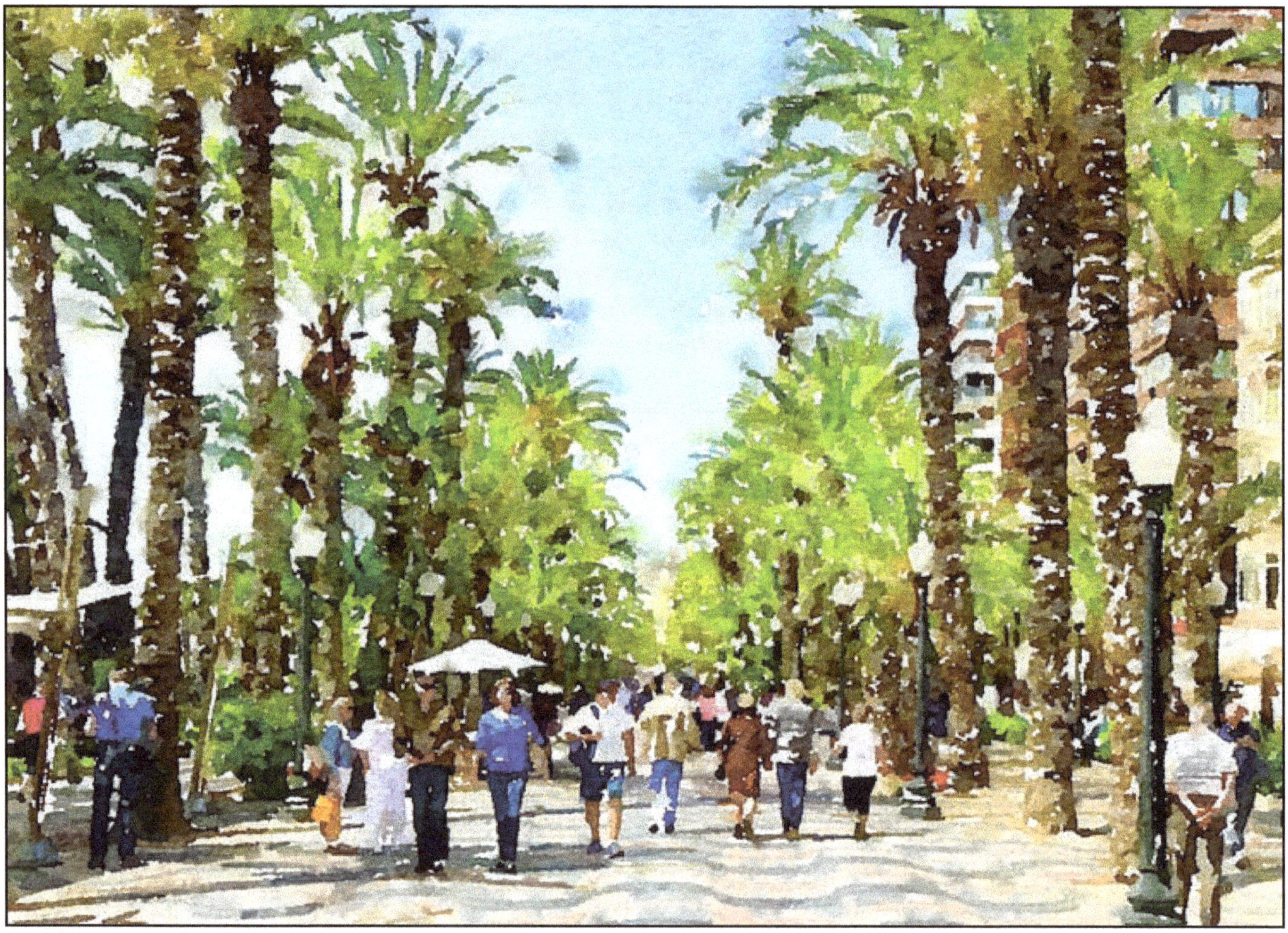

▲'Palm Promenade' (2018), Alicante, Spain [EES(AL)1801].

'The Basilica' (2016), Cadiz, Spain [EES(CA)1601].▼

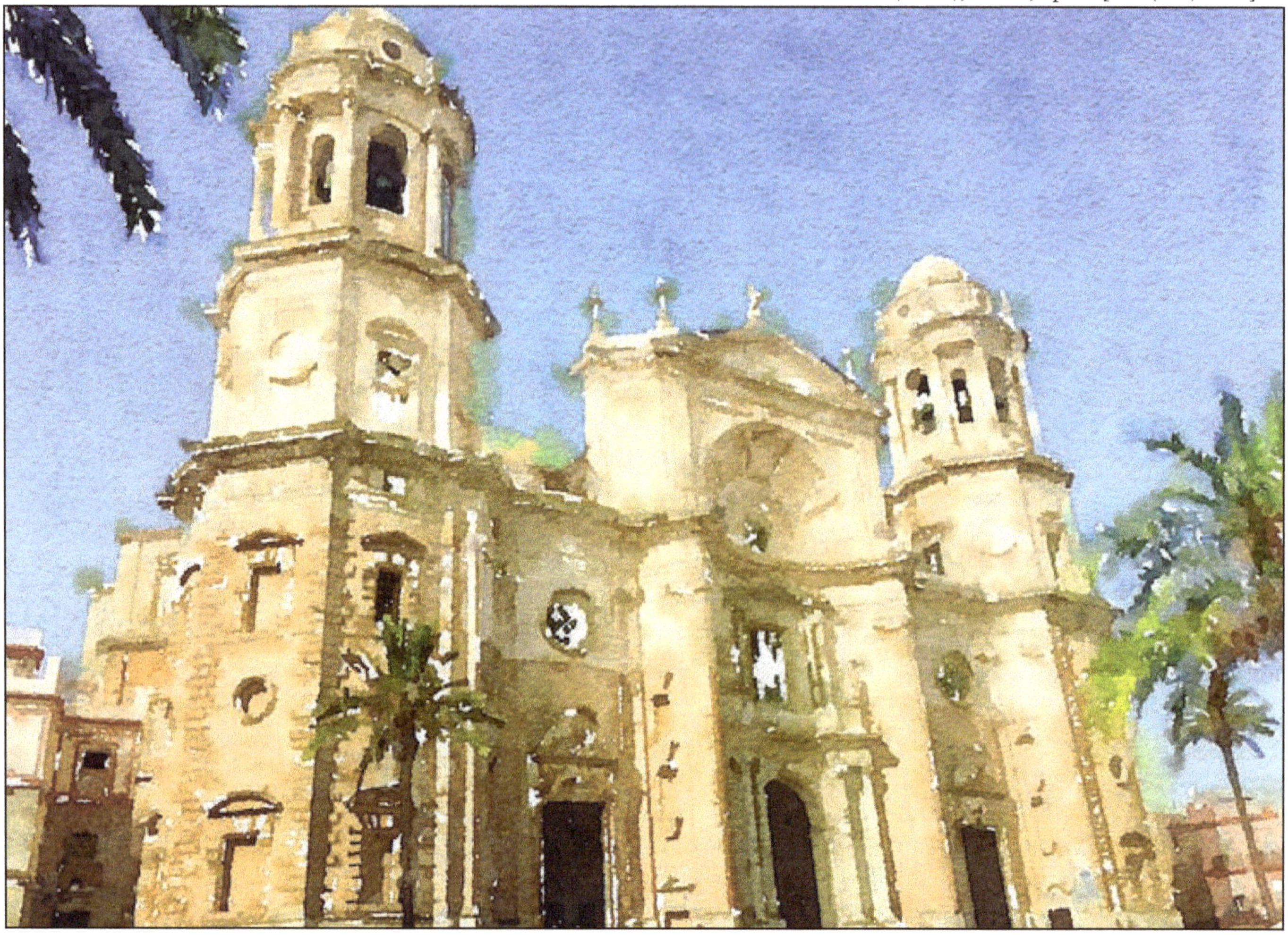

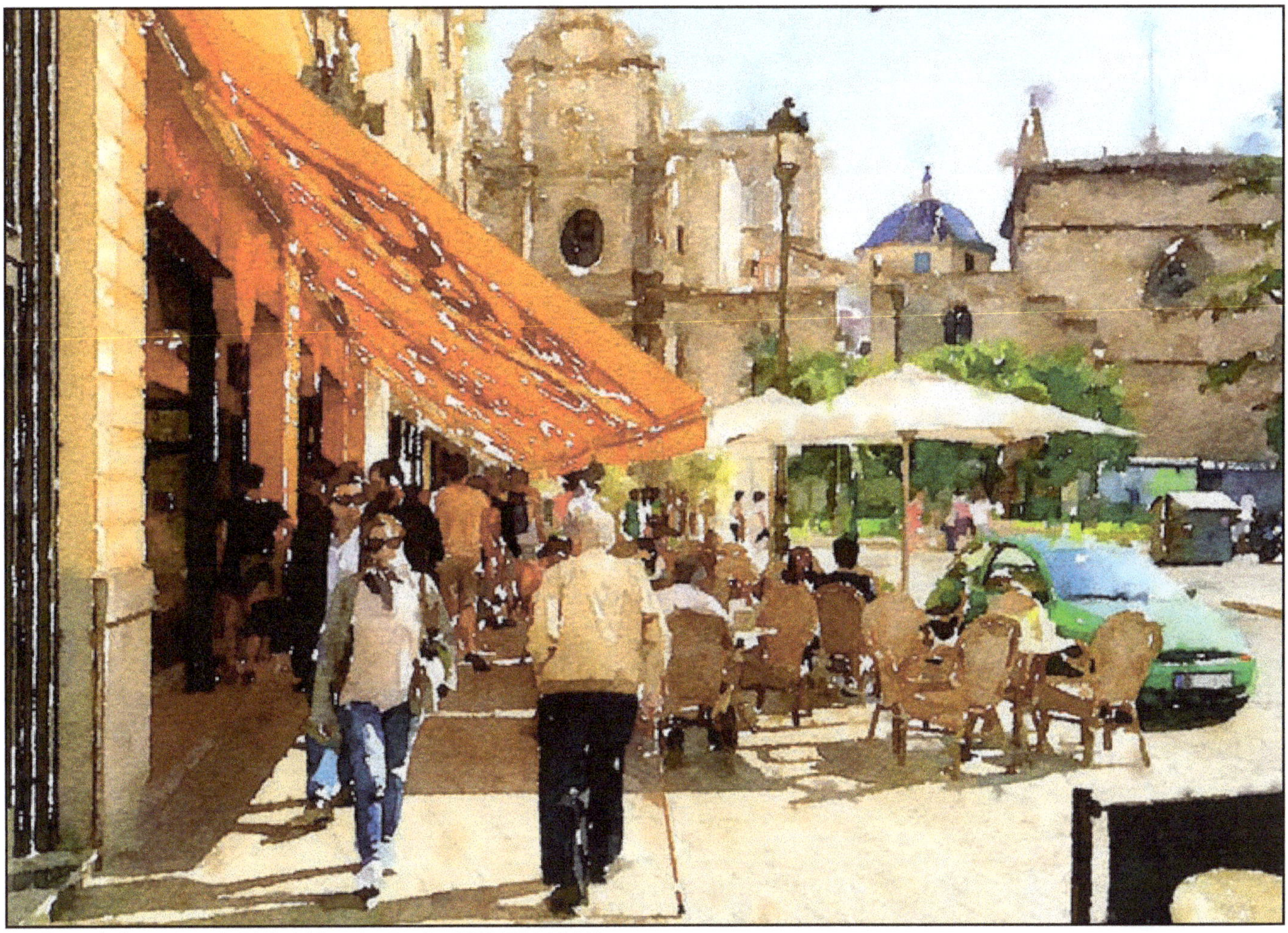

▲'Placa de la Reina' (2018), Valencia, Spain [EES(VA)1801].

'Santa Cruz, La Palma' (2018), Canary Islands, Spain [EES(CI)1801].▼

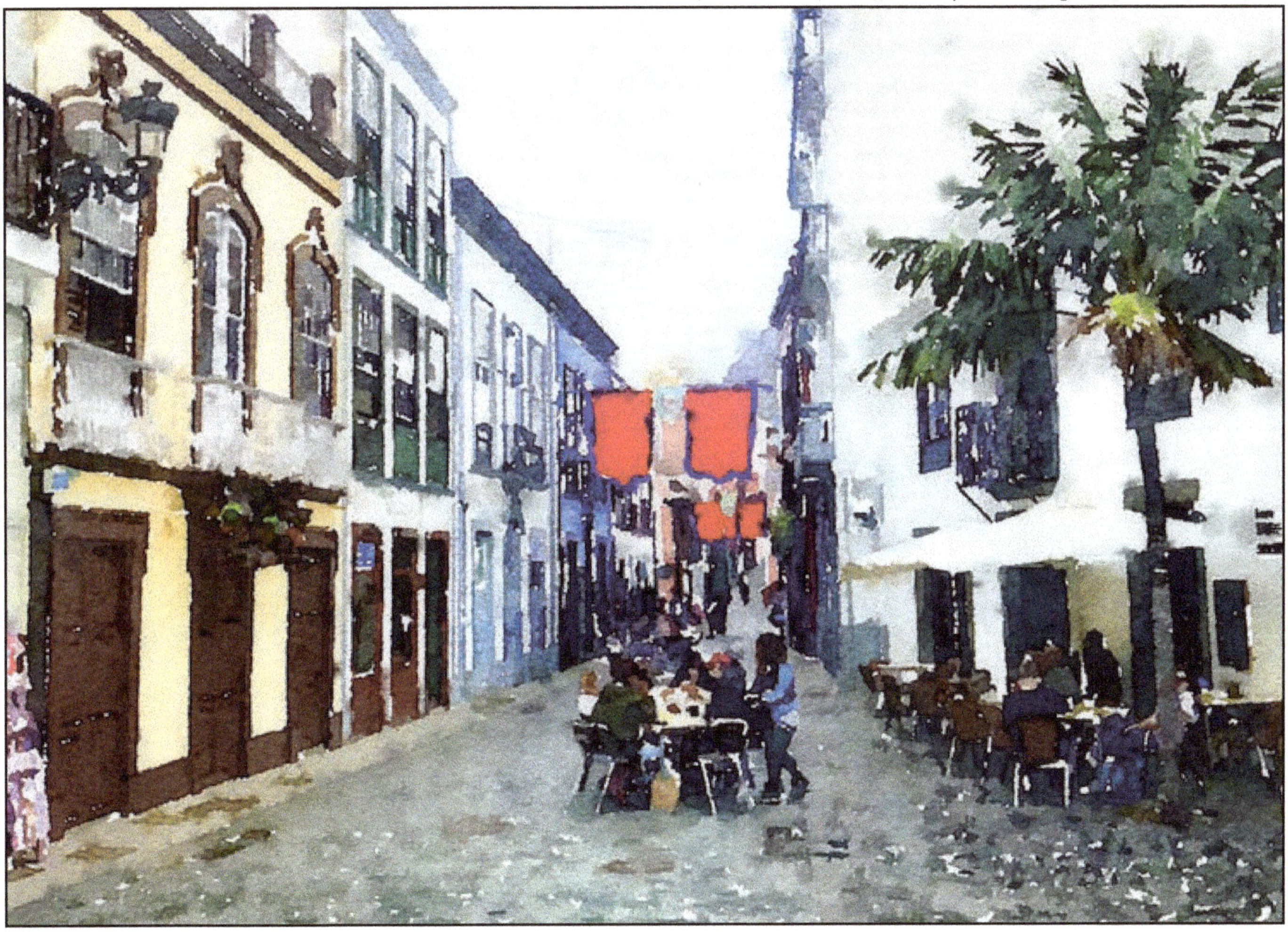

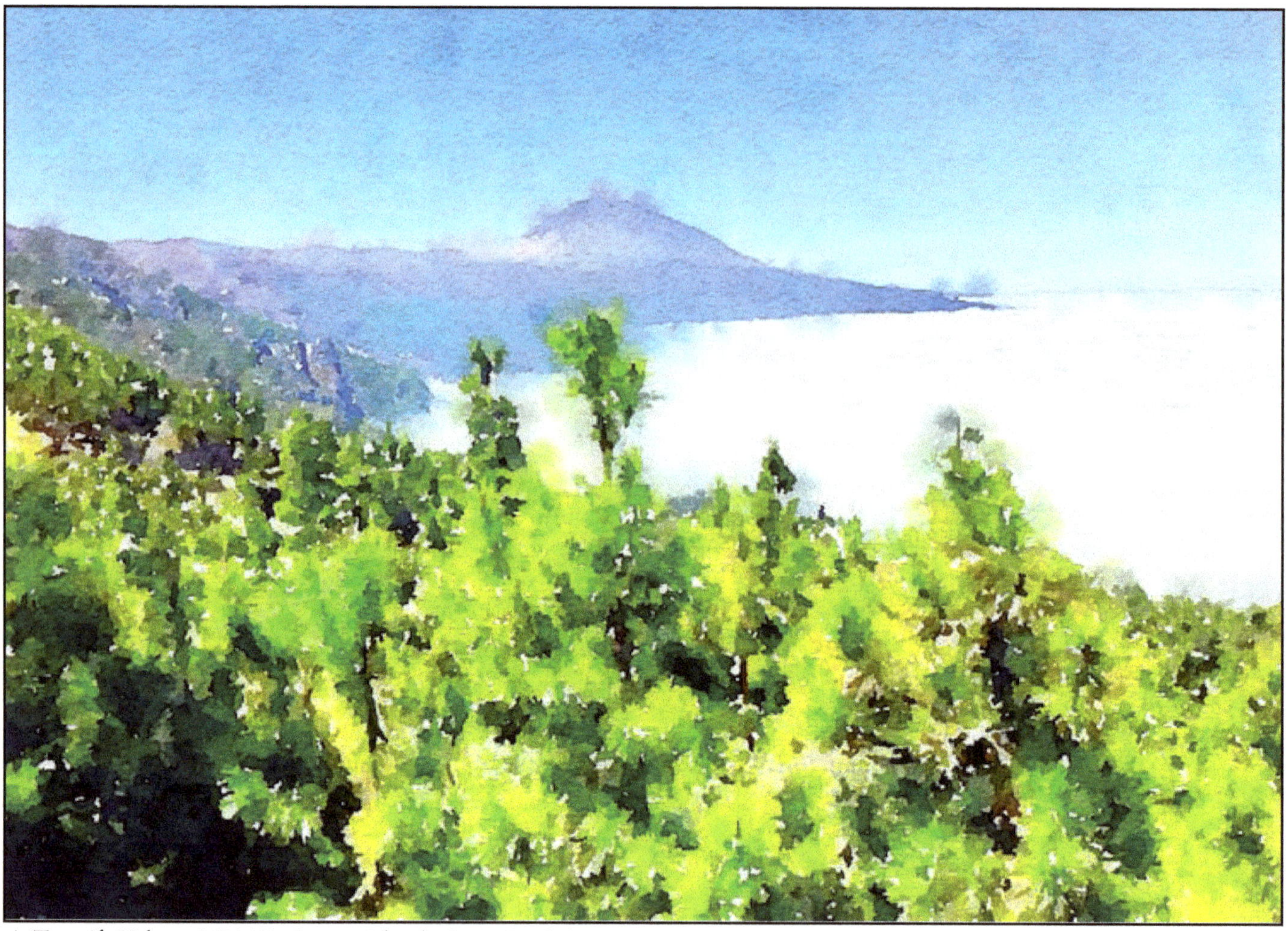

▲'Tenerife Volcano' (2018), Canary Islands, Spain [EES(CI)1802].

'Las Palmas, Gran Canaria' (2018), Canary Islands, Spain [EES(CI)1803].▼

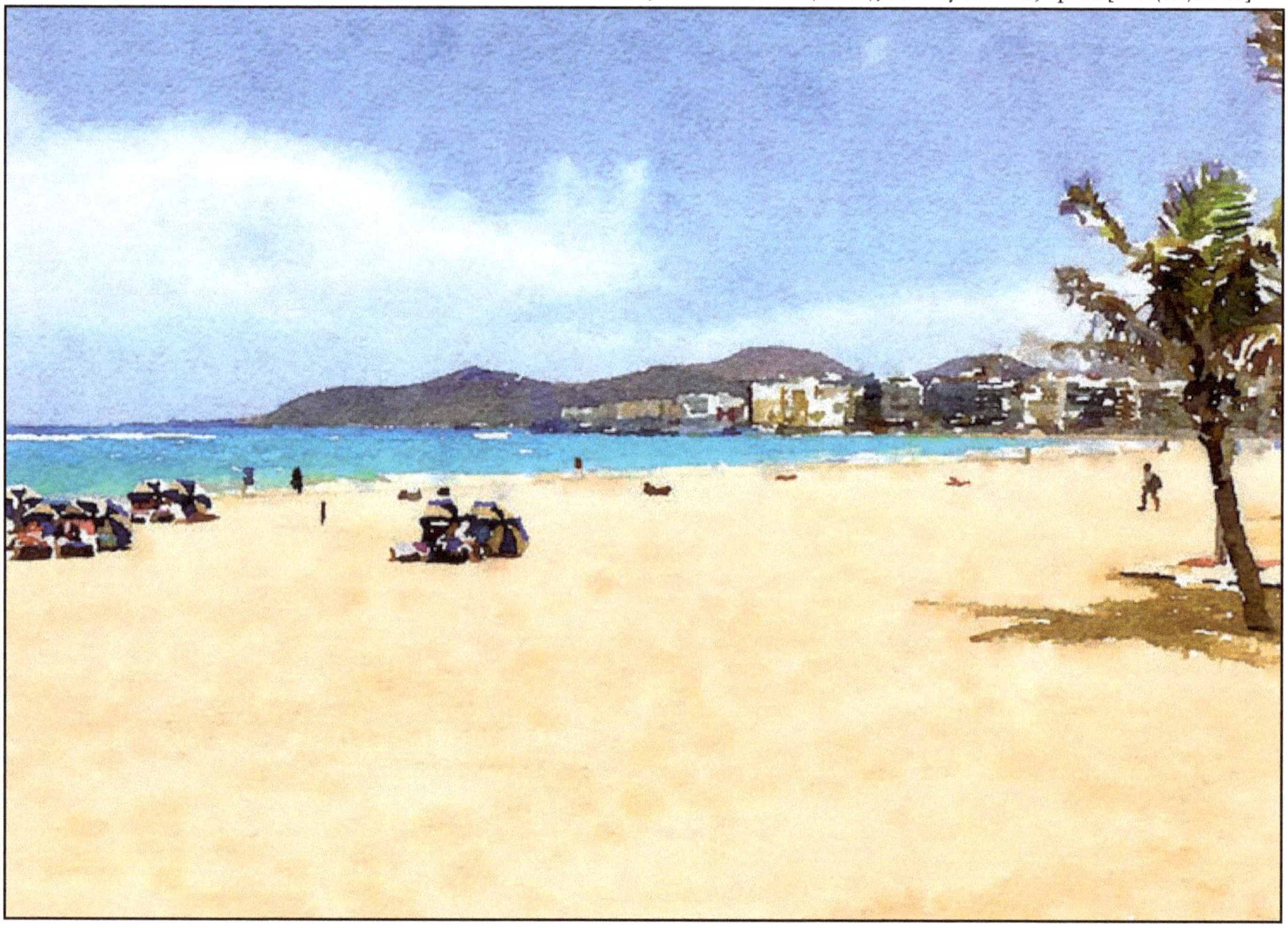

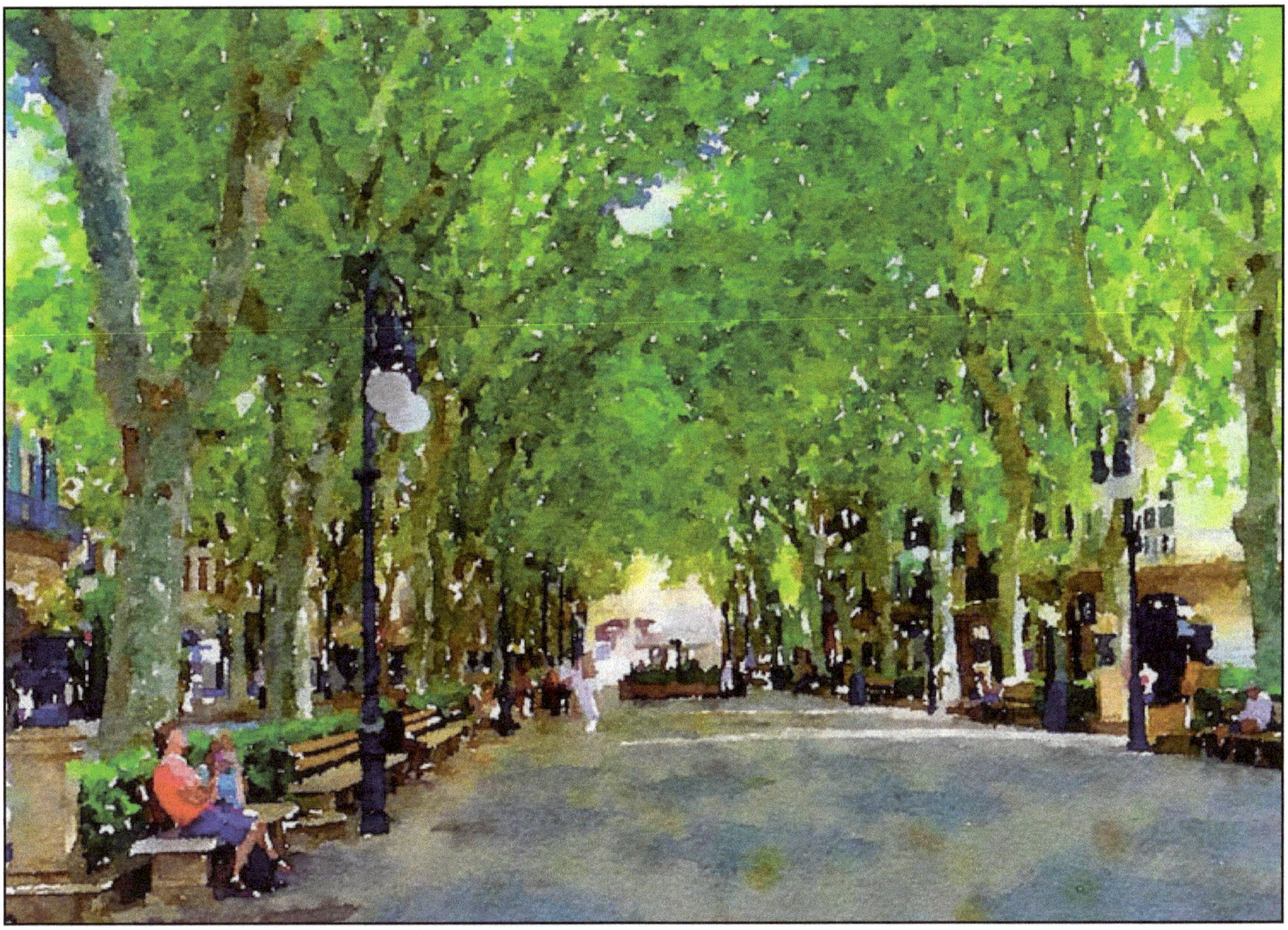

▲'Palma Boulevard' (2016), Majorca, Spain [EES(MA)1601].

'Platja de Muro' (2016), Majorca, Spain [EES(MA)1602].▼

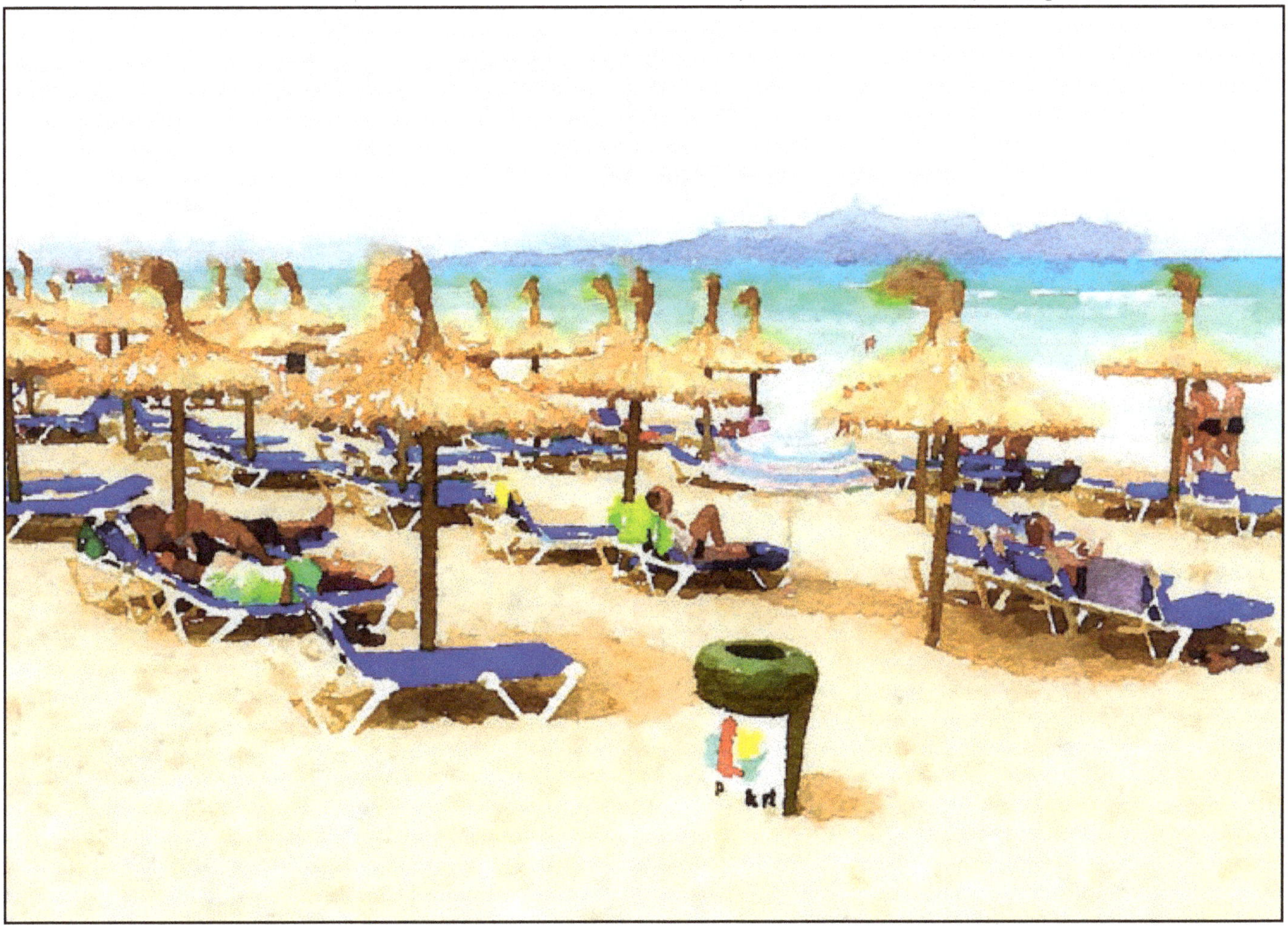

Switzerland...

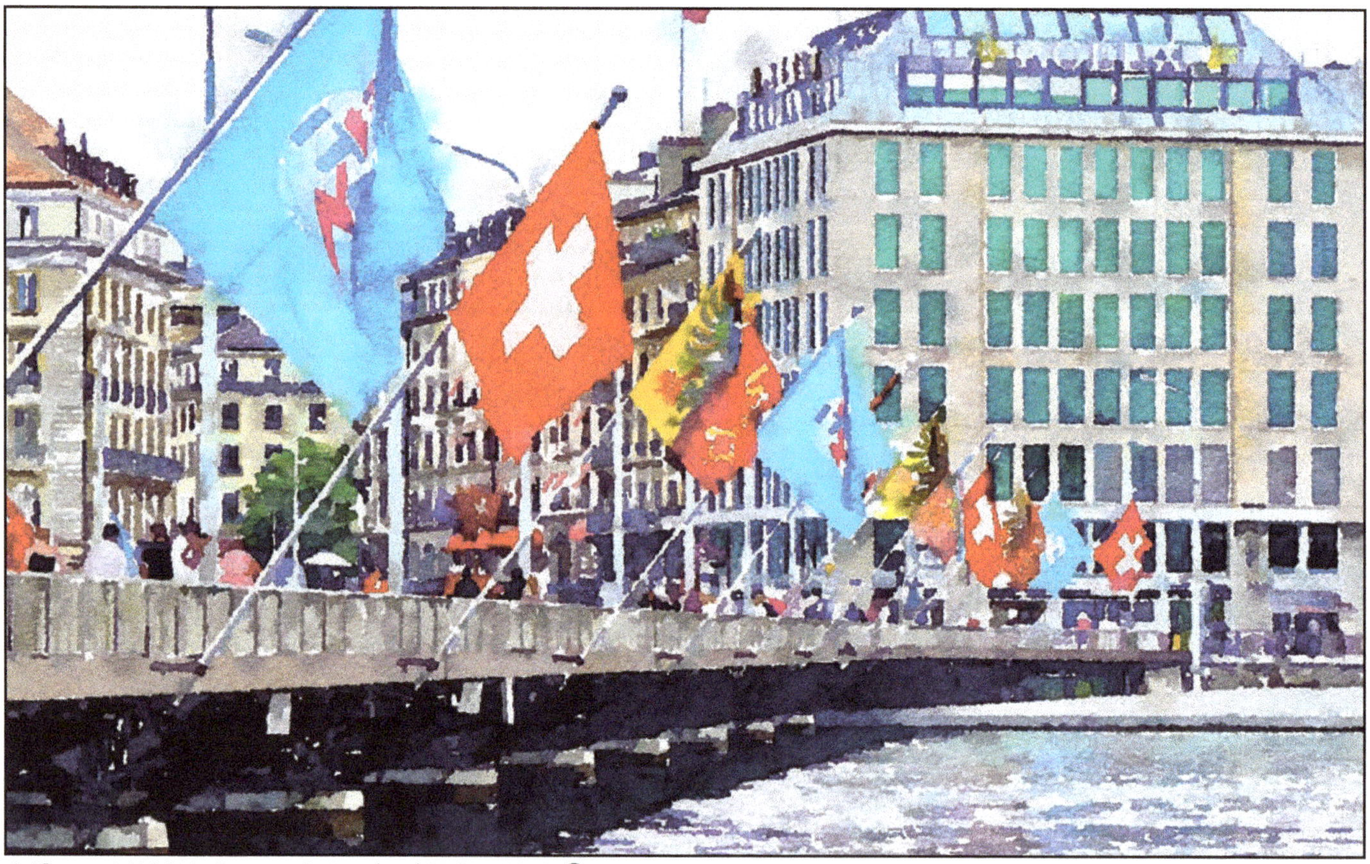

▲'Geneva' (2019), Geneva, Switzerland [ECH1901]. ⊘

'The Gardens At Lugano' (2008), Lugano, Switzerland [ECH0801].▼

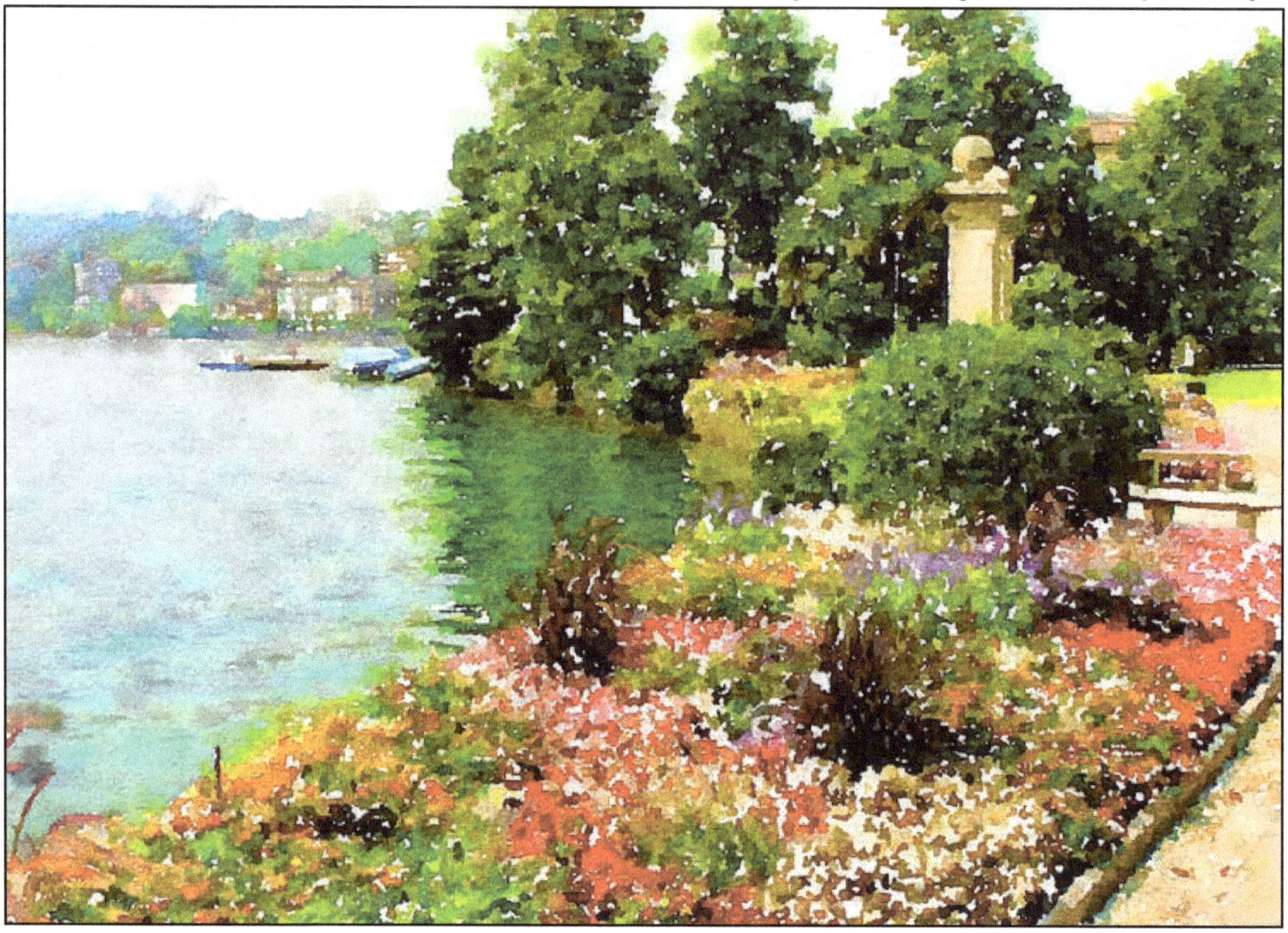

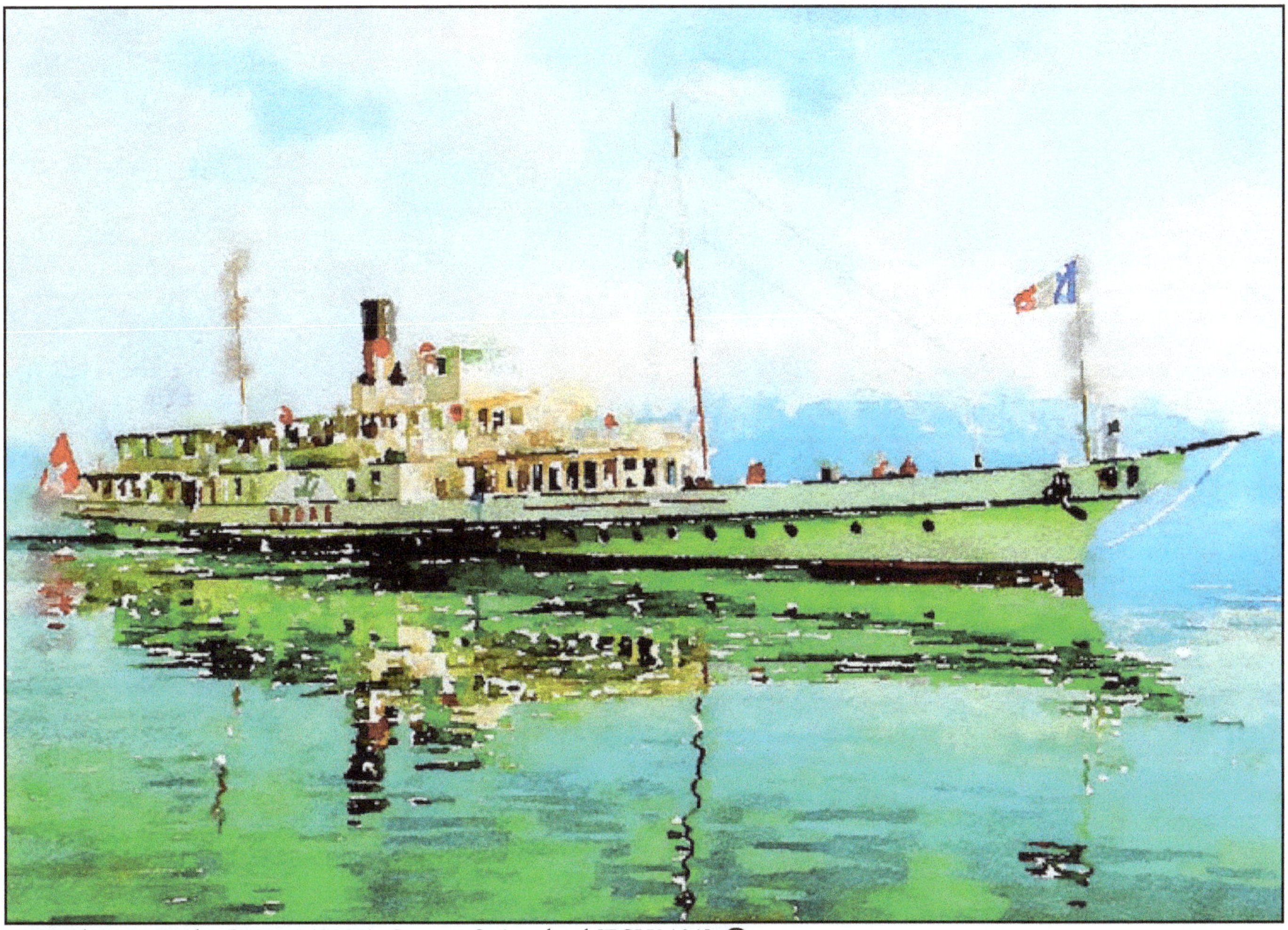

▲'SS Rhone on Lake Geneva' (2021), Geneva, Switzerland [ECH2101]. ⊘

'Lake Geneva' (2021), Geneva, Switzerland [ECH2102]. ⊘▼

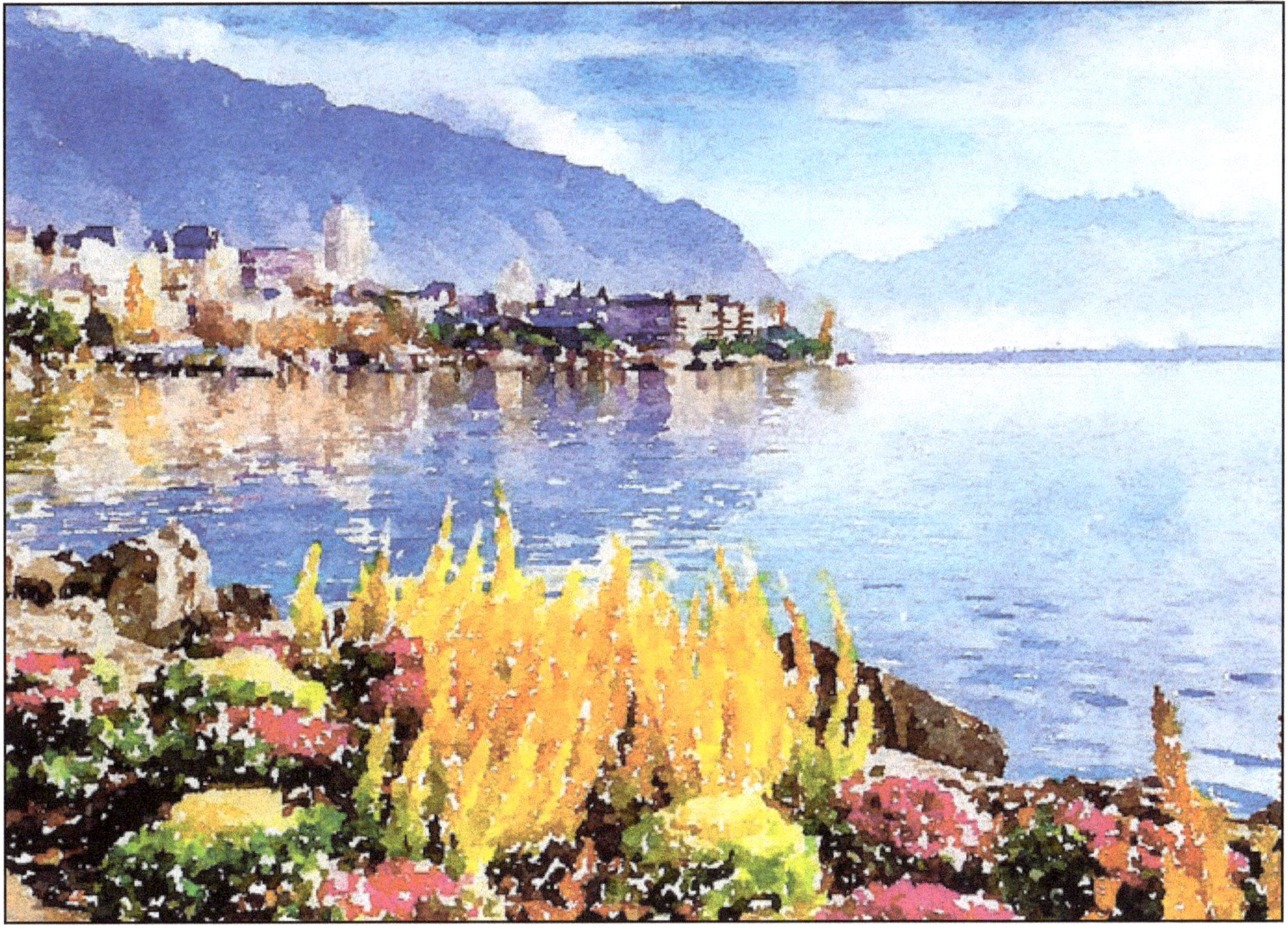

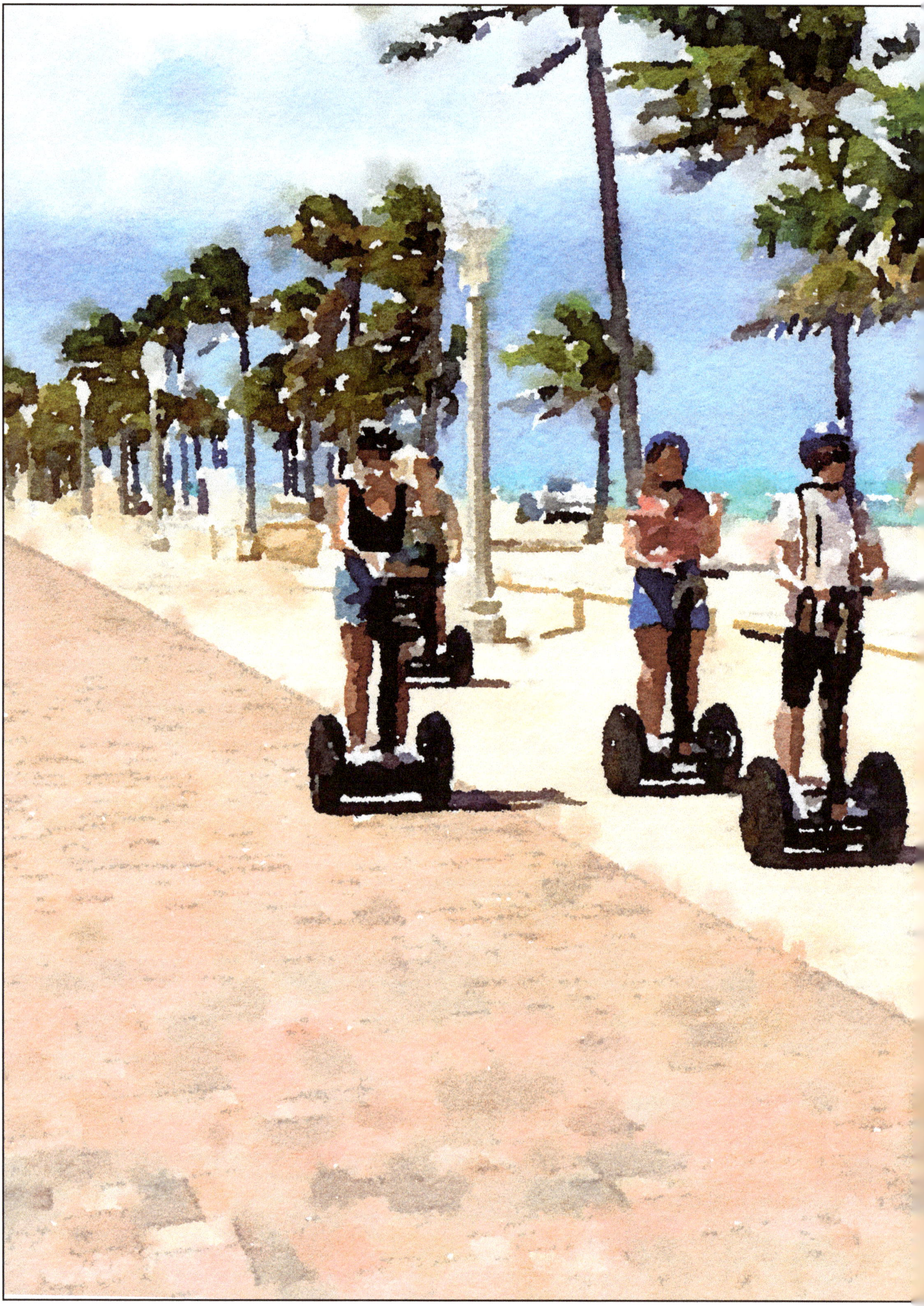

NTH AMERICA

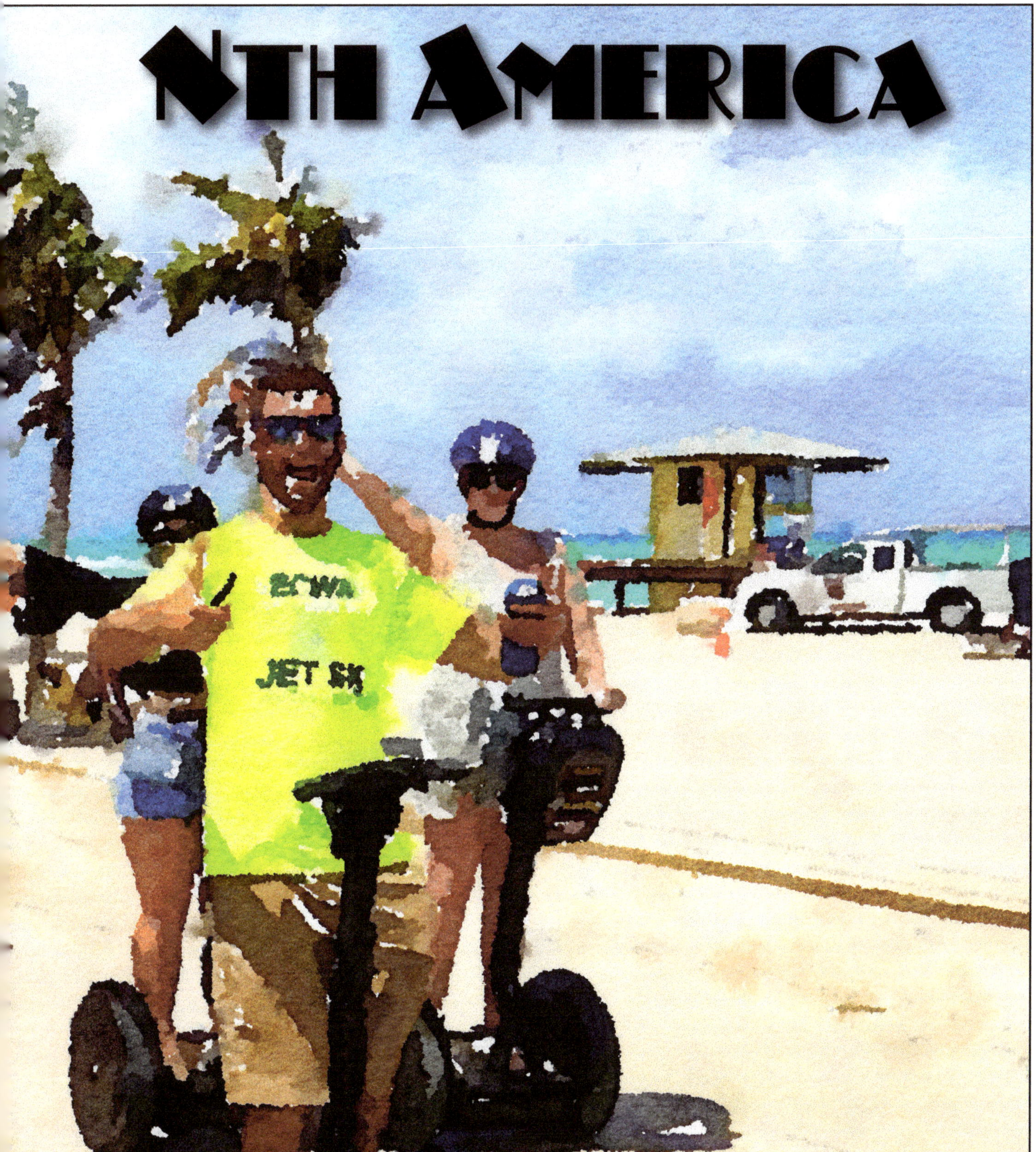

'Florida Fun' (2018), Fort Lauderdale Beach, Florida [NUS)FL)1802].

Canada...

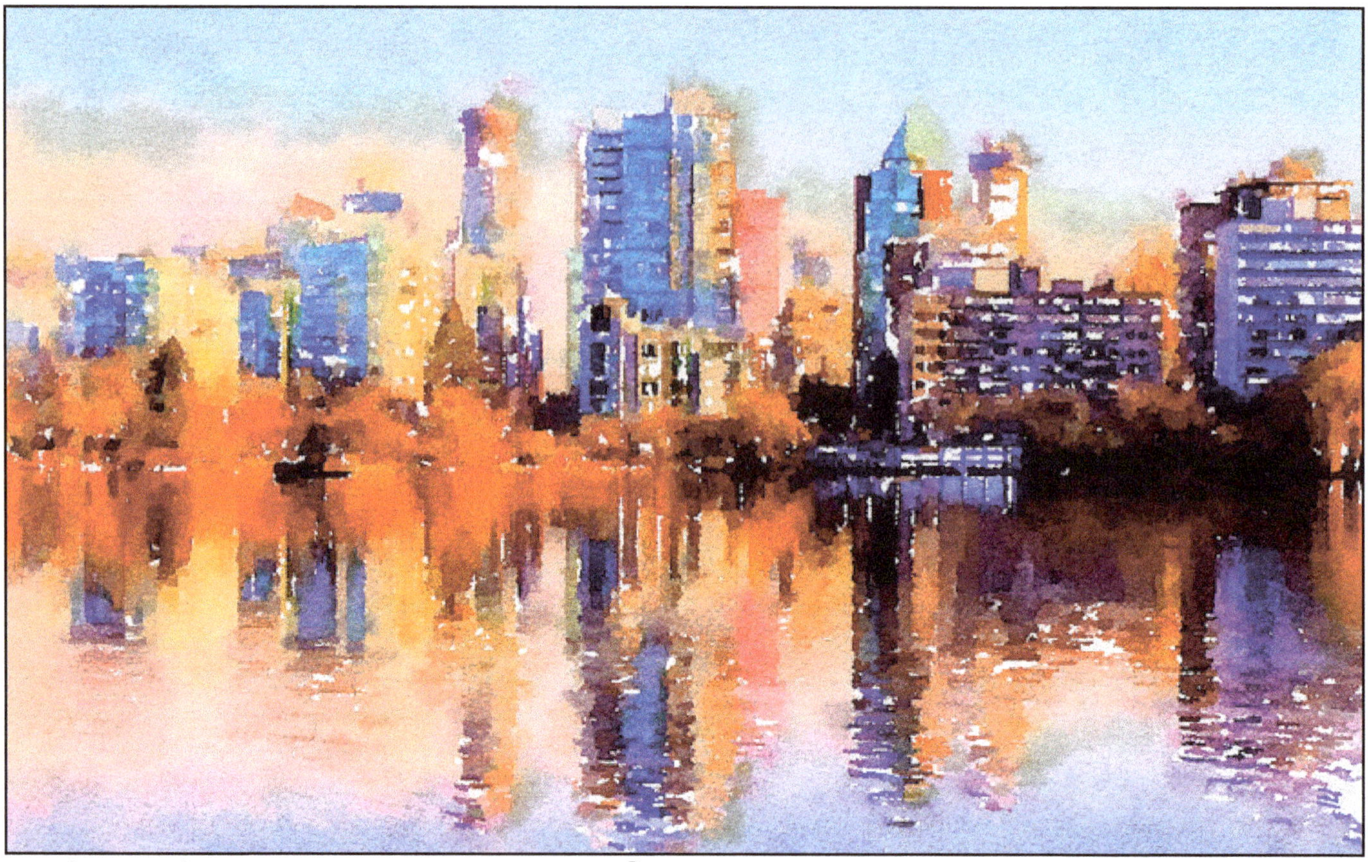

▲'Reflections Of Vancouver' (2021), Canada [NCA2102]. ©

'Parliament' (2015), Ottawa, Canada [NCA1501].▼

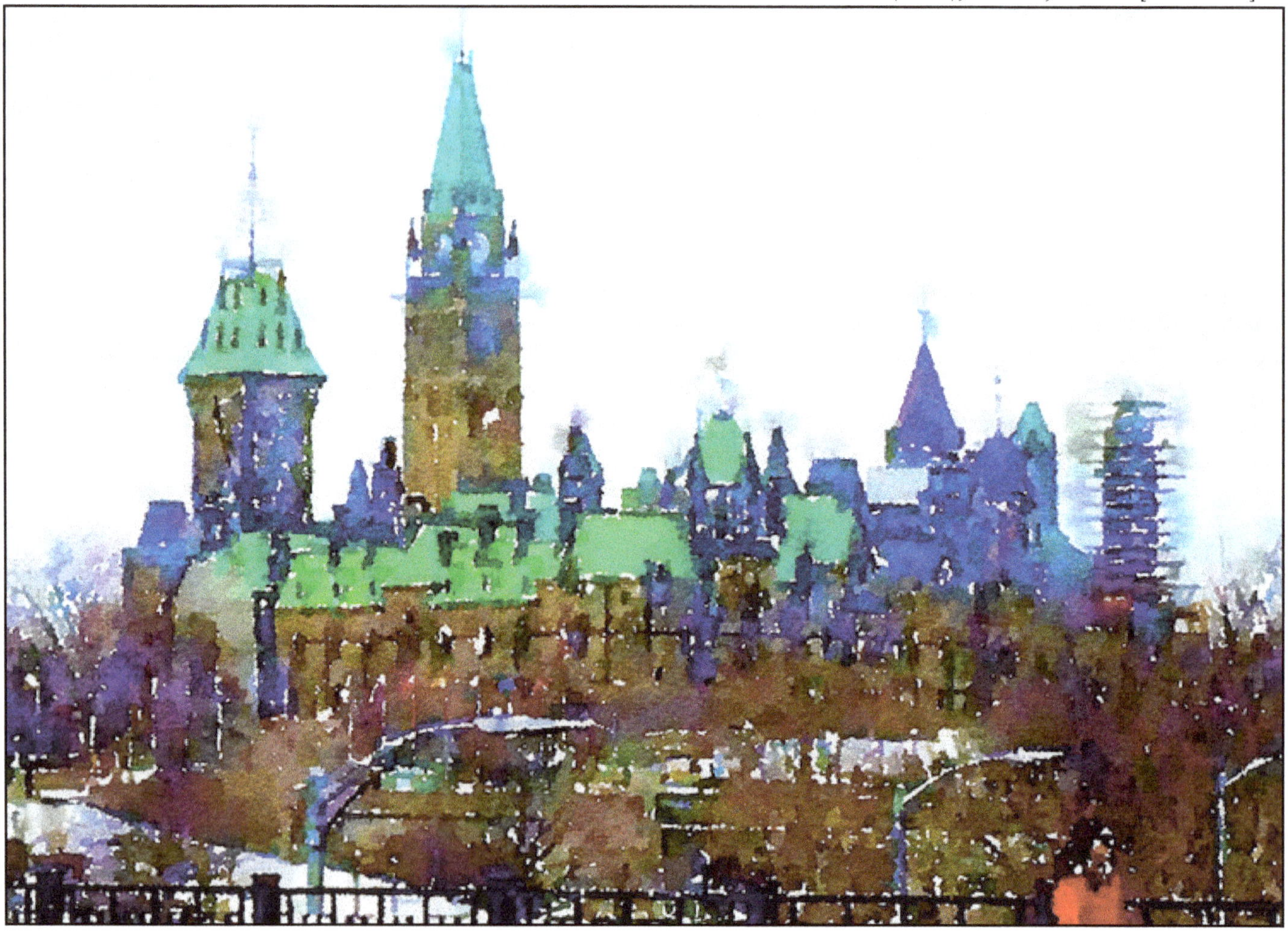

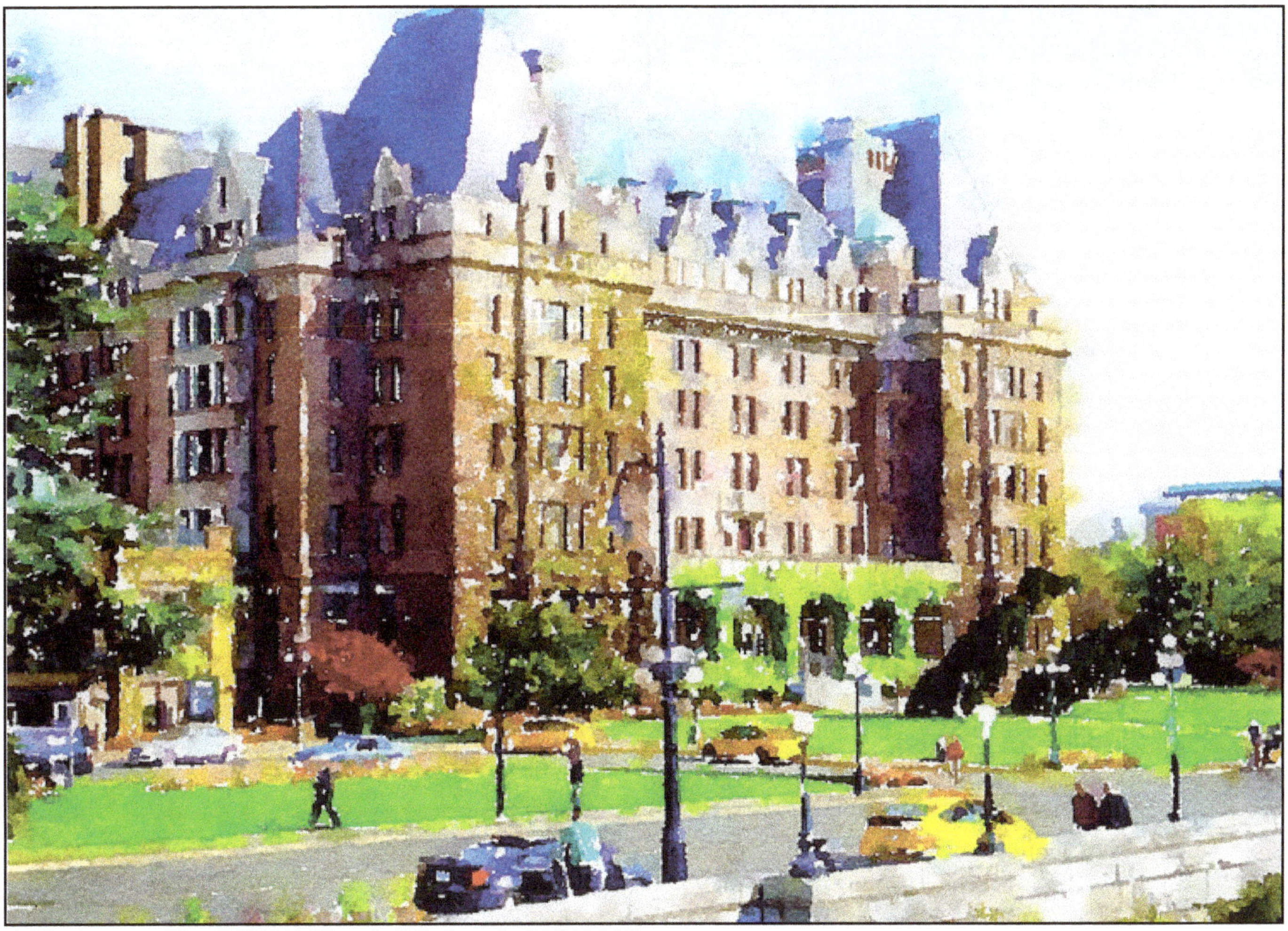

▲'The Empress Hotel' (2021), Victoria BC, Canada [NCA2103].

'Dawn Over Parliament' (2021), Ottawa, Canada [NCA2101]. ⓔ ▼

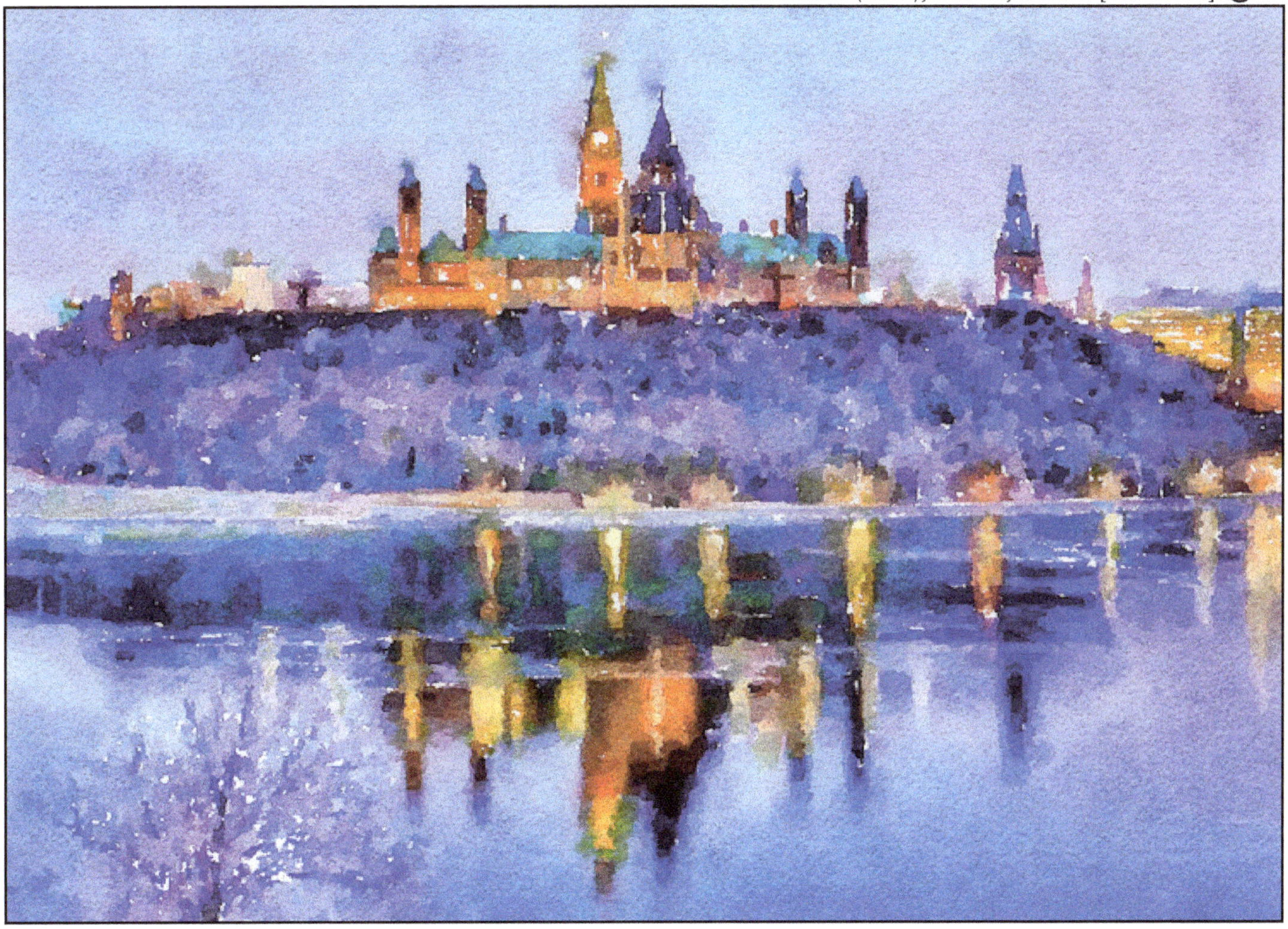

Puerto Rico...

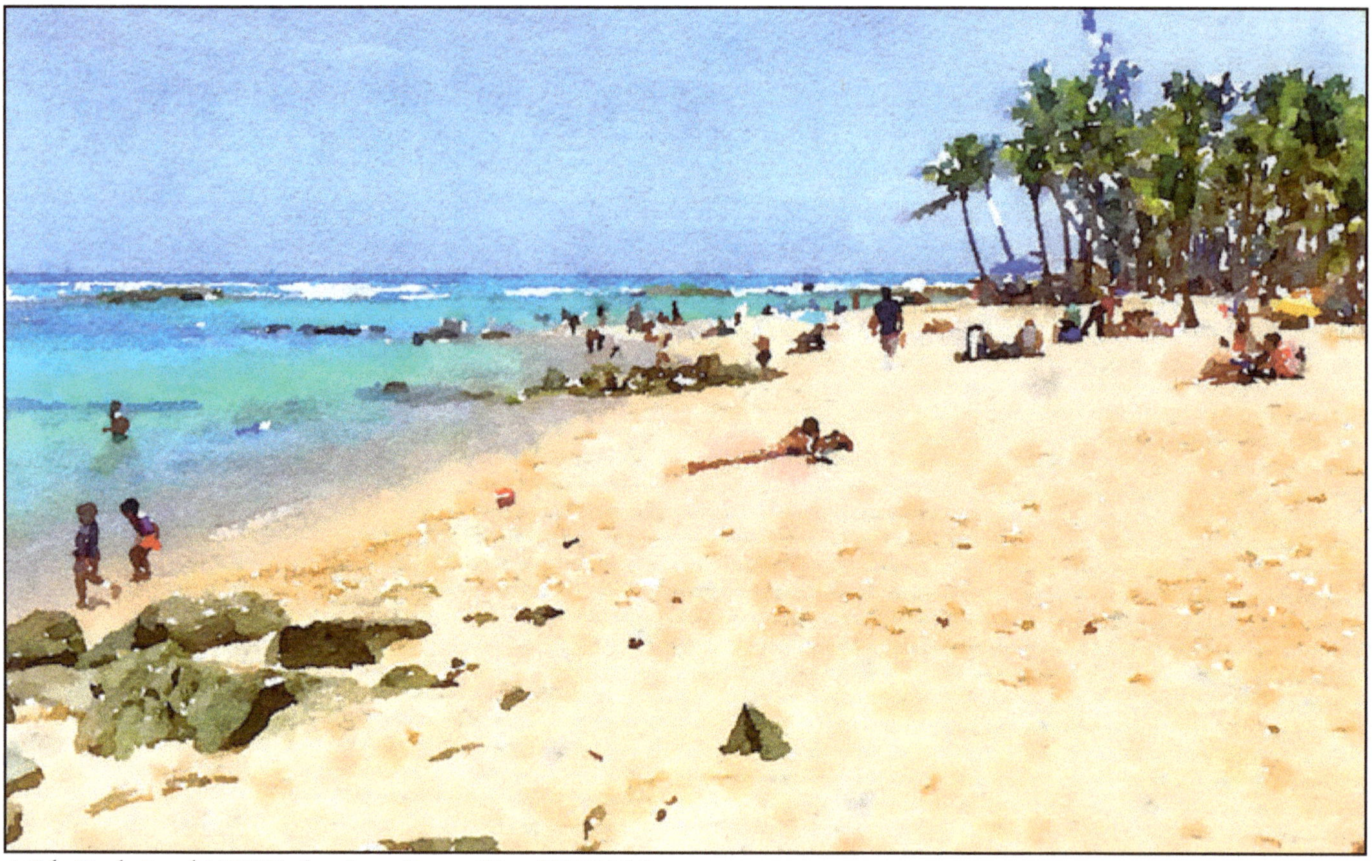

▲'Isle Verde Beach' (2018), San Juan, Puerto Rico [NPR1804].

'San Juan Summer' (2018), Puerto Rico [NPR1801].▼

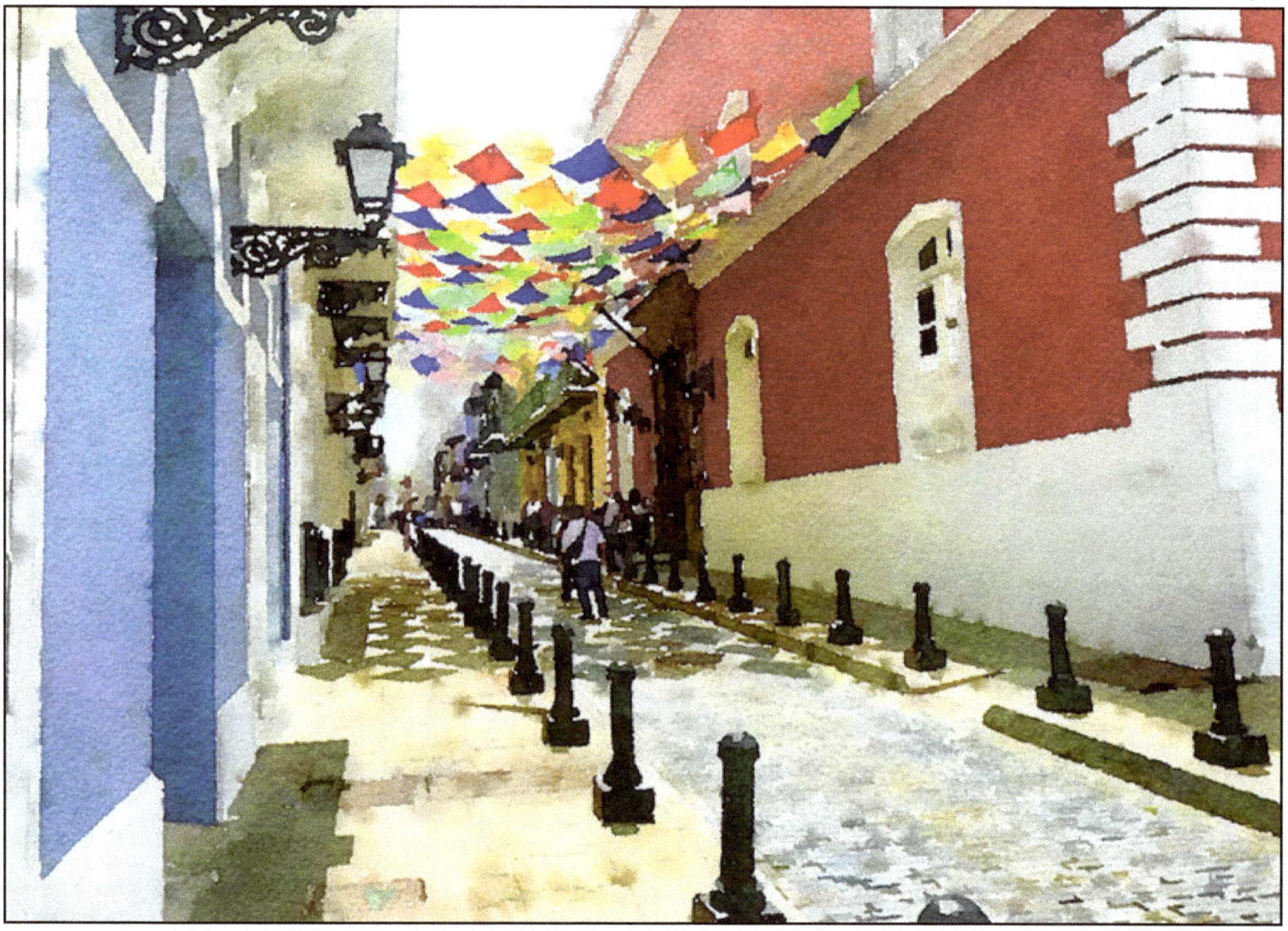

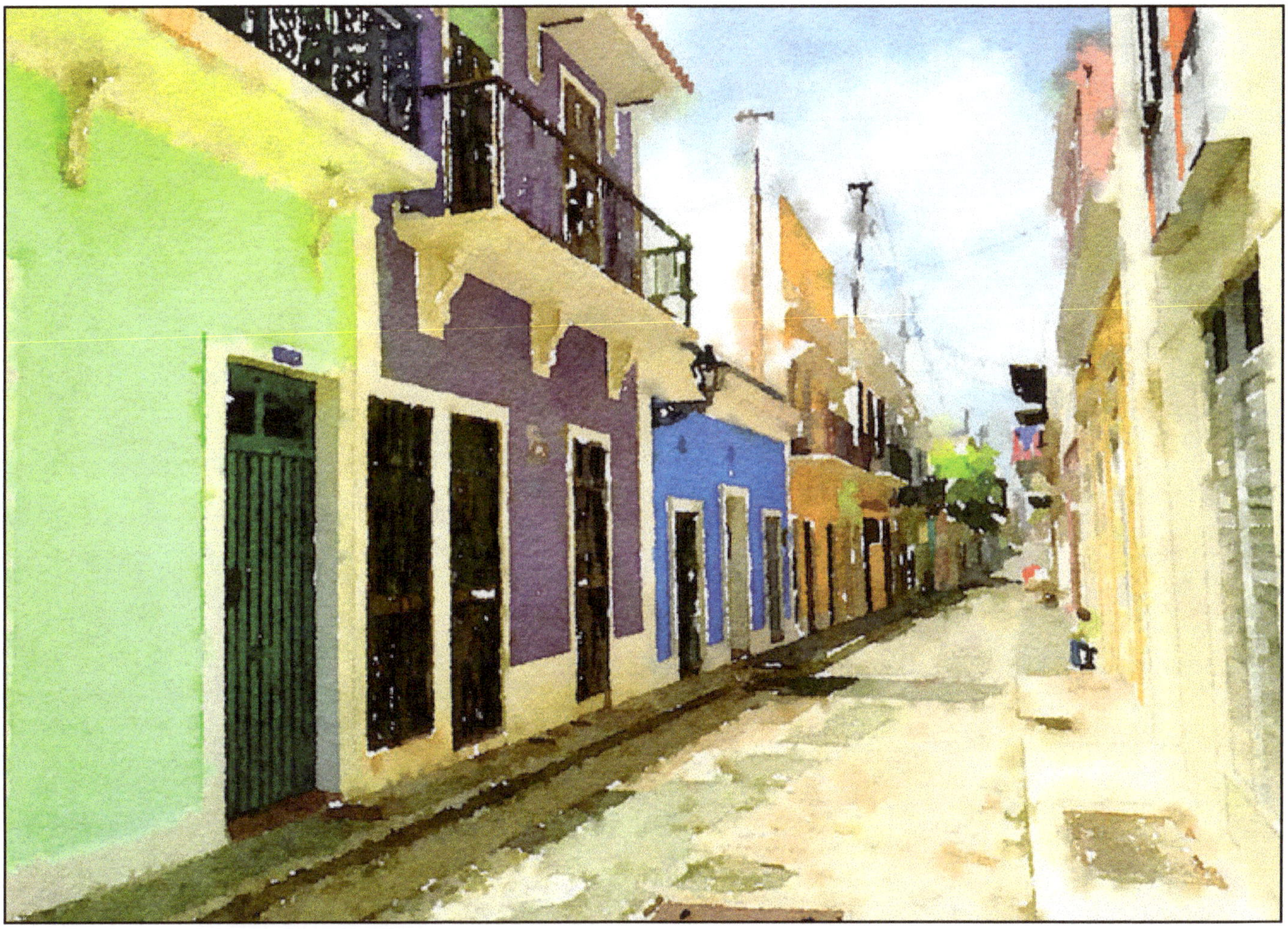

▲'Calle de la Cruz' (2018), San Juan, Puerto Rico [NPR1803].

'San Juan Nights' (2018), Puerto Rico [NPR1802].▼

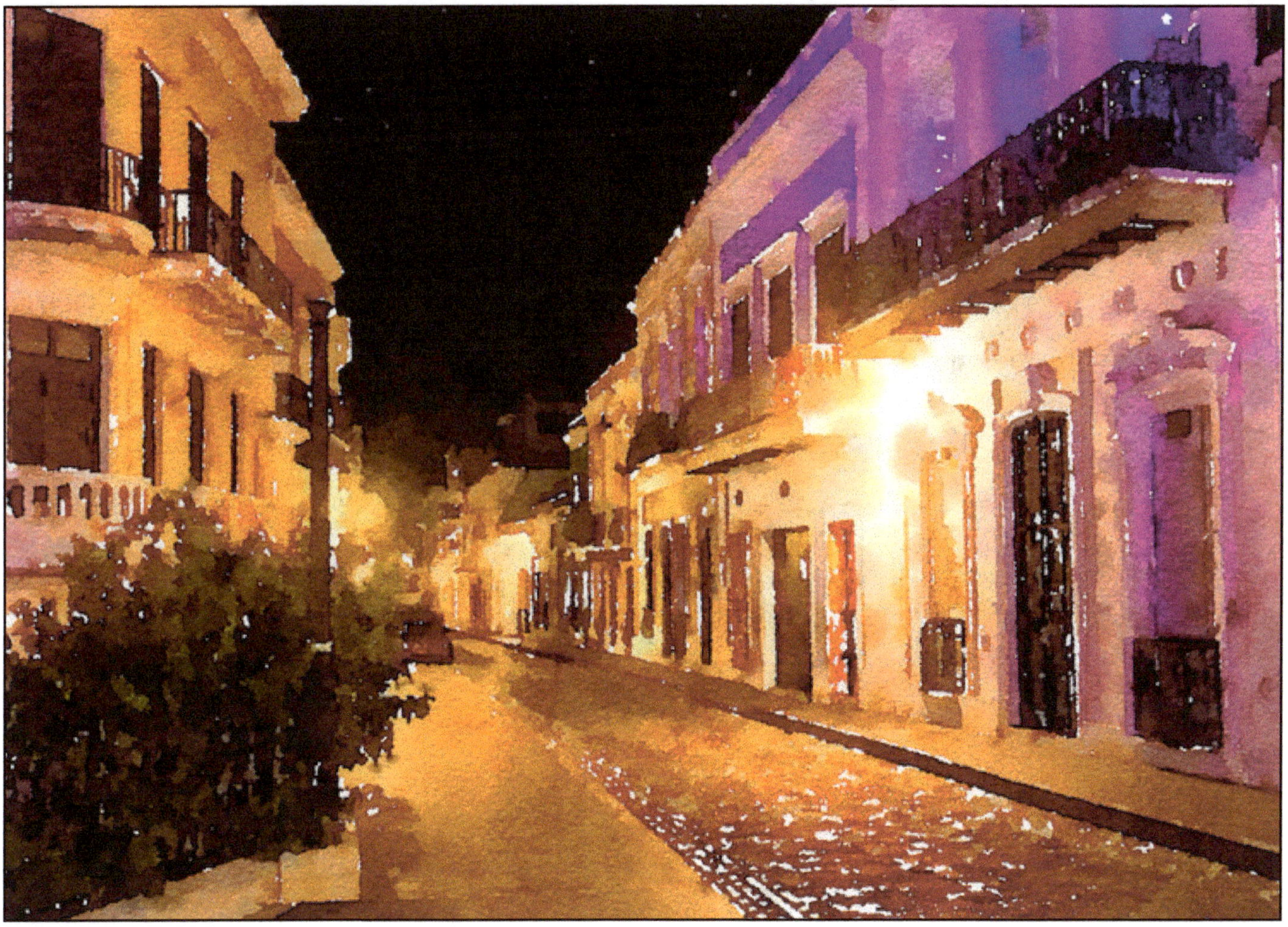

United States...

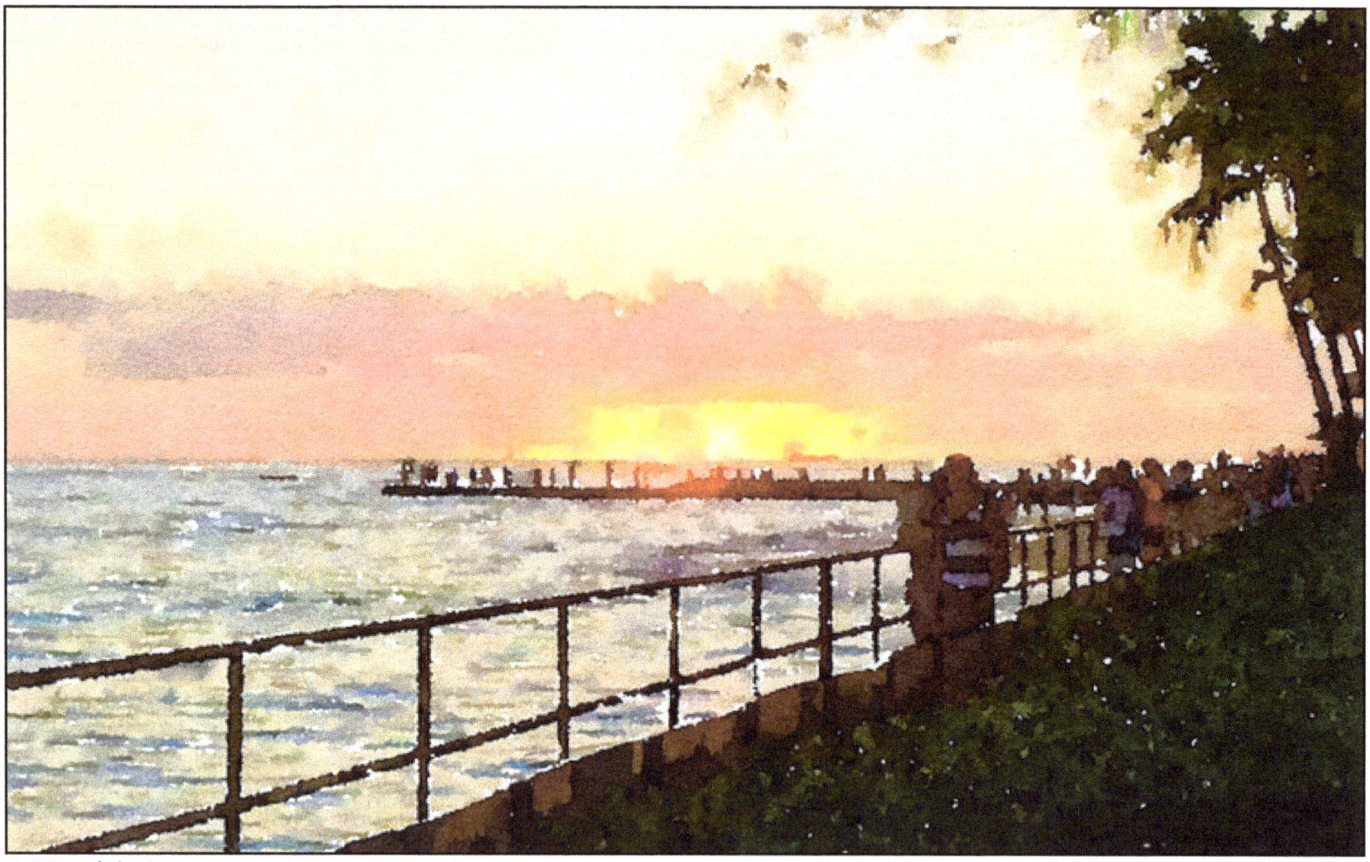

▲'Honolulu Sunset' (2014), Hawaii [NUS(HA)1401].

'Hawaii Sands' (2014), Honolulu, Hawaii [NUS(HA)1402].▼

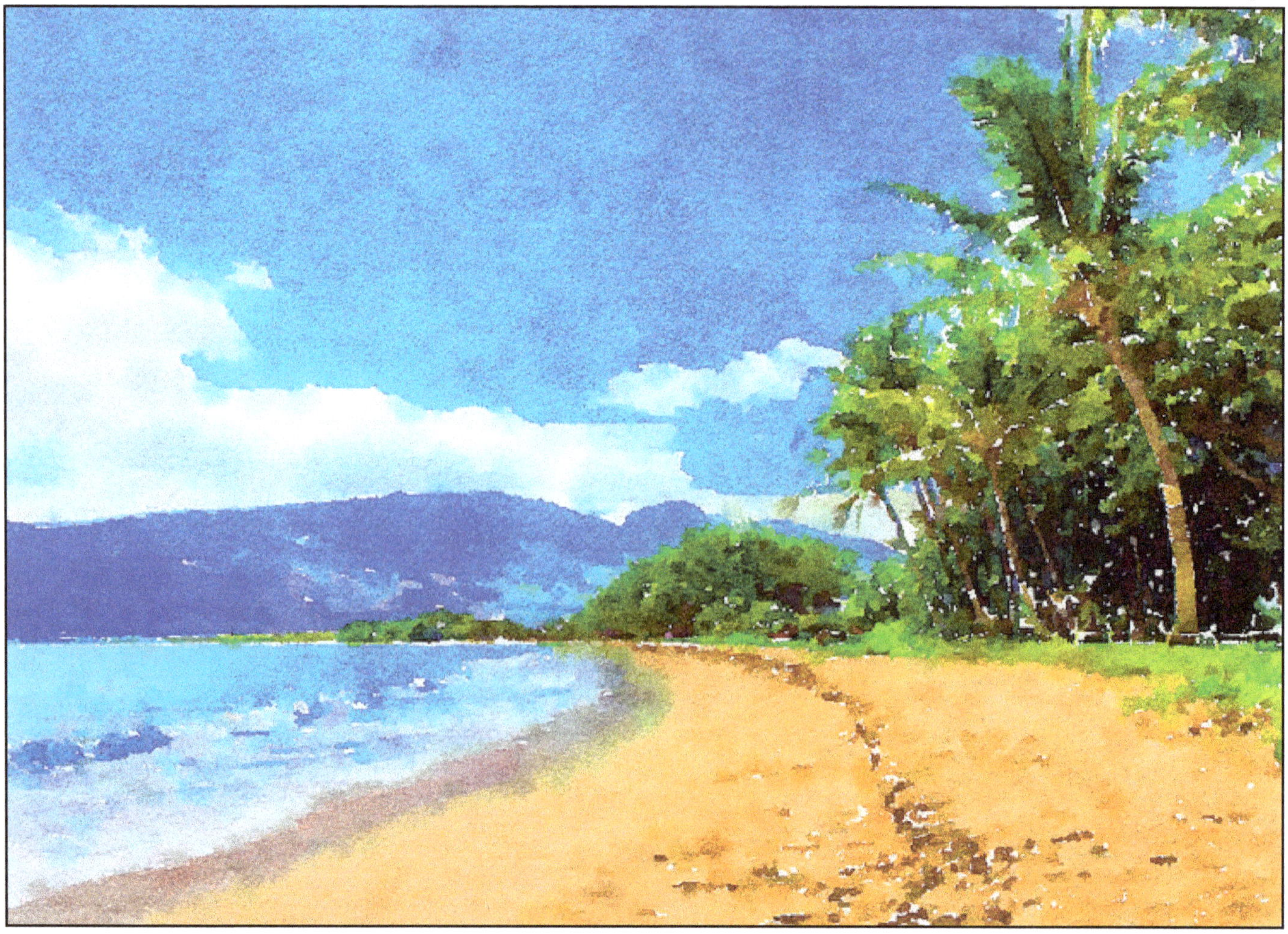

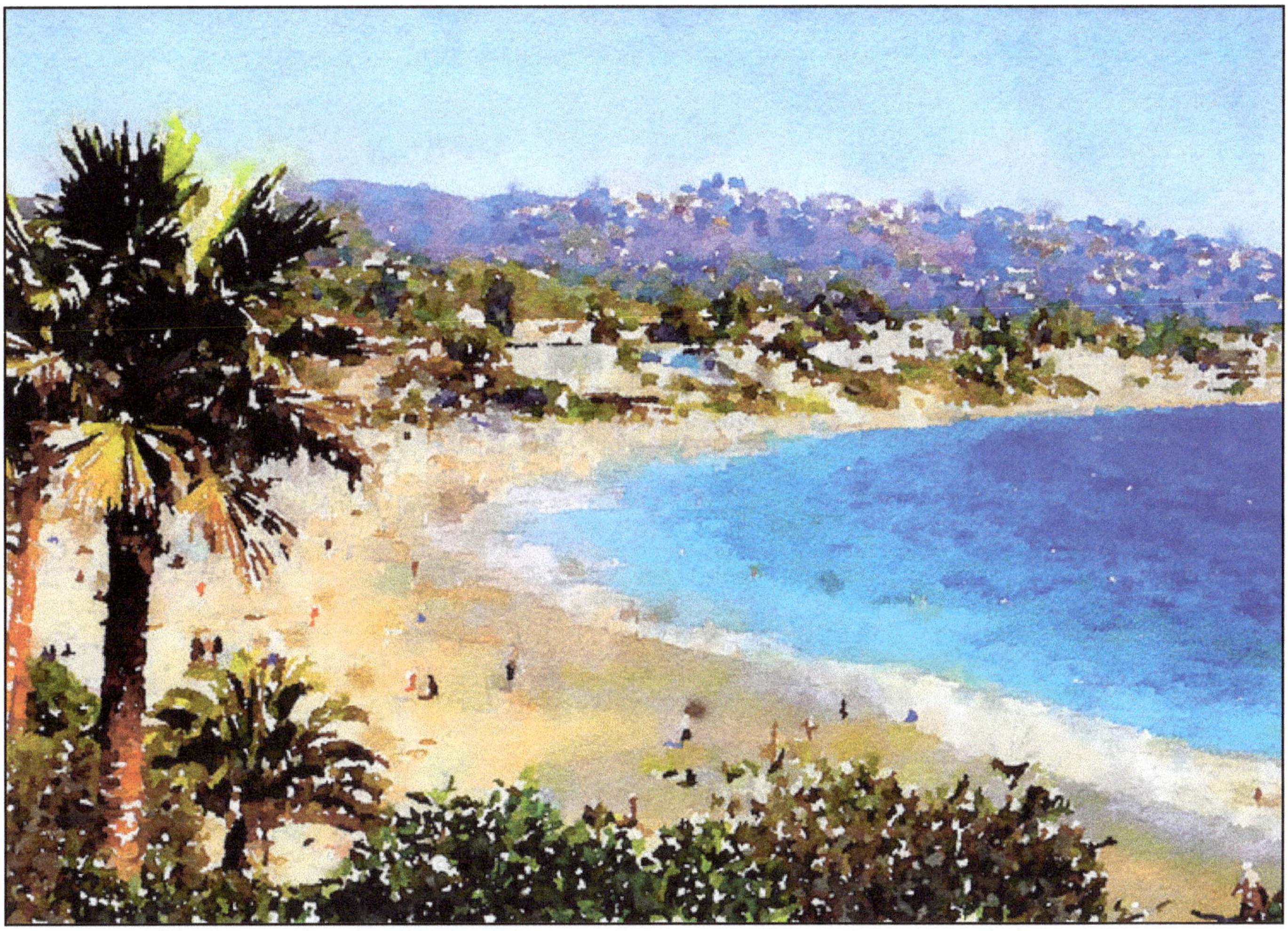

▲'Laguna Beach' (2015), California [NUS(CF)1502].

'Laguna Beach & Bay' (2015), California [NUS(CF)1501].▼

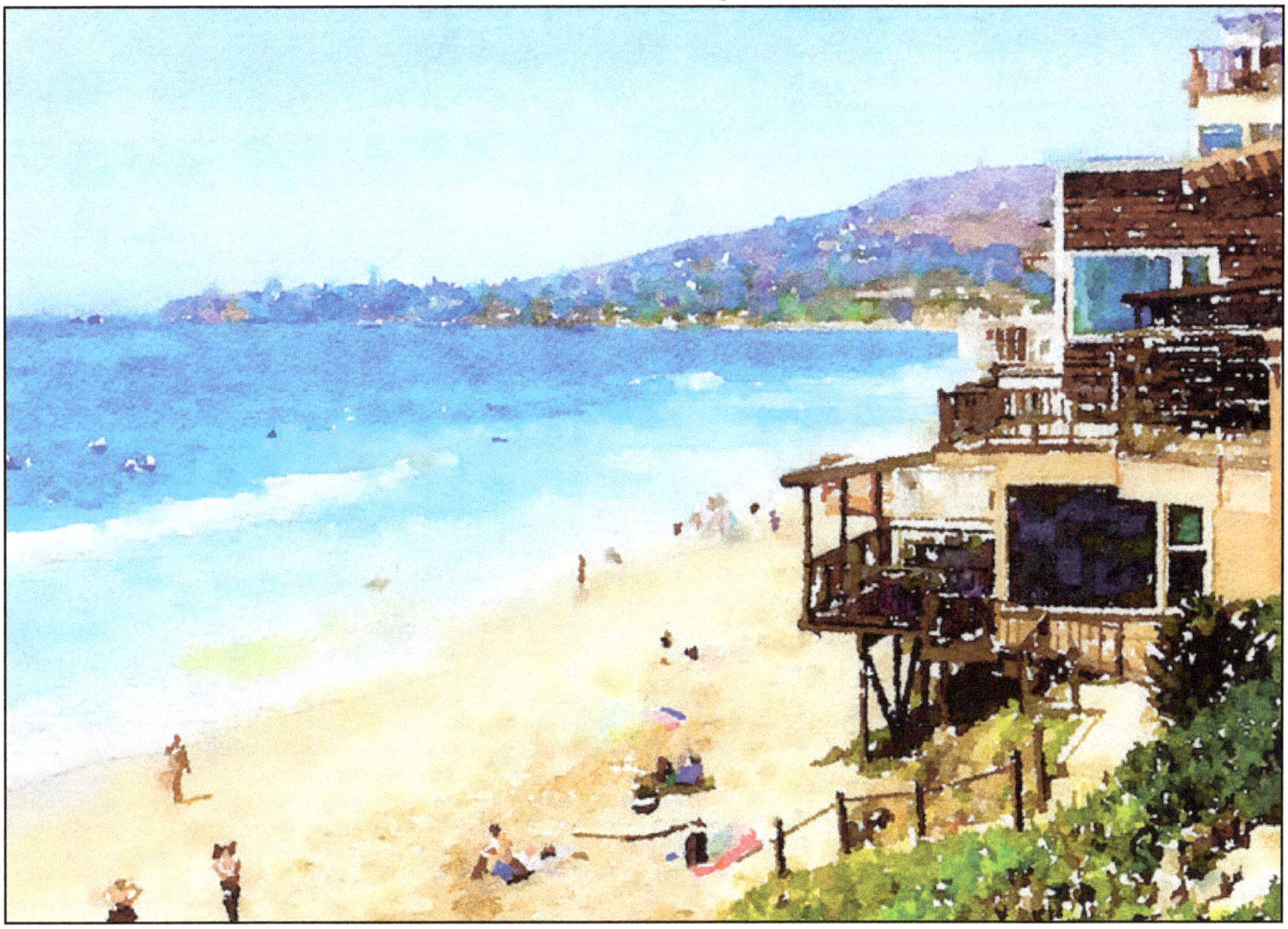

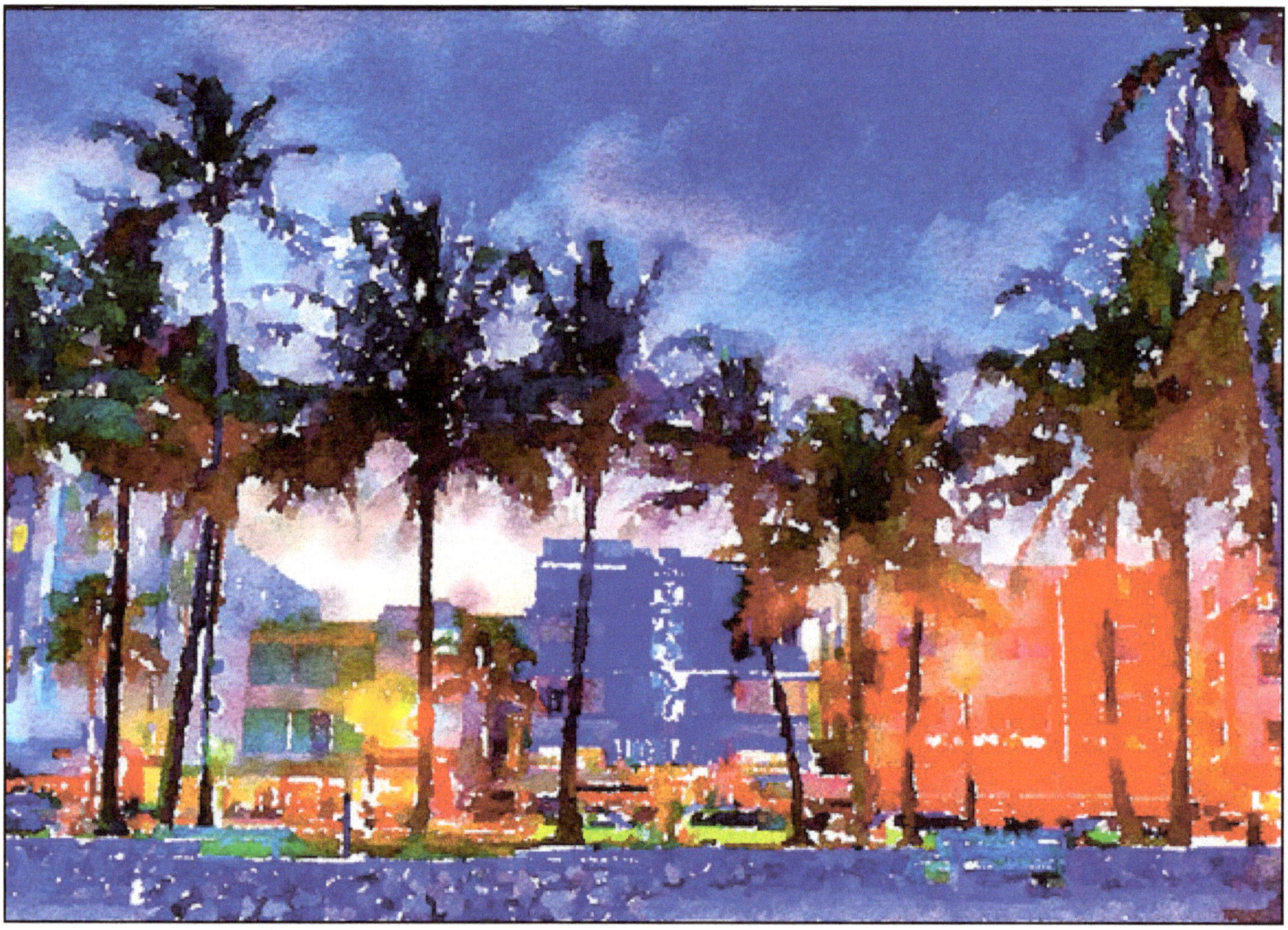

▲'Downtown Miami Beach' (2018), Florida [NUS(FL)1801].

'Strand Theatre' (2018), Key West, Florida [NUS(FL)1804].▼

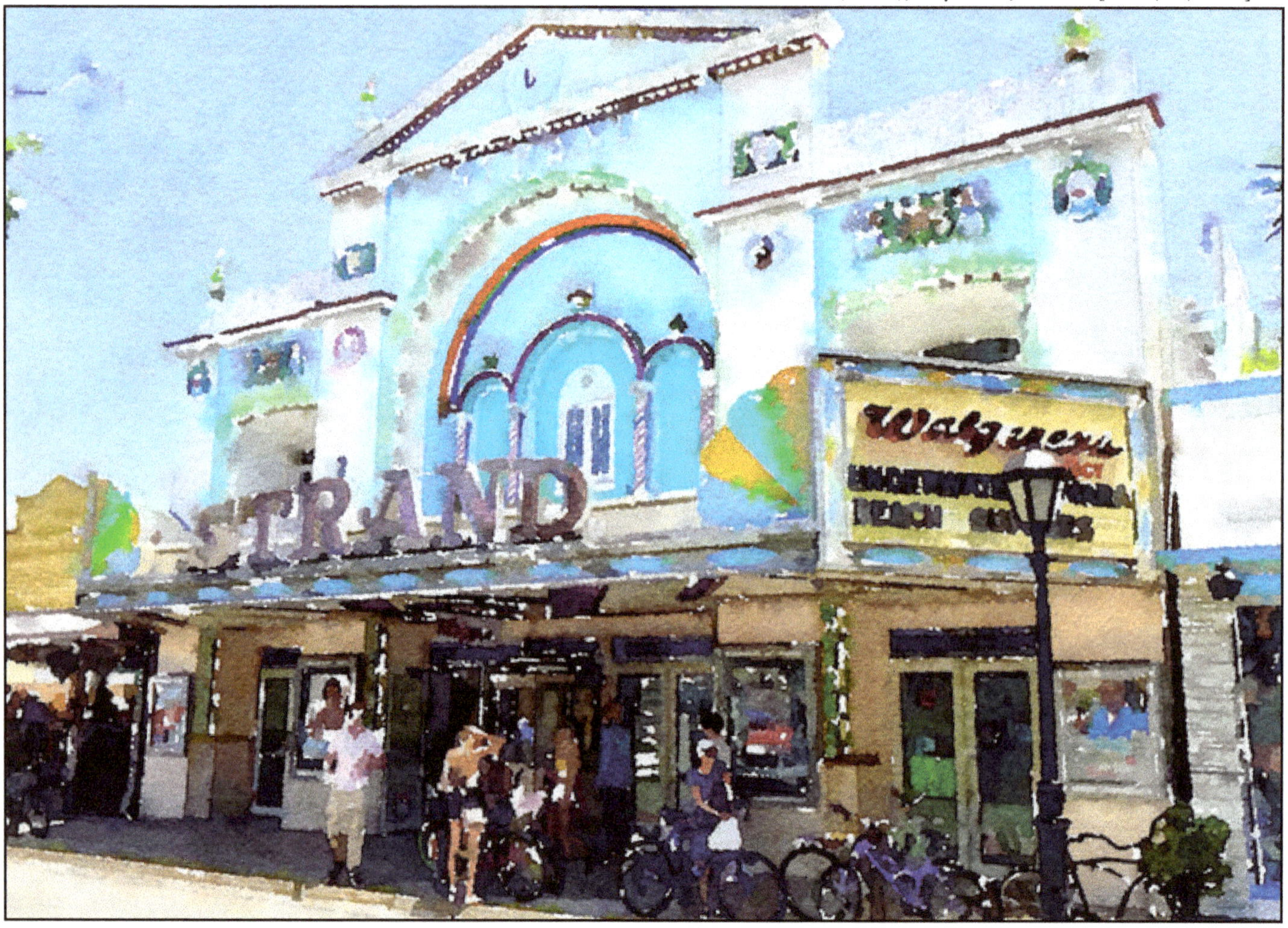

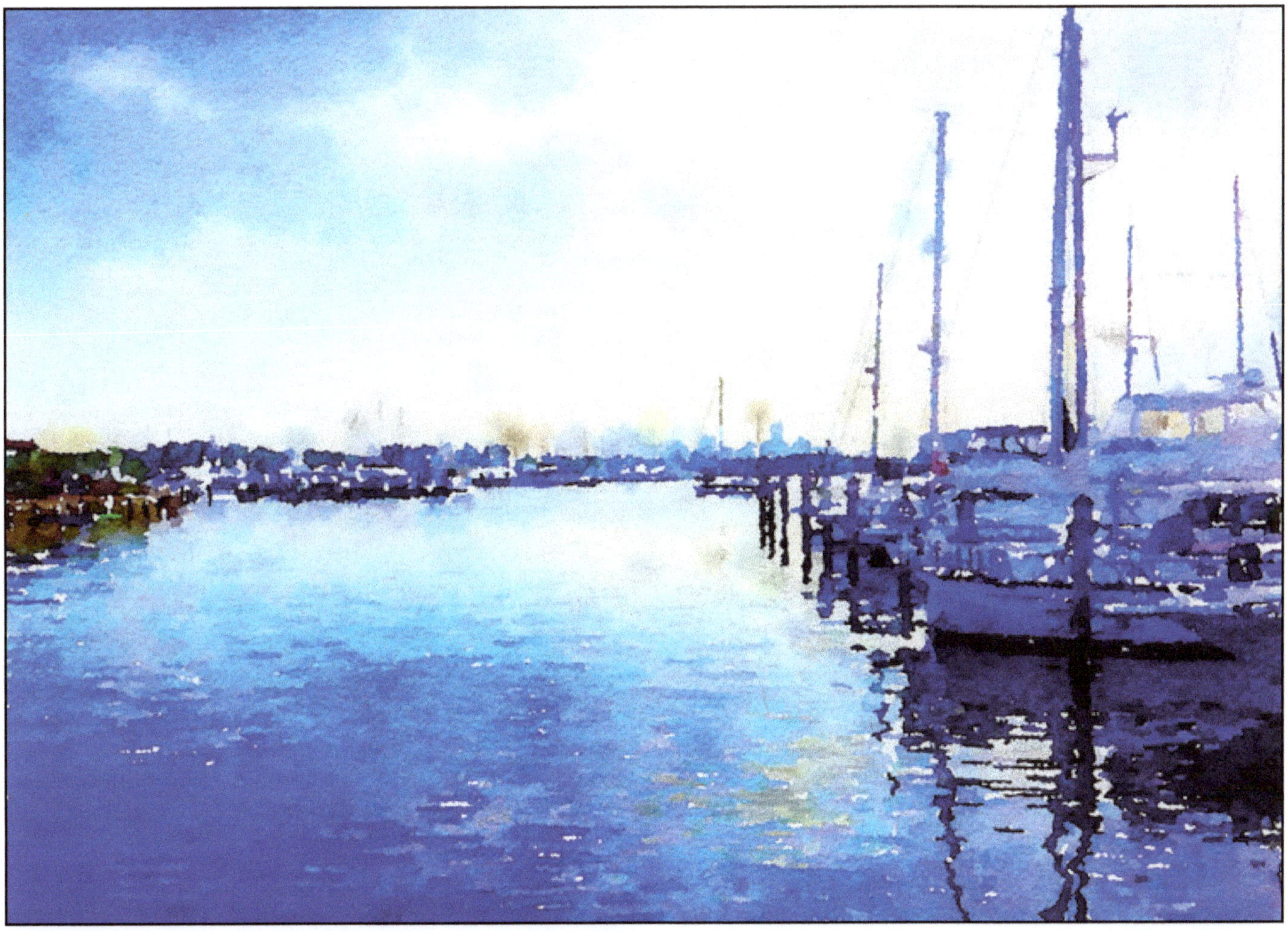

▲'Miami Keys' (2015), Coconut Grove, Florida [NUS(FL)1501].

'West Palm Beach' (2018), Florida [NUS(FL)1803].▼

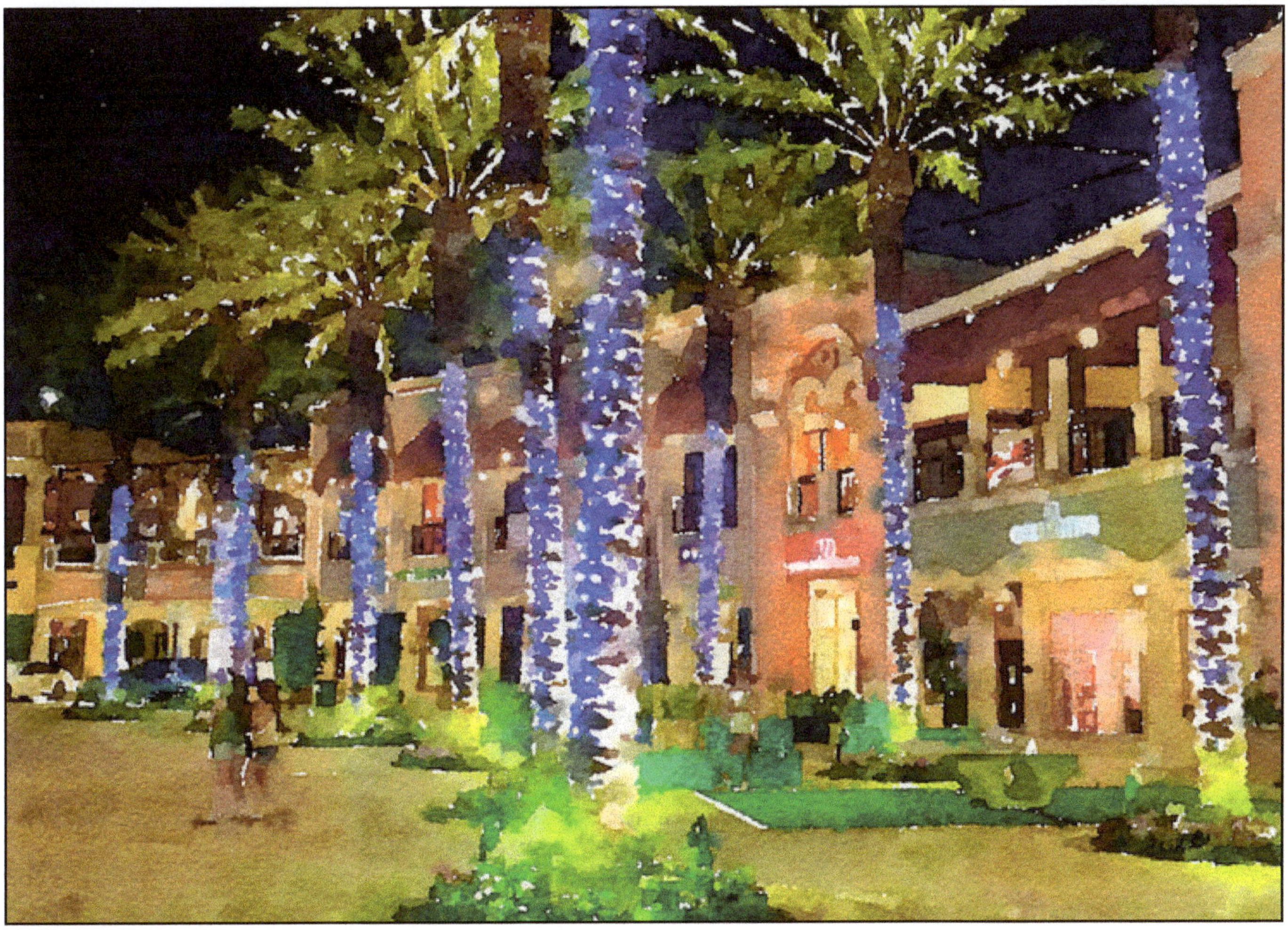

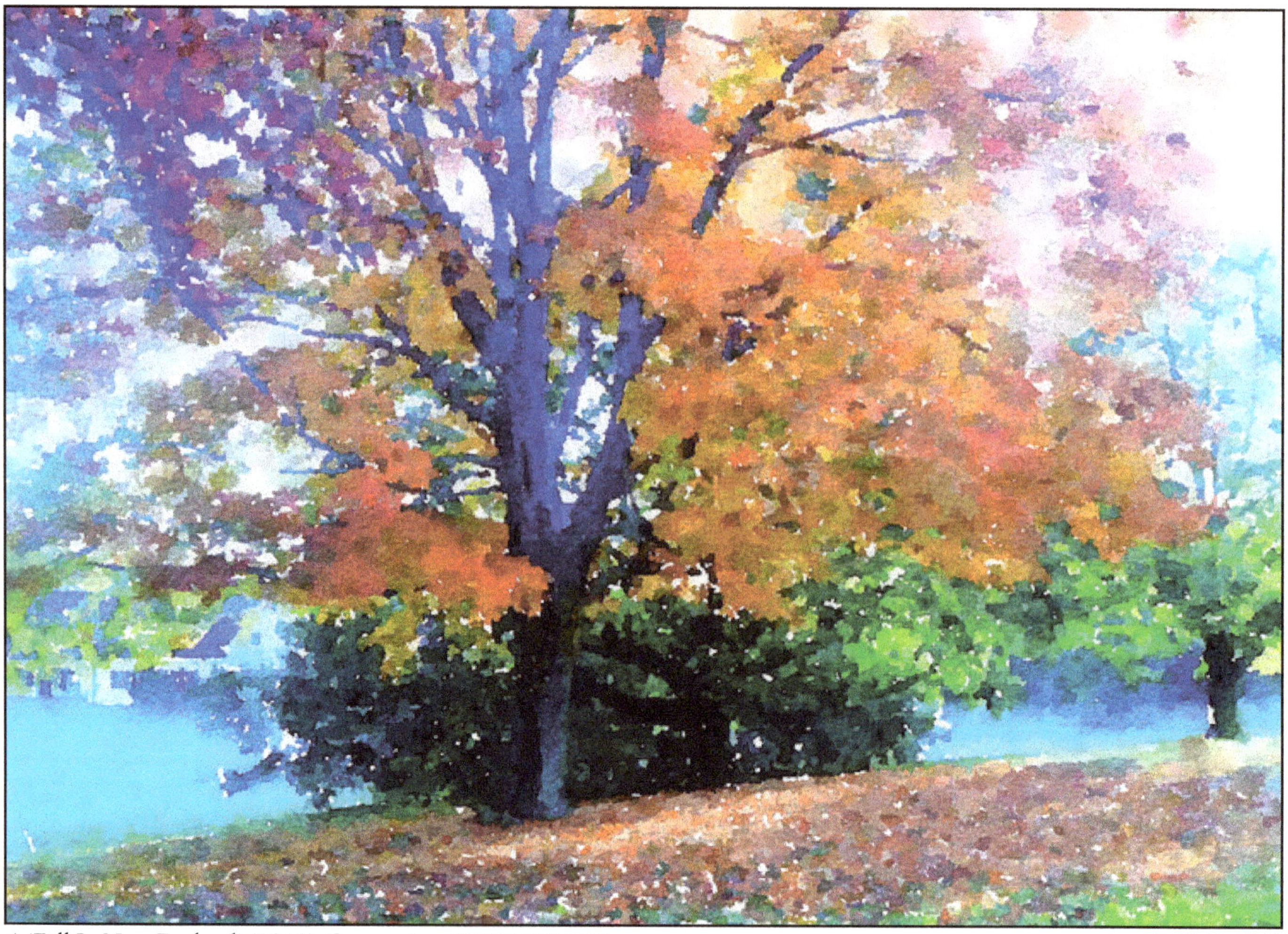

▲'Fall In New England' (2010), Connecticut [NUS(NE)1002].

▼'New England Birch' (2010), Connecticut [NUS(NE)1001].

'Flame Trees' (2010), Connecticut [NUS(NE)1003].▼

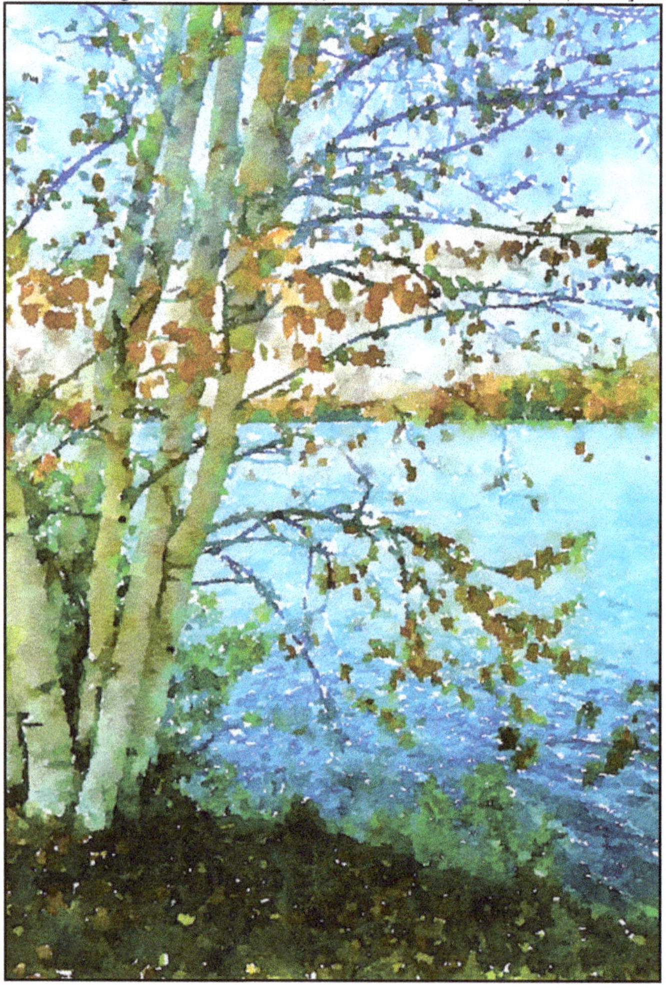

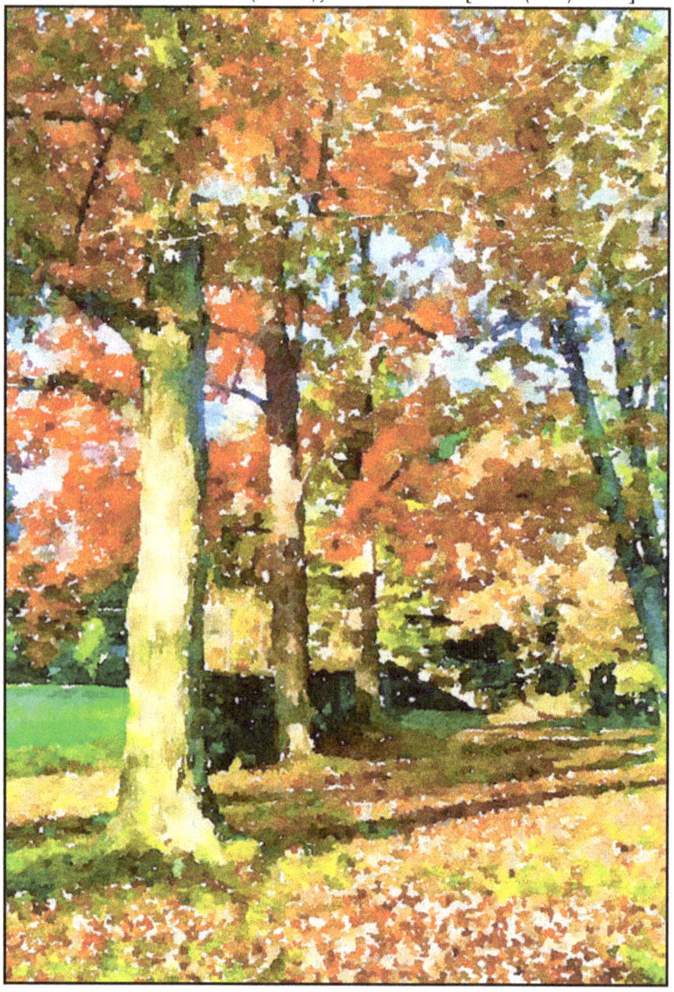

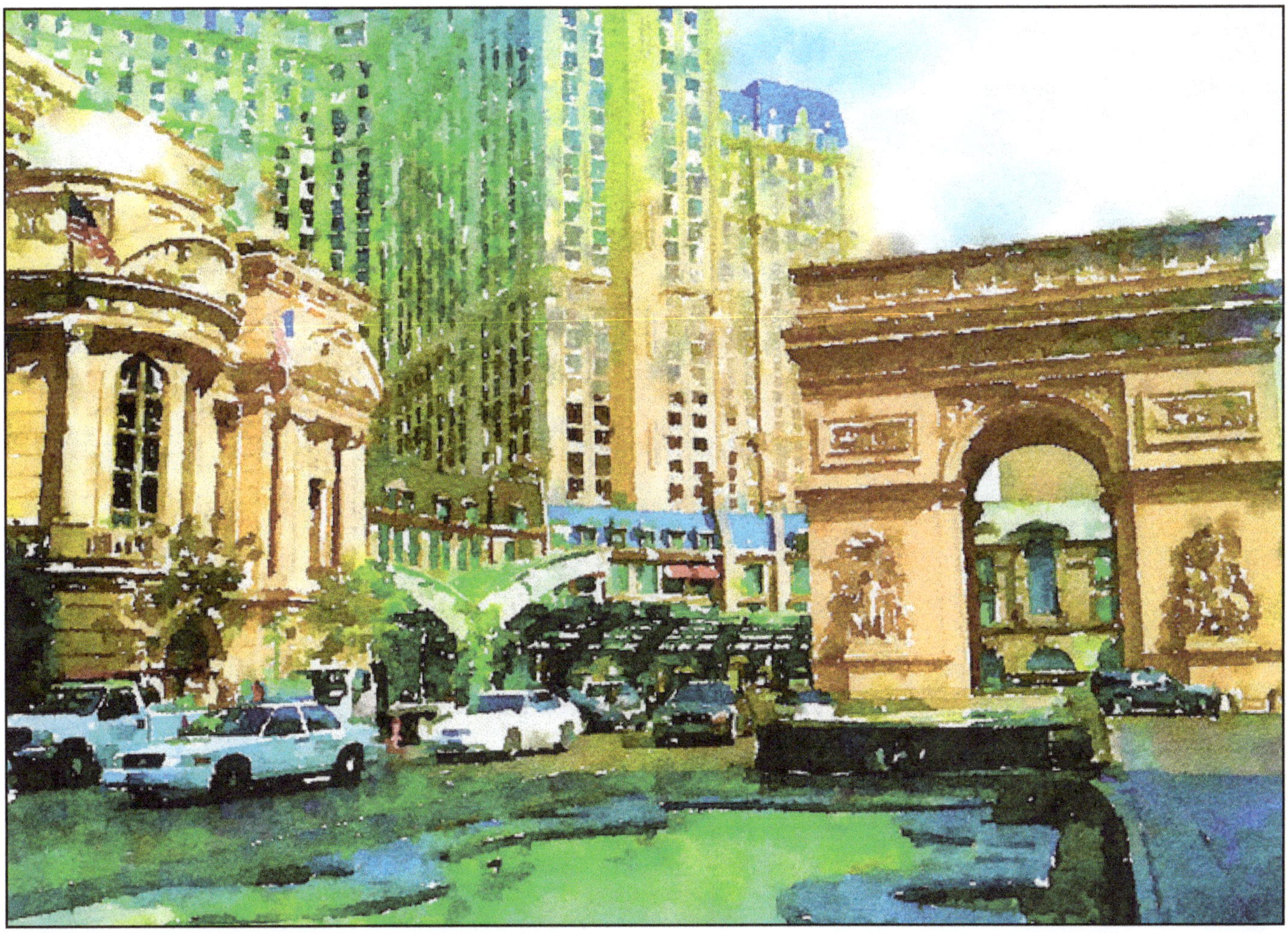

▲'The Forum' (2010), Las Vegas, Nevada [NUS(NV)1001].

'The Strip' (2021), Las Vegas, Nevada [NUS(NV)2101]. ⊘▼

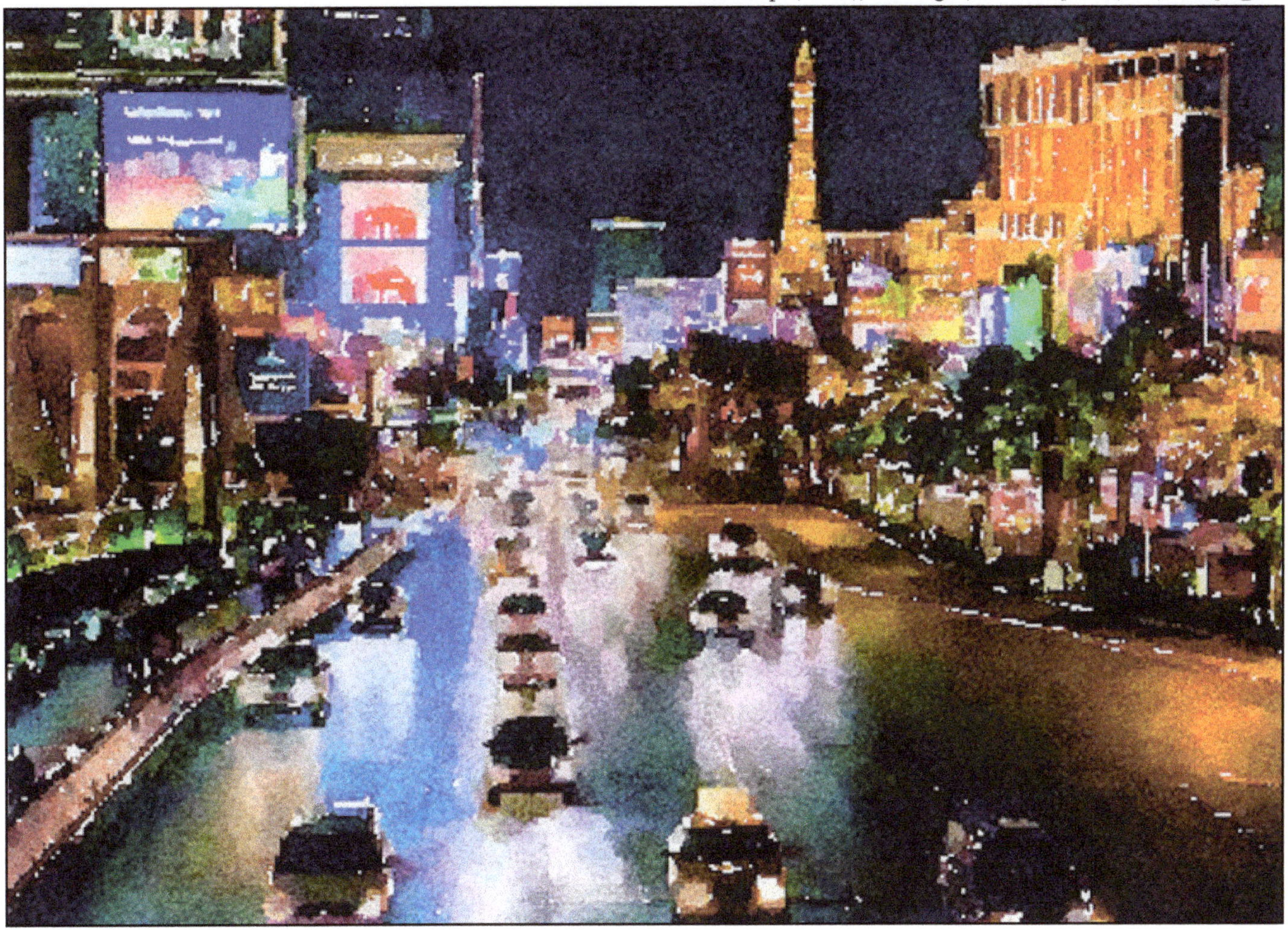

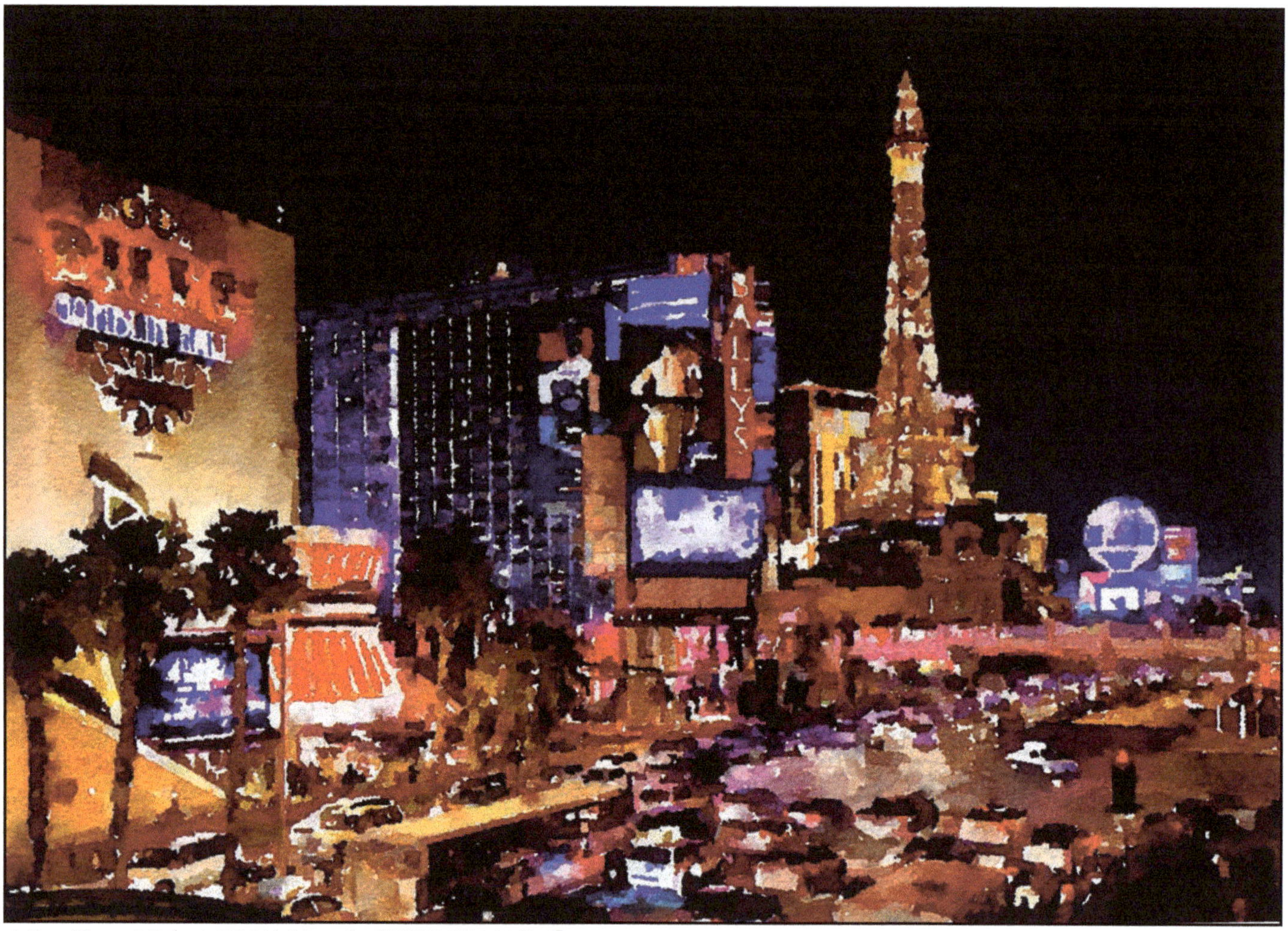

▲'Las Vegas Nights' (2021), Nevada [NUS(NV)2102]. ⓔ

'NYC Skyline' (2021), New York [NUS(NY)2101]. ⓔ▼

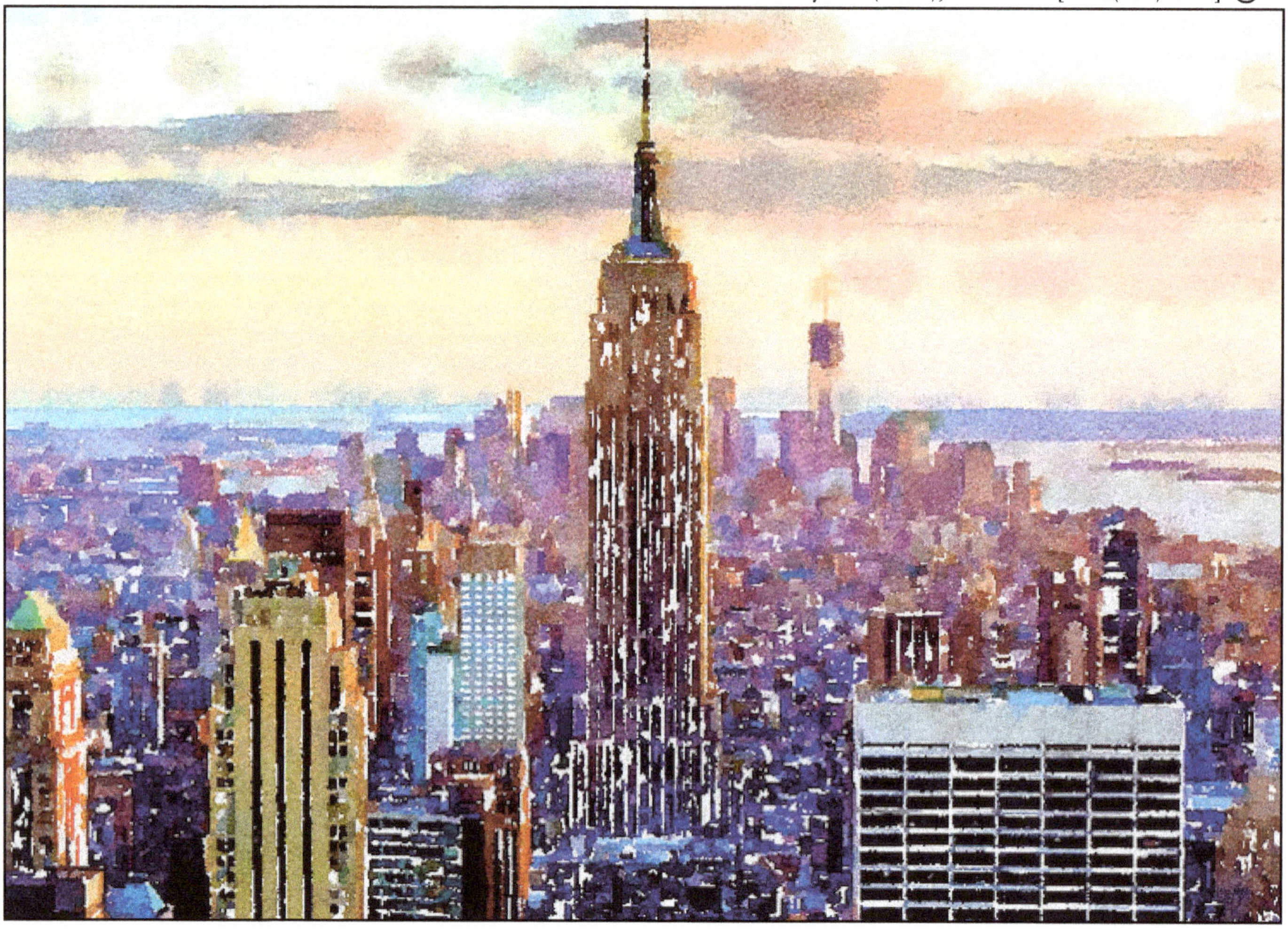

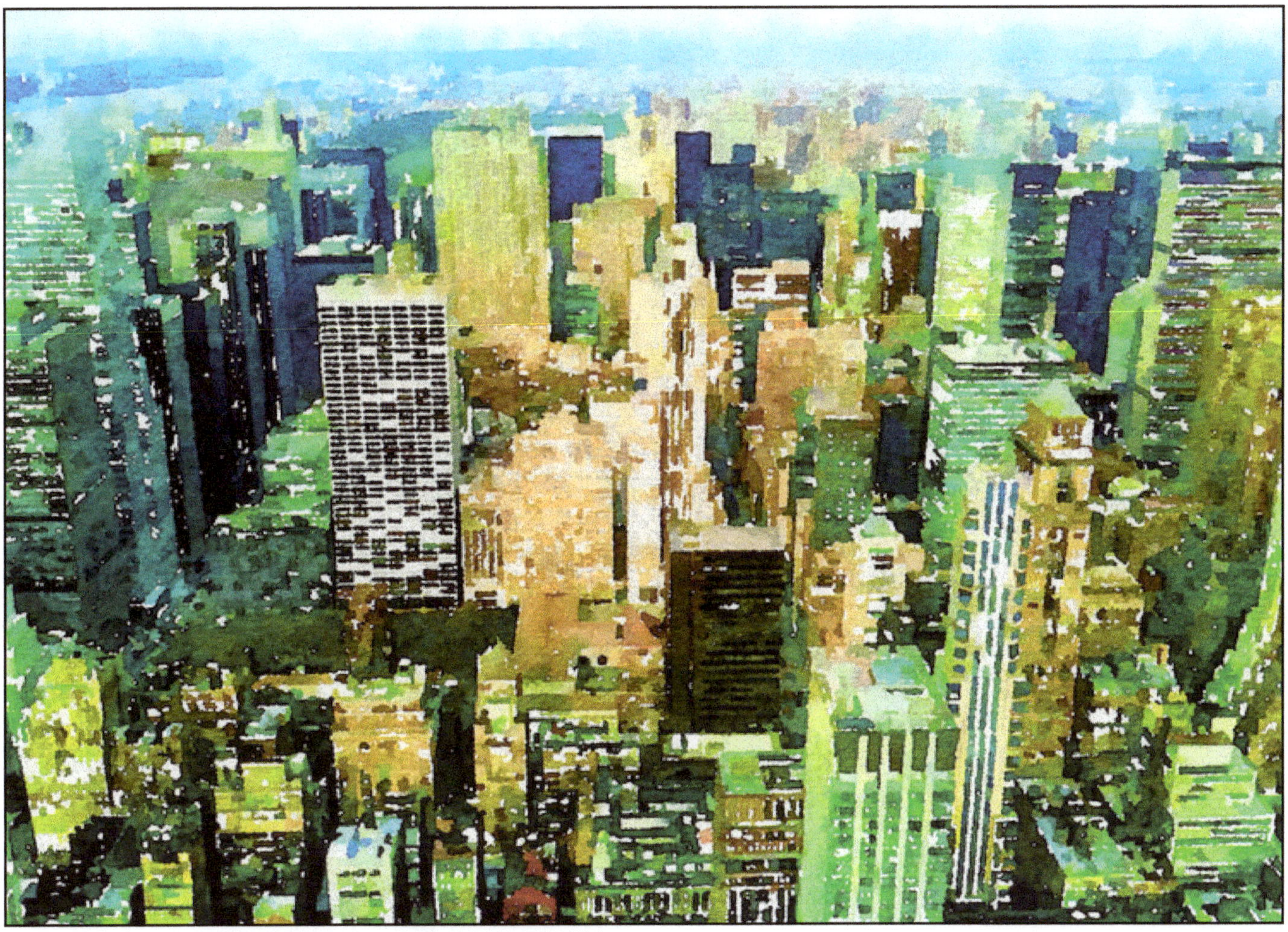

▲'Top Of The Big Apple' (2010), New York [NUS(NY)1001.

'Times Square' (2021), New York [NUS(NY)2102]. ⊘▼

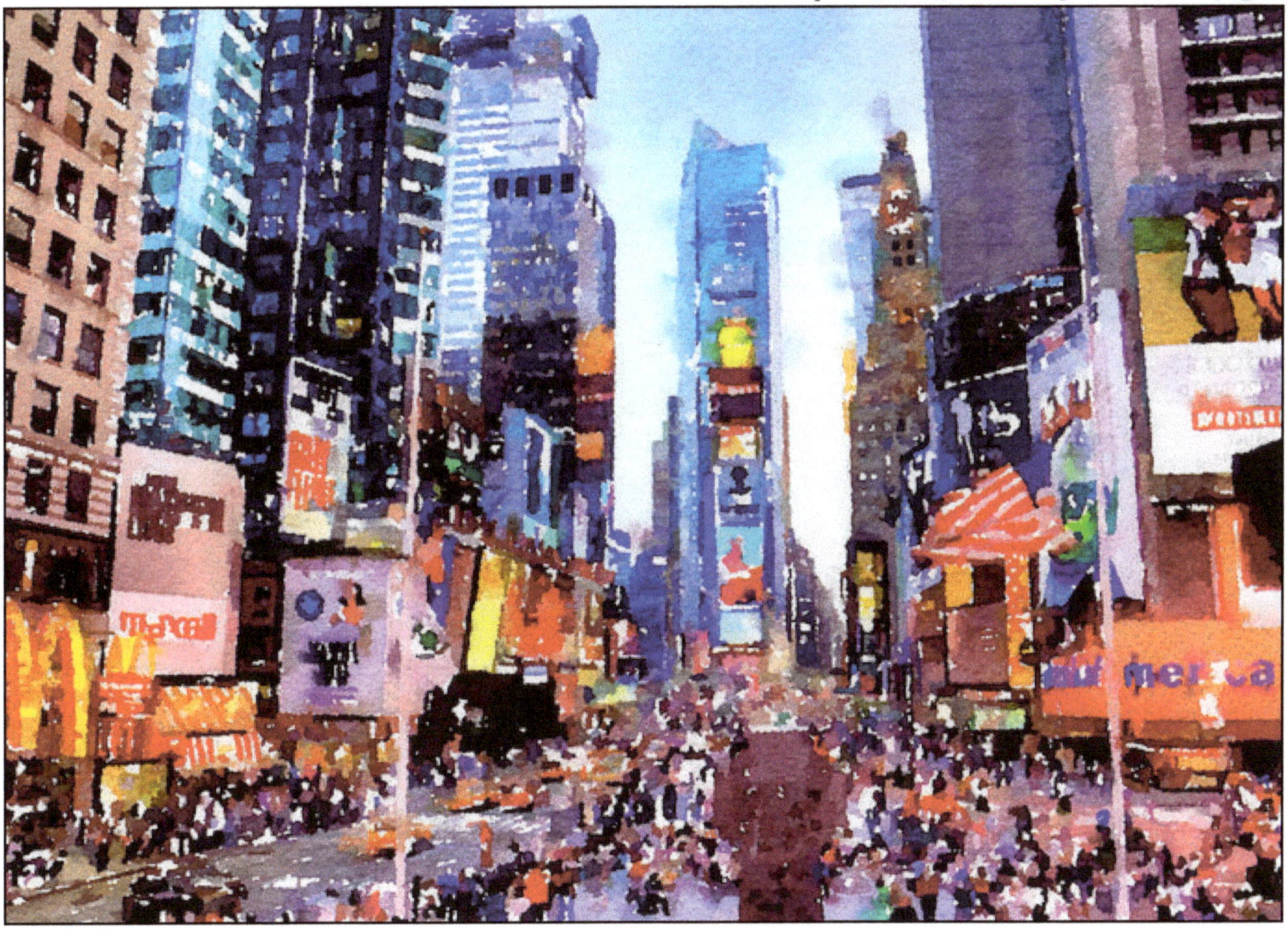

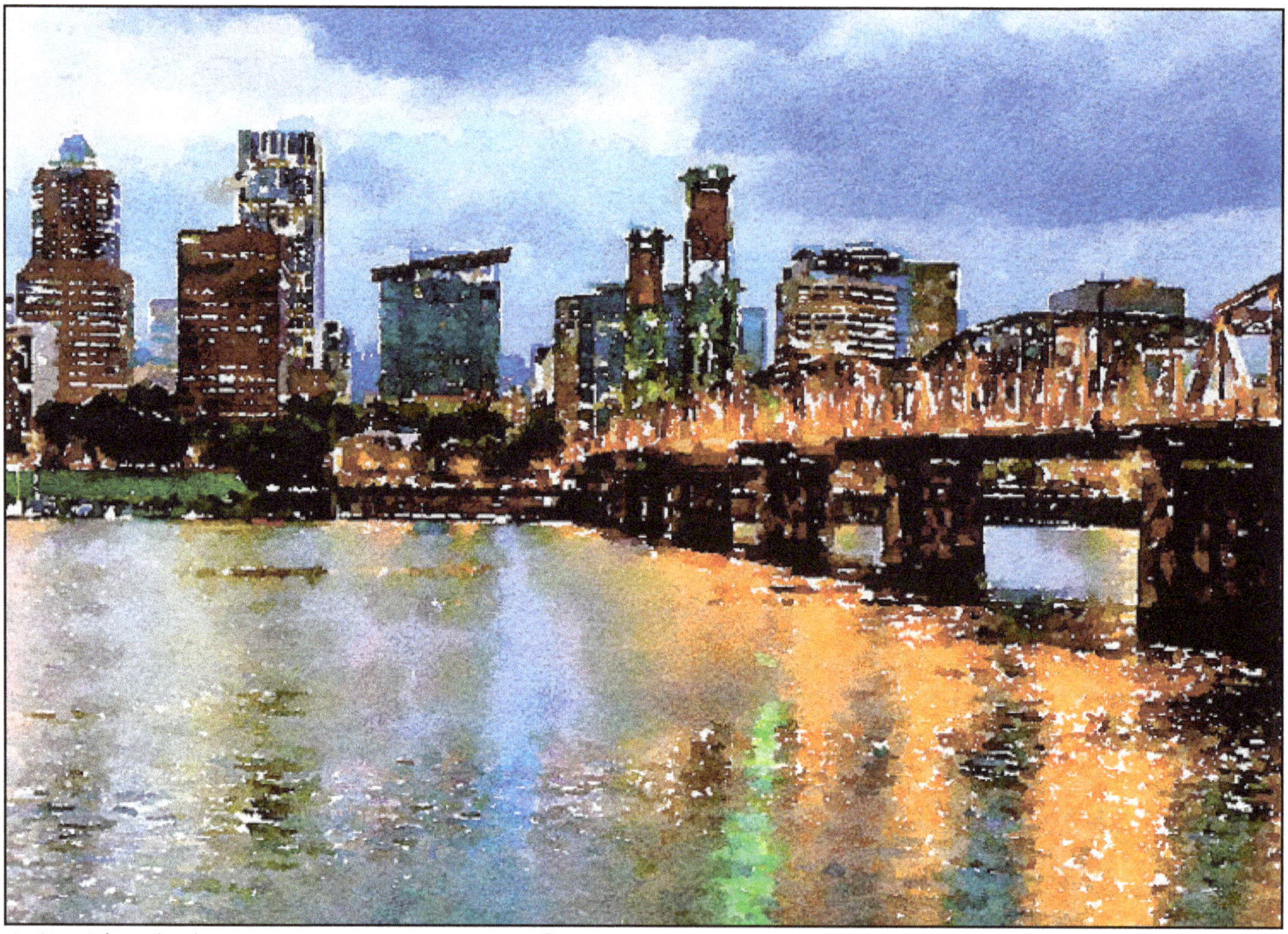

▲'City Of Portland' (2021), Oregon [NUS(OR2101]. ⊘

'Boarding The Max' (2015), Portland, Oregon [NUS(OR)1501].▼

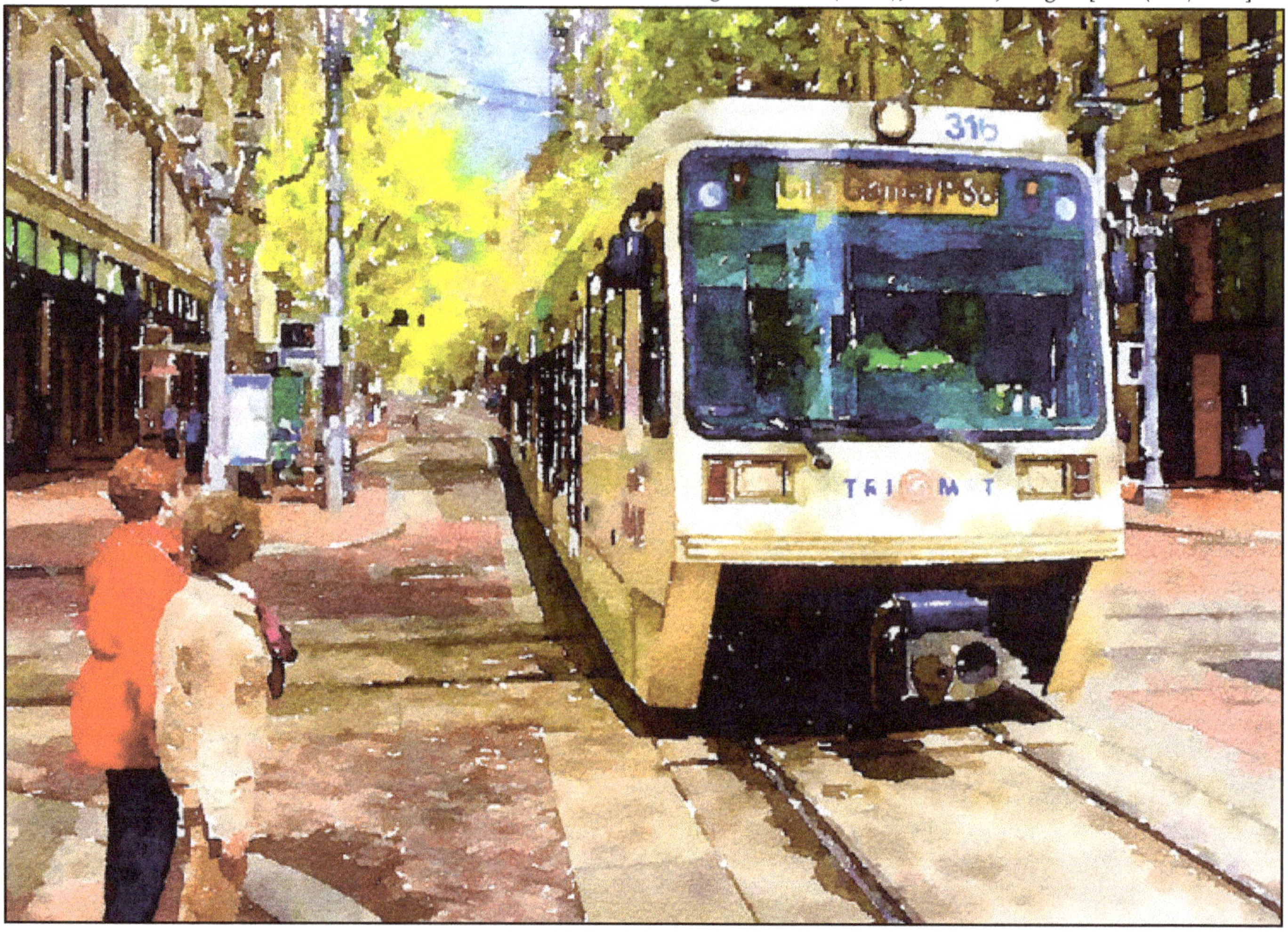

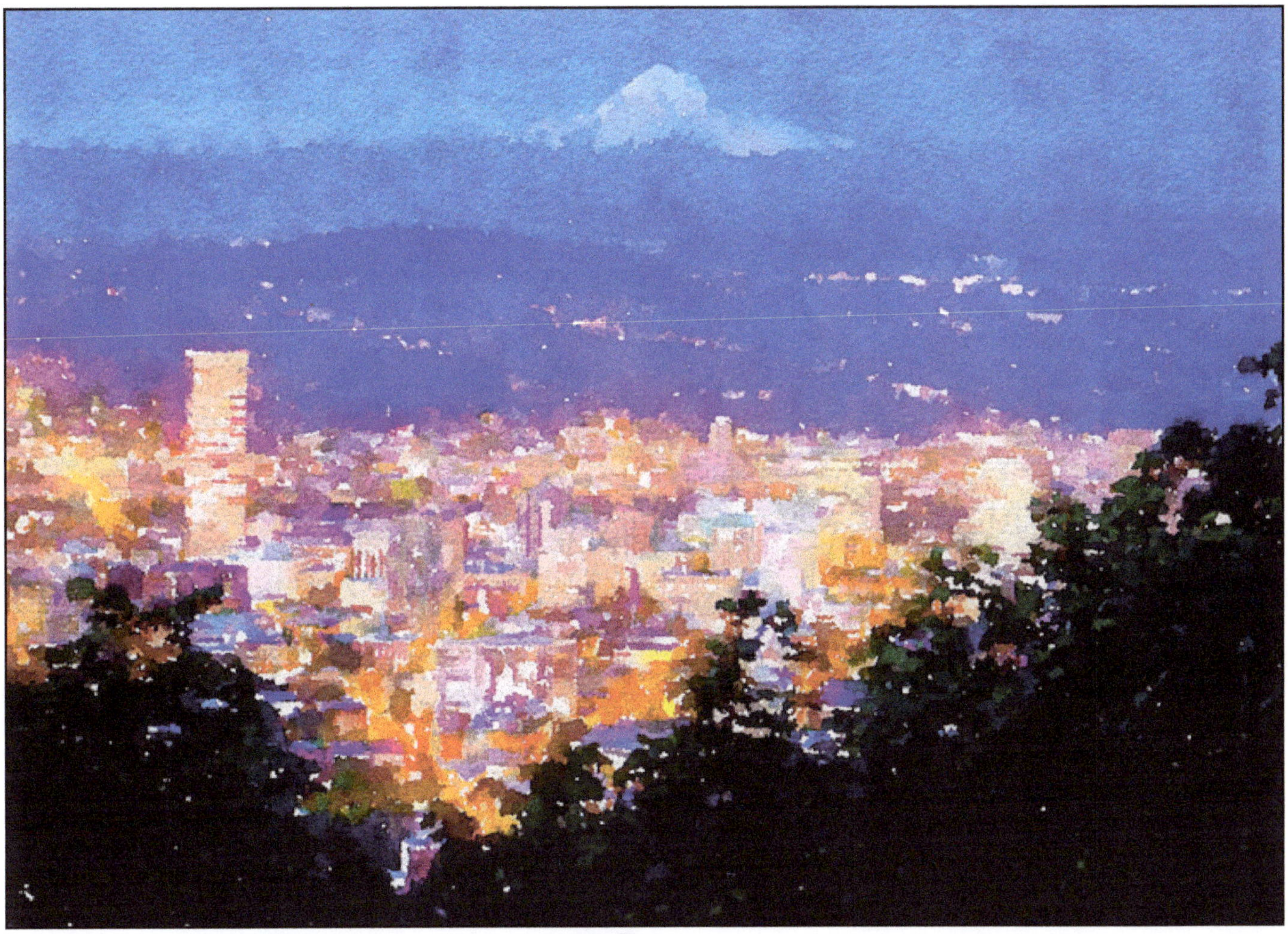

▲'Twilight Time' (2021), Portland, Oregon [NUS(OR2102]. ⊘

'Fall On The Willamette' (2021), Portland, Oregon [NUS(OR2103]. ⊘▼

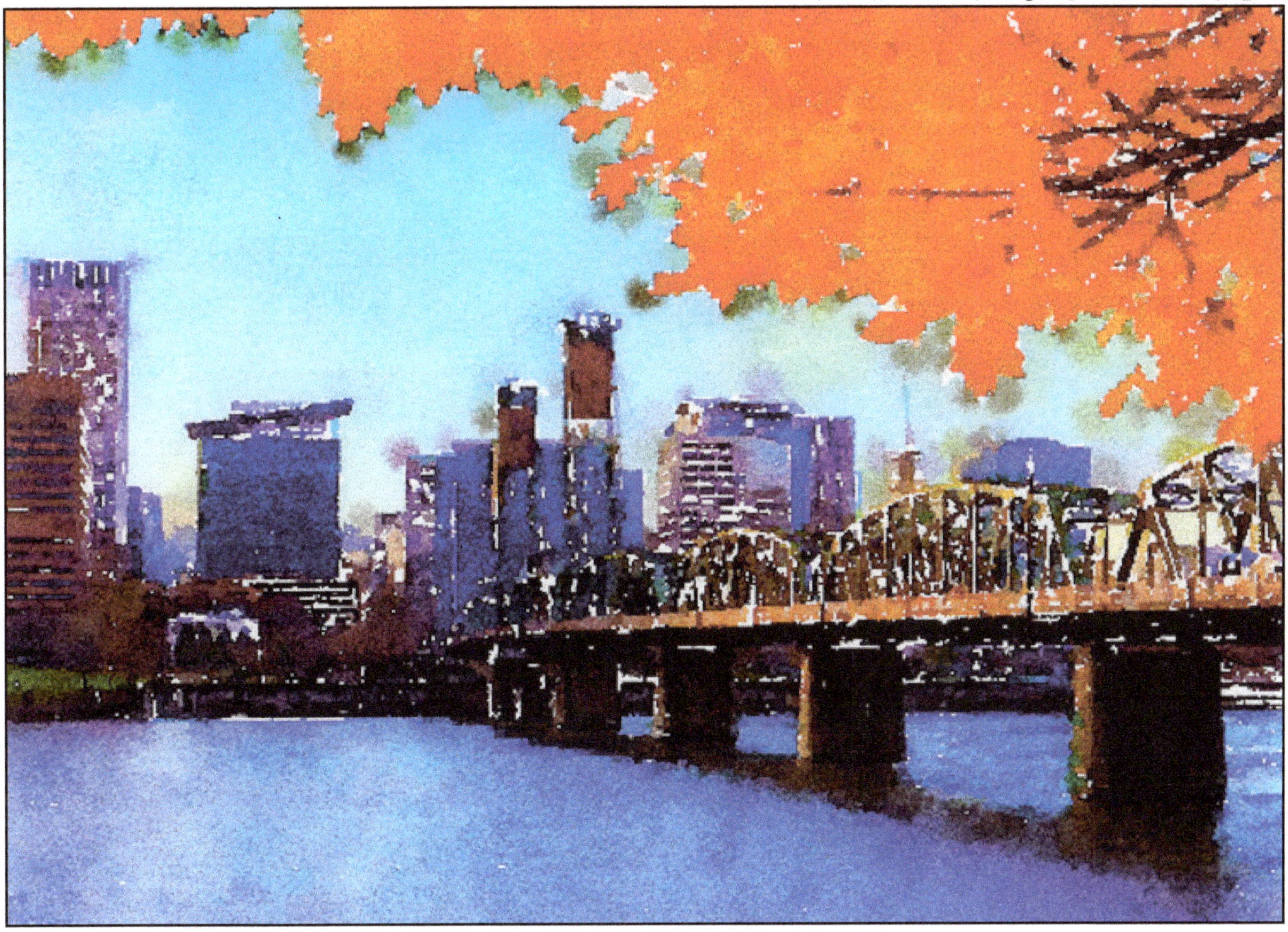

OCEANIA

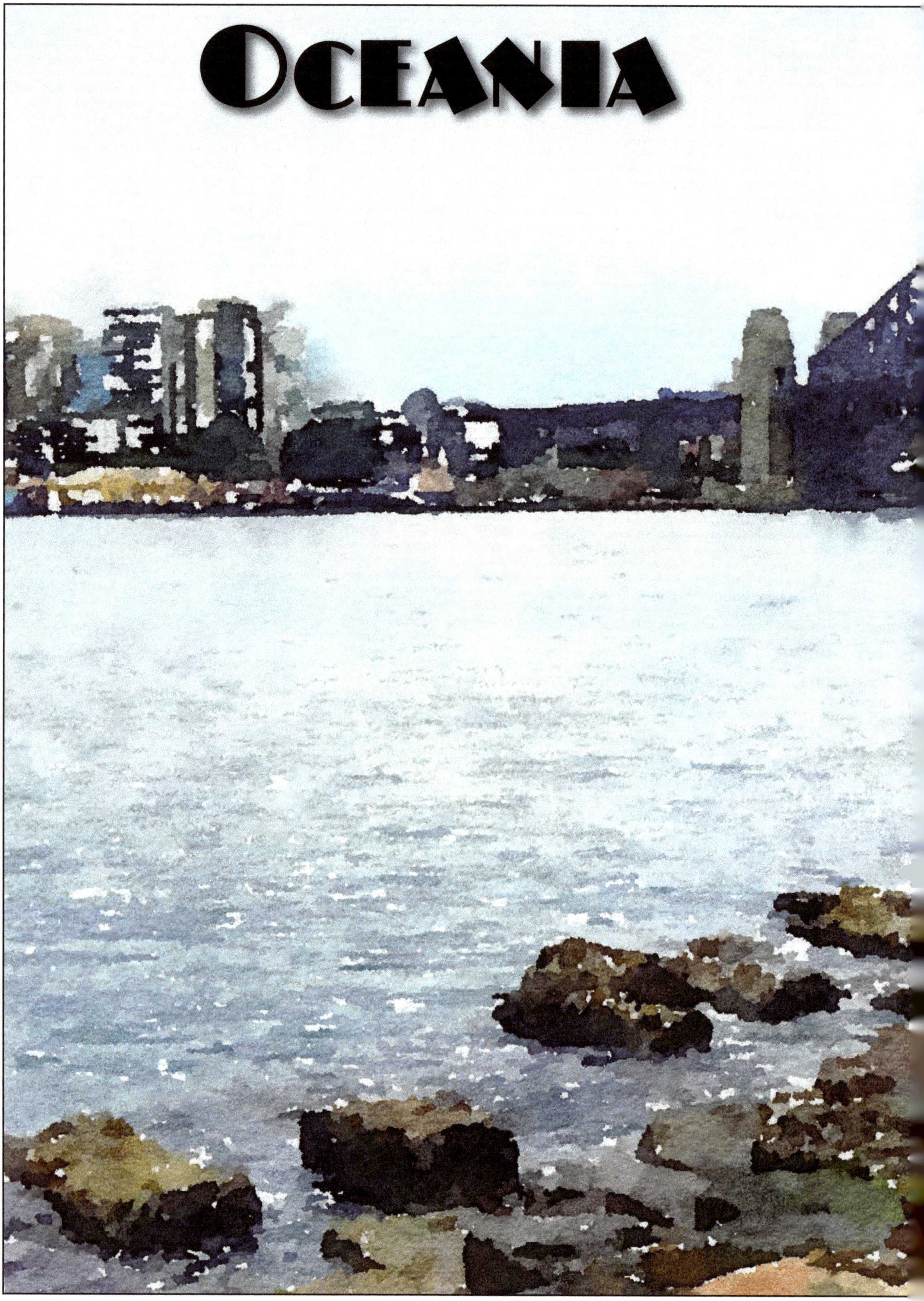

'Sydney Harbour Bridge' (2017), Walsh Bay, Sydney [ALSY1704].

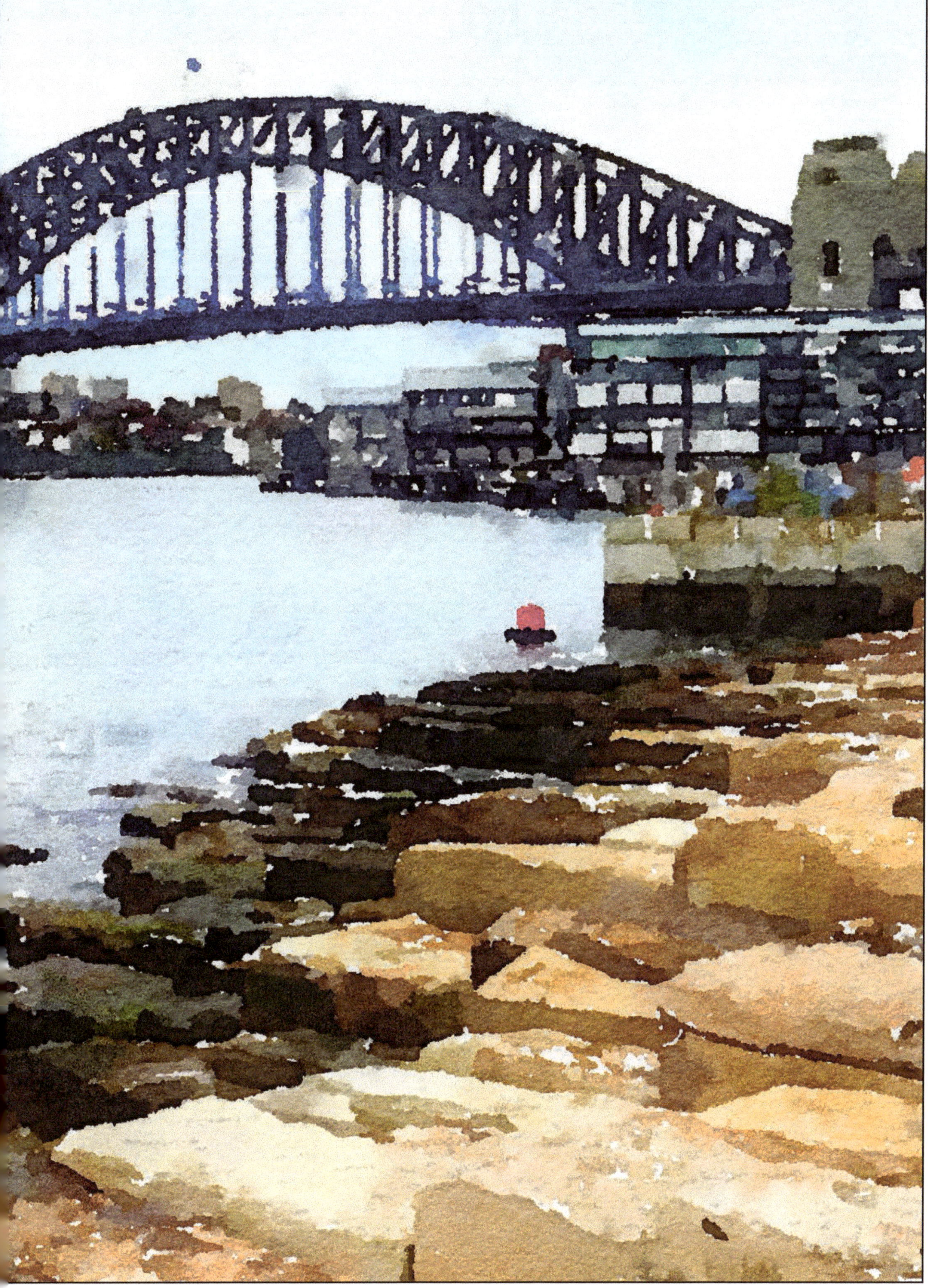

In addition to my international journeys, I regularly travel and photograph the 'wide brown land' of Australia, selecting my very best works for this catalogue. The Australian section has been split into 'landscapes' and 'seascapes', with a sub-division by rural and urban.

The rural interior of Australia has amazing appeal with outstanding regions like the Blue Mountains in New South Wales, the Kimberley in Western Australia, Far North Queensland, the Flinders Ranges in South Australia and virtually all of Tasmania.

Nonetheless, having grown up around the water and been an avid participant in swimming, life saving and water polo, my interest and passion has unashamedly been focused upon the sea, which explains the high proportion of seascapes throughout this book. The constantly evolving relationship between the natural elements of sun, sand and sea, and their stark contrast with the human world, particularly at the beach, is one of the purest, most enjoyable pastimes imaginable...

Rural Landscapes...

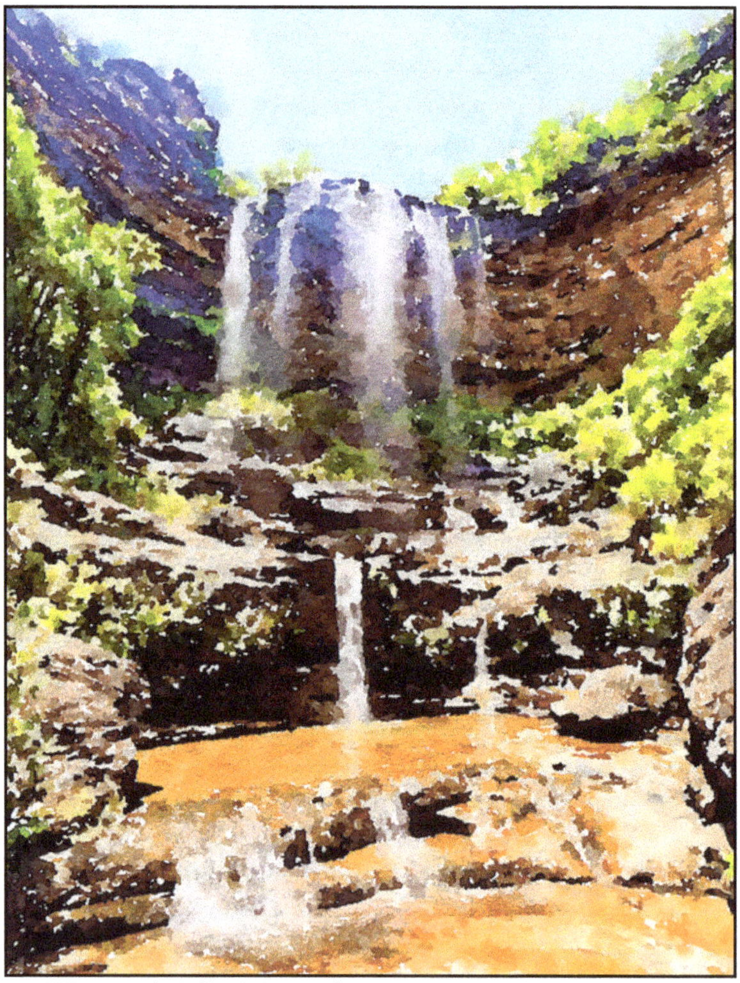

'Wentworth Falls' (2015), Blue Mountains, NSW [ALBM1501].▲

▼'Wolgan Valley' (2012), Blue Mountains, NSW [ALBM1201].

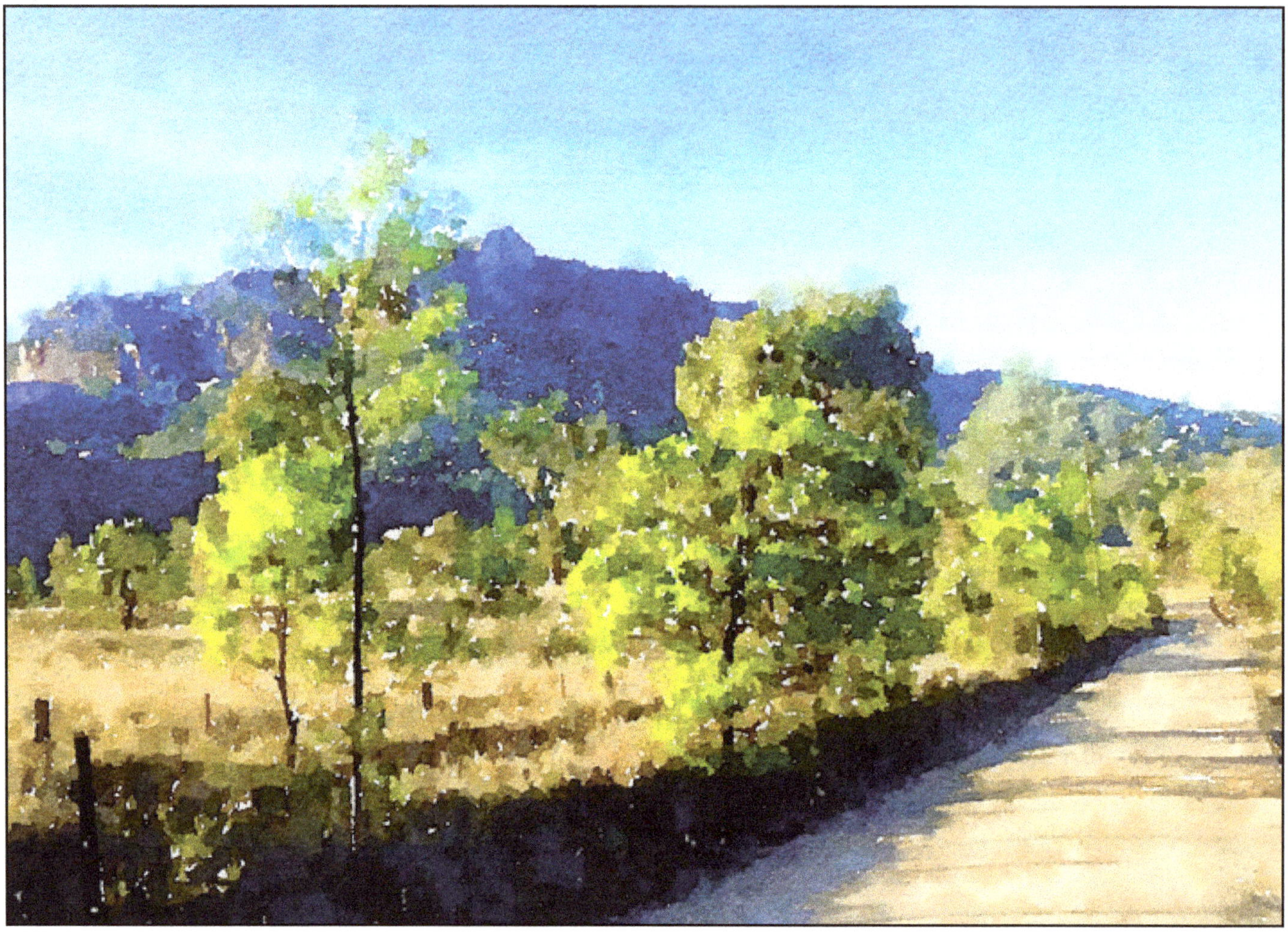

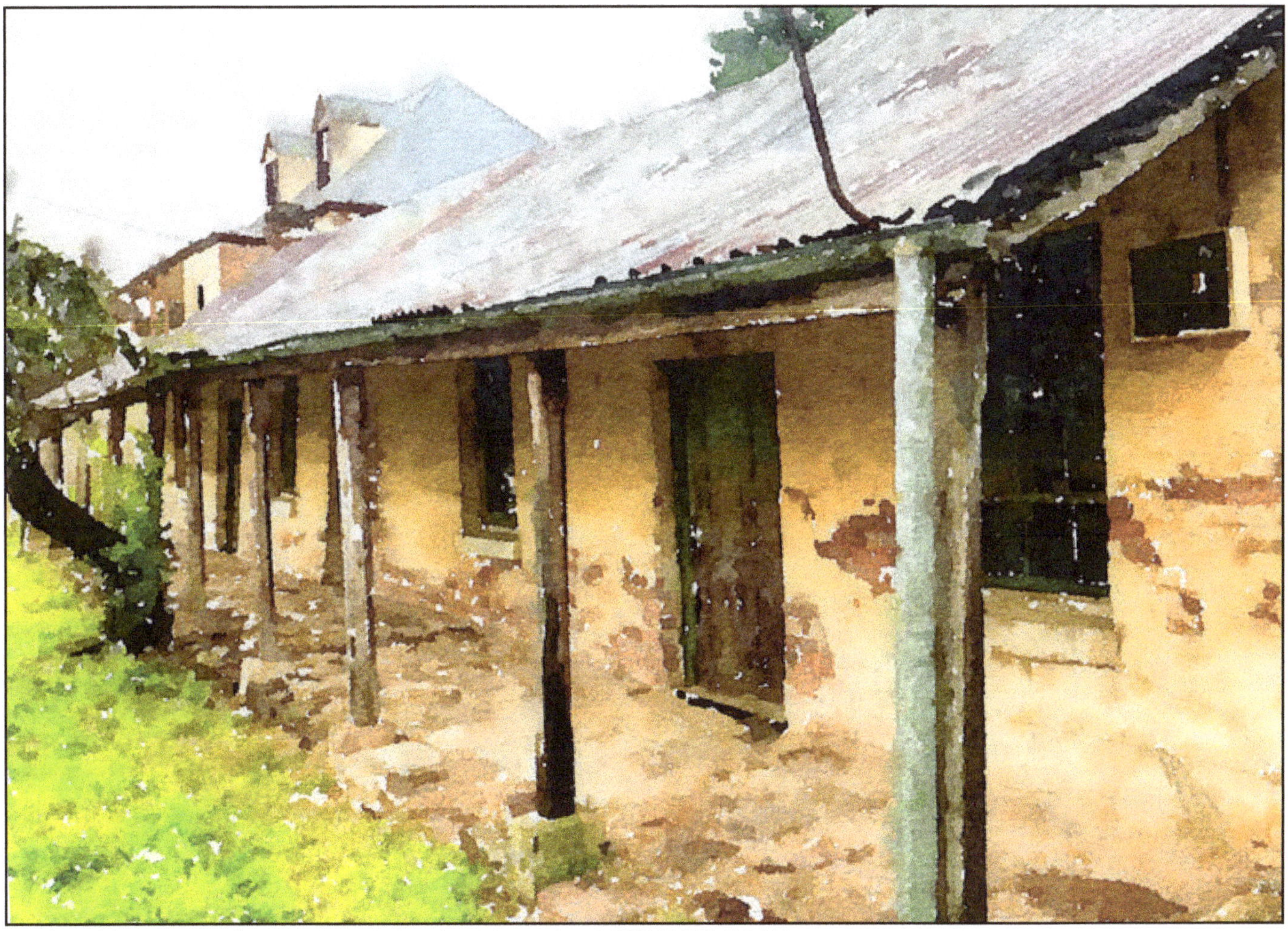

▲'The Old Inn at Hartley (1840)' (2018), Blue Mountains, NSW [ALBM1801].

'A Wilderness State Of Mind' (2019), Katoomba, NSW [ALBM1903].▼

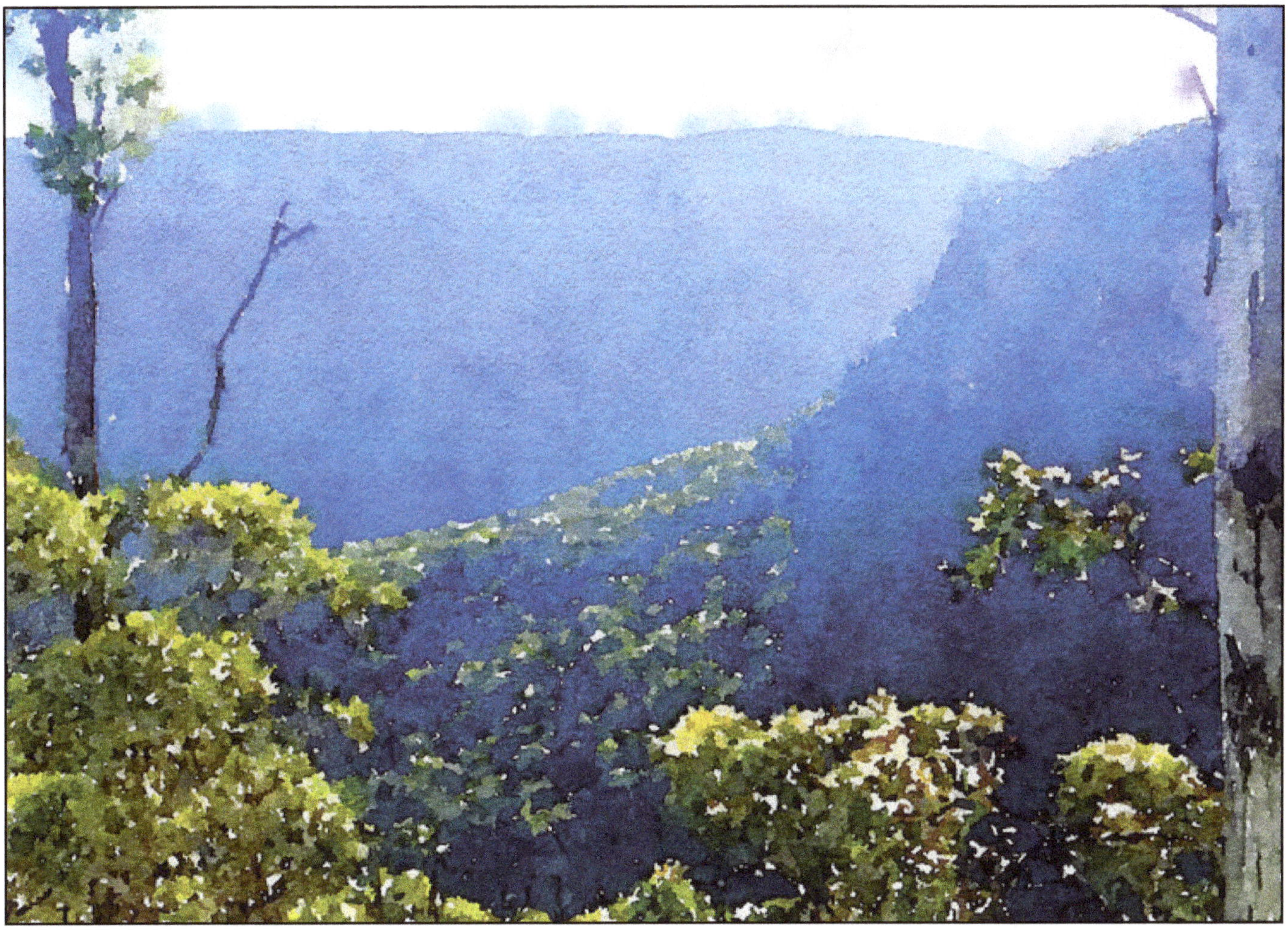

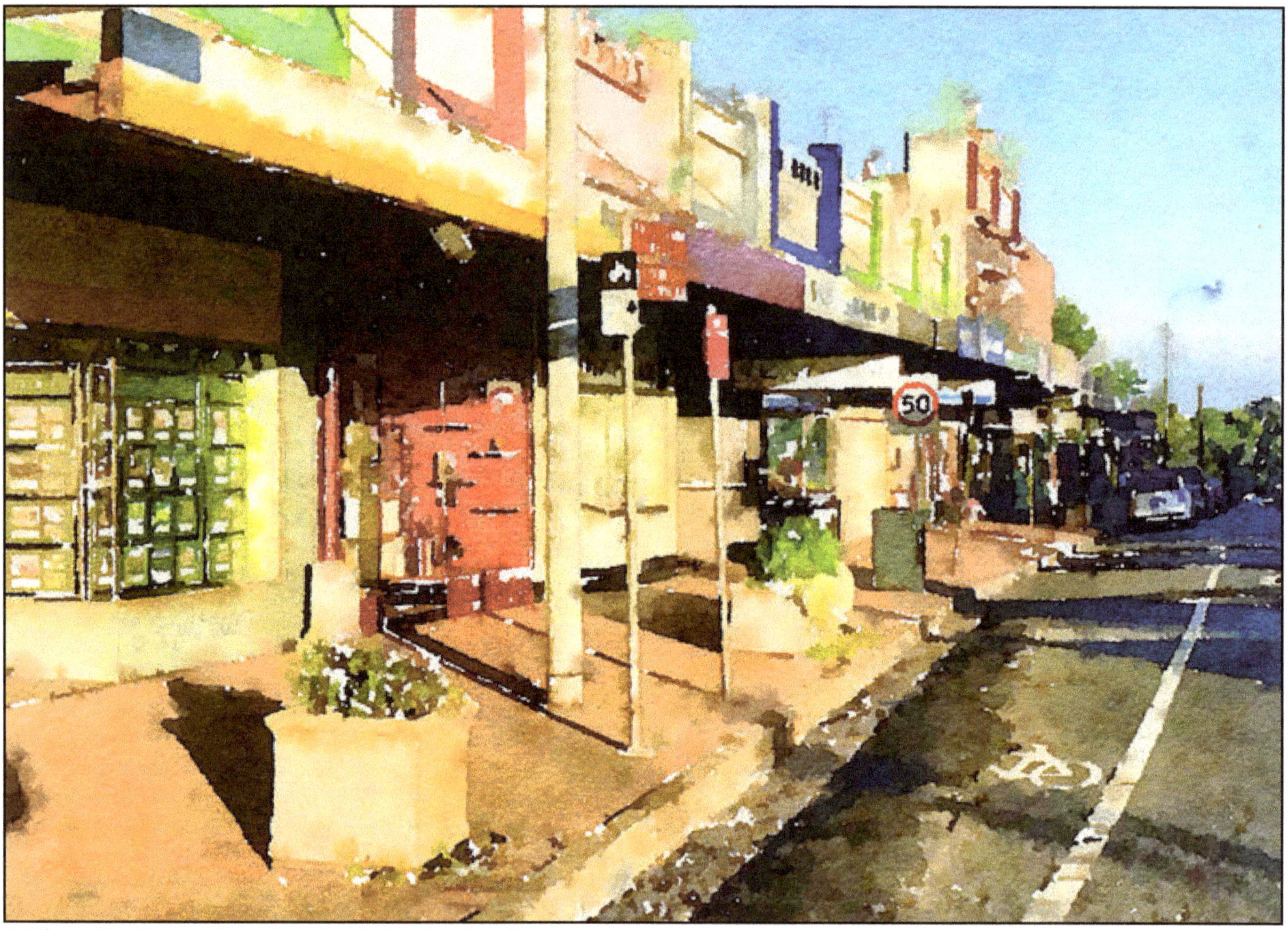

▲'Shops On Govetts Leap Road' (2019), Blackheath, NSW [ALBM1901].

'The Comet Inn (1879)' (2019), Blue Mountains, NSW [ALBM1902].▼

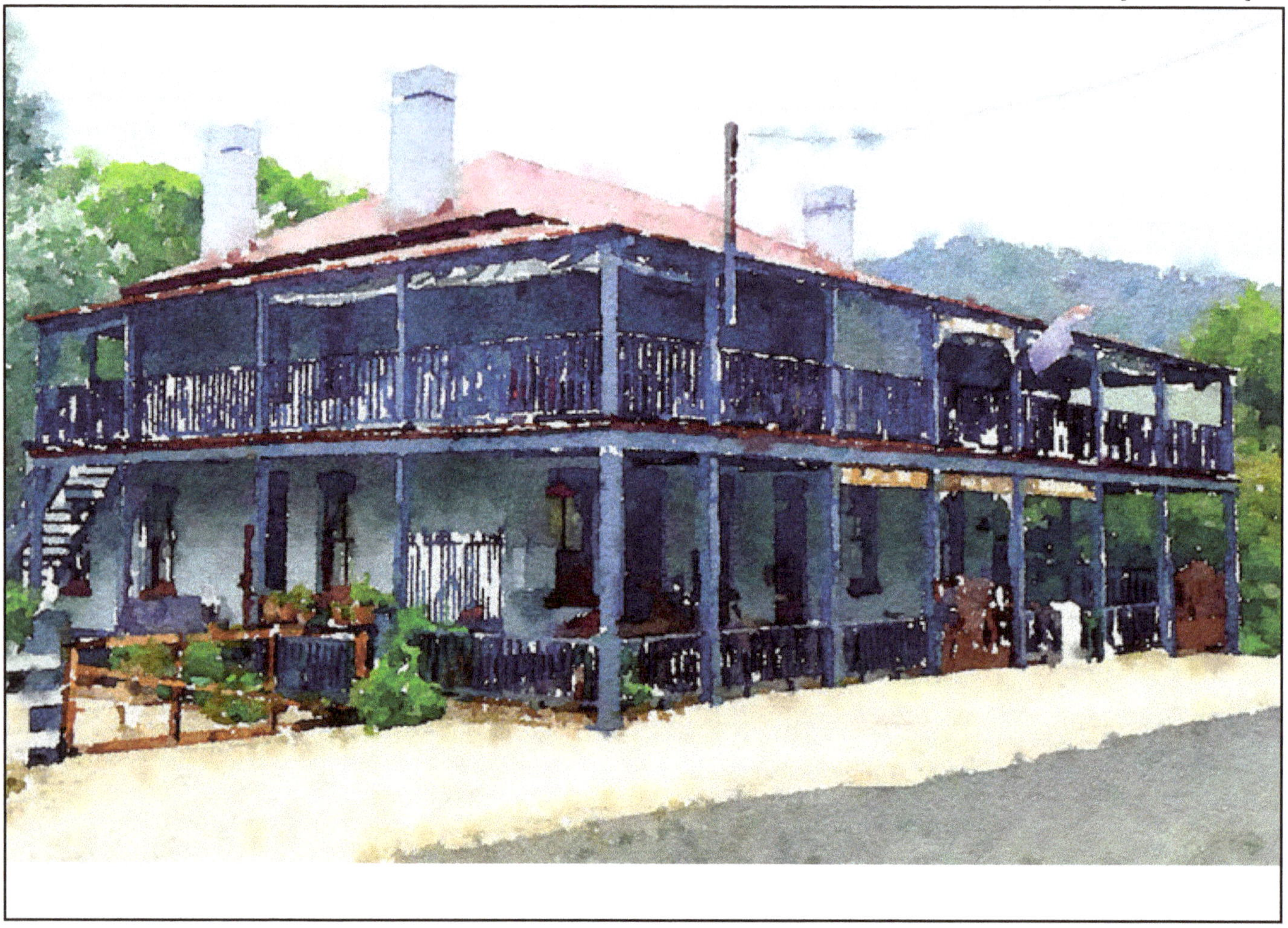

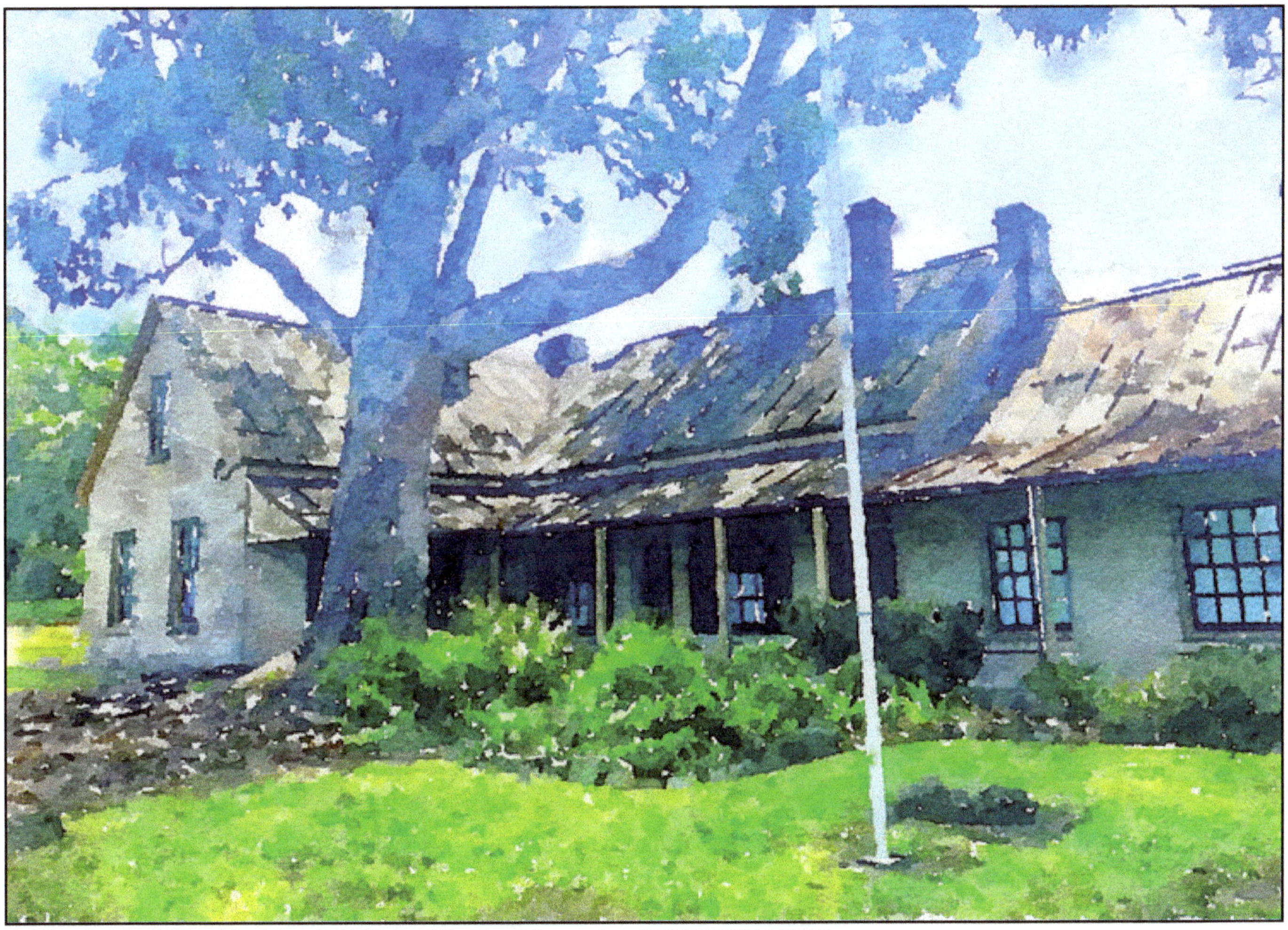

▲'The Original Woodford Inn (1835)' (2019), Blue Mountains, NSW [ALBM1905].

'The Old Inn' (2019), Woodford, NSW [ALBM1904].▼

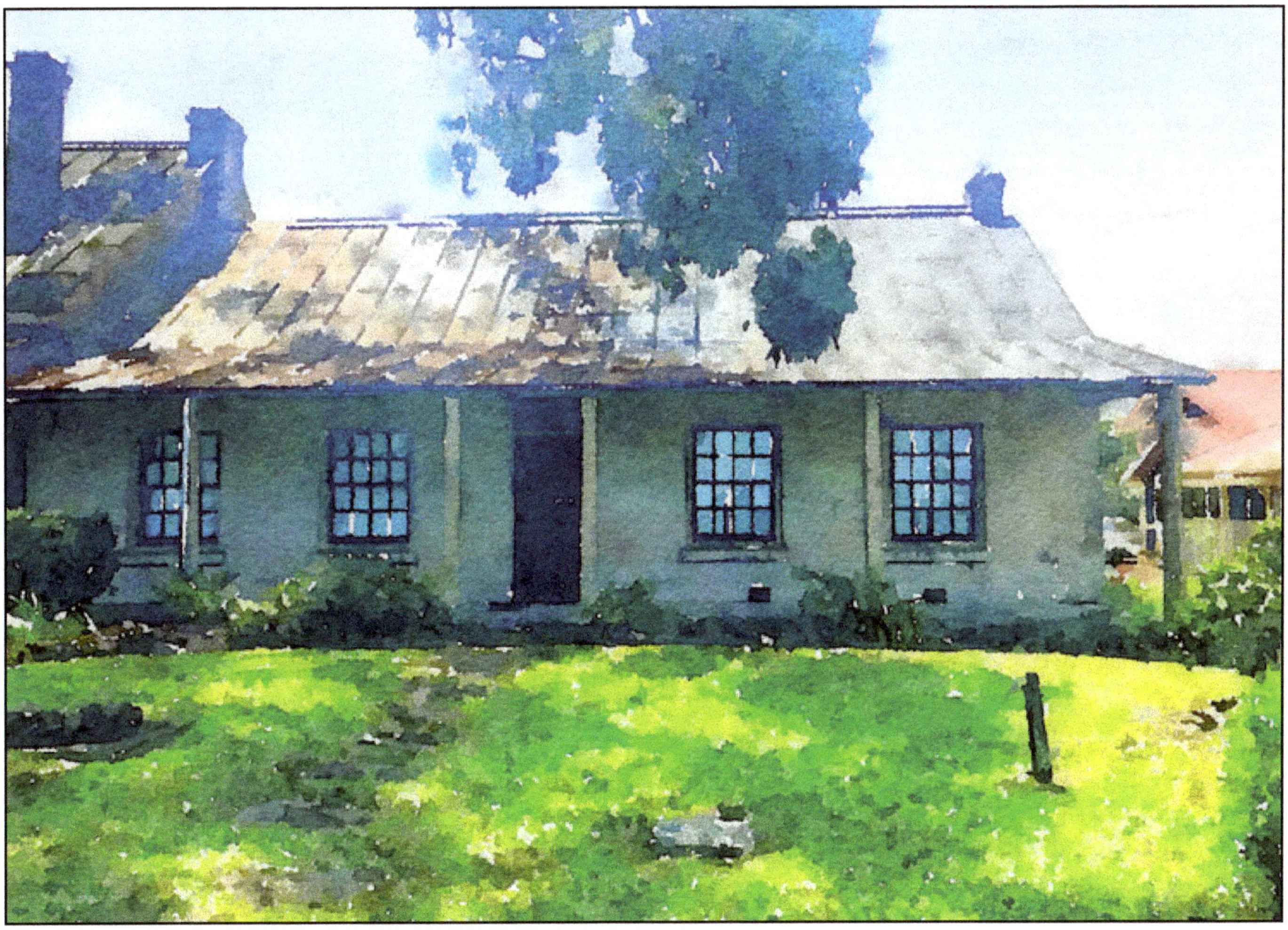

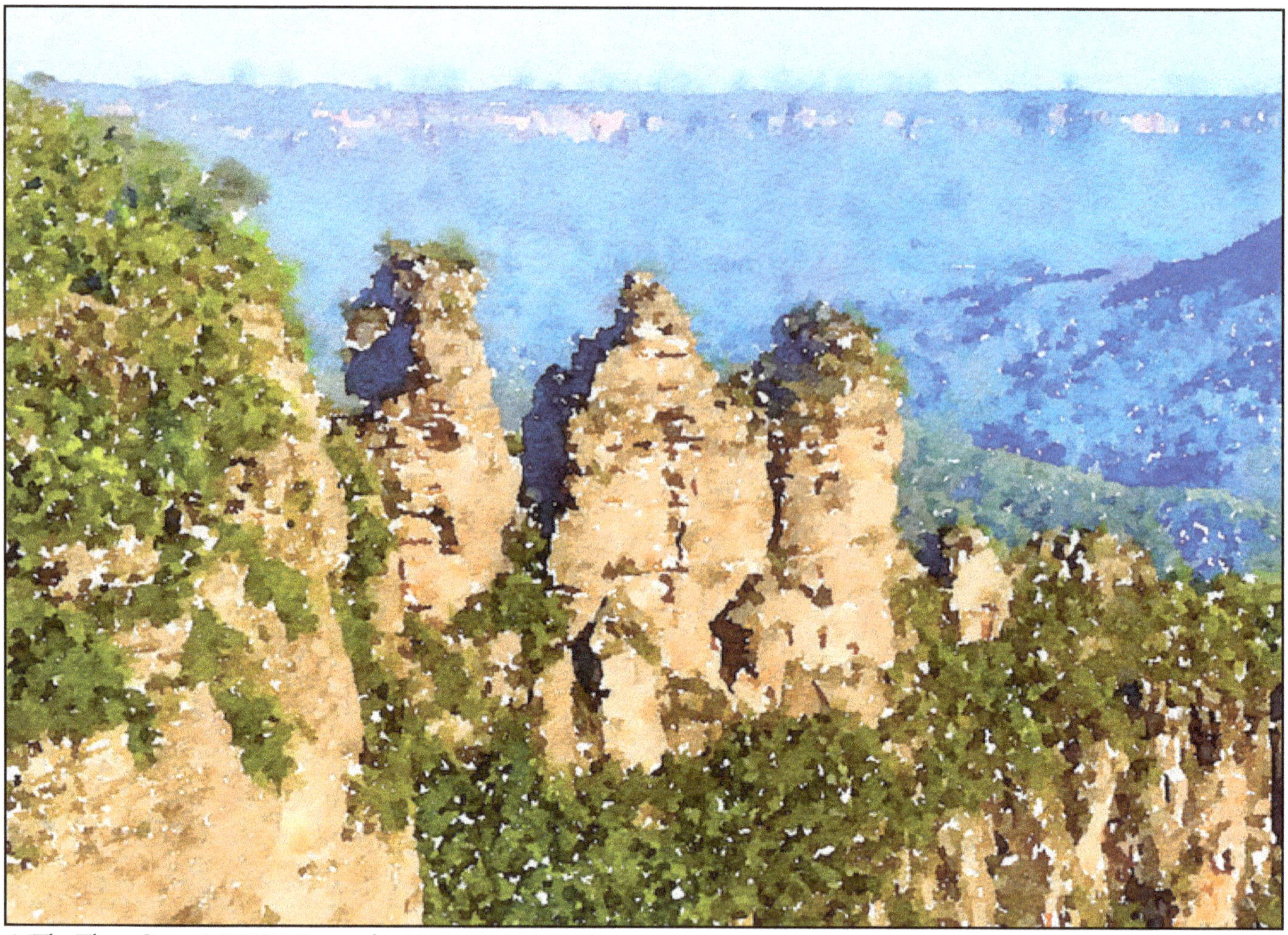

▲'The Three Sisters' (2019), Katoomba, NSW [ALBM1907].

'Plane Tree Tunnel' (2019), Wentworth Falls, NSW [ALBM1906].▼

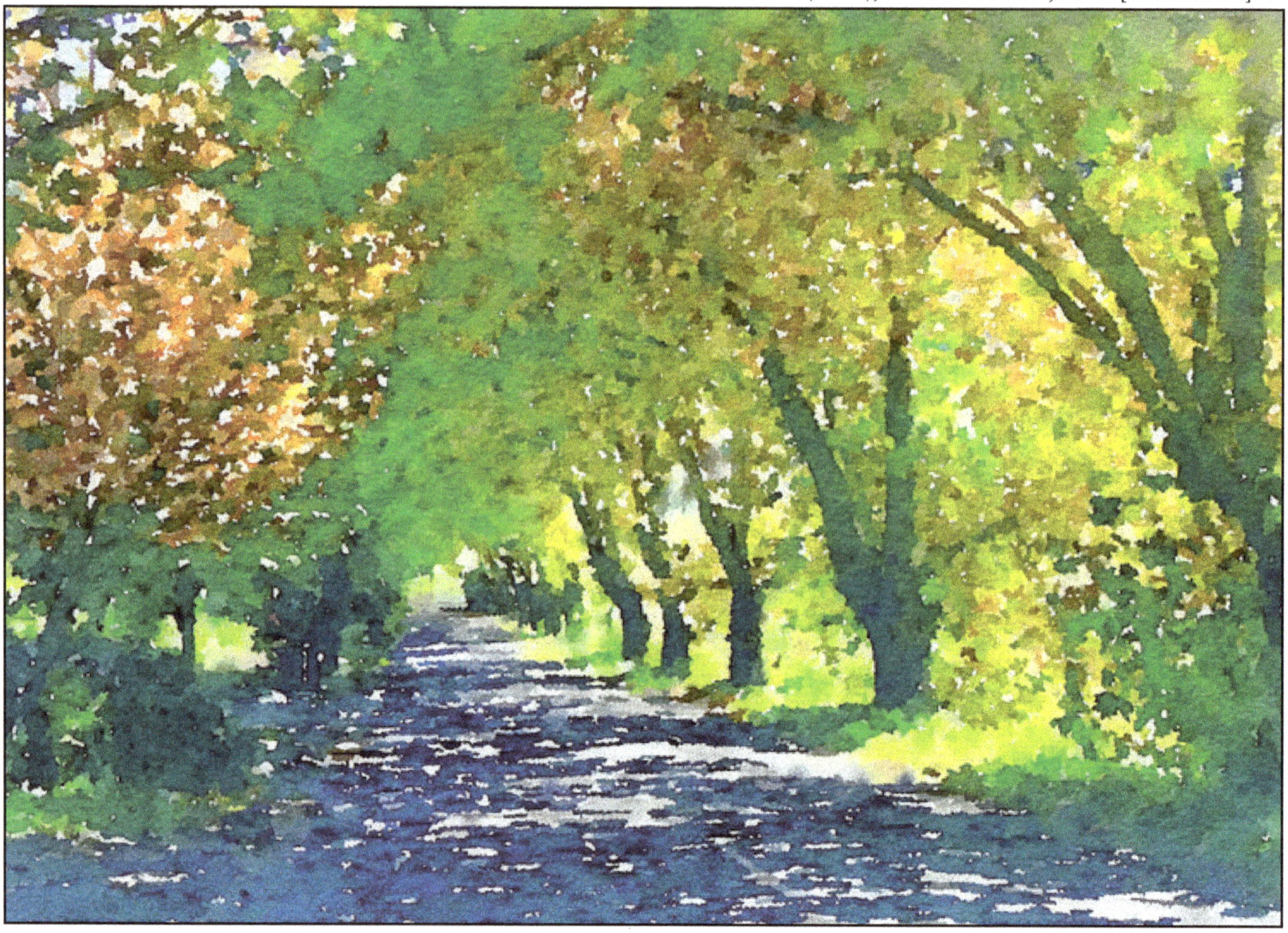

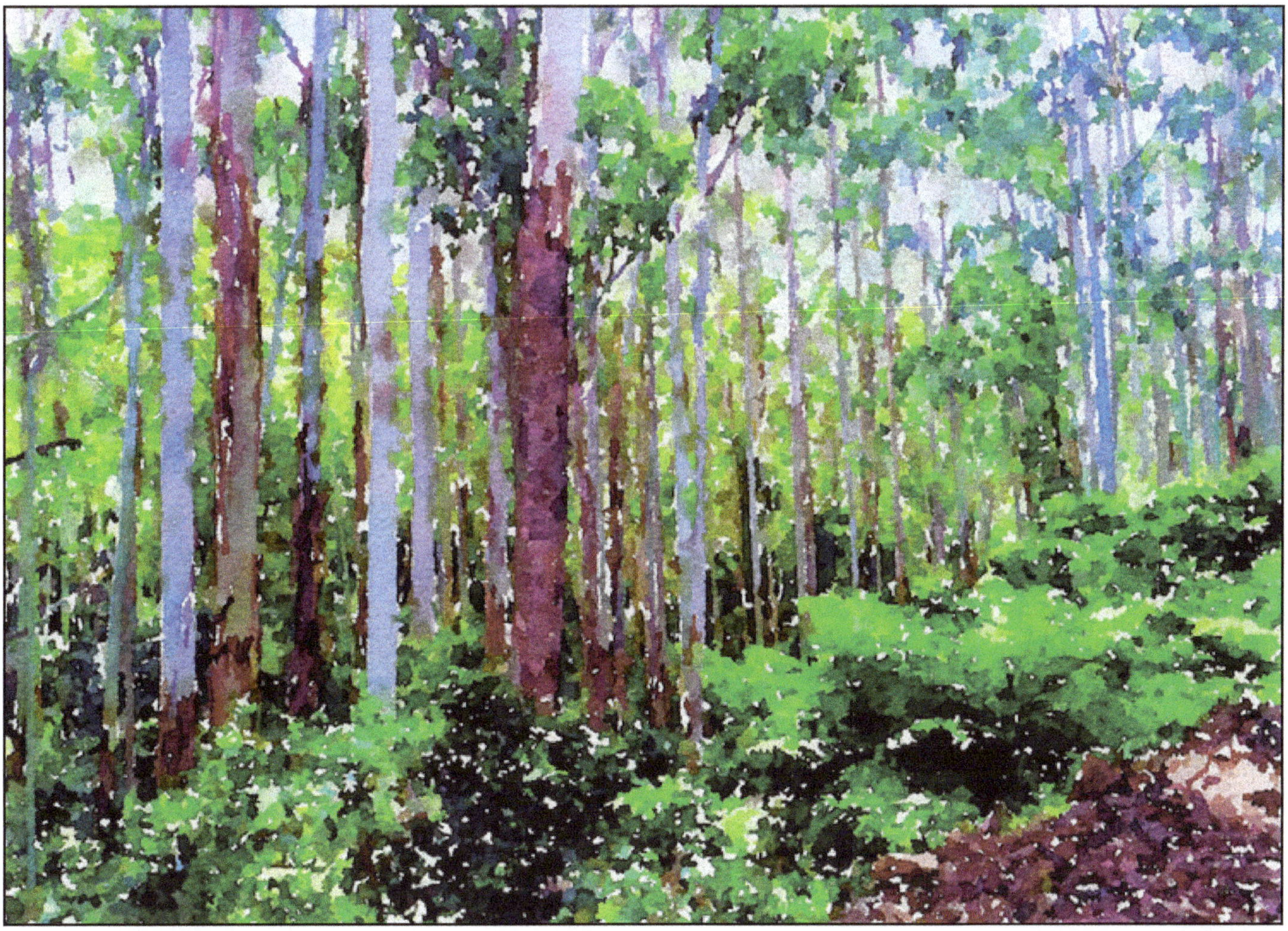

▲'North Coast Blue Gums' (2015), Comboyne, NSW [ALNS1501].

'Sunrise On The Murray' (2019), Albury, NSW [ALNS1901].▼

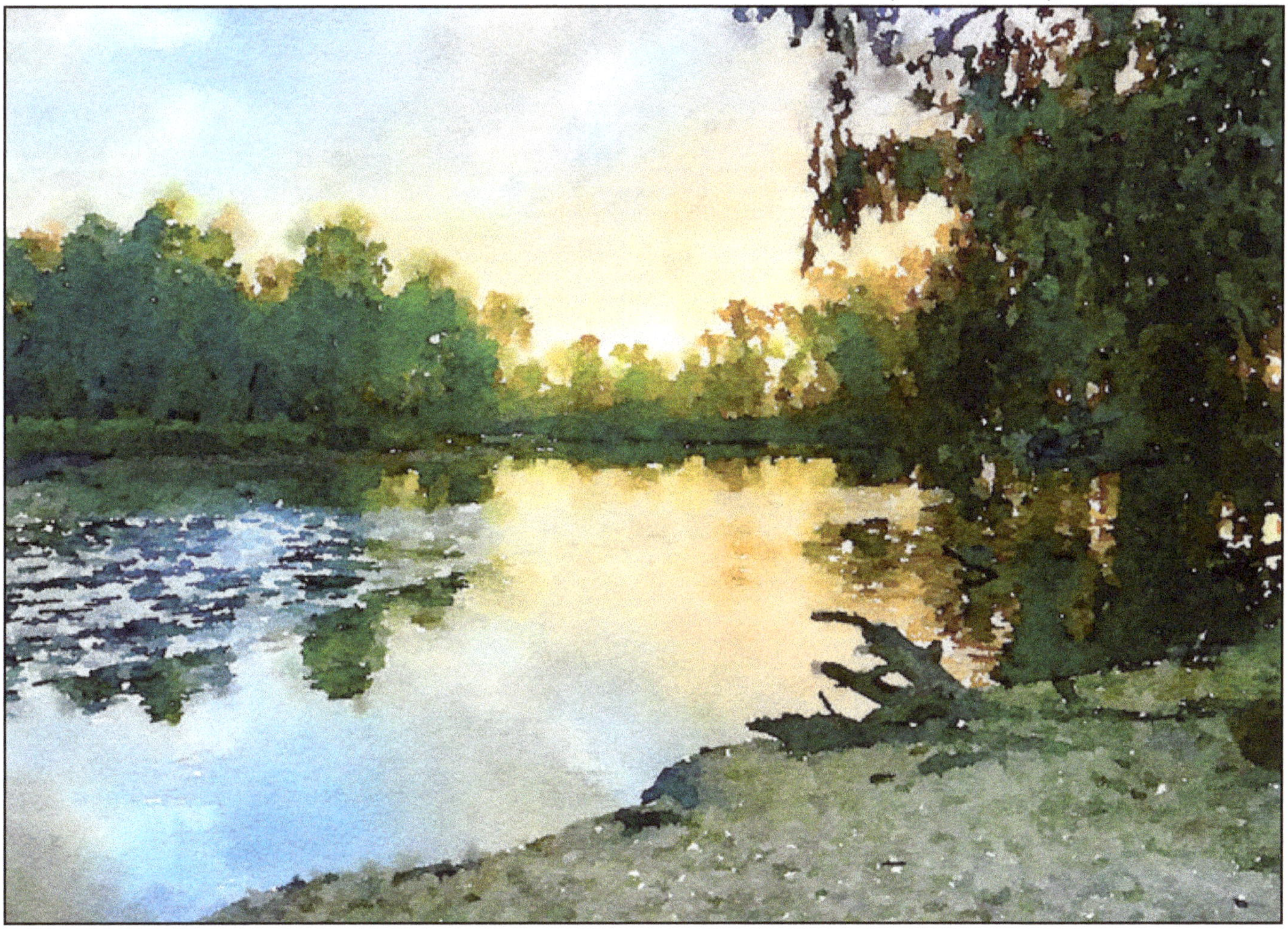

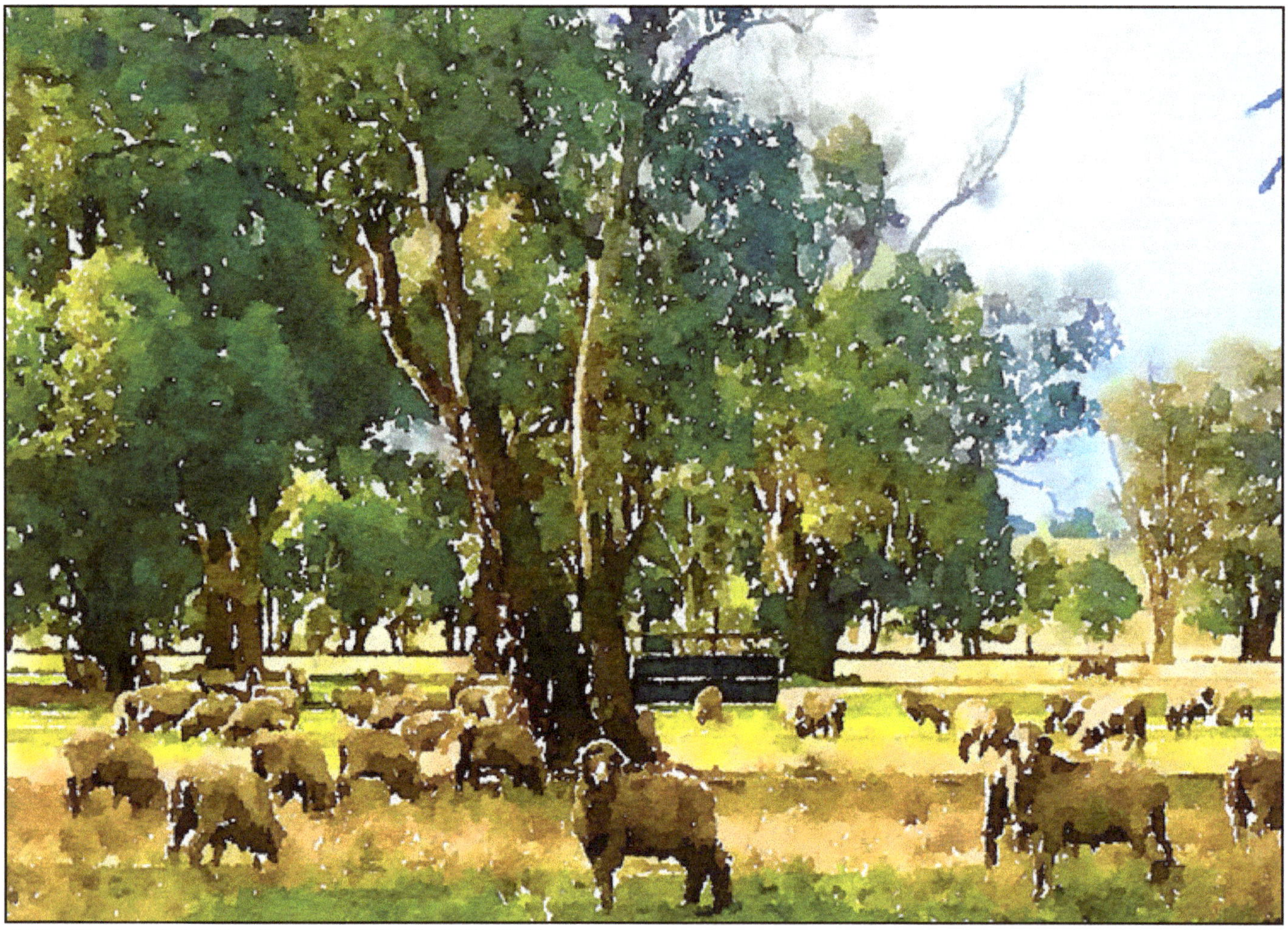

▲'On The Land' (2019), Crowther, NSW [ALNS1902].

'Grazing Country' (2019), Crowther, NSW [ALNS1903].▼

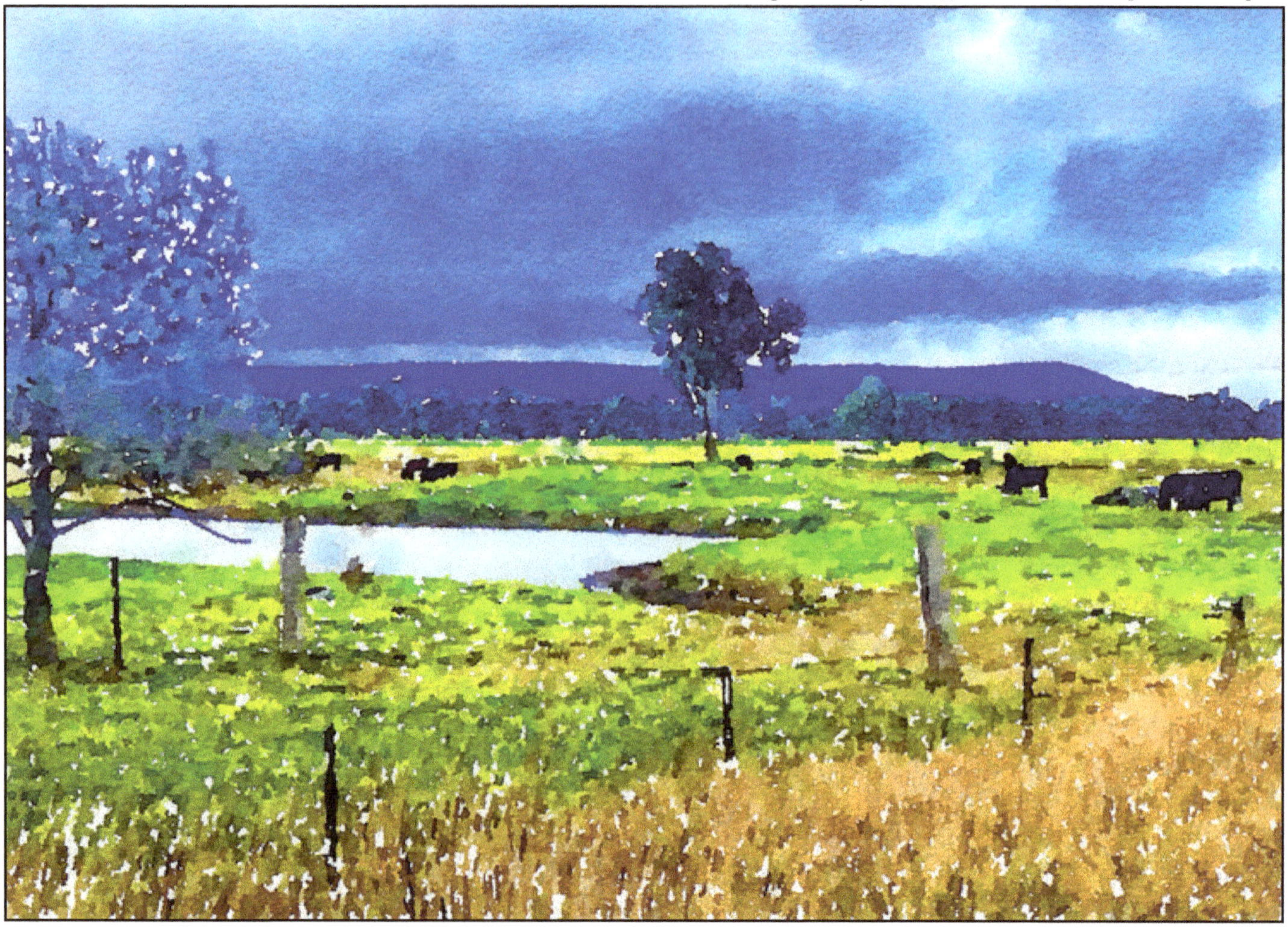

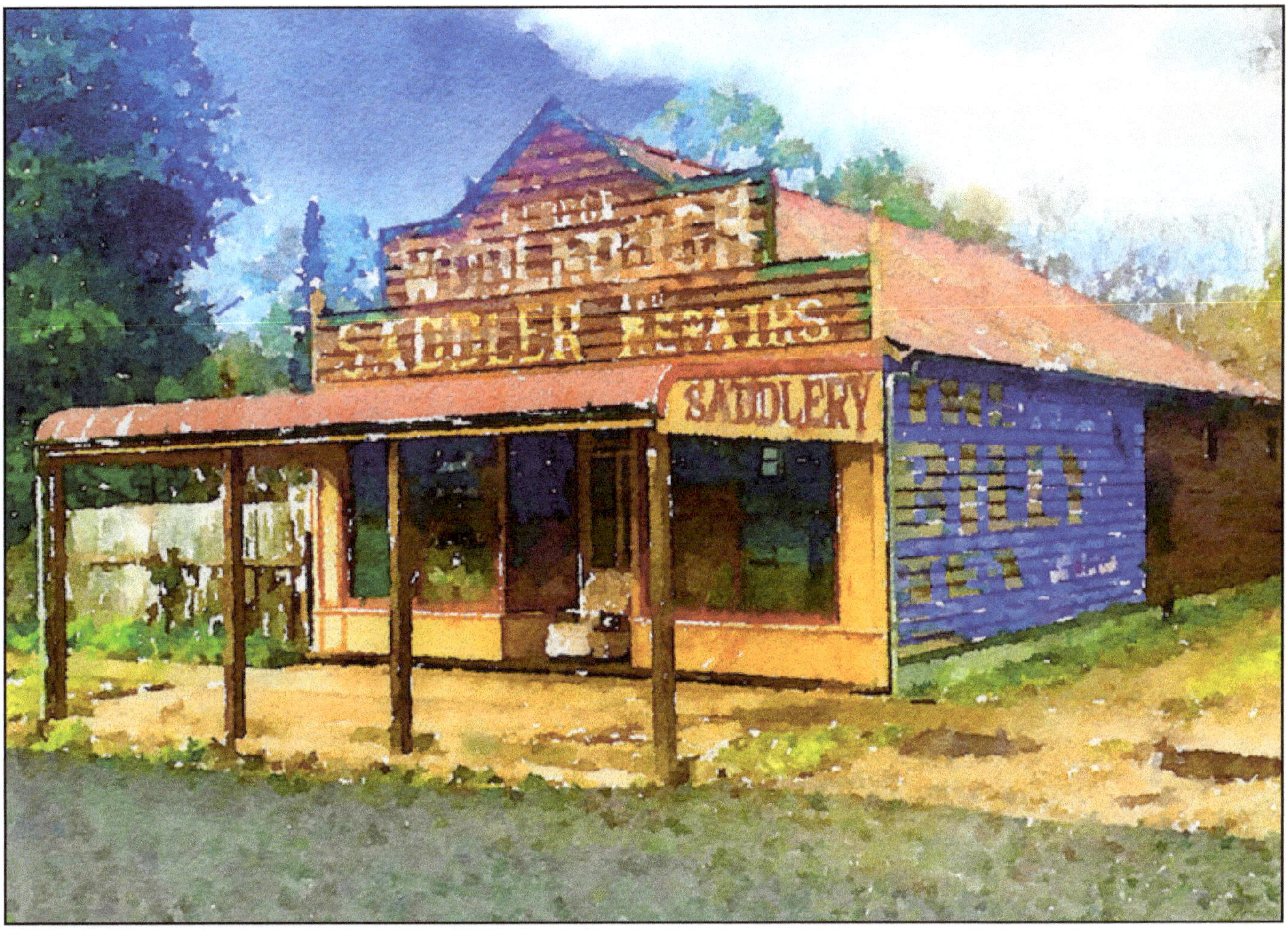

▲'The Saddlery' (2019), Carcoar, NSW [ALNS1904].

'Bush Home' (2019), Millthorpe, NSW [ALNS1905].▼

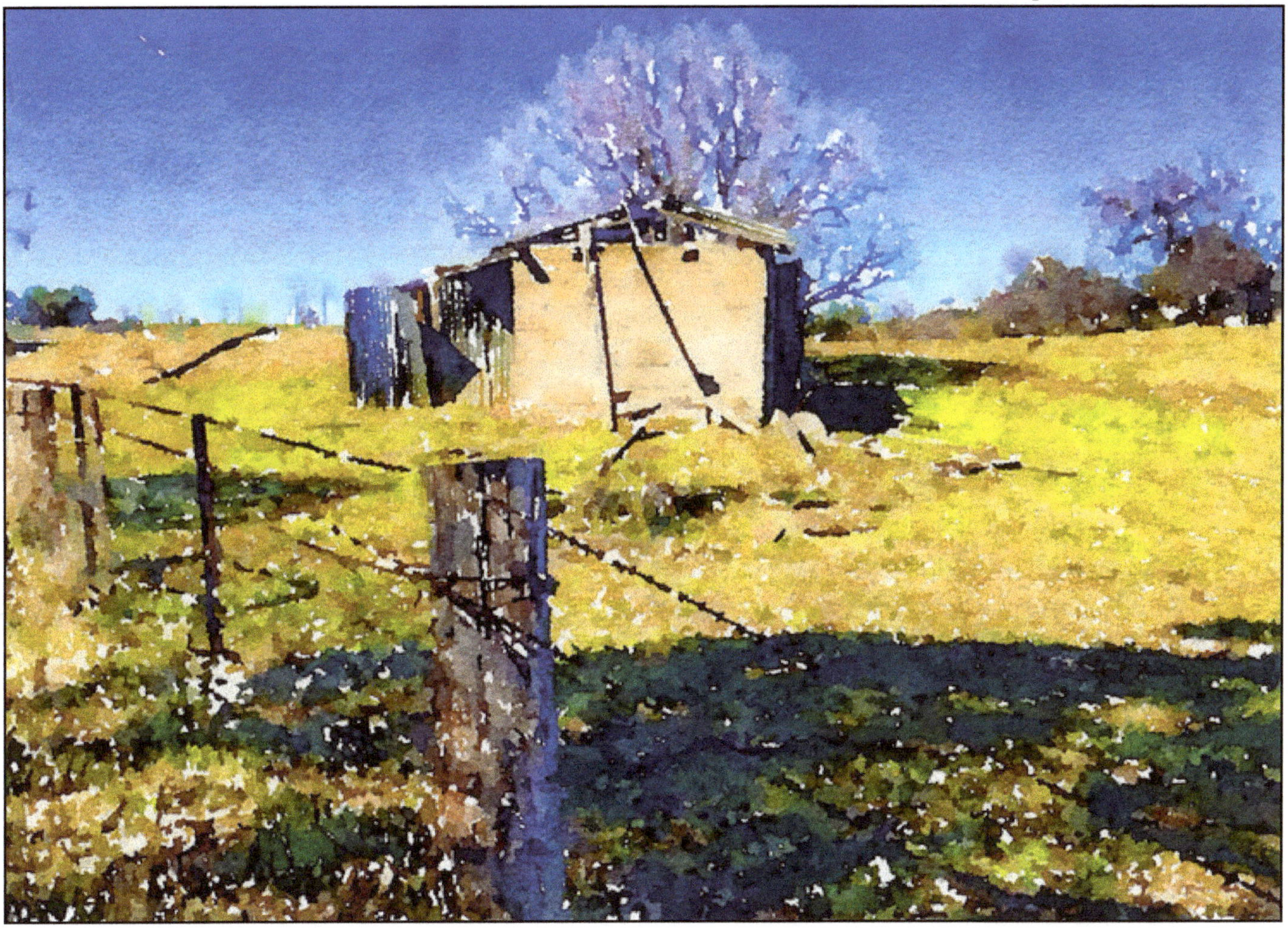

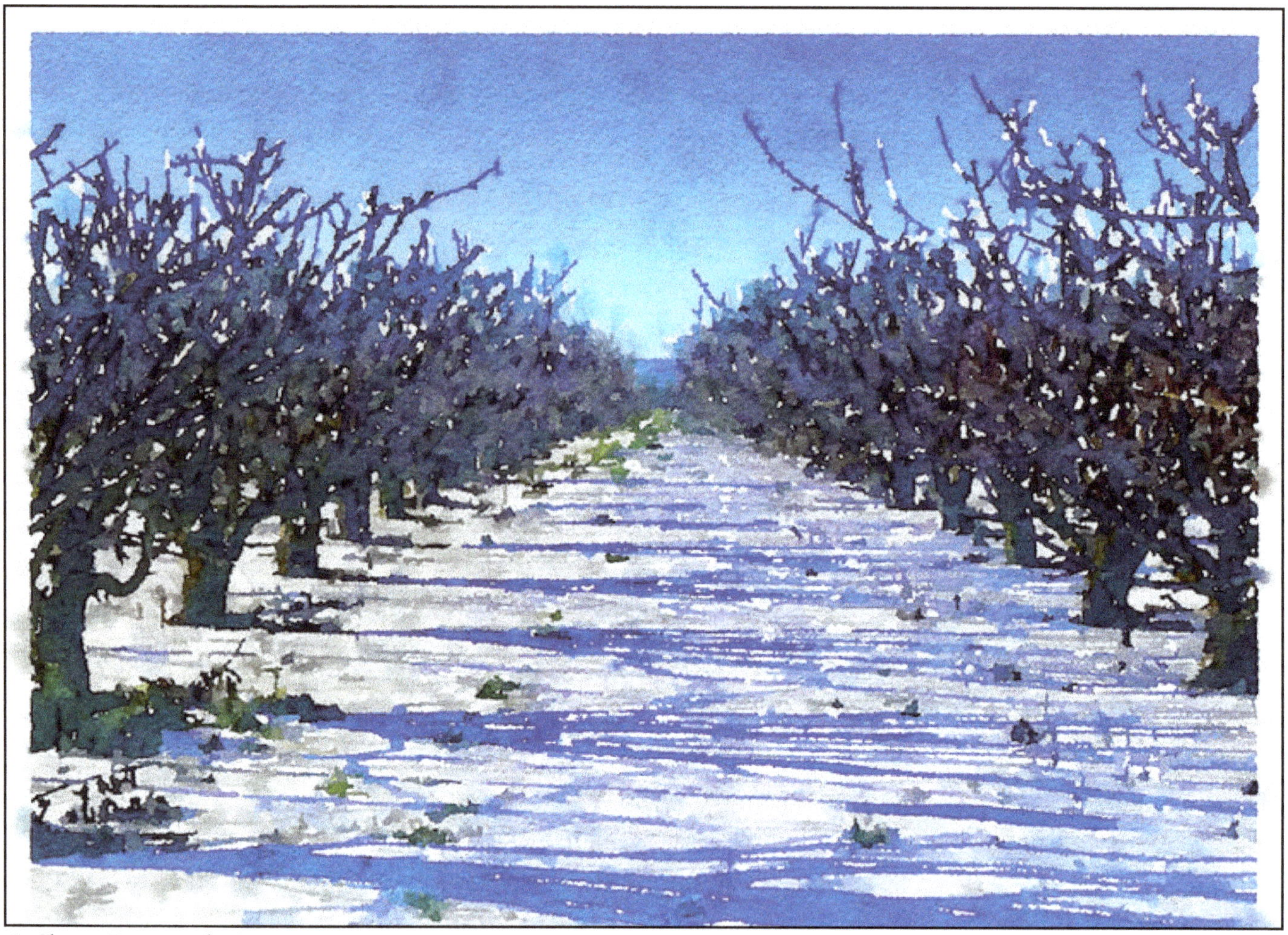

▲'Cherry Trees In The Snow' (2019), Orange, NSW [ALNS1906].

'Outback Windmill' (2019), Lucknow, NSW [ALNS1907].▼

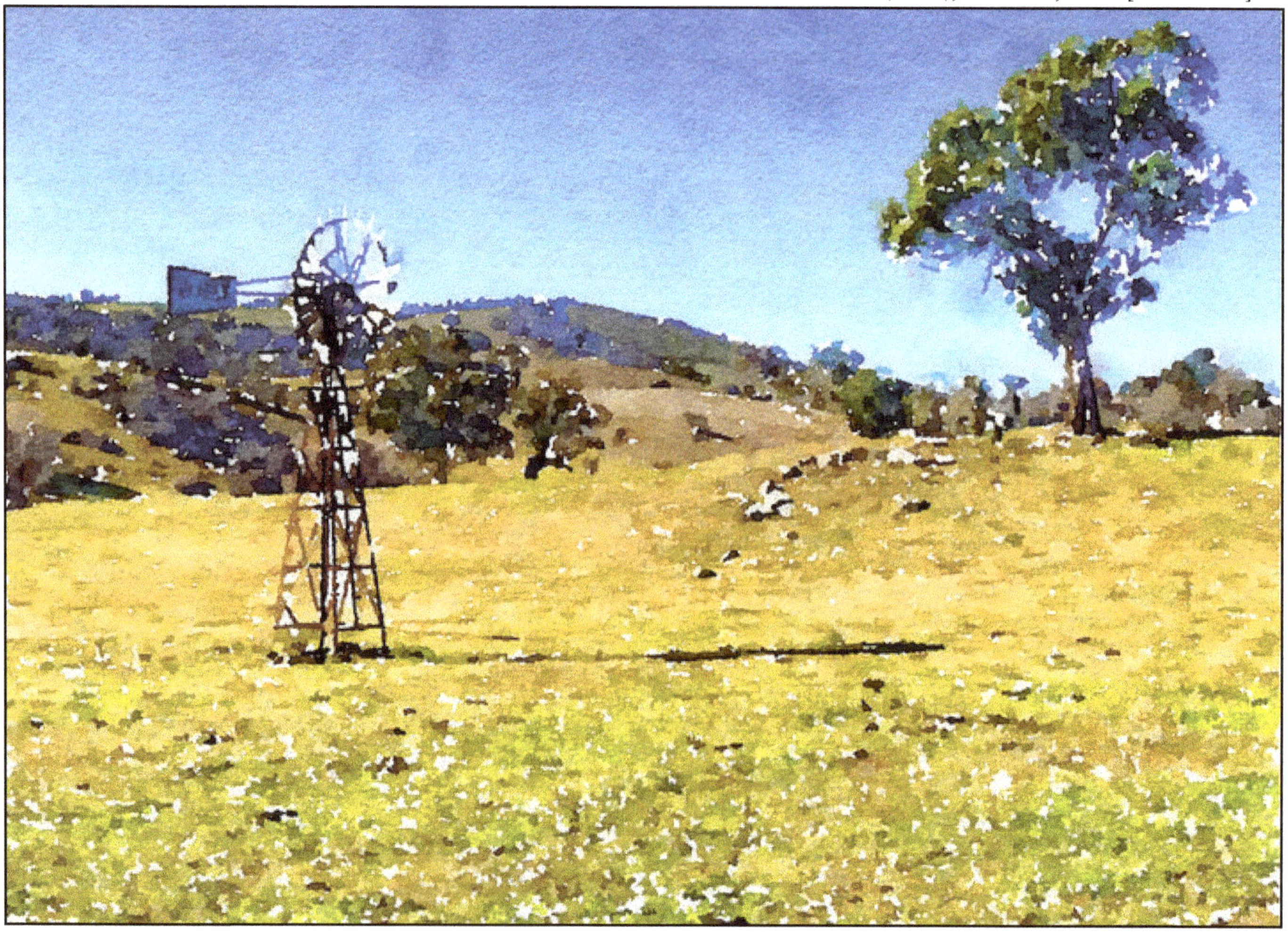

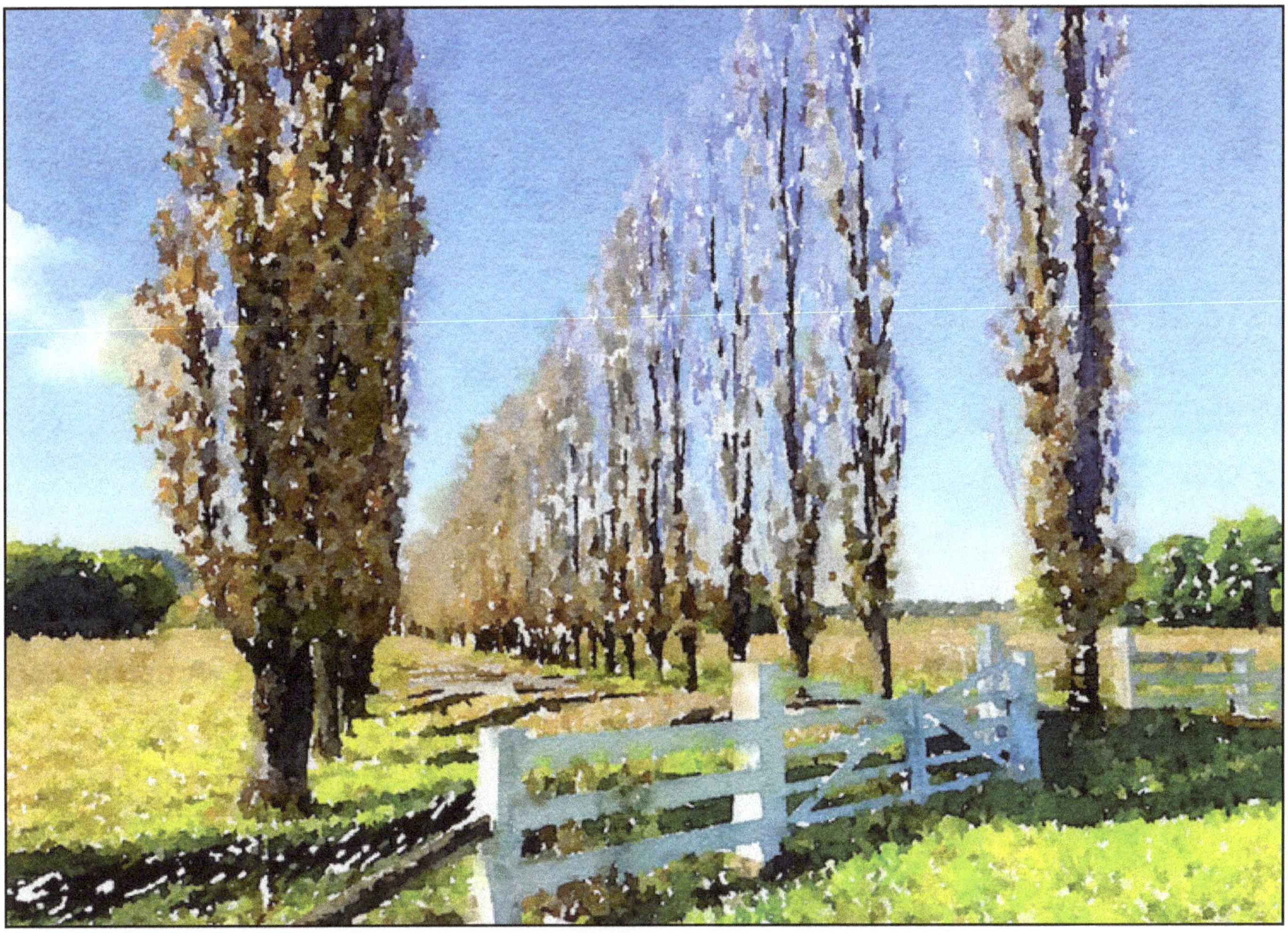

▲'New England Poplars' (2021), Glen Innes, NSW [ALNS2101].

'The Town Hall' (2021), Glen Innes, NSW [ALNS2102].▼

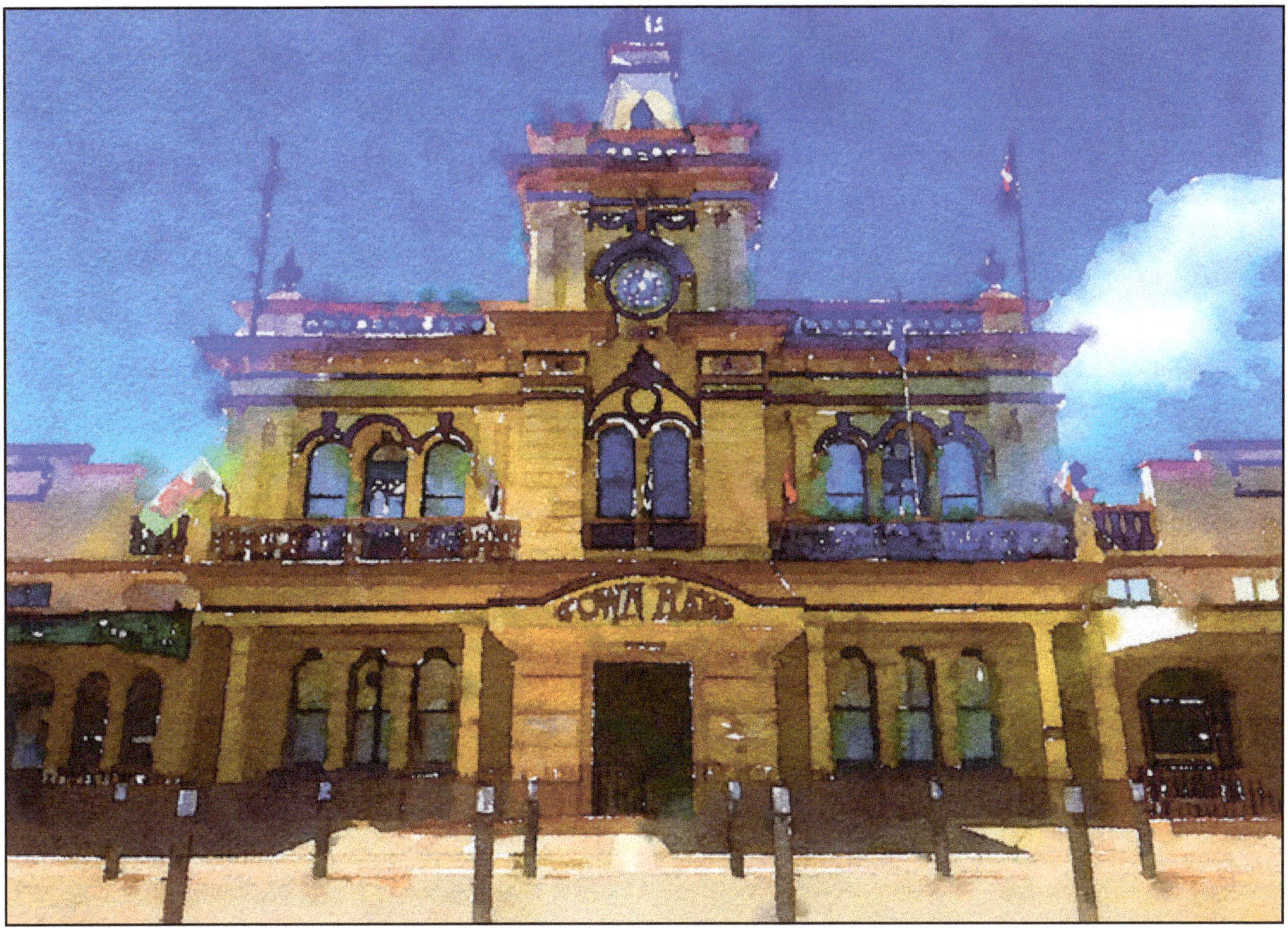

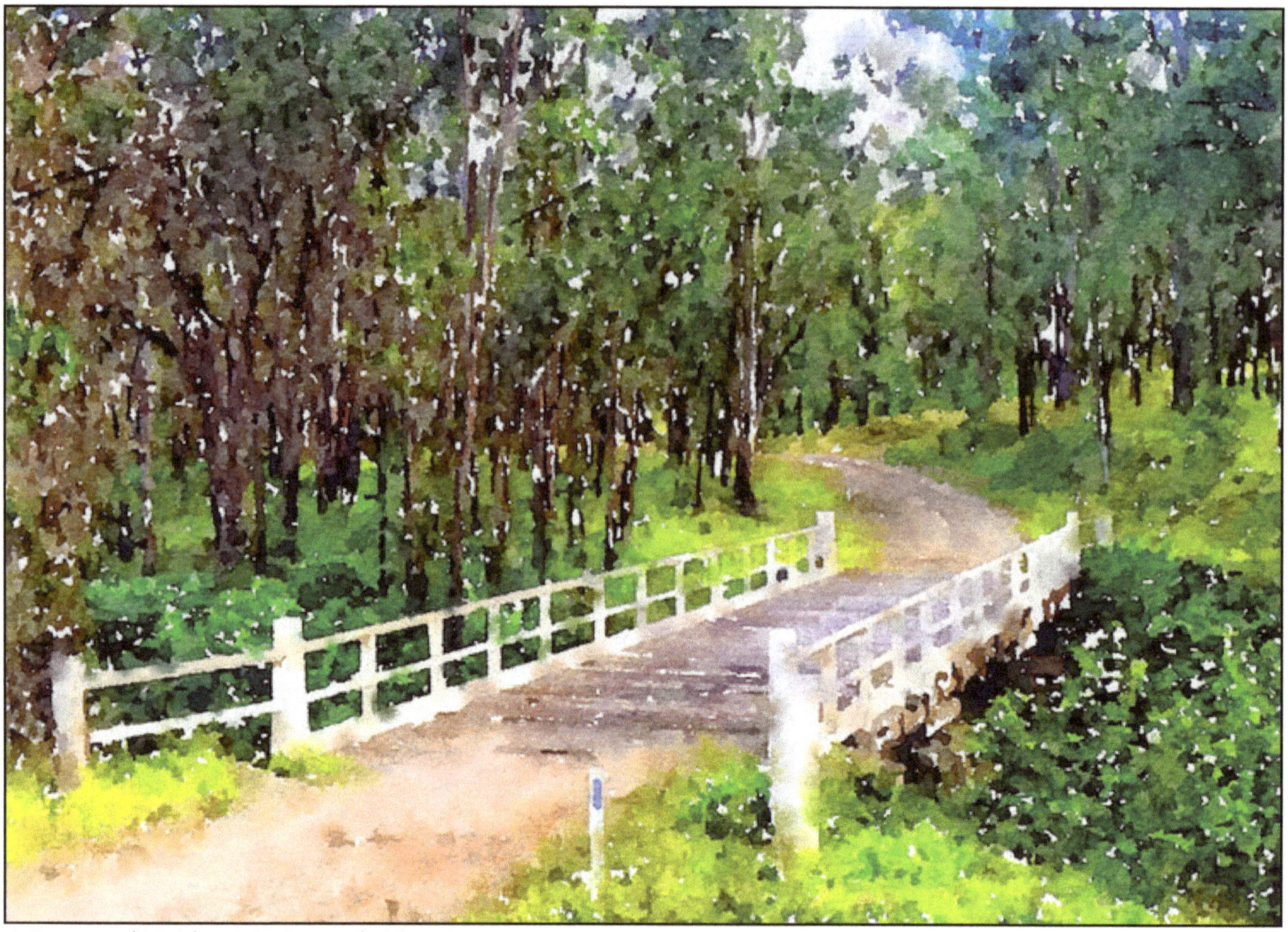

▲'Buccarumbi Bridge' (2021), Nymboida, NSW [ALNS2103].

'North Coast Forest' (2021), Buccarumbi, NSW [ALNS2104].▼

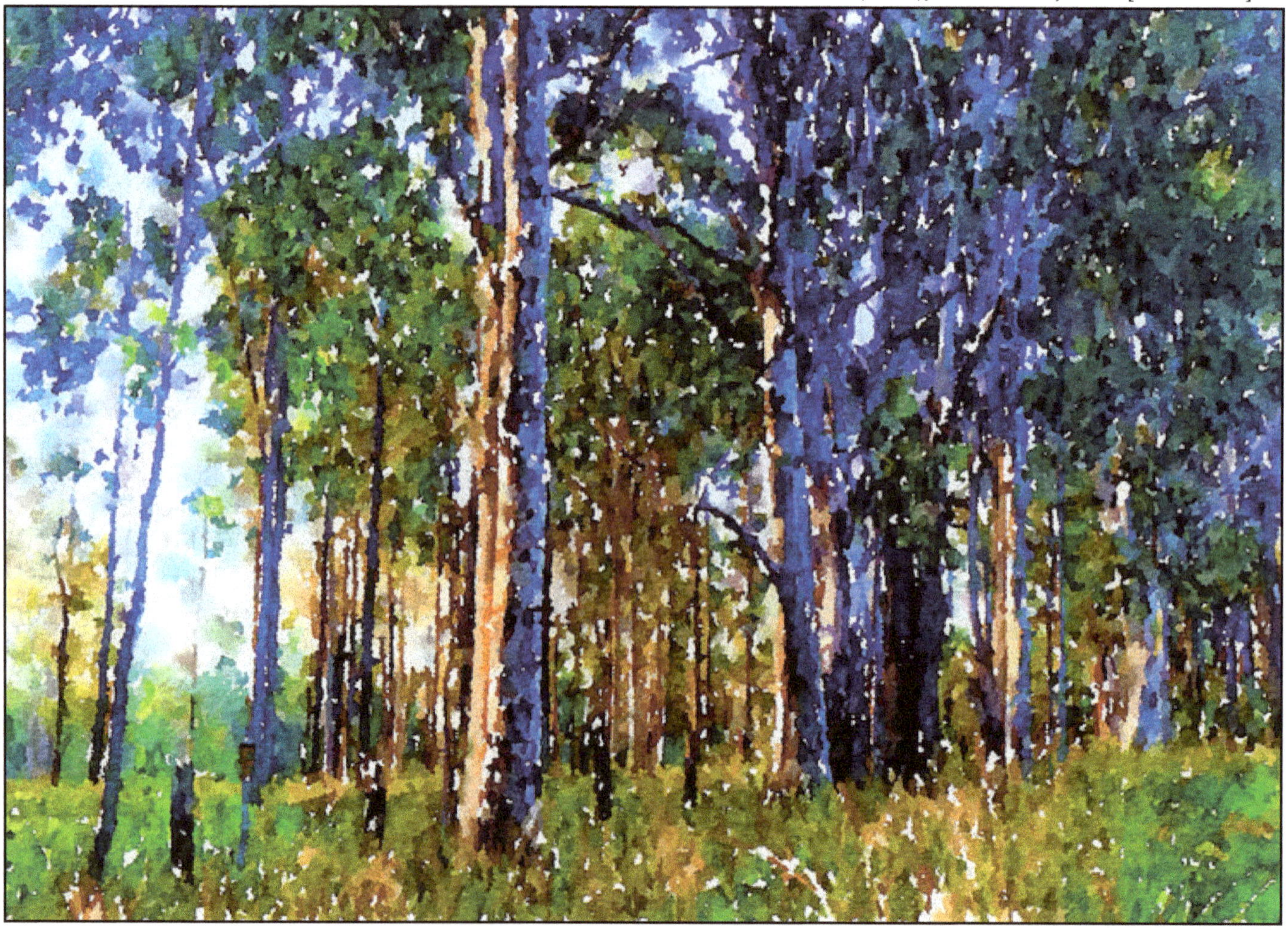

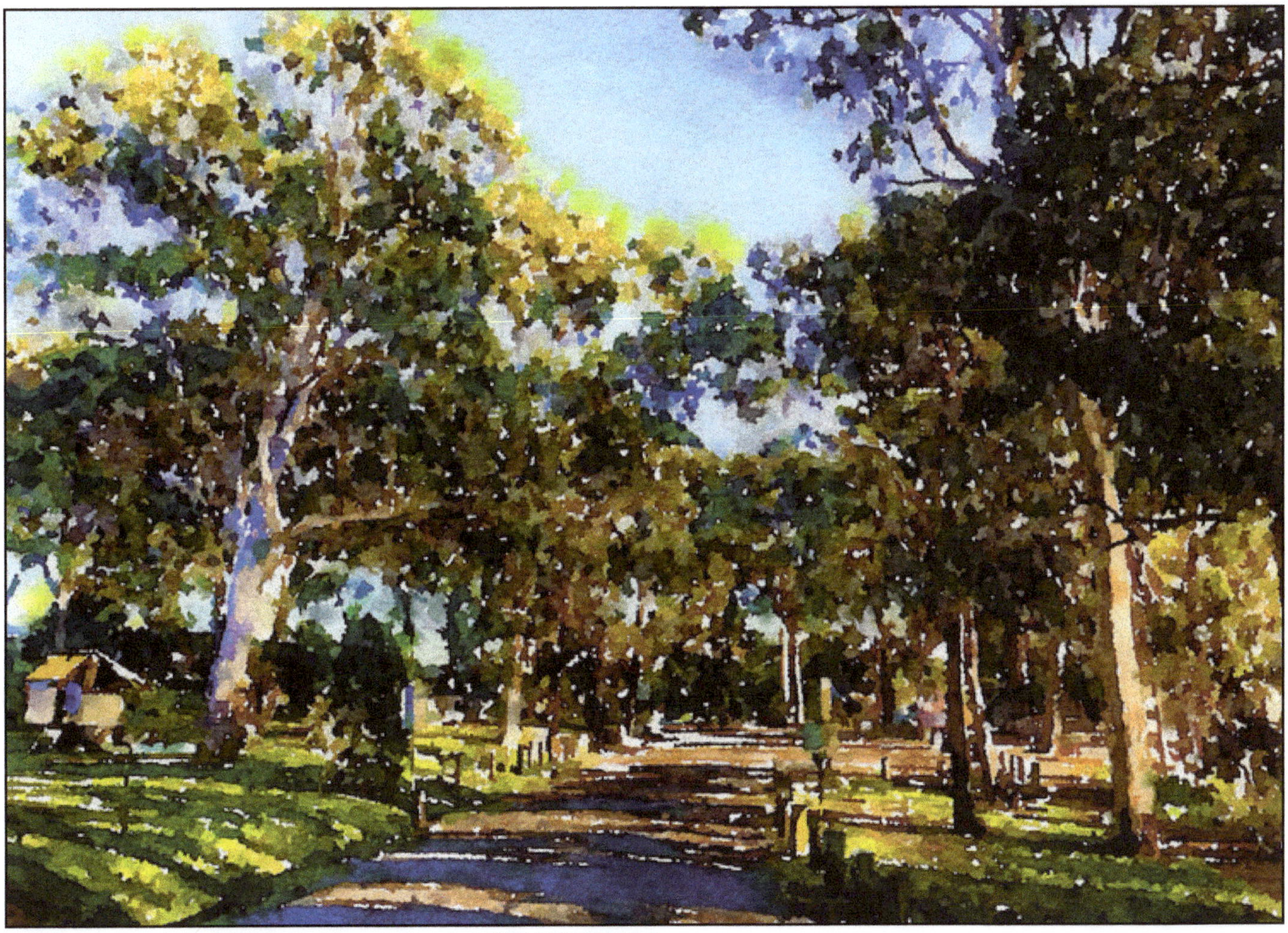

▲'Moonie Beach Park' (2021), Moonie Beach, NSW [ALNS2106].

'The Footbridge' (2021), Moonie Beach, NSW [ALNS2105].▼

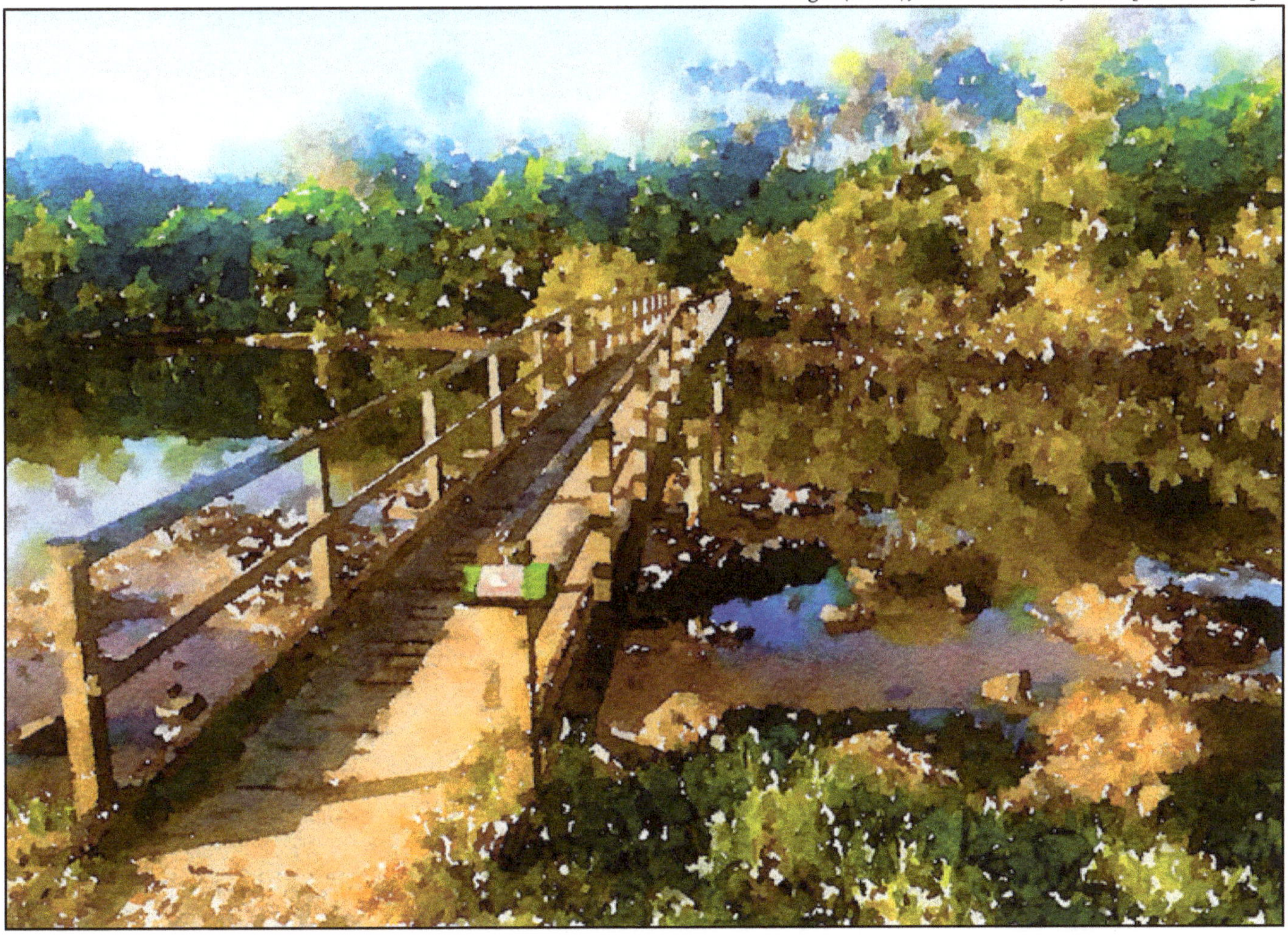

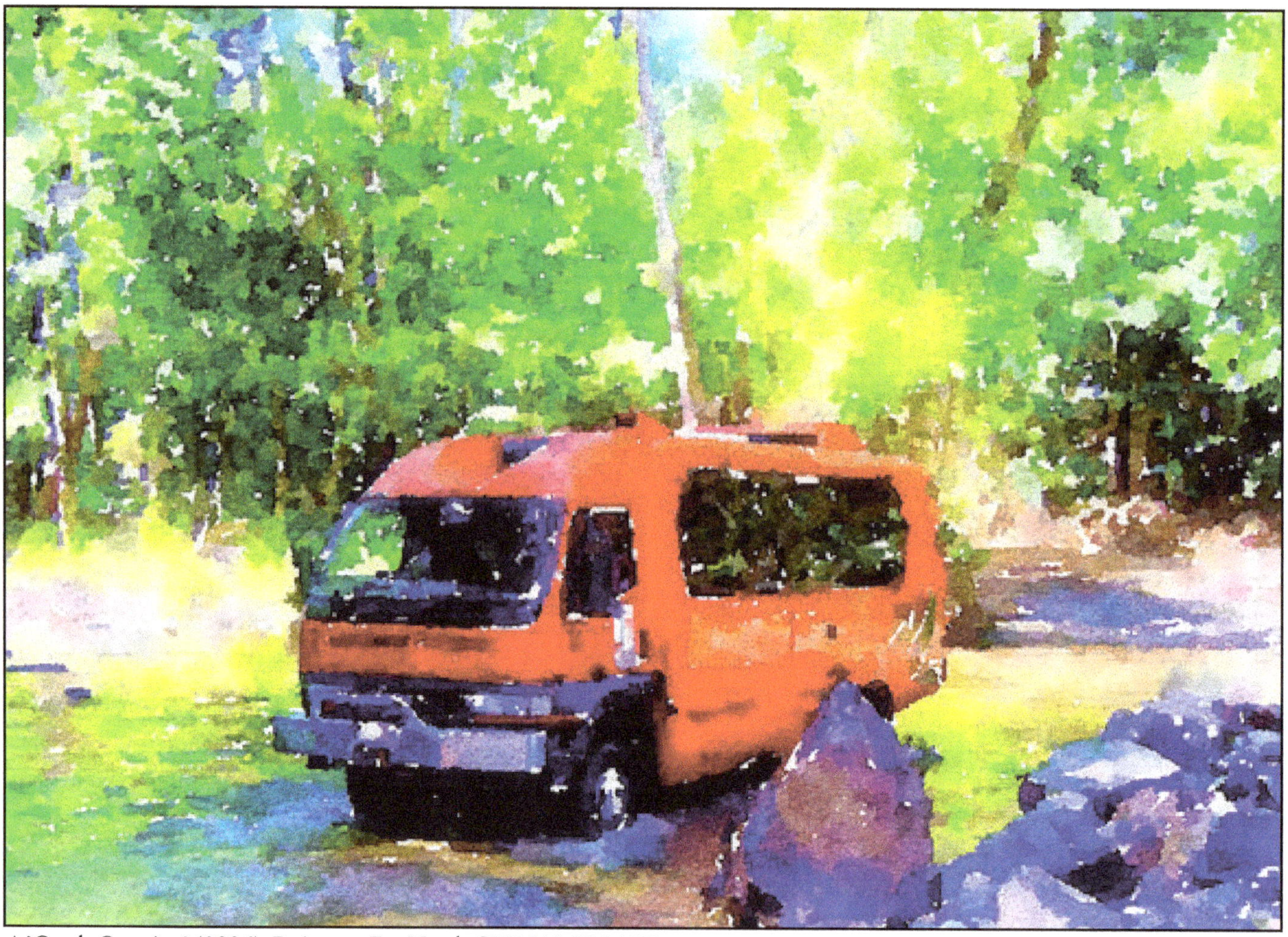

▲'Creek Crossing' (2006), Daintree, Far North QLD [ALQL0602].

'Bloomfield River 2' (2006), Daintree, Far North QLD [ALQL0603].▼

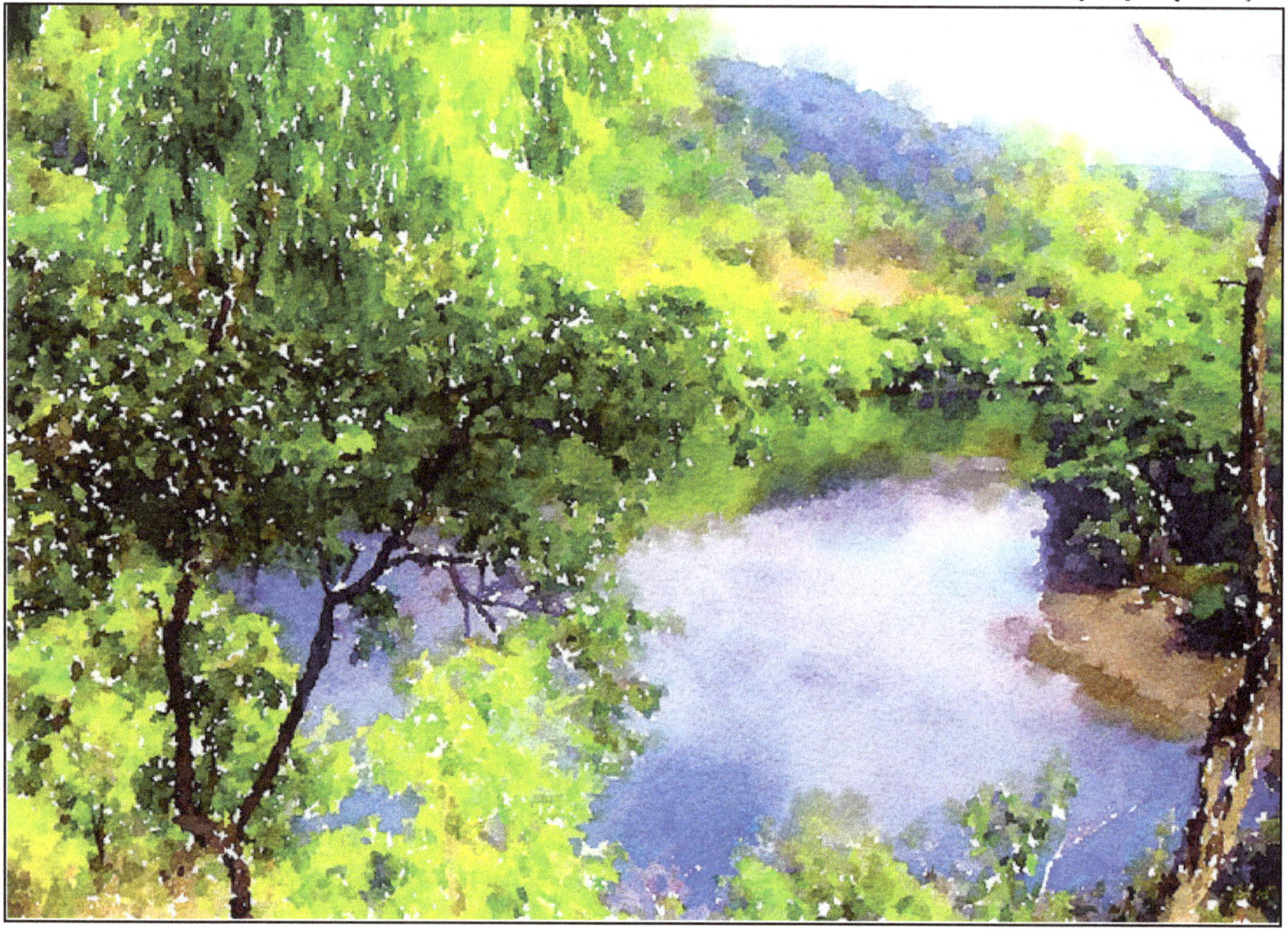

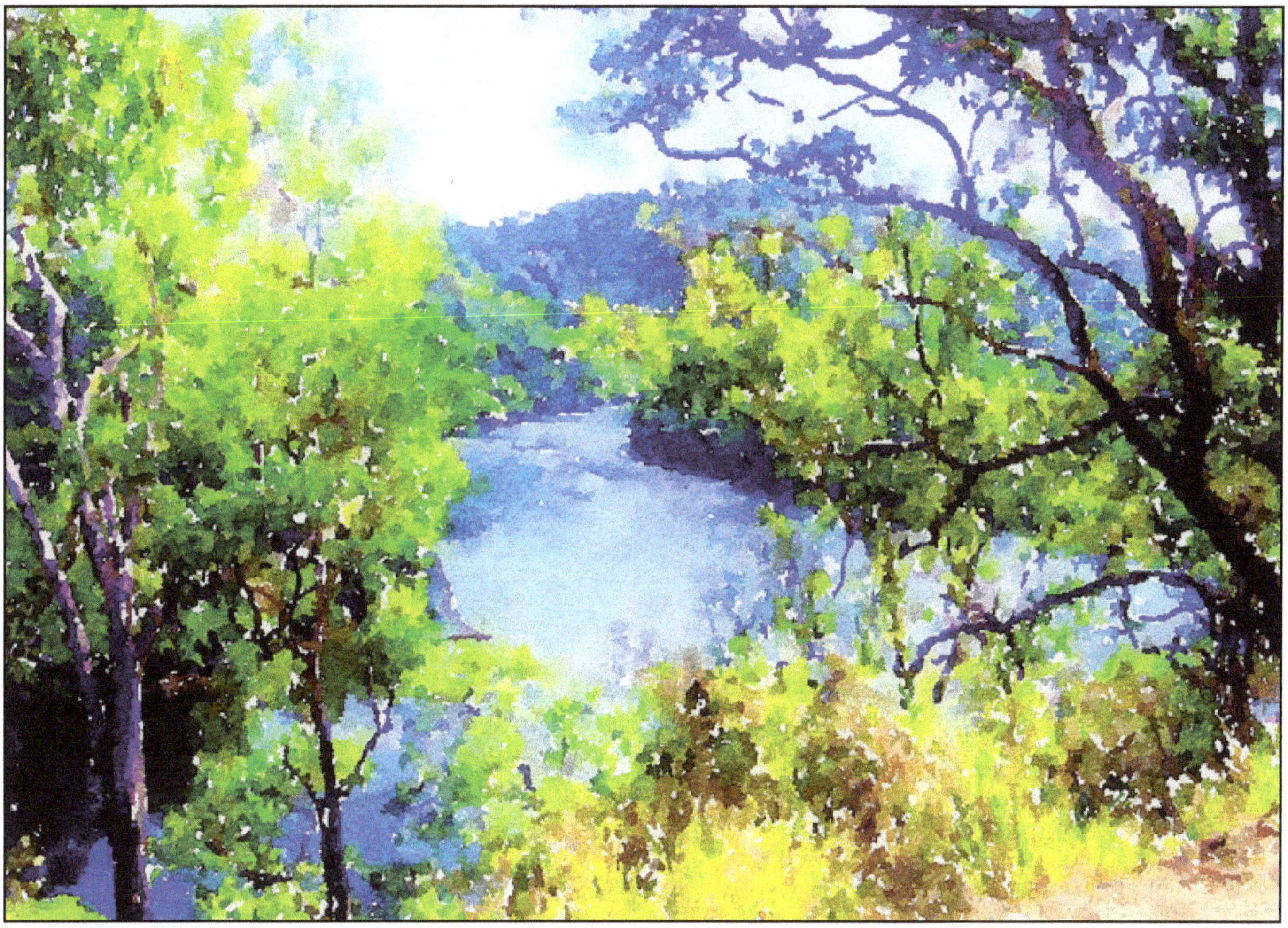

▲'Bloomfield River 1' (2006), Daintree, Far North QLD [ALQL0601].

'Daintree Creek' (2006), Far North QLD [ALQL0604].▼

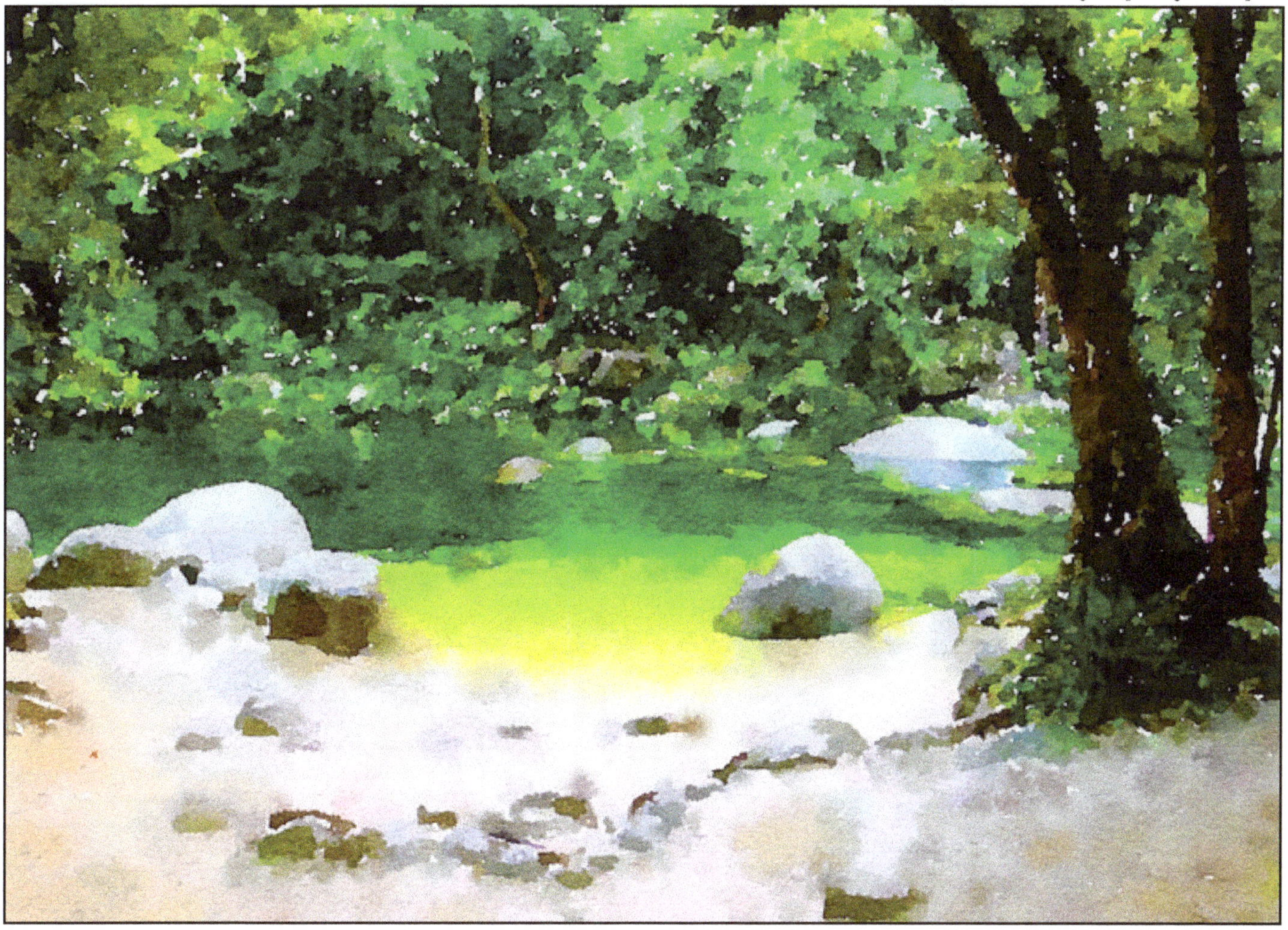

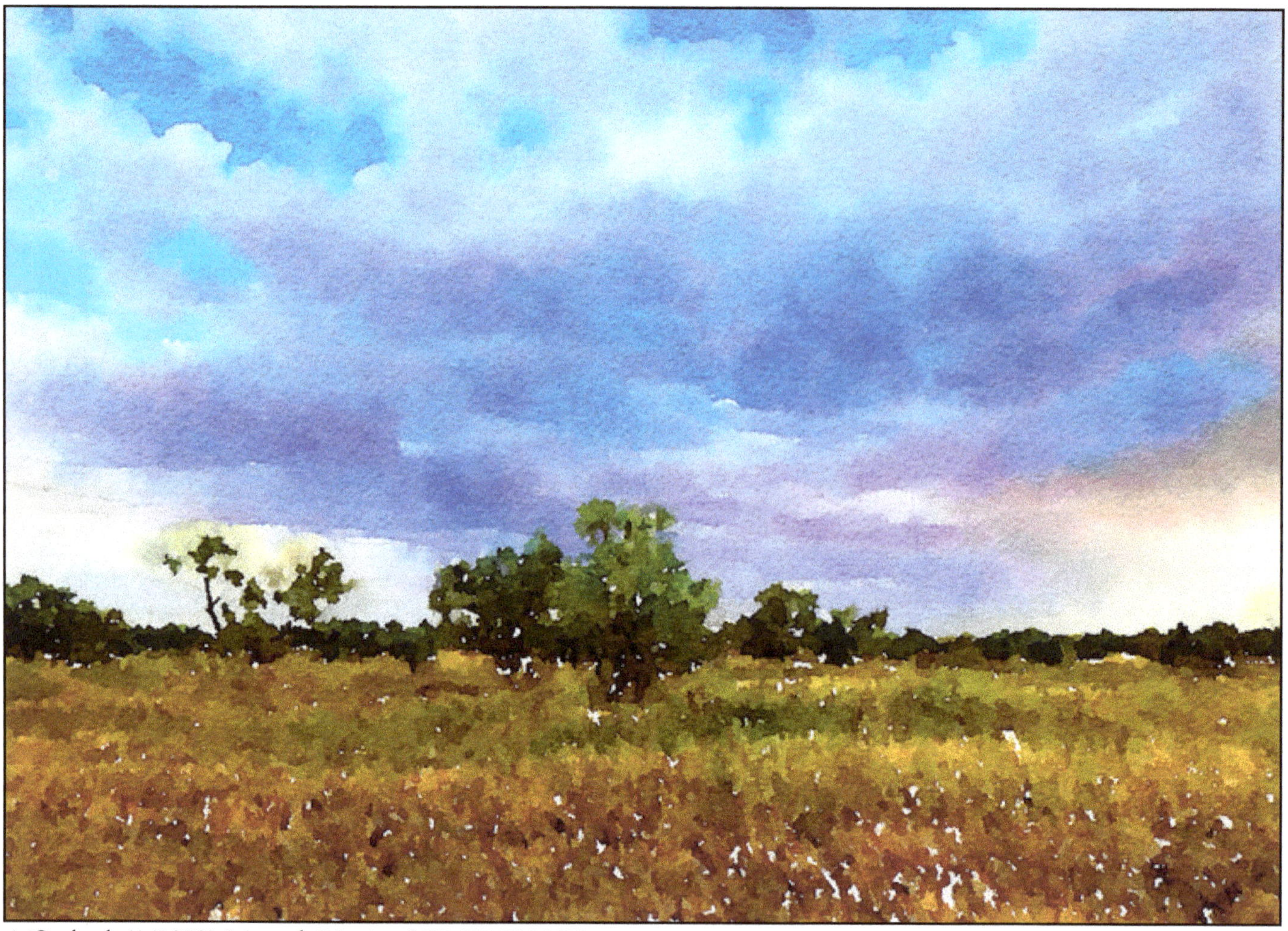

▲'Outback 1' (2020), Murweh District, QLD [ALQL2002].

'Outback 2' (2020), Murweh District, QLD [ALQL2001].▼

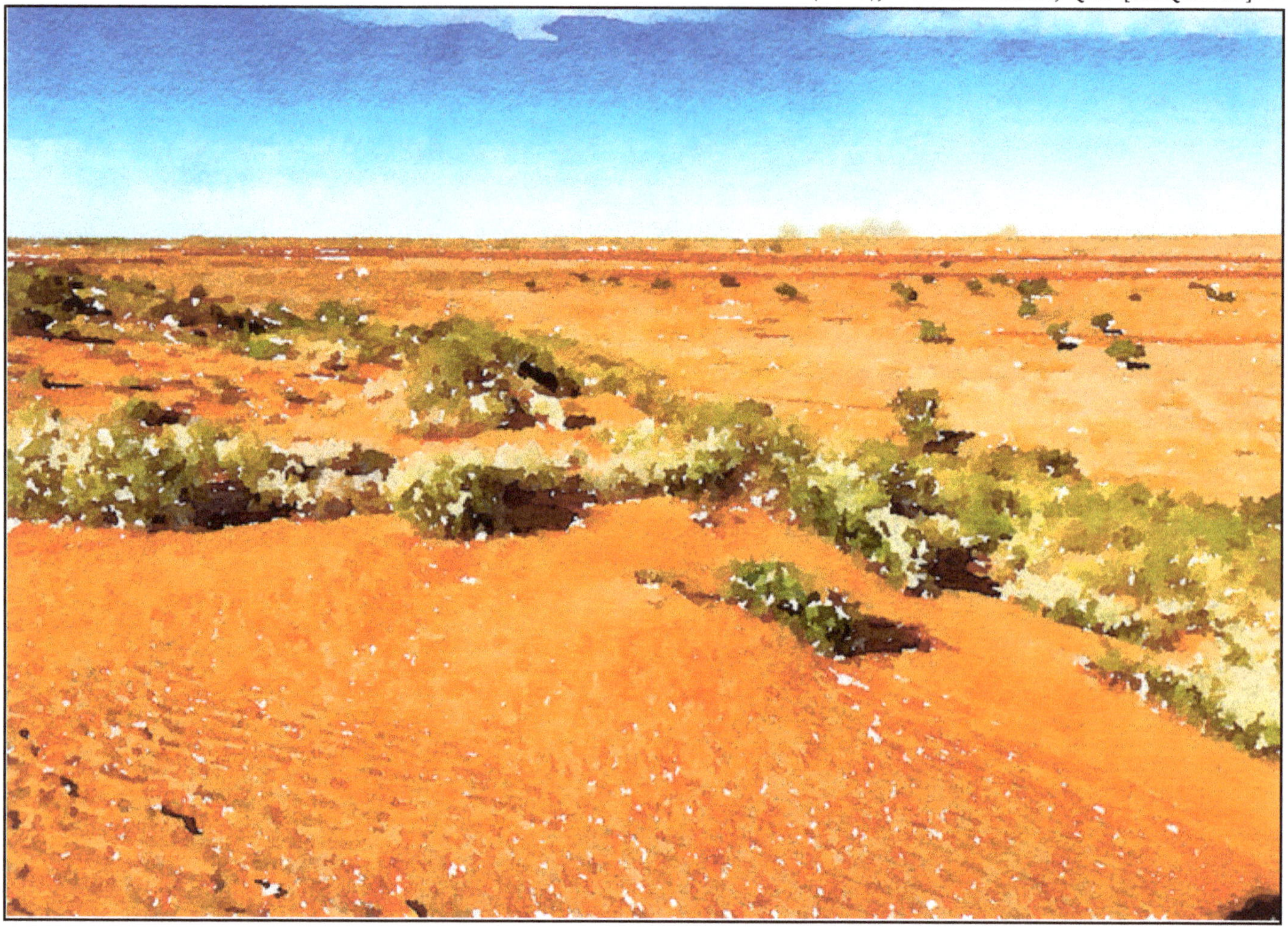

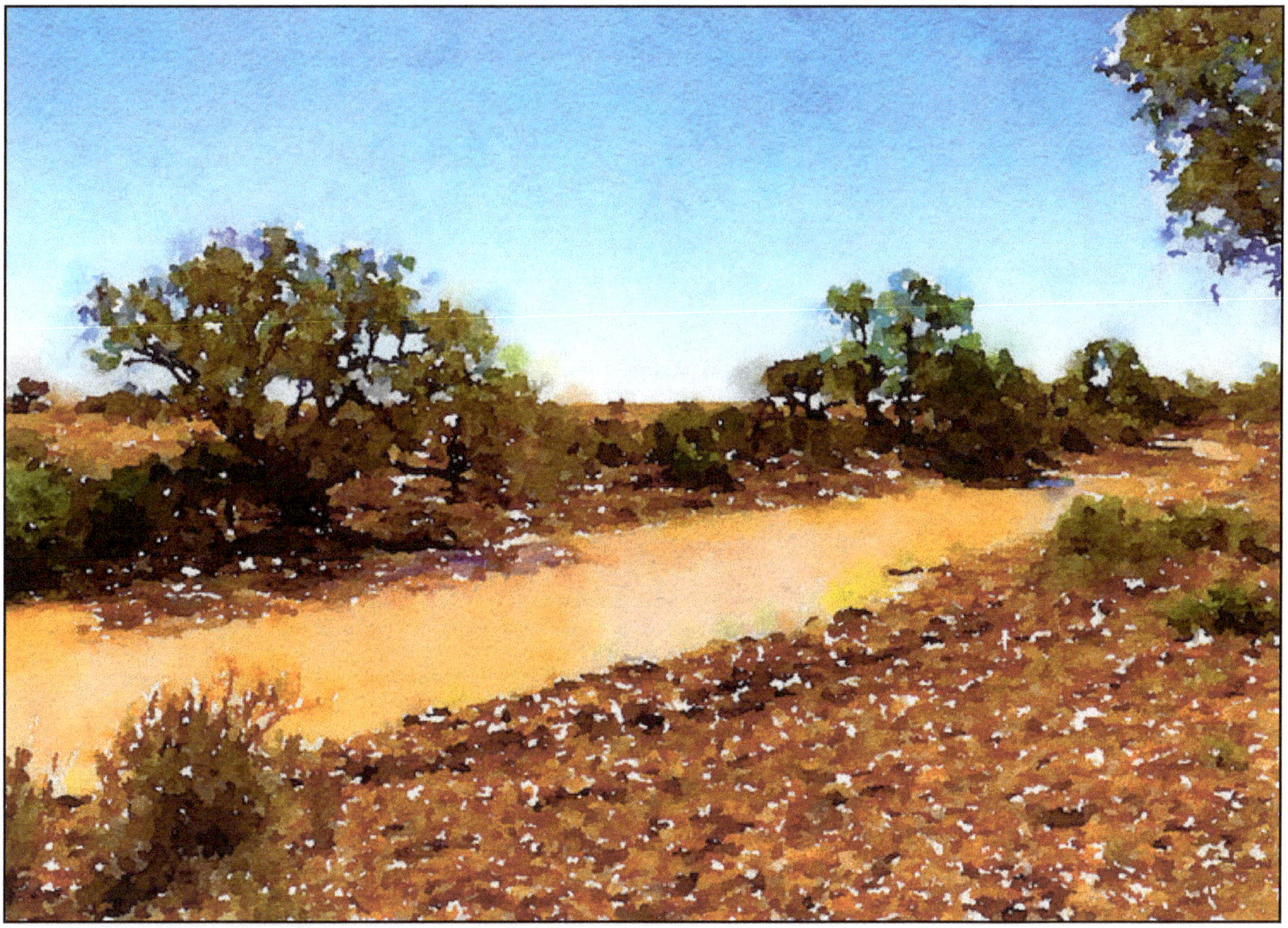

▲'Outback 3' (2020), Murweh District, QLD [ALQL2003].

'Outback 4' (2020), Murweh District, QLD [ALQL2004].▼

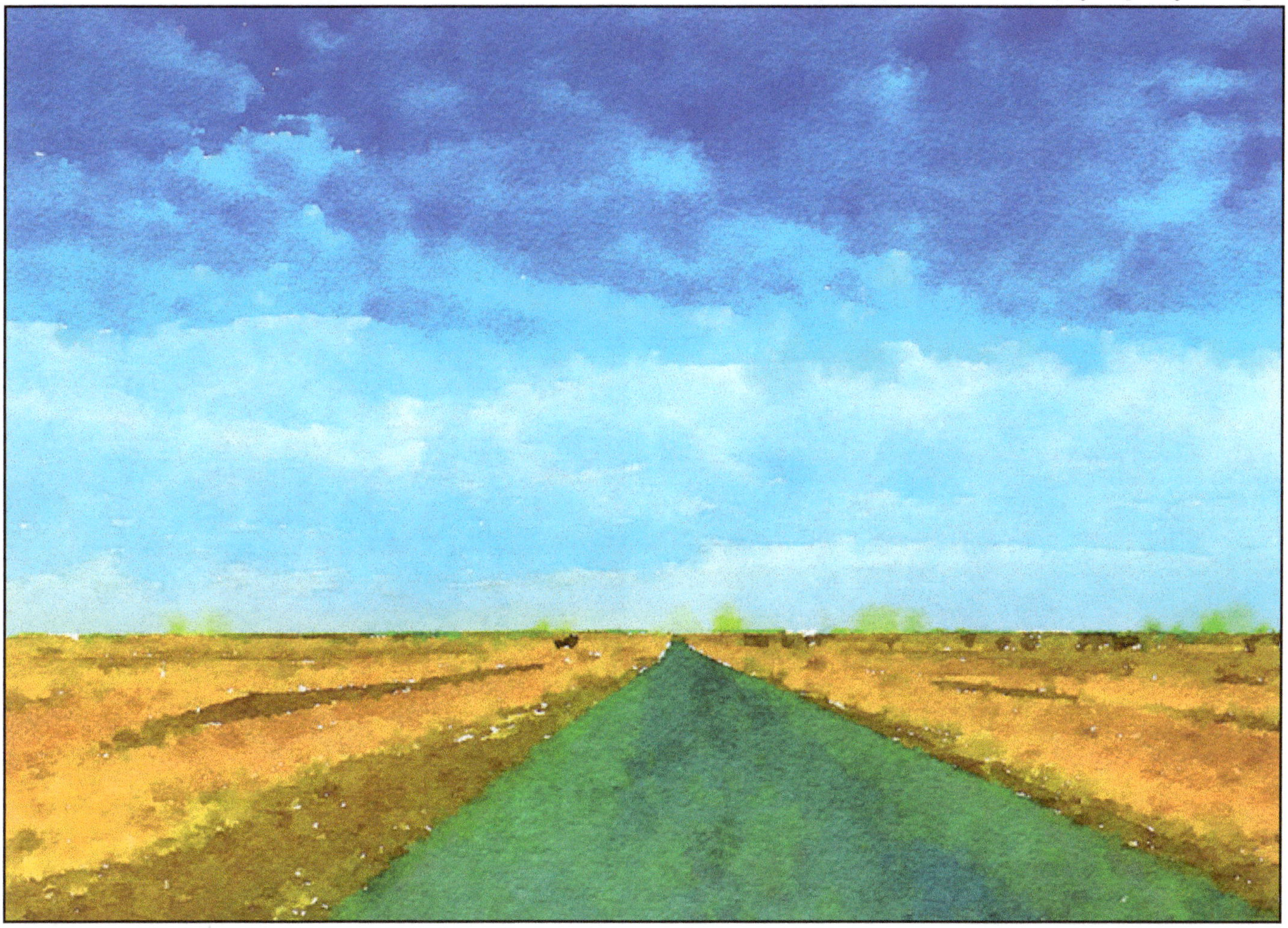

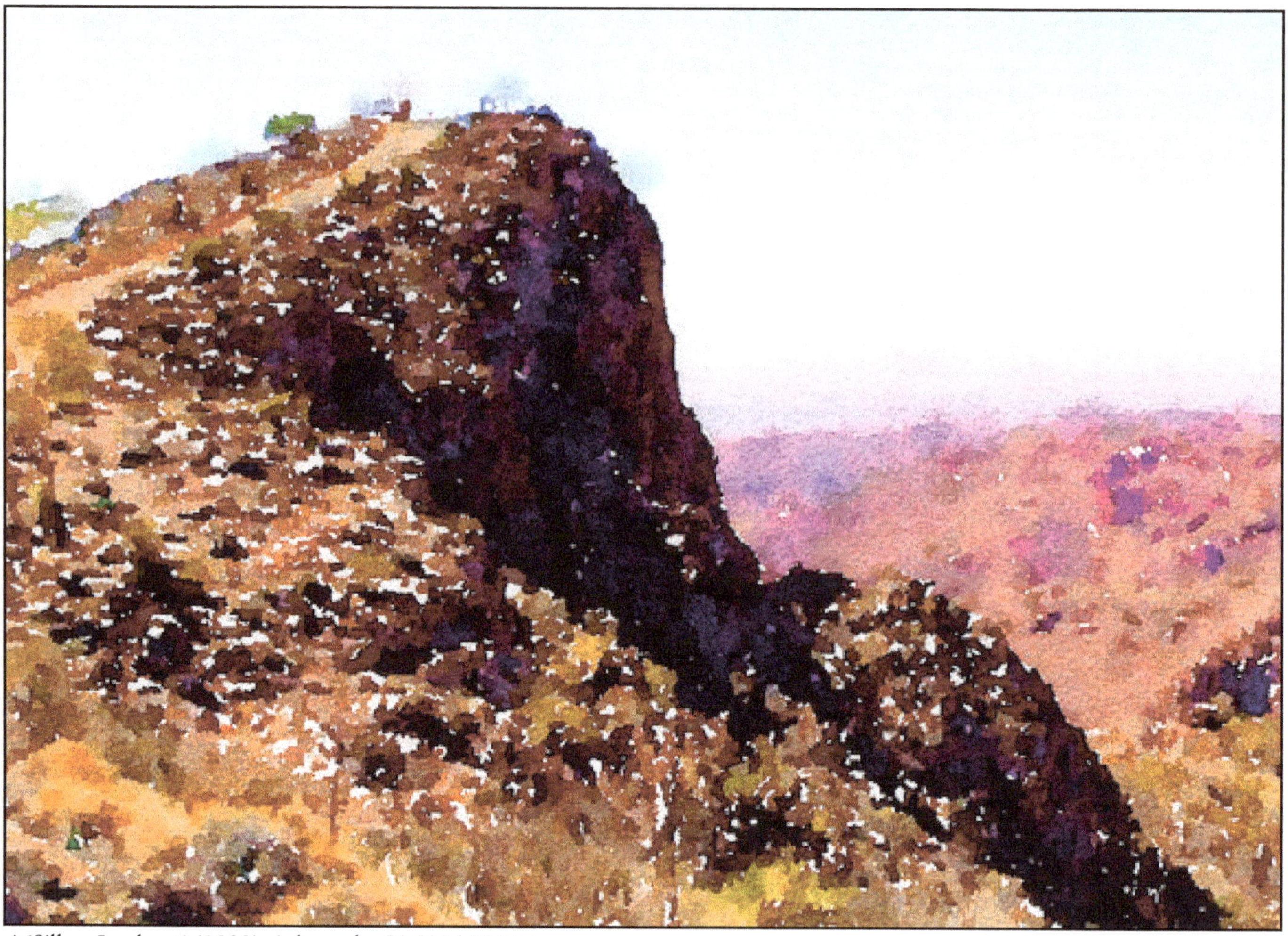

▲'Sillers Lookout' (2008), Arkaroola, SA [ALSA0801].

▼'SA Eucalypt' (2008), Wilpena Pound, SA [ALSA0802].

'Morialta Falls' (2021), SA [ALSA2101]. ⊘▼

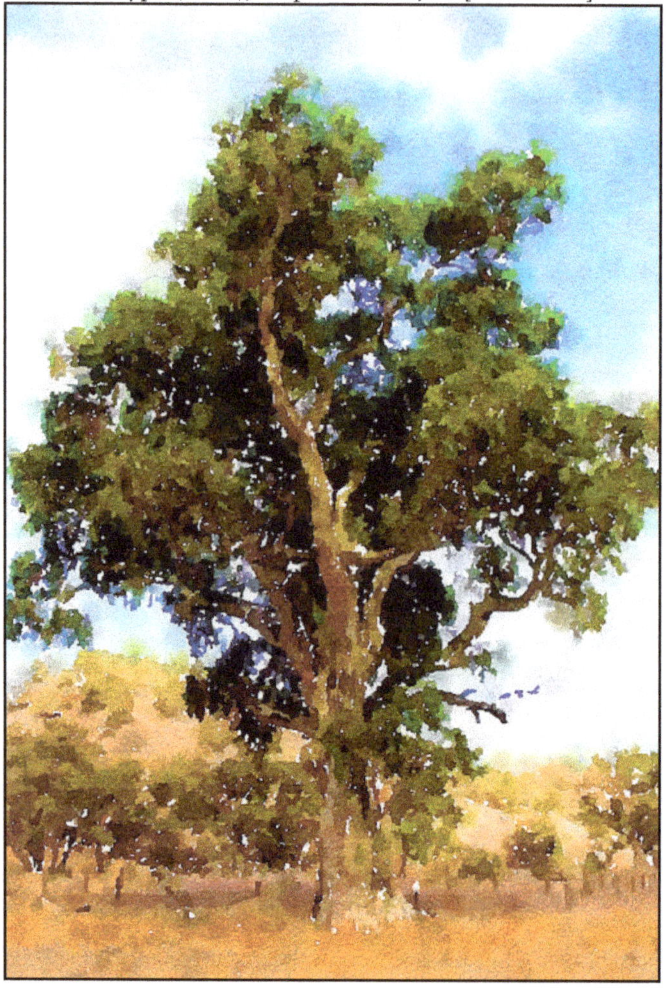

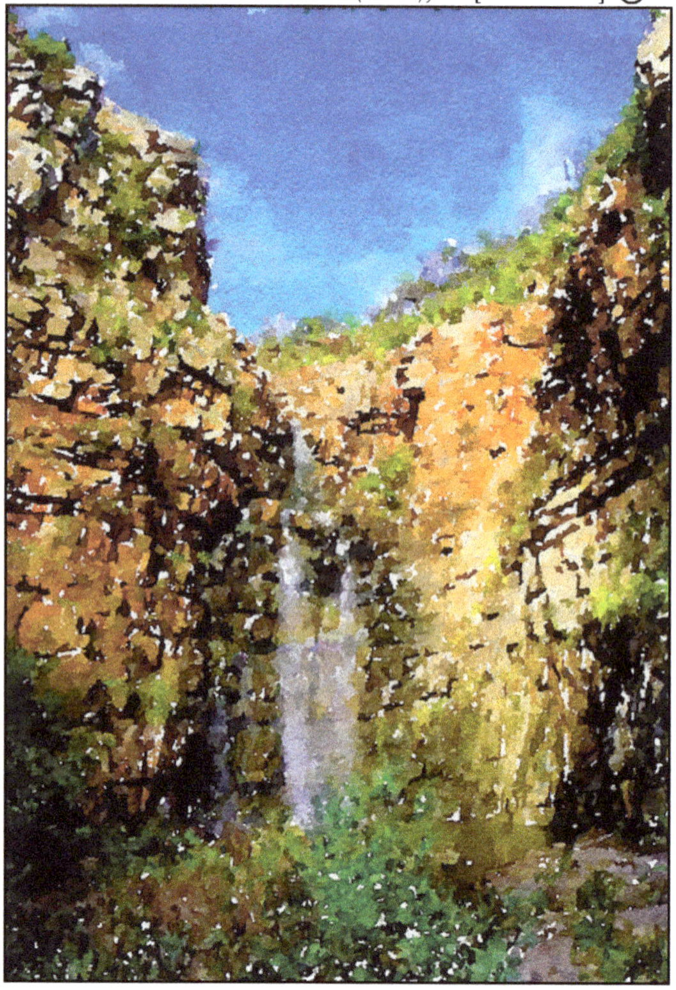

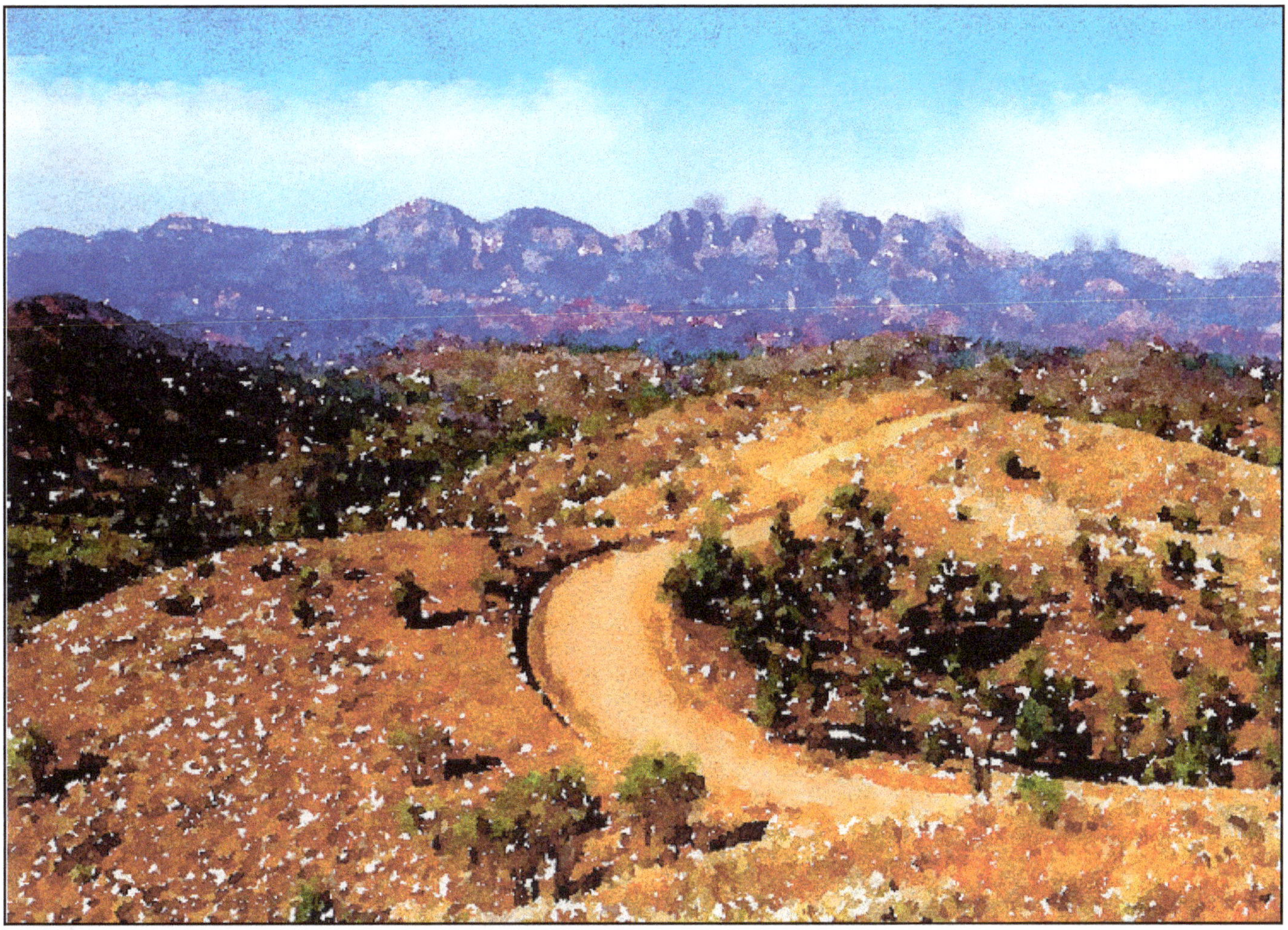

▲'Flinders Ranges' (2021), Blinman Road, SA [ALSA2102].

'Sunset At The Prairie Hotel' (2008), Parachilna, SA [ALSA0803].▼

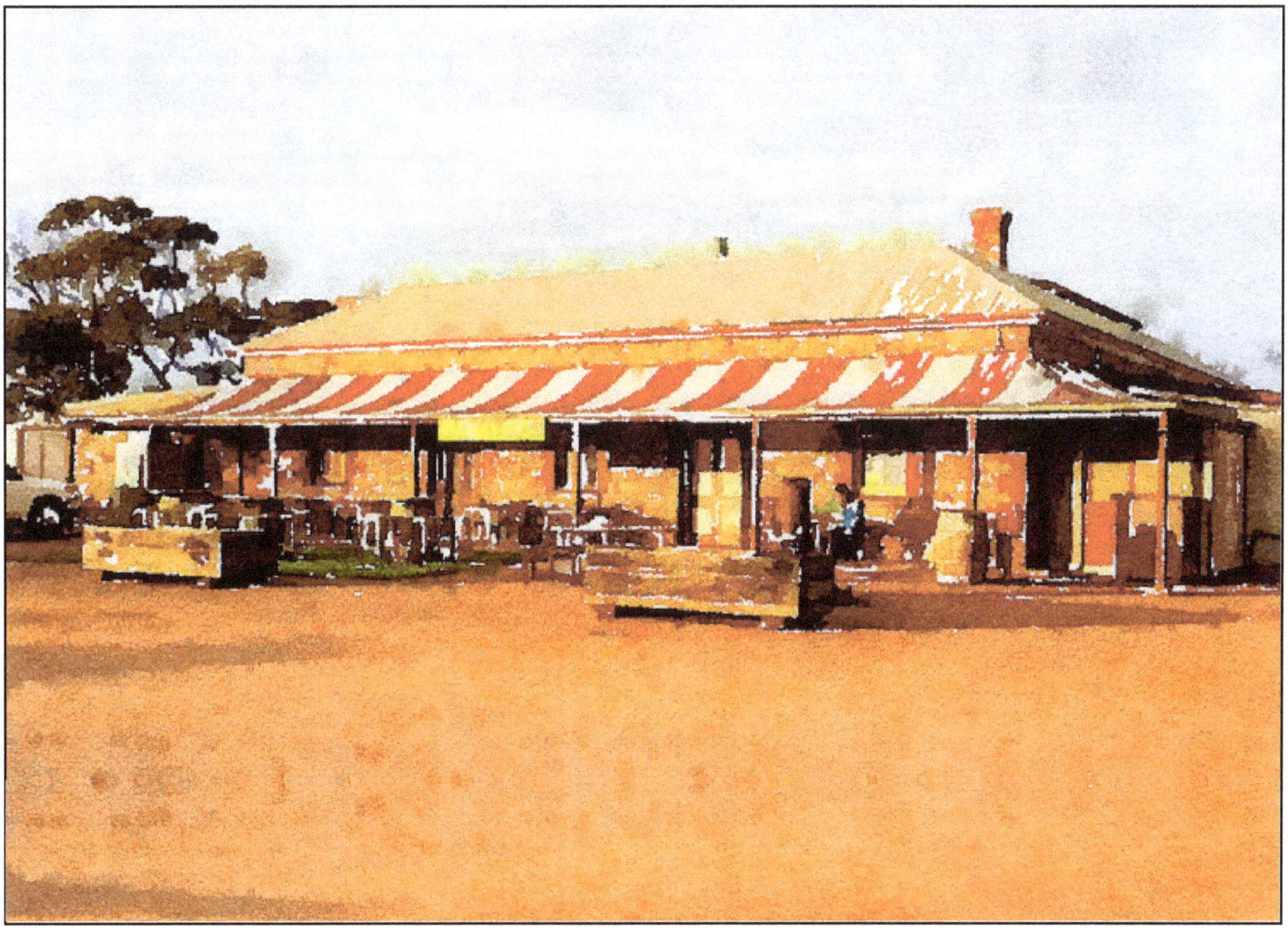

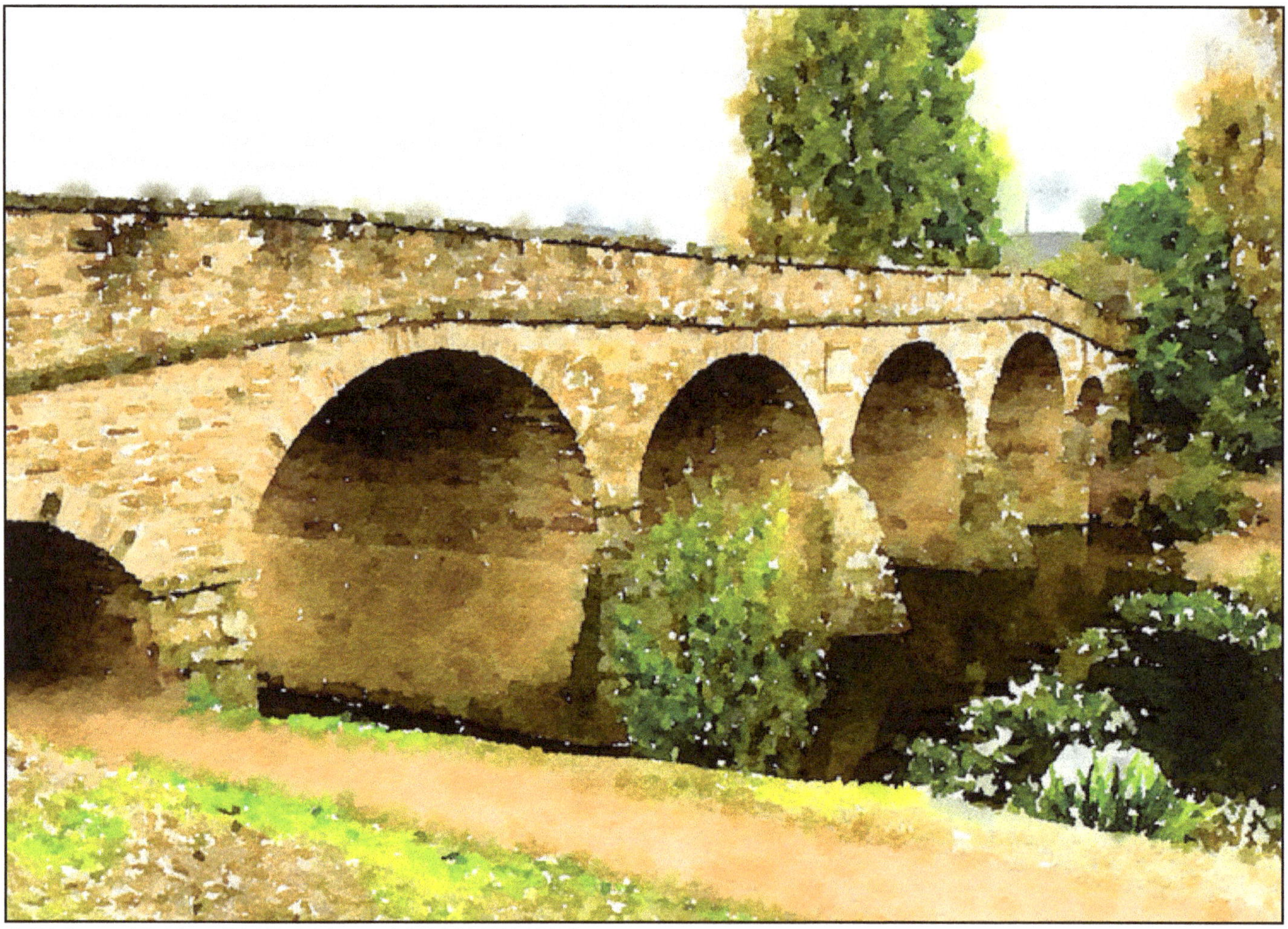

▲'Richmond Bridge' (2019), Richmond, TAS [ALTA1902].

'Tasmanian Forest' (2019), Lake Leake, TAS [ALTA1905].▼

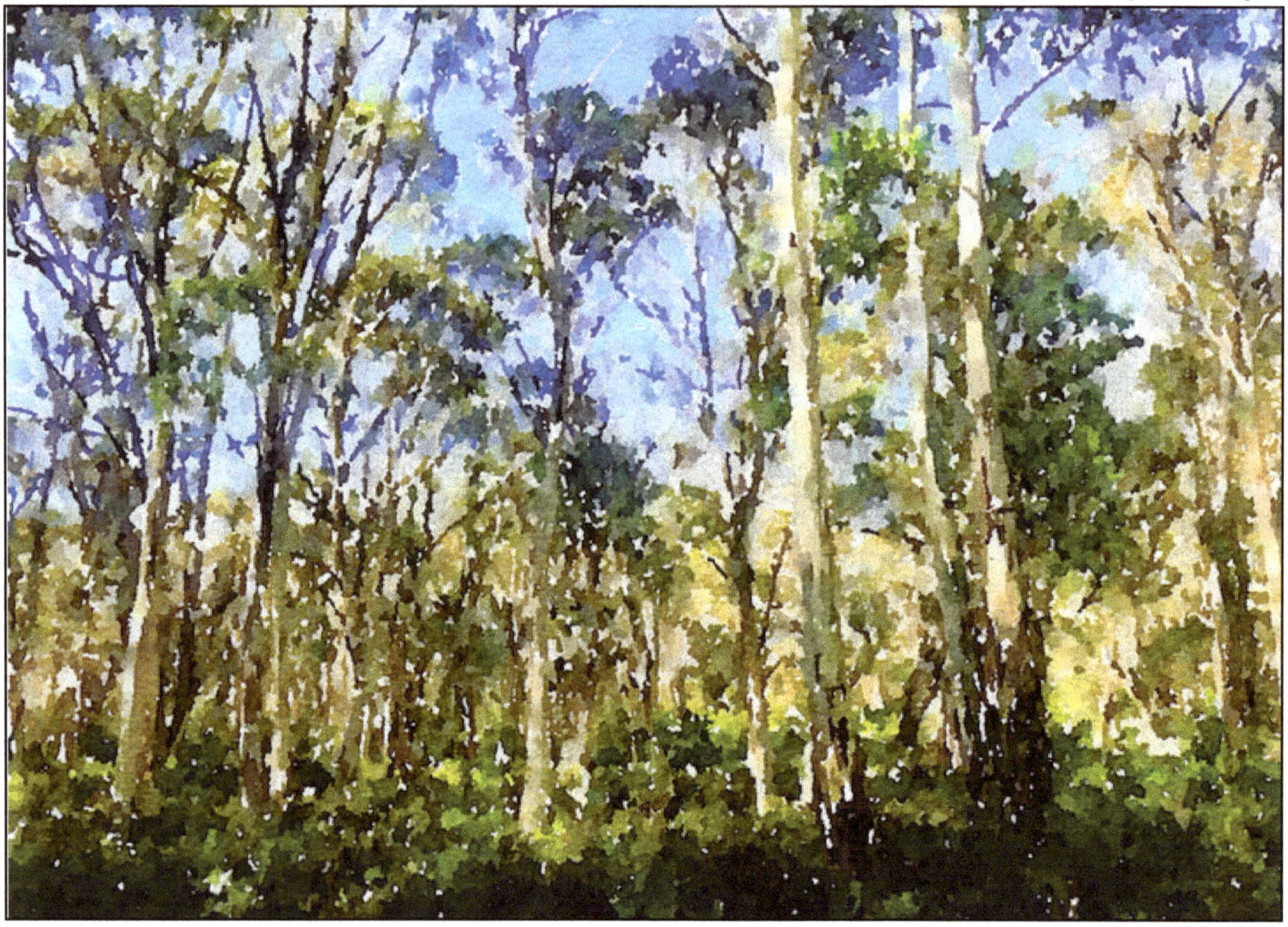

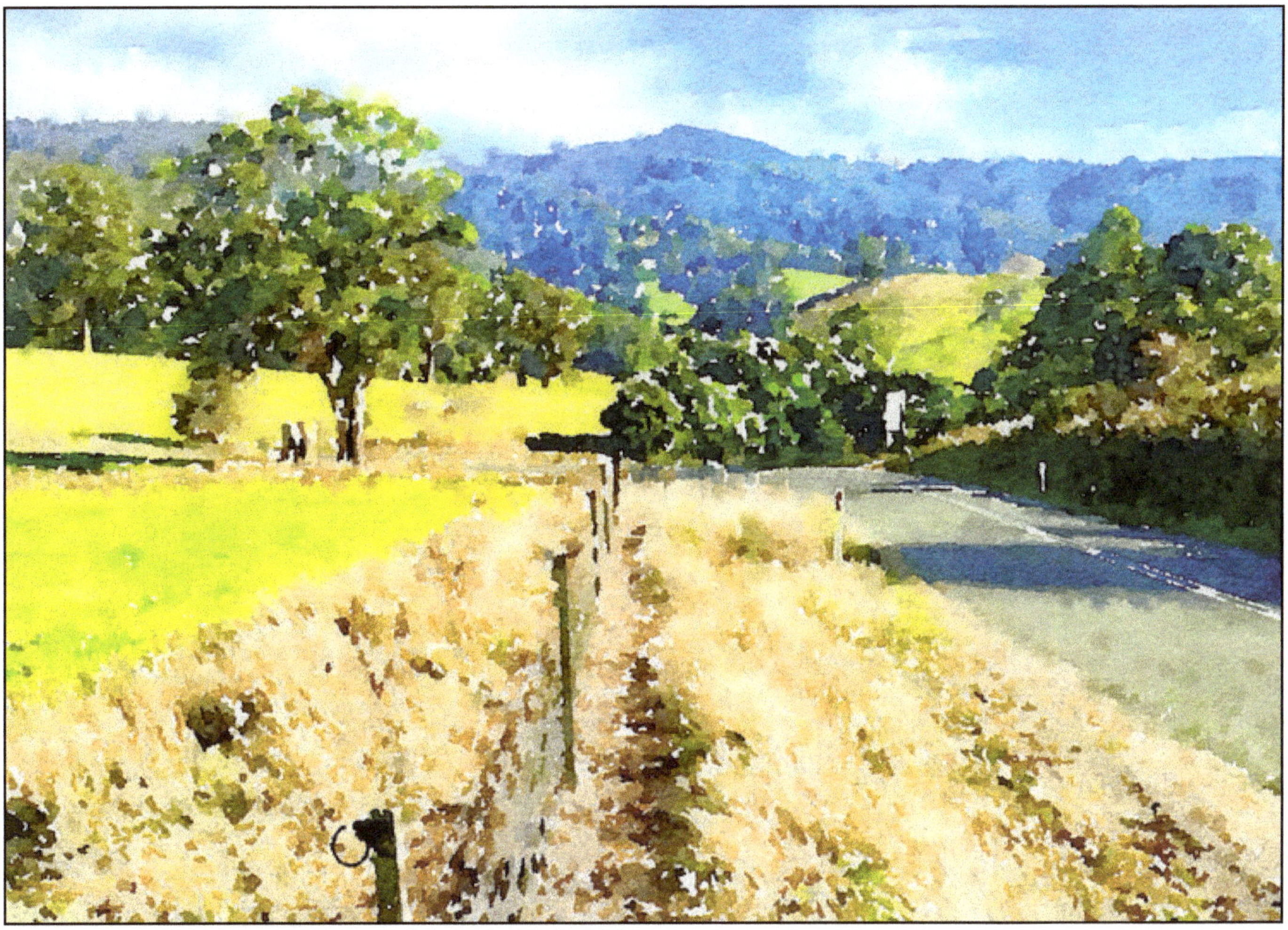

▲'Mountain & Meadow' (2019), Scottsdale, TAS [ALTA1906].

'The Convict Bridge' (2019), Ross, TAS [ALTA1903].▼

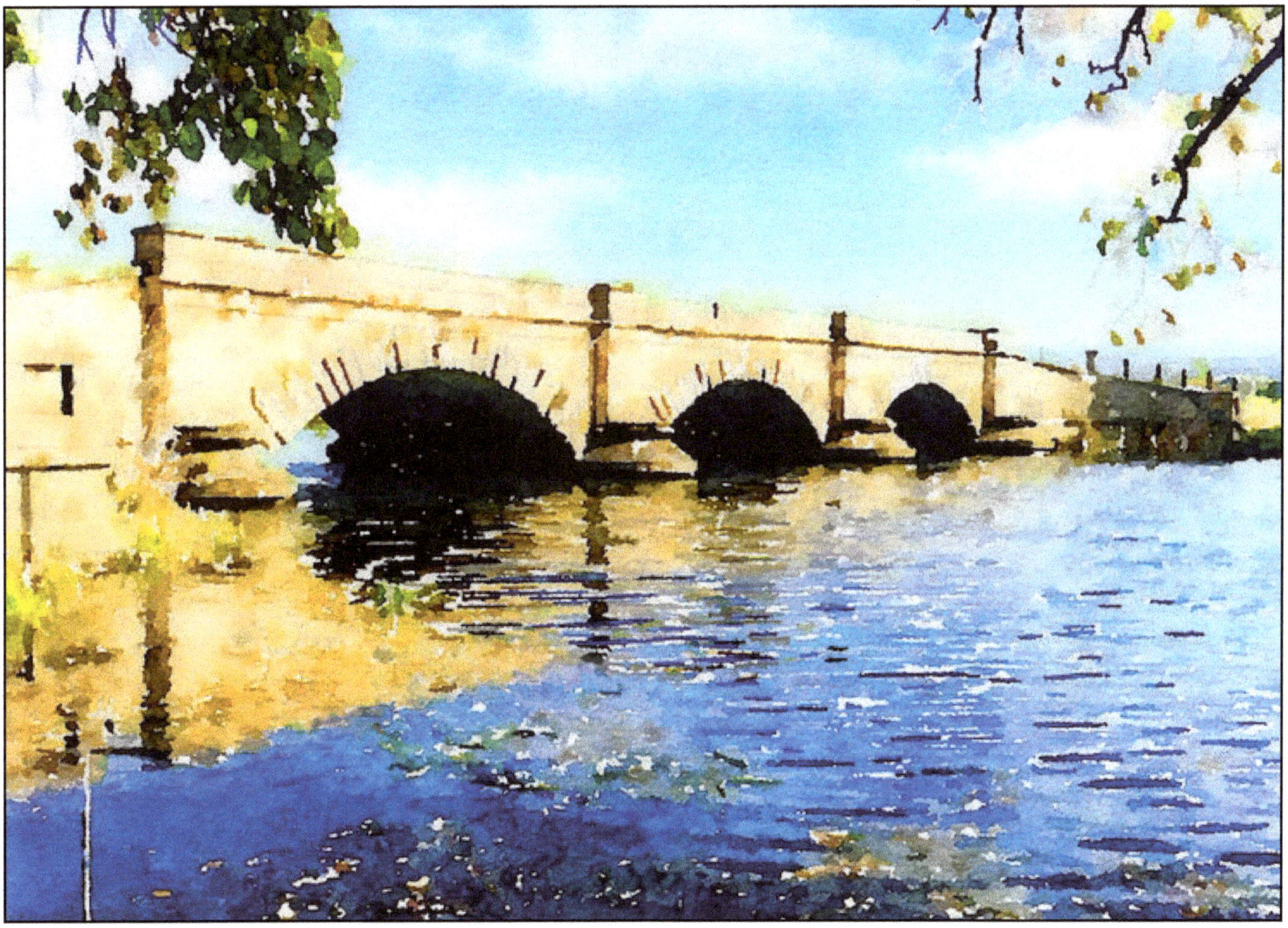

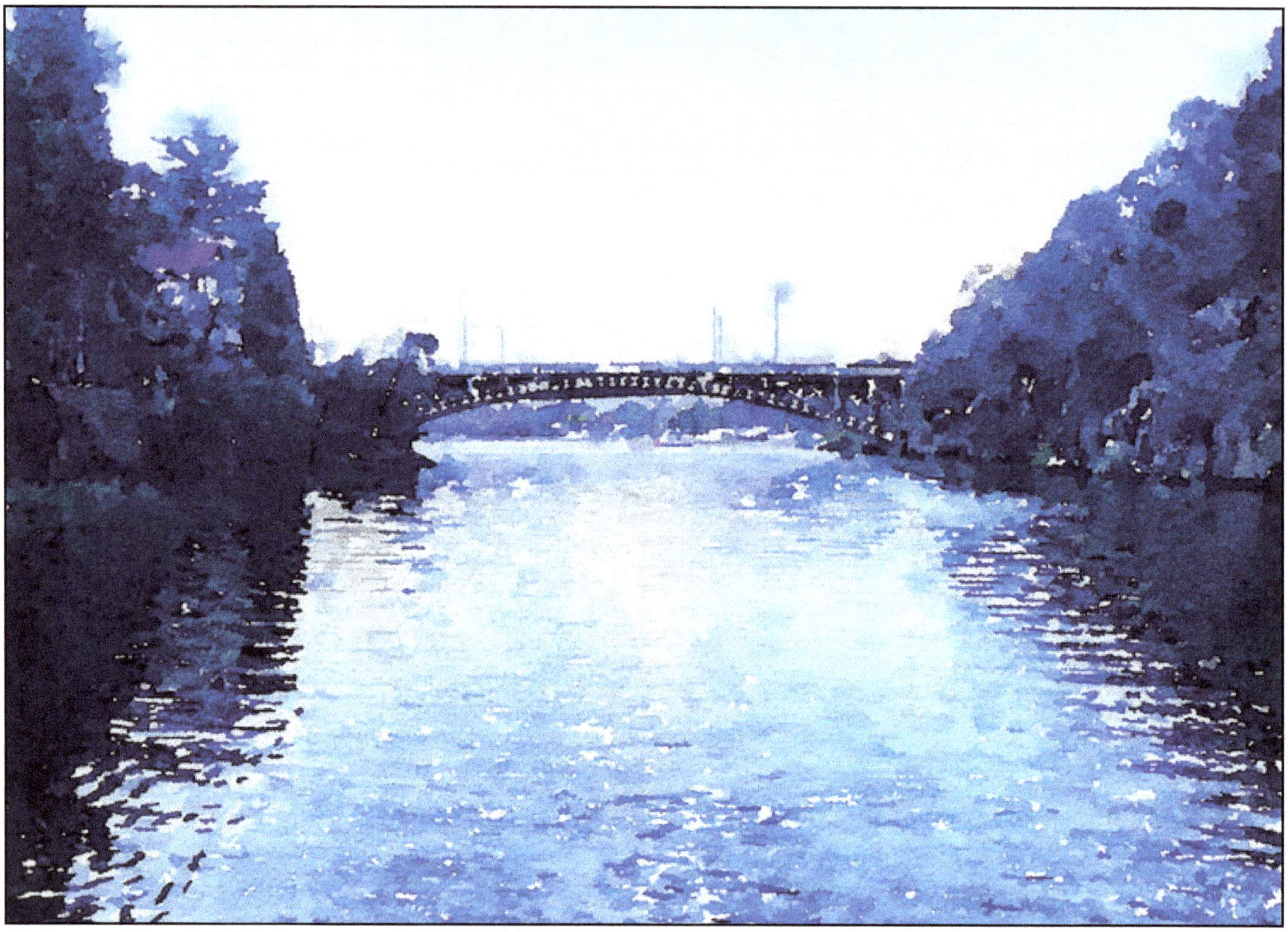

▲'Cataract Gorge' (2019), Launceston, TAS [ALTA1907].

'Sheep Pond' (2019), Westbury, TAS [ALTA1908].▼

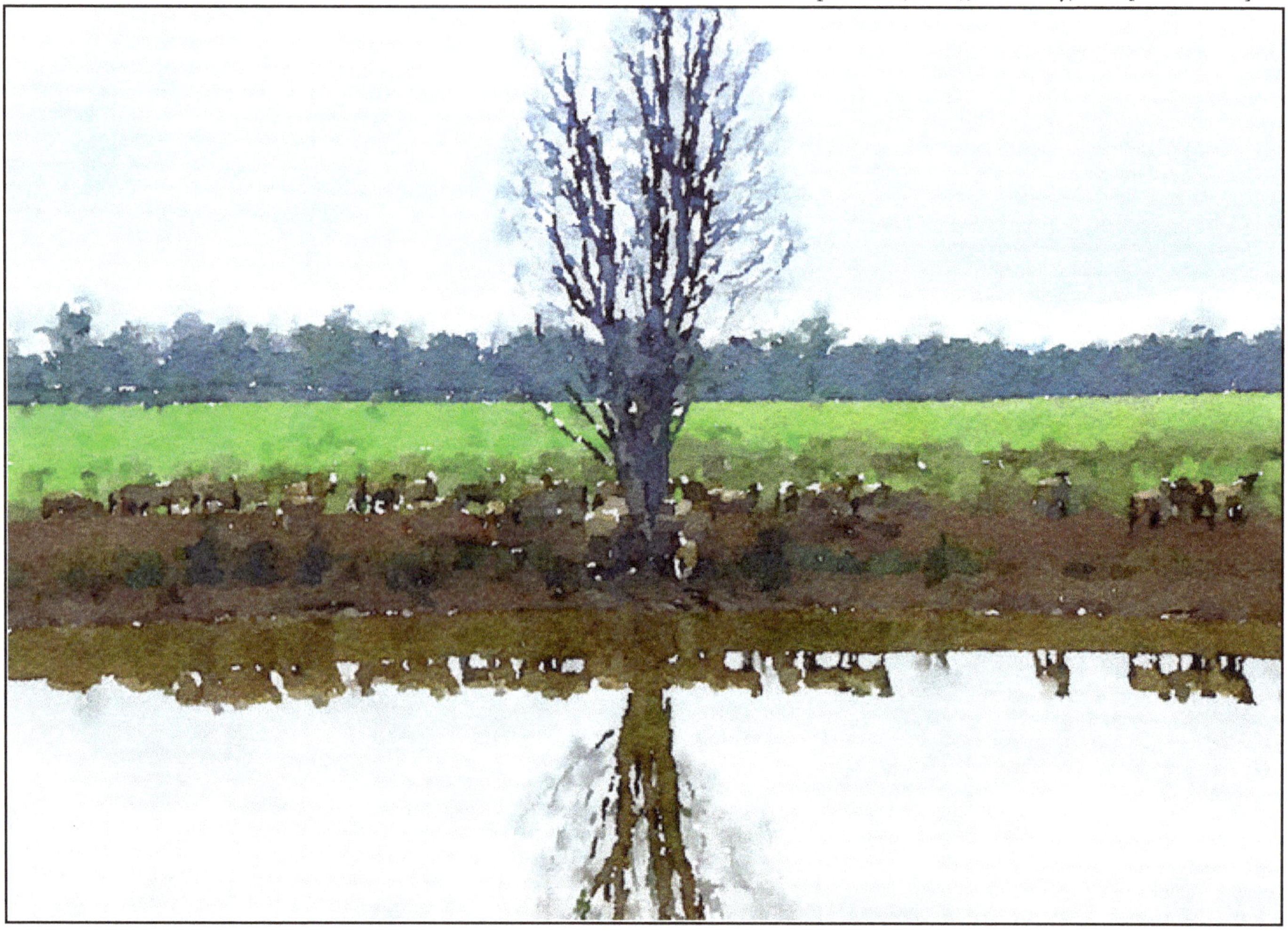

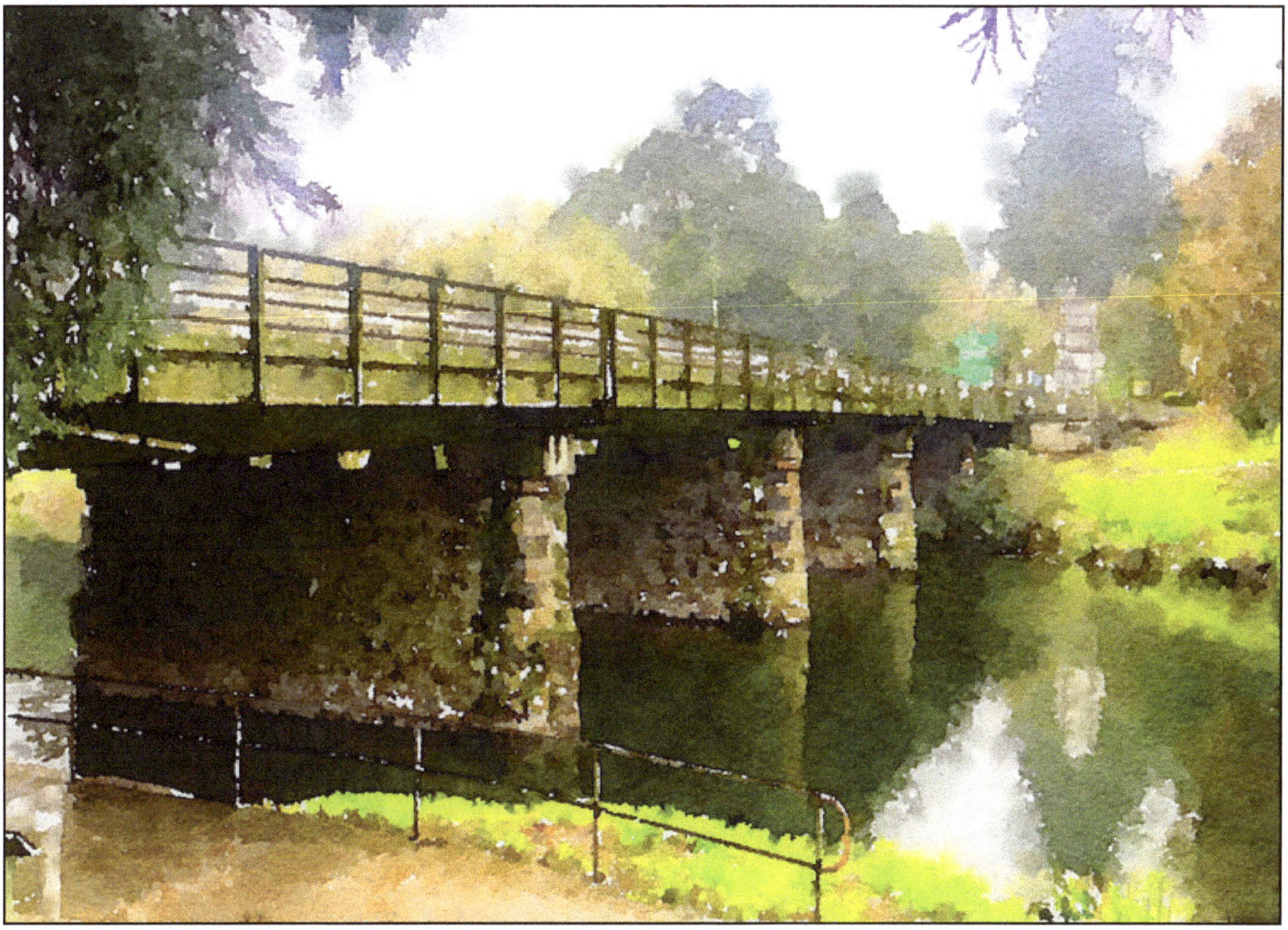

▲'The Meander River Bridge' (2019), Deloraine, TAS [ALTA1909].

'Lake MacIntosh' (2019), Tullah, TAS [ALTA1910].▼

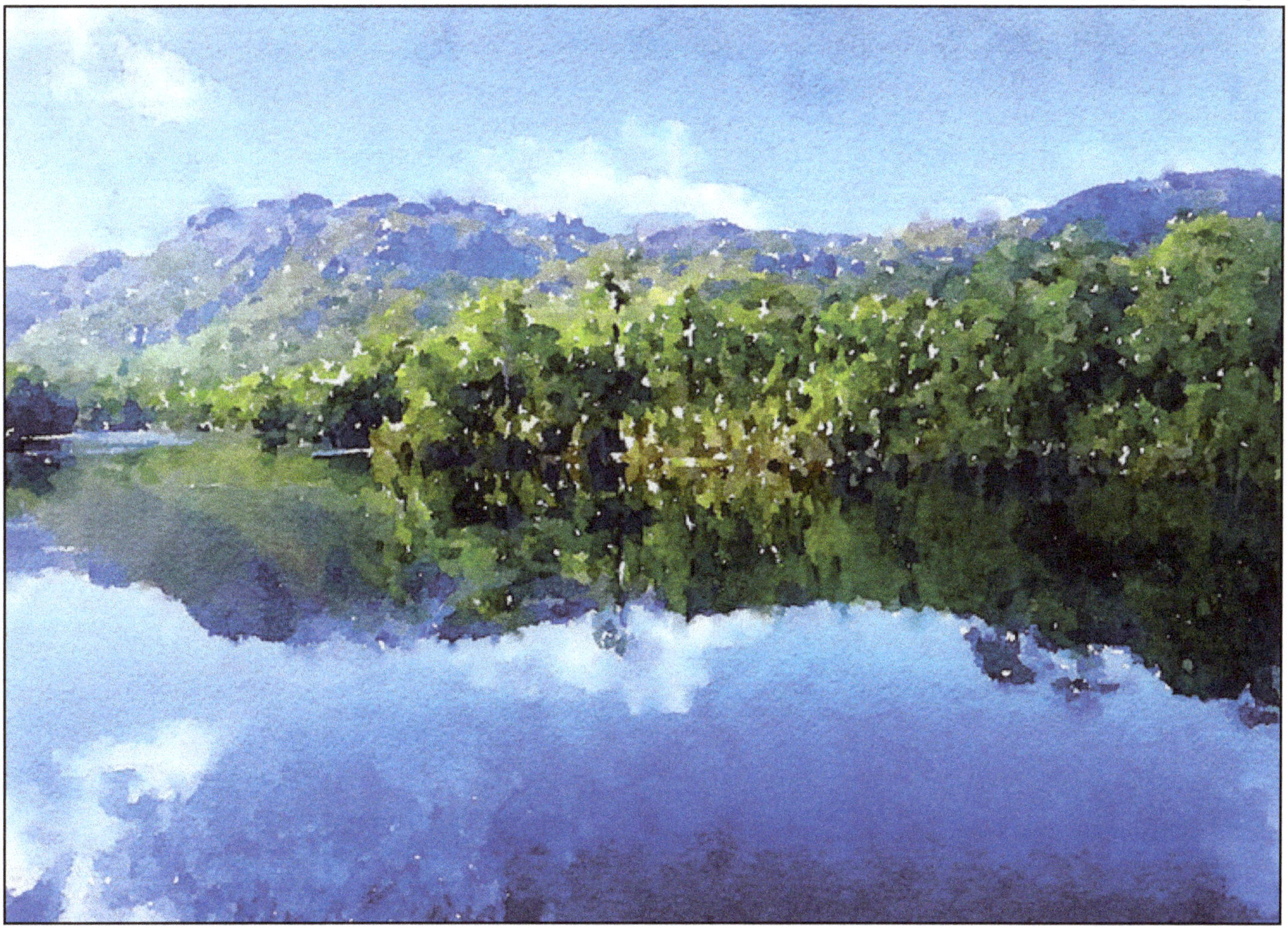

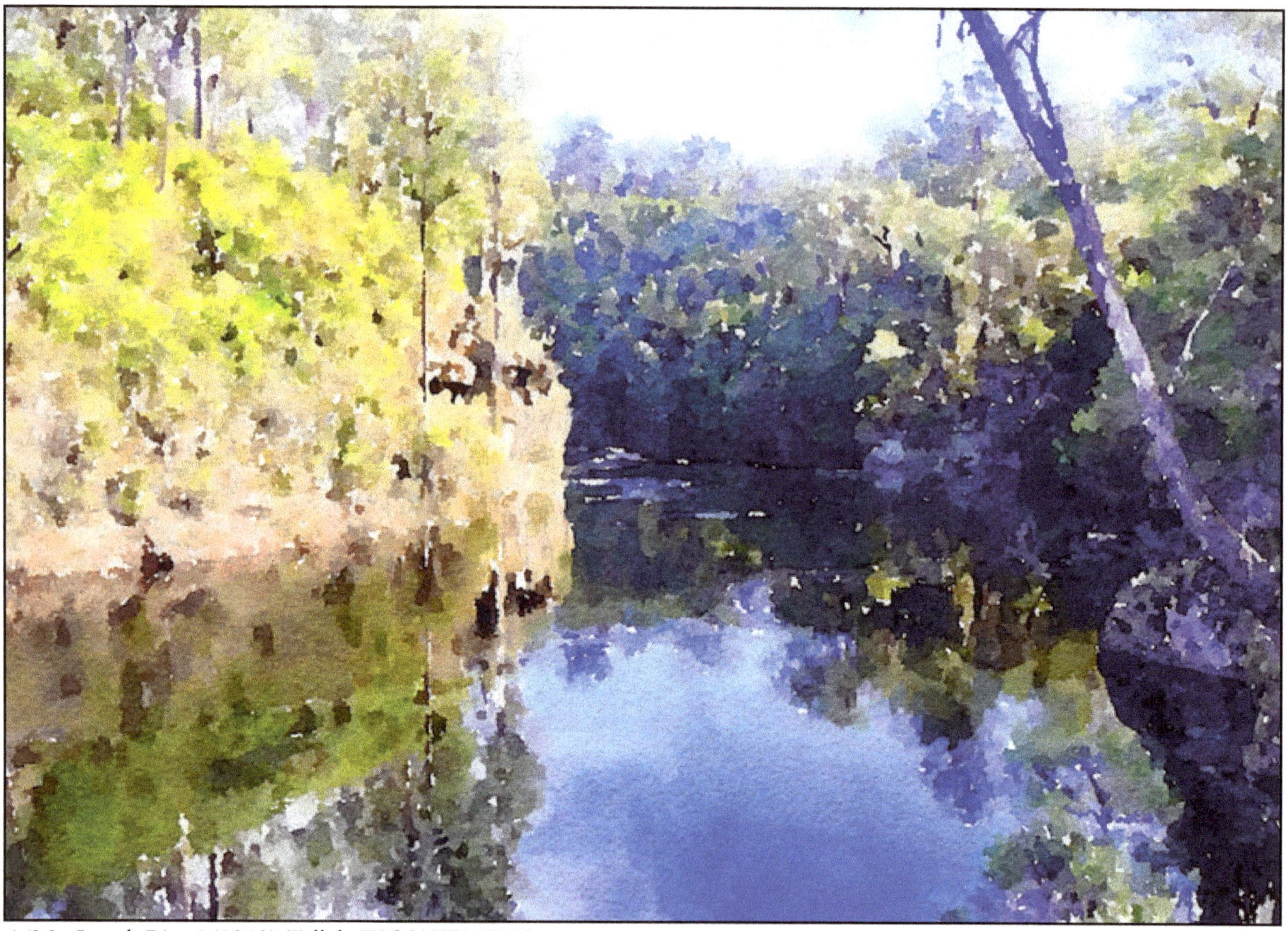

▲'MacIntosh River' (2019), Tullah, TAS [ALTA1911].

'Lake Rosebery 1' (2019), Tullah, TAS [ALTA1912].▼

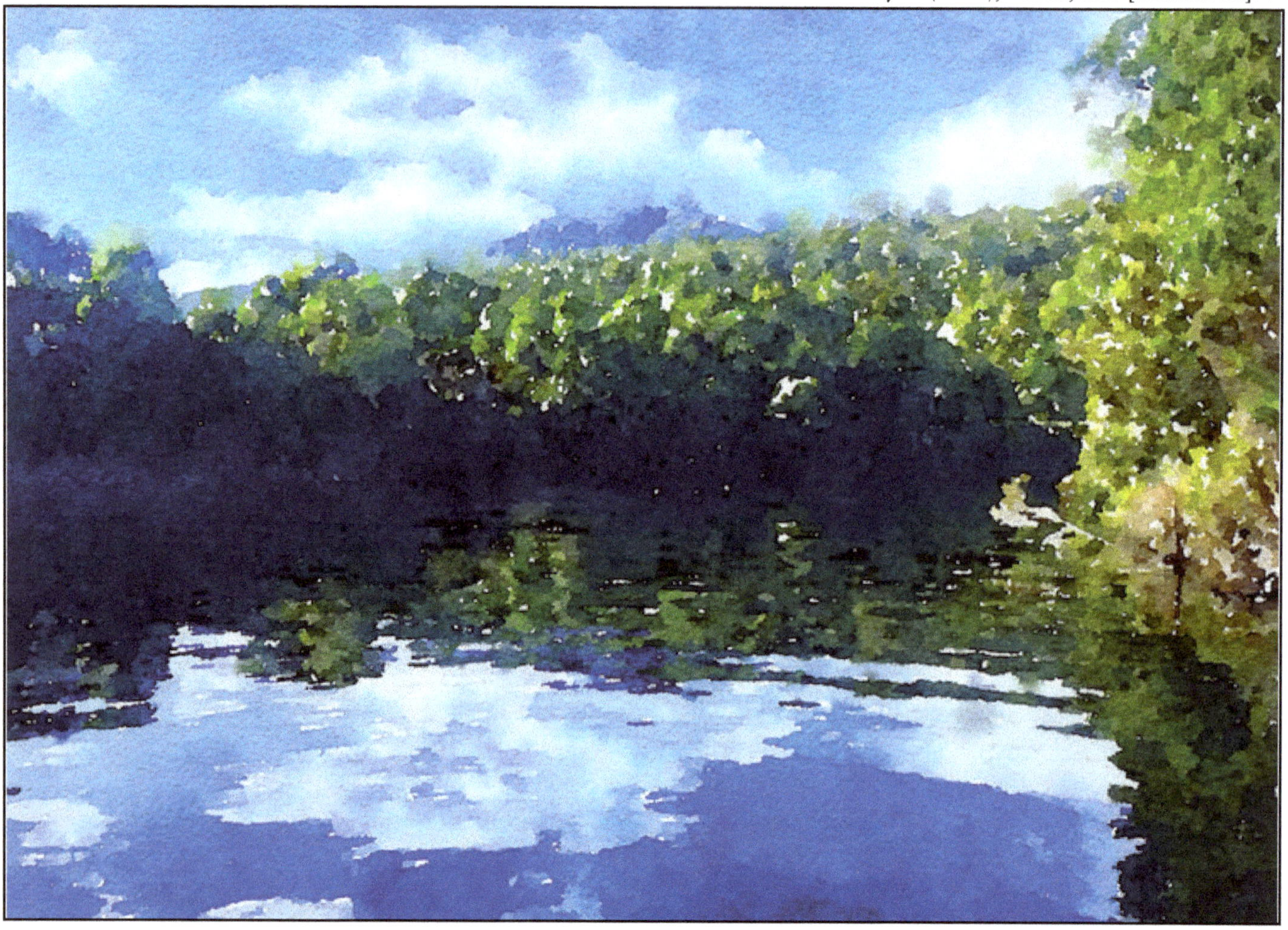

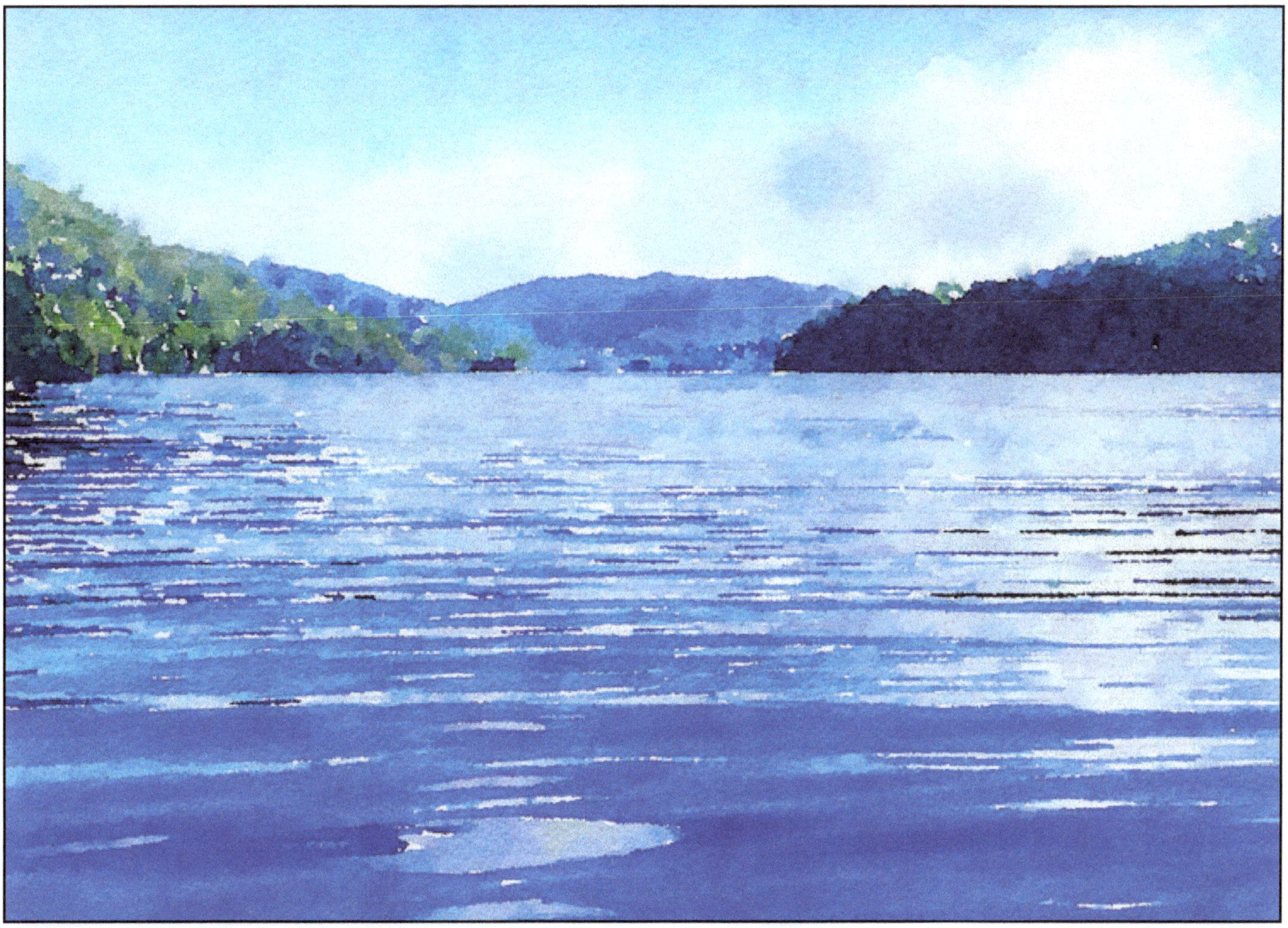

▲'Lake Rosebery 2' (2019), Tullah, TAS [ALTA1913].

'Tungatinah Lagoon' (2019), Tarraleah, TAS [ALTA1914].▼

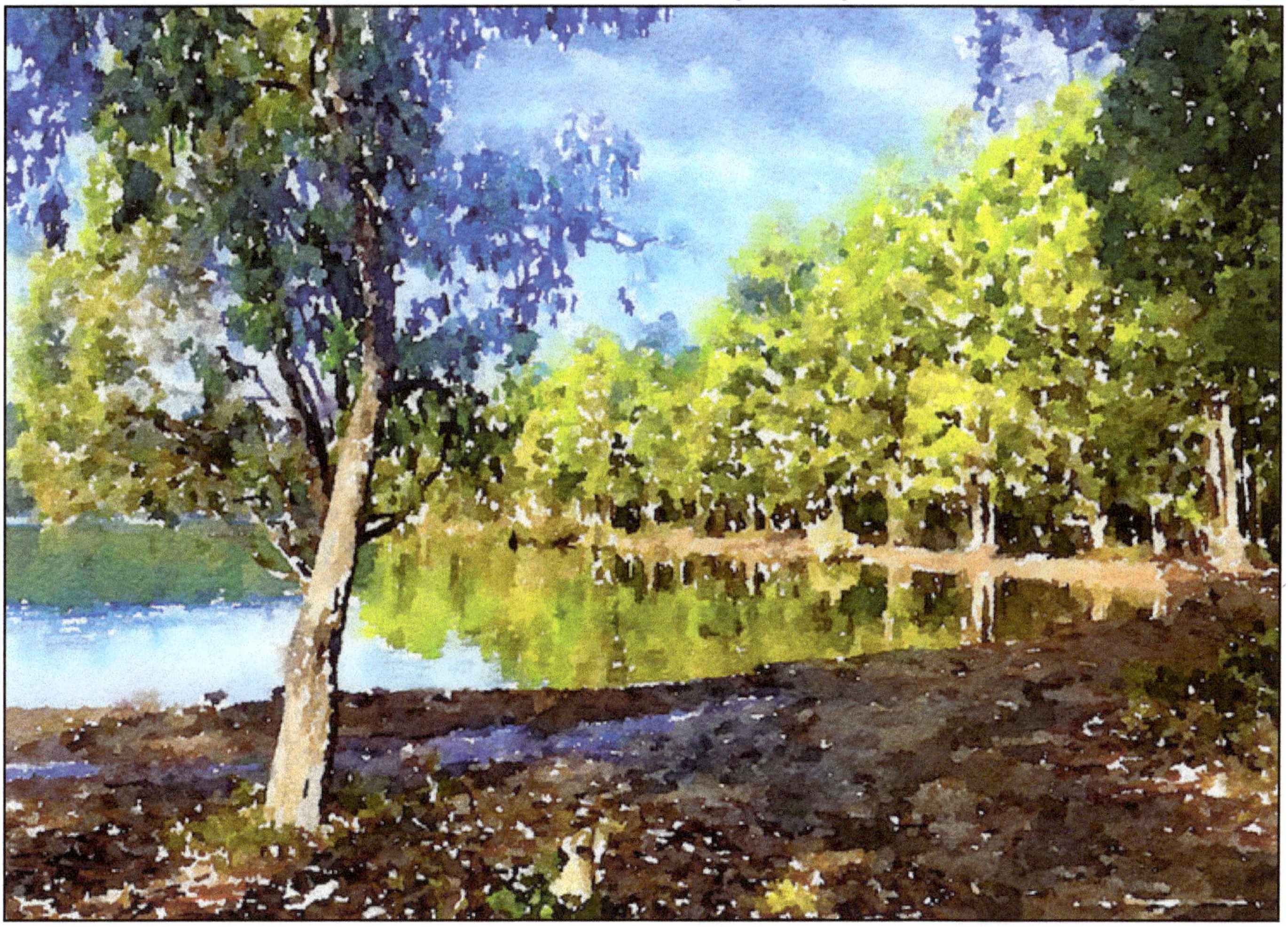

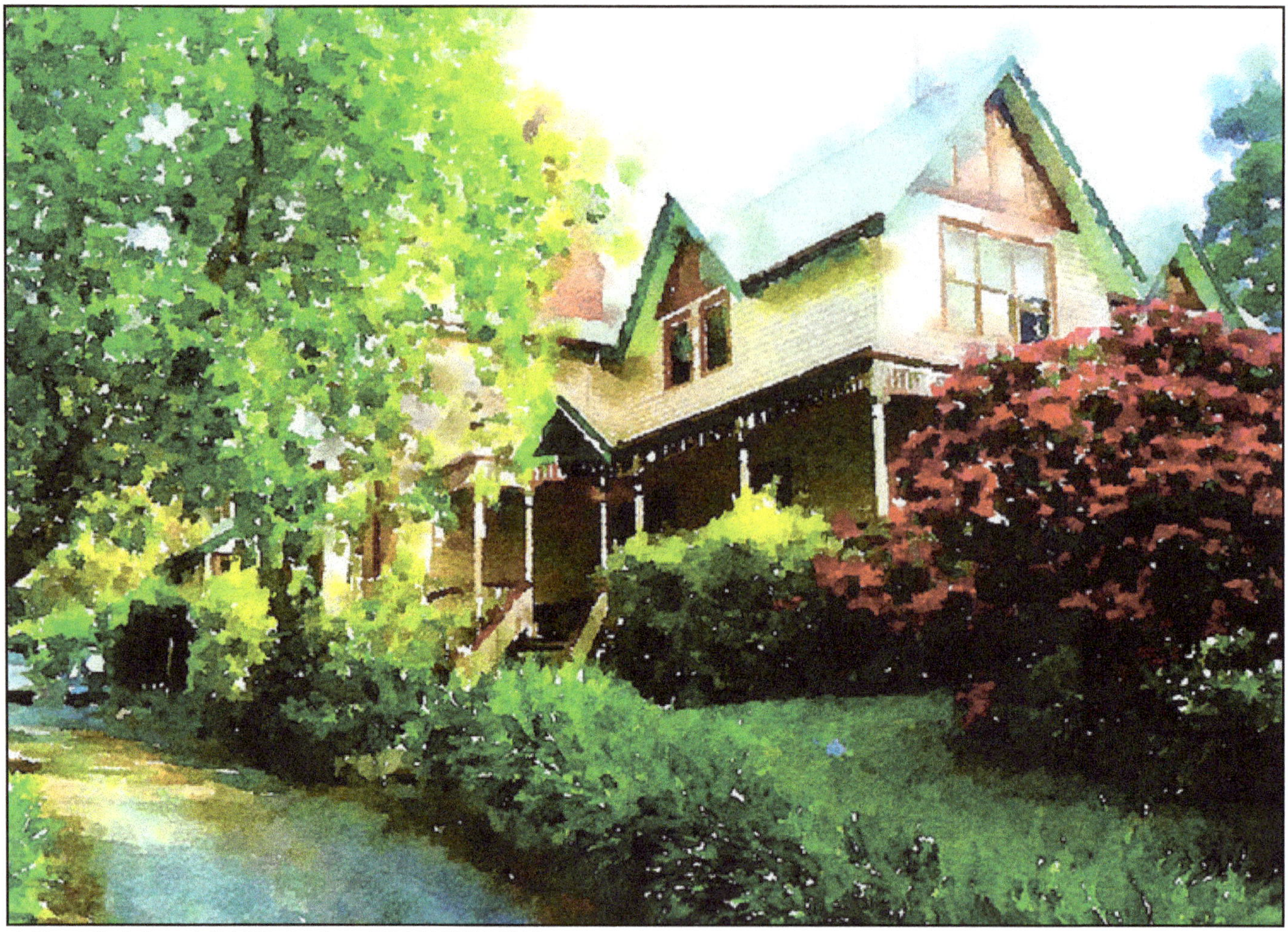

▲'Franklin Manor' (2009), Strahan, TAS [ALTA0901].

'Daylesford Lake' (2019), Victoria [ALVC1901]. ⊘▼

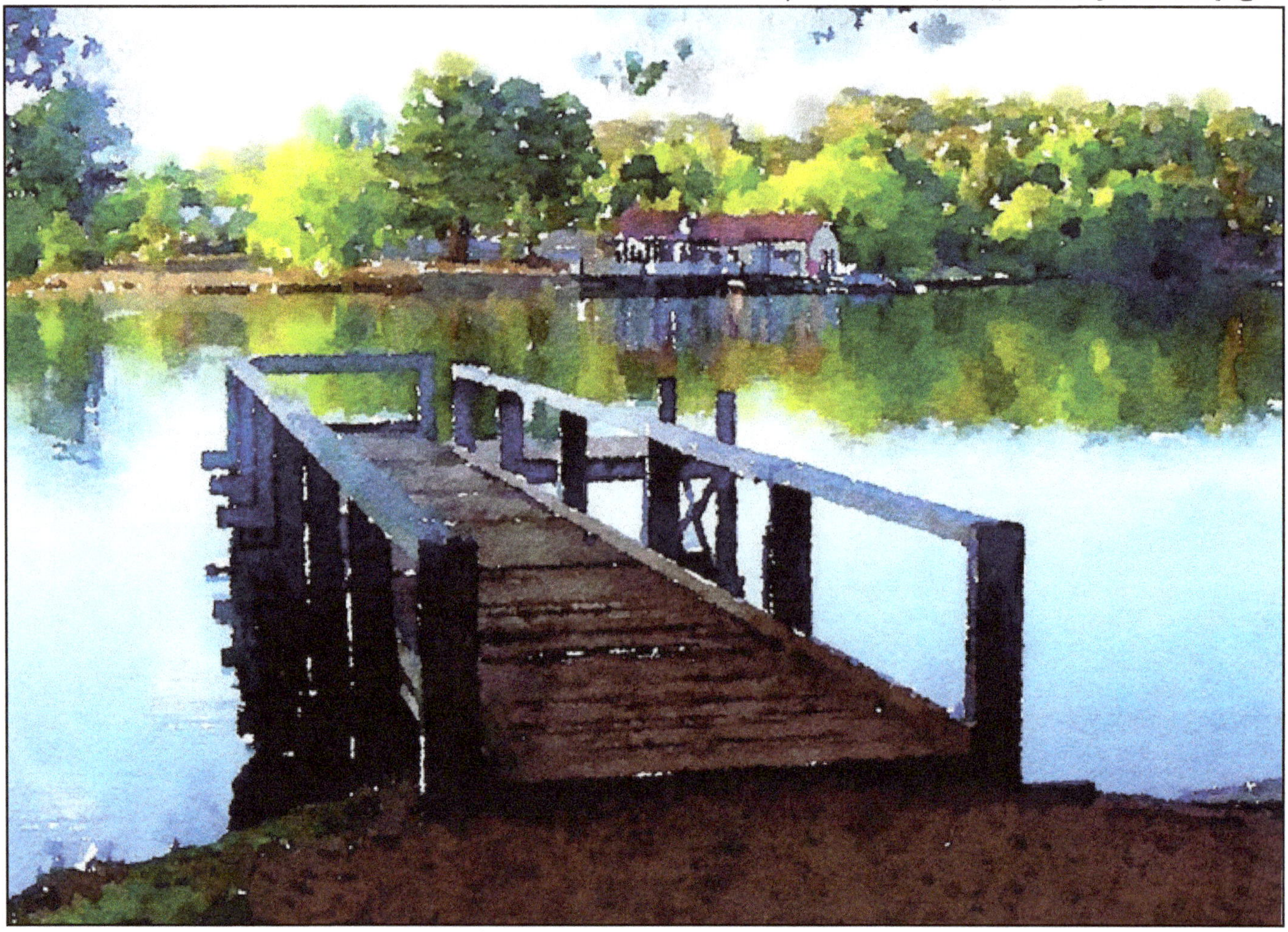

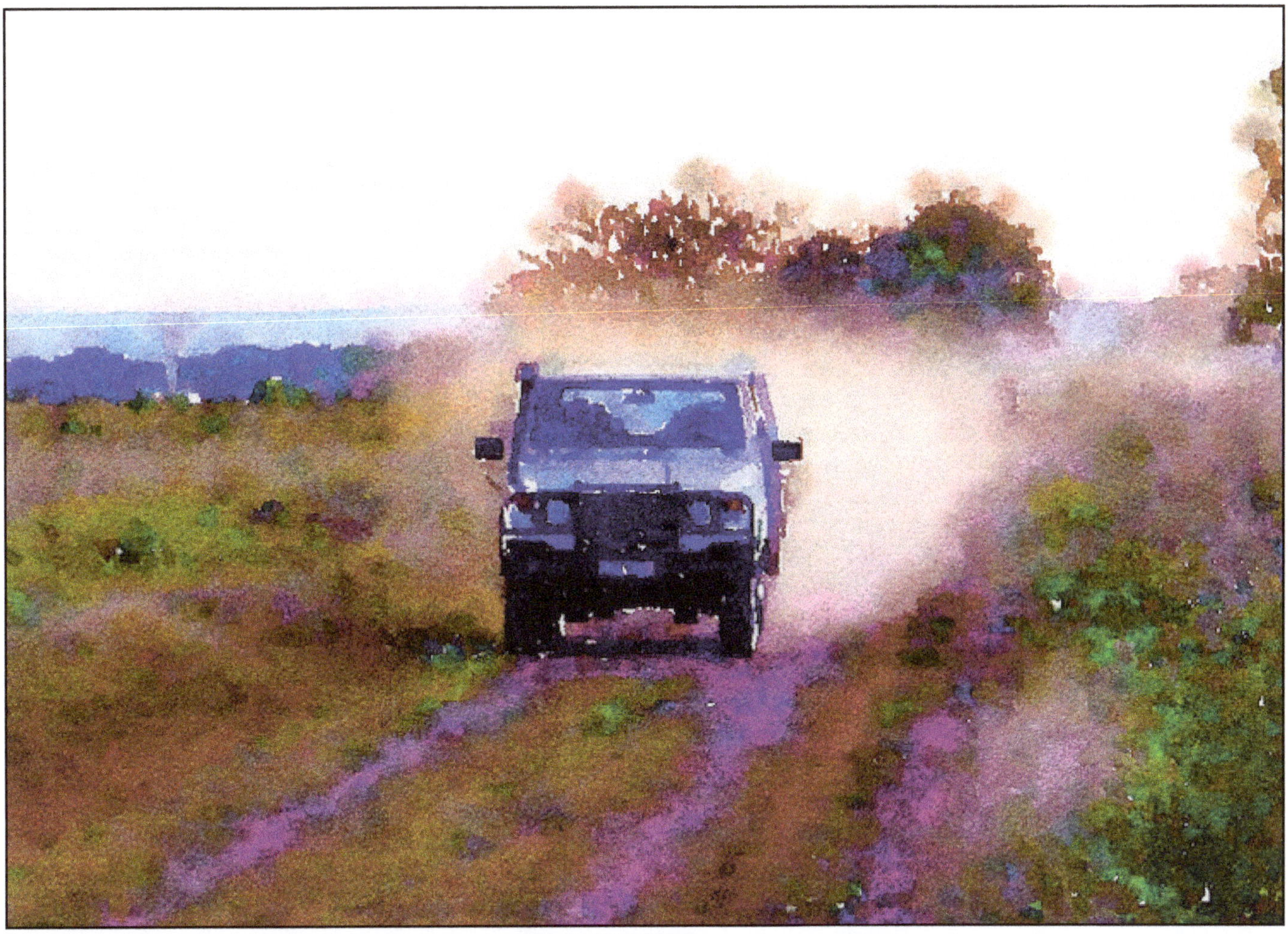

▲'Colours Of Country' (2008), Bullo River Station, WA [ALWA0801].

'Mornington Conservation Park' (2008), Kimberley District, WA [ALWA0802].▼

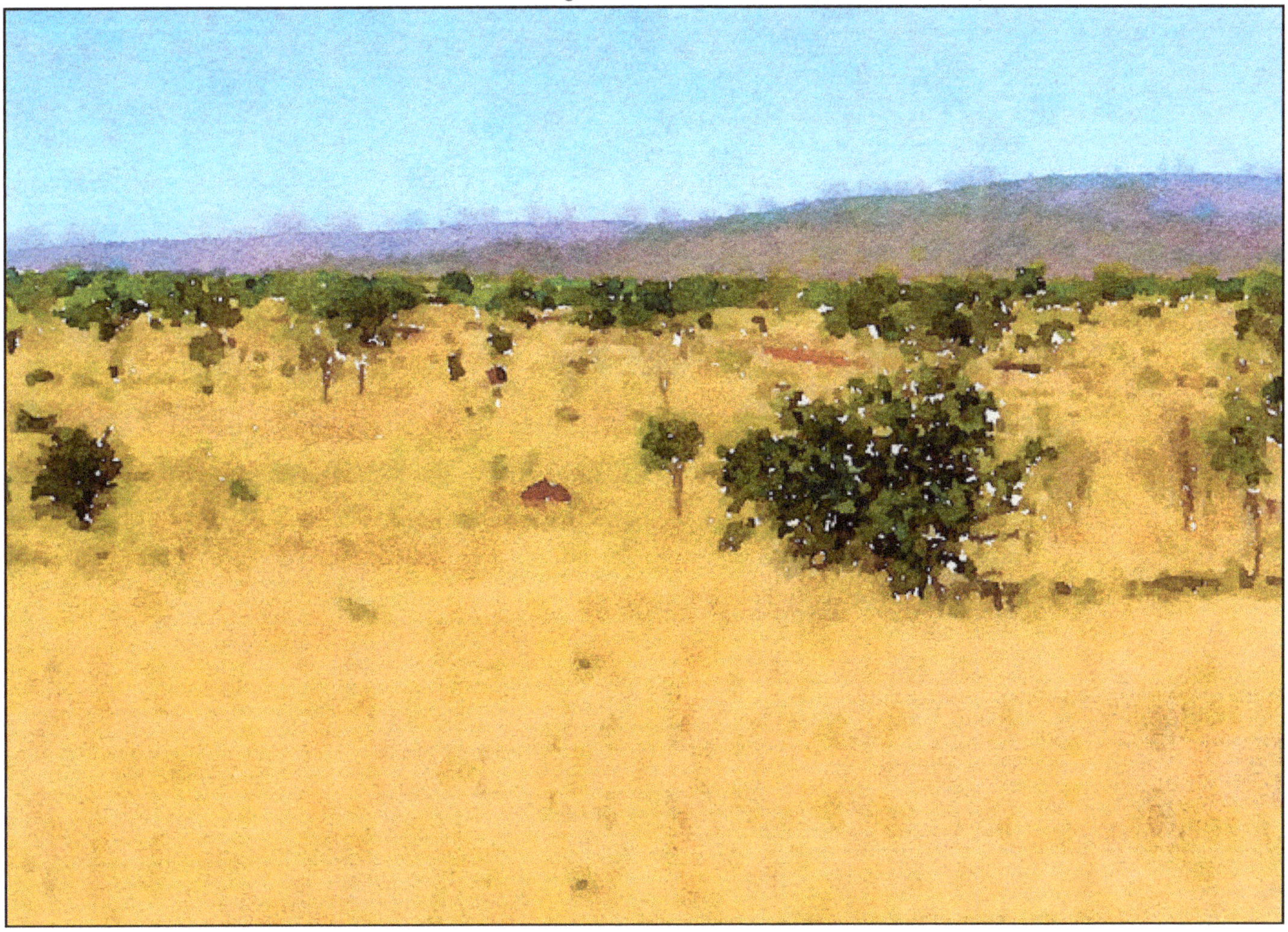

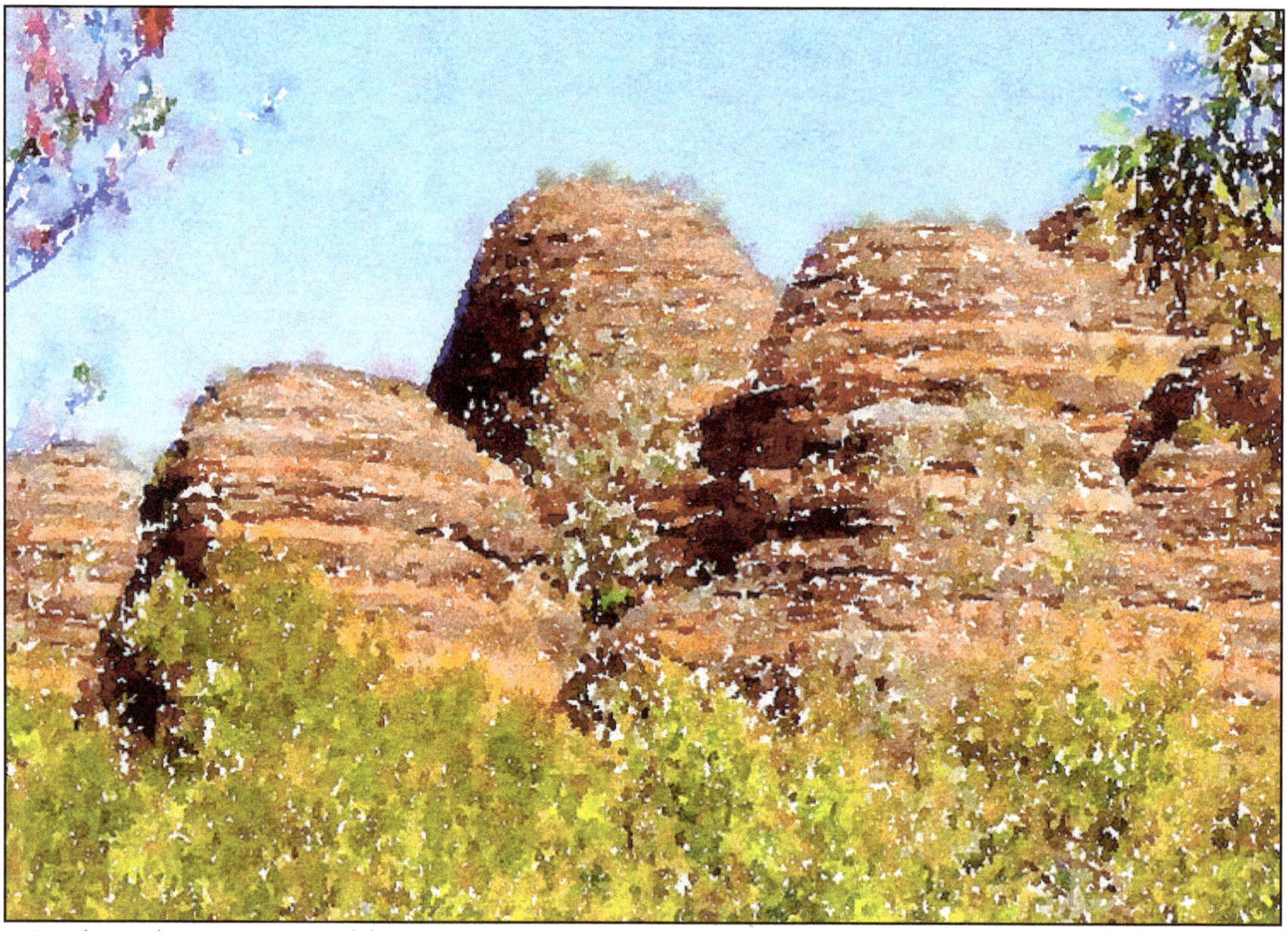

▲'Bungle Bungles 1' (2008), Purnululu NP, WA [ALWA0803].

'Amalia Gorge' (2008), El Questro, WA [ALWA0804].▼

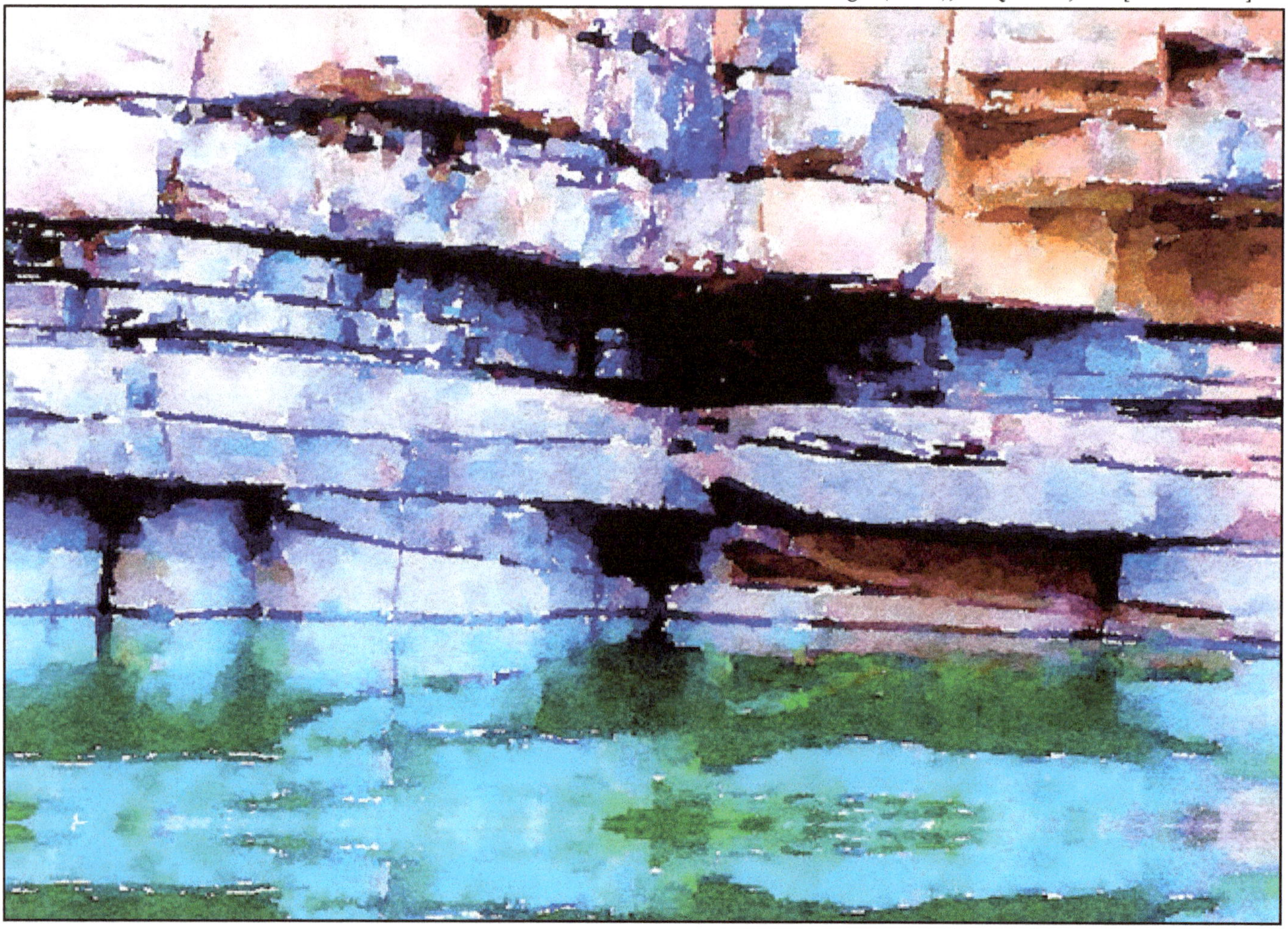

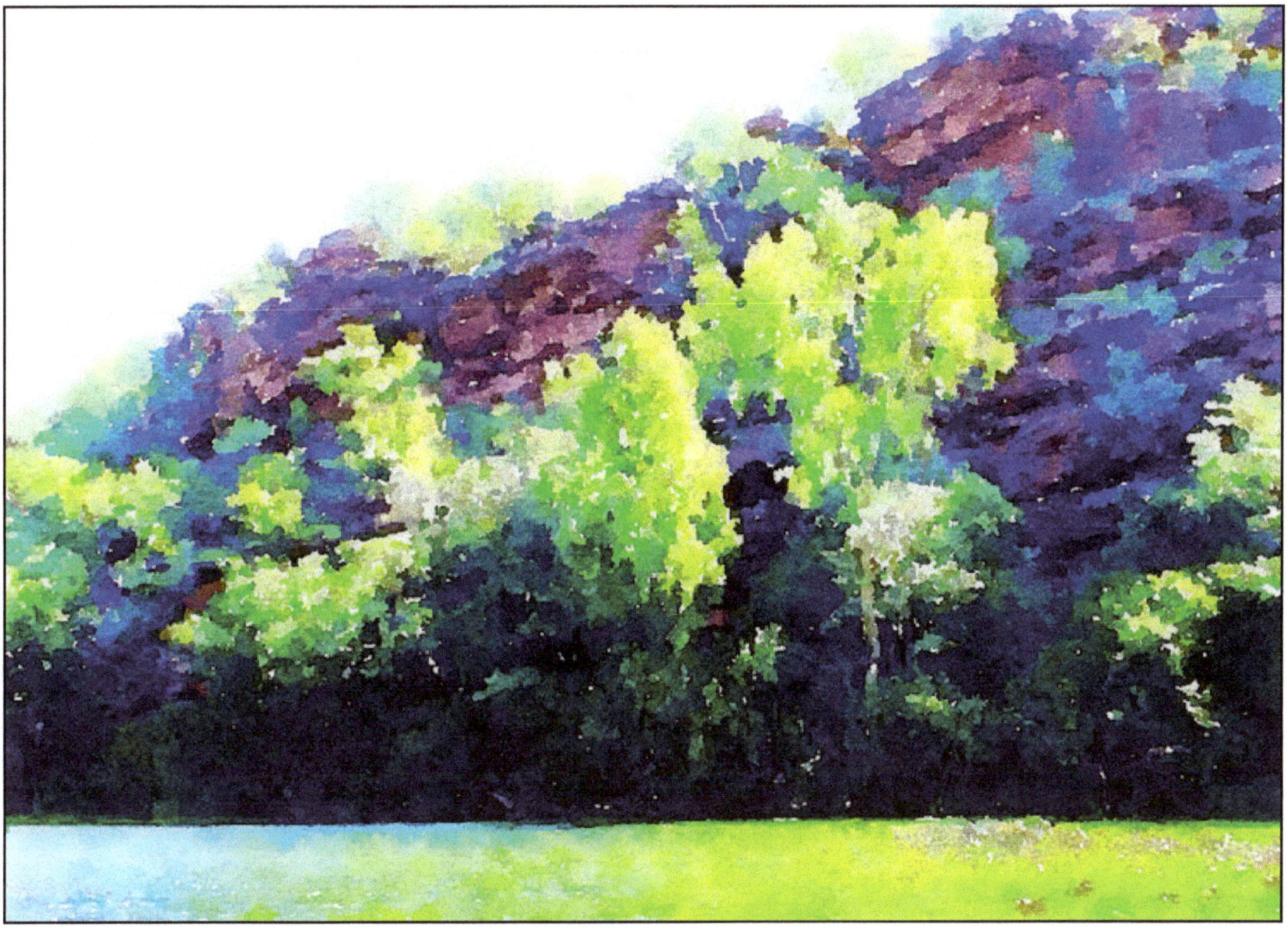

▲'The Rainbow Rocks' (2008), Bullo River Station, WA [ALWA0806].

'Bungle Bungles 2' (2008), Purnululu NP, WA [ALWA0805].▼

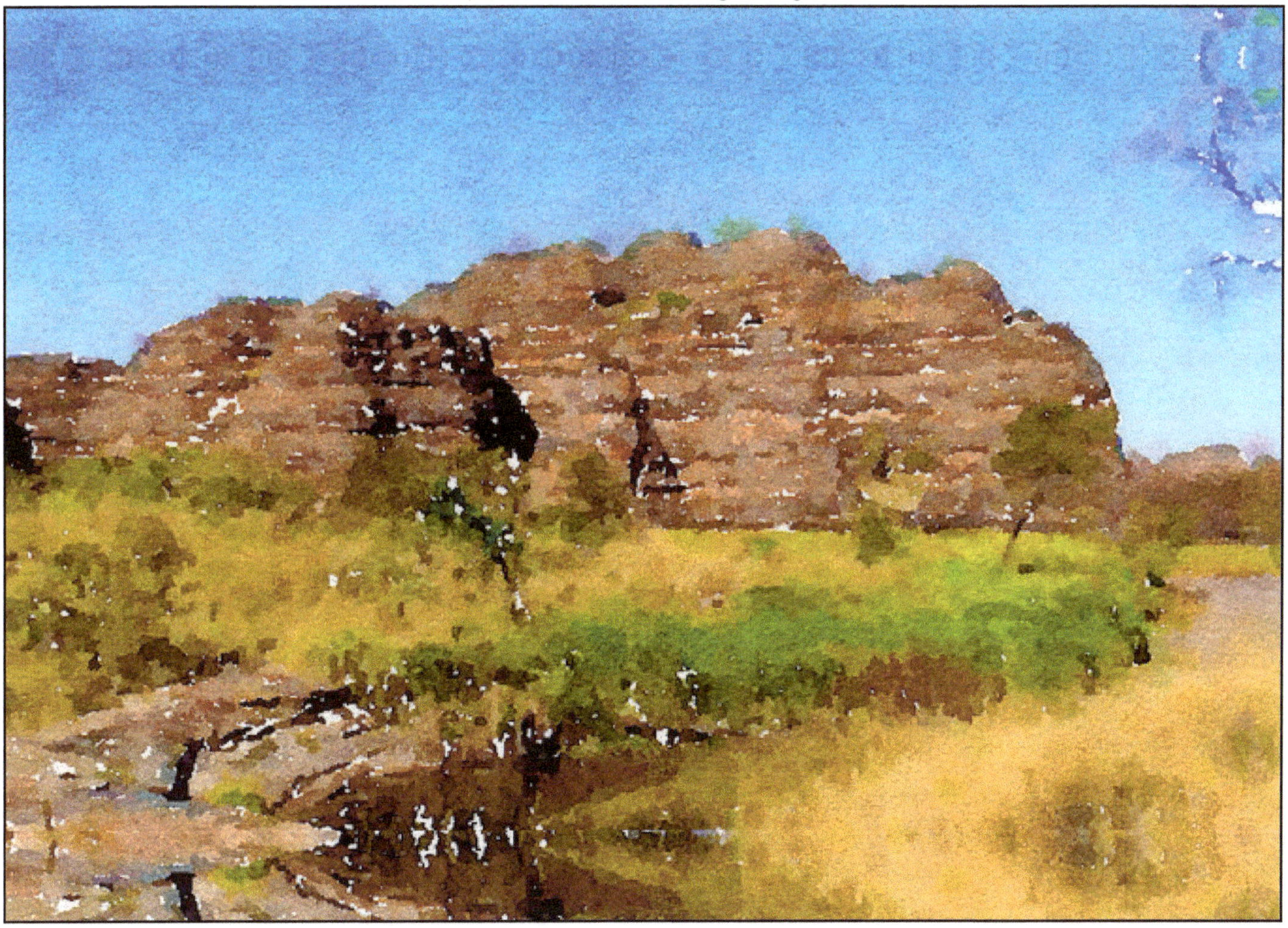

Urban Landscapes...

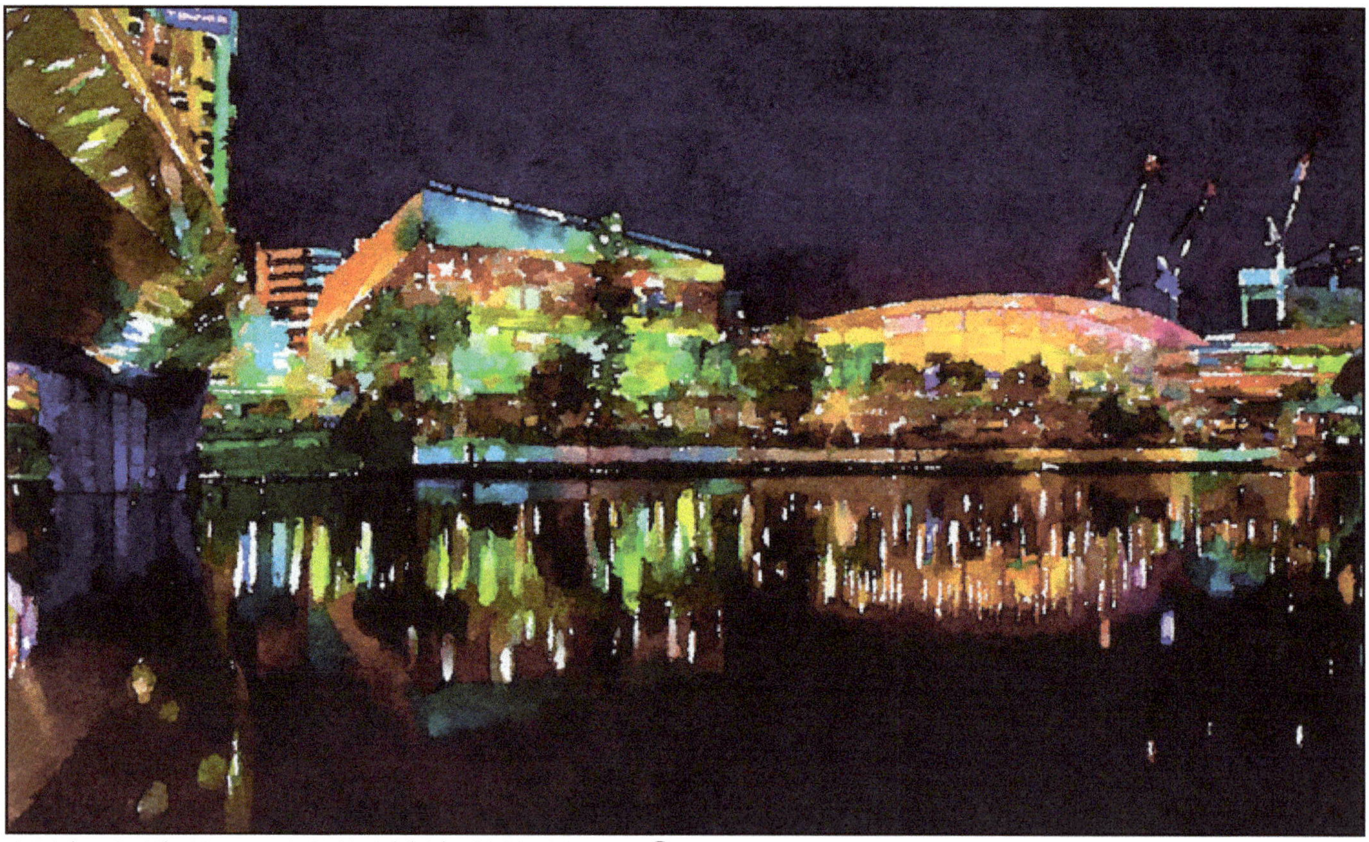

▲'Lights On The Torrens' (2021), Adelaide, SA [ALSA2103].

'View From Mt Ainslie' (2020), Canberra, ACT [ALCA2001].▼

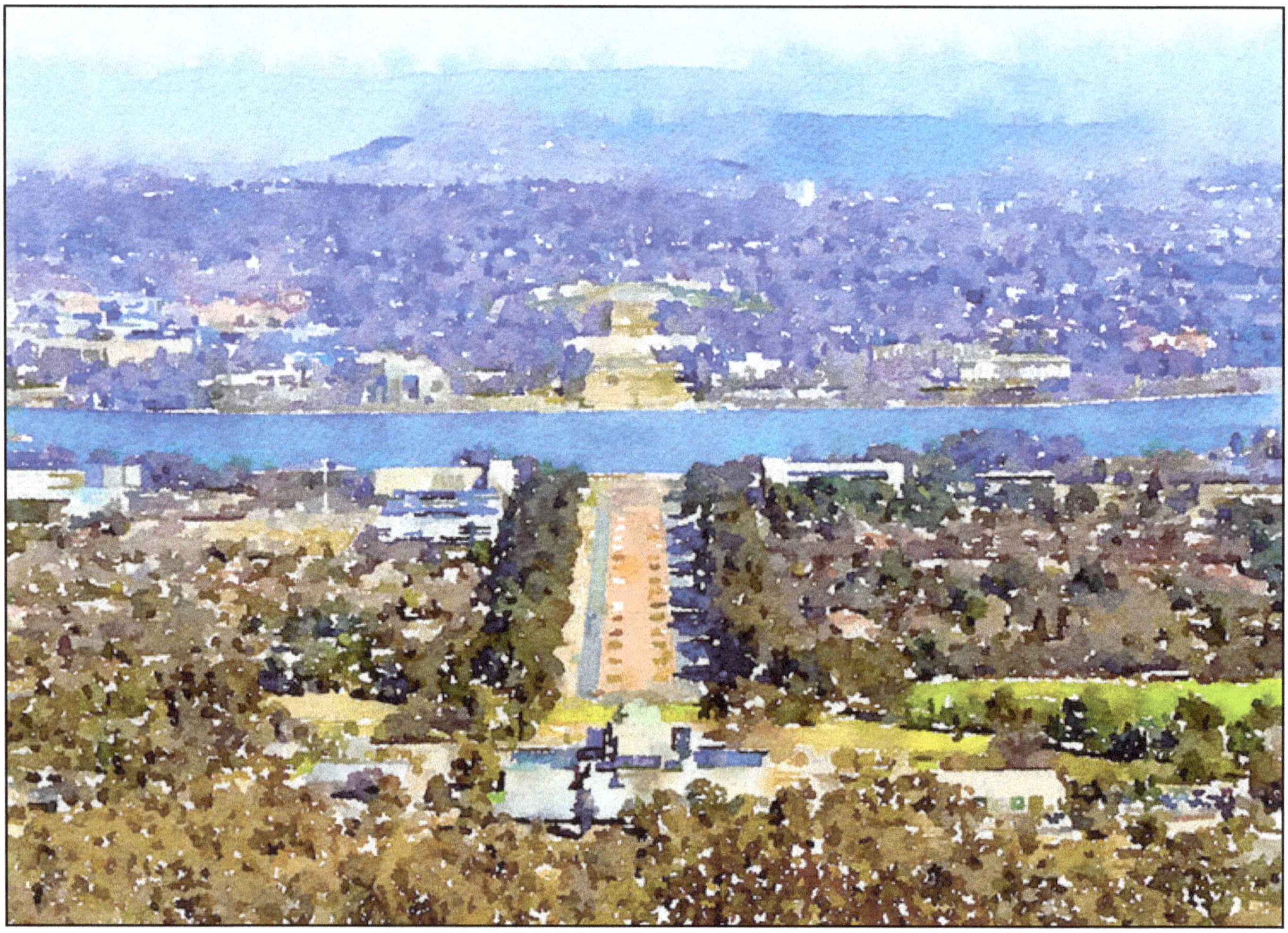

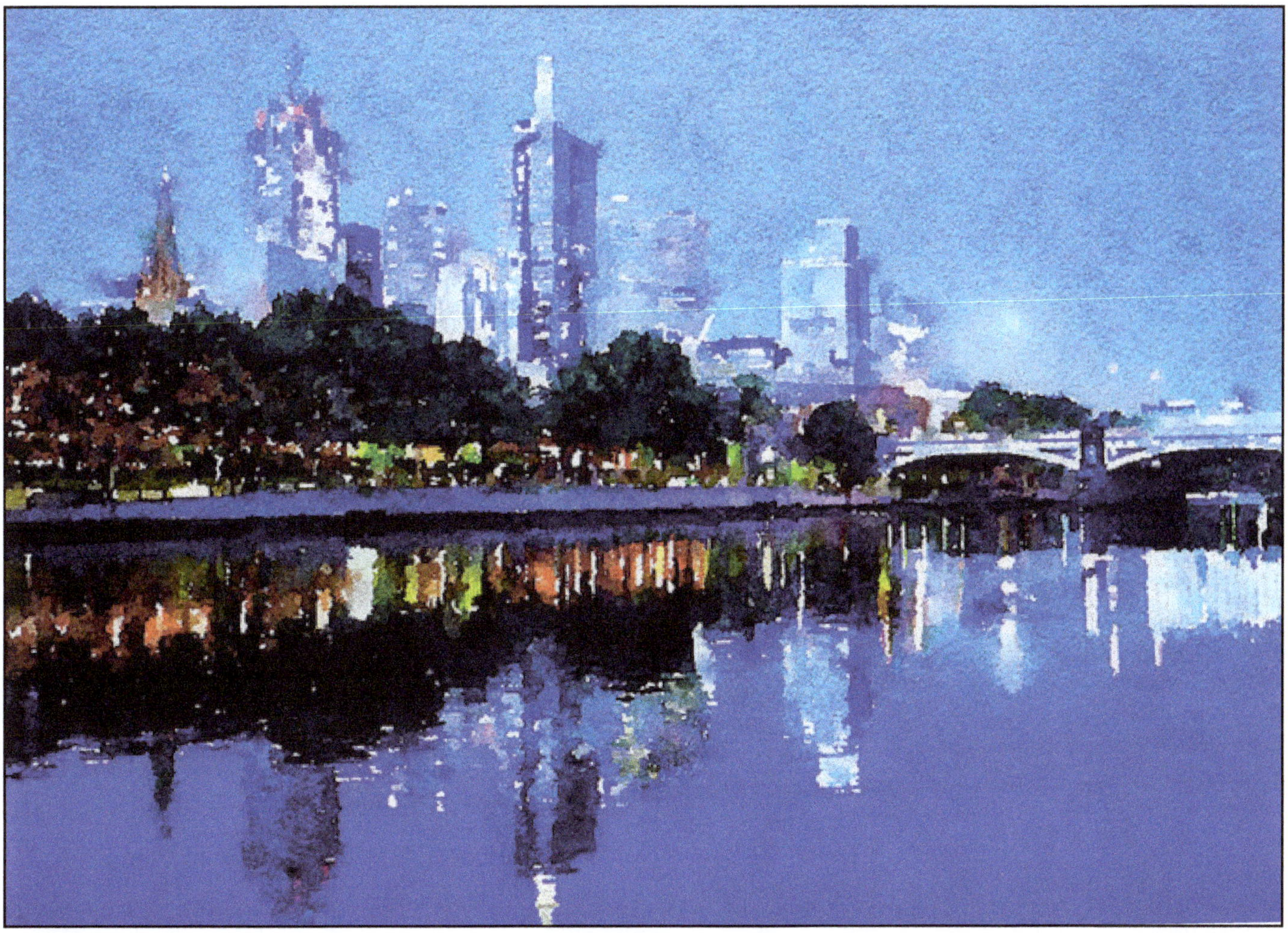

▲'Towers Over The Yarra' (2019), Melbourne, VIC [ALML1901].

'Trams On Swanston Street' (2012), Melbourne, VIC [ALML1201].▼

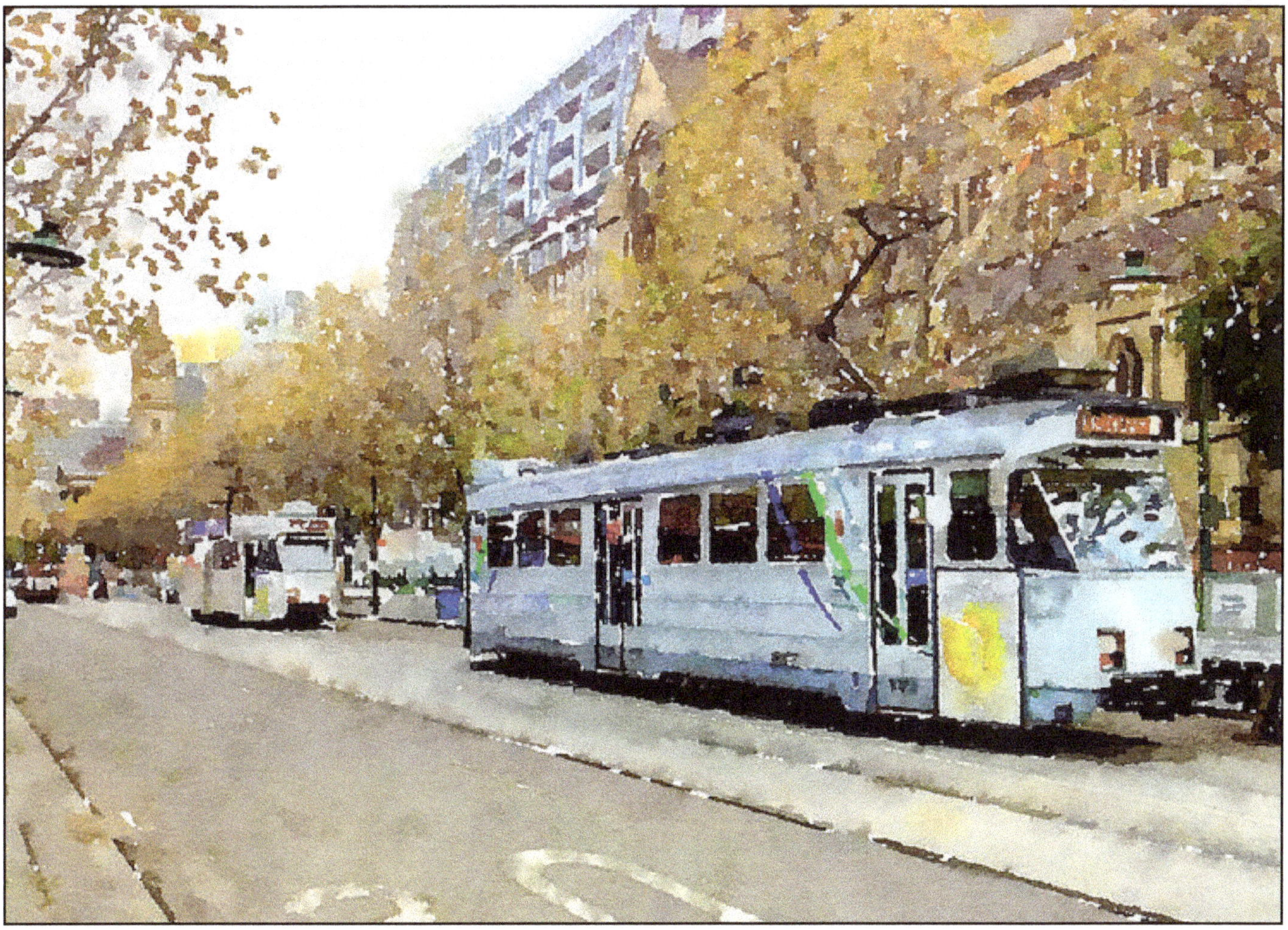

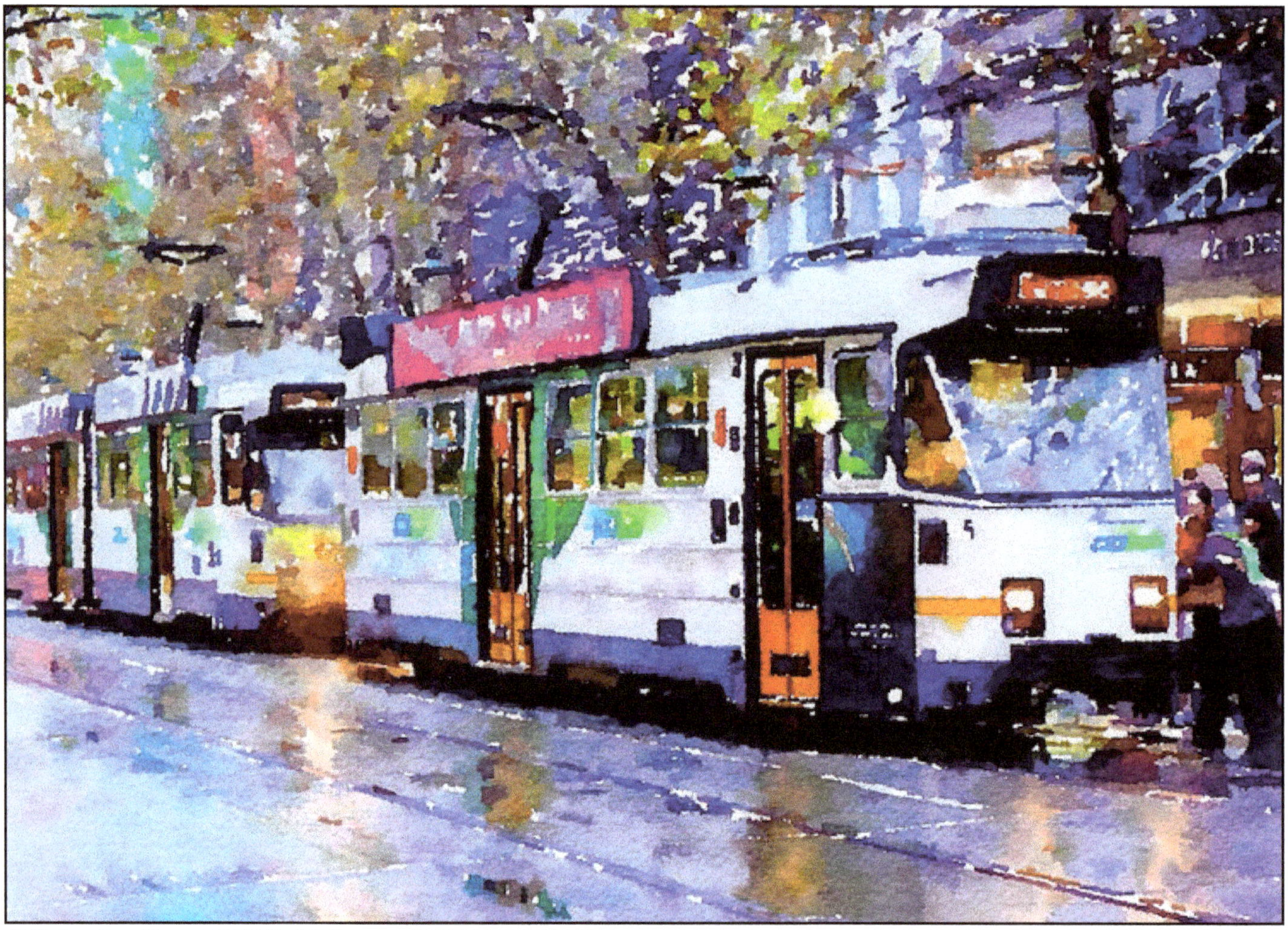

▲'Rainy Day Trams' (2019), Melbourne, VIC [ALML1902].

'The Emerald City' (2019), Melbourne, VIC [ALML1903].▼

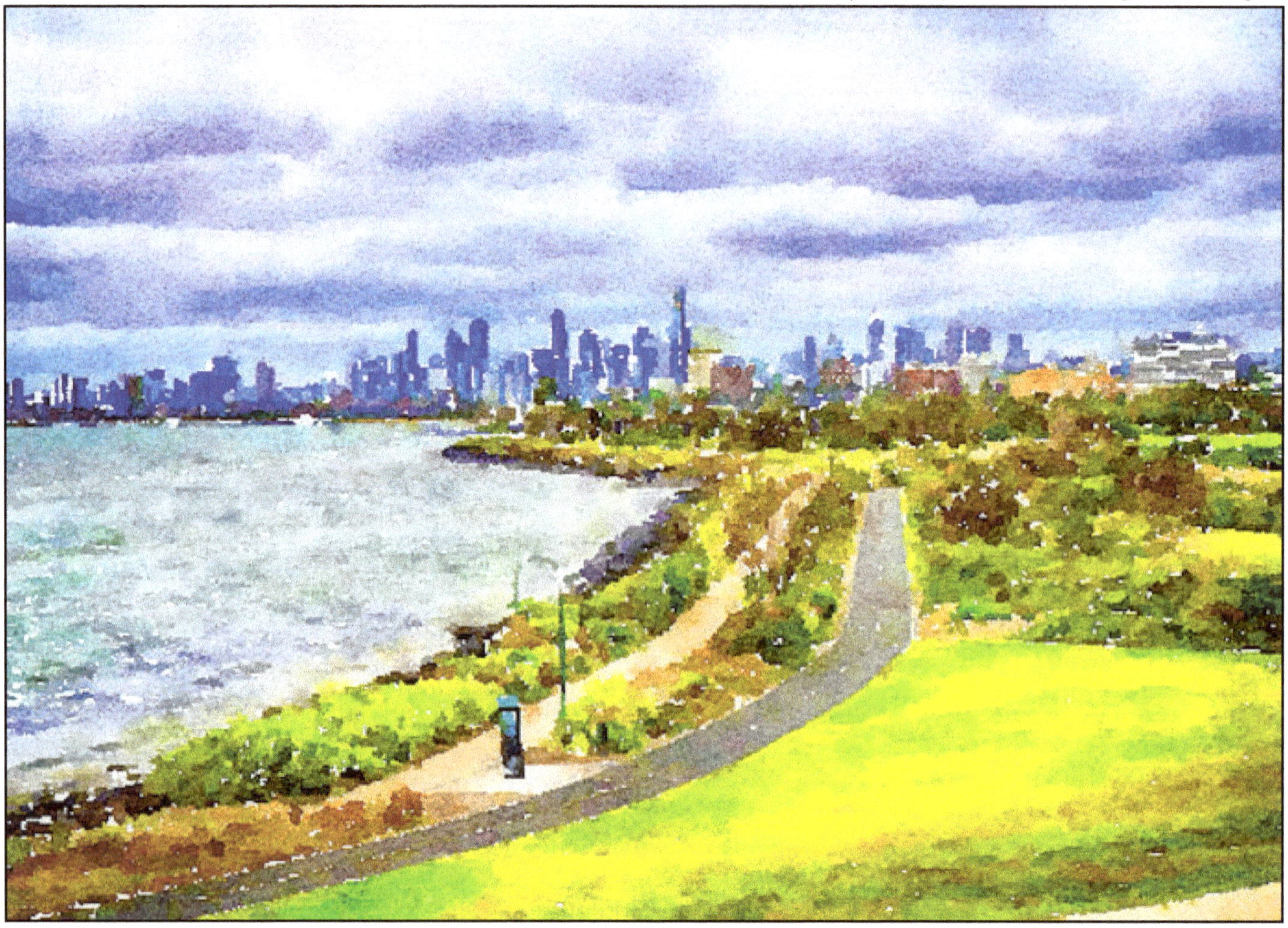

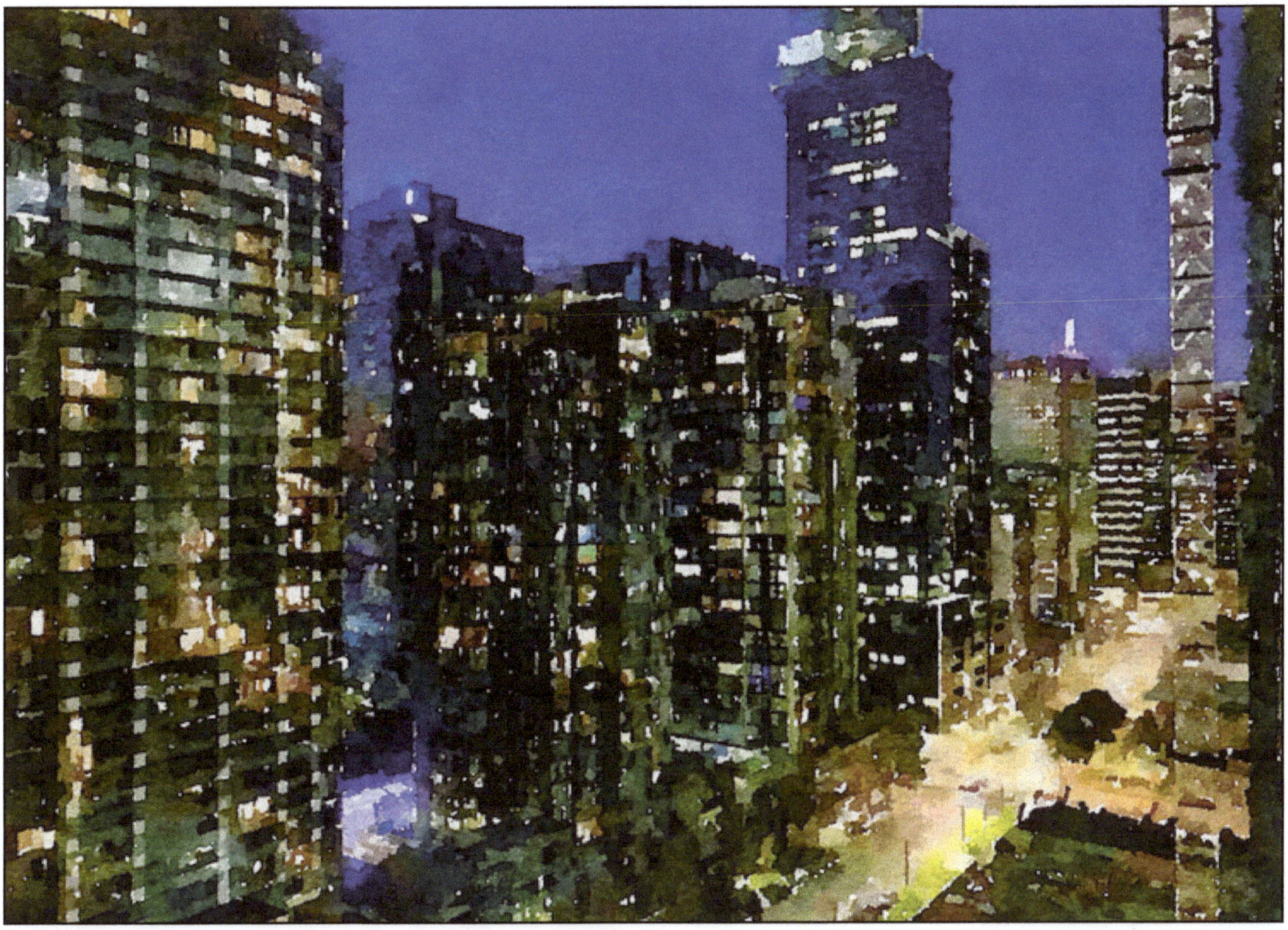

▲'Apartment Overload' (2019), Melbourne, VIC [ALML1904].

'Yarra River Lights' (2019), Melbourne, VIC [ALML1905].▼

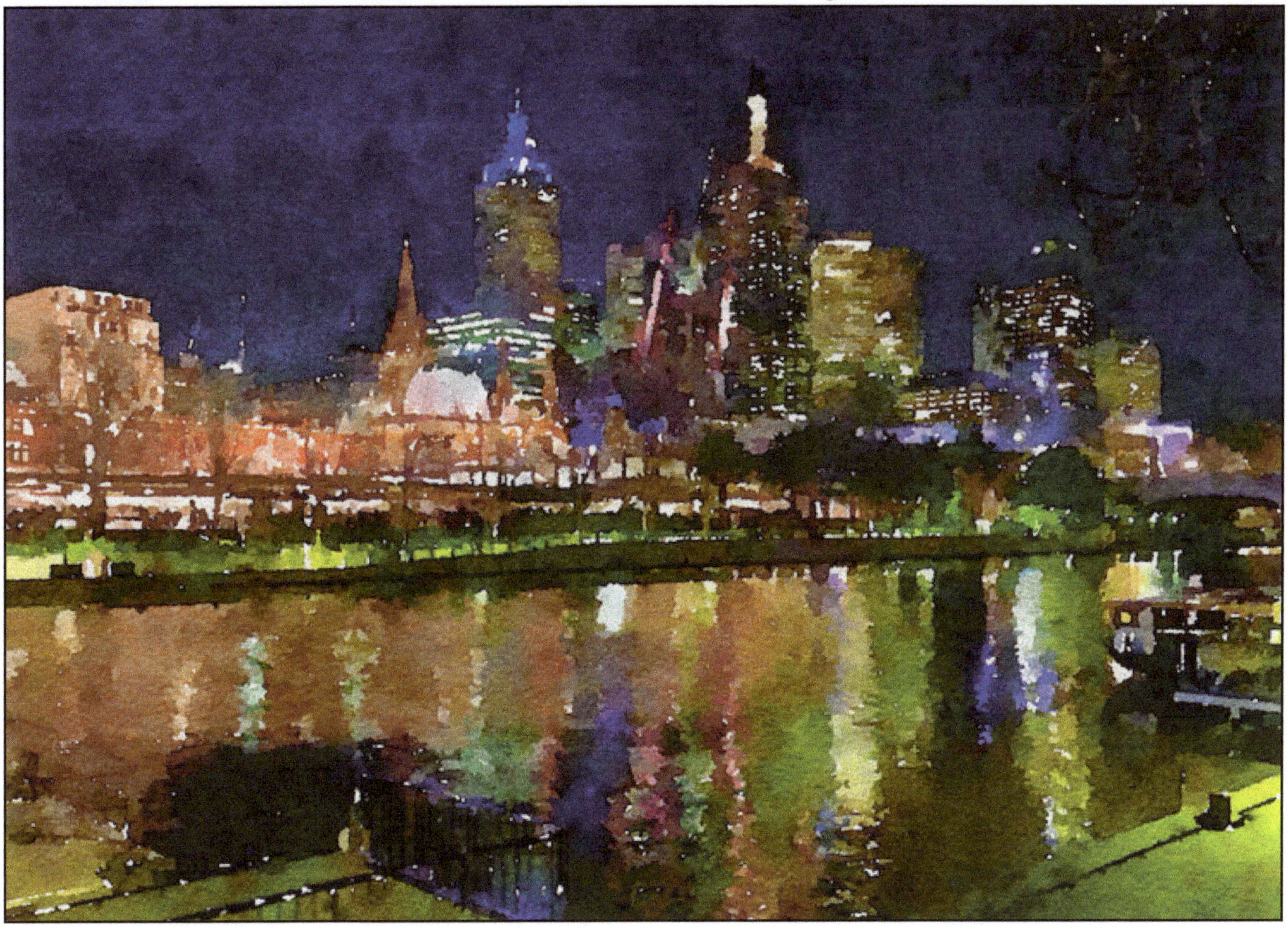

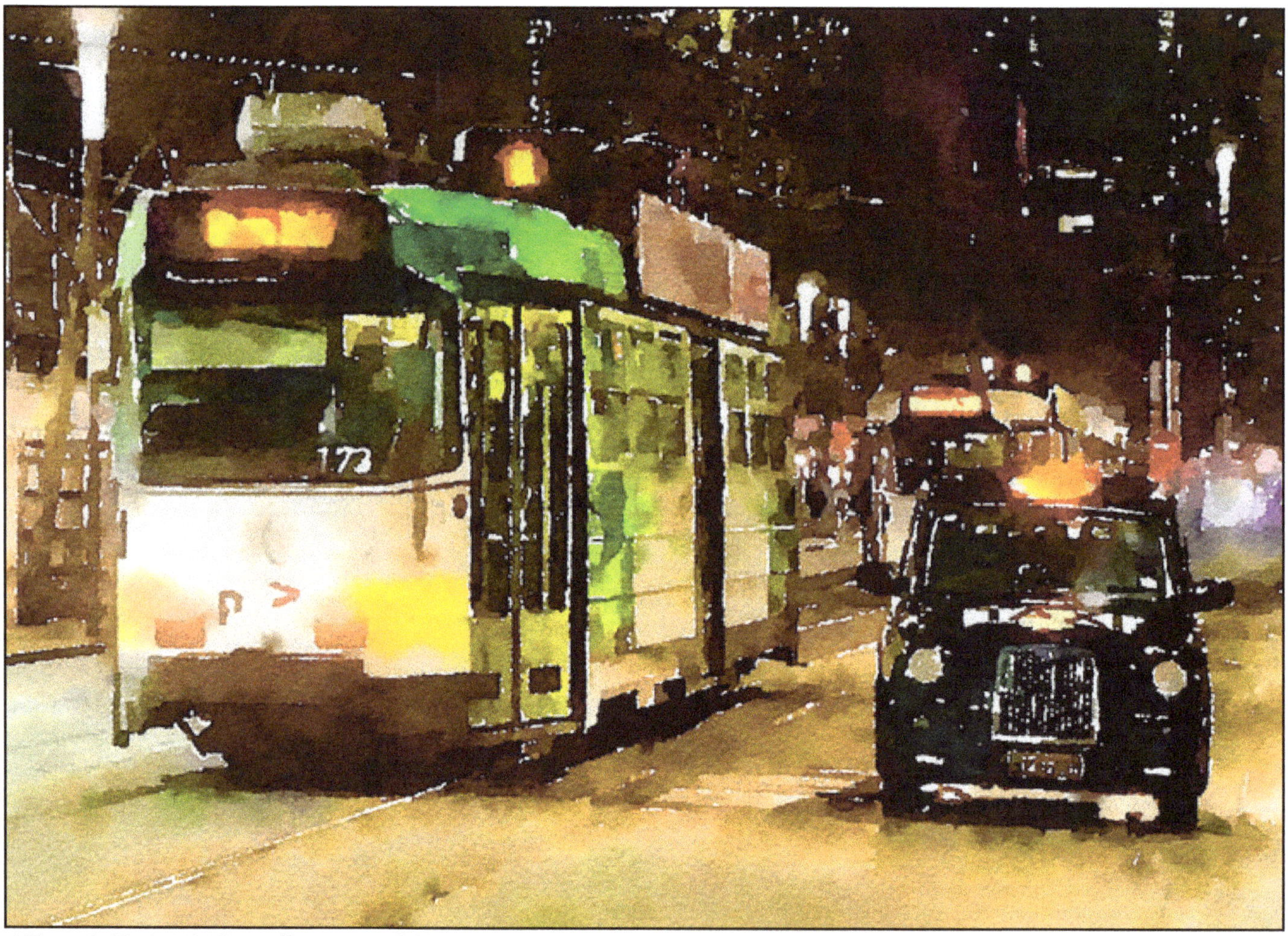

▲Tram & Taxi' (2019), Melbourne, VIC [ALML1906].

'Salamanca Markets' (2019), Hobart, TAS [ALTA1901].▼

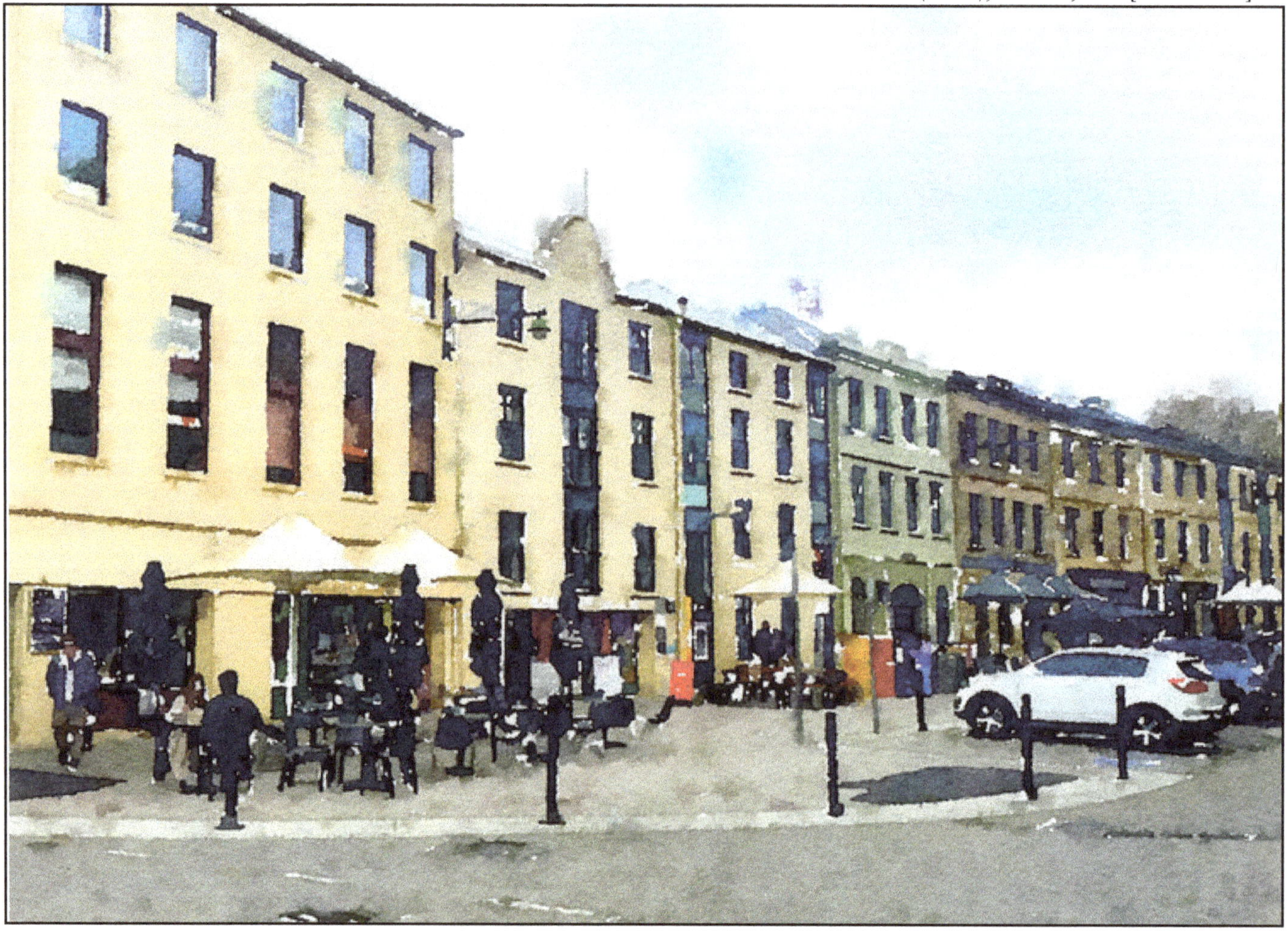

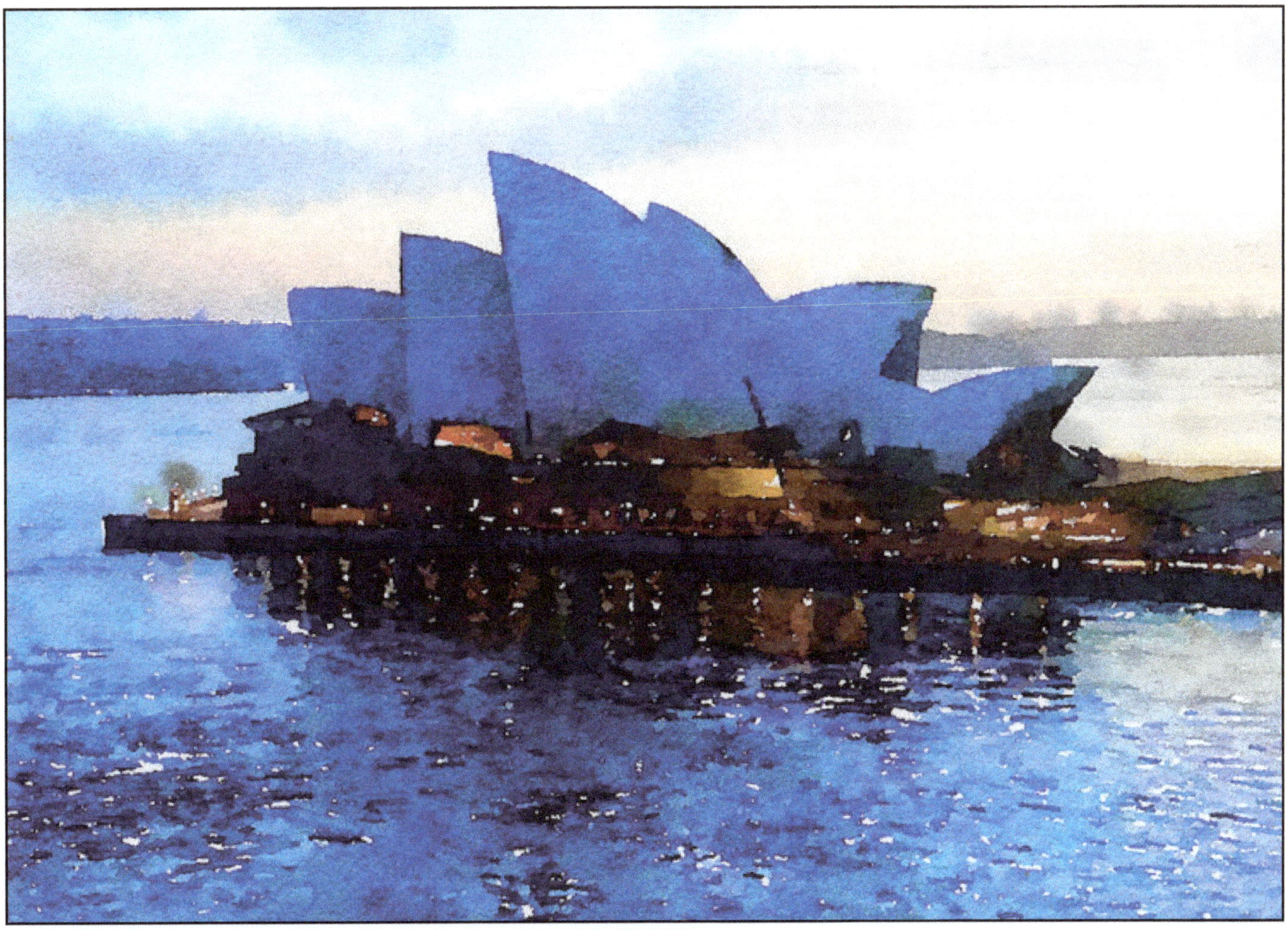

▲'Sunrise Over The Opera House' (2020), Sydney, NSW [ALSY2002].

'Dawes Point & The Bridge' (2020), Sydney, NSW [ALSY2001].▼

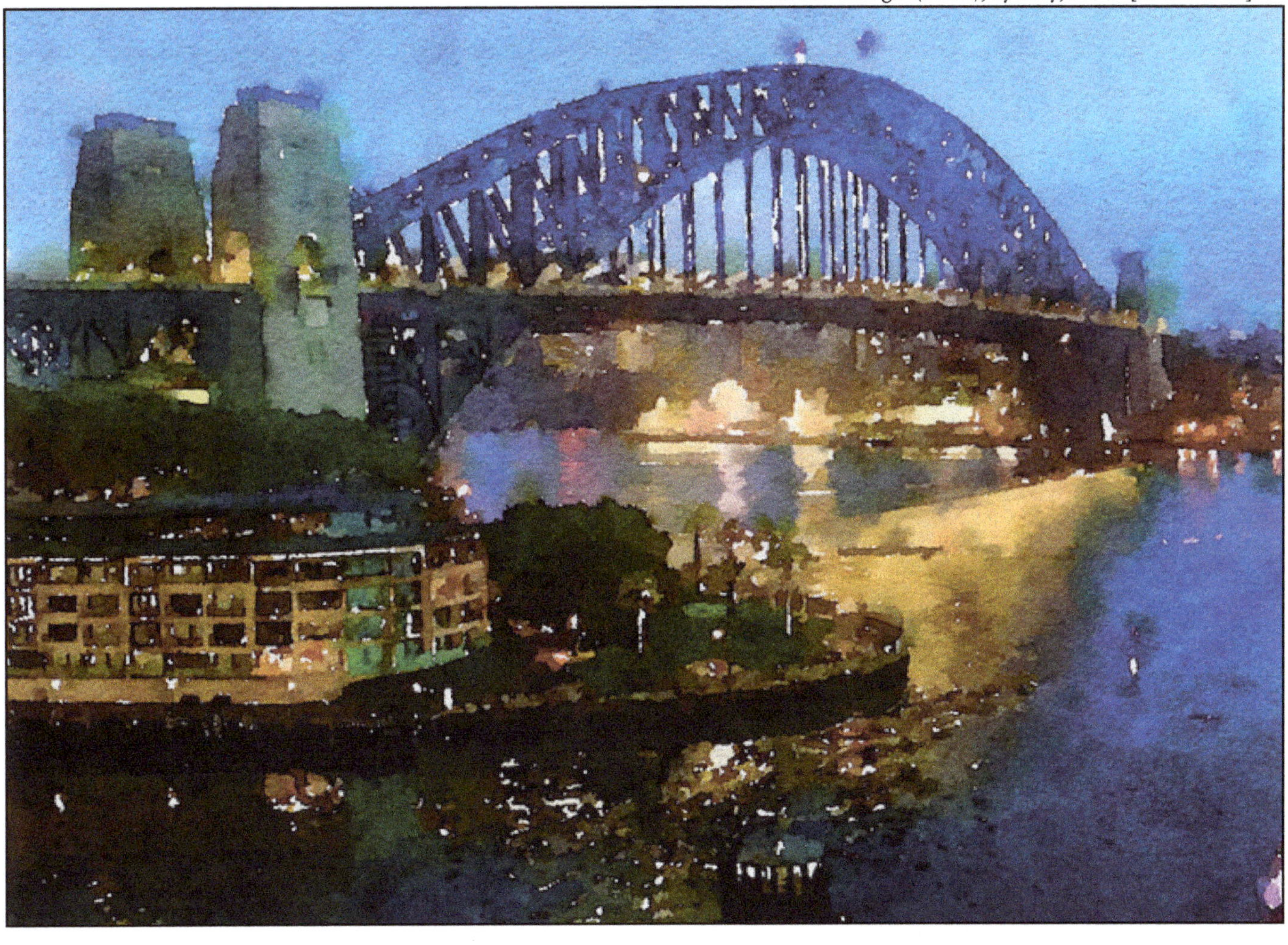

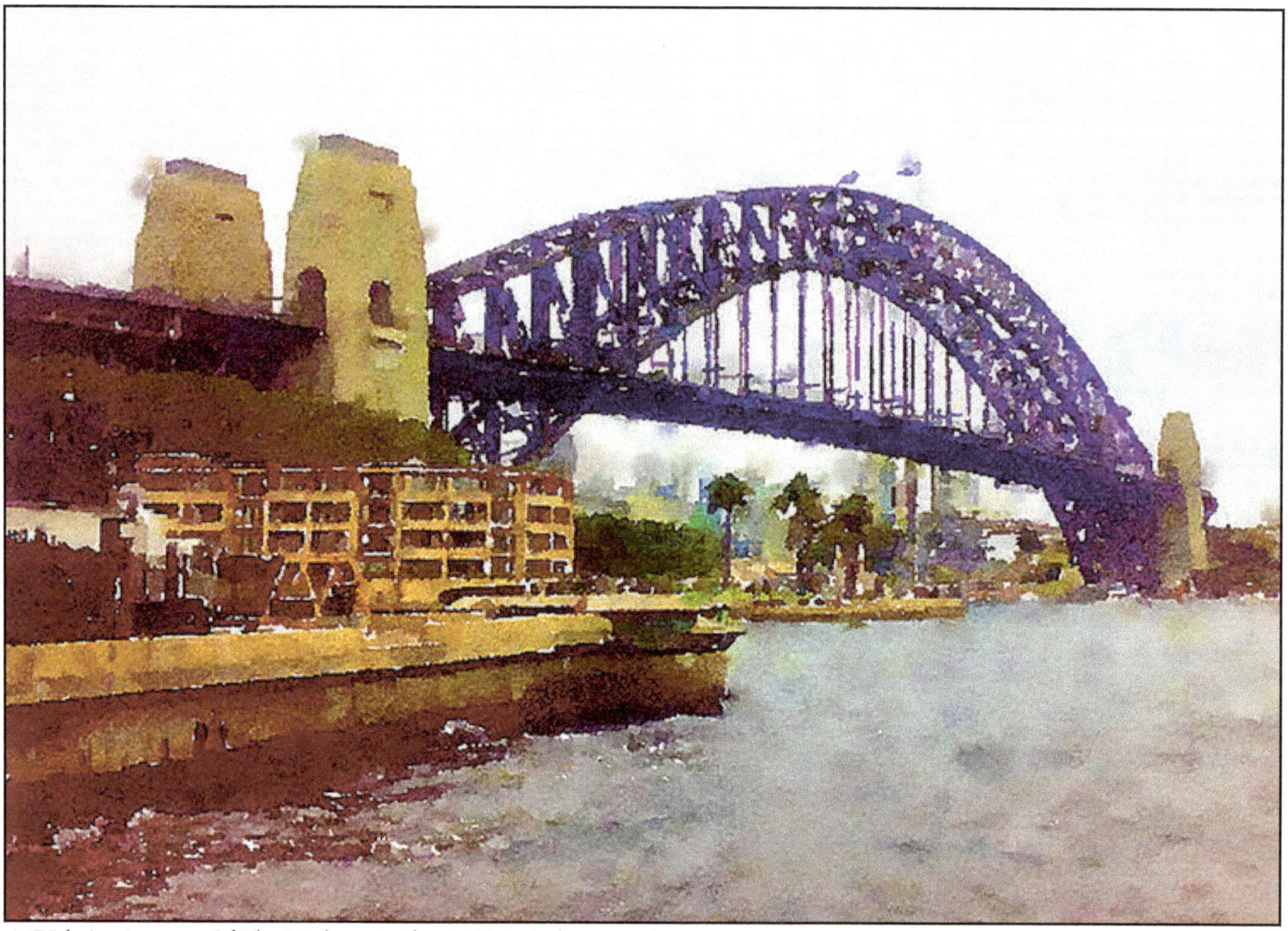

▲'75th Anniversary Of The Harbour Bridge' (2007), Sydney, NSW [ALSY0701].

'Vivid Reflections' (2015), Sydney, NSW [ALSY1501].▼

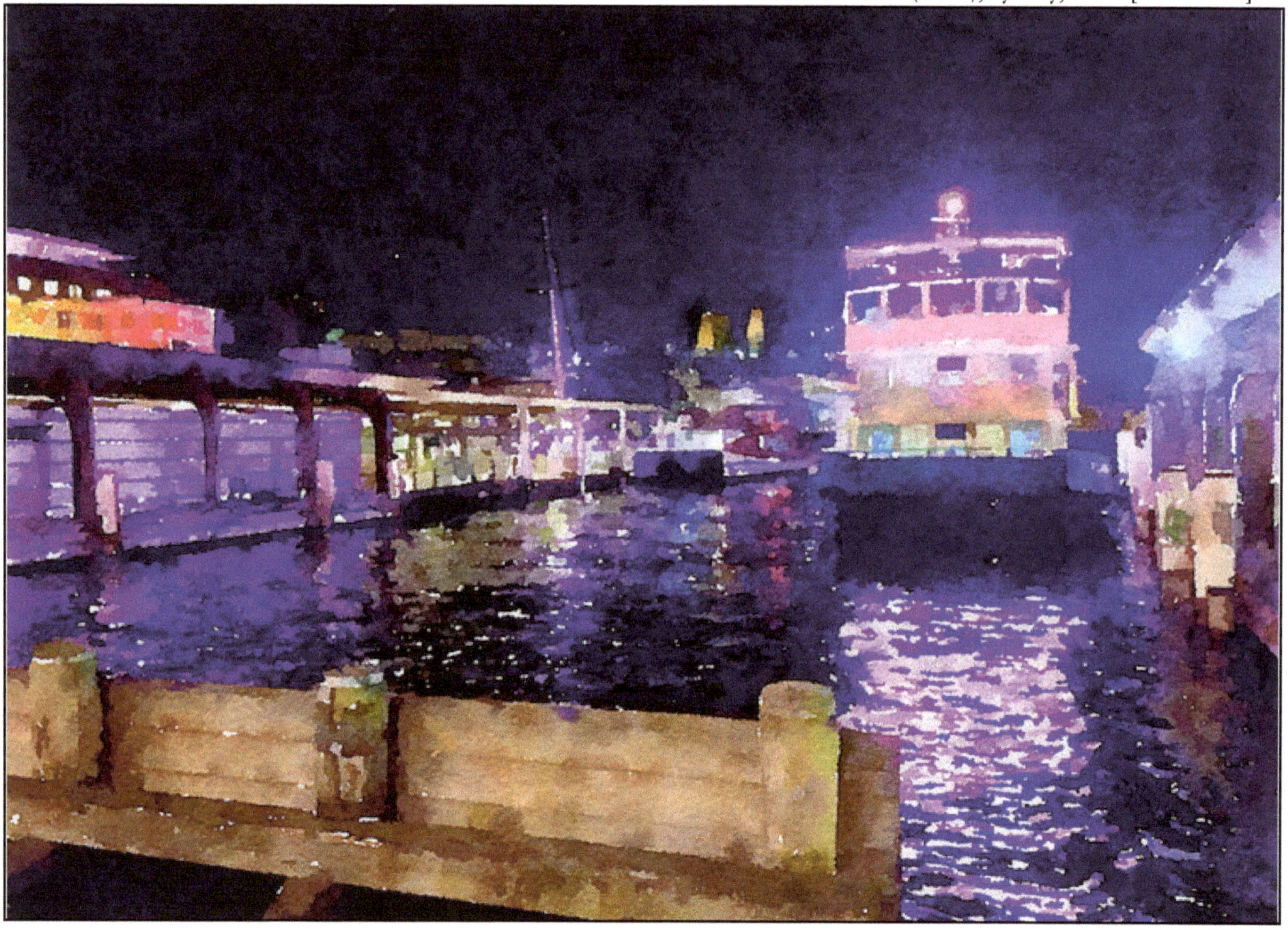

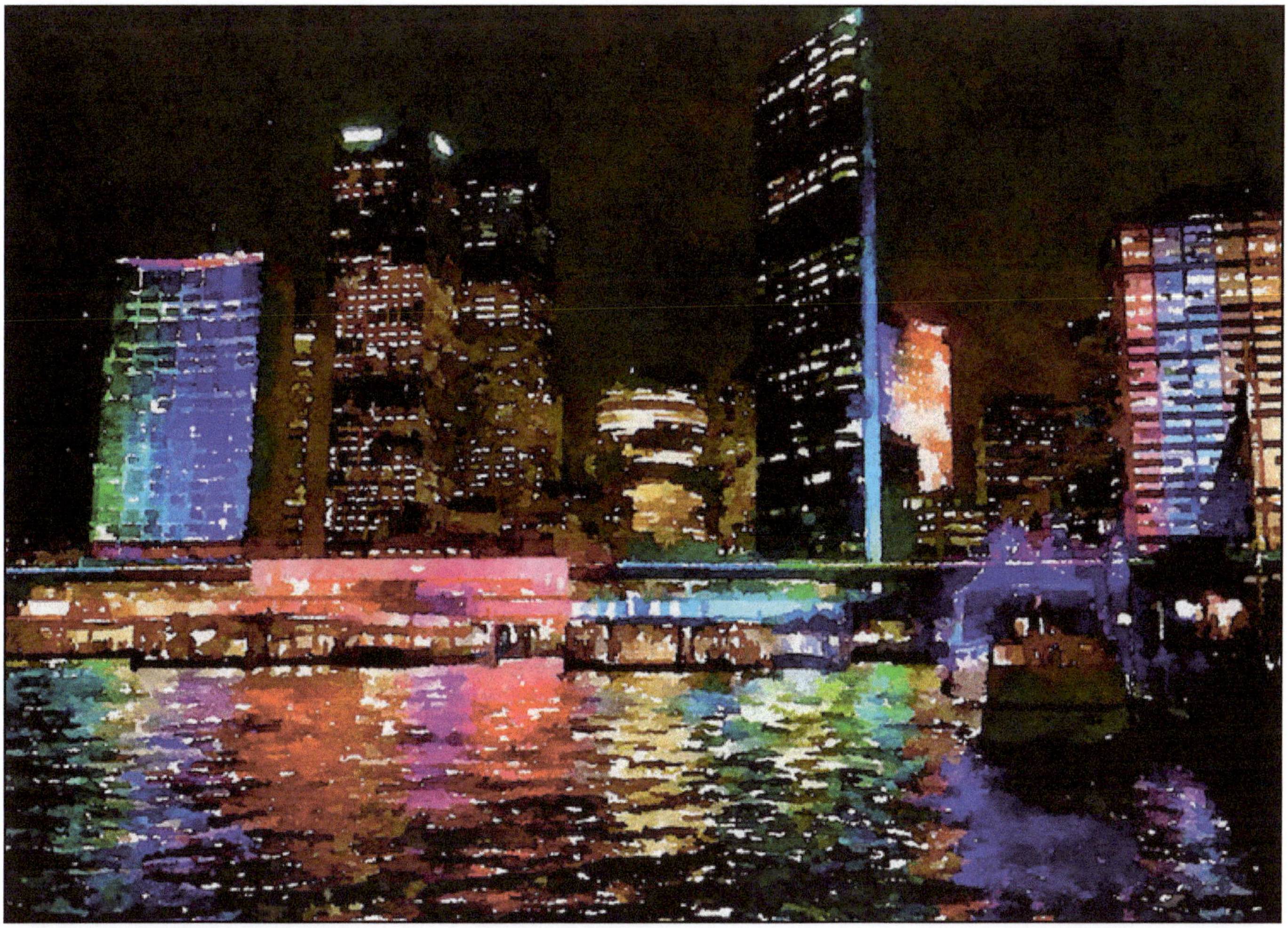

▲'Sydney Lights Up At Vivid' (2015), Sydney, NSW [ALSY1502].

'The Crimson Bridge' (2017), Sydney, NSW [ALSY1705].▼

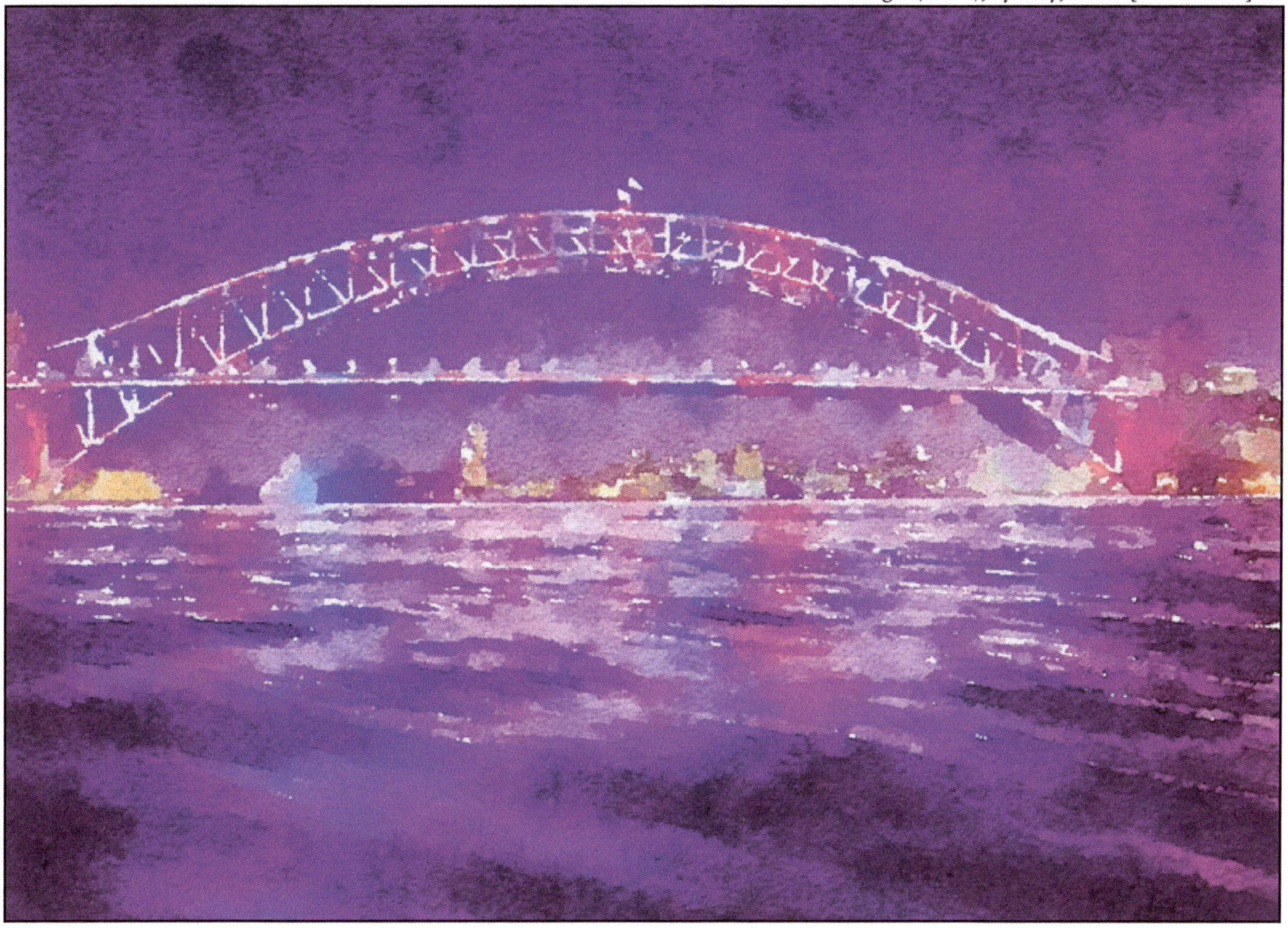

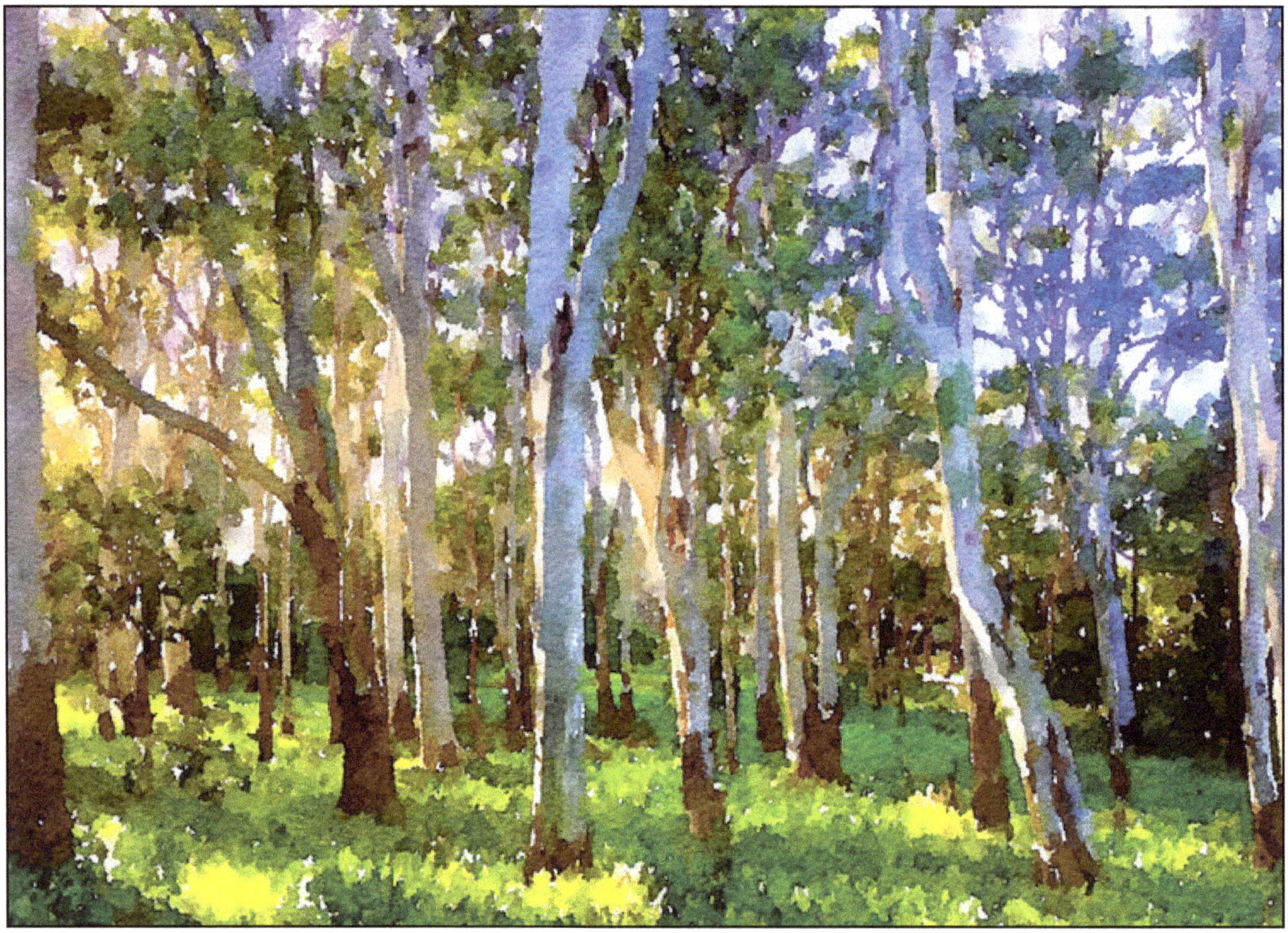

▲'Morning In The Bluegums' (2016), Centennial Park, NSW [ALSY1601].

'Musgrave Pond' (2017), Centennial Park, NSW [ALSY1702].▼

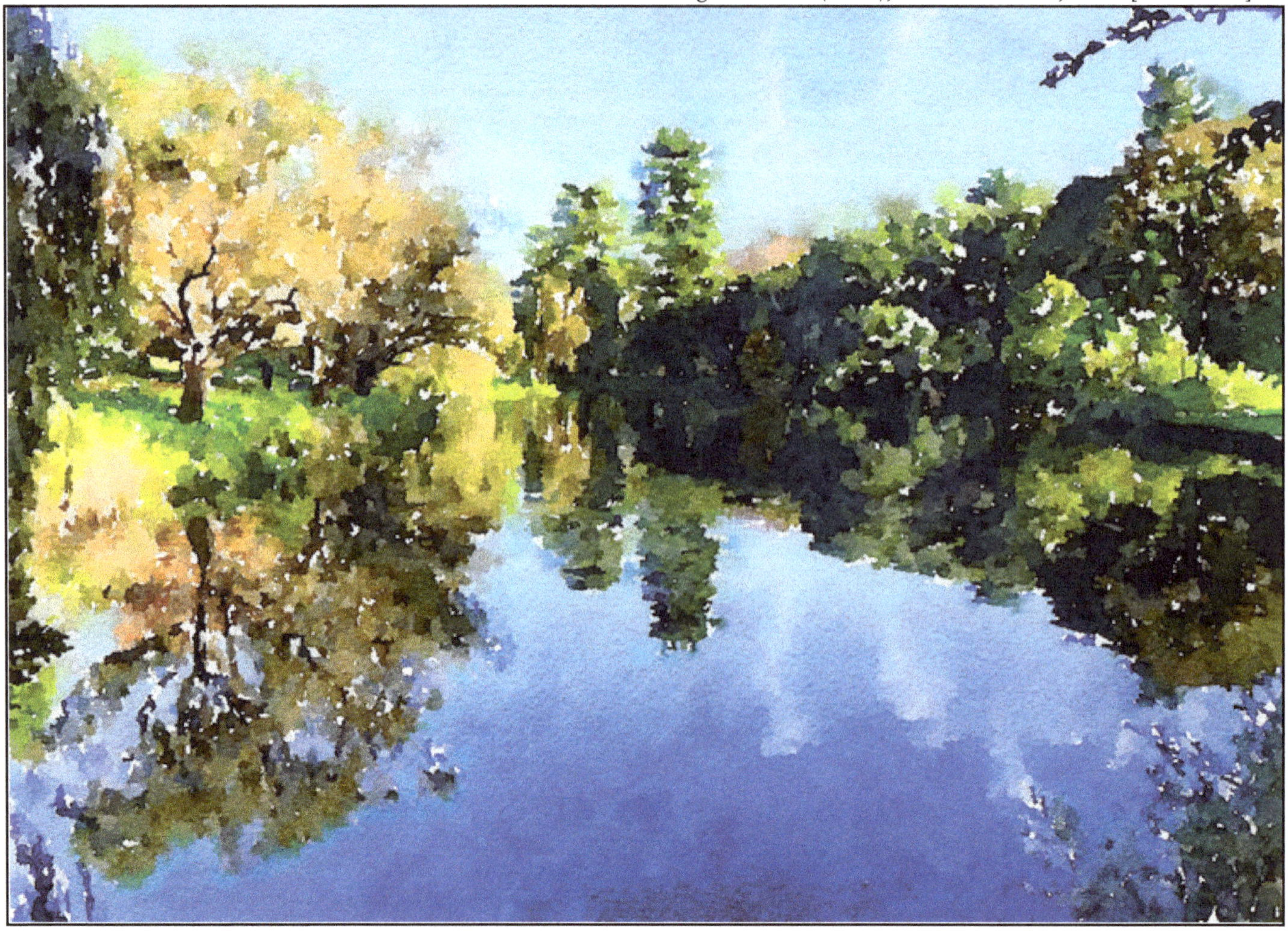

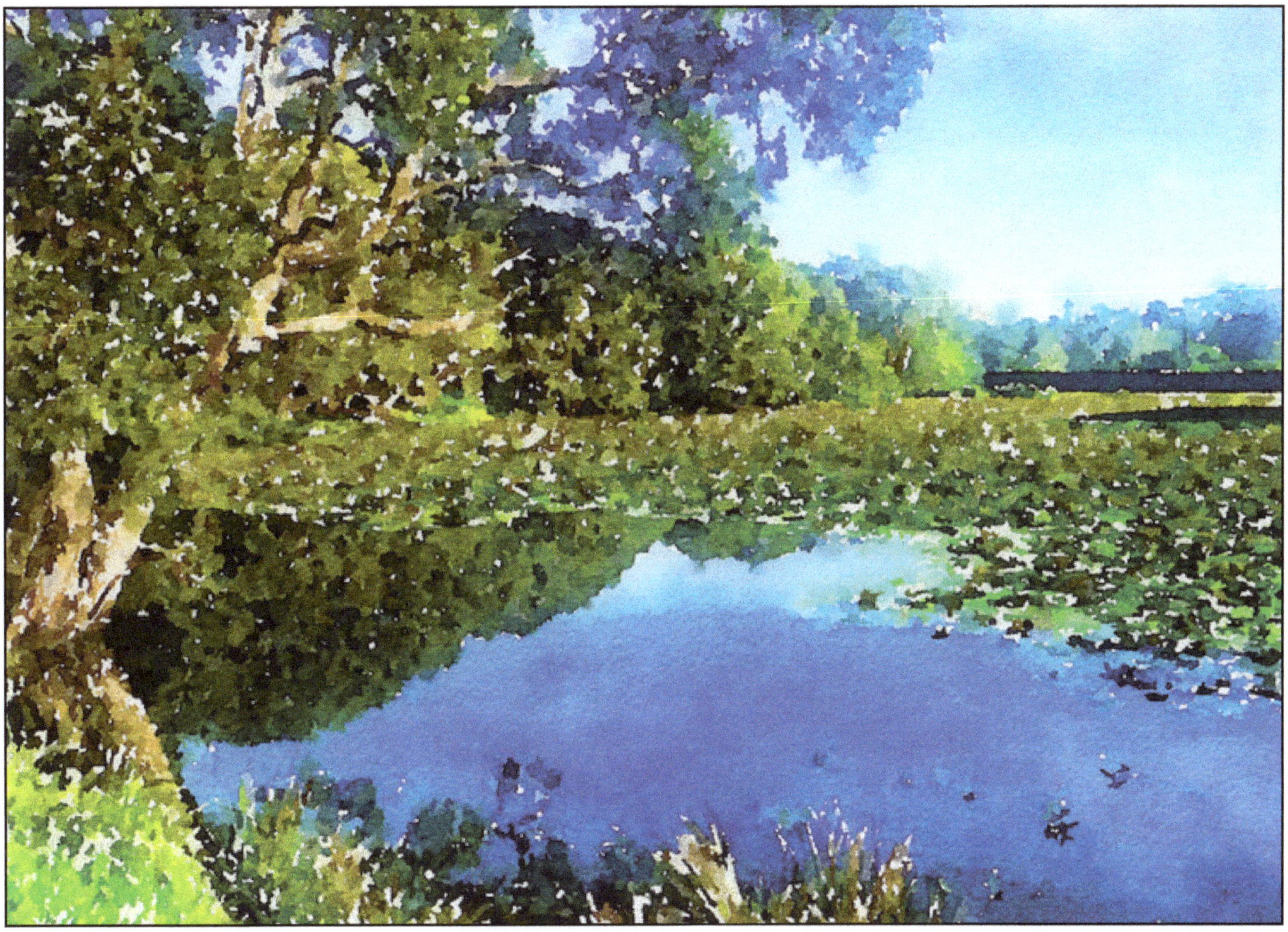

▲'Busby's Pond' (2019), Centennial Park, NSW [ALSY1910].

'Early Morning Rays' (2019), Centennial Park, NSW [ALSY1913].▼

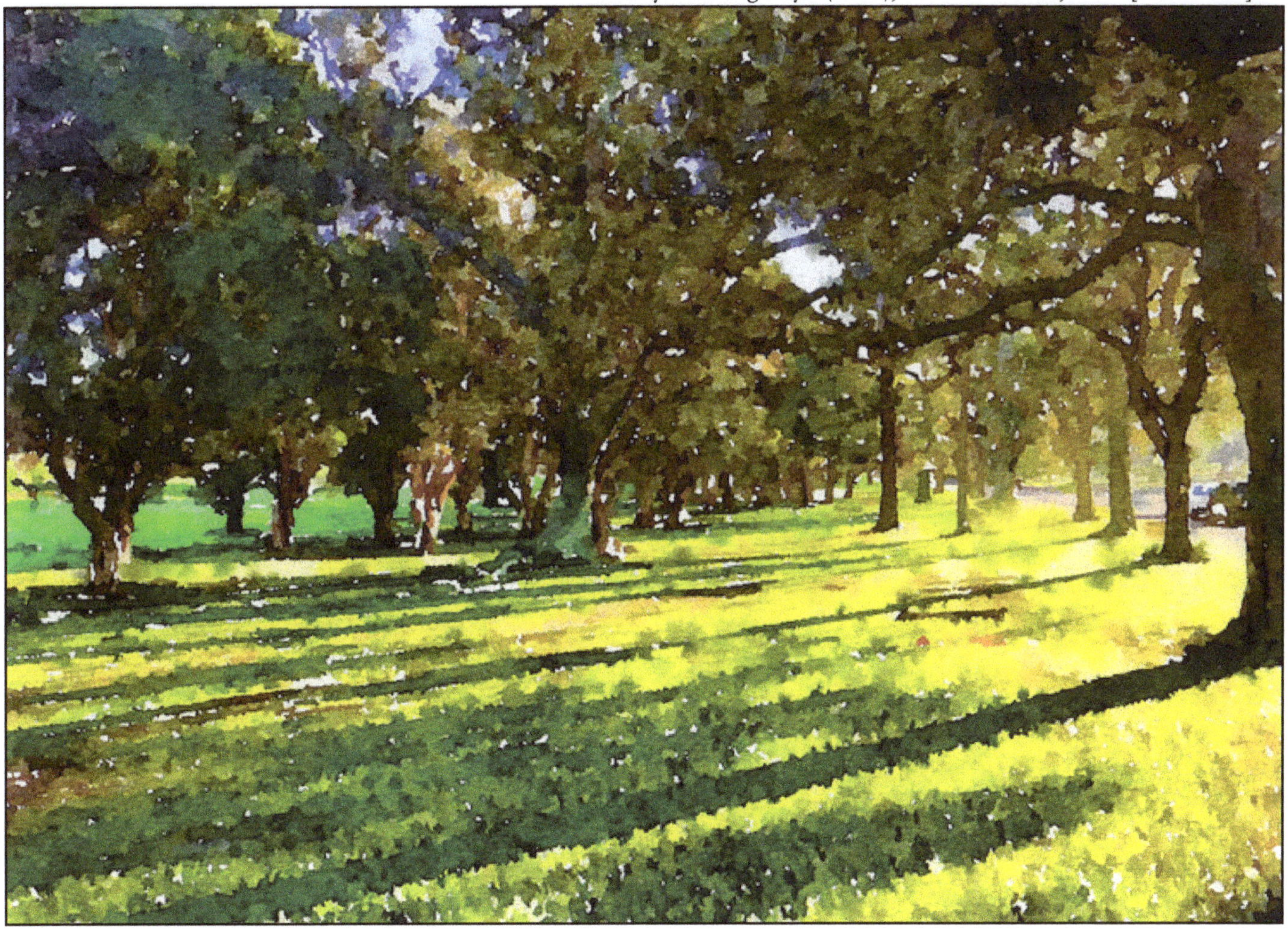

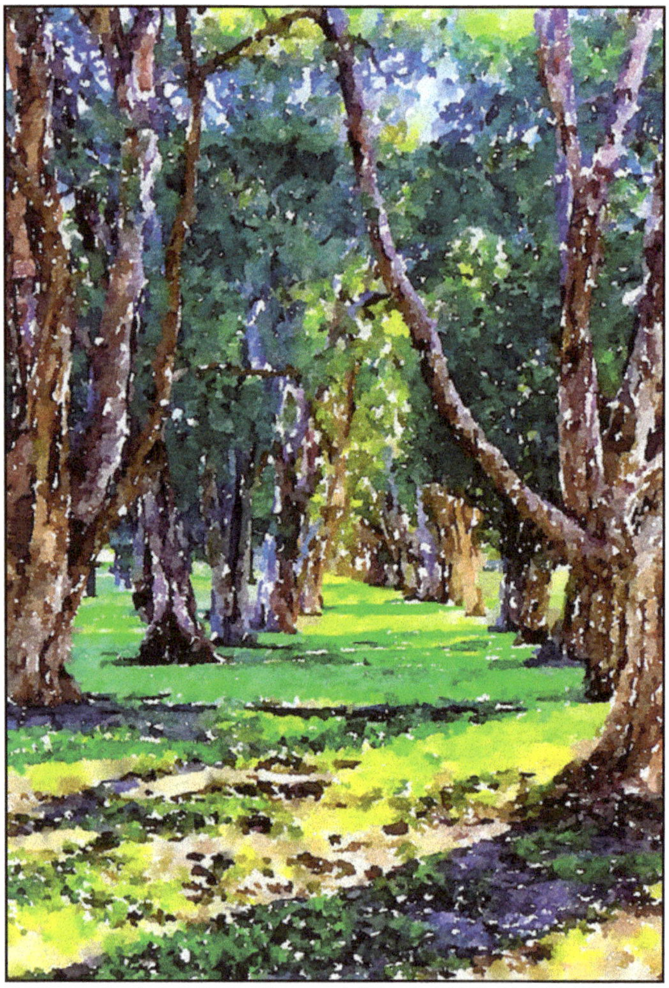

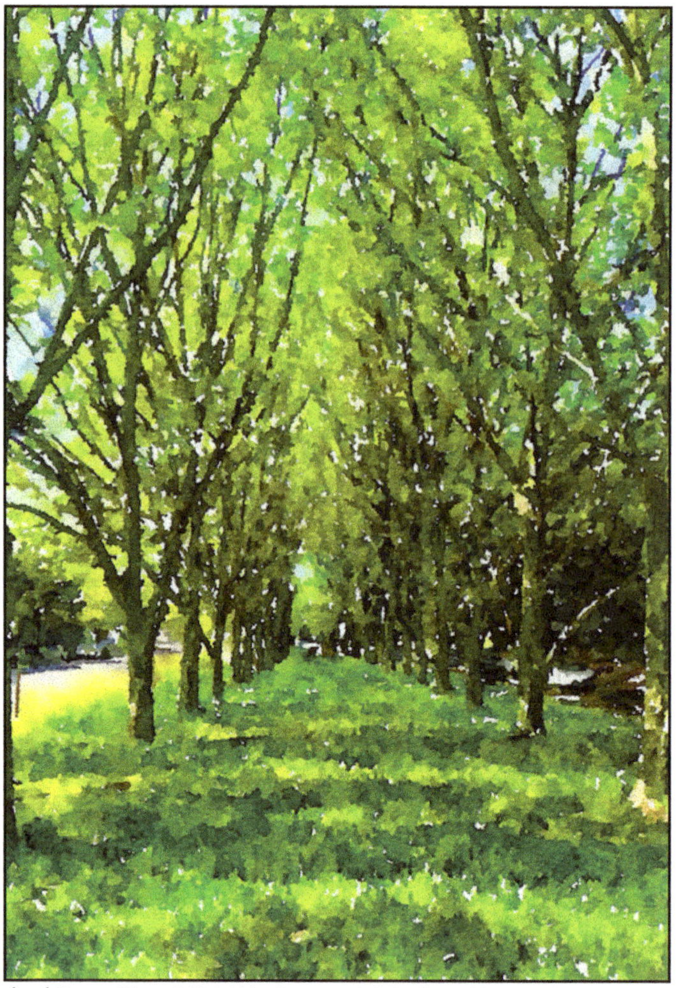

▲'Paper Barks' (2017), Centennial Park, NSW [ALSY1701].

'Oxford Street Trees' (2019), Centennial Park, NSW [ALSY1902].▲

'Central Station' (2019), Sydney, NSW [ALSY1905]. ▼

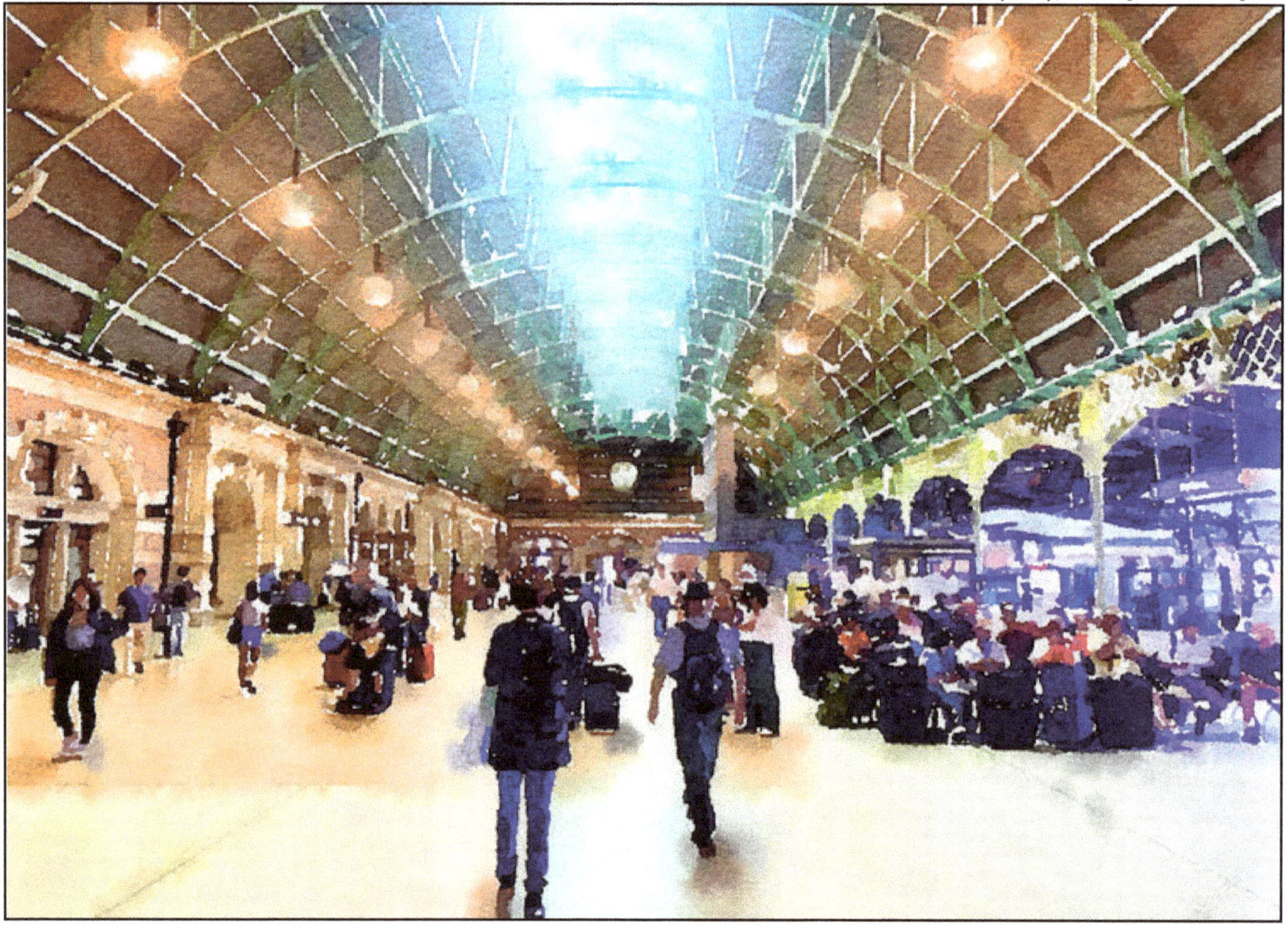

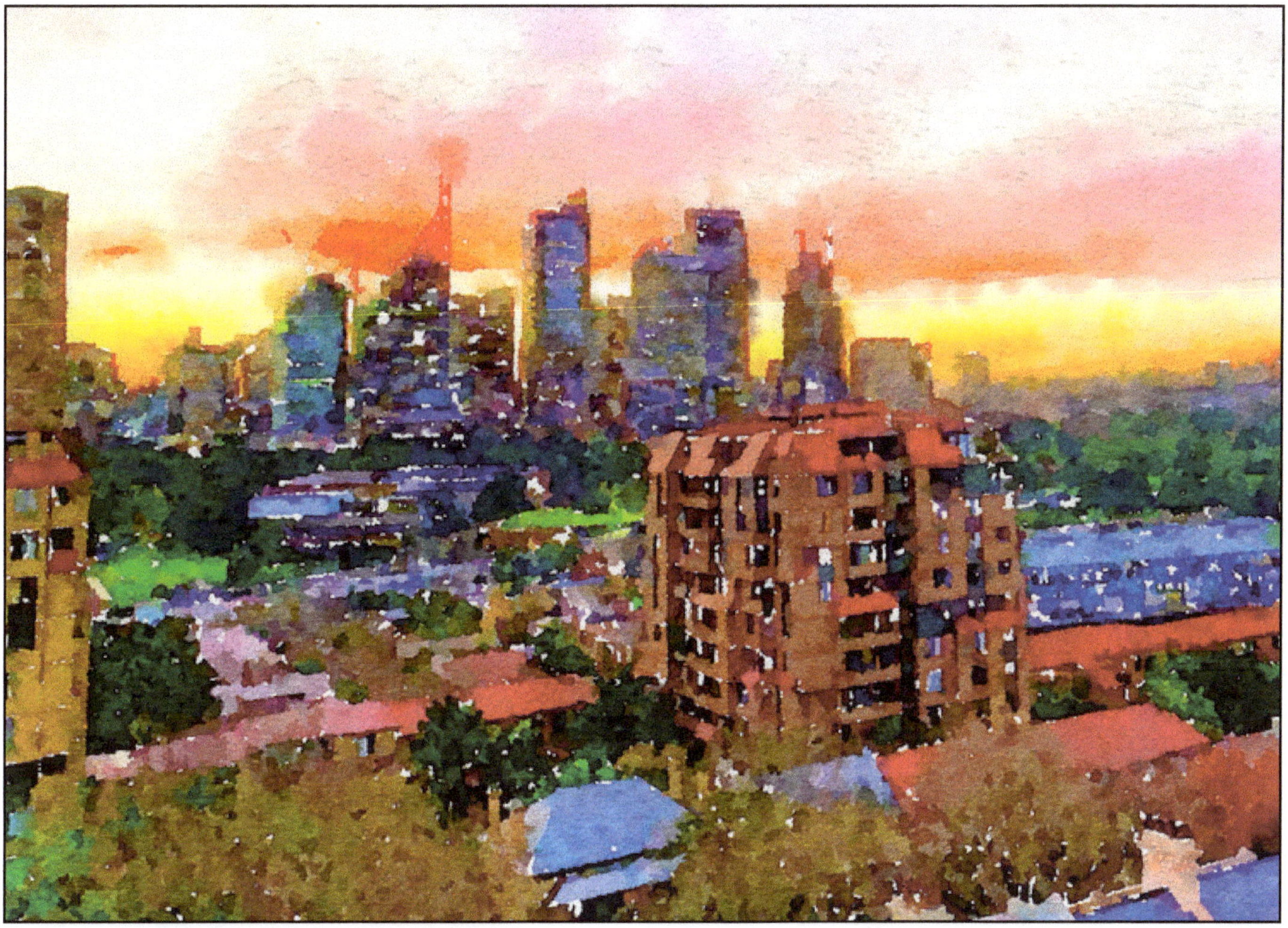

▲'City Sundown' (2019), Sydney, NSW [ALSY1903].

'William Street Terraces' (2019), Paddington, NSW [ALSY1904].▼

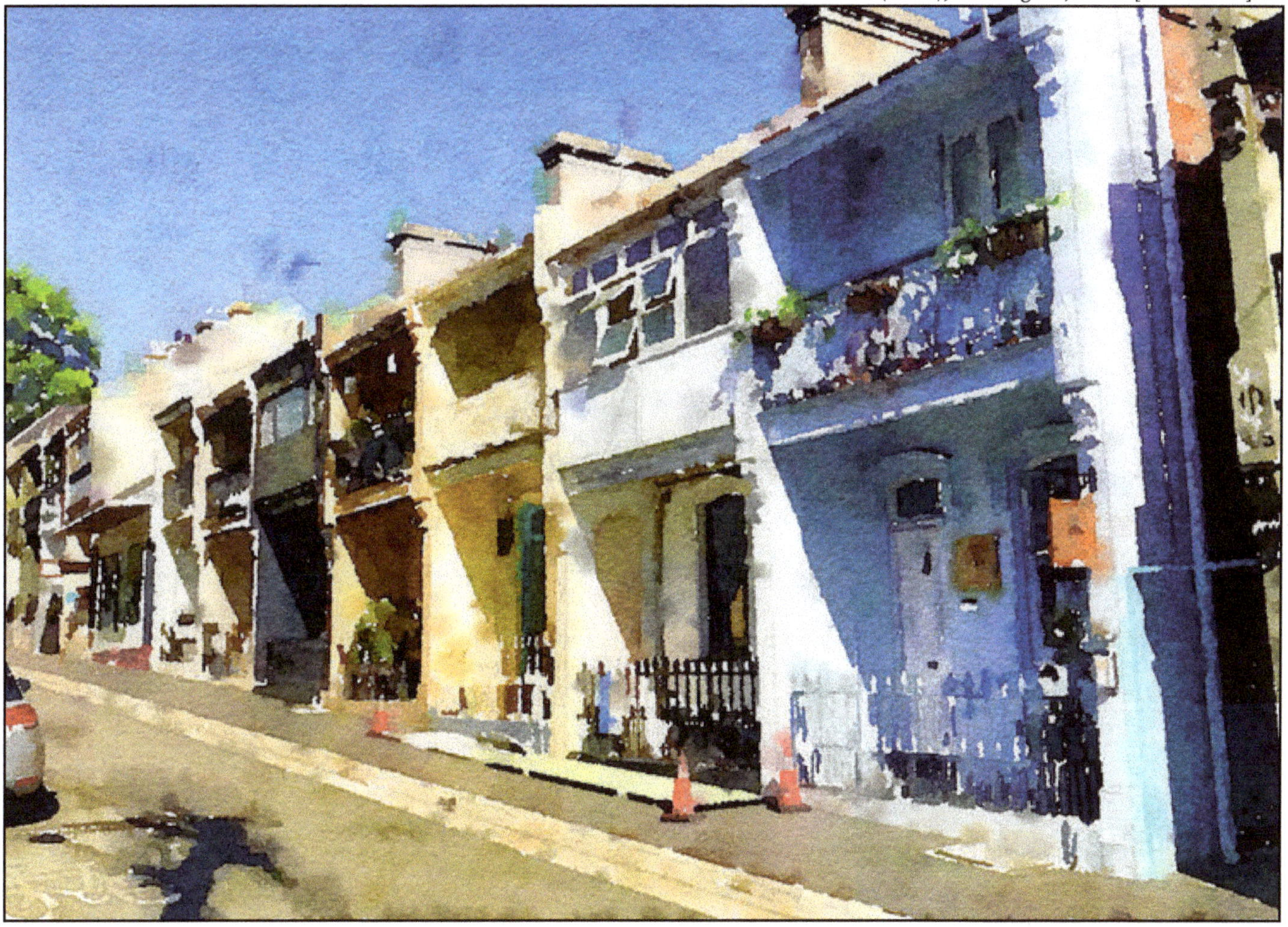

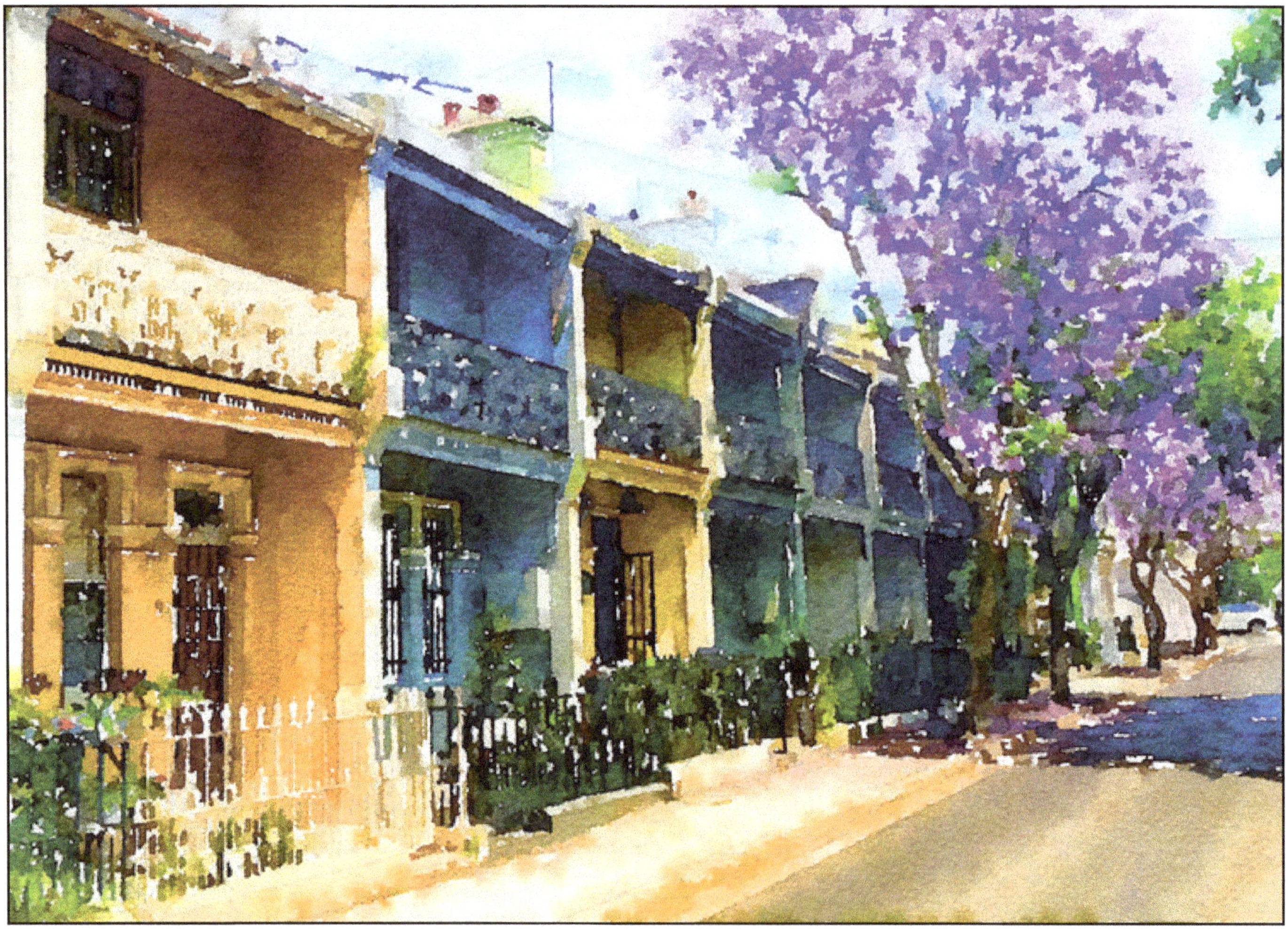

▲'Paddington Blooms 1' (2019), Paddington, NSW [ALSY1906].

'Jacarandas on Oxford Street' (2019), Paddington, NSW [ALSY1901].▼

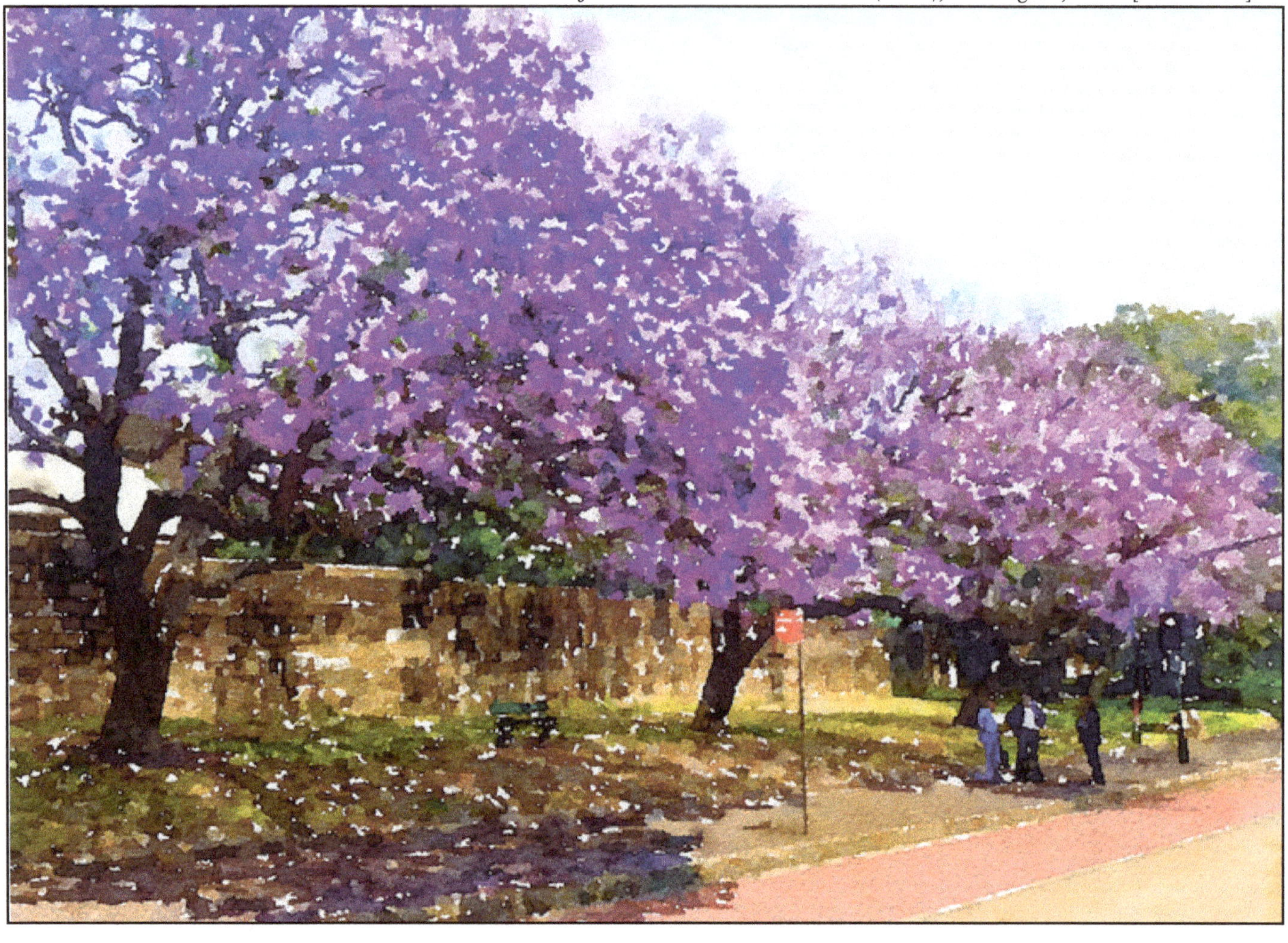

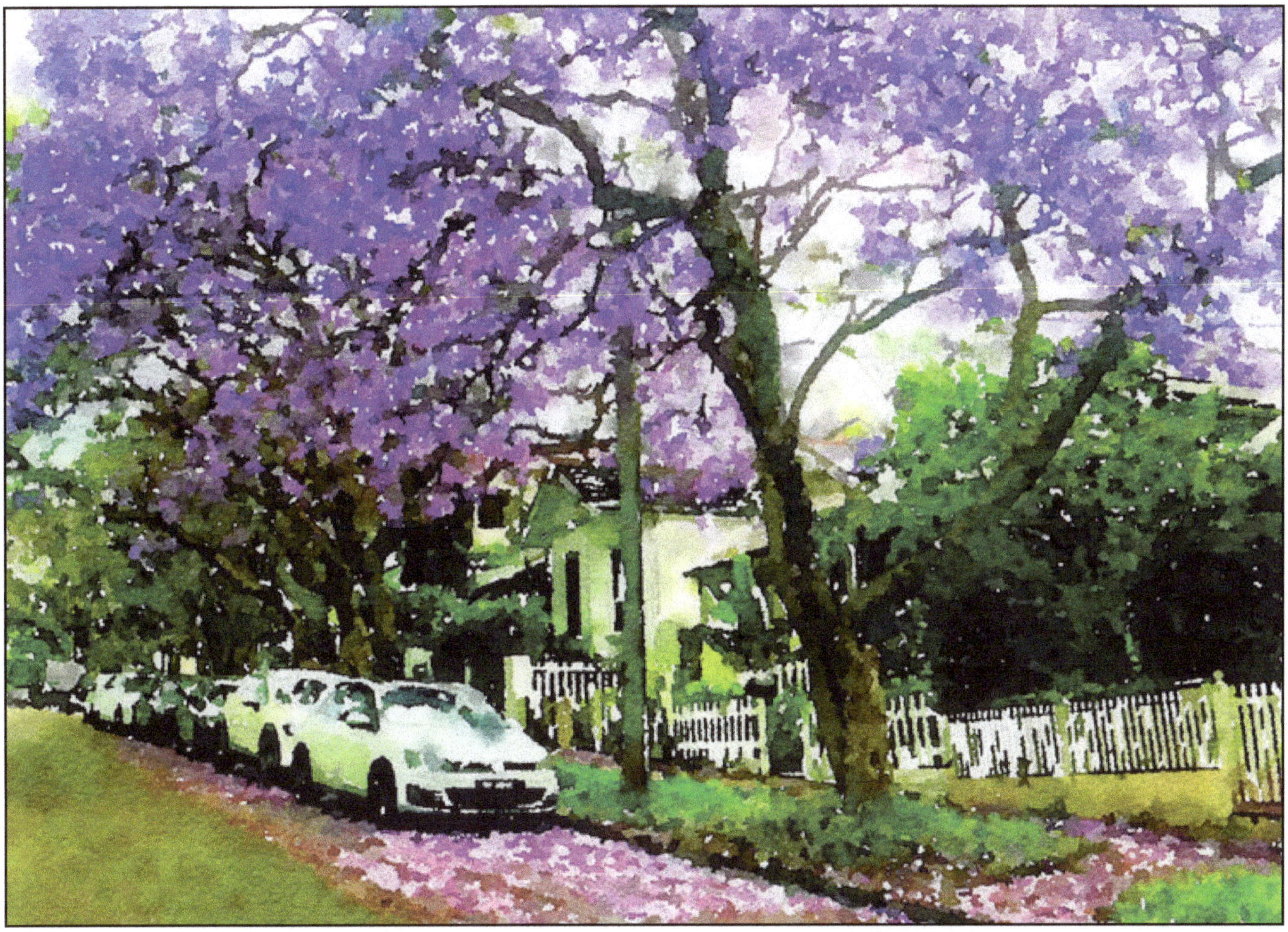

▲'Blooming Jacarandas' (2019),Woollahra, NSW [ALSY1909].

'Paddington Blooms 2' (2019), Paddington, NSW [ALSY1907].▼

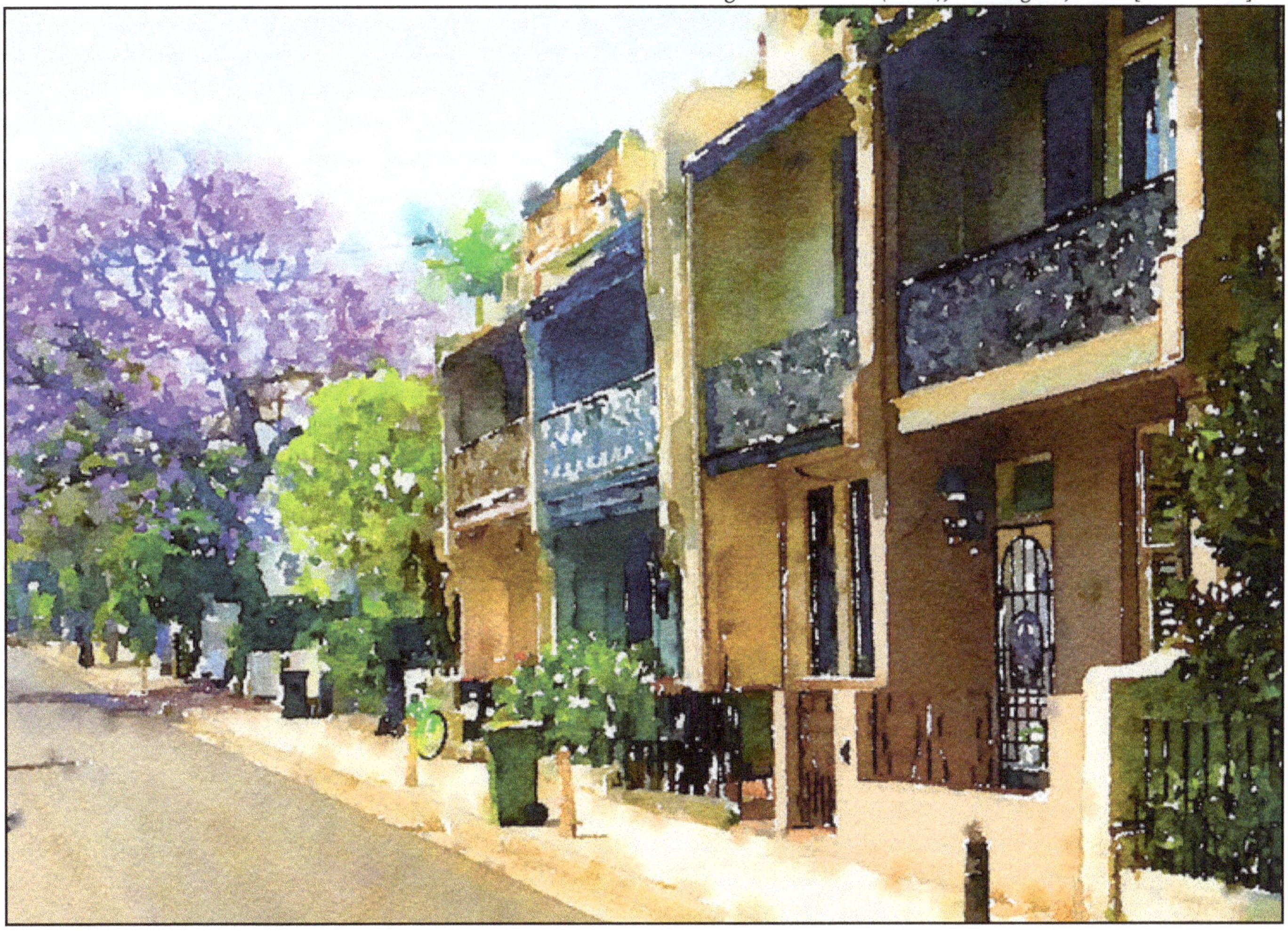

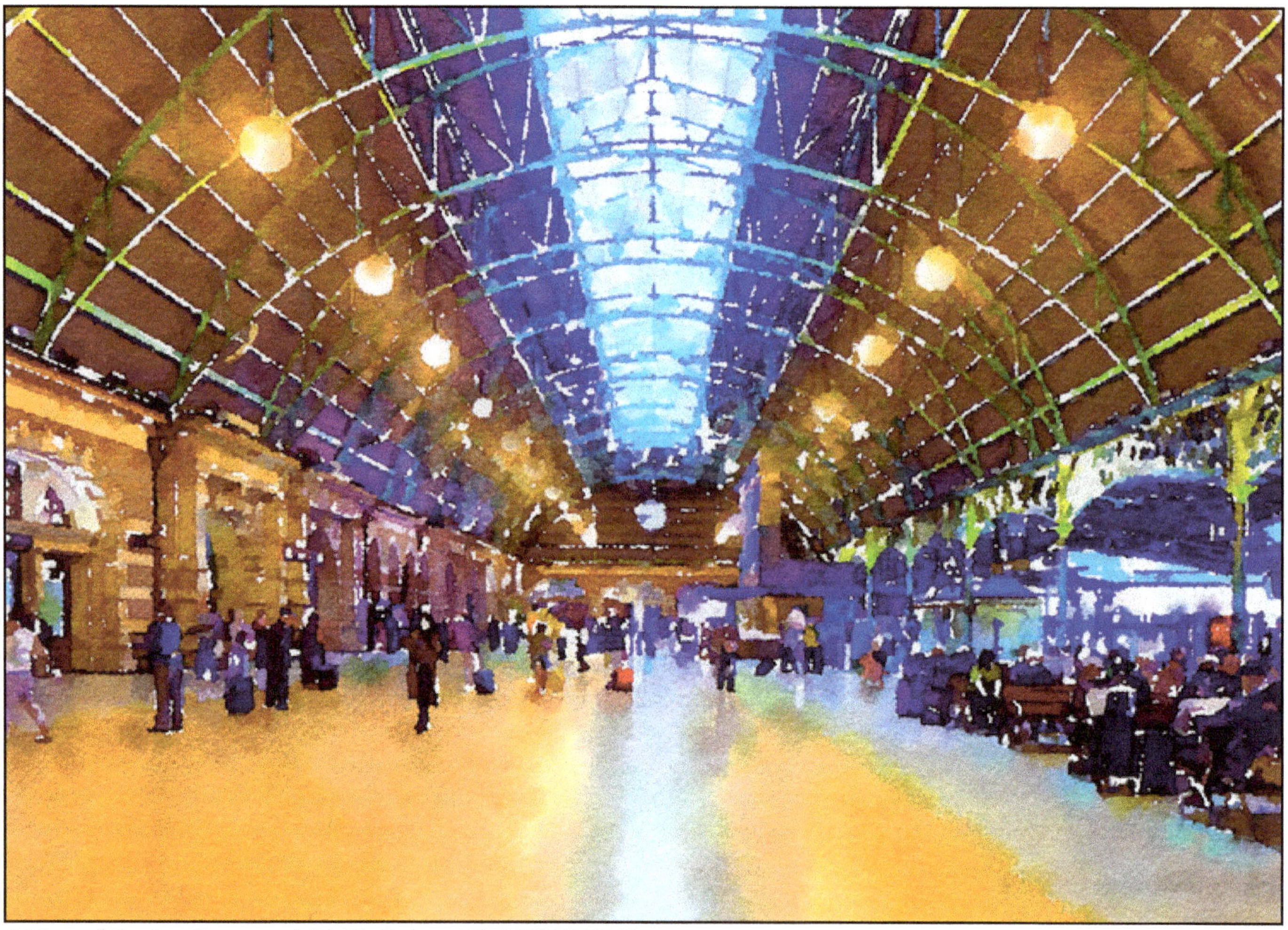

▲'Central Station Concourse' (2019), Sydney, NSW [ALSY1908].

'Opera House 2' (2019), Sydney, NSW [ALSY1916]. ⓔ▼

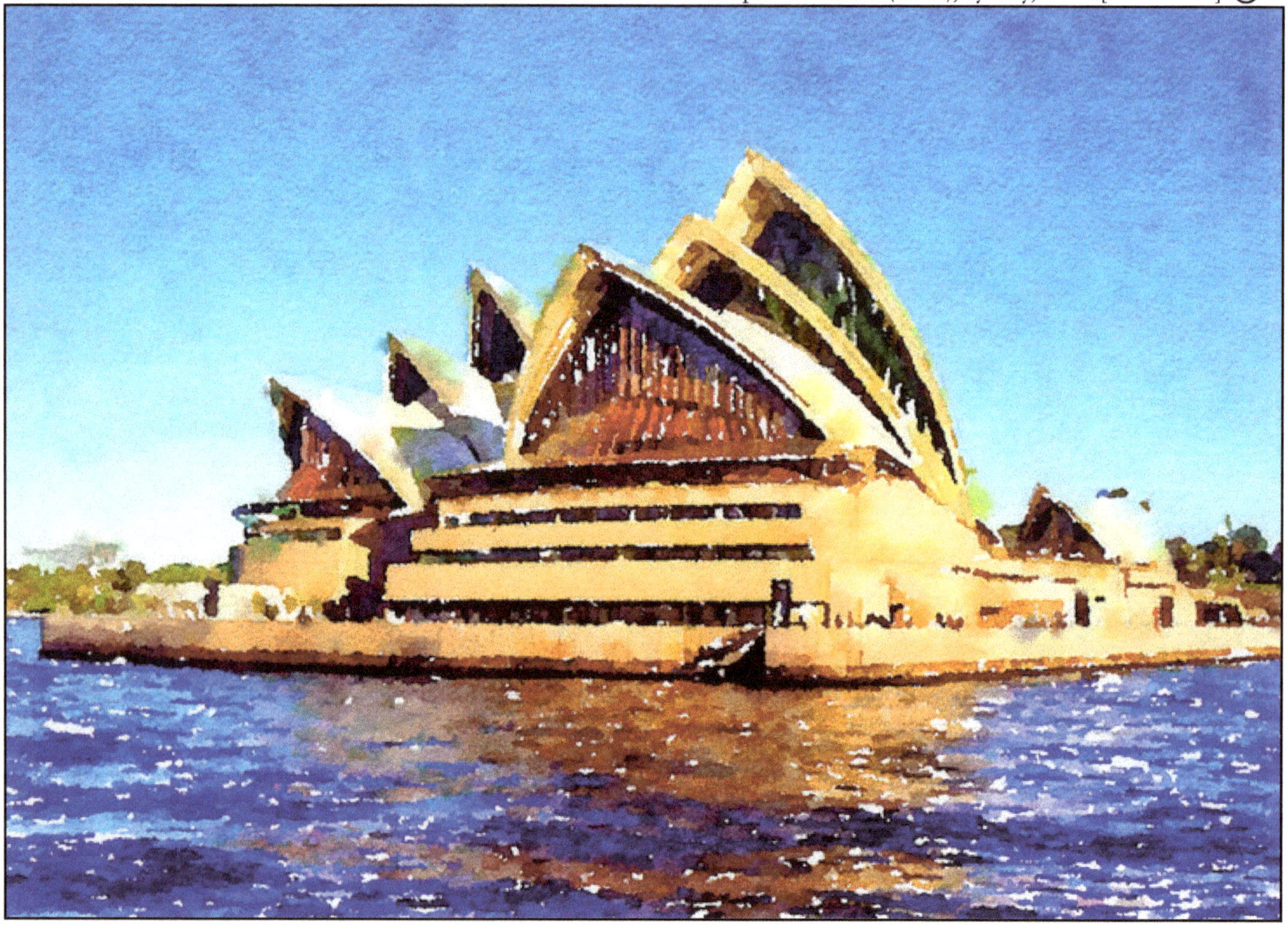

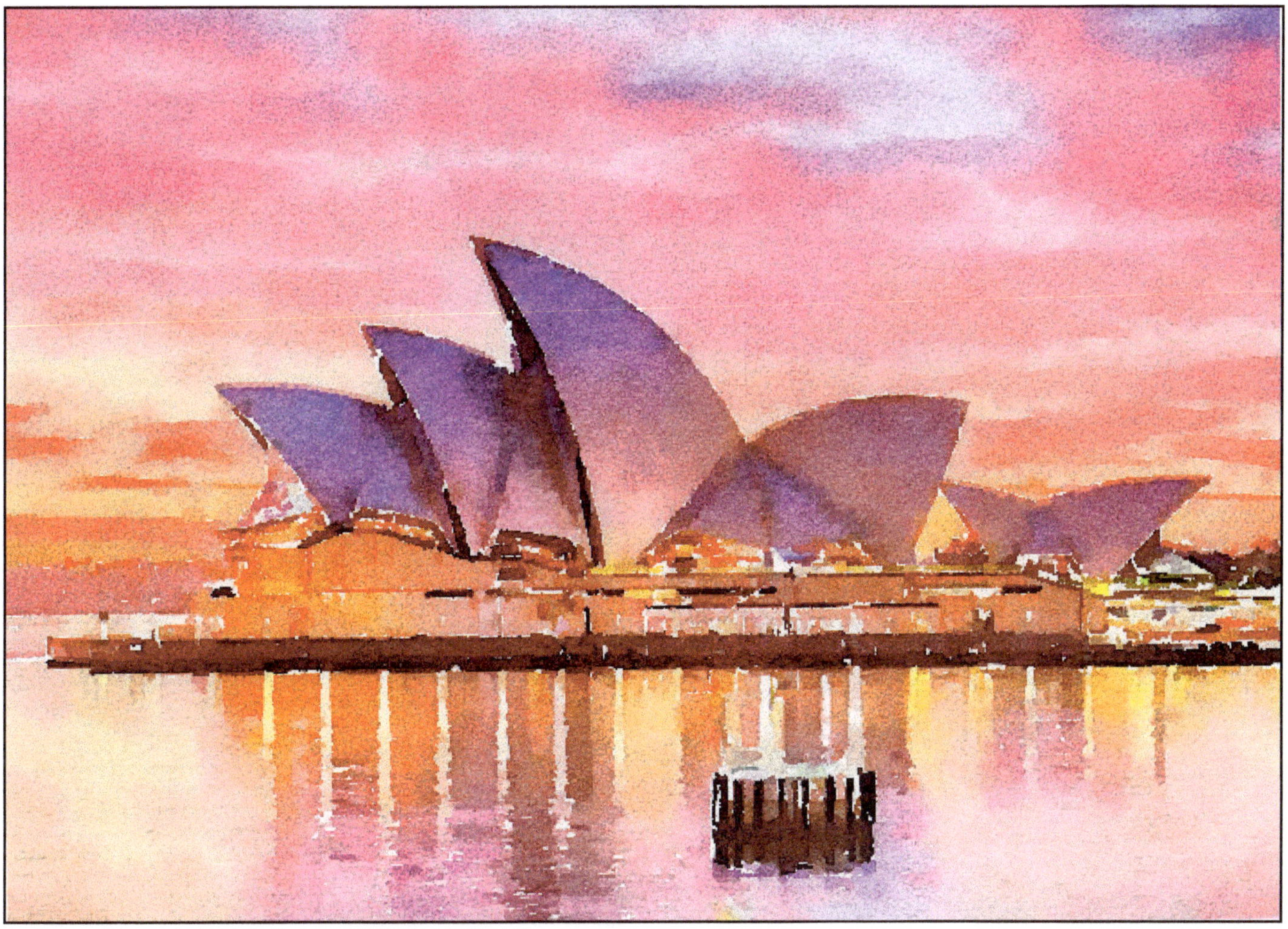

▲'Opera House 1' (2019), Sydney, NSW [ALSY1915].

'War Memorial At Sundown' (2019), Sydney, NSW [ALSY1914].▼

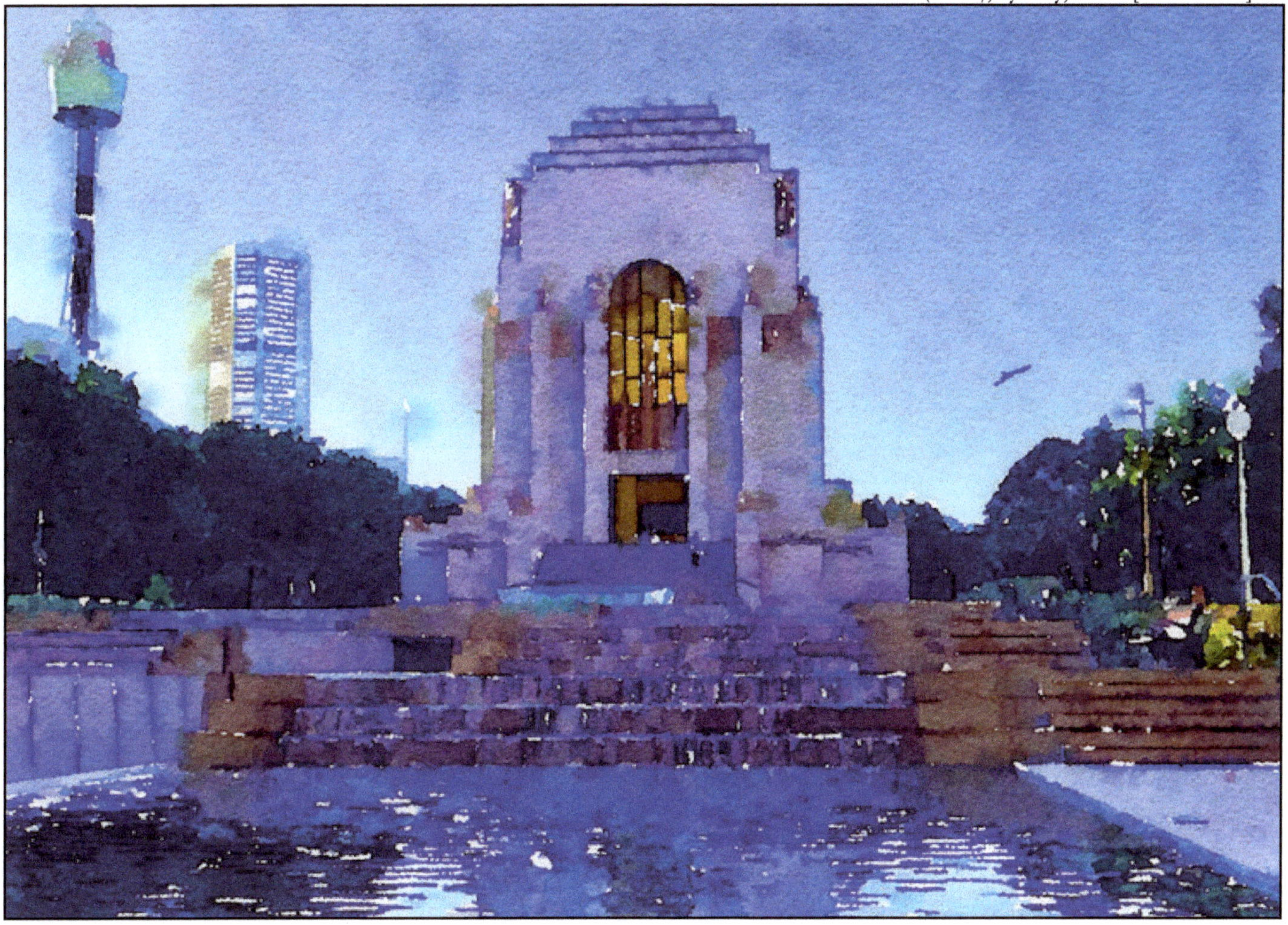

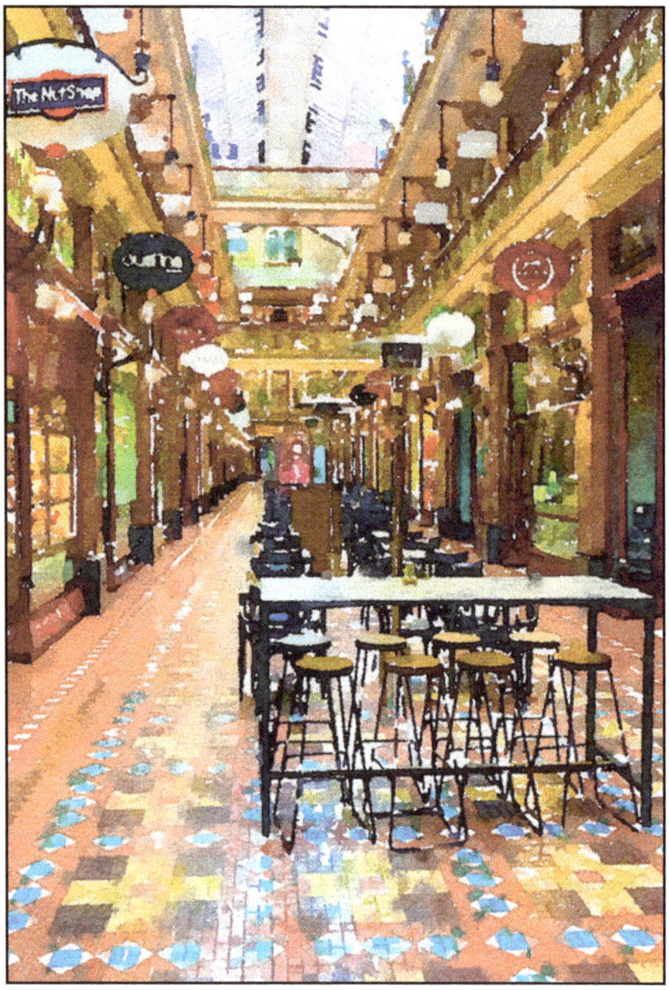

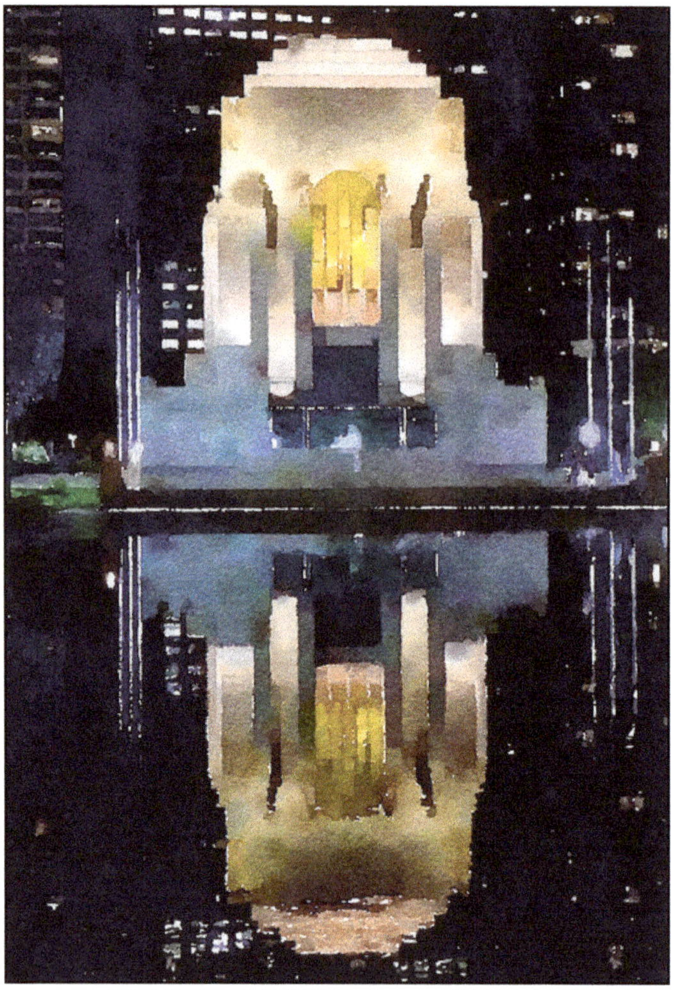

▲'Strand Arcade' (2017), Sydney, NSW [ALSY1703].

'War Memorial' (2019), Sydney, NSW [ALSY1912].▲

'Harbour Celebrations' (2019), Sydney, NSW [ALSY1911]. ⊘▼

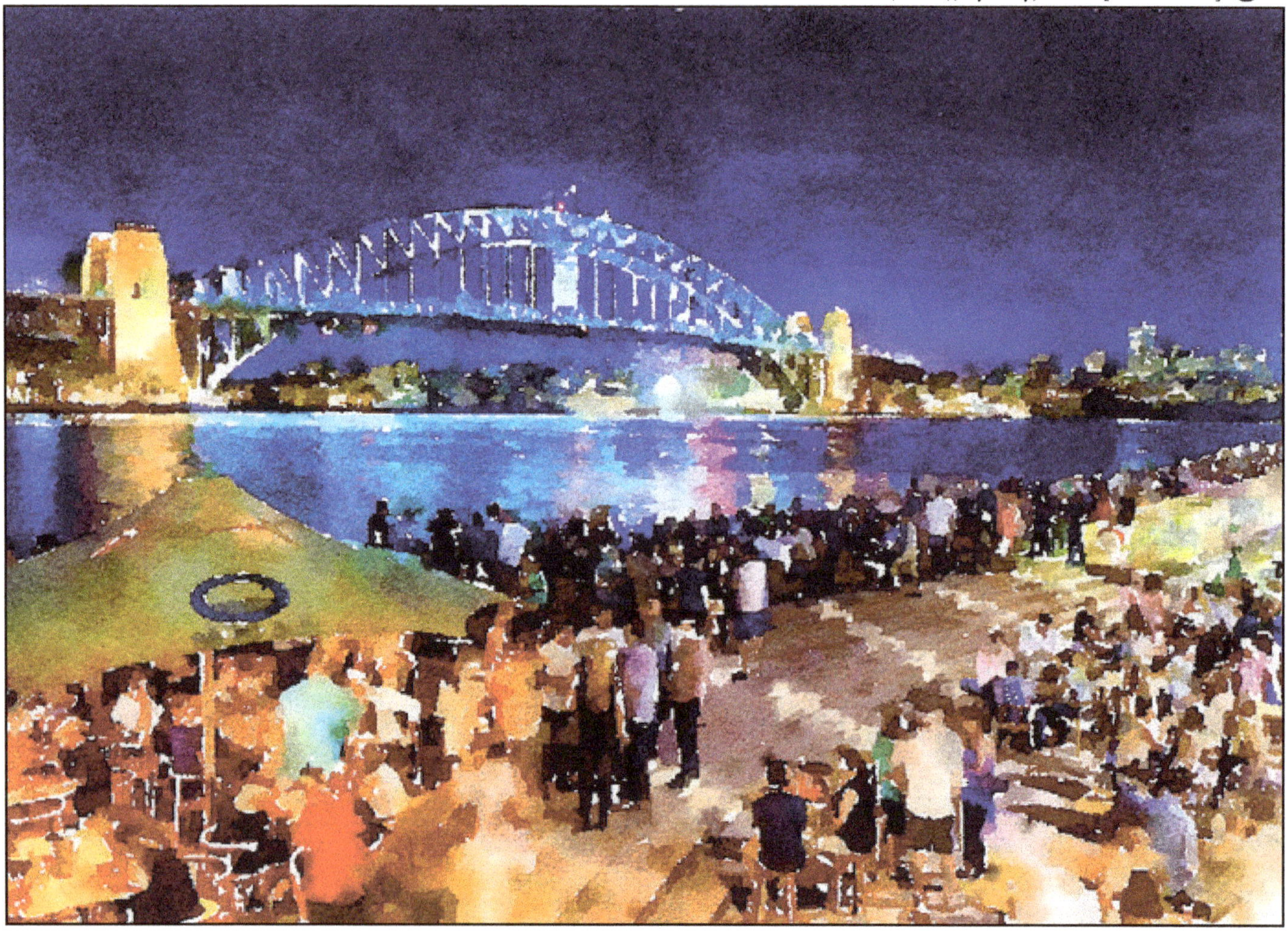

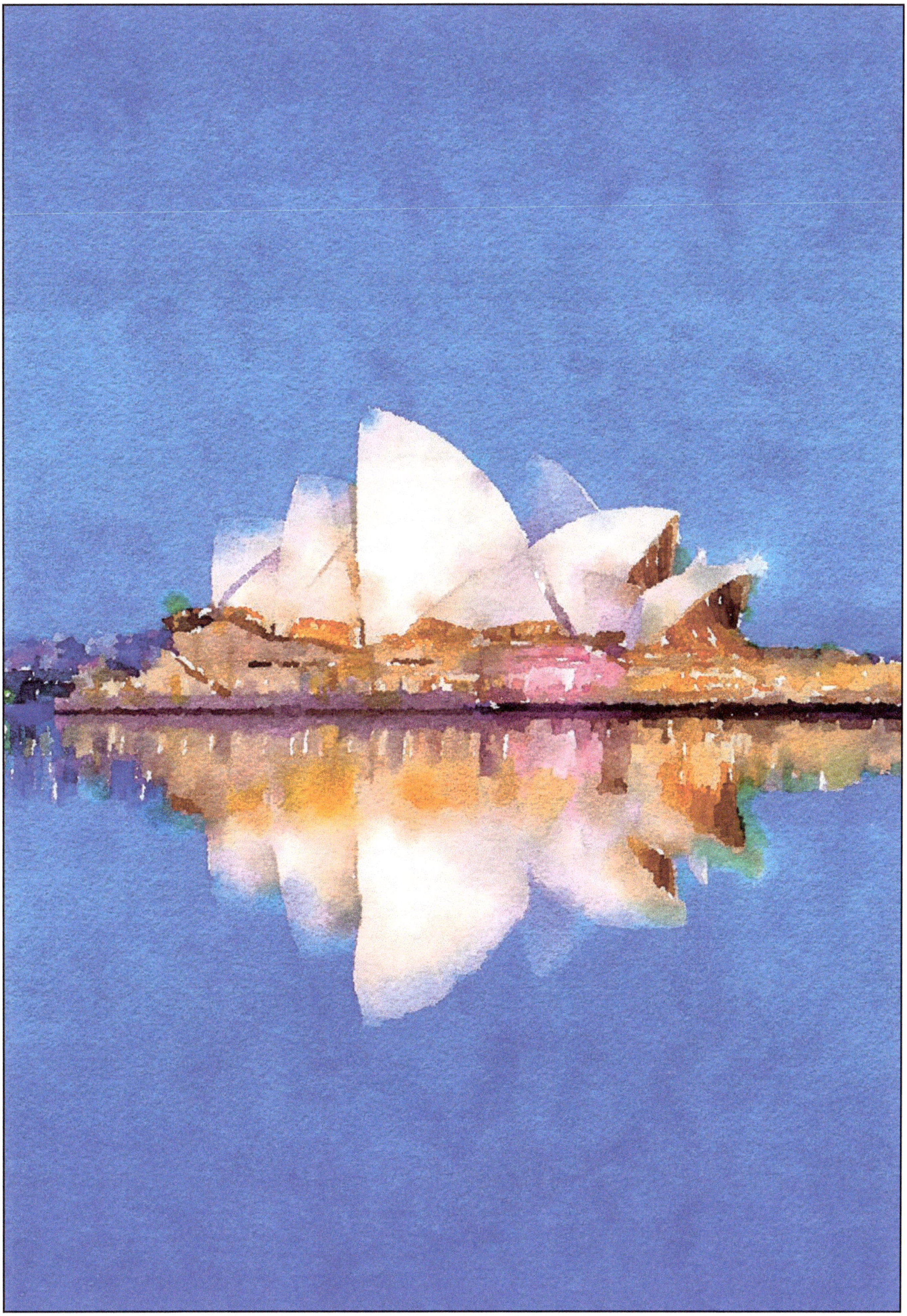

▲'Opera House' (2019), Sydney, NSW [ALSY1917]. ©

Rural Seascapes...

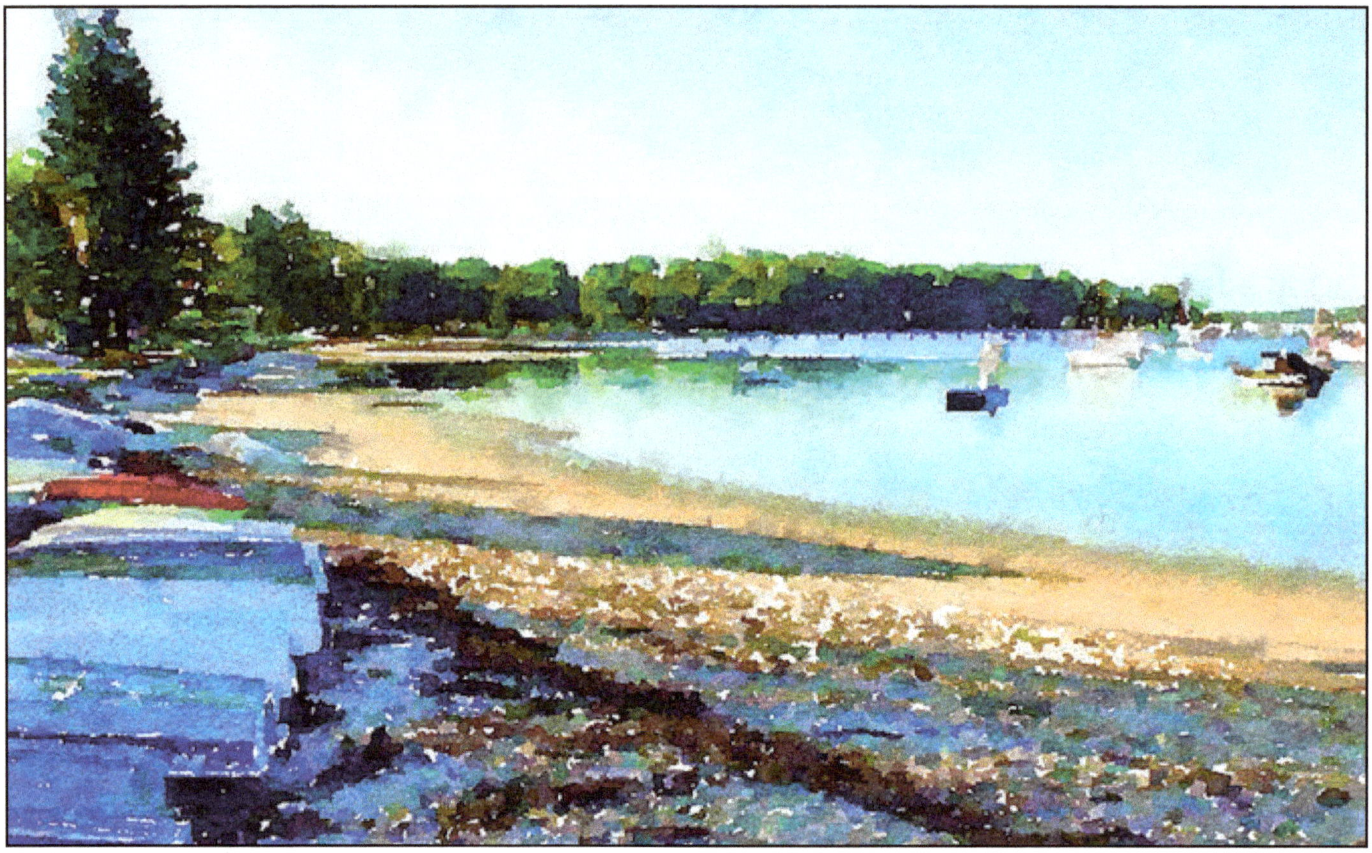

▲'The Beach At Shoal Bay' (2008), Port Stephens, NSW [ASNS0802].

'The Moorings' (2008), Corlette, NSW [ASNS0801].▼

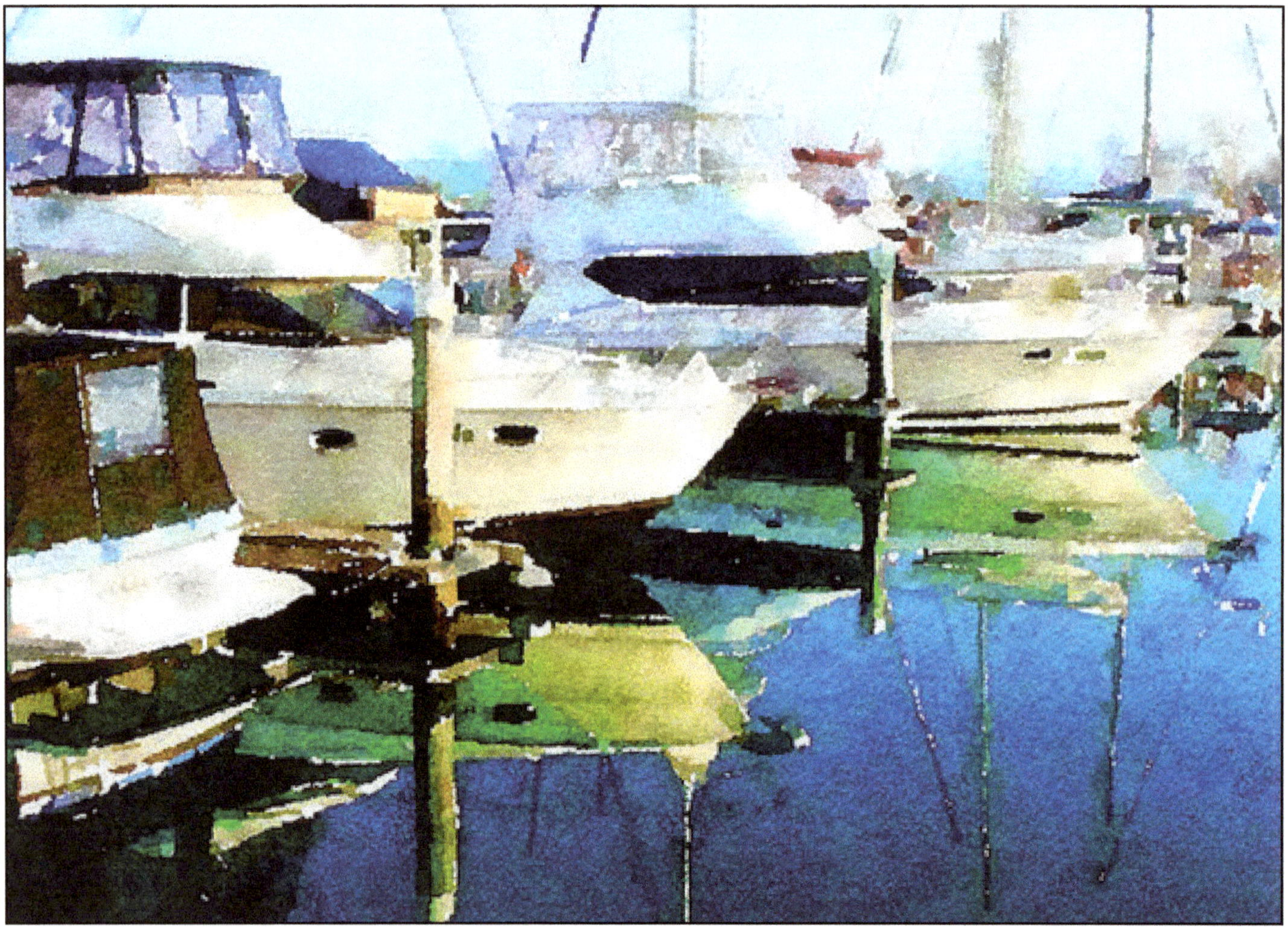

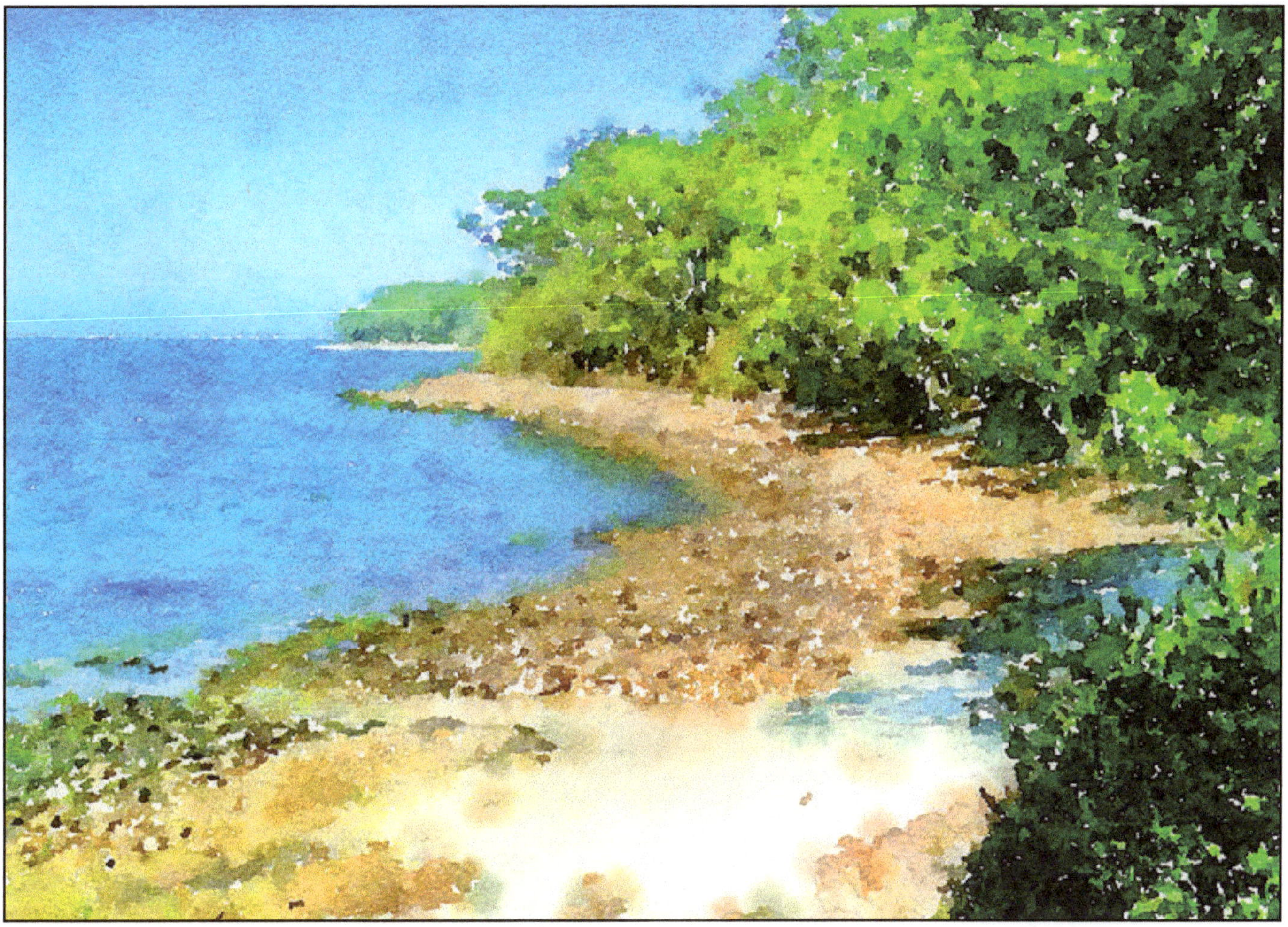

▲'The Rocky Shoreline' (2008), Corlette, NSW [ASNS0803].

'Sunset At Soldiers Point' (2010), Port Stephens, NSW [ASNS1001].▼

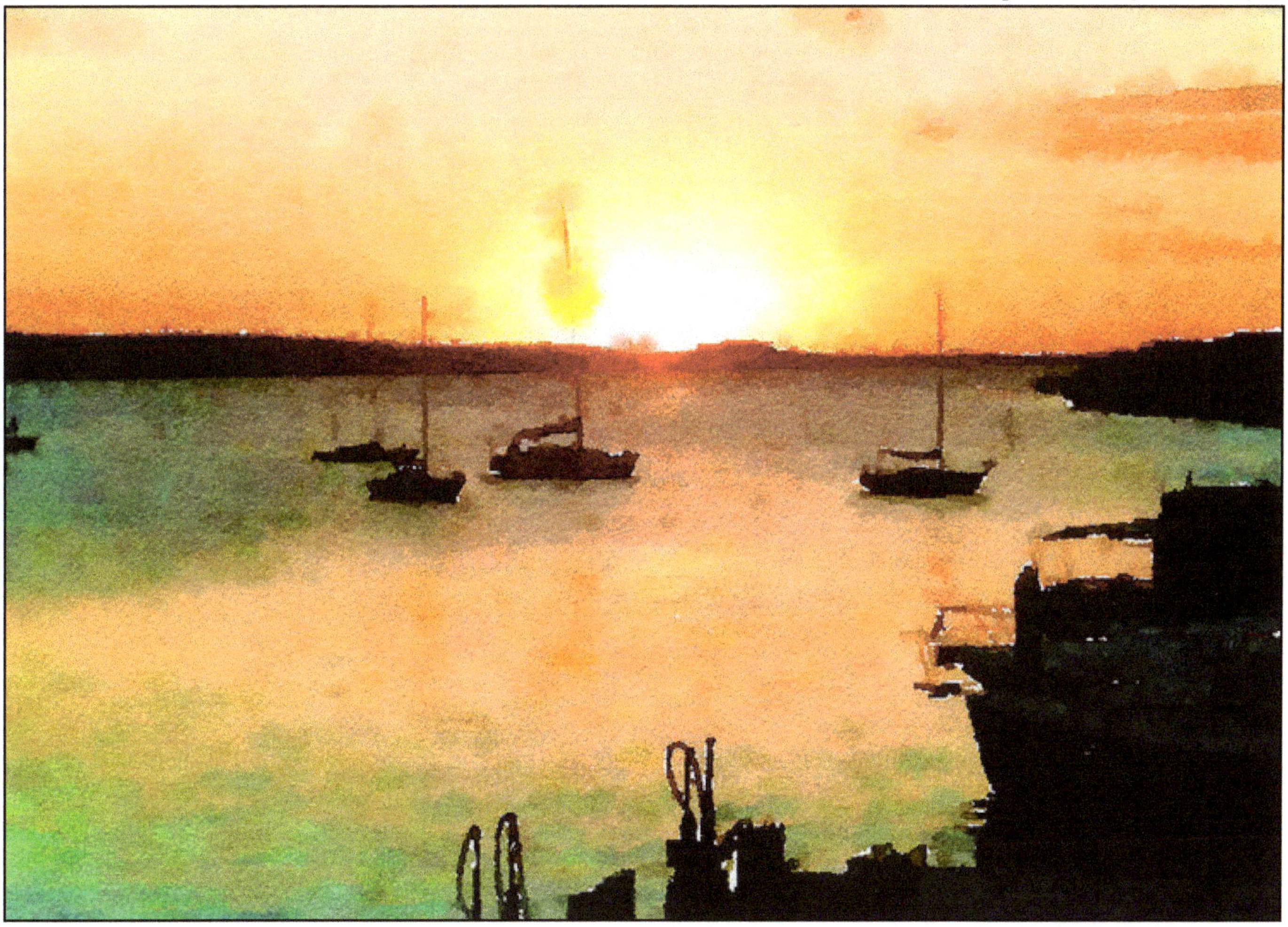

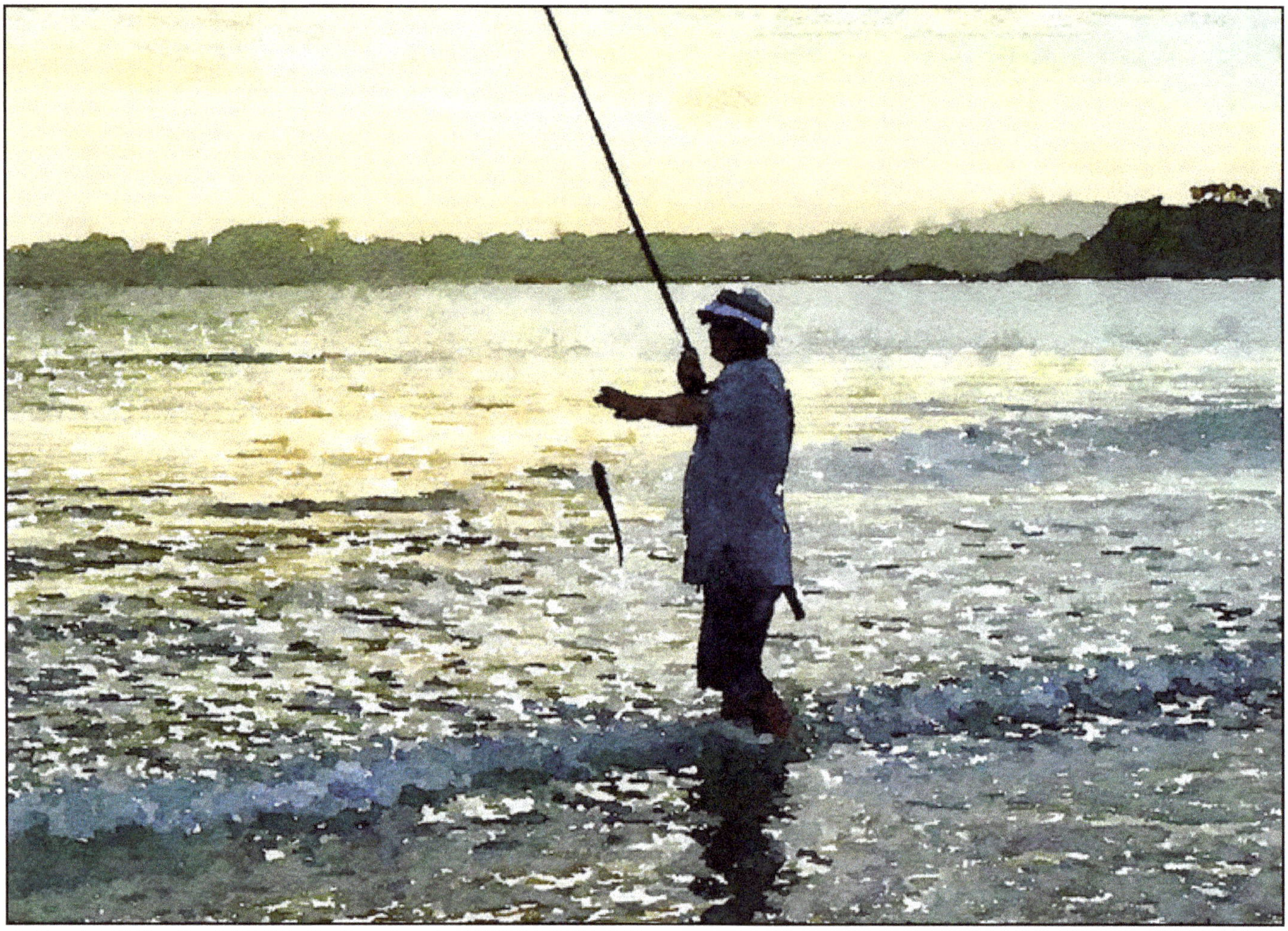

▲'Catch Of The Day' (2018), Barlings Beach, NSW [ASNS1801].

'The Three Fisherman' (2018), Barlings Beach, NSW [ASNS1802].▼

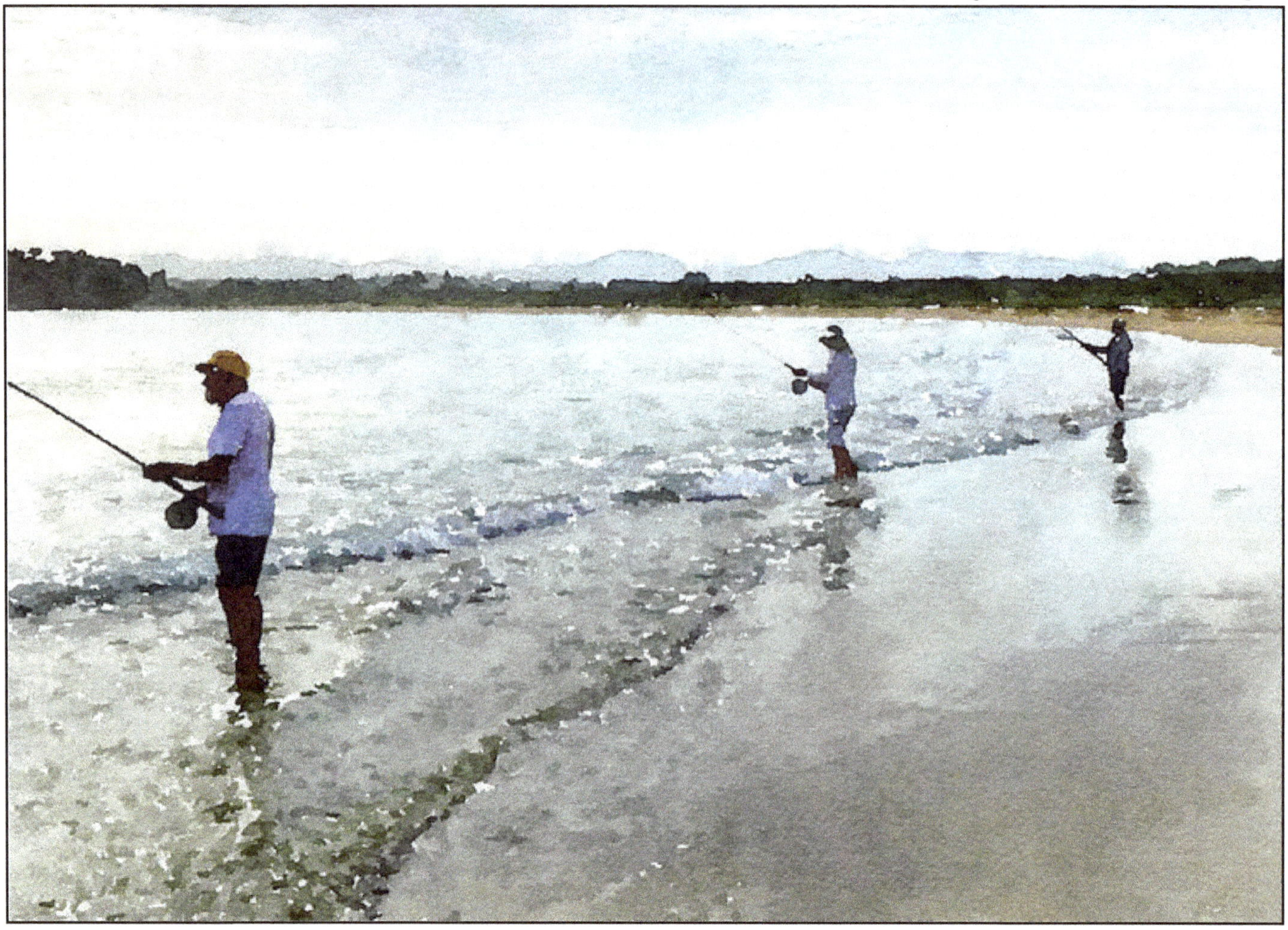

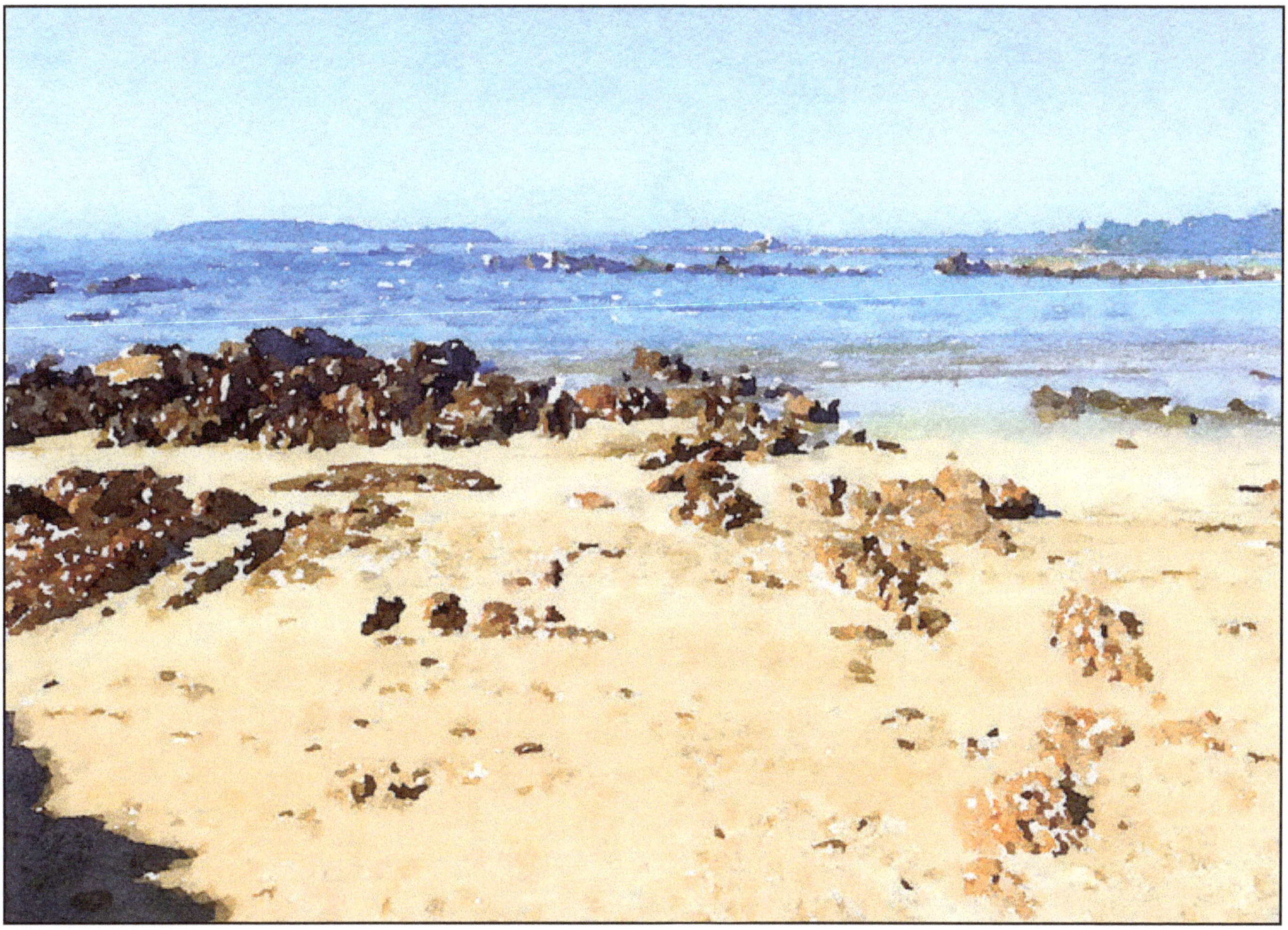

▲'Tomakin Rocks' (2018), Tomakin Beach, NSW [ASNS1803].

'Misty Clarence Morning' (2021), Grafton, NSW [ASNS2101].▼

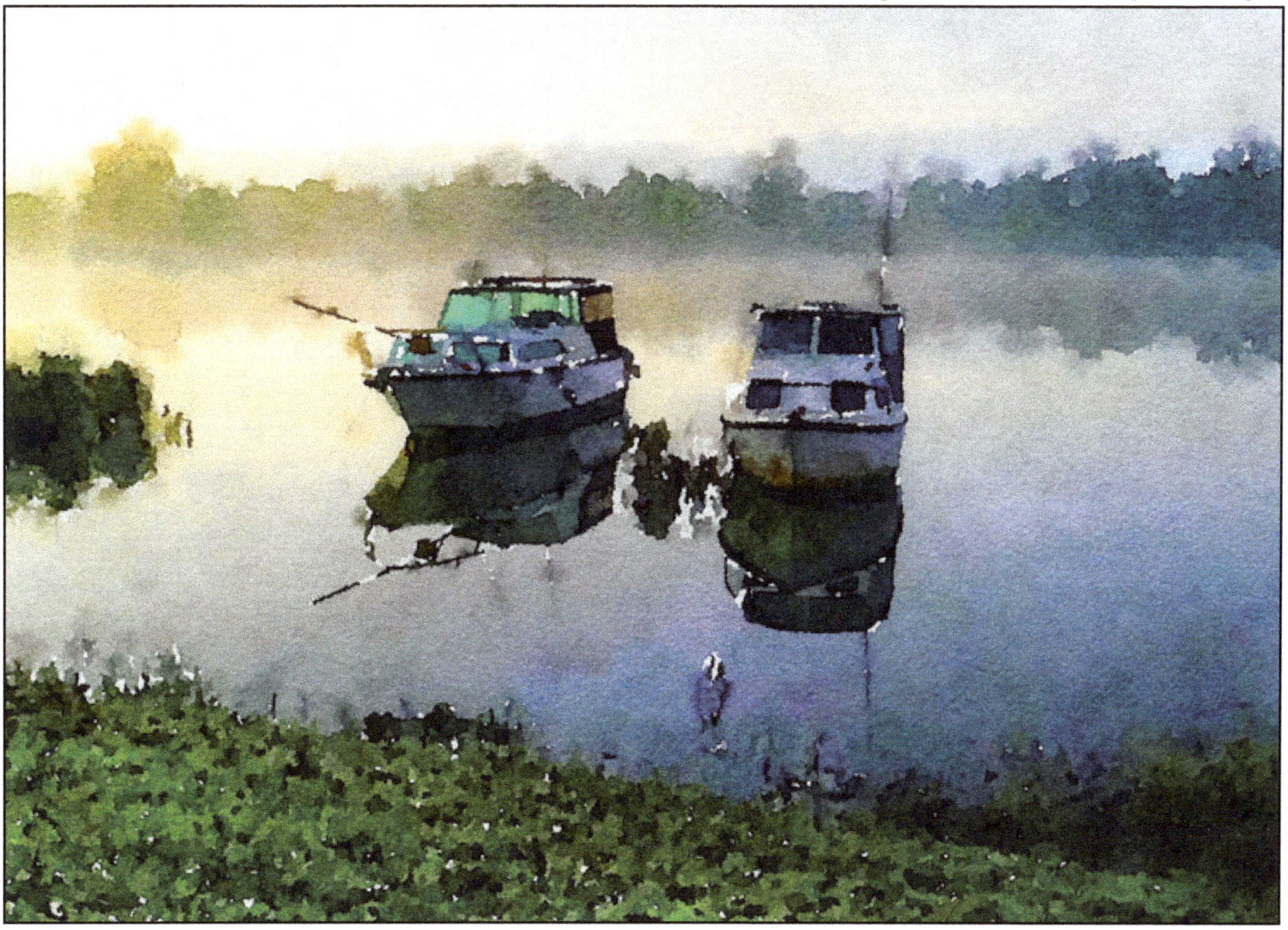

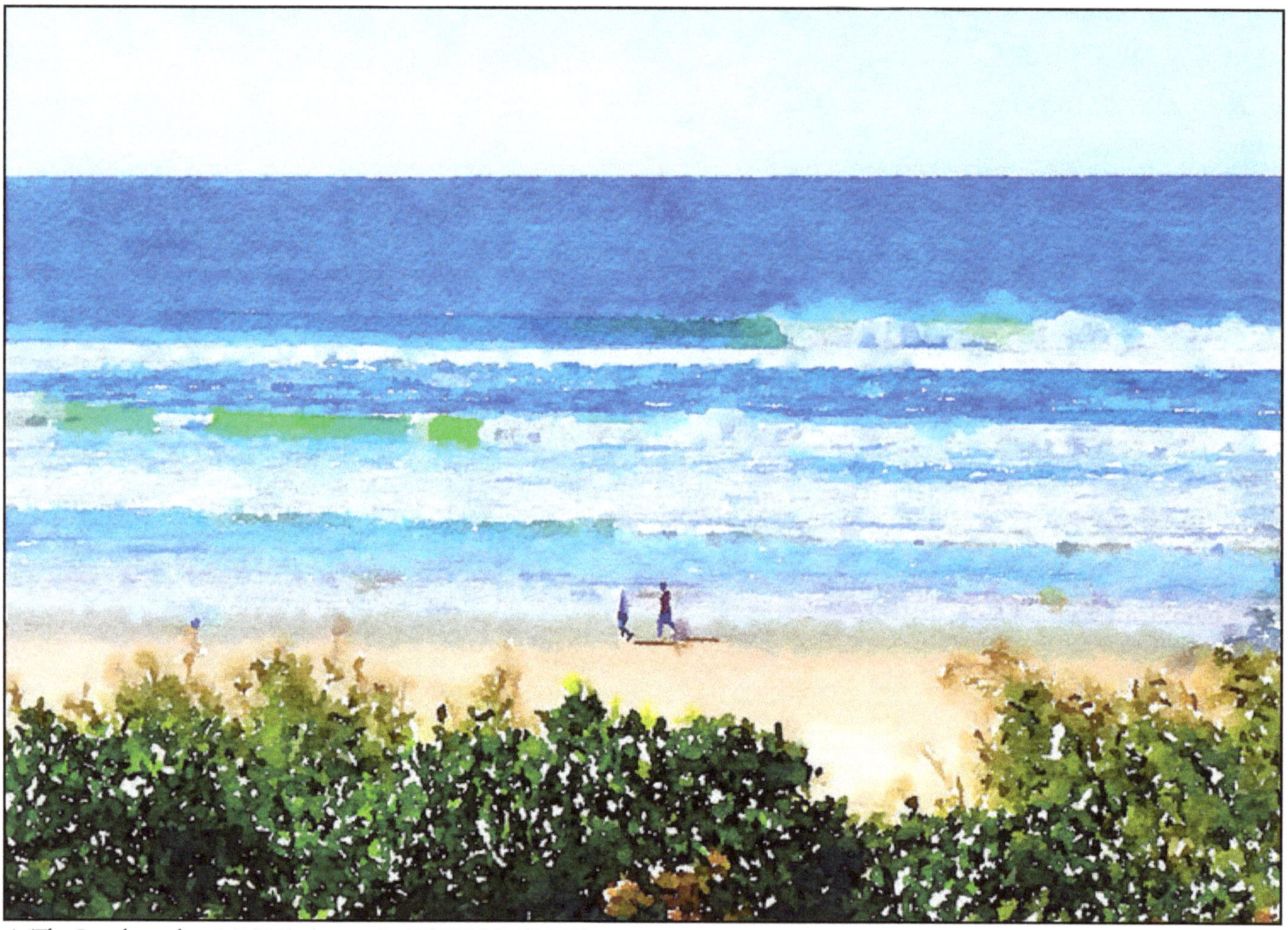

▲'The Beachcombers' (2021), Angourie, NSW [ASNS2102].

'The Creek' (2021), Moonie Beach, NSW [ASNS2103].▼

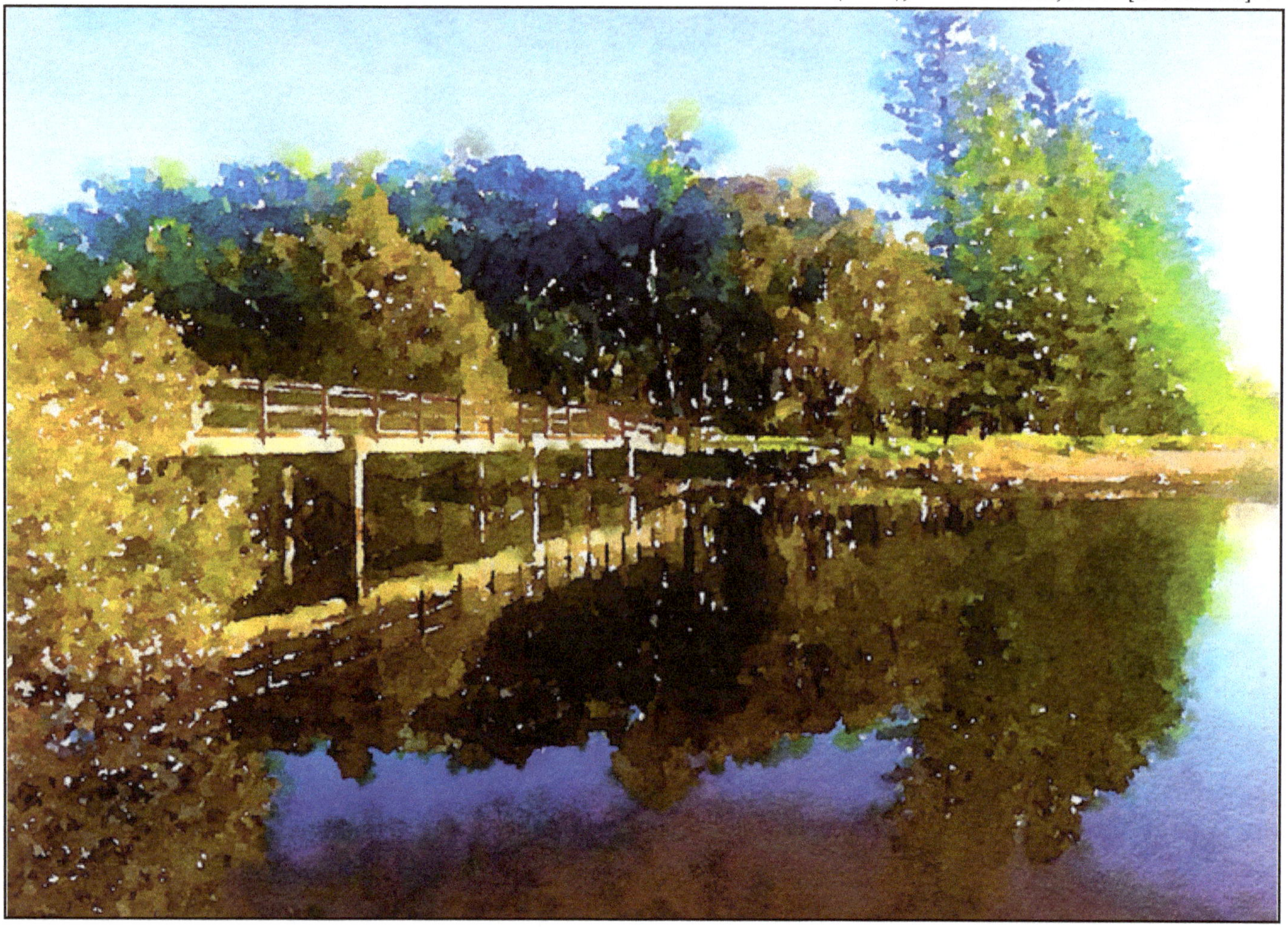

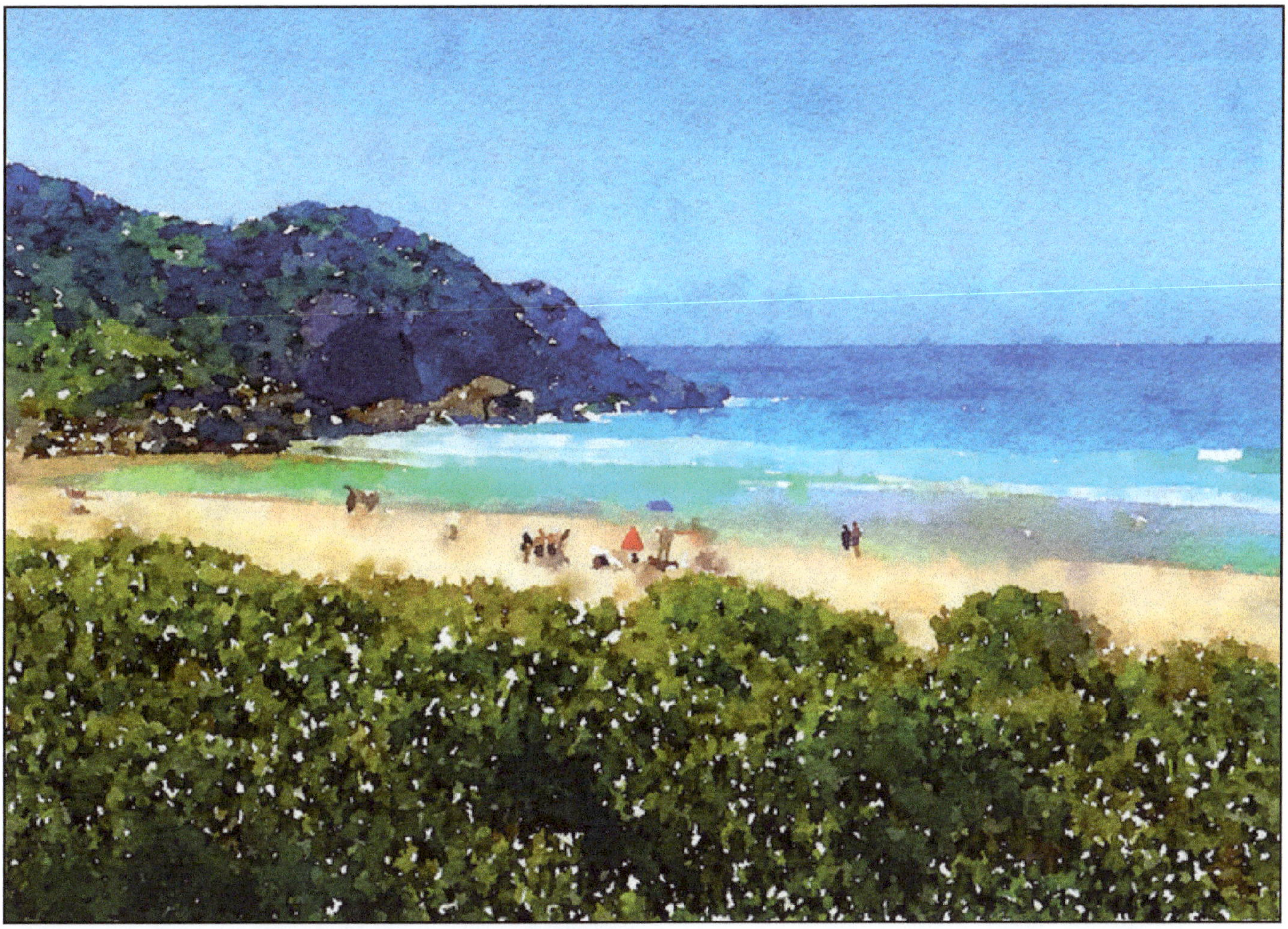

▲'Boomerang Beach' (2021), Pacific Palms, NSW [ASNS2105].

'The Quay Lights' (2021), Forster, NSW [ASNS2104].▼

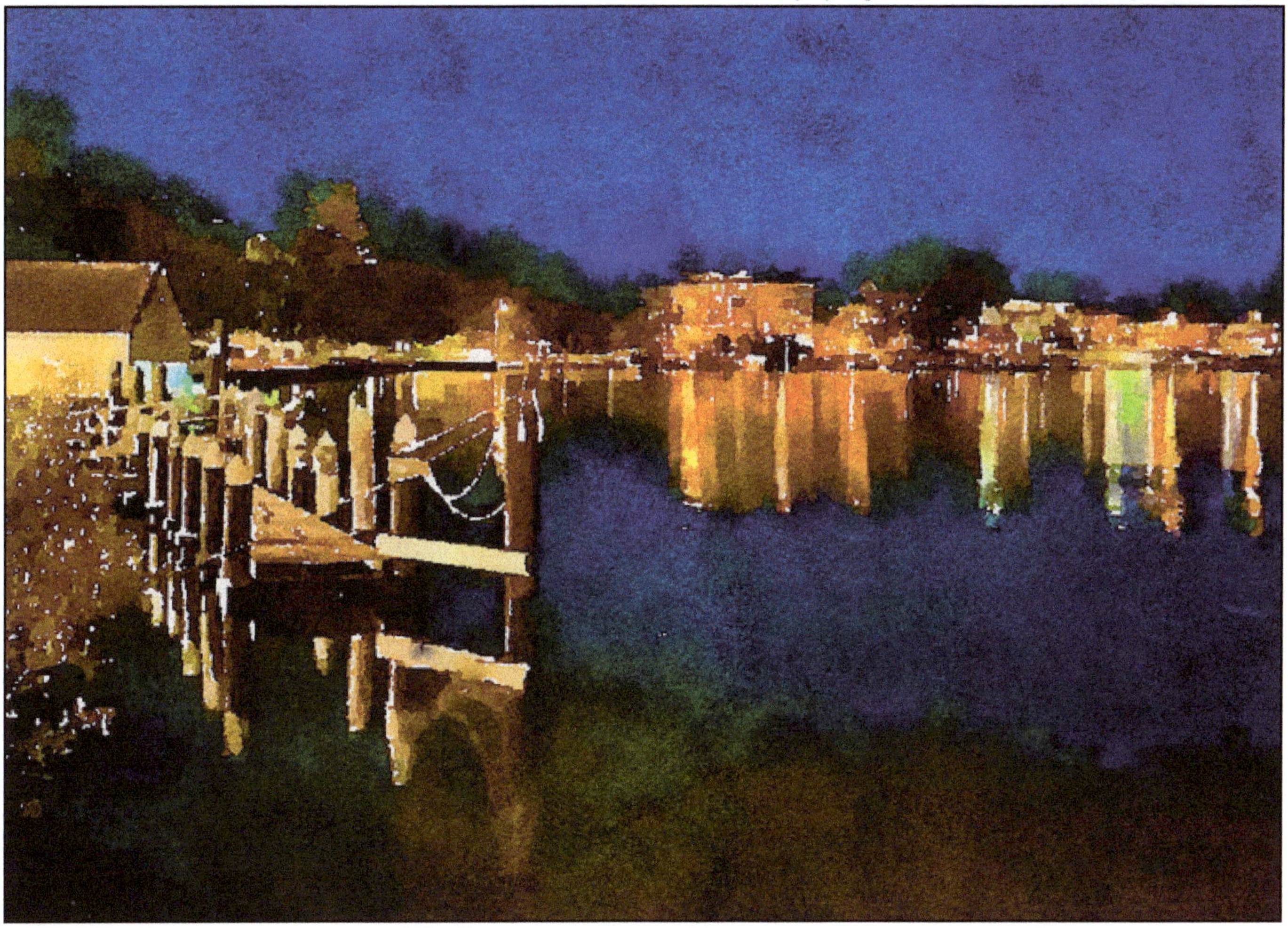

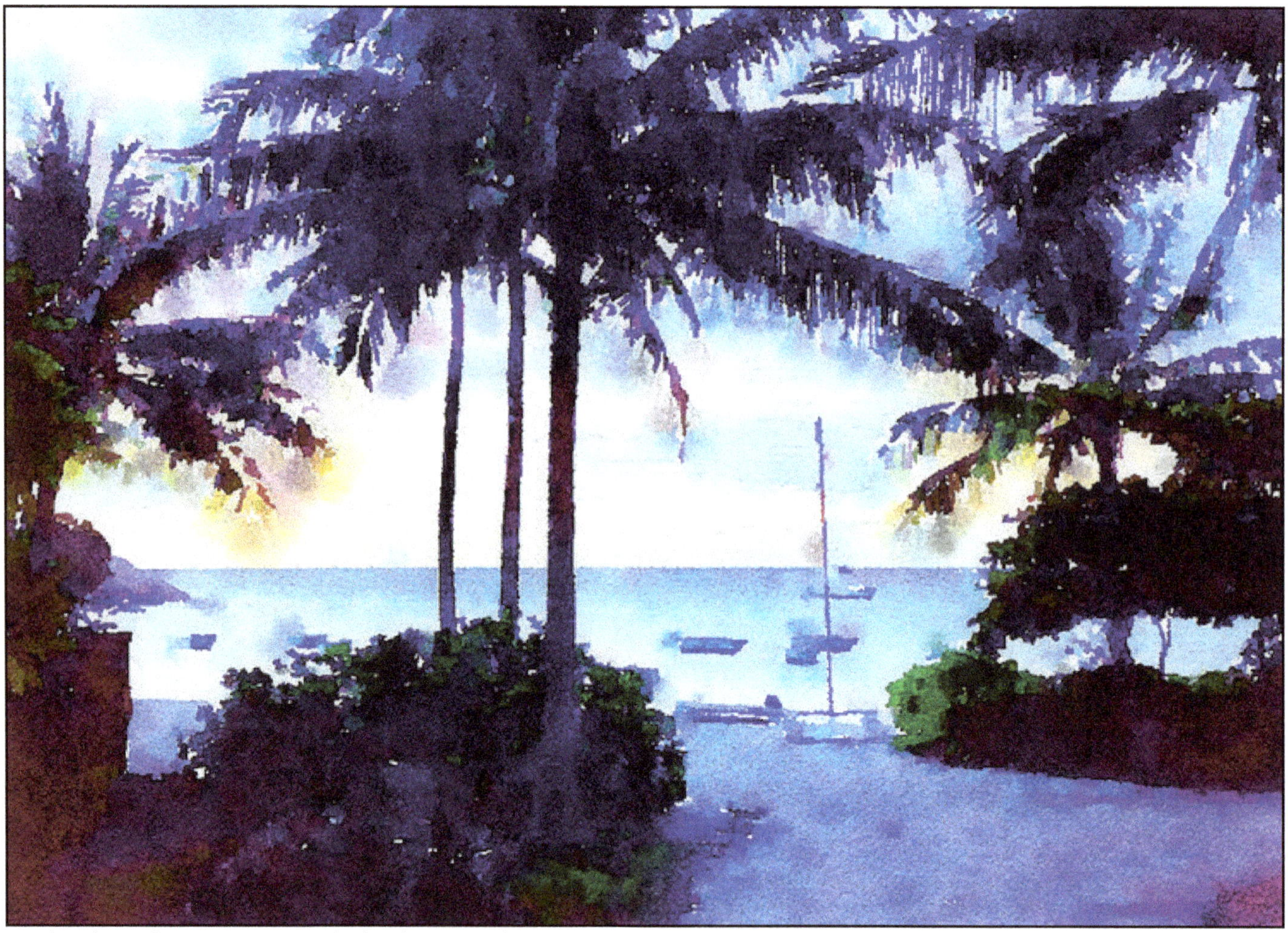

▲'The Blue Palms' (2009), Lizard Island, Far North QLD [ASQL0901].

'Kewarra Beach & Double Island' (2011), Cairns, Far North QLD [ASQL1101].▼

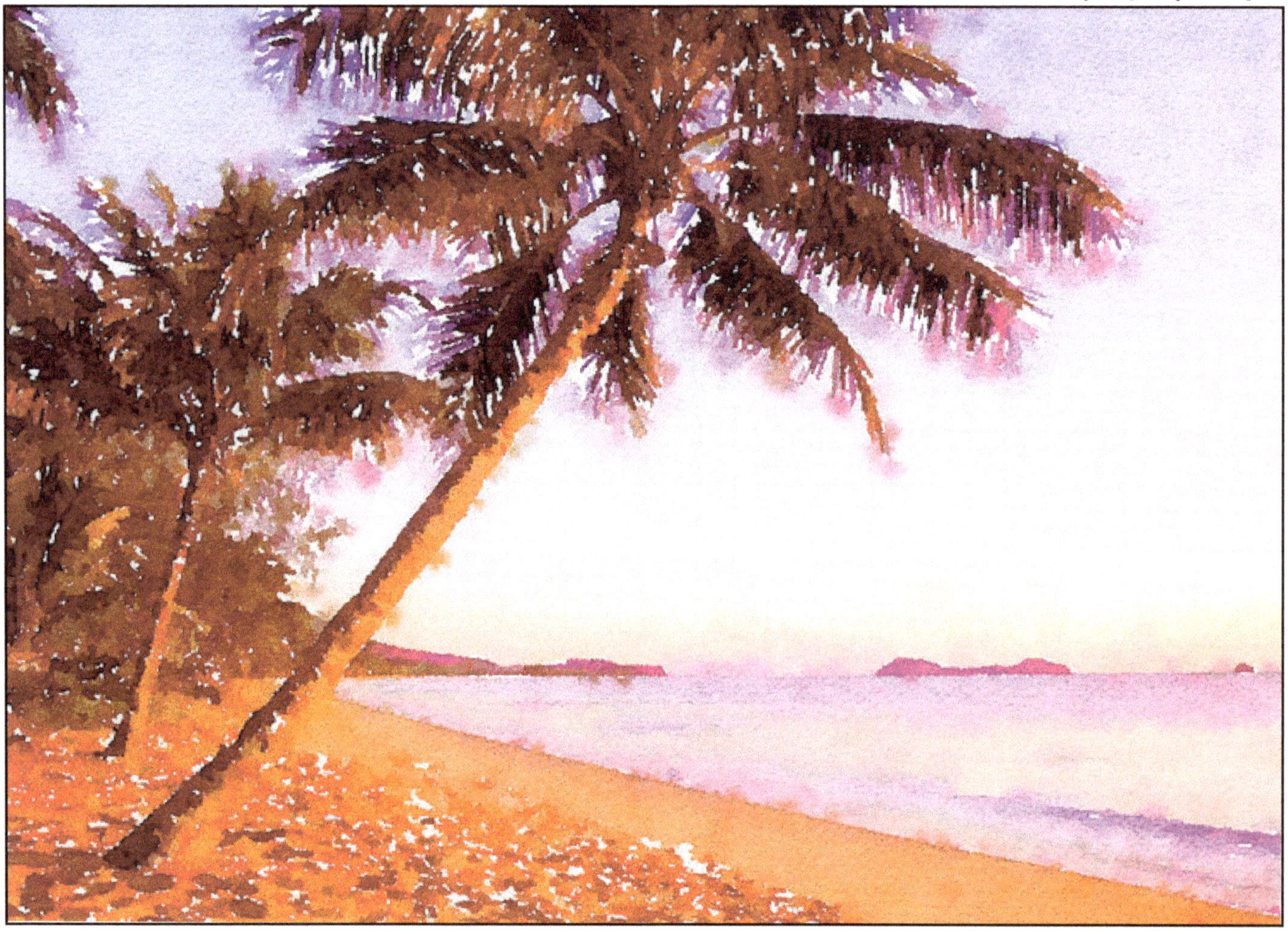

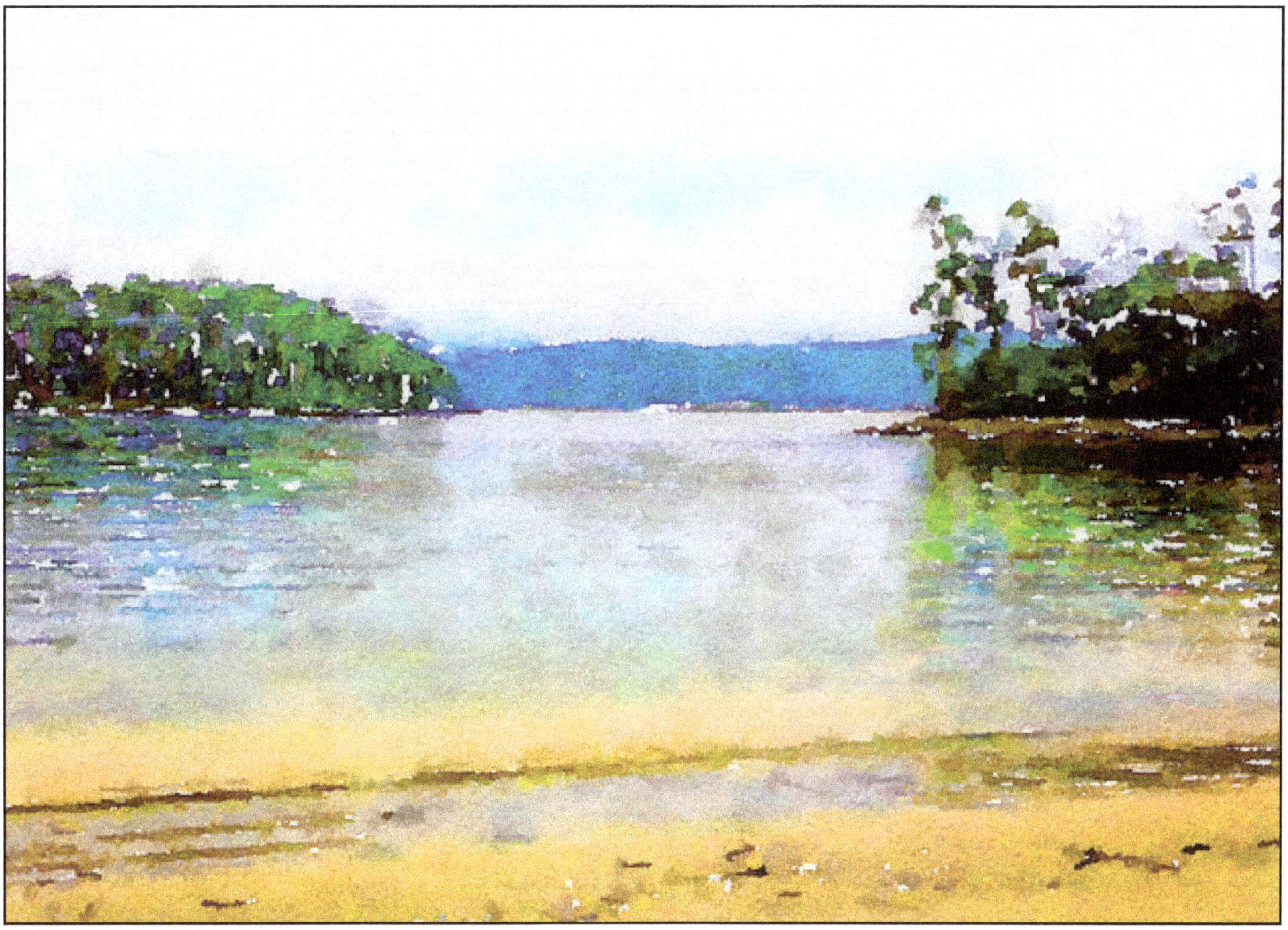

▲'Stewarts Bay' (2007), Port Arthur, TAS [ASTA0701].

'The Granite Monolith' (2009), Freycinet, TAS [ASTA0901].▼

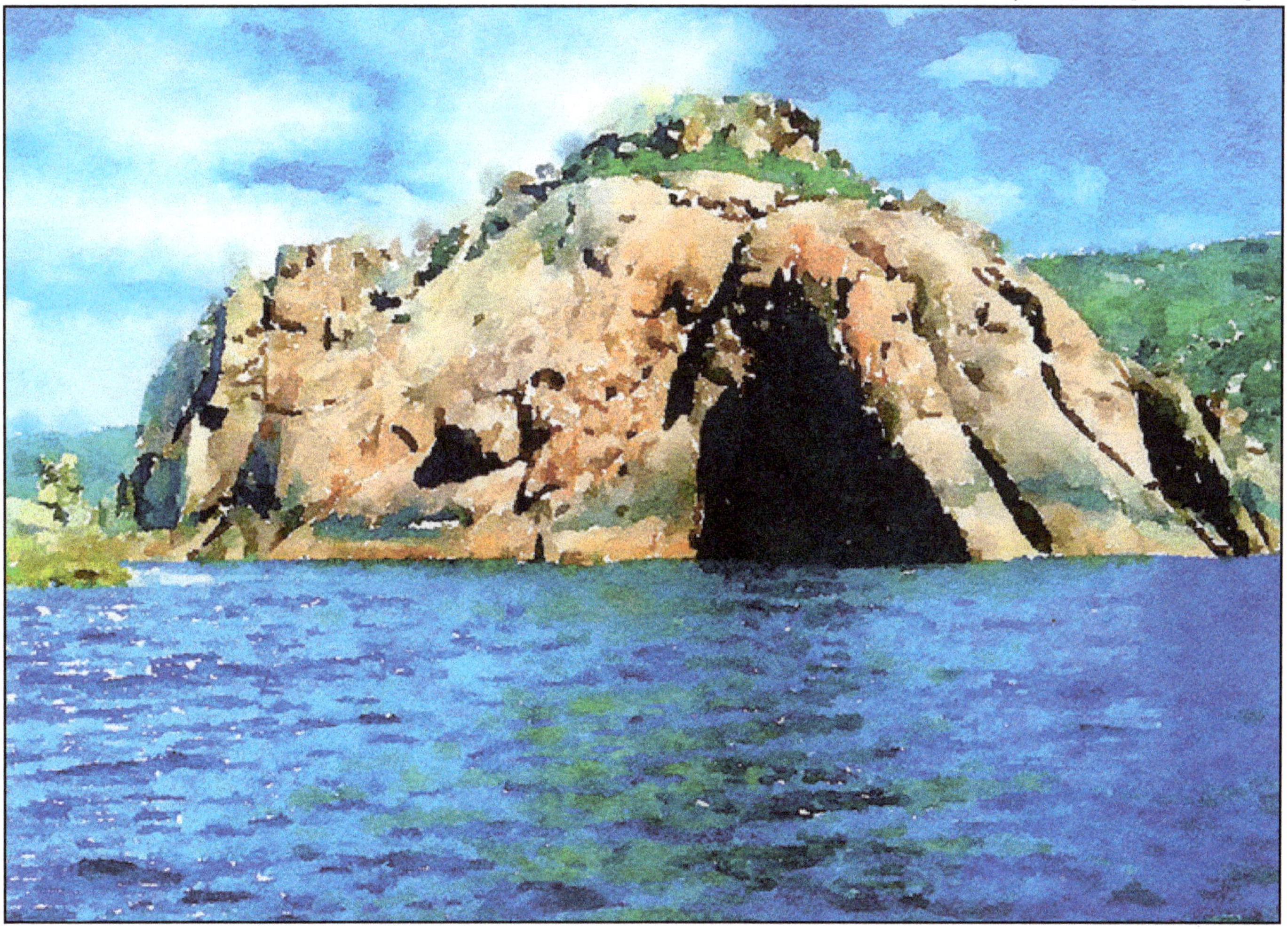

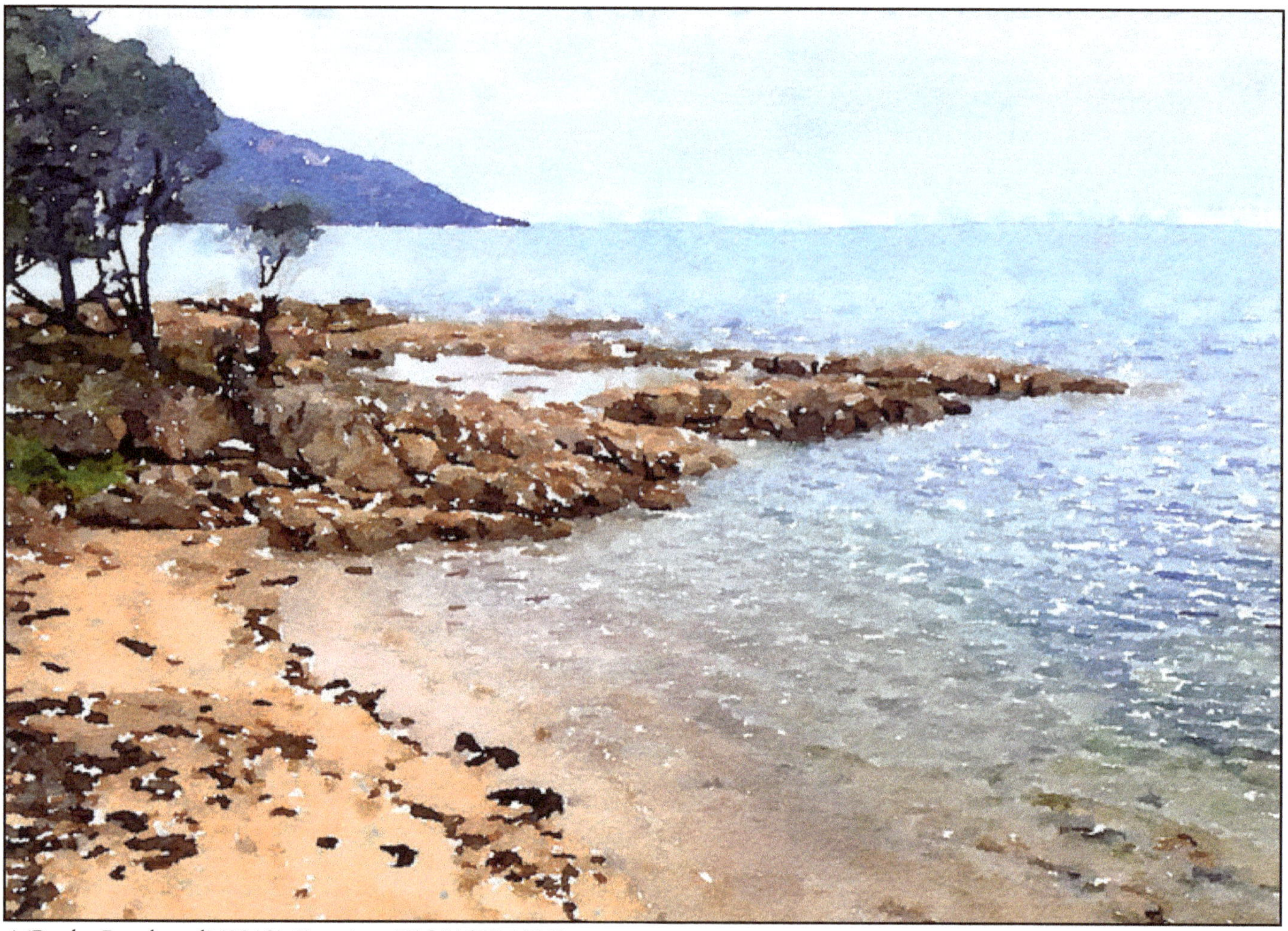

▲'Rocky Roadstead' (2019), Freycinet, TAS [ASTA1902].

'Bicheno Boulders' (2019), Bicheno, TAS [ASTA1903].▼

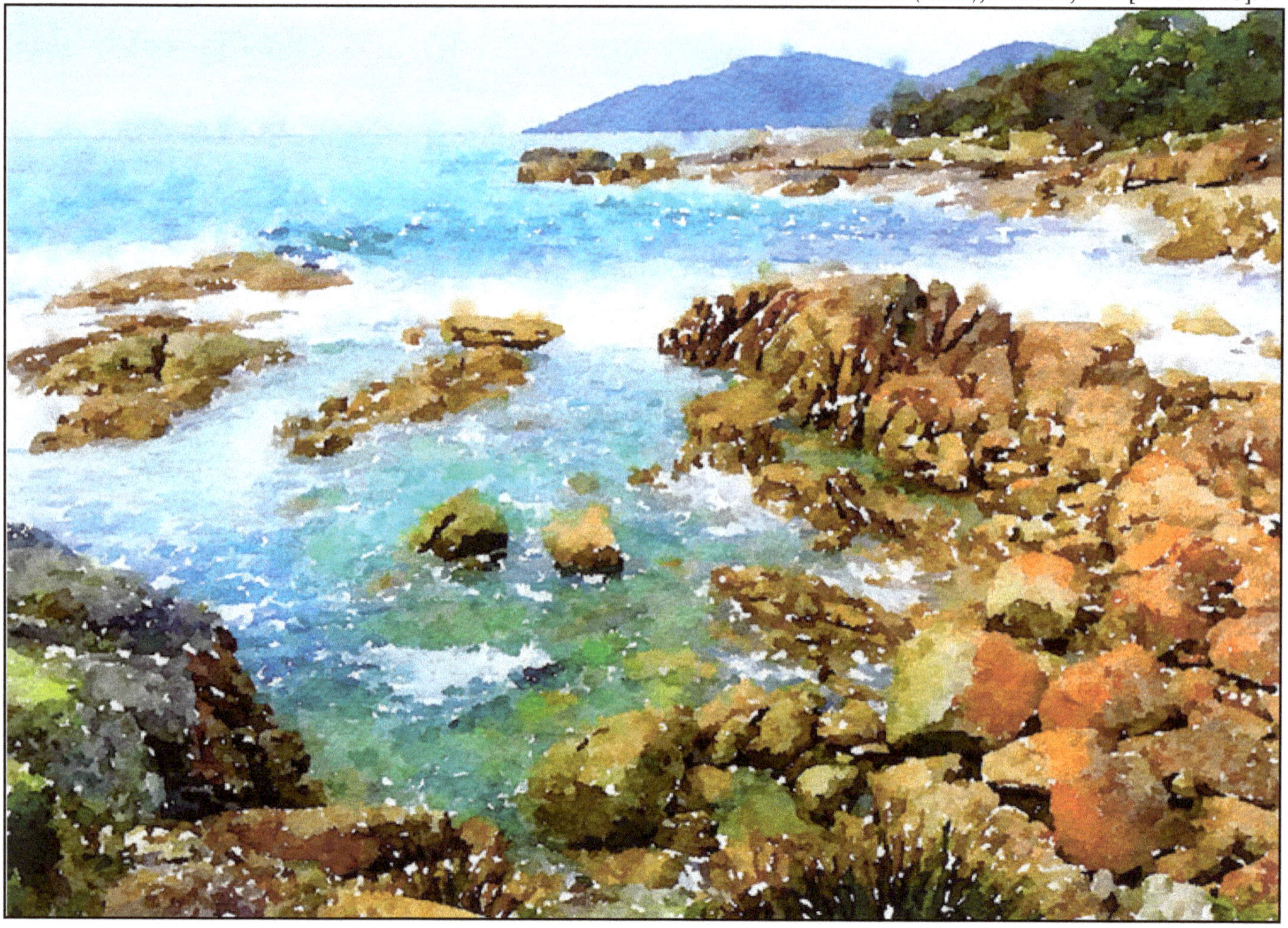

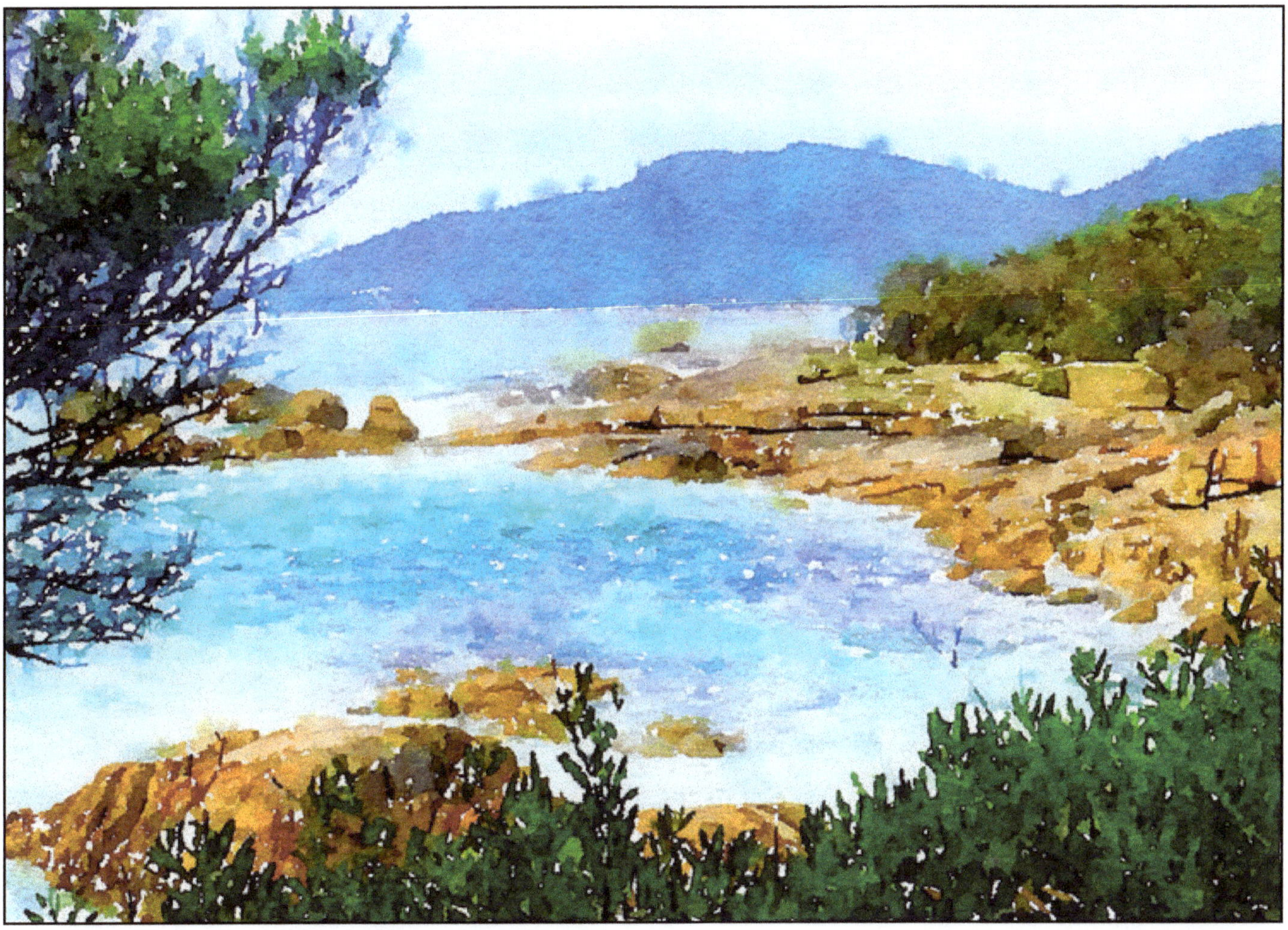

▲'Red Rocks Of Bicheno' (2019), Bicheno, TAS [ASTA1904].

'The Harbour' (2019), Strahan, TAS [ASTA1905].▼

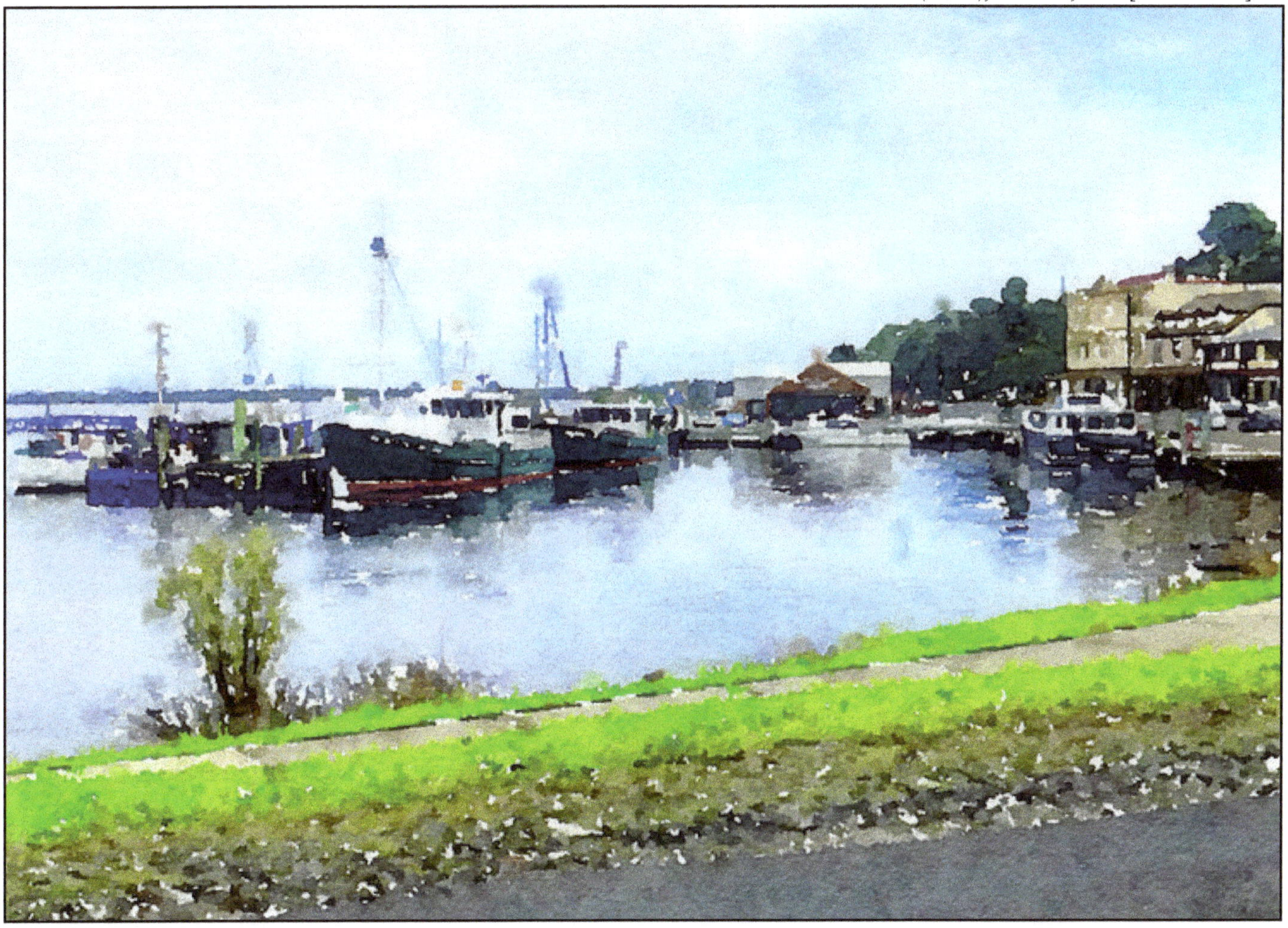

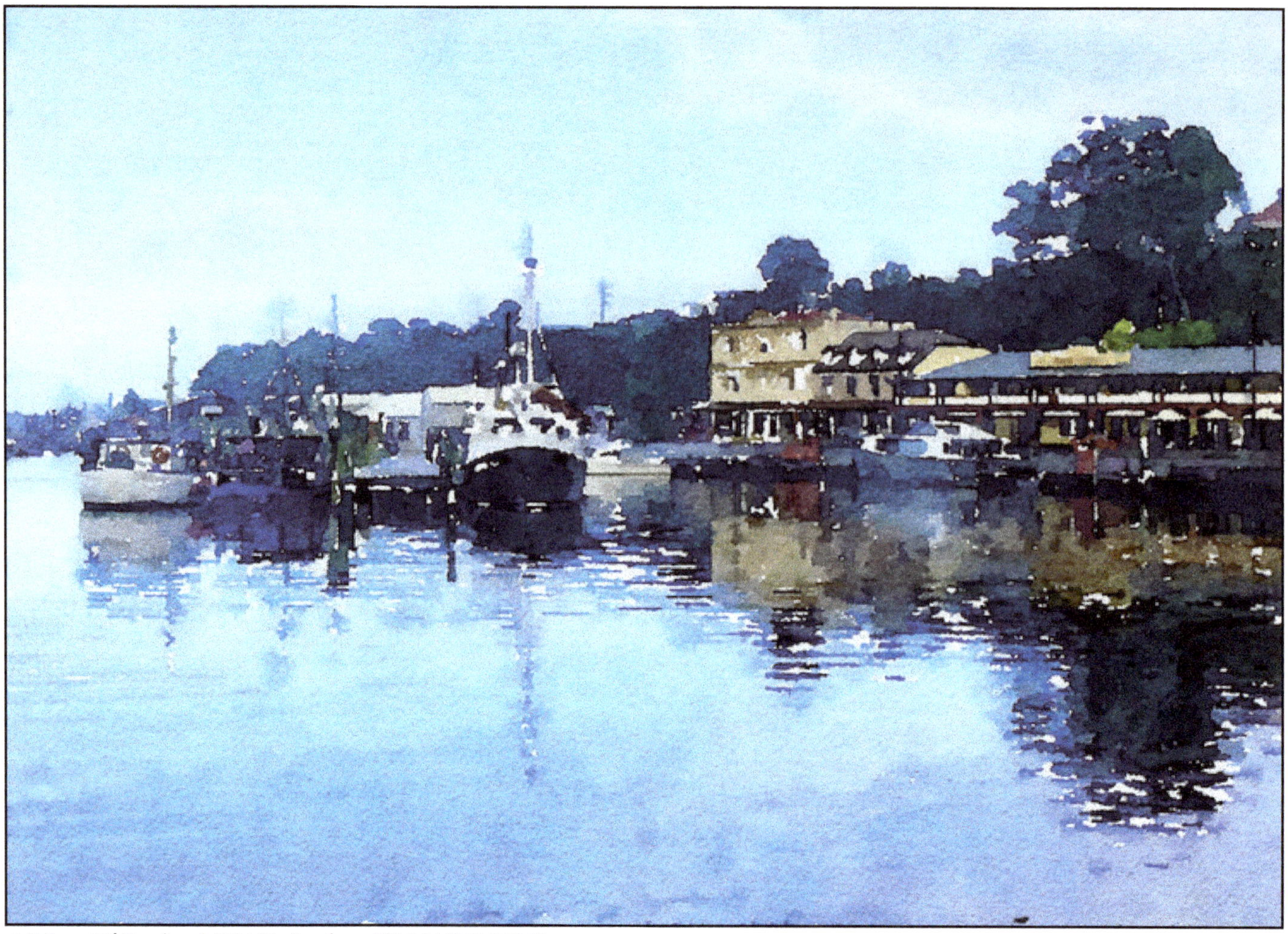

▲'View Of Strahan' (2019), Strahan, TAS [ASTA1906].

'Glassy Morning' (2019), Strahan, TAS [ASTA1907].▼

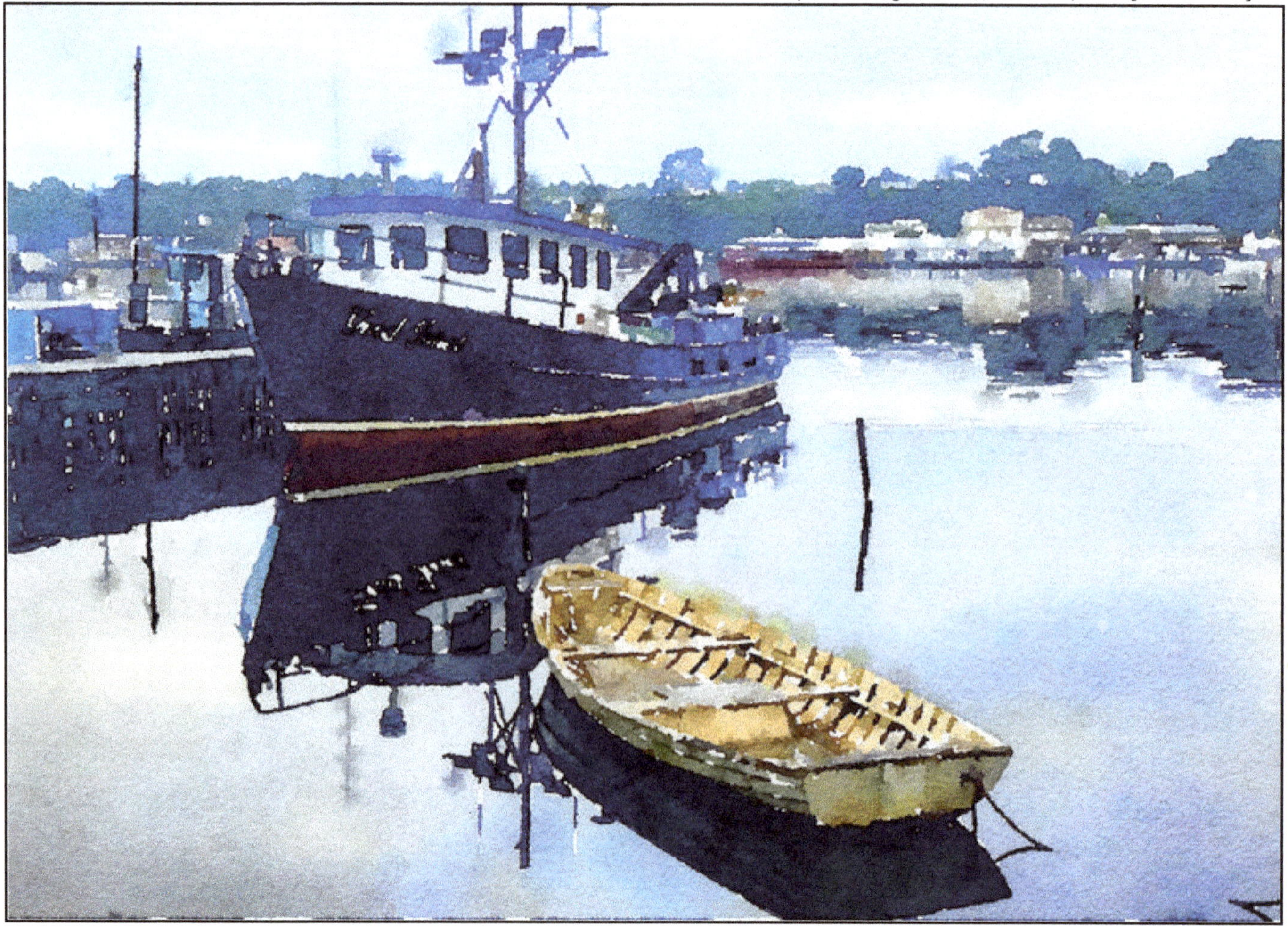

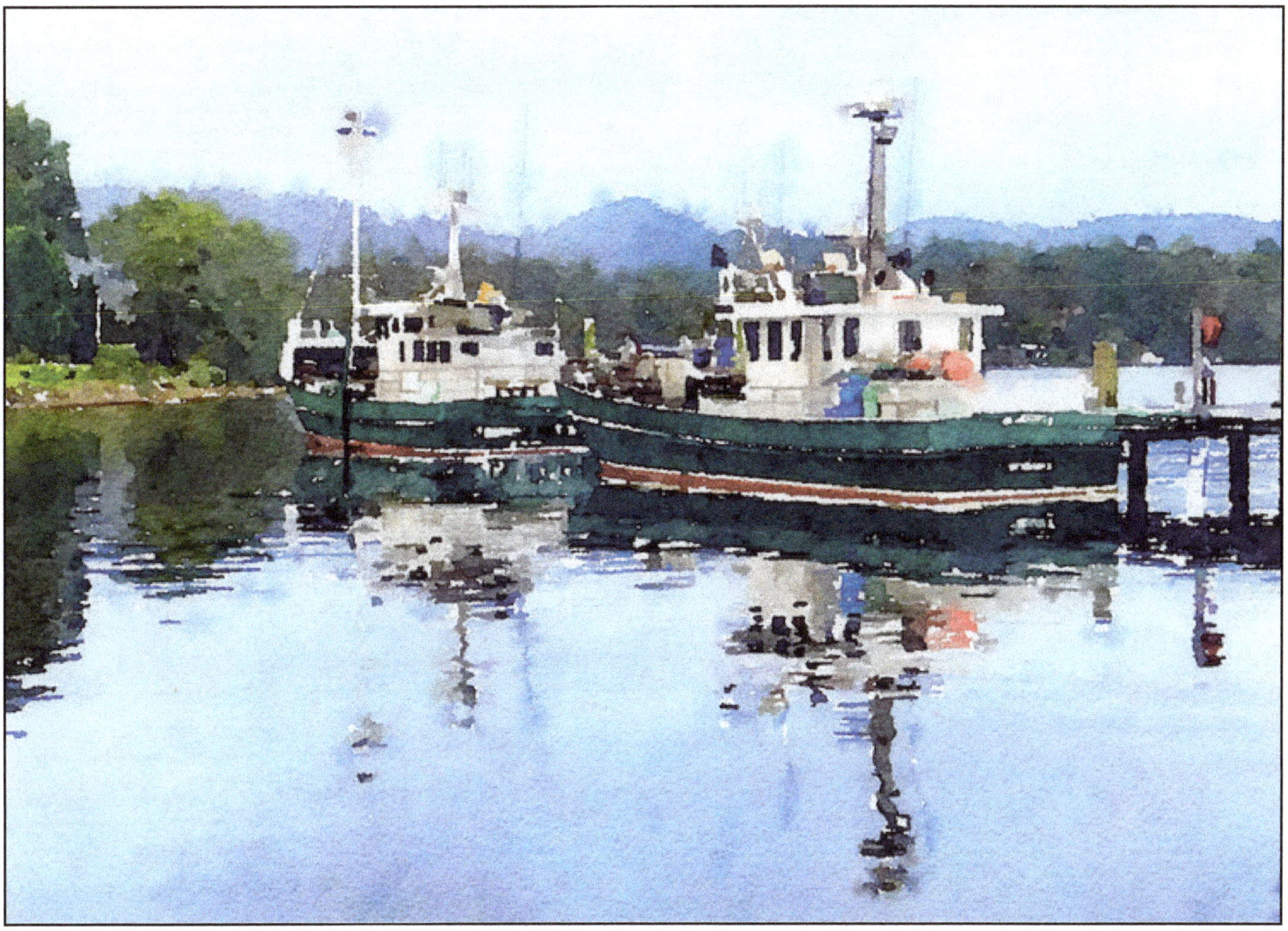

▲'The Port Of Strahan' (2019), Strahan, TAS [ASTA1908].

'Stillness' (2019), Strahan, TAS [ASTA1909].▼

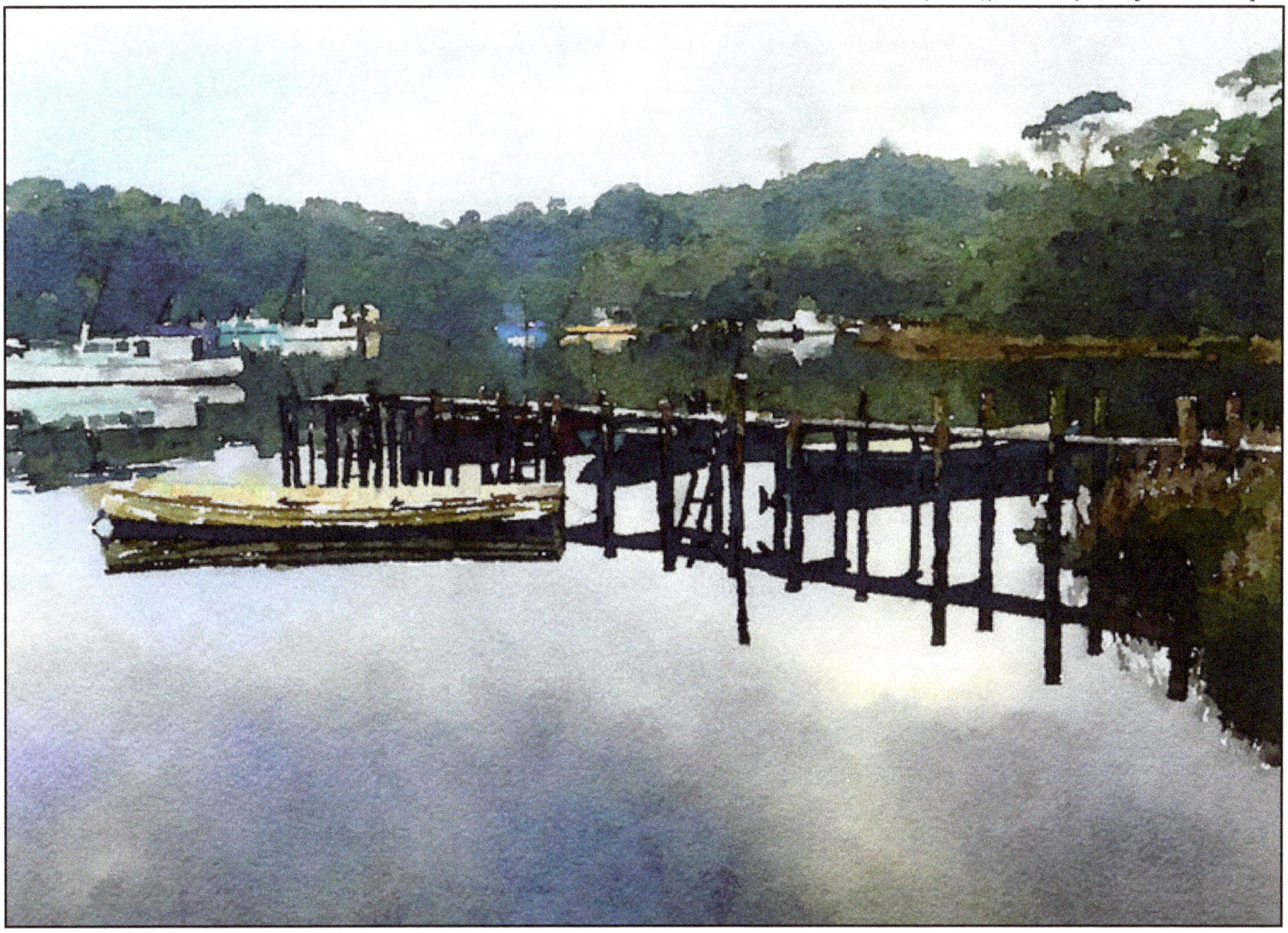

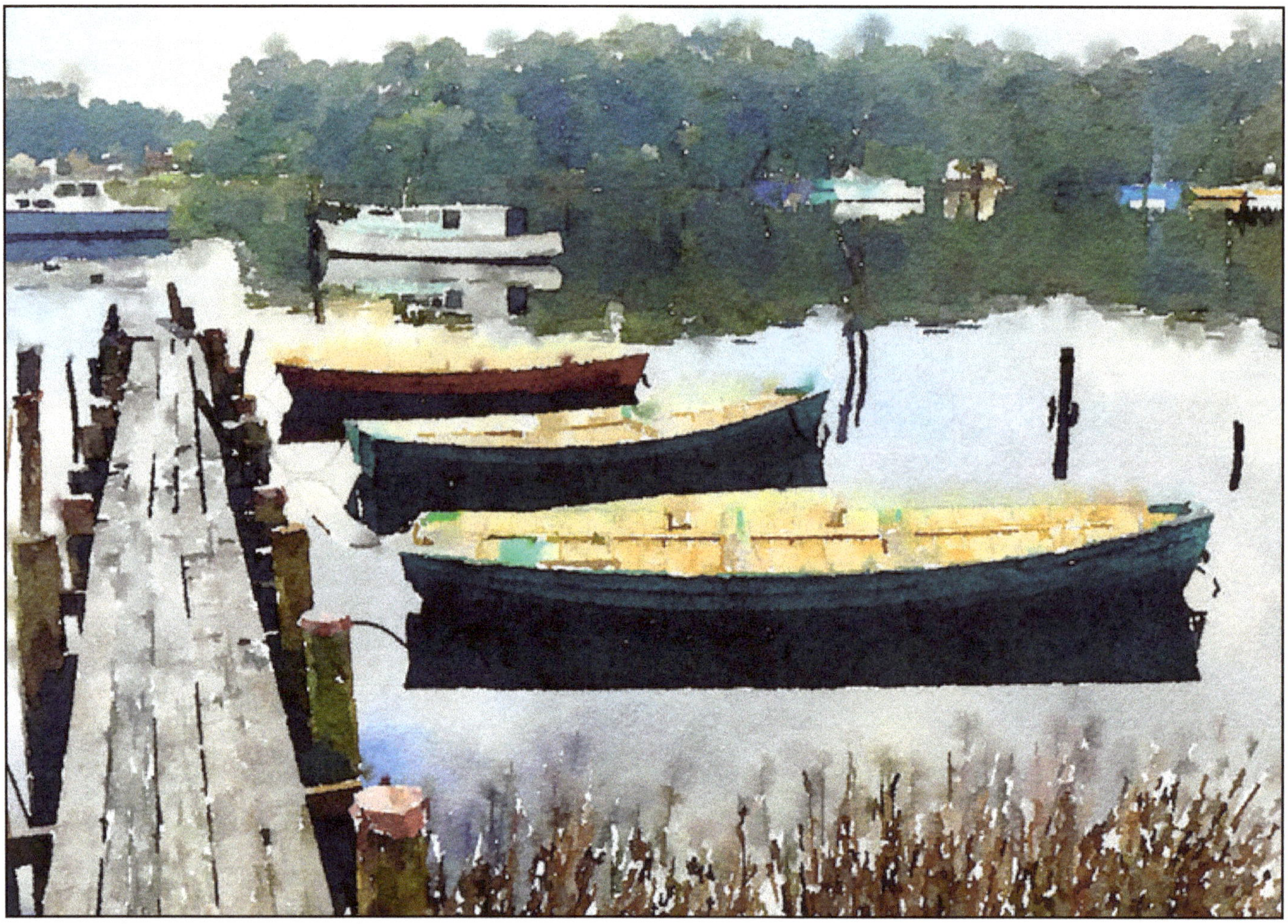

▲'Mirrored Moorings' (2019), Strahan, TAS [ASTA1910].

'Reflections Of Strahan' (2019), Strahan, TAS [ASTA1911].▼

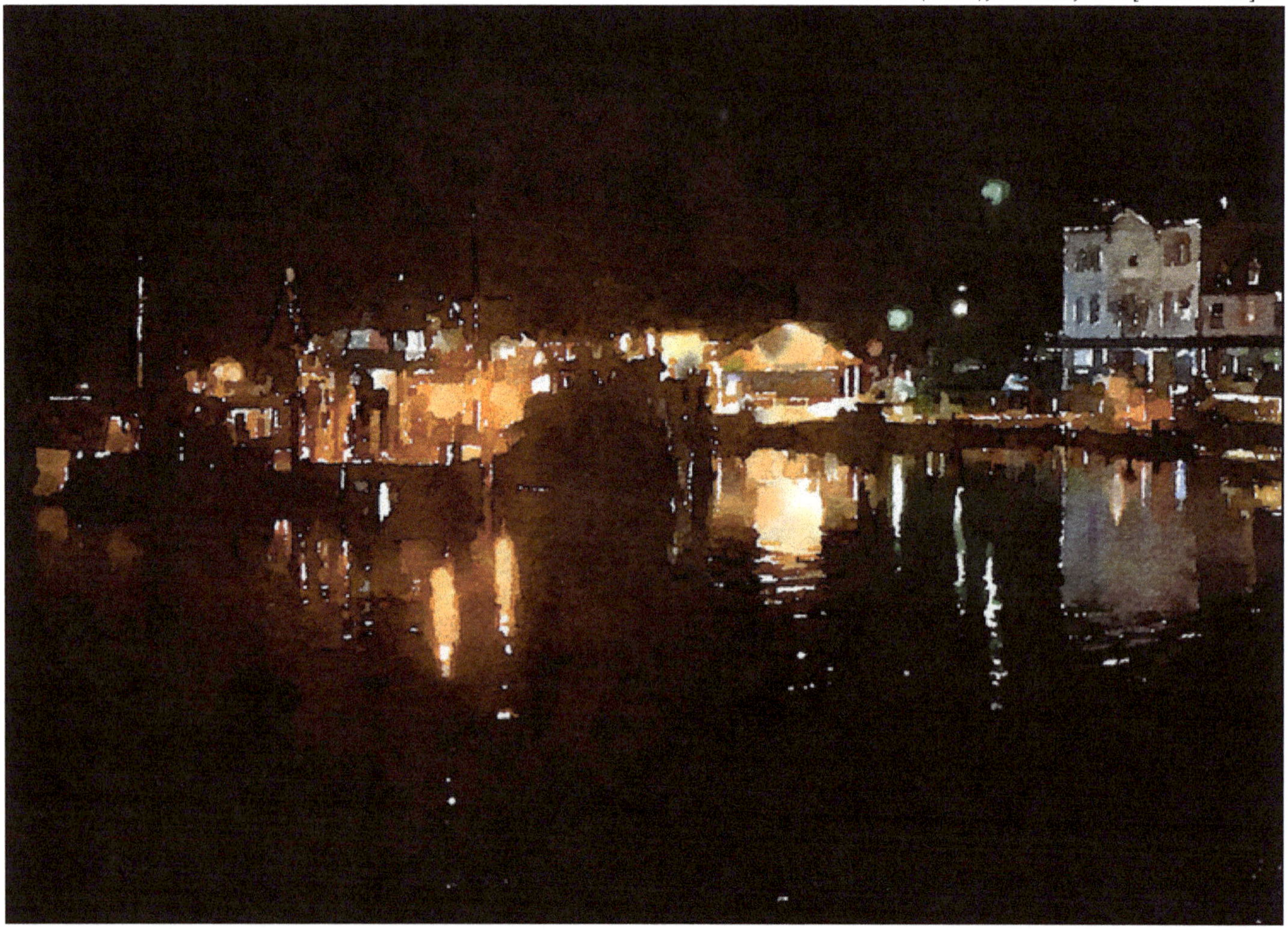

Urban Seascapes...

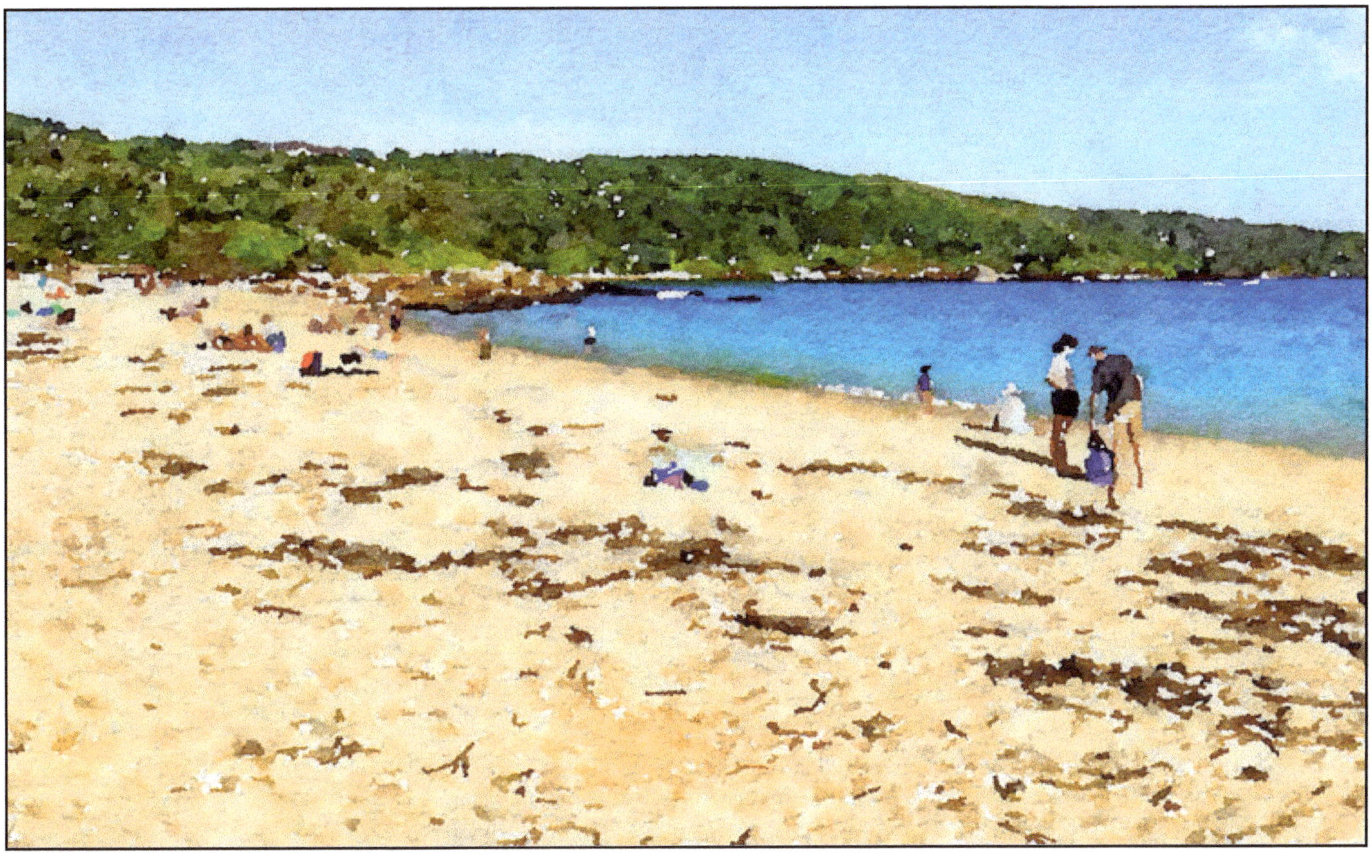

▲'Congwong Beach' (2019), La Perouse, Sydney [ASBO1902].

'Bare Island Bridge' (2019), La Perouse, Sydney [ASBO1901].▼

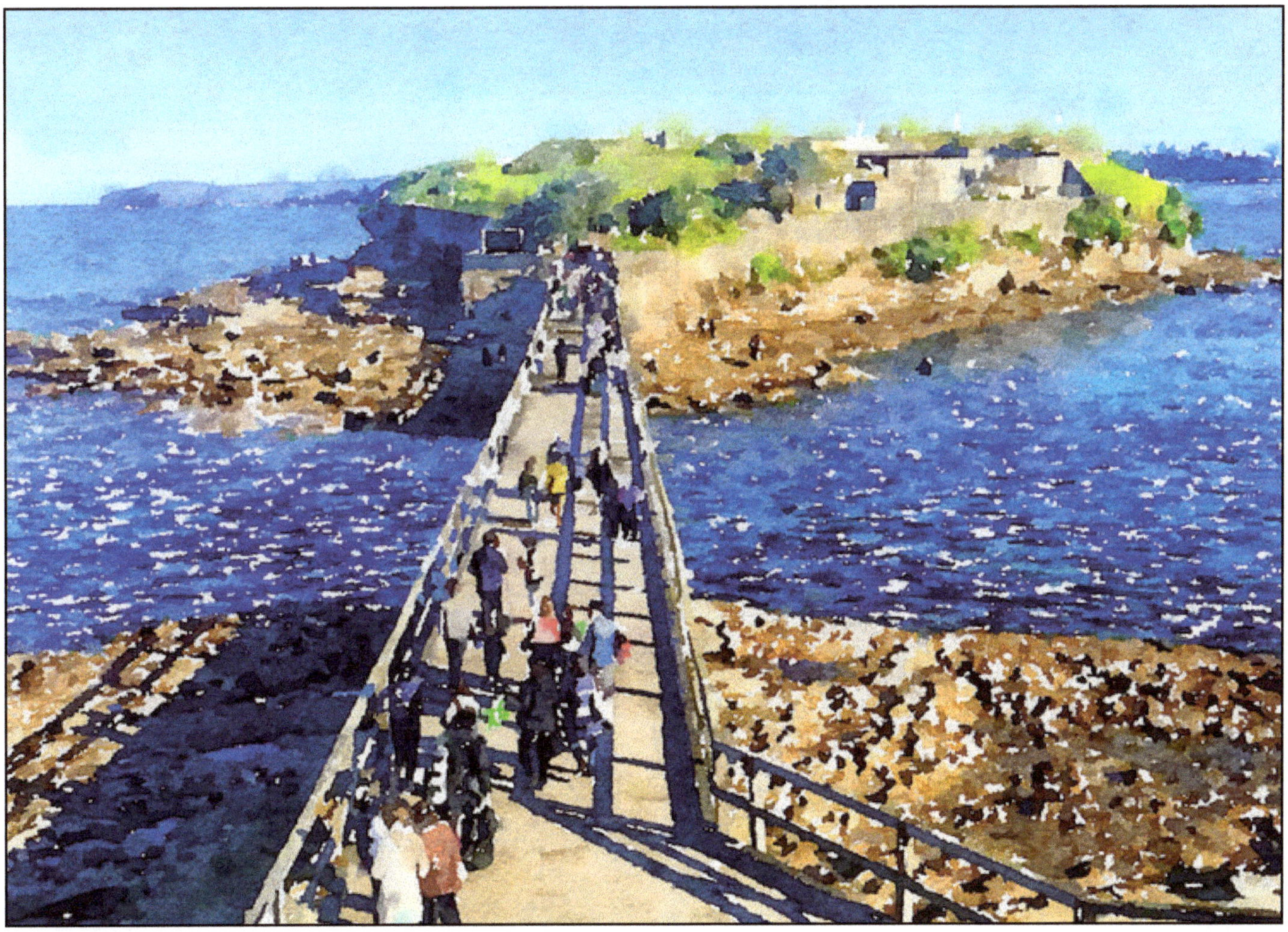

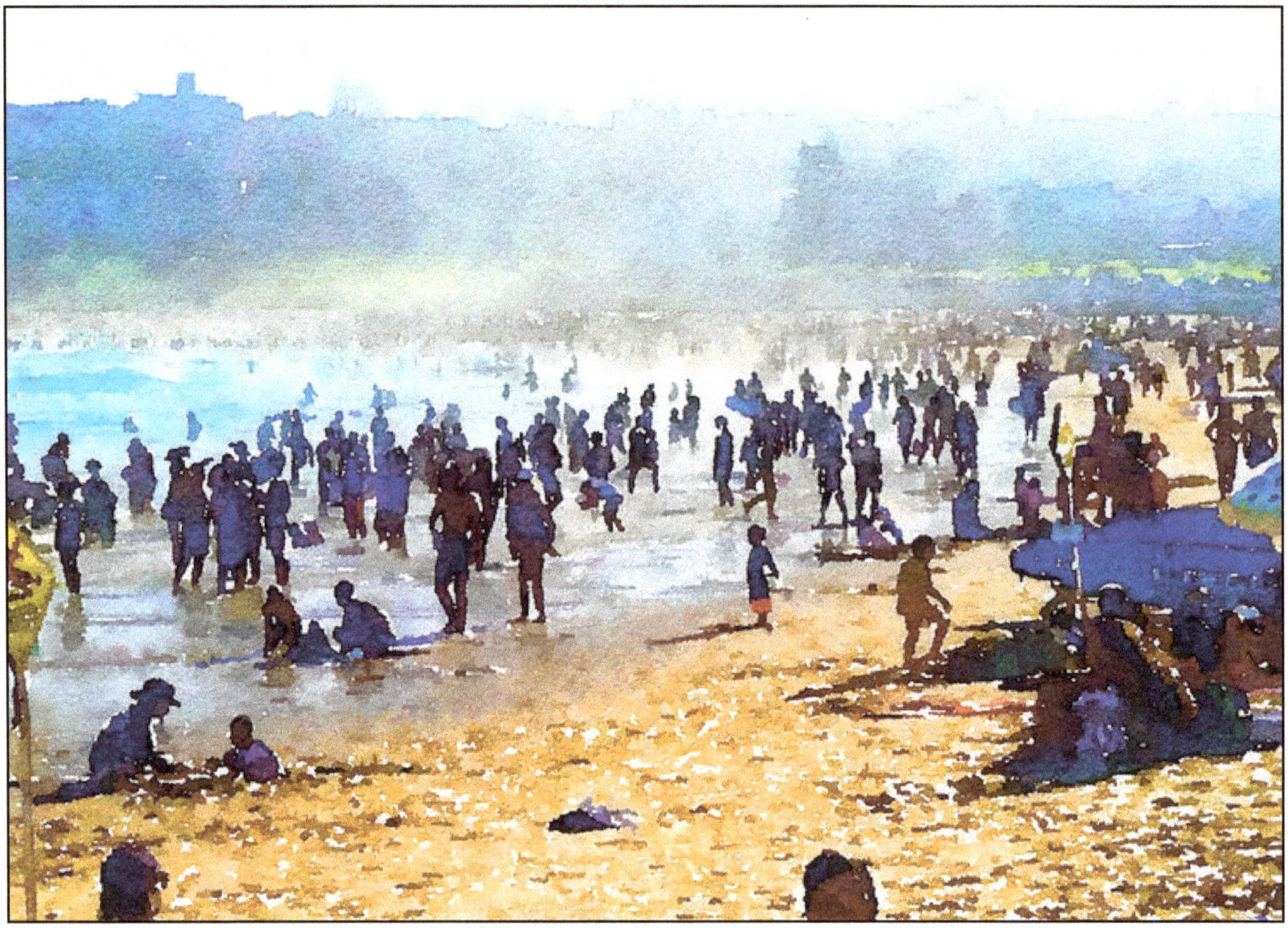

▲'Cooling Off' (2018), Bondi Beach, NSW [ASBB1801].

'Life Is Different At The Beach' (2018), Bondi Beach, NSW [ASBB1802].▼

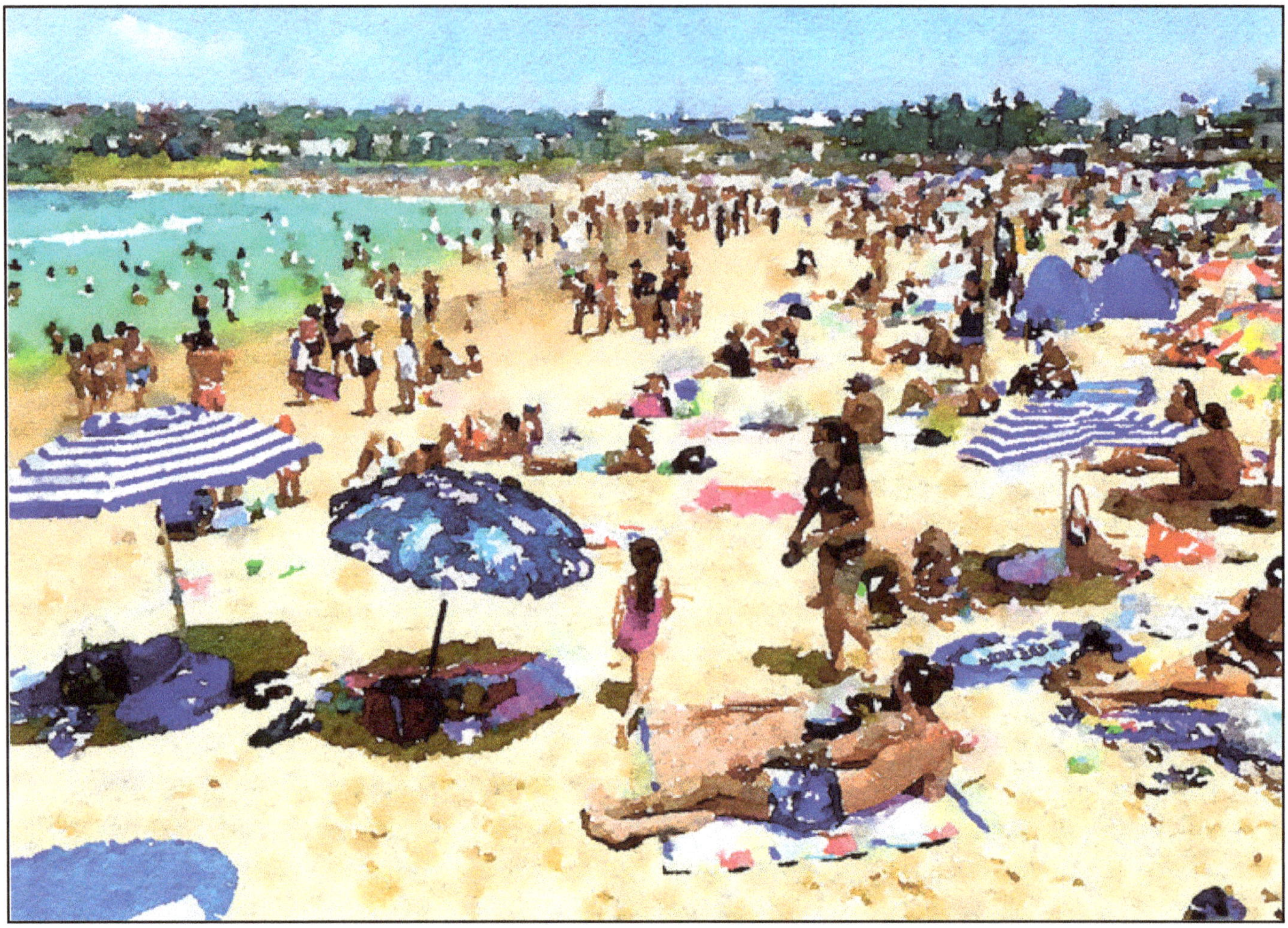

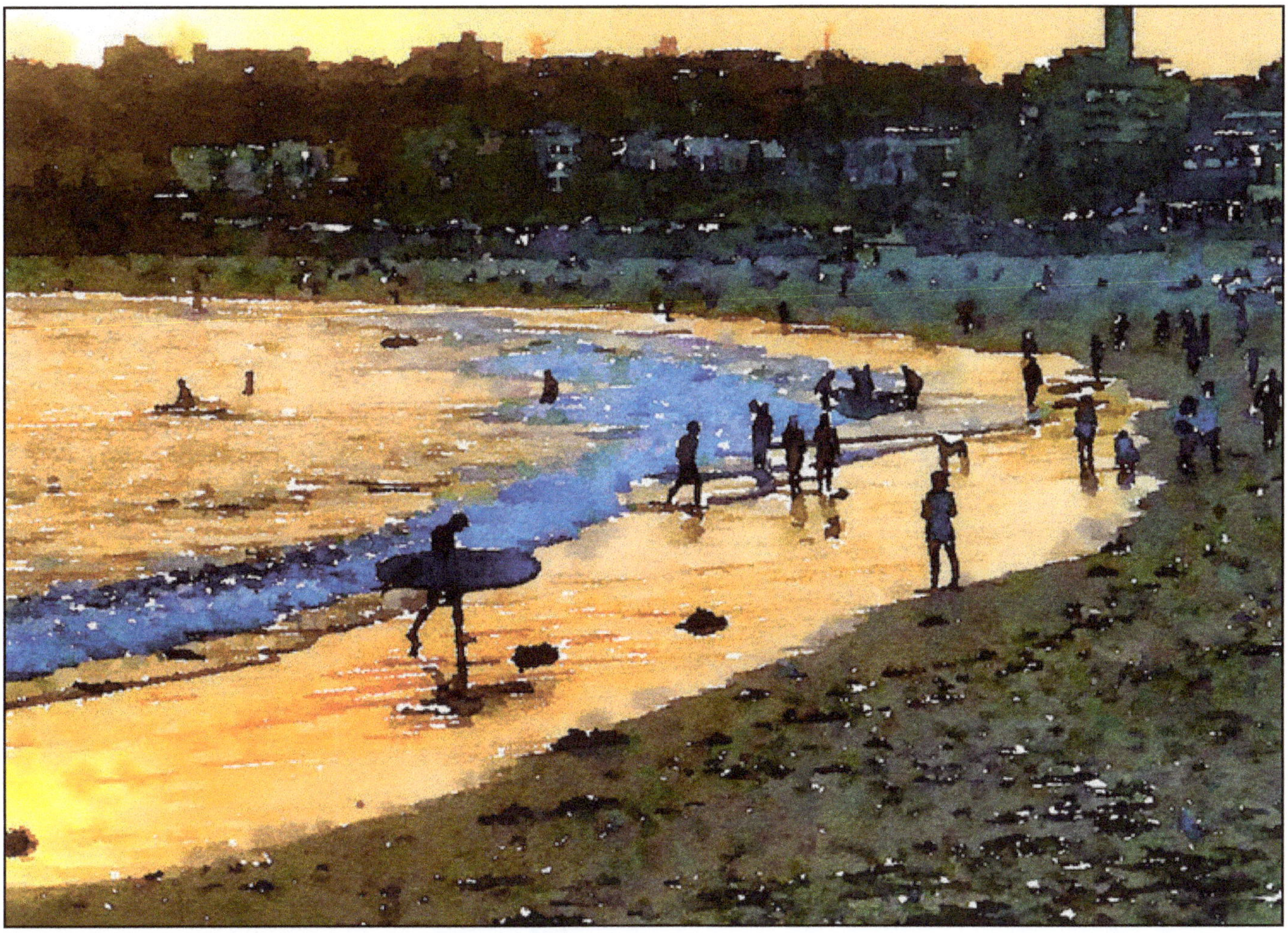

▲'Coming Out Of Your Shell' (2019), Bondi Beach, NSW [ASBB1901].

'Emerald Sets' (2007), Bondi Beach, NSW [ASBB0701].▼

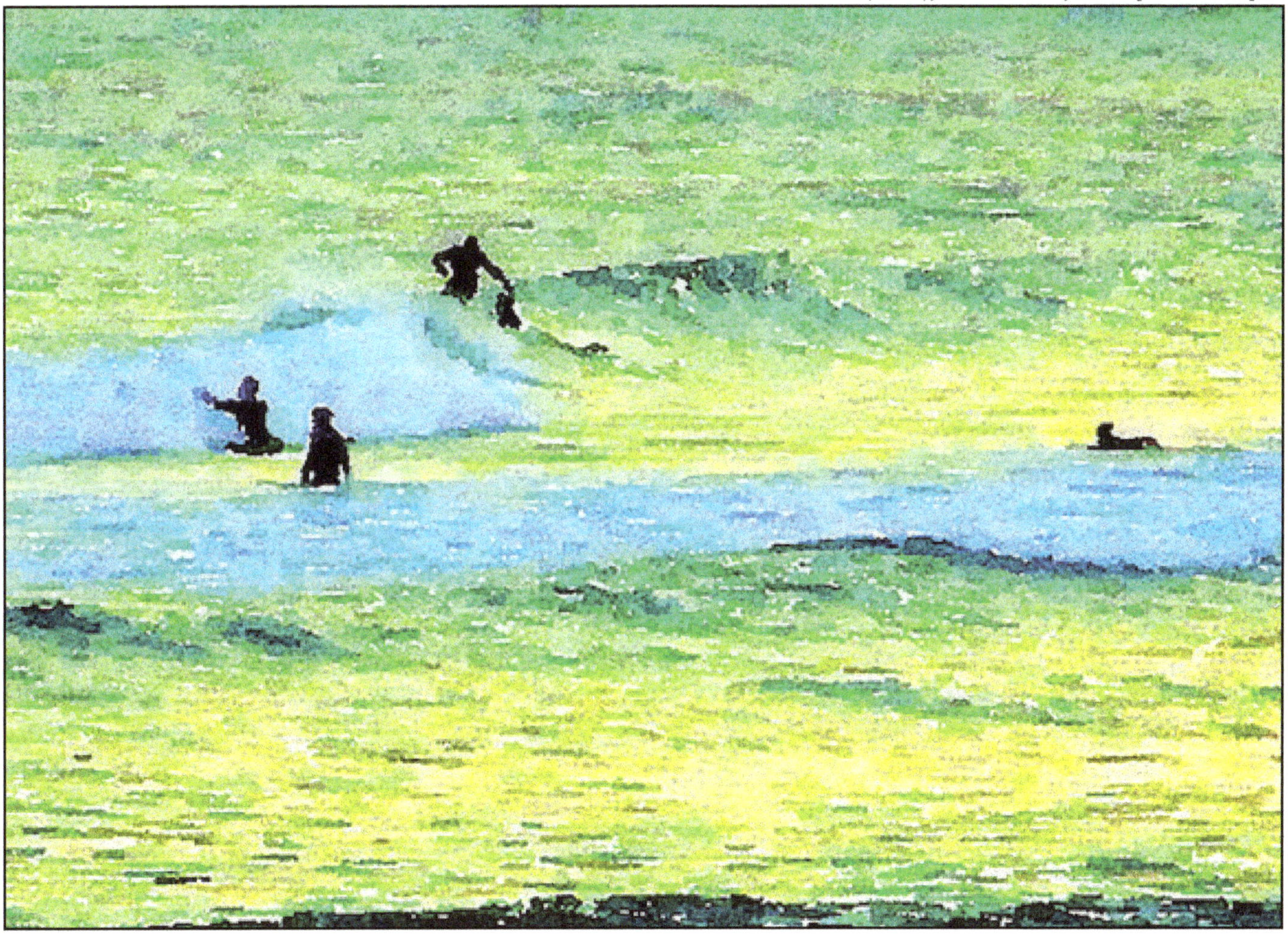

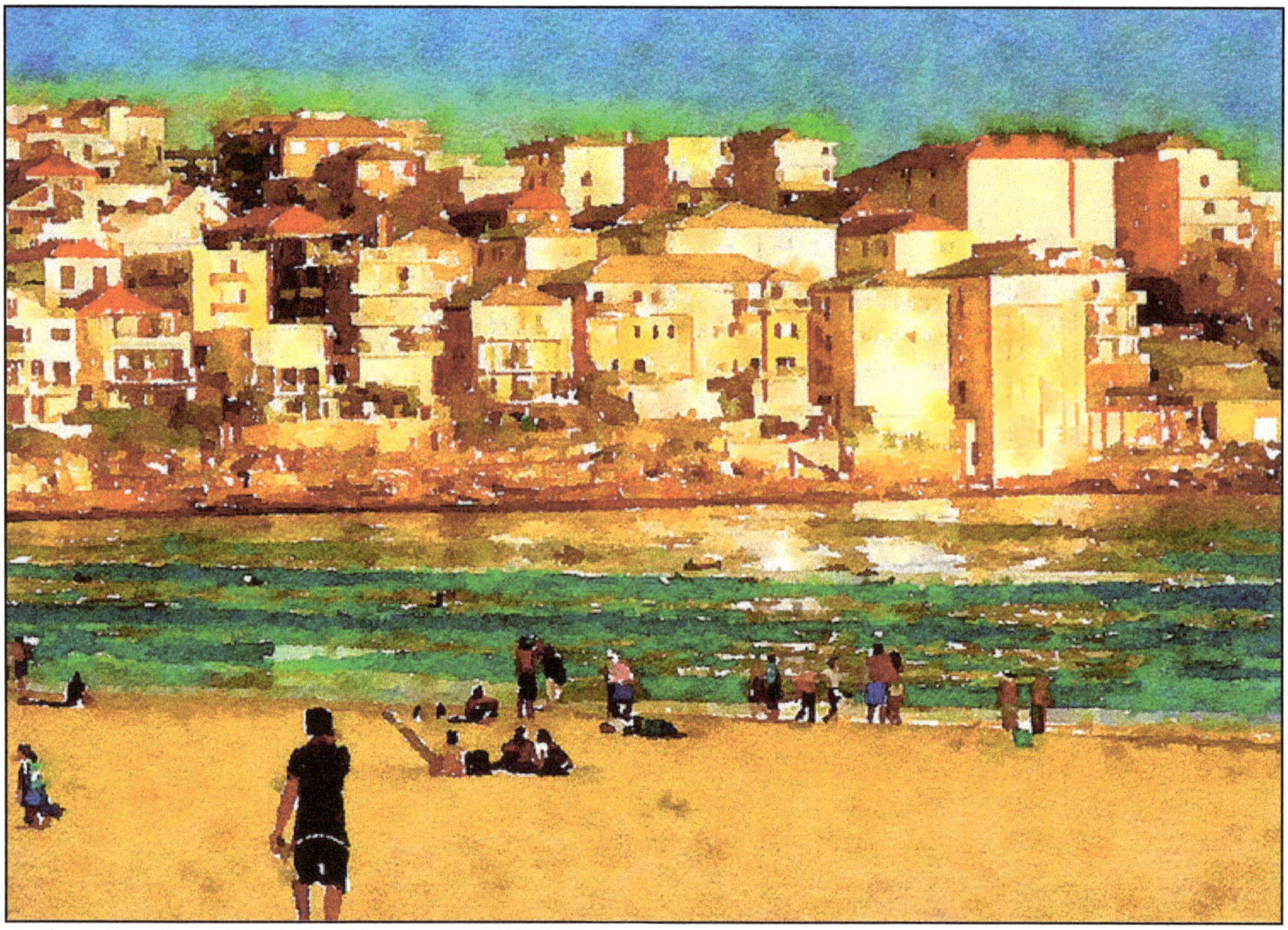

▲'The Golden Hour' (2007), Bondi Beach, NSW [ASBB0702].

'Bondi Lifesaving Club' (2019), Bondi Beach, NSW [ASBB1905].▼

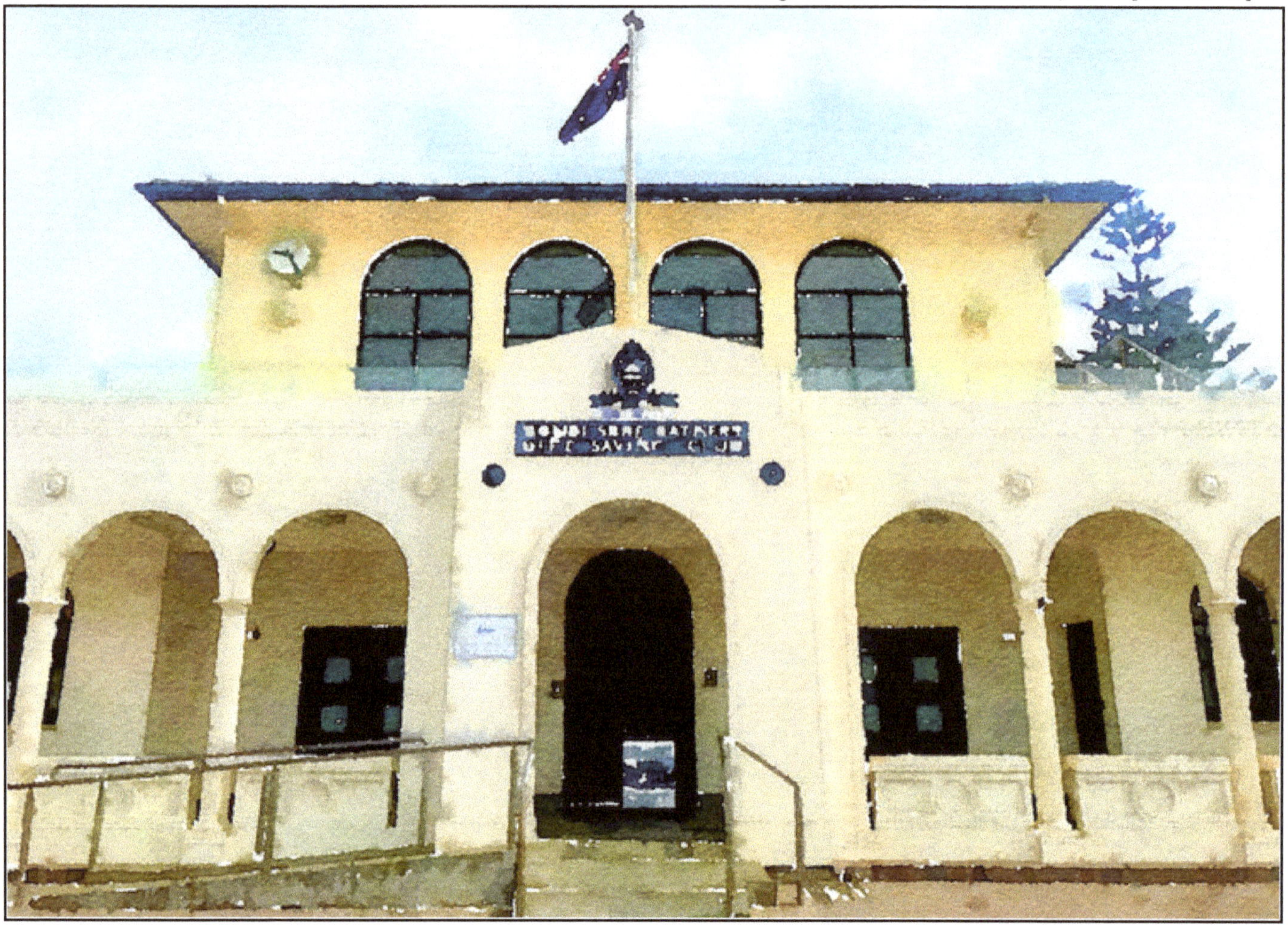

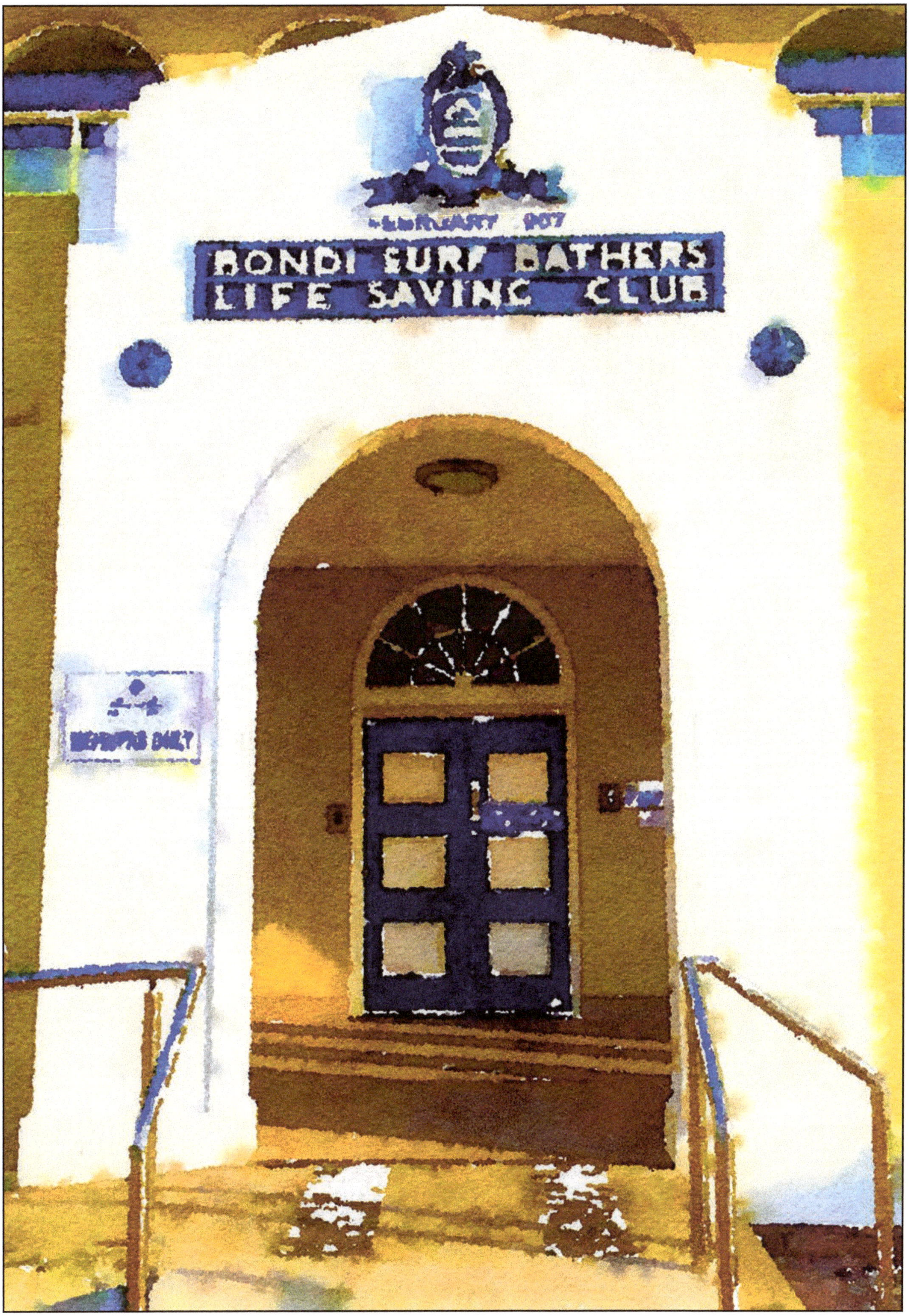

▲'Bondi SBLSC' (2015), Bondi Beach, NSW [ASBB1501].

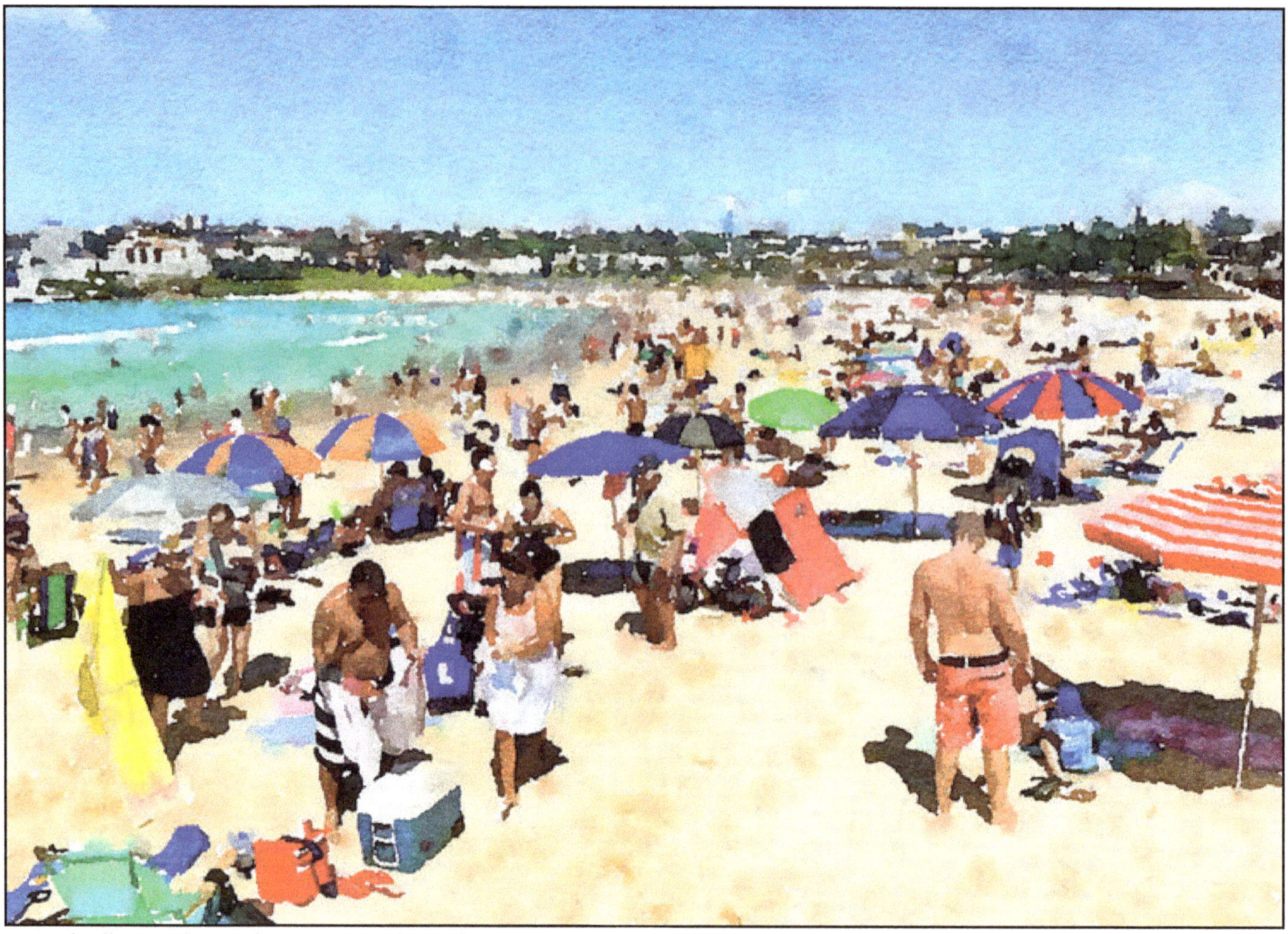

▲'Sunbrellas In The Sand' (2017), Bondi Beach, NSW [ASBB1701].

'Just The Two Of Us' (2018), Bondi Beach, NSW [ASBB1803].▼

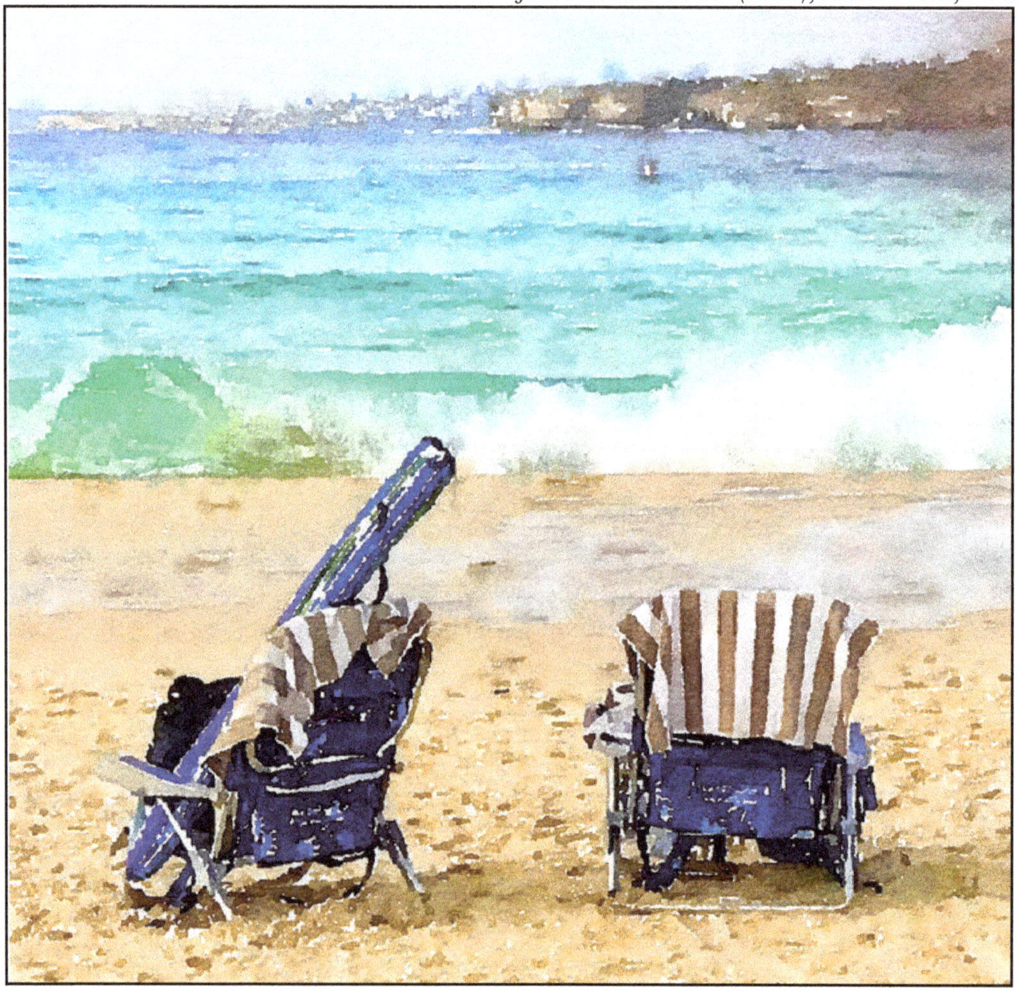

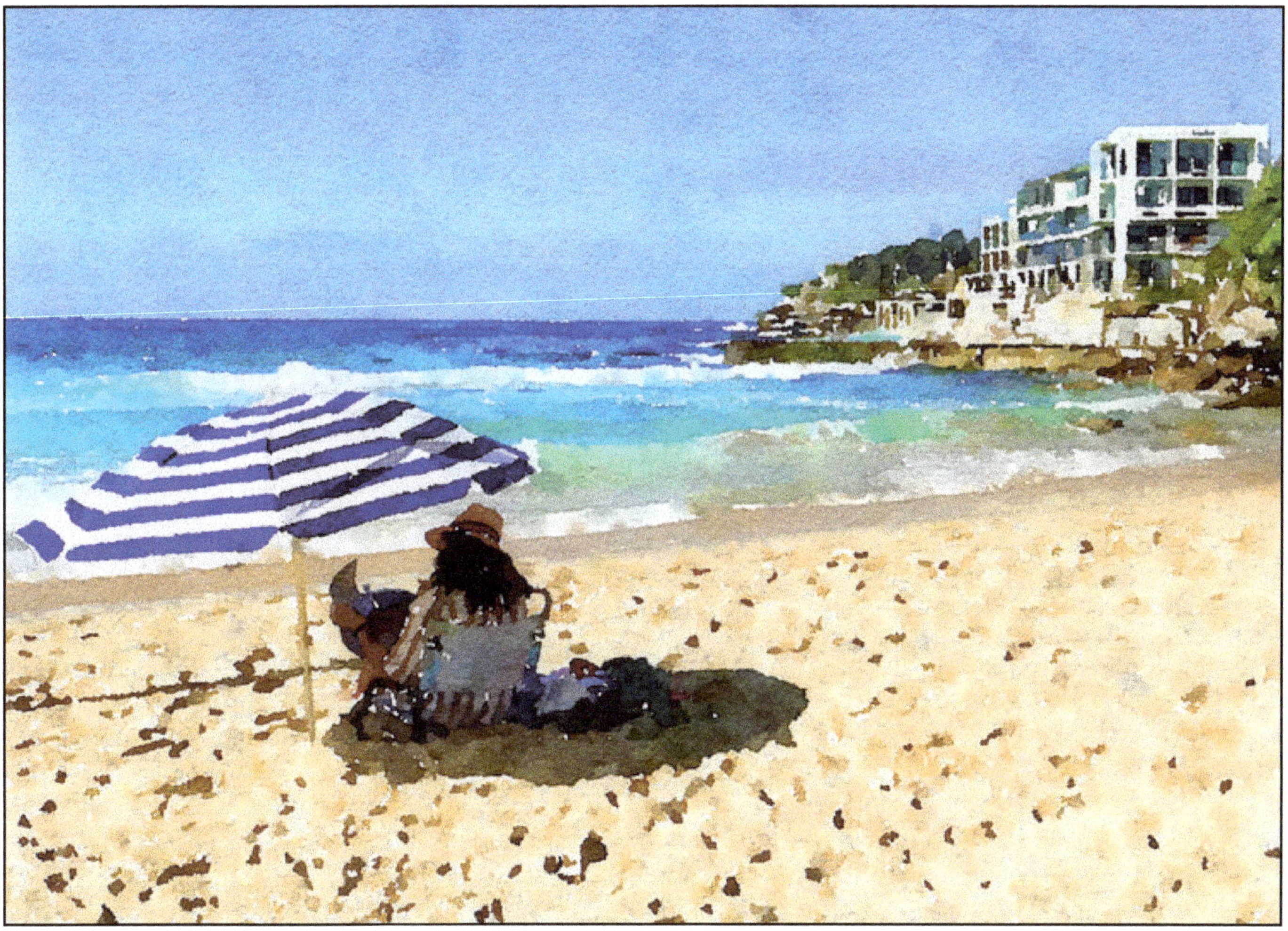

▲'Bliss At Bondi' (2019), South Bondi Beach, NSW [ASBB1902].

'The Icebergs Club' (2019), Bondi Beach, NSW [ASBB1903].▼

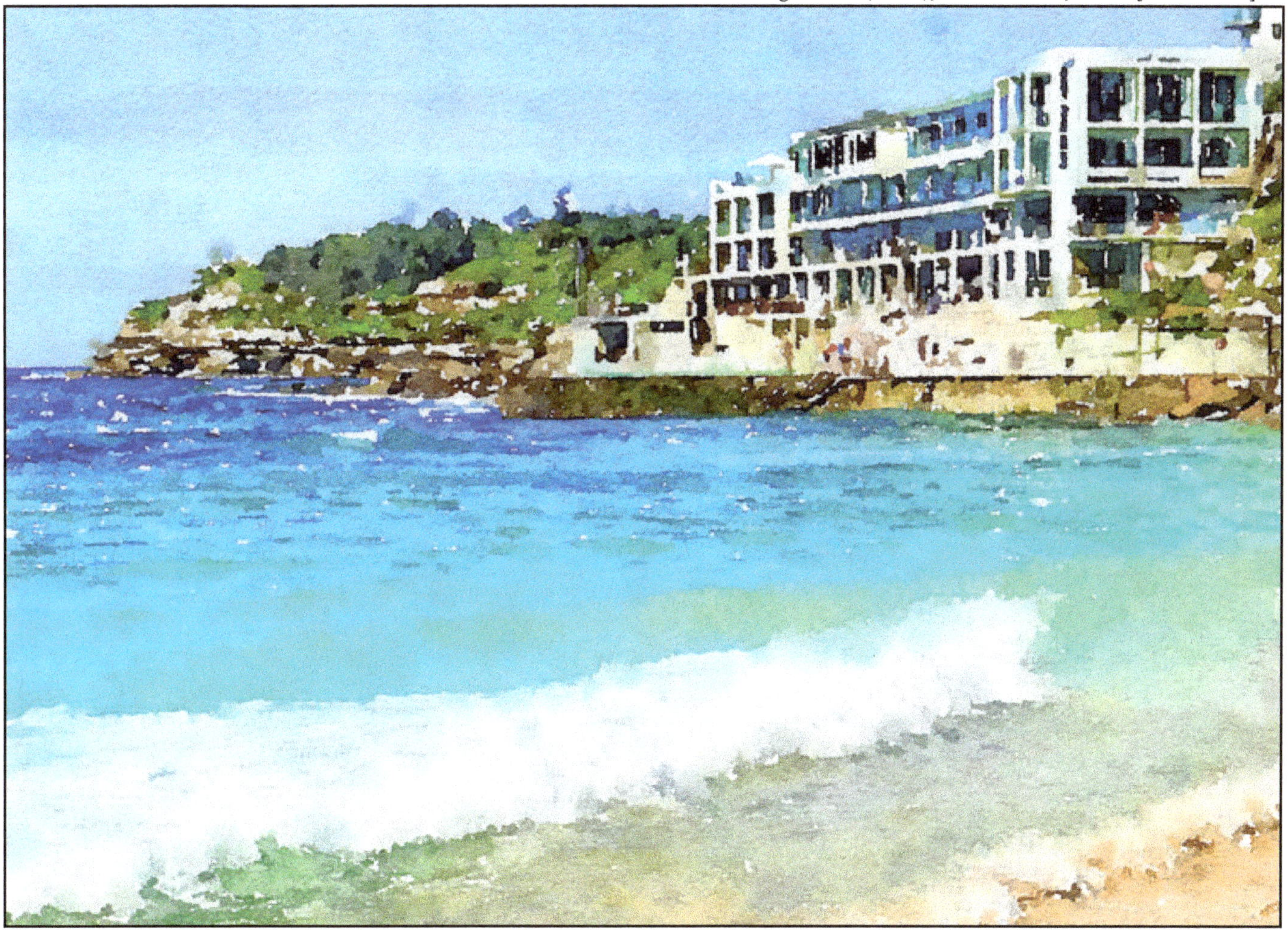

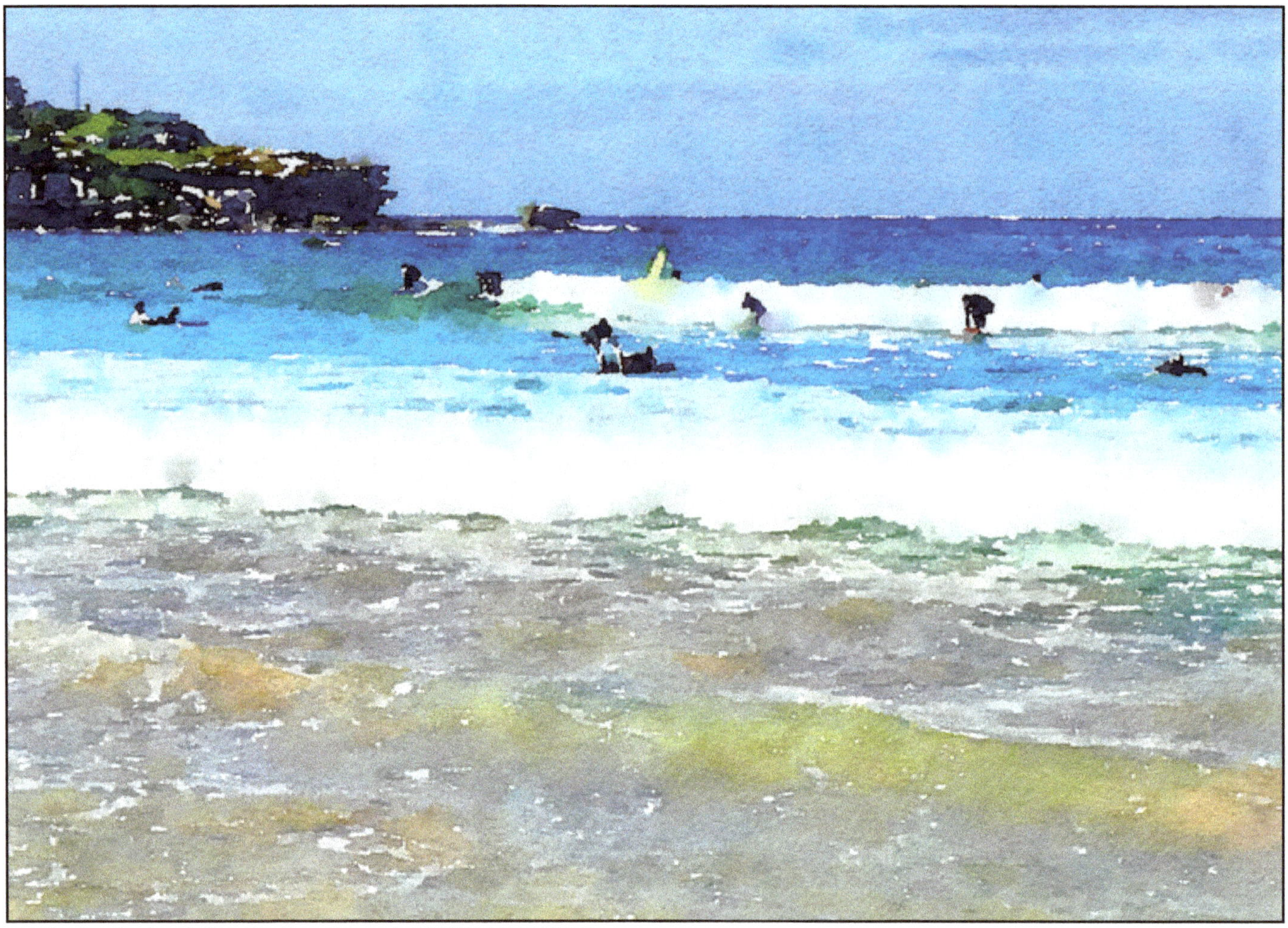

▲'The Surf School' (2019), Bondi Beach, NSW [ASBB1904].

'Walking The Prom' (2019), Bondi Beach, NSW [ASBB1907].▼

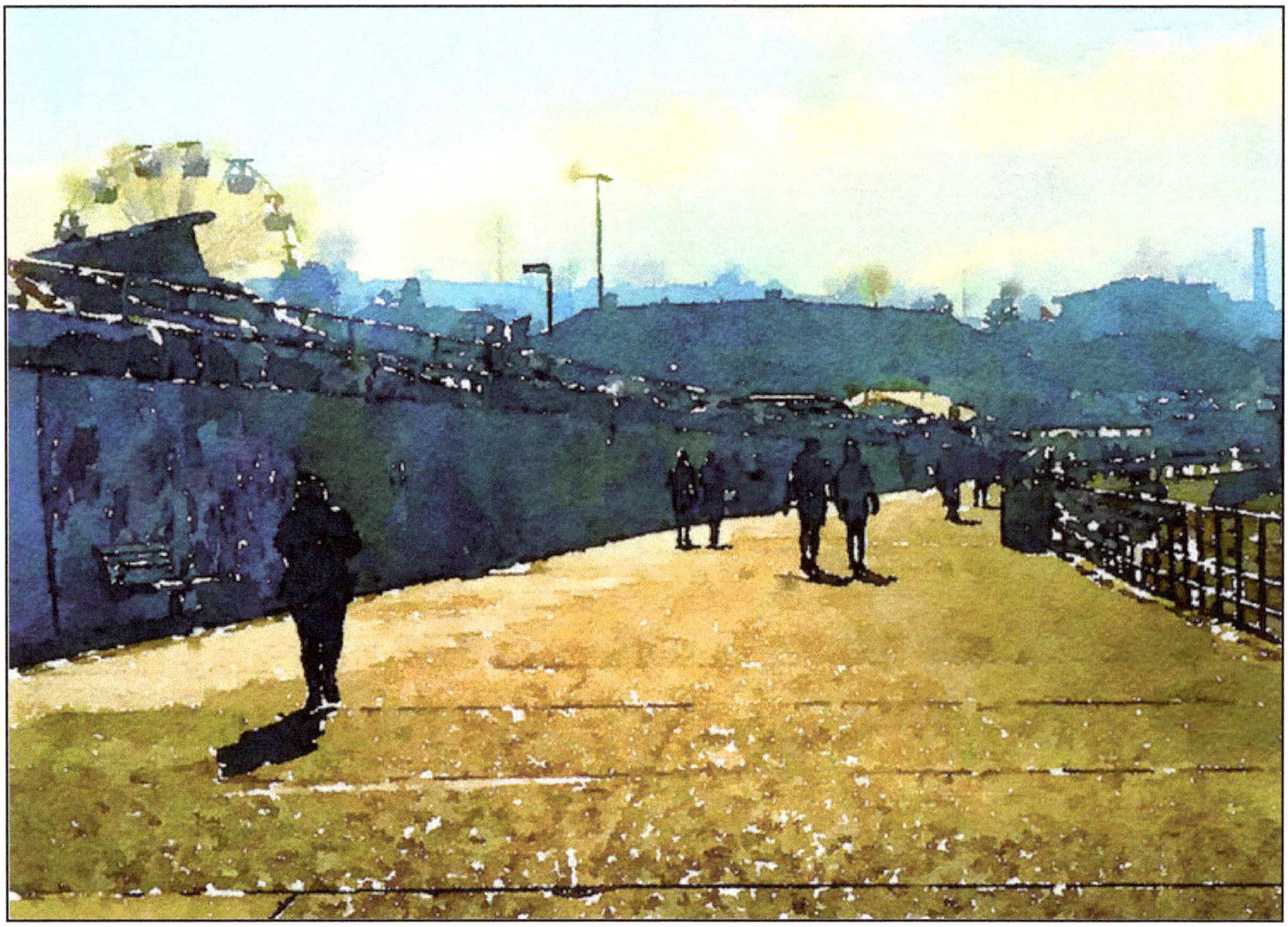

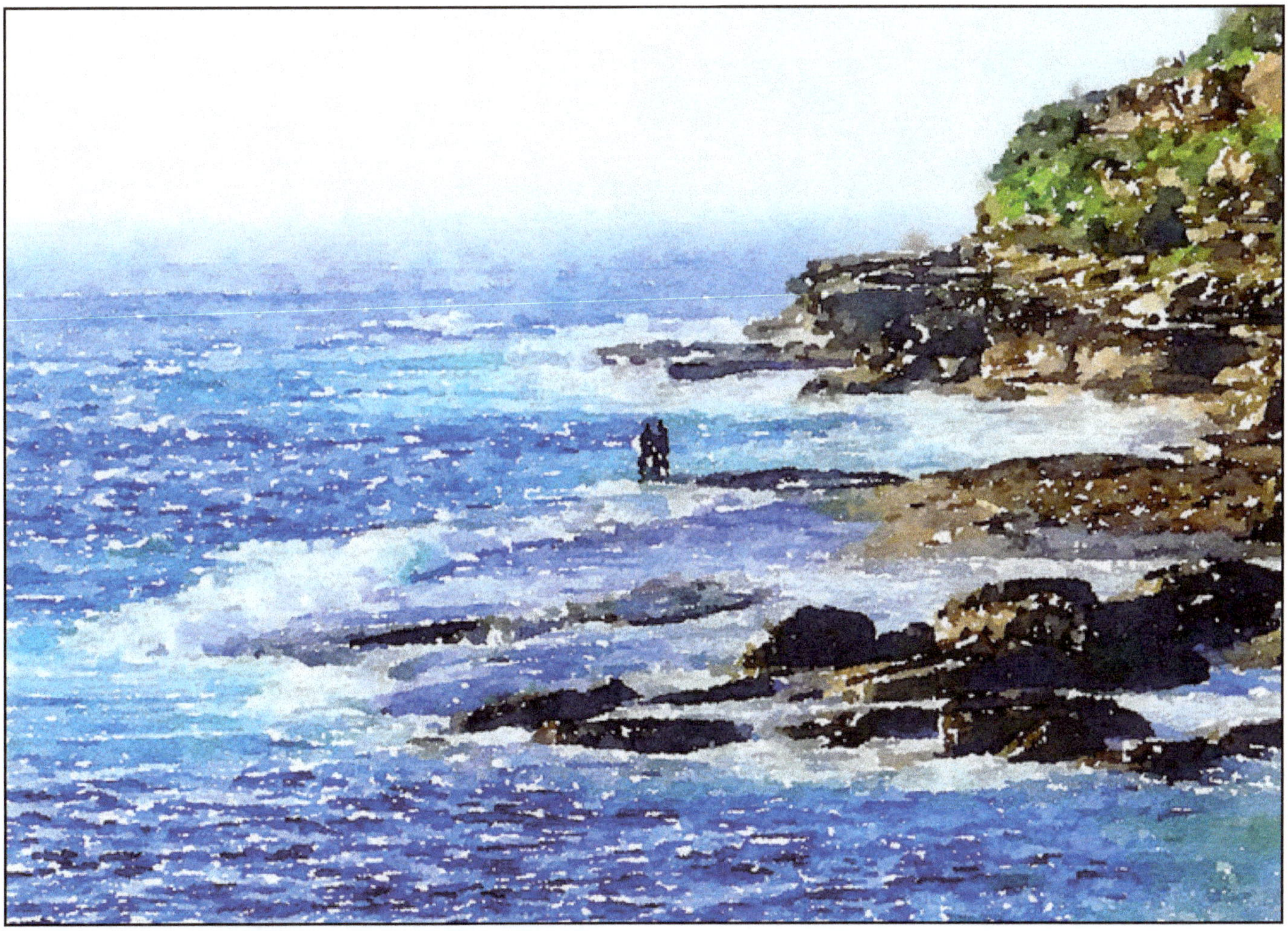

▲'Fishing The Boot' (2019), South Bondi, NSW [ASBB1906].

'Go With The Flow' (2019), Bondi Beach, NSW [ASBB1910].▼

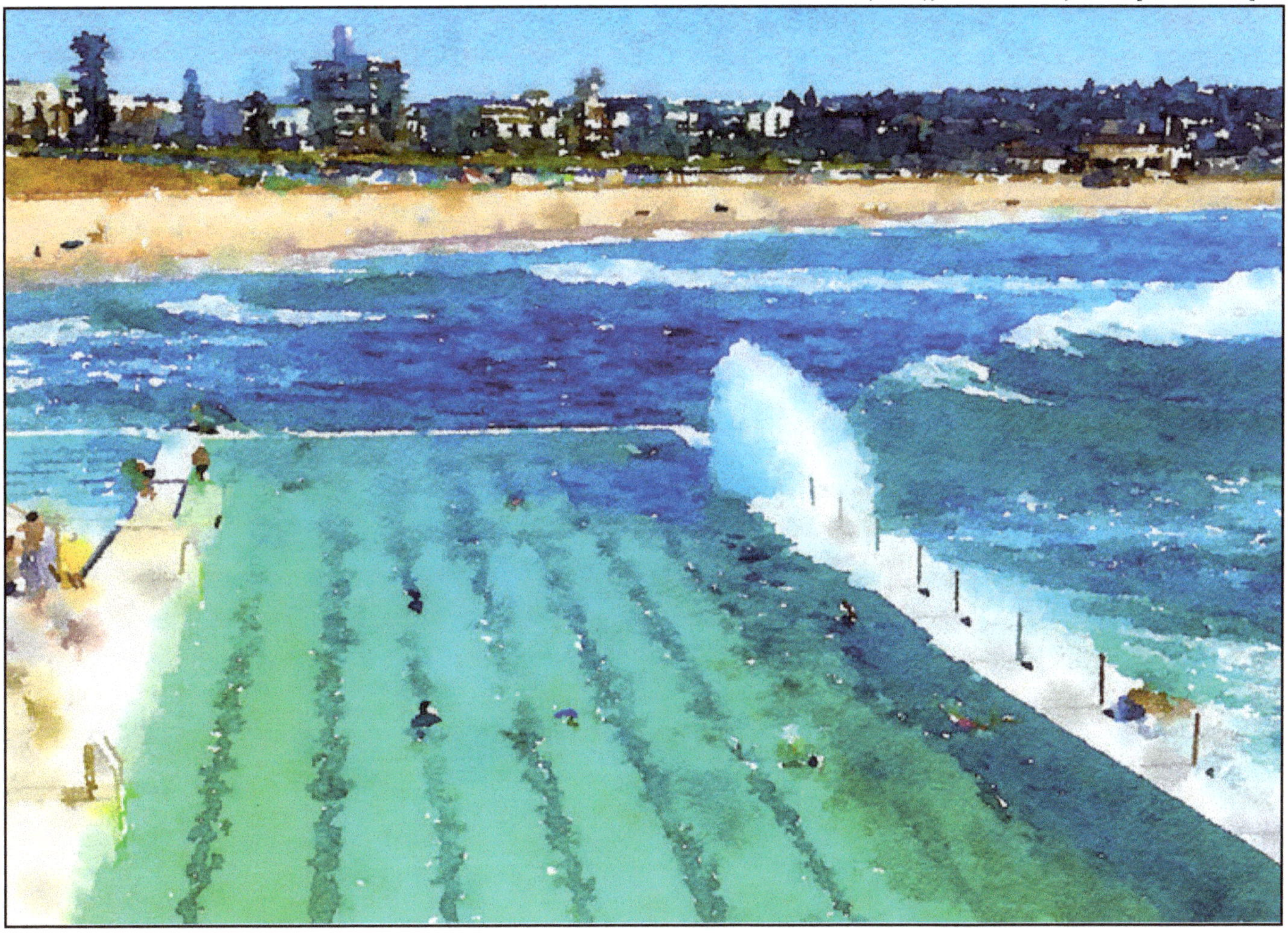

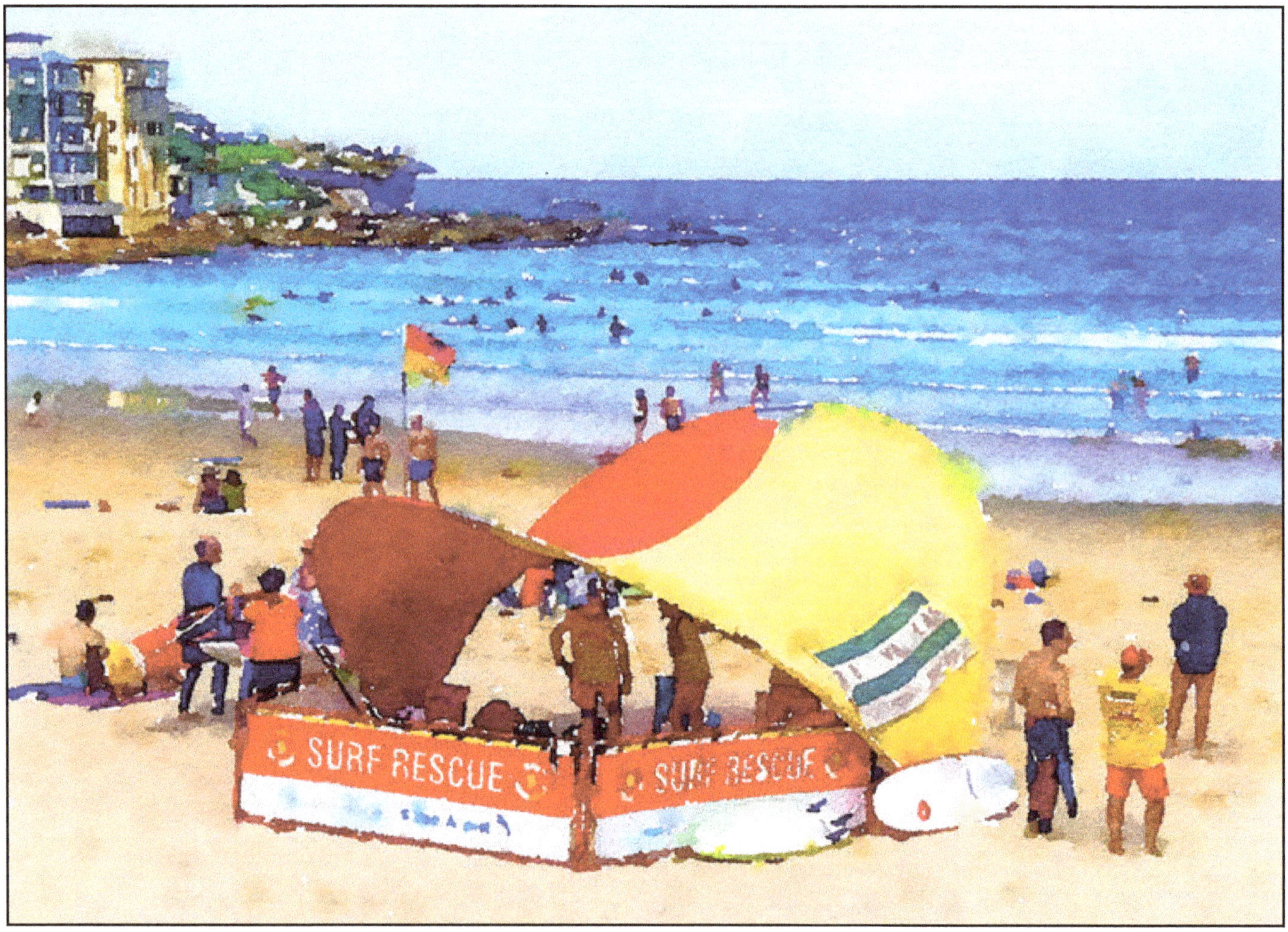

▲'On Patrol' (2019), Bondi Beach, NSW [ASBB1908].

'The Start Of Summer' (2019), Bondi Beach, NSW [ASBB1909].▼

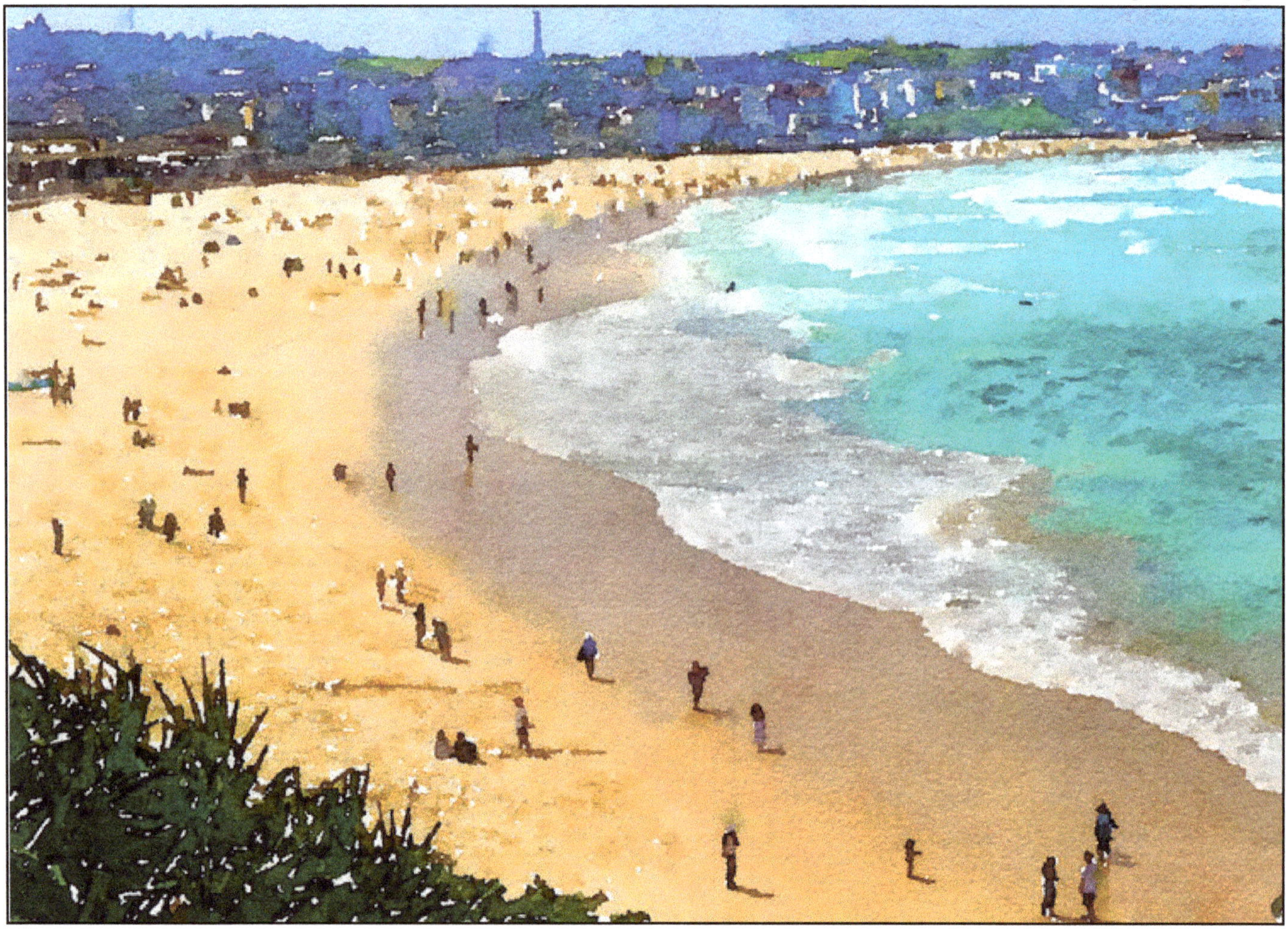

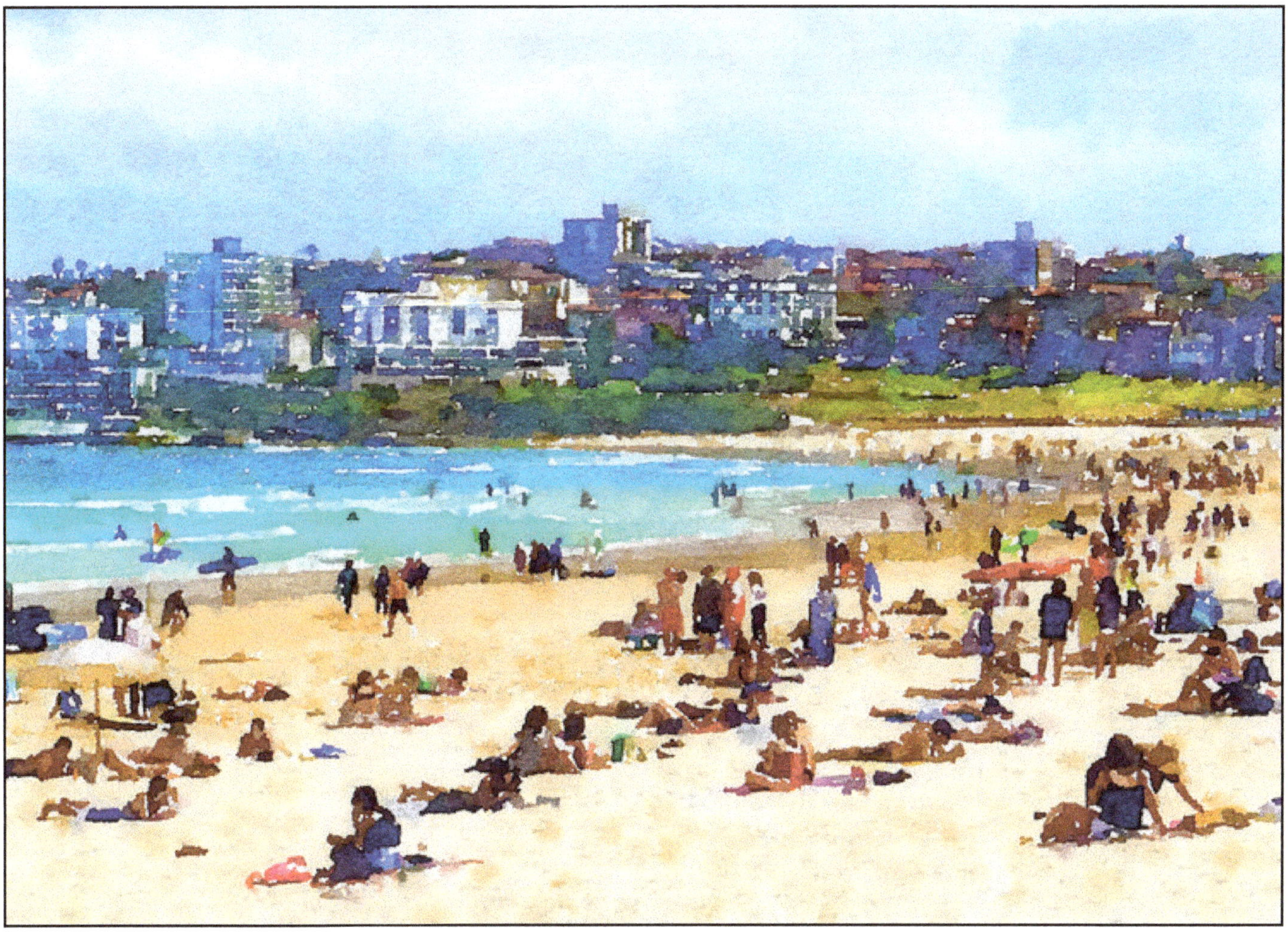

▲'The Sand Society' (2019), Bondi Beach, NSW [ASBB1911].

'Sun, Sand & Sea' (2020), Bondi Beach, NSW [ASBB2003].▼

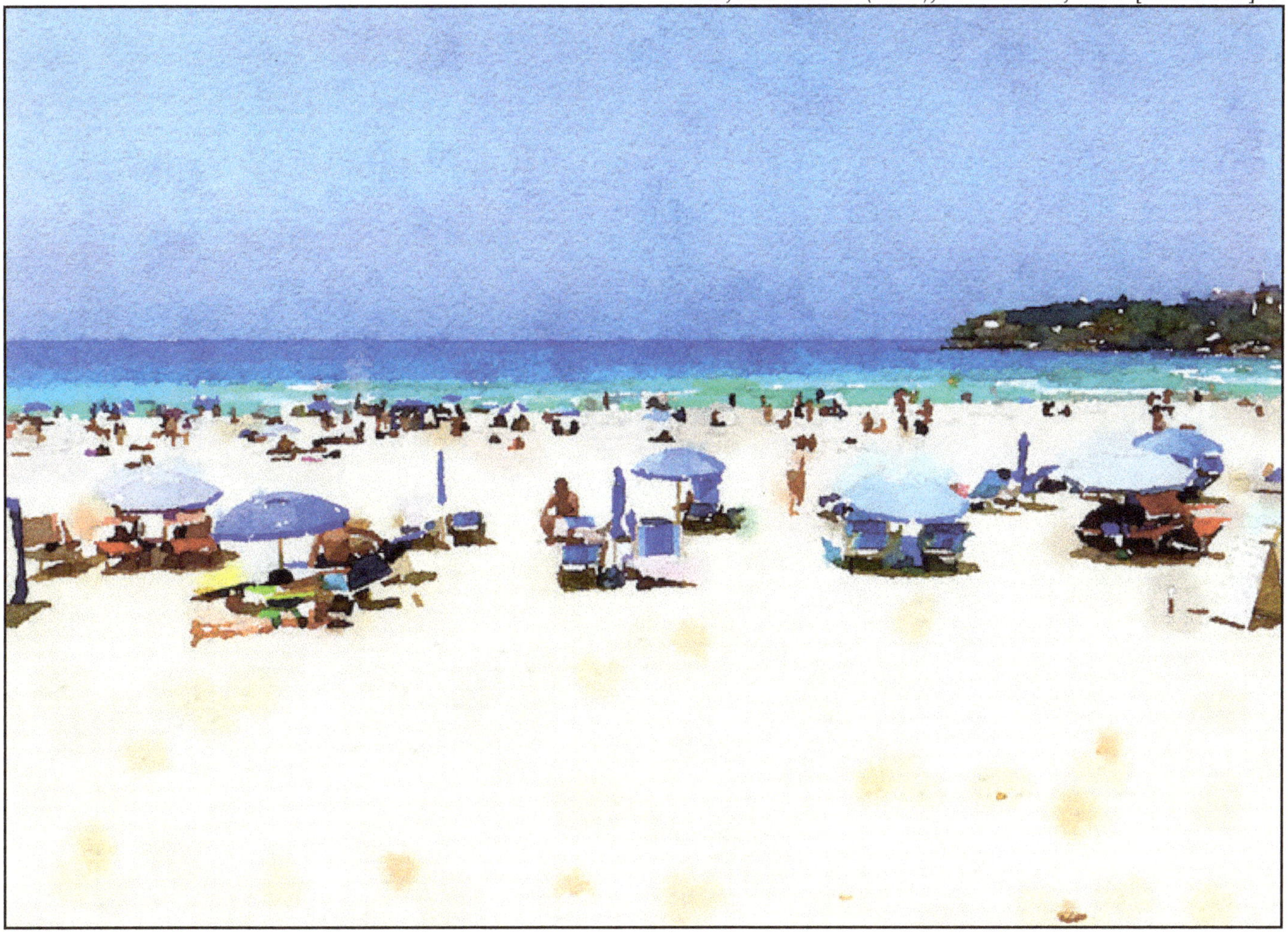

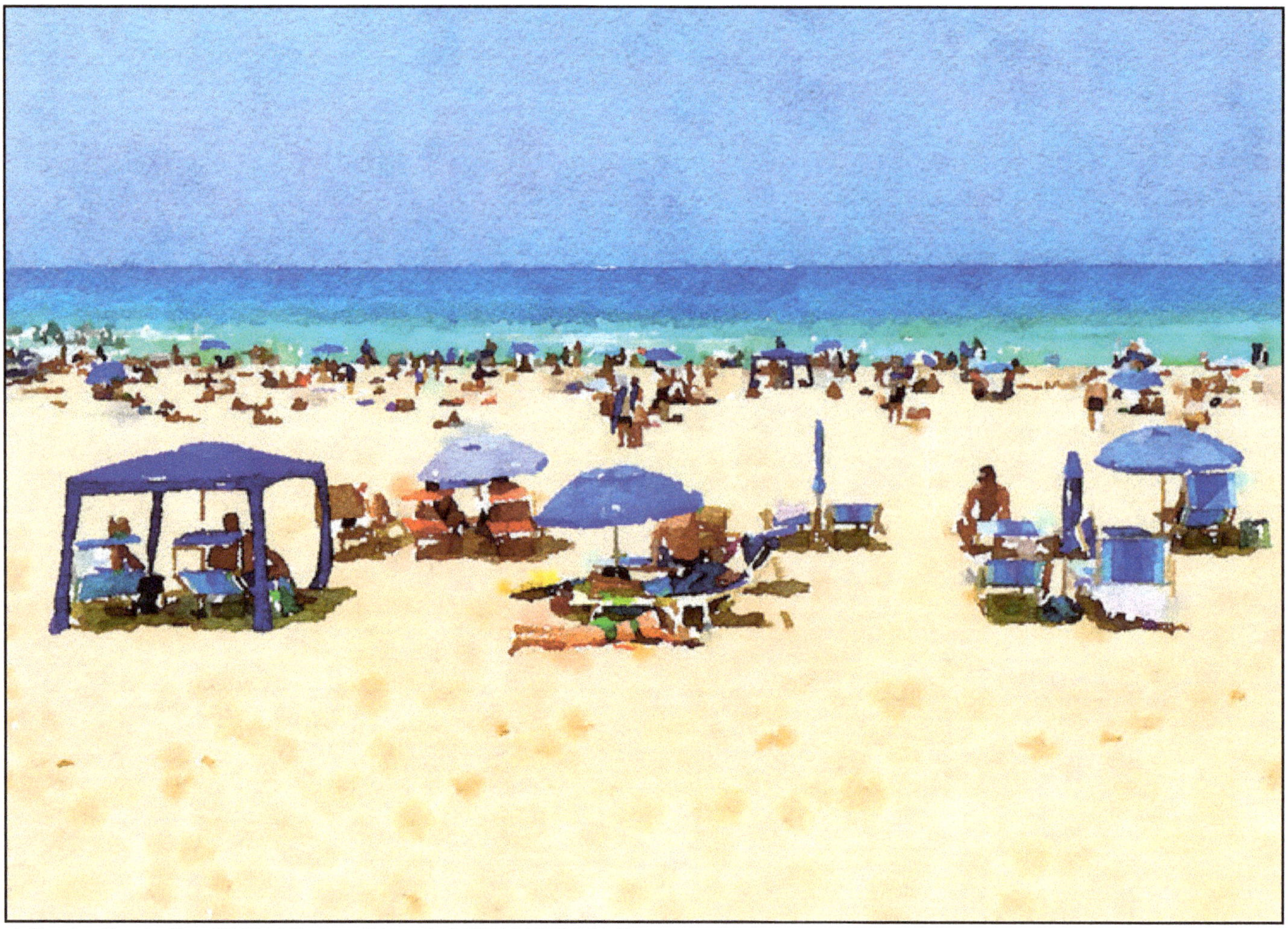

▲'Sunbrellas At Bondi' (2020), Bondi Beach, NSW [ASBB2001].

'Searching for Space' (2020), Bondi Beach, NSW [ASBB2002].▼

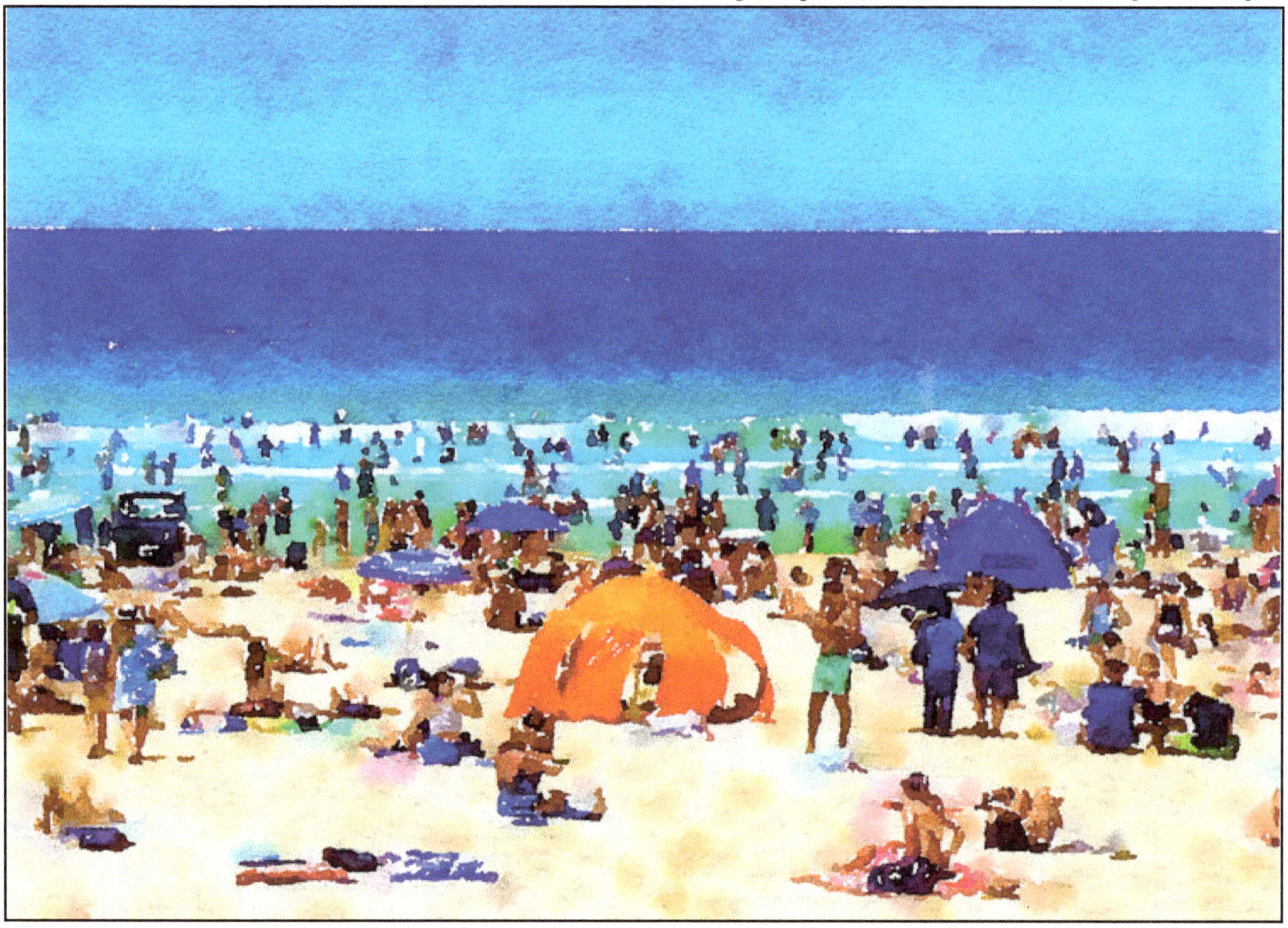

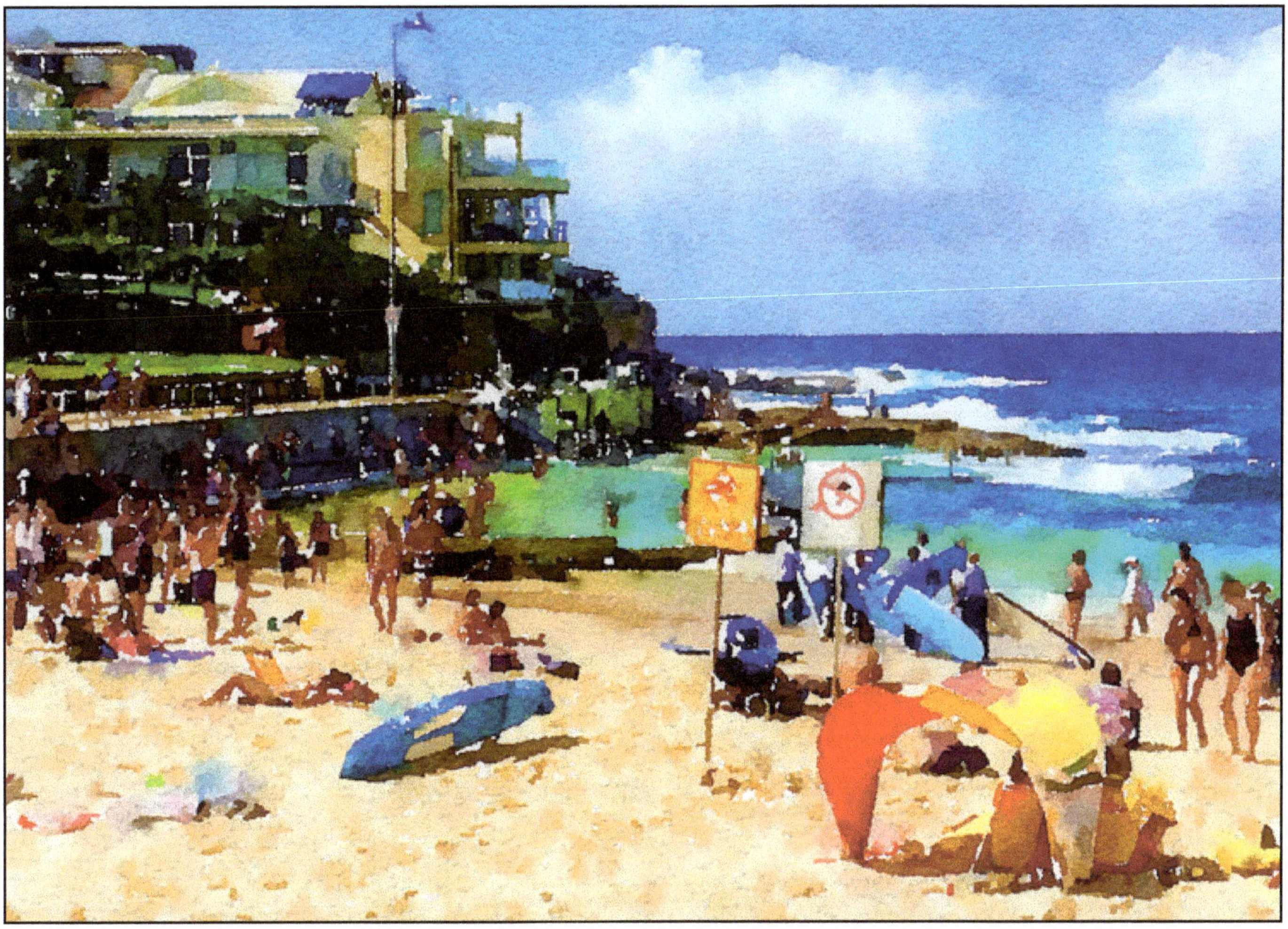

▲'Saltwater Fixes Everything' (2016), Bondi Beach, NSW [ASBB1601].

'Bondi Break' (2020), Bondi Beach, NSW [ASBB2004].▼

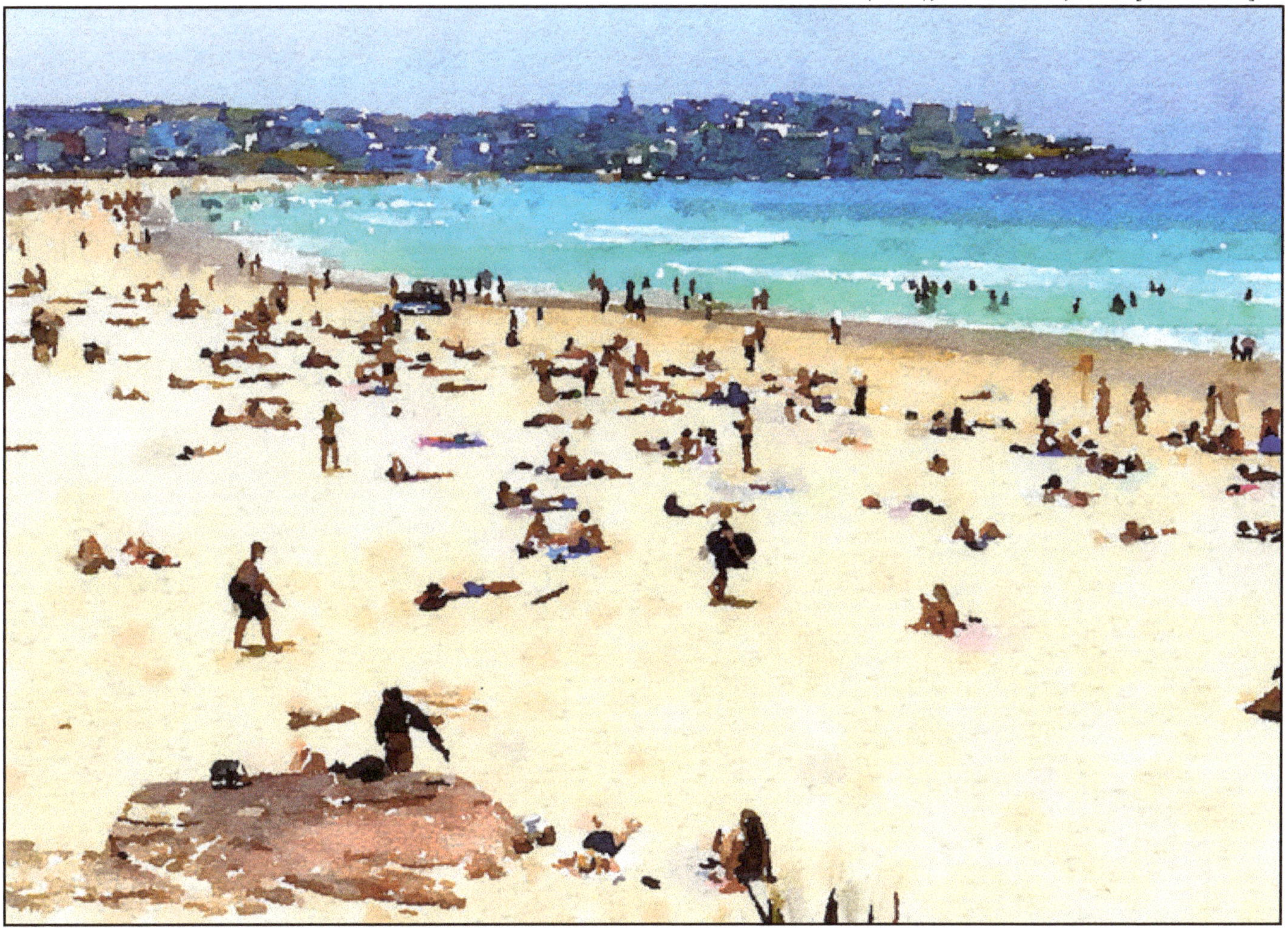

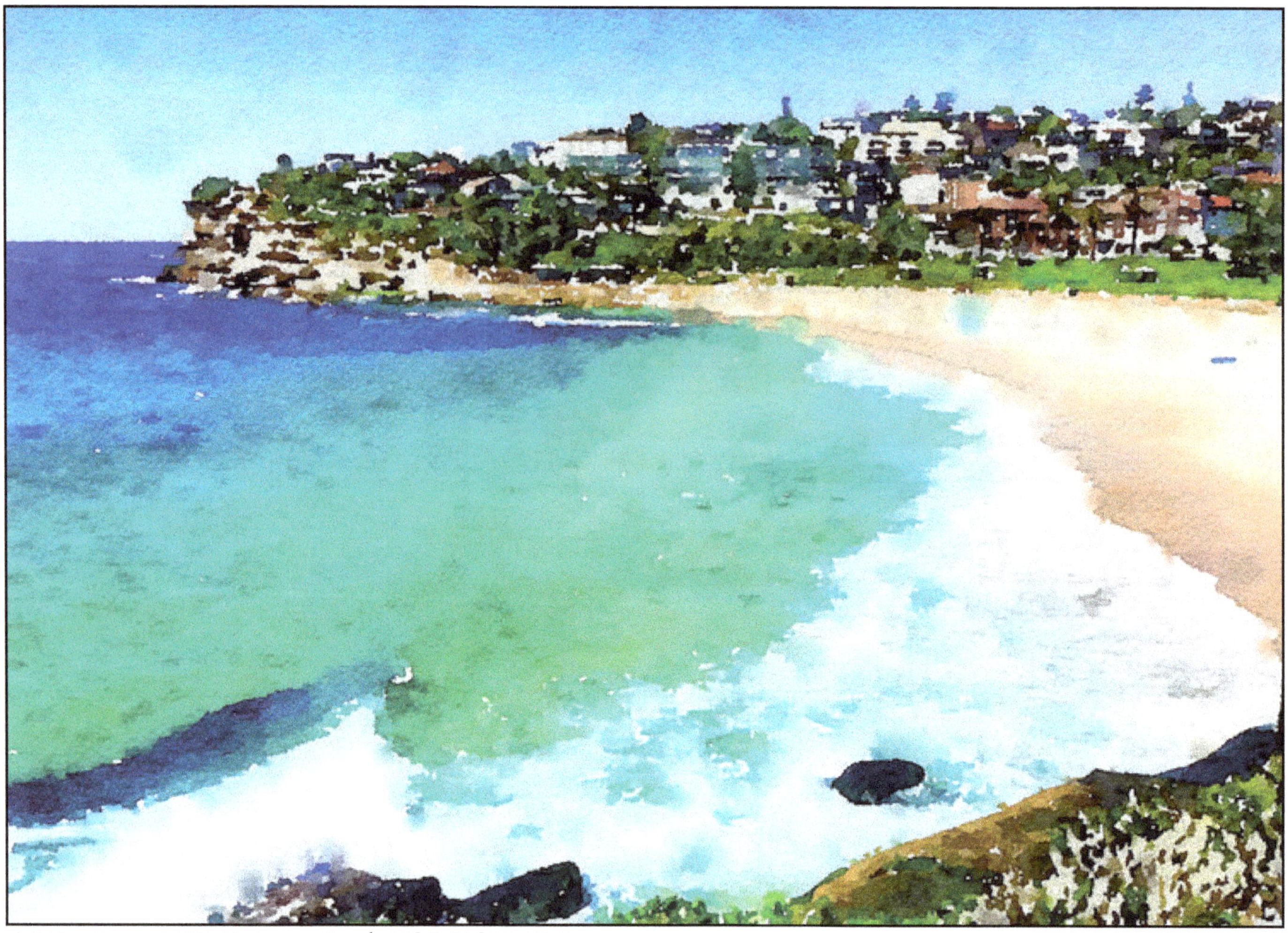

▲'Briny Bronte' (2020), Bronte Beach, NSW [ASBR2001].

'Morning At Bronte' (2019), Bronte Beach, NSW [ASBR1901].▼

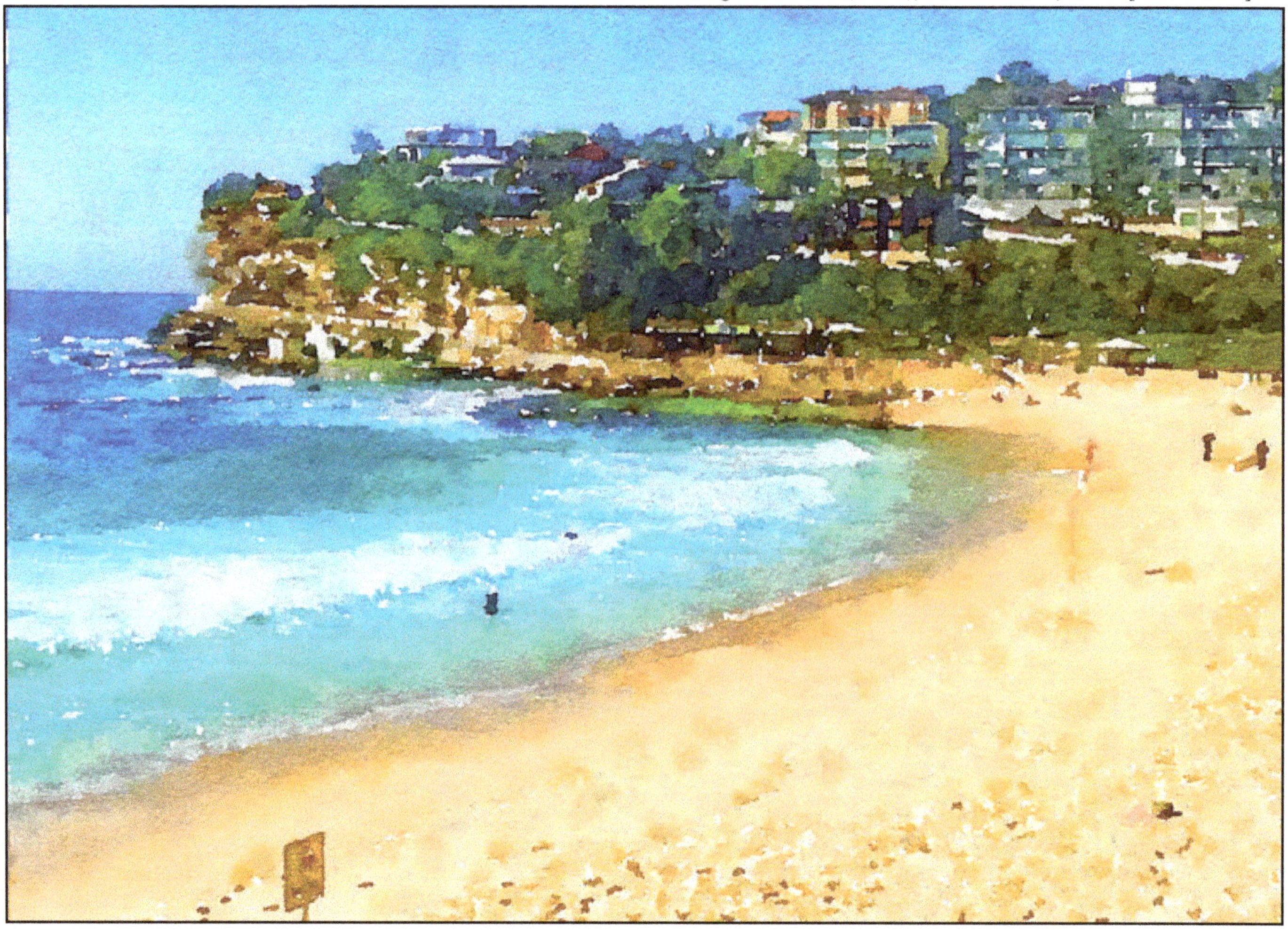

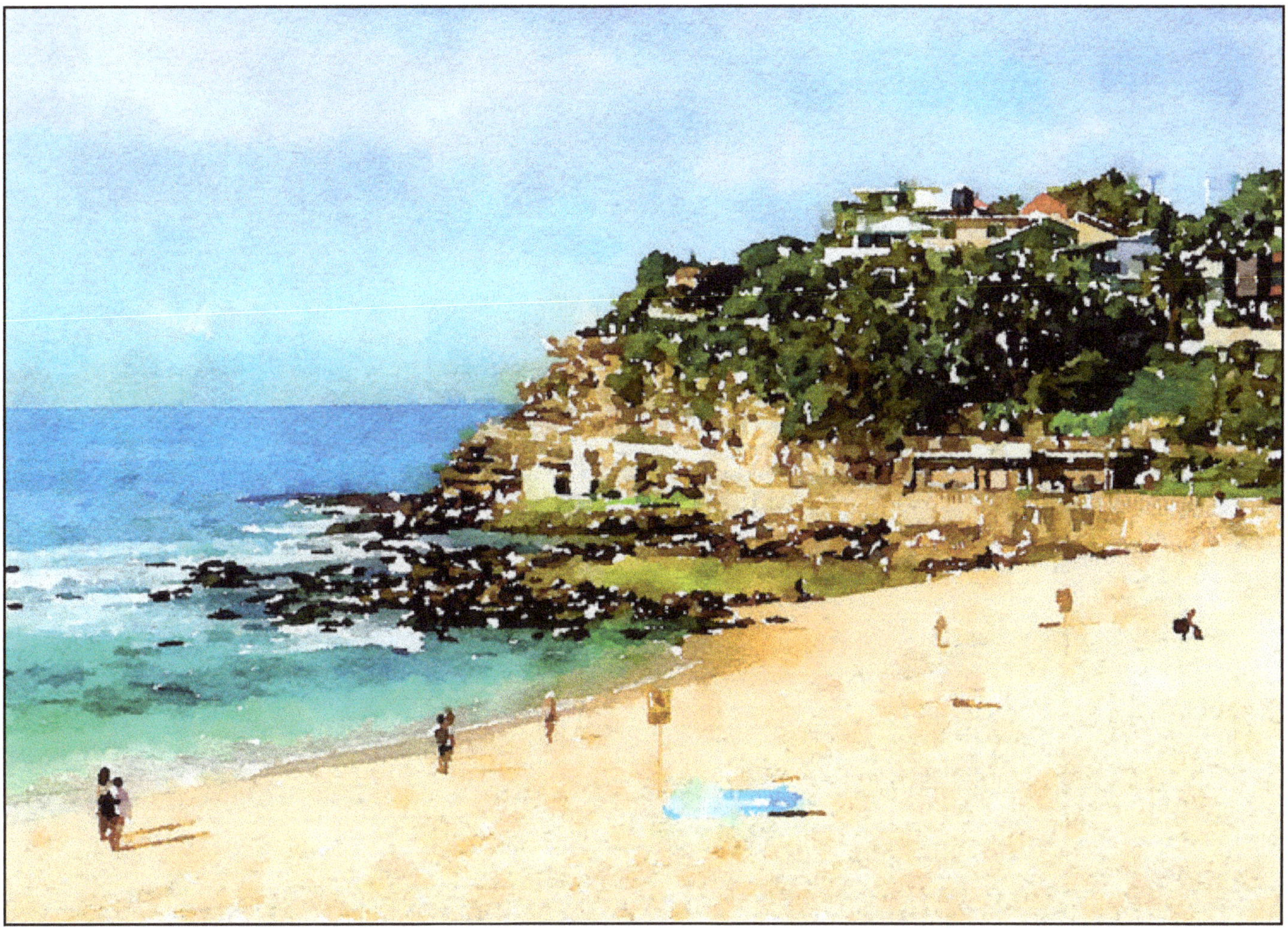

▲'Low Tide At Bronte' (2017), Bronte Beach, NSW [ASBR1701].

'Serenity' (2019), Bronte Beach, NSW [ASBR1902].▼

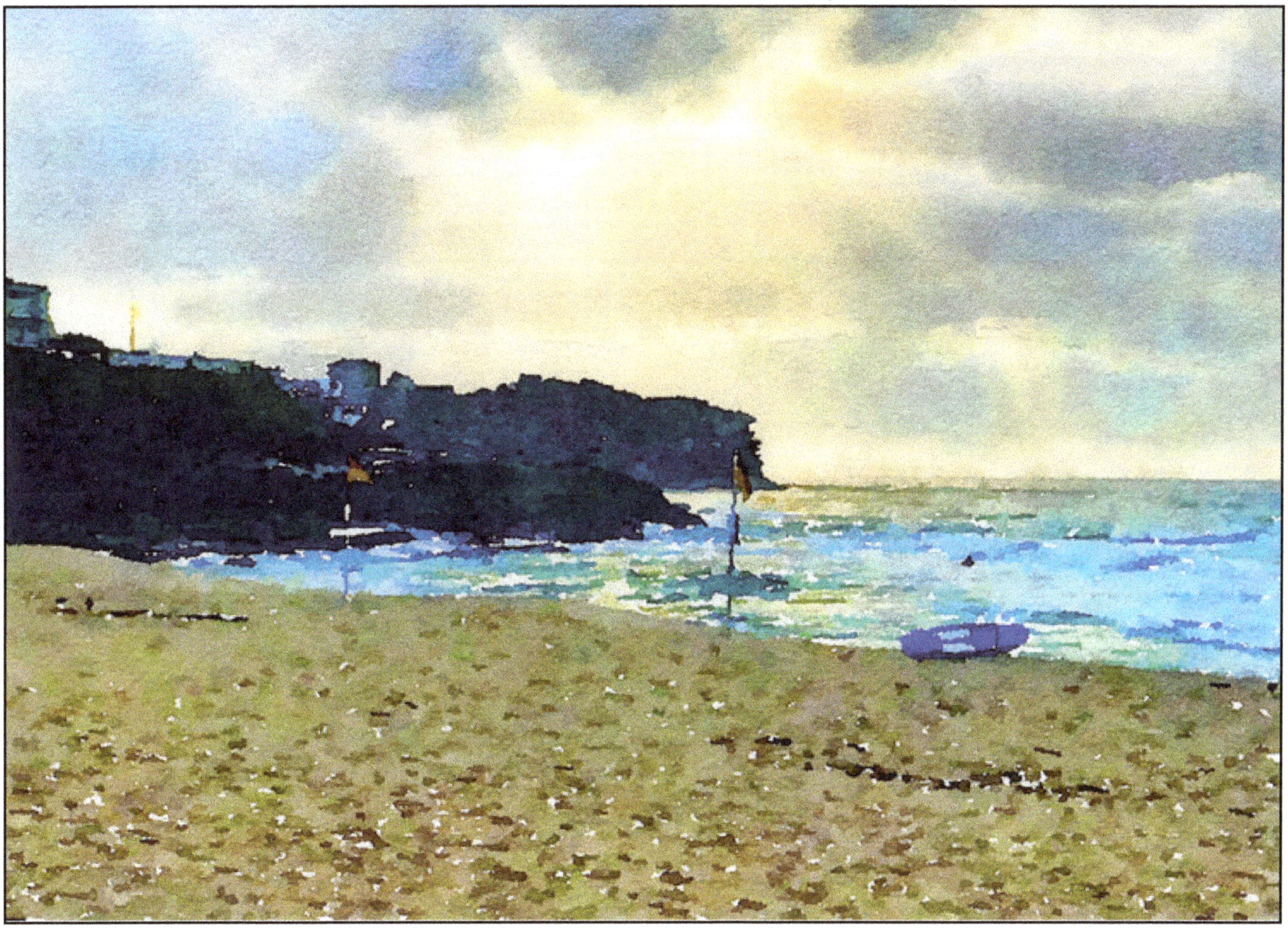

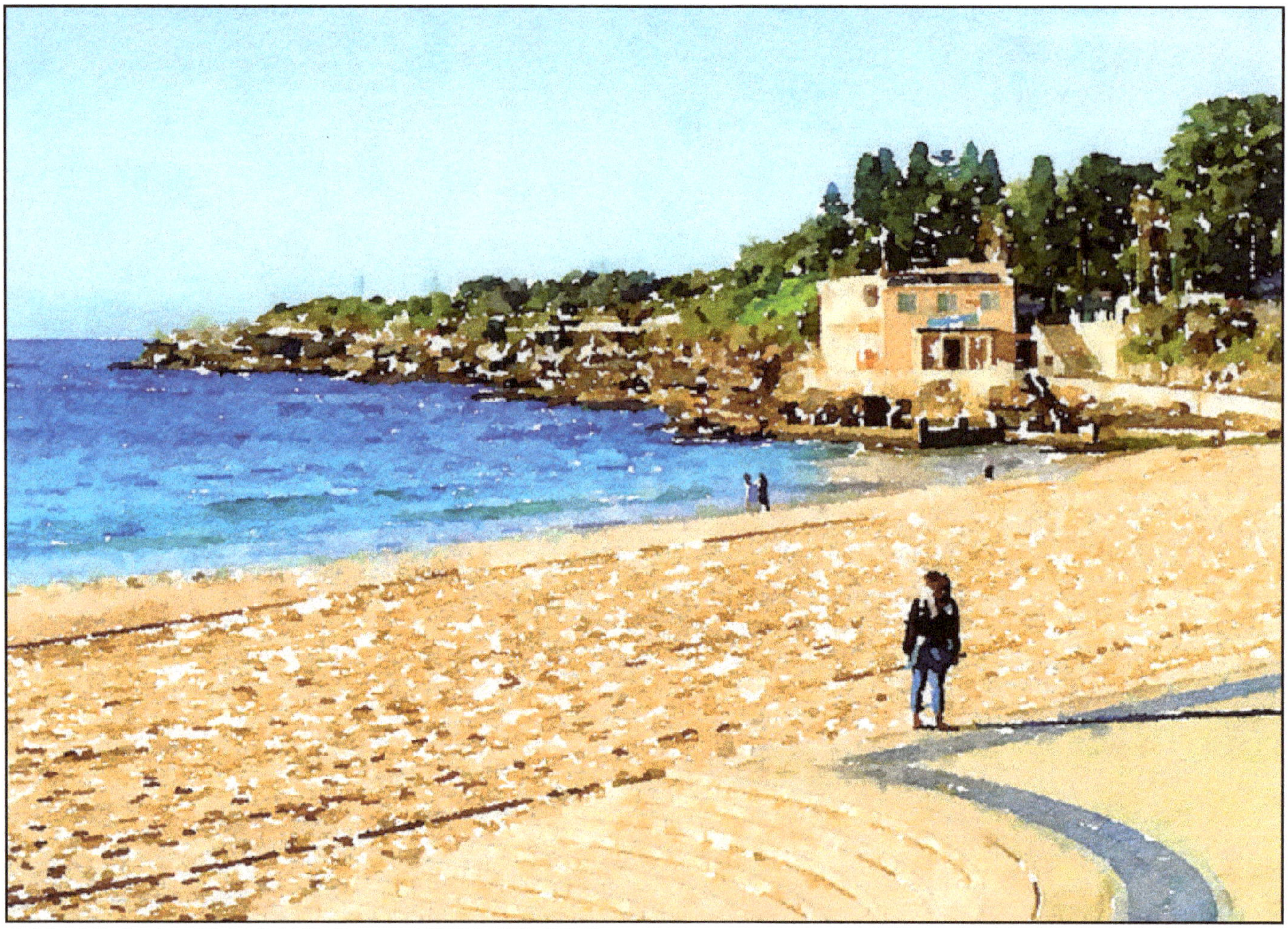

▲'The Life Saving Club' (2017), Coogee, NSW [ASCB1701].

'Coogee Beach Storm' (2021), Sydney, NSW [ASCB2101]. ⊘▼

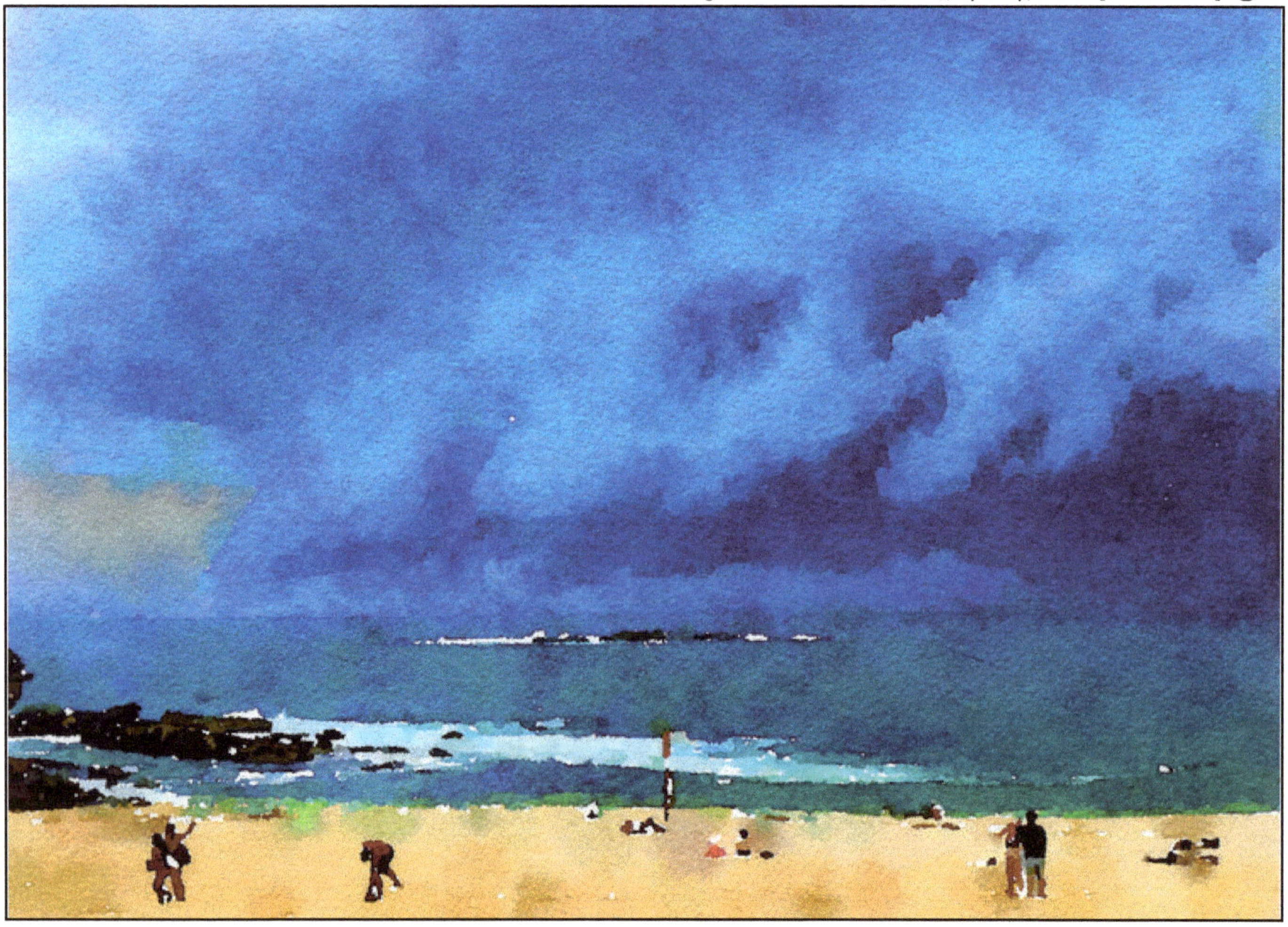

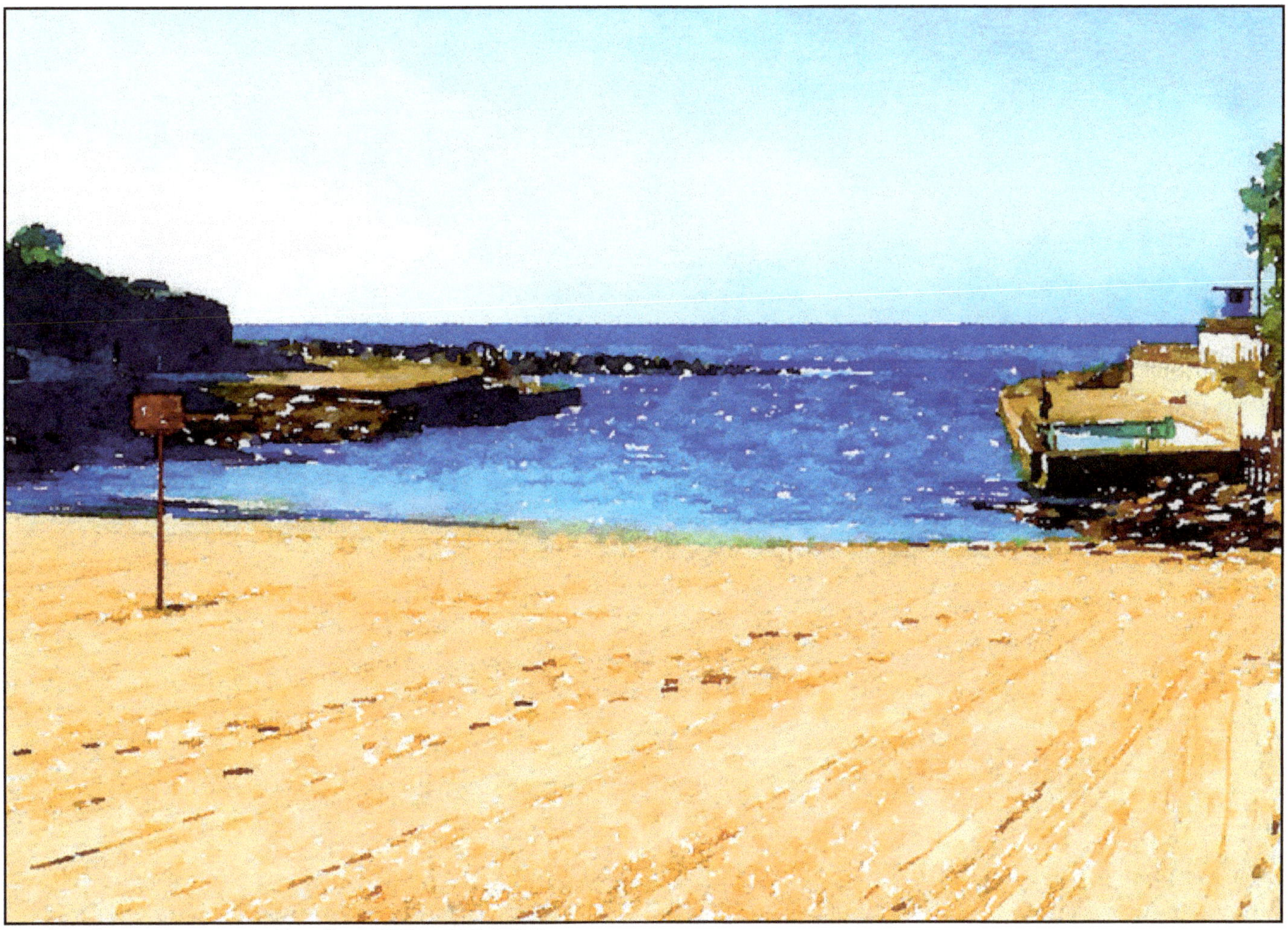

▲'Clovelly Beach' (2017), Clovelly, NSW [ASCL1701].

'Welcoming The Dawn' (2019), Clovelly, NSW [ASCL1901].▼

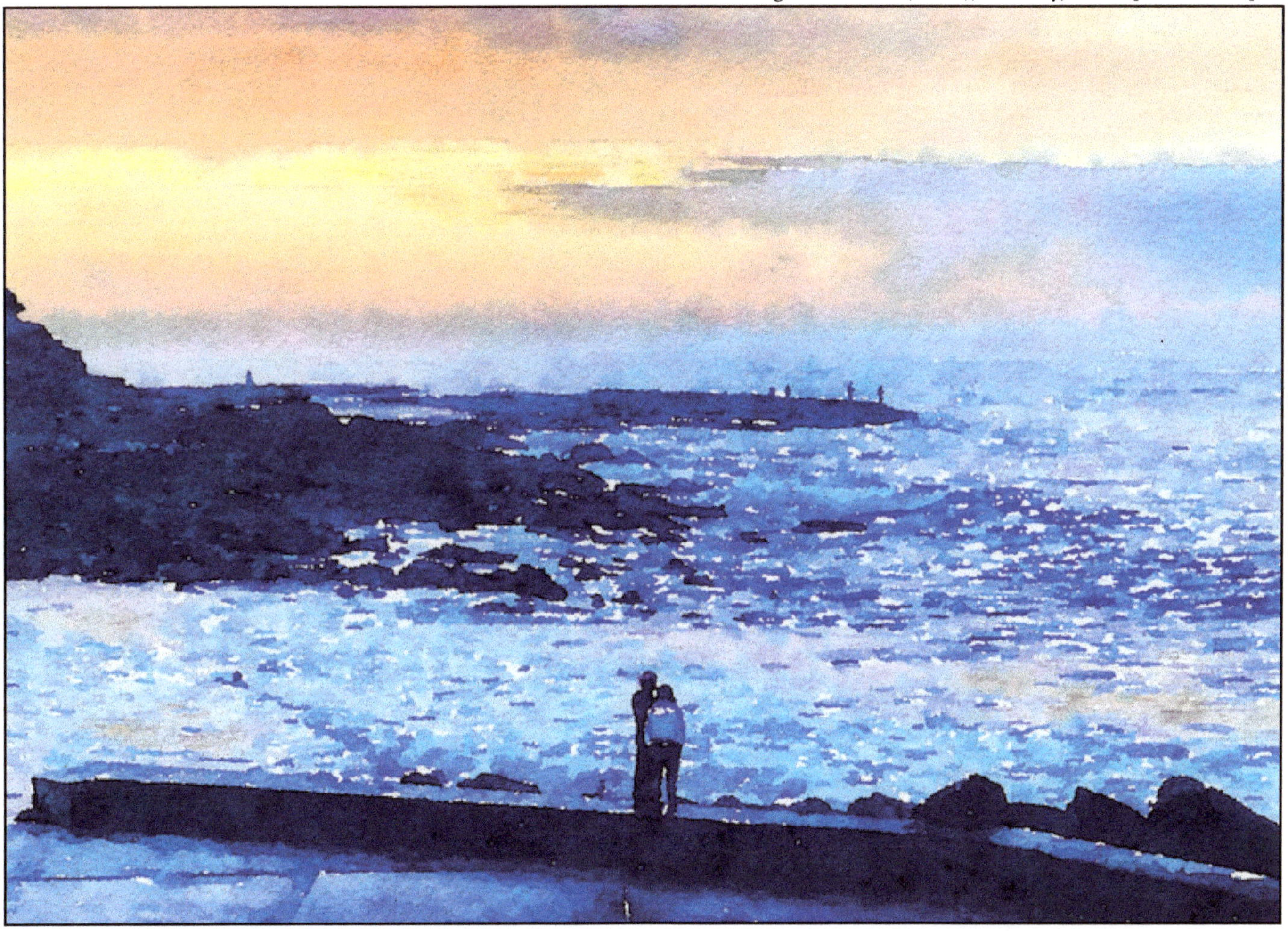

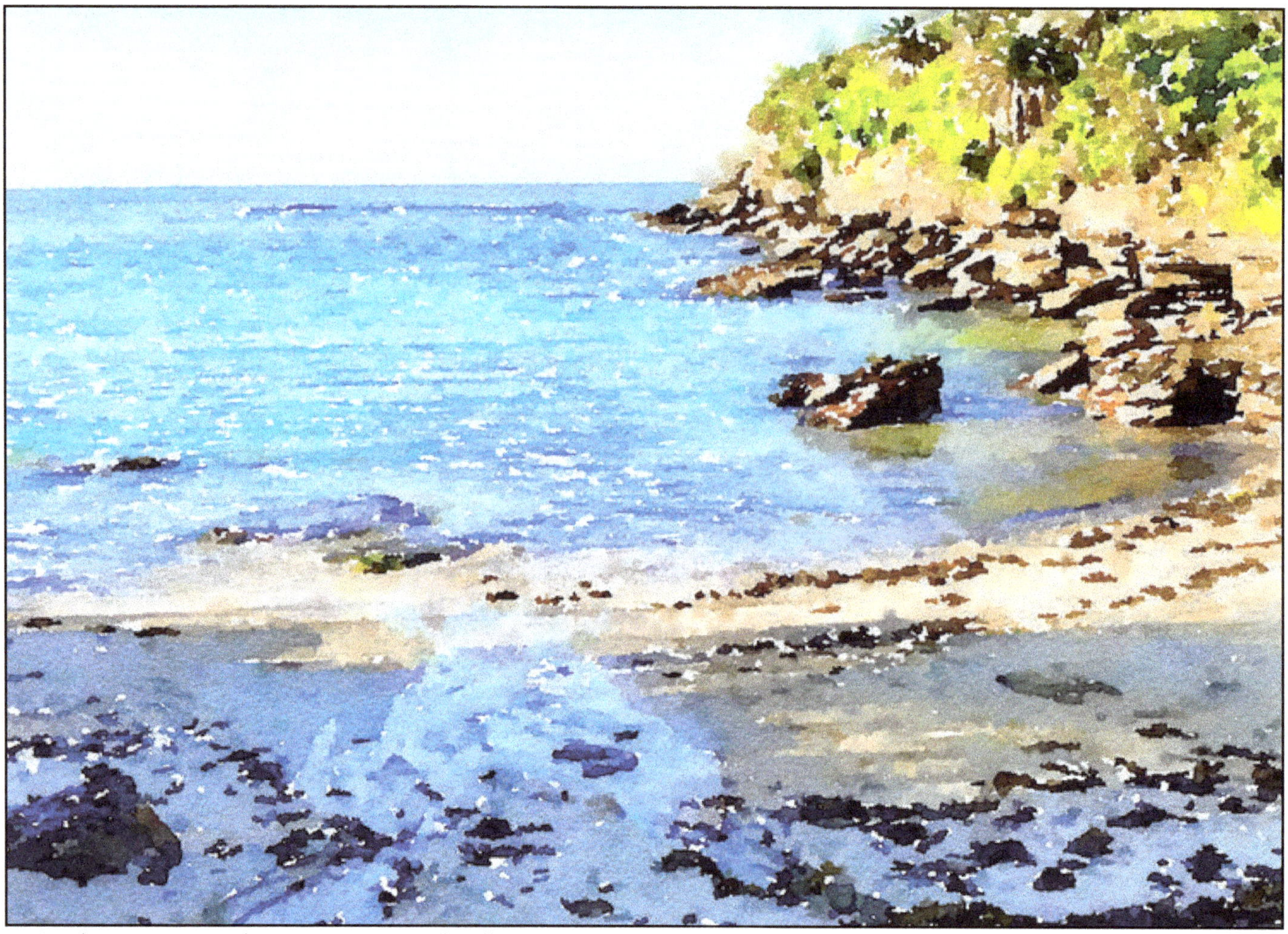

▲'Gordons Bay & Beach' (2017), Coogee-Clovelly, NSW [ASGB1701].

'Gordon's Bay' (2019), Coogee-Clovelly, NSW [ASGB1901].▼

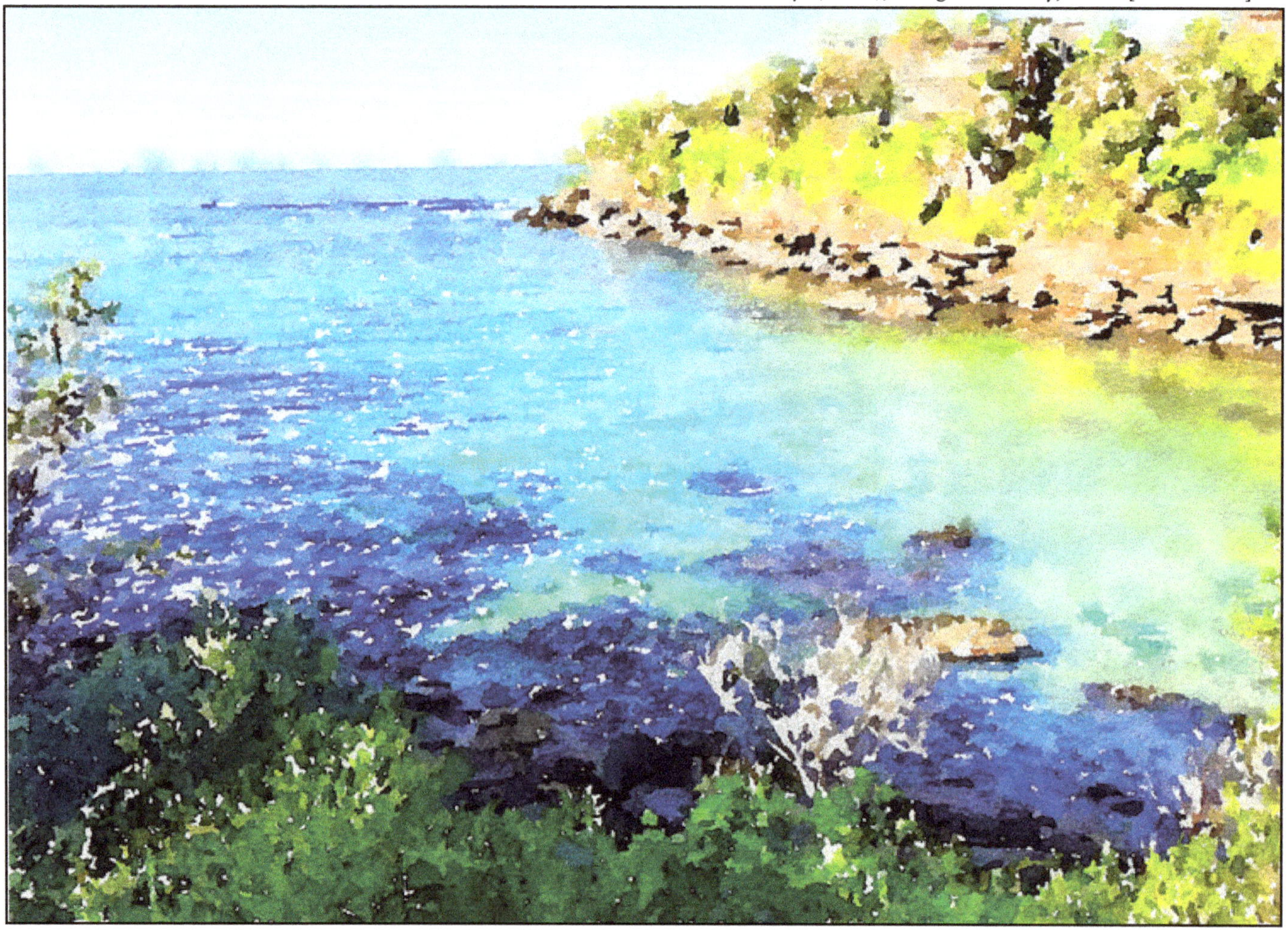

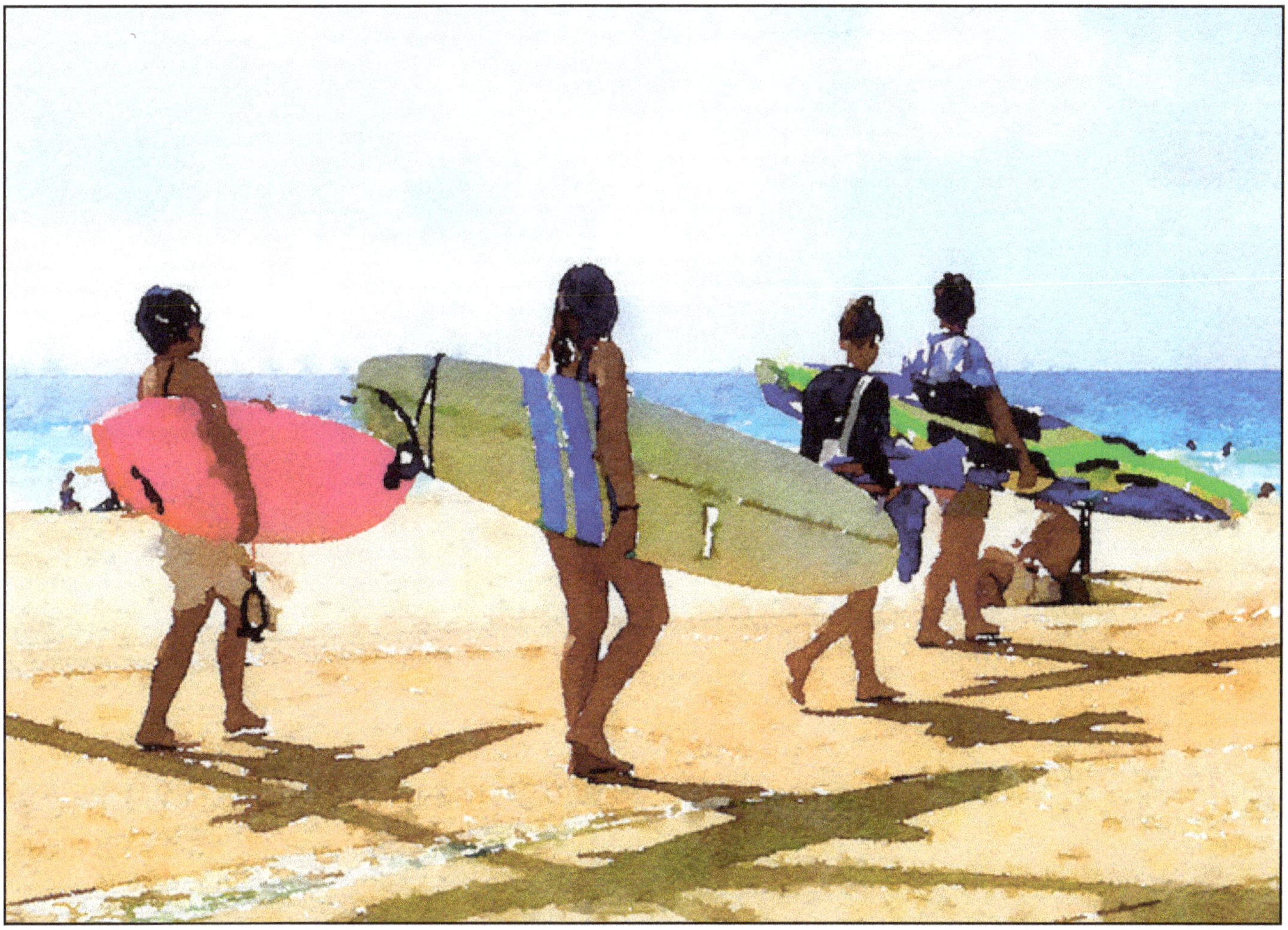

▲'Surfing The Promenade' (2018), Maroubra, NSW [ASMA1801].

'The Waves Of Change' (2018), Maroubra, NSW [ASMA1802].▼

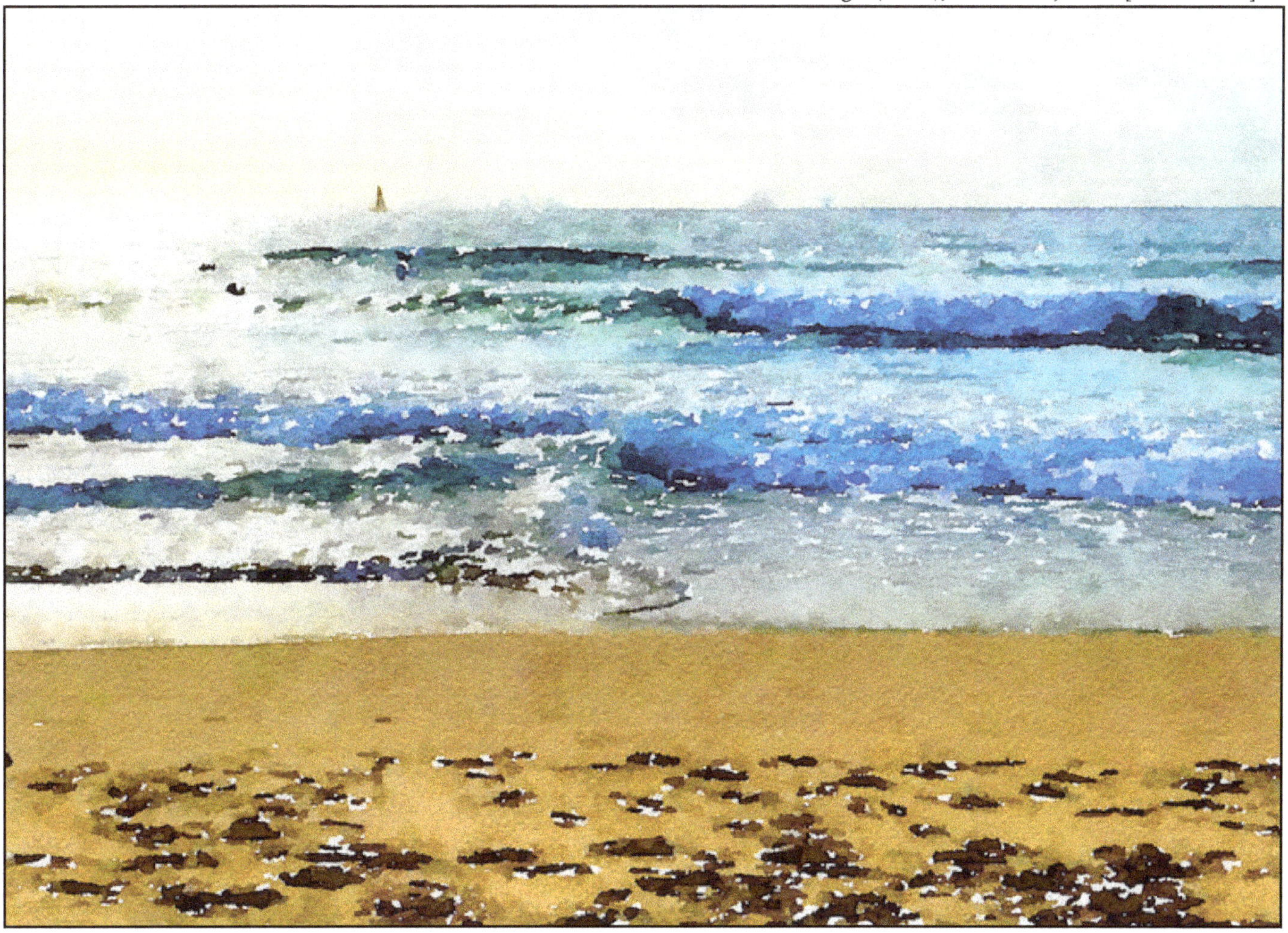

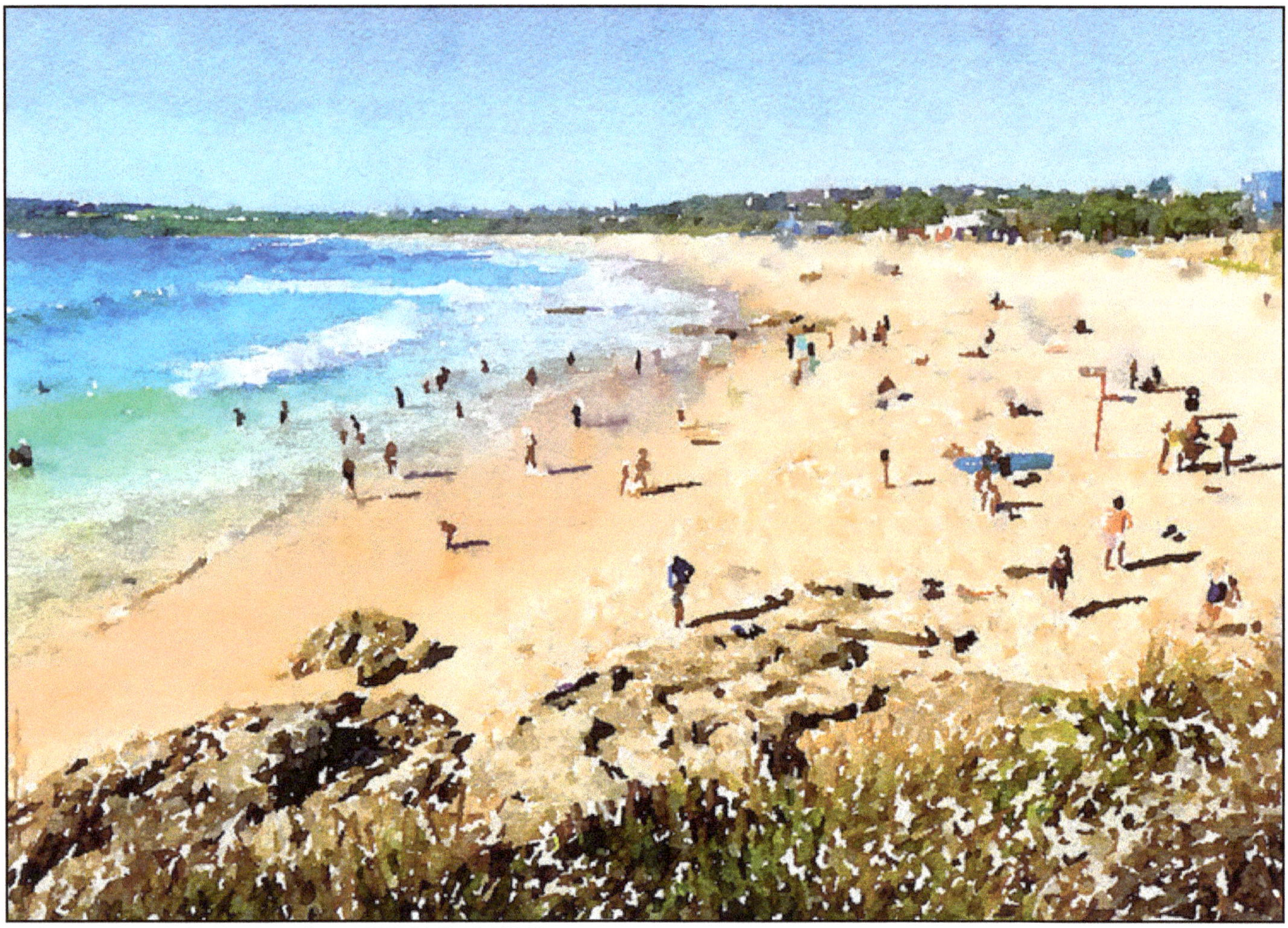

▲'A New Day' (2018), Maroubra, NSW [ASMA1803].

'The Mahon Pool' (2018), Maroubra, NSW [ASMA1806].▼

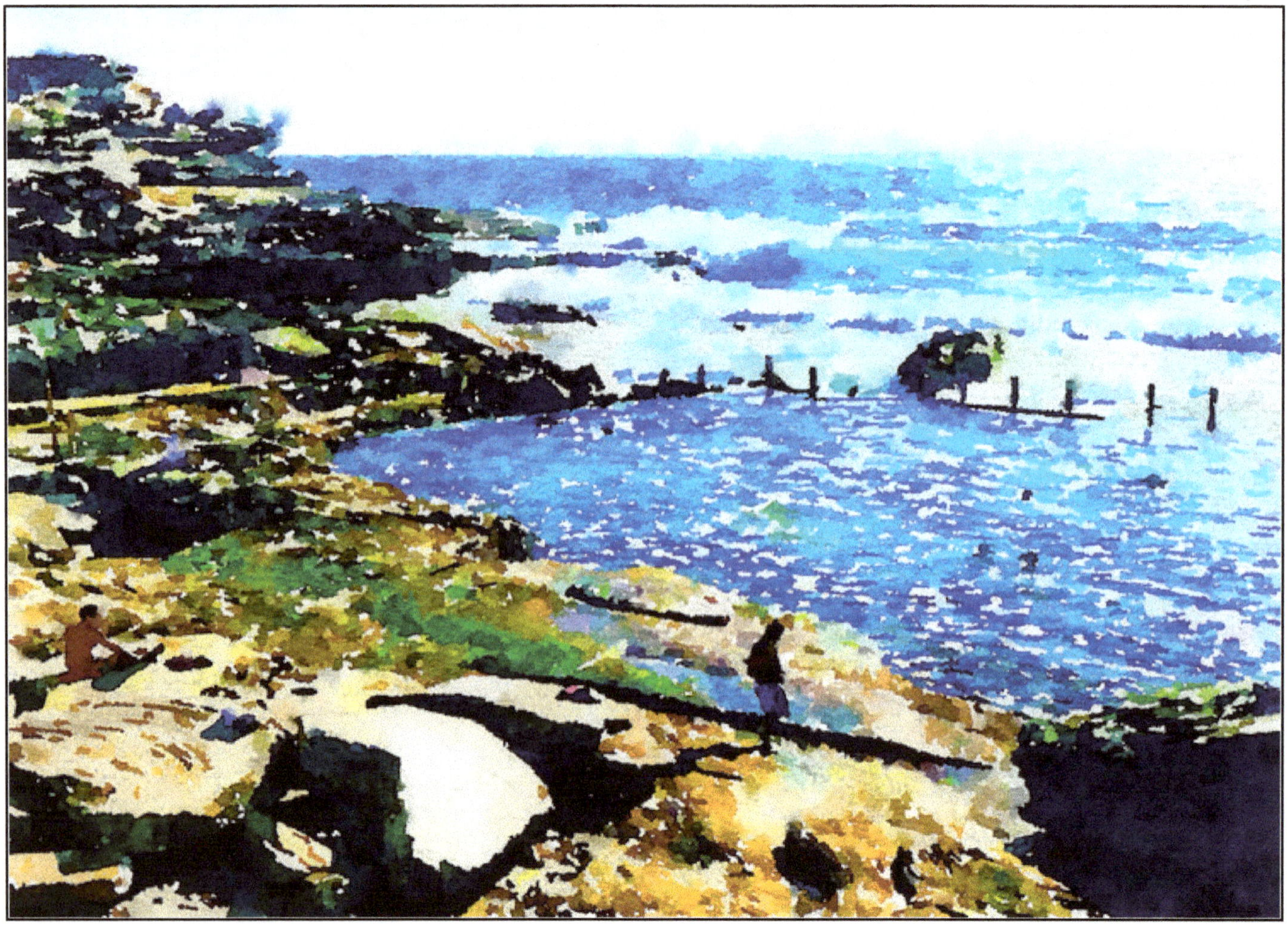

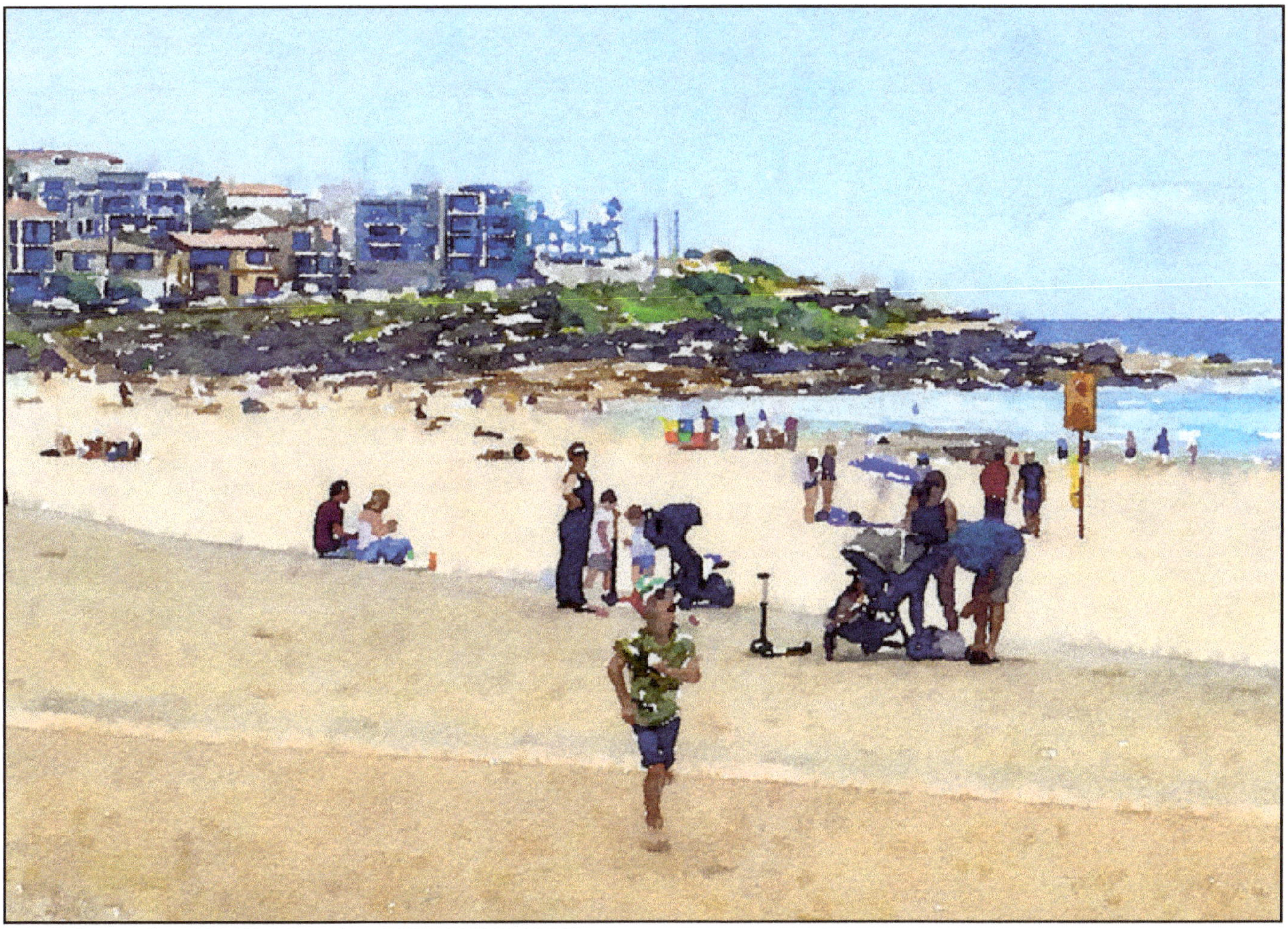

▲'Beach Breather' (2018), Maroubra, NSW [ASMA1805].

'Golden Sands' (2018), Maroubra, NSW [ASMA1804].▼

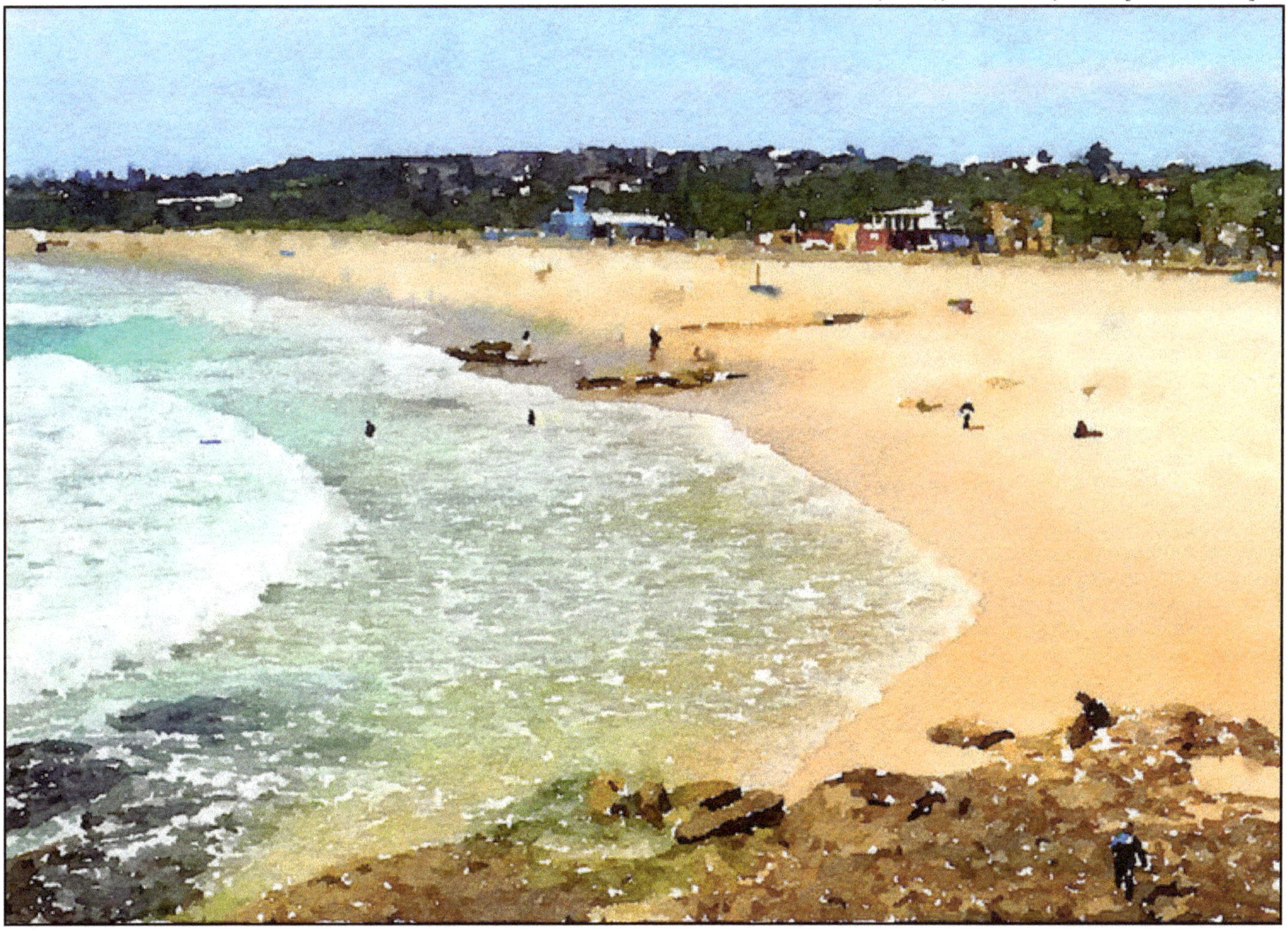

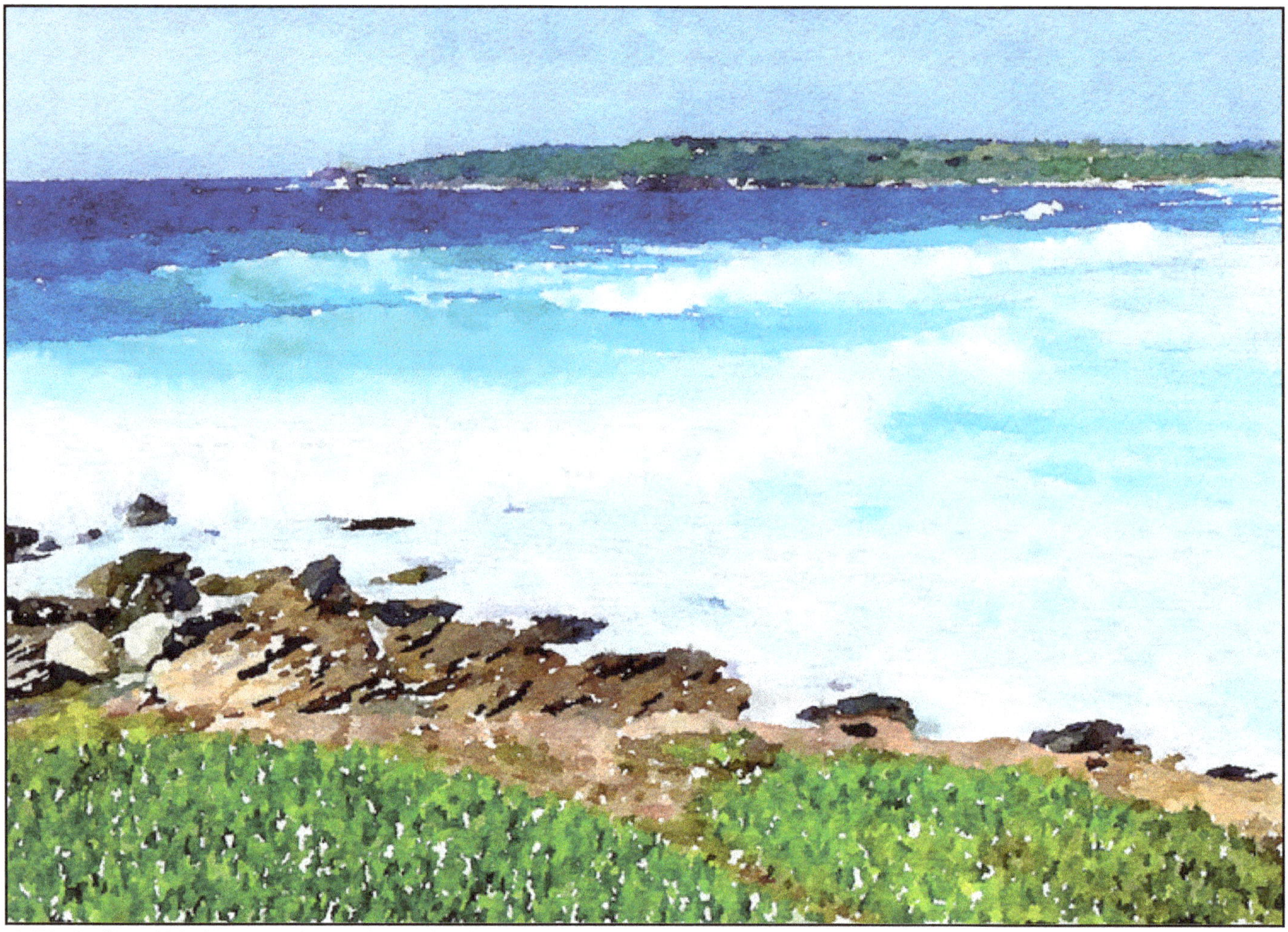

▲'Big Rollers' (2019), Maroubra, NSW [ASMA1901].

'Morning At The Mahon' (2019), Maroubra, NSW [ASMA1902].▼

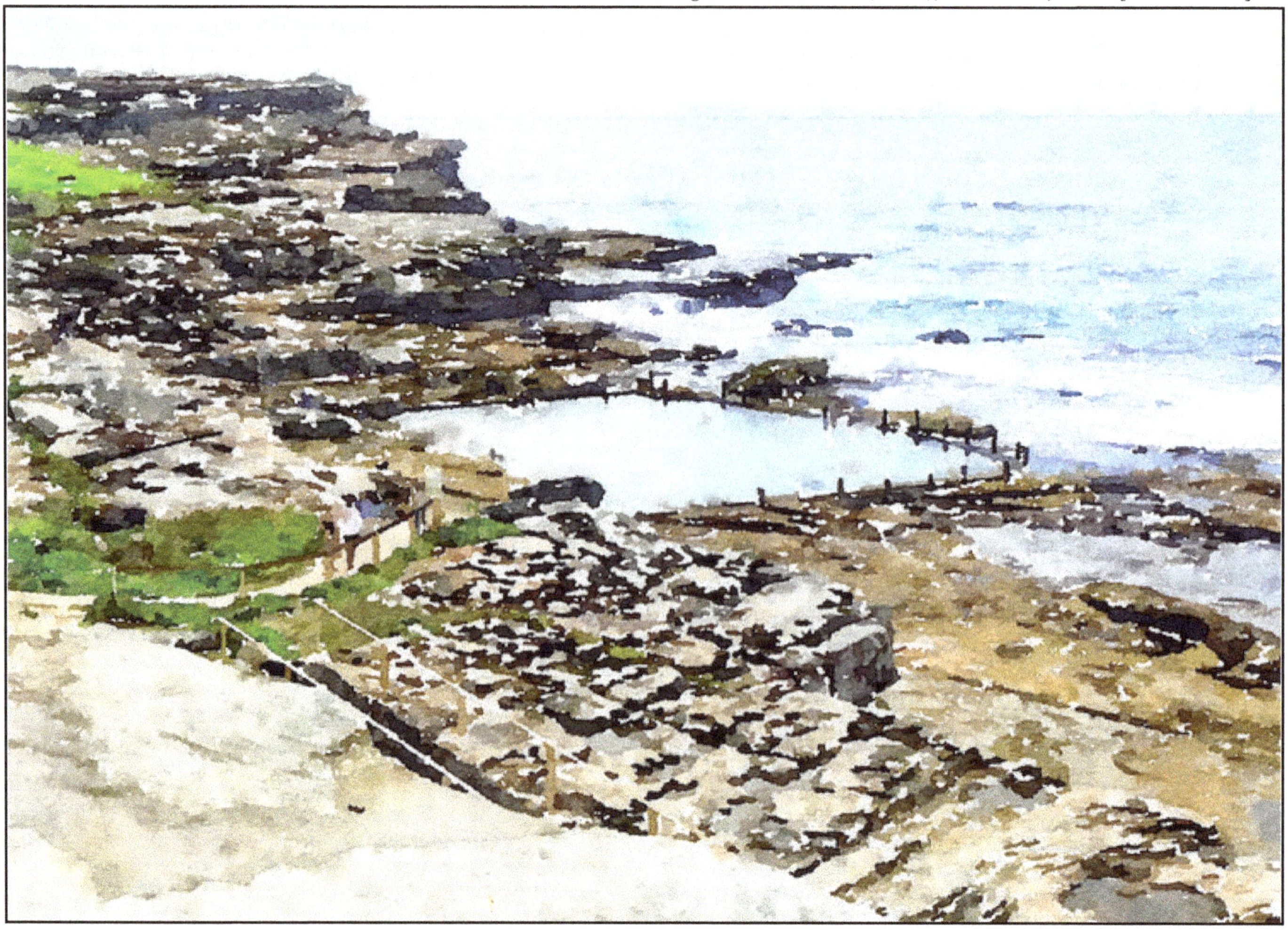

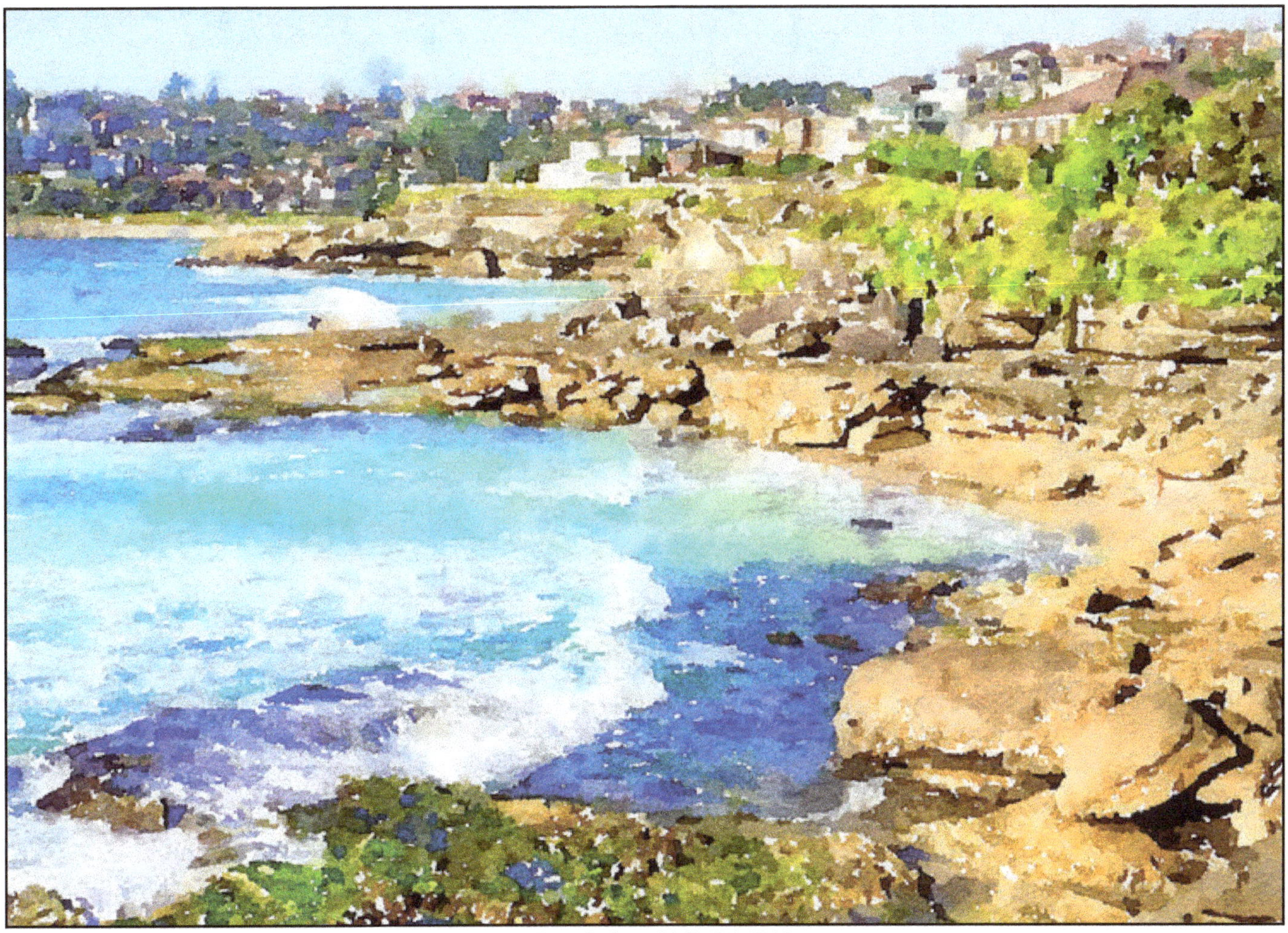

▲'The Unique MacKenzies Bay' (2015), MacKenzies Bay, Sydney [ASMB1501].

'Alone At MacKenzies' (2011), MacKenzies Bay, Sydney [ASMB1502].▼

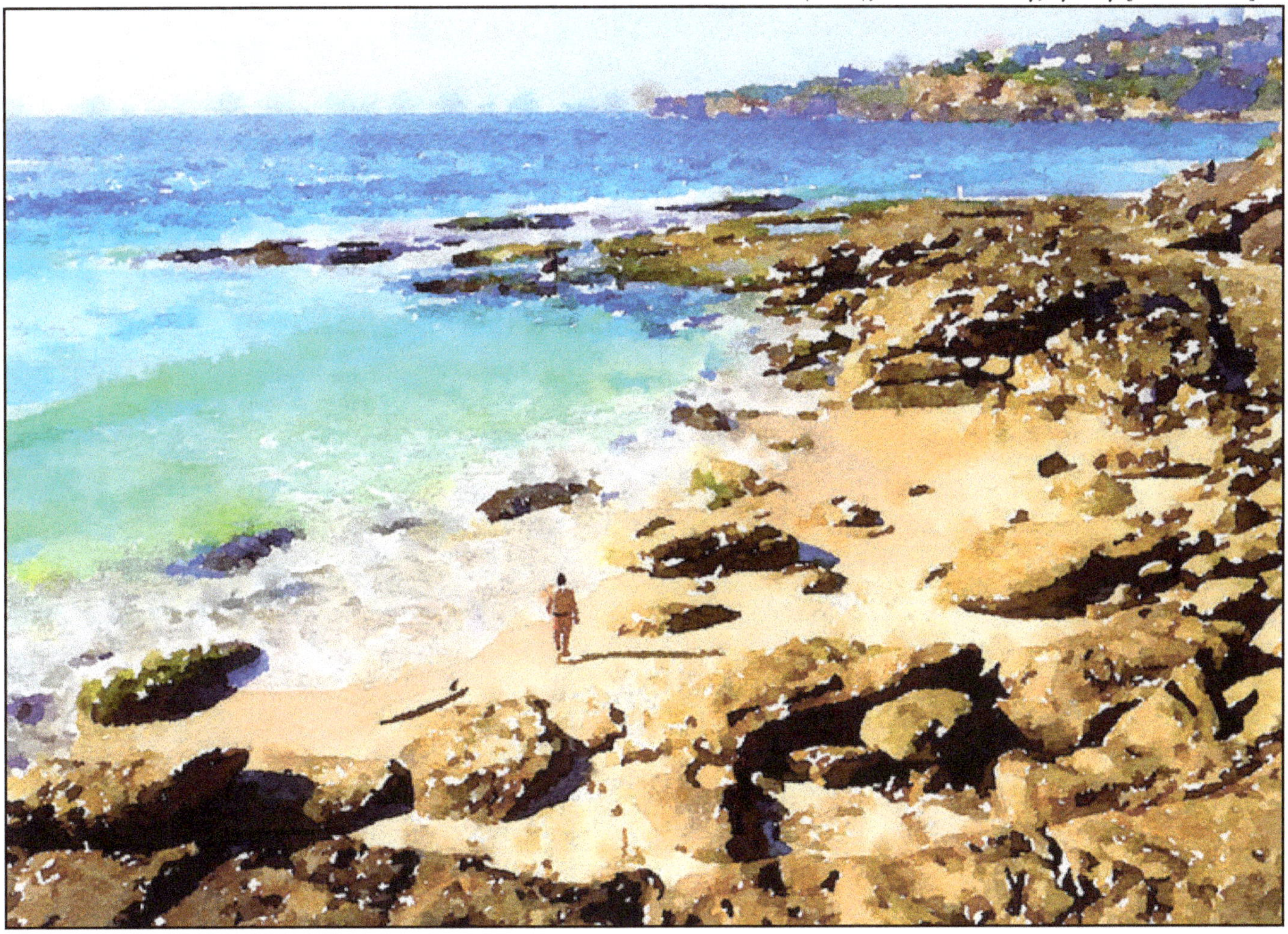

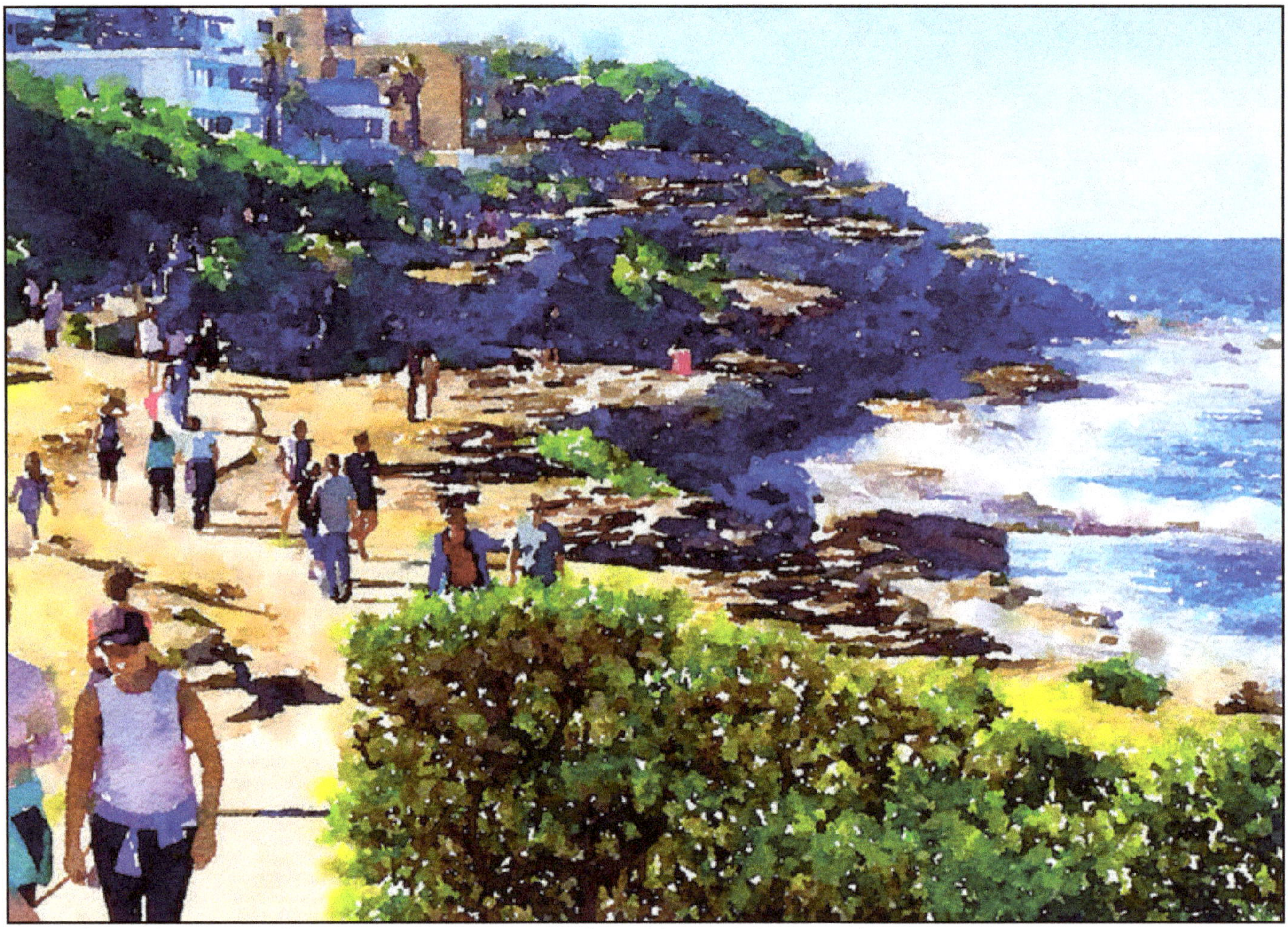

▲'On the Bondi-Bronte Walk' (2015), MacKenzies Bay, Sydney [ASMB1503].

'MacKenzies Break' (2019), MacKenzies Bay, Sydney [ASMB1901].▼

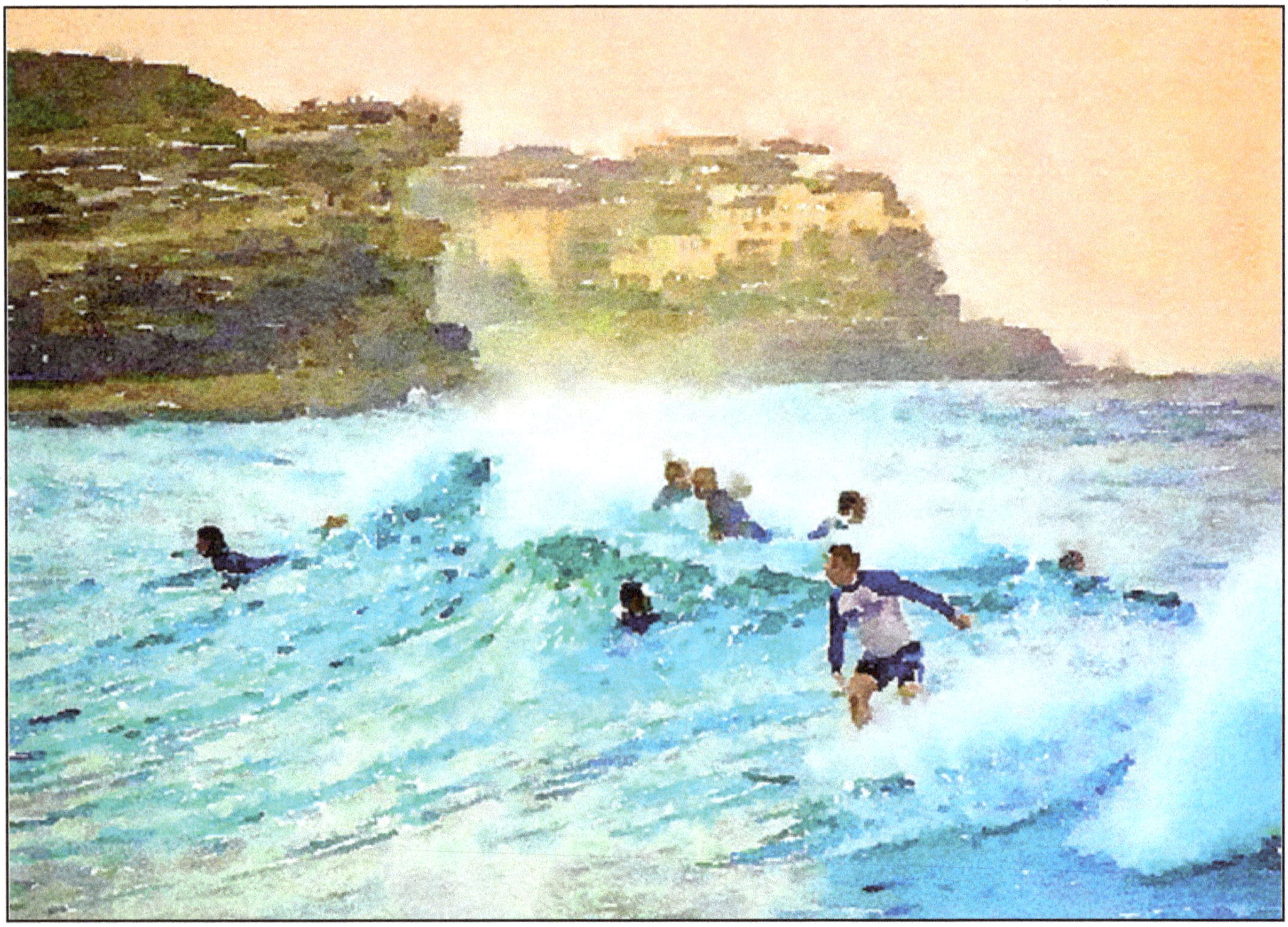

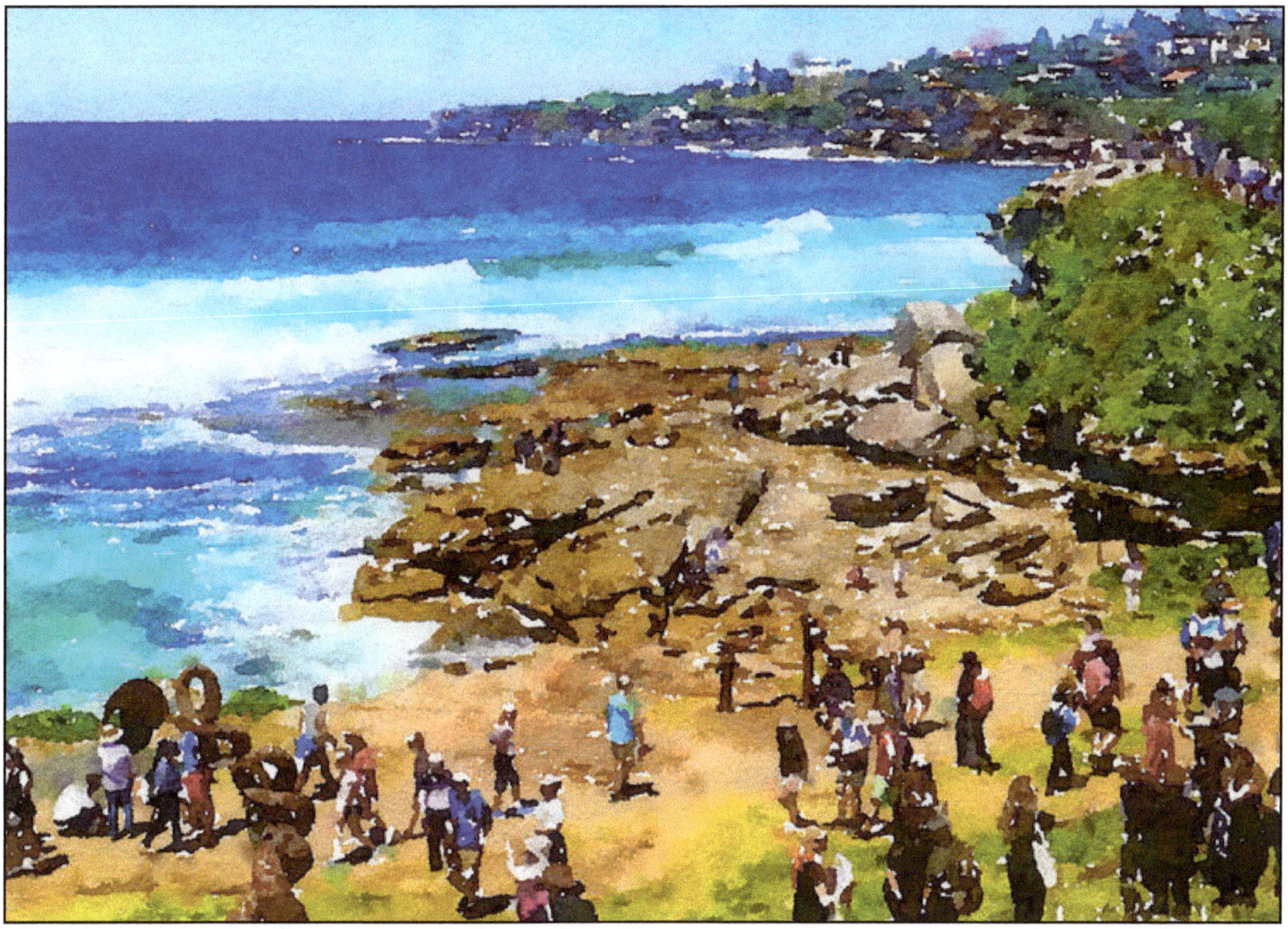

▲'Paradise Found' (2019), MacKenzies Bay, Sydney [ASMB1902].

'The Return Of MacKenzies' (2020), MacKenzies Bay, Sydney [ASMB2001].▼

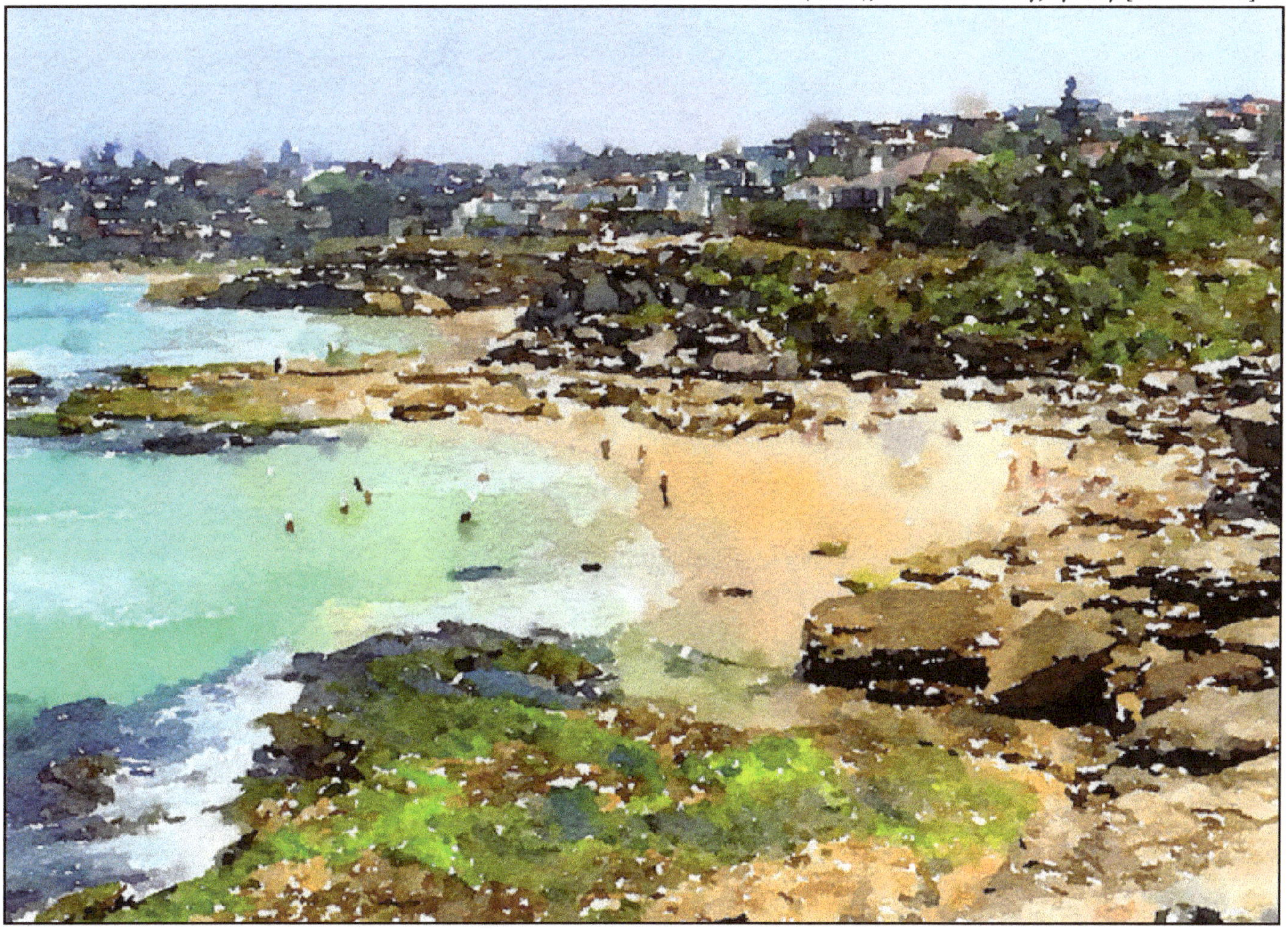

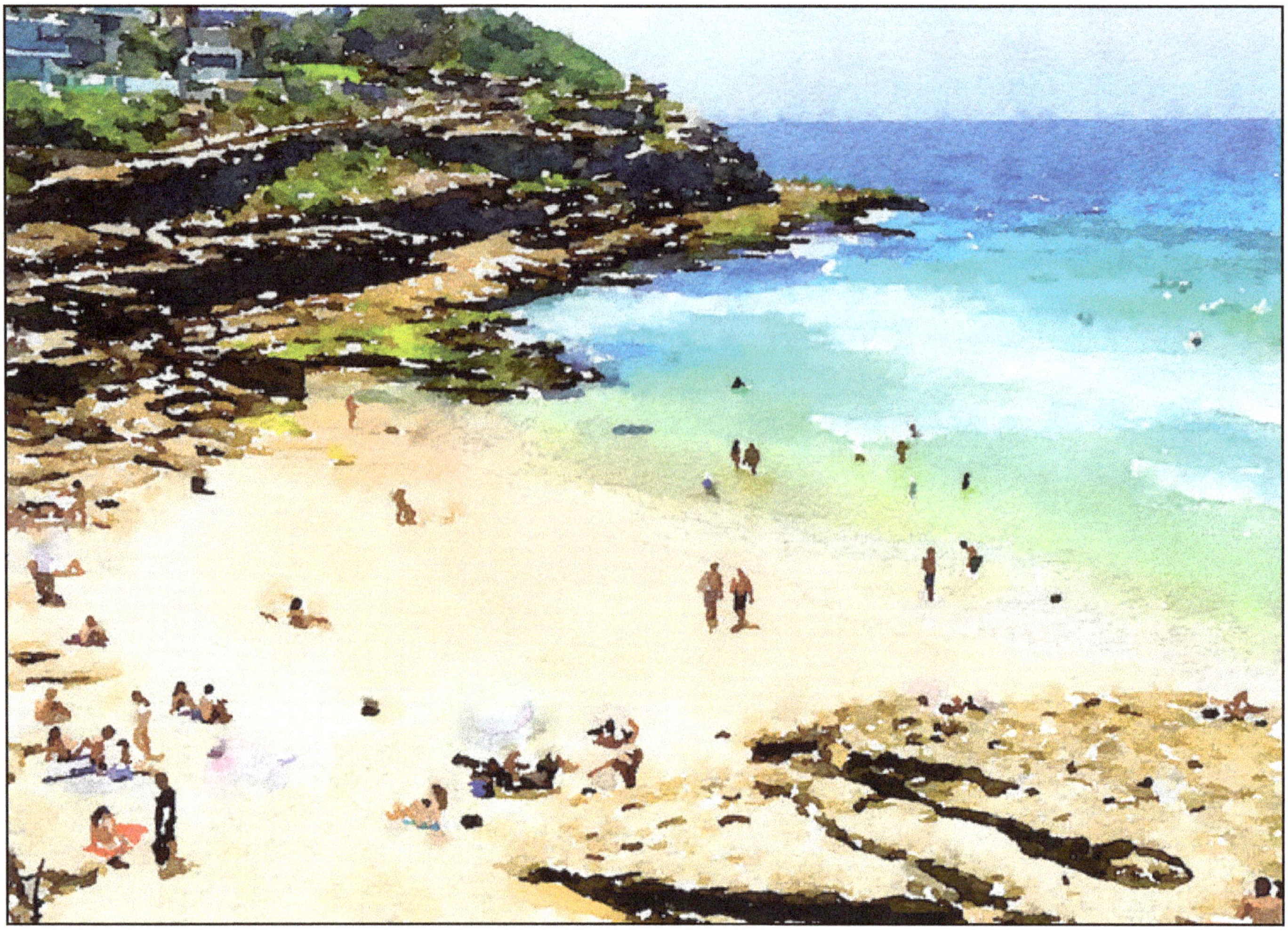

▲'MacKenzies Beach 1' (2020), MacKenzies Bay, Sydney [ASMB2003].

'The Eastern Cliffwalk' (2019), Clovelly, NSW [ASCL1902].▼

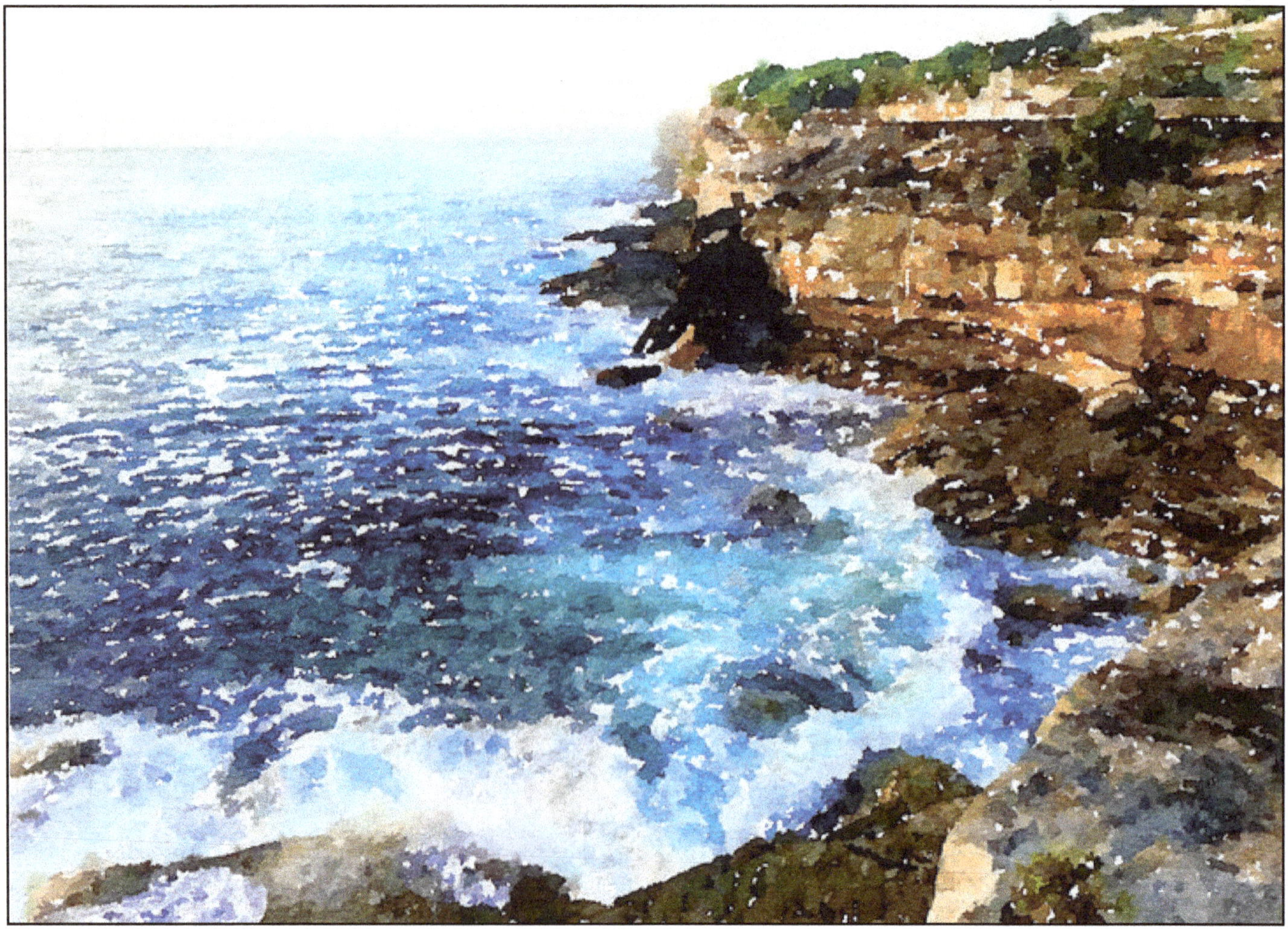

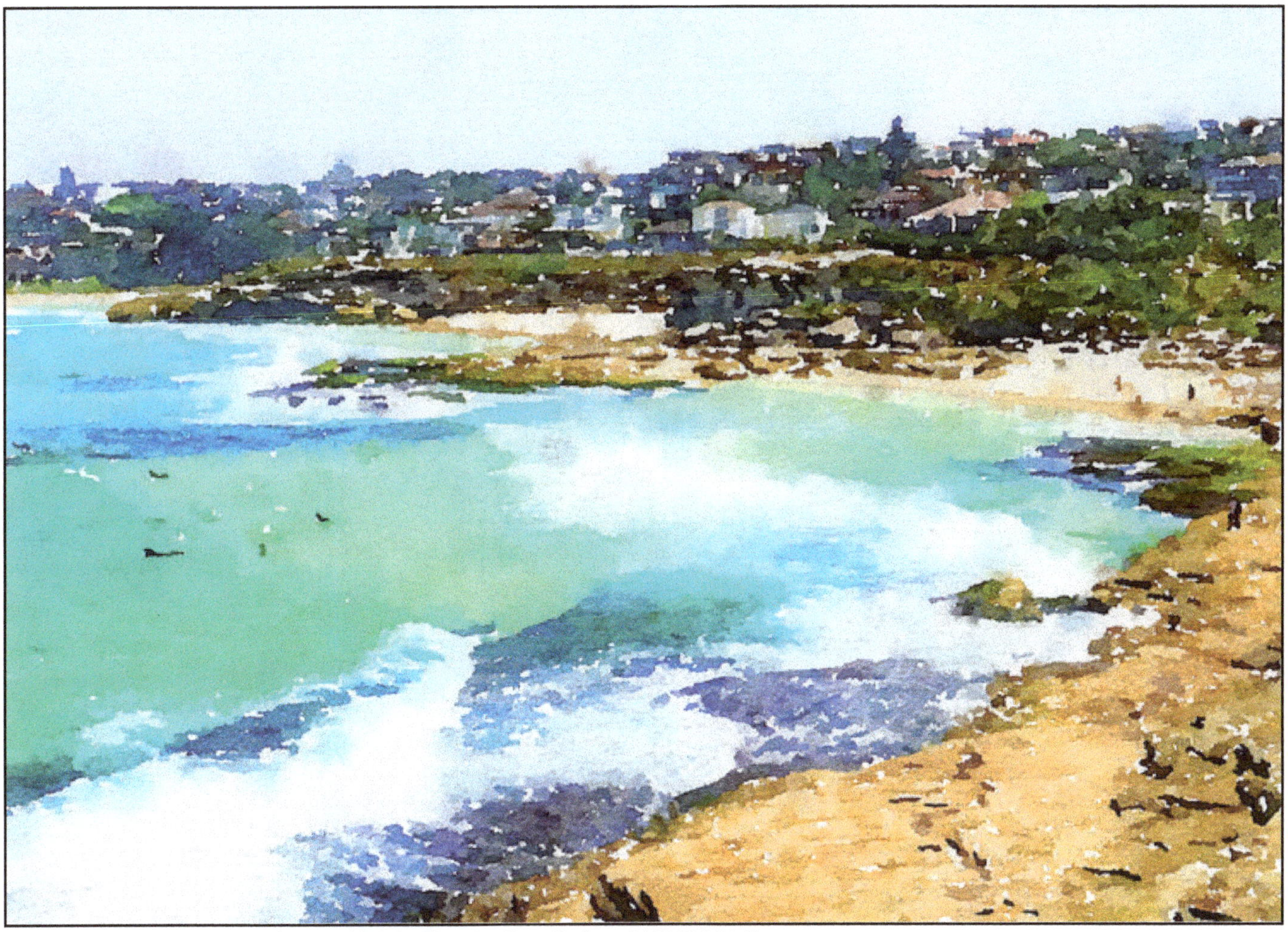

▲'MacKenzies Bay & Beach' (2020), MacKenzies Bay, Sydney [ASMB2004].

'MacKenzies Beach 2' (2020), MacKenzies Bay, Sydney [ASMB2002].▼

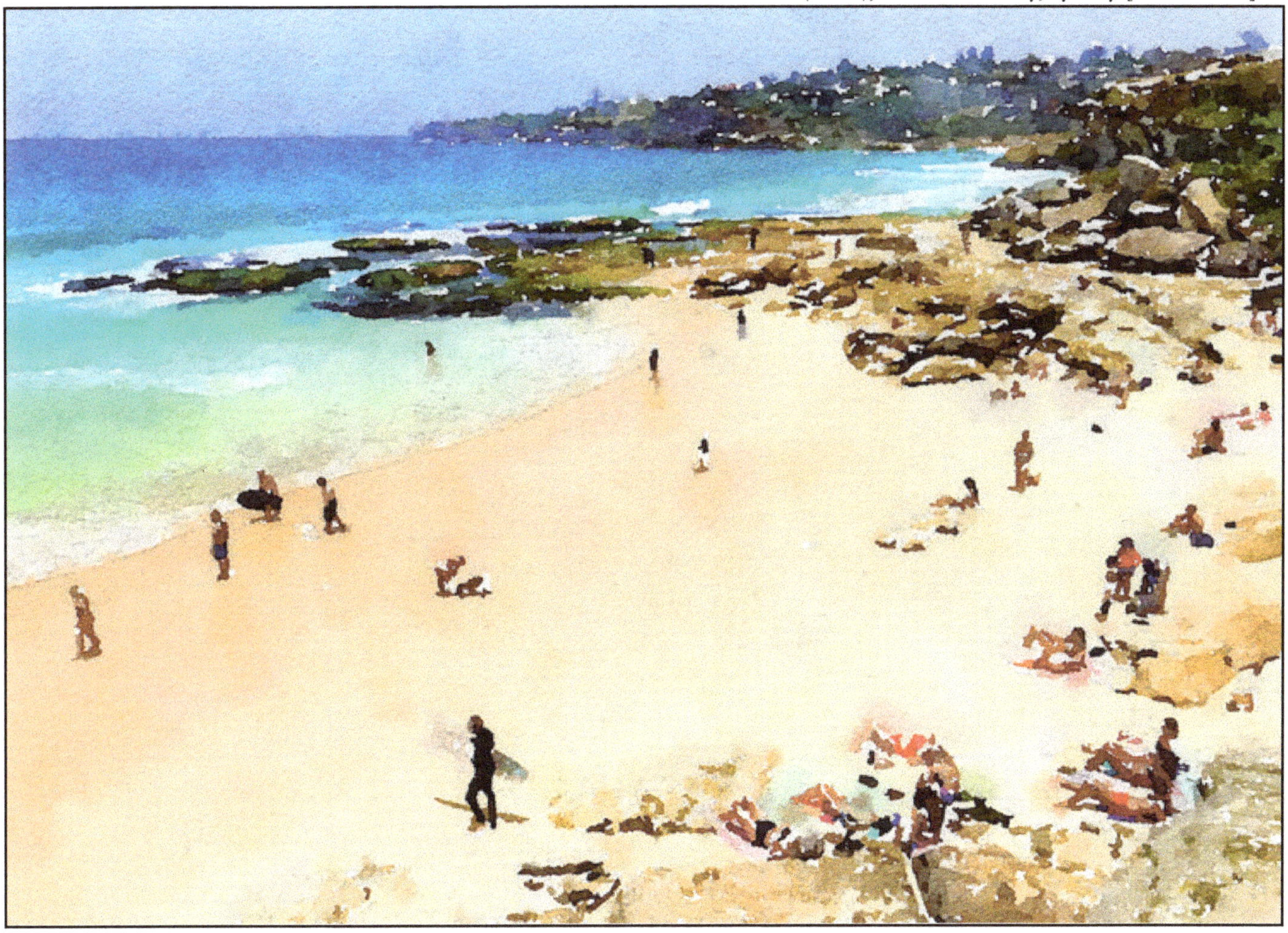

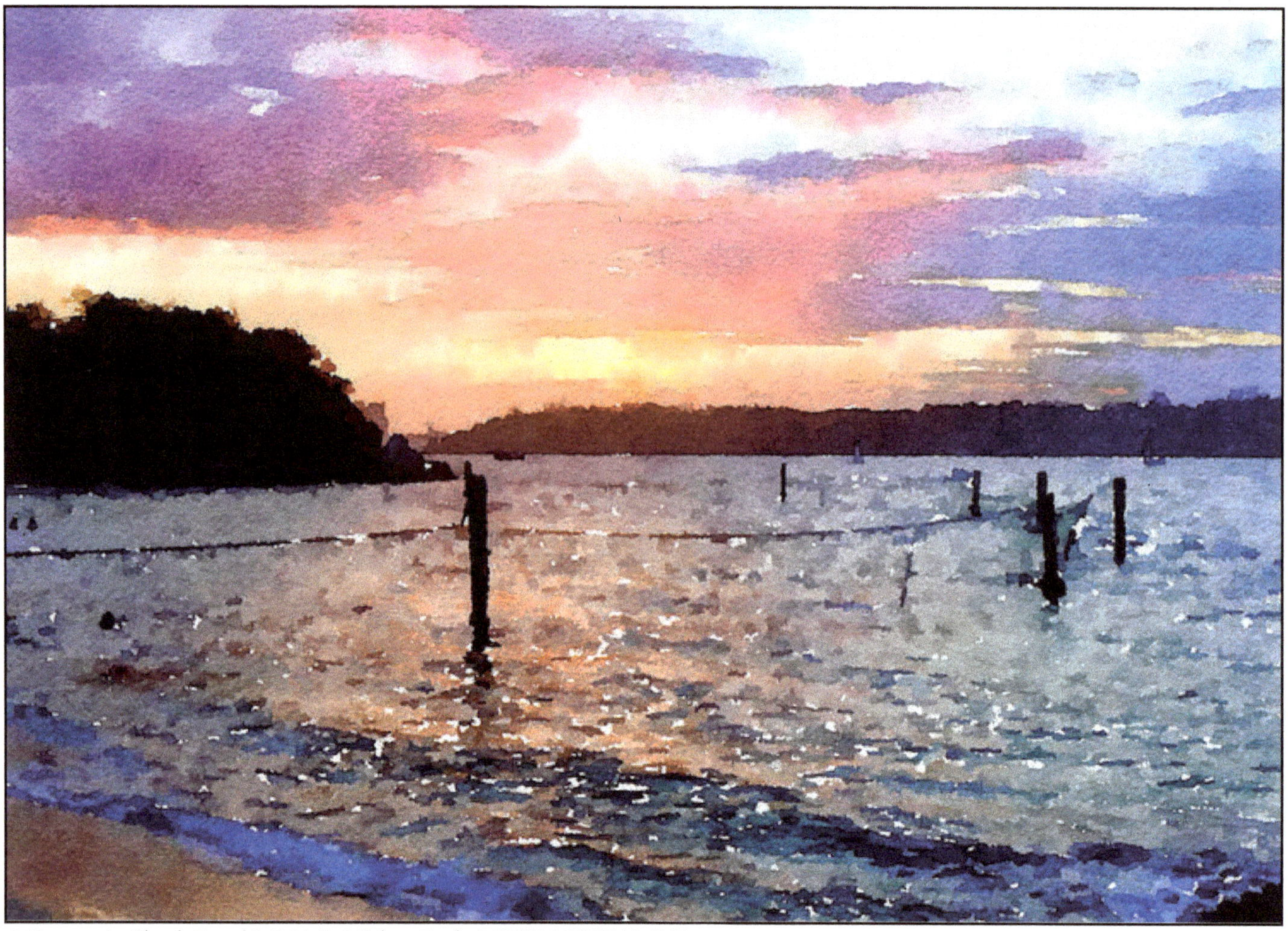

▲'Sunset At Shark Beach' (2016), Nielsen Park, NSW [ASY(SB)1601].

'Fern Bay & Snapper Island' (2020), Drummoyne, NSW [ASY(SH)2001].▼

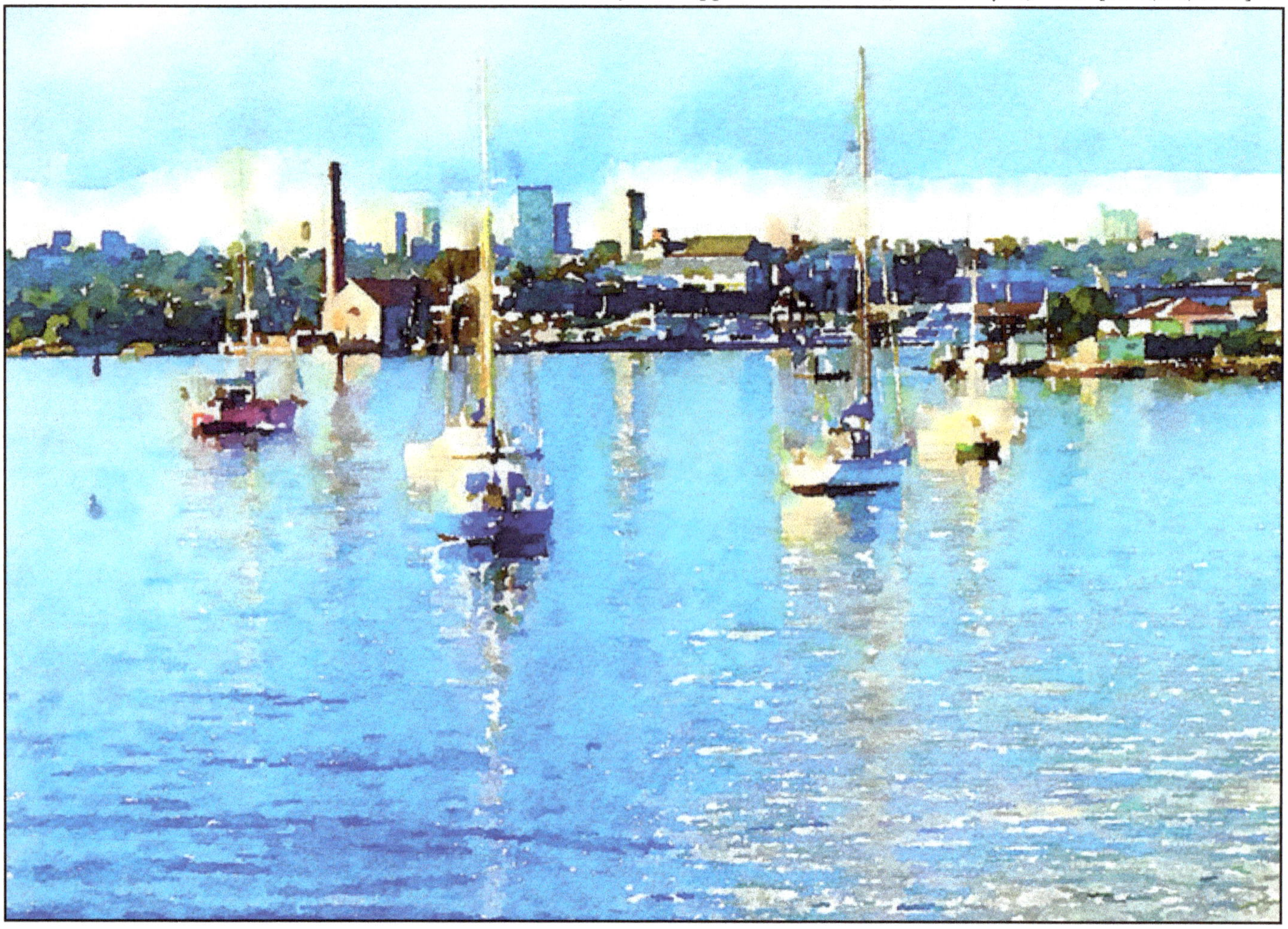

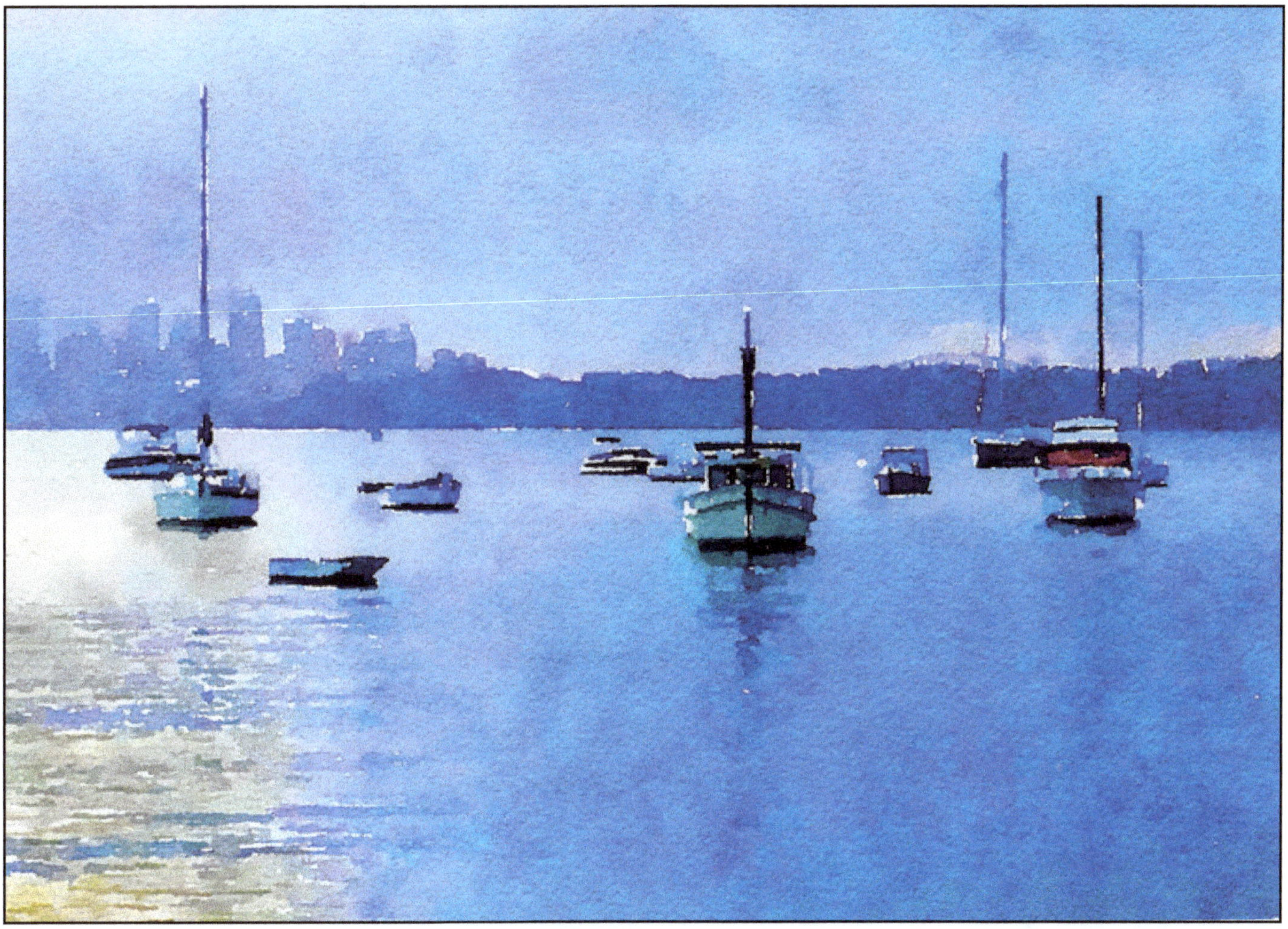

▲'Watsons Bay Twilight' (2016), Watsons Bay, NSW [ASY(WB)1601].

'Sunset Is My Favourite Colour' (2016), Watsons Bay, NSW [ASY(WB)1602].▼

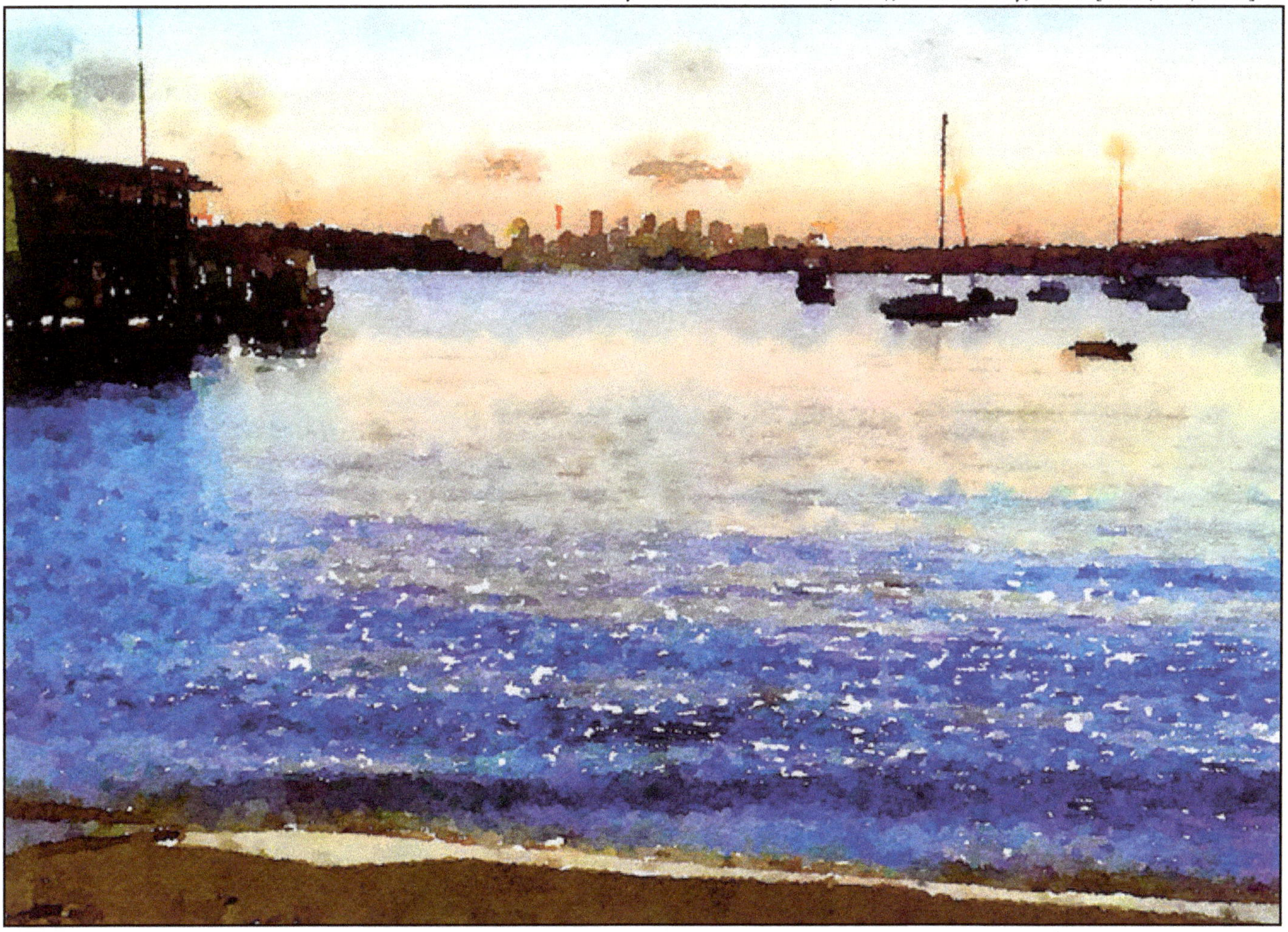

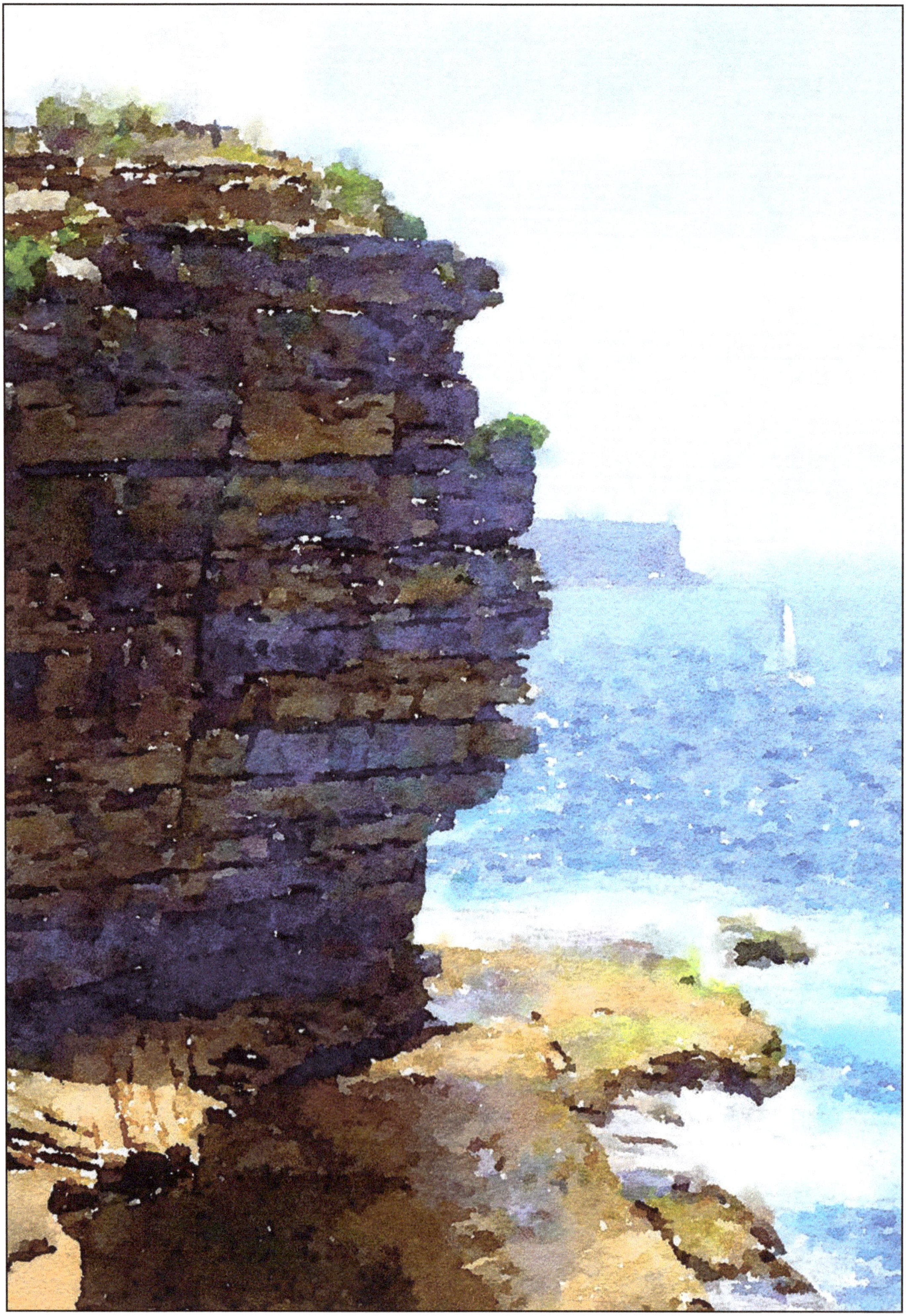

▲'View North From The Gap' (2015), Watsons Bay, NSW [ASY(WB)1501].

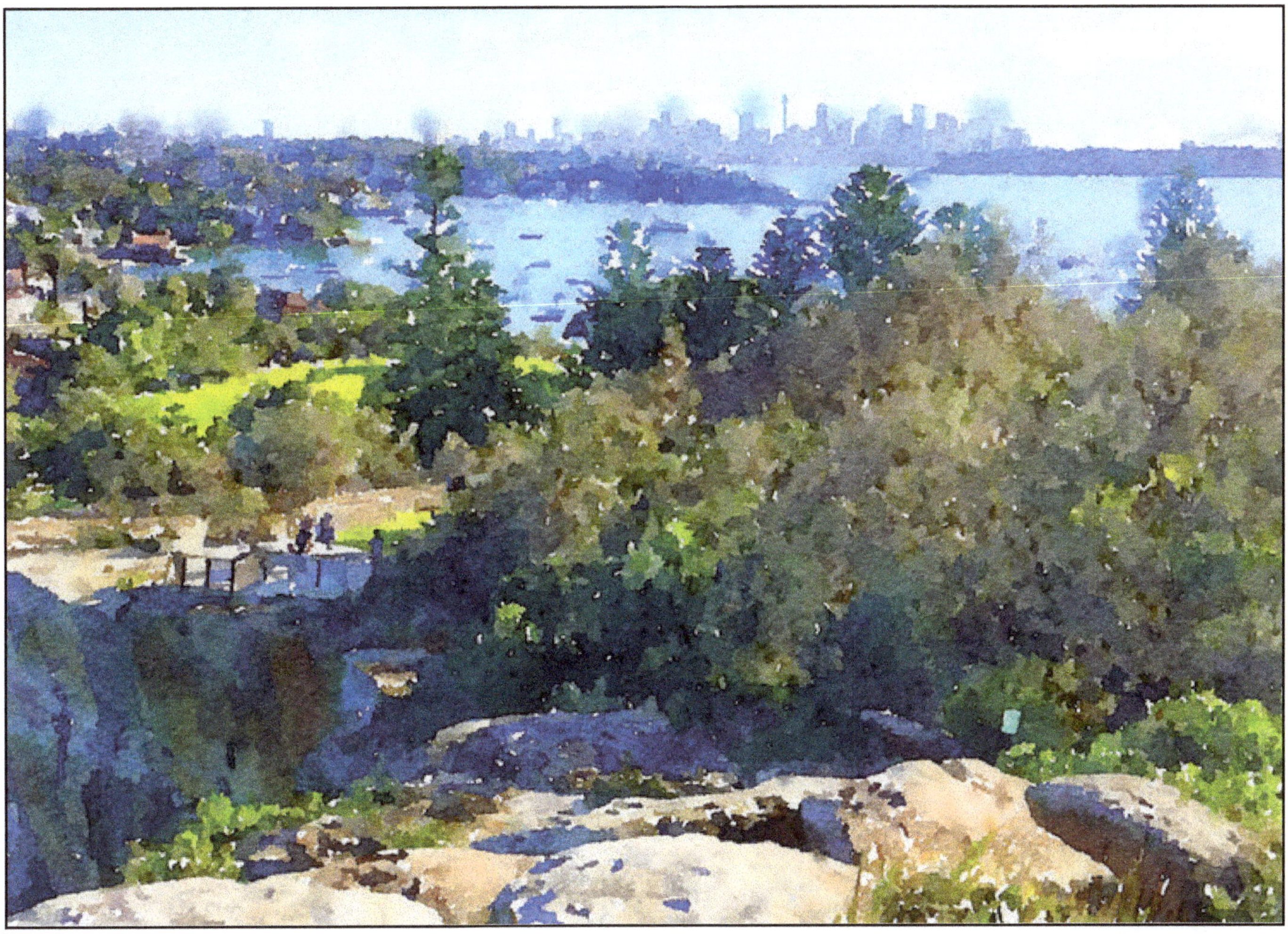

▲'Vistas Of Port Jackson' (2016), Watsons Bay, NSW [ASY(WB)1603].

'Everybody's On' (2019), Tamarama Beach, NSW [ASTB1918].▼

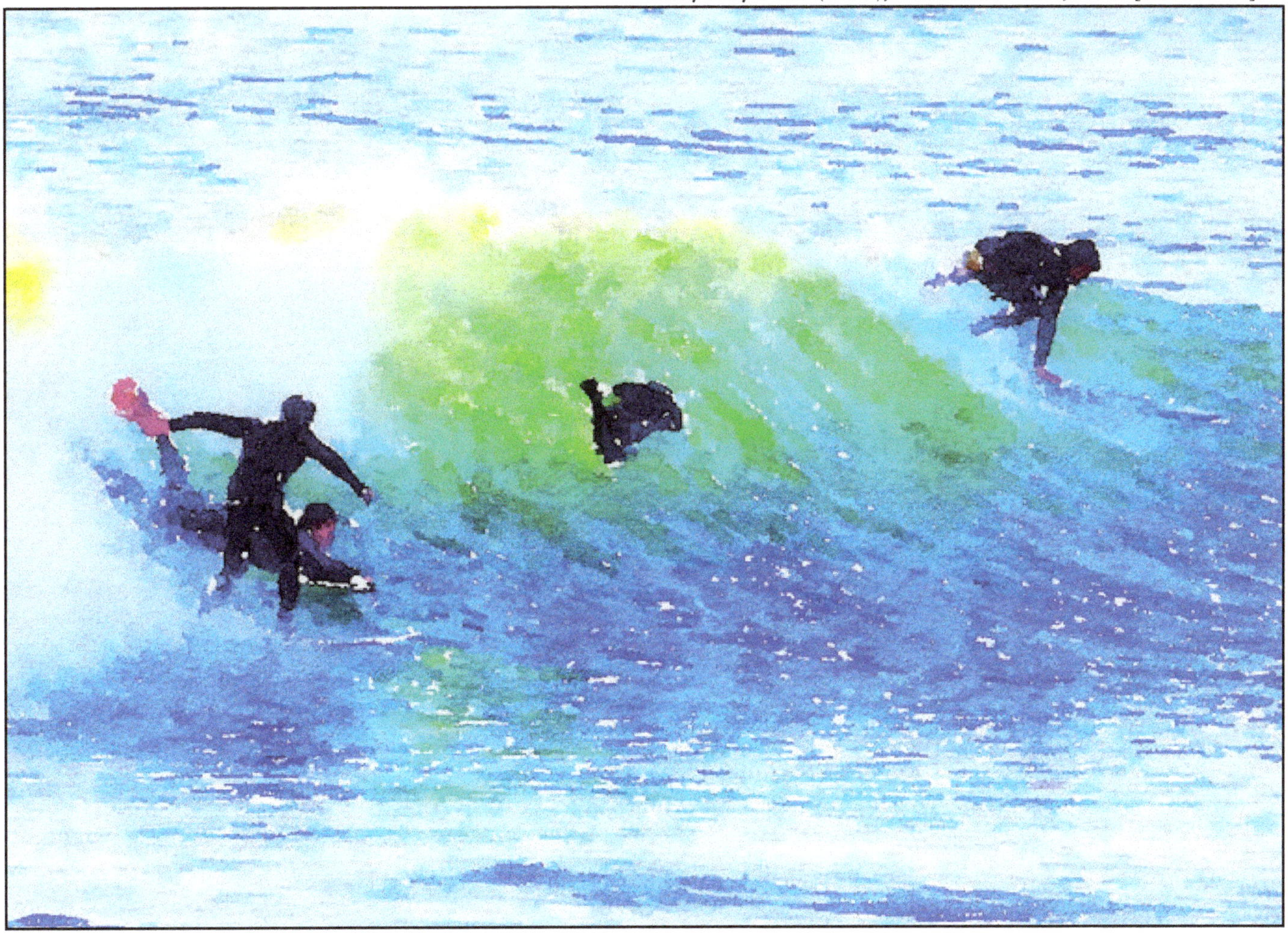

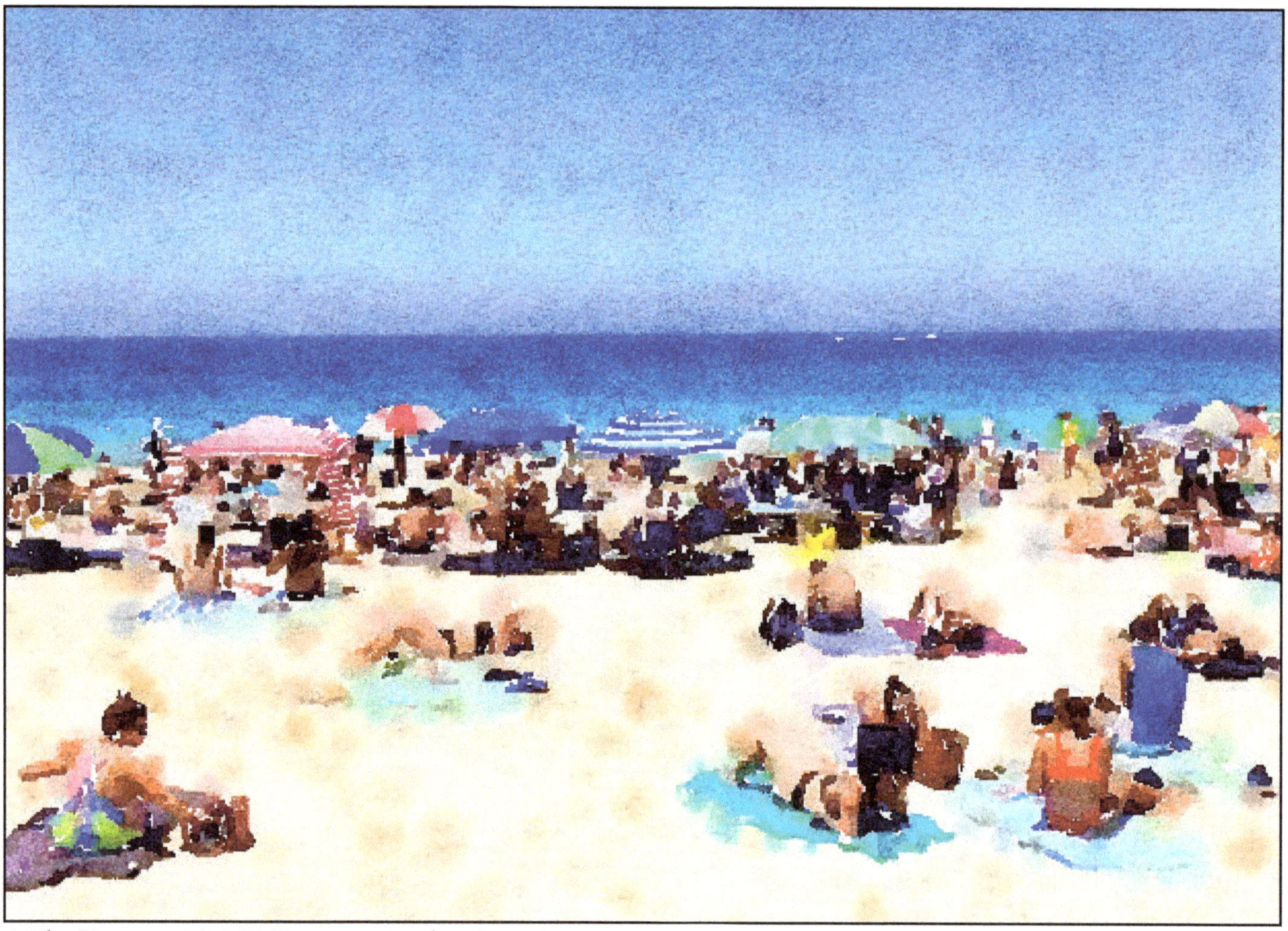

▲'Blue Tamarama' (2017), Tamarama Beach, NSW [ASTB1701].

'Shadows From The Overhang' (2017), Tamarama Beach, NSW [ASTB1702].▼

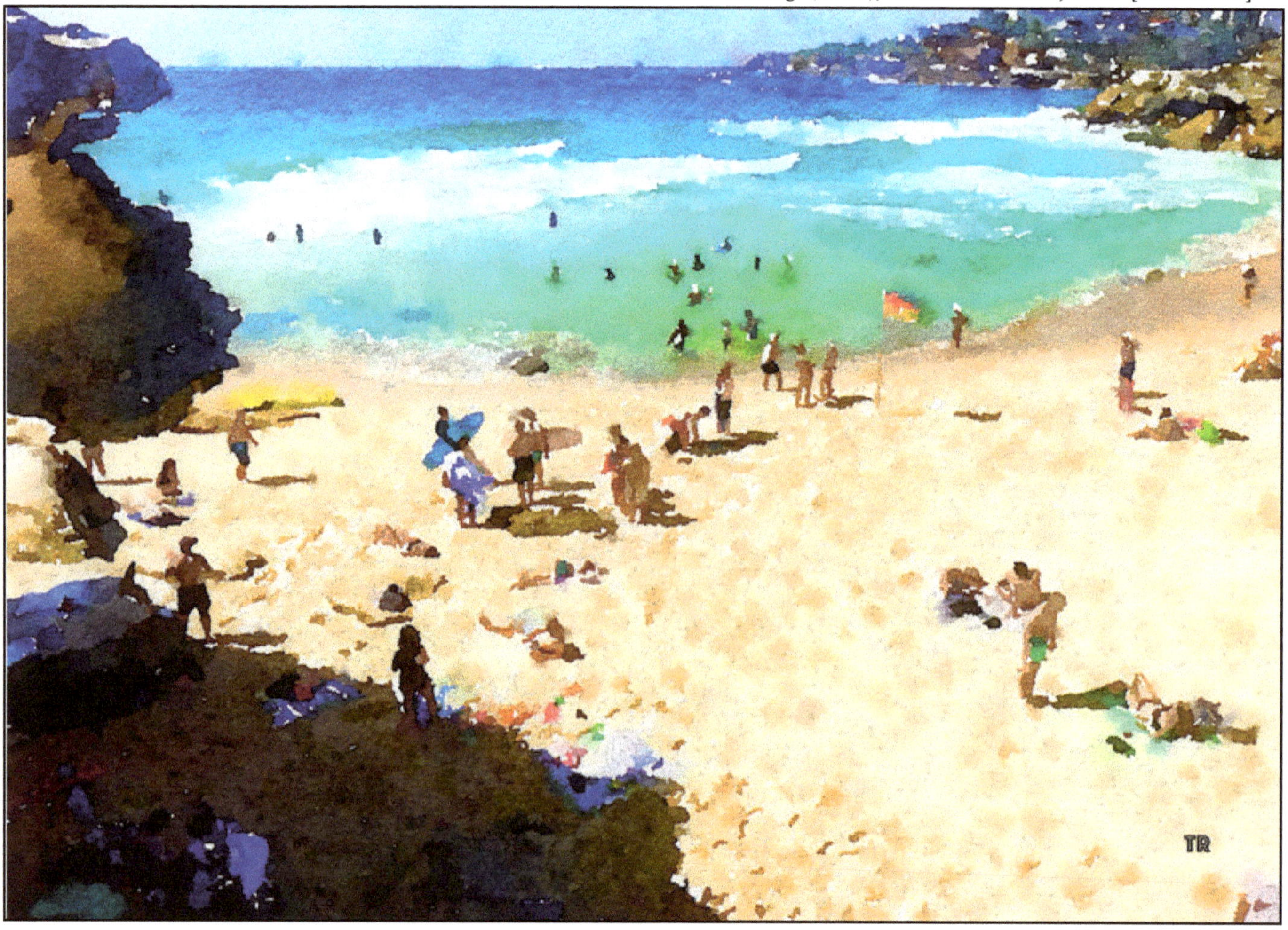

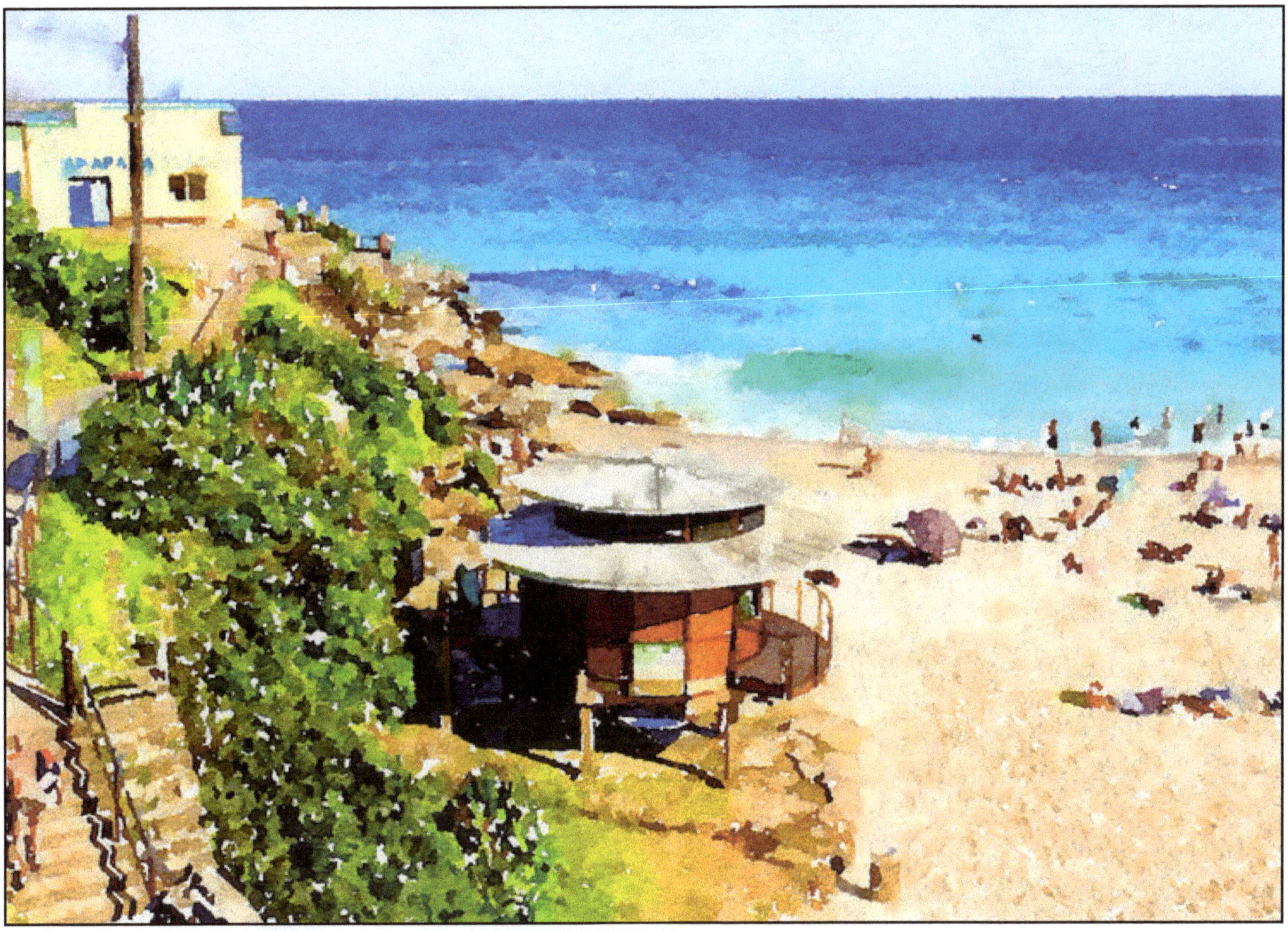

▲'The Lifeguard Post' (2017), Tamarama Beach, NSW [ASTB1703].

'A Day At Glamarama' (2018), Tamarama Beach, NSW [ASTB1801].▼

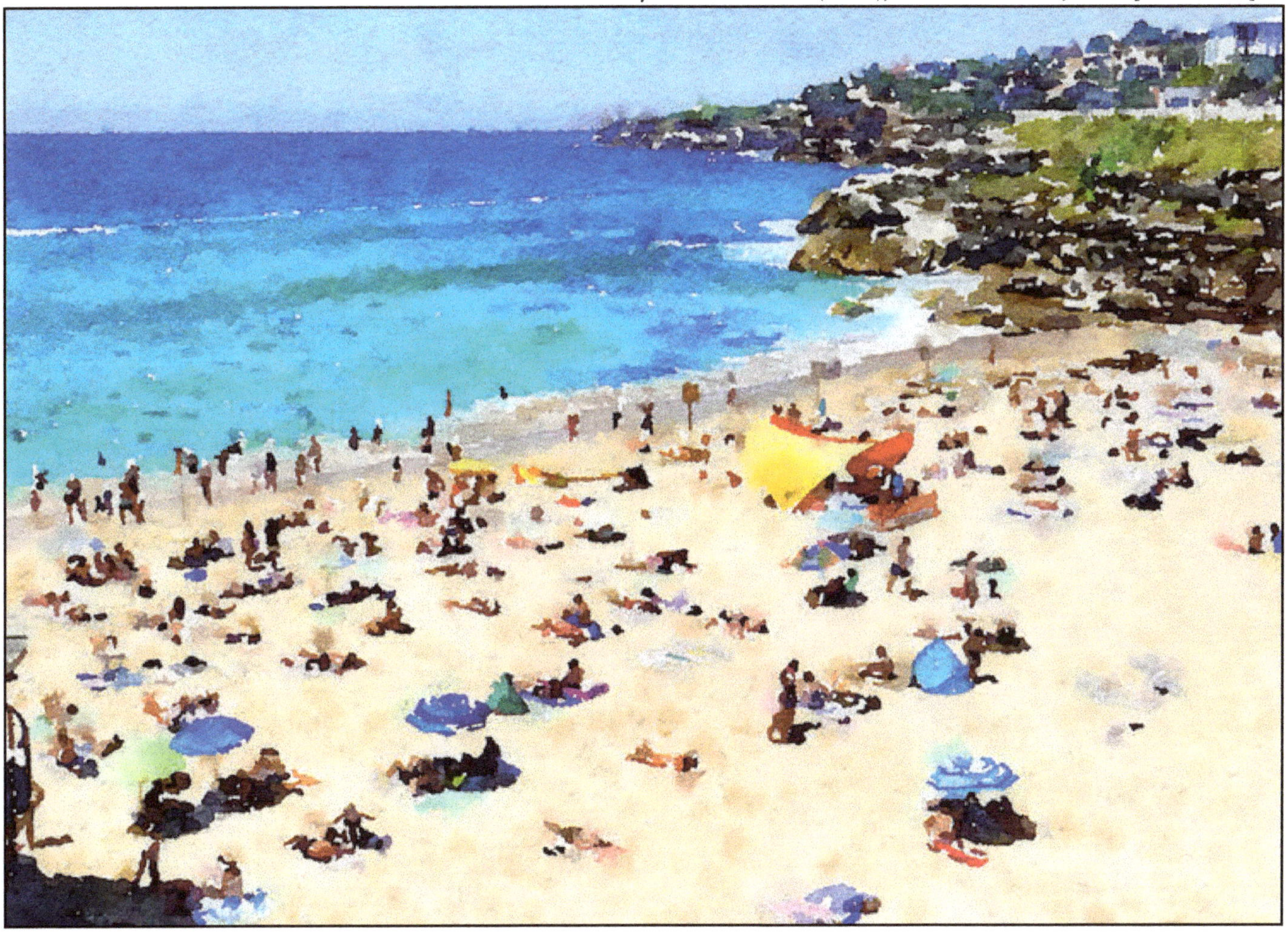

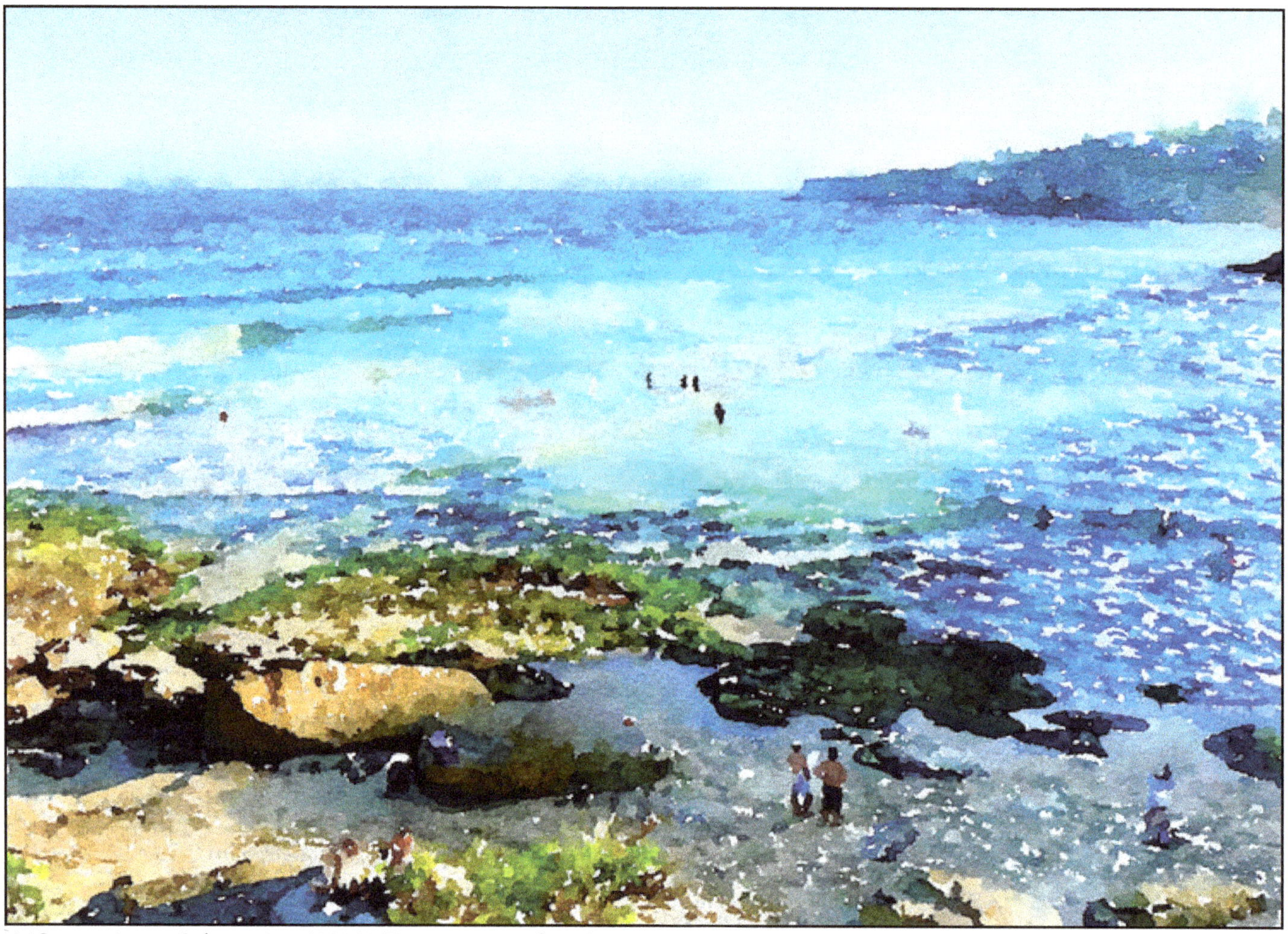

▲'Conversion to Submersion' (2018), Tamarama Beach, NSW [ASTB1802].

'Call Of The Ocean' (2019), Tamarama Beach, NSW [ASTB1901].▼

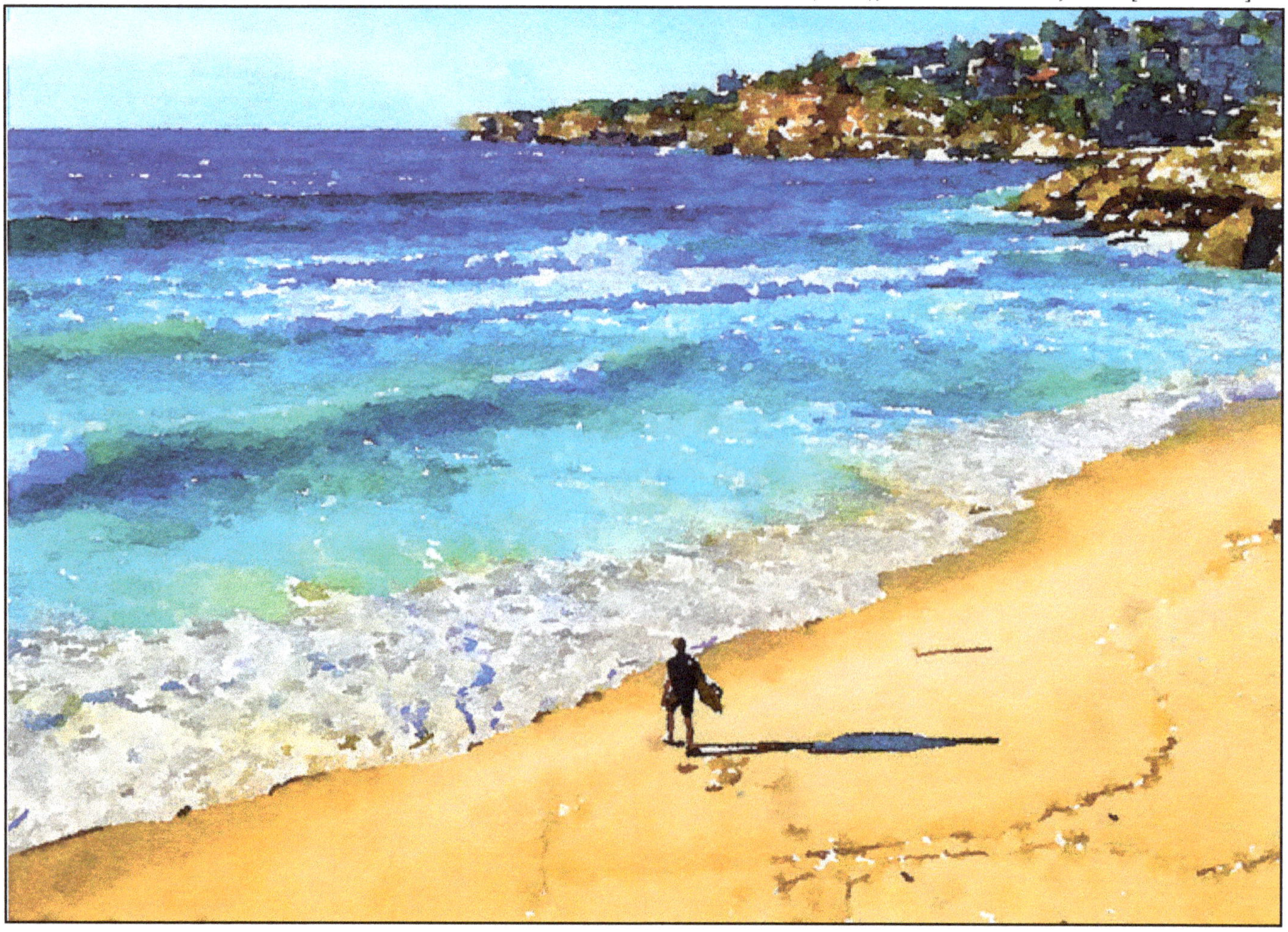

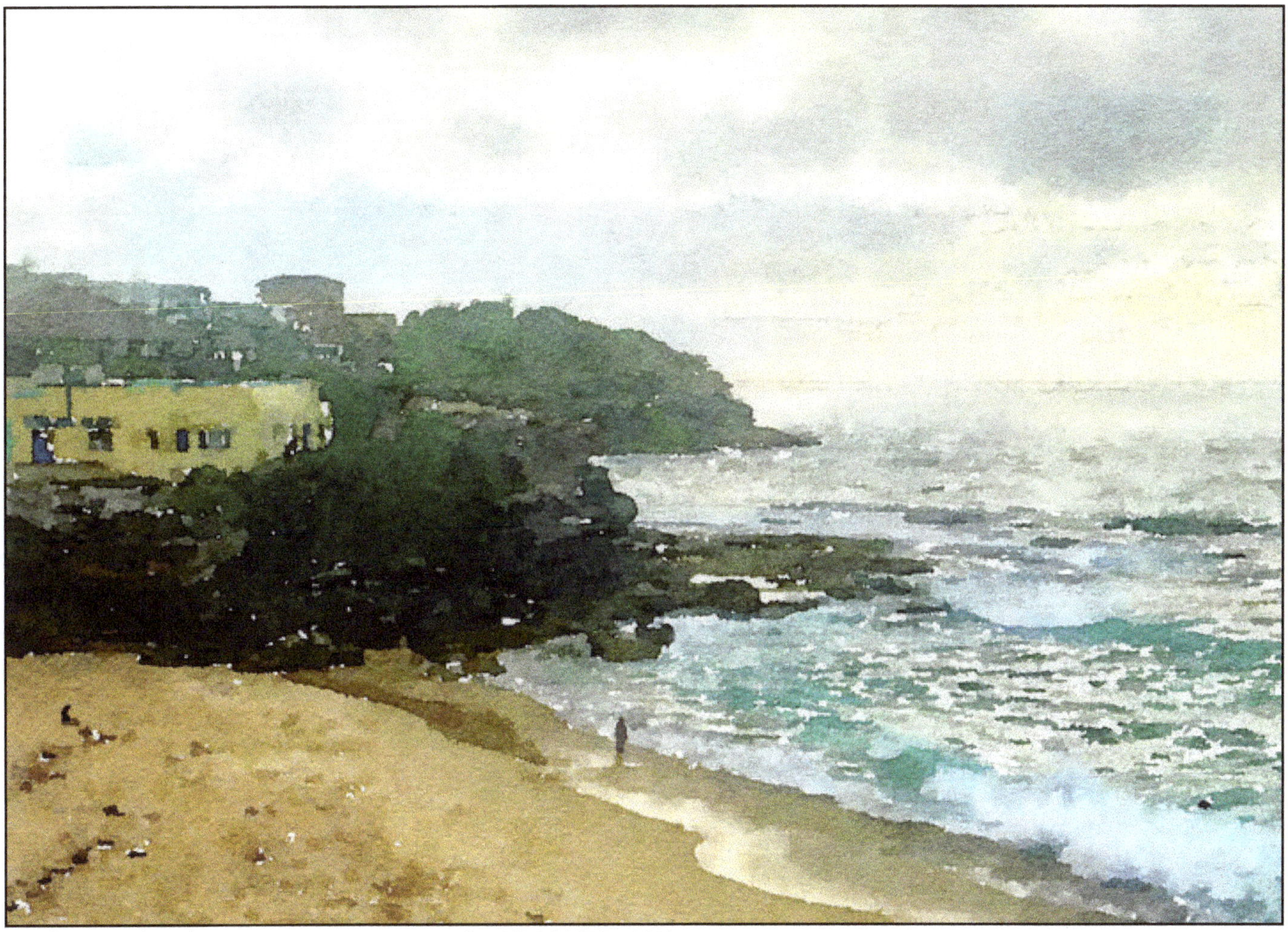

▲'Close To The Edge' (2019), Tamarama Beach, NSW [ASTB1902].

'Ocean Breezes' (2019), Tamarama Beach, NSW [ASTB1903].▼

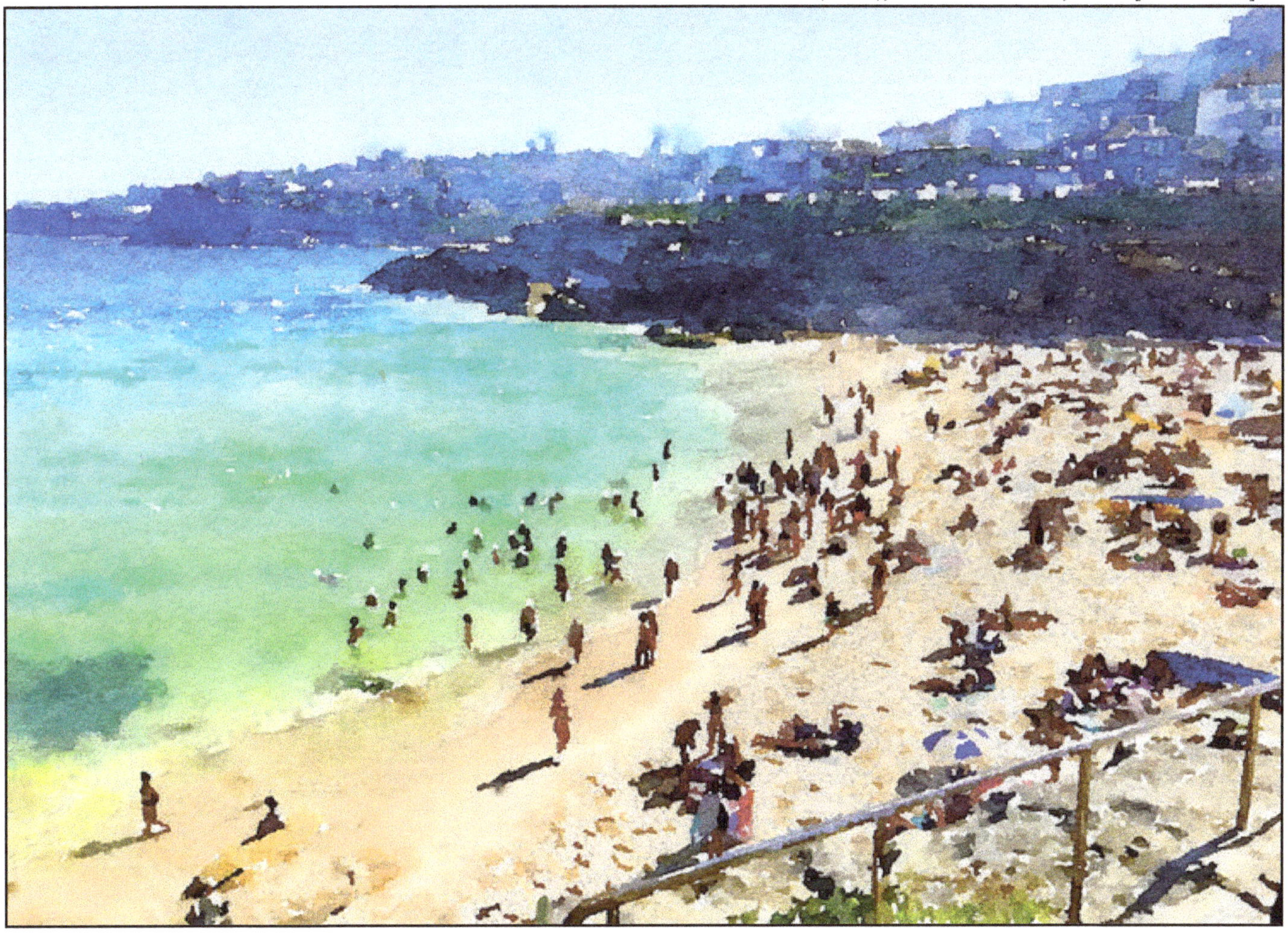

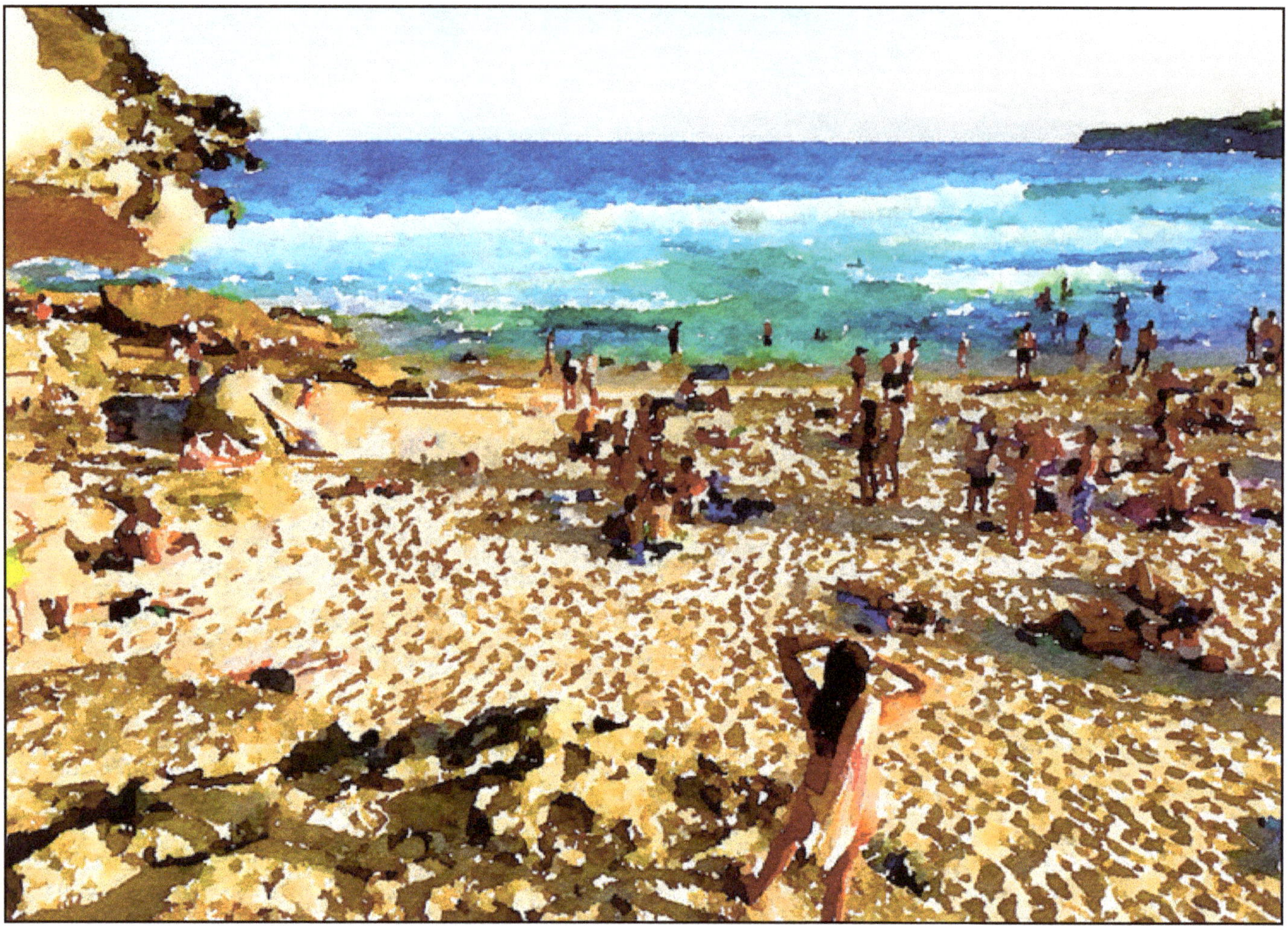

▲'Evening Escape' (2019), Tamarama Beach, NSW [ASTB1904].

'Shades Of Tamarama' (2019), Tamarama Beach, NSW [ASTB1905].▼

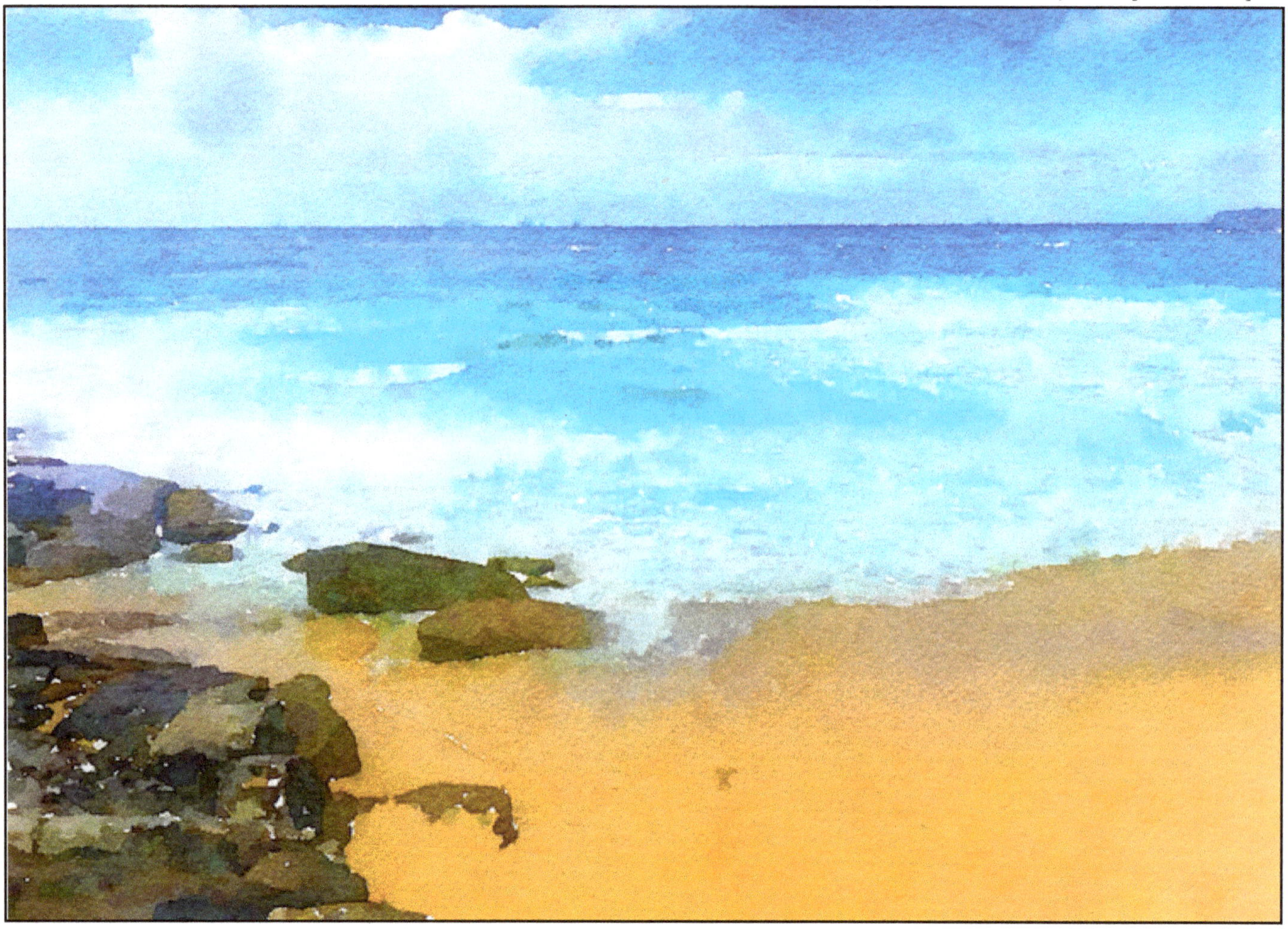

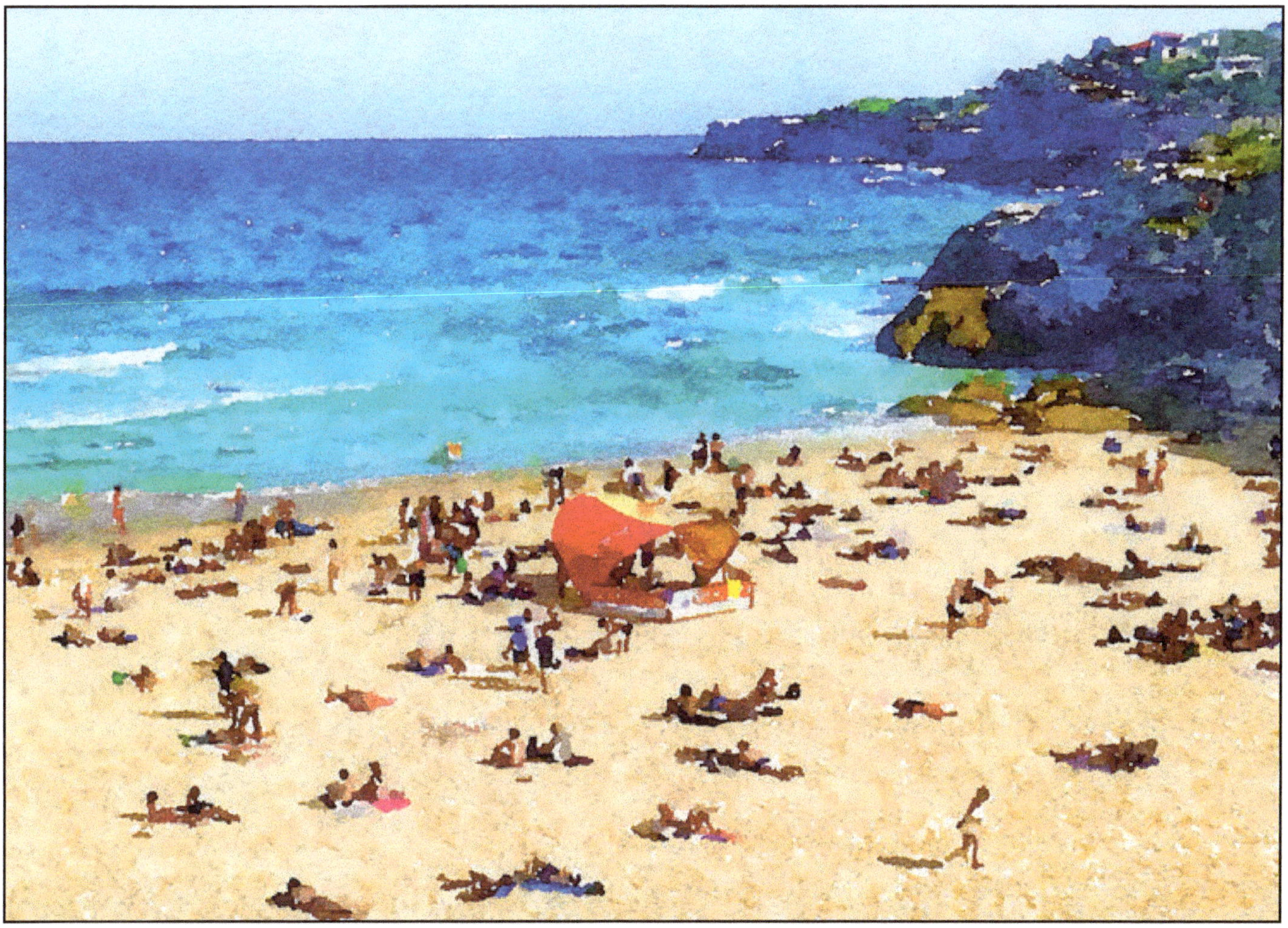

▲'The Fortunate Few' (2019), Tamarama Beach, NSW [ASTB1906].

'Tamarama Tides' (2019), Tamarama Beach, NSW [ASTB1907].▼

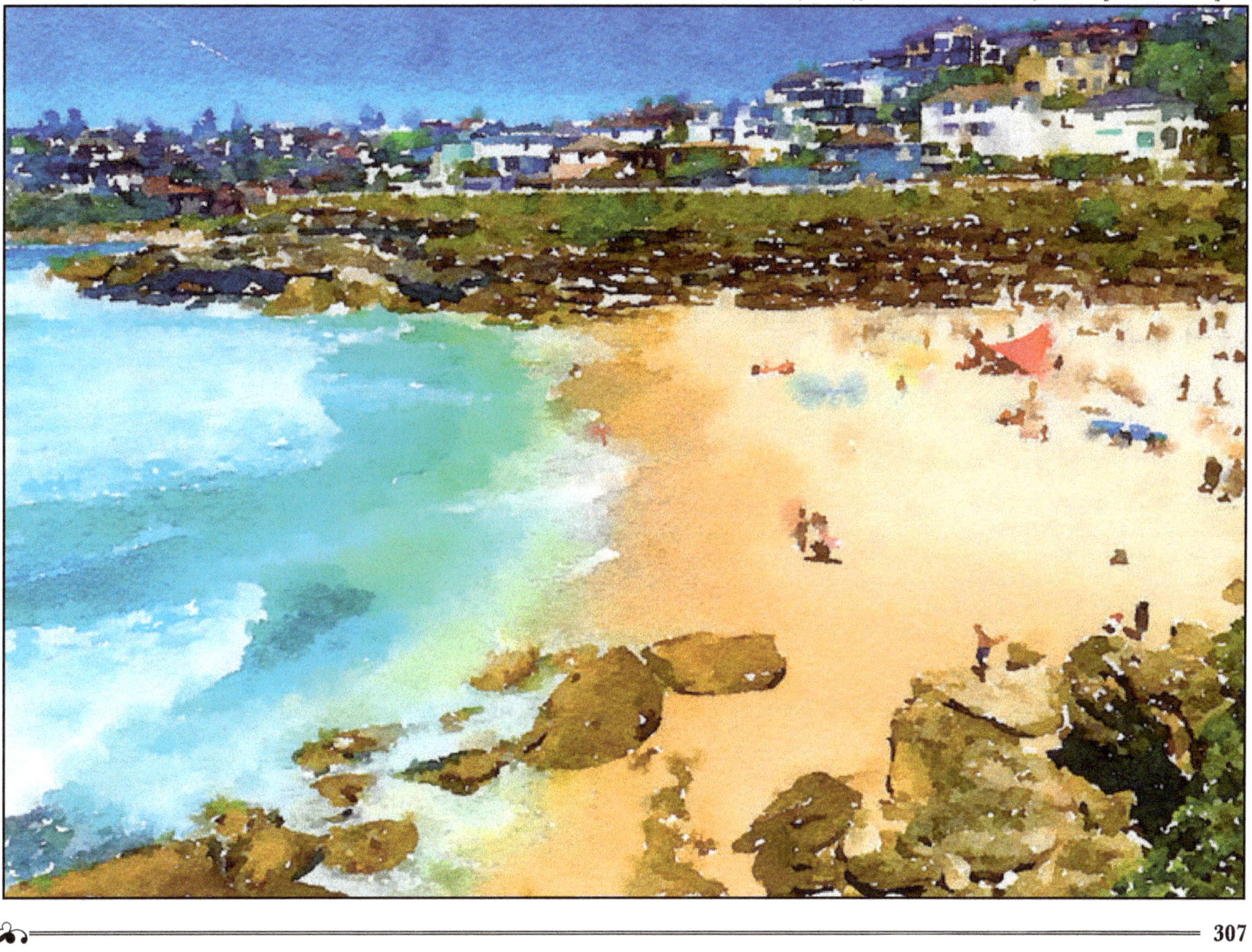

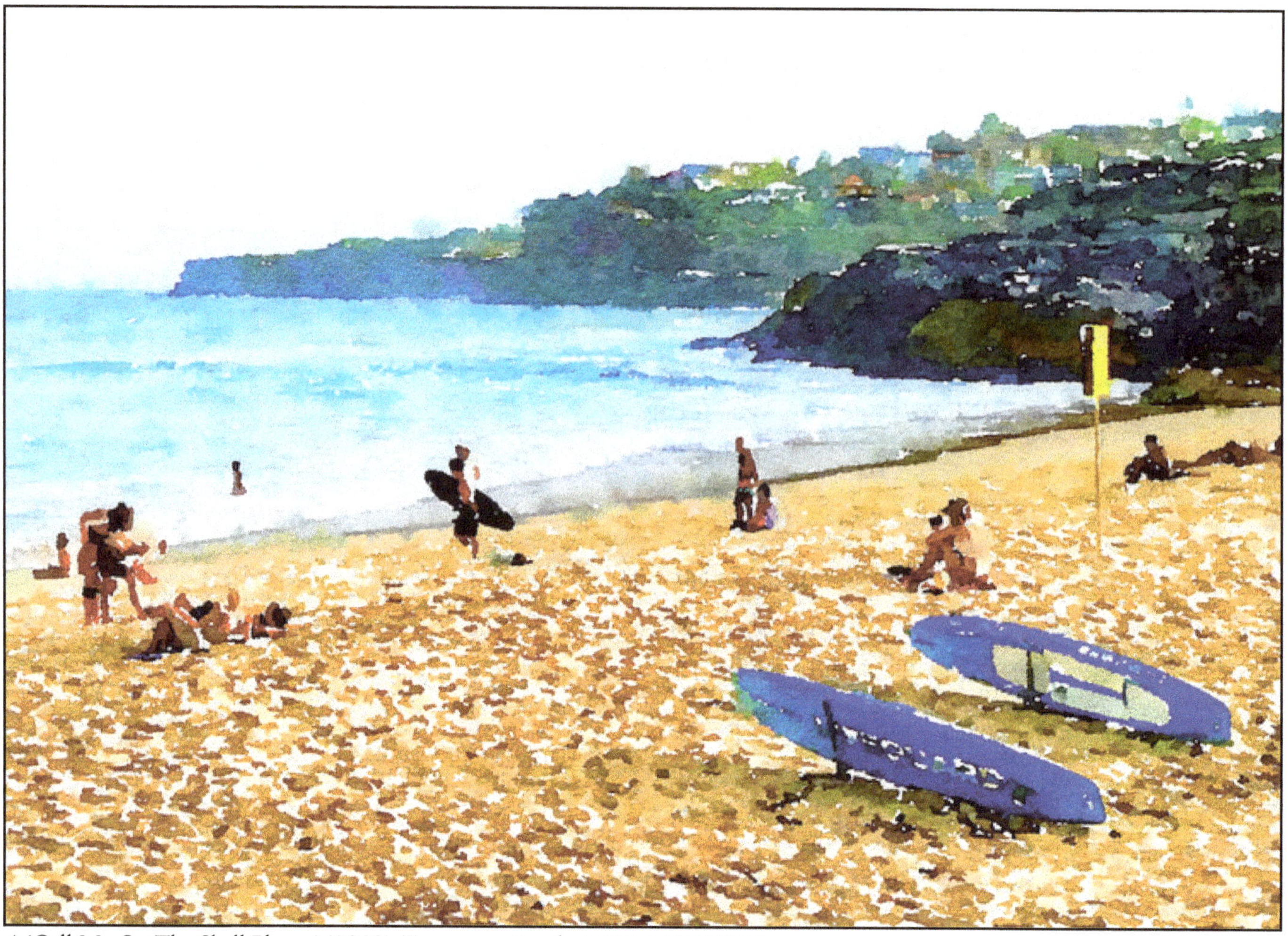

▲'Call Me On The Shell Phone' (2019), Tamarama Beach, NSW [ASTB1908].

'Corners On The Reef' (2019), Tamarama Beach, NSW [ASTB1909].▼

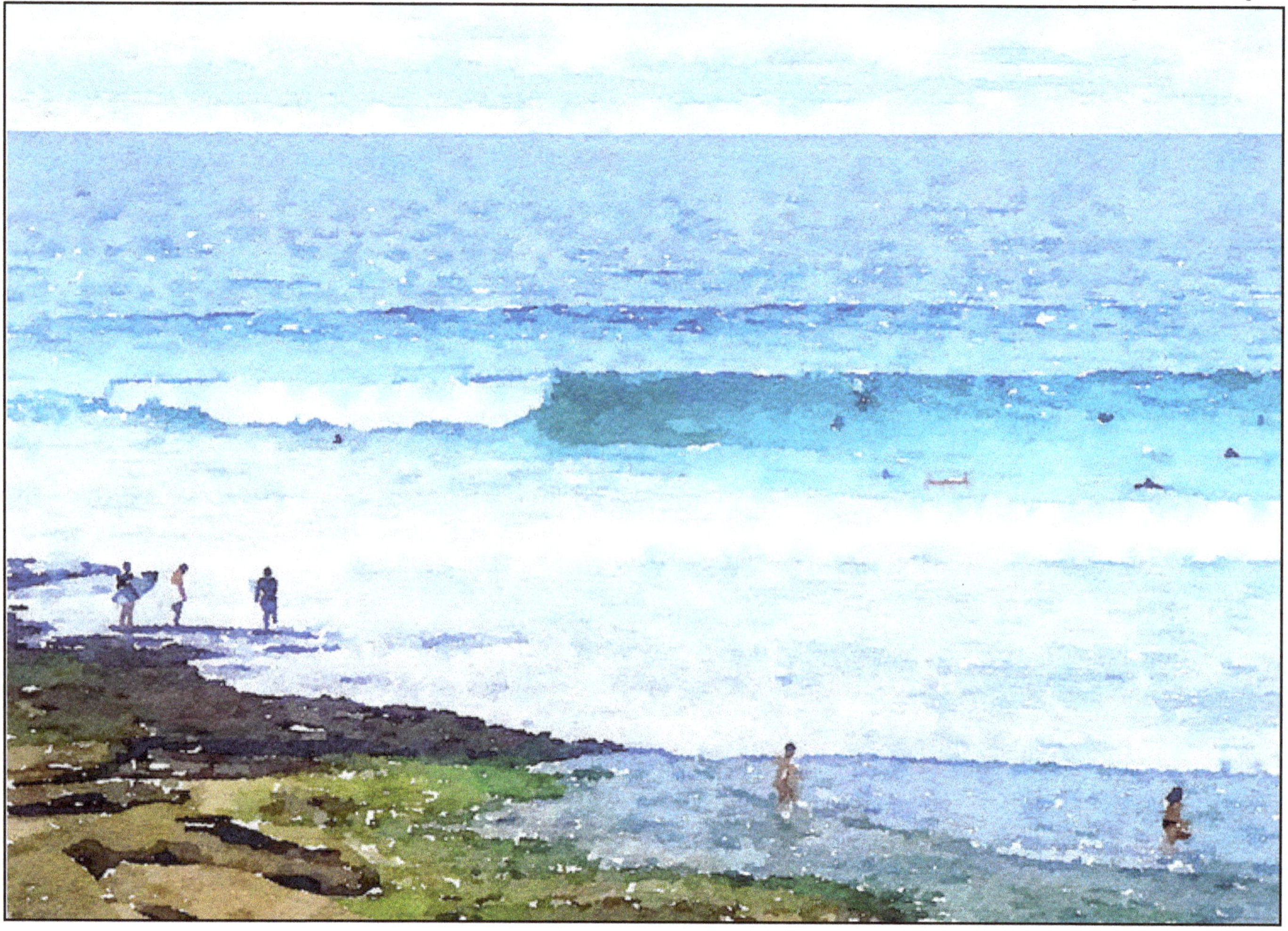

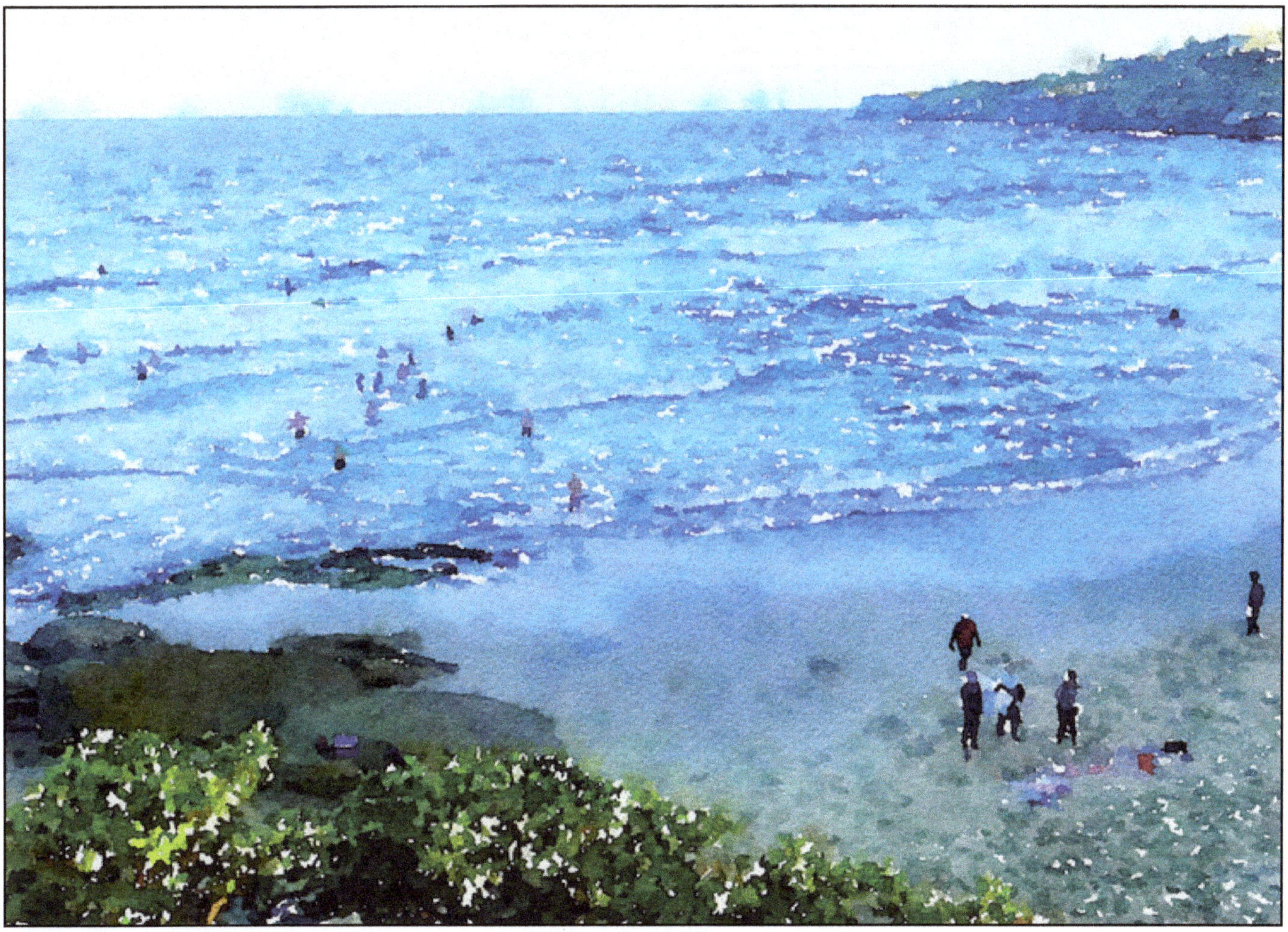

▲'Last Waves of the Day' (2019), Tamarama Beach, NSW [ASTB1910].

'Safety In Numbers' (2019), Tamarama Beach, NSW [ASTB1911].▼

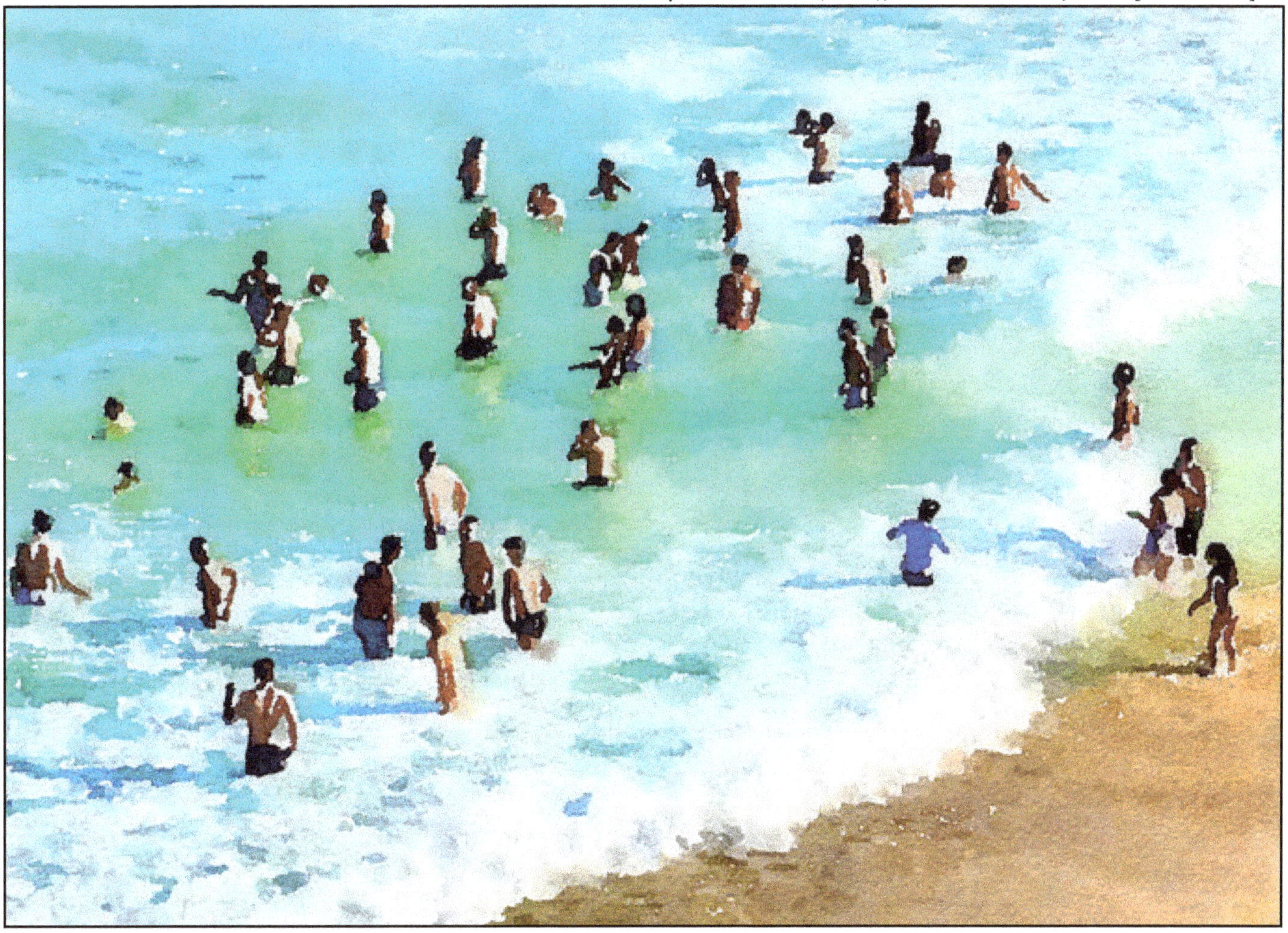

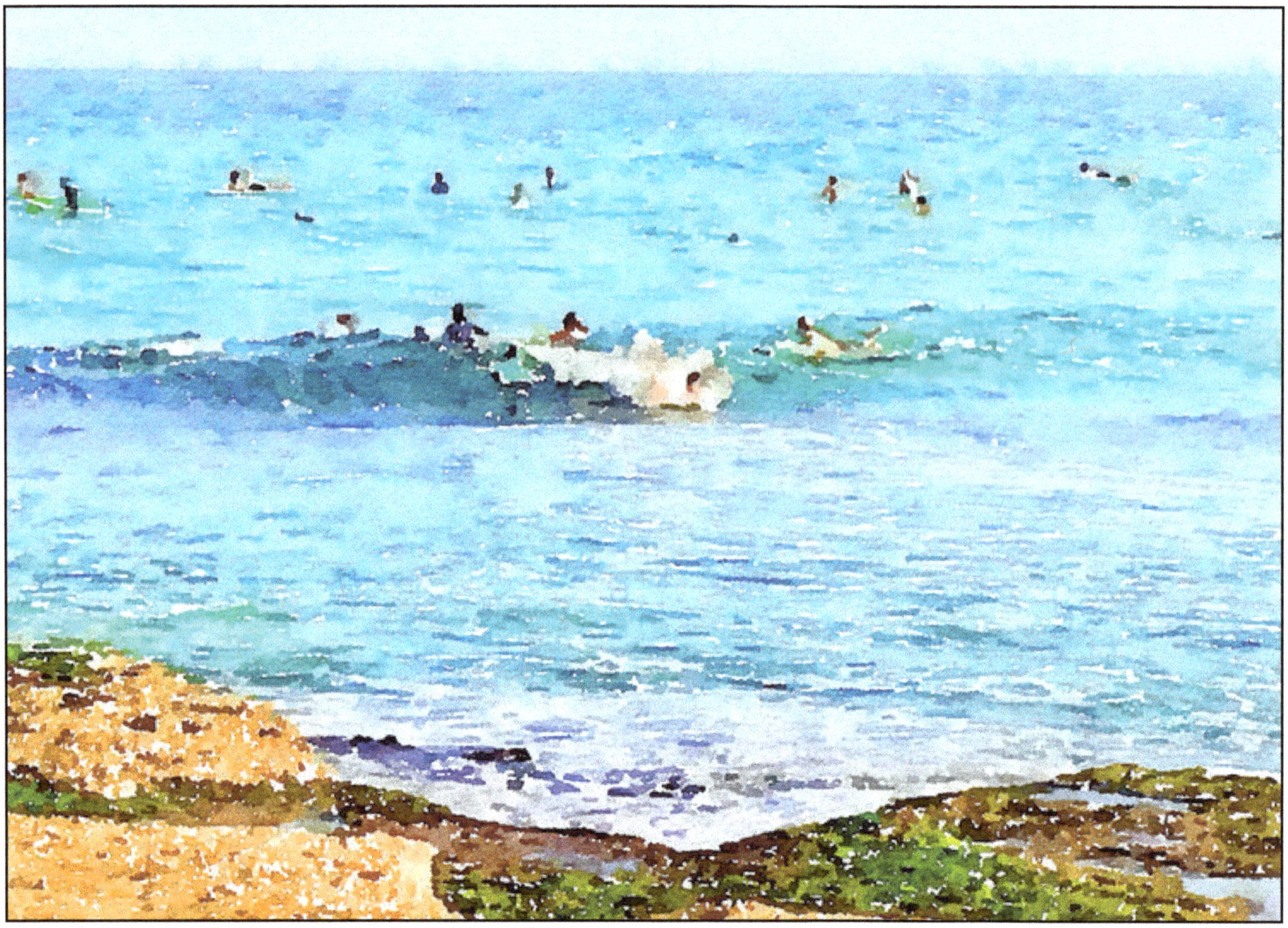

▲'Reef Riders' (2019), Tamarama Beach, NSW [ASTB1912].

'The Rock Overhang' (2019), Tamarama Beach, NSW [ASTB1913].▼

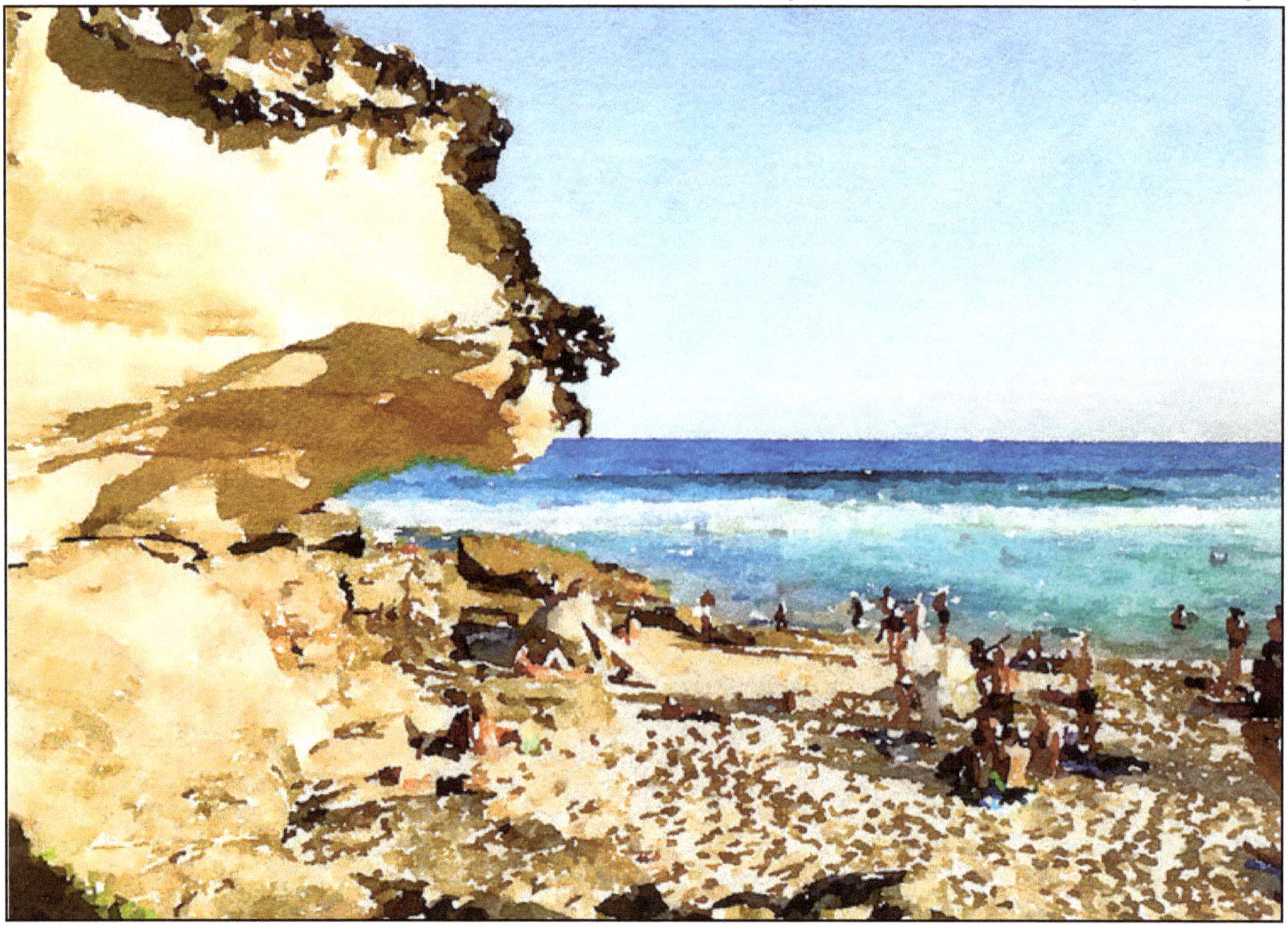

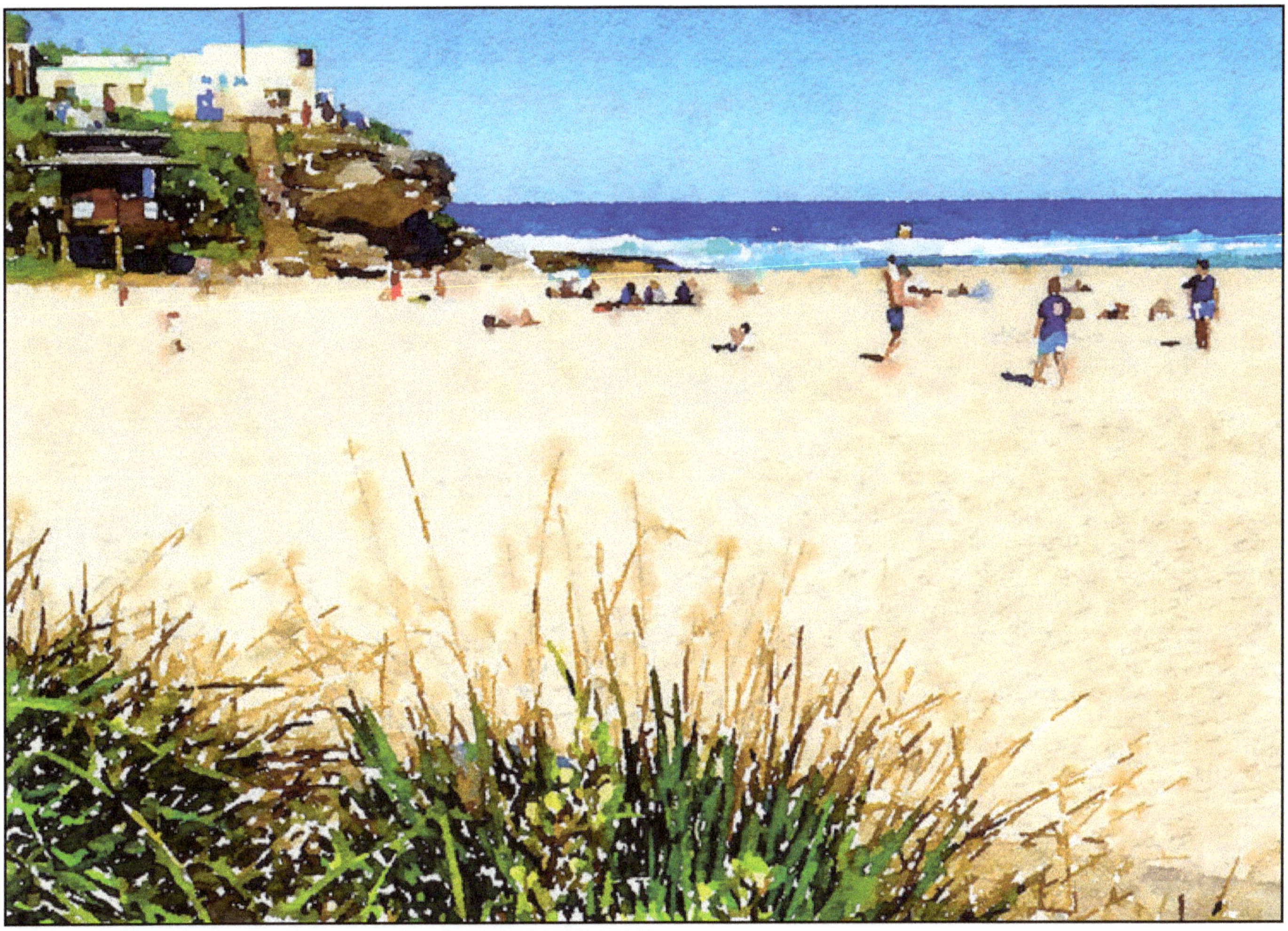

▲'The Sand People' (2019), Tamarama Beach, NSW [ASTB1914].

'Magic Morning' (2019), Tamarama Beach, NSW [ASTB1915].▼

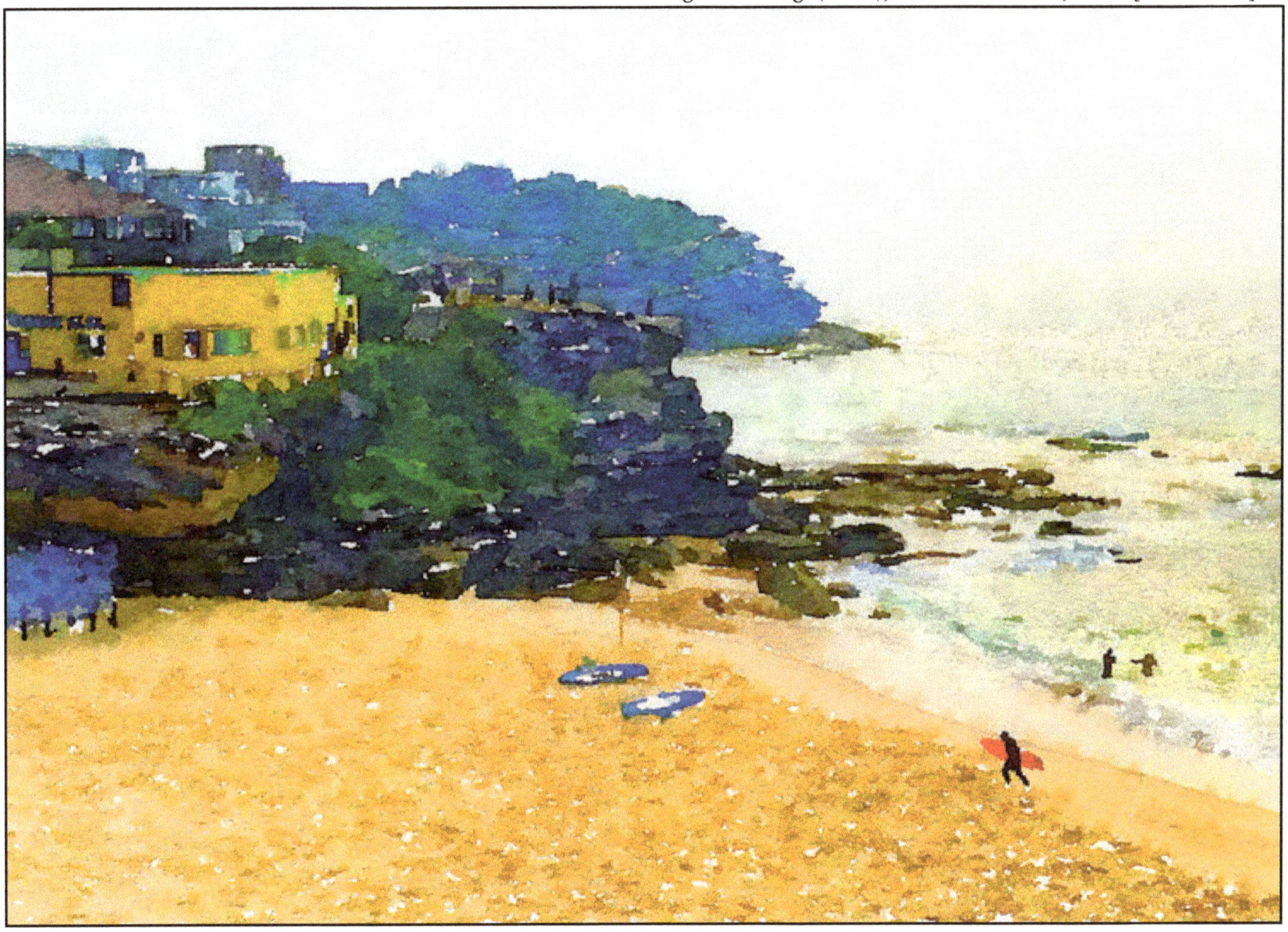

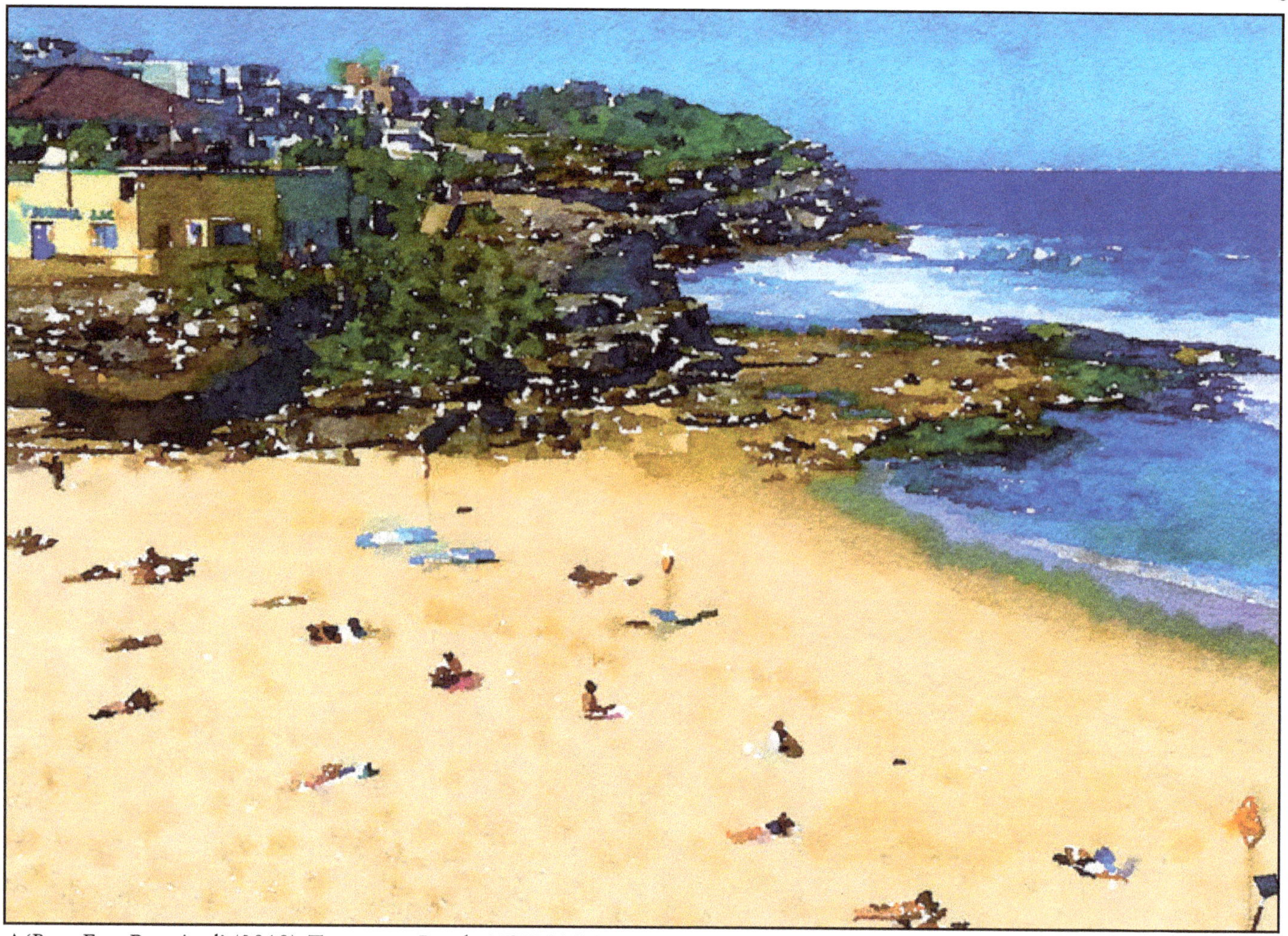

▲'Bare Feet Required' (2019), Tamarama Beach, NSW [ASTB1916].

'Tamarama Time' (2019), Tamarama Beach, NSW [ASTB1917].▼

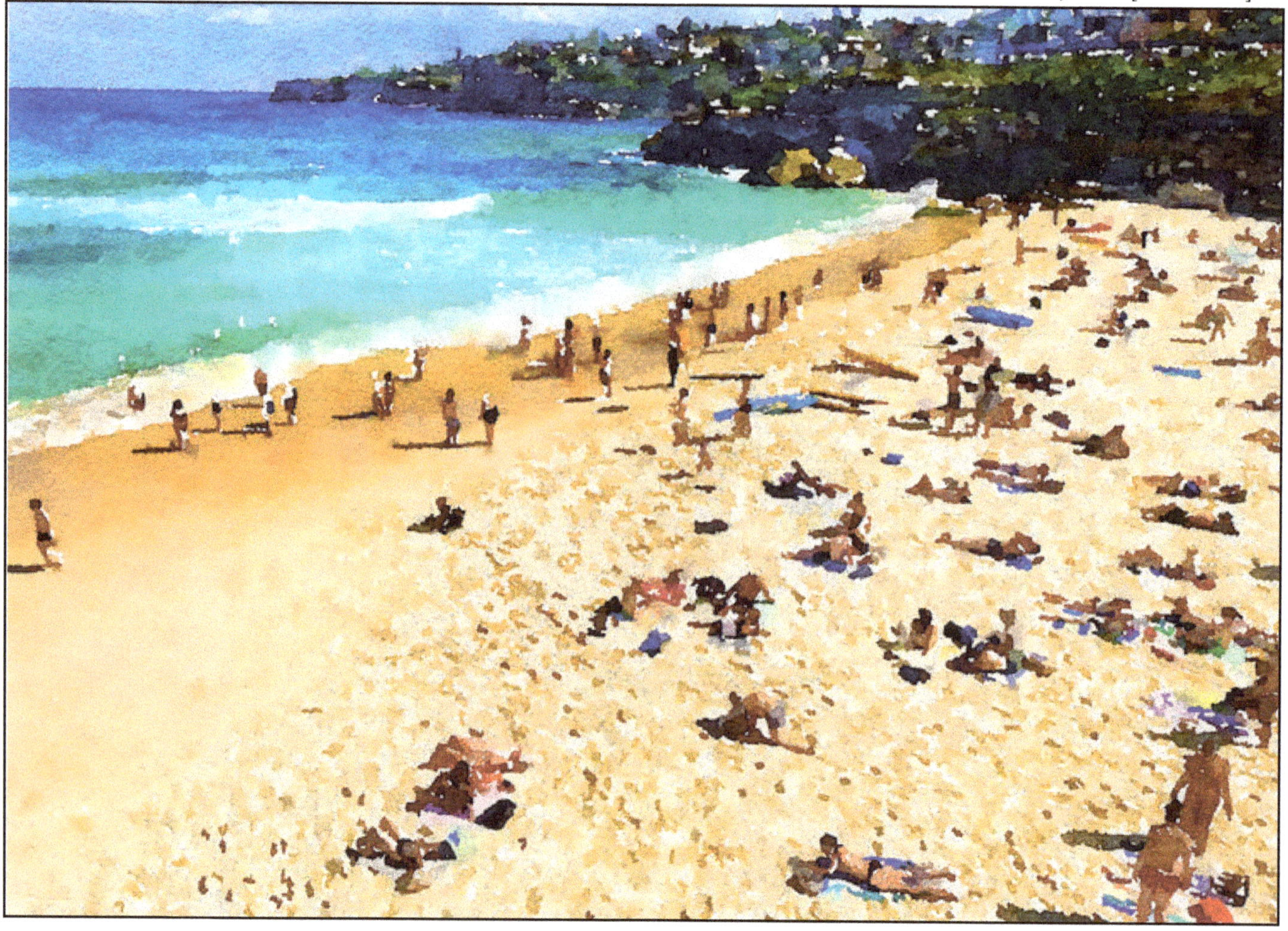

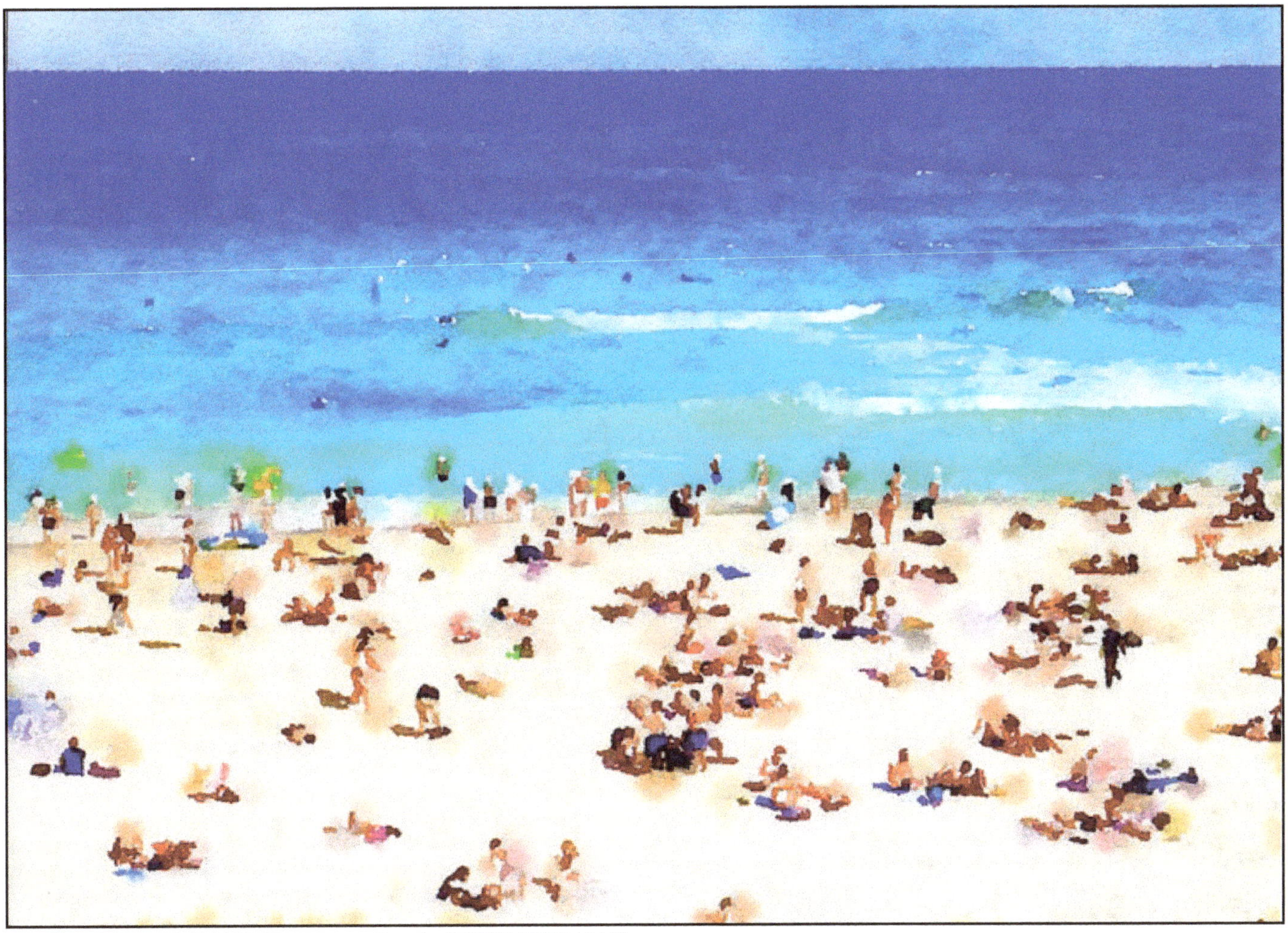

▲'Life's A Beach' (2019), Tamarama Beach, NSW [ASTB1919].

'Broken Break' (2020), Tamarama Beach, NSW [ASTB2001].▼

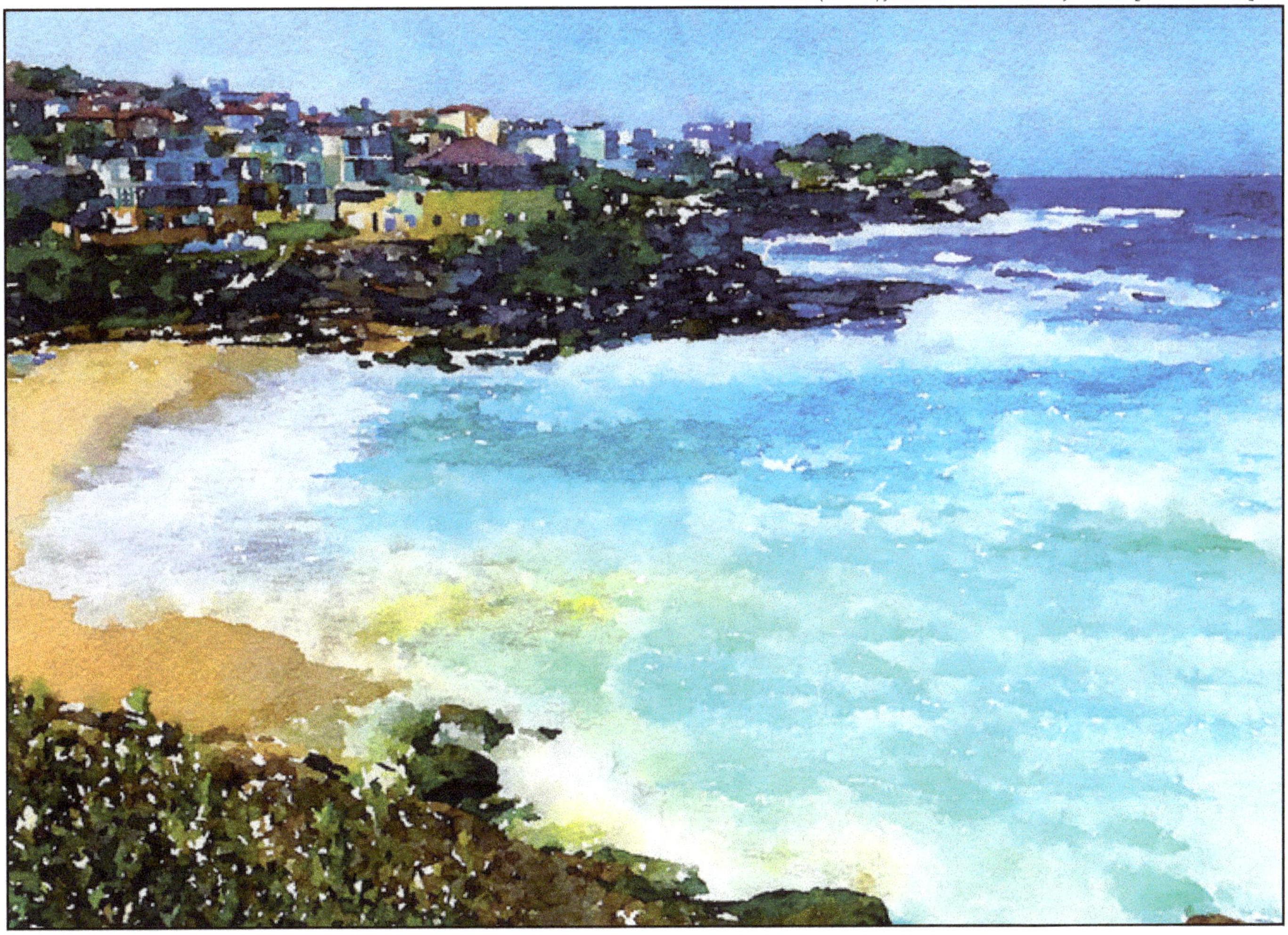

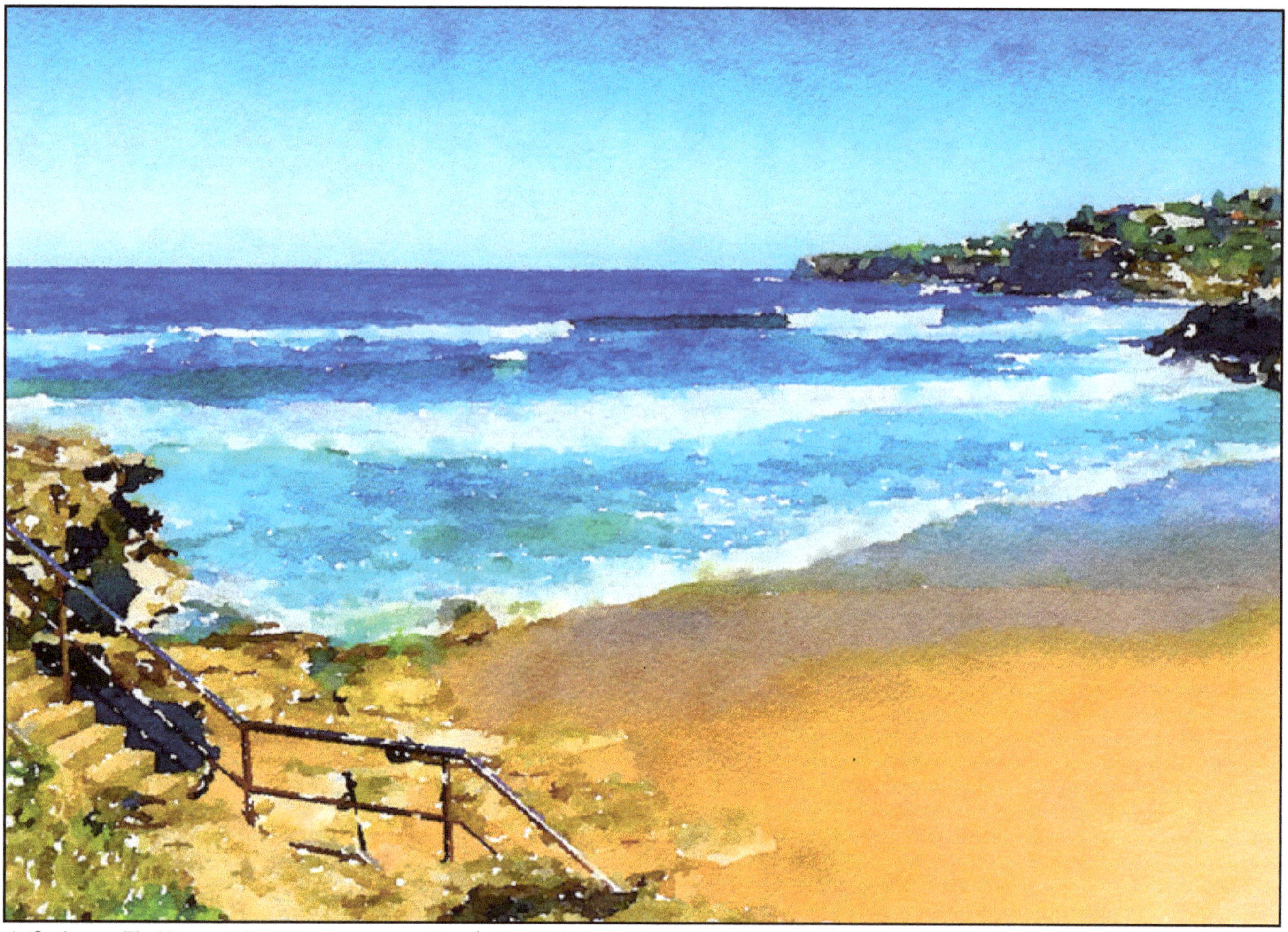

▲'Stairway To Heaven' (2020), Tamarama Beach, NSW [ASTB2002].

'Tamarama Towers' (2020), Tamarama Beach, NSW [ASTB2003].▼

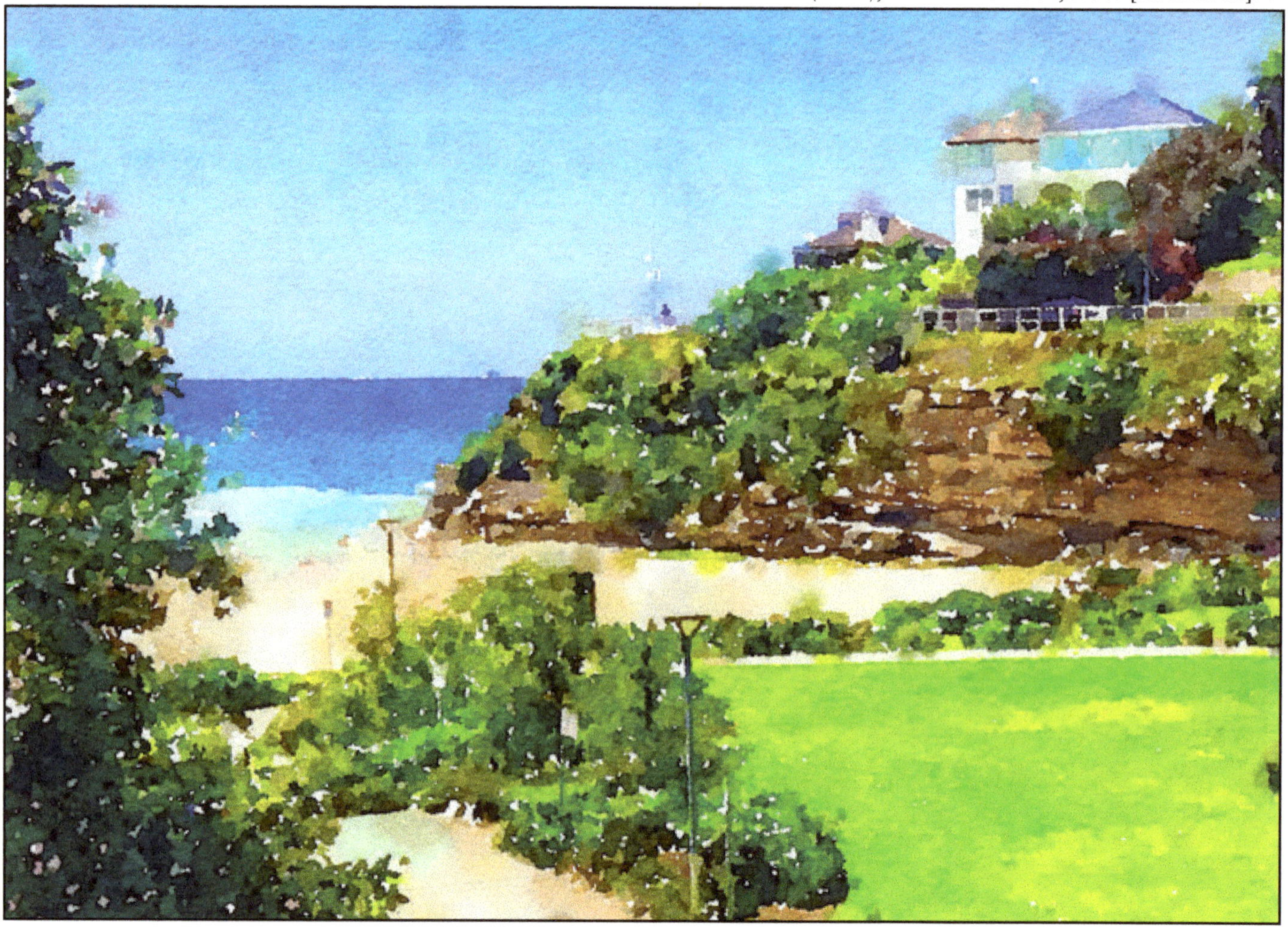

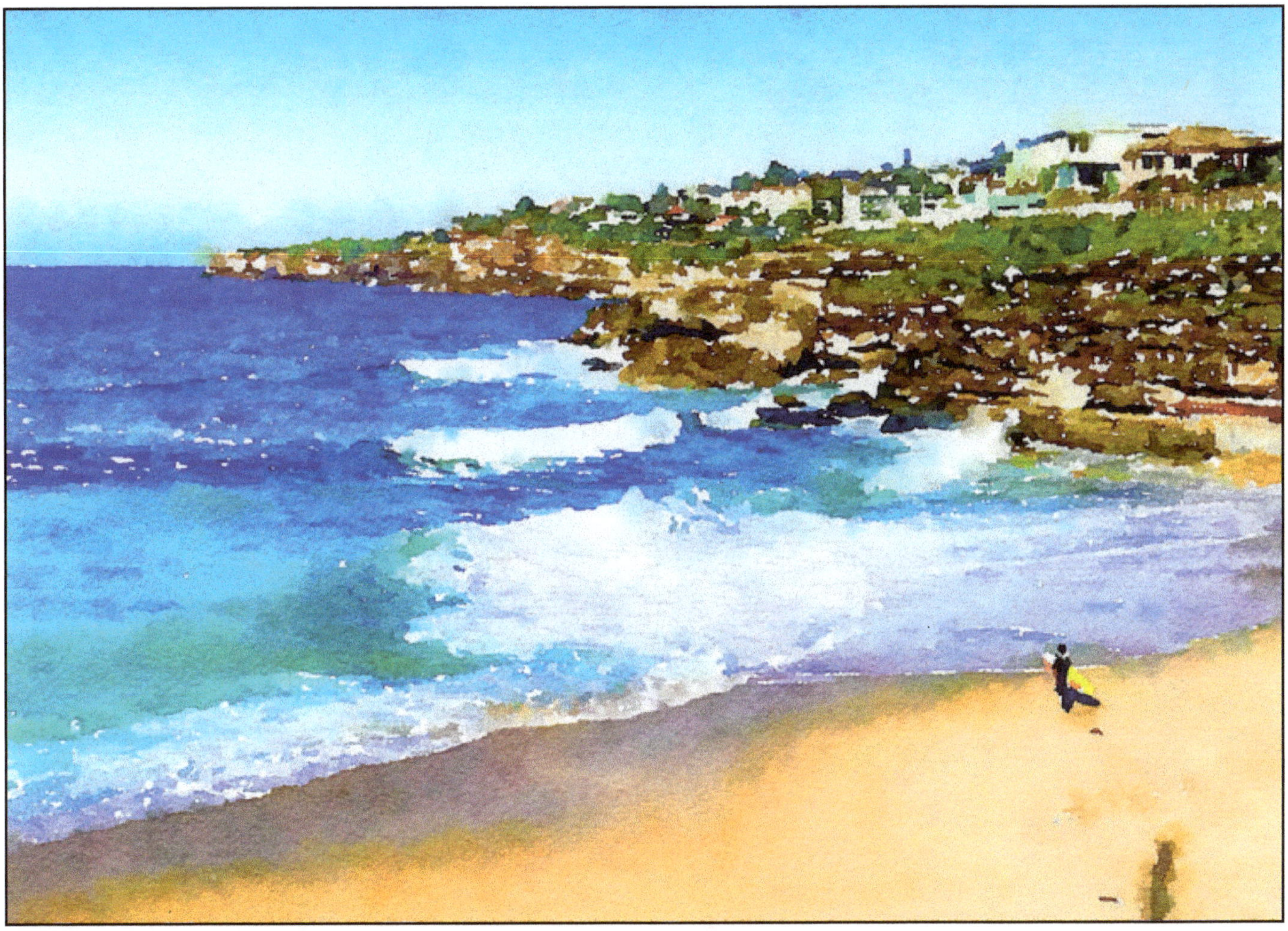

▲'Paying Respect' (2020), Tamarama Beach, NSW [ASTB2004].

'Tamarama Foam' (2020), Tamarama Beach, NSW [ASTB2005].▼

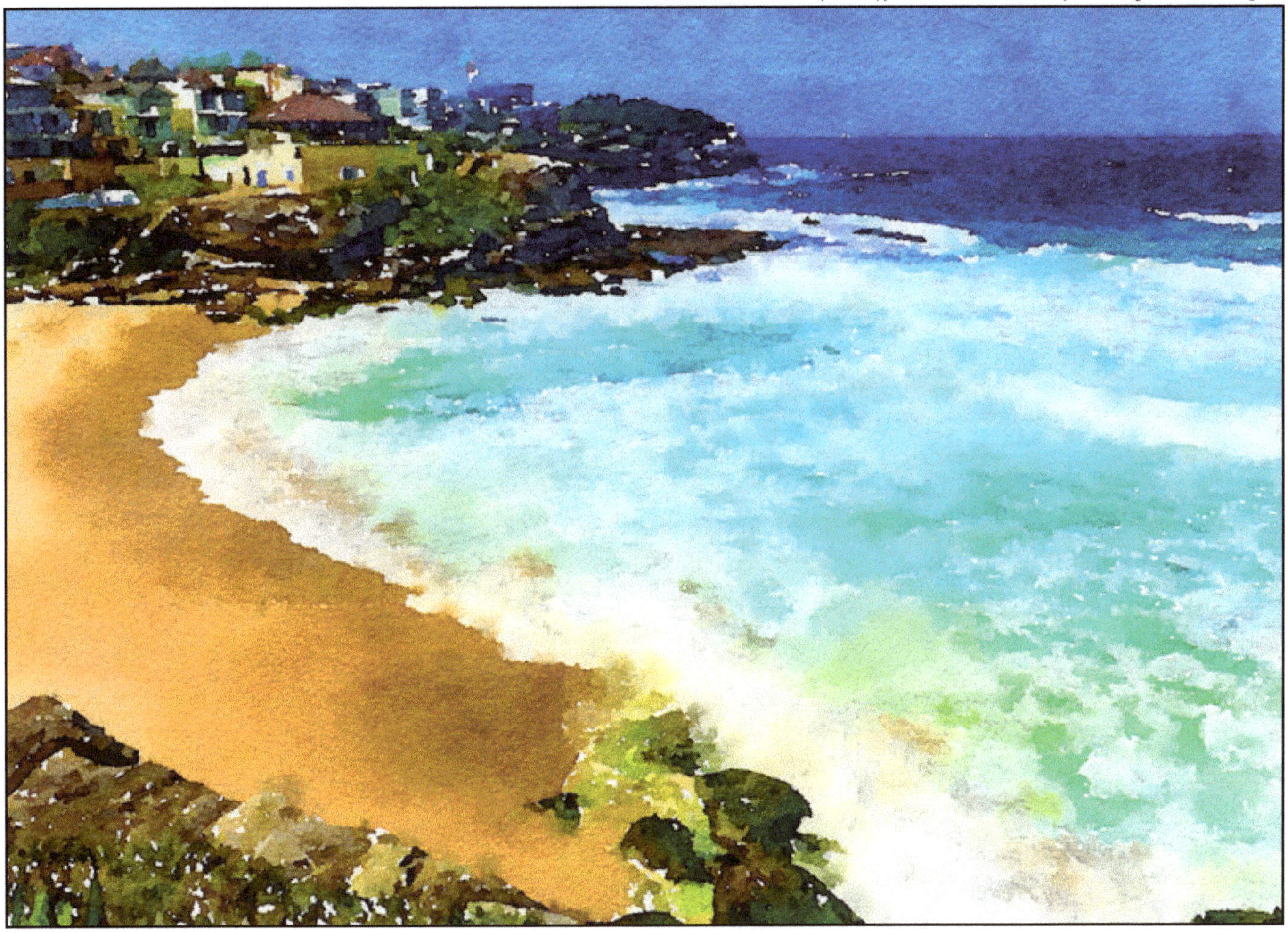

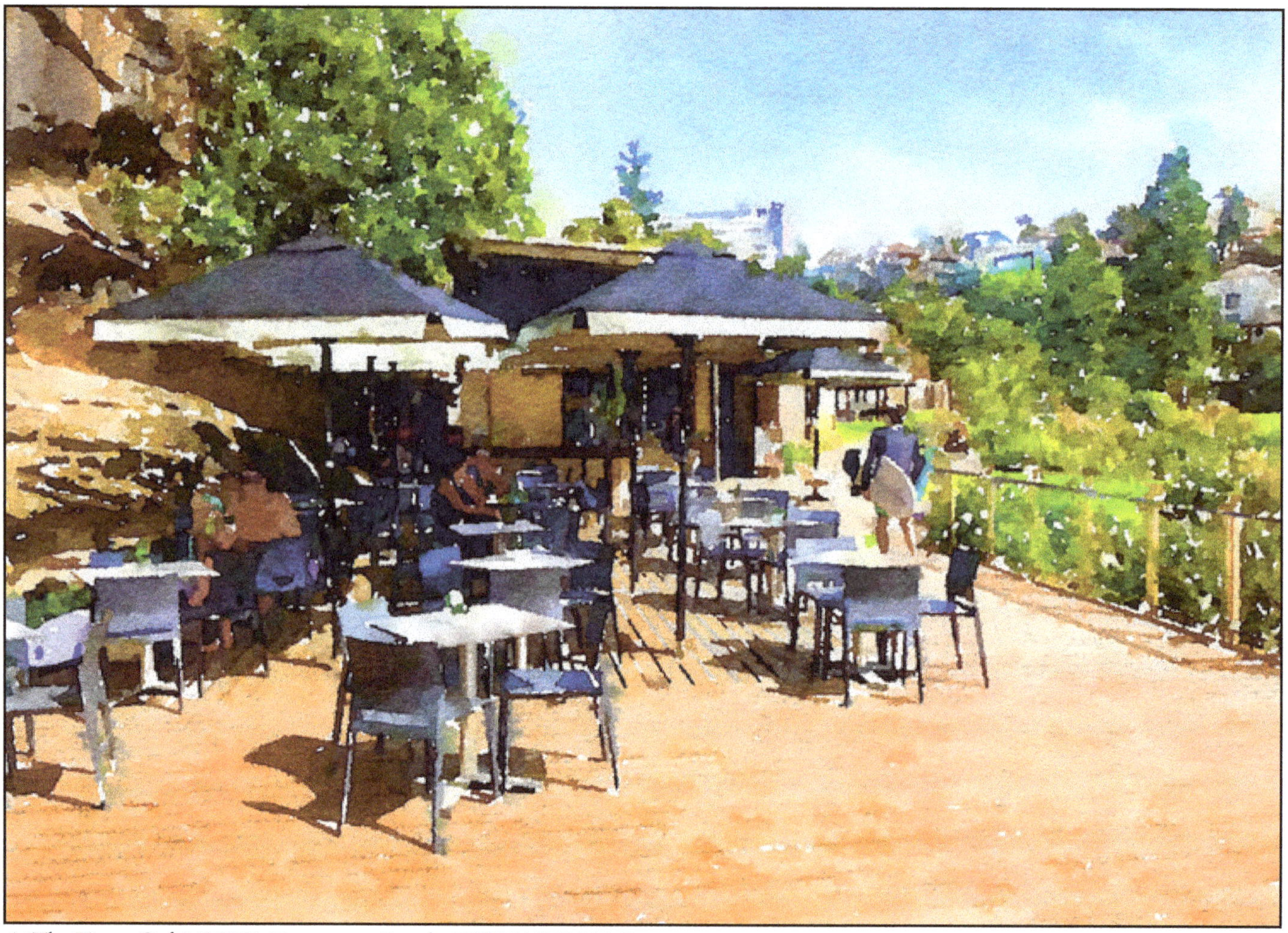

▲'The Tama Cafe' (2020), Tamarama Beach, NSW [ASTB2006].

'Tamarama Panarama' (2021), Tamarama Beach, NSW [ASTB2101]. ⊘▼

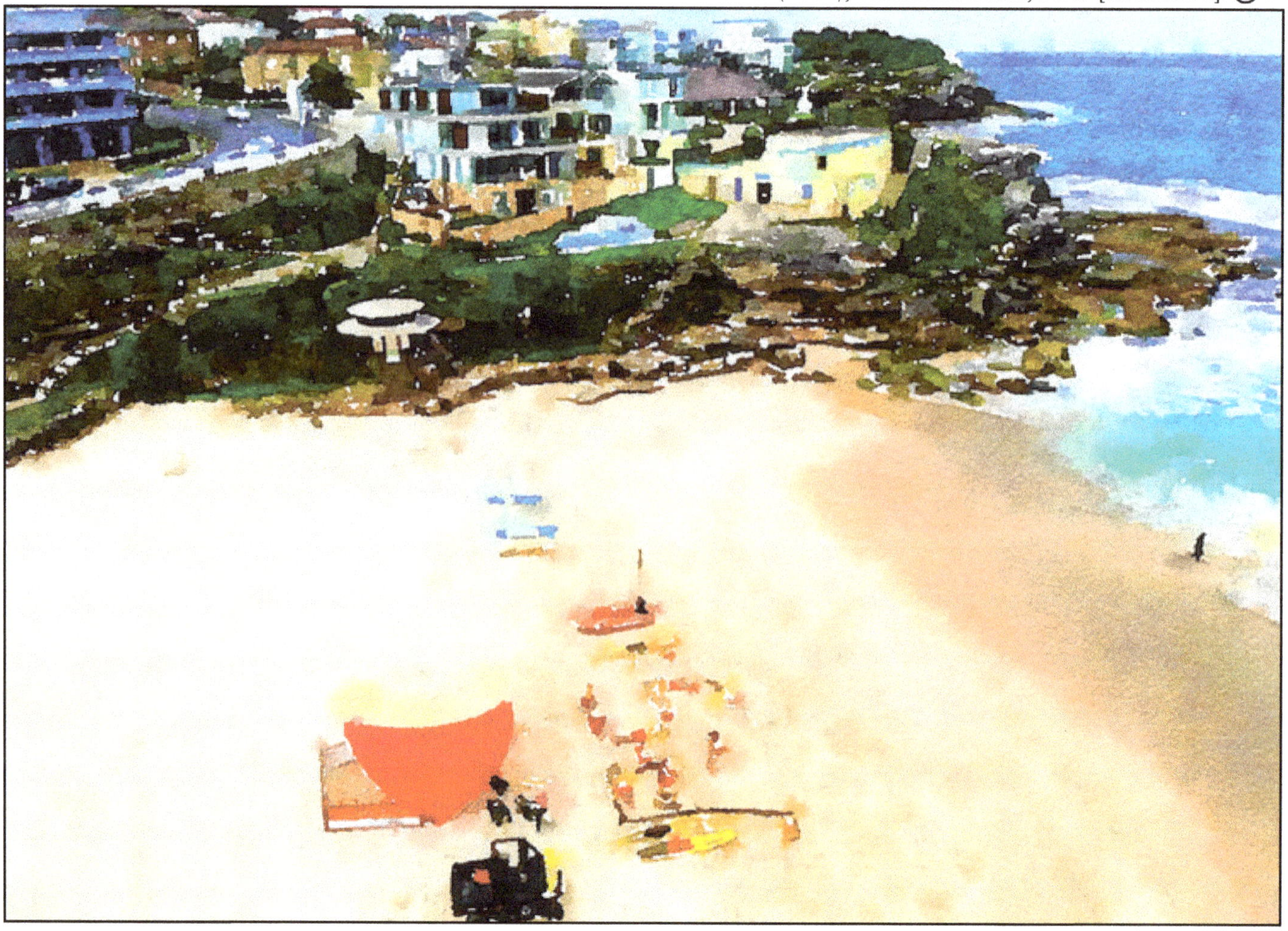

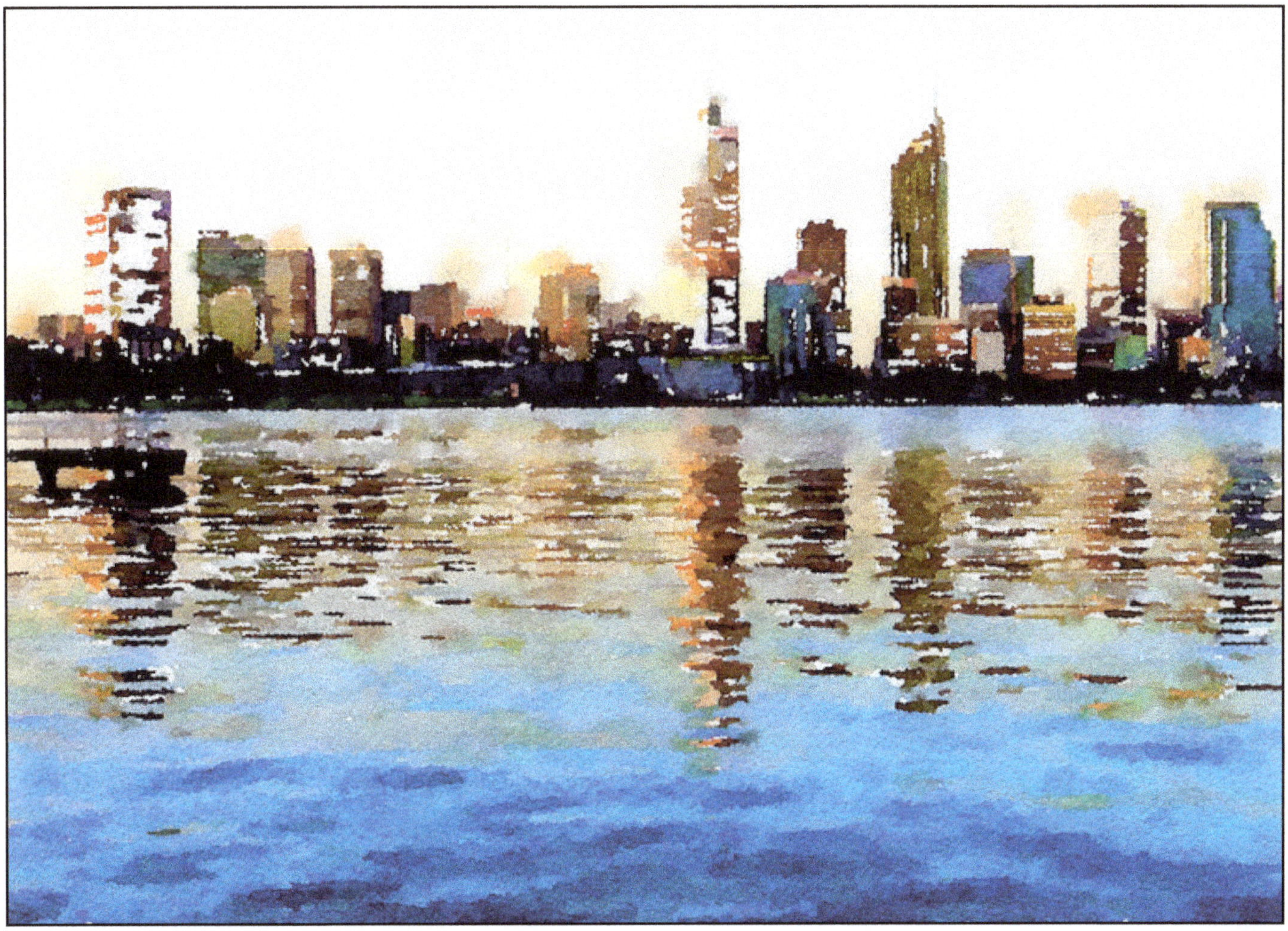

▲'Swan River & Perth' (2021), Perth, WA [ASWA2101].

'Cottesloe Beach & Pavilion' (2007), Perth, WA [ASWA0701].▼

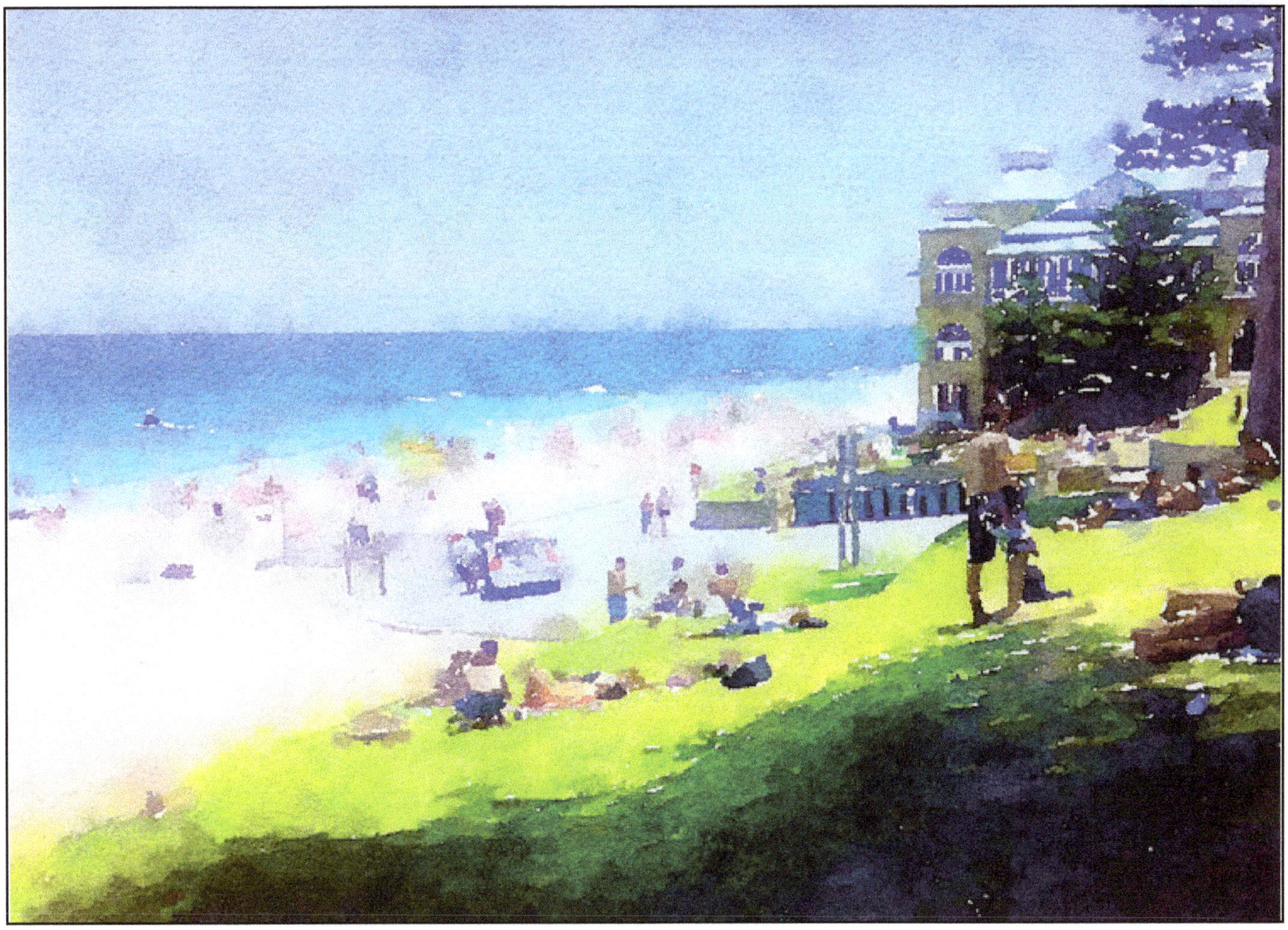

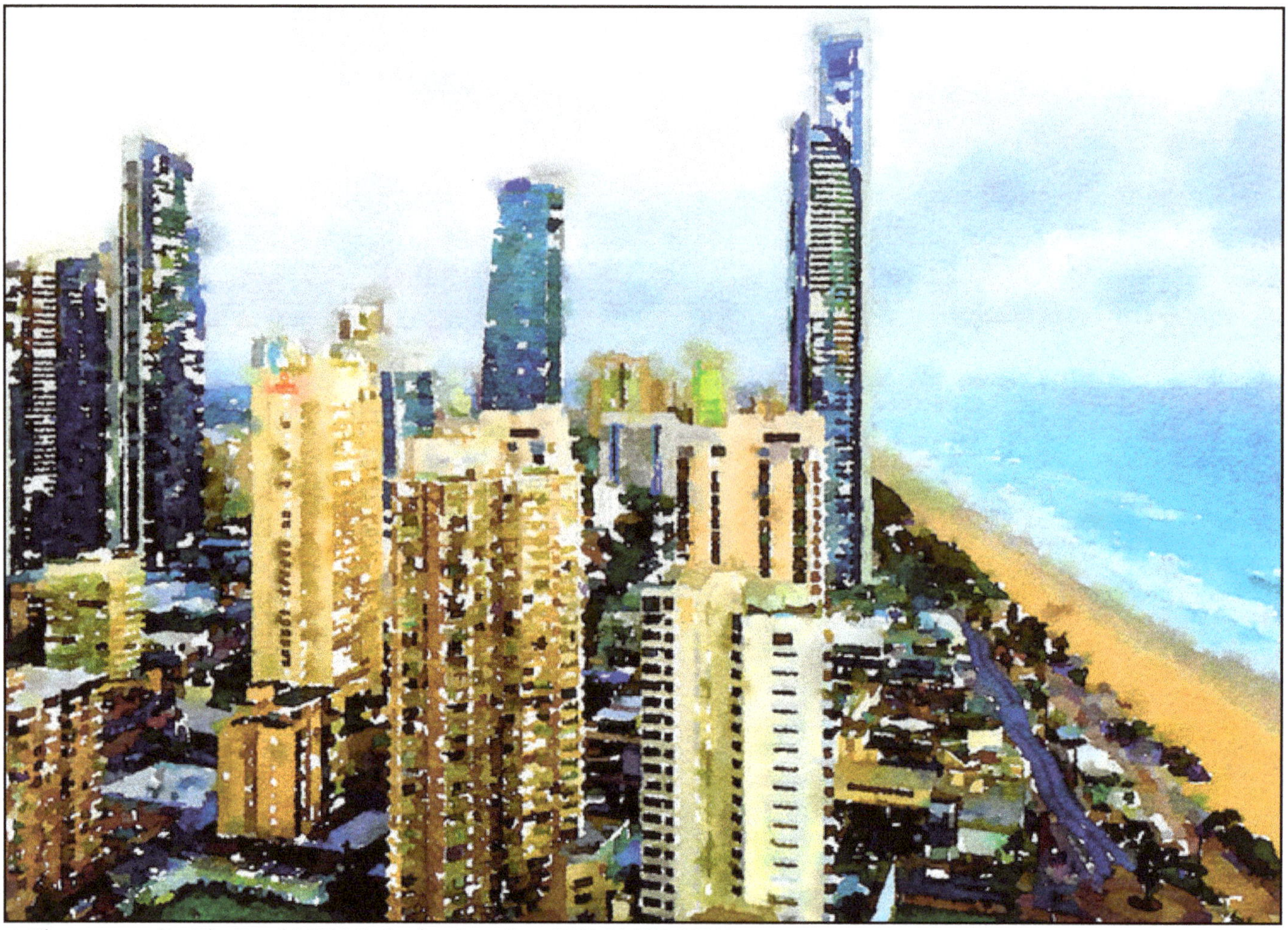

▲'Skyscrapers On The Beach' (2015), Surfers Paradise, QLD [ASQL1501].

'The Twinkling Towers' (2015), Surfers Paradise, QLD [ASQL1502].▼

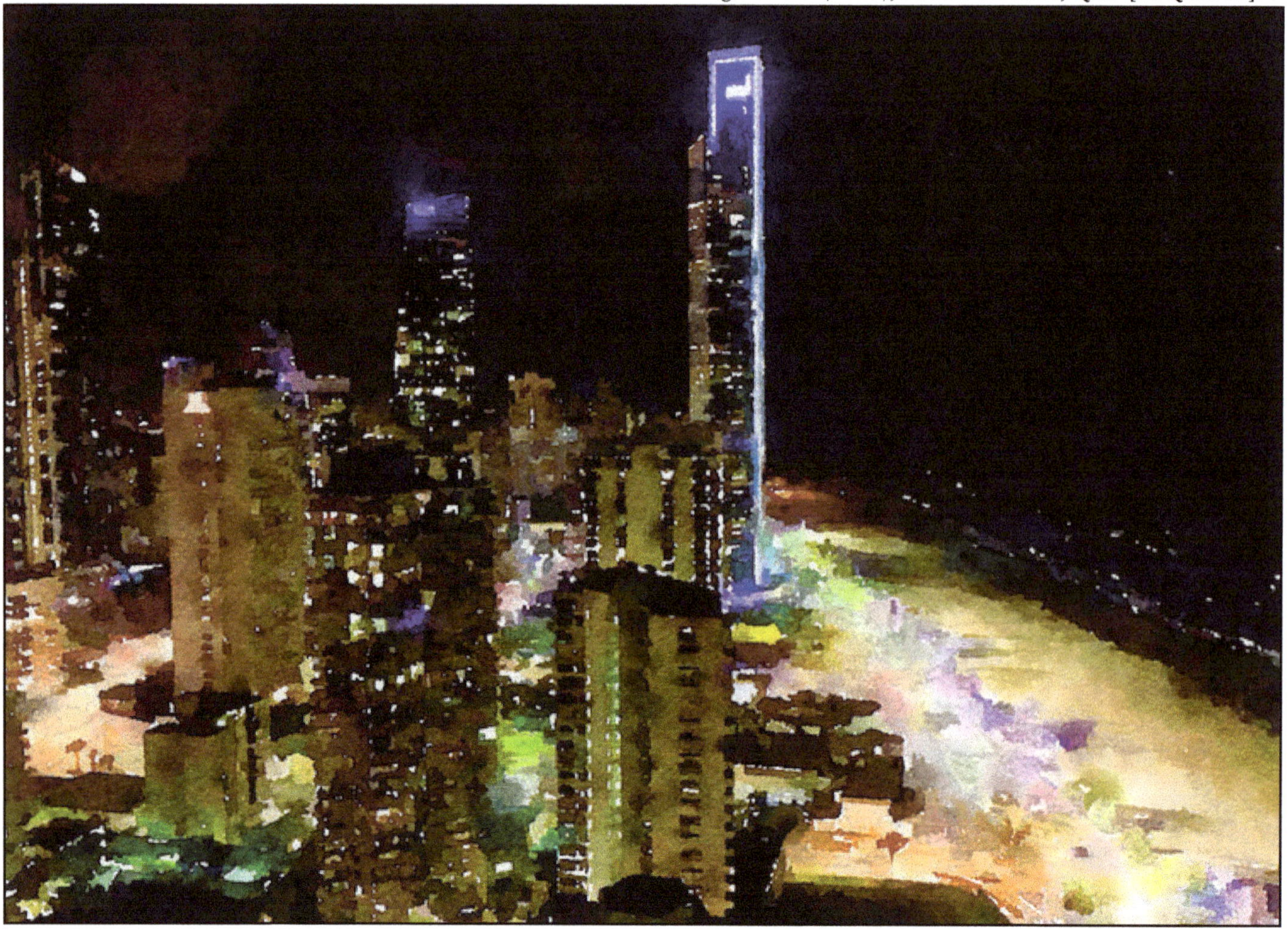

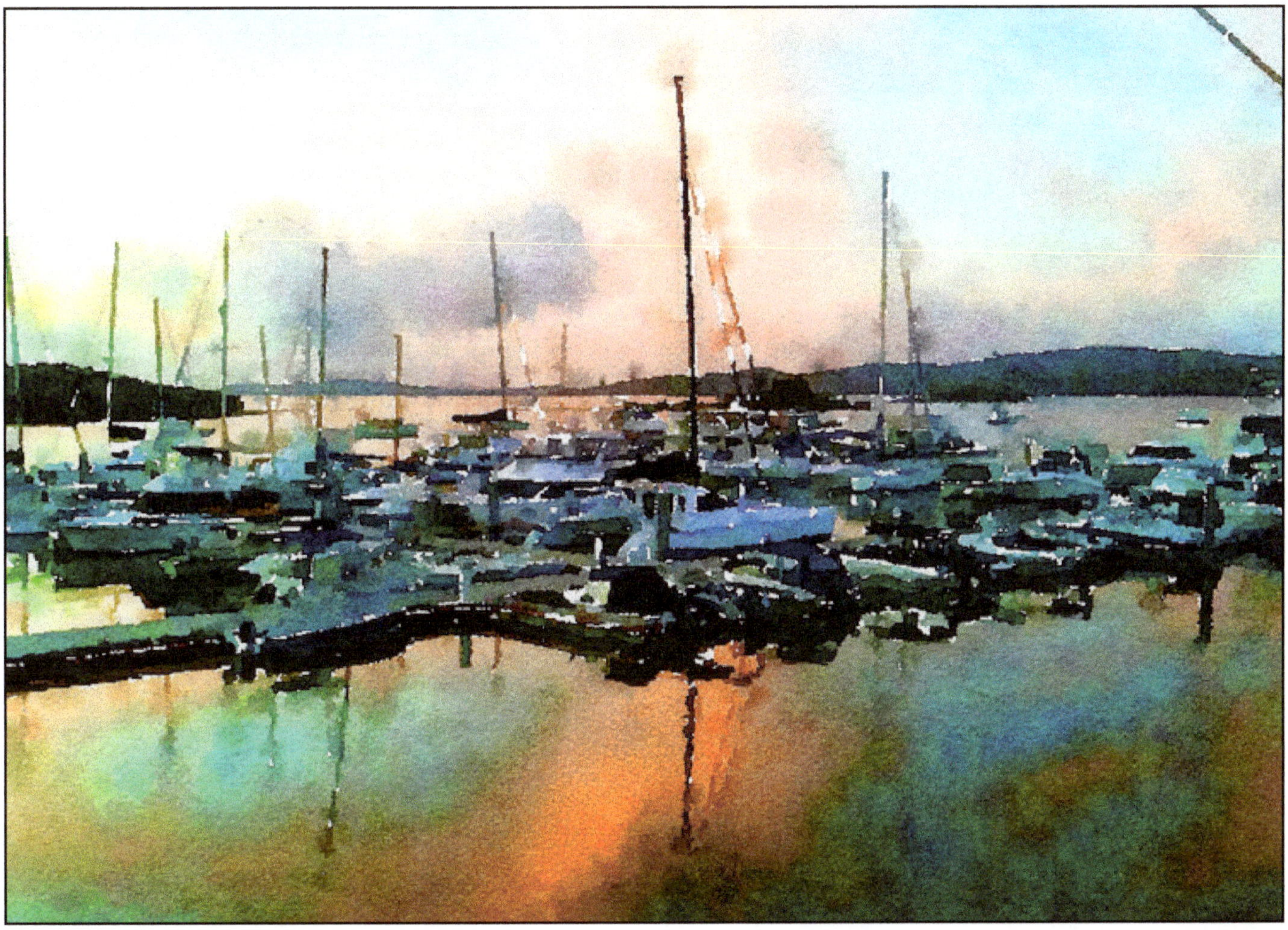

▲'Marina Masts' (2010), Hobart, QLD [ASTA1001].

'Sandy Bay Marina' (2019), Hobart, TAS [ASTA1901].▼

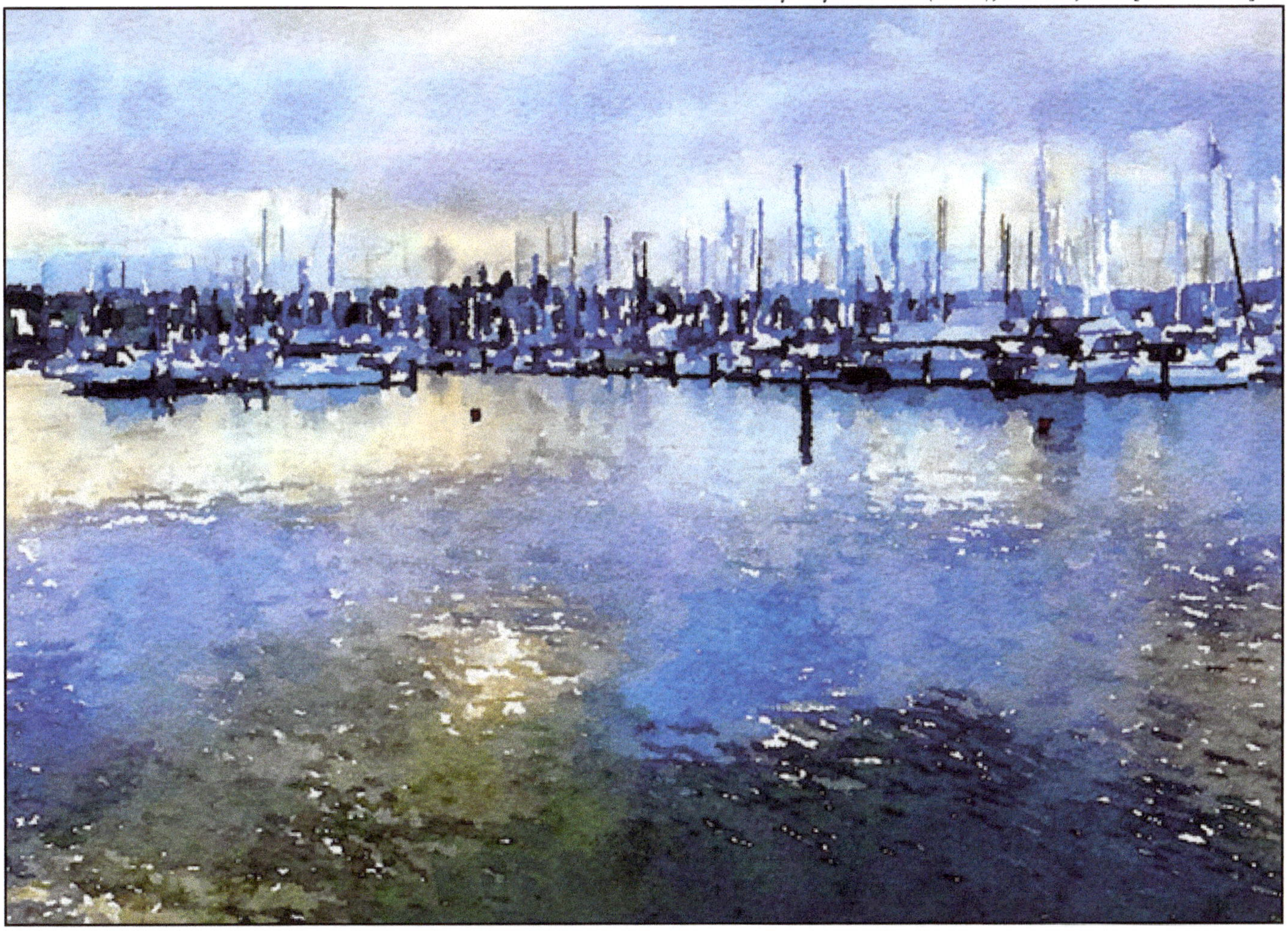

New Zealand...

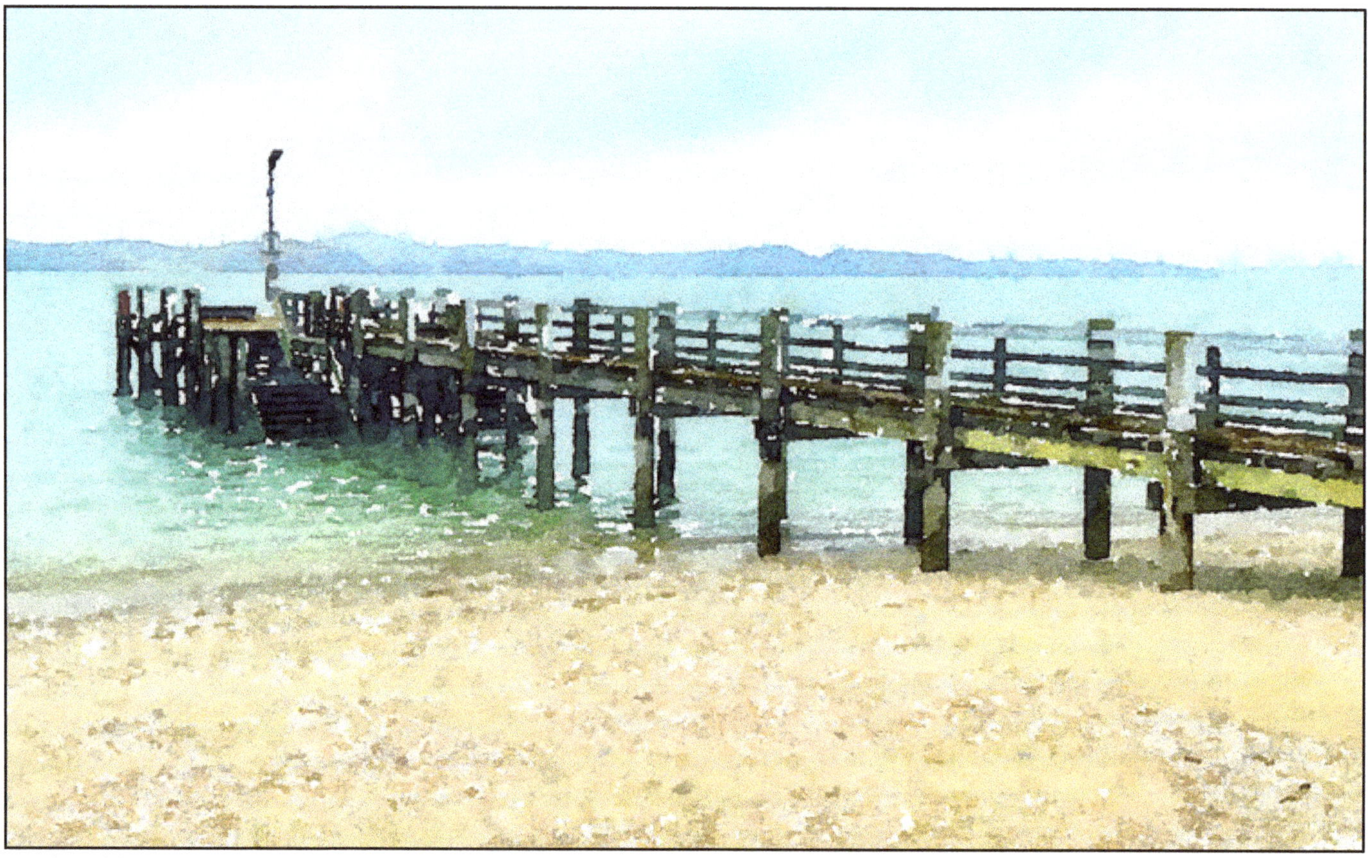

▲'The Old Wooden Pier' (2019), Maraetai, New Zealand [ONZ(NI)1902].

'Waiomanu Beach' (2019), Maraetai, New Zealand [ONZ(NI)1903].▼

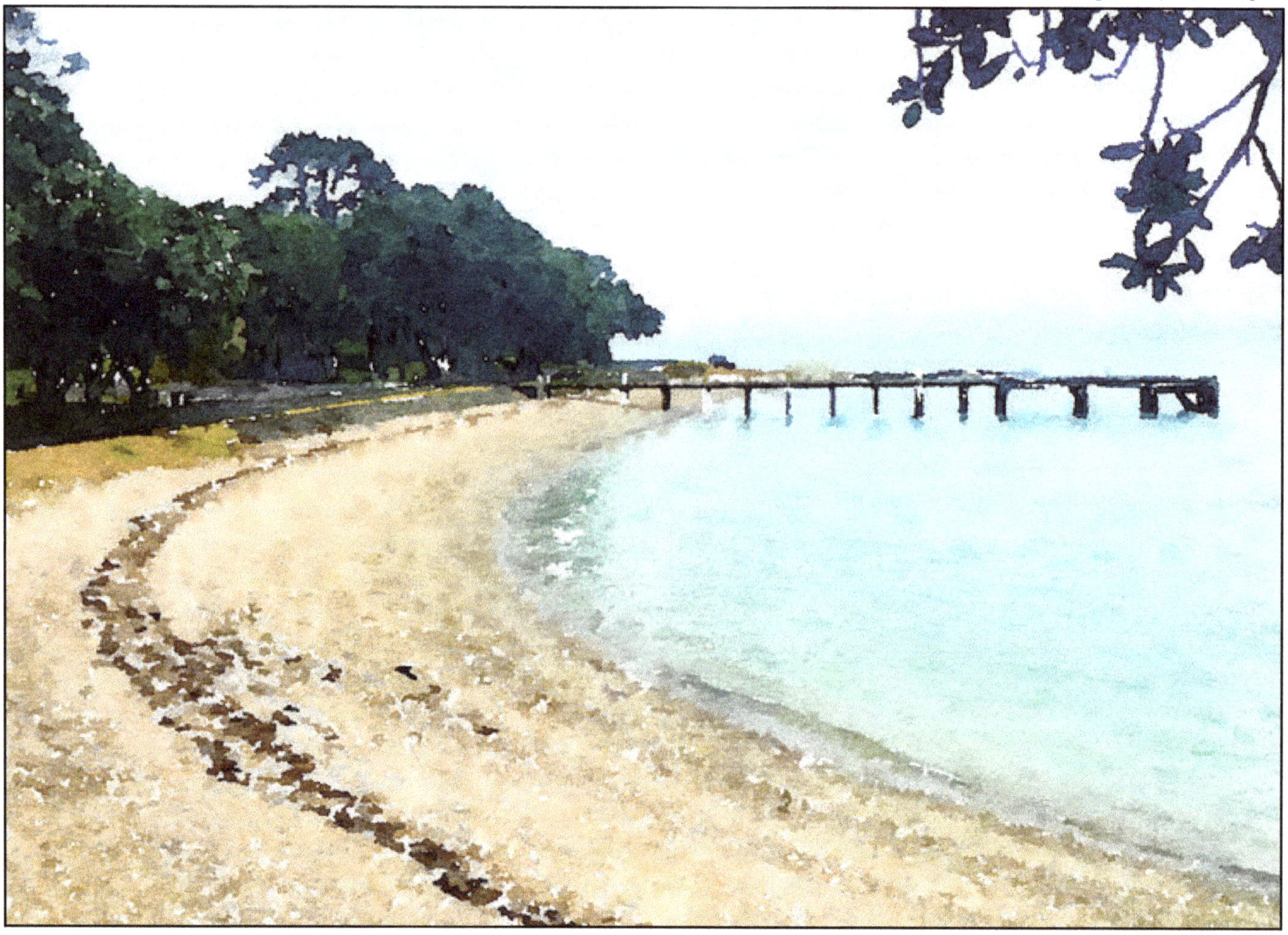

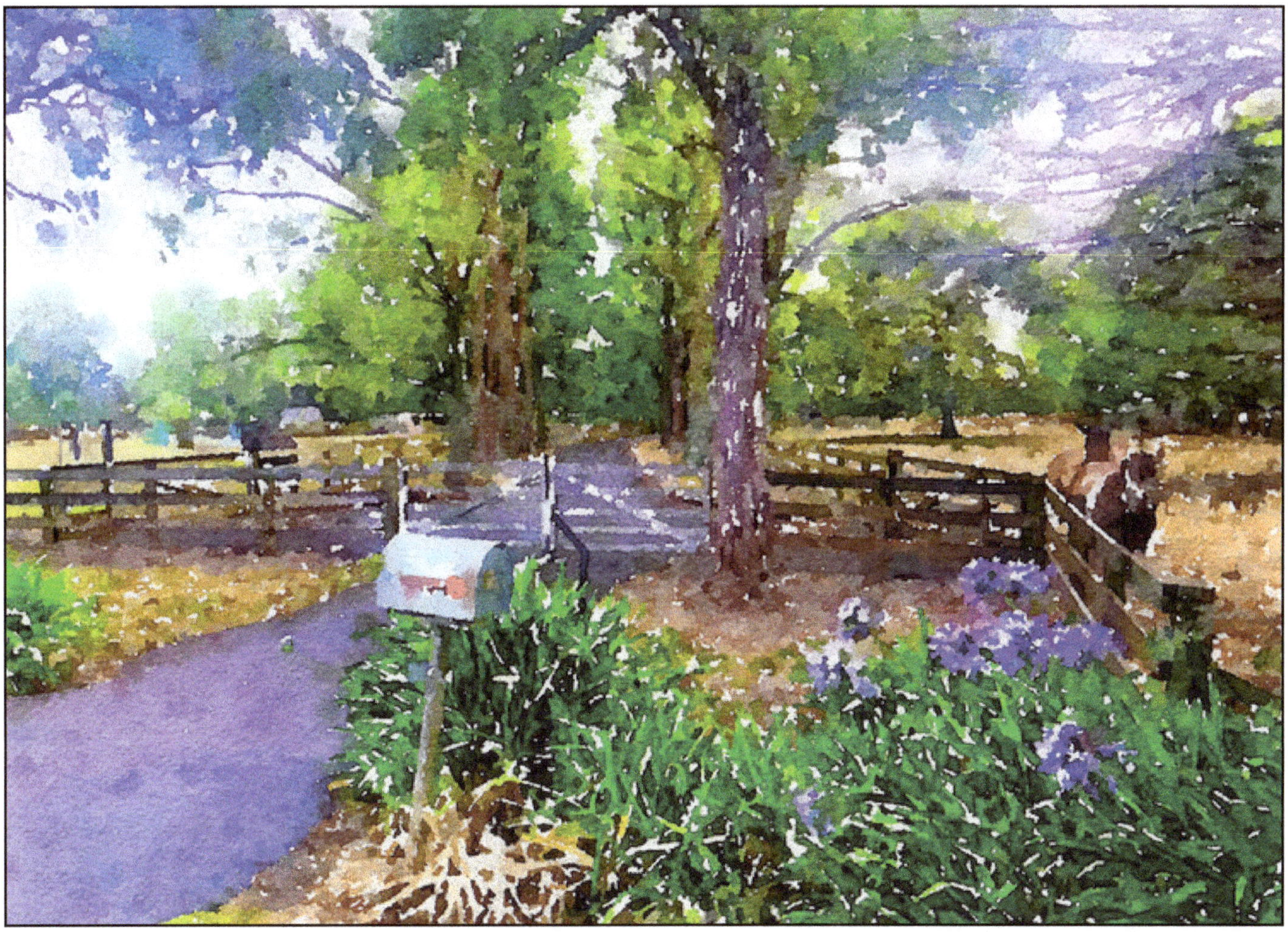

▲'Ardmore Farm' (2020), New Zealand [ONZ(NI)2001].

'Sunrise Over Auckland' (2019), New Zealand [ONZ(NI)1901].▼

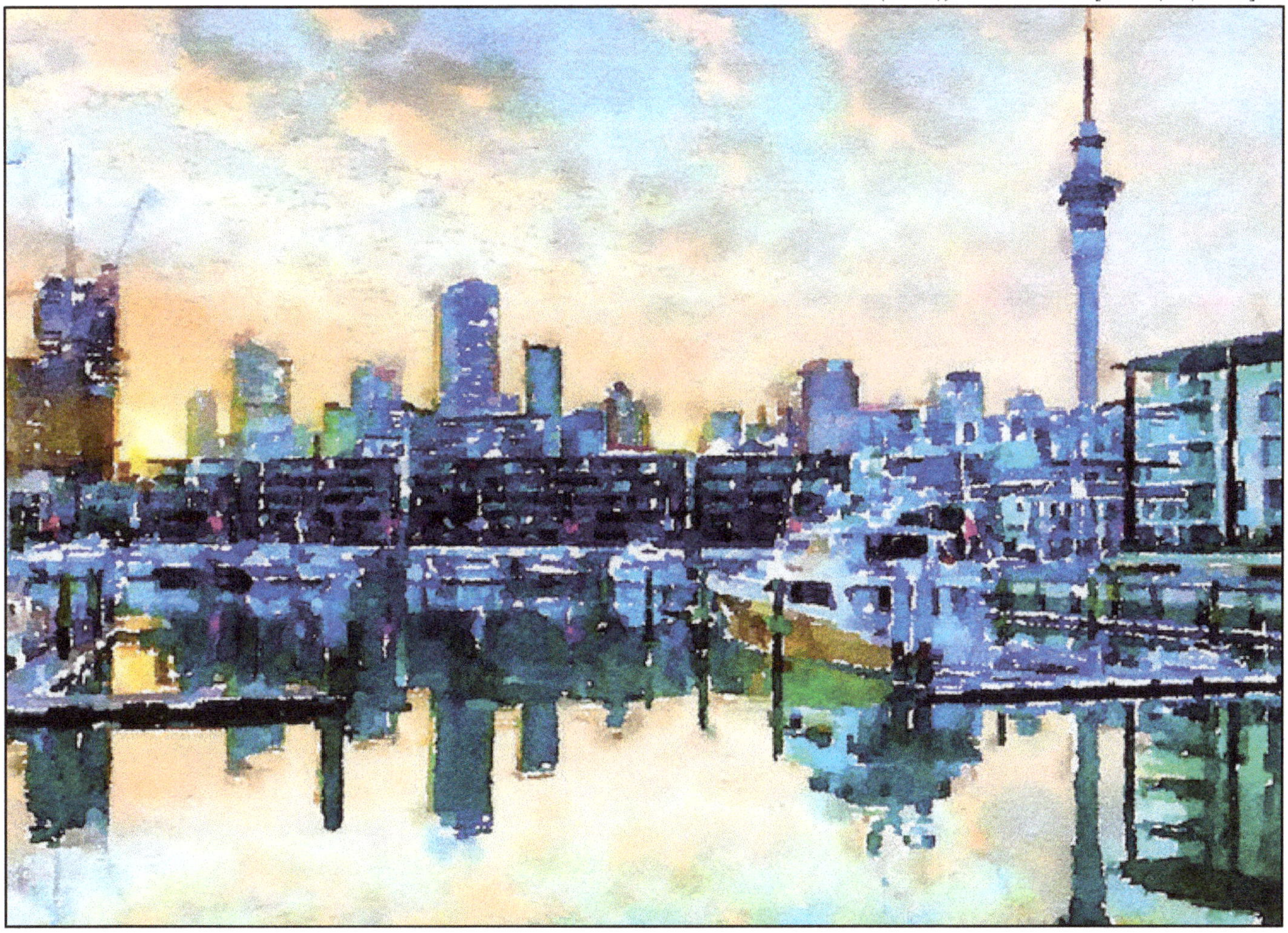

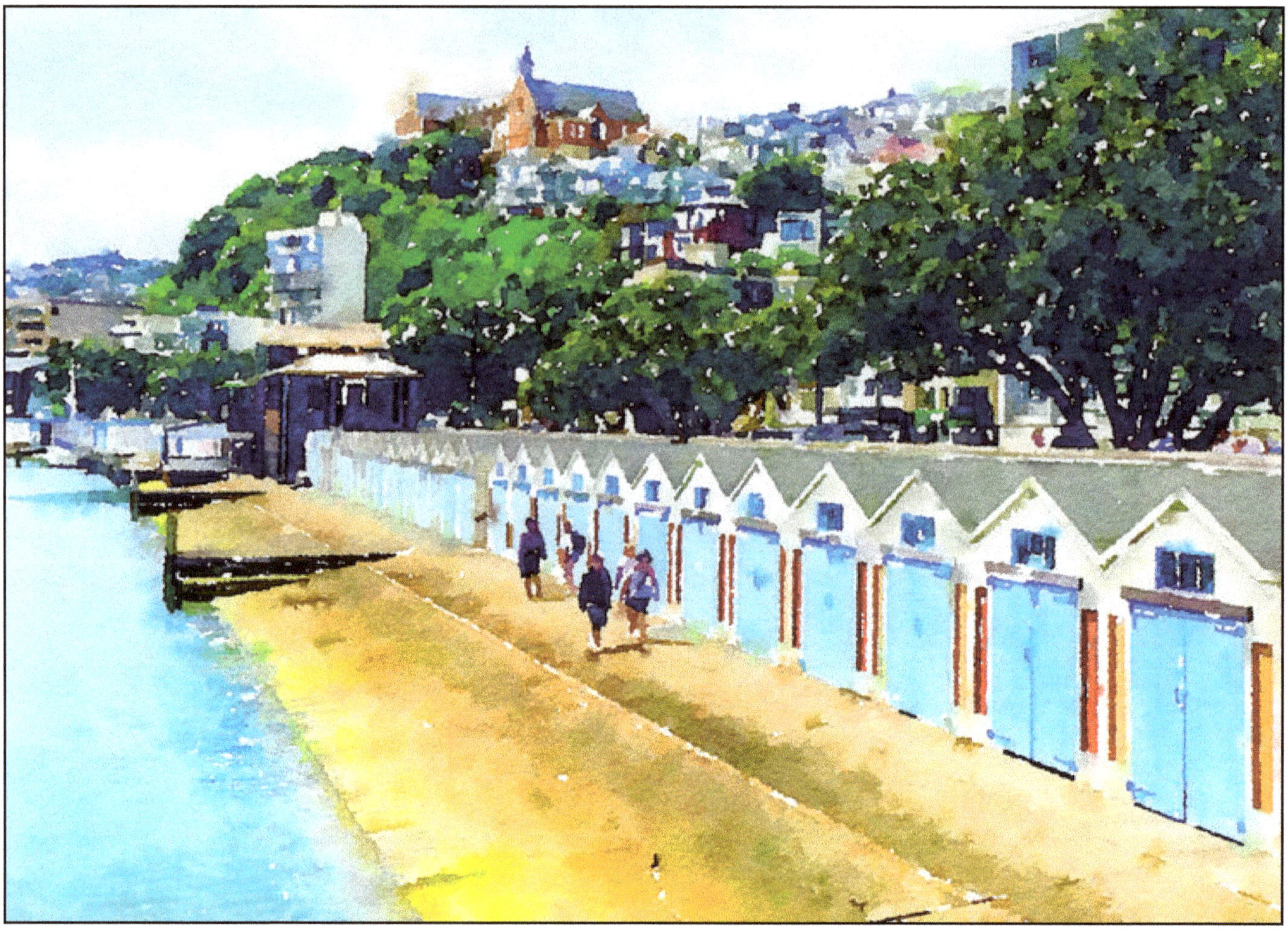

▲'Oriental Bay' (2020), Wellington, New Zealand [ONZ(NI)2002].▼

'Wellington Station' (2020), New Zealand [ONZ(NI)2003].▼

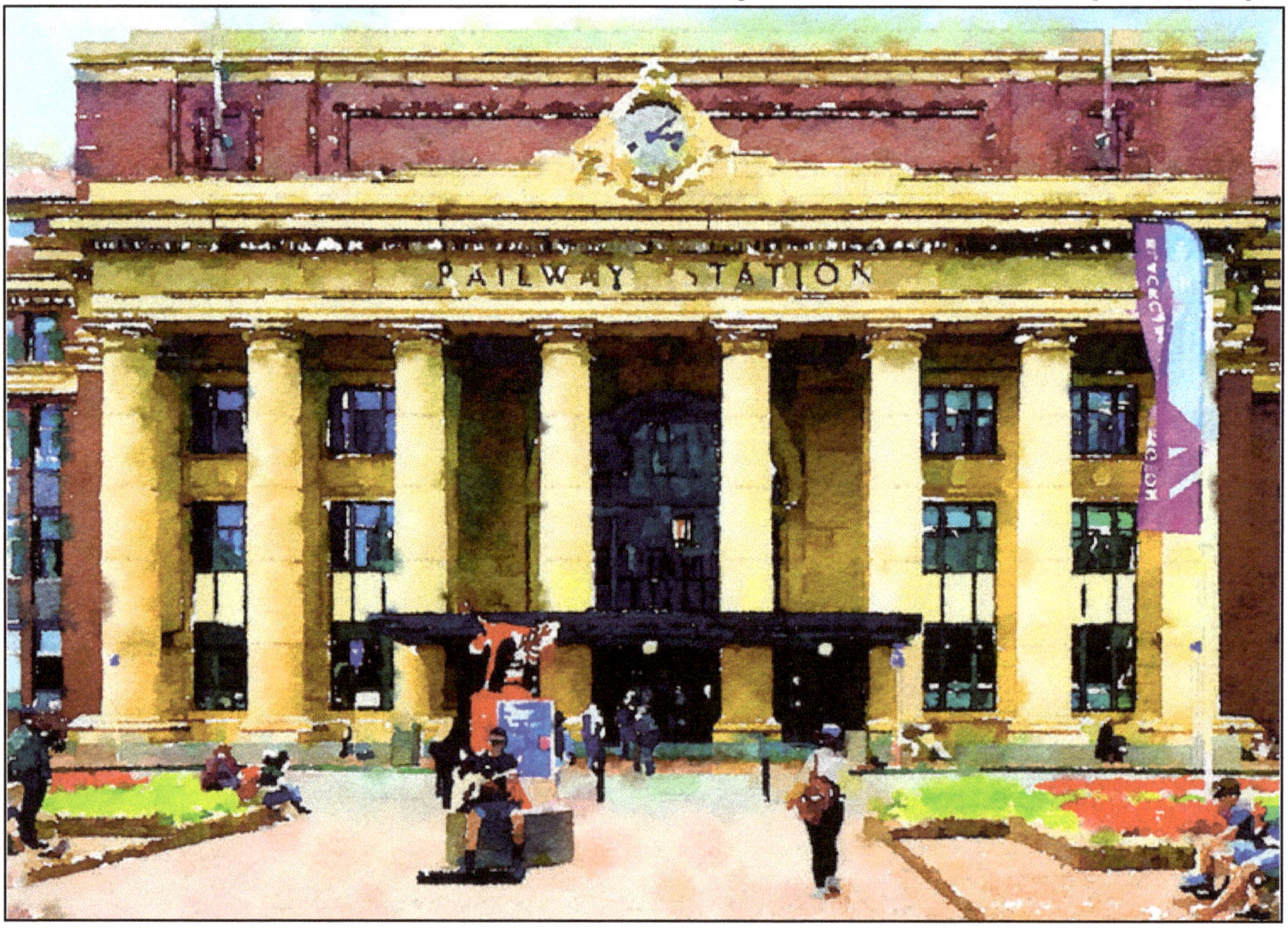

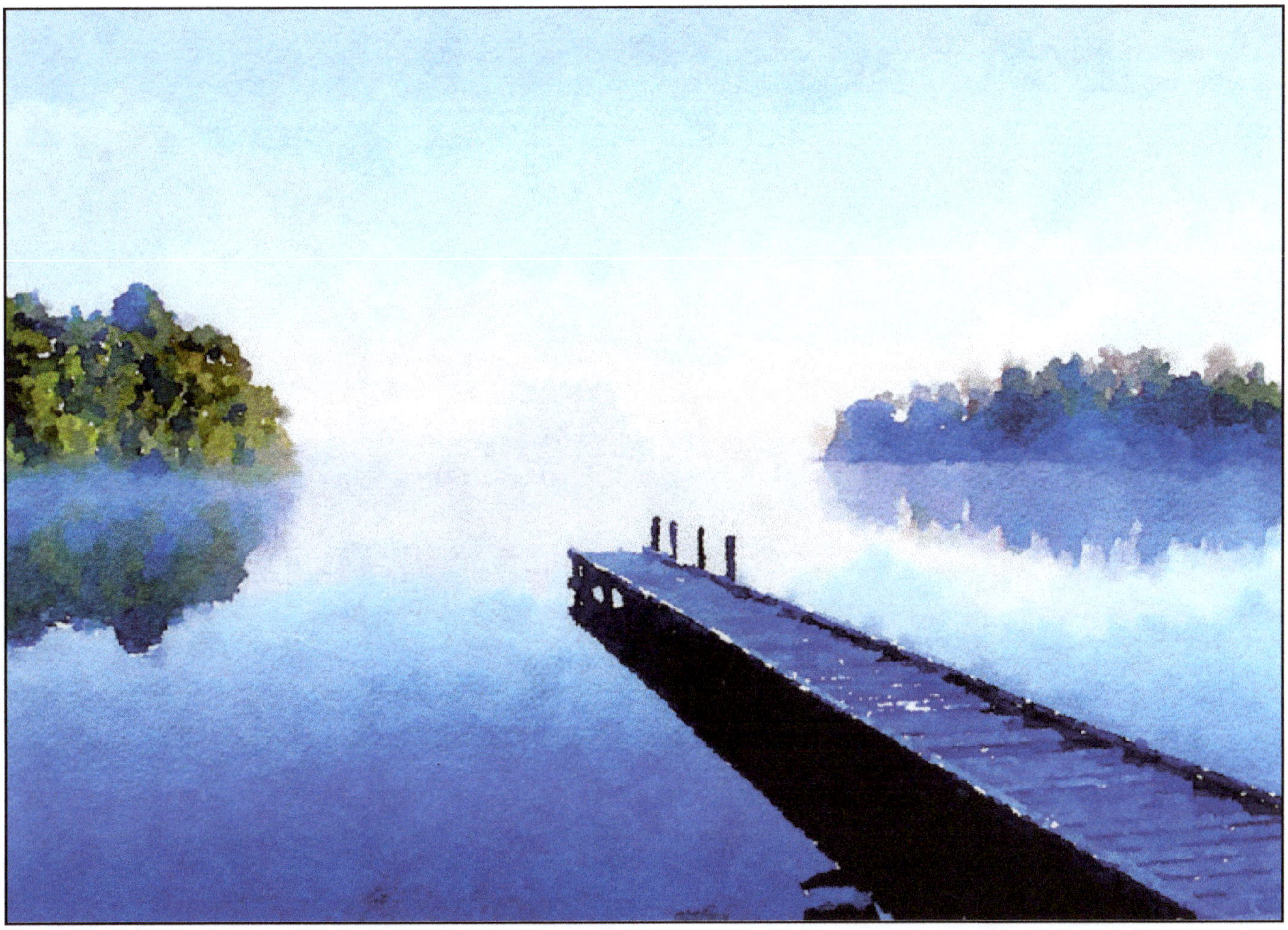

▲'Lake Mapourika' (2019), New Zealand [ONZ(SI)1901]. ©

'Milford Sound' (2020), New Zealand [ONZ(SI)2001].▼

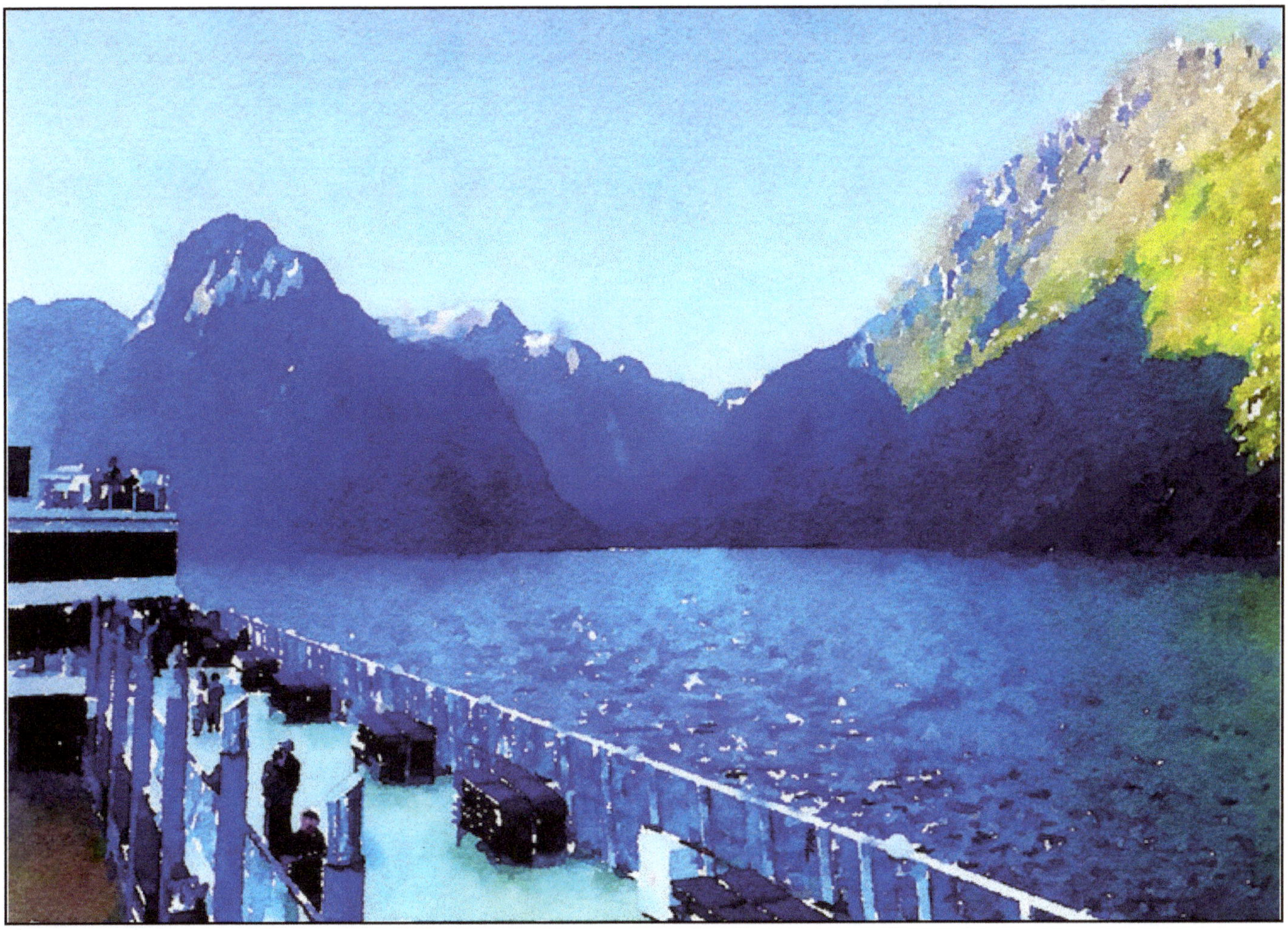

Pacific Islands...

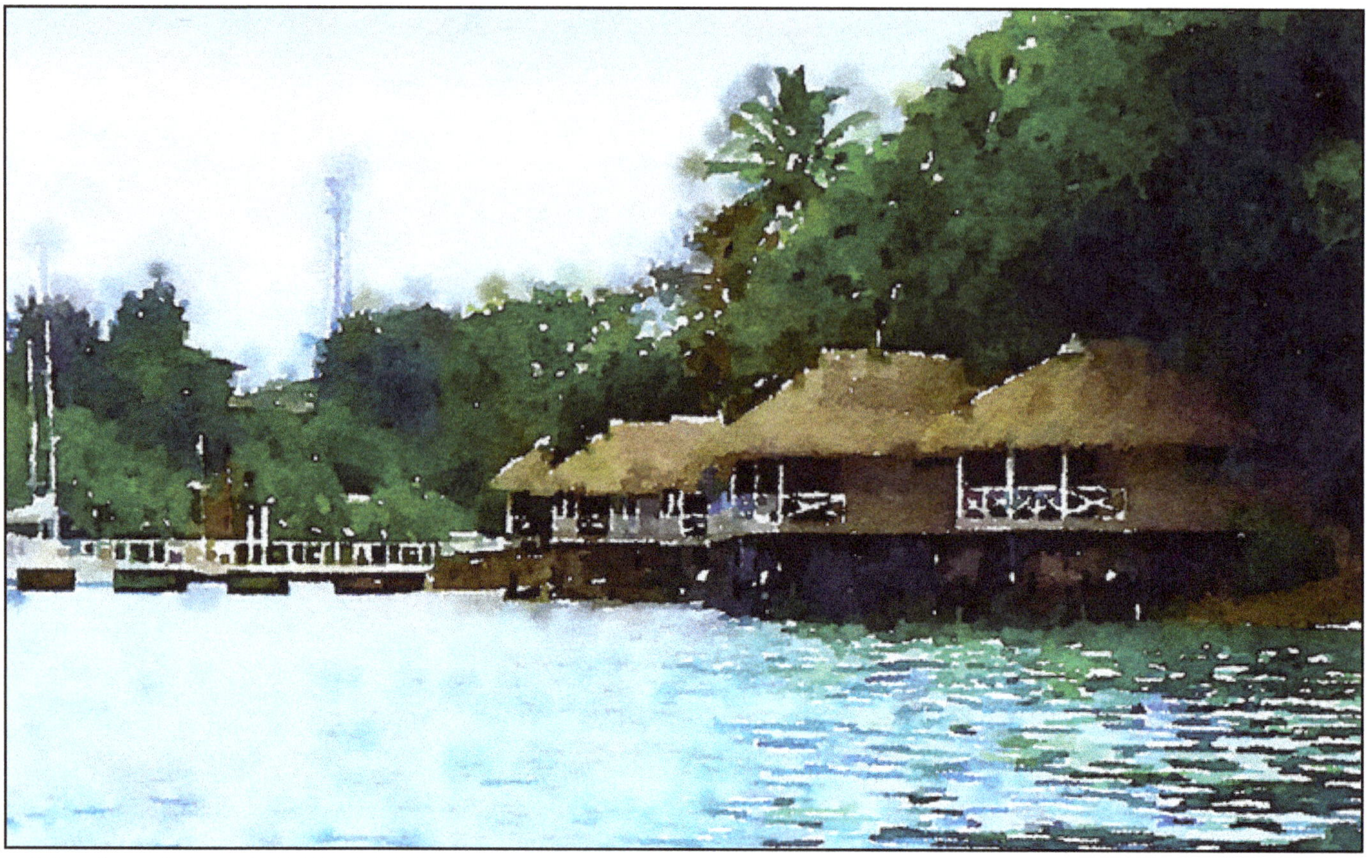

▲'Waterfront Cabanas' (2014), Fiji [OPI1403].

'Anse Vata Bay' (2014), New Caledonia[OPI1404].▼

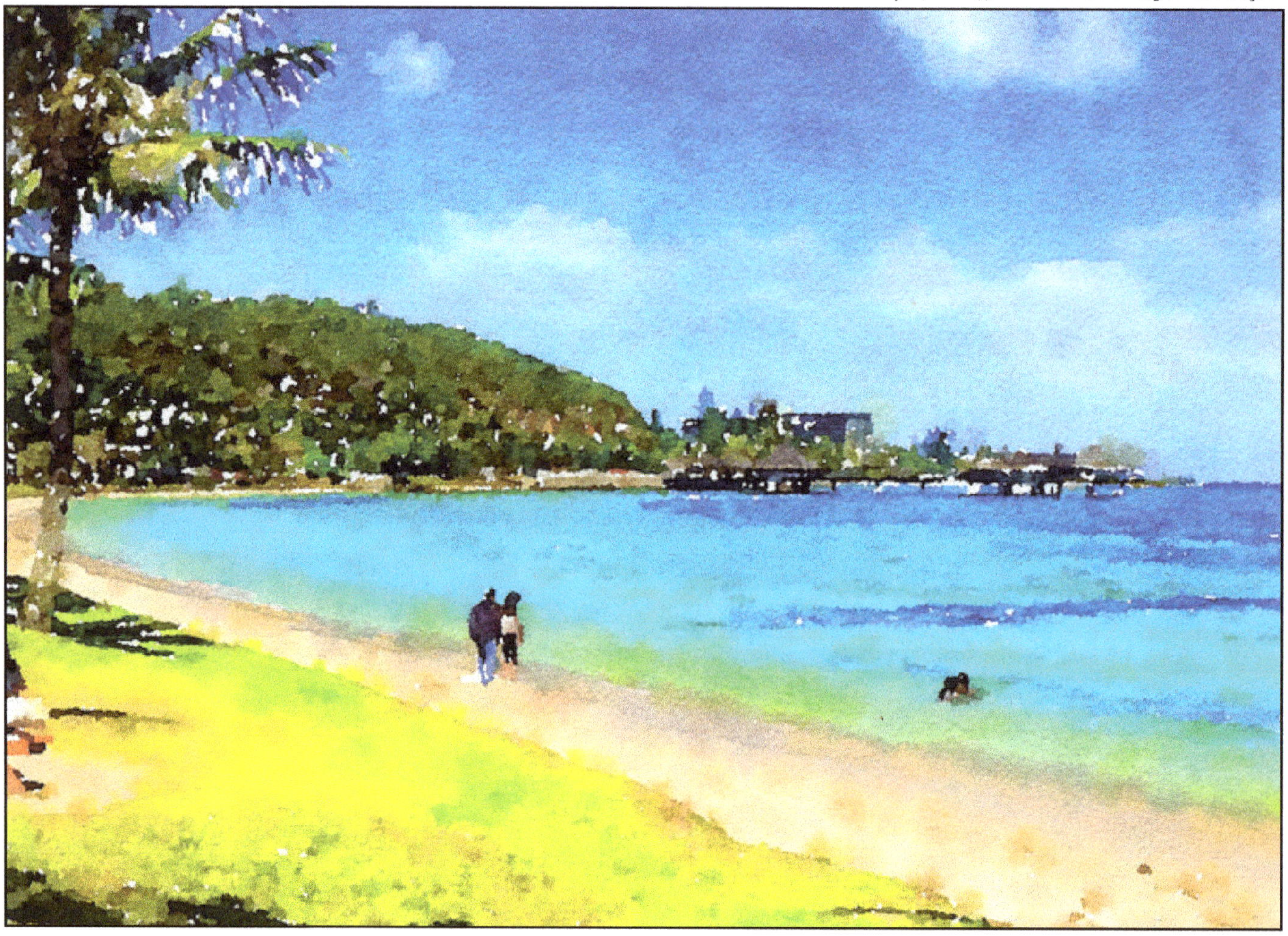

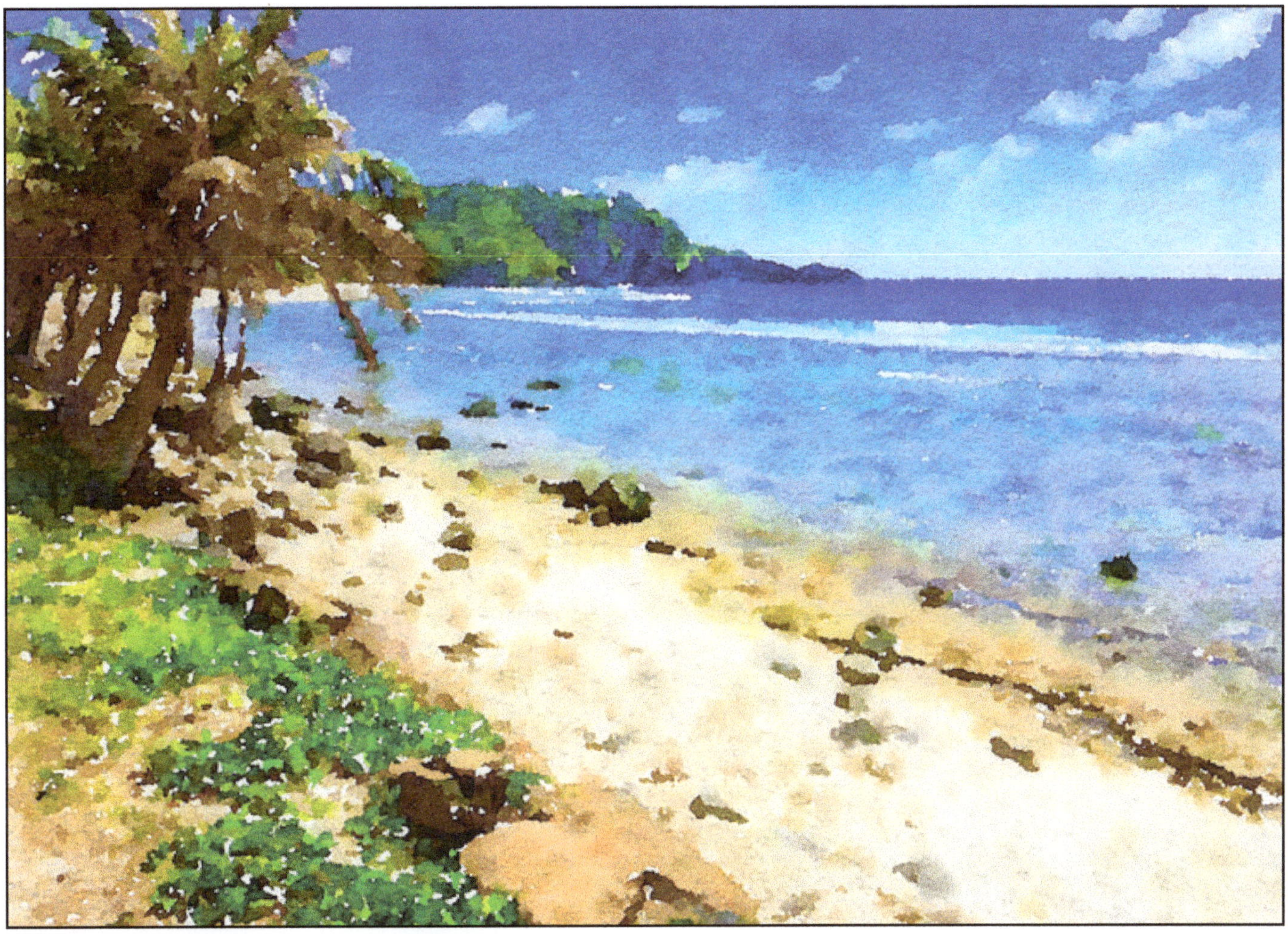

▲'Tifa Point' (2014), American Samoa [OPI1401].

'Faga'itua Bay' (2014), American Samoa [OPI1402].▼

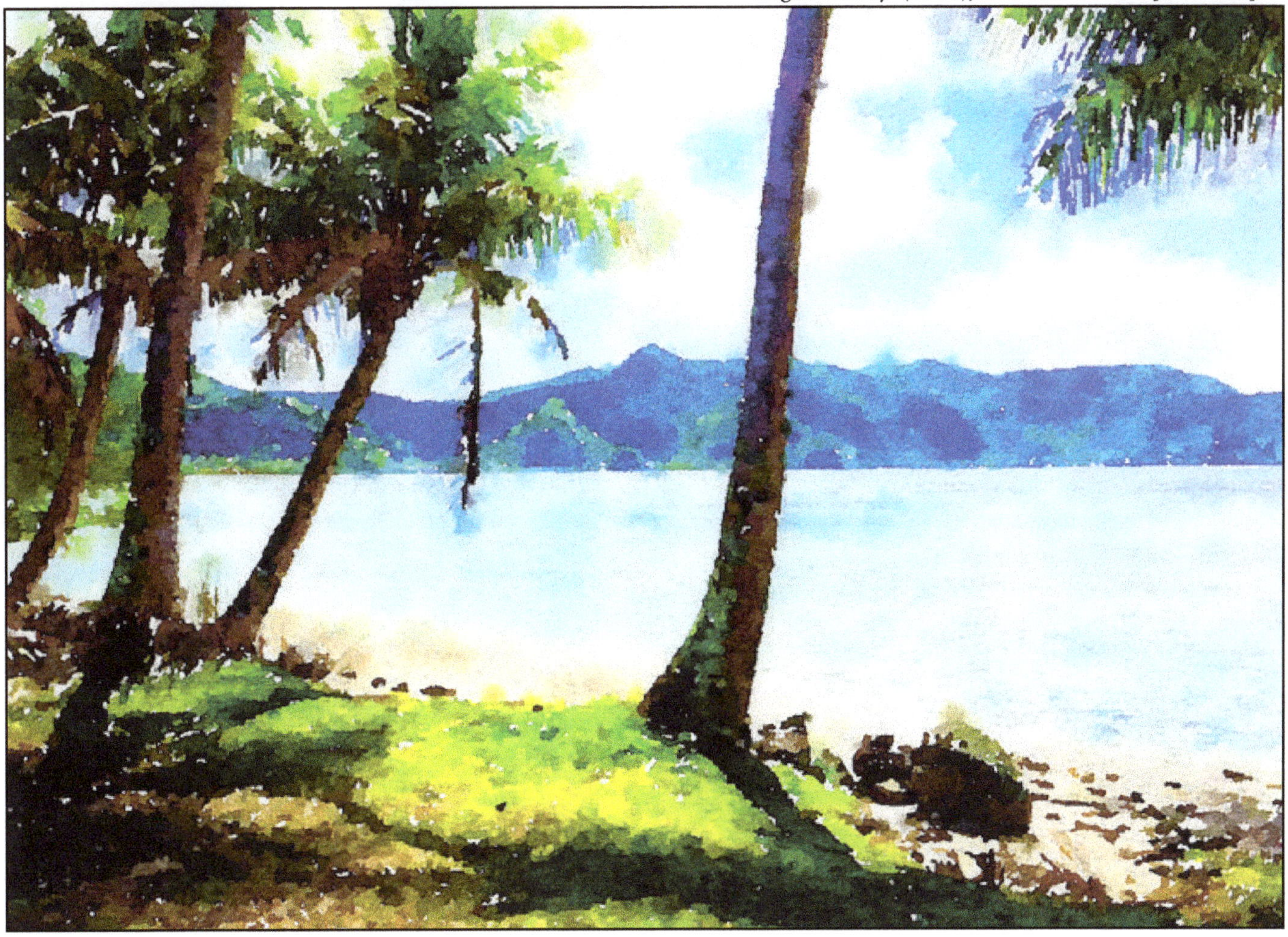

ABSTRACTS

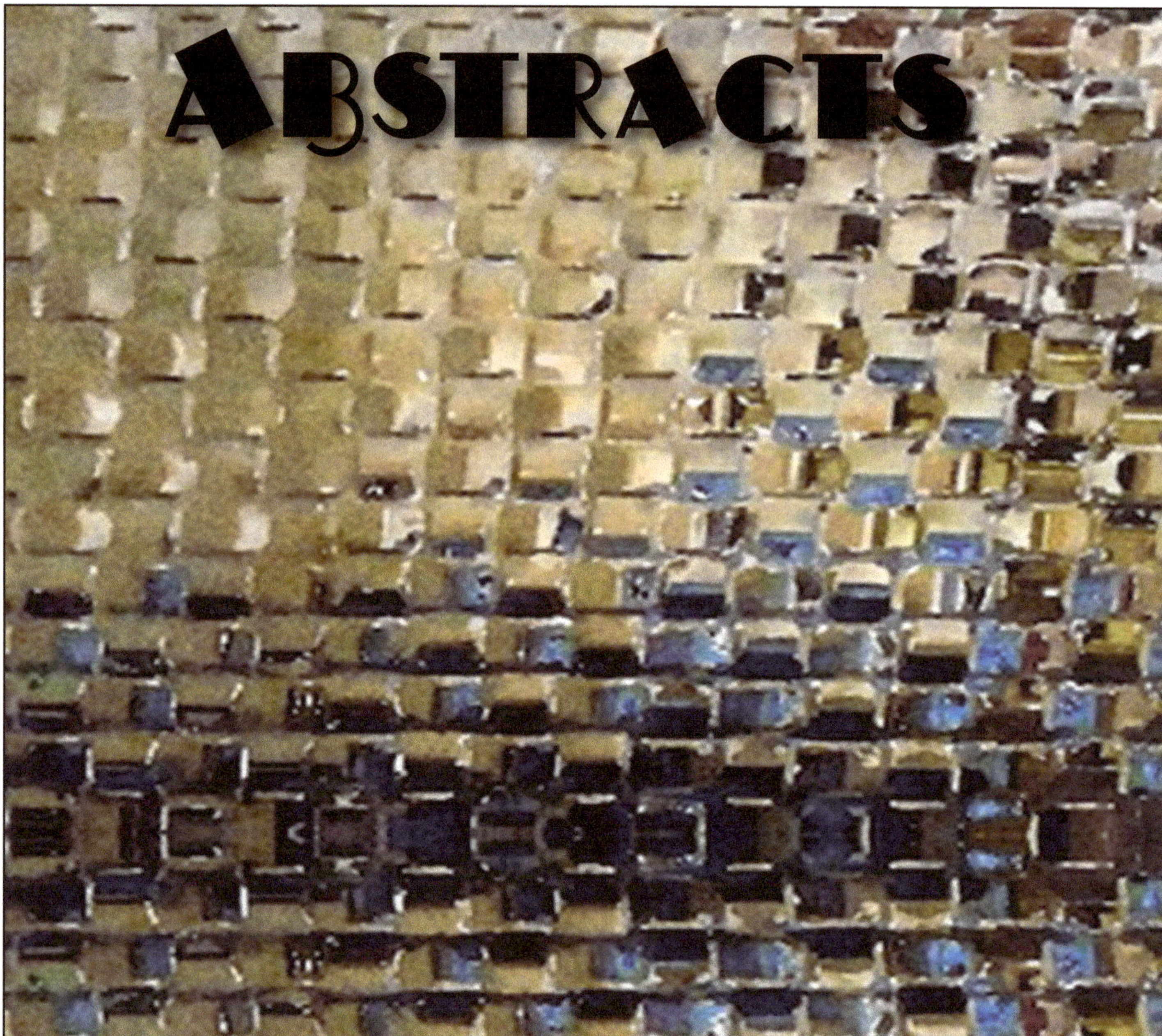

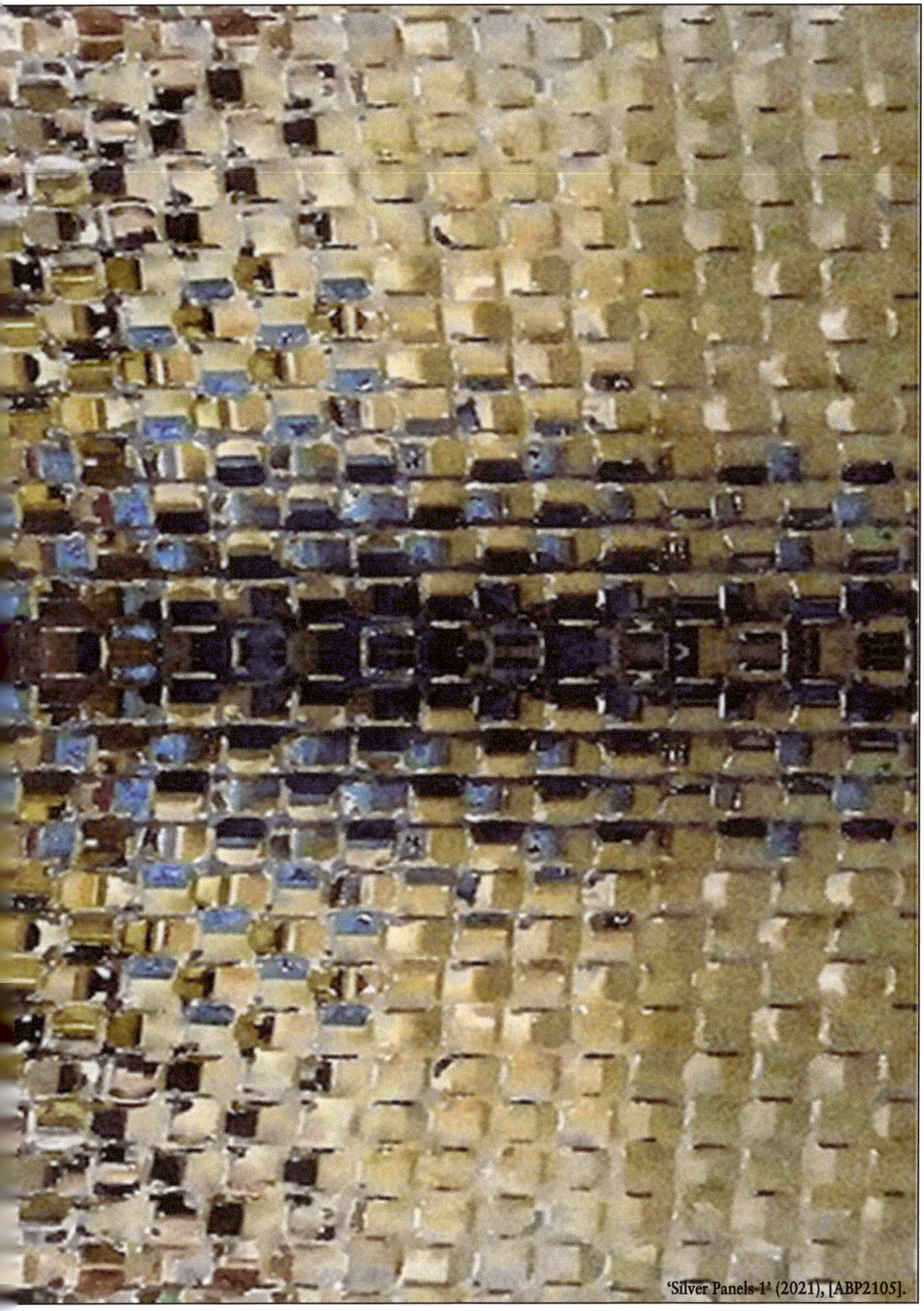

'Silver Panels-1' (2021), [ABP2105].

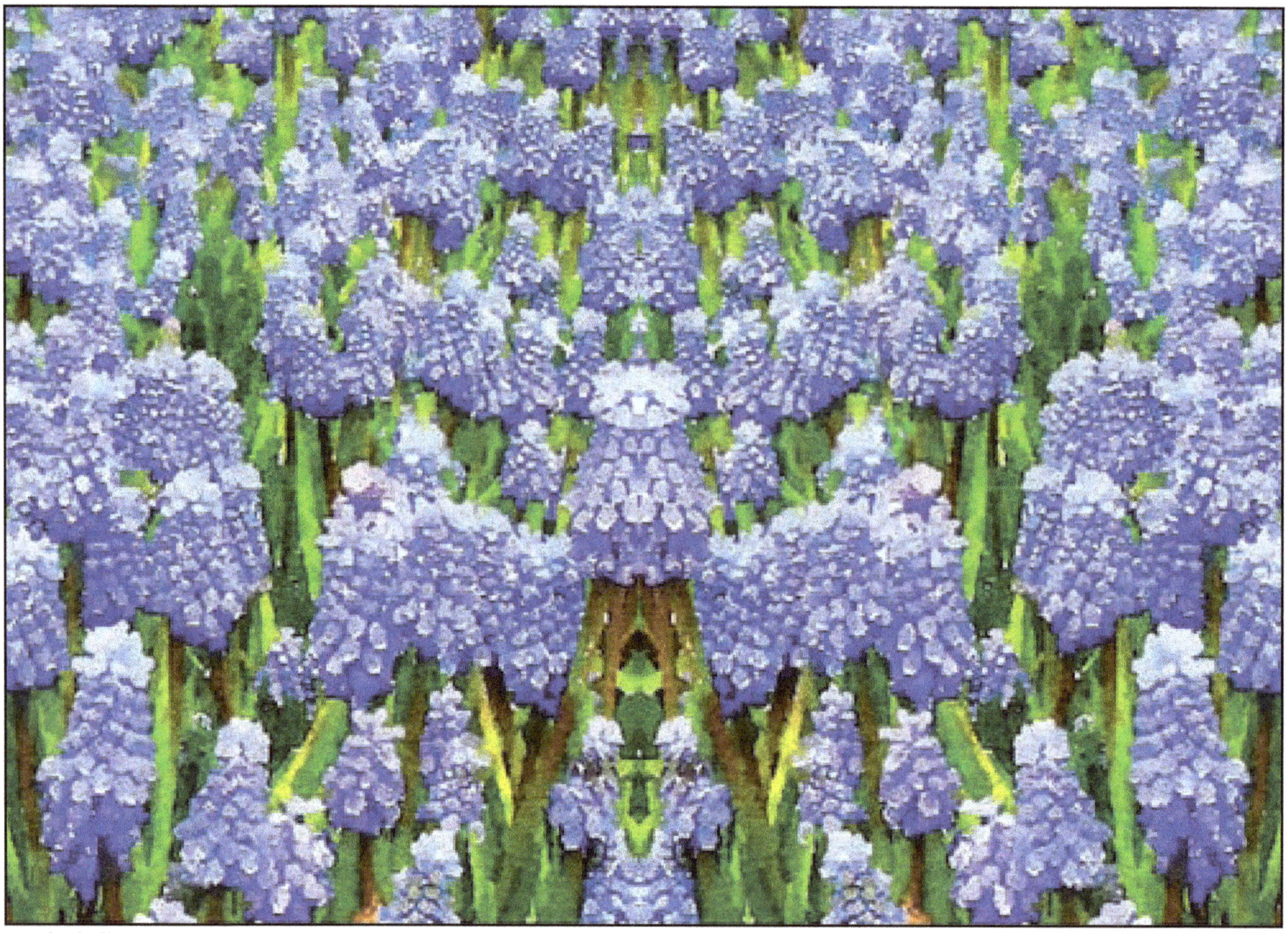

▲'Bluebells' (2021), [ABN2102].

'Cotton Cups' (2021), [ABN2103].▼

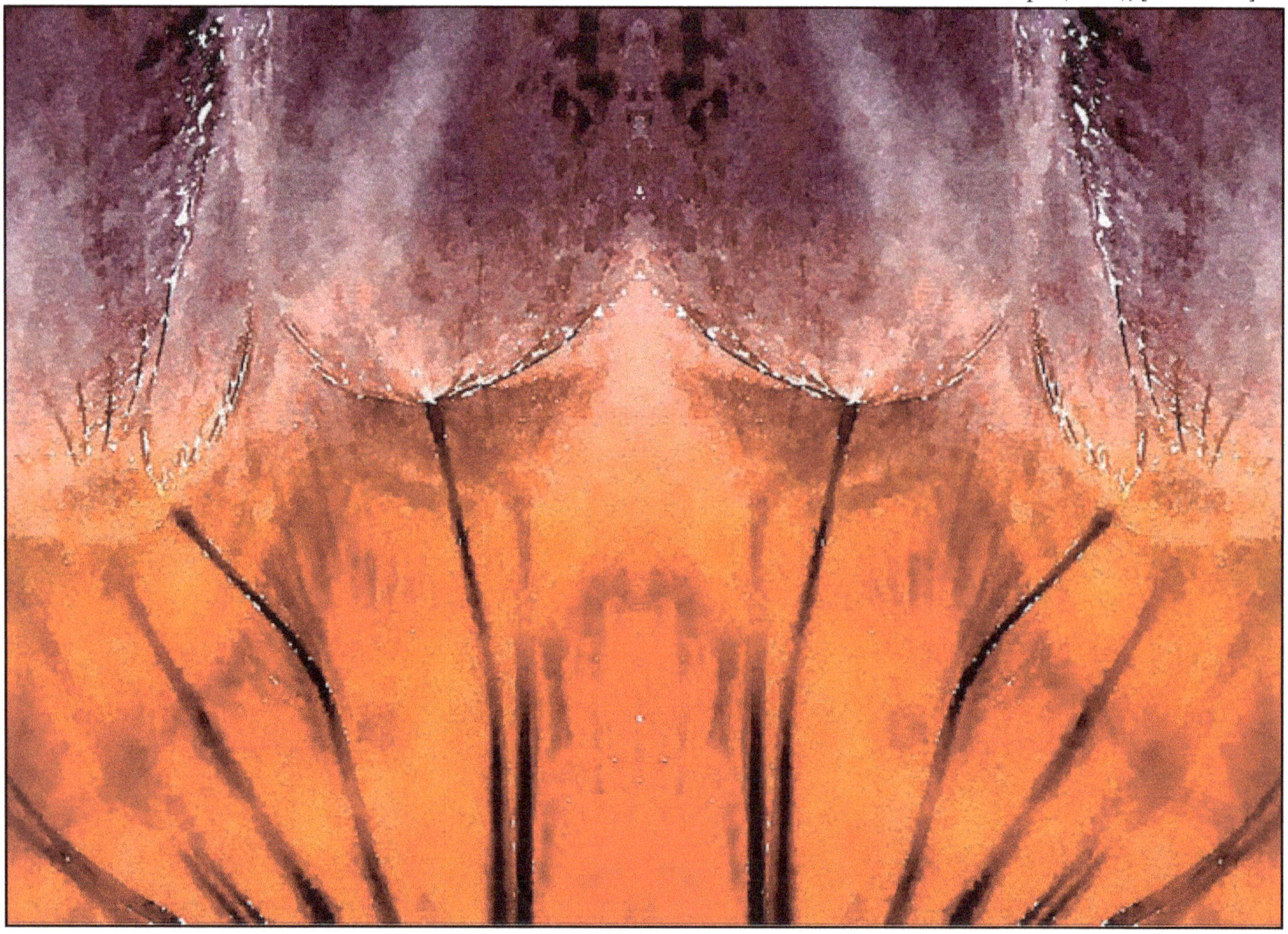

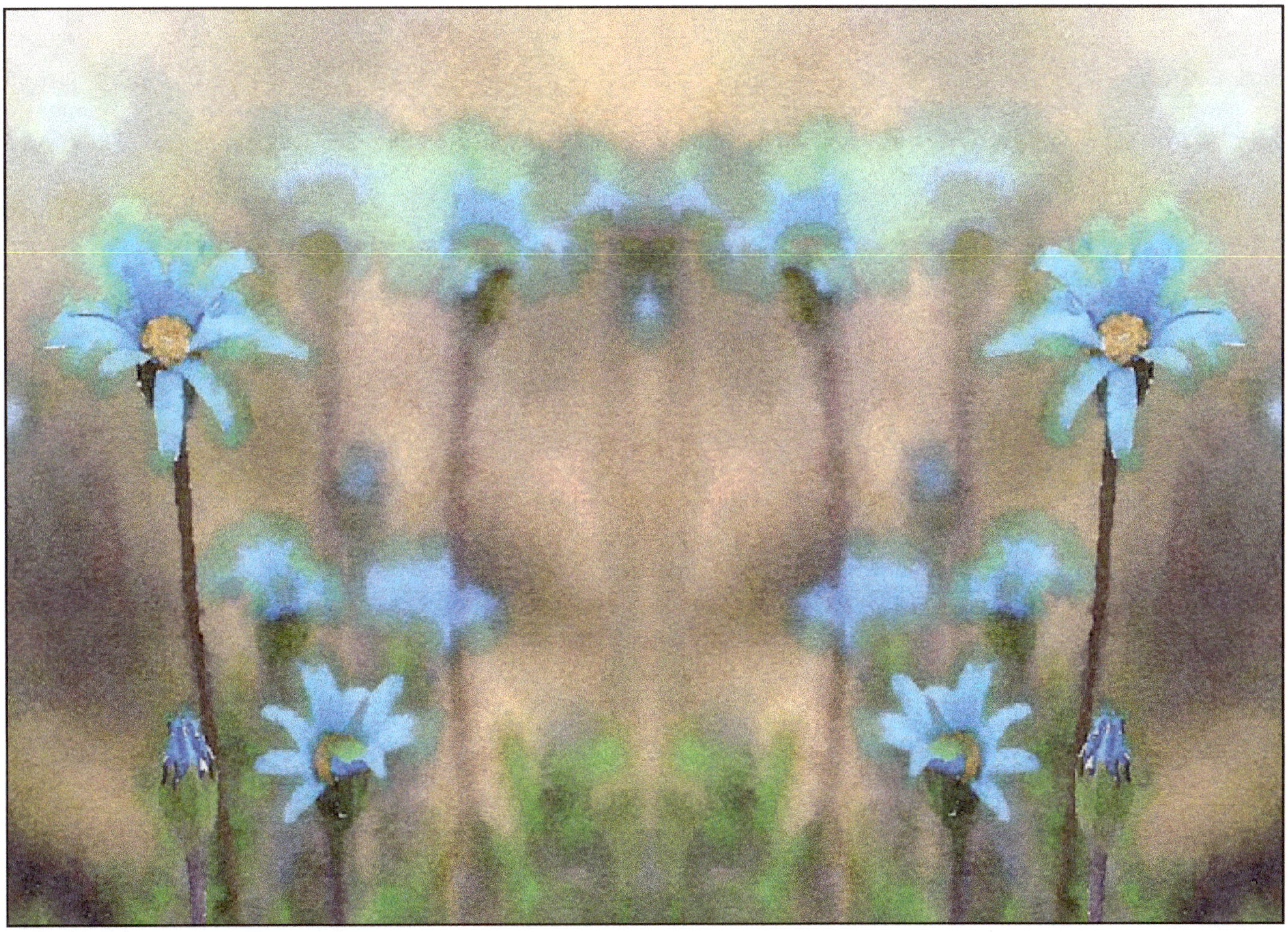

▲'Teal Petals' (2021), [ABN2104].

'Floral Spray' (2021), [ABN2105].▼

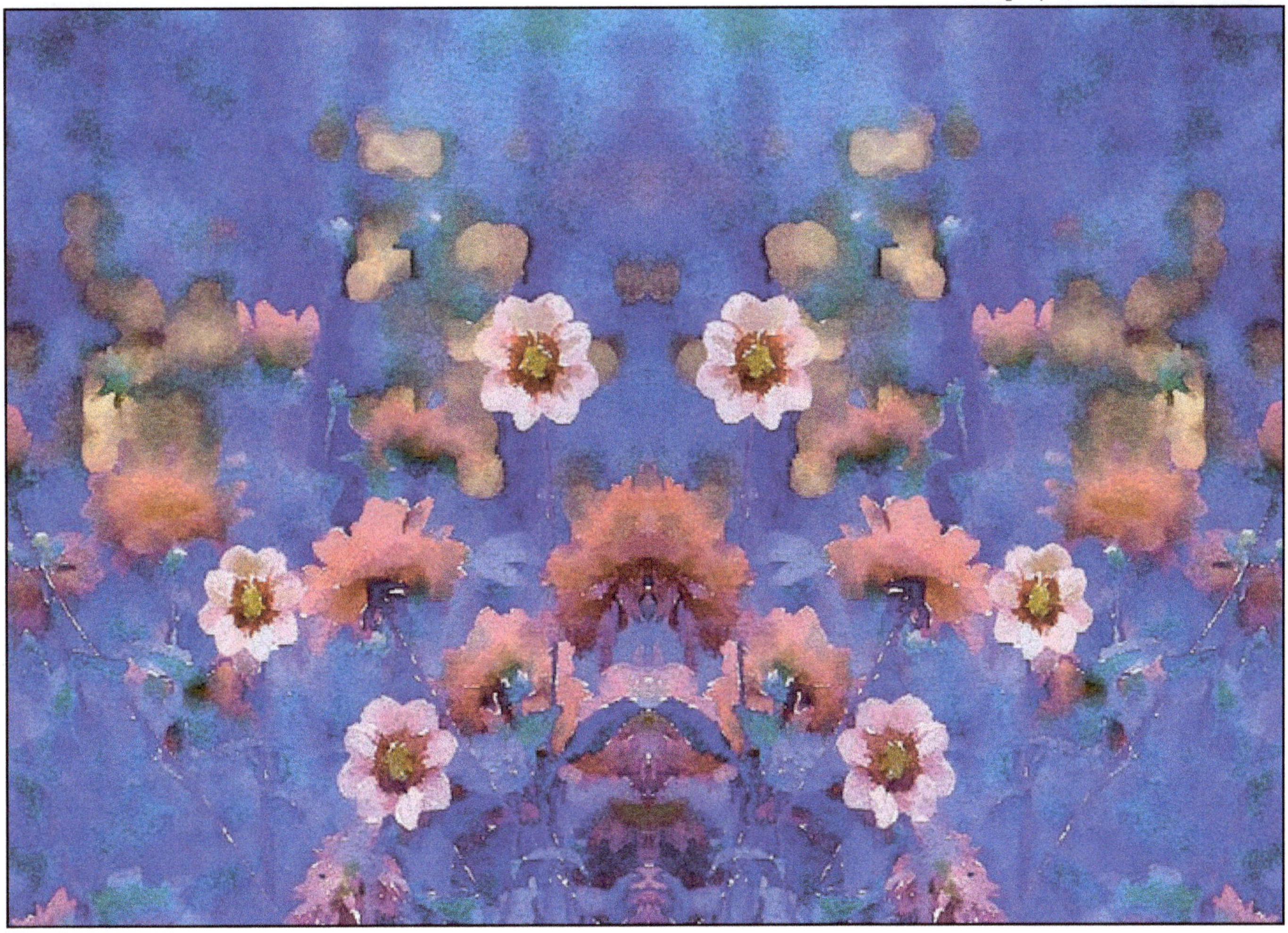

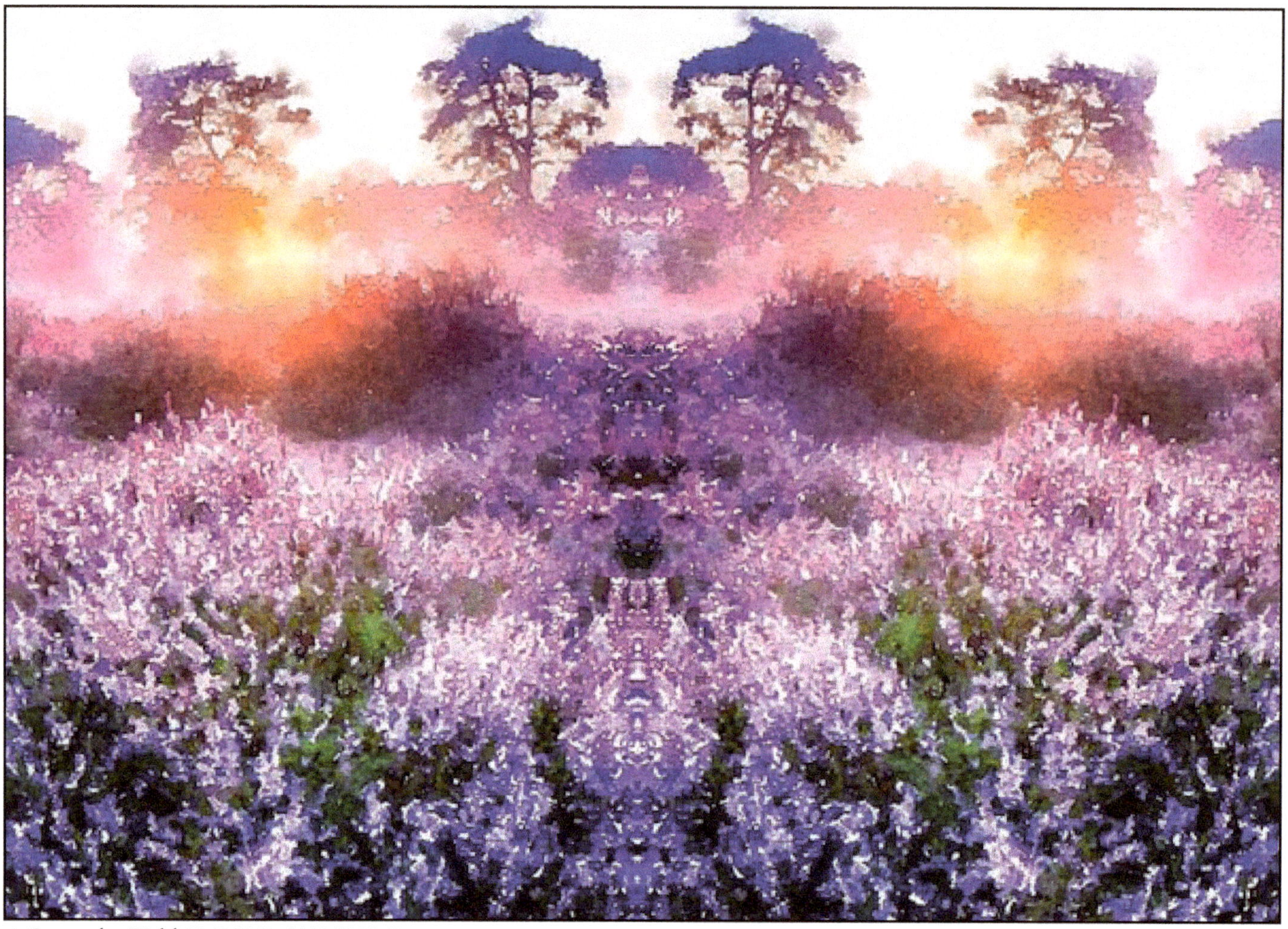

▲'Lavender Field 2' (2021), [ABN2106].

'The Crimson Forest' (2021), [ABN2107].▼

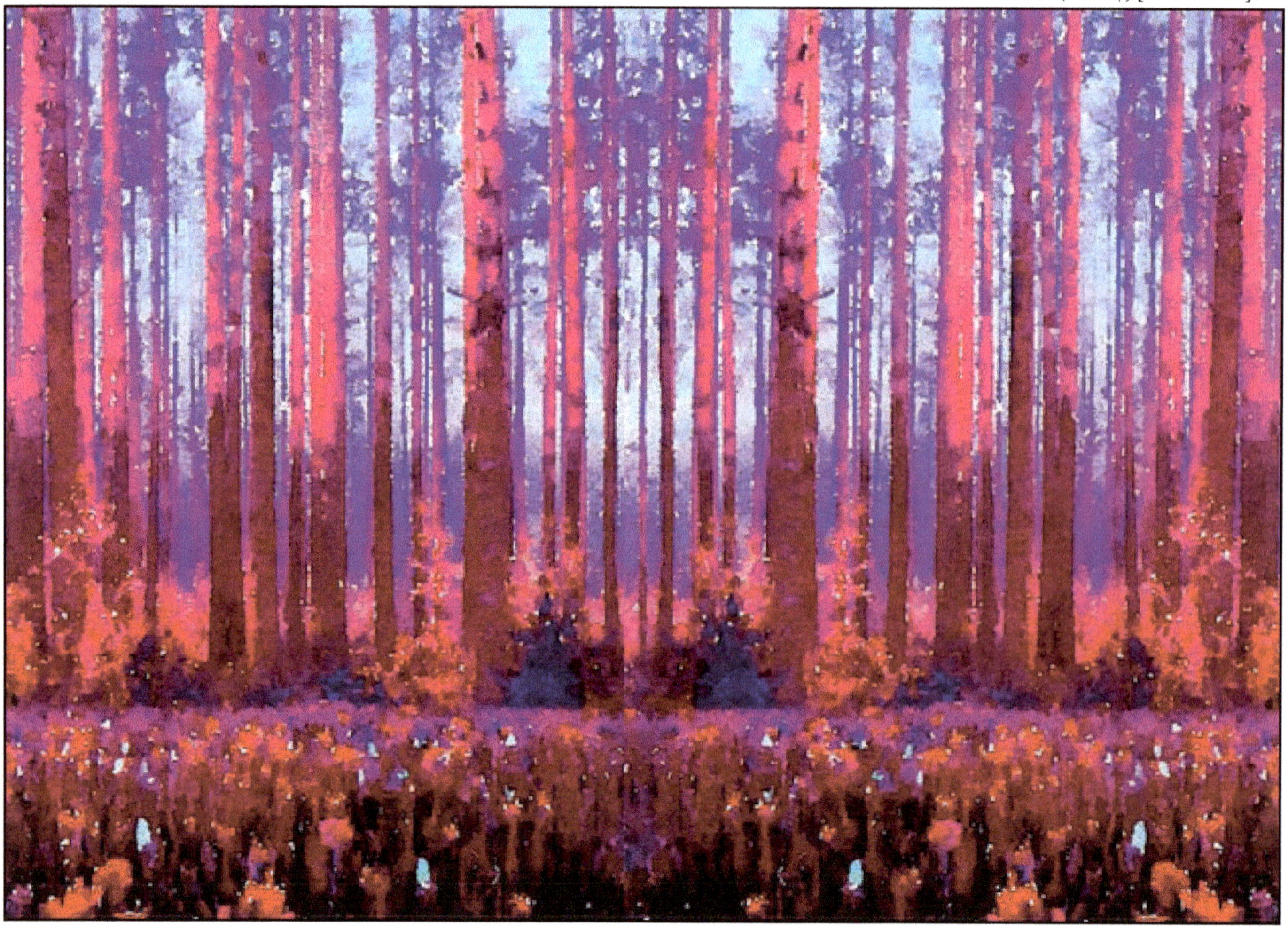

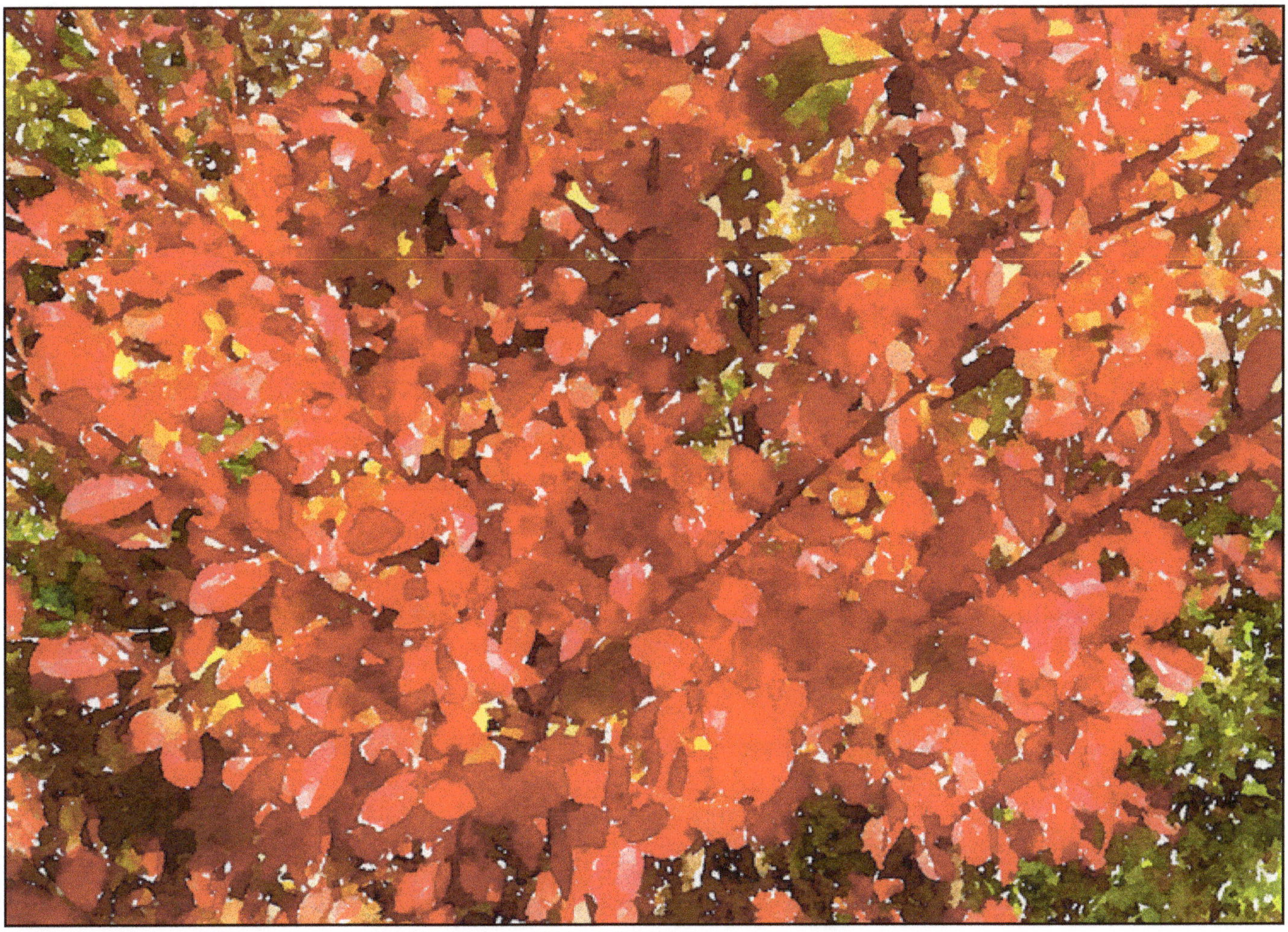

▲'The Red Leaves Of Runnymeade' (2019), Hobart, TAS [ABN1901].

'Alonissos Stones' (2016), Alonissos, Greece [ABP1601].▼

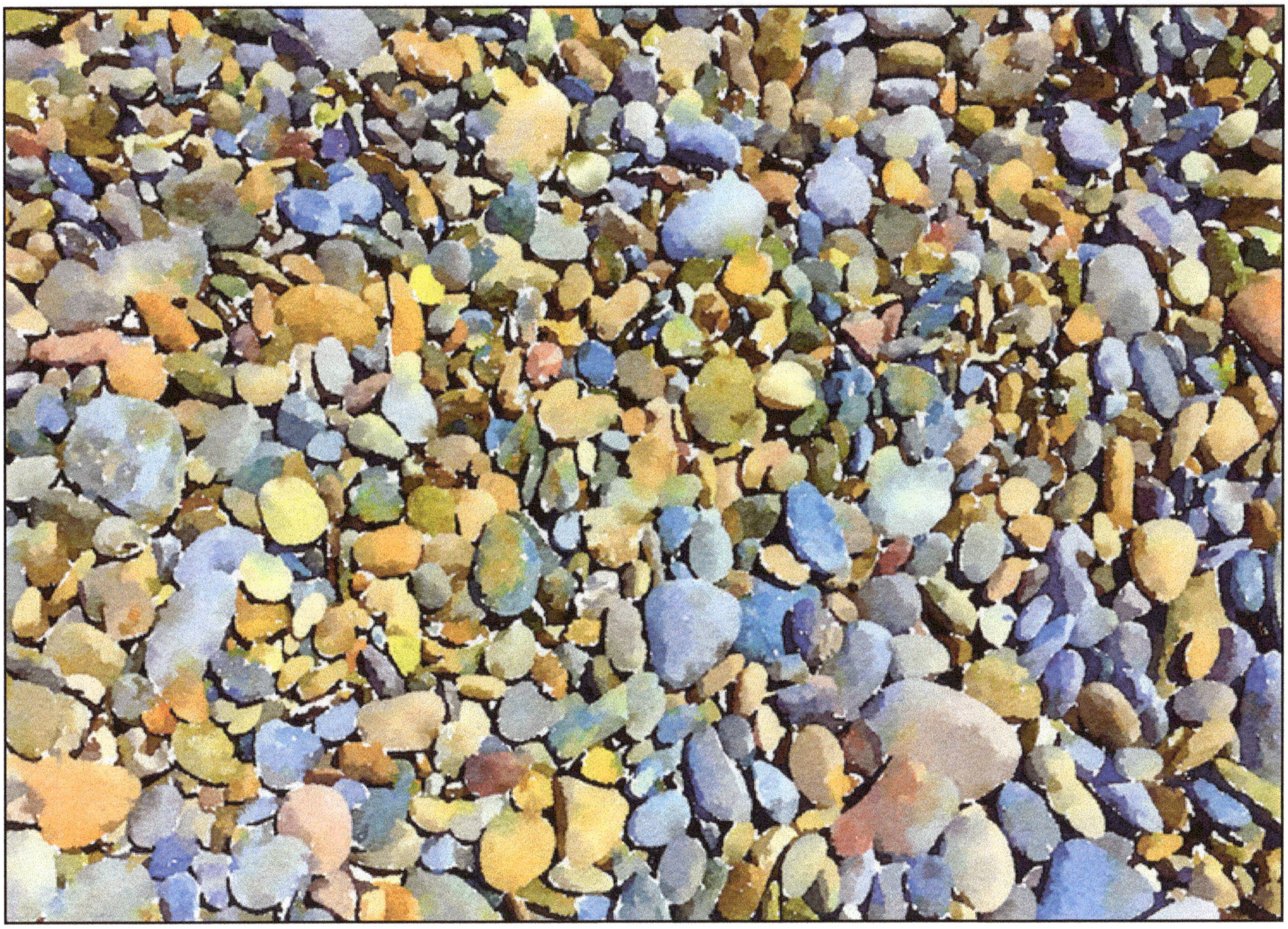

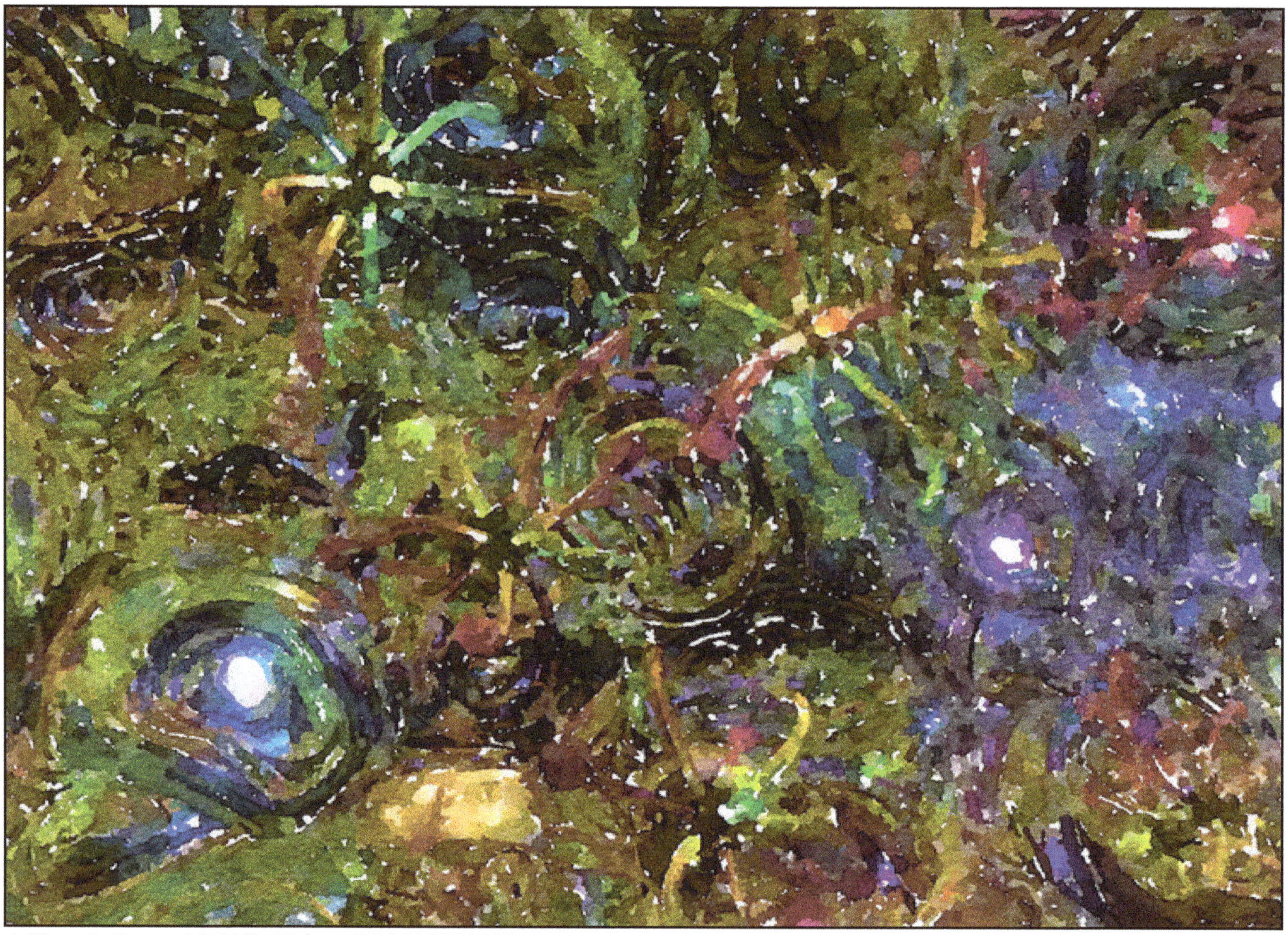

▲'Cosmic Dancer' (2019), Hobart, TAS [ABP1901].

'Celestial Blush 3' (2021), [ABP2104].▼

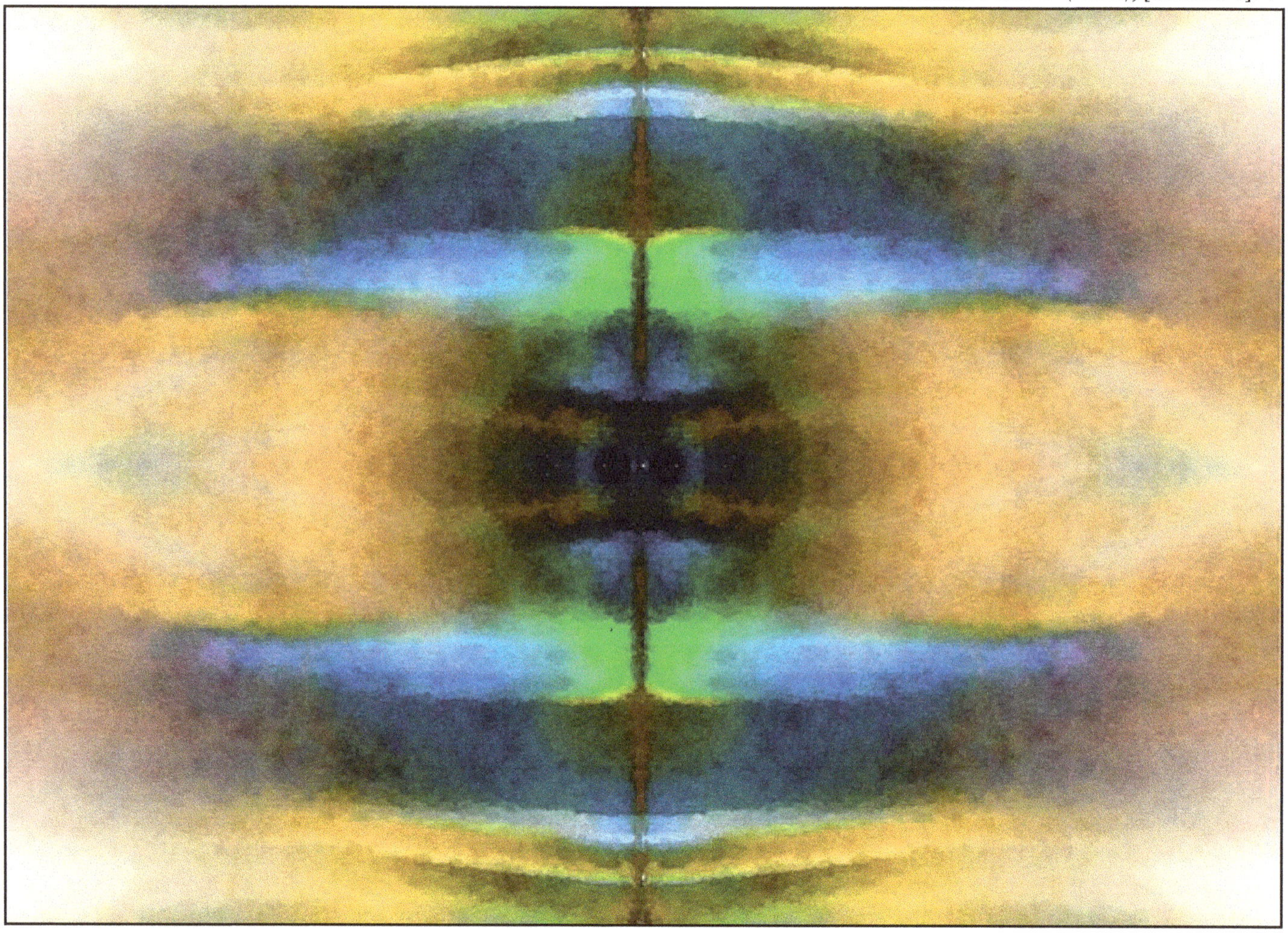

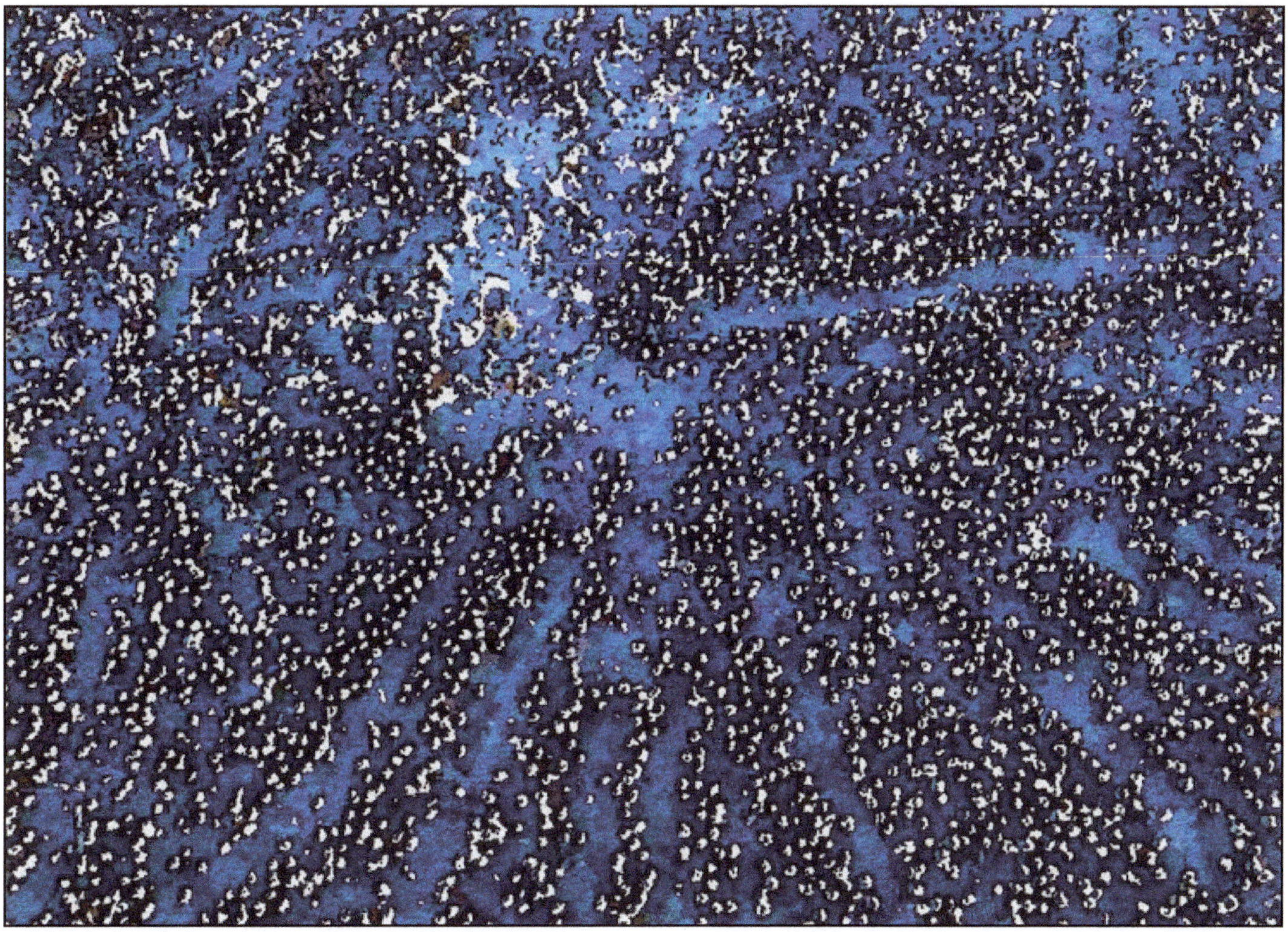

▲'The Crab Nebula 1' (2021), Yamba, NSW [ABP2101].

'The Crab Nebula 2' (2021), Yamba, NSW [ABP2102]▼

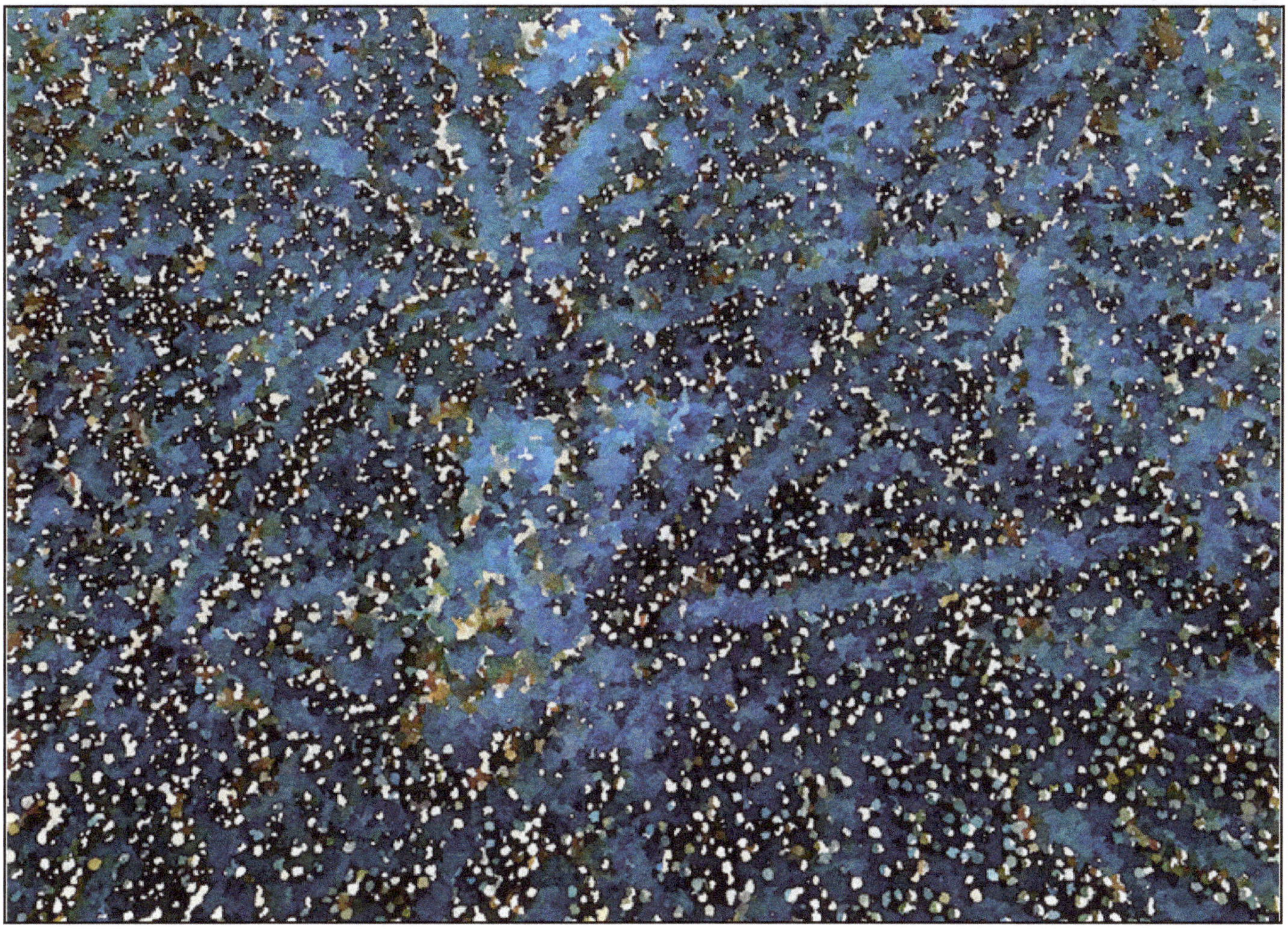

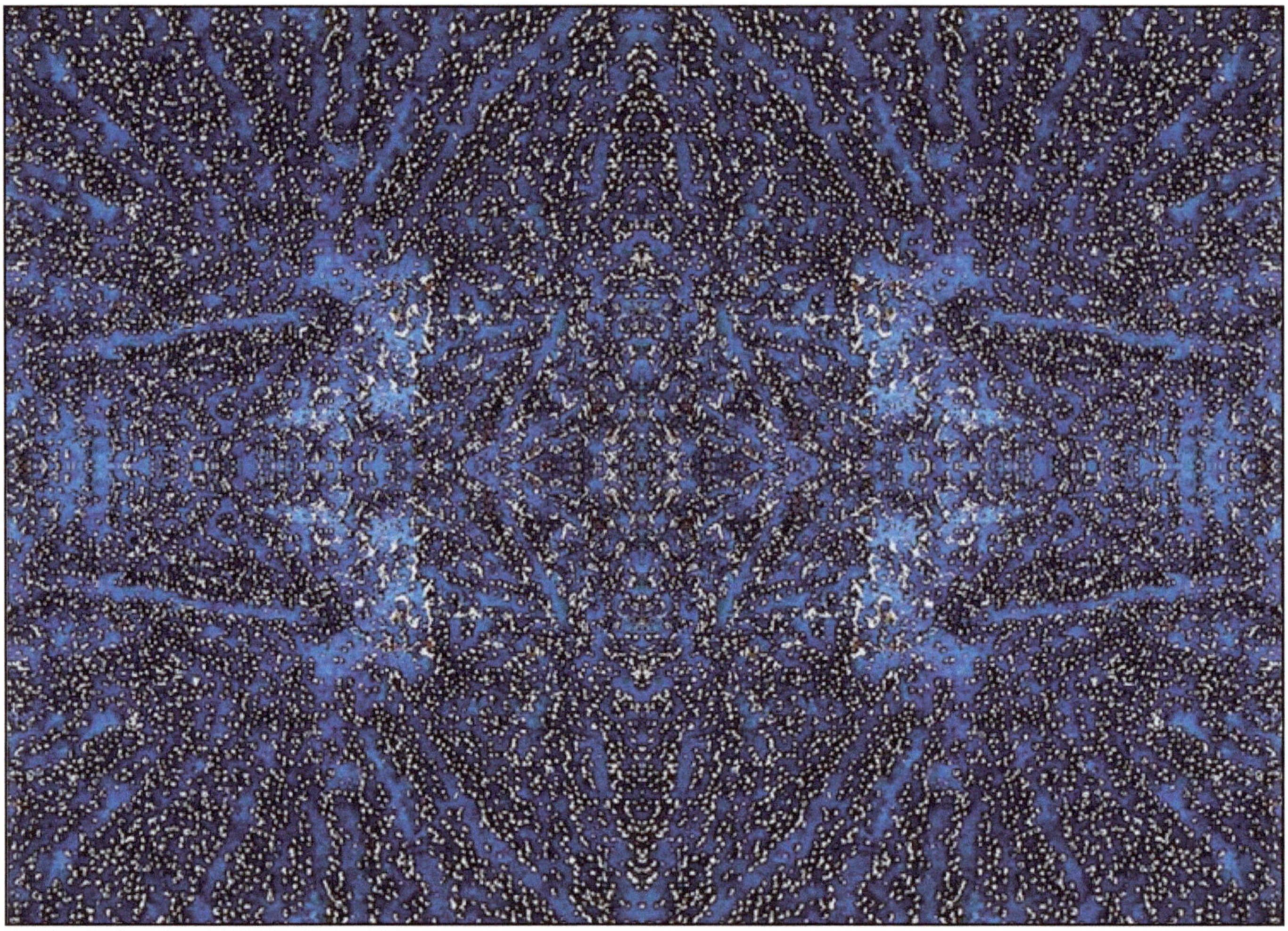

▲'The Crab Galaxy' (2021), [ABP2103].

'Crimson Tide' (2021), [ABP2112].▼

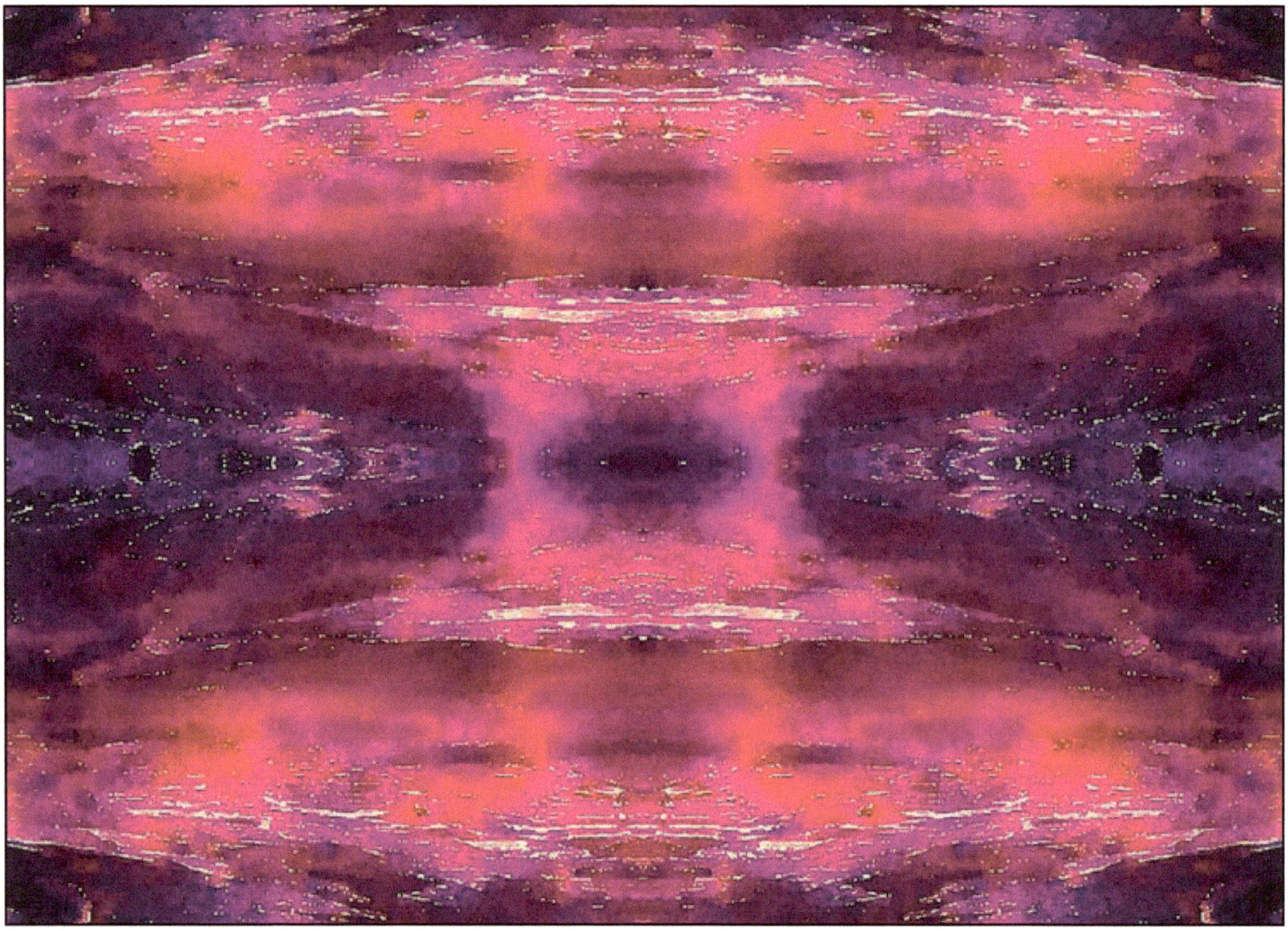

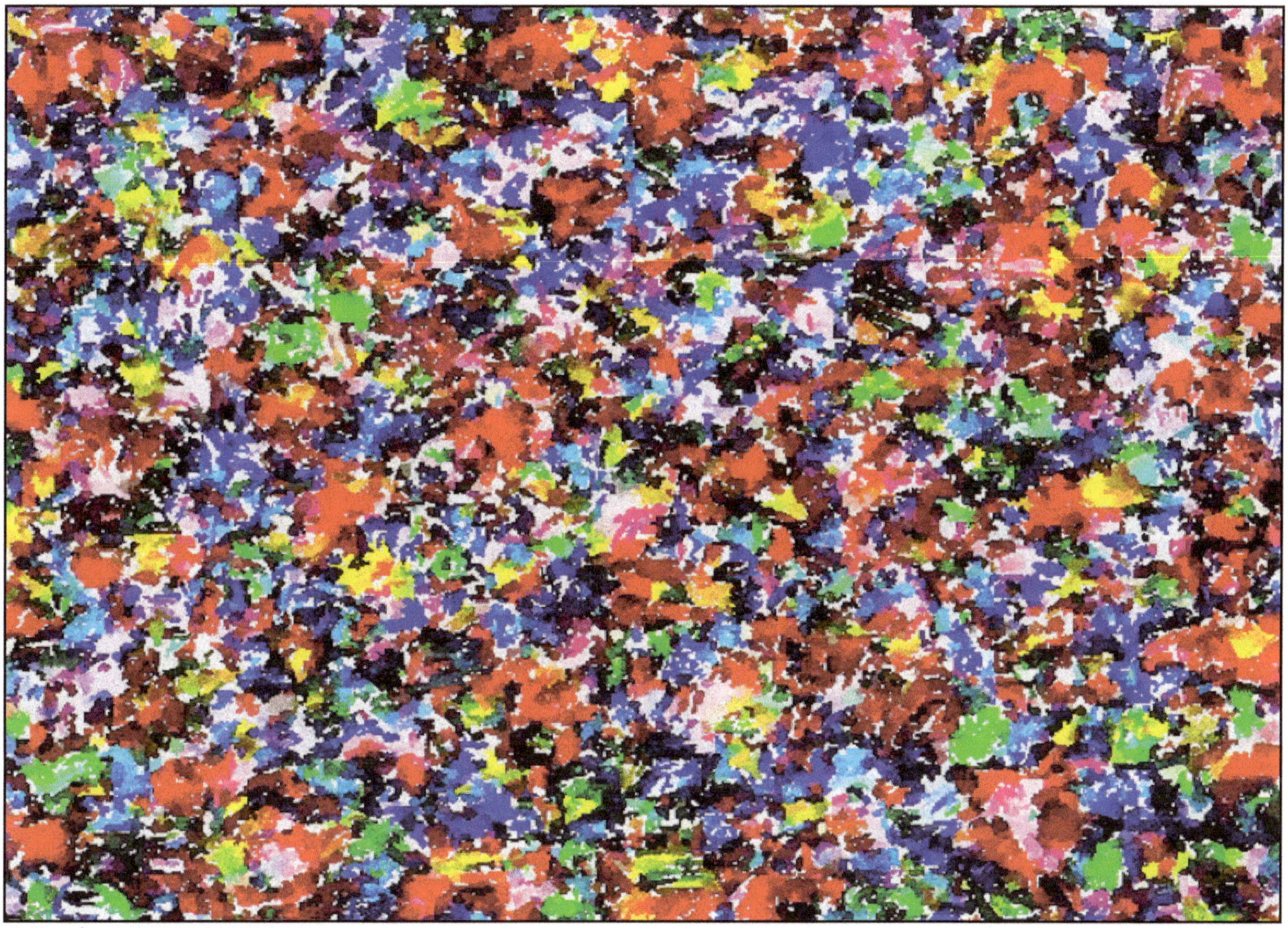

▲'Confetti' (2021), [ABP2111].

'Silver Panels 2' (2021), [ABP2106].▼

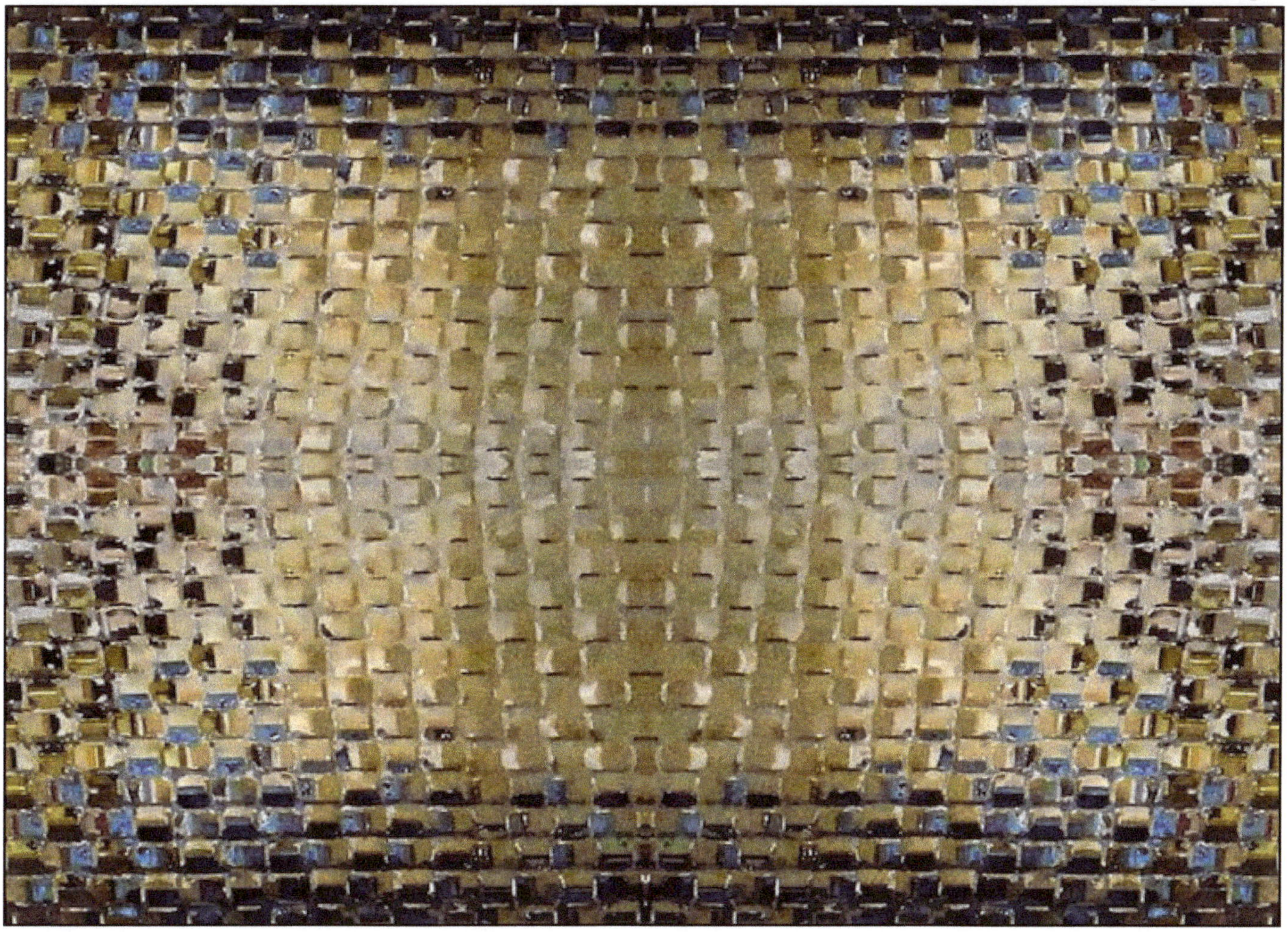

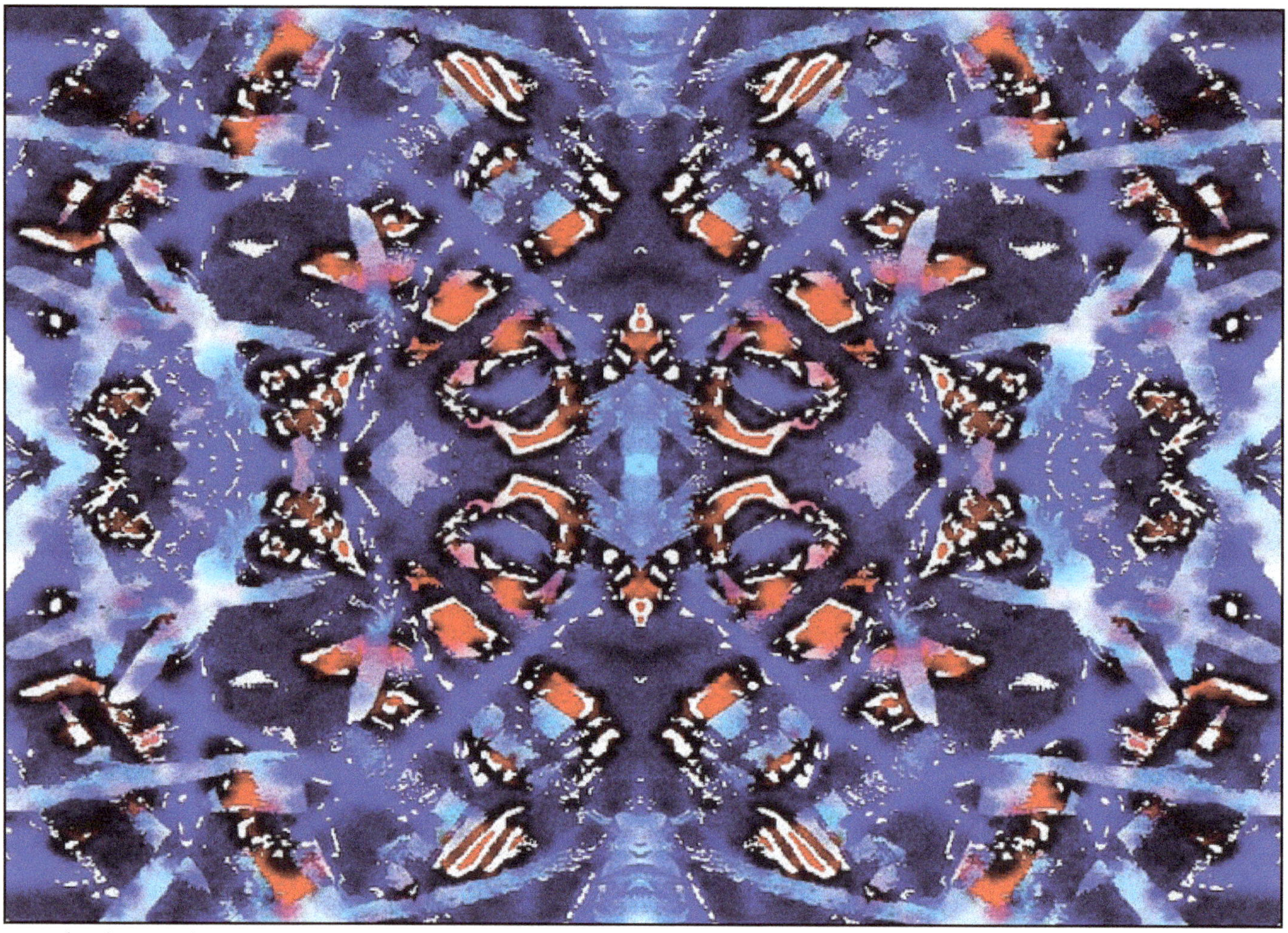

▲'Red, White & Blue 4' (2021), [ABP2107].

'Fireworks 1' (2021), [ABP2108].▼

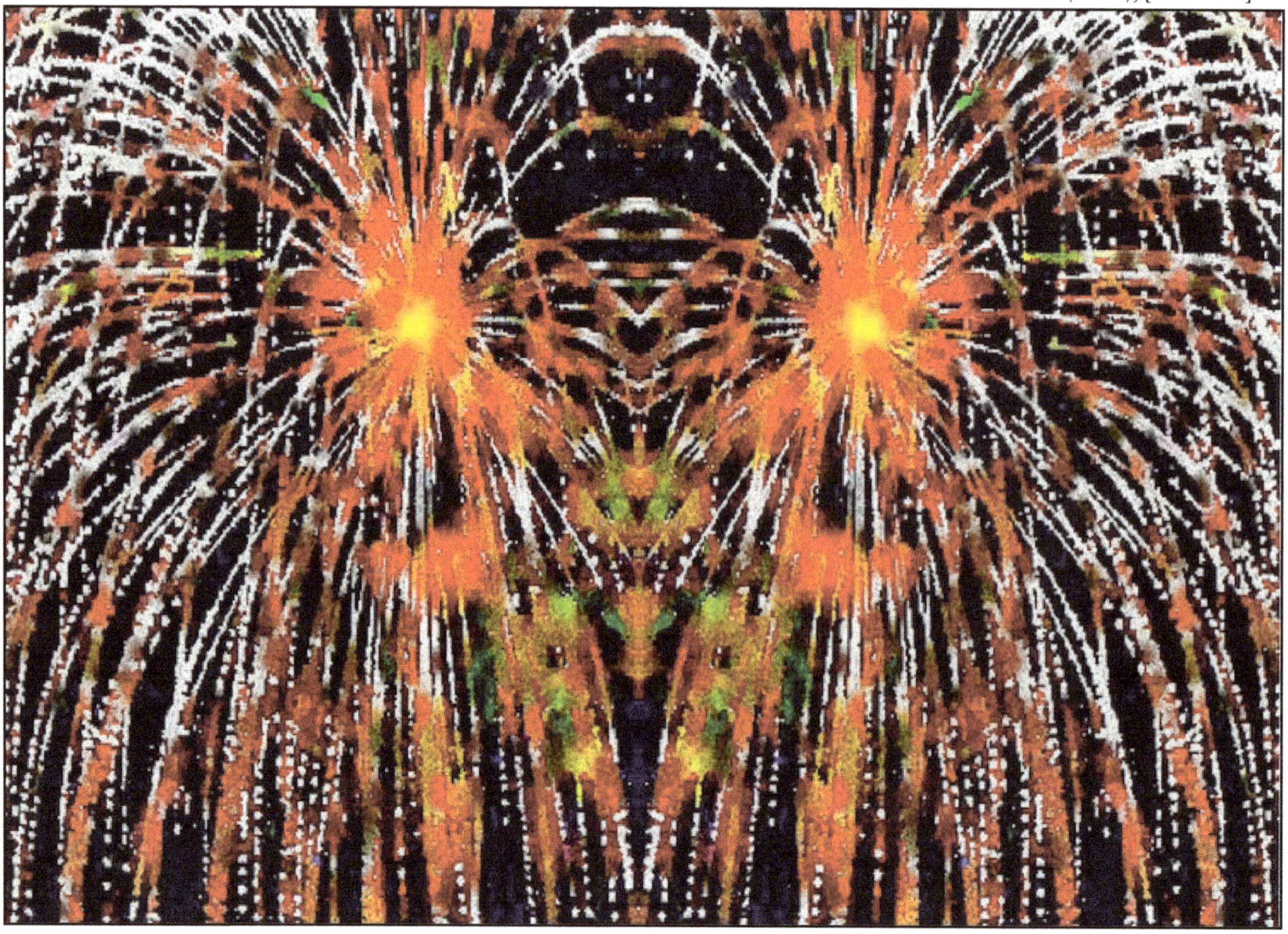

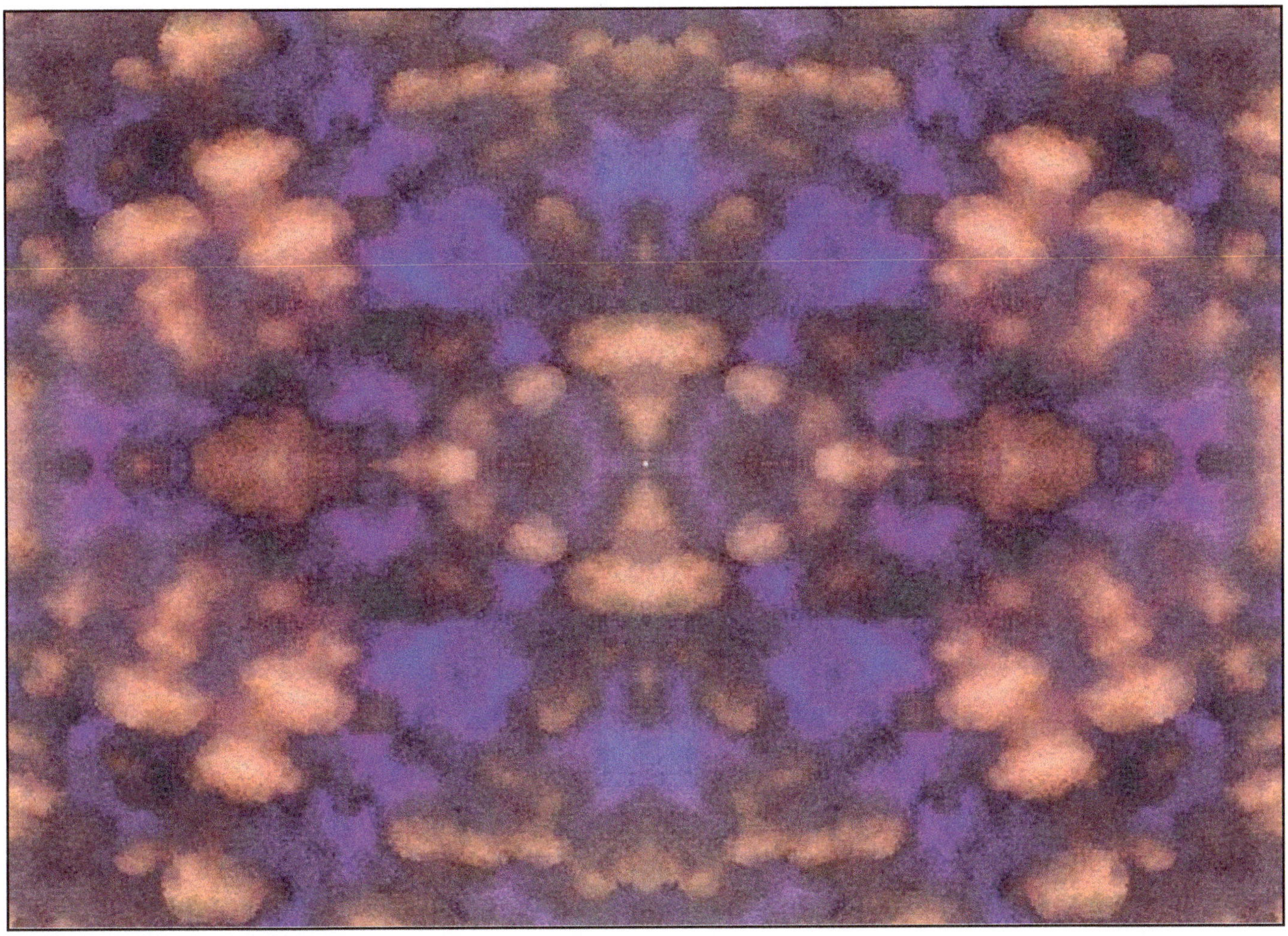

▲'Cloud One' (2021), [ABP2109].

'Cloud Two' (2021), [ABP2110].▼

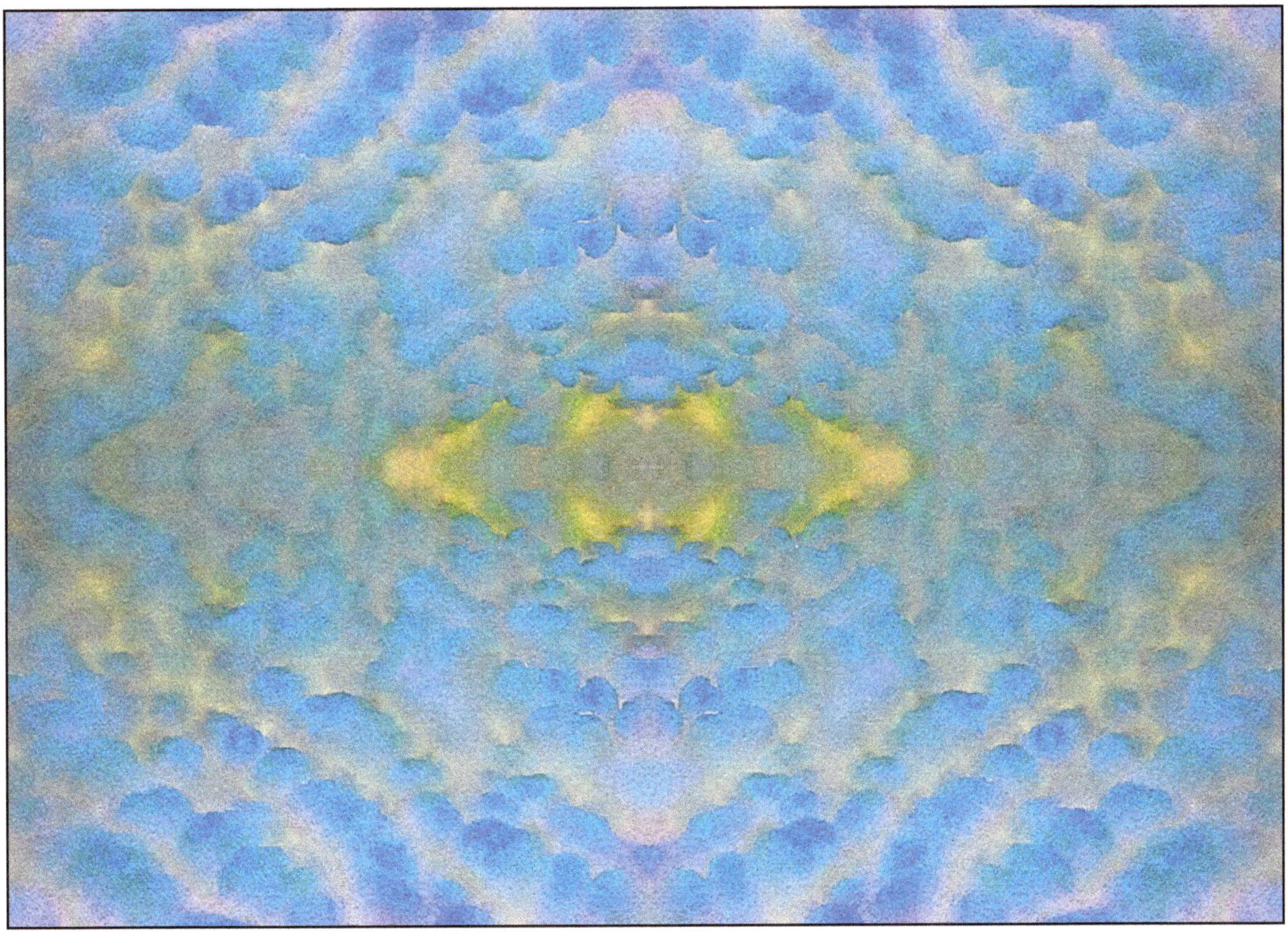

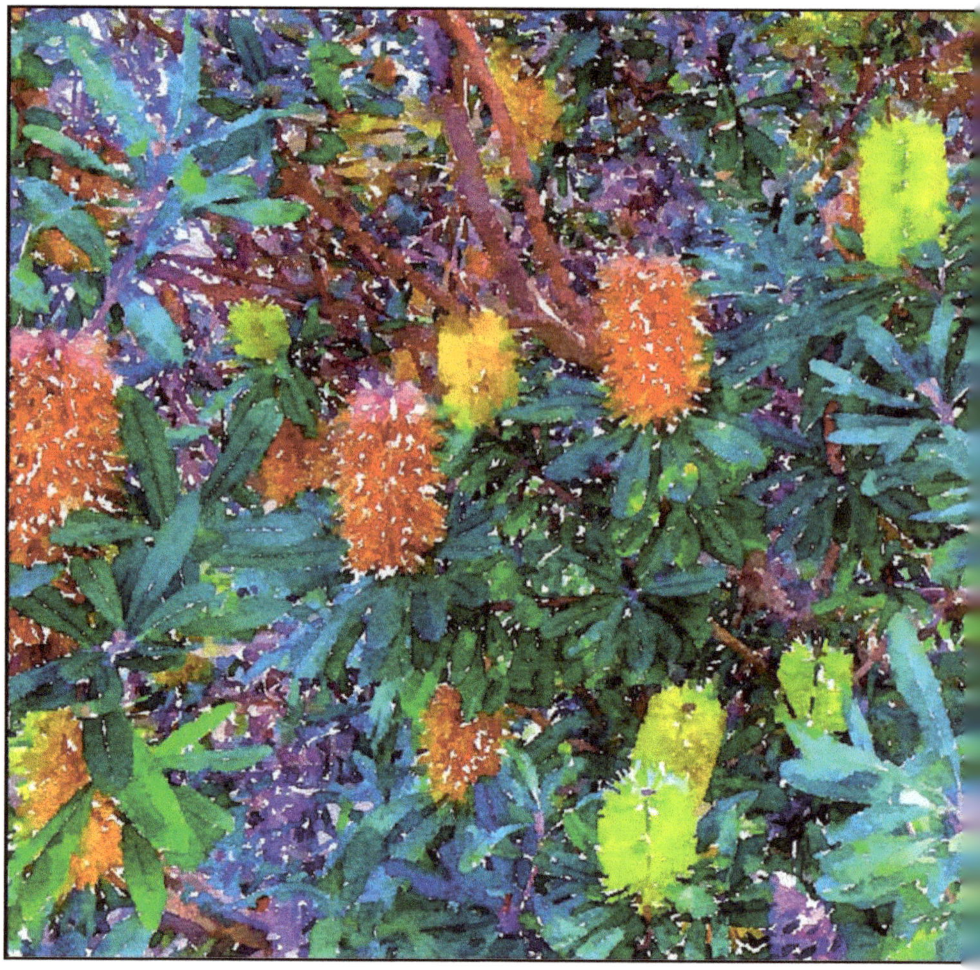

REFERENCES

Page 9, Claude Monet, (1877). "Arrival of the Normandy Train, Gare Saint-Lazare," Paris, FR, Public Domain.

Page 22, Basile Morin, (6 Jun 2019). "Colorful street signs in Kabukicho, Shinjuku," Tokyo, JP, CC Attribution-Share Alike 4.0 Int. license.

Page 23, Author Unknown, (Date Unknown). "Reflections Of Tokyo," Tokyo, JP, Public Domain.

Page 24, Flickr - Laurie Nevay, (1 May 2016). "Skyline view from Seoul City," South Korea, Seoul, KR, CC Attribution-Share Alike 2.0 Generic license.

Page 27, Peggychoucair, (13 Oct 2016). "Lebanon, Mediterranean, Beach, Tyr," LB, Pixabay - Free For Commercial use.

Page 28, Véronique Dauge, (19 Apr 2017). "Byblos-Lebanon," Byblos, LB, CC Attribution-Share Alike 3.0 IGO license.

Page 31, CEphoto-Uwe Aranas, (23 Dec 2015). "Pilars of the Taipei Bridge," Taipei, TW, CC Attribution-Share Alike 3.0 Unported license.

Page 83, pixabairis, (27 May 2015). "Gibraltar Rock," Gibraltar, GI, Pixabay - Free For Commercial use.

Page 146, Author Unknown, (Date Unknown). "Dolomiti, Italy, Mountain, Alps, Nature," Dolomites, IT, CC Zero - CC0.

Page 146, Fshoq, (7 Aug 2018). "Panorama of Dolomites and Val Gardena," Italy, Dolomites, IT, Attribution-4.0 International (CC BY 4.0).

Page 162, Elena Deniakina, (Date Unknown). "Valletta Skyline: A view of Valletta from the sea," Valletta, MT, CC0 Public Domain.

Page 184, C messier, (24 Aug 2017). "Sagrada Familia from Placa de Gaudi" [Cranes digitally removed], Barcelona, ES, CC Attribution-Share Alike 4.0 Int. license.

Page 192, 495796, (16 Sep 2015). "Geneva Flags," Geneva, CH, Pixabay - Free For Commercial use.

Page 193, SofiLayla, (12 Apr 2008). "SS Rhone On Lake Geneva," Geneva, CH, Pixabay - Free For Commercial use.

Page 193, Author Unknown, (Date Unknown). "Lake Geneva," Geneva, CH, Public Domain.

Page 196, 12019, (9 Aug 2017). "Vancouver, Sea Ocean," Vancouver, CA, Pixabay - Free For Commercial use.

Page 197, tsaiproject, (13 Feb 2012). "Parliament Hill (Posterior view of the Parliament of Canada)," Ottawa, CA, Attribution. 2.0 Generic (CC BY 2.0).

Page 205, Author Unknown, (Date Unknown). "The Las Vegas 'Strip' At Night," Las Vegas, NV, Public Domain.

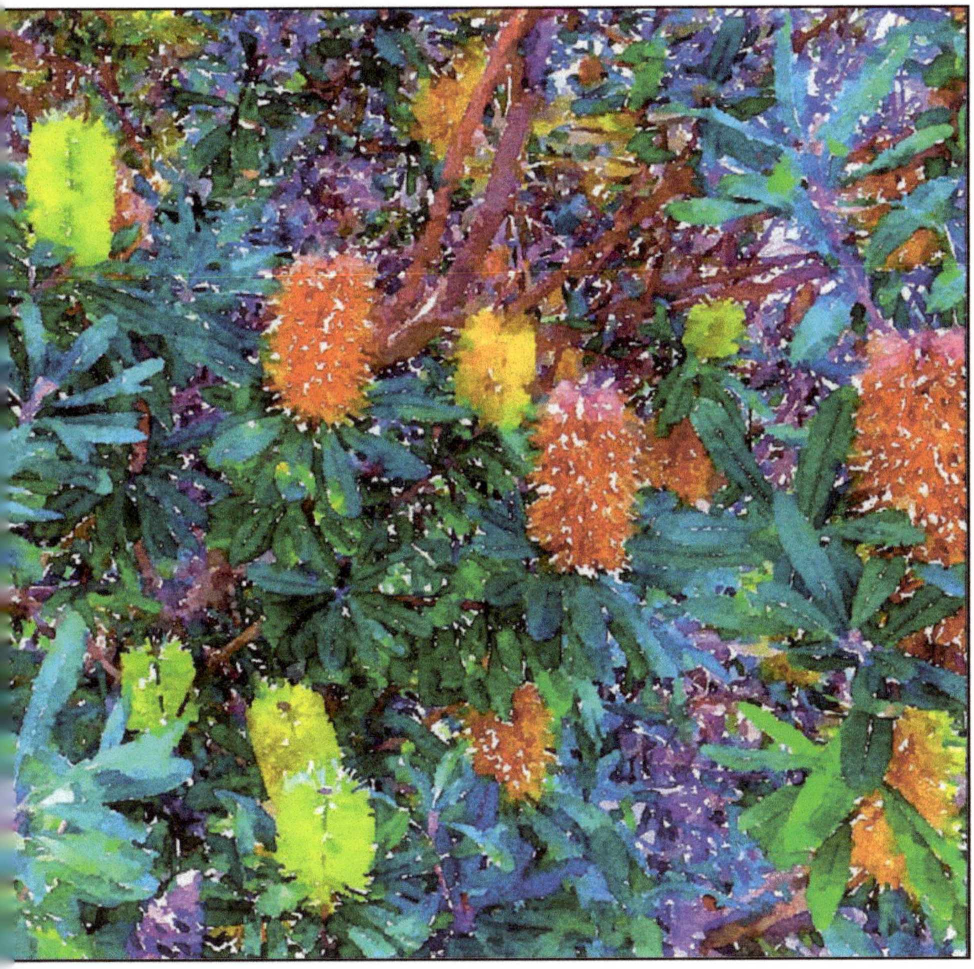

◀'Banksias' (2021), [ABN2101].

While the majority of images in this catalogue were processed directly from the artists original photographs, a small number were digitised from copyright free sources, with an acknowledgement where possible of each individual contributor being listed below.

Page 206, Dietmar Rabich, (26 Jul 2012). "The Strip In Las Vegas," Nevada, Las Vegas, NV, CC Attribution-Share Alike 4.0 Int. license.
Page 206, Terabass, (13 Sep 2009). "Times Square, New York," New York, NY, CC Attribution-Share Alike 3.0 Unported license.
Page 207, Sam valac, (28 Aug 2012). "Empire State - New York City," New York, NY, Attribution-2.0 Generic (CC BY 2.0).
Page 208, Author Unknown, (Date Unknown). "Portland, Oregon," Portland, OR, Public Domain.
Page 209, Author Unknown, (Date Unknown). "Portland At Dusk," Portland, OR, Public Domain.
Page 209, Author Unknown, (Date Unknown). "Fall In Portland," Portland, OR, Public Domain.
Page 228, Peter Neaum, (1 Jul 2011). "First Falls, Morialta Conservation Park," Morialta, SA, CC Attribution-3.0 Unported license.
Page 229, Jacqui Barker, (25 Dec 2012). "Razorback Lookout," Flinders Ranges, SA, CC Attribution-2.0 Generic license.
Page 236, Graham Manning, (Feb 2007). "Daylesford Lake looking across to boat house," Daylesford Lake, VIC, CC Attribution-Share Alike 3.0 Unported license.
Page 240, Travellers photobook, (16 Apr 2016). "Lights On The Torrens," Available at www.flickr.com/photos/neelelora/albums, Adelaide, SA, CC Attribution-2.0 Generic license.
Page 254, Thomas Schoch, (24 Jul 2005). "Sydney Opera House," Sydney, NSW, CC Attribution-Share Alike 2.5 Generic license.
Page 256, Author Unknown, (Date Unknown). "Opera House 1," Sydney, NSW, Public Domain.
Page 257, Author Unknown, (Date Unknown). Sydney Opera House, NSW, Sydney, NSW, Public Domain.
Page 286, ShorebreakOz, (6 Nov 2015). Coogee Beach just as the Storm of the Year hits," Coogee, NSW, CC Attribution-Share Alike 4.0 Int. license.
Page 316, Author Unknown, (Date Unknown). "Tamarama Panarama," Tamarama, NSW, Public Domain.
Page 323, Richard Palmer, (16 Jul 2004). "Morning mist on Lake Mapourika," Lake Mapourika, NZ, CC Attribution-Share Alike 3.0 Unported license.

CPSIA information can be obtained
at www.ICGtesting.com
Printed in the USA
LVHW072248311021
702018LV00015B/1832

9 781925 909128